Que's Computer User's Dictionary

Bryan Pfaffenberger, Ph.D.
School of Engineering and Applied Science
University of Virginia

Technical Review by
Walter R. Bruce III
Timothy S. Stanley

Que® Corporation
Carmel, Indiana

Acknowledgments

No one individual could possibly undertake a task of this magnitude, and in creating this dictionary, I had some terrific co-workers. I thank Lloyd Short for convincing me that my breadth of knowledge was sufficient to undertake this project, as daunting as it seemed.

After the first draft reached Carmel, Ind., it was tackled by a world-class editorial team. I particularly thank the two technical editors, Walter R. Bruce and Timothy S. Stanley; if this book is said to have merit, their distinguished contribution and expertise should be recognized in the next breath.

I also thank my editors, Kelly D. Dobbs, Jo Anna Arnott, Fran Blauw, Jeannine Freudenberger, Cheryl Robinson, and Daniel Schnake. They saved me from my self in innumerable ways. Very special thanks are due, last but not least, to Karen Bluestein, who in desktop publishing this book labored long hours.

Que gave me the freedom to attempt a totally new kind of dictionary, a user's dictionary: it's a dictionary written from the user's viewpoint, and it's about computing from the user's perspective. Academic types and lexicographers may find this approach wrong-headed or even to pose a danger to Civilization for having obfuscated nice, tidy, academic distinctions, but I am the proper target for their ire, not those who aided me so much as I pursued my goal. If computer users find this dictionary of value in defining the world of computing as they see it, I will be more than satisfied.

Publishing Director
Lloyd J. Short

Product Director
Karen A. Bluestein

Developmental Editor
Shelley O'Hara

Production Editor
Kelly D. Dobbs

Editors
Jo Anna Arnott
Fran Blauw
Jeannine Freudenberger
Cheryl Robinson
Daniel Schnake

Production
Tami Hughes
Jodi Jensen
Lori Lyons
Dennis Sheehan

Preface

Personal computing technology brings computing tools to ordinary people. Personal computing, however, also brings a new and daunting terminology to daily life.

These terms aren't just the unfamiliar terms of data processing and management information science—the kind of words defined in other computer dictionaries. These terms are the unfamiliar terms of personal computing, such as *page mode interleaved memory*, *parameter RAM*, and *zero wait states*. Personal computer users are faced with seemingly unanswerable questions every day—Do you want your new '386 to use cache memory or will a disk cache do? Do you prefer an ST506 hard disk over a SCSI-compatible drive?

The language of personal computing is distinct for reasons other than the arrival of complicated new hardware. Today's user also must learn terms derived from new applications of computing technology, such as desktop publishing and presentation graphics.

To use a page layout program effectively, for example, you should understand at least some of the terms of professional typesetting, such as the difference between *points* and *picas*. To use a presentation graphics package, you should understand the difference between the *categories axis* and the *values axis*. In both cases, understanding these distinctions is all but essential to the productive and intelligent use of these programs.

Terms like these often are not defined in other computer dictionaries, which have two aims. First, other computer dictionaries include any and all computer terms, even if they derive from academic computer science and mainframe computing. Second, these dictionaries exclude terms not intrinsically computer-related, even if some of these terms (such as *pica* or *values axis*) are germane to computer applications. These aims stem from the academic purpose of such dictionaries; they strive to define the scope of computer science by a comprehensive survey of its distinctive language.

Que's Computer User's Dictionary is different; the purpose of this book is practical, and the focus is personal computing. Any and all terms relevant to Macintosh and IBM personal computing are included, even if some of these terms are not intrinsically computer-related. Mainframe data processing or academic computer science terms that personal computer users are not likely to encounter are excluded. This dictionary is a *user's* dictionary.

The emphasis on practicality leads to another unique feature of this dictionary: the many tips and cautions. What is the point of learning what ASCII sort order means, unless you are warned that this sort order violates standard publication guidelines and that you may have to move some sorted items if you let the computer sort text for you? This dictionary's aims are practical. The information contained should be of practical value to you, the user.

I hope that this dictionary helps you not only to understand this new language but, even more, to apply the terms you learn more productively and effectively. Every word of this book was written with this intention.

Introduction

From the user's point of view, the language of computing is a language of user appropriation—a language about those aspects of computing technology that the user can obtain, apply, and modify. The social and economic significance of personal computing lies in precisely this fact; ordinary people have appropriated the technology that, just twenty years ago, was the exclusive possession of large organizations and highly trained data processing professionals.

Appropriating a technology, however, brings with it the task of appropriating its language. You don't fly an airplane, for example, without having at least some grasp of terms such as "pitch," "yaw," and "stall."

The language of user computing is, for example, necessarily a language of adapters and expansion busses. If personal computers were closed devices, which prevented the user from adding plug-in adapters, the language wouldn't involve terms such as AT bus and Extended Industry Standard Architecture (EISA). But computers are open devices, which is one of the keys to marketing a successful personal computer, as every firm in the industry has discovered.

In the same league technically are such hardware matters as memory and microprocessors. Like it or not, you need to understand the differences between 16-bit and 32-bit computers, between Intel 80286 and 80386 microprocessors, and between the real mode and the protected mode.

With the profusion of systems and system vendors, you must have a working knowledge of available systems to make intelligent choices. Other technical questions include the selection of display adapters, monitors, and printers, and the ports and interfaces by which these peripheral devices are connected. Do you want a digital monitor—or will an analog monitor do, or could it even be better for some purposes? What about keyboards, mice, and other input devices? Unlike the characters on Star Trek, we cannot simply talk to these machines and have them do complex tasks. To make meaningful comparisons among devices, you also must know the language of measurements in computing. For a given device, you apply the yardsticks of hertz (Hz) or megahertz (MHz), of bytes or megabytes (M), of characters per inch (cpi) or dots per inch (dpi).

The day-to-day business of managing the computer brings with it another large body of terms. These terms include the language of disks, disk drives, and secondary storage devices just as another set of terms exists for files and file formats and another for operating systems and utilities. The trend toward user-friendliness is well established; however, and one cannot ignore the new language of user interfaces and windowing environments. Marching to a different drummer, Macintosh people have developed their own, unique terminology for many of these matters.

All the technical minutiae aside, the language of user computing is supremely a language of applications. Most users have jobs to do—professional, technical, managerial, and executive jobs. For these users, what matters most is the language of the "Big Three" applications: database management, spreadsheets, and word processing. Most users are using, or planning to use, graphics and desktop publishing applications, which means that they eventually must learn the language of fonts and typography.

The capability of sharing information with others via linked computers also introduces another set of terms. Gone are the days when personal computers were exclusively stand-alone devices, insulated from the rest of the computing world. Today's personal computers are linked via communications to other computers worldwide, and in growing numbers of organizations, local area networks are linking personal computers to each other and even with large corporate mainframes.

The language of user computing isn't simply a language of off-the-shelf devices and ready-to-run software packages. Computers are programmable, and well over half of the subscribers to a popular personal computing magazine revealed that they occasionally or frequently program their machines. The language of programming and of programming languages represents the final stage of user appropriation, in which users truly make the technology their own.

This dictionary surveys the language of computing from the user's point of view. Its principle of inclusion is simple: if the term is relevant to the user, it belongs in the dictionary. If the term is relevant to academic computer science, data processing, scientific computing, or corporate mainframe computing but is not relevant to users, it does not belong in this dictionary. (Other dictionaries cover such terms but do not do a comprehensive job of covering the language of user computing).

Users have not merely appropriated and modified computer technology but also have appropriated and modified its language. In the language of user computing, more than a few mainframe and data processing terms have taken on a new gloss. For personal computer users, the term operating system means something very different than it does to the technicians who run mainframes. For users, an operating system is a way of maintaining and customizing a system in an orderly way that suits the applications they run. For mainframe people, an operating system is a way of running other people's work through the computer with the optimum allocation of system resources. A dictionary that is not sensitive to the distinctive semantics of user computing wouldn't be of much use to users.

Any attempt to define the language of user computing is akin to trying to change a tire on a moving truck. Hardly a week goes by without the introduction, replete with talk of "revolution," of some new computer system based on a new microprocessor, or a self-described "path-breaking" new program that will turn the entire industry on its ear. No doubt you will find the names of some chips, computers, and programs are missing from this dictionary. This dictionary is necessarily an artifact of its history, and I have not attempted to include most of today's software packages and systems; I have tried to include only the best sellers or programs that are innovative or important in some way.

The concepts of user computing change more slowly than the changing faces of systems and software packages. One of the most widely hyped "new" applications, hypertext, was envisioned more than twenty years ago. Even if this dictionary doesn't list your favorite new application or the snazziest new microprocessor, you will find that the underlying concepts are surprisingly stable, and this dictionary should prove of lasting value to you.

Using This Dictionary To Learn Computer Concepts

If you are new to personal computing, you can use this dictionary as a way to learn the fundamental concepts of user computing. Disregarding specific brands and products, the following is a quick overview of some of the more important conceptual entries, broken down by subject category:

- **Adapters and busses**—adapter, address bus, bus, expanded memory, expansion slot, Extended Industry Standard Architecture (EISA), Micro Channel Bus, network interface card, open architecture, open bus system, and video adapter
- **Applications**—communications program, database management, database management program, desktop publishing (DTP), draw program, paint program, presentation graphics, spreadsheet program, and word processing program
- **Artificial intelligence and expert systems**—expert system, knowledge base, and knowledge representation
- **Communications**—asynchronous communication, communications program, electronic mail, modem, and terminal emulation.
- **Database management**—data field, data independence, data integrity, data manipulation, data record, database, database design, database management, database management program, database management system (DBMS), database structure, relational database management, relational database management program, record-oriented database management program, and table-oriented database management program

- **Desktop publishing**—page description language (PDL), page layout program, and PostScript
- **Disks, disk drives, and secondary storage**—CD-ROM, disk drive, floppy disk, hard disk, optical disk, and secondary storage
- **Display adapters and monitors**—analog monitor, Color Graphics Adapter (CGA), color monitor, digital monitor, Enhanced Graphics Adapter (EGA), Hercules Graphics Adapter, monitor, monochrome display adapter (MDA), monochrome monitor, and Video Graphics Array (VGA)
- **Files and file formats**—binary file, file, file format, file name, graphics file format, and text file
- **Fonts and typography**—bit-mapped font, body type, display type, font, font family, outline font, printer font, screen font, and typeface
- **Graphics**—analytical graphics, animation, bit-mapped graphic, draw program, multimedia, paint program, and presentation graphics program
- **Keyboards, mice, and other input devices**—character, cursor-movement keys, extended character set, input, keyboard, keyboard layout, mouse, and trackball
- **Macintosh**—desktop, Finder, graphical user interface (GUI), icon, and System
- **Measurements**— access time, benchmark, dots per inch (dpi), kilobyte, megabyte, megahertz (MHz), pica, point, response time, and transfer rate.
- **Memory**—base memory, bit, byte, cache memory, dynamic random-access memory (DRAM), expanded memory, extended memory, firmware, memory, primary storage, random access, random-access memory (RAM), read-only memory (ROM), secondary storage, sequential access, storage, virtual memory, and word
- **Microprocessors**—8-bit computer, 16-bit computer, 32-bit computer, central processing unit (CPU), chip, digital, digital computer, instruction cycle, instruction set, integrated circuit, microprocessor, numeric coprocessor, protected mode, real mode, and wait state
- **Networks**—baseband, broadband, bus network, connectivity, connectivity platform, contention, distributed processing system, electronic mail, file

server, local area network (LAN), multiplexing, network architecture, network interface card, network operating system, peer-to-peer network, platform independence, ring network, star network, token-ring network, workgroup, and workstation

- **Operating systems and utilities**—argument, argument separator, background, backup, backup utility, basic input-output system (BIOS), batch file, boot, cold boot, command processor, command-line operating system, context switching, crash, current directory, current drive, delimiter, extension, file name, graphical user interface (GUI), hard disk backup program, interactive processing, load, multitasking, system disk, system file, system prompt, system software, tree structure, warm boot, and wild card

- **Ports and interfaces**—interface, parallel port, port, RS-232, and serial port

- **Printers**—built-in font, cartridge, continuous paper, daisywheel printer, dot-matrix printer, downloadable font, friction feed, imagesetter, laser printer, letter-quality printer, nonimpact printer, page description language (PDL), parallel printer, plotter, PostScript, PostScript laser printer, print engine, printer driver, printer font, resolution, serial printer, thermal printer, toner, and tractor feed.

- **Programming**—algorithm, assembly language, branch control structure, case branch, control structure, conventional programming, debugging, DO/WHILE loop, extensible, FOR/NEXT loop, high-level programming language, IF/THEN/ELSE, instruction, interpreter, loop, loop control structure, low-level programming language, machine language, macro, modular programming, nested structure, object code, object-oriented programming language, procedural language, program, sequence control structure, software command language, source code, structured programming, subroutine, and variable

- **Programming languages**—BASIC, C, Pascal, SmallTalk, bundled software, character-based program, command-driven, copy protection, default setting, documentation, freeware, graphics-based program, groupware, integrated program, menu-driven, public domain software, run-time version, shareware, software, and vaporware

- **Spreadsheets**—absolute cell reference, active cell, automatic recalculation, built-in function, cell, cell address, cell pointer, cell protection, constant, edit mode, entry line, forecasting, formula, key variable, label, macro, model, range, range expression, range name, recalculation method, relative cell reference, spreadsheet program, value, what-if analysis, worksheet, and worksheet window

- **Systems and system vendors**—clone, closed bus system, compatibility, desktop computer, hardware, hardware platform, high end, home computer, laptop computer, low end, mainframe, microcomputer, minicomputer, multiuser system, open architecture, open bus system, personal computer, portable computer, and professional workstation

- **User interface and windowing systems**—application program interface, graphical user interface (GUI), mouse, pull-down menu, scroll bar/scroll box, user interface, window, windowing environment

- **Word processing**—attribute, base font, block, block move, boilerplate, document base font, document format, embedded formatting command, emphasis, forced page break, format, hanging indent, hard space, hidden codes, indentation, initial base font, insert mode, justification, leading, mail merge, off-screen formatting, on-screen formatting, Overtype mode, proportional spacing, scroll, selection, soft carriage return, soft page break, style sheet, what-you-see-is-what-you-get (WYSIWYG), word processing, word processing program, and word wrap

1-2-3   See *Lotus 1-2-3.*

3-D spreadsheet program   See *three-dimensional spread-sheet.*

3 1/2-inch disk   A floppy disk originally developed by Sony Corporation and used as a secondary storage medium for personal computers. The magnetic disk is enclosed in a hard plastic case.

Introduced to personal computing by the Apple Macintosh computer and later used in IBM's Personal System/2 machines, 3 1/2-inch disks represent a significant improvement over 5 1/4 floppies, which are susceptible to fingerprint damage because of the open access hole. 3 1/2-inch disks, unlike their larger predecessors, cover the access holes with an aluminum gate, which is opened by the disk drive only after the disk is inserted. 3 1/2-inch disks also are easier to write-protect; instead of covering up a notch hole with a piece of tape, you move a little plastic lever in the back of the disk.

Under DOS, 3 1/2-inch disk drives offer storage capacities of 720K (double density) or 1.44M (high density). DOS Version 3.2 began supporting the 720K disks, and DOS Version 3.3 began supporting the 1.44M disks. Macintosh computers format 3 1/2 disks with a storage capacity of 800K (double density) or 1.4M (high density).

▲ **Caution:** If your IBM PC-compatible computer has 3 1/2-inch disk drives, specify 3 1/2-inch disks when purchasing software. Ordinarily, software publishers distribute their products on 5 1/4-inch disks, but 3 1/2-inch disks often are made available—if you ask for them. In some cases, the only way you can get 3 1/2-inch disks from a software publisher is to send in a coupon, but some companies are faster than others in sending the 3 1/2-inch disks to you. Because computers with 3 1/2-inch drives prohibit you from exchanging data with colleagues who have 5 1/4-inch drives, many computers are sold with a 5 1/4-inch drive and a 3 1/2-inch drive. Organizations find that having such a computer around the office is convenient.

4th Dimension A relational database program developed by Acius, Inc., for Macintosh computers.

A sophisticated product with networking capabilities, 4th Dimension is of special interest to organizations with large mainframe databases. A special version of Oracle, a connectivity platform, enables 4th Dimension to search Oracle, DB2, and SQL databases. See *connectivity platform* and *ORACLE.*

5 1/4-inch disk A floppy disk enclosed in a flexible plastic envelope and used as a secondary storage medium for personal computers.

The most widely used secondary storage technology   medium in personal computing, 5 1/4-inch disks are inexpensive and used as a distribution medium for commercial software.

▲ **Caution:** The open access hole of 5 1/4-inch disks is an invitation for fingerprints, which can make the disk unreadable. Handle 5 1/4-inch disks with caution, and when they are not in use, store them in the protective envelope.

8-bit computer A computer that uses a central processing unit (CPU) with an 8-bit data bus and processes one byte (eight bits) of information at a time.

8-bit computers represent the minimal configuration of computing equipment; in binary numbers, eight bits represent all letters of the alphabet and the numbers 0 through 9. The first microprocessors used in personal computers, such as the MOS Technology 6502, Intel 8080, and Zilog Z-80, found their way into 8-bit computers such as the Apple II, the MSAI 8080, and the Commodore 64.

Millions of these computers are still in use for educational and home-computing applications, but the best business and professional software is available for 16-bit and 32-bit personal computers such as the IBM Personal Computer and the Apple Macintosh. See *bus, central processing unit (CPU), CP/M,,* and *microprocessor.*

16-bit computer A computer that uses a central processing unit (CPU) with a 16-bit data bus and processes two bytes (16 bits) of information at a time.

▲ **Caution:** Many computers, such as the original IBM Personal Computer and IBM Personal Computer XT and compatibles, which are billed as 16-bit computers, do not use a true 16-bit structure. These machines use the Intel 8088.

The 8088 can process two bytes at a time internally, but the external data bus is only eight bits wide. IBM chose to use the Intel 8088 to take advantage of the many inexpensive, off-the-shelf peripherals developed for 8-bit computers. The IBM Personal Computer AT, introduced in 1984, used a microprocessor with a true 16-bit structure; the data bus that extends beyond the microprocessor also is 16 bits wide. See *Intel 8088*, *Intel 8086*, and *Intel 80286*.

32-bit computer   A computer that uses a central processing unit (CPU) with a 32-bit data bus and processes four bytes (32 bits) of information at a time.

▲ **Caution:** Personal computers advertised as 32-bit machines, such as the Macintosh Plus, the Macintosh SE, and IBM PC compatibles based on the 80386SX microprocessor, are not true 32-bit computers. These computers use microprocessors (such as the Motorola 68000 and Intel 80386SX) that can process four bytes at a time internally, but the external data bus is only 16 bits wide.

The designers of these machines chose the external 16-bit data bus so that they could take advantage of inexpensive, off-the-shelf peripherals developed for 16-bit computers. True 32-bit machines use a true 32-bit data bus and 32-bit peripherals and cost substantially more than computers that do not extend the 32-bit structure beyond the bounds of the microprocessor. See *Intel 80386SX*, *Intel 80386*, *Intel 80486*, *Motorola 68000*, *Motorola 68020*, and *Motorola 68030*.

286   See *Intel 80286*.

386   See *Intel 80386*.

386SX   See *Intel 80386SX*.

486   See *Intel 80486*.

8086   See *Intel 8086*.

8088   See *Intel 8088*.

68000   See *Motorola 68000*.

68020   See *Motorola 68020*.

68030   See *Motorola 68030*.

a

A Programming Language   See *APL*.

abandon   To clear a document, spreadsheet, or other work from the computer's memory without saving it to disk. The work is irretrievably lost.

abort   To cancel, or terminate, a program, command, or procedure while in progress.

Abs key   In Lotus 1-2-3, the F4 function key that cycles a cell reference through the four possible combinations: absolute cell reference (A1), mixed cell references ($A1 and A$1), and relative cell reference (A1).

absolute cell reference   A spreadsheet cell reference that does not adjust when you copy a formula. Use an absolute cell reference to keep the reference the same when being copied.

   For example, the following Lotus 1-2-3 formula contains a relative cell reference (B12) and an absolute cell reference (A6). The formula tells 1-2-3 to multiply B12 by the contents of cell A6 and place the result in the current cell:

        +B12*A6

   When you copy this formula to the next row down and the next column right, 1-2-3 changes the formula to +C13*A6. The relative cell reference is adjusted, but the absolute cell reference stays the same.

➔ **Tip:** Use absolute cell references to establish a single cell location for key variables for your worksheet. A key variable is a constant, such as a tax rate. See *key variable, low-level format,* and *relative cell reference.*

absolute value   The magnitude of a number, regardless of its algebraic sign (positive or negative), equal to the positive value of a number. The absolute value of -357, for example, is 357. In Lotus 1-2-3 and similar spreadsheet programs, the @ABS built-in function returns the absolute value of a number.

accelerator board   An adapter containing a microprocessor faster or more advanced than the one that powers your computer. If you have a Macintosh based on the Motorola 68000 chip, for example, you can purchase an accelerator board containing the faster 68030 chip. If you have an IBM PC-compatible computer based on the Intel 8088 microprocessor, you can purchase an accelerator board containing the faster 80286 or 80386 microprocessor.

▲ **Caution:** Adding an accelerator board can speed a sluggish computer, but the speed gains are most apparent for tasks carried out within the microprocessor, such as sorting or calculating. An accelerator board does little to improve the speed of disk-related operations, such as retrieving a file. If you frequently use a program (such as a database program) that makes heavy use of the disk drive, a faster hard disk probably leads to a more noticeable speed improvement than an accelerator board. If you are using an IBM PC-compatible computer based on the Intel 8088 chip, you cannot use the faster drives designed for the 16-bit data bus of the AT-class computers. Therefore, 8088 users are advised to forget accelerator boards—save your money for an 80286- or 80386-based computer. See *bus* and *hard disk.*

accent   A mark that forms one of the accented characters of many languages other than English. The following accents are used frequently:

´ Acute	˘ Breve	ç Cedilla
∧ Circumflex	¨ Diaeresis	` Grave
¯ Macron	˜ Tilde	¨ Umlaut

You enter accents in two ways. First, you can use a dead key that enters the accent character without advancing the cursor to the next character. You then press the letter, character, and the two keystrokes form the accented character. Second, you can use a key code to enter the character and the accent at the same time. On a Macintosh computer you can use both techniques. To enter the vowel e with an acute accent, you press Option-e (a dead key that enters an acute accent character) and then press e, and the accented character (é) appears.

▲ **Caution:** If you plan to work in foreign languages on an IBM PC-compatible computer, make sure that your printer can print the entire 254 extended character set that includes many accented characters. Not all compatibles can print the extended characters.

access To retrieve data or program instructions from a secondary storage device or some other on-line computer device.

To the dismay of English teachers everywhere, the noun access is now used as a verb, as in "I cannot access that file." English usage authorities usually disparage the conversion of nouns into verbs, but this usage is sufficiently common to be included in a dictionary such as this one.

access arm In a disk drive, the mechanical device that moves the magnetic read/write heads back and forth across the surface of the disk.

Without an access arm, the disk drive would act like a record player's arm as it moves sequentially along the grooves of an LP record and would take a long time to reach information stored away from the head's current location. See *random access* and *sequential access.*

access code An identification number or password used to gain access to a computer system.

access hole An opening in a floppy disk's case. The access hole permits the disk drive's read/write head to make contact with the surface of the disk. Only when this contact occurs can you perform read/write operations, in which the computer retrieves information from or stores new information on the disk.

access mechanism   In a disk drive, the mechanism used for moving the read/write head over the surface of the disk so that data may be accessed. Synonymous with *actuator*. See *disk drive* and *read/write head*.

Access System menu   In Lotus 1-2-3, the menu that appears when you type **lotus** at the DOS prompt. This menu enables you to start Lotus 1-2-3, install the program, or choose the Translate option (see fig. A.1).

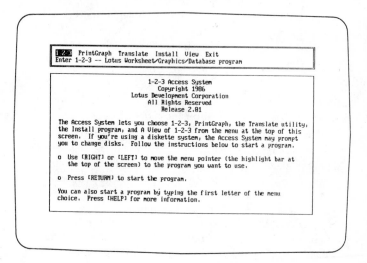

Fig. A.1. The Access System menu of Lotus 1-2-3.

→ Tip: You can bypass the Access menu by typing 123 at the DOS prompt.

access time   The time that elapses between the time the operating system issues an order for data retrieval and the time the data is ready for transfer from the disk.

Typical access times for personal computer hard disks range between 9 ms (fast) and 100 ms (slow). For disk-intensive applications like database management programs or book-length word processing projects, the difference between a fast and a slow disk drive is noticeable to the user.

The access time of a disk drive is determined by the following: seek time (the time the disk heads take to move to the correct track), settle time (the time the heads take to settle down after reaching the correct track), and latency (the time required for the correct sector to swing around under the head).

For hard disks, access times usually are measured in microseconds (ms).

▲ **Caution:** If you are using an IBM PC-compatible computer based on an 80286, 80386, or 80486 microprocessor, make sure that the hard disk's access time is 28 ms or better. When you run these computers under DOS, much of the speed improvement over earlier 8088-based machines is attributable to the faster hard disk. See *hard disk* and *operating system.*

accounting package   A set of personal computer programs intended to help a small-business owner automate a firm's accounting functions.

Accounting packages do not comprise a large share of the total market for personal computer software for a couple of reasons. First, most small-business owners have none of the accounting knowledge required to use most available programs and prefer to leave the accounting to a professional. Second, using these programs without a point-of-sale system that automatically posts receipts to the ledgers is pointless. You have to type all the figures at the end of the day.

Despite these drawbacks, you may have good reasons to use a simple accounting program. Even if you don't perform all accounting functions yourself, your accountant needs to see a ledger showing all your business transactions. If some of these transactions can be posted automatically to a computer ledger from PCs that handle sales invoices and other transactions, you have simplified your life immensely. See *integrated accounting package* and *modular accounting package.*

accumulator   A temporary storage location in a central processing unit (CPU). The accumulator holds intermediary values during a computation or stores input/output information.

Many processing operations require an accumulator. Computer multiplication, for example, frequently is done by a series of additions; the accumulator holds the intermediate values until the process is completed. See *central processing unit (CPU)*.

accuracy   The exactness of a measurement, unlike precision (the number of decimal places to which the accuracy is computed).

acoustic coupler   A modem with cups that fit around the earpiece and mouthpiece of a standard telephone headset. The cups contain a microphone and a speaker that convert the computer's digital signals into sound and vice versa. With the increasing use of modular telephone connections, direct-connect modems have supplanted acoustic modems in general use. See *direct-connect modem* and *modem*.

acoustical sound enclosure   A sound insulation cabinet designed to accommodate noisy impact printers and reduce the noise such printers release into the environment. See *impact printer*.

acronym   A word formed by joining the first letters (sometimes other letters) of a series of words such as BASIC (Beginners' All-purpose Symbolic Instruction Code) and WYSIWYG (what-you-see-is-what-you-get).

active area   In a Lotus 1-2-3 worksheet, the area bounded by cell A1 and the lowest rightmost cell containing data.

active cell   In a spreadsheet, the cell in which the cursor currently is positioned. Synonymous with *current cell*.

active database   In database management, the database file that currently is in use and present in random-access memory (RAM).

active file   The worksheet currently in memory when working with Lotus 1-2-3 and other spreadsheet programs.

▲ **Caution:** Versions of Lotus 1-2-3 prior to Release 2.2 do not warn you when you attempt to leave the active file without saving your work. When you load a worksheet from disk into memory, Lotus 1-2-3 does not update the disk file until you issue the /File Save command. If you quit 1-2-3 without saving your work, the file on disk remains unchanged.

In some cases, leaving the file unchanged is desirable. For example, many users like to perform what-if analyses, which involves entering hypothetical values as the key variables of the worksheet. You don't want to save these changes, because the data is imaginary. Early versions of Lotus and other spreadsheet programs left the decision of whether to save a session's changes to the user. Most users, however, want to be reminded when they are about to lose changes. Versions of Lotus since Release 2.2, therefore, detect changes and warn the user if they are about to be lost at the end of a session. See *what-if analysis.*

active index   In database management programs, the index file currently being used to determine the order in which data records are displayed on-screen. See *index.*

active window   In an application program or operating system that displays multiple windows, the window in which the cursor is positioned and text appears when you type.

Early windowing environments tiled the windows so that none overlapped, but too often the windows were too small for convenient use. In more recent windowing applications, the active window floats above the others (see fig. A.2). See *windowing environment.*

activity light   A small red or yellow light on the computer's front panel that signals when a disk drive is reading or writing data.

actuator   See *access mechanism.*

Ada   A high-level programming language developed by the U.S. Department of Defense and required for all military programming applications.

Named for Lady Augusta Ada Byron, a friend of Charles Babbage and arguably the world's first female computer scientist, the Ada language stems from the military's need for a

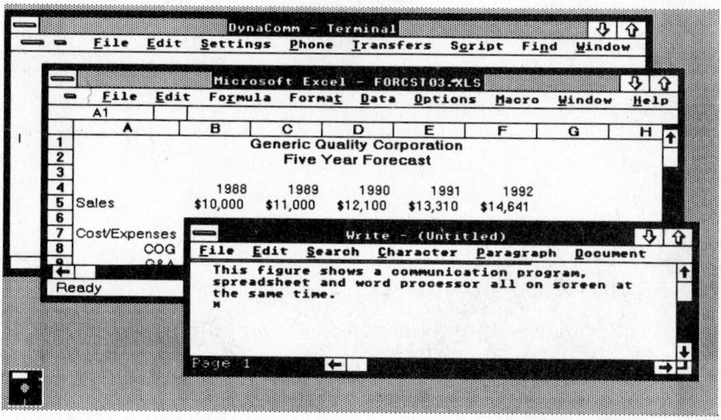

Fig. A.2. An active window superimposed on other windows.

standard computer language capable of real-time process control (the operation of a highly complex device like a missile). In the early 1970s, more than 400 languages were being used to develop systems acquired by the military, and the expense of maintaining so many incompatible systems was mounting. A committee was appointed to create a new standard language, and the final specification was published in 1980.

With roots in Pascal and Modula-2, Ada uses the principles of structured programming, such as program modules that can be compiled separately (like those of Modula-2). Ada programs are designed to be highly readable so that they are easier to maintain.

Ada has attracted a great deal of criticism from computer scientists who believe that no single programming language can succeed at all tasks. Ada is a highly structured language for general-purpose programming and a specialized language for real-time process control. As a result, Ada is an extremely large language; the compiler requires several hundreds of thousands of code lines. To critics, Ada's unmanageable size is an invitation to disaster because large programs are likely to contain errors that cannot be detected. However, the language's success is ensured. The U.S. Department of Defense requires contractors to use Ada or demonstrate why the language cannot be used.

▲ **Caution:** Ada is now available for personal computers, but if you decide to learn the language, make sure that you choose a compiler that has been certified by the Department of Defense. This agency rigidly controls the Ada standard and accepts no code that has not been created by a compiler that meets the department's standards. See *compiler, Modula-2, Pascal*, and *structured programming.*

adapter   A circuit board that plugs into a computer's expansion bus and gives the computer additional capabilities.

Popular adapters for personal computers include display adapters, that produce video output; memory expansion adapters; input-output adapters that provide the computer with serial ports, parallel ports, and game ports; internal modems, and clock/calendar boards. Increasingly, this circuitry is being included on the motherboard of personal computer systems. The motherboard of IBM's PS/2 computer, for example, includes ports and a VGA display adapter for high-resolution video output. See *circuit board, clock/calendar board, display adapter, expansion bus, internal modem, motherboard, open bus system, parallel port*, and *serial port.*

ADB   See *Apple Desktop Bus*

add-in program   An accessory or utility program designed to work with an application program and extend its capabilities.

A popular add-in program for Lotus 1-2-3 is Allways (Funk Software) that adds desktop publishing features to 1-2-3's report capabilities. Allways prints Lotus spreadsheets with a variety of fonts, lines, shadings, and other formatting features, such as boldface and underline. See *Allways* and *Oracle.*

address   A computer system location identified by a name, number, or code label. The address can be specified by the user or by a program. See *memory address.*

address bus   An internal electronic channel from the microprocessor to random-access memory (RAM), along which the
addresses of memory storage locations are transmitted.

The address bus is necessary so that the microprocessor
can locate program instructions and data stored in memory.
Like a post office box, each memory location has a distinct
number or address; the address bus provides the means by
which every location in the memory can be activated independently.

→ **Tip:** The width of the address bus determines the maximum size of the computer's main memory because the number of wires in the address bus determines the maximum
number of possible memory locations. Computers use binary
numbers internally, and because address information is sent
along the address bus in parallel (one number per lane of the
freeway), the address bus needs many wires to handle a big
binary number. Early IBM personal computers used address
buses 20 bits wide (20 wires); these computers could identify
and use a maximum of 2^{20} memory locations (1M of RAM).
With an address bus width of 24 bits, more recent IBM PC-
compatible computers can address a maximum of 16M of
RAM. However, the standard operating system of IBM PC-
compatible computers, DOS, may not be able to use more
than 640K of RAM. See *expanded memory, extended
memory, OS/2,* and *Windows.*

ADM3A   A terminal developed by Lear Siegler and used in the
late 1970s and early 1980s. The ADM3A is included in the list
of terminals that communication programs can emulate. See
communications program, terminal, and *terminal emulation.*

Adobe Illustrator   Pronounced "uh-doe´-bee." A professional
illustration program for Macintosh and IBM PC-compatible
computers. Adobe Illustrator produces object-oriented images and prints them on PostScript laser printers.

Introduced in 1987, this highly regarded program went
several steps beyond existing painting and drawing programs, such as MacPaint and MacDraw, by offering Post-
Script output, Bézier curves, an autotrace tool, precision cod-

ing for color printing, and many other features for professional illustration. See *autotrace*, *Bézier curves*, *Freehand*,
object-oriented graphic, and *PostScript*.

Adobe Type Manager (ATM)   Pronounced "uh-doe´-bee." For
Macintosh computers, a utility program that displays outline
fonts without distortion.

Normally, the Macintosh uses bit-mapped fonts for the
screen display. For desktop publishing applications, however, this display technique has drawbacks. If you try to
display a font in a size not matched by a complete set of bit-
mapped characters in the System Folder, you see grossly
distorted characters on-screen. Adobe Type Manager tackles
this problem by using outline font technology to display
fonts. Because outline fonts are constructed from mathematical formulas, they can be scaled to any size without
distortion.

▲ **Caution:** Adobe Type Manager has its drawbacks. The
program affects the appearance of Adobe fonts only. Even
Adobe fonts are not affected unless you have in the System
Folder a special screen display file for each font you want to
display. The program comes with Times Roman and Helvetica; the user must purchase an expensive add-in program to
obtain screen fonts for the rest of the typefaces normally included with PostScript laser printers.

aftermarket   The market for software and peripherals created
by the sale of large numbers of a specific brand of computer.

agate   Pronounced "ag´-it." A 5.5-point type size frequently
used in newspaper classified advertising but too small for
most other uses.

aggregate function   In database management programs, a
command that performs arithmetic operations on all of a
field's values in all the records within a database or in one
view of the database. For example, dBASE performs the following aggregate functions:

Average	Computes the arithmetic mean of the values
Sum	Adds all the values
Minimum	Finds the smallest value

Maximum	Finds the largest value
Count	Counts the number of records that meet the specified criteria

aggregate operator   In a database management program, a command that instructs the program to perform an aggregate function.

Suppose that you are the owner of a video tape rental store and you want to know how many tapes are more than two weeks late. Because the date is May 19, you want to know how many rentals were due on May 5 or earlier (less than 05/06/90). The following dBASE expression finds the information:

```
COUNT FOR due_date <05/06/90
```

You will see a response such as

```
2 records
```

See *aggregate function.*

AI   See *artificial intelligence.*

AIX   An IBM version of the UNIX operating system. AIX runs on PS/2 computers equipped with the Intel 80386 micropro-cessor, IBM workstations, minicomputers, and mainframes.

Aldus PageMaker   See *PageMaker.*

alert box   In a graphical user interface, a cautionary window that appears on-screen warning you that the command you have given may result in lost work or other errors (see fig. A.3).

algorithm   A specific set of well-defined, simple mathematical and logical procedures that can be followed to solve a prob-lem in a finite number of steps.

An algorithm is a recipe for finding the right answer to a difficult problem by breaking the problem down into simple, easy steps. You already have learned many algorithms—for example, the ones you learned for grade-school arithmetic. You use algorithms every day in recipes, when mowing the lawn, placing a long-distance telephone call, and packing a grocery bag.

algorithm 16

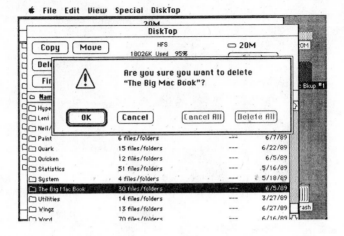

Fig. A.3. An alert box.

Not every list of instructions constitutes an algorithm, however. An algorithm must satisfy the following three basic criteria:

- The list of instructions must be finite and short enough that they can be carried out.

- Each instruction must be executable; you must be able to perform the actions or operations named.

- The algorithm must enable execution to end at some point.

The British logician Alan Turing proved that any mathematical or logical problem capable of a solution, and for which a solution is known to exist, can be solved by the algorithmic approach. Every known solvable problem can be attacked by a computer; the solution is a matter of finding the correct algorithm.

The computer programs you use every day embody one or more algorithms. Someone, somewhere, had to sit down and puzzle through the problem of how to get that font to appear on-screen and print with typographical beauty on your laser printer. At one time, the problem was unsolved, and many people thought that it never would be solved. A good deal of thought and work went into expressing the procedure as a computer-readable algorithm.

alias   A secondary or symbolic name for a file or computer device. In a spreadsheet, for example, a range name such as Income is an alias for a range such as A3...K3.

aliasing   In computer graphics, the undesirable jagged or stair-stepped appearance of diagonal lines in computer-generated graphic images. Synonymous with the *jaggies*. See *antialiasing*.

alignment   1. The adjustment of tolerances within a disk drive's mechanism so that read/write operations occur without error. 2. In word processing, the horizontal arrangement of lines on the page with respect to the left and right margins (flush left, centered, flush right, or justified).

   ▲ **Caution:** Because a jolt can knock a disk drive out of alignment, be careful not to drop or knock your computer around when moving the machine. A drive slightly out of alignment may have trouble reading disks, especially those formatted by a different computer. If your machine cannot read an important disk, don't assume that the disk is bad—possibly another computer can read the disk.

all points addressable (APA) graphics   See *bit-mapped graphic*.

Allways   A Lotus 1-2-3 add-in program that adds desktop publishing capabilities to the popular spreadsheet program's report functions.

alpha test   The first stage in the testing of computer software before commercial release. Alpha tests usually are conducted within a company. See *beta test*.

alphanumeric characters   Any character you can type, including upper- and lowercase letters A through Z, numbers 0 through 9, punctuation marks, and special keyboard symbols. See *data type*.

Alt key   On IBM PC-compatible keyboards, a key that programs frequently use in combination with other keys to generate commands. In Microsoft Word, for example, Alt-B boldfaces the selected text.

ALU See *arithmetic/logic unit (ALU)*.

American National Standards Institute (ANSI) Pronounced "ann´-see." An organization devoted to the development of voluntary standards that will enhance the productivity and international competitiveness of American industrial enterprises. ANSI committees have developed standard versions of computer languages such as COBOL and FORTRAN.

American Standard Code for Information Interchange (ASCII) Pronounced "ass´-kee." A standard computer character set devised in 1968 to enable efficient data communication and achieve compatibility among different computer devices.

The standard ASCII code consists of 96 displayed upper- and lowercase letters, plus 32 non-displayed control characters. An individual character code is composed of seven bits plus one parity bit for error checking. The code permits the expression of English-language textual data but is inadequate for many foreign languages and technical applications. Because ASCII code includes no graphics characters, most modern computers use an extended character set containing needed characters. See *extended character set*.

Amiga Pronounced "uh-mee´-guh." A personal computer developed by Commodore International and based on the Motorola 68000 microprocessor. The Amiga is used for home computing applications.

With outstanding color graphics and multichannel stereo sound, the Amiga is considered by some to be the computer of choice for playing computer games and composing music. The machine has found little acceptance as a business computer, however, because of the lack of business software for the machine.

The Amiga is not compatible with the Macintosh computer, which uses the same microprocessor but a different operating system. See *Musical Instrument Digital Interface (MIDI)*.

ampersand Pronounced "am´-per-sand." A character (&) sometimes used in place of the English "and;" originally a ligature of "et," the Latin for and.

analog   A form of measurement or representation in which an indicator is varied continuously, often to reflect ongoing changes in the phenomenon being measured or represented.

Analog representation is used, for example, in a thermometer: the hotter the patient, the longer the mercury. Analog techniques also are used for the reproduction of music in standard LP records and audio cassettes. See *digital*.

analog computer   A computer that draws a comparison, or analogy, between the computer representation and the object being represented, making the object easy to measure. Analog computation is used widely in laboratory settings to monitor on-going, continuous changes and record these changes in charts or graphs. See *digital computer*.

analog device   A computer peripheral that handles information in continuously variable quantities rather than digitizing the information into discrete, digital representations.

An analog monitor, for example, can display thousands of colors with smooth, continuous gradations.

analog/digital converter   An adapter that enables a digital computer (such as an IBM Personal Computer) to accept analog input from laboratory instruments. Analog/digital converters are frequently used for the real-time monitoring of temperature, movement, and other continuously varied conditions. See *analog*, *digital*, and *real time*.

analog monitor   A monitor that accepts a continuously varied video input signal and consequently is capable of displaying continuously varied colors. See *digital monitor* and *Video Graphics Array (VGA)*.

analog transmission   A communications scheme that uses a continuous signal varied by amplification. See *broadband* and *digital transmission*.

analogical reasoning   A form of understanding in which the dynamics of a phenomenon are comprehended by studying a model of the phenomenon.

analytical graphics   The preparation of charts and graphs to aid a professional in the interpretation of data.

Many spreadsheet program's graphs fall into this category: they are useful for clarifying trends in worksheet numbers, but you don't want to show them to the company's stockholders. Many presentation graphics packages can accept and enhance graphs created by spreadsheet programs. See *presentation graphics*.

anchor cell   In Lotus 1-2-3, the cell in which the pointer is anchored as you press the cursor-movement keys to define a range.

animation   The creation of the illusion of movement in a computer program by recording a series of images that show slight incremental changes in one of the displayed objects and playing these images back fast enough that the eye perceives smooth movement. See *cell animation* and *MacroMind Director*.

annotation   Synonymous with *remark*.

ANSI   See *American National Standards Institute (ANSI)*.

ANSI screen control   A set of standards developed by the American National Standards Institute (ANSI) to control the display of information on computer screens. See *ANSI.SYS*.

ANSI.SYS   In DOS and OS/2, a configuration file containing instructions needed to display information, following the recommendations of the American National Standards Institute.

➔ **Tip:** Some programs require that you include the instruction `DEVICE = ANSI.SYS` in a CONFIG.SYS file, which must be present on the disk you use to start your computer. See *CONFIG.SYS*.

answer mode   See *auto-dial/auto-answer modem*

answer/originate   In data communications, the property of a communications device so that the device can receive (answer) and send (originate) messages.

antialiasing   The automatic removal or reduction of stair-step distortions in a computer-generated graphic image. See *aliasing*.

antistatic mat   A mat or pad placed on or near a computer device. This pad absorbs static electricity, which can damage semiconductor devices if the devices are not properly grounded.

antivirus program   See *vaccine.*

APA graphics   See *bit-mapped graphic.*

API   See *application program interface (API).*

APL (A Programming Language)   A high-level programming language well suited for scientific and mathematical applications.

APL uses Greek letters and requires a display device that can display these letters. Used on IBM mainframes, the language is now available for IBM PC-compatible computers. See *high-level programming language.*

append   To add data at the end of a file or a database. In database management, for example, to append a record is to add a new record, which is placed after all existing records (preserving the chronological order of data entry).

APPEND   In DOS, an external command that lists the directories DOS should consult when searching for a data file.

After you divide your hard disk into directories, DOS looks for data files only in the current directory; if DOS cannot find the file, you see the message `File not found`. However, the file may be present in another directory on the same disk. With the APPEND command, you tell DOS which directories to consult when the system cannot find a data file in the current directory. In OS/2's protected mode, this command is called DPATH. See *external command*, and *PATH.*

Apple II   A series of 8-bit personal computers developed by Apple Computer. These computers are based on the MOS Technology 6502 microprocessor.

Apple II computers feature built-in sound and graphics and an integer version of the BASIC language encoded on a read-only memory (ROM) chip. Apple IIs are widely used in homes and primary and secondary schools.

Originally released in 1977, the Apple II featured 4K of random-access memory (RAM) and a cassette recorder for secondary storage. Lines of 40 characters were displayed on a television screen.

1979's Apple II+ was designed to work with up to 64K of RAM, an optional floppy disk drive, and floating-point BASIC. In 1983, the Apple IIe increased the amount of RAM to a maximum of 128K. A portable version of the machine, the Apple IIc, was released in 1984.

An open-architecture computer, the Apple II is remarkable for the huge variety of software and peripherals available for the machine. The software pool is especially strong for educational and home applications, although serious business programs are available for Apple IIs.

By 1986, however, it became clear that the Apple II's 8-bit technology could not continue to compete with 16-bit IBM PC-compatible computers. The 1986 release of the Apple IIGS, a 16-bit version of the Apple II, renewed sales, but by 1990, it was clear that the Apple II series was approaching the end of its life as a viable product for the company.

Apple Computer   A major manufacturer of personal computers located in Cupertino, CA.

Founded by Steve Wozniak and Steve Jobs in 1976, Apple Computer grew out of the activities of the San Francisco Bay Area hobbyists to become one of the largest corporations in the United States. Wozniak, a member of the Homebrew Computer Club and a Hewlett-Packard engineer, worked with Jobs to develop the Apple I, a hobbyists' computer that required a good deal of technical expertise to develop into a working computer system.

This machine sold far more successfully than they had hoped, and Wozniak and Jobs developed its successor—the Apple II—one of the first complete, ready-to-run personal computer systems made available to the public. Wozniak chose the MOS Technology 6502, an 8-bit microprocessor for the Apple I and II because this chip was available for significantly less money than the chip most hobbyists preferred, the Intel 8080.

Equipped with sound and color graphics, the Apple II was welcomed not only by home computer hobbyists but also by educators, and the machine soon became the personal computer of choice for elementary and secondary school applications in computer-assisted instruction.

Featuring an open architecture design, the Apple II demonstrated that such a system can increase its own chances of success by encouraging third-party firms to develop adapter boards and peripherals. By 1979, dozens of firms were manufacturing such equipment, which broadened the computer's range of applications. VisiCalc,.the first electronic spreadsheet program, was released for the Apple II, and equipped with this program, thousands of Apple II computers found their way into large and small businesses.

The Apple II's success was followed by what most analysts agree was a major design and manufacturing misstep, the Apple III, released in 1980. The Apple III, which also used the MOS Technology 6502 microprocessor, did not represent a significant technological advance over its predecessor. Worse, the machine was released without proper testing and had serious manufacturing flaws. This machine was not even fully compatible with Apple II software.

Although the manufacturing problems were corrected, the Apple III damaged the company's reputation. Fortunately for the company, Apple II computers continued to sell well in home and educational markets. Apple's failure to develop an innovative computer for business applications, however, created a vacuum in the marketplace, into which IBM stepped with its 1981 Personal Computer, the open architecture design of which is reminiscent of the Apple II. Apple could not respond to the IBM PC's challenge, and in the years to follow, its market share eroded as IBM and IBM PC-compatible computers grew in popularity.

Searching for innovative technology, Jobs learned of the remarkable team of computer scientists and electrical engineers assembled at Xerox's Palo Alto Research Laboratory (PARC). The PARC researchers developed a sophisticated approach to human-computer interaction that include virtually all the components of the graphical user interface: the use of the mouse as an editing and control device, the representation of computer functions using on-screen icons, pull-down menus, dialog boxes, the on-screen display of typefaces and graphics, and the use of laser printers for high-quality personal computer output.

Industry analysts, however, believe that Xerox's management did not fully comprehend the significance of the technology the PARC researchers developed, and the company failed to market the technology effectively. Correctly sensing the promise of PARC technology, Jobs lured away several PARC researchers and assigned them to the development of a new business computer, the Lisa.

Released in 1983, the Lisa was a pioneering personal computer that featured a graphical user interface and a set of integrated application programs. Critically acclaimed, the machine (priced in excess of $10,000) was far too expensive for its market, and sales were disappointing.

In 1984, however, Apple released the Macintosh, which for $2,500 offered a significant fraction of Lisa technology at highly competitive prices. Technically innovative in many respects, the Macintosh soon proved to have significant design defects: the machine was equipped originally with only 128K of random-access memory (RAM) and one 400K disk drive, making the machine unsuitable for business applications. In addition, the Mac used a closed architecture, a significant—and unwise—departure from the open architectural principles that Apple had pioneered (and which had contributed strongly to the success of the IBM Personal Computer).

Subsequently, Jobs recruited John Sculley, formerly the CEO of Pepsi, to head the firm. Internal conflict, partly over the Macintosh and issues regarding the company's direction, resulted in Sculley's expulsion of Jobs from Apple Computer in 1986, and the firm's future seemed uncertain. But help was to come from the unanticipated rise of a new application for computing technology: desktop publishing.

With the release of Aldus PageMaker, the first page layout program for personal computers, and the development of the Apple LaserWriter, Apple's graphical user interface was positioned to place the Macintosh in the forefront of desktop computing. The LaserWriter established the Macintosh as a computer for serious business enterprises.

Subsequent product releases such as the Mac SE with a hard disk, and the open-architecture Macintosh II, renewed Apple's fortunes, although the company failed to regain the market share lost to IBM in the early 1980s.

By 1990, however, Apple's focus on sophisticated, high-end desktop publishing systems contributed to a neglect of low-end systems, and as Apple II sales declined, the company waited too long to develop an inexpensive Macintosh for the home and educational markets. Apple lost sales to inexpensive IBM PC-compatible machines.

In the meantime, more powerful IBM PC-compatible computers arrived. These computers were based on the Intel 80386 and 80486 microprocessors and equipped with high-resolution graphical user interfaces. Industry experts predicted that Apple would soon lose its technological edge in the high end of the marketplace.

Apple's periodic problems and management debacles make for business headlines and best-selling tell-all books, but the company's achievements should not be forgotten. With its motto of developing computers for the rest of us, Apple has played a leading role in bringing computing technology to people who would not otherwise have access to that technology.

The Macintosh user interface, in particular, is one of the great achievements of U.S. industrial design, and this achievement came during a period that has witnessed the steady erosion of American innovativeness and competitiveness in world markets. See *Apple II*, *graphical user interface*, *Macintosh*, and *open architecture*.

Apple Desktop Bus (ADB)   An interface standard for connecting keyboards, mice, trackballs, and other input devices to Apple's Macintosh SE, Macintosh II, and IIGS computers. These computers come with an ADB port capable of a maximum data transfer rate of 4.5 kilobits per second. Up to 16 devices can be connected to one ADB port.

Apple Desktop Interface   A set of user interface guidelines developed by Apple Computer (published by Addison-Wesley) and intended to ensure that all Macintosh applications appear and work in similar ways.

Apple File Exchange   A utility program provided with each Macintosh computer that enables Macs equipped with suitable disk drives to exchange data with IBM PC-compatible computers.

Apple Macintosh   See *Macintosh*.

AppleShare   A network operating system developed by Apple Computer, Inc. AppleShare transforms a Macintosh computer into a file server for an AppleTalk network. The Macintosh used for this purpose cannot be used for other applications; the computer becomes a "slave" of the network. See *AppleTalk, local area network (LAN)*, and *LocalTalk*.

AppleTalk   A local area network standard developed by Apple Computer, Inc. AppleTalk is capable of linking as many as 32 Macintosh computers, IBM PC-compatible computers, and peripherals like laser printers. Every Macintosh computer has an AppleTalk port, through which the machine can be connected to an AppleTalk network using a bus topology. Most AppleTalk networks are simple; they link a few Macintosh computers with a LaserWriter printer.

A significant advantage of AppleTalk is that the network also can accommodate IBM PC-compatible computers; several companies manufacture adapters that provide AppleTalk ports for IBM PC compatible computers. Microsoft Mail, an application developed by Microsoft Corporation, enables electronic mail to be sent among all users of an AppleTalk network, including users of IBM PC-compatibles.

Another advantage of AppleTalk is that almost anyone can quickly set up an AppleTalk network. In many offices, AppleTalk networks are used for sharing access to a laser printer.

AppleTalk also is priced right. Because every Macintosh includes an AppleTalk network port, the only hardware required for an AppleTalk network is connectors and cable. The physical connections among the computers and peripherals are made by Apple's LocalTalk hardware. Each device has a LocalTalk connector, a small box containing a transformer that insulates the computer or peripheral from electrical interference and provides plugs for the network interface.

The LocalTalk boxes are connected by ordinary telephone wire (called twisted-pair cable) with standard modular connectors.

AppleTalk networks are slow compared to high-speed systems like EtherNet. AppleTalk is capable of transmitting up to 320 bits per second, but EtherNet and other networks using network interface cards that connect directly to the computer's high-speed internal bus are capable of speeds of up to 20M bits per second. However, AppleTalk's simplicity and low cost make it an attractive option for networks of modest size and use.

→ **Tip:** If you are considering an AppleTalk installation, you can save money and extend an AppleTalk network's capabilities by using PhoneNet hardware (Farallon Computing, Inc.). After equipping each node with a PhoneNet connector (instead of the LocalTalk connector), you can wire the network using ordinary telephone cabling, considerably cheaper than LocalTalk cable. In some circumstances, you can use existing telephone wiring to create the network. A PhoneNet network can transmit data 3,000 feet, three times the extent of a LocalTalk network; Farallon also offers repeaters and other devices that make even larger networks possible. See *AppleShare, bus Network, local area network (LAN), LocalTalk, node, repeater,* and *twisted-pair cable.*

AppleWorks   A popular integrated software package developed by Apple Computer for the Apple II series. The program includes a word processor, a spreadsheet, a file manager, business graphics, and a telecommunications package.

application   The use of a computer for a specific purpose, such as writing a novel, printing payroll checks, or laying out the text and graphics of a newsletter. This term also is used to refer to a software program that accomplishes a specific task.

application heap   In a Macintosh computer, the area set aside for user programs. Synonymous with *base memory.*

application program interface (API)   System software that provides resources on which programmers can draw to create user interface features, such as pull-down menus and windows, and to route programs or data to local area networks (LANs).

An application program interface greatly benefits the user. With an API, all programs written for a computer can draw from a common repertoire of command names, menus, windows, dialog boxes, keyboard commands, and other interface features. Such standards substantially lower the cost of learning a new program and lead to measurable increases in the number of programs a typical user is likely to use. For example, Macintosh users typically use more programs and use their computers for longer portions of the workday than do users of DOS systems. The Macintosh was the first personal computer to use the API concept. See *Presentation Manager* and *DESQView*.

application software Programs that perform specific tasks, such as word processing or database management; unlike system software that maintains and organizes the computer system and utilities that assist you in maintaining and organizing the system. Synonymous with *application package*. See *database management program*, *page layout program*, *spreadsheet program*, *system software*, *utility program*, and *word processing program*.

architecture The overall design by which the individual hardware components of a computer system are interrelated.

This term frequently is used to describe the internal data-handling capacity of a computer. The 8-bit architecture of the Intel 8088 microprocessor, for example, is determined by the 8-bit data bus that transmits only one byte of data at a time. See *data bus* and *microprocessor*.

archival backup A backup procedure in which a hard disk backup program backs up all files on the hard disk by copying them to floppy disks or some other backup medium. See *hard disk backup program* and *incremental backup*.

archive A compressed file that is designed for space-efficient backup storage and contains one or more files.

In IBM PC-compatible computing, the most popular program for compressing and decompressing files is ARC, a shareware program created by Systems Enhancement Associates. The program is available from many bulletin board systems; look for files named ARCxxx, where xxx is the version number. A recent version is ARC500. In the Macintosh world, the file compression utility of choice is Stuffit, a shareware program created by Raymond Lau.

Almost all bulletin board systems store files in archives, because archived files take up considerably less space. You cannot use the files stored in the archive until you have used the file compression program to extract them. See *file compression utility*.

archive attribute   In DOS and OS/2, a hidden code, stored with a file's directory entry, that indicates whether the file has been changed since the last backup operation.

When you archive a file by using the BACKUP command, DOS turns off the archive attribute. When the archive attribute is off, these commands may be instructed to ignore the file. However, when you use an application program to modify the file after the archive attribute has been turned off, DOS turns on the archive attribute. The next time you use the BACKUP command, therefore, you can instruct the command to back up only the modified file. A file's archive attribute enables you to back up or copy only the files you have changed since the last backup procedure.

→ **Tip:** You can view and modify a file's archive attribute by using the ATTRIB command.

ARCnet   Pronounced "ark net." A high-speed local area network developed by Datapoint Corporation and widely used for office automation applications. See *local area network*.

area graph   In presentation graphics, a line graph in which the area below the line is filled in to emphasize the change in volume from one time period to the next. The x-axis (categories axis) is the horizontal axis, and the y-axis (values axis) is the vertical axis.

When more than one data series is displayed, each series is shown in a distinctive cross-hatching pattern (see fig. A.4). See *column graph, line graph, presentation graphics, x-axis*, and *y-axis*.

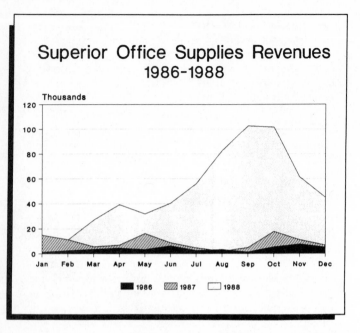

Fig. A.4. An area graph.

argument   Words, phrases, or numbers you enter on the same
line as a command or a statement to expand or modify the
command or statement. The command acts on the argument.

In the dBASE expression, **USE customer**, USE is the command, and customer is the argument. In Lotus 1-2-3, the arguments of built-in functions are enclosed in parentheses, as
in **@SUM(B1..B3)**.

→ **Tip:** Think of the command as a verb and the argument
as an object of the verb. See *argument separator* and *parameter.*

argument separator   In spreadsheet programs and programming languages, a comma or other punctuation mark
that sets off one argument from another in a command or
statement.

Many commands, such as the built-in functions of spreadsheet programs, require you to provide information, called
an argument, that the program needs to execute the com-

mand. For example, the @CTERM function in Lotus 1-2-3 requires three arguments: interest, future value, and present value. You must specify all three arguments, separated by commas:

@CTERM(.012,14000,9000)

The argument separator is essential in commands that take more than one argument. Without the separator, the program cannot tell one argument from another.

➜ **Tip:** If you are having trouble getting a command or function to work, make sure that you know exactly how many arguments the command or function requires and that you have separated the arguments with the correct separator. Some programs don't allow spaces after the separator. If you are used to pressing the space bar after typing a comma, you may have to delete unnecessary spaces.

arithmetic operator   A symbol that tells the program how to perform an arithmetic operation, such as addition, subtraction, multiplication, and division.

In almost all computer programs, addition is represented by a plus sign (+), subtraction by a hyphen (-), multiplication by an asterisk (*), and division by a slash (/). See *comparison operators* and *logical operator.*

arithmetic/logic unit (ALU)   The portion of the central processing unit (CPU) devoted to the execution of fundamental arithmetic and logical operations on data.

ARPANET   A wide-area network supported by the U.S. Defense Advanced Research Projects Agency (DARPA) and intended to support advanced scientific research.

Access to ARPANET is restricted to a small group of advanced researchers as its broader communication functions are being taken over by NSFNET. See *wide-area network.*

array   One of the fundamental data structures in computer programming; a single- or multidimensional table that the program treats as one data item.

arrow keys   See *cursor-movement keys.*

artificial intelligence (AI)　A computer science field that attempts to improve computers by endowing them with some of the characteristics associated with human intelligence, such as the capability to understand natural language and to reason under conditions of uncertainty. See *expert system.*

ascender　In typography, the portion of the lowercase letters b, d, f, h, k, l, and t that rises above the height of the letter x. The height of the ascender varies in different typefaces. See *descender.*

ascending order　A sort in which items are arranged from smallest to largest (1, 2, 3) or from first to last (a, b, c). Ascending order is the default sort order for virtually all applications that perform sorting operations. See *descending sort.*

ASCII　See *American Standard Code for Information Interchange (ASCII).*

ASCII character set　Pronounced "ass´-kee." A character set consisting only of the characters included in the original 128-character ASCII standard. See *extended character set.*

ASCII file　Pronounced "ass´-kee." A file that contains only characters drawn from the ASCII character set. See *binary file.*

ASCII sort order　Pronounced "ass´-kee." A sort order determined by the sequence used to number the standard ASCII character set.

When you use the greater than (>) or less than (<) logical operators, the strings are compared character-by-character to determine which string has the greater or lesser value. A character with a high-order designation is greater than a character with a low-order designation. The order of alphanumeric characters is as follows:

Lower Order

(space)!"#$%&'(apostrophe)( )*+,(comma)-.(period)
/0...9:;<=>?@ABC...XYZ[\]^abc...xyz

Higher Order

▲ **Caution:** Programs that sort data in ASCII sort order may violate publication guidelines—all capitalized words, for instance, come before words beginning with lowercase letters—so you may have to perform some manual rearrangement of the data. In addition, ASCII sorts may not handle foreign language characters properly. See *dictionary sort.*

aspect ratio   In computer graphics, the ratio of the horizontal dimension of an image to the vertical dimension. In sizing a graphic, maintaining the height-to-width ratio is important to avoid distortions.

assembler   A program that transforms an assembly language program into machine language so that the computer can execute the program. See *assembly language* and *compiler.*

assembly language   A low-level programming language in which each program statement corresponds to an instruction that the processing unit can carry out.

Assembly languages are procedural languages; they tell the computer what to do in precise detail. They are only one level removed in abstraction from machine language, the language of 0s and 1s that the processing unit actually reads to carry out its operations. Assembly language differs from machine language only in the use of codes that represent the major functions the machine carries out.

Assembly languages have many disadvantages. Programming in assembly language is tedious; the programmer must specify in detail exactly what procedure is to be followed to accomplish a task, and as many as two dozen lines of code may be required to add two numbers. Assembly language programs are extremely difficult to write and exhibit no obvious structure or modularity beyond that imposed by the procedure and dictated by the processing unit. Assembly language programs also are not transferred easily from one type of computer to another. They are designed for the specific capabilities and instruction sets of a given processing unit.

If you program in assembly language, the code is compact and operates quickly. If you program in a high-level language, such as BASIC or Pascal, when the compiler translates the code into assembly language code, it does not do so as efficiently as an operator would. Some programs, such as operating systems, must run at the maximum speed possible. By programming in assembly language, a programmer can ensure that a program performs efficiently. Most operating system programs, therefore, are written in assembly language. Assembly language programs also consume less memory space than compiled programs written in a high-level language.

For application program development, assembly language has the advantage of producing fast programs. Lack of portability, however, limits the market for these programs. Professional software developers, therefore, prefer to develop programs in C, which combines the structure of a modern high-level language with the speed and efficiency of assembly language programming. See *BASIC, C, compiler, high-level programming language, machine language, Pascal,* and *procedural language.*

assign   To give a value to a named variable.

ASSIGN   In DOS and OS/2, an external command that reroutes to another drive requests for disk operations on a specific drive. Although ASSIGN still is supported by DOS, the preferred command is SUBST.

    → **Tip:** ASSIGN is used infrequently. ASSIGN is needed, however, when a poorly designed application program insists on using a nonexistent drive (such as drive B in a hard disk system) for disk operations. Using the ASSIGN command, you can reroute requests for operations on drive B to drive C.

    ▲ **Caution:** Do not use BACKUP, CHKDSK, DISKCOMP, DISKCOPY, FDISK, FORMAT, JOIN, LABEL, RECOVER, RESTORE, or SYS with an assigned or substituted drive. The operation will not work, and you may lose data. See *external command.*

assignment statement   In computer programming, a program statement that places a value into a variable. In BASIC, for example, the statement LET A=10 places the value 10 into the variable A. See *BASIC.*

asterisk   In DOS and OS/2, a wild-card symbol that stands for one or more characters, unlike the question mark wild card, which stands for only one character.

asynchronous communication   Pronounced "ay-sink´-roh-nuss." A method of data communication in which the transmission of bits of data is not synchronized by a clock signal but is accomplished by sending the bits one after another, with a start bit and a stop bit to mark the beginning and end of the data unit.

Computer information is conveyed in two ways. Synchronous communication sends data in parallel along a bus, with each wire corresponding to one bit of information in a binary number. Synchronous communication can be compared to sending eight cars side-by-side down a freeway. The cars travel together, and they arrive at the same time. Asynchronous communication comes into play when you have only two wires. The bits are sent one after the other, with a start bit and a stop bit. Asynchronous communication can be compared to sending eight cars, one after the other, down a one-lane road, with a motorcycle policeman at the beginning and end of the procession.

Because the telephone company relies on two-wire cables, asynchronous communication is synonymous with telecommunications. See *bus, modem, synchronous communication,* and *Universal Asynchronous Receiver/Transmitter (UART).*

AT   See *IBM Personal Computer AT.*

AT bus   The 16-bit expansion bus used in the IBM Personal Computer AT, as distinguished from the 8-bit bus of the original IBM Personal Computer and the 32-bit bus of computers using the Intel 80386 and 80486 microprocessors. Most 80386 and 80486 machines contain AT-compatible slots. See *expansion bus, IBM Personal Computer, IBM Personal Computer AT, Intel 80386, Intel 80486,* and *Micro Channel Bus.*

ATM   See *Adobe Type Manager (ATM).*

attenuation   In local area networks, the loss of signal strength when the system's cables exceed the maximum range stated in the network's specifications. The attenuation of a signal prevents successful data communications. The maximum length of a network's cable can be extended by using a device called a repeater. See *local area network* (LAN) and *repeater*.

ATTRIB   In DOS and OS/2, an external command that displays, sets, or clears a file's read-only attribute or archive attribute.

If a file is read-only, you cannot alter or erase the file. If you want to alter or erase the file, you can turn off this attribute. The file's archive attribute is set by the BACKUP command. The archive attribute tells DOS whether the file has been changed since the last archival copy was made. See *external command* and *file attribute*.

attribute   In many word processing and graphics programs, a character emphasis, such as boldface and italic, and other characteristics of character formatting, such as typeface and type size. In WordPerfect, for example, attributes include appearance attributes (boldface, underline, double underline, italic, outline, shadow, small caps, strikeout, and redline) and size attributes. See *archive attribute* and *file attribute*.

audit trail   In an accounting program, an automatic program feature that keeps a record of transactions so that you can locate the origin of specific figures that appear on reports.

authoring language   A computer-assisted instruction (CAI) application that provides tools for creating instructional or presentation software.

A popular authoring language for Macintosh computers is HyperCard, provided free with every Macintosh computer. Using HyperCard, educators can develop instructional programs quickly and easily. HyperCard applications can control video disk players and CD-ROM drives, making the application useful as a front end for large text or video databases.

AutoCAD   Pronounced "auto´-cad." A computer-aided design (CAD) program developed by AutoDesk and widely used for professional CAD applications. See *computer-aided design (CAD)*.

auto-dial/auto-answer modem   A modem capable of generating tones to dial the receiving computer and of answering a ringing telephone to establish a connection when a call is received. See *modem*.

AUTOEXEC.BAT   In DOS, a batch file consulted by DOS when the system is started or restarted.

AUTOEXEC.BAT is not mandatory for IBM PC-compatible computers, but when you are running a hard disk loaded with several applications and a computer to which you have attached several peripherals, the file is all but essential for efficient operation. Common ingredients in AUTOEXEC.BAT are PATH command statements that tell DOS where to find application programs and the names of system-configuration programs, such as MODE, that set up your computer for the use of peripherals, such as a serial printer and mouse. Such commands and programs do not remain in your computer's memory when you shut off the power. You must enter all this information manually at the start of every operating session. AUTOEXEC.BAT does the task for you.

You may want to include in your AUTOEXEC.BAT file a method to display a neat list of available applications and the command(s) needed. For example, if you routinely use Lotus 1-2-3, WordStar, dBASE III Plus, CHART-MASTER, and Microsoft Project, you can create a batch file called MENU.BAT with the following lines:

```
ECHO OFF
CLS
:START
.
.
ECHO  ***********Welcome to the PC *************
ECHO  = = = = = = = = = = = = = = = = = = = = = =
ECHO          Available applications
ECHO          To run:              Type:
ECHO
ECHO          WordStar 4           WS
ECHO          1-2-3                WS
ECHO          dBASE III Plus       DB
ECHO          CHART-MASTER         CM
ECHO          Microsoft Project    PROJ
ECHO  ********************************************
CLS
MENU
```

WS, LOTUS, DB, CM, and PROJ are the names of batch files set up to switch to the appropriate subdirectory, call up the correct program, and so on. This batch file enables you to see at a glance the choice of applications available and the commands to start each application.

See *batch file*, *CONFIG.SYS*, *MODE*, and *PATH*.

automatic font downloading   The transmission of disk-based, downloadable printer fonts to the printer, done by an application program as the fonts are needed to complete a printing job. See *downloading utility* and *printer font*.

automatic hyphenation   See *hyphenation*.

automatic mode switching   The automatic detection and adjustment of a display adapter's internal circuitry to adjust the video output of a program on an IBM PC-compatible computer. Most Video Graphics Array (VGA) adapters, for example, switch to adjust to CGA, MDA, EGA, or VGA output from applications.

automatic recalculation   In a spreadsheet, a mode in which cell values are recalculated every time any cell is changed in the worksheet.

▲ **Caution:** Automatic recalculation slows your work because the program recalculates the worksheet every time you add a new label, value, or formula. Unless you are working with a large spreadsheet, though, automatic recalculation is still better than manual recalculation. After you switch to manual recalculation, the computed values become inaccurate as you add new data to the worksheet. If you forget to recalculate (or to turn automatic recalculation back on), you could print a spreadsheet with erroneous results. See *background recalculation* and *manual recalculations*.

automation   The replacement of human skill by automatic machine operations.

Automation brings the specter of technological job displacement, in which skilled humans suddenly find themselves without employment as machines take over the jobs they once performed. You can look at automation in another way, however. Automation also can distribute the skills formerly possessed only by highly paid experts and make those skills available to many.

Word processing software is an excellent example of the potential of automation to distribute skills; a secretary can expertly center text on the page and proofread spelling so that letters and reports contain no spelling or typographical errors. A high-quality word processing program such as WordPerfect is, in part, an automated secretary, and its economic significance lies partly in the fact that the program brings secretarial expertise to people and small businesses that could not afford such expertise in the past.

Using such technology, a small firm can compete more effectively. In academia, for example, to get tenure, you sometimes need a research grant. Hiring a secretary used to be the only way you could keep up with the mass of paperwork involved in networking effectively, publishing articles, and building a solid case for tenure. Personal computer technology has altered the power equation in the academic game and is performing the same role for small businesses and entrepreneurs.

The potential of personal computing technology to distribute expert skill is one of the major reasons for its success in the marketplace. Equipped with a desktop computer and a variety of application programs, virtually anyone can carry out a sophisticated financial analysis, create a presentation-quality business chart, and publish an attractive newsletter or brochure.

Why pay an artist and typesetter $2,000 every six months to produce a newsletter, when the same job can be done by adding the one-time expense of a $400 page layout program and a $2,000 laser printer to an existing desktop computer system? Experts are quick to point out that untrained people often make mistakes when they attempt such applications. Learning basic guidelines for producing quality output sometimes is easier than mastering layout and design skills, such as the use of an X-ACTO knife and T-square.

autorepeat key   A key that repeatedly inputs a character as long as you press and hold down the key.

autosave   See *timed backup*.

autostart routine   A set of instructions contained in ROM that tells the computer how to proceed when the power is switched on.

In most personal computers, the operating system must be loaded from disk at the beginning of every operating session. One of the autostart routine's instructions tells the disk drive how to position the read/write head over the portion of the disk on which the operating system is stored.

autotrace   In a graphics program, such as Adobe Illustrator, a command that transforms an imported bit-mapped image into its object-oriented counterpart.

The bit-mapped images created by a paint program, such as MacPaint, can print at the maximum resolution of the Macintosh screen (72 dots per inch). Object-oriented graphics, however, print at the printer's maximum resolution (up to 300 dots per inch for laser printers). Using the autotrace tool, you can transform low-resolution graphics into art that prints at substantially higher resolution. See *bit-mapped graphic*, *object-oriented graphic*, and *paint program*.

A/UX   Apple Computer's version of the UNIX operating system. To use A/UX, you need a Macintosh with a Motorola 68020 or 68030 microprocessor and 4M of random-access memory (RAM). See *UNIX*.

AUX   In DOS, an abbreviation for auxiliary port, the communications (COM) port DOS uses by default (normally COM1).

auxiliary storage   See *secondary storage*.

axis   See *x-axis*, *y-axis*, and *z-axis*.

b

background   In computers that can do more than one task at a time, the environment in which low-priority operations (such as printing a document or downloading a file) are carried out while the user works with an application in the foreground.

In a computer system that lacks multitasking capabilities, the background task is carried out during brief pauses in the execution of the system's primary (foreground) task(s). Many word processing programs use this technique to provide background printing. See *multitasking* and *multiple loading operating system*.

background communication   Data communication, such as downloading a file, accomplished in the background while the user concentrates on another application in the foreground. See *multitasking* and *multiple loading operating system*.

background noise   The random or extraneous signals that infiltrate a communications channel, unlike the signals that convey information.

background printing   The printing of a document in the background while a program is active in the foreground.

→ **Tip:** Background printing can bring major productivity benefits if you frequently print lengthy documents or use a slow printer. Without background printing, you cannot use your computer system while the document is printing. With background printing, you can continue to work while the document prints.

Background printing can work four ways. First, some word processing programs, such as Microsoft Word, provide a background printing command that enables the user to print one document while editing another. Second, commercially available print spooling programs extend background printing to all or most of your applications. Third, some operating systems, such as OS/2, provide background printing by enabling you to bring another application to the foreground while printing in the background. Fourth, you can add a print buffer to your system. A print buffer is a hardware device that connects your computer and the printer. The buffer contains memory chips that store the computer's output until the printer is ready. Your computer thinks that it is hooked up to a super-fast printer and sends the output at the maximum speed possible. You return to your work, and the buffer feeds the output to the printer. See *multitasking*, *PRINT*, *print queue*, and *print spooling program*.

background processes   In a multitasking operating system, the operations occurring in the background (such as printing or downloading a program from a bulletin board) while you work with an application program in the foreground.

background recalculation   In spreadsheet programs, such as Lotus 1-2-3, an option that enables you to make changes to a large spreadsheet while the program performs recalculations in the background.

backlit display   See *liquid crystal display* (LCD).

backplane   The rear panel of a computing device where you find receptacles for peripheral devices and power cords.

backspace   A key that deletes the character to the left of the cursor's position, or the act of moving one space to the left by using the cursor-movement keys.

backup   A copy of a program or document file made for archival purposes. See *global backup* and *incremental backup*.

   ▲ **Caution:** Hard disks fail, and when they do, they often take some of or all the data and documents with them. Regular backup procedures are required for successful use of a hard disk system.

backup   To copy a data or program file to a removable secondary storage device so that it can be kept in a safe off-site location.

BACKUP   In DOS and OS/2, an external command that makes a backup copy of one or more files and preserves a record of their directory locations.

   For efficient and effective use of the computer, regular backup procedures are essential. Too many personal computer users fail to make backup copies of their work; sooner or later, they see hours or even days of work evaporate after a system crash or accidental erasure. Backup procedures are essential for users of hard disks because hard disks may fail catastrophically, taking some or all of your work with them.

   Users of IBM PC compatible computers can choose between commercial backup programs or the tools provided by

DOS, such as the BACKUP command. Commercial backup
utilities are much easier to use. If the command-driven interface of DOS doesn't give you trouble, however, DOS can be
effective in a regular backup procedure.

For archival purposes, the BACKUP command has several
advantages over the COPY command. Unlike COPY,
BACKUP copies the file's directory location with the file's
contents. If you accidentally delete the original file or if the
file is corrupted, you use the RESTORE command to retrieve
the backup copy from the archive. RESTORE places the file
in the directory from which the file was copied. Another
benefit of BACKUP is that, unlike COPY, BACKUP prompts
the user to insert an additional disk, or disks, if the files will
not fit on one backup disk.

By including command parameters (symbols that modify
the command's operation), you can use BACKUP to copy
only files that have been changed since the last backup procedure or only files that have been changed since a specified
date.

BACKUP also differs from the XCOPY command, which
does not split a large file over more than one disk.

➔ **Tip:** Hard disk users should not back up copies of all
the program files—you still have your original program disks
stored safely away, and you can re-install your software after
a disk crash. Concentrate on backing up your spreadsheets,
documents, databases, and other data files. Don't forget to
back up program configuration files containing the options
you have chosen for an application program. See *archive
attribute, ATTRIB, backup utility, command parameters, configuration file, external command,* and *XCOPY.*

backup utility   A utility program that makes it easier to back
up program and data files from a hard disk to a backup medium, such as floppy disks.

A good backup utility can back up an entire hard disk on a
series of floppies; the program prompts you when one disk
is full and the next one is needed.

DOS and the Macintosh operating system include backup
utilities, but the DOS BACKUP command is not particularly

easy to use, and the Mac's HD Backup program does not perform incremental backups. (An incremental backup is a copying operation that backs up only the files that have been modified since the last backup procedure.) Backup utilities are popular options in both environments. See *incremental backup*.

backward chaining In an expert system, a commonly used method of drawing inferences from IF..THEN rules. A backward chaining system starts with a question and searches through the system's rules to determine which ones enable the system to solve the problem and what data is needed.

Expert systems simulate the expertise of a professional in fields like medical diagnosis, property assessment, identification of an unknown substance's toxicity, and acceptability of life insurance applications. These programs engage the user, who is not an expert in these fields, in a dialog.

In a backward chaining system, the user begins with a question, such as "How much is this property worth?" The program then searches the IF..THEN rules stored in the knowledge base. As the search goes on, the program prompts the user to supply additional data by asking questions such as "Does the house need a new roof?" (Unlike a database, a knowledge base contains more than data—a knowledge base contains propositions about the subject, phrased in IF..THEN rules, such as "IF the house needs a new roof, THEN deduct $3,000 from the asking price.")

This technique is backward because the user begins with the question and supplies the necessary data in response to the program's queries. In a forward chaining system, the user begins by supplying all the data. Because backward chaining systems are more interactive, they are preferred for applications designed for use by people who aren't computer experts. See *forward chaining* and *knowledge base*.

backward search In database management or word processing, a search that begins at the cursor's location and proceeds backward toward the beginning of a database or document (rather than the default forward search).

bad break   An improperly hyphenated line break. See *automatic hyphenation.*

bad page break   In word processing and desktop publishing, an inappropriate or unattractive soft page break that has been inserted by the word processing or page layout program.

A common flaw in documents produced on computers, bad page breaks should be caught by a final careful proofreading before a document goes out the door. Headings can be widowed at the bottom of pages, units of text that should be kept together (such as tables) are split, and single lines of text (orphans) can be left at the top of a page.

The best policy is to use block protection features that prevent bad page breaks from occurring. These features are found in high-quality word processing programs, such as WordPerfect and Microsoft Word.

▲ **Caution:** Don't fix bad page breaks by inserting hard page breaks. Suppose that you place a hard page break just before a heading so that it prints with the text below. If you later revise your document, adding a great deal of text before the hard page break, the break is no longer needed but is forcing a bad page break. Use Block Protect or a similar feature. Block protection is used only if the program would place a soft page break within that block. See *block protection, orphan,* and *widow.*

bad sector   An area of a floppy or hard disk that will not reliably record data.

Almost all hard disks have some bad sectors as a result of manufacturing defects. If you run a disk diagnostic program such as CHKDSK and the diagnostic program reports a few bad sectors, don't worry. The operating system locks these sectors out of reading and writing operations. Aside from the loss of a few bytes of storage, you can use the disk as if the bad sectors did not exist.

▲ **Caution:** Bad sectors on floppy disks present serious problems. Most operating systems reject new disks containing bad sectors. If an attempt to format a floppy disk fails, discard the disk. If a bad sector appears after the disk has been used, you almost can be certain that the data on that sector has been corrupted, probably by dust or a fingerprint. The entire disk may be unusable. Users of IBM PC-compatible computers may be able to salvage a portion of the disk by using utility programs, such as Norton Utilities or PC Tools. As a last resort, users may use the DOS RECOVER command if the file that corrupted the bad sector is a text file. Macintosh computer users should try using a program called Disk First Aid, provided with every Macintosh computer. See *bad track table.*

bad track table   A list attached to or packaged with a hard disk. The bad track table lists the bad sectors or the defective areas of the disk.

Almost every hard disk comes off the assembly line with some defects. During the low-level format, these defective areas of the disk are locked out so that system software cannot access them. See *low-level format.*

bandwidth   The transmission capacity of a communication channel, measured in bits per second (bps).

In local area networks, bandwidth is a measurement of network speed. In monitors, bandwidth is a measurement of the monitor's maximum resolution; the higher the bandwidth, the more dense the resolution on-screen.

bank switching   A way of expanding memory beyond an operating system's or microprocessor's limitations by switching rapidly between two banks of memory chips. See *expanded memory.*

bar code   A printed pattern of wide and narrow vertical bars used to represent numerical codes in machine-readable form.

Bar codes are printed on almost every product sold in supermarkets. These bar codes conform to the Universal Product Code (UPS), a standard bar code format that lists the product maker's identification number and a product number. When the bar code is dragged past an optical scanner at the check-out counter, the point-of-sale computer matches the product number with its database of price lists and rings up the correct amount.

Equipped with a bar code reader and the appropriate software, personal computers can be used for the development of bar-code applications. For example, an audio-visual office can attach bar-code labels to all pieces of equipment, so that checking out this equipment becomes a simple matter. You pass the reader over the bar code label, and the equipment number is posted to the database of checked-out equipment. Bar code applications can be major timesavers when you need to maintain inventory control. See *bar code reader*.

bar code reader   An input device equipped with a stylus that scans bar codes; the device then converts the bar code into a number displayed on-screen. See *bar code*.

bar graph   In presentation graphics, a graph with horizontal bars, commonly used to show the values of independent items. The x-axis (categories axis) is the vertical axis, and the y-axis (values axis) is the horizontal axis.

Properly, the term bar graph is used only for graphs with horizontal bars (see fig. B.1). If the bars are vertical, the graph is a column graph. In practice, however, the term bar graph is used for both. In professional presentation graphics, bar graphs are used to display the values of discrete items (apples, oranges, grapefruit, and papaya), and column graphs are used to show the changes in one or more items over time (for example, apples vs. oranges in January, February, March, and so on). See *column graph, line graph, paired bar graph, x-axis,* and *y-axis*.

base font   The default font a word processing program uses for a document unless you specifically instruct the program otherwise. You can choose a default base font for all documents or for just the document you are currently editing.

→ **Tip:** If your word processing program enables you to use many fonts, you should understand how the base font is selected. In WordPerfect 5.1, you set the base font in three ways. The primary way is to choose an initial base font from the Select Printer Edit menu. However, you can override this setting by choosing a document base font from the Format Document menu or by placing a base font code in your document. Establishing base fonts doesn't mean that you

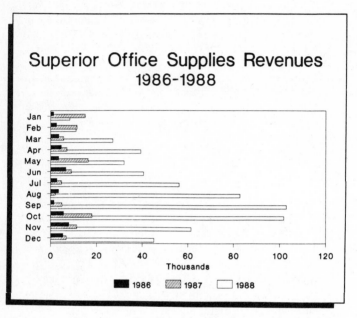

Fig. B.1. A bar graph.

cannot change fonts within the document; the base font is the default font, the one the program uses unless you give explicit commands to the contrary. In Microsoft Word 5.0 (IBM version), the base font is monospaced Courier. You can override the base font by redefining the Normal style in each document's style sheet. See *default font, document base font,* and *initial base font.*

base memory   In a computer's random-access memory (RAM), the portion of the memory map set aside for user programs.

   The base memory of IBM PC-compatible computers running under DOS is 640K, although the actual usable amount is smaller because the base memory also contains the DOS operating system.

baseband   In local area networks, a communications method in which the information-bearing signal is placed directly on the cable in digital form without modulation.

A computer's signals can be conveyed over cables in two ways: by analog signals or by digital signals. Analog signals, such as the signals that travel from a high-fidelity amplifier to its speakers, are continuous signals that vary in a wave-like pattern. The number of variations or cycles per second is the signal's frequency, measured in Hertz (Hz). Digital signals are discrete signals that alternate between high current or low current.

Because a computer's signals are digital signals, they must be transformed by a process called modulation before they can be conveyed over an analog-signal network. A modem performs this task. An analog communication network is called a broadband network.

Digital communication networks are called baseband networks. The advantage of a baseband network is that considerably less circuitry is required to convey the signal to and from the computer. In addition, because many baseband networks can use twisted-pair (ordinary telephone) cables, baseband networks are cheaper to install than broadband networks that require coaxial cable. However, a baseband system is limited in its geographic extent and provides only one channel of communication at a time. Most personal computer local area networks are baseband networks. See *analog*, *broadband*, *digital*, and *twisted-pair cable*.

baseline   In typography, the lowest point characters reach (excluding descenders). For example, the baseline of a line of text is the lowermost point of letters like a and x, excluding the lowest points of p and q.

BASIC   Pronounced "basic." An easy-to-use (but widely criticized) high-level programming language available on personal computers.

Developed in 1964 by John G. Kemeny and Thomas E. Kurtz, two Dartmouth College professors, BASIC (Beginner's All-Purpose Symbolic Instruction Code) was designed to make computer programming accessible to people who are not computer scientists. Like predecessors FORTRAN and ALGOL (the forerunner of Pascal), BASIC is a procedural language that tells the computer what to do step-by-step. A program consists of lines of text, with each line containing one or more statements. Unlike its predecessors, BASIC programs run in an interactive environment, complete with a text editor, debugger, and interpreter that translates and executes the BASIC source code line-by-line. You develop a program interactively, trying alternatives and testing program integrity each step of the way. The result is a process of program construction highly conducive to learning. More recently created compilers transform BASIC code into stand-alone executable programs.

BASIC may be easy to learn, but many computer scientists question whether the language is worth the effort. Like other interpreted languages, BASIC programs execute slowly, making the language a poor choice for professional applications. Some computer scientists argue that BASIC is a poor choice even for educational purposes. Early versions of BASIC lacked the control structures needed for structured programming. Students who learned BASIC also were learning bad programming techniques, such as the use of the GOTO statement, which in early versions was the fundamental building block for the control of program flow. A GOTO statement transfers program control to a specified line number, producing spaghetti code in which even the programmer has difficulty visualizing all the interlinks. The result is a program that most people find impossible to read if the program is longer than two or three dozen lines.

Newer versions that include modern control structures and named subroutines have appeared. These subroutines make GOTO statements superfluous. Line numbers are optional in these newer versions of BASIC. Examples of modernized BASIC include Microsoft's QuickBASIC and Borland's TurboBASIC. Both versions include compilers that make the production of professional executable object code programs possible. Although these modern versions of BASIC are hardly the language of choice for professional program development, some commercially viable software (and a great many shareware programs) are written in a compiled BASIC. C is far more popular for professional program development. See *C, compiler, control structure, debugger, interpreter, Pascal, procedural language, QuickBASIC,* and *structured programming.*

BASICA   Pronounced "basic A´." An interpreter for the Microsoft BASIC programming language. BASICA is supplied on
the DOS disk provided with IBM personal computers. See
GWBASIC.

basic input-output system (BIOS)   Pronounced "buy´-ose." A
set of programs encoded in read-only memory (ROM) in IBM
PC-compatible computers. These programs facilitate the
transfer of data and control instructions between the computer and peripherals, such as disk drives.

   The BIOS programs of IBM Personal Computers, XTs, ATs,
and PS/2s are copyrighted. PC-compatible manufacturers,
such as Compaq Corporation, must create a BIOS that emulates the IBM BIOS without actually using IBM's code. Companies that manufacture IBM PC-compatible computers can
choose to create the BIOS emulation themselves or purchase
an emulation from other companies, such as Phoenix Technologies.

basis weight   A measurement of the weight of one sheet based
on the weight of one ream (500 sheets) of uncut (17-inch-by-
22-inch) paper. Common basis weights are 16 and 20
pounds.

batch file   A file containing a series of DOS commands executed one after the other, as if you typed them. Batch files
are useful when you repeatedly need to type the same series
of DOS commands. Almost all hard disk users have an
AUTOEXEC.BAT file, a batch file that DOS loads at the start
of every operating session. See *AUTOEXEC.BAT.*

   A practical example of a batch file may prevent you from
formatting your hard disk. Under DOS, the FORMAT.COM
program is activated when you type FORMAT at the prompt.
You can disguise this program by renaming it
XFORMAT.COM with the following command:

   `RENAME FORMAT.COM XFORMAT.COM`

   If someone types FORMAT nothing drastic happens because no such program file exists on the hard disk. The following batch file is called FORMAT.BAT:

```
ECHO OFF
IF %1. == . GOTO :NONE
IF %1 == C: GOTO :NOCAN
IF %1 == c: GOTO :NOCAN
XFORMAT %1
GOTO END
:NONE
ECHO You did not specify the drive (B:)
ECHO e.g. FORMAT B:
ECHO Please try the command again.
GOTO END
:NOCAN
ECHO You don't really mean to do that—format
ECHO the C drive—do you?
:END
```

With the renamed file and batch file in place, typing FOR-
MAT B: causes DOS to use the batch file, not FORMAT.COM.

batch processing   A mode of computer operation in which
program instructions are executed one after the other without user intervention.

Batch processing efficiently uses computer resources in a
multiuser system, but batch processing is not convenient for
users. Often, you discover a programming or data input error
only after the computer has run the job and spewed out
reams of useless printout. In interactive processing, you see
the results of your commands on-screen, so that you can correct errors and make necessary adjustments before completing the operation. See *interactive processing* and *multiuser
system.*

baud   Pronounced "bawd." A measure of the number of times
per second that switching can occur in a communications
channel. See *baud rate.*

baud rate   The transmission speed of an asynchronous communications channel.

Technically, baud rate refers to the maximum number of
changes that can occur per second in the electrical state of a
communications circuit. Under RS-232C communications
protocols, 300 baud is likely to equal 300 bits per second
(bps), but at higher baud rates, the number of bits per sec-

ond transmitted is actually higher than the baud rate because one change can represent more than one bit of data. For example, 2400 bps is usually sent at 600 baud.

In personal computing, baud rates are frequently cited to measure the speed of modems. Although 1200-baud modems are standard, most frequent users of telecommunications prefer 2400-baud modems. With serial printers, you must set up your computer's serial port so that the computer sends the printer signals at the correct speed. The Apple LaserWriter, for example, requires serial transmissions at 9600 baud. Under DOS, you set the serial transmission speed by using the MODE command. See *asynchronous communication, LaserWriter, MODE, modem, serial port, serial printer,* and *telecommunications,*

BBS   See *bulletin board system (BBS).*

BCD   See *binary coded decimal (BCD).*

bells and whistles   An application program's or computer system's advanced features.

Many people say bells and whistles, such as mail-merging capabilities in a word processing program, aren't desirable for novices and recommend programs that lack such features. If advanced features do not clutter up the user interface, however, you should buy full-featured software you can grow into. A feature that seems hopelessly advanced right now may turn out to be vital.

Microsoft Word 4.0 for the Macintosh offers the best of both worlds. You can choose a user interface that hides the program's complexity by including only a few features on the program's menus. You also can choose a standard interface that includes the advanced features. See *mail merge.*

benchmark   A standard measurement used to test the performance of different brands of equipment.

In computing, standard benchmark tests (such as Dhrystones and Whetstones) do not provide accurate measures of a system's actual performance in an end-user computing environment. Most of these tests are CPU-intensive; they put the central processing unit through a mix of instructions, such as floating-point calculations, but do not test the performance of system components such as disk drives and internal communications.

The speed of these components greatly affects the performance of end-user application programs. Benchmarks developed for personal computers, such as the Norton SI, include the performance of peripherals. See *Norton SI*, and *throughput.*

benchmark program A utility program used to measure a computer's processing speed so that its performance can be compared to that of other computers running the same program.

Benchmark programs provide some indication of the number-crunching prowess of a central processing unit (CPU), but the results they generate may be close to meaningless. Users run application programs. What counts for users is a system's throughput, its capability to push data not only through the CPU but also through all the system's peripheral components, including its disk drives. A computer with a fast processor (and a numeric coprocessor) performs well on benchmarks, but if the computer is equipped with a sluggish hard disk and lacks cache memory, the performance may disappoint the user. See *cache memory, central processing unit (CPU), throughput,* and *utility program.*

Berkeley UNIX A version of the UNIX operating system, developed by the University of California at Berkeley, that takes full advantage of the virtual memory capabilities of Digital Equipment Corporation (DEC) minicomputers.

The Berkeley version of UNIX, often called BSD (Berkeley System Distribution) UNIX, was developed initially to take full advantage of the technical capabilities of VAX minicomputers. Enhancements also were added, and many thought that Berkeley UNIX would become a de facto standard. AT&T's promotion of its own UNIX System 5, however, has relegated Berkeley UNIX to a subsidiary role. Berkeley UNIX still is preferred in technical, academic, and educational environments, in which the system's features meet special needs. See *UNIX.*

Bernoulli box   Pronounced "ber-noo´-lee." An innovative removable mass storage system developed by Iomega Corporation for IBM PC-compatible and Macintosh computers.

Bernoulli boxes have removable cartridges containing flexible disks capable of holding up to 44M of programs and
data. Unlike floppy disk drives, however, these disks spin at
high speeds; the latest Bernoulli boxes are capable of up to
22 ms access time. The Bernoulli box is named for the Swiss
scientist who predicted the dynamics of a rapidly spinning,
flexible disk around a fixed object. Bernoulli said that owing
to the force of air pressure, the disk would bend around the
object (read/write head) just enough to maintain a slight
space between the object and the disk. Unlike hard disks,
which use a massive, fixed platter, this design is resistant to
head crashes, in which the read/write head collides with and
ruins the disk. Crashes often are caused by shock, but you
can drop a Bernoulli cartridge to the floor without damaging
the disk or data. Bernoulli cartridges also are removable and
relatively inexpensive. Therefore, you can use Bernoulli
boxes to create a virtually unlimited mass storage system. See
hard disk and *secondary storage*.

beta site   Pronounced "bay´-tah." The place where a beta test
occurs. When developing a program or a version of an existing program, a company chooses beta sites where the program is subjected to demanding, heavy-duty usage. This
process reveals the program's remaining bugs and shortcomings.

beta test   Pronounced "bay´-tah." The second stage in the testing of computer software before the commercial release.
Beta tests usually are conducted outside the company manufacturing the software. See *alpha test*.

Bézier curve   Pronounced "bez´-ee-ay." A mathematically generated line that can display nonuniform curves.

Bézier curves are named after the French mathematician
Pierre Bézier, who first described their properties. In a Bézier
curve, the location of two midpoints—called control
handles—is sufficient to describe the overall shape of an irregular curve. In computer graphics applications, you manipulate the control handles normally shown as small boxes

on-screen. By clicking on these points and dragging with the mouse, you manipulate the complexity and shape of the curve.

bibliographic retrieval service   An on-line information service that specializes in maintaining huge computerized indexes to scholarly, scientific, medical, and technical literature.

The databases offered by these services are almost identical to the indexes available in the reference section of major university libraries. Most databases do not contain the text of the works cited—only the bibliographic citation and an abstract that may not contain useful information. To get the full benefit of the literature, you have to retrieve the original document. These service firms offer the original documents, but the price is stiff.

The two leading information firms are BRS Information Technologies (Latham, NY) and DIALOG Information Services (Menlo Park, CA). Serving mainly corporate and institutional customers, these companies' fees are steep—well over an average of $1 per minute. Personal computer users can access, at substantially lower rates, special menu-driven night and weekend versions of these services, BRS/After Dark and Knowledge Index.

➜ **Tip:** Before signing on, find out whether your local library makes databases available on CD-ROM disks. If so, you can search these databases for free. Because no clock is ticking away, you can make full use of the interactive searching potential of this information. See *on-line information service.*

biform   In typography, a typeface, such as Peignot, that combines lowercase and small-cap characters to form the lowercase alphabet (see fig. B.2).

ABCDEFGHIJKLMNOPQRSTUVWXYZ
abcdefghijklmnopqrstuvwxyz 1234567890

Fig. B.2. Example of the Peignot typeface.

Big Blue   Slang for International Business Machines Corp., which uses blue as its corporate color.

binary coded decimal (BCD)   A method of coding long decimal numbers so that they can be processed with precision in a computer using an 8-bit data word.

Most personal computers process data in 8-bit chunks called bytes, but that size causes problems for number crunching. When working with binary numbers, the biggest number that can be represented with 8 bits is 256. The data word length must be increased to about 60 bits to work effectively with binary numbers. That increase is exactly what numeric coprocessors are for.

Some programs get around the 8-bit limitation by using BCD notation, a way of coding decimal numbers in binary form without really translating them into binary. You cannot fit 260 into 8 bits, but you can fit the codes for 2, 6, and 0 into 3 adjacent bytes. A 3-digit decimal number takes up 3 bytes of storage; larger numbers can be accommodated by increasing the number of bytes set aside in memory to store the number. Therefore, you have no limit to the precision that can be achieved in coding and processing numbers.

binary file   A file containing data or program instructions in a format other than that of a text file, so that special software is required to display the file. See *text file*.

binary numbers   A number system with a base (or radix) of 2, unlike the number systems most people use, which have bases of 10 (decimal numbers), 12 (measurement in feet and inches), and 60 (time).

Binary numbers are preferred for computers for precision and economy. Constructing an electronic circuit that can detect the difference between 2 states (high current and low current) is easy and inexpensive; building a circuit that detects the difference among 10 states is much more difficult and expensive.

binary search   A search algorithm that avoids a slow sequential search by starting in the middle of the sorted database and determining whether the desired record is above or below the midpoint. Having reduced the number of records to be searched by 50 percent, the search proceeds to the middle of the remaining records, and so on, until the desired record is found.

binding offset   An extra-wide margin that shifts text away from the edge of the page when the document is bound.

You use binding offsets only for documents printed or reproduced on both sides of the page (duplex printing); the margin is increased on the right side of verso (left, even-numbered) pages and the left side of recto (right, odd-numbered) pages. See *gutter.*

➔ **Tip:** If you are planning to bind a document printed or reproduced on only one side of the page, don't use a binding offset. Just increase the left margin to make room for the binding.

BIOS   See *basic input-output system (BIOS).*

bit   The basic unit of information in a binary numbering system (BInary digiT).

Computers work with binary numbers, and the internal circuit can represent one of the two numbers in a binary system: 1 or 0. These basic either/or, yes/no units of information are called bits. Because building a reliable circuit that tells the difference between a 1 (represented by high current) and a 0 (represented by low current) is easy and inexpensive, computers are accurate in their internal processing capabilities. Computers typically make fewer than one internal error in every 100 billion processing operations. Note, however, that such internal errors have nothing to do with programming errors, which are much more common and account for almost all computer glitches. See *byte.*

bit map   The representation of a video image stored in a computer's memory. Each picture element (pixel) is represented by bits stored in the memory.

Bit-mapped graphics are notorious consumers of memory. Up to 1M of video memory may be required to store a bit map for a high-resolution screen display. See *block graphics* and *pixel.*

bit-mapped font   A screen or printer font in which each character is composed of a pattern of dots. Bit-mapped fonts represent characters with a matrix of dots. To display or print bit-mapped fonts, the computer or printer must keep a full representation of each character in memory.

"Font" should be taken literally as a complete set of characters of a given typeface, weight, posture, and size. For example, if you want to use Palatino (Roman) 12 and Palatino Italic 14, you must load two complete sets of characters into memory. Bit-mapped fonts cannot be scaled up or down without introducing grotesque stair-case distortions, called aliasing. Distortions are clearly visible when you attempt to scale Macintosh bit-mapped screen fonts to a size not represented by a corresponding font in the System Folder.

Because the computer's or printer's memory must contain a complete set of characters for each font you use, bit-mapped fonts consume enormous amounts of disk and memory space. Outline fonts, however, are constructed from mathematical formulas and can be scaled up or down without distortion. Outline fonts are considered technically superior. Printers that can print outline fonts, therefore, are more expensive. These fonts require processing circuitry to decode the formulas and memory to store the bit map constructed from the formulas. See *aliasing, LaserJet, LaserWriter, outline font, printer font,* and *screen font.*

bit-mapped graphic   A graphic image formed by a pattern of pixels (screen dots) and limited in resolution to the maximum screen resolution of the device being used. Bit-mapped graphics are produced by paint programs, such as MacPaint, SuperPaint, GEM Paint, PC Paintbrush, and some scanners.

Considered inferior to object-oriented graphics for most applications, bit-mapped graphics tie the printed resolution to the resolution of the video display currently in use, even if the printer is capable of higher resolution. Macintosh Systems, for example, display bit-mapped graphics with a resolution of 72 dpi, even though LaserWriter printers can print at 300 dpi. Such graphics may be afflicted with aliasing, rough diagonal lines attributable to the square shape of the pixels. The irregular patterns are visible when the image includes a straight diagonal line (see the W in fig. B.3). However, a skillful illustrator can create beautiful air-brush effects with paint packages.

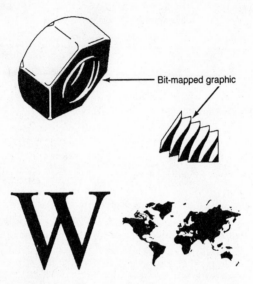

Bit-mapped graphic

Fig. B.3. Aliasing is visible in the diagonal lines of a bit-mapped graphic.

Bit-mapped graphics have other drawbacks. Unlike object-oriented and encapsulated PostScript (EPS) graphics, bit-mapped graphics consume considerable memory and disk space. Resizing a bit-mapped graphic image without introducing distortions is almost impossible. Scaling up the graphic produces a chunky effect because the lines thicken proportionately; scaling down causes the bits to run together, resulting in an inky effect. Unlike object-oriented graphics, in which each object, such as a line, can be edited or moved independently, bit-mapped graphic images are difficult to edit or modify. See *aliasing, encapsulated PostScript (EPS) file, object-oriented graphic, paint program, pixel, resolution,* and *scanner.*

BITNET A wide-area network that links over 1,000 colleges and universities in the U.S., Canada, and Europe.

BITNET (Because It's Time Network) was developed by EDUCOM, a non-profit educational consortium, for scholarly communication. Services provided include electronic mail and file transfer. BITNET is used heavily by geographically separated scholars who are working jointly in a narrowly defined research area.

The service is used by scholars fortunate enough to work at host institutions, but scholars at institutions that are not BITNET members frequently complain that they are shut out of an important network of informal scholarly communication.

bits per second (bps)   In asynchronous communications, a measurement of data transmission speed.

In personal computing, bps rates frequently are used to measure the performance of modems and other serial communications devices, such as serial ports. The bps rates are enumerated incrementally using a doubling scheme: 110 bps; 150 bps; 300 bps; 600 bps; 1,200 bps; 2,400 bps; 4,800 bps; 9,600 bps; 19,200 bps; 38,400 bps; 57,600 bps, and 115,200 bps. See *asynchronous communication, baud,* and *modem.*

black letter   In typography, a family of typefaces derived from German handwriting of the medieval era.

Black letter typefaces often are called Fraktur (after the Latin word fractus, meaning broken) because the medieval scribes who created this design lifted their pens from the line to form the next character—fracturing the continuous flow of handwriting (see fig. B.4).

𝕬𝕭𝕮𝕯𝕰𝕱𝕲𝕳𝕵𝕶𝕷𝕸𝕹𝕺𝕺𝕻𝕼𝕽𝕾𝕿𝖀𝕬𝕭𝖂𝖃𝖄𝖅
𝖆𝖇𝖈𝖉𝖊𝖋𝖌𝖍𝖎𝖏𝖋𝖑𝖒𝖓𝖔𝖕𝖖𝖗𝖘𝖙𝖚𝖇𝖜𝖝𝖞𝖟 1234567890

Fig. B.4. An example of a Fraktur typeface.

blank cell   In a spreadsheet program, a cell that contains no values, labels, or formatting different from the worksheet's global formats.

blessed folder   The Macintosh's System Folder, equivalent to a DOS subdirectory and containing files loaded at the beginning of an operating session.

The Macintosh operating system, the System, consults this folder when the computer cannot locate a program file. The blessed folder is like a DOS directory named in the PATH command. A major limitation of the Macintosh operating system, however, is that the System Folder is the only folder the System consults when it cannot find a file. Macintosh users, therefore, are obliged to place all the configuration files required by their application programs in this folder, which can quickly grow so large that keeping track of its contents is difficult. See *System* and *System Folder.*

board   See *adapter* and *circuit board.*

block   1. A unit of information processed or transferred. The unit may vary in size. In communications, a unit of information passed from one computer to another is a block. For example, using XMODEM, a communications protocol for transferring files, 128 bytes is considered a block. Under DOS, a block transferred from a disk drive is 512 bytes. 2. In word processing, a unit of text highlighted to be moved, copied, or otherwise affected by a block operation.

Techniques for marking blocks vary. The earliest word processing programs required the user to enter a keyboard command at the beginning and end of the block. More recent programs enable the user to mark the block by using a process called selection, in which the cursor-movement keys are used to highlight the marked text in reverse video. When the block is marked, block operations are possible, such as copying, moving, deleting, formatting, or saving the block to a named file.

block definition   See *selection.*

block graphics   When working with IBM PC-compatible computers, graphics formed on-screen by graphics characters in the extended character set.

The graphics characters in the IBM extended character set are suitable for creating on-screen rectangles but not for fine detail. Because the block graphics characters are handled the same way as ordinary characters, the computer can display block graphics considerably faster than bit-mapped graphics. See *bit-mapped graphic.*

block move   A fundamental editing technique in word processing in which a marked block of text is cut from one location and inserted in another.

Writing experts agree that the major determinant of a written work's quality is its logical coherence: the ideas and facts must be presented in a logical progression. To achieve coherence, restructuring larges amounts of text often is necessary.

Because word processing software enables a writer to restructure large text domains with ease, some writing teachers thought the technology would lead to improved writing. But writers, particularly beginning writers, need to be reminded that major surgery is often necessary to perfect a document's organization.

➔ **Tip:** Learn how to carry out a block move with the word processing software you are using. The technique should be second nature so that you do not hesitate to use it. Remember that a well-organized document, in which the ideas and facts are presented in logical order, impresses people. Synonymous with *cut and paste.*

block operation   The act of transferring a chunk or block of information from one area to another. In word processing, an editing or formatting operation performed on a marked block of text, such as copying, deleting, moving, or underlining. See *block move.*

block protection   In word processing and page layout programs, the prevention of soft page breaks within a block of text. See *bad page break.*

body type   The font (normally 8- to 12-point) used to set the paragraphs of the text (distinguished from the typefaces used to set headings, subheadings, captions, and other typographical elements).

➔ **Tip:** Serif typefaces, such as Century, Garamond, and Times Roman, are preferred over sans serif typefaces for body type because they are more legible. See *display type, sans serif, serif,* and *Times Roman.*

boilerplate   A standard passage of text used over and over in letters, memos, or reports.

➜ **Tip:** Use boilerplate to achieve big gains in your writing productivity. If your job involves answering routine inquiry letters, develop boilerplate responses to questions on such matters as warranty, sales terms, and the like, and attach these passages to glossaries (named storage areas for boilerplate text and other frequently used items, such as logos). Then, you can write a letter just by inserting two or three glossaries and adding a few personalized touches. See *glossary.*

boldface   A character emphasis visibly darker and heavier in weight than normal type. See *emphasis* and *weight.*

bomb   In the Macintosh environment, an error that causes a system crash.

Bookman   See *ITC Bookman.*

Boolean operator   See *logical operator.*

boot   To initiate an automatic routine that clears the memory, loads the operating system, and prepares the computer for use.

The term boot is derived from the saying "pulling yourself up by your own bootstraps." Personal computers must do just that because random-access memory (RAM) does not retain program instructions when the power is shut off.

Buried within the computer's read-only memory (ROM) circuits is an autostart program that comes into play when the power is switched on (a cold boot). Unlike RAM, ROM circuits retain data and program instructions without requiring power. The autostart program instructs the computer's disk drives to search for the disk containing the computer's operating system.

After a system crash occurs, you usually must reboot the computer. With most systems, you can perform a warm boot that restarts the system without the stress on electronic com-

ponents caused by switching the power off and on again.
See *cold boot* and *warm boot*.

boot record   The first track on an IBM PC-compatible disk
(track 0). After you turn on the power, the boot-up software
in ROM instructs the computer to read this track to begin
loading DOS. See *boot*.

bowl   In typography, the curved strokes that enclose or partially enclose the counter (the blank space inside).

bozo bit   A simple copy protection scheme made possible by
the System, the operating system of Macintosh computers.
The System stores each file with a file attribute (the bozo bit)
that, when turned on, prevents you from copying the file by
dragging the icon to another disk.

→ **Tip:** To gain the file-attribute control denied by the
Macintosh operating system, users should equip themselves
with a utility package. For example, DiskTop (CE Software)
and Symantec Tools (Symantec) can display and change file
attributes. See *copy protection*, *file attribute*, and *System*.

bps   See *bits per second (BPS)*.

branch control structure   A control structure in which program control branches in two or more directions, depending
on the results of a conditional test. Synonymous with *selection*. See *case branch*, *control structure*, and *if/then/else* .

break   A user-initiated signal that interrupts processing or the
reception of data. See *Ctrl-Break*.

BREAK   In DOS and OS/2, an internal command that determines when DOS searches for a Ctrl-Break or Ctrl-C keyboard command to stop a program's execution.

The BREAK command has two options: on and off. By default, BREAK is off, meaning that your system runs somewhat
faster, but you have fewer opportunities to interrupt the execution of a program (during standard input, output, print,
and auxiliary device operations). When you turn on BREAK,
DOS checks for a Ctrl-Break or Ctrl-C keystroke with every
DOS operation. See *internal command*.

breakout box   A testing device inserted into a communications cable that enables each electrical line to be tested independently.

bridge   In local area networks, a device that enables two networks (even ones dissimilar in topology, wiring, or communications protocols) to exchange data.

broadband   In local area networks, an analog communications method characterized by high bandwidth. The signal usually is split, or multiplexed, to provide multiple communications channels.

A broadband system uses analog transmissions. Because the microcomputer is a digital device, a device similar to a modem is required at either end of the transmission cable to convert the digital signal to analog and back again.

Broadband communications can extend over great distances and operate at extremely high speeds. A broadband network can, like a cable TV network, convey two or more communication channels at a time (the channels are separated by frequency). Therefore, a broadband network can handle voice and data communications. See *analog* , *analog transmission*, *bandwidth*, *baseband*, and *digital*.

brownout   A period of low-voltage electrical power caused by unusually heavy demand.

Brownouts can cause computers to operate erratically or to crash. If brownouts frequently cause your computer to crash, you may need to purchase an uninterruptible power supply (UPS) to work with your machine. See *uninterruptible power supply (UPS)*.

Browse mode   In a database management program, a program mode in which data records are displayed in a columnar format for quick on-screen review (see fig. B.5). Synonymous with *list* view or *table* view in some programs. See *edit mode*.

brush style   In typography, a typeface design that simulates script drawn with a brush or broad-pointed pen (see fig. B.6).

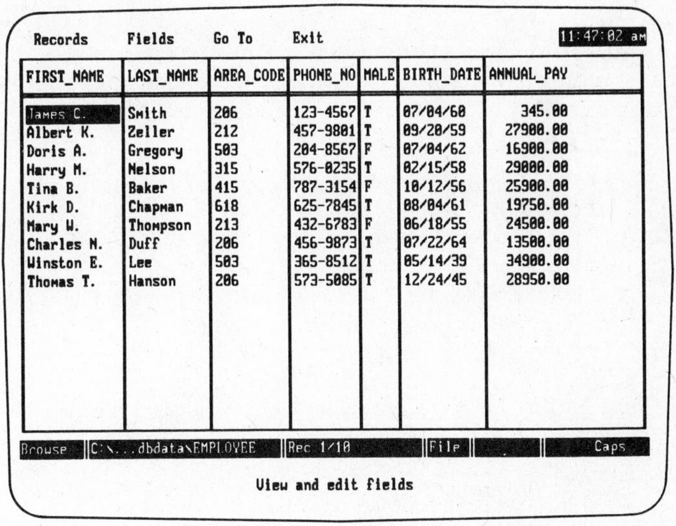

```
┌─────────────────────────────────────────────────────────────────────┐
│  Records      Fields     Go To     Exit                  11:47:02 am  │
│ ┌──────────┬──────────┬─────────┬─────────┬────┬──────────┬─────────┐ │
│ │FIRST_NAME│LAST_NAME │AREA_CODE│PHONE_NO │MALE│BIRTH_DATE│ANNUAL_PAY│ │
│ ├──────────┼──────────┼─────────┼─────────┼────┼──────────┼─────────┤ │
│ │James C.  │Smith     │206      │123-4567 │T   │07/04/60  │   345.00 │ │
│ │Albert K. │Zeller    │212      │457-9801 │T   │09/20/59  │ 27900.00 │ │
│ │Doris A.  │Gregory   │503      │204-8567 │F   │07/04/62  │ 16900.00 │ │
│ │Harry M.  │Nelson    │315      │576-0235 │T   │02/15/58  │ 29000.00 │ │
│ │Tina B.   │Baker     │415      │787-3154 │F   │10/12/56  │ 25900.00 │ │
│ │Kirk D.   │Chapman   │618      │625-7845 │T   │08/04/61  │ 19750.00 │ │
│ │Mary W.   │Thompson  │213      │432-6783 │F   │06/18/55  │ 24500.00 │ │
│ │Charles N.│Duff      │206      │456-9873 │T   │07/22/64  │ 13500.00 │ │
│ │Winston E.│Lee       │503      │365-8512 │T   │05/14/39  │ 34900.00 │ │
│ │Thomas T. │Hanson    │206      │573-5085 │T   │12/24/45  │ 28950.00 │ │
│ │          │          │         │         │    │          │          │ │
│ │          │          │         │         │    │          │          │ │
│ └──────────┴──────────┴─────────┴─────────┴────┴──────────┴─────────┘ │
│ Browse  C:\...dbdata\EMPLOYEE    Rec 1/10      File            Caps    │
│                       View and edit fields                            │
└─────────────────────────────────────────────────────────────────────┘
```

Fig. B.5. Viewing records in Browse mode.

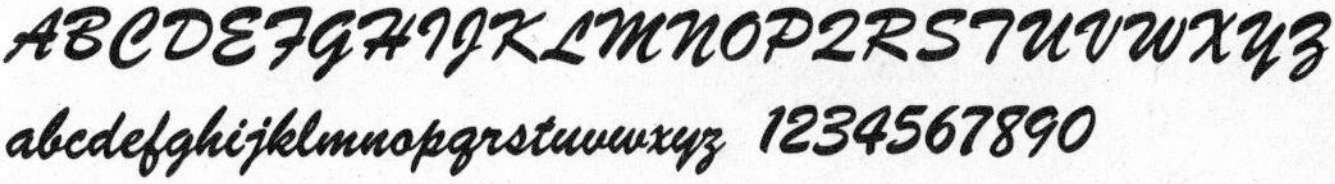

ABCDEFGHIJKLMNOPQRSTUVWXYZ
abcdefghijklmnopqrstuvwxyz 1234567890

Fig. B.6. An example of a brush style typeface,
Brush Script .

buffer A unit of memory given the task of holding information temporarily, especially when such temporary storage is needed to compensate for differences in speed between computer components. See *print buffer*.

BUFFERS In DOS and OS/2, a CONFIG.SYS file command that specifies how many disk buffers DOS sets aside each time you boot the system.

Disk buffers speed your system's operation by storing in memory information that ordinarily is read from disk. However, because each buffer reduces the available memory space by 500 bytes, specifying too many buffers can slow your computer's performance by saturating the memory. By default, DOS uses 2 to 15 buffers, depending on how much memory you have installed in your system.

▲ **Caution:** Some application programs require a minimum number of buffers. If a program requires 20 buffers, for example, the program cannot operate unless a file called CONFIG.SYS is on the start-up disk and contains the instruction **BUFFERS=20**. Most application programs that require this file create the file or add the appropriate statement to the file when you install the program. See *buffer* and *CONFIG.SYS*.

bug A programming error that causes a program or a computer system to perform erratically, produce incorrect results, or crash.

Bugs can have serious consequences. Five days before the first manned moon attempt, a bug was discovered in NASA's program. This bug would have performed trajectory calculations based on the assumption that the moon's gravity was repulsive rather than attractive. If the bug had not been discovered, the astronauts probably would not have returned to earth safely.

The term bug was coined when a real insect was discovered to have fouled up one of the circuits of the first electronic digital computer, the ENIAC.

built-in font A printer font encoded permanently in the printer's read-only memory (ROM).

All laser printers offer at least one built-in font family. You should purchase a printer with a range of built-in fonts, including (at the minimum) a Roman-style serif font (such as Times Roman or Dutch) and an attractive, clean sans serif font (such as Helvetica or Swiss). PostScript-compatible laser printers have a nice range of built-in fonts from Adobe Systems, Inc. These fonts include Avant Garde, Bookman, New Century Schoolbook, Palatino, and Zapf Chancery. See *cartridge font*, *downloadable font*, and *screen font*.

built-in function In a spreadsheet program, a ready-to-use formula that performs mathematical, statistical, trigonometric, financial, calendrical, logical, and other calculations.

A built-in function is prefaced by a special symbol (usually @) and followed by a keyword (such as AVG or SUM) that describes the formula's purpose. Most built-in functions require one or more arguments. In Lotus 1-2-3, for example, the @ROUND function requires you to provide the number to be rounded (or a cell reference) and the number of decimal places to which the number should be rounded. The following built-in function rounds the value in cell C5 to two decimal places: @ROUND(C5,2).

When a built-in function has more than one argument, you must use argument separators, the comma in the preceding example, so that the program can tell one part of the expression from the others. See *argument, argument separator,* and *keyword.*

bulk storage   A secondary storage device (usually using magnetic tape) that can store one terabyte of data or more. Synonymous with *mass storage.*

bullet   An open or closed circle (•), about the height of a lowercase letter, used to set off items in a list.

Often combined with a hanging indent, bullets are effective for listing items whose content is roughly equal in emphasis or significance. If you want to list items that vary in their significance or are arranged chronologically, choose a numbered list. See *hanging indent.*

bulleted list chart   In presentation graphics, a text chart used to communicate a series of ideas or to enumerate items of equal weight (see fig. B.7). See *presentation graphics.*

bulletin board system (BBS)   A private telecommunications utility, usually set up by a personal computer hobbyist for the enjoyment of other hobbyists.

Bulletin boards used to be great fun. Late at night, you loaded your communication software, dialed a BBS, left messages, uploaded and downloaded public domain software and shareware, and played Space Invaders. The advent of computer viruses took away a great deal of the BBS's appeal. Anyone using a personal computer with a hard disk for professional purposes should download software from a BBS with great caution. If you want to explore bulletin boards,

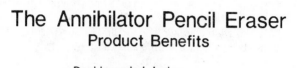

The Annihilator Pencil Eraser
Product Benefits

- Double-ended design

- Brazilian rubber fabrication

- Rubber formula A-27 produces easily removed ball-shaped flecks.

- Rubber formula A-27 lasts 70% longer.

Fig. B.7. A bulleted list chart.

use a dual-floppy computer and keep the downloaded software away from your main system. See *communication program, virus,* and *telecommunication.*

bundled software   Software included with a computer system as part of the system's total price.

burn-in   A power-on test of a computer system performed on behalf of the customer.

     Semiconductor components such as memory chips and microprocessors tend to fail at two times: early or late in their lives but seldom during the middle. Responsible computer retailers, therefore, burn in systems for 24 to 48 hours before releasing the systems to customers. Defective chips are likely to fail during the burn-in period.

bus   An internal pathway along which signals are sent from one part of the computer to another.

Personal computers have a bus design with three pathways:

- The data bus sends data back and forth between the memory and the microprocessor.

- The address bus identifies which memory location will come into play.

- The control bus carries the control unit's signals.

The data bus and address bus are wired in parallel so that all the bits in a binary number can travel simultaneously, like 8 cars side-by-side on a 16-lane freeway. See *expansion bus.*

bus mouse   A mouse connected to the computer by an adapter inserted into an available expansion slot. See *serial mouse.*

bus network   In local area networks, a decentralized network in which a single connecting line, the bus, is shared by a number of nodes, including workstations, shared peripherals, and file servers (see fig. B.8).

Fig. B.8. Bus topology.

In a bus network, a workstation sends a message to all other workstations. Each node in the network, however, has a unique address, and its reception circuitry constantly monitors the bus to determine whether a message is being sent to the node. A message sent to the Laser Printer node, for example, is ignored by the other nodes in the network.

➔ **Tip:** Bus networks have a significant advantage over competing network topologies (star networks and ring networks); the failure of a single node does not disrupt the rest of the network. Most commercial local area networks, such as AppleTalk and EtherNet, use a bus topology. Extending a bus network also is a simple matter. You lengthen the bus and add nodes, up to the system's maximum. The signal, however, cannot travel more than about 1,000 feet without an added device called a repeater. See *bus Network*, *network topology*, *node*, and *repeater*.

byte Pronounced "bite." Eight contiguous bits, the fundamental data word of personal computers.

Storing the equivalent of one character, the byte provides a basic comprehensible unit of measurement for computer storage. Because a single page of double-spaced text contains about 1,375 characters, about 1,500 bytes are required to store the page (allowing for spaces, control characters, and other needed information). Because many bytes of memory are required to store information in a computer, byte counts tend to involve very large numbers—many personal computers have millions of bytes of memory. Because computer architecture is based (for the most part) on binary numbers, bytes are counted in powers of two. The most frequently used units are kilobyte (K), or 2^{10} = 1,024 bytes, and megabyte (M) (2^{20} = 1,048,576).

The terms kilo (in kilobyte) and mega (in megabyte) are misleading: they derive from decimal (base 10) numbers. Kilo suggests 1,000, and mega suggests 1,000,000. Many computer scientists criticize these terms for their inherent inaccuracy and irrelevance to computer architecture. By any standard, 2^{10} and 2^{20} are logical places to establish benchmarks for measurement, and the fact that they are close to 1,000 and 1,000,000 (respectively) gives those who think in decimal numbers a nice handle on the measurement of memory. See *bit* and *kilobyte (K)*.

C

C A high-level programming language widely used for professional programming. C is highly portable and produces efficient, fast-running programs.

Developed by Dennis Ritchie of Bell Laboratories in 1972, C is a descendant of an earlier language called B. Most major professional software companies prefer C over other programming languages. A general-purpose procedural language like FORTRAN, BASIC, and Pascal, C combines the virtues of high-level programming languages with the efficiency of an assembly language.

The program's syntax encourages the creation of well-structured programs using modern control structures. At the same time, the programmer can embed instructions that directly address the processor's internal management of individual data bits. Because these instructions perform computations at the processing unit's highest speed, compiled C programs run significantly faster than programs written in other high-level programming languages. You can think of C, in fact, as a modular and structured framework for the expression of assembly language instructions. The framework of the program expresses the algorithm for the application; the assembly language instructions reach the bit-by-bit representation of data inside the processing unit to enhance the speed and efficiency of the program's operations.

Assembly language programs usually are not portable to other processing environments because assembly language programs are tied to a specific processing unit's design. A C program is rewritten easily and quickly so that the program runs on a new computer, if the target environment has a C compiler. The language's portability is an important factor in its widespread adoption by professional programmers, who hope to find the widest possible market for their products. The portability of C is evident in UNIX. This operating system (also developed at Bell Laboratories) was written in C and is portable across all processor architectures. Most UNIX systems include C compilers.

Despite C's many advantages, the language is formidable for beginners. Unlike BASIC and Pascal, which originated as teaching languages, C was designed as a tool for advanced professional programmers. Therefore, the syntax and terminology are designed for efficiency rather than readability.

C's dominance in the professional programming world is all but ensured, and not merely because of its efficiency and portability. AT&T's Bell Laboratories was prohibited from copyrighting C or UNIX because of the antitrust regulations in effect before the breakup of the Bell System. Therefore, C compilers and UNIX are in the public domain and have been adopted by virtually all colleges and universities. The result is a steady stream of computer science graduates well versed in the C language and the UNIX operating system. See *algorithm, assembly language, control structure, high-level programming language, portable computer, procedural language, syntax*, and *UNIX*.

C++ A high-level programming language developed by AT&T's Bell Laboratories. Based on its predecessor, C, C++ is an object-oriented programming language that combines the benefits of C with the modularity of object-oriented programming. The language has been chosen by several large software publishers for major development projects. See *C* and *object-oriented programming language*.

cache memory Pronounced "cash." A special fast section of random-access memory (RAM) set aside to store the most frequently accessed information stored in RAM.

A cache memory is a special section of ultra-fast RAM chips (such as static RAM chips). This section is controlled by a cache controller chip, such as the Intel 82385. Cache memory dramatically improves the speed of a computer because the microprocessor need not wait for the slower dynamic random-access memory chips (DRAM) to catch up. With a cache memory and cache controller, even a fast 80386 microprocessor can operate without wait states. Cache memory is distinguished from a disk cache, an area of ordinary RAM set aside to store information frequently accessed from disk drives.

→ **Tip:** To assemble a very fast computer system, choose a system with the Intel 82385 cache controller and at least 32K of static cache memory (64K is preferable). See *disk cache, static random-access memory RAM*, and *wait state*.

CAD See *computer-aided design*.

CADD See *computer aided design and drafting*.

CAI See *computer-aided instruction*.

calculated field In a database management program, a data field that contains the results of calculations performed on other fields.

In a database that stores students' grades for a training course, for example, you can create a field that totals the scores of tests and quizzes. You can place the calculated field on the on-screen data form or on the report form so that the calculated total appears when you print. Synonymous with *derived field*. See *data field* and *field*.

call   In programming, a statement that directs the flow of program control to a subroutine, procedure, or function.

CALL   In DOS and OS/2, a batch command that tells DOS to carry out instructions in another specified batch file and then return to the original batch file and resume carrying out its instructions. See *batch file*.

callout   The text (often accompanied by arrows) used to point out and identify parts of an illustration.

camera-ready copy   A printed and finished manuscript or illustration ready to be photographed by the printer for reproduction.

cap height   The height of a capital letter from the baseline. See *baseline*.

Caps Lock key   A toggle key that locks the keyboard so that uppercase letters are entered without you pressing the Shift key.

Some keyboards have a light that shows when you toggle the keyboard into the uppercase mode. If the keyboard has no light, you must look at what you are typing before you know which mode you have selected. Some programs display a message when you are in uppercase mode.

▲ **Caution:** Unlike the Caps Lock key of a typewriter, the keyboard's Caps Lock key has no effect on the number and punctuation keys. To use the punctuation marks on the row of number keys, you must press Shift whether or not you have pressed Caps Lock.

card   An electronic circuit board designed to fit into the slots of a computer's expansion bus. Synonymous with *adapter*. See *expansion bus*.

caret Pronounced "carrot." A symbol (^) commonly found over the 6 key on computer keyboards. The caret sometimes is used to stand for the Ctrl key in computer documentation, as in "Press ^C."

carriage return See *Enter/Return.*

carrier sense multiple access with collision detect (CSMA/CD) In local area networks, a widely used method for controlling a computer's access to the communication channel. With CSMA/CD, each component of the network (called a node) has an equal right to access the communication channel. If two computers try to access the network at the same time (an unlikely occurrence), the network uses a random number to decide which computer gets on to the network.

This channel access method works well with relatively small- to medium-sized networks (two or three dozen nodes). This method is used by the two most popular network architectures: EtherNet and AppleTalk. When you have many workstations, and network traffic volume is high, however, many data collisions occur. The entire system can become overloaded and lock up, with each station behaving as if it is trying to access the system and failing because the system is in use. Large networks, therefore, use alternative channel access methods, such as polling and token passing. See *AppleTalk, EtherNet, local area network (LAN), node, polling,* and *token passing.*

Cartesian coordinate system Pronounced "car-tee´-zhun." A method, created by the seventeenth-century French mathematician René Descartes, of locating a point in a two-dimensional space by defining a vertical x-axis and a horizontal y-axis.

A mouse uses the Cartesian coordinate system to locate the pointer on-screen. In some graphics applications, you can display the coordinates so that the pointer can be located precisely.

cartridge In secondary storage, a removable module containing secondary storage media such as magnetic tape and magnetic disks. In computer printers, a removable module that expands the printer's memory or font capabilities.

cartridge font   A printer font supplied in the form of a read-only memory (ROM) cartridge that plugs into a receptacle on Hewlett-Packard LaserJet printers and clones.

Hewlett-Packard LaserJet printers rely heavily on cartridge fonts that have some merits over their chief competition, downloadable fonts. Unlike downloadable fonts, the ROM-based cartridge font is immediately available to the printer and does not consume space in the printer's random-access memory (RAM), which can be used up quickly when printing documents loaded with graphics.

Hewlett-Packard's cartridges generally contain only two to four typefaces, but other firms have cartridges available with as many as 25 fonts in several typefaces.

➔ **Tip:** If you plan to print documents containing several typefaces, buying one cartridge that contains all the typefaces you use is better than buying several cartridges, each of which contains only one or two typefaces. With the multi-typeface cartridge, you do not need to change cartridges in the middle of a printing operation. See *font* and *typeface*.

case branch   In programming, a branch control structure that specifically enumerates several if/then/else branch options.

The following pseudocode example demonstrates how a menu with three options can be kept on-screen until the user gives one of the three correct responses.

```
WHILE response = false
    ASK choice "Load (R)eport, (L)etter, or
        (M)emo template?"
    BEGIN CASE
        CASE choice = "R"
            LOAD REPORT.DOC
            SET response = true
        CASE choice = "L"
            LOAD LETTER.DOC
            SET response = true
        CASE choice = "M"
            LOAD MEMO.DOC
            SET response = true
    END CASE
ENDWHILE
```

In English, the program reads as follows: Define a new variable, called response and set the variable to false. Create a variable called choice and show an on-screen message asking whether the user wants to load a report, letter, or memo template. Place the user's typed response in the choice variable. If the response equals false, examine the user input. If the user types R, load the REPORT.DOC file and set the response to true. If the user types L, load the LETTER.DOC file and set the response to true. If the user types M, load the MEMO.DOC file and set the response to true. When the response contains true, quit.

The menu in the ASK statement stays on-screen until the user presses one of the three acceptable inputs: R, L, or M (upper- or lowercase). Any other input doesn't match one of the cases and doesn't set the response to true. As long as the response remains false, the menu stays on-screen. See *control structure* and *pseudocode*.

case-sensitive Responsive to the difference between upper- and lowercase letters. DOS is not case-sensitive; you can type DOS commands in upper- or lowercase letters.

case-sensitive search A search in which the program attempts to match the exact pattern of upper- and lowercase letters in the search string. A case-sensitive search for Porter, for example, matches Porter but not PORTER, porter, or pOrter.

catalog In dBASE, a list of related database files you have grouped together so that they are distinguished easily from others.

Like all relational database management programs, dBASE can work with more than one file at a time. Frequently, the results of relational operations (such as a join) produce a new file. In addition, you create several indexes and other files that support the application. The Catalog menu helps you track all these related files in a unit. See *dBASE*, *join*, and *relational database management system (RDBMS)*.

cathode ray tube (CRT) A computer monitor that uses an electron gun (cathode) to emit a beam of electrons that paint the phosphors on the screen as the beam sweeps across.

CBT   See *computer-based training.*

CD   See *compact disk (CD)* or *CHDIR.*

CDEV   See *control panel device (CDEV).*

CD-ROM   Pronounced "see dee rahm´." A read-only optical storage technology that uses compact disks.

CD-ROM disks can store up to 650M of data, all of which can be made available interactively on the computer's display. CD-ROM currently is used to produce encyclopedias, dictionaries, and software libraries available to personal computer users. New compression techniques enable you to pack up to 250,000 text pages on one CD-ROM disk. See *compact disk* and *optical storage.*

CD-ROM disk drive   A read-only disk drive designed to access and read the data encoded on compact disks and transfer this data to a computer.

With audio compact disk players selling for as little as $99, personal computer users often are appalled at the high price of CD-ROM drives. The two devices, however, are dissimilar. A CD-ROM disk drive contains circuitry optimized to locate data at high speeds; CD players need to locate only the beginning of audio tracks, which they play sequentially. As the number of these drives increases, the prices of CD-ROM drives will drop to more reasonable levels. See *compact disk.*

cell   In a spreadsheet, the rectangle formed by the intersection of a row and column. You can place constants, labels, or formulas in cells. See *constant, label,* and *formula.*

cell address   In a spreadsheet, a code that identifies a cell's location on the worksheet by specifying the cell's row and column (A3, B9, C2, and so on). When used in a formula, the cell address becomes a cell reference. See *cell reference* and *formula.*

cell animation   An animation technique in which a background painting is held in place while transparent sheets of celluloid are moved over the background painting, producing the illusion of movement.

Cell animation is much easier than drawing a new background for every frame in the animation sequence. A Macintosh animation program that uses a computerized version of cell animation is MacroMind Director. See *MacroMind Director.*

cell definition   The actual contents of a cell in a spreadsheet, as displayed on the entry line.

The cell definition may differ from what is displayed in the worksheet. If you place a formula in the cell, the program displays the value generated by the formula rather than the formula itself (see fig. C.1).

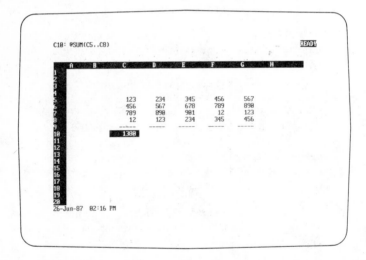

Fig. C.1. Value returned by the formula shown on the entry line.

▲ **Caution:** You easily can corrupt a spreadsheet by typing a value in a cell that contains a formula. As you look at the worksheet, unless the pointer is resting on the cell, you have no way to tell whether a cell's value is a constant (a number you typed directly into the cell) or a value produced by a formula. If you mistakenly think that the value is a constant, you may change the value and erase the formula stored in the cell. Then, the worksheet may not generate the correct answer—but you don't know why. This mistake is a common source of incorrect results.

You can guard against this problem by using cell protection and by keeping your eye on the entry line as you move the cursor through the worksheet. The entry line always shows the current cell definition, displaying precisely what is in the cell—including any formula. See *cell protection, entry line, formula,* and *value.*

cell format   In a spreadsheet, the way the program displays values and labels on-screen.

You can format labels and values two ways: first, by choosing a global format that affects all the cells of a worksheet; second, by choosing a range format that affects one or more cells in a rectangular block. Label formats for character-based programs like Lotus 1-2-3 are limited to label alignment; graphics spreadsheets can use multiple typefaces and type sizes. Numeric formats include currency (dollar signs, commas, and two decimal places), fixed (user-specified number of decimal places), and general (all significant digits displayed). See *character-based program, current cell, global format, graphics spreadsheet, label, label alignment, numeric format, range format,* and *value.*

cell pointer   In Lotus 1-2-3, the rectangular highlight that indicates the location on-screen of the current cell, where values and labels appear after you type them and press Enter. Synonymous with *cursor.*

cell protection   In a spreadsheet program, a format applied to a cell, a range of cells, or an entire file. The format prevents you from altering the contents of protected cells.

cell reference   In a spreadsheet formula, a cell address that specifies the location of a value to be used to solve the formula. Cell references are the keys to a spreadsheet program's power and usefulness. A spreadsheet program would not be very useful if you had to write formulas with constants, such as 2+2. Because formulas are not visible on the worksheet, you would have to edit the formula to perform the exploratory what-if recalculations that make spreadsheets useful. Using cell references instead of values, you write the formula as B1+B2. B1 and B2 are cell addresses. When used in a formula, they instruct the program to go to the named cell (such as B1) and to use the value appearing in that cell. If you want to change the constants, you don't have to edit the formula; you type a new constant in cell B1 or cell B2.

Cell references enable the user to create an intricate pattern of links among the cells in a worksheet. A cell reference also can refer to a cell containing a formula. The value produced by the formula is referenced. Because the formula may contain its own cell references to other cells, which can themselves contain formulas, the worksheet can contain an unbroken chain of mathematical links. A change made to any constant in such a worksheet affects intermediate values and, ultimately, the bottom line. See *cell address, constant, formula, recalculation, value,* and *what-if analysis.*

central mass storage   See *file server.*

central processing unit (CPU)   The computer's internal storage, processing, and control circuitry, including the arithmetic-logic unit (ALU), the control unit, and the primary storage.

Only the ALU and control unit are wholly contained on the microprocessor chip; the primary storage is elsewhere on the motherboard or an adapter on the expansion bus. See *adapter, arithmetic/logic unit (ALU), control unit, expansion bus, microprocessor, motherboard,* and *primary storage.*

CGA   See *Color Graphics Adapter (CGA).*

CGM   See *computer graphics metafile (CGM).*

chained printing   The printing of separate files as a unit by placing at the end of the first file commands that direct the program to continue printing the second file, and so on.

Full-featured word processing programs such as Microsoft Word enable chained printing with continuous pagination and in some cases the generation of a complete table of contents and index for the combined document.

chamfer   Pronounced "cham´-fer." In desktop publishing and presentation graphics, a beveled edge between two intersecting lines.

channel access   In local area networks, the method used to gain access to the data communication channel that links the computers. Three common methods are contention, polling, and token ring. See *contention, local area network (LAN), polling,* and *token-ring Network.*

character   Any letter, number, punctuation mark, or symbol that can be produced on-screen by pressing a key.

character-based program   In IBM PC-compatible computing, a program that relies on the IBM PC's built-in character set and block graphics rather than taking advantage of a windowing environment to display on-screen fonts and bit-mapped graphics. See *Lotus 1-2-3, Microsoft Windows,* and *windowing environment.*

character graphics   See *block graphics.*

character-mapped display   A method of displaying characters in which a special section of memory is set aside to represent the display; programs generate a display by inserting characters into the memory-based representation of the screen. The whole screen, therefore, remains active, not just one line, and the user or the program can modify characters anywhere on-screen. See *teletype display (TTY).*

character mode   A display mode in which the video image is constructed from the computer's built-in character set, which may include block graphics. Character mode, however, cannot display bit-mapped graphics. Synonymous with *text mode.* See *bit-mapped graphics, block graphics,* and *character set.*

character set   The fixed set of keyboard codes that a particular computer system uses. See *American Standard Code for Information Interchange (ASCII), code page,* and *extended character set.*

characters per inch (cpi)   The number of characters that fit within a linear inch in a given font. Standard units drawn from typewriting are pica (10 cpi) and elite (12 cpi).

characters per second (cps)   A measurement of the speed of a communications or printing device.

CHCP   In DOS and OS/2, an internal command that selects the code page (character set) currently in use. See *code page* and *internal command.*

CHDIR (CD)   In DOS and OS/2, an internal command that changes the current directory.

Hard disk users must master this command to use computers effectively. DOS places a maximum limit of 512 files for each directory, but today's 40M and larger hard disks can hold many more files. Almost all hard disk users divide disks into directories and subdirectories. The CHDIR (or CD) command permits users to switch from one directory to another quickly.

➜ **Tip:** Typing CHDIR commands is a hassle because you must type the directory symbol, a backslash, before you type the directory name. The location of this symbol is one of the least standardized elements of IBM PC-compatible computer keyboards. More than likely, you have to hunt for the key. In some situations, however, you can omit the backslash. To change to a directory immediately below the current directory, you need type only CHDIR and the directory name, as in the following example:

    CHDIR MEMOS

To change to the parent directory, the directory immediately above the current directory, you need only type CHDIR and the parent directory symbol, two periods, as in the following example:

    CHDIR..

See *directory, internal command, parent directory,* and *subdirectory.*

check boxes   In a graphical user interface, a square option box, which the user clicks to select or deselect an option from a group of options in an on-screen dialog box. See *dialog box* and *radio button.*

checksum   In data communications, an error-checking technique in which the number of bits in a unit of data is summed and transmitted along with the data. The receiving computer then checks the sum.

If the sum differs, an error probably occurred in transmission. A commonly used personal computer communications protocol called XMODEM uses the checksum technique. See *XMODEM.*

chip   A miniaturized electronic circuit mass-produced on a tiny chip or wafer of silicon.

The electronic age began in earnest with the 1947 invention of the transistor, a switching and amplifying device that replaces huge, power-hungry, and unreliable vacuum tubes. As important as the transistor was, it did not solve the biggest problem facing any firm that wanted to manufacture complex electronic components: the necessity of wiring all those components together.

Various automated procedures were devised, but in the end, at least some of the wiring and soldering had to be done manually. Complex electronic devices, therefore, were very expensive.

In the late 1950s, Jack Kilby (an engineer at Texas Instruments) and Robert Noyce (an engineer at Fairchild Semiconductor) discovered that they could create an integrated circuit, a chip made out of semiconducting materials that could duplicate the function of several transistors and other electronic components.

Semiconductors, materials such as silicon, can be chemically altered in a process called doping so that their conductive properties are improved or reduced. By doping a chip of silicon in a series of layers, each with differing conductive properties, the equivalent of one or more transistors can be created.

The first integrated circuits contained only a few components, but an impressive and sustained drive of technological development created chips containing thousands, tens of thousands, and more components on one tiny chip. The same techniques now can generate 16 million components on a chip so tiny that it can be placed on the tip of your finger.

Of even greater economic and social significance than the chip's miniaturization is the fact that it can be mass-produced. After a chip is designed, the circuit pattern is transferred to a series of lithographic plates called photomasks. The photomasks then are used to coat the chip with materials that, when exposed to light, lay down a pattern of hardened and unhardened areas. Acid is applied to etch out the unhardened areas, and then chemicals are forced into these areas to alter the silicon's conductive properties.

Through multiple applications of the photomask, a chip with several layers of silicon with varying conductive properties is created, and the result is the equivalent of a complex electronic circuit. The process is largely automated, and chips can be produced at low prices.

Today's Intel 80486 microprocessor, for example, sells for a few hundred dollars, but this microprocessor is the electronic equivalent of a mainframe computer priced at several million dollars just 20 years ago. The achievement of chip-manufacturing technology has made the diffusion of computer technology throughout society possible.

Memory chips and microprocessors are the two chips most applicable to user's needs, but many kinds of special-purpose chips are manufactured for a variety of applications. These chips include microprocessor support chips, chips for the control of disk drives, and chips for generating video displays. See *integrated circuit* and *microprocessor.*

CHKDSK   Pronounced "check-disk." In DOS and OS/2, an external command that checks the directory and file allocation table (FAT) of the disk and reports disk and memory status. This command also reports the amount of free memory space available for application programs.

CHKDSK also detects lost chains, or portions of program or data files that have become detached from the rest of the original file. DOS does not store a program file in contiguous portions of a disk; the file may be broken up into sections distributed here and there. The file allocation table tracks the linkages. However, the information required to track these linkages may be lost, and the result is a lost chain—or several of them.

➜ **Tip:** Use CHKDSK with the /F parameter (load the program by typing CHKDSK /F). If the command finds lost chains, you are given the option of converting them to files. Examine these files using the TYPE command to see whether they contain information you want to save. If they don't, erase them to free up disk space. See *directory, file allocation table (FAT), lost chain, parameter,* and *TYPE.*

Chooser   A Macintosh desktop accessory (DA) supplied by Apple Computer with the Mac's operating system (the System). The Chooser governs the selection of printer drivers, programs that control communication with the printer. The Chooser displays the icons of the printer drivers currently installed in the System Folder.

A major contrast between character-based DOS and the Macintosh operating system is that the Macintosh provides printer drivers at the operating system level, but in DOS computers, character-based programs must provide their own printer drivers. This arrangement is inconvenient for the user (not all programs offer a wide range of drivers) and costly for software developers, who must develop dozens of drivers for each application program. A Chooser printer driver works with any Mac application. Following the Mac's lead, the windowing environments for DOS and OS/2—Microsoft Windows and Presentation—provide printer drivers for all programs designed to take advantage of their graphical user interfaces. See *character-based program, printer driver, System,* and *System Folder.*

chord   In desktop publishing and presentation graphics, a line segment that connects the end points of an arc.

circular reference   In a spreadsheet, an error condition caused by two or more formulas referencing each other. For example, a circular reference occurs when the formula +B5 is placed in cell A1 and the formula +A1 is placed in cell B5.

Circular references do not always result in errors. They can be used deliberately, for example, to create an iterative function in a spreadsheet: each recalculation increases the values of the two formulas. However, circular references frequently arise from unintentional typing errors. Unintended circular references may produce erroneous results.

→ **Tip:** If you see an error message informing you that a circular reference exists in your worksheet, track down the circular reference. Eliminate any unwanted circular references before placing confidence in the spreadsheet's accuracy.

circuit board   A flat plastic board on which electrically conductive circuits have been laminated. Synonymous with printed circuit board. See *adapter* and *motherboard.*

CISC   See *complex instruction set computer (CISC).*

clear   To remove a document or other work from the computer's random-access memory (RAM) so that you can start with a fresh, blank workspace. Synonymous with *abandon.*

click   To press and quickly release a mouse button.

client   In a local area network, a workstation with processing capabilities, such as a personal computer, that can request information or applications from the network's file server. See *client-server network, file server,* and *local area network (LAN).*

client-based application   In a local area network, an application that resides on a personal computer workstation and is not available for use by others on the network.

   Client-based applications do not make sharing common data easy, but they are resistant to the system-wide failure that occurs when a server-based application becomes unavailable after the file server crashes. See *client-server network, file server, local area network (LAN),* and *server-based application.*

client-server network   A method of allocating resources in a local area network so that computing power is distributed among the personal computers in the network, but some shared resources are centralized in a file server. See *file server* and *peer-to-peer network.*

clip art   A collection of graphics images, stored on disk and available for use in a page layout or presentation graphics program.

The term clip art is derived from graphics design tradition; portfolios of printed clip art are sold and actually clipped out by layout artists to enhance newsletters, brochures, and presentation graphics. Now available on disk, clip art collections can be read by most page layout or presentation graphics programs (see fig. C.2).

Fig. C.2. T/Maker clip art.

clipboard   A temporary storage place in memory (called a buffer). The clipboard stores text or graphics that have been cut or copied from one location in a document to be pasted into another location in the same or another document (see fig. C.3). The same temporary parking place is used to store text and graphics while copying or moving them from one application to another. See *buffer.*

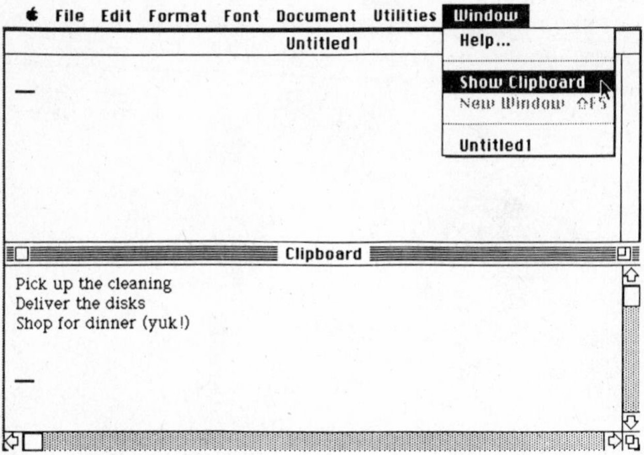

*Fig. C.3. The clipboard temporarily stores text or
graphics during cut-and-paste operations.*

Clipper A compiler developed by Nantucket Systems, Inc., for
the dBASE software command language (IBM version). Considered by many application developers to be superior to the
compiler offered by dBASE's publisher, Ashton-Tate. See
compiler and *dBASE.*

clock An electronic circuit that generates evenly spaced pulses
at speeds of millions of cycles per second; the pulses are
used to synchronize the flow of information through the
computer's internal communication channels.

   Some computers also contain a circuit that tracks hours,
minutes, and seconds. See *clock speed* and *clock/calendar
board.*

clock/calendar board An adapter that includes a battery-
powered clock for tracking the system time and date and is
used in computers that lack such facilities on their motherboards. See *adapter* and *motherboard.*

clock speed   The speed of the internal clock of a microprocessor that sets the pace (measured in megahertz [MHz])
at which operations proceed within the computer's internal
processing circuitry.

Each successive model of microprocessor has produced a
faster clock speed. The original microprocessor of IBM Personal Computers, the Intel 8088, operated at a speed of 4.77
MHz. The chip powering the original IBM Personal Computer AT, the Intel 80286, operated at 6 MHz, with more recent versions operating at up to 25 MHz. The Intel 80386 microprocessor operates at speeds ranging from 16 to 33 MHz.

Clock speed affects performance but is not the only determinant. Faster clock speeds bring noticeable gains in CPU-intensive tasks, such as recalculating a spreadsheet. Disk-intensive application programs perform slowly, however, if the
disk drives are sluggish. See *Intel 8088*, *Intel 80286*, and
Intel 80386.

clone   A functional copy of a hardware device, such as a non-
IBM PC-compatible computer that runs software and uses
peripherals intended for an IBM PC-compatible computer, or
of a program, such as a spreadsheet program that reads Lotus
1-2-3 files and recognizes most or all of the commands.

Only one year after the IBM PC hit the market, a Texas
company, COMPAQ, released the first IBM PC-compatible
computer. The COMPAQ was designed to be 100-percent
compatible with IBM software and accessory devices, such as
displays and printers. Additional companies followed COM-
PAQ with 100-percent compatible computers; these companies, including AT&T, Tandy, Zenith, Epson, and Dell, experienced great success. At first, these computers were known
collectively as clones, conveying the connotation of a cheap
imitation. Many IBM PC-compatible computers actually improved on the original, however, so the term clone is no
longer fair.

Why did IBM permit so many companies to copy its personal computer? The original IBM PC was designed to use
off-the-shelf components—such as disk drives, microprocessors, and power supplies—that non-IBM companies had developed for earlier personal computers. These same compo-

nents could be assembled by anyone with the requisite technical know-how. In addition, IBM purchased the PC's operating system, PC DOS, from Microsoft Corporation, which was free to sell virtually the same system (MS-DOS) to clone manufacturers. The only part of the computer that IBM actually copyrighted was a small amount of internal programming code, which other computer companies could emulate without actually copying. In 1987, IBM threatened to sue several small clone makers who, according to IBM, had actually copied the code verbatim.

Partly to counter the compatible market, IBM attempted to close the architecture of its personal computers by the 1986 release of the PS/2 series. A key feature of the PS/2 line is its Micro Channel bus architecture, which has certain technical advantages over the method used to communicate data within previous PCs. But, the Micro Channel bus created a closed environment for PC add-on boards and accessories; the older boards and accessories do not work on a Micro Channel machine, and any company developing products for Micro Channel machines needs to obtain a license from IBM.

Compatible makers have not emulated the Micro Channel standard, preferring instead to stick with the tried-and-true PC architecture. To take full advantage of the 32-bit bus structure of the Intel 80386 and 80486 microprocessors, these manufacturers (dubbed the "Gang of Nine") have created a bus standard called Extended Industry Standard Architecture (EISA). Computers conforming to the EISA standard can accept existing adapters while taking full advantage of these powerful new microprocessors.

Clones also exist in the software world, but unlike hardware clones, software clones have attracted a great deal of litigation. In early cases, the courts tended to support clone makers as long as the program code was not a verbatim copy of the original. More recently, however, courts have taken the view that a copyright infringement occurs if a program emulates the "look and feel" of another program, even if the code differs. On this basis, Lotus Development Corporation sued Paperback Software International, claiming that Paperback's VP-Planner copied the look and feel of Lotus 1-2-3. In a move that astonished industry observers, Apple Computer sued Microsoft Corporation, claiming that Microsoft Windows copied the look and feel of the Macintosh user interface. These and other cases will require years of litigation to resolve, but few firms have attempted software clones recently. The cost of litigation can ruin a small company, even if that company wins. See *Extended Industry Standard Architecture (EISA)*, *Micro Channel BUS*, and *PS/2*.

closed bus system   A computer design in which the computer's internal data bus does not contain receptacles and is not easily upgraded by users. See *open bus system*.

CLS   In DOS and OS/2, an internal command that clears the screen and places the cursor in the home position (upper left corner). See *internal command*.

cluster   In a floppy disk or hard disk, a unit of storage that includes one or more sectors.

When DOS stores a file on disk, DOS breaks down the file's contents and distributes them among dozens or even hundreds of clusters drawn from hither and thither all over the disk. The file allocation table (FAT) tracks how all the sectors on a disk are connected. See *CHKDSK*, *file allocation table (FAT)*, *file fragmentation*, and *sector*.

CMOS   See *Complementary Metal-Oxide Semiconductor (CMOS)*.

coaxial cable   Pronounced "co-acks´-ee-uhl." In local area networks, a high-bandwidth connecting cable in which an insulated wire runs through the middle of the cable. Surrounding the insulated wire is a second wire made of solid or mesh metal.

Coaxial cable is much more expensive than twisted-pair cable (ordinary telephone wire), but coaxial cable can carry more data. Coaxial cables are required for high-bandwidth broadband systems and for fast baseband systems like EtherNet. See *bandwidth*, *broadband*, *local area network (LAN)*, and *twisted pair cable*.

COBOL   Pronounced "co´-ball." A high-level programming language specially designed for business applications.

Short for COmmon Business Oriented Language, COBOL is a compiled language that originated in a 1959 committee representing business, government, defense, and academic organizations. Released in 1964, the language was the first to introduce the data record as a principal data structure. Because COBOL is designed to store, retrieve, and process corporate accounting information and to automate such functions as inventory control, billing, and payroll, the language quickly became the language of choice in businesses. COBOL programs are verbose but easy to read because most commands resemble English. The programmer, therefore, hardly can help documenting the program, and program maintenance and enhancement are easy even if personnel change frequently. COBOL is the most widely used programming language in corporate mainframe environments.

Versions of COBOL are available for personal computers, but the language's strengths for corporate computing are of little relevance to stand-alone workstations. Business applications for personal computers far more frequently are created and maintained in the dBASE command language that taps the flexible data record capabilities of this popular database management system. See *dBASE* and *high-level programming language*.

code   To express a problem-solving algorithm in a programming language. See *algorithm*.

code page   In DOS and OS/2, a table of 256 codes for an IBM PC-compatible computer's character set.

Code pages are classed as two kinds:

1. Hardware code page, the character set built into the computer's ROM

2. Prepared code page, a disk-based character set you can use to override the hardware code page

Prepared code pages contain character sets appropriate for foreign languages. (Supported by DOS 4.0, for example, are Canadian French, Danish, Finnish, French, German, Italian, Latin American Spanish, Dutch, Norwegian, Portuguese, Peninsular Spanish, U.K. English, and U.S. English.) To override the hardware code page, use the CHANGE CODE PAGE (or CHCP) command. See *character set* and *CHCP*.

codes   See *hidden codes*.

cold boot A system start-up initiated by turning on the system's power switch. See *boot* and *warm boot*.

cold link A connection established between two files or data items so that a change in one is reflected by a change in the second. A cold link requires user intervention and action, such as opening both files and using an updating command, to make sure that the change occurs. See *warm link*.

collate Pronounced "co´-late." Synonymous with *sort*.

collating sequence See *sort order*.

collision In local area networks, a garbled transmission that results from simultaneous transmissions by two or more workstations to the same network cable. See *local area network*. (LAN)

color In typography, the tone quality of the printed portion of the page, which should be perceived by the eye as an overall shade of gray without interruption from rivers, bad word breaks, poor character spacing, or uneven line spacing.

To maintain good color, use consistent word spacing, avoid widows and orphans, use kerning as necessary (especially for display type), and avoid hyphen ladders. See *hyphen ladder*, *kerning*, *orphan*, *river*, and *widow*.

Color Graphics Adapter (CGA) A bit-mapped graphics display adapter for IBM PC-compatible computers. This adapter displays four colors simultaneously with a resolution of 200 pixels horizontally and 320 pixels vertically or displays one color with a resolution of 640 pixels horizontally and 200 vertically.

CGAs can drive composite color monitors and RGB monitors, but screen resolution produced by CGA adapters is inferior to that of EGA and VGA adapters. See *bit-mapped graphic*, *composite color monitor*, *Enhanced Graphics Adapter (EGA)*, *RGB monitor*, and *Video Graphics Array (VGA)*.

color monitor A computer display device that can display an image in multiple colors, unlike a monochrome monitor that displays one color on a black or white background.

color separation   The creation of a multicolor graphic by creating several layers, with each layer corresponding to one of
the colors that will be printed when the graphic is reproduced by a professional printer. See *Pantone Matching System* .

column   In character-based video displays, a vertical one-char-
acter-wide line down the screen. In a spreadsheet, a vertical
block of cells, identified (in most programs) by a unique alphabetical letter. In a relational database management program, column is sometimes used synonymously with field.

column graph   In presentation and analytical graphics, a
graph with vertical columns. Column graphs commonly are
used to show the values of items as they vary at precise intervals over a period of time (see fig. C.4). The x-axis (categories axis) is the horizontal axis, and the y-axis (values axis) is
the vertical axis.

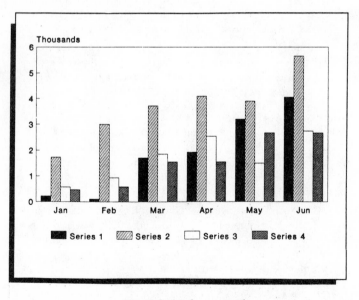

Fig. C.4. A column graph.

Technically, bar graph refers only to graphs with horizontal bars; if the bars are vertical, the graph is a column graph.

In practice, however, bar graph is used to name both types. In professional presentation graphics, bar graphs are used to display the values of discrete items (apples, oranges, grape-fruit, and papaya), and column graphs are used to show the change in one or more items over time (for example, apples vs. oranges in January, February, March, and so on).

Column graphs also should be differentiated from line graphs, which suggest a continuous change over time. Column graphs suggest that the information was obtained at intervals. In this sense, column graphs are more honest than line graphs in some cases, because a line graph suggests that you are making data observations all along instead of once a month or once every two weeks.

When displaying more than one data series, clustering the columns (see fig. C.5) or overlapping them (see fig. C.6) is helpful to the audience. With caution, you also can create a three-dimensional effect to differentiate the columns, but choose this option only if it really helps clarify the data (see fig. C.7). See *bar graph, line graph, histogram, stacked-column graph, x-axis,* and *y-axis.*

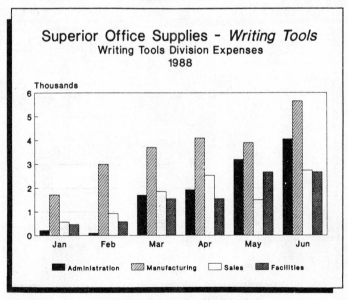

Fig. C.5. Clustered columns.

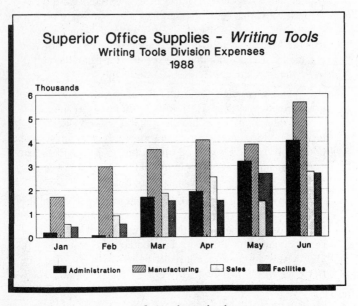

Fig. C.6. Overlapped columns.

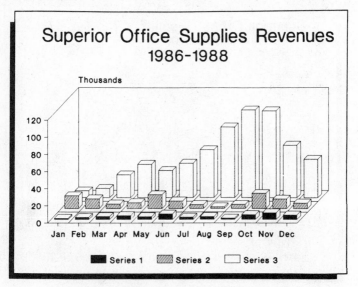

Fig. C.7. A three-dimensional column graph.

column indicator   In word processing programs, an on-screen status message that shows the current number of horizontal spaces, or columns, the cursor has moved across the screen.

column text chart   In presentation graphics, a text chart used to show related text items side-by-side in two or three columns (see fig. C.8).

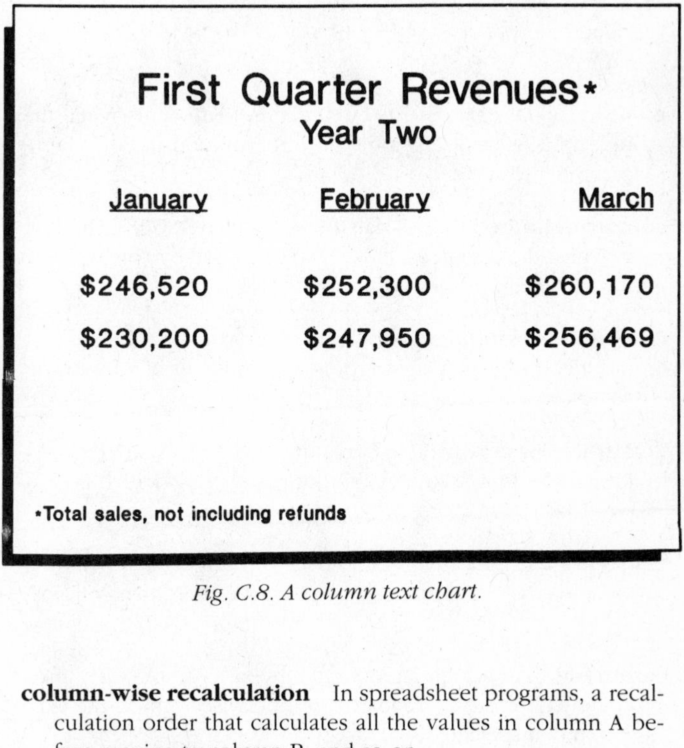

First Quarter Revenues*
Year Two

January	February	March
$246,520	$252,300	$260,170
$230,200	$247,950	$256,469

*Total sales, not including refunds

Fig. C.8. A column text chart.

column-wise recalculation   In spreadsheet programs, a recalculation order that calculates all the values in column A before moving to column B, and so on.

  ▲ **Caution:** If your spreadsheet program does not offer natural recalculation, use column-wise recalculation for worksheets in which columns are summed and the totals are forwarded. Row-wise recalculation may produce an erroneous result. See *natural recalculation, optimal recalculation,* and *row-wise recalculation.*

COM   In DOS and OS/2, a code that refers to a serial port. You use this code in commands like MODE, which configures the communications parameters of a serial port. The code COM1:, for example, refers to the system's first serial port.

▲ **Caution:** When referring to a serial port in an DOS command, don't forget to type the colon (COM1:, COM2:, COM3:). See *communications parameters*, *MODE*, and *serial port*.

COM file   In DOS and OS/2, an executable program file designed to operate in a specific part of the base memory. See *EXEC file*.

combinatorial explosion   A condition that occurs when the possibilities to be examined are too numerous for a large computer to solve.

comma-delimited file   A data file, usually in ASCII file format, in which the data items have been separated by commas. See *ASCII*, *file format*, and *tab-delimited*.

combinatorics   The study of methods of counting the number of objects of a particular type, or the number of ways to do something.

COMDEX   An acronym for Communications and Data Processing Exposition. A large computer trade show, which is held twice yearly.

come down gracefully   The process of bringing a system to a complete halt by command or automatic shutdown with losing any data.

command   A user-initiated signal given to a computer program that initiates, terminates, or otherwise controls the execution of a specific operation.

In command-driven programs, the user must memorize the command statement and its associated syntax and type the command. In a menu-driven program, the user chooses a command from an on-screen menu. See *command-driven program, graphical user interface,* and *menu-driven program.*

COMMAND.COM　In DOS, an essential system disk file that contains the command processor. This file must be present on the start-up disk for DOS to run.

command-driven program　A system, utility, or application program that requires you to memorize keyboard commands and to rely on your memory to type command statements with the correct syntax and nomenclature. See *graphics user interface* and *menu-driven program.*

command language　See *software command language.*

command-line operating system　A command-driven operating system, such as DOS, that requires you to type commands at the keyboard.

command processor　The portion of a command-line operating system that handles user input and displays messages, such as prompts, confirmation messages, and error messages. See *command-line operating system.*

comments　See *remarks.*

communications parameters　In telecommunications and serial printing, the settings (parameters) that customize serial communications for the hardware you are contacting. See *baud rate, communications protocol, data bits, duplex, MODE, parameters, parity, serial communications,* and *stop bits.*

communications program　An application program that turns your computer into a terminal for transmitting data to and receiving data from distant computers through the telephone system.

　　A good communications program includes a software command language that you can use to automate cumbersome protocols (such as Xmodem and Kermit), terminal emulation of two or more popular mainframe terminals (such as the DEC VT100), and on-screen timing so that you can keep track of time charges and facilities for storing and retrieving telephone numbers.

➔ **Tip:** For communications software, most users need not fork over big bucks for a commercial program: several excellent shareware communications programs are available. Examples include PC-Talk and QMODEM for IBM PC-compatible computers. See *terminal* and *terminal emulation*.

communications protocol   A list of communications parameters (settings) and standards that govern the communication of information between computers using telecommunications. Both computers must have the same settings and follow the same standards for error-free communication to take place.

When you use a modem to access a bulletin board or information service, such as CompuServe, you must choose the correct communications protocol—the one established by the host computer system. Your communications program enables you to choose the necessary parameters, including baud rate, data bits, duplex, parity, and stop bits. The baud rate usually is determined by your modem's capabilities. Most communications services use eight data bits and one stop bit; full duplex is also common. Before you attempt to establish communication with an on-line service, read the documentation to find out which communications parameters to use. The setting are displayed prominently at the beginning of the documentation.

You may have to specify an additional parameter called handshaking. This parameter establishes the way one computer tells the other device when to wait. Almost all computers and many peripheral devices use XON/XOFF handshaking, the default for most communications programs.

➔ **Tip:** If you are having trouble establishing communication with an on-line service, press Enter twice and try these settings:

> Parity: No
> Data bits: 8
> Stop bits: 1
> Duplex: Full

If you cannot see what you are typing, switch to half duplex. If the preceding settings don't work, hang up and dial again with these settings:

> Parity: Even
> Data bits: 7
> Stop bits: 1
> Duplex: Full or half

If you are using half duplex and see the echoed characters (HHEELLOO), switch to full duplex. See *asynchronous communications, baud rate, communications parameters, communications program, data bits, duplex, file transfer protocol, full duplex, half duplex, handshaking, mode, modem, parity,* and *stop bits.*

comp   In desktop publishing, a complete mock-up of a page layout design, showing what the final printed page will look like.

COMP command   In DOS and OS/2, an external command that compares two or more text files to see whether they are identical.

This command is useful for determining whether two files are identical but cannot produce a complete list of the differences. The COMP command can list only the first 10 differences. Commercially available file-comparison programs, such as DocuComp, can list all the differences between two word processing documents. This capability is ideal for collaborative writing, during which you may need to look at two versions of a document. A program like DocuComp enables you to pinpoint the differences between the two versions. See *external command.*

compact disk (CD)   A plastic disk, 4.75 inches in diameter, that uses optical storage techniques to store up to 72 minutes of music or 650M of digitally encoded computer data.

In an optical storage medium, digital data is stored as microscopic pits and smooth areas with different reflective properties. A precisely controlled beam of laser light shines on the disk so that the reflections can be detected and translated into digital data.

Compact disks provide read-only secondary storage. The computer can read information from the disk, but you cannot change this information or write new information to the disk. Therefore, this storage medium accurately is termed CD-ROM (read-only memory). Erasable optical disk drives are now available and are expected to have a major impact on secondary storage techniques in the 1990s. In the meantime, however, compact disks are expected to become popular for the distribution of huge databases to personal computer users who have systems equipped with CD-ROM disk drives. Currently, the disks tend to be very expensive because the market is small, but as CD-ROM disk drives become available at lower prices, the price of the disks should drop too. The average computer user eventually may work with a system capable of displaying, in an on-screen window, the contents of huge databases, such as the complete works of William Shakespeare or the *Encyclopedia of Science and Technology*. See *CD-ROM disk drive, erasable optical disk drive, optical disk,* and *secondary storage*.

company network   A wide-area computer network, such as DEC ENET (the internal engineering network of Digital Equipment Corporation), that often has automatic gateways to cooperative networks such as ARPANET or BITNET for functions such as electronic mail and file transfer.

COMPAQ Computer Corporation   Pronounced "com´-pack." A Houston company that manufacturers high-performance IBM PC-compatible desktop and portable computers.

The first maker of IBM Personal Computer clones, COMPAQ's first computers were portable versions of the popular PC. The company sold over $100 million worth of computers in its first year in business (1983), setting a U.S.

record Subsequently, the firm became known as the maker of technically sophisticated, high-end machines that featured fast clock speeds and other technical improvements.

COMPAQ was the first manufacturer to develop and market a desktop computer based on the Intel 80386 micro-processor, and the firm played a leading role in the devel-opment of the Extended Industry Standard Architecture (EISA), an alternative to IBM's proprietary micro channel bus. See *Extended Industry Standard Architecture (EISA)* and *Intel 80386.*

comparison operator   See *relational operator.*

compatibility   The capability of a peripheral, a program, or an adapter to function with or substitute for a given make and model of computer. Also, the capability of one computer to run the software of another company's computer.

▲ **Caution:** To be truly compatible, a program or device should operate on a given system without modification; all features should operate as intended, and a computer claim-ing to be compatible with another should run all the other computer's software without modification.

➔ **Tip:** In IBM PC-compatible computing, a frequently used index of 100-percent IBM compatibility is a computer's capability to run Microsoft Flight Simulator. See *clone.*

compiler   A program that reads the statements written in a human-readable programming language, such as Pascal or Modula-2, and translates the statements into a machine-read-able executable program.

Compiled programs run significantly faster than inter-preted ones because the entire program has been translated into machine language and need not share memory space with the interpreter. See *interpreter* and *machine language.*

Complementary Metal-Oxide Semiconductor (CMOS) A chip fabricated to duplicate the functions of other chips, such as memory chips or microprocessors. A CMOS chip draws less power.

CMOS chips are used in battery-powered portable comput-ers. See *chip.*

complex instruction set computer (CISC) A central processing unit (CPU) that can recognize as many as 100 or more instructions, enough to carry out most computations directly.

Most microprocessors are CISC chips. The use of RISC technology is becoming increasingly common, however, in professional workstations and is expected to migrate to personal computers in the early 1990s. See *central processing unit (CPU)* and *reduced instruction set computer (RISC)*.

compose sequence A series of keystrokes that enables a user to enter a character not found on the computer's keyboard.

In Lotus 1-2-3, for example, pressing Alt-F1 followed by typing 233 enters a lowercase e with an acute accent.

composite See *comp.*

composite color monitor A monitor that accepts a standard analog video signal that mixes red, green, and blue signals to produce the color image.

The composite video standard of the National Television Standards Committee uses a standard RCA-type connector, found on the Color Graphics Adapter (CGA). Display quality is inferior to that of RGB monitors. See *RGB monitor.*

composite video A standard for video signals in which the red, green, and blue signals are mixed together.

The standard, regulated by the U.S. National Television Standards Committee (NTSC), is used for television. Some computers have composite video outputs that use a standard RCA phono plug and cable such as on the backplane of a high-fidelity system. See *composite color monitor* and *RGB monitor.*

compressed file A file that a file compression utility has written to a special disk format that minimizes the storage space required. See *file compression utility.*

CompuServe Pronounced "comp´-yoo-serve." The largest and most successful personal computer information service.

Essentially a for-profit version of a bulletin board system (BBS) coupled with the resources of an on-line information service, CompuServe offers file downloading, electronic mail, current news, up-to-the-minute stock quotes, an on-line encyclopedia, and conferences on a variety of topics. However, the character-based command-line user interface is technically antiquated and challenging to novice users. If you are interested in using CompuServe, consider using a front-end program like CompuServe Navigator. See *bulletin board system (BBS)*, *on-line information service*, and *Prodigy*.

computation   The successful execution of an algorithm whose steps are finite, executable, and capable of termination. A computation is not only a numerical operation; a successfully completed textual search or sort also is a computation. See *algorithm*.

computer   A machine capable of following instructions to alter data in a desirable way and to perform at least some of these operations without human intervention.

Do not think that computers are devices for performing only calculations, although that function is one of many computer tasks. Computers represent and manipulate text, graphics, symbols, and music, as well as numbers. See *analog computer* and *digital computer*.

computer-aided design (CAD)   Pronounced "cad." The use of the computer and a computer-aided design program as the environment for the design of a wide range of industrial artifacts, ranging from machine parts to modern homes.

Computer-aided design has become a mainstay in a variety of design-related fields, such as architecture, civil engineering, electrical engineering, mechanical engineering, and interior design. But, computer-aided design has been dominated until recently by expensive dedicated minicomputer systems. CAD applications are graphics and calculation-intensive, requiring fast processors and high-resolution video displays. CAD programs often include sophisticated statistical analysis routines that help designers optimize their applications, as well as extensive symbol libraries. All these features require huge amounts of processing power, and that requirement kept CAD off early personal computers.

Like many other professional computer applications based on expensive mainframe or minicomputer systems, however,

CAD is migrating to powerful personal computers, such as those based on the Intel 80386 and Motorola 68030 micro-processors. CAD software for personal computers blends the object-oriented graphics found in draw programs with precision scaling in two and three dimensions. Drawings can be produced with an intricate level of detail. See *draw programs, Intel 80386, Motorola 68030,* and *object-oriented graphics.*

computer-aided design and drafting (CADD)　Pronounced "cad." The use of a computer system for industrial design and technical drawing.

CADD software closely resembles computer-aided design (CAD) software but has additional features that enable the artist to produce drawings conforming to engineering conventions.

computer-assisted instruction (CAI)　The use of instructional programs to perform instructional tasks, such as drill and practice, tutorials, and tests.

Unlike human teachers, a CAI program doesn't get bored or frustrated with a slow student and is blind to distinctions of gender and race. Ideally, CAI could use sound, graphics, and on-screen rewards to engage a student in learning—with huge payoffs. In practice, however, a great deal of CAI software is badly designed: the software is stilted, boring, and emphasizes drill and practice, often in a way that suggests remedial instruction.

With standard programming techniques, creating quality instructional software is a big job, which accounts for CAI's dearth. With the advent of multimedia, however, CAI may be entering a new era. Standard computer configurations, such as a character-based PC equipped with a printer, reduce the appeal of CAI programs; they are visually drab and lack information density. Multimedia machines equipped with compact disks, video, and sound, however, may function to open new worlds to students by placing immense reservoirs of knowledge and experience in every classroom. Authoring languages, such as HyperTalk, make developing high-quality instructional software much easier. By using techniques that allow interactive exploration of a subject, multimedia promises to engage learners in a kind of creative exploration not possible with standard computer configurations. See *authoring language*, *multimedia*, and *HyperTalk*.

computer-based training (CBT)   The use of computer-aided instruction (CAI) techniques to train adults for specific skills, such as operating a numerically controlled lathe.

computer graphics metafile (CGM)   An international graphics file format that stores object-oriented graphics in device-independent form so that you can exchange CGM files among users of different systems (and different programs).

Personal computer programs that can read and write to CGM file formats include Harvard Graphics and Ventura Publisher. See *device independence* and *object-oriented graphics*.

computer system   A complete computer installation—including peripherals, such as disk drives, a monitor, and a printer—in which all the components are designed to work with each other.

CON   In DOS and OS/2, the device name that refers to the keyboard and monitor.

For example, the command

```
COPY CON C:AUTOEXEC.BAT
```

creates a file called AUTOEXEC.BAT and stores in this file all the characters you type after giving the command. To finish copying text from the keyboard, press Ctrl-Z and then press Enter.

concatenation   Pronounced "con-cat´-en-ay´-shun." The combination of two or more units of information, such as text or files, so that they form one unit.

➜ **Tip:** In DOS, you easily can combine two or more files by using a straightforward (but little-known) variation of the COPY command. Normally, the COPY command copies the source file (the first file named) to the target file (the second file named). To combine files, you list all the source files separated by plus signs. The following command combines all the DOC files into one backup file:

```
COPY REPORT1.DOC+REPORT2.DOC
+REPORT3.DOC REPORT.BAK
```

See *COPY command.*

concordance file   A file containing the words you want a
word processing program to include in the index the program constructions.

   To index a document, you have only one choice with most
programs: you must mark each occurrence of each word
throughout the manuscript. Then, the program includes
these words (with page references) in the index, constructed
and appended to the document. This operation is tedious
because an important word may appear on more than one
page.

   The best word processing programs, such as WordPerfect,
use a concordance file to simplify the manual part of indexing. Instead of marking the words manually throughout the
document (many of them more than once), you create a new
file that contains one sample of each word you want indexed. When you give the command that starts the indexing
operation, the program uses the concordance file as a guide
and performs the marking operation.

concurrency management   The capability of an application
written for use on a local area network (LAN) to ensure that
data files are not corrupted by simultaneous modification or
multiple input.

concurrent processing   See *multitasking.*

condensed type   Type narrowed in width so that more characters will fit into a linear inch. In dot-matrix printers, condensed type usually is set to print 17 characters per inch
(cpi). See *characters per inch (cpi).*

CONFIG.SYS   In DOS and OS/2, an ASCII text file that contains configuration commands.

   DOS consults this file at system start-up. If no CONFIG.SYS
file is on the start-up disk, DOS uses the default configuration values. Most programs work well with the default
configuration settings. Nonstandard peripherals and some

application programs, however, may require that a CONFIG.SYS file be present in the root directory so that these configurations are modified.

The following list is an overview of the configuration commands:

- DEVICE. Specifies the driver DOS requires to use a peripheral device. If you are using a mouse, for example, you need to create a CONFIG.SYS file with a statement such as DEVICE = MOUSE.SYS. The file called MOUSE.SYS must be present in the root directory. If your mouse doesn't work, check to see whether you have erased CONFIG.SYS. If you recently installed another program, you may have erased your old CONFIG.SYS; you will have to put the DEVICE statement back into the file by using your word processing program.

  Some programs require you to place the following command in your configuration file: **DEVICE = ANSI.SYS**. ANSI is an acronym for American National Standards Institute, and the file ANSI.SYS (on every DOS disk) contains procedures for controlling the display of information. The file called ANSI.SYS must be present in the root directory.

- BUFFERS. Determines the number of areas DOS sets aside in memory to store disk data temporarily. The default setting varies with the version of DOS. Some application programs require you to specify more buffers than the DOS default number. You may need to add a statement such as BUFFERS = 15 before these programs will work.

- FILES. Determines the number of files that can be open at the same time. The default setting is 8 files.

If the preceding material seems too technical, don't worry: the peripherals and programs that require CONFIG.SYS statements usually create them automatically when you follow the standard installation procedure. Knowing about these commands is worthwhile, however, especially if you accidentally erase CONFIG.SYS or—as sometimes happens—if an installation program erases the existing CONFIG.SYS and substitutes its own.

▲ **Caution:** If an application program you are using has written a CONFIG.SYS file to your start-up disk, do not erase the CONFIG.SYS file. If you do, the program may not run, or some features may be disabled. If you erase CONFIG.SYS accidentally, repeat the program's installation procedure. See *American National Standards Institute (ANSI), ANSI.SYS, American Standard Code for Information Interchange (ASCII), buffer, driver, mouse, peripheral,* and *root directory.*

configuration file   A file, created by an application program, that stores the choices you make when you install the program so that they are available the next time you start the program. In Microsoft Word, for example, the file MW.INI stores the choices you make from the Options menu.

▲ **Caution:** More than a few users have inadvertently erased configuration files by erasing unidentifiable files in an attempt to free up disk space. Avoid erasing the configuration file your program creates. If you do, the program probably will revert to the default settings chosen by its programmers. These settings may or may not prove suitable for your system and application needs. In the extreme, the program may not function at all, and you may have to re-install it.

connectivity   The extent to which a given computer or program can function in a network setting.

connectivity platform   A program or utility designed to enhance another program's capability to exchange data with other programs through a local area network. Oracle for the Macintosh, for example, provides HyperCard with the connectivity required to search for and retrieve information from large corporate databases. See *HyperCard* and *local area network (LAN).*

console   A display terminal, consisting of a monitor and keyboard.

In multiuser systems, console is synonymous with *terminal*, but console also is used in personal computer operating systems to refer to the keyboard and display.

constant   In a spreadsheet program, a number you type directly into a cell or place in a formula.

You see two kinds of numbers in a worksheet's cells. Constants are numbers you type on the entry line. These numbers do not change unless you edit the cell contents or type a new value in the cell. The second kind of number is the value produced by a hidden formula. You cannot tell the difference between a constant and a value produced by a formula just by looking at the worksheet. If you place the pointer on the cell, however, the actual cell definition—including a formula if present—appears on the entry line.

▲ **Caution:** If you type a constant in a cell with a value produced by a formula, you erase the formula in the cell. This mistake is a common cause of major errors in spreadsheet calculations.

→ **Tip:** You should avoid entering constants in formulas. Suppose that you have created a worksheet in which each column computes a commission of 5 percent. You enter this constant into 15 formulas. If you decide to compute the commission at 6 percent, you must change all 15 formulas.

A better solution is to place the constant in one cell, called a key, and place this cell at the top of the worksheet. You then reference this cell in the formulas. This way, you make only one change instead of 15 if you change the constant. See *cell definition* and *key variable*.

contention   In local area networks, a channel access method in which access to the communication channel is based on a first-come, first-served policy. See *carrier sense multiple access with collision detect (CSMA/CD)*.

context switching   The immediate activation of a program loaded into random-access memory (RAM) along with one or more other programs in a multiple loading operating system.

Unlike true multitasking, a multiple loading operating system, such as the Macintosh system equipped with MultiFinder, enables you to load more than one program at a time, but while you are using the foreground program, the background program stops executing. For a stand-alone computer, multiple loading operating systems provide a high level of functionality because you can switch rapidly from one program to another. When combined with a graphical user interface and cut-and-paste facilities provided by a clipboard, context switching enables you to move data rapidly and easily from one application to another. See *multiple-loading operating system* and *multitasking*.

context-sensitive help   In an application package, a user-assistance mode that displays on-screen documentation relevant to the command, mode, or action the user currently is performing.

Context-sensitive help is a desirable program feature because it reduces the time and keystrokes needed to get on-screen help. In WordPerfect, for example, if you press Help (F3) after pressing Format (Shift-F8), you see a help screen explaining the options available on the Format menu. Without context-sensitive help, you have to locate the desired information manually from an index or menu.

contiguous   Adjacent; placed one after the other.

continuous paper   Paper manufactured in one long strip, with perforations separating the pages, so that the paper can be fed into a printer with a tractor-feed mechanism.

continuous tone   An illustration, whether black-and-white or color, in which tones change smoothly and continuously from the darkest to the lightest, without noticeable gradations.

Control-Break   In DOS and OS/2, a keyboard command that suspends the execution of a program at the next available break point.

control code   In the American Standard Code for Information Interchange (ASCII), a code reserved for hardware-control purposes, such as advancing a page on the printer. There are 32 ASCII control codes.

Control (Ctrl) key   In IBM PC-compatible computing, a key frequently pressed with other keys for program commands. In WordStar, for example, pressing Ctrl-Y deletes a line.

control panel   1. In Lotus 1-2-3, the top three lines of the display screen. The top line contains the current cell indicator, the mode indicator, and the entry line. The second and third lines contain menus and prompts. 2. In the Macintosh, Windows, and OS/2 Presentation Manager, a utility menu that lists user options for hardware devices, such as the mouse, monitor, and keyboard.

control panel device (CDEV)   Pronounced "see-dev." A Macintosh utility program placed in the System Folder that appears as an option in the Control Panel.

control structure   A logical organization for an algorithm that governs the sequence in which program statements are executed.

Control statements govern the flow of control in a program. They specify the sequence in which the program's steps are to be carried out. Early programs offered only a few control structures, such as a simple sequence interrupted occasionally by GOTO statements. A major trend in the design of programming languages, however, has been toward the nearly universal adoption of more modern control structures. These control structures include branch structures that cause a special set of instructions to be executed if a specified situation is encountered, loop structures that execute over and over until a condition is fulfilled, and procedure/function structures that set aside distinct program functions or procedures into separate modules, which are invoked from the main program.

The use of sequential, branch, and loop structures to express an algorithm is more than just a good practice; this technique is valid for important scientific reasons. A brilliant mathematical proof demonstrated that these three structures are adequate for the procedural expression of any known algorithm. The use of control structures tends to make a program more readable by humans, and readability is important in organizational settings, where someone other than the original programmer may be called on to maintain or enhance the program. Readability is enhanced, too, by avoiding GOTO statements that tend to produce a jumble of untrackable program interconnections, called spaghetti code by the detractors of BASIC (which uses GOTO statements).

In personal computing, you are likely to use control structures even if you do not plan to learn a high-level programming language. Most software command languages, including macro commands, include control structures, such as do/while loops, case branches, for/next loops, if/then/else branches, and repeat loops. See *branch control structure, case branch, DO/WHILE loop, FOR/NEXT loop, high-level programming language, IF/THEN/ELSE branch, loop control structure,* and *structured programming.*

➔ **Tip:** Take a hint from professional programmers: make your macros more readable (for yourself and others) and avoid spaghetti code by sticking to the three basic control structures—sequential, branch, and loop—for all program functions. Avoid GOTO statements; instead, use a named procedure and mark the procedure clearly so that you can find it if you need to update or debug it.

control unit   A component of the central processing unit (CPU) that obtains program instructions and emits signals to carry them out. See *arithmetic/logic unit (ALU)* and *central processing unit (CPU).*

controller card   An adapter that connects disk drives to the computer. Most personal computer controller cards contain circuitry to connect one or more floppy disks and hard disks. See *adapter.*

conventional programming   The use of a procedural programming language, such as BASIC, FORTRAN, or assembly language, to code an algorithm in machine-readable form.

In conventional programming, the programmer must be concerned with the sequence in which events occur within the computer. Nonprocedural programming languages enable the programmer to focus on the problem, without worrying about the precise procedure the computer must follow to solve the problem. See *nonprocedural language* and *procedural language.*

cooperative network   A wide-area computer network, such as BITNET or UUCP, in which the costs of participating are borne by the linked organizations. See *BITNET, commercial network, company network, research network,* and *UUCP.*

coprocessor   A microprocessor support chip optimized for a specific processing operation, such as handling mathematical computations or displaying images on the video display. See *microprocessor* and *numeric coprocessor.*

copy   The text of a publication, exclusive of all graphics, before the text is formatted and laid out for publication.

COPY   In DOS and OS/2, an internal command that copies one or more files. When you copy a file, you can change its name. See *BACKUP command, internal command,* and *XCOPY.*

copy editing   A rigorous and exact critique of copy to make sure that it conforms to the publisher's standards for facts, grammar, spelling, clarity, coherence, usage, and punctuation.

copy fitting   In desktop publishing, a method used to determine the amount of copy (text) that, using a specified font, will fit into a given area on a page or in a publication.

copy protection   The inclusion in a program of hidden instructions intended to prevent you from making unauthorized copies of software. Because most copy-protection schemes impose penalties on legitimate owners of programs, such as forcing them to insert a specially encoded "key disk" before using a program, most business software publishers have given up using these schemes. Copy protection is still common, however, in recreational and educational software.

corrupted file   A file that contains scrambled and unrecoverable data.

cost-benefit analysis   A projection of the costs and benefits of installing a computer system. The analysis compares the costs of operating an enterprise with and without the computer system and calculates the return (if any) on the original investment.

▲ **Caution:** Cost-benefit analyses often involve overly optimistic assumptions about the tangible cost savings of installing a computer system. A word processing program may enable you to revise a document faster, but the technology invites the user to keep working on the document until it is close to perfect, and the user may spend more time than he or she would have originally.

Computerization also may prove more costly than standard methods if the enterprise must carry out its business in an inefficient or unprofitable way. More than a few businesses have failed after installing expensive accounting and inventory systems that proved to be inflexible as the businesses' needs changed.

counter   In typography, the space enclosed by the fully or partially enclosed bowl of a letter. See *bowl*.

Courier   A monospace typeface, commonly included as a built-in font in laser printers, that simulates the output of office typewriters. For example: `This is Courier type`.

courseware   Software developed for computer-assisted instruction (CAI) or computer-based training (CBT) applications.

cpi   See *characters per inch (cpi)*.

CP/M   An operating system for personal computers that uses the 8-bit Intel 8080 and Zilog Z-80 microprocessors.

CP/M (Control Program for Microprocessors) was created in the late 1970s as floppy disk drives became available for early personal computers. Designed for computers with as little as 16K of random-access memory (RAM), CP/M is a command-line operating system that requires users to observe a fussy syntax as they type system commands. CP/M is still widely used, however, on the more than four million 8-bit computers (such as Morrow, Kaypro, and Osborne) still in existence.

CP/M closely resembles MS-DOS; in fact, MS-DOS is a clone of CP/M and was designed to facilitate the translation of 8-bit CP/M business software so that the software would run in the new 16-bit IBM Personal Computer environment.

IBM originally approached CP/M's publisher, Digital Research, to write the operating system for its new computer, but as the result of a now legendary communication breakdown, Microsoft Corporation got the job instead.

CPM   See *critical-path method.*

cps   See *characters per second.*

CPU   See *central processing unit (CPU).*

crash   An abnormal termination of program execution, usually (but not always) resulting in a frozen keyboard or an unstable state. In most cases, you must reboot the computer to recover from a crash.

criteria range   In spreadsheet programs that include data management functions, the range that tells the program which records to retrieve from a database. The range contains the conditions you specify to govern how a search is conducted.

critical-path method (CPM)   In project management, a technique for planning and timing the execution of tasks that relies on the identification of a critical path: a series of tasks that must be completed in a timely fashion if the entire project is to be completed on time. Project management software helps the project manager identify the critical path.

cropping   A graphics editing operation in which edges are trimmed from a graphic to make it fit into a given space or to remove unnecessary parts of the image.

cross-hatching   The black-and-white patterns added to areas within a pie, bar, or column graph to distinguish one data range from another.

▲ **Caution:** Avoid the overuse of cross-hatching, and be careful of a common and serious flaw of computer-generated graphics: Moiré vibrations, which result from visual interference between cross-hatching patterns. If your graph seems to flicker, reduce the cross-hatching. See *Moiré vibrations.*

cross-reference   In word processing programs, a code name referring to material previously discussed in a document.

When printed, the reference is changed so that the correct page number of this material appears in its place.

Cross-references, such as "See the discussion of burnishing methods on page 19," are helpful to the reader, but they can become a nightmare if you add or delete text. Therefore, the best word processing programs (such as WordPerfect and Microsoft Word) contain cross-reference features. Instead of typing the cross-reference, you mark the original text and assign a code name to the marked text, such as BURNISH. Then, you type the code name (not the page number) when you want to cross-reference the original text. When you print your document, the program substitutes the correct page number for the code name. If you discover after printing that you need to add or delete text, the code names are still there, and you can perform the edit and print again without worrying about the cross-references.

crosstalk　　The interference generated by cables that are too close to one another.

You sometimes hear crosstalk on the telephone. When speaking long-distance, hearing other voices or entire conversations in the background of your conversation is not uncommon.

Crosstalk　　A popular communications program developed by DCA/Crosstalk Communications for IBM PC-compatible computers.

CRT　　See *cathode ray tube (CRT)*.

CSMA/CD　　See *carrier sense multiple access with collision detection*.

Ctrl　　See *Control (Ctrl) key*.

Ctrl-Break　　In DOS, a keyboard command that cancels the last command you gave.

current cell　　In a spreadsheet program such as Lotus 1-2-3, the cell in which the pointer is positioned. Synonymous with *active cell*.

current cell indicator   In Lotus 1-2-3, a message that displays the address of the cell in which the pointer is positioned. If the cell has contents, the program also displays the cell format, its protection status, the column width, and the cell definition.

current directory   The directory that DOS or an application uses to store and retrieve files.

Within an application, the current directory is normally the one from which you start that application program. Some programs, however, enable you to change the current directory so that you can save data files in a directory other than the one in which the program's files are stored. Synonymous with *default directory*.

current drive   The drive the operating system uses for an operation unless you specifically instruct otherwise. Synonymous with default drive.

current graph   In Lotus 1-2-3, the graph that the program creates when you choose /Graph View and retains in memory until you save the graph or quit the worksheet.

cursor   An on-screen blinking character that shows where the next character will appear when you press a key. See *pointer*.

cursor-movement keys   The keys that move the on-screen cursor.

With most programs, the arrow keys on the numeric keypad move the cursor in the directions of the arrows. You can move the cursor one character left or right or one line up or down. Like the keys in the typing area, these keys are autorepeat keys. If you hold down the key, the cursor keeps moving in the direction indicated.

The newest keyboards often include a separate cursor keypad with keys that perform the same function as the arrow keys on the numeric keypad.

Some programs configure additional keys so that they move the cursor. These keys include Home, End, Tab, Shift-Tab, PgUp, and PgDn.

Cursor movement is distinguished from scrolling by some programs. The Macintosh version of Microsoft Word, for example, has scrolling commands that display a different portion of the document without moving the cursor. More commonly, however, scrolling commands move the cursor as well as display a different portion of the document. See *arrow keys* and *scroll.*

cut and paste   See *block move.*

cut-sheet feeder   A paper-feed mechanism that feeds separate sheets of paper into the printer, where a friction-feed mechanism draws the paper through the printer.

You can purchase cut-sheet feeding mechanisms as optional accessories for dot-matrix and letter-quality printers, but they are standard equipment with laser printers and high-quality inkjet printers. See *friction feed mechanism* and *tractor feed mechanism.*

cylinder   In disk drives, a unit of storage consisting of the set of tracks that occupy the same position.

On a double-sided disk, a cylinder includes track 1 of the top and the bottom sides. On hard disks in which several disks are stacked on top of one another, a cylinder consists of the tracks in a specific location on all the disks.

d

daisywheel printer   An impact printer that simulates the typescript produced by an office typewriter.

"Daisywheel" refers to the mechanism used to produce the printout: the characters are mounted in a circular pattern and connected to a hub with spokes, resembling a daisy. To produce a character, the printer spins the wheel until the desired character is in place. Then, the printer strikes the inked ribbon with the character, transferring the image to paper. Because the daisywheels can be removed and replaced, these printers can print multiple typefaces.

However, changing fonts within a document is tedious because the daisywheel must be changed manually.

Once the ultimate in printing technology, daisywheel printers have all but disappeared from the market, due to the development of inexpensive laser printers. A laser printer can change fonts and typefaces within a document. See *impact printer.*

DASD Pronounced "daz´-dee." Acronym for Direct Access Storage Device. A storage device such as a magnetic disk that can write anywhere on its surface.

data Factual information stored on magnetic media that can be used to generate calculations or to make decisions.

data communication The transfer of information from one computer to another.

The transfer can occur via direct cable connections, as in local area networks or via telecommunications links involving the telephone system and modems. See *local area networks (LAN)* and *telecommunications.*

data deletion In a database management program, an operation that deletes records according to specified criteria.

Some database programs do not actually delete the records in such operations; they merely mark the records so that they are not included in data retrieval operations. Therefore, you usually can restore the deleted records if you make a mistake.

data dictionary In a database management program, an on-screen listing of all the database files, indexes, views, and other files relevant to a database application.

data-entry form In a database management program, an on-screen form that makes entering and editing data easier by displaying only one data record on-screen at a time. The data fields are listed vertically as in the following example:

```
TITLE        Barney, the Loyal Puppy
CATEGORY     Children
RATING       G
RENTED TO    325-1234
DUE DATE     12/31/90
```

dBASE, for example, displays a standard data-entry form
when you add records (see fig. D.1). You also can create a
custom data-entry form (see fig. D.2).

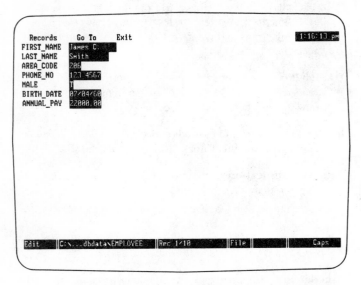

Fig. D.1. Standard data-entry form in dBASE.

data field In a database management program, a space for a
specified piece of information in a data record. In a table-oriented database management program, in which all retrieval
operations produce a table with rows and columns, data
fields are displayed as vertical columns.

In the following example, the headings in all capital letters
are the data field titles. The information typed into these
fields is to the right of the headings.

TITLE	Harold, the Friendly Dinosaur
CATEGORY	Children
RATING	PG
RENTED TO	325-9178
DUE DATE	12/31/90

See *database, field definition,* and *table-oriented database
management program.*

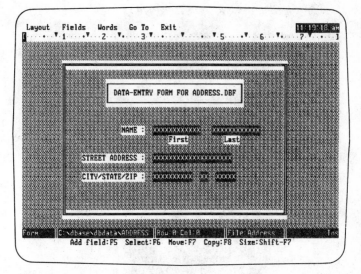

Figure D.2 Custom data-entry form in dBASE.

data file   A disk file containing the work you create with a program, unlike a program file that contains instructions for the computer.

data independence   In database management, the storage of data so that users can gain access to the data without knowing where the data is located.

Ideally, you should be able to say to the computer, "Give me information on Acme International." You should not have to say, "Go to record #1142 and match the text string Acme International." Many recent database management programs include command languages, called query languages, that enable you to phrase questions without worrying about the data's physical location. Even the best query languages require you to know some procedures, such as which database to search, but databases are evolving toward complete data independence. In the future, anyone using a corporate computer will be able to send a query out on a network, searching the company's shared databases and the small, personal ones on some of the computers connected to the network. See *query language* and *Structured Query Language (SQL)*.

data insertion In a database management program, an operation that appends new records to the database.

data integrity The accuracy, completeness, and internal consistency of the information stored in a database.

A good database management program ensures data integrity by making it difficult (or impossible) to accidentally erase or alter data. Relational database management programs help to ensure data integrity by eliminating data redundancy. See *data redundancy*.

data interchange format (DIF) file In spreadsheet programs and some database programs, a standard file format that enables the exchange of data among different brands or versions of spreadsheet programs.

Originally developed by Software Arts, the creators of VisiCalc, DIF is supported by Lotus 1-2-3 and other spreadsheet programs that can read spreadsheets saved in the DIF format.

data manipulation In database management, the four fundamental database manipulation operations are *data retrieval*, *data modification*, *data deletion*, and *data insertion*.

data mask See *field template*.

data modification In database management, an operation that updates one or more records according to specified criteria.

You specify the criteria for the update using a query language. For example, the following statement, written in a simplified form of Structured Query Language (SQL), instructs the program to update the inventory database by finding records in which the supplier field contains "CC" and incrementing the value in the price data field by 15 percent.

```
UPDATE inventory
    SET price = price * 1.15
    WHERE supplier = "CC"
```

See *query language* and *Structured Query Language (SQL)*.

data privacy   In local area networks, the limiting of access to a file so that other participants in the network cannot display its contents. See *encryption, field privilege, file privilege*, and *password protection.*

data processing   Preparing, storing, or manipulating information with a computer. See *word processing.*

data record   In a database management program, a complete unit of related data items expressed in named data fields. In a relational database, data record is synonymous with row.

A data record contains all the information related to a unit of related information in the database. In a video store's database, for example, the data record lists the following information for each tape the store stocks: title, category (horror, adventure, and so on), rating (G, PG, PG-13, and so on), the telephone number of the customer, and the due date. Most programs display data records in two ways, as data-entry forms and as data tables.

In a table-oriented relational database-management program, which displays the results of all retrieval operations as a table with rows and columns, the data records are displayed as horizontal rows.

data redundancy   In database management, the repetition of the same data in two or more data records.

Generally, you should not enter the same data in two different places within a database—someone may mistype just one character, destroying accurate retrieval. To the computer, Acme is not Acmee. Suppose that one data record contains the supplier name Meg Smith, and another has Megan Smith. The program fails to retrieve both data records if you search for all the records with Megan Smith in the Supplier Name field. Integrity is a serious issue for any database management system.

Relational database management programs can reduce the data redundancy problem. Suppose that you are running a retail operation, and you have created a simple inventory database to help you track items in stock. In the Supplier field, you type USPI instead of Ultra-Sophisticated Products International. USPI appears in several records, such as the following:

PRODUCT:	Minoan Pattern Plate
STOCKING LEVEL:	5
CURRENT STOCK:	4
REORDER AT:	1
PRICE:	12.99
SUPPLIER:	USPI
PRODUCT:	Minoan Pattern Bowl
STOCKING LEVEL:	10
CURRENT STOCK:	10
REORDER AT:	3
PRICE:	9.98
SUPPLIER:	USPI

In a second database, you list the suppliers:

SUPPLIER	USPI
COMPANY NAME	Sophisticated Products Intl.
ADDRESS	123 Shady Lane
CITY	Merchantville
STATE	IL
ZIP	61899

Because the full name and address of the company appear once in both databases, the address cannot be typed two different ways. Of course, you still can mistype the code USPI, but a short code is easier to type, and errors are easier to catch.

data retrieval In database management programs, an operation that retrieves information from the database according to the criteria specified in a query.

A database management program is useless if the program displays all the information at once. You must be able to access only needed information. The following query, written in simplified Structured Query Language (SQL), instructs a program to choose data from the first_name, last_name, phone_no, and due_date fields of the Rentals database, when the due date field contains a date equal to or earlier than May 5, 1990. The query then instructs the program to sort the displayed data by the due date, so that those custom ers with the most overdue tapes are at the top of the list.

```
SELECT first_name, last_name, phone_no, due_date
FROM rentals
WHERE due_date =< 05/05/90
ORDER BY due_date
```

The result of this query is a data table:

first_name	last_name	phone_no	due_date
ANGELINA	BAKER	499-1234	03/19/90
TERRENCE	TARDY	499-9876	04/30/90
BERMUDA	JAKE	499-5432	05/06/90

A program that displays data tables as the result of retrieval operations is a table-oriented database-management program. Record-oriented database management programs are less useful because they display all the information on all the data records retrieved.

data table   In a database management program, an on-screen view of information in a columnar (two-dimensional) format, with the field names at the top.

Data tables provide a good way to summarize the data contained in a database for convenient viewing. Most database management programs display data tables as the result of sorting or querying operations (see fig. D.3). See *data-entry form*.

data type   In a database management program, a definition that governs the kind of data that you can enter in a data field.

In dBASE, for example, you can choose among the following data types:

- Character (or text) field. You can place any character you can type at the keyboard into a character field, including numbers. But numbers are treated as strings (text), and the program cannot perform computations on strings. A character field can contain approximately one line of text.

- Memo field. A memo field can contain more text than a character field. Memo fields are used to store extensive notes about the information contained in a record.

- Numeric field. Stores numbers in such a way that the program can perform calculations on them.

- Logical field. Stores information in a true/false, yes/no format.

- Date field. Stores dates so that the program can recognize and compare them.

See *field template*.

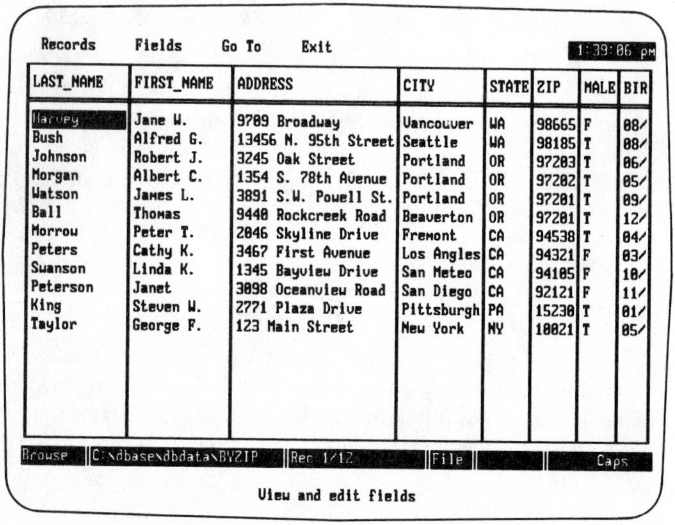

Records	Fields	Go To	Exit				1:39:06 PM

LAST_NAME	FIRST_NAME	ADDRESS	CITY	STATE	ZIP	MALE	BIR
Harvey	Jane W.	9789 Broadway	Vancouver	WA	98665	F	08/
Bush	Alfred G.	13456 N. 95th Street	Seattle	WA	98185	T	08/
Johnson	Robert J.	3245 Oak Street	Portland	OR	97283	T	06/
Morgan	Albert C.	1354 S. 78th Avenue	Portland	OR	97282	T	05/
Watson	James L.	3891 S.W. Powell St.	Portland	OR	97281	T	09/
Ball	Thomas	9440 Rockcreek Road	Beaverton	OR	97281	T	12/
Morrow	Peter T.	2046 Skyline Drive	Fremont	CA	94538	T	04/
Peters	Cathy K.	3467 First Avenue	Los Angles	CA	94321	F	03/
Swanson	Linda K.	1345 Bayview Drive	San Mateo	CA	94185	F	10/
Peterson	Janet	3098 Oceanview Road	San Diego	CA	92121	F	11/
King	Steven W.	2771 Plaza Drive	Pittsburgh	PA	15230	T	01/
Taylor	George F.	123 Main Street	New York	NY	10021	T	05/

Browse	C:\dbase\dbdata\BYZIP	Rec 1/12		File			Caps

View and edit fields

Fig. D.3. Data displayed in columnar format after a sort in dBASE.

database   A collection of related information about a subject organized in a useful manner that provides a base or foundation for procedures such as retrieving information, drawing conclusions, and making decisions.

Any collection of information that serves these purposes qualifies as a database, even if the information is not stored on a computer. In fact, important predecessors of today's sophisticated business database systems were files kept on index cards and stored in file cabinets.

Information is usually divided into distinct data records, each with one or more data fields. For example, a video store's record about a children's film may include the following information:

TITLE	The Blue Fountain
CATEGORY	Children
RATING	G
RETAIL PRICE	$24.95
RENTED TO	325-1234
DUE DATE	12/31/90

A data record is a form that includes headings that prompt the user to fill in specific information. You can create a database without dividing the record into distinct fields, but headings make accidental omissions more obvious and make retrieval operations function more quickly. See *data field* and *data record*

database design   The choice and arrangement of data fields in a database so that fundamental errors (such as data redundancy and repeating fields) are avoided or minimized. See *data redundancy* and *repeating field.*

database driver   In Lotus 1-2-3 Release 3.0, a program that enables 1-2-3 to exchange data with database programs such as dBASE.

database management   Tasks related to creating, maintaining, organizing, and retrieving information from a database. See *data manipulation.*

database management program   An application program that provides the tools for data retrieval, modification, deletion, and insertion. Such programs also can create a database and produce meaningful output on the printer or on-screen. In personal computing, three kinds of database management programs exist: flat-file, relational, and text-oriented.

Using computers for database management is easier than traditional methods. A computer can sort the records in a few seconds and in several different ways. For example, in a video store's database, you can sort the records by title, category, rating, availability, and so on. Furthermore, a database management program can select just those records that meet the criteria you specify in a query. The results of sorts or selections can be displayed on-screen or printed in a report. See *flat-file database management program, relational database management program,* and *text-oriented database management program.*

database management system (DBMS)   1. In mainframe computing, a computer system organized for the systematic management of a large collection of information. 2. In personal computing, a program such as dBASE with similar information storage, organization, and retrieval capacities, sometimes including simultaneous access to multiple databases through a shared field (relational database management). See *flat-file database management* .

database structure   In database management, a definition of the data records in which information is stored, including: the number of data fields; a set of field definitions that for each field specify the type of information, the length, and other characteristics; and a list of field names.

In the following example, the database structure includes six fields:

```
TITLE            The Blue Fountain
CATEGORY         Children
RATING           G
RETAIL PRICE     $24.95
RENTED TO        325-1234
DUE DATE         12/31/90
```

The first field is a text field that can accommodate up to 60 characters. The last field is a date field that accepts only eight characters entered in the date format (mm/dd/yy).

▲ **Caution:** Rare is the database structure that does not require alterations after you start entering data. You may not have left enough room for data in a character field, or more likely, you need to add fields to store essential data. However, many database management programs do not enable you to redefine the database structure, or if they do, these programs require a cumbersome procedure that may corrupt the data. If you are using such a program, perform exhaustive tests on sample data before typing hundreds of data records. See *data type*.

DATE   In DOS and OS/2, a command that displays the current system date and prompts you to enter a new date.

dBASE   A popular database management system (DBMS) for personal computers.

Database management systems are mainstays in corporate computing systems, but until the development of dBASE II for 8-bit CP/M computers and 16-bit IBM Personal Computers in 1981, these systems were virtually unknown in personal computing. dBASE II, the brainchild of C. Wayne Ratliffe, a Jet Propulsion Laboratory engineer, and marketed by Ashton-Tate, included relational database management capabilities and other sophisticated DBMS features.

Unfortunately, the power of dBASE II came with a price; the program's notorious dot prompt presented the user with a blank screen with no hints about what to do next. However, by learning dBASE's powerful, cryptic software command language, you could build and maintain a database application. System developers often use this full-fledged, high-level programming language to create custom database applications.

dBASE III, introduced in 1984 for IBM Personal Computers, took better advantage of the IBM PC-compatible environment and included many powerful features, such as the capability to work with larger databases. The 1986 release of dBASE III Plus, with a user-friendly, menu-driven Assistant, confirmed dBASE's position as the supreme database management product for IBM PC-compatible computers.

However, dBASE clones soon appeared and took market share away from Ashton-Tate by offering faster program compilation and other features. Ashton-Tate faltered with the 1988 release of dBASE IV, an ambitious product that was to include Structured Query Language (SQL) for database queries as well as the standard dBASE language, an improved menu-driven user interface, and completely redesigned report generation facilities.

Version 1.0 of dBASE IV contained bugs that introduced errors into certain calculations, and more than a year passed before the company succeeded in releasing a corrected version (1.1).

dBASE Mac, a version of the program for the Macintosh computer, attracted criticism because the program cannot read traditional dBASE file formats or use the powerful dBASE command language. See *Clipper*, *dot prompt*, *FoxBASE +*, and *software command language*.

DBMS   See *database management system (DBMS)*.

debugger   A utility often included in program compilers or interpreters that helps programmers find and fix syntax errors and other errors in the source code. See *compiler*, *interpreter*, *source code*, and *syntax error*.

debugging   The procedure of locating and correcting errors in a program.

decimal tab   In a word processing or page layout program, a tab stop configured so that values align at the decimal point.

declarative language   A programming language that frees the programmer from specifying the exact procedure the computer needs to follow to accomplish a task. Instead, you tell the program what you want to accomplish.

For example, Structured Query Language (SQL) enables a user to perform a search by asking to see a list of records showing specific information rather than by telling the computer to search all records for those with the appropriate entries in specified fields. See *data independence* and *procedural language*.

decryption   The process of deciphering data from an encrypted form so that the data can be read. See *encryption*.

dedicated file server   In a local area network, a file server dedicated to providing services to the users of the network and running the network operating system.

Not all file servers are dedicated so that they cannot be used for other purposes. In peer-to-peer networks, for example, all the networked computers are potential file servers, although they are being used for stand-alone applications.

default directory   See *current directory.*

default extension   The three-letter extension an application program uses to save and retrieve files, unless you override the default by specifying another file name.

→ **Tip:** If the program you are using supplies a default extension, use the default instead of your own extension. Many programs, such as Lotus 1-2-3 and Microsoft Word, assign extensions if you do not provide one. When saving a file with Microsoft Word, for example, the program assigns the extension DOC. During retrieval operations, such programs display a list of the files with the default extension, making retrieving a file easier. If you give the file an extension that differs from the default extension, however, the file does not appear on the list. You still can retrieve the file, but you must remember the file's name without any help from the program. See *extension* and *file name.*

default font   The font that the printer uses unless you instruct otherwise. See *initial base font.*

default numeric format   In a spreadsheet program, the numeric format that the program uses for all cells unless you choose a different one. See *numeric format.*

default setting   A command option a program uses unless you specify another setting. In Lotus 1-2-3, for example, the default column width is 9 characters.

→ **Tip:** An important step toward the mastery of an application program is learning the program defaults. You should learn how to change defaults so that the program works the way you want. Most programs save the changes you make so that they are in effect for the next working session, but some options may not be saved under any circumstances. Micro-soft Word, for example, saves the printer driver you select, but it does not save settings like the number of copies to be printed (the default is always one). If the program saved the number of copies, you may inadvertently print unwanted copies of a document the next time you choose the Print command.

default value A value an application program chooses when you do not specify one.

defragmentation A procedure in which all the files on a hard disk are rewritten so that all parts of each file are written to contiguous sectors. The result is a significant improvement—up to 75 percent or more—in the disk's speed in retrieval operations. During normal operations, the files on a hard disk become fragmented, so that parts of a file are written all over the disk, slowing down retrieval operations.

The defragmentation process is accomplished by a com-mercial utility program. Popular defragmentation programs include DiskExpress and PowerUP for the Macintosh and DOS Rx for IBM PC-compatible computers.

DEL See *ERASE.*

Delete key A key that erases the character at the cursor.

→ **Tip:** Use the Backspace and Delete keys to correct mis-takes as you type. If you discover you have made a typing error, press Backspace to erase the error and retype. Use the Delete key to erase a character at the cursor.

delimiter A symbol that marks the end of one section of a command and the beginning of another section.

demo A program designed to emulate some of the functions of an application program for marketing purposes.

demodulation In telecommunications, the process of receiv-ing and transforming an analog signal into its digital equiva-lent that can be used by a computer. See *modulation* and *telecommunications.*

demon   In computer programming, a section of a program or a standalone program that waits until an event occurs before running.

     Demons can circumvent copy-protection schemes. One widely used copy-protection scheme prevents unauthorized copies of a program by requiring the user to insert the original program disk, which the program checks for an authorization code. When the request for the code occurs, the demon runs. Pretending to be the original program disk, the demon passes along the correct code. See *copy-protection* .

density   A measurement of the amount of information (in bits) that can be packed reliably into a square inch of a magnetic secondary storage device, such as a floppy disk. See *double density, high density, and single density.*

derived field   See *calculated field.*

descender   The portion of a lowercase letter that hangs below the baseline. Five letters of the alphabet have descenders: g, j, p, q, and y.

descending sort   A sort that reverses the normal ascending sort order. Instead of sorting A, B, C, D and 1, 2, 3, 4; a descending sort lists D, C, B, A and 4, 3, 2, 1.

descriptor   In database management, a term used to classify a data record so that all records sharing a common subject can be retrieved as a group.

     In a video store's database, for example, the descriptor Adventure appears in the data records of all action-oriented films. See *identifier.*

desk accessory (DA)   In a graphical user interface, a set of utility programs that assist with day-to-day tasks such as jotting down notes, performing calculations on an on-screen calculator, maintaining a list of names and phone numbers, and displaying an on-screen clock (see fig. D.4).

     ➔ **Tip:** Many Macintosh users equip their systems with Suitcase II (Fifth Generation Systems) or MasterJuggler (Al-soft) INIT utility programs that can install an unlimited number of desk accessories. See *Font/DA Mover, graphical user interface,* and *utility programs.*

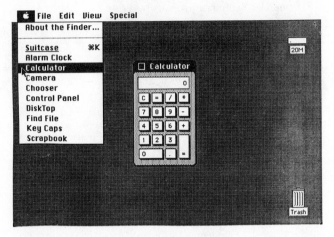

Fig. D.4. Desk accessories.

desktop In a graphical user interface, a computer representation of your day-to-day work, as if you are looking at an actual desk littered with folders full of work to do (see fig. D.5). See *graphical user interface.*

desktop computer A personal computer or professional workstation designed to fit on a standard-sized office desk and equipped with sufficient memory and secondary storage to perform business computing tasks. See *laptop computer.*

desktop publishing (DTP) The use of a personal computer as an inexpensive production system for generating typeset-quality text and graphics. Desktop publishers often merge text and graphics on the same page and print pages on a high-resolution laser printer or typesetting machine (see fig. D.6.).

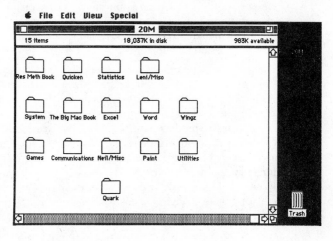

Fig. D.5. Macintosh desktop.

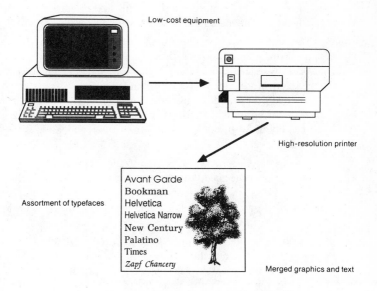

Fig. D.6. Elements of desktop publishing.

One of the fastest-growing applications in personal computing, desktop publishing offers cost-saving, productivity, and time-saving advantages that have helped speed the proliferation of desktop computers.

Using traditional methods, a business may find itself paying up to $2,000 per page to prepare camera-ready copy for a technical manual. Such costs may amount to as much as 15 percent of the total manufacturing costs in such industries. A typical document-production project also involves the timely cooperation of layout artists, typesetters, proofreaders, and printers, many of whom are employed by outside firms on a contract basis. But they may not cooperate, and their work may not be completed on time. Traditional methods also make last-minute changes expensive or impossible.

Because one person can produce typeset-quality text and graphics with a personal computer, desktop publishing enables an organization to reduce publication costs by as much as 75 percent, eliminate delays attributable to tardy subcontractors and miscommunication, and make last-minute changes without encountering additional costs or delays.

The capability to make last-minute changes is a key advantage of this technology that should not be underestimated. Several five-star restaurants, for example, use Macintoshes and laser printers to produce daily menus. Freed from dependence on printed menus, these restaurants can experiment with new dishes, adjust the menu to the changing availability of fresh foods, and ensure that every menu looks fresh and clean.

For documents crucial to an organization's public image, however, laser-produced output may not be of high enough quality. For such documents, desktop-published output needs to be produced on a linotronic typesetting machine or a RIP.

Desktop publishing's origins are in the early history of word processing software. Some of the earliest word processing programs were devised by computer programmers to assist them in preparing manuals for the programs they had written.

These programs included such features as automatic table of contents and index generation, automatic pagination, automatic spelling correction, and other productivity-enhancing features. Printed on low-resolution printers, these manuals were poorly suited to public distribution. Research at Xerox Corporation's Palo Alto Research Laboratories, however, demonstrated the technical feasibility of high-quality document production using WYSIWYG (what-you-see-is-what-you-get) software and laser printers. But with a price tag of $25,000 or more, these early systems could not compete with the traditional document production process for most firms.

The rapid growth of desktop publishing as a personal computer application was made possible by four key innovations: the availability of reasonably inexpensive personal computers capable of displaying text and graphics simultaneously, like the Macintosh; the development of page layout programs like PageMaker; the development of page description languages like PostScript, and the introduction of moderately priced laser printers with a variety of typefaces, like the LaserWriter. Suddenly, a high-quality desktop publishing system could be obtained for less than $10,000. Because these innovations originated in the Macintosh environment, the Macintosh took an early lead in this area.

The necessary technology has become available for IBM PC-compatible computers, although the 640K RAM barrier of DOS imposes severe limitations on the size of documents that can be produced and the number of features page layout programs offer. Ventura Publisher, a popular page-layout program for IBM PC-compatible computers, requires the installation of extended memory before such features as automatic hyphenation can be used.

▲ **Caution:** Despite the many advantages of desktop publishing in organizational settings, desktop publishing has limitations. Laser printers produce output with a resolution of 300 or 400 dpi, which appears professionally typeset to the untrained eye. Type printed at 300 dpi is a major improvement over the low-resolution output of dot-matrix printers (about 120 dpi), but 300 dpi still is considered coarse by typesetting standards.

Professional typesetting equipment has resolutions of 1200 dpi and more (see fig. D.7). However, page layout programs can produce output in a form that can be read by professional typesetting equipment. If high-resolution output is desired for a project, you can engage a professional typesetting firm to produce high-resolution output from a disk.

A A A

Fig. D.7. Characters printed at 120, 300, and 1200 dots per inch.

A more serious drawback of desktop publishing is that the use of a page layout program does not guarantee that a document meets professional design standards. By observing a few rules, however, virtually anyone can produce a price list, brochure, or report that does not embarrass an organization.

When preparing a brochure or newsletter, for example, the designer should choose a typeface that sets the tone of the piece effectively and then stick with the typeface. No more than two typefaces should be used. White space should be used effectively for emphasis, balance, and proportion. Graphics should be relevant to a key point made in the text, clearly-printed, and tasteful. Rules and borders should be used conservatively.

Keep the layout simple; for any document that will be seen by the public, engage a professional designer to critique the design before printing. See *dots per inch (dpi), extended memory, laser printer, page description language (PDL), page layout program, PageMaker, PostScript, resolution,* and *typeface.*

DESQview   A windowing environment developed by Quarterdeck Office Systems for IBM PC-compatible computers.

Comparable to Microsoft Windows, DESQview provides a graphical user interface for DOS and the capability to load more than one program and execute tasks simultaneously. DESQview can take full advantage of the Intel 80386 microprocessor's protected mode and extended memory, even while running under DOS.

DESQview has gained increased use as an alternative to upgrading to OS/2. In response to DESQview's success, Microsoft Corporation, the publisher of MS-DOS and OS/2, has released Version 3 of Microsoft Windows that includes most of DESQview's capabilities. See *extended memory, Intel 80386, Microsoft Windows, Operating System/2 (OS/2),* and *protected mode.*

destination file   In many DOS commands, the file that data or program instructions are copied into. See *source file.*

device   Any hardware component or peripheral, such as a printer, modem, monitor, or mouse, that can receive and/or send data.

device driver   A program that extends the operating system's capabilities by enabling the operating system to work with a specific hardware device (such as a printer).

In DOS and OS/2, device drivers are files with the extension SYS. To use a device driver, you must enter a configuration command that identifies the file containing the driver. You place the command in the CONFIG.SYS file. The following command, for example, tells DOS to use a mouse driver:

```
DEVICE = MOUSE.SYS
```

DOS does not need DEVICE commands to work with most keyboards, monitors, and printers. You use DEVICE commands, however, to install a mouse and files that set up RAM disks.

▲ **Caution:** After you install a mouse on your system, beware of accidentally erasing the CONFIG.SYS file. If you do, the mouse will not work.

device name   In DOS and OS/2, the abbreviation that refers to a peripheral device. See *CON, LPT,* and *PRN.*

diacritical marks   Marks added to characters to represent their phonetic value in a foreign language, such as accents. See *accent*.

diagnostic program   A utility program that tests computer hardware and software to determine whether they are operating properly.

> **→ Tip:** Most computers initiate a diagnostic check at the start of every operating session. A particular focus of attention is the memory. If any errors are found, you see an error message, and the computer does not proceed. If you run into this problem, try starting the computer again. If you see the error message again, you may have to replace a memory chip. Because the error message specifies the location of the faulty chip, be sure to write down the number you see on-screen.

dialog box   In a graphical user interface, an on-screen message box that conveys or requests information from the user (see fig. D.8). See *graphical user interface*.

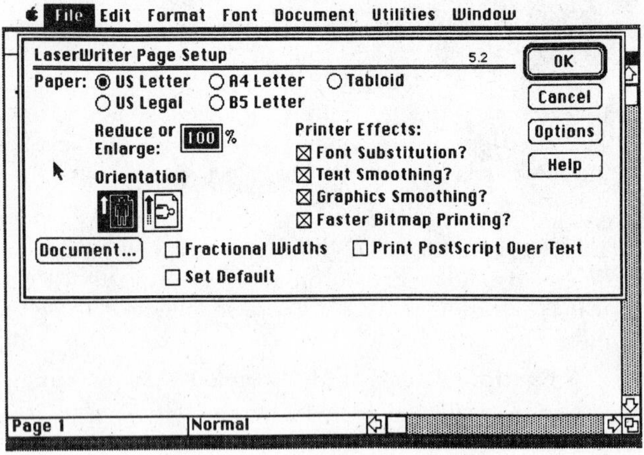

Fig. D.8. A typical Macintosh dialog box.

dictionary sort   A sort operation that ignores the case of characters as data is rearranged. See *sort* and *sort order*.

DIF   See *data interchange format (DIF) file* .

digital   A form of representation in which discrete (separate)
objects (digits) are used to stand for something so that counting and other operations can be performed precisely.

Information represented digitally can be manipulated to
produce a calculation, a sort, or some other computation. In
an abacus, for example, quantities are represented by positioning beads on a wire. A trained abacus operator can
perform calculations at high rates of speed by following an
algorithm, a recipe for solving the problem. In digital electronic computers, two electrical states correspond to the 1s
and 0s of binary numbers, and the algorithm is embodied in
a computer program. See *algorithm, analog, binary
numbers, computation*, and *program.*

digital computer   A computer that represents information using digits, or objects clearly separate and different from each
other and performs computations on this information using
at least partly automatic procedures. See *analog computer*
and *computer.*

Digital Darkroom   An image-enhancement program developed by Silicon Beach Software for Macintosh computers.
The program uses computer processing techniques to edit
and enhance scanned black-and-white photographic images.

digital monitor   A cathode-ray-tube (CRT) display that accepts digital output from the display adapter and converts
the digital signal to an analog signal.

Digital monitors cannot accept input unless the input conforms to a prearranged standard, such as the IBM Monochrome Display Adapter (MDA), Color Graphics Adapter
(CGA), or Enhanced Graphics adapter (EGA). All these
adapters produce digital output.

Digital monitors are fast and produce sharp, clear images.
However, they have a major disadvantage: unlike analog
monitors, they cannot display continuously variable colors.
Simple digital color monitors can display colors in two
modes, on and off; more complex color digital monitors rec-

ognize more intensity modes. For the Video Graphics Array (VGA) standard, IBM chose to use analog monitors so that continuously variable images can be displayed on-screen. See *analog monitor, Color Graphics Adapter (CGA), digital, Enhanced Graphics Adapter (EGA), monochrome display adapter (MDA),* and *Video Graphics Array (VGA).*

digital transmission   A data communications technique that passes information encoded as discrete, on-off pulses. Unlike analog transmission, which uses a continuous wave form to transmit data, digital transmission does not require the use of digital-to-analog converters at each end of the transmission. However, analog transmission is faster and can carry more than one channel at a time. See *analog transmission.*

dingbats   Ornamental characters such as bullets, stars, and flowers used to decorate a page. See *Zapf Dingbats.*

DIP (Dual In-line Package) switch   A switch, usually hidden on an internal circuit board, used to choose operating parameters, such as the amount of memory that should be recognized by the operating system or the printer file format the printer should expect.

"Dual in-line package" refers to the switch's plastic housing designed to be attached directly to a circuit board. The trend in computer and peripheral design is to make such switches more accessible by placing them on the exterior of the component's case or to eliminate them entirely in favor of more easily manipulated controls.

direct-connect modem   A modem that makes a direct connection to the telephone line via modular connectors, unlike an acoustic coupler modem designed to cradle a telephone headset. See *acoustic coupler.*

directory   An index to the files stored on a disk or a portion of a disk that can be displayed on-screen.

The contents of a disk are not obvious to the eye. A good operating system keeps an up-to-date record of the files stored on a disk, with ample information about the file's content, time of creation, and size.

In DOS and OS/2, the DIR command displays a disk directory. A typical directory display appears as follows:

```
Volume in Drive A has no label
Directory of A:\
ANSI       SYS     1651   3-21-86    0:01a
DRIVER     SYS     1102   3-21-86    7:47a
RAMDRIVE SYS       6462   7-07-86   12:00p
CONFIG     SYS       15   1-17-89    3:37p
COMMAND COM       23612   9-30-86   12:00p
APPEND     COM     1725   3-21-86   11:00p
ASSIGN     COM     1523   3-21-86    4:50p
CLOCK      COM      505   2-10-87   12:00p
FORMAT     COM    11597   9-30-86    9:00a
SYS        COM     4607   8-01-87   12:00p
ATTRIB     EXE     8234   3-21-86   12:00p
CHKDSK     EXE     9680   3-21-86   12:00p
DEBUG      EXE     5647   3-21-86    8:19p
13 File(s) 12876 bytes free
```

This disk directory contains the following information:

- Volume label. When formatting a disk, you can name it; the name is called a volume label. You also can name the disk later using the VOL command. If you give the disk a volume label, you see the name at the top of the directory when you use the DIR command.

- File name. DOS file names have two parts, the file name and the extension. The first two columns of the directory table show the file name and the extension of each file on the disk.

- File size. The third column of the disk directory table shows the size of each file (in bytes).

- Date last modified. The fourth column of the disk directory shows the date on which the file was last modified.

- Time last modified. The fifth column of the disk directory shows the time when the file was last modified.

- Space remaining. The number of bytes of storage space left on the disk is shown at the bottom of the directory. This information is important because you cannot write a file to a disk with insufficient room.

➜ **Tip:** If your computer is not equipped with a clock/cal-endar board, be sure to set the system time and system date manually when you start the computer. DOS and OS/2 use this information to create the date and time listings in disk directories. If the date and time are not set, the dates listed for files are incorrect.

See *clock/calendar board* and *subdirectory.*

directory markers   In DOS and OS/2, symbols displayed in a subdirectory's on-screen directory that represent the current directory (.) and the parent directory (..). See *current directory, directory, parent directory,* and *subdirectory.*

disk   See *floppy disk* and *hard disk.*

disk buffer   See *disk cache.*

disk cache   Pronounced "cash." An area of random-access memory (RAM) set aside by the operating system to store fre-quently accessed data and program instructions. A disk cache can improve the speed of disk-intensive applications such as database management programs. If the central proc-essing unit (CPU) must wait for this information from disk, processing speed slows noticeably.

When the CPU repeatedly is accessing the same infor-mation, you can obtain modest speed gains by placing the frequently-accessed information in a buffer (a temporary storage place in memory). Although using a disk cache does not eliminate disk accesses, the number of accesses is re-duced. See *central processing unit (CPU), RAM cache,* and *random-access memory (RAM).*

disk drive   A secondary storage medium such as a floppy disk drive or a hard disk. This term usually refers to floppy disk drives.

A floppy disk drive is an economical secondary storage medium that uses a removable magnetic disk. Like all mag-netic media, a floppy disk can be recorded, erased, and re-used over and over. The recording and erasing operations are performed by the read/write head that moves laterally over the surface of the disk—giving the drive its random-access capabilities.

Although floppy disk drives are inexpensive, they are too slow to serve as the main secondary storage medium for today's personal computers; for business applications, a minimum configuration is one hard disk and one floppy disk drive. (The floppy disk drive is needed to copy software and disk-based data onto the system and for backup operations.) See *floppy disk*, *random access*, *read/write head*, and *secondary storage*.

disk operating system   See *operating system*.

disk optimizer   See *defragmentation*.

DISKCOMP   In DOS and OS/2, an external command that compares two disks on a track-by-track basis to see whether the contents are identical. See *external command*.

DISKCOPY   In DOS and OS/2, a command that copies the contents of one disk to another on a track-for-track basis.

   ➔ **Tip:** Unlike the COPY command, which copies one or more files, DISKCOPY makes an exact duplicate of an entire disk, including the hidden files containing DOS or OS/2. If you are copying a disk that contains DOS, therefore, use DISKCOPY instead of COPY.

display   See *monitor*.

display type   A typeface, usually 14 points or larger and differing in style from the body type, that is used for headings and subheadings. See *body type*.

distributed processing system   A computer system designed for multiple users that provides each user with a fully functional computer. Unlike a stand-alone system, however, a distributed system is designed to make communication among the linked computers and shared access to central files easier.

In personal computing, distributed processing takes the form of local area networks, in which the personal computers of a department or organization are linked via high-speed cable connections.

Distributed processing offers some advantages over multiuser systems because each user is given a fully functional workstation instead of a remote terminal without processing circuitry. If the network fails, you can still work. You also can select software tailored to your needs. A distributed processing system can be started with a modest initial investment; you need only two or three workstations and, if desired, a central file server. More workstation nodes can be added as needed.

A multiuser system, however, requires a major initial investment in the central computer, which must be powerful enough to handle system demands as the system grows. Multiuser systems have advantages such as point-of-sale terminals, in which little is to be gained by distributing processing power and much to be gained by making sure that all information is posted to a central database. See *file server, local area network (LAN)*, and *multiuser system*.

DO/WHILE loop   In programming, a loop control structure that continues to carry out its function while an external condition is satisfied.

In the following pseudocode example, a database management program's software command language is used to write a short program that prints all the records in the file. In English, the program says, "Open the database called videos. Get ready to route output to the printer. Check to see whether you have reached the end of the file. If you have not reached the end of the file, do the following: print the title, rating, and category, and then skip two lines. Turn off printer output, close the database called videos, and quit."

```
USE videos
SET printer on
DO WHILE end_of_file = false
    PRINT title
    PRINT rating
```

```
      PRINT category
      SKIP 2 lines
ENDDO
SET printer off
CLOSE videos
QUIT
```

The external condition is supplied by the variable called end_of_file. When the program reaches the last record, this variable is set to true, so that the DO/WHILE loop stops. At this point, the sequential control structure takes over again, and the program moves on to the next statement (SET printer off). See *case branch*, *loop control structure*, *sequence control structure*, *software command language*, and *syntax*.

document base font   The default font that a word processing program uses, unless you override the program by choosing a different font. Unlike an initial base font that affects all documents, the document base font affects only one document.

You can choose Times Roman as the initial base font for all documents, for example, but override this choice by choosing Helvetica as the document base font for a letter you are currently writing. You can choose other fonts within this letter, but the program uses Helvetica unless you give an explicit command to the contrary. See *initial base font.*

document comparison utility   A utility program that compares two documents created with a word processing program. If the two documents are not identical, the program displays the differences between them, line-by-line.

Document comparison utilities are useful in collaborative writing. Suppose that you create a document, keep a copy, and send one file to the person working with you on the project. This person makes changes and returns an altered version of the file to you.

Using a document comparison utility, you can see the differences between the two documents on-screen. In figure D.9, for example, altered or added passages are shown in reverse video, and the original version is shown in strike-through text. See *redlining*.

In the old days, writers had to stop editing days before a document was due and start combing through the main text to prepare the document references. One of WordPerfect 5's handiest features is that it speeds up that process. ~~One of WordPerfect 5's handiest features is that it speeds up the process of assembling document references.~~ With a little foresight and planning, you can work on a document right down to a few hours before a deadline, confident that as your main text changes, the document references will keep right up with it.

This chapter shows you how to create lists, tables of contents, tables of authorities, and indexes. You also learn to use automatic cross-referencing, which lets you change the structure of your document and automatically maintain accurate references to footnotes, pages and sections. ~~which lets you change the structure of your document and automatically maintain accurate references to certain spots in a document.~~ Finally, you learn to use the Document Compare feature so that you can show someone else what was omitted from, ~~you learn to use the Document Compare feature so that you can see what was omitted from,~~ or added to, a document, without having to mark all those changes yourself.

Fig. D.9. Two versions of a document compared by a document comparison utility.

document format   In a word processing program, a set of formatting choices that affect the page layout of all pages of the document you are currently working on. Examples of document formats include margins, headers, footers, page numbers, and columns.

document processing   The application of computer technology to every stage of the in-house production of documents, such as instruction manuals, handbooks, reports, and proposals.

A complete document processing system includes all the software and hardware needed to create, organize, edit, and print such documents. Because these documents generally are reproduced from camera-ready copy, a document processing system's word processing software should be able to generate indexes and tables of contents. See *word processing program* and *desktop publishing (DTP)*.

documentation   The instructions, tutorials, and reference information that provide users with the information required to use a computer program or computer system effectively. Documentation can appear in printed media or in on-line help systems.

DOS   Pronounced "doss." Acronym for disk operating system; used to refer to PC-DOS and MS-DOS, the operating systems of IBM Personal Computers and compatibles. See *MS-DOS*.

DOS prompt   In DOS, a letter representing the current disk drive and the greater-than symbol (C>) that informs the user when the operating system is ready to receive a command. This default DOS prompt can be changed. See *prompt*.

dot-matrix printer   An impact printer that forms text and graphics images by pressing the ends of pins against a ribbon.

A dot-matrix printer forms an image of text or graphics by hammering the ends of pins against a ribbon. The ends of these wires form a character made up of a pattern (a matrix) of dots. Dot-matrix printers are fast, but the output they produce is generally poor quality because the character is not fully formed. These printers also can be extremely noisy. Some dot-matrix printers use 24 pins instead of 9, and the quality of their output is better.

Many of today's dot-matrix printers offer a near-letter quality (NLQ) mode that sacrifices speed to produce substantially improved output. In the NLQ mode, the printer passes over a line several times, offsetting the dots to form a solid character.

Better dot-matrix printers can produce printout in more than one type style and size (called a font). Fonts are measured in points (1/72 of an inch). A standard type size is 12 points, producing 6 lines per vertical inch on the page, but you usually can choose sizes ranging from 8 to 24 points.

▲ **Caution:** In IBM PC-compatible computing, no one, widely accepted standard exists for printer control commands. De facto standards have been established by Epson and IBM. Many dot-matrix printers recognize the Epson or IBM commands, but others do not. If you plan to purchase a dot-matrix printer, make sure that your software includes a printer driver for the model. See *impact printer*, *near-letter quality (NLQ)*, and *nonimpact printer*.

dot pitch   The size of the smallest dot that a monitor can display on-screen. Dot pitch determines a monitor's maximum resolution.

To keep the electron beam from spilling over and activating the wrong part of the screen, color monitors use a shadow mask, a metal sheet with fine perforations. These perforations are arranged so that the beam strikes one hole at a time, corresponding to one dot on-screen. The smaller the hole in the shadow mask, the higher the resolution.

➔ **Tip:** High-resolution monitors use dot pitches of approximately 0.31 mm or less; the best monitors use dot pitches of 0.28 mm or less.

dot prompt   In dBASE, the prompt—a lone period on an otherwise empty screen—for the command-driven interface of the program.

dots per inch (dpi)   A measure of screen and printer resolution that counts the dots that the device can produce per linear inch.

➔ **Tip:** In expressing the resolution of display devices, the custom is to state the horizontal measurement before the vertical one. A Super-VGA monitor with a resolution of   1024 x 768, for example, can display 1024 dots per inch horizontally and 768 dots per inch vertically.

double density   A widely used recording technique that packs twice as much data on a floppy or hard disk as the earlier single-density standard. See *high density, modified frequency modulation (MFM) recording, run length limited (RLL) recording,* and *single density.*

Dow Jones News/Retrieval Service   An on-line information service from Dow Jones, the publishers of the *Wall Street Journal* and *Barron's*, that offers a computer-searchable index to financial and business publications and up-to-date financial information (such as stock quotes). See *on-line information service.*

downloadable font   A printer font that must be transferred from the computer's (or the printer's) hard disk drive to the printer's random-access memory before the font can be used.

Often called soft fonts, downloadable fonts are the least convenient of the three types of printer fonts you can use. Downloading can consume as much as 5 or 10 minutes at the start of every operating session.

Purchase a printer with a variety of built-in typefaces or a cartridge that contains several typefaces in a variety of sizes. These fonts are immediately available for printing, because they are resident in the printer's (or cartridge's) ROM.

Downloaded fonts take up room in your printer's memory, leaving less room for page-makeup operations and potentially causing out-of-memory problems. You may have to add another megabyte or two of expensive printer memory to avoid such difficulties. However, downloadable fonts are available in hundreds of typefaces, and what they lack in convenience they make up for in versatility.

The hard disk need not be the computer's. High-end PostScript-compatible laser printers such as the Apple LaserWriter NTX come with SCSI ports for hard drives.

Downloadable fonts usually are provided in the form of a font family, with a range of type styles and sizes with the same typeface design. Bit-mapped fonts cannot be resized— a bit-mapped Helvetica 14 font cannot be printed at 12 or 16 points. Outline fonts, however, consist of a mathematical font representation (written in a page-description language like PostScript) that the printer can resize. Therefore, you are not   limited to a narrow range of font sizes. Only printers with the necessary internal circuitry are capable of decoding and printing outline fonts.

You can download fonts at the start of the operating session using a downloading utility or while using a word processing or page layout program (such as Microsoft Word, WordPerfect, or PageMaker) capable of downloading fonts as needed.

Some laser printers (such as the Hewlett-Packard LaserJet) categorize fonts as permanent or temporary. Permanent fonts are downloaded at the beginning of the operating session and remain in the printer's memory throughout the session. (They are not really permanent, however, because they are erased—along with everything in the printer's memory— when you shut the printer off.)

Permanent fonts consume memory space. Temporary fonts, in contrast, are downloaded as needed during a printing operation and deleted from memory to make room for other fonts as font changes occur in the document. Temporary fonts do not hold memory, but temporary fonts interrupt printing with downloads that can make the whole operation tedious.

➔ **Tip:** When you finish printing a document that required several downloadable fonts you no longer need, switch your printer off and on before proceeding—especially if the next document contains graphics. The power interruption clears the printer's memory and makes room for the computations needed to generate the graphic image. See *bit-mapped font built-in font, cartridge font, downloading utility, font, font family, outline font, page description language (PDL),* and *PostScript.*

downloading   The reception and storage of a program or data file from a distant computer through data communications links. See *file transfer protocol* and *modem.*

downloading utility   A utility program that transfers downloadable fonts from your computer's (or printer's) hard disk to the printer's random-access memory (RAM).

Downloading utilities usually are provided free by the publishers of downloadable fonts. You may not need the utility if the word processing or page layout program you are using has downloading capabilities built in, such as Word-Perfect, Microsoft Word, Ventura Publisher, and PageMaker.

downward compatibility Hardware or software that runs without modification when used with earlier computer components or software versions. VGA monitors, for example, are downwardly compatible with the original IBM PC, if you use an 8-bit VGA adapter that fits in the PC's 8-bit expansion bus.

dpi See *dots per inch (dpi)*.

DRAM See *dynamic random-access memory (DRAM)*.

draw program A computer graphics program that uses object-oriented graphics to produce line art.

A draw program stores the components of a drawing, such as lines, circles, and curves, as mathematical formulas rather than as a configuration of bits on-screen. Unlike images created with paint programs, line art created with a draw program can be sized and scaled without introducing distortions.

Draw programs differ from paint programs in another way: they produce output that prints at a printer's maximum resolution. Popular draw programs include MacDraw and SuperPaint for the Macintosh. See *object-oriented graphic* and *paint program*.

drive See *disk drive*.

drive designator In DOS and OS/2, an argument that specifies the drive to be affected by the command. For example, the command **FORMAT B:** instructs DOS to format the disk in drive B.

driver A disk file that contains information needed by a program to operate a peripheral such as a monitor or printer. See *device driver*.

drop cap An initial letter of a chapter or paragraph enlarged and positioned so that the top of the character is even with the top of the first line and the rest of the character descends into the second and subsequent lines (see fig. D.10). See *stickup initial*.

This is a 24 point
Helvetica Big First
Char. with Space For
Big First: Normal.
Ventura automatically
aligns the top of the
character with the top of
the first line of text and
calculates the number
of lines to indent.

This is a 24 point
Helvetica Big First
Char. with Space For
Big First: Custom. You
set the number of lines
to indent and Ventura
aligns the baselines of
the First Char. and the
last indented line of text.

Fig. D.10. Drop caps created with Ventura Publisher.

drop out type   White characters printed on a black background.

drop shadow   A shadow placed behind an image, slightly offset horizontally and vertically, that creates the illusion that the topmost image has been lifted off the surface of the page.

dual y-axis graph   In presentation and analytical graphics, a line or column graph that uses two y-axes (values axes) when comparing two data series with different measurement scales (see fig. D.11).

    Dual y-axis graphs are useful when you are comparing two different data series that must be measured with two different values axes (apples and oranges). In figure D.11, for example, production costs are measured in dollars per carton, and sales are measured in thousands of cartons. See *paired bar graph.*

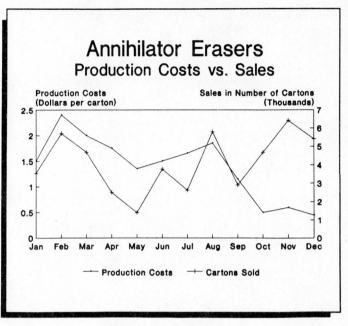

Fig. D.11. Dual y-axis graph.

dumb terminal   See *terminal.*

dump   To transfer the contents of memory to a printing or secondary storage device.

Programmers use memory dumps while debugging programs to see exactly what the computer is doing when the dump occurs. See *screen dump.*

duplex   See *full duplex* and *half duplex.*

duplex printing   Printing or reproducing a document on both sides of the page, so that the verso (left) and recto (right) pages face each other after the document is bound.

A document begins on an odd-numbered recto page; verso pages have even numbers. See *binding offset.*

Dvorak keyboard   Pronounced "dih-vor´-ack." An alternative keyboard layout in which 70 percent of the keystrokes are made on the home row (compared to 32 percent with the standard QWERTY layout).

The home row is the row of keys your fingers rest on when you are ready to start typing. Ideally, most of the characters you type are positioned on the home row, but not in the QWERTY method. Because you can configure a computer keyboard any way you want, you can equip your computer with a Dvorak keyboard.

➔ **Tip:** If you are just learning how to touch-type, consider a Dvorak keyboard because it is easier and faster. Every time you use a QWERTY keyboard, however, you must go back to the hunt-and-peck method.

dynamic link   A method of linking data shared by two programs. When data is changed in one program, the data is likewise changed in the other when you use an update command. See *warm link*.

dynamic random-access memory (DRAM)   A random-access memory (RAM) chip that represents memory states by using capacitors that store electrical charges.

Because the capacitors eventually lose their charges, DRAM chips must be refreshed continually (hence "dynamic").

Dynamic RAM chips vary in their access time, the speed with which the central processing unit (CPU) can obtain information encoded within them. These access times are rated in nanoseconds (billionths of a second); a chip marked -12, for example, has an access time of 120 ns. Such access times may seem remarkably fast, but they actually may be insufficient for today's fast microprocessors that must be programmed with wait states so that memory can catch up.

➔ **Tip:** If you are using an Intel 80286- or 80386-based computer with a fast clock speed (such as 25 or 33 MHz), you need the fastest DRAM chips you can obtain. Chips rated

120 ns are too slow; make sure that your computer is equipped with chips rated at 80 ns or better.

See *central processing unit (CPU)*, *Intel 80286*, *Intel 80386*, *nanosecond (NS)*, *static random-access memory (RAM)*, and *wait state*.

E-mail   See *electronic mail*.

EARN   See *European Academic Research Network (EARN)*.

EBCDIC   See *Extended Binary Coded Decimal Interchange Code* (EBCDIC).

ECHO   In DOS and OS/2, a batch command that displays a message when the batch file is executed.

When DOS or OS/2 starts executing a batch file, the operating system turns on echo mode. When echo is on, all the commands in the batch file are displayed on-screen as they are carried out.

➔ **Tip:** To suppress the display of batch file commands as they are carried out, place the following batch command on the first line of your batch file:

    ECHO off

To display a message while echo is off, start the message line with an ECHO statement as follows:

    ECHO Put the backup disk in Drive A

See *batch file*.

echoplex   An asynchronous communications protocol in which the receiving station acknowledges and confirms the reception of a message by echoing the message back to the transmitting station. See *full duplex* and *half duplex*.

Edit mode   A program mode that makes correcting text and data easier (see fig. E.1).

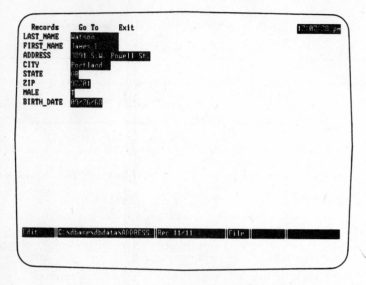

```
 Records     Go To     Exit                              12:07:28 pm
LAST_NAME  Watson
FIRST_NAME James T.
ADDRESS    7891 S.W. Powell St.
CITY       Portland
STATE      OR
ZIP        97201
MALE       T
BIRTH_DATE 09/26/68




 Edit   C:\dbase\dbdata\ADDRESS  Rec 11/11        File
```

Fig. E.1. Data record displayed in edit format.

In Lotus 1-2-3, for example, you type **EDIT** to correct a cell definition. After you type **EDIT**, the program echoes the current cell definition on the entry line, and you can use editing keys to correct errors or add characters.

editor   See *text editor*.

edits   In a word processing program, the changes made to a document (including insertions, deletions, block moves, and formatting).

EDLIN   Pronounced "ed´-lin." In DOS, the line editor provided with the operating system for light text-creation and editing duties.

A line editor is a primitive word processing program that forces you to work with text line-by-line. Although EDLIN may be suitable for creating a small batch file, EDLIN is cumbersome and difficult to use. For most purposes, a word processor is better for creating text files.

EGA   See *Enhanced Graphics Adapter (EGA).*

EISA   See *Extended Industry Standard Architecture (EISA).*

electronic mail   The use of electronic communications media to send textual messages (such as letters, memos, and reports).

Electronic mail may involve a one-to-one communication, in which one person sends a private message to another person; or a one-to-many communication, in which one person sends a message to many people connected to the network.

Electronic mail is a store-and-forward technology; unlike a telephone call, the recipient need not be present. The system stores the message and, if the system is a good one, informs the recipients that a message is waiting when they log on to the system.

Electronic mail services are provided privately and publicly. Private electronic mail is possible in local area networks. Mail can be exchanged only among users of the network. Public electronic mail is provided by an on-line information service such as CompuServe or GEnie, or an electronic mail service such as MCI Mail. Mail can be exchanged among users who can log onto the information service using a modem and a communications program. See *communications program, local area network (LAN),* and *modem.*

elite   A typeface that prints twelve characters per inch. See *pitch.*

em dash   A continuous dash equal in width to one em, the width of the capital letter M in a given typeface.

Em dashes often are used to introduce parenthetical remarks. The following sentence contains an em dash: The butler—or someone who knows what the butler knows—must have done it. See *en dash.*

em fraction   A single-character fraction that occupies one em of space and uses a diagonal stroke (¼).

Em fractions are used when fractions appear occasionally within body text, but they are not available in some fonts.

A true em fraction is one character and should be distinguished from a piece fraction made from three or more characters (1/4). See *en fraction*.

embedded formatting command   A text formatting command placed directly in the text to be formatted that does not affect the appearance of the text on-screen.

Considered by many to be an undesirable formatting technique in word processing programs, embedded commands cannot be seen until the document is previewed on-screen or printed. Studies in work environments show that using word processors with embedded commands may take longer to produce documents than using typewriters. Synonymous with *off-screen formatting*. See *hidden codes*, *on-screen formatting*, and *what-you-see-is-what-you-get (WYSIWYG)*.

emphasis   The use of a non-Roman type style, such as underlining, italic, bold typefaces, and small caps, to highlight a word or phrase.

Word processing and page layout programs provide many more ways to emphasize text than typewriters do, but with the increase in options has come an increase in abuse. Emphasis often is overused by inexperienced writers.

Good taste in page layout design calls for restraint in the use of emphasis. Because underlining is a signal to the typesetter to set the text in italic, underlining is redundant in documents prepared using desktop publishing techniques. Many programs include outline and shadow characters that should be used only rarely. See *type style*.

EMS   See *Expanded Memory Specification (EMS)*.

emulation   The duplication of the functional capability of one device in another device.

In telecommunications, for example, a personal computer emulates a dumb terminal for on-line communication with a distant computer. See *dumb terminal*.

en   A unit of measurement in typesetting that equals half the width of an em space, the width of the capital letter M in the current typeface.

en dash A continuous dash equal in width to one half em, the width of the capital letter M in the current typeface.

En dashes are used in place of the English words to or through, as in pp. 63–68 or January 9–14. See *em dash*.

en fraction A single-character fraction that occupies one en of space and uses a horizontal stroke. See *em fraction*.

encapsulated PostScript (EPS) file A high-resolution graphic image stored using instructions written in the PostScript page description language.

The EPS standard enables the device-independent transfer of high-resolution graphic images between applications. EPS graphics are of outstanding quality and can contain subtle gradations in shading, high-resolution text with special effects, and graceful curves generated by mathematical equations.

The printout resolution is determined by the printing device's maximum capabilities; on laser printers, EPS graphics print at 300 dpi, but on Linotronic typesetters, resolutions of up to 2540 dpi are possible. EPS images can be sized without sacrificing image quality (see fig. E.2).

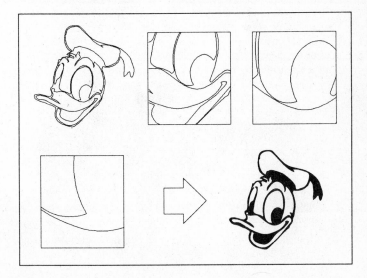

Fig. E.2. EPS graphics can be scaled to any size without image distortion.

The major drawback of EPS graphics is that a PostScript-compatible laser printer is required to print them, and with most application programs, the image is not visible on-screen unless a PICT- or TIFF-format screen image has been attached to the EPS file.

Programs capable of creating, displaying, and editing EPS graphics include Adobe Illustrator (Adobe Systems) and Aldus Freehand (Aldus Corporation). You create the image using on-screen graphics tools, and the program saves the image as a text file containing PostScript instructions.

As an alternative to expensive PostScript printers, developers have created programs that interpret and print EPS files on standard dot-matrix printers or nonPostScript laser printers. One such program is GoScript (LaserGo, Inc.). See *PostScript.*

encryption   The process of enciphering or encoding data so that the data cannot be read by users who do not possess the necessary password. See *decryption.*

End key   A key on IBM PC-compatible keyboards with varying functions from program to program.

Frequently, the End key is used to move the cursor to the end of the line or the bottom of the screen, but the assignment of this key is up to the programmer.

end user   The person who benefits, directly or indirectly, from the capabilities of a computer system and uses these capabilities to perform a professional, managerial, or technical task, such as analyzing a company's finances, preparing a publication-quality report, or maintaining an inventory of items in stock.

In corporate data processing during the 1950s and 1960s, end users typically had little or no data processing or computer expertise themselves and were kept at arm's length from computer resources. One significant outcome of the personal computer has been to distribute computer tools to people who previously could not gain access to such tools.

With the distribution of tools has come the distribution of computer expertise. Today's end user possesses sufficient expertise to carry out routine system maintenance tasks and to run application programs. Increasing numbers of end-users modify application programs by writing macros and using software command languages.

endnote A footnote positioned at the end of the document rather than the bottom of the page.

Many word processing programs enable the user to choose between footnotes and endnotes.

Enhanced Expanded Memory Specification (EEMS) A technique to expand the memory of IBM PC-compatible computers running under DOS with a 640K limitation on random-access memory.

EEMS was introduced by AST, Quadram, and Ashton-Tate to improve the performance of the Lotus-Intel-Microsoft (LIM) Expanded Memory Specification. The introduction of LIM Version 4.0, however, has resolved many of the performance issues that motivated the release of EEMS, and the LIM standard is the dominant one. See *extended memory* and *Lotus-Intel-Microsoft Expanded Memory Specification (LIM EMS)*.

Enhanced Graphics Adapter (EGA) A color bit-mapped graphics display adapter for IBM PC-compatible computers that displays up to 16 colors simultaneously with a resolution of 640 pixels horizontally by 350 pixels vertically.

→ **Tip:** For slightly more than the cost of a good EGA adapter and monitor, you can buy the superior VGA technology that preserves the correct aspect ratio of on-screen graphics. See *Color Graphics Adapter (CGA)* and *Video Graphics Array (VGA)*.

Enhanced Graphics Display A color digital monitor designed to work with the IBM Enhanced Graphics Adapter (EGA).

Enhanced System Device Interface (ESDI) An interface standard for hard disk drives. Drives using the ESDI standard transfer data at 10 megabits per second, twice as fast as the earlier ST-506 interface standard.

➜ **Tip:** ESDI drives are substantially more expensive than drives conforming to other interface standards. If your system uses an 80286, 80386, or 80486 microprocessor, and if the system's clock speed is approximately 12 (MHz) or higher, an ST-506 drive may slow down your system's performance. See *ST-506 drive*.

Enter/Return   A key that confirms a command, sending the command to the central processing unit (CPU). In word processing, the Enter/Return key starts a new paragraph.

On early IBM PC keyboards, this key is labeled with a hooked left arrow. On more recent IBM keyboards, and the keyboards of most IBM PC compatibles, Enter or Return is printed on the key.

▲ **Caution:** Most IBM PC-compatible keyboards have two Enter/Return keys. The first is located to the right of the typing area, and the second is located at the lower left of the numeric keypad. These two keys have identical functions in most, but not all programs. Synonymous with *carriage return*.

entry line   In a spreadsheet program, the line in which the characters you type appear. The program does not insert the characters into the current cell until you press Enter.

If the cell has contents, the entry line displays the current cell definition.

environment   The hardware and/or operating system for application programs, such as the Macintosh environment.

EOF   Acronym for *end of file*.

EOL   Acronym for *end of line*.

equation typesetting   Embedded codes within a word processing document that cause the program to print multiline equations, including mathematical symbols such as integrals and summation signs.

The best word processing programs, such as WordPerfect and Microsoft Word, provide commands and symbols that enable technical writers to create multiline equations. You write the equation by embedding special codes for such

symbols as radicals and integrals. You then use a command
that displays the equation on-screen as it will print.

erasable optical disk drive   A read/write secondary storage
medium that uses a laser and reflected light to store and retrieve data on an optical disk.

Unlike CD-ROM and write-once retrieve-many (WORM)
drives, erasable optical disk drives can be used like hard
disks are used; you can write and erase data repeatedly. Storage capacities are enormous; current drives store up to 650
megabytes of information.

However, erasable optical disk drives are expensive and
much slower than hard disks and are not expected to displace magnetic secondary storage media soon. Like CD-
ROM, erasable optical disk drives are used in organizations
that need on-line access to huge amounts of supplementary
information, such as engineering drawings or technical documentation. See *CD-ROM disk drive*, *optical disk*, *secondary
storage*, and *write-once read-many (WORM)*.

erasable programmable read-only memory (EPROM)
A read-only memory (ROM) chip that can be programmed
and reprogrammed.

The erasability of EPROM chips matters to computer
manufacturers, who often find that they need to reprogram
ROM chips containing bugs. PROM chips, which cannot be
reprogrammed, must be discarded when a programming error is discovered.

EPROM chips are packaged in a clear plastic case so that
the contents can be erased using ultraviolet light. To reprogram the EPROM chip, a PROM programmer is necessary.

➜ **Tip:** Because of the slight possibility that EPROM chips
may be damaged by ultraviolet light, you should avoid
exposing your computer's innards to bright sunlight. See *programmable read-only memory (PROM)* and *read-only
memory (ROM)*.

ERASE   In DOS and OS/2, an internal command that deletes a
file from the disk directory.

➜ **Tip:** The ERASE command does not actually remove the
file from the disk. If you have accidentally erased the only

copy of a valuable file, do not write any additional files to the disk. Obtain an undelete program such as the one packaged with Norton Utilities. Undelete programs can restore the disk directory entry and files if you have not saved anything on the disk since the erasure occurred. See *internal command.*

ergonomics   The science of designing machines, tools, and computers so that people find them easy and healthful to use.

error handling   The way a program copes with errors, such as the failure to access data on a disk or a user's failure to press the appropriate key.

A poorly written program may fail to handle errors at all, leading to a system lockup. The best programmers anticipate possible errors and provide information that helps the user solve the problem. See *error trapping.*

error message   In interactive computing, an on-screen message informing the user that the program is unable to carry out a requested operation.

Early computing systems assumed users to be technically sophisticated, and frequently presented cryptic error messages such as

```
EXECUTION TERMINATE-ERROR 19869087
```

Applications for general use should display more helpful error messages that include suggestions about how to solve the problem, such as

```
You are about to lose work you have
not saved. Click OK if you want to
abandon this work. Click Cancel to
return to your document.
```

error trapping   A program or application's capability to recognize an error and perform a predetermined action in response to that error.

Esc   A key that can be implemented differently by application programs. Esc usually is used to cancel a command or an operation.

escape code   A combination of the Esc code and an ASCII character that, when transmitted to a printer, causes the printer to perform a special function, such as print characters in boldface type.

EtherNet   Pronounced "ee´-thur-net." A local area network hardware standard, originally developed by Xerox Corporation, capable of linking up to 1,024 nodes in a bus network.

A high-speed standard using a baseband (single-channel) communication technique, EtherNet provides for a raw data transfer rate of 10 megabits per second, with actual throughputs in the 2 to 3 megabits per second range. EtherNet uses carrier sense multiple access/collision detection techniques to prevent network failures when two devices attempt to access the network at the same time.

▲ **Caution:** Several firms such as 3Com and Novell manufacture local area network hardware that uses EtherNet protocols, but the products of one firm often are incompatible with the products of another. See *AppleTalk, bus network,* and *local area network (LAN).*

ETX/ACK handshaking   See *handshaking.*

European Academic Research Network (EARN)   A European wide-area network fully integrated with BITNET. See *BITNET.*

even parity   In asynchronous communications, an error-checking technique that sets an extra bit (called a parity bit) to 1 if the number of 1 bits in a one-byte data item adds up to an even number. The parity bit is set to 0 if the number of 1 bits adds up to an odd number. See *asynchronous communication, odd parity,* and *parity checking.*

event-driven program   A program designed to react to user-initiated events, such as clicking a mouse, rather than forcing the user to go through a series of prompts and menus in a predetermined way.

Macintosh application programs are event-driven. Unlike conventional programs that have an algorithm for solving a problem, the central feature of a Mac program is the main event loop that forces the program to run in circles while waiting for the user to do something like click the mouse.

evocative typeface In typography, a display type design intended to evoke an era or place (see fig. E.3).

ABCDEFGHIJKLMNOPQRSTUVWXYZ
1234567890

Fig. E.3. The Bracelet typeface evokes the American West.

Excel A graphics-based spreadsheet program developed by Microsoft Corporation that incorporates some of the features of page layout programs.

Available for the Macintosh and IBM PC-compatibles running Windows or Presentation Manager, Excel combines an excellent spreadsheet program and presentation graphics package with user-selectable typefaces, color, and shading. Excel provides the tools to create and analyze spreadsheets, and to desktop publish the results. See *character-based program* and *Lotus 1-2-3*.

execute To carry out the instructions in an algorithm or program.

Expanded Memory Specification (EMS) See *Lotus-Intel-Microsoft Expanded Memory Specification (LIM EMS)*.

expanded memory In IBM PC-compatible computers, a method of getting beyond the 640K DOS memory barrier by swapping programs and data in and out of the main memory at high speeds.

When the IBM Personal Computer was designed, many people thought that 640K was more than enough memory for any application. (The first IBM PCs were available with as little as 16K of RAM.) The IBM PC architecture and DOS, the PC's operating system, were designed to use a maximum of 640K of RAM.

By the mid-1980s, however, people realized that the 640K RAM barrier was imposing severe limitations on many new programs. Spreadsheets, for example, reserve all available memory space for the active worksheet, and the computer can run out of memory after filling in even a small fraction of the available cells. Many users also want to load several programs into RAM simultaneously and switch from one to the other at a keystroke.

Expanded memory uses a programming trick to get beyond the 640K RAM barrier. A peephole of 64K of RAM is set aside so that program instructions and data can be paged in and out in 64K chunks. When the computer requires a 64K chunk not currently paged in, expanded memory software finds and inserts the chunk into the peephole. Such swapping (bank switching) occurs so quickly that the computer seems to have more than 640K RAM.

If your computer uses the 8088, 8086, or 80286 microprocessor and you want to take advantage of expanded memory, equip your computer with an expanded memory board conforming to the Lotus-Intel-Microsoft Expanded Memory System. If you are using an 80836 or 80486 computer with more than one megabyte of extended RAM, you can take advantage of this additional RAM under DOS by using a memory management program such as Quarterdeck's Expanded Memory Manager (QEMM/386) or Microsoft Expanded Memory Manager 386.

▲ **Caution:** Software cannot work with expanded memory unless designed to do so. Most popular application packages such as WordPerfect and Lotus 1-2-3 work with LIM 4.0 expanded memory, but less popular programs and shareware may not function in EMS unless you are using a windowing environment such as Quarterdeck's DESQview or Microsoft Windows.

See *extended memory* and *Lotus-Intel-Microsoft Expanded Memory System (LIM EMS).*

expanded type   Type that has been increased laterally so that fewer characters are contained per linear inch.

expansion bus   An extension of the computer's data bus and address bus that includes a number of receptacles (slots) for adapter boards.

Because each generation of microprocessors has a wider data bus, the expansion bus of IBM PC-compatible computers has changed. The original IBM Personal Computer and XT, based on the 8/16-bit 8088 chip, used an expansion bus with 62-pin expansion slots; the IBM Personal Computer AT, based on the 16-bit 80286, uses the same 62-pin expansion slot plus a supplemental, 36-pin expansion slot.

Non-IBM PC compatibles based on the 32-bit Intel 80386 microprocessor require a 32-bit data bus structure to connect with primary storage. Because even these computers use 16-bit peripherals such as disk drives and video displays, however, some of them set aside adequate room for memory expansion on the motherboard and use the standard, AT-style expansion bus for peripherals. Some machines have expansion slots for full 32-bit memory boards.

▲ **Caution:** If you are buying an 80386 computer and plan to run OS/2, you need as much as 8 megabytes of memory, if you plan to run several applications at once. Make sure that the motherboard of your computer has adequate room for expansion if the computer does not offer 32-bit memory expansion slots.

With the advent of true 32-bit microprocessors such as the Intel 80386, the 32-bit data bus is extended throughout the machine, and the full performance benefits of 32-bit chips are realized. However, two competing standards have emerged for 32-bit expansion busses. See *address bus*, *bus*, *Extended Industry Standard Architecture (EISA)*, *Micro Channel Bus*, *microprocessors*, and *motherboard*.

expansion slot   A receptacle connected to the computer's expansion bus, designed to accept adapters. See *adapter*.

expert system   A computer program containing much of the knowledge used by an expert in a specific field that assists nonexperts as they attempt to cope with problems.

Expert systems contain a knowledge base that expresses an expert's knowledge in a series of IF...THEN rules and an inference engine capable of drawing inferences from the knowledge base. The system engages you in a dialogue, prompting you to supply information needed to assess the situation.

After the information is provided, the system's inference engine consults the rules and attempts to come to a conclusion. Most expert systems express such conclusions with a confidence factor, ranging from speculation to educated guess to firm conclusion.

Creating an expert system is more difficult than it appears. A surprisingly high proportion of expertise is based on experientially learned rules of thumb, such as cleaning the video board contacts with an ink eraser if the computer does not start.

Some of these rules are little more than hunches or guesses rarely verbalized. In knowledge acquisition, interviewers attempt to glean such knowledge from experts so that the knowledge can be placed into an expert system. Research efforts now are focused on creating expert systems capable of acquiring the necessary knowledge without so much assistance.

Expert systems that rely on IF...THEN rules are severely limited in their performance capabilities. Like the BASIC programming language, the formulation of knowledge in the form of IF... THEN rules results in chaos because the total number of interrelationships among program statements quickly grows beyond the programmer's comprehension. An expert system containing 10,000 or more IF... THEN rules, therefore, is likely to perform in an erratic and unstable manner. Yet, most significant areas of human expertise involve far more than 10,000 rules.

Owing to their performance limitations, rule-based expert systems are not likely to displace human professionals such as physicians or attorneys. However, expert systems have proven commercially viable for limited applications, in which the number of rules falls within the technology's capabilities. A major life insurance firm, for example, uses an expert system to perform a preliminary analysis on life insurance applications. The system's judgments then are subject to review by an expert. See *PROLOG*.

exploded pie graph   A pie graph in which one or more of the slices has been offset slightly from the others (see fig. E.4). See *pie graph*.

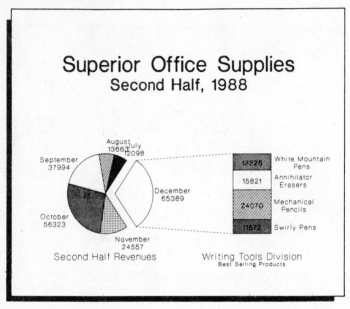

Fig. E.4. An exploded pie graph with a legend.

export   To output data in a form that another program can read.

Most word processing programs can export a document in ASCII format, which almost any program can read and use. See *import*.

Extended Binary Coded Decimal Interchange Code (EBCDIC)   A standard computer character set coding scheme used to represent 256 standard characters.

IBM mainframes use EBCDIC coding, and personal computers use American Standard Code for Information Interchange (ASCII) coding. Communications networks that link personal computers to IBM mainframes must include a translating device to mediate between the two systems.

extended character set   In IBM PC-compatible computing, a 254-character set based in the computer's read-only memory (ROM) that includes, in addition to the 128 ASCII character codes, a collection of foreign language, technical, and block graphics characters.

The characters with numbers above ASCII code 128 sometimes are referred to as higher-order characters.

▲ **Caution:** You can produce the foreign language, technical, and graphics characters on-screen by holding down the Alt key and typing the character's code on the numeric keypad. But, you may not be able to print these characters unless your printer is designed to print the entire IBM extended character set. The popular Epson printers do not print higher-order characters because they use that space for italic characters.

Extended Industry Standard Architecture (EISA)   A 32-bit expansion bus design introduced by a consortium of IBM PC-compatible computer makers to counter IBM's proprietary Micro Channel Bus.

Unlike Micro Channel, the EISA bus is downwardly compatible with existing 16-bit peripherals such as disk drives and display adapters. See *Micro Channel Bus* and *expansion bus*.

extended memory   In an IBM PC-compatible computer with an 80286 or 80386 microprocessor, the random-access memory (RAM) above one megabyte that is set aside for DOS and internal system uses.

Any 80286 or 80386 computer can be equipped with memory above 1M; you can equip a 286 with 15 additional megabytes, and a 386 with a total of 4 gigabytes.

But, under DOS, which is locked into the real mode of these microprocessors, programs must execute in base memory (640K maximum). However, a memory management program, such as Quarterdeck's QEMM-386, can configure this additional memory as expanded memory. To realize the full benefit of extended memory, however, you must use an operating system (such as OS/2) that takes full advantage of the 80286 and 80386 chips' protected mode. See *expanded memory, memory-management program, Operating System/2, protected mode, random-access memory (RAM),* and *real mode.*

extensible   In a programming language, a quality of the language so that you can create, save, and use new commands.

extension   A three-letter suffix to a DOS file name that describes the file's contents.

> **→ Tip:** Use extensions to categorize files, not to name them. Because DOS gives you only eight characters for file names, you may be tempted to use the extension as part of the name (LETTER3.JOE). Doing so, however, makes grouping files more difficult for backup and other operations. If all your document files have the same extension (DOC or TXT, for example), you can use the DOS wild-card feature to back up all these files with one command.

external command   In DOS and OS/2, a command that cannot be used unless the program file is present in the current drive or directory.

If you try to use the BACKUP command and see the message `Bad command or file name`, for example, you must switch to the directory or disk containing your DOS files. See *internal command.*

external command (XCMD)   In HyperTalk programming, a user-defined command (written in a language like Pascal or C) that uses built-in Macintosh routines to perform tasks not normally available within HyperCard.

A popular XCMD is ResCopy, written by Steve Maller of Apple Computer and widely available in public domain or shareware stack-writing utilities. ResCopy enables a HyperTalk programmer to copy external commands and external resources from one program or stack to another. Using ResCopy, even a novice HyperTalk programmer can add resources to a HyperCard stack by copying resources from another stack. See *external function (XCFN)* and *ResEdit.*

external function (XCFN) In HyperTalk programming, a program function (written in a language like Pascal or C) that is external to HyperTalk but returns values to the program. The values can be used within the HyperTalk program.

For example, Resources, an XCFN written by Steve Maller of Apple Computer and widely available in public domain or shareware stack-writing utilities, returns a list of all named resources in a file of a specified type. See *external command (XCMD)*.

external hard disk A hard disk equipped with its own case, cables, and power supply. External hard disks generally cost more than internal hard disks of comparable speed and capacity.

external modem A modem equipped with its own case, cables, and power supply. External modems are designed to plug into the serial port of a computer. See *internal modem*.

external table In Lotus 1-2-3 Release 3, a database created with a database management program (such as dBASE III) that Lotus 1-2-3 directly can access using the /Data External command.

f

facing pages The two pages of a bound document that face each other when the document is open.

The even-numbered page (verso) is on the left, and the odd-numbered page (recto) is on the right. See *recto* and *verso*.

Fastback Plus A popular hard disk backup utility developed by Fifth Generation Systems for IBM PC-compatible computers.

FASTOPEN In DOS, an external command that keeps directory information in memory so that DOS can quickly find and open files you frequently need. See *external command*.

fault tolerance   The capability of a computer system to cope with internal hardware problems without interrupting the system's performance. Fault tolerant designs typically use back-up systems automatically brought on-line when a failure is detected.

The need for fault tolerance is indisputable whenever computers are assigned critical functions, such as guiding an aircraft to a safe landing or ensuring a steady flow of medicants to a patient. Fault tolerance also is beneficial for non-critical, everyday applications.

fax   The transmission and reception of a printed page between two locations connected via telecommunications.

Short for FACSimile, fax has taken the business world by storm. A fax machine scans a sheet of paper and converts its image into a coded form that can be transmitted via the telephone system. A fax machine on the other end receives and translates the transmitted code and prints a replica of the original page.

→ **Tip:** Personal computer users who already have modems can add fax adapters to their systems for far less money than the cost of a fax machine. You can send and receive files. However, most fax adapters cannot process graphics.

feathering   Adding an even amount of space between each line on a page or column to force vertical justification.

female connector   A computer cable terminator and connection device with receptacles designed to accept the pins of a male connector. See *male connector.*

field   See *data field.*

field definition   In a database management program, a list of the attributes that define the type of information that the user can enter into a data field. The field definition also determines how the field's contents appear on-screen.

In dBASE, the field definition includes the following:

- Field name. A 10-character, one-word field name that appears as a heading in data tables and as a prompt on data-entry forms.

- Data type. A definition that governs the type of data you can enter into a field.

- Field width. The maximum number of characters the field accommodates.

- Number of decimal places. The number of decimal places to appear if the field is a numeric field.

- Index attribute. If you turn on the index attribute, the program includes this field when constructing an index to the database.

- Field mask.

See *data type* and *field template.*

field name   In a database management program, a name given to a data field that helps you identify the field's contents.

→ **Tip:** Field names are important from the user's standpoint, because they describe the data contained in each data field. You see the field names on data-entry forms and data tables. Ideally, the field names you choose are descriptive—if you name a field MX388SMRPS, nobody will know what the name means.

In dBASE, field names are restricted to one word consisting of a continuous series of characters. You can write two- or three-word field names by separating the words with underscore characters as in the following:

```
FIRST_NAME
LAST_NAME
PHONE_NO
```

In dBASE, field names are limited to 10 characters. Some programs do not impose such stringent limitations. Even so, you should keep field names short. When you display data in a columnar format, therefore, you see more columns of data on-screen. However, do not make the names so short that they become cryptic.

field privilege   In a database management program, a database definition that establishes what a user can do with the contents of a data field in a protected database. See *data field* and *file privilege.*

field template In database management programs, a field definition that specifies which kind of data can be typed in the data field. If you try to type data into a field that does not match the field template, the program displays an error message. Synonymous with data mask. See *data type*.

➔ **Tip:** Field templates should be used as often as possible. They help to prevent users from adding inappropriate information to the database.

In dBASE, you can specify the following field templates for each character field in the database structure:

X	Accepts any character
A	Accepts alphabetic letters (a-z, A-Z)
#	Accepts numbers (0-9)
N	Accepts alphabetic letters, numbers, or an underscore character
Y	Accepts Y (for Yes) or N (for No)
L	Accepts T (for True) or F (for False)
!	Converts all inputted characters to uppercase

For numeric fields, you can specify the following templates:

9	Accepts numbers and + or - signs, and requires the user to type the number of characters specified (for example, 99999 requires that the user type five numbers)
#	Accepts numbers, space, and + or - signs
*	Displays leading zeros as asterisks
$	Displays leading zeros as dollar signs
,	Displays numbers larger than 999 with commas
.	Displays a decimal point

file A named collection of information stored as an apparent unit on a secondary storage medium such as a disk drive.

Although a file appears to be whole, the operating system may distribute the file among dozens or even hundreds of noncontiguous sectors on the disk, storing the linkages (chains) among these sectors in a file allocation table. To the user, however, files appear as units on disk directories and are retrieved and copied as units. See *file allocation table (FAT)* and *secondary storage.*

file allocation table (FAT)   A hidden table on a floppy disk or hard disk that stores information about how files are stored in distinct (and not necessarily contiguous) sectors. See *file fragmentation.*

file attribute   A hidden code stored with a file's directory that contains its read-only or archive status and other information about the file. See *archive attribute, bozo bit, invisible file, locked file,* and *read-only attribute.*

file compression utility   A utility program that compresses and decompresses infrequently used files so that they take up 40 to 50 percent less room on a hard disk. The utility decompresses these files when they are needed. File compression utilities commonly are used for two purposes: to decompress files that have been downloaded from a bulletin board system (BBS) and to make room on a hard disk by compressing all files opened for a specified period (such as one week). See *archive.*

file conversion utility   A utility program that converts files created with one word processing program so that the files can be read by another word processing program. One popular conversion utility is Word for Word, which can convert files among 30 file formats.

file defragmentation   See *defragmentation.*

file deletion   The removal of a file name from a directory without actually removing the contents of the file from the disk.

You should understand how personal computers erase files for two reasons: security and the recovery of accidentally deleted files.

When you erase a file with a DEL or ERASE statement, the operating system does not actually destroy the data or program instructions stored on the disk; the operating system merely deletes the name of the file from the disk directory so that the space the file occupies is made available for future storage operations.

This procedure brings up the security angle: others can recover sensitive data from your system, even if you think you have erased the information. To prevent the recovery of such data, you can use a shareware program such as Complete Delete (Macintosh) that totally erases the information on disk.

The fact that file deletions do not actually erase the data on disk can be helpful if the deletion was accidental. An undelete utility, widely available as shareware and in utility program packages such as Symantec Utilities (Macintosh environment) and Norton Utilities (IBM PC-compatible environment), can restore a deleted file if no other information has been written over the file.

➜ **Tip:** If you accidentally delete a file, stop working. Do not perform any additional operations that write information to the disk. Use an undelete utility immediately. See *shareware*, *undelete utility*, and *utility program*.

file format   The patterns and standards a program uses to store data on disk.

Few programs store data in ASCII format; most use a proprietary file format that other programs cannot read. For example, Microsoft Word cannot read files created with WordPerfect, and WordPerfect cannot read files created with Microsoft Word. The use of proprietary file formats stems from marketing strategy (ensuring that customers continue to use the company's program). Proprietary file formats also enable programmers to include special features that standard formats may not allow.

➜ **Tip:** If you are stuck with some documents your program cannot read, you can use a data conversion service or a file conversion utility. To locate a data conversion service, look in the Yellow Pages or in the back advertising sections of popular personal computer magazines. See *file conversion utility*, *file format*, *native file format*, and *proprietary file format*.

file fragmentation   The inefficient allocation of files in non-contiguous sectors on a floppy disk or hard disk. Fragmentation occurs because of multiple file deletions and write operations.

When DOS writes a file to disk, the operating system looks for available clusters. If you have created and erased many files on the disk, few files are stored in contiguous clusters; the disk drive's read/write head must travel longer distances to retrieve the scattered data. A process known as defragmentation can improve disk efficiency by as much as 50 percent by rewriting files so that they are placed in contiguous clusters. See *defragmentation*.

file locking   On a local area network, the setting of a file attribute so that the file cannot be used by more than one person at a time. See *file attribute* and *local area network (LAN)*.

file management program   See *flat-file database management program*.

file name   A name assigned to a file so that the operating system can find the file. You assign file names when the files are created. Every file on a disk must have a unique name.

In DOS and early versions of OS/2, file names have two parts: the file name and the extension. These names must conform to the following rules.
- Length. You may use up to eight characters for the file name and up to three characters for the extension. The extension is optional.
- Delimiter. If you use the extension, you must separate the file name and extension by typing a period (no spaces).
- Legal characters. You may use any letter or number on the keyboard for file names and extensions. You also may use the following punctuation symbols:

      ' ~ ! @ # $ ^ & ( ) _ - { }

▲ **Caution:** One of the shortcomings of DOS and the early versions of OS/2 is the eight-character restriction on file names. (OS/2 Versions 1.2 and 2 enable you to use lengthier file names.) You are given little room to express the contents of a file. Yet, the file name must express the file's contents well enough so that you recognize the file in a disk directory. Obviously, a file name such as @12AX97.TBT is not going to mean much to you a few months later. Good file-naming practice restricts the use of extensions to describe the type of file (not the contents). Files labeled with the extensions COM and EXE are program files. Files labeled DOC and TXT are word processor or text files. Files labeled WK1 or WKS are spreadsheet (worksheet) files, and so on.

In the Macintosh environment, you can use up to 32 characters for file names, and file names can contain any character (including spaces) with the exception of the colon (:). The colon is restricted because the Mac's Hierarchical File System (HFS) uses the colon to construct path names. For example, the path name Proposals:Foundations:Proposal No. 1 describes the location of the file Proposal No. 1. This file is in the Foundations folder within the Proposals folder.

➔ **Tip:** The Mac's Open and Save dialog boxes can display only 22 characters; the last 10 characters of longer file names are truncated. Because seeing the entire file name when retrieving or saving files is convenient, knowledgeable Mac users restrict file names to 22 characters.

file privilege   In dBASE, an attribute that determines what a user can do with a protected database on a network. The options are DELETE, EXTEND, READ, and UPDATE. See *field privilege.*

file recovery   The restoration of an erased disk file. See *undelete utility.*

file server   In a local area network, a computer that provides users of the network with access to shared data and program files. Generally, the file server is a personal computer, although the file server may be a proprietary system designed specifically for use as a file server.

File servers normally cannot run application programs. In most systems, the file server comes with a large hard disk, multiuser programs, and the network operating system. See *local area network (LAN)* and *workstation.*

filespec   In DOS, a complete specification of a file's location, including a drive letter, path name, file name, and extension, such as `C:\REPORTS\REPORT1.WK1`.

file transfer protocol   In asynchronous communications, a standard that governs the error-free transmission of program and data files via the telephone system. See *Kermit* and *XMODEM*.

file transfer utility   A utility program that transfers files between different hardware platforms, such as the IBM Personal Computer and the Macintosh, or between a desktop and a laptop computer.

Popular file transfer utilities include MacLink Plus, which links PCs and Macs via their serial ports, and Brooklyn Bridge, which links desktop IBM computers with IBM PC-compatible laptops.

FileMaker II   A popular flat-file database management program for the Macintosh (Claris Corp.). See *4th Dimension*.

FILES   In DOS, a configuration command that specifies the number of files that can be open simultaneously.

By default, DOS can work with up to eight files at a time. However, some applications require a CONFIG.SYS statement, such as `FILES=15`, that increases this number. Usually, the program's installation software adds such a statement to your CONFIG.SYS file or creates the file if it does not exist.

fill   In spreadsheet programs, an operation that enters a sequence of values (numbers, dates, times, or formulas) in a worksheet.

In Lotus 1-2-3, you use the /Data Fill command to fill a range with values, beginning with the start value (the number 1-2-3 uses to start filling the range), the step value (the number Lotus 1-2-3 uses to increment each number placed in the range), and the stop value (the highest number placed in the range).

➔ **Tip:** You can use /Data Fill to enter a column or row of dates automatically. If you enter @DATE(91,11,1) as the start value, 14 (days) as the step value, and @DATE(92,10,1) as the stop value, 1-2-3 enters dates at two-week intervals between November 1, 1991 and October 1, 1992 in the column or row.

filter command   In DOS and OS/2, a type of command that takes input from a device or a file, changes or reduces the input, and sends the result to an output device or printer. See *FIND*, *MORE*, and *SORT*.

FIND   In DOS and OS/2, an external filter command that displays all the lines from a file or files containing (or not containing) a string of specified characters and writes these lines to the screen, a file, or an output device.

Finder   A file and memory management utility, provided by Apple, for Macintosh computers. This utility enables you to run one application at a time. See *Multi Finder*.

Often mistakenly referred to as the Macintosh's operating system, the Finder is nothing more than a shell that can be replaced by other shell programs such as XTreeMac. Although the Finder's intuitive and easy-to-use icons and menus have contributed to the Mac's success, the program's limitations quickly become apparent on systems equipped with large hard disks. A new version of the Finder, to be shipped with System 7, is expected to solve many problems.

firmware   Broadly, the system software permanently stored in a computer's read-only memory (ROM) or elsewhere in the computer's circuitry. Firmware cannot be modified by the user.

fixed disk   See *hard disk*.

fixed numeric format   In spreadsheet programs, a numeric format in which values are rounded to the number of decimal places you specify. See *numeric format*.

Fkey   Macintosh utility program executed by pressing the Command and Shift keys with a number key from 0 to 9 (the keys that simulate the function keys on IBM PC keyboards).

Four Fkey utilities are included with the Macintosh system software:

Cmd-Shift-1	Eject the disk in the internal drive
Cmd-Shift-2	Eject the disk in the external drive
Cmd-Shift-0	Eject the disk in the third drive, if any
Cmd-Shift-3	Save the current screen as a MacPaint file
Cmd-Shift-4	Print the current screen

Additional Fkey utilities (and software to manage them) are available through shareware and commercial sources.

flame   In electronic mail, to lose one's self-control and write a communication that uses derogatory, obscene, or inappropriate language. (Slang term.)

flat-file database management program A database management program that stores, organizes, and retrieves information from one file at a time. Such programs lack relational database management features. See *data integrity* and *relational database management.*

flatbed scanner   An optical graphics digitizer that can transform a full-page (8 1/2-by-11-inch) graphic into a digitized file.

floating-point calculation   A method for storing and calculating numbers so that the location of the decimal is not fixed but floating (the decimal moves around as needed so that significant digits are taken into account in the calculation). Floating-point calculation can be implemented in numeric coprocessors or in software, improving the accuracy of computer calculations.

▲ **Caution:** Floating-point notation helps computers perform calculations more accurately. But an inherent limitation to any computer's capability to deal with large and small numbers still exists. Some programs set aside more memory than others for number storage; any program has a range of numbers that it can handle accurately. One program can handle any number from -10^{20} to 10^{20}, but smaller or larger numbers produce erroneous results.

A good program states the range of acceptable numbers in the manual. Some programs do not inform you what the range is and enable you to enter numbers that are truncated without your knowledge. These programs can produce erroneous results when used for any calculation involving very large or small numbers. See *numeric coprocessor.*

floppy disk   A removable and widely used secondary storage medium that uses a magnetically sensitive flexible disk enclosed in a plastic envelope or case.

Floppy disks are the usual way in which programs and text files are communicated from one computer to another. At one time, they also were the only medium for secondary storage for personal computers, but the availability of inexpensive hard disks has relegated floppy disks to the sidelines.

Hard disk are preferred for many reasons: floppy disk drives are slower, and the disks are damaged more easily and offer less storage. However, floppy disks are essential for getting programs and data into your computer and for backup purposes.

A floppy disk is a magnetically coated, flexible disk of plastic. The disk rotates within a flexible or firm plastic envelope (see fig. F.1). The access hole (head slot) provides an opening so that the drive's read/write head can perform recording and playback operations on the disk's surface, within the magnetically-encoded tracks and sectors created when disks are formatted. You can use the write-protect notch to keep the drive from erasing the data on the disk; when the notch is covered, the drive cannot perform erase or write operations.

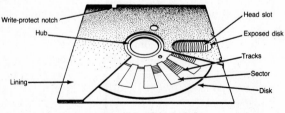

Fig. F.1. Floppy disk.

Most floppy disks used in personal computing come in two sizes: 5 1/4 and 3 1/2 inches. Floppy disks are available in single-sided or double-sided and standard double density or high density. Single-sided disks are rarely used, and high density disks are becoming more popular than double-density disks. 5 1/4-inch disks, with flimsy sleeves and open access holes, are more susceptible to damage; 3 1/2-inch disks come in rigid plastic cases and have a sliding door that covers the access hole. (The drive opens the door after you insert the disk.)

5 1/4-inch and 3 1/2-inch disks are used in IBM PC-compatible computing. The single-sided disks used in the original IBM Personal Computer held only 160K; the drives introduced soon after accommodated 320K on a double-sided disk.

In 1983, changes in the formatting procedure introduced with PC-DOS Version 2.0 increased the figure to 360K for double-sided disks. With the IBM Personal Computer AT came MS-DOS 3.0 and the capability to store 1.2M on a high-density 5 1/4-inch disk. Later IBM PC-compatible computers came with 3 1/2-inch drives capable of storing 720K or 1.44M with high-density disks. Macintoshes use 3 1/2-inch disks. The original Macintosh stored 400K on single-sided disks; this figure was doubled to 800K when double-sided disk drives were introduced. A floppy drive high density (FDHD) drive capable of storing 1.4M on high-density floppies was introduced in 1988; this technically-sophisticated drive can read and write DOS disks, giving Mac users an easy way to exchange data with users of IBM PC-compatible computers.

▲ **Caution:** 5 1/4-inch disks are more susceptible to damage than 3 1/2-inch disks; avoid pressing down hard with a ball-point pen as you label the disk and be wary of fingerprints on the actual surface of the disk (easy to touch through the open access hole). Always keep 5 1/4-inch disks in protective envelopes when they are not being used and do not leave the disk in the drive when the computer is turned off; the disk may accumulate dust. Although less susceptible than 5 1/4-inch disks, 3 1/2-inch disks can be damaged. Keep both types of disks away from moisture, dust, and strong magnetic fields. See *access hole, double density, hard disk, high density, read/write head, single-sided disk,* and *write-protect notch.*

flow　To import text into a specific text area on a page layout so that the text wraps around graphics and fills in specified columns. Page layout programs can import text in this way. See *page layout program.*

flow chart　A chart that contains symbols referring to computer operations, describing how the program performs.

font　Pronounced "fahnt." One complete collection of letters, punctuation marks, numbers, and special characters with a consistent and identifiable typeface, weight (Roman or bold), posture (upright or italic), and font size.

Technically, font still refers to one complete set of characters in a given typeface, weight, and size, such as Helvetica italic 12. But the term often is used to refer to typefaces or font families.

Two kinds of fonts exist: bit-mapped fonts and outline fonts. Each comes in two versions, screen fonts and printer fonts. See *bit-mapped font, font family, outline font, posture, printer font, screen font, typeface, type size,* and *weight.*

Font/DA Mover　In the Macintosh environment, a utility program provided by Apple Computer that enables the user to install bit-mapped screen fonts and desk accessories in the System Folder.

After screen fonts are installed, they appear in the Font menu and the desk accessories appear in the Apple menu.

font family　A set of fonts in several sizes and weights that share the same typeface.

The following list describes a font family in the Helvetica typeface:

Helvetica Roman 10
Helvetica bold 10
Helvetica italic 10

Helvetica Roman 12
Helvetica bold 12
Helvetica italic 12
Helvetica bold italic 12

font ID conflict   In the Macintosh environment, a system error caused by conflicts between the identification numbers assigned to the screen fonts stored in the System Folder.

The Macintosh System and many Macintosh applications recognize and retrieve fonts by the identification number assigned to them, not by name. But, the original Macintosh operating system enabled you to assign only 128 unique numbers to fonts, so that you inadvertently could assemble a repertoire of screen fonts with conflicting numbers, causing printing errors. With System 6.0, a New Font Numbering Table (NFNT) scheme was introduced that enables you to assign 16,000 unique numbers, reducing—but not ruling out—the potential for font ID conflicts.

font metric   The width and height information for each character in a font. The font metric is stored in a width table.

font smoothing   In high-resolution laser printers, the reduction of aliasing and other distortions when text or graphics are printed.

font substitution   Substituting an outline font for printing in place of a bit-mapped screen font.

In the Macintosh environment, the LaserWriter printer driver substitutes the outline fonts Helvetica, Times Roman, and Courier for the screen fonts Geneva, New York, and Monaco. However, spacing may be unsatisfactory. Better results are obtained by using the screen font equivalent to the printer font.

Fontographer   A computer typography program developed for Macintosh computers.

Using Fontographer, a graphic artist can create custom-designed screen fonts and printer fonts that use outline font technology and print at the maximum resolution possible. See *outline font*, *printer font*, and *screen font*.

footer In a word processing or page layout program, a short version of a document's title or other text positioned at the bottom of every page of the document. See *header*.

footnote In a word processing or page layout program, a note positioned at the bottom of the page.

Most word processing programs with footnoting capabilities number the notes automatically, and renumber them if you insert or delete a note. The best programs can float lengthy footnotes to the next page so that no more than half the page is taken up by footnotes.

➔ **Tip:** If you are writing business reports or scholarly work that requires excellent footnoting capabilities, make sure that you can format the footnotes properly. For example, many publishers require double-spacing of all text, even footnotes, and some word processors cannot perform this task. See *endnote*.

footprint The space occupied by a computer's case on a desk.

FOR In DOS and OS/2, a batch command that sets up a for/next loop control structure, in which a command is repeated the number of times you specify.

The syntax of the FOR command is daunting, but the concept is simple. The following is an example of a FOR command that backs up to drive A any drive B file with extension DOC:

FOR %%p in (B:*.DOC) do COPY B:%%p A:

The symbol %%p is a replaceable parameter, a symbol that DOS replaces with information you supply. The information in this command is located within the parentheses (B:*.DOC). Using a wild card, this expression tells DOS to find a file with the extension DOC. If a DOC file is found, DOS fills in the replaceable parameter with the full name of the file and copies the file to drive A. DOS repeats this procedure for every DOC file found. See *batch file command*, *FOR/NEXT loop*, *GOTO*, and *syntax*.

forced page break A page break inserted by the user; the page always breaks at this location. See *hard page break*.

forecasting Using a spreadsheet program, a method of financial analysis that involves the projection of past trends into the future.

▲ **Caution:** Implementing a forecast with a spreadsheet program is easy, but beware that a forecast is only a model of reality, and any model is only as good as the assumptions that it is based on. Your forecast may project stable or slightly declining revenues into the next three months, but you may have failed to take into account a seasonal variable that could stimulate sales. Your forecast may lead you to underestimate the inventory you actually need.

foreground task In a computer capable of multitasking, a job done in priority status before subordinate, or background, tasks are executed. The foreground task generally is the one you see executing.

FORMAT In DOS and OS/2, an external command that prepares a disk to accept files.

As it comes out of a package, a new, unformatted disk contains a patternless ocean of magnetic particles. Before your computer can use the disk, the disk must be formatted.

During the formatting operation, your computer's disk drive encodes a magnetic pattern consisting of tracks and sectors. The tracks are arranged concentrically around the disk's center, like the tracks of an LP album. The sectors are created by drawing electronic lines from the disk's center to its edge.

With MS DOS, the lines divide each track into nine sectors. Each sector can store 512 bytes of information. With double-sided, double-density disks, DOS creates 40 tracks, so that each side contains 360 sectors. Because 512 bytes equals 1/2K, each disk side holds 180K, and the disk holds 360K.

➜ **Tip:** If you use a dual-floppy computer that lacks a hard disk, you may want to place DOS on several disks so that you can use these disks to boot your computer. To place DOS on a disk as the disk is being formatted, use the /S parameter. For example, to format the disk in drive B and copy the system tracks to that disk, use the following command:

FORMAT B: /S

Most hard drives are formatted at the factory.

▲ **Caution:** Version 3.1 and earlier versions of DOS may carry out an unintended format of a hard disk if not used with caution. Suppose that you have copied the FORMAT program to a directory on drive C, and without thinking, you type **FORMAT** and press Enter. Because you have not specified a drive name, DOS uses the current drive. If the current drive is C, these versions of DOS begin a formatting operation on the hard disk, erasing everything. If you are using an early version of DOS, always specify the drive designator after FORMAT, as in the following example.

FORMAT A:

Synonymous with initialize. See *external command, floppy disk,* and *hard disk.*

format   Any method of arranging information for storage, printing, or displaying.

The format of floppy disks and hard disks is the magnetic pattern laid down by the formatting utility. Programs often use proprietary file formats for storing data on disk. Because of these special formats, some programs cannot read files saved by other programs. WordPerfect, for example, cannot read files prepared with Microsoft Word.

In a spreadsheet program, the format is the style and physical arrangement of labels, values, and constants in a cell. Numeric formats include the display of decimal places, and currency symbols. Alignment formats for labels include flush left, centered, and flush right.

In a database management program, the physical arrangement of field names and data fields in a data entry form are displayed on-screen. In a word processing program, document formats include the style and physical arrangement of all document elements, including characters (typeface, type size, weight, posture, and emphasis), lines and paragraphs (alignment, leading), and page design elements (folios, margins, headers, and footers).

In a graphics program, the format is the way in which text and numbers are displayed within charts and graphs and the way in which graphics are stored on disk. See *Browse mode, edit mode,* and *graphics mode.*

format file   In dBASE, a file that stores the formats you have chosen for a custom data-entry form.

formatting   An operation that establishes a pattern for the storage or printing of data.

In operating systems, an operation that prepares a floppy disk for use in a particular computer system by laying down a magnetic pattern. See *format, high-level format,* and *low-level format.*

formula   In a spreadsheet program, a cell definition that defines the relationship between two or more values. In a database management program, an expression that instructs the program to perform calculations on numeric data contained in one or more data fields.

To enter values in a spreadsheet formula, you enter constants, cell references, or a combination. For example, 2+2 is a valid formula, as is A2+A4 and A4+38.9.

To express the formula in a way that most spreadsheets can recognize, you must convert the formula to spreadsheet notation. Spreadsheet notation differs from mathematical formulas.

One key difference between the usual way you write formulas and spreadsheet notation lies in the operators, the symbols that indicate the arithmetic operation, such as addition, subtraction, multiplication, and division. The operators for addition and subtraction are the same: plus (+) and minus (-). However, you indicate multiplication by using an asterisk (*) and division by using a slash (/). You type a caret (^) before an exponent. See *calculated field, cell definition, precedence,* and *value.*

FOR/NEXT loop   A loop control structure that carries out a procedure the number of specified times.

The following pseudocode example shows how you can use a page layout program's macro command language to locate and kern (adjust the spacing) two troublesome letter pairs, av and aw, which look awkward if not moved closer together.

Suppose that the two letter pairs occur 10 times in a document. In English, the macro reads, "Set the count to 1, and find av or aw. After a match has been found and the characters have been selected (highlighted in reverse video), kern the selection. Then, set the count to the previous count plus 1. Keep doing this until the count equals 10."

```
FOR count = 1 to 10
    FIND av OR aw
    KERN selection
    NEXT count
END
```

See *loop control structure* and *pseudocode*.

FORTH   A high-level programming language that offers direct control over hardware devices.

Developed in 1970 by an astronomer named Charles Moore to help him control the equipment at the Kitt Peak National Radio Observatory, FORTH—short for FOuRTH-generation programming language—quickly spread to other observatories but has been slow to gain acceptance as a general-purpose programming language. FORTH sometimes is preferred, however, for laboratory data acquisition, robotics, machine control, arcade games, automation, patient monitoring, and interfaces with musical devices.

FORTRAN   A high-level programming language well suited to scientific, mathematical, and engineering applications.

Developed by IBM in the mid-1950s and released in 1957, FORTRAN—short for FORmula TRANslator—was the first compiled high-level programming language. The nature of

FORTRAN shows the predominance of scientific applications in the early history of computing; the language enables you to describe and solve mathematical calculations in a way similar paper procedures. Still highly suited to such applications, FORTRAN is widely used in scientific, academic, and technical settings. For anyone familiar with BASIC, FORTRAN is immediately recognizable. Indeed, FORTRAN was BASIC's progenitor. FORTRAN shares BASIC's unfortunate limitations as a general-purpose programming language (such as the tendency to produce spaghetti code). However, recent versions of FORTRAN are more structured and have fewer limitations. See *BASIC, high-level programming language, modular programming, Pascal,* and *structured programming.*

forward chaining   In expert systems, an inference technique that regulates the order in which conclusions are drawn from the knowledge base.

A forward chaining system starts with the data and works forward through its rules to determine whether additional data is required and how to draw the inference. See *backward chaining, expert system,* and *knowledge base.*

FoxBASE +   A dBASE III-compatible database management system developed by Fox Software, Inc., for Macintosh and IBM PC-compatible computers.

FoxBASE improves on dBASE by offering a highly regarded compiler for the dBASE software command language. With this compiler, FoxBASE users can create custom, stand alone database applications. The latest version of this program is called FoxPRO. The Macintosh version of the program is compatible with dBASE III files.

fragmentation   See *file fragmentation.*

free-form text chart   In presentation graphics, a text chart used to handle information difficult to express in lists, such as directions, invitations, and certificates (see fig. F.2). See *text chart.*

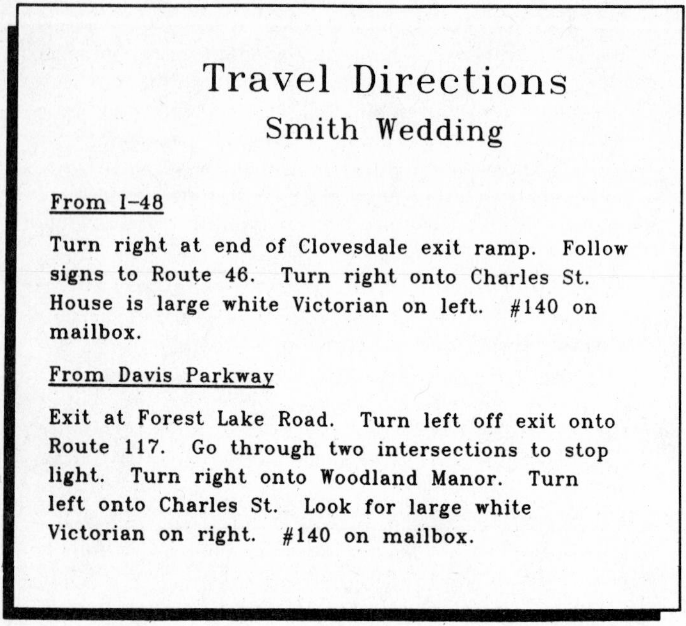

Travel Directions
Smith Wedding

From I-48

Turn right at end of Clovesdale exit ramp. Follow signs to Route 46. Turn right onto Charles St. House is large white Victorian on left. #140 on mailbox.

From Davis Parkway

Exit at Forest Lake Road. Turn left off exit onto Route 117. Go through two intersections to stop light. Turn right onto Woodland Manor. Turn left onto Charles St. Look for large white Victorian on right. #140 on mailbox.

Fig. F.2. A free-form text chart.

Freehand A professional illustration program for Macintosh computers that produces object-oriented images.

Freehand shares many of Adobe Illustrator's features, such as Bézier curves, an autotrace tool, precision coding for color printing, and many other features for professional illustration. Freehand does not require a PostScript printer. See *Adobe Illustrator, autotrace, Bézier curve, object-oriented graphic,* and *PostScript.*

freeware Copyrighted programs that have been made available without charge for public use. See *public domain software,* and *shareware.*

frequency division multiplexing In local area networks, a technique for transmitting two or more signals over one cable by assigning each to its own frequency. This technique is used in broadband (analog) networks. See *broadband*, *local area network (LAN)*, and *multiplexing*.

frequency modulation (FM) recording   An early, low-density method of recording digital signals on computer media such as tape and disks. Synonymous with single-density recording. See *modified frequency modulation (MFM) recording*.

friction feed   A printer paper-feed mechanism that draws individual sheets of paper through the printer using pressure exerted on the paper by the platen.

Friction-feed mechanisms usually require you to position the paper manually. For a document of more than one or two pages in length, however, manual feeding can be tedious. See *cut-sheet feeder* and *tractor feed*.

front end   A program designed to provide a user-friendly interface to computer resources available on another computer or in a large database.

Front-end programs are available for searching on-line bibliographic database services such as DIALOG and information services such as CompuServe. Unlike ordinary communications programs, front ends include specific commands and controls for specific on-line systems. Front ends also have been developed for the interactive use of videodisks. See *communications program*.

full duplex   An asynchronous communications protocol in which the communications channel can send and receive signals at the same time. See *asynchronous communication*, *communications protocol*, *echoplex*, and *half duplex*.

full justification   The alignment of multiple lines of text along the left and the right margins. See *justification*.

▲ **Caution:** Word processing programs justify both margins by placing extra spaces between words. Because such spacing irregularities destroy the color of a block of text, full justification is rarely advisable. Research also has shown that text formatted with a ragged right margin is more readable than fully justified text. See *color*.

FullWrite Professional   An innovative (but complex and sluggish) word processing program for the Macintosh that fully integrates text with object-oriented graphics.

function key   A programmable key (conventionally numbered F1, F2, and so on) that provides special functions, depending on the software you are using. See *Fkey*.

g

gas plasma display   See *plasma display*.

gateway   In distributed computing, a device that connects two dissimilar local area networks or that connect a local area network to a wide-area network, a minicomputer, or a mainframe. A gateway has its own processor and memory and may perform protocol conversion and bandwidth conversion.

Gateways typically are found in large organizations in which more than one local area network protocol is installed. For example, a gateway called FastPath (Kinetics) provides a link between AppleTalk and EtherNet networks. See *bridge* and *local area network (LAN)*.

general format   In most spreadsheet programs, the default numeric format in which values are displayed with all significant (nonzero) decimal places, but without commas or currency signs.

general-purpose computer   A computer whose instruction set is sufficiently simple and general that a wide variety of algorithms can be devised for the computer.

GEnie   An on-line information service developed by General Electric that, like CompuServe, offers many of the attractions of a bulletin board system (BBS) and up-to-date stock quotes, home shopping services, and news updates. See *on-line information service*.

gigabyte   A unit of memory measurement approximately equal to one billion bytes (1,073,741,824). One gigabyte equals 1,000 megabytes.

global backup   A hard disk backup procedure. Everything on the hard disk, including all program files, is backed up onto a medium such as floppy disks. See *incremental backup*.

global format   In a spreadsheet program, a numeric format or label alignment choice that applies to all cells in the worksheet. With most programs, you can override the global format by defining a range format for certain cells.

→ **Tip:** If you are working on a financial spreadsheet, the values in your worksheet may require dollar signs and two decimal places. You should choose this global format, therefore, when you begin the worksheet. You can override the global format in sections of the worksheet in which dollar signs are not required by creating a range format. See label alignment, numeric format, and range format.

glossary   In a word processing program, a storage utility that stores frequently used phrases and boilerplate text and inserts them into the document when needed. See *boilerplate*.

GOTO   In DOS and OS/2, a batch command that tells DOS to jump to a specified label in a batch file and carry out the commands listed in that label.

In batch files, the GOTO command frequently is used with the IF statement to set up a branching control structure. The following example of a batch file checks to see whether a file exists on drive A before copying the file to that drive:

```
IF exist a:%1 GOTO warn
COPY %1 A:
:warn
ECHO A:%1 exists.
```

This batch file uses replaceable parameters. If you save the file using the file name SAFECOPY.BAT, you can type the following command to use this batch file.

```
SAFECOPY filename.ext
```

The system replaces the %1 symbols in the batch file with the file name you type, such as LETTER.DOC. Executing the batch file commands in sequence, the system checks to see whether a file with this name already exists on drive A. If the file does not already exist, the next command (COPY) is executed. But, if the file does exist, the system jumps to the :warn label and quits executing the batch file (without performing the copying operation). See *batch file* and *FOR*.

grabber hand   In graphics programs and HyperCard, an on-screen image of a hand that you can position with the mouse to move selected units of text or graphics from place to place on-screen.

graphical user interface (GUI)   Pronounced "gooey." A user interface that uses the mouse and a bit-mapped graphics display to make basic computer operations substantially easier for novices.

Standard features of the graphical user interface include alert boxes, a clipboard, desk accessories, the desktop metaphor, dialog boxes, scroll boxes, on-screen display of fonts, "what-you-see-is-what-you-get" (WYSIWYG) on-screen page representation, and multiple on-screen windows.

The graphical user interface has been criticized for slowing down the computer and insulating users from the nitty-gritty details of the operating system. Microprocessors such as the Intel 80386 and Motorola 68030, however, can run GUIs at speeds sufficient to satisfy most users, and the nitty-gritty details of the operating system ought to be transparent to the user.

Early versions of the Macintosh's operating system provided no way for users to establish paths to folders, requiring them to guide an application to the right folder manually if the application could not find a file, but this problem was a shortcoming of the old system's design, not of graphical user interfaces in general. With Microsoft's endorsement of GUI in Microsoft Windows and Presentation Manager, GUI clearly defines the future of personal computing.

graphics In personal computing, the creation, modification, and printing of computer-generated graphic images.

The two basic types of computer-produced graphics are object-oriented graphics (also called vector graphics) and bit-mapped graphics (often called raster graphics).

Object-oriented graphics programs, often called draw programs, store graphic images in the form of mathematical representations that can be sized and scaled without distortion. Object-oriented graphics programs are well suited for architecture, computer-aided design, interior design, and other applications in which precision and scaling capability are more important than artistic effects.

Bit-mapped graphic programs, often called paint programs, store graphic images in the form of patterns of screen pixels. Unlike draw programs, paint programs can create delicate patterns of shading that convey an artistic touch, but any attempt to resize or scale the graphic may result in unacceptable distortion. See *bit-mapped graphic*, *draw program*, *object-oriented graphic*, and *paint program*.

graphics file format In a graphics program, the way in which information needed to display the graphic is arranged and stored on disk.

Little standardization exists for graphics file formats. Your graphics program may be unable to read the files created by another graphics program. The situation is in many ways similar to the profusion of file formats among word processing programs. Many popular programs such as AutoCAD, GEM Draw, Lotus 1-2-3, Windows Paint, and PC Paintbrush generate files in proprietary file formats that other programs can read only if they have been specially equipped to do so.

The Macintosh environment has a standard file format called PICT that uses routines drawn from the Mac's Quick-Draw toolbox, a set of image-producing programs stored in the Mac's read-only memory (ROM). But, this format is not satisfactory for many applications. Additional formats include the MacPaint file format for 72 dpi bit-mapped graphics, tagged image file format (TIFF) files for scanned images stored at up to 300 dpi, and Encapsulated PostScript (EPS) Graphics that produce high-resolution graphics on PostScript laser printers.

In the IBM PC environment, many programs can recognize TIFF and EPS files. The graphics file format of Lotus 1-2-3 charts and graphs, stored in files with the PIC extension, is widely recognized by presentation graphics packages; many of these programs are designed to read and enhance charts created with Lotus 1-2-3.

Also widely recognized is the Hewlett-Packard Graphics Language (HPGL), a graphics format created for HP plotters, and some programs recognize the Computer Graphics Metafile (CGM) format. Microsoft Windows and OS/2, unlike DOS, establish graphics file format conventions, and programs designed to run under Windows or OS/2 must adhere to this format. See *Encapsulated PostScript (EPS) file*, *file format*, *QuickDraw*, and *Tagged Image File Format (TIFF)*.

Graphics mode   A video adapter display mode that can include free-form graphics images. See *character mode*.

graphics scanner   A graphics input device that transforms a picture into an image displayed on-screen.

graphics spreadsheet   A spreadsheet program that displays the worksheet on-screen, using bit-mapped graphics instead of relying on the computer's built-in character set.

Graphics spreadsheets such as Lotus 1-2-3/G and Microsoft Excel make available desktop publishing tools such as multiple typefaces, type sizes, rules, and screens (grayed areas). Printouts also can combine spreadsheets and business graphs on one page. See *Lotus 1-2-3* and *Microsoft Excel*.

graphics tablet   A graphics input device that enables you to draw with an electronic pen on an electronicall sensitive table. The pen's movements are relayed to the screen.

gray scale   In computer graphics, a series of shades from white to black (see fig. G.1.).

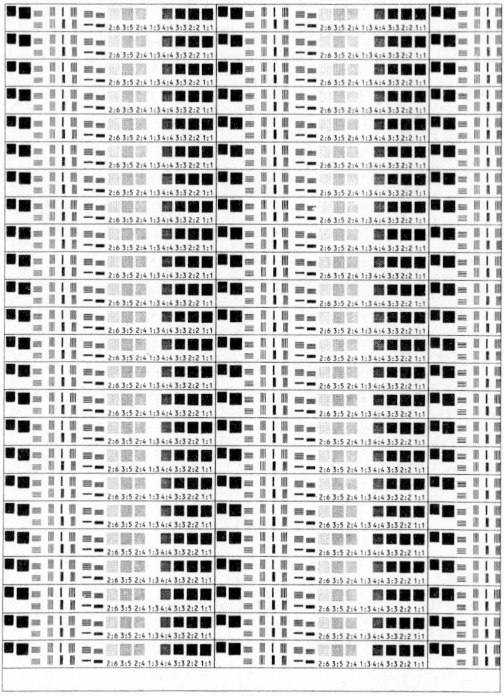

Fig. G.1. Gray scale registration self-test.

Greek text   A block of text used to represent the positioning and point size of text in a designer's composition of a design.

Greek text is used to simulate the appearance of the document so that the aesthetics of the page design can be assessed. Standard Greek text used by typesetters actually looks more like Latin:

Lorem ipsum dolor sit amet...

Some word processing and page layout programs use a print preview feature analogous to Greeking.

groupware   Application programs that increase the cooperation and joint productivity of small groups of co-workers.

An example of groupware is ForComment (Broderbund Software), designed to make collaborative writing easier. The program enables each member of the group to insert comments and make changes to the text, subject to the other members' approval.

guide In a page layout program, a nonprinting line that appears as a dotted line on-screen, showing the current location of margins, gutters, and other page layout design elements.

gutter In typography, the space between columns in a multiple-column page layout.

GW-BASIC A version of the BASIC programming language often licensed to PC-compatible computers.

GW-BASIC is nearly identical to the BASIC interpreter distributed with IBM PCs, but each manufacturer is free to customize the language.

h

hacker A technically sophisticated computer enthusiast who enjoys making modifications to programs or computer systems.

Hackers can be seen at virtually any college or university computer lab, where they spend inordinate amounts of time trying to master a computer system. Often described as addicted to computers, hackers nevertheless learn skills that prove valuable to organizations.

half duplex An asynchronous communications protocol in which the communications channel can handle only one signal at a time. The two stations alternate their transmissions. Synonymous with local echo. See *asynchronous communication, communications protocol, echoplex,* and *full duplex.*

half-height drive A disk drive that occupies half of the standard space allotted for a disk drive in the original IBM Personal Computer.

halftone   A copy of a photograph prepared for printing by breaking down the continuous gradations of tones into a series of discontinuous dots. Dark shades are produced by dense patterns of thick dots, and lighter shades are produced by less dense patterns of smaller dots.

A black-and-white photograph is a continuous-tone image of varying shades of gray. Photographs do not photocopy well; the fine gradations of gray tones are lost. To print a photograph in a newspaper or magazine, the photograph is copied using a halftone screen in front of the film. The screen breaks up the image into patterns of dots of varying size, depending on the intensity of the light coming from the photograph.

Halftones are usually superior to digitized photographs for professional-quality reproduction. Even professionals who use the latest desktop publishing technology may prefer to leave space for halftones and paste them in after printing the document. See *scanner and Tagged Image File Format (TIFF)*

handle   In an object-oriented graphics program, the small black squares that surround a selected object, enabling you to drag, size, or scale the object (see fig. H.1). See *object-oriented graphic, draw program.*

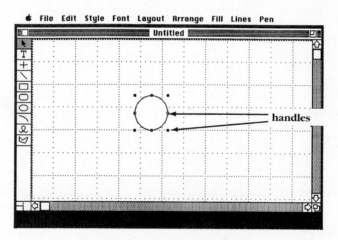

Fig. H.1. Handles on a selected object.

handler   In object-oriented programming, the program instructions (called a script) embedded within an object. The instructions are designed to trap messages that begin within
the object.

In HyperTalk, for example, one such object is a button that
you place on a card in a HyperCard stack. Within the button
is a set of programming instructions (the script) designed to
intercept certain user-initiated messages, such as the click of
a mouse. After a click is trapped, the code carries out a procedure, such as displaying another card. See *object-oriented
programming language* and *event-driven programming*.

handshaking   A method for controlling the flow of serial communication between two devices, so that one device transmits only when the other device is ready.

In hardware handshaking, a control wire is used as a signal line to indicate when the receiving device is ready to receive a transmission; software handshaking uses a special
control code.

Hardware handshaking is used for devices such as serial
printers, because the device is nearby and a special cable can
be used. For long-distance serial communication, software
handshaking must be used when the telephone system is involved. (Because the telephone system uses only two wires,
hardware handshaking is impossible). The two software
handshaking techniques are ETX/ACK, which uses the ASCII
character Ctrl-C to pause in data transmission, and XON/
XOFF, which uses Ctrl-S to pause and Ctrl-Q to resume transmission.

hanging indent   A paragraph indentation in which the first
line is flush with the left margin, but subsequent lines (called
turnover lines) are indented.

hard copy   Printed output, distinguished from data stored on
disk or in memory.

hard disk   A secondary storage medium that uses several non-
flexible disks coated with a magnetically sensitive material
and housed, together with the recording heads, in a hermeti-
cally sealed mechanism. Typical storage capacities range
from 10 to 140M.

Developed by IBM in 1973, the hard disk often is called a Winchester disk after the code name assigned to the development project. Early hard disks were extremely expensive. With the rise of a mass personal computer aftermarket in the early 1980s, however, hard disks have been manufactured in huge quantities and now are available for as little as $200. Because hard drives are almost a necessity for efficient use of personal computers today, they have become a standard element in computer systems.

A hard disk is a complex storage subsystem that includes the disks, the read/write head assembly, and the electronic interface that governs the connection between the drive and the computer (see fig. H.2).

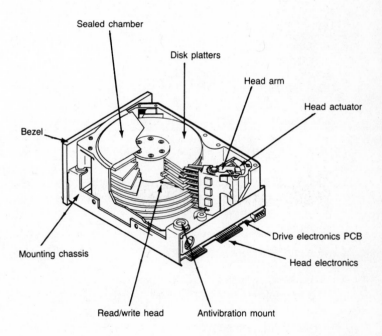

Fig. H.2. The components of a hard disk drive.

The disks, numbering from three to five, revolve 60 times per second (3600 rpm); the read/write head floats on a thin pocket of air just above the magnetically encoded surface of the disk, so that no wear occurs on the disk itself. Less expensive hard drives use 5 1/4-inch disks, but the trend is toward 3 1/2-inch disks, because the read/write heads have shorter distances to move.The technology used to position the read/write heads least expensive hard disks uses stepper motors that move the heads one step at a time over the disk. However, stepper motors gradually lose their alignment, necessitating an annual reformatting procedure to make sure that the disk remains aligned with the read/write heads. More expensive drives use voice coil motors that are more reliable and less likely to go out of alignment.

Hard drive interface standards include ST506, RLL, ESDI, and SCSI. With typical storage spaces of 20M to 40M, hard disks have ample room for storing several major application programs, system software, and data files. Because most hard disks are not removable, however, you should develop a regular backup procedure. Hard disks occasionally fail, and they may take the data with them.

Some hard drives use removable cartridges, a significant advantage over normal hard drives. See *Bernoulli box.*

hard disk backup program   A utility program that backs up hard disk data and programs onto floppy disks.

➔ **Tip:** The best backup programs perform incremental backups, in which the program backs up only those files that have changed since the last backup procedure. See *utility program.*

hard drive   See *hard disk.*

hard hyphen   A hyphen specially formatted so that a program does not introduce a line break between the hyphenated words.

Hyphenated proper nouns, such as Radcliffe-Brown and Evans-Pritchard, should not be interrupted with line breaks. A hard hyphen prevents the insertion of a line break between the two hyphenated words.

➜ **Tip:** Use a hard hyphen for hyphenated names, even if the names are not positioned near the end of a line. Remember, you may add or delete text in the paragraph later, and these changes are likely to push the name to the end of the line. Synonymous with nonbreaking hyphen. See *soft hyphen.*

hard space   In a word processing program, a space specially formatted so that the program does not introduce a line break at the space's location.

hard wired   A processing function built into the computer's electronic circuits rather than facilitated by program instructions.

Computer science theorists regard the ideal computer to be one containing only general-purpose logic circuits that can perform no specific task without program instructions. To improve computer performance, computer designers depart from this philosophy and include circuits designed to perform specific functions, such as multiplication or division, at higher speeds. These functions are hard wired.

This term also refers to the program instructions contained in the computer's read-only memory (ROM) or firmware. See *read-only memory (ROM).*

hardware   The electronic components, boards, peripherals, and equipment that make up your computer system—distinguished from the programs (software) that tell these components what to do.

hardware platform   A computer hardware standard, such as IBM PC-compatible or Macintosh personal computers, in which a comprehensive approach to the computer solution of a problem can be based. See *platform independence.*

hardware reset   A soft reboot performed by pressing a restart button after the computer system has been turned on. See *programmer's switch.*

Harvard Graphics   A full-featured presentation graphics program (Software Publishing Corp.) for IBM PC-compatible computers.

　　With the capability to produce a wide variety of text charts (including organization charts), column charts, bar graphs, line graphs, area graphs, pie graphs, and combination charts, Harvard Graphics is an exceptionally versatile and easy-to-use program.

　　You can type data into the program or import data from a Lotus 1-2-3 spreadsheet. After a chart or graph is created, it can be enhanced with the program's built-in clip art or vector graphics drawing program. You can produce output in the form of on-screen slide shows or rout the output to a film recorder or printer.

　　The program requires little knowledge of graphics presentation principles because it guides the user through each step of the process and produces output that meets high standards of aesthetics and professional graphics.

Hayes command set   A standardized set of instructions used to control modems.

　　Common Hayes commands include the following:

AT	Attention (used to start all commands)
ATDT 322-1234	Dial the number with touch tones
+++	Enter command mode during communication session
ATH	Hang up

　　See *modem.*

Hayes-compatible modem   A modem that recognizes the Hayes command set. See *Hayes command set* and *modem.*

head   See *read/write head.*

head crash   A serious malfunction that occurs when a hard disk's read/write head comes into contact with the rapidly spinning disk, resulting in the loss of data or even the destruction of the read/write head and disk.

▲ **Caution:** You can cause a head crash by dropping or jolting a computer while its hard disk is running. Never attempt to pick up or move a computer while a hard disk is operating. Prudent users always shut down their systems by using a command (ship or park) that places the read/write head in an area where head crashes cannot occur. The parked drive is less susceptible to damage if the computer is moved, jostled, or shipped.

head seek time   See *access time.*

header   Repeated text (such as a page number and a short version of a document's title) that appears at the top of each page in a document.

Some programs include odd headers and even headers, enabling you to define mirror image headers for documents printed with duplex printing (both sides of the page). For example, you may want to place the page number on the outside corner of facing pages.

Word processing programs vary significantly in the flexibility of header commands. The best programs, such as WordPerfect and Microsoft Word, enable you to suppress the printing of a header on the first page of a document or a section of a document and to change headers within the document. Synonymous with running head. See *footer.*

Helvetica   A sans serif typeface frequently used for display type applications and occasionally for body type.

Sans serif fonts have their origins in 19th-century reactions to the ornate typefaces currently in use. Helvetica, a 20th-century creation, is rooted in the work of the influential Bauhaus school, founded in 1919 by the German architect Walter Bauhaus. Bauhaus-influenced typographers fled to Switzerland to escape Nazi persecution. They developed Helvetica in the 1950s.

Like much modern architecture, Helvetica reflects the Bauhaus ideal: clean, simple functionality, uncluttered by sentiment or decoration.

One of the most widely used fonts in the world, Helvetica is included as a built-in font with many laser printers. Figure H.3 shows Helvetica type.

ABCDEFGHIJKLMNOPQRSTUVWXYZ
abcdefghijklmnopqrstuvwxyz 1234567890

Fig. H.3. An example of Helvetica.

Far less mannered than ITC Avant Garde, Helvetica is an excellent choice for display type. Helvetica also is suitable for body type in brochures, price lists, and brief reports, especially when an organization wants to portray itself as a well-organized, modern operation.

Hercules Graphics Adapter A single-color display adapter for IBM PC-compatible computers. The Hercules Graphics Adapter displays text and graphics on an IBM monochrome monitor with a resolution of 720 pixels horizontally and 320 pixels vertically.

▲ **Caution:** The Hercules (and Hercules-compatible) display adapter works only with graphics software that includes drivers for its non-IBM display format. Software designed to work with the Color Graphics Adapter (CGA), for example, does not display graphics on systems equipped with Hercules cards unless the software specifically includes a Hercules driver. Many shareware, public-domain, and low-priced graphics programs do not include the necessary driver and do not work with Hercules-equipped systems. However, Hercules display adapters work with all programs that display monochrome text. See *monochrome display adapter (MDA)*.

hertz (Hz) A unit of measurement of electrical vibrations; one Hz equals one cycle per second. See *megahertz (MHz)*.

heuristic   Pronounced "hyur-iss´-tick." A method of solving a problem by using rules of thumb acquired from experience. Heuristics rarely are stated formally in textbooks, but they are part of the knowledge human experts use in problem solving. See *expert system* and *knowledge base.*

Hewlett-Packard Co. (HP)   A major manufacturer of mini-computers, personal computers, plotters, laser printers, and scientific and technical instruments.

     The company's headquarters are located in Palo Alto, CA. See *LaserJet* and *Vectra.*

hexadecimal   A numbering system that uses a base (radix) of 16.

     Unlike decimal numbers (base 10), hexadecimal numbers require 16 digits: 0, 1, 2, 3, 4, 5, 6, 7, 8, 9, A, B, C, D, E, and F. When counting in hexadecimal, you don't carry over to the next place until you reach the first number past F (in decimal, you carry over when you reach the number past 9).

     Programmers use hexadecimal numbers as a convenient way of representing binary numbers. Using binary numbers is inconvenient because they use a base or radix of 2, and you must carry over to the next place when you reach the first number past one. Binary numbers, therefore, grow in length quickly. In binary, for example, the decimal number 16 requires four places (1111).

     Binary numbers are ideally suited to the devices used in computers, but these numbers are hard to read.

     For any four-digit set of binary numbers, you have 16 possible combinations of 1s and 0s. Hexadecimal numbers, therefore, provide a convenient way for programmers to represent four-digit clumps of binary numbers

Binary	Hex	Binary	Hex
0000	0	1000	8
0001	1	1001	9
0010	2	1010	A
0011	3	1011	B
0100	4	1100	C
0101	5	1101	D
0110	6	1110	E
0111	7	1111	F

hidden codes   The hidden text formatting codes embedded in a document by an on-screen formatting program.

Even a what-you-see-is-what-you-get (WYSIWYG) word processing program, in which formatting commands directly affect the appearance of the text on-screen, generates and embeds codes in your text as a result of formatting commands. The codes are necessary because the screen imaging technique may have no connection to the technique used to generate output to the printer. Most word processing programs hide these codes completely, making formatting operations completely transparent to the user. In WordPerfect, you can view and edit the codes.

hidden file   A file with file attributes set so that the file name does not appear on the disk directory. You cannot display, erase, or copy hidden files.

Hierarchical File System (HFS)   A Macintosh disk storage system, designed for use with hard disks, that enables you to store files within folders so that only a short list of files appears in the dialog boxes.

The previous Macintosh Filing System (MFS) enabled you to organize files into folders in the Finder. In Open and Save dialog boxes, the names of all the files on the disk appeared without any hierarchical organization.

HFS is analogous to the directory/subdirectory organization of DOS disks but with one important exception: with DOS, you can define default paths that applications follow to locate data files and program files. In HFS, no such path definition facilities exist, with the exception of the System Folder consulted when an application searches for a data or program file. Mac users, therefore, must guide applications manually through the structure of nested folders when a program cannot find a file.

➜ **Tip:** Because Macintosh users often have to assist an application manually as it tries to find a program or data file, you should avoid the temptation of nesting too many levels of folders. Using two or three nested levels reduces the amount of pointing or clicking when searching for a file; using five or six, however, increases the tedium. To automate the process, consider purchasing a file-location utility such as Findswell (Working Software). See *APPEND* and *PATH*.

high density   A storage technique for secondary storage media such as floppy disks. This technique requires the use of extremely fine-grained magnetic particles. High-density disks are more expensive to manufacture than double-density disks. High-density disks, however, can store one megabyte or more of information on one 5 1/4- or 3 1/2-inch disk. Synonymous with *quad density.*

high-density disk   See *floppy disk.*

high end   A product among the highest-priced models available in a manufacturer's line of products.

high-level format   A formatting operation that creates housekeeping sections on a disk. These sections, including the boot record and file allocation table, track free and in-use areas of the disk.

When you use the DOS FORMAT command to format a floppy disk, the computer performs a low-level format in addition to the logical format. When you use a hard disk, however, DOS performs just the logical format.

If a low-level format has not been performed at the factory, you must run a program (probably provided on a floppy disk that comes with the hard disk) that performs the absolute format. See *boot record, file allocation table (FAT),* and *low-level format.*

high-level programming language   A programming language such as BASIC or Pascal that crudely resembles human language.

Each statement in a high-level language corresponds to several machine language instructions. Therefore, writing programs more quickly in a high-level language than in a low-level language like Assembly is possible. However, programs written in a high-level language run slower. See *assembly language, low-level programming language,* and *machine language.*

high/low/close/open graph   In presentation graphics, a line graph in which a stock's high value, low value, closing price, and average value are displayed (see fig. H.4). The x-axis (categories axis) is aligned horizontally, and the y-axis (values axis) is aligned vertically.

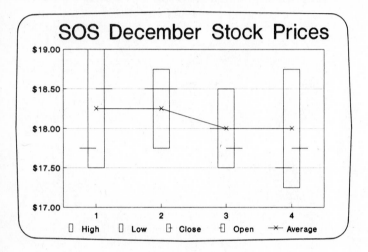

Fig. H.4. A high/low/close/open graph.

Another application for a high/low/close graph is a record of daily minimum, maximum, and average temperatures. Synonymous with HLCO chart. See *line graph* and *column graph*.

highlight   A character, word, text block, or command displayed in reverse video on-screen. This term sometimes is used synonymously with *cursor.*

highlighting   The process of marking characters or command names in reverse video on-screen.

hinting   In digital typography, the reduction of the weight of a typeface so that small-sized fonts print without blurring or losing detail on 300-dpi printers.

histogram   A stacked column graph in which the columns are brought together to emphasize variations in the distribution of data items within each stack (see fig. H.5).

By stacking the data items in a column, you emphasize the contribution each makes to the whole (as in a pie graph). By placing the columns adjacent to one another, the eye is led to compare the relative proportions of one data item as the item varies from column to column.

In figure H.5, note the variation in sales expenses and the sudden appearance (and subsequent steady rise) in administrative and facilities expenses. Synonymous with stepped column graph.

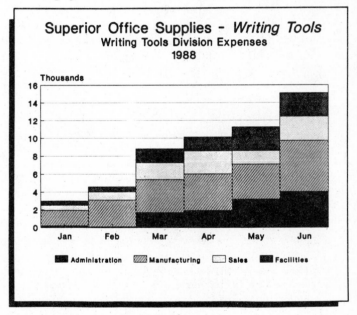

Fig. H.5. A histogram.

home computer   A personal computer specifically designed and marketed for home applications, such as educating children, playing games, balancing a checkbook, paying bills, and controlling lights or appliances.

A home computer usually has less memory, less secondary storage, and a slower microprocessor than a business computer.

In the late 1970s, people predicted that home computers would improve the quality of family life by providing convenient and sophisticated tools for education, finance management, and other household chores, but the low-powered machines marketed for such purposes typically lacked the software and memory required to carry out tasks effectively.

In 1978, a Wall Street Journal reporter was given a home computer for six months and assigned to use the machine for recipes, taxes, education, and so on. He concluded that the machine was most adept at gathering dust in the closet.

Millions of home computers, however, were sold—including the Commodore 64, an 8-bit home computer based on the same MOS Technology 6502 chip used in the Apple II. (The Commodore 64, however, does not run Apple II programs.) Most of these computers were used infrequently, and did not materially alter the patterns of American family life.

By 1984, the market for home computers had collapsed, and most of the personal computers that found their way into homes were more powerful business computers, such as the IBM Personal Computer. Most of these machines were used as a means of extending the work day by enabling users to accomplish tasks such as word processing and financial analysis at home.

Now, it is clear that home computing applications actually require as much processing power and memory as business applications do—and perhaps more. Easy-to-use home computing applications are best implemented with a graphical user interface that requires a powerful microprocessor and as much as a megabyte or more of internal memory.

Now that such machines are in homes, home computing applications may become a reality. For example, the idea that people would balance their checkbooks by using their computer remained something of a joke until Intuit Software successfully marketed a best-selling checkbook-management program called Quicken. Compared to early home computing programs, Quicken is in a different league in every possible sense: programming sophistication, the quality of the user interface, the capacity for virtually unlimited numbers of transactions, the features you actually need to carry out home financial tasks, speed, and ease of use. Quicken requires a business computer such as an IBM PC-compatible or Macintosh computer.

American companies may have failed to place useful home computers in every American home, but a Japanese firm may have succeeded at precisely this task. Unknown to most video-game addicts is the fact that the Nintendo game system is based on a general-purpose, 8-bit computer specifically designed to serve as the platform for other computer applications besides playing video games. Among the possible applications are home education, telecommunications, and home financial management. Whether the firm can market such applications, however, remains to be seen.

Home key   A key on IBM PC-compatible keyboards that has varying functions from program to program.

Frequently, the Home key is used to move the cursor to the beginning of the line or the top of the screen, but the assignment of this key is up to the programmer.

host   In a computer network, the computer that performs centralized functions such as making program or data files available to workstations in the network.

HP LaserJet   See *LaserJet.*

HyperCard   An authoring language bundled with the Macintosh that makes storing and interactively retrieving on-screen cards containing text, bit-mapped graphics, sound, and animation easier. HyperCard was developed in 1984 by Bill Atkinson at Apple Computer.

A HyperCard application, a stack, is a collection of one to several thousand cards. On each card, you find a background layer, consisting of buttons, graphics, and fields that several or all cards in the stack share and the card layer that contains the buttons, graphics, and fields unique to the card.

You interact with the stack by clicking the buttons. Each button has an associated script, written in HyperTalk, that specifies the procedure to follow when a button is clicked. Clicking a button may display another card in the stack or initiate an animation sequence that may include sound.

HyperCard comes with several prewritten stacks, but the program's significance is that it provides you with a way to create your own HyperCard applications.

The Macintosh is a formidable machine even for accomplished programmers, and the Mac received a great deal of criticism from hobbyists and users who wanted to develop their own applications without spending inordinate amounts of time. HyperCard answers these criticisms by providing a complete application development environment for nonprogrammers.

The range of applications is limited to those that can be displayed as HyperCard stacks. However, what many people would like to do with computers is related to the storage and retrieval of textual and graphic information, and HyperCard provides excellent tools for such applications.

The result is not a database management system in the traditional sense, but what Apple calls hypermedia, a way of displaying information by embedding linkages within the system and giving people the tools to explore these links interactively.

Because HyperCard is so well suited to the creation of instructional software, one could call HyperCard an authoring language. A major area of application development lies in the use of HyperCard as a front end for huge external information resources encoded on CD-ROM and interactive laser disks.

HyperCard also is serving as the platform for the development of multimedia applications, many with an educational emphasis. However, HyperCard can be used to create stand alone applications. Commercial applications include a musical composition program, an appointment/calendar system, an employee payroll and check-writing program, and a game that enables you to explore a huge labyrinth of interconnected rooms. See *authoring language, front end, hypermedia, HyperTalk, script,* and *stack.*

hypermedia   A computer-assisted instructional application such as HyperCard that is capable of adding graphics, sound, video, and synthesized voice to the capabilities of a hypertext system.

In a hypertext system, you select a word or phrase and give a command to see related text. In a hypermedia system, such a command reveals related graphics images, sounds, and even snippets of animation or video. See *hypertext.*

HyperScript   The software command language provided with Wingz, an innovative Macintosh spreadsheet program developed by Informix, Inc. Using HyperScript, even a novice programmer can develop spreadsheets by using on-screen buttons containing scripts for specific, customized spreadsheet functions. These scripts are the equivalent of macros in programs such as Lotus 1-2-3, but they are much easier to develop and use.

HyperScript resembles HyperTalk, the object-oriented programming language supplied with HyperCard. See *HyperCard, HyperTalk,* and *object-oriented programming language.*

HyperTalk   A software command language for the Macintosh HyperCard application that fully implements object-oriented programming principles. See *object-oriented programming language* and *SmallTalk.*

hypertext   The nonsequential retrieval of a document's text. The reader is free to pursue associative trails through the document by means of predefined or user-created links.

A hypertext application seeks to break away from a sequentially oriented text presentation of information and to provide the reader with tools to construct his own connections among the component texts of the document. A hypertext application is a form of nonsequential writing.

In a true hypertext application, the user can highlight virtually any word in a document and immediately jump to other documents containing related text. Commands also are available that enable the user to create his own associative trails through the document.

Computer technology helps when constructing a hypertext application. If this book were presented in hypertext format, for example, you could click your mouse on one of the cross references, and a window would pop up displaying the cross-referenced entries.

hyphen ladder   A formatting flaw caused by the repetition of hyphens at the end of two or more lines in a row.

Hyphen ladders attract the eye and disrupt the text's readability.

➔ **Tip:** If you insert hyphens throughout a document, proofread the results carefully. Hyphenation utilities cannot prevent hyphen ladders. If hyphen ladders occur, adjust word spacing and hyphenation manually.

hyphenation   In word processing and page layout programs, an automatic operation that hyphenates words on certain lines to improve word spacing.

When used with caution and manual confirmation of each inserted hyphen, a hyphenation utility can improve the appearance of a printed work by improving the line spacing. Automatic hyphenation is especially helpful with newspaper columns or narrow margins. An unhyphenated, lengthy word such as "collectivization" can introduce ugly word spacing irregularities into your document.

▲ **Caution:** Do not count on automatic hyphenation utilities to do the job perfectly: you should confirm each hyphen. Some programs break fundamental hyphenation rules, such as leaving fewer than two characters on one side of the hyphen or hyphenating a one-syllable word. No automatic hyphenation utility can cope effectively with homographs, two words spelled the same but that have different meanings and pronunciations. See the following:

in-val-id	in-va-lid
min-ute	mi-nute
put-ting	putt-ing

Watch out for hyphen ladders, an unsightly formatting error that occurs when three or more sentences in a row are hyphenated. You may need to use additional, manual hyphenation to finish the job. The automatic hyphenation utility consults an on-disk hyphenation database, but this file probably contains only a fraction of the words in your manuscript. See *hard hyphen, hyphen ladder,* and *soft hyphen.*

i

IBM 8514/A display adapter   A video adapter for IBM Personal System/2 computers that, with the on-board video graphics array (VGA) circuitry, produces a resolution of 1024 dots horizontally and 768 dots vertically. The adapter also contains its own processing circuitry that reduces demand on the computer's central processing unit (CPU).

For IBM PC-compatibles using the 16-bit AT bus rather than IBM's proprietary Micro Channel Bus, VGA adapters are available with the 1024-by-768 high-resolution mode. See *super VGA* and *video adapter.*

IBM PC-compatible computer   A personal computer—dubbed a clone by industry analysts—that runs all or almost all the software developed for the IBM Personal Computer (whether in PC, XT, or AT form) and accepts the IBM computer's cards, adapters, and peripheral devices. See *clone.*

IBM Personal Computer   A personal computer based on the Intel 8088 microprocessor.

Personal computers existed before the IBM Personal Computer, but the release of the IBM PC in 1981 legitimized the fledgling personal computer industry and ensured the technology's acceptance in the business community.

No longer a plaything for hobbyists, the personal computer became a serious business tool—or so many people concluded, because those magic three letters, IBM, appeared on the nameplate.

The story of the PC's development is an interesting chapter in technological innovation. IBM had been burned in the past by failing to recognize the market potential of small computers. The company thought that no market existed for minicomputers, leaving the market open for start-up firms such as Digital Equipment Corporation (DEC) and Hewlett-Packard (HP). Both companies cashed in under the umbrella created by IBM's disinterest in small-scale computer technologies.

IBM was not about to permit this setback to occur again and made an early decision to move into the personal computer market (then dominated by Apple Computer, Radio Shack, and 8-bit CP/M computers). Recognizing that a bureaucracy can frustrate an innovation effort, the team assigned to develop the PC was given substantial autonomy. Looking at the success of the Apple II, the team decided to emulate Apple's example by creating an open bus, open architecture system that would attract droves of third-party suppliers.

The computer developed by this team (at the Entry Level Systems Division in Boca Raton, Fla.) was by no means a state-of-the-art device. The PC used the Intel 8088 microprocessor instead of the faster Intel 8086, largely because the 8088 can take advantage of the 8-bit peripherals and microprocessor support chips that worked with the 8088 (but not with the 8086).

IBM also did not attempt to develop an operating system for the new computer. Instead, the firm hired Microsoft Corporation to develop an operating system that would enable CP/M programs to be quickly and easily modified to run on the new PC, because hundreds of business programs were available for CP/M computers.

Microsoft bought an operating system under development by a small Seattle firm, and dubbed the system MS-DOS (Microsoft Disk Operating System). Few people realized that MS-DOS is little more than a clone of CP/M. Therefore, the IBM PC fairly may be said to represent the technology of the late 1970s, not the early 1980s.

The future of IBM PC-compatible computing is much in doubt due to the limitations of MS-DOS. The 1981 machine is almost laughable by today's standards. It was released with a total of 16K of random-access memory (RAM), expandable to 64K on the motherboard. The monochrome display adapter (MDA) and monochrome monitor are incapable of displaying bit-mapped graphics—only the 254 characters (including block graphics characters) in the extended character set can be displayed. The disk drive, however, held an astonishing 160K of data, much more than the 50K to 90K drives in widespread use at the time.

Recognizing the limitations of the original IBM PC, the company introduced the PC-2 in 1983. This model came with 64K of RAM expandable to 256K on the motherboard without additional memory cards. Its disk drives used both sides of disks (they stored 320K). Also introduced was the Color Graphics Adapter (CGA) and an RGB color monitor.

IBM's choice of an open architecture and open bus for the PC quickly engendered a huge support industry as third-party vendors created memory cards, video adapters, and other accessories for the system. A major step forward was the Hercules Graphics Adapter that displayed bit-mapped graphics on the monochrome monitor.

By 1984, clones (non-IBM computers that claimed compatibility with the IBM PC) had appeared on the market, and because of their lower price, quickly gained market share. IBM countered with enhanced versions of the PC called the IBM Personal Computer XT in 1983 and the IBM Personal Computer AT in 1984.

These models were not successful in stemming the tide of clones, however, and in 1987, IBM introduced the IBM PS/2 line, abandoning the open bus architecture of the PC in favor of the proprietary Micro Channel Bus.

Because few clone manufacturers have decided to obtain the necessary license to create Micro Channel machines, the world of IBM PC-compatible computing has split into two camps: on one side is IBM, with is proprietary technology, and on the other is a consortium of clone manufacturers (led by Compaq Corporation) that continues to advocate the open architecture and open bus principles of the original IBM PC. See *Extended Industry Standard Architecture (EISA)* and *Micro Channel Bus.*

IBM Personal Computer AT   A personal computer, based on the Intel 80286 microprocessor, that was introduced in 1984.

The AT (short for Advanced Technology) significantly improved on the performance of PCs and XTs. Using the 80286 microprocessor and a 16-bit data bus, the computer's throughput was approximately 50 to 75 percent better than the fastest XT's.

Widely emulated by clones, the AT standard lives on in the form of AT compatibles, now available at bargain prices. See *Intel 80286*.

IBM Personal Computer XT   A personal computer, based on the Intel 8088 microprocessor and including a hard disk, that was introduced in 1983.

In addition to its hard disk, the XT (short for eXtended Technology) added a heftier power supply, additional expansion slots, and room for up to 640K of random-access memory (RAM) on the motherboard.

The XT standard lives on in 8088-based compatible machines called Turbo XTs because they offer a clock speed of approximately 10 MHz, twice that of the original XT. See *Intel 8088*.

IBM Personal System/2   A series of personal computers introduced in 1987 based on the Intel 8086, 80286, and 80386 microprocessors. Most PS/2s contain a proprietary expansion bus format. See *Micro Channel Bus*.

icon   In a graphical user interface, an on-screen symbol that represents a program file, data file, or some other computer entity or function.

In figure I.1, for example, are icons representing a paint/draw program, the files created by this program, and a configuration file. In the lower right corner is the trash can, where you can drag unwanted files for erasure.

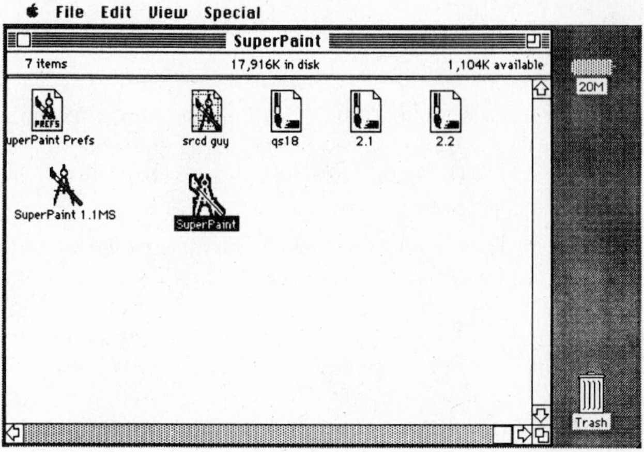

Fig. I.1. On-screen icons representing program and data files.

identifier   In database management, an identifier is used to specify the uniqueness of the information contained in the data record.

For example, the descriptor Norway appears in the data record of the only travel film that depicts scenery from that country.

IF   In DOS and OS/2, a batch command that sets up a conditional branch control structure. See *GOTO*.

IF/THEN/ELSE   A branch control structure that tests a variable or data to see whether a condition is true. If the condition is true, the program branches to option A, but if the condition is false, the program branches to option B.

The following example tests to see whether a file exists. If the file exists, the program instructs the computer to open the file. If the file does not exist, the program instructs the computer to create a file.

```
IF file_exists = true
    THEN open_file
    ELSE create_new_file
ENDIF
```

illegal character   A character that cannot be used according to the syntax rules of command-driven programs and programming languages. Such characters usually are reserved for a specific program function.

For example, with DOS, you cannot assign a file name to a file if the name includes an asterisk (*). The asterisk is reserved for use as a wildcard symbol. Commas also are illegal characters for file names. DOS uses commas as an argument separator in commands requiring two or more arguments.

imagesetter   A professional typesetting machine that generates very high-resolution output on photographic paper or film.

Popular imagesetters include the Agfa Compugraphic, Linotronic, and Varityper models that recognize PostScript commands. All are capable of resolutions of 1200 dots per inch (dpi) or more, unlike the 300-dpi resolution of laser printers. They also are quite expensive, selling for $30,000 and up.

If you have a PostScript-compatible word processor or page layout program, you can take a disk to a service bureau that owns one of these machines to obtain high-resolution output.

imaging model   The method of representing output on-screen.

In character-based programs, a connection may not exist between the screen and printer fonts. The screen font appears to be a monospaced typewriter font, but the printer font in use may be a proportionally spaced font with a different typeface.

In a graphical user interface, the goal is to use a unified imaging model, so that the text displayed on-screen closely resembles the text printed. See *graphical user interface* and *screen font.*

impact printer   A printer that forms an image by pressing a physical representation of a character against an inked ribbon, forming an impression on the page.

Impact printers are noisy, but they can produce multiple copies of business forms using carbons. See *dot-matrix printer, letter-quality printer,* and *nonimpact printer.*

import   To load a file created by one program into a different program.

Harvard Graphics, for example, can import the PIC files created by Lotus 1-2-3.

incremental backup   A backup procedure in which a hard disk backup program backs up only the files changed since the last backup procedure. See *archival backup.*

indentation   The alignment of a paragraph to the right or left of the margins set for the entire document.

▲ **Caution:** Do not use the space bar or Tab key to indent text. If a printer uses proportional typefaces, the text does not align properly. You also cannot change the indentation of all the lines with just one command; you must change each one individually.

Most word processing programs include commands that indent text from the left, right, or both margins (see fig. I.2). You also can create a hanging indent.

index   In database management programs, a compact file containing information (called pointers) about the physical location of records in a database file. When searching or sorting the database, the program uses the index rather than the full database. Such operations are faster than sorts or searches performed on the actual database.

In word processing programs, an index is an appendix that lists important words, names, and concepts in alphabetical order, with the page numbers where the terms appear. With most word processing programs, you must mark terms to be included in the index the program constructs. See *active index, concordance file, sort,* and *sort order.*

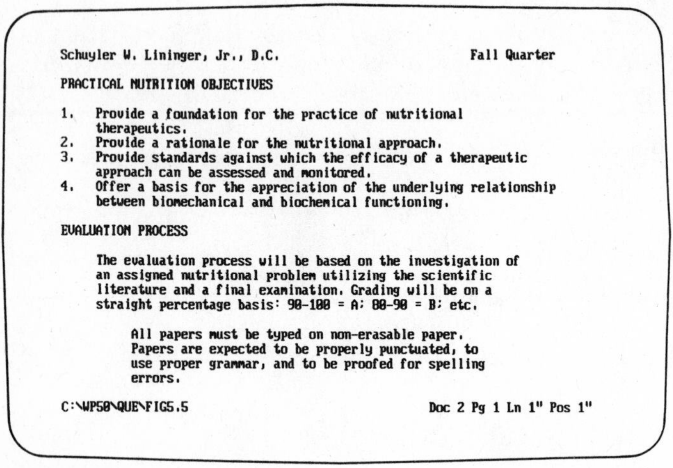

```
Schuyler W. Lininger, Jr., D.C.                        Fall Quarter

PRACTICAL NUTRITION OBJECTIVES

1.  Provide a foundation for the practice of nutritional
    therapeutics.
2.  Provide a rationale for the nutritional approach.
3.  Provide standards against which the efficacy of a therapeutic
    approach can be assessed and monitored.
4.  Offer a basis for the appreciation of the underlying relationship
    between biomechanical and biochemical functioning.

EVALUATION PROCESS

    The evaluation process will be based on the investigation of
    an assigned nutritional problem utilizing the scientific
    literature and a final examination. Grading will be on a
    straight percentage basis: 90-100 = A; 80-90 = B; etc.

        All papers must be typed on non-erasable paper.
        Papers are expected to be properly punctuated, to
        use proper grammar, and to be proofed for spelling
        errors.

C:\WP50\QUE\FIG5.5                          Doc 2 Pg 1 Ln 1" Pos 1"
```

*Fig. I.2. Text indented from the left margin and from
    both margins.*

infection   The presence within a computer system of a virus
or Trojan Horse. The infection may not be obvious to the
user; many viruses, for example, remain in the background
until a specific time and date, when they display prank messages or erase data.

information service   See *bibliographic retrieval service, bulletin board system (BBS)*, and *on-line information service*.

inheritance   In object-oriented programming, the passing of a
message up through the levels of objects until an object is
reached that traps the message.

In HyperTalk, for example, the lowest-level object is a button. If the user produces a message by clicking the button,
and the button contains no programming code (called a handler) that traps this message, the message is passed up to the
next level of the hierarchy, the card. If the card contains no
handler, the message is passed to the next level, the stack. If

the stack contains no handler, the message is passed to the highest level, HyperCard. See *object-oriented programming language.*

INIT   In the Macintosh environment, a utility program that executes during a system start or restart.

Examples of INITs are SuperClock, which displays the current system date and time in the menu bar, and Adobe Type Manager, which uses outline-font technology to display Adobe screen fonts.

▲ **Caution:** Like terminate-and-stay resident (TSR) programs in the IBM environment, INITs can conflict with each other and cause system crashes. If your system is behaving erratically, try removing INITs one at a time from the System Folder and restarting your system; you may be able to determine if an INIT is the culprit.

initial   In typography, an enlarged letter at the beginning of a chapter or paragraph.

Initials set down within the copy are drop caps, and initials raised above the top line of the text are stickup caps (see fig. I.3).

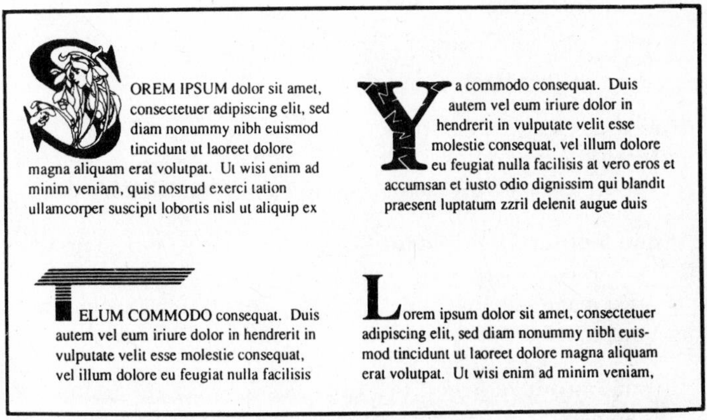

OREM IPSUM dolor sit amet, consectetuer adipiscing elit, sed diam nonummy nibh euismod tincidunt ut laoreet dolore magna aliquam erat volutpat. Ut wisi enim ad minim veniam, quis nostrud exerci tation ullamcorper suscipit lobortis nisl ut aliquip ex

a commodo consequat. Duis autem vel eum iriure dolor in hendrerit in vulputate velit esse molestie consequat, vel illum dolore eu feugiat nulla facilisis at vero eros et accumsan et iusto odio dignissim qui blandit praesent luptatum zzril delenit augue duis

ELUM COMMODO consequat. Duis autem vel eum iriure dolor in hendrerit in vulputate velit esse molestie consequat, vel illum dolore eu feugiat nulla facilisis

Lorem ipsum dolor sit amet, consectetuer adipiscing elit, sed diam nonummy nibh euismod tincidunt ut laoreet dolore magna aliquam erat volutpat. Ut wisi enim ad minim veniam,

Fig. I.3. Drop caps and stickup caps.

▲ **Caution:** You can create initials with many word processing and page layout programs, but to avoid a common formatting error, make sure that the letter aligns precisely at the base of a line of text.

initial base font   The default printer font used by word processing programs to print all documents unless you instruct otherwise.

You can override the initial base font for a particular document by choosing a document base font, and you can override this choice by formatting individual characters or blocks of characters within the document. See *document base font*.

initialization   The process of formatting a disk so that it is ready for use. See *format*.

inkjet printer   A nonimpact printer that forms an image by spraying ink from a matrix of tiny jets.

Inkjet printers are quiet and can produce excellent results. Hewlett-Packard's DeskJet and DeskWriter printers can produce text and graphics at resolutions of 300 dpi, rivaling the output of laser printers to the untrained eye.

▲ **Caution:** The ink used by most inkjet printers is water-soluble and smears easily. See *nonimpact printer*.

input   The information entered into the computer for processing purposes.

input device   Any peripheral that assists you in getting data into the computer, such as a keyboard, mouse, trackball, voice recognition system, graphics tablet, or modem.

input/output (I/O) system   One of the chief components of a computer system's architecture, the channels and interfaces that make the flow of data and program instructions into and out of the central processing unit (CPU) go smoothly.

input/output redirection   In DOS and OS/2, the routing of input and output operations to a file, the printer, or another device instead of the console (keyboard and monitor). See *filter command, FIND, pipe, redirection,* and *SORT*.

Ins key In IBM PC-compatible keyboards, a programmable key frequently (but not always) used to toggle between the insert mode and overtype mode in applications with text entry. See *Insert mode* and *Overtype mode.*

Insert mode In word processing programs, a program mode (usually toggled with the Ins key) that makes inserted text push the existing text right and down. See *Overtype mode.*

installation program A utility program provided with an application program that assists you in installing the program on a hard disk and configuring the program for use.

▲ **Caution:** In IBM PC-compatible computing, installation programs sometimes must change the CONFIG.SYS configuration file or the AUTOEXEC.BAT startup file on your hard disk. Some programs execute this procedure in a well-mannered way: they append instructions to the existing files.

Other installation programs, however, are ill-mannered, and actually delete files without asking you and write new ones in their place. If an old program stops working just after you install a program, the newly installed program may be the offender. You may have to reinstall the old program.

instruction In computer programming, a program statement interpreted or compiled into machine language that the computer can understand and execute.

instruction cycle The time it takes a central processing unit (CPU) to carry out one instruction and move on to the next.

instruction set A list of keywords describing all the actions or operations that a central processing unit (CPU) can perform. See *complex instruction set computer (CISC)* and *reduced instruction set computer (RISC).*

integer A whole number without any decimal places.

integrated accounting package An accounting program that includes all the major accounting functions: general ledger, accounts payable, accounts receivable, payroll, and inventory.

Unlike modular accounting packages, integrated programs update the general ledger every time an accounts payable or accounts receivable transaction occurs. You do not need to periodically batch update the general ledger.

One such integrated accounting program is Plains and Simple (Great Plains Software). This program is designed to emulate the way small-business users keep the books in their businesses, rather than forcing them to think like accountants.

integrated circuit   A semiconductor circuit that contains more than one transistor and other electronic components.

ENIAC, the first North American electronic computer, occupied a room of 1,500 square feet, about the size of a three-bedroom apartment. Weighing in at a hefty 30 tons, the 1946 machine required 18,000 vacuum tubes that functioned as the main switching devices.

Vacuum tubes once were common in radios and televisions, in which they amplified a signal. Within the tube, a weak current (such as one retrieved from a radio broadcast) acts to shape a stronger one. Vacuum tubes also are useful as switching devices—and are called valves in Britain—which is how they were used in the ENIAC.

But vacuum tubes have many liabilities: they get hot; they burn out frequently; and they draw huge amounts of current. When the ENIAC's power was switched on, the computer drew so much current that the lights throughout the neighborhood dimmed. The only way technicians could keep the computer running was to have teams of university students running around with shopping carts full of vacuum tubes, ready to replace the tubes that blew during processing sessions.

By the late 1950s, the vacuum tube gave way to the transistor, an amplifying and switching device invented in 1947. Even in the late 19th century, scientists had known that certain substances, called semiconductors, had electronic characteristics, such as the capability to transform alternating current into direct current. Silicon and germanium are two semiconducting materials. Semiconducting materials lie on the border between conductors, which transmit electricity well, and insulating materials, which do not transmit electricity at all.

The conducting properties of semiconductors also can be altered by introducing impurities. Impurities, such as arsenic, are introduced in a process called doping. If you dope a wafer of silicon so that some areas conduct and some areas do not, you can make some interesting things happen. In fact, you can make a tiny flake of silicon behave exactly like a big, expensive, hot, and power-hungry vacuum tube.

Even transistorized computers could not solve what engineers called the tyranny of numbers: they could envision wonderfully complex electronic devices, but it was an uneconomic proposition to create one so complex that years of work were necessary just to hand-wire the transistors together.

The engineers interested in semiconductors, however, were not ready to quit. If you can dope up a chip of silicon to produce a transistor, why not go further—why not place two or more transistors and other electronic devices on the same chip?

Such a chip, an integrated circuit, debuted in 1959, but its reception was chilly. At that time, producing integrated circuits was difficult and expensive. Unless a mass market arose for the new chips, their production costs would remain prohibitive for circuit designers.

The integrated circuit may have remained a curiosity for many years if it had not been for two historical events. First, in 1957, the Soviet Union launched the first artificial satellite, Sputnik, and set off a major U.S. campaign to catch up with Soviet science and space technology. Second, in 1961, President Kennedy announced a major U.S. effort to land a human being on the moon.

Both events eventually created a huge domestic market for integrated circuits, which were necessary for the space effort. Unlike the Soviets, who developed huge booster rockets to launch crude, heavy circuitry into space, the U.S. space program was in a catch-up mode and had to make do with relatively small boosters, which meant reducing weight in every possible way. With the assistance of huge amounts of federal research funding, electronic firms invested in major research and development projects to increase the complexity of integrated circuits.

The research efforts paid off; in the early 1960s, the number of transistors possible on a chip doubled each year, and the price of integrated circuits declined rapidly. By the mid-1960s, integrated circuits were in all kinds of electronic devices, ranging from stereo amplifiers and hearing aids to spacecraft and nuclear missiles.

But what no one predicted was how far this amazing process of technological development was to go. In 1965, an engineer noted that if the number of transistors on a single chip kept doubling each year, by 1975 one chip would have 65,000 transistors. In 1965, that idea seemed ridiculous. But no one had realized how much room is in the microscopic realm within a semiconductor chip. Today's Intel 80486 packs more than a million transistors into about one-sixteenth square inch of silicon.

integrated program   A program that combines two or more software functions, such as word processing and database management.

When Symphony (Lotus Development Corp.) and Framework (Ashton-Tate) were released in 1984, many thought these programs had ushered in a new era in personal computing. Both programs contained a spreadsheet, a database management program, a word processing program, a telecommunications program, and an analytical graphics program.

Every program within each package had a consistent user interface, so that you could switch from one program to the next without having to learn a new set of commands and menus. These programs facilitated the movement of data from one program to another.

For most users, however, the gains achieved by the consistent user interface were not worth the sacrifice involved—neither package's set of programs measured up to the

stanards of the best stand-alone programs. Most users preferred to assemble their own repertoire of programs.

Apple Computer's Lisa and Macintosh computers introduced the idea of using an application programming interface (API) that any program can access, with built-in routines
for generating screen menus, scroll bars, dialog boxes, alert
boxes, and other user interface amenities. The use of an API
creates an environment in which programs share a common
core of identical commands and menus, departing from the
core only to implement unique program functions.

Along with a copy-and-paste buffer called a clipboard, the
API approach offers the advantages of software integration
plus an attractive addition: the user can assemble precisely
the repertoire of programs that he or she wants, and they all
function together effectively and effortlessly.

With the introduction of a multiple-loading operating system for the Macintosh called MultiFinder, Macintosh users
achieved precisely the level of context-switching functionality that Symphony and Framework users possessed.

The Macintosh example shows that the goal of software
integration is correct, but the way to implement software integration is at the level of the operating system. With OS/2
and Presentation Manager, IBM PC-compatible computing is
moving in the same direction.

One exception to this trend is the success of entry-level
programs such as Microsoft Works. Such programs make
operations like label printing and mail merging easier than
with stand-alone programs. See *application programming
interface (API)*, *clipboard*, and *Macintosh*.

Intel 8086   A microprocessor introduced in 1978 with a full 16-
bit data bus structure.

Although the 8086 communicates with the rest of the computer more quickly than the 8088, the 8086 was not chosen
for the first IBM Personal Computer because of the high cost
of 16-bit peripherals and microprocessor support chips.

By the time such peripherals became available at low
prices, however, Intel had developed the Intel 80286 microprocessor, which addresses 16 megabytes of memory (in
contrast to the 8086's one megabyte).

Few personal computers, therefore, have used the 8086 chip. One exception is the use of the 8086 for the unsuccessful lower-end models of the PS/2 line, such as the Model 25. See *IBM Personal System/2, Intel 8088*, and *Intel 80286*.

Intel 8088   A microprocessor introduced in 1978 with an 8-bit external data bus and an internal 16-bit data bus structure used in the original IBM Personal Computer.

Although the Intel 8088 can process 16 bits at a time internally, the 8088 communicates with the rest of the computer 8 bits (1 byte) at a time. This design compromise was deliberate; Intel designers wanted to introduce 16-bit microprocessor technology and take advantage of the inexpensive 8-bit peripherals (such as disk drives) and 8-bit microprocessor support chips.

Capable of addressing up to 1 megabyte of random-access memory, the original 8088 operated at 4.77 MHz, a speed now considered too slow for business and professional applications. Later versions of the chip have pushed its clock speed to approximately 10 MHz; such chips power IBM PC-compatible computers known as Turbo XTs. See *Intel 8086*.

Intel 80286   A microprocessor introduced in 1984 with a 16-bit data bus structure and the capability to address up to 16 megabytes of random-access memory (RAM).

The Intel 80286 powered the high-performance IBM Personal Computer AT. The chip requires 16-bit peripherals that are more expensive than the 8-bit peripherals used in machines such as the original IBM PC, but by the time of the AT's introduction, such peripherals were available.

The 80286 has a split personality: in its real mode, the chip runs DOS programs in an 8086 emulation mode and cannot use more than 1 megabyte of RAM (under DOS, the limit is 640K), but in its protected mode, the 80286 can use up to 16 megabytes. However, DOS cannot take advantage of this mode.

➔ **Tip:** If you are planning to run OS/2, avoid the 80286 in favor of the 80386, the 80386SX, or the 80486, which have superior memory-management capabilities. OS/2 programs can take advantage of the 32-bit architecture of these chips. The 80286 runs Microsoft Windows, but not as well as as the newer microprocessors. See *Microsoft Windows.*

Intel 80287/Intel 80387   Numeric coprocessors designed to work (respectively) with the Intel 80286 and 80386. See *numeric coprocessor* and *Weitek coprocessor.*

Intel 80386   A microprocessor introduced in 1986 with a 32-bit data bus structure and the capability to address up to four gigabytes of main memory directly.

The Intel 80386 represented a revolutionary advance over its predecessors. Not only did the chip introduce a full 32-bit data bus structure to IBM PC-compatible computing, the 80386 also brought technical advances like a much-improved memory architecture.

Because this full 32-bit chip requires 32-bit microprocessor support chips, computers using the 80386 are more expensive than their 16-bit predecessors.

The 80386 includes a mode that enables the operating system to divide memory into separate blocks of 640K, so that DOS applications can run concurrently. You can, for example, run Lotus 1-2-3 and WordPerfect at the same time. To use this mode, however, requires special software such as DESQview/386 or Windows/386. See *Microsoft Windows.*

Intel 80386SX   A microprocessor introduced in 1988 with all the electronic characteristics of the Intel 80386, except that the chip has a 16-bit external data bus structure that enables it to use the inexpensive peripherals developed for the Intel 80286.

The 80386SX is like the Intel 8088 because it processes data internally twice as fast as it communicates with the rest of the computer. However, this compromise enables the computer to use the significantly cheaper 16-bit peripherals and microprocessor support chips.

➜ **Tip:** If you are thinking about purchasing a 286 computer, consider a 386SX computer instead. The prices are comparable, and the 386SX is equipped to handle 386 software.

Intel 80486 A microprocessor introduced in 1989 with a full 32-bit data bus structure and the capability to address 64 gigabytes of main memory directly.

The 80386 represents a technological leap over the 80286, but the 80486 is only an incremental step over the 80386. Packing more than one million transistors into one tiny silicon chip, the 80486 incorporates the mathematical processing circuitry that formerly was segregated on a coprocessor, such as the Intel 80387.

Intel 82385 A cache controller chip that governs cache memory in fast personal computers using the Intel 80386 and 80486 microprocessors. See *cache memory.*

interactive processing A method of using the computer in which the computer's processing operations are monitored directly on a video display, so that the user can catch and correct errors before the processing operation is completed.

Interactive processing is so characteristic of personal computing that forgetting the old days, when batch processing was the only way one could use the computer, is easy. Certain features of today's programs, however, hearken back to the early days. Word processing programs, for example, sometimes require you to embed formatting commands into the text, rather than showing you their effects directly on-screen. See *batch processing.*

interactive videodisc A computer-assisted instruction (CAI) technology that uses a computer to provide access to up to two hours of video information stored on a videodisc.

Like CD-ROM, videodiscs are read-only optical storage media, but they are designed specifically for the storage and random-access retrieval of images, including stills and continuous video.

An interactive videodisc application includes a computer program that serves as a front end to the information stored on the videodisc, a cable that links the computer to the videodisc player, and a videodisc that contains the appropriate images.

The user uses the front end program to explore the contents of the videodisc. For example, with a videodisc of paintings in the National Gallery of Art, the user can demand, "Show me all the renaissance paintings that depict flowers or gardens." A well-designed front end can lead the viewer through a series of vivid instructional experiences under the viewer's complete control.

With interactive videodisc technology, television viewing promises to become a less passive activity. See *computer-assisted instruction (CAI)* and *videodisc.*

interface   An electronic circuit that governs the connection between two hardware devices and helps them exchange data reliably. Synonymous with port.

interleave factor   The ratio of physical disk sectors on a hard disk that are skipped for every sector actually used for write operations.

If the interleave factor is 6:1, the disk writes to a sector, skips six sectors, writes to a sector, skips six sectors, and so on. The interleave factor is set by the hard disk manufacturer, but the factor can be changed by system software capable of performing a low-level format.

An interleave factor greater than 1:1 slows down the transfer rate so that the computer can keep up with the disk drive. Synonymous with sector interleave.

▲ **Caution:** Do not attempt to change the interleave factor of your hard disk unless you know what you are doing. In almost all cases, the interleave factor set by the disk manufacturer is optimal for your disk drive and computer.

interleaved memory   A method of speeding access to dynamic random access memory (DRAM) chips by dividing RAM into two large banks or pages and storing bit pairs in alternate banks; the microprocessor accesses one bank while the other is being refreshed. See *Page-mode RAM* and *static random-access memory (RAM).*

internal command   In DOS and OS/2, a command such as DIR or COPY that remains in memory and is always available when the DOS or OS/2 prompt is visible on-screen. See *external command*.

internal font   See *printer font*.

internal hard disk   A hard disk designed to fit within a computer's case and to use the computer's power supply.

→ **Tip:** Because internal hard disks do not require their own power supply, case, or cables, they generally cost less than external hard disks of comparable quality.

internal modem   A modem designed to fit into the expansion bus of a personal computer. See *external modem* and *modem*.

interpreter   A translator for a high-level programming language that does not create an executable version of a program; instead, an interpreter translates and runs the program at the same time.

Interpreters run a program more slowly than compilers, because a compiler does all the translating before the program is run.

However, interpreters are excellent for learning how to program, because if an error occurs, the interpreter shows you the likely place (and sometimes even the cause) of the error. You can correct the problem immediately and execute the program again. In this way, you learn interactively how to create a successful program. If a compiler is available for the programming language you are using, you can compile the program to make it run faster. See *compiler*.

interrupt   A microprocessor instruction that halts processing momentarily so that input/output or other operations can take place. When the operation is finished, processing resumes.

In a hardware interrupt, the instruction is generated within the computer as the control unit manages the flow of signals within the machine. In a software interrupt, a program generates an instruction that halts processing so that a specific operation can take place.

invisible file   See *hidden file*.

I/O   See *input/output (I/O) system*.

italic   A posture of a serif typeface that slants to the right and commonly is used for emphasis. See *oblique* and *Roman*.

ITC Avant Garde   Pronounced "ah-vahnt gard´." A sans serif typeface frequently used for display type applications.

Modern in appearance, Avant Garde—a design owned by the International Typeface Corporation (ITC) and licensed to Adobe Systems—is more mannered than Helvetica and should be used when a touch of informality is desired (see fig. I.4). ITC Avant Garde is included as a built-in font with many PostScript laser printers.

abcdefghijklmnopqrstuvwxyz
ABCDEFGHIJKLMNOPQRSTUVWXYZ
1234567890 .,;:'"&!?$

Fig. I.4. The ITC Avant Garde typeface .

ITC Bookman   A serif typeface frequently used for body type.

Bookman, a design owned by the International Typeface Corporation (ITC) and licensed to Adobe Systems, conveys a contemporary feeling and has widely spaced characters that make Bookman easy to read even in text-intensive documents (see fig. I.5). ITC Bookman is included as a built-in font with many PostScript laser printers.

abcdefghijklmnopqrstuvwxyz
ABCDEFGHIJKLMNOPQRSTUVWXYZ
1234567890 .,;:"&!?$

Fig. I.5. The ITC Bookman typeface .

ITC Zapf Chancery   Pronounced "zaff chance´-er-ee." An italic typeface that imitates hand calligraphy.

Zapf Chancery, a design owned by the International Typeface Corporation (ITC) and licensed to Adobe Systems, is included as a built-in font with many PostScript laser printers (see fig. I.6).

abcdefghijklmnopqrstuvwxyz
ABCDEFGHIJKLMNOPQRSTUVWXYZ
1234567890 .,;:"&!?$

Fig. I.6. The ITC Zapf Chancery typeface.

iteration   The repetition of a command or program statement. See *loop control structure*.

j

jaggies   See *aliasing*.

job   A unit of work to be performed by the computer, especially one that does not require human intervention (such as printing a file or group of files).

This term originates from the world of mainframe data processing, in which an end user does not directly use the computer but submits a request for a job to be carried out by the data processing staff, much as one requests a print job from the printing department.

The term job, however, is not unknown in personal computing. In WordPerfect, for example, you can define a print job in which one or more documents are printed in the background.

job control language (JCL)   In mainframe computing, a programming language that enables programmers to specify batch processing instructions, which the computer then carries out.

The acronym JCL refers to the job control language used in IBM mainframes.

job queue   A series of tasks automatically executed, one after the other, by the computer.

In mainframe data processing during the 1950s and 1960s, the job queue was literally a queue: you brought your stack of keypunch cards to the computer room, where technicians told you how many jobs were ahead of yours and how long you had to wait. When you went back, you saw reams of spurious printout full of error messages, and you had to go through the queue all over again.

With the rise of interactive, multiuser computing, and personal computing, you do not need to line up to get your work done. The term is still used, however, to describe the assignment of a specific order in which tasks are executed (usually in the background, while you are performing other tasks). In WordPerfect, for example, you can assign a job number to several files to be printed, and the program prints them in the order you assign.

join   In a relational database management program, a data retrieval operation in which a new data table is constructed from data in two or more existing data tables.

To illustrate how a join works (and why join operations are desirable in database applications), consider a database design that minimizes data redundancy. Suppose that for your video store, you create a database table called RENTALS that lists the rented tapes with the phone number of the person renting the tape and the due date:

TITLE	PHONE_NO	DUE_DATE
Alien Beings	499-1234	05/07/90
Almost Good	499-7890	05/08/90

You also create another database table, called CUSTOMERS, in which you list the name, telephone number, and credit card number of all your customers:

PHONE_NO	F_NAME	L_NAME	CARD_NO
499-1234	Terrence	Jones	1234-4321-098
499-1234	Jake	Smith	9876-1234-980

Suppose that you want to find out whether any of your customers are more than two weeks late returning a tape. You want to know the title and due date of the movie and the phone number, name, and charge card number of the customer. You need to join information from two databases.

The following Structured Query Language (SQL) command retrieves the information you need:

```
SELECT title, due_date, phone_no
FROM rentals, customers
WHERE due_date=<05/07/90
```

This command tells the program to display the information contained in the data fields called title, due_date, and phone_no for those records in which the data field due_date contains a date equal to or earlier than May 7, 1990. The result is the following display:

TITLE	DUE_DATE	PHONE_NO
Alien Beings	05/07/90	499-1234
Almost Home	05/05/90	499-7890

JOIN   In DOS and OS/2, an external command that connects a disk drive to a directory on a second drive so that the directory appears to be stored on the first drive.

▲ **Caution:** JOIN sometimes is used in systems with two hard drives to create one directory structure for both drives, but after the drives are joined, the use of BACKUP, DISKCOPY, FORMAT, and RESTORE can lead to unpredictable results. See *ASSIGN* and *external command.*

joystick   A cursor-control device widely used for computer games and some professional applications, such as computer-aided design.

jump line   A message at the end of part of an article in a newsletter, magazine, or newspaper, indicating the page on which the article is continued.

Page layout programs include features that make using jump lines for newsletters easier.

jumper An electrical connector that enables an end user to customize a circuit board. The jumper is a small rectangle of plastic with two or three receptacles. You install a jumper by pushing it down on two- or three-prong pins sticking up from the circuit board's surface.

justification The alignment of multiple lines of text along the left margin, the right margin, or both margins.

The term justification often is used to refer to full justification, or the alignment of text along both margins.

K See *kilobyte*.

Kermit 1. An asynchronous communications protocol that makes the error-free transmission of program files via the telephone system easier. 2. A public-domain communications program that contains the Kermit protocol.

Developed by Columbia University and placed in the public domain, Kermit is used by academic institutions, because unlike XMODEM, Kermit can be implemented on mainframe systems that transmit seven bits per byte. See *asynchronous communication*, *communications protocol*, and *XMODEM*.

kernal In an operating system, the core portions of the program that perform the most essential operating system tasks, such as handling disk input and output operations and managing the internal memory.

The kernal can be used with a variety of external shells that vary in their user-friendliness. The shell handles the task of communicating with the user.

kerning   The reduction of space between certain pairs of characters in display type, so that the characters print in an aesthetically pleasing manner.

Kerning is rarely necessary for body type, but may be required for headlines and titles. Some page layout programs include an automatic kerning feature, relying on a built-in database of letter pairs that require kerning (such as AV, VA, WA, YA, and so on). Manual kerning is possible with most page layout and some word processing programs (see fig. K.1).

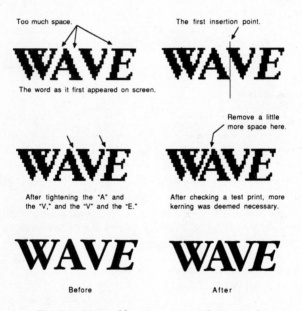

Fig. K.1. Manual kerning steps with PageMaker.

key assignments   The functions given to specific keys by a computer program.

Most of the keys on a personal computer keyboard are fully programmable, meaning that an application programmer can use them in different ways. The best programs, however, stick to standards in key assignments.

One such standard is the use of the F1 key on IBM PC-compatible keyboards for initiating on-screen help. A program that violates these standards raises the cost of training users and restricts their ability to export their skills to other application programs.

key status indicator   An on-screen status message displayed by many application programs that informs you which, if any, toggle keys are active on the keyboard.

The earliest IBM PC keyboards lacked indicator lights that informed you when you had pressed a toggle key such as Num Lock or Caps Lock. If you inadvertently press Num Lock, for example, the arrow keys on the numeric keypad do not control the cursor; they enter numbers instead. To make up for this oversight, many application programs provide on-screen indicators that flash when you press Num Lock, Scroll Lock, or Caps Lock.

key variable   In a spreadsheet program, a constant placed in a cell at the upper left corner of the spreadsheet and referenced throughout the spreadsheet using absolute cell references.

➔ **Tip:** The use of key variables is essential to good spreadsheet design. If you place a key variable, such as a tax or commission rate, in one cell and reference this rate using absolute cell references throughout the spreadsheet, you need make only one change if the rate changes. If you place the constant in all the formulas, you have to change every cell to update your spreadsheet.

keyboard   The most frequently used input device for all computers.

The keyboard provides a set of alphabetical, numeric, punctuation, symbol, and control keys. When an alphanumeric or punctuation key is pressed, the keyboard sends a coded input signal to the computer, which echoes the signal by displaying a character on-screen. See *autorepeat key, keyboard layout,* and *toggle key.*

keyboard buffer   A small area of primary storage set aside to
hold the codes of the last keystrokes you pressed on the keyboard so that the computer can continue to accept your typing even if the computer is busy.

keyboard layout   A personal computer's keyboard provides
an excellent example of how computer technology has had
to adapt to people (rather than people adapting to computers). A PC's keyboard layout uses the standard QWERTY layout that typewriters have used for a century. A superior
layout is the Dvorak keyboard, designed in the 1930s by
August Dvorak, a professor of education at the University of
Washington. The Dvorak keyboard is designed so that more
than two-thirds of the words you type only require the home
row keys. (For QWERTY keyboards, the figure is 32 percent.)

The world's typing speed record—170 words per minute—
was set on a Dvorak keyboard. Equipping a PC with a
Dvorak keyboard is easy, but surprisingly few people do so.
The old QWERTY habit is still too strong.

Early IBM Personal computers used a standard 83-key layout that attracted a good deal of criticism because of the odd
key layout, such as placing the backslash key between the Z
and the Shift keys (see fig. K.2). Many people also considered the Enter key too small. Toggle keys such as Scroll
Lock, Num Lock, and Caps Lock lacked lights, and you could
not tell if one was active.

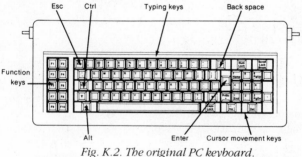

Fig. K.2. The original PC keyboard.

In response to this criticism, IBM introduced a new 84-key
layout with the release of the IBM Personal Computer AT
(see fig. K.3). The AT keyboard uses the standard Selectric

typewriter key layout for the typing area, with three indicators that light up when you press Scroll Lock, Num Lock, or Caps Lock. The new 84th key, called Sys Req, is used only when you are running an operating system other than DOS.

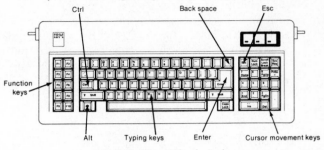

Fig. K.3. The AT keyboard.

The latest standard is an enhanced, 101-key layout (see fig. K.4). The 12 function keys (instead of 10) are lined up above the number keys. The 101-key layout also has a separate cursor-control keypad.

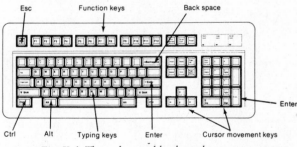

Fig. K.4. The enhanced keyboard.

The 101-key standard includes a relocated Ctrl key that touch typists dislike. The Ctrl key is used with other keys to give commands. In the earlier keyboard, Ctrl was situated left of the A key, within easy reach of your left pinky. In the 101-key layout, however, Ctrl is at the lower left, requiring a contorted movement to reach it. Many IBM PC-compatible computers use a corrected 101-key layout that places the Ctrl key back beside the A.

The original Macintosh keyboard contained only 58 keys. This keyboard lacked a numeric keypad and arrow keys, which the Apple engineers thought were unnecessary because of the Mac's extensive use of the mouse.

Widely criticized, this keyboard was replaced by a 78-key keyboard for the Macintosh Plus. This keyboard included a numeric keypad and arrow keys. With the release of the Macintosh SE and Macintosh II computers, Apple created a new interface standard for input peripherals called the Apple Desktop Bus (ADB). Today's ADB keyboards include the 81-key Apple keyboard with Control and Escape keys, and the 105-key Apple Extended Keyboard, which includes function keys.

▲ **Caution:** Increasingly, you may choose among several keyboard alternatives when you purchase a personal computer system. Some keyboards require extremely awkward fingerings for certain operations, such as holding down the Ctrl key and pressing another key to give a keyboard command. Before buying a keyboard, try holding down the Ctrl, Alt, or Command keys and pressing various alphanumeric keys.

Fast typists should make sure that the keyboard has N-key roll-over, enabling you to strike an additional key even while the previous key is still engaged at the end of a stroke. To find out whether a keyboard has N-key roll-over, hold down the A key. Then, press S D F in rapid succession. You probably will see several characters owing to the keyboard's autorepeat feature, but you also should see the s d and f.

keyboard template   A plastic card with adhesive that can be pressed onto the keyboard to explain the way a program configures the keyboard.

Many applications provide keyboard templates, which are helpful when you are learning the program.

keystroke   The physical action of pressing down a key on the keyboard so that a character is entered or a command is initiated.

➔ **Tip:** Programs vary in the number of keystrokes they require to perform basic and oft-repeated operations, such as highlighting text for a block move. Other things being equal, a program that requires fewer keystrokes for such tasks probably is more convenient to use.

keyword　In programming languages (including software command languages), a word describing an action or operation that the computer can recognize and execute.

kilobit　1,024 bits of information. See *kilobyte (K)*.

kilobyte (K)　Pronounced "kill´-oh-bite." The basic unit of measurement for computer memory, equal to 1,024 bytes.

The prefix kilo suggests 1,000, but this world contains twos, not tens: $2^{10} = 1,024$. Because one byte is the same as one character in personal computing, a memory of 1K can contain 1,024 characters (letters, numbers, or punctuation marks).

Early personal computers (mid-1970s) offered as little as 16K or 32K of random-access memory (RAM); memory chips were expensive. In IBM PC-compatible computing, 640K is considered a standard figure (the maximum under DOS); today, Macintosh computers are equipped with at least 1M of RAM.

kludge　Pronounced "kloodge." An improvised, technically inelegant solution to a problem.

knowledge acquisition　In expert system programming, the process of acquiring and systematizing knowledge from experts.

A major limitation of current expert system technology is that knowledge cannot be acquired by the systems directly; the knowledge must be acquired by engineers and, in a slow and painstaking process, systematized so that the knowledge can be expressed in the form of computer-readable rules. See *expert system* and *knowledge engineer*.

knowledge base　In an expert system, the portion of the program that expresses a expert's knowledge, often in IF-THEN rules (such as "If the tank pressure exceeds 600 pounds per square inch, then sound a warning.").

knowledge domain   In artificial intelligence, an area of problem-solving expertise.

Current artificial intelligence technology works well only in sharply limited knowledge domains, such as the configuration of one manufacturer's computer systems, the repair of a specific robotic system, or investment analysis for a limited range of securities. See *artificial intelligence (AI)*.

knowledge engineer   In expert system programming, a specialist whose profession is to elicit the knowledge possessed by an experts in a knowledge domain and to express this knowledge in a form that an expert system can use. See *expert system* and *knowledge domain*.

knowledge representation   In expert system programming, the method used to encode and store the knowledge in a knowledge base.

Although several alternative knowledge representation schemes have been proposed and implemented in systems currently under development, most commercially available expert system environments use the production system approach. In this approach, knowledge is represented in the form of production rules, which have the following form:

> IF {condition} THEN {action}

A given rule may have multiple conditions as in the following example:

> IF {a person has raised intraocular pressure}
> AND {the person has left quadratic pain}
> THEN {immediate hospitalization is indicated}

Although several alternative knowledge representation schemes have been proposed and implemented in systems currently under development, most commercially available expert system environments use the production system approach. In this approach, knowledge is represented in the form of production rules, which have the following form:

IF {condition} THEN {action}

A given rule may have multiple conditions as in the following example:

IF {a person has raised intraocular pressure}
AND {the person has left quadratic pain}
THEN {immediate hospitalization is indicated}

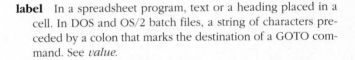

label In a spreadsheet program, text or a heading placed in a cell. In DOS and OS/2 batch files, a string of characters preceded by a colon that marks the destination of a GOTO command. See *value*.

label alignment In a spreadsheet program, the way labels are aligned in a cell (flush left, centered, flush right, or repeating across the cell).

→ **Tip:** In Lotus 1-2-3, you can control the alignment of a label as you type it by beginning the label with a prefix. Usually optional, the label prefix specifies how 1-2-3 aligns the label within the cell:

Label Prefix	*Alignment*
'	Flush left
^	Centered
''	Flush right
\	Repeating across the cell

See *label* and *label prefix*.

label prefix In a spreadsheet program, a punctuation mark at the beginning of a cell entry that tells the program that the entry is a label and specifies how the program should align the label within the cell.

Most programs enter the label prefix—often an apostrophe—when you begin the cell entry with an alphabetical character.

➔ **Tip:** If you begin a cell entry with a number, the program interprets the number as a value rather than a label.
However, you can make a number into a label by starting the
entry with the label prefix. In Lotus 1-2-3, for example, if you
type '1991, the program interprets the entry as a label and
formats the label flush left.

LAN Pronounced "lan." See *local area network (LAN)*.

landscape orientation The rotation of a page design to print
text and/or graphics horizontally across the longer axis of the
page. See *portrait orientation*.

laptop computer A lightweight, battery-powered, portable
computer that uses a lightweight display device such as a liquid crystal display.

True laptops that weigh less than twelve pounds are different from luggables, portable computers that are too heavy to
be carried around like a briefcase. The better laptops use
backlit or gas-plasma screens that are easier to read, but
these brighter screens consume more electricity, and require
more frequent recharges.

large-scale integration (LSI) In integrated circuit technology,
the fabrication on one chip of up to 100,000 discrete transistor devices. See *very large scale integration (VLSI)*.

laser font See *outline font*.

laser printer A high-resolution printer that uses a version of
the electrostatic reproduction technology of copying machines to fuse text and graphic images to the page.

Although laser printers are complex machines, understanding how they work is not difficult. The printer's controller circuitry receives the printing instructions from the computer and, for each page, constructs a bit map of every dot
on the page (about 1M of memory is required to ensure adequate storage space for graphics images). The controller ensures that the print engine's laser transfers a precise replica
of this bit map to a photostatically sensitive drum or belt.
Switching on and off rapidly, the beam travels across the

drum, and as the beam moves, the drum charges the areas exposed to the beam. The charged areas attract toner (electrically charged ink) as the drum rotates past the toner cartridge.

In a write-black engine, the beam charges the areas that print, and does so with a positive charge that attracts toner. In a write-white engine, the beam charges the areas not printed, giving the areas a negative charge that repels toner. Because of this technique, write-black engines show details of images better than write-white engines, but write-white engines print denser images. An electrically charged wire pulls the toner from the drum onto the paper, and heat rollers fuse the toner to the paper. A second electrically charged wire neutralizes the drum's electrical charge.

Alternative technologies include light-emitting diode (LED) imaging printers that use a dense array of LEDs instead of a laser to generate the light that exposes the drum, and liquid crystal shutter (LCS) printers that use a lattice-like array of liquid crystal gateways to block or transmit light as necessary. See *print engine* and *resolution.*

LaserJet   A series of laser printers manufactured by Hewlett-Packard and widely used in IBM PC-compatible computing.

Introduced in 1984, the LaserJet offered only one built-in font (the monospace Courier), but its 300-dpi resolution and capability to accept font cartridges helped to launch desktop publishing. The LaserJet Plus, introduced in 1985, offered sufficient internal random-access memory (RAM) so that the printer could accept downloadable fonts, further increasing its versatility as a desktop typesetter.

The LaserJet Series II was introduced in 1987 with additional built-in fonts, a larger paper tray, and additional memory. The LaserJet IIP Personal Laser Printer was added in 1989 and brought the street cost of laser printing technology below $1,000 for the first time.

Although LaserJet printers are popular, they are not Post-Script-compatible; therefore, they use bit-mapped fonts rather than the more versatile outline fonts that can be scaled to any type size without downloading additional fonts. Applications running under DOS cannot display the user's typeface and type size choices on-screen.

Many people, therefore, prefer PostScript laser printers such as the Apple LaserWriter for professional desktop publishing applications. However, the LaserJet brings a high level of laser-printing functionality to personal-computer users at a low cost, and by adding an internal adapter or cartridges, you can upgrade LaserJets so that they can print PostScript files. See *laser printer.*

LaserWriter   A series of PostScript laser printers manufactured by Apple Computer and used with Macintosh and IBM PC-compatible computers.

Introduced in 1985 with a list price of nearly $8,000, the Apple LaserWriter was the first commercial laser printer to offer a built-in interpreter for the PostScript page description language. Capable of using the sophisticated and scalable outline fonts created by Adobe Systems, Inc., and other firms, the LaserWriter is well-integrated with the Macintosh family of computers because a standard Postscript-compatible printer driver is available for any application to use. (For an IBM PC compatible running DOS, an application cannot produce PostScript-compatible output unless the application includes a PostScript-compatible driver.)

Coupled with the Mac's capability of displaying screen fonts that suggest the typeface and type size changes, the LaserWriter gave the Macintosh an early lead in desktop publishing.

Designed to be connected to the Macintosh through inexpensive AppleTalk network connections, Apple envisioned the LaserWriter as a shared peripheral, designed for use by a small workgroup of four to seven individuals. A standard serial port is included, however, for direct connection to IBM PC-compatible computers.

The LaserWriter II series, introduced in 1987, featured a better print engine, more memory, and faster output. At the top of the line is the LaserWriter II NTX, which includes 11 Adobe typefaces (a total of 35 fonts), a 68020 microprocessor running at 16.7 MHz, and a SCSI output port for a dedicated hard disk. The LaserWriter II SC, the least expensive printer in the LaserWriter line, is not a PostScript printer and therefore relies on bit-mapped fonts for its output.

The LaserWriter has been imitated—many PostScript laser printers are functionally identical. Although LaserWriter printers are much cheaper now than they were originally, they can cost as much or more than a well-equipped personal computer. LaserWriters will never be as inexpensive as LaserJets, because unlike LaserJets, PostScript-compatible printers must have their own microprocessing circuitry and require large amounts of RAM. Non-PostScript outline font technologies, however, promise to lower prices by circumventing Adobe Systems' licensing fees. See *AppleTalk, laser printer,* and *PostScript laser printer.*

latency   In disk drives, the delay caused by the disk rotating so that the desired data is positioned under the read/write head.

launch   To start a program.

layer   In some illustration and page-layout applications, an on-screen sheet on which text or graphics can be placed independent of other sheets.

In SuperPaint, for example, you can create illustrations on two layers: a paint layer for bit-mapped graphics and a draw layer for object-oriented graphics. In FreeHand, you can draw or paint on up to 200 transparent layers. Commands typically named Bring to Front or Send to Back enable you to bring a background layer forward so that you can edit that layer.

layout   1. In desktop publishing, the process of arranging text and graphics on a page. 2. The arrangement of data items on a data record or the arrangement of page design elements, such as text and graphics, on a printed page.

LCD   See *liquid crystal display (LCD).*

leader   In word processing, a row of dots or dashes that provides a path for the eye to follow across the page.

Leaders often are used in tables of contents to lead the readers' eye from the entry to the page number. Most word processing programs enable the user to define tab stops that insert leaders when the Tab key is pressed.

leading   Pronounced "ledding." The space between lines of type, measured from baseline to baseline. Synonymous with line spacing.

The term originated from letterpress-printing technology, in which thin lead strips were inserted between lines of type to control the spacing between lines.

leading zero   The zeros added in front of numeric values so that a number fills up all required spaces in a data field. For example, three leading zeros are in the number 00098.54.

Most of today's database management programs do not require leading zeros; they are symbolic of previous generations of software, which often forced the user to enter data to conform to the program's limitations.

LED   See *light emitting diode (LED)*.

left justification   The alignment of text along only the left margin. Synonymous with *ragged-right alignment*.

legend   In presentation graphics, an area of a chart or graph that explains the meaning of the patterns or colors used in the presentation.

letter-quality printer   An impact printer that simulates the fully formed text characters produced by a high-quality office typewriter.

The print technology used is a spin-off of office typewriter technology. Many letter-quality printers use daisywheels or printing mechanisms in which the character images are positioned on the ends of spokes of a plastic or metal hub that rotates quickly as printing occurs. You change fonts by changing the daisywheel.

A major drawback of letter-quality printers is that they cannot print graphics. This fact ensures a brisk market for dot-matrix printers that, despite their poorer quality for text output, can print charts and graphs. With the arrival of laser printers, the market for letter-quality printers has all but disappeared.

▲ **Caution:** If you plan to purchase a letter-quality printer, make sure that your software includes a printer driver for the specific brand and model you are buying. In IBM PC-compatible computing, no single, widely accepted standard for printer control commands exists. De facto standards are established by Diablo and Qume letter-quality printers. Many letter-quality printers recognize the Epson or IBM commands, but others do not. See *impact printer*.

library   A collection of programs kept with a computer system and made available for processing purposes. The term often refers to a collection of library routines written in a given programming language such as C or Pascal. See *library routine*.

library routine   In programming, a prewritten and well-tested subroutine, procedure, or function in a given programming language.

The library routine handles tasks that all or most programs need, such as reading data from disk. The programmer can draw on this library to develop programs quickly.

ligature   In typography, two or more characters designed and cast as a distinct unit for aesthetic reasons.

Five letter combinations beginning with f (fi, ff, fl, ffi, and ffl) and two dipthongs (ae and oe) commonly are printed as ligatures. Some outline fonts available for PostScript laser printers include ligatures for professional typesetting applications. See *outline font* and *PostScript laser printer*.

light emitting diode (LED)   A small electronic device made from semiconductor materials. An LED emits light when current flows through it.

LEDs are used for small indicator lights, but because they draw more power than liquid crystal displays (LCD), they rarely are used for computer displays.

light pen   An input device that uses a light-sensitive stylus to enable you to draw on-screen, on a graphics tablet, or select items from menus.

LIM EMS   See *Lotus-Intel-Microsoft Expanded Memory System (LIM EMS)*.

line   1. In programming, one program statement. 2. In data communications, a circuit that directly connects two or more electronic devices.

line adapter   In data communications, an electronic device that converts signals from one form to another so that the signals can be transmitted.

A modem is a line adapter that converts the computer's digital signals to analog equivalents so that these signals can be transmitted via the telephone system.

line art   In computer graphics, a drawing that does not contain halftones so that it can be reproduced accurately by low- to medium-resolution printers. See *halftone*.

line chart   See *line graph*.

line feed   A signal conveyed that tells the printer when to start a new line.

line graph   In presentation and analytical graphics, a graph that uses lines to show the variations of data over time or to show the relationship between two numeric variables (see fig. L.1). In general, the x-axis (categories axis) is aligned horizontally, and the y-axis (values axis) is aligned vertically. A line graph, however, may have two y-axes. See *bar graph*, *presentation graphics*, *x-axis*, and *y-axis*.

line spacing   See *leading*.

link   To establish a connection between two files or data items so that a change in one is reflected by a change in the second.

A cold link requires user intervention and action, such as opening both files and using an updating command, to make sure that the change has occurred; a warm link occurs automatically. See *cold link* and *warm link*.

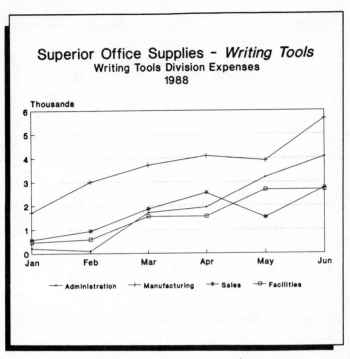

Fig. L.1. A line graph showing a trend over time.

linked list   See *list.*

linked pie/column chart   See *linked pie/column graph.*

linked pie/column graph   In presentation graphics, a pie graph paired with a column graph so that the column graph displays the internal distribution of data items in one of the pie's slices (see fig. L.2).

Use linked pie/column graphs to demonstrate an internal breakdown of the values making up one of a pie's slices. For example, in a pie graph showing total expenditures for a quarter, the linked column graph could display a breakdown of physical plant expenditures (such as salaries, equipment, maintenance, insurance, and so on).

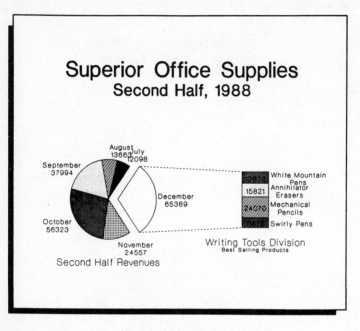

Fig. l.2. A linked pie/column graph.

liquid crystal display (LCD)   A low-power display technology used in laptop computers and small, battery-powered electronic devices such as meters, testing equipment, and digital watches. The display device uses rod-shaped crystal molecules that change their orientation when an electrical current flows through them. When no current exists, the crystals seem to disappear. When energized, they direct light to a polarizing screen, producing a darkened area.

LCD displays are flat and draw little power, but they are not bright enough for sustained use without causing eyestrain. A compromise design uses a backlit screen. This design improves the LCD screen's readability but draws more power.

LISP   Pronounced "lisp." A high-level programming language, often used for artificial intelligence research, that makes no distinction between the program and the data. This language is considered ideal for the manipulation of text.

One of the oldest programming languages still in use, LISP (short for list processing) was developed by John McCarthy and his colleagues at the Massachusetts Institute of Technology in the early 1960s.

LISP is a declarative language; the programmer does not write a series of instructions that tells the computer what to do; instead, the programmer composes lists that declare the relationships among symbolic values. Lists are the fundamental data structure of LISP, and the program performs computations on the symbolic values expressed in lists. A variable is declared in the following way:

```
(SETQMAP(NATION(STATE(COUNTY(CITY
(ZONE(STREET(HOUSE)))))))))
```

Because LISP is a symbolic processing language, this expression is evaluated by the LISP interpreter, which returns a value—in this case, the variable map is bound to the following hierarchical list:

```
(NATION(STATE(COUNTY(CITY(ZONE(STREET
(HOUSE))))))).
```

Because each LISP statement produces a value that can be passed to other statements, no inherent distinction exists between data and program instructions; on the contrary, each LISP statement is potentially an item of data that another LISP statement can consider. Writing LISP programs that modify themselves or writing new programs is easy. By using recursion, moreover, you can build complex applications.

Not all of these applications lie in the field of artificial intelligence research. LISP was used to write EMACS—a respected mainframe text editor that has influenced the design and implementation of personal computer word processing packages such as WordPerfect and Sprint.

A distinctive feature of LISP, as this example suggests, is the use of parentheses to express the logical structure of the program. Critics of LISP say the use of parentheses makes the language difficult to read.

Like other public domain programming languages, LISP has appeared in a number of mutually unintelligible versions. A standardization effort, however, resulted in Common LISP, which defines a fully configured, current version of the language that is widely accepted. See *declarative language*, *interpreter*, and *recursion*.

list   In programming, a data structure that lists and links each data item with a pointer showing the item's physical location in a database.

Using a list, a programmer can organize data in various ways without changing the physical location of the data. For example, a database can be displayed on-screen so that it appears to be sorted in alphabetical order, even though the actual physical data records still are stored in the order in which they were entered.

live copy/paste   A warm-link technique introduced in the Macintosh System 7.0 that updates linked data shared by two or more applications.

In a document such as a report or a worksheet, you begin by selecting the text or data that you want updated in other files, and you publish that data by saving it to a special disk file. Then you identify the documents that subscribe to the publication and show where in these documents the publication should appear.

If you change the publication, the other documents contain notices that an update has occurred and ask you to confirm the insertion of the update in the document. Live copy/paste works in network settings and within one computer. See *warm link*.

load   To transfer program instructions or data from a disk into the computer's random-access memory (RAM).

local area network (LAN)   The linkage of personal and other computers within a limited area by high-performance cables so that users can exchange information, share peripherals, and draw on the resources of a massive secondary storage unit (called a file server).

Local area networks offer the advantages of a distributed computing system in which computational power is distributed to users without sacrificing their ability to communicate (see fig. L.3).

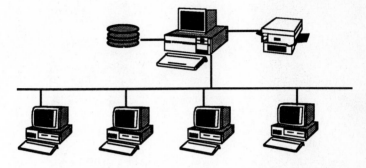

Fig. L.3. A personal computer local area network.

Ranging tremendously in size and complexity, LANs may link only a few personal computers to an expensive, shared peripheral, such as a laser printer. More complex systems use central computers called file servers and enable users to communicate with each other via electronic mail to share multiuser programs and to access shared databases.

Some of the largest and most complex LANs are found on university campuses and in large corporations. Such networks may be composed of several smaller networks interconnected by electronic bridges. Unlike a multiuser system, in which each user is equipped with a dumb terminal that may lack processing capabilities; each user in a LAN possesses a workstation containing its own processing circuitry. High-speed cable communication links connect these workstations.

LANs are not without their disadvantages when compared to multiuser systems, however. Multiuser systems may be highly appropriate for vertical applications such as point-of-sale systems, in which it is unnecessary to provide each node with its own processing circuitry and software.

In addition, much of the software developed for multiuser systems has its origins in vertical application development, such as the creation of software for hospital management, and as such, it represents the accumulation of years of experience in managing specific organizations with computers.

A set of standards (network protocols) governs the flow of information within the network. These standards determine when and how a node may initiate a message. Network protocols also handle conflicts that occur when two nodes begin transmitting at the same time. Common network protocols for personal computers include AppleTalk and EtherNet.

The basic physical components of a LAN are cables, a network interface card, a file server (which includes the central mass storage), and personal computers or workstations linked by the system.

Three alternative network topologies (methods for interconnecting the network's workstations) exist: bus networks, ring networks, and star networks. In addition, two methods for communicating information via the network's cables exist: baseband and broadband. See *AppleTalk, baseband, broadband, bus network, EtherNet, file server, multiuser system, ring network,* and *star network.*

local echo   See *half duplex.*

LocalTalk   The physical connectors and cables manufactured by Apple Computer for use in AppleTalk networks.

locked file   In a local network, a file attribute that prevents applications or the user from updating or deleting the file.

logarithmic chart   See *logarithmic graph.*

logarithmic graph   In analytical and presentation graphics, a graph displayed with a y-axis (values axis) incremented exponentially in powers of 10.

On an ordinary y-axis, the 10 is followed by 20, 30, 40, and so on. On a logarithmic scale, however, 10 is followed by 100, 1,000, 10,000, and so on.

→ **Tip:** Use a logarithmic scale when one of the data series has very small values, and others have large values. In an ordinary graph, you almost cannot see the data series with small values (see fig. L.4); on a logarithmic chart, the small values show up much better (see fig. L.5). See *analytical graphics* and *presentation graphics*.

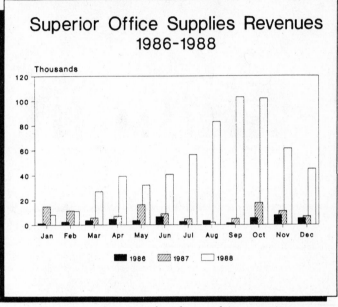

Fig. L.4. A column graph with an ordinary y-axis.

logic board   See *motherboard.*

logical drives   The disk drives of a computer system that present themselves to the user as identical devices which retrieve and store data using the same file-management commands. See *physical drive.*

logical format   See *high-level format.*

logical operator   A symbol used to specify the logical relationship of inclusion or exclusion between two quantities or concepts.

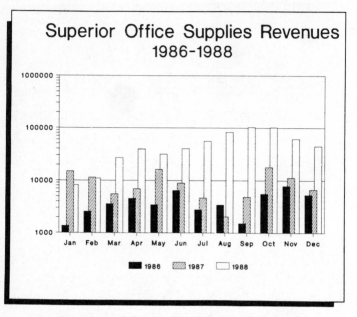

Fig. L.5. A column graph with a logarithmic y-axis.

In query languages, the inclusive operator (OR) broadens the number of data records retrieved, and the exclusive operators (AND, NOT) restrict the number retrieved.

Suppose that you specify a query that asks "Show me the titles of all the videotapes in which the field RATING contains PG OR PG-13." You see a list of the titles with either rating; the program retrieves records that meet either of the criteria you specify.

To illustrate the restrictive effect of the AND operator, consider the following example: you ask, "Show me the titles of all the videotapes in which the field CATEGORY contains Adventure AND the field RATING includes PG." Only those records that meet both of the criteria you specify in your query appear on-screen.

The NOT operator is also restrictive, as in the following example: "Show me the titles of all the videotapes in which the field CATEGORY contains Adventure, but NOT the ones in which the field RATING includes R. Synonymous with *Boolean operator.*

log-in security   In local area networks, a validation process that requires users to type a password before gaining access to the system. See *local area network (LAN)* and *password protection.*

Logo   A high-level programming language well-suited to teaching fundamental programming concepts to children.

Developed at the Massachusetts Institute of Technology in the 1960s with the National Science Foundation, Logo is the creation of computer scientist Seymour Papert. A special version of LISP, Logo was designed as an educational language to illustrate the concepts of recursion, extensibility, and other fundamental concepts of computing in an environment that did not require the use of mathematics. The language also provides an environment in which children can develop their reasoning and problem-solving skills.

A key feature of Logo is turtle graphics, in which a graphic representation of a turtle creates graphic images under program control. Program instructions tell the turtle to put down the pen and move forward, backward, left, or right. After the child succeeds in writing a program that defines a shape such as a rectangle, he or she can save the program as a new command; this teaches the concept of extensibility. Through recursion, children can create and print beautiful geometric diagrams.

log on   The process of establishing a connection with, or gaining access to, a computer system or peripheral device.

A log-on procedure is used to contact host computers via telecommunications or network links. In operating systems, a log-on procedure is used to activate a disk drive.

log off   The process of terminating a connection with a computer system or peripheral device in an orderly way.

lookup function   A procedure in which the program consults stored data listed in a table or file.

lookup table   In a spreadsheet program, a range of cells set apart from the rest of the worksheet and dedicated to a lookup function, such as determining the correct tax rate based on annual income.

loop   In programming, a set of program instructions that execute repeatedly until a condition is satisfied. See *loop control structure*.

loop control structure   A control structure in which a block of instructions repeats until a condition is fulfilled. See *DO/WHILE loop* and *FOR/NEXT loop*.

lost chain   In DOS and OS/2, a section of a file once connected with other sections, but the file allocation table (FAT) no longer contains the information needed to reconstruct the linkages.

➔ **Tip:** Use the CHKDSK command to determine whether you have lost chains on your disk. If any are detected, choose the on-screen option that converts lost chains into files. Use the TYPE command to examine the files. Erase the files if they do not contain useful data.

Lotus 1-2-3   A spreadsheet program for IBM PC-compatible computers that integrates database management and analytical graphics capabilities.

Introduced in 1982 by Lotus Development Corporation, Lotus 1-2-3 supplanted VisiCalc, the original spreadsheet program, by offering all of VisiCalc's functions and adding to database and graphics functions.

Developed by Mitchell D. Kapor, Lotus 1-2-3 is sometimes credited with being responsible for the success of the IBM personal computer. Many people bought IBM PCs (equipped with Hercules Graphics Adapters) so that they could run

1-2-3 and transform spreadsheet data into vivid, on-screen charts and graphs.

Like dBASE, the popular database management system for IBM PC-compatible computers, many clones have imitated Lotus 1-2-3. Lotus countered this competition by successful product introductions in 1989.

Version 3.0, designed for computers with the Intel 80286 and Intel 80386 microprocessors, requires at least 1M of RAM under DOS (640K of conventional memory and 384K of expanded memory) or 3M of RAM under OS/2. This version of the program features three-dimensional worksheets and other advanced features.

To address the much larger market of users still running computers with the Intel 8088 microprocessor, Lotus also released Version 2.2, which lacked three-dimensional capabilities but included many features offered by the clone programs. Borland International's Quattro Pro, however, provides three-dimensional functions to users of 640K systems and is expected to erode some of the market for Version 2.2.

Despite these successful product introductions, Lotus 1-2-3 is still a character-based program and does not produce presentation-quality output without the use of an add-on program such as Allways, also published by Lotus Development Corporation. Competition has appeared in the form of programs such as Excel that run in a bit-mapped graphics mode under Microsoft Windows. Lotus 1-2-3/G— a new, graphics-based spreadsheet—answers those challenges.

Lotus-Intel-Microsoft Expanded Memory Specification (LIM EMS) An expanded memory standard that enables the programs that recognize the standard to work with more than 640K RAM under DOS.

The LIM Version 4.0 standard, introduced in 1987, supports up to 32M of expanded memory and enables programs to run in expanded memory (as well as providing space for the storage of data).

▲ **Caution:** Software cannot work with expanded memory unless specifically designed to do so. Most popular application packages such as WordPerfect, Lotus 1-2-3, and dBASE work with LIM 4.0 expanded memory, but less popular programs and shareware may not function in EMS unless you use a windowing environment such as Quarterdeck's DESQview or Microsoft Windows. See *expanded memory* and *extended memory.*

low-level format   The physical pattern of magnetic tracks and sectors created on a disk during formatting. This operation, sometimes called a physical format, is different from the high-level format that establishes the housekeeping sections that track free and in-use areas of the disk.

When you format a floppy disk using the DOS FORMAT command, the computer establishes an absolute and a relative format on the disk.

➜ **Tip:** If you have just purchased a new hard disk for your system, remember that the DOS FORMAT command does not perform a physical format on a hard disk. On hard disks, FORMAT performs only a high-level format. In most cases, the factory has performed the absolute format. If you attempt to use FORMAT on the disk and the format fails, however, you first must perform a low-level format using a program that the hard disk manufacturer provides. See *high-level format.*

low-level programming language   In computer programming, a language, such as machine language or assembly language, in which the programmer must pay strict attention to the exact procedures occurring in the computer's central processing unit (CPU). See *assembly language, high-level programming language,* and *machine language.*

low resolution   In output devices, such as monitors or printers, the lack of sharpness produced by a display or printing technology that does not generate enough dots per inch to resolve an image fully.

A low-resolution display, for example, displays characters and graphics with jagged edges.

LPT   In DOS, a device name that refers to one of the parallel ports to which parallel printers can be connected.

LSI   See *large-scale integration (LSI)*.

m

M   See *megabyte (M)*.

MacBinary   A file transfer protocol for Macintosh computers that enables Macintosh files to be stored on non-Macintosh computers without losing icons, graphics, and information about the file (such as the creation date). Most Macintosh communication programs send and receive files in MacBinary.

Mace Utilities   A package of utility programs developed by Paul Mace and sold by Fifth Generation Systems for IBM PC-compatible computers.

Similar to Norton Utilities, this package includes a remarkable file recovery program that, under some conditions, can recover files if you accidentally reformat a hard disk.

machine language   The language recognized and executed by the computer's central processing unit (CPU). The language is symbolized by 0s and 1s and is extremely difficult for people to use and read. See *assembly language* and *high-level programming language*.

Macintosh   A family of personal computers introduced by Apple Computer in 1984 that features a graphical user interface.

During the 1970s, the Xerox Palo Alto Research Center (PARC) attracted what were unquestionably some of the greatest minds in computer design. In an organizational context well suited to technical innovation, the PARC scientists generated an astonishing series of innovations: a WYSIWYG word processor called Bravo that inspired Microsoft Word, desktop publishing with laser printers, local area networks for workgroups, and the graphical user interface with pull-down menus and a mouse.

Visiting PARC in the early 1980s, Steve Jobs of Apple Computer was so impressed that he hired several PARC scientists. At Apple, they joined a team that created the Lisa—a $10,000 computer released in 1983.

The Lisa, however, was a commercial flop. Well-received and considered a milestone in computer design, the Lisa was too expensive for its market. In the meantime, IBM was running away with Apple's market share in personal computing with the phenomenal success of the IBM personal computer.

In response, a team at Apple wanted to bring PARC-like technology to the masses, in the form of a computer named Macintosh.

The people at Apple developed the Mac with a utopian idealism and a near-religious fervor for changing the world; this computer was to be the "computer for the rest of us."

Yet, the machine the team produced departed significantly from the open-architecture and open-bus philosophy that had done so much to ensure the popularity of Apple's previous product, the Apple II. With a sealed case that users could not open without a special tool, the Mac seemed to be designed to bring user-friendly technology to people, but also to keep the market for expensive peripherals and accessories in Apple's hands.

With the release of the open-bus Macintosh II in 1987, Apple tacitly admitted that the closed-bus architecture of the early Mac was a mistake. By 1989, a healthy support industry had grown up around the Macintosh, with many suppliers providing adapters, monitors, and printers for Macintosh computers.

The earliest Mac had other problems beside the sealed case. Jobs is said to have stated that the average personal computer user did not want a fast computer or a lot of memory—and given that the original Mac was equipped with only 128K of RAM and only one 400K disk drive, the computer reflected this philosophy.

In other ways, however, the Macintosh was technologically advanced. The Mac was the first computer to offer a 32-bit microprocessor, the Motorola 68000, running at a clock speed of 7.8 MHz (a modest improvement over the Intel 8088's 4.77 MHz). A striking innovation was the original Mac's medium-resolution monitor that displayed 512-by-312 black pixels on a paper-white background. Perhaps most importantly, the Mac's application program interface (API) and mouse gave programmers a standard that reduced the learning time for programs.

Although the Macintosh sold well at first, the original Mac never found a mass market, especially in the business context. Pressures inside Apple led to Jobs' departure, and under the leadership of Apple's CEO, John Sculley, Apple made the necessary changes: the Macintosh received more memory (512K in the Mac 512 and 1M in the Mac Plus), hard disks, facilities for communication with corporate mainframes, and a library of business software.

What ensured the Mac's entrance into the business world, however, was the 1986 release of the LaserWriter printer, coupled with the PageMaker page-layout program and high-resolution outline fonts. This technology made desktop publishing possible, and with a major technological advantage over IBM PC-compatible computers, the Macintosh made significant inroads into the world of corporate computing in the closing years of the 1980s.

Because of the brisk market for inexpensive clones, however, 12 IBM PC-compatible computers existed for every Mac in use. A series of successful product innovations in 1989, including high-performance Mac II computers based on the Motorola 68030 microprocessor and the release of a portable

Macintosh, ensured the computer's continuing place in organizational and home computing. See *graphical user interface* and *Motorola 68000*.

Macintosh II   An open-bus, high-performance personal computer introduced by Apple Computer in 1987.

The earliest Mac II featured a Motorola 68020 microprocessor, but computers using the Motorola 68030 running at 15.67 MHz soon replaced the 68020. The Macintosh II computers include the extremely popular Macintosh IIc, and the high-performance Macintosh IIcxi that features a clock speed of 25 MHz.

The Mac II was a significant departure from the Mac's previous closed-bus architecture. For the first time, users could assemble a system using video cards, monitors (including color monitors), and even keyboards derived from non-Apple suppliers. See *Motorola 68030*.

Macintosh Plus   A personal computer introduced by Apple Computer in 1986 with 1M of RAM (upgradable to 8M), a 800K disk drive, and an output port for a SCSI-format hard disk.

The entry-level Macintosh Plus uses the original Mac's microprocessor, the Motorola 68000, and seems slow and outmoded by the standards of more advanced Macs.

▲ **Caution:** Macs using the 68000 microprocessor cannot take advantage of virtual memory and certain other advanced features of Apple's System 7. The sure path to upward compatibility is to purchase a Mac with the Motorola 68030 microprocessor, such as the Macintosh IIcx or Macintosh SE/30. See *Motorola 68000* and *System*.

Macintosh SE   A personal computer introduced by Apple Computer in 1987 with 1M of RAM (expandable to 8M), and two 800K disk drives (or one floppy disk and one hard disk).

The original SE uses a Motorola 68000 microprocessor, but a later version—the high-performance SE/30—features the Motorola 68030 running at 15.67 MHz. See *Motorola 68030*.

MacPaint   The first (and now widely imitated) paint program created for the original Macintosh computer.

macro   A stored list of two or more application program commands that, when retrieved, replays the commands to accomplish a task. Macros automate tedious and often-repeated tasks (such as saving and backing a file up to a floppy) that would otherwise require the user to press several command keys or choose several options from menus.

Some programs provide a macro-recording mode, in which the program records your keystrokes; you then save the recording and play it back when you want. Other programs provide a built-in macro editor that enables you to type and edit the macro commands instead of recording them. Such facilities often amount to a full-fledged software-command language, including a full set of modern control structures such as DO/WHILE loops, IF/THEN/ELSE branches, and other advanced features.

Full-featured application programs such as Microsoft Word, WordPerfect, and Lotus 1-2-3 include macro capabilities. Commercially-available macro programs such as SuperKey or AutoMac III provide macro capabilities for programs that lack them. See *IF/THEN/ELSE* and *DO/WHILE loop.*

MacroMind Director   An animation-development program (MacroMind, Inc.) for Macintosh computers that creates animated sequences including graphics, text, and sound.

MacWrite   The first Macintosh word processing program—an easy-to-use and fast program designed for novice users.

The new version, MacWrite II (from Claris Corporation, an Apple spin-off), is substantially slower, but includes many new features.

magnetic disk   In secondary storage, a random-access storage medium that is the most popular method for storing and retrieving computer programs and data files. In personal computing, common magnetic disks include 5 1/4-inch floppy disks, 3 1/2-inch floppy disks, and hard disks of various sizes.

The disk is coated with a magnetically sensitive material. Like a record player's arm, the magnetic read/write head moves laterally across the surface of the spinning disk, accessing locations of the disk under the disk drive's automatic control. Unlike a record, however, the information stored on a magnetic disk can be repeatedly erased and rewritten, like any other magnetic storage medium. See *3 1/2-inch disk*, *5 1/4 -inch disk*, *disk*, *hard disk*, and *random access*.

magnetic media   In secondary storage, the use of magnetic techniques to store and retrieve data on disks or tapes coated with magnetically sensitive materials.

Like iron filings on a sheet of waxed paper, these materials are re-oriented when a magnetic field passes over them. During write operations, the read/write head emits a magnetic field that re-orients the magnetic materials on the disk or tape so that they are positively or negatively charged, corresponding to a bit of data. During read operations, the read/write head senses the magnetic polarities encoded on the tape.

magnetic tape   In secondary storage, a high-capacity mass storage and backup medium.

Although magnetic tape drives must use slow sequential access techniques, magnetic tape is inexpensive and offers a cost-effective way to store massive amounts of data; one role of tape can store up to 100 megabytes of data. Magnetic tape drives are available for IBM Personal Computers and compatibles. See *sequential access*.

mail merge   A utility common in full-featured word processing programs that draws information from a database—usually a mailing list—to print multiple copies of a document. Each copy contains one or part of one of the database records and text that does not vary from copy to copy.

The most common application of the mail merge utility is

the generation of personalized form letters. A personalized form letter contains text that you send to all recipients, but mail merge has personalized the letter with the correspondent's name and address. You also may personalize the salutation.

In a mail-merge application, you use the word processing program to create the database, called the secondary file or data document, and you create a primary file (sometimes called a main document) that contains the text you want to send. In place of the correspondent's name and address, however, you type codes that refer to fields in the name-and-address database. Finally, you give a command that prints one copy of the primary file for each record in the database.

→ **Tip:** Most programs enable you to perform conditional merging that prints an optional passage of text if a database record meets a specified condition.

mailbox   In electronic mail, a storage location that holds messages addressed to an individual until he or she accesses the system. An on-screen message informs the user that mail is waiting.

mainframe   A multiuser computer designed to meet the computing needs of a large organization.

Originally, the term mainframe referred to the metal cabinet that housed the central processing unit (CPU) of early computers. The term came to be used generally to refer to the large, central computers developed in the late 1950s and 1960s to meet the accounting and information-management needs of large organizations. The largest mainframes can handle thousands of dumb terminals and use gigabytes of secondary storage.

Rather than differentiating such machines by size alone, experts increasingly differentiate them by function: a mainframe meets the computing needs of an entire organization, and a minicomputer meets the needs of a department within an organization. By accepting this definition, one must concede that a minicomputer should be termed a mainframe if a small business uses it as its sole computing resource. The boundaries between the two types of computers are blurring. See *minicomputer, personal computer*, and *workstation*.

main program   In programming, the part of the program containing the master sequence of instructions, unlike the subroutines, procedures, and functions that the main program calls.

main storage   *See random-access memory (RAM).*

male connector   In computer cables, a cable terminator and connection device in which the pins protrude from the connector's surface. See *female connector*.

management information system (MIS)   A computer system, usually based on a mainframe or minicomputer, designed to provide management personnel with up-to-date information on the organization's performance.

manual recalculation   In a spreadsheet program, a recalculation method that suspends the recalculation of values after you change them until you press a key that forces recalculation to take place.

Most spreadsheet programs recalculate all values within the spreadsheet after you change the contents of an individual cell. If you are using a slow computer and creating a large spreadsheet, you may want to choose the Manual Recalculation mode as you enter data.

▲ **Caution:** After you enter data or labels in the Manual Recalculation mode, be sure to recalculate the spreadsheet and turn automatic recalculation on again. If you do not, you may forget that you chose manual recalculation, and the spreadsheet may display an incorrect result after you make additional changes.

The latest generation of spreadsheet software offers background recalculation, in which the keyboard does not lock up as recalculation occurs. With these spreadsheet programs, such as Lotus 1-2-3 Release 3, you do not need to risk using manual recalculation. See *automatic recalculation.*

map   A representation of data stored in memory. See *bit map.*

mapping   The process of converting data encoded in one format or device to another format or device.

In database management, for example, the database index provides a way of mapping the actual records (which are stored on disk in a fixed order) to the display screen in ways useful to the user.

mask   A pattern of symbols or characters that, when imposed on a data field, limits the kinds of characters that the user can type into the field.

In a database management program, for example, the mask Az enables the user to type any alphabetical character, uppercase or lowercase, but not numbers or other symbols.

master boot record   See *boot record.*

mass storage   See *secondary storage.*

master document   In WordPerfect, for example, a method of linking two or more documents so that the program paginates all the documents as a unit and produces one table of contents and an index. See *chained printing.*

masthead   In desktop publishing, the section of a newsletter or magazine that gives the details of its staff, ownership, advertising, subscription prices, and so on.

math coprocessor   See *numeric coprocessor.*

MD   See *MKDIR (MD).*

mean time between failures (MTBF)   The statistical average operating time between the start of a component's life and the time of its first electronic or mechanical failure.

➔ **Tip:** You should not take MTBF figures too seriously

when comparison shopping. The figures stem from laboratory tests performed under extreme conditions; the results then are statistically extrapolated to determine the MTBF. Little pressure exists for manufacturers to use an extrapolation procedure that revises the MTBF figure downward.

mechanicals   In desktop publishing, the final pages or boards with pasted-up galleys of type and line art, sometimes with acetate or tissue overlays for color separations and notes, which you send to the offset printer. See *camera-ready copy* and *desktop publishing (DTP)*.

media   The plural of medium. See *secondary storage medium*.

megabyte (M)   Pronounced "megga´-bite." A unit of memory measurement equal to approximately one million bytes (1,048,576 bytes).

megaflop   A benchmark used to rate professional workstations and scientific mainframe or minicomputers; a megaflop is equal to one million floating point operations per second.

megahertz (MHz)   A unit of measurement equal to one million electrical vibrations or cycles per second. Commonly used to compare the clock speeds of computers.

One million cycles per second sounds impressive, but it actually takes microprocessors three or four clock cycles to execute one instruction. A 1 MHz computer, in fact, is too slow by today's standards; even the 4.77 MHz clock speed of the original IBM personal computer is considered sluggish. Clock speeds of 16 MHz, 20 MHz, 25 MHz, and even 33 MHz are increasingly common in personal computing. See *clock speed* and *hertz (Hz)*.

membrane keyboard   A flat and inexpensive keyboard covered with a dust- and dirt-proof plastic sheet on which only the two-dimensional outline of computer keys appears.

The user presses the plastic sheet and engages a switch hidden beneath. Accurately typing on a membrane keyboard is more difficult, but such keyboards are needed in restaurants or other locations where users may not have clean hands.

memory   The computer's primary storage (random-access memory, or RAM, for example), as distinguished from its secondary storage (disk drives, for example). See *primary storage* and *secondary storage.*

memory address   A code number that specifies a specific location in a computer's random-access memory. See *random-access memory (RAM).*

memory cache   See *cache memory.*

memory controller gate array   Synonymous with MultiColor Graphics Array (MCGA), a video display standard of the lowend IBM Personal System/2.

memory-management program   A utility program that increases the apparent size of random-access memory (RAM) by making expanded memory, extended memory, or virtual memory available for the execution of programs.

Memory-management programs include utilities provided with expanded memory boards, windowing environments such as Microsoft Windows, and virtual memory programs that set aside a portion of a hard disk and treat it as a RAM extension.

memory map   An arbitrary allocation of segments of a computer's primary storage that defines which areas the computer can use for specific purposes.

Although the Intel 8088 microprocessor can use 1M of RAM, a portion of this potential memory space is reserved for the system's use of such functions as the keyboard buffer and display adapters. User programs may use the remaining 640K of base memory.

This decision, although arbitrary, is irrevocable if DOS is involved, because DOS and its application programs cannot operate unless the memory map remains exactly the way it was laid out when IBM designed the personal computer.

memory word   See *word.*

memory-resident program   See *terminate-and-stay-resident (TSR) program.*

menu   An on-screen display that lists the choices available to the user. See *pull-down menu.*

menu-driven program   A program that provides you with menus for choosing program options so that you do not need to memorize commands. See *command-driven program.*

MFM   See *modified frequency modulation (MFM) recording.*

micro   See *microcomputer.*

Micro Channel Bus   A proprietary 32-bit expansion-bus architecture introduced by IBM for its high-end PS/2 computers. The Micro Channel Bus is not downwardly compatible with previous bus architectures.

Given the achievement of 32-bit microprocessors such as the Intel 80386 and 80486, the AT expansion bus, with its 16-bit data bus structure, was destined to receive competition from a true, 32-bit expansion bus.

Almost all non-IBM 80386 computers use a 32-bit bus structure only on the motherboard, where the RAM is linked to the microprocessor. Outside the motherboard, these computers use the 16-bit AT expansion bus, for which a huge supply of cheap peripherals is available. But the improvement of PCs clearly calls for a 32-bit expansion bus. In an attempt to define a 32-bit bus standard, IBM introduced Micro Channel Architecture (MCA) in 1987 and used the Micro Channel Bus on its high-end PS/2 models.

The MCA standard is not downwardly compatible with existing peripherals and adapters designed for the AT expansion bus. Some industry analysts, therefore, believe MCA was designed primarily to recapture for IBM part of the lucrative market for peripherals and adapters. But the MCA bus has many technical advantages, including the capability of using 32-bit peripherals, higher speed, greater reliability, and even the capability of using more than one central processing unit (CPU) in one computer.

IBM has offered the technology to clone makers under a licensing scheme, but few have taken IBM up on the offer. Instead, the major manufacturers of IBM-compatibles have

offered their own 32-bit bus design, called Extended Industry
Standard Architecture (EISA), which has most of MCA's benefits but also is compatible with peripherals and adapters designed for the AT expansion bus. See *Extended Industry
Standard Architecture (EISA)*.

micro manager   The person responsible for managing the
acquisition, modification, and maintenance of an organization's personal computers. The micro manager also trains
users to use application programs.

micro-to-mainframe   The linkage of personal computer to
mainframe or minicomputer networks.

microcomputer   Any computer with its arithmetic-logic unit
(ALU) and control unit contained on one integrated circuit
called a microprocessor.

When personal computers first appeared in the mid- to
late-1970s, people often referred to them as microcomputers,
because their CPUs were microprocessors. Microcomputers
were designed as single-user machines. For the first time,
microcomputers placed the processing circuitry entirely under the end user's control. Many computing professionals,
however, did not take microcomputers seriously at first. For
them, "microcomputer" had the connotation of an amusing
toy.

Since the mid-1980s, the distinction between minicomputers (as multiuser computers) and microcomputers (as
single-user computers) has become blurry. Many microcomputers are substantially more powerful than the mainframes of just 10 years ago. You can transform some of
today's more powerful microcomputers into minicomputers
by equipping them with remote terminals. Also, many of
today's minicomputers use microprocessors.

An attempt was made recently to put a mainframe on one
large chip but failed. Theoretically, however, it is possible,
and someday, someone will succeed. Technological change
has made the distinction between microcomputers and minicomputers all but meaningless.

Differentiating among these machines by the function they are designed to perform makes the most sense.

- Centralized Computing Systems. Designed for use by several users simultaneously, most mainframe and minicomputer systems meet the needs of an organization or a department within an organization. The emphasis in such computer systems is on keeping programs, data, and processing capabilities under central control, so that end users gain access to these systems through remote terminals.

- Stand-alone Computers. Designed for single-user applications, a stand-alone computer such as a personal computer is a self-contained, standalone microcomputer that does not rely on external resources such as a central database. A PC is ideal for personal, home, or private use by an individual who does not need to share computing resources with other people.

- Distributed Computing Systems. In a distributed system, the object is to get computing power to the user without giving up the means to share external computing resources, such as access to a central database. An example of a distributed computing system is a network of professional workstations.

  A professional workstation is an advanced microcomputer that contains the advanced display and processing circuitry needed by professionals such as engineers, financial planners, and architects. Because their computers are linked in a computer communication network, these professionals can send messages to each other using their computers, share expensive printers, and create a common pool of data and programs.

Today's advanced personal computers are powerful enough to migrate around these categories with ease. You can use most powerful PCs, for example, as centralized systems with remote terminals. These machines are as powerful as the professional workstations of five years ago, and can work smoothly in a distributed computing system.

microdisk   See *3 1/2-inch disk.*

microprocessor   An integrated circuit that contains the arith-
metic/logic unit (ALU) and control unit of a computer's central processing unit (CPU). See *Intel 8088, Intel 8086, Intel
80286, Intel 80386, Intel 80386SX, Intel 80486, Motorola
68000, Motorola 68020,* and *Motorola 68030*

Microsoft Corporation   A major personal computer software
firm located in Bellevue, Washington.

Founded in 1975 by two ex-college students, Bill Gates
and Paul Allen, Microsoft's first product was a BASIC interpreter for the Altair 8080 microcomputer. The firm did well
with BASIC, but its early success was only a prelude to the
rapid growth that followed IBM's selection of Microsoft to
develop the operating system for the IBM Personal Computer.

This system, called PC DOS when sold directory to IBM
and separately marketed by Microsoft as MS-DOS, is now the
most popular computer operating system in the world.
Microsoft has released an operating system, OS/2, for the
new generation of personal computers based on the Intel
80286 and Intel 80386 and later microprocessors. Linked with
a graphical user interface package, Presentation Manager,
that functions as a shell for OS/2, the operating system has
been slow to gain acceptance.

Microsoft has met with market success with several pro-
gramming languages and application programs. Microsoft
Word is second only to WordPerfect in the world of IBM and
IBM PC-compatible word processing programs, and Excel,
Microsoft's graphics spreadsheet program, dominates the
Macintosh software market. See *MS-DOS, Microsoft Word,*
and *Microsoft Excel.*

Microsoft Excel   A graphics-oriented spreadsheet program
developed by Microsoft Corporation for IBM PC-compatible
computers (running Microsoft Windows) and the Macintosh
computer.

Unlike character-based spreadsheets such as Lotus 1-2-3
Release 2.2 or 3.0, Excel enables the user to use multiple

typefaces, type sizes, object-oriented graphics, shading, and even color; you can include business charts and graphs in the output.

The IBM PC-compatible version has made modest inroads against Lotus 1-2-3; in the Macintosh environment, in which Lotus 1-2-3 is at the time of this writing not available, Microsoft Excel almost completely dominates the spreadsheet market. See *Wingz*.

Microsoft Windows A windowing environment and application user interface (API) for DOS that brings to IBM-format computing some of the graphical user interface features of the Macintosh, such as pull-down menus, multiple typefaces, desk accessories (a clock, calculator, calendar, and notepad, for example), and the capability of moving text and graphics from one program to another via a clipboard (see fig. M.1).

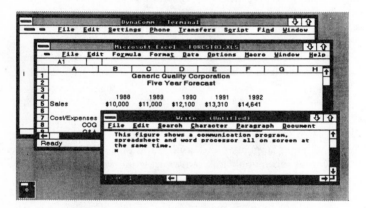

Fig. M.1. The Windows desktop with several open applications.

The history of Windows betrays the reluctance of users and software developers to move to OS/2, the Microsoft operating system created to replace MS-DOS. Originally, Windows was to be little more than a preview of OS/2's

Presentation Manager. Windows ran the few applications specifically developed for it in a graphical user interface environment, but—like DOS—Windows was tied to the 640K random-access memory limit.

Windows used expanded memory schemes such as the Lotus-Intel-Microsoft Specification 4.0, but the new generation of IBM-format programs needed the technically superior protected mode of the Intel 80286 and 80386 microprocessors, with their 16M of undifferentiated memory space. Microsoft had taken the position that protected-mode programs must be developed for OS/2 and Presentation Manager.

As windowing systems such as DESQview (QuarterDeck Systems) appeared, however, with the capability of running DOS programs in protected mode; Microsoft released a new version of Windows (3.0) that runs DOS applications in protected mode.

The future of OS/2 is in even more doubt—the major incentive for developing OS/2 programs was that OS/2 provided access to the protected mode. Because such access is possible under DOS, however, which millions of people already use, less incentive exists to develop OS/2 applications. DOS may be far from dead.

→ **Tip:** Microsoft Windows comes in different versions according to the microprocessor of your computer. Windows/386 is more powerful than Windows/286, for the following reasons:

- Windows/386 can run several programs simultaneously for true multitasking.

- Windows/386 enables you to cut and paste data between applications.

- The 640K barrier for DOS does not apply to Windows/386.

If you are planning to use Microsoft Windows, do not buy a computer with a 80286 microprocessor. Opt for an 80386, an 80386SX, or an 80486 microprocessor. See *Presentation Manager.*

Microsoft Word   A full-featured word processing program for IBM PC compatibles and the Macintosh computer.

Inspired by an on-screen formatting program called Bravo, developed during the 1970s at Xerox's Palo Alto Research Center (PARC), Microsoft Word brings the what-you-see-is-what-you-get philosophy of word processing to the IBM PC-compatible and Macintosh environments.

With its natural affinities to the Macintosh graphical user interface, the Macintosh version of Microsoft Word has assumed a position of dominance. WordPerfect still leads in the PC market, however.

Version 5 of the PC version of the program offers a list of features competitive with WordPerfect and many features normally associated with page-layout programs, such as the capability of positioning text or graphics on the page so that text flows around. Word for Windows, a new version for the PC similar to the Macintosh version, may escalate the battle for best word processor.

Microsoft Works   An easy-to-use integrated program for Macintosh computers and IBM PC compatibles that offers a word processor with a spelling checker, a spreadsheet with business charts, a flat-file database manager, a macro-recording utility and a telecommunications utility. An object-oriented drawing program is available in the word processor and spreadsheet modes.

Although each of its modules is no match for a full-featured, stand-alone program (such as WordPerfect, Lotus 1-2-3, or dBASE), Works packs an amazing amount of functionality into one package. Each module includes the most frequently used features, omitting the complexity of advanced program functions.

You also can move data around with ease within the program, and the object-oriented drawing program makes printing of attractive-looking output easier. Applications that can be challenging with full-featured programs, such as printing form letters and labels or including a chart in a business report, are easy to accomplish in Works. See *flat-file database management program*, *integrated program*, and *object-oriented graphic*.

MIDI   See *Musical Instrument Digital Interface (MIDI)*.

MIDI port   A port that enables a personal computer to be connected directly to a musical synthesizer.

migration   The movement of users (especially organizational users) from one hardware platform to another.

million instructions per second (MIPS)   Pronounced "mips." A benchmark method for measuring the rate at which a computer executes microprocessor instructions. A computer capable of 0.5 MIPS can execute 500,000 instructions per second.

     ▲ **Caution:** MIPS ratings are associated with sophisticated mainframes and supercomputers; only recently has the performance of personal computers improved to the point that their processing speed can be described in MIPS. However, MIPS measurements inadequately state a computer system's throughput—a performance measurement that takes into account the speed of internal data transfer to and from the memory and the speed of important peripherals such as disk drives. See *benchmark*, *Norton SI*, and *throughput*.

millisecond (ms)   A unit of measurement, equal to one-thousandth of a second, commonly used to specify the access time of hard disk drives. See *access time*.

minicomputer   A multiuser computer designed to meet the needs of a small company or a department. A minicomputer is more powerful than a personal computer but not as powerful as a mainframe. Typically, about 4 to 100 people use a minicomputer simultaneously.

MIPS   See *million instructions per second (MIPS)*.

MIS   See *management information system (MIS)*.

mixed cell reference   In a spreadsheet program, a cell reference in which the column reference is absolute but the row reference is relative ($A9) or in which the row reference is absolute but the column reference is relative (A$9). See *cell reference* and *relative cell reference*.

mixed column/line chart   See *mixed column/line graph.*

mixed column/line graph   In presentation and analytical graphics, a graph that displays one data series using columns and another data series using lines (see fig. M.2).

You use a line graph to suggest a trend over time; a column graph groups data items so that you can compare one to another. In figure M.1, for example, the trend of increased manufacturing costs, displayed by a line, is compared to expenses in three other divisions. As the figure shows, administration costs—once insignificant—have increased disproportionately to other expenses.

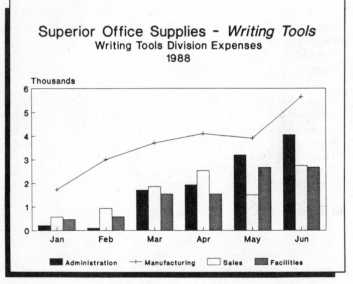

Fig. M.2. A mixed column/line graph.

MKDIR (MD)   In DOS and OS/2, the internal command that creates a subdirectory. See *subdirectory.*

MODE   In DOS and OS/2, an external command that sets the mode of operation for the video display and sets the communication parameters for printers and other devices connected through the serial port.

Often, you do not need to use the MODE command for controlling the video display, because most application programs select the correct mode. You must use the MODE command, however, if you are attempting to connect a serial printer to your computer. For details on how to use the MODE command, consult your printer manual.

➔ **Tip:** Place the MODE command in your AUTOEXEC .BAT file (if you are using DOS) or in your STARTUP.CMD file (if you are using OS/2). See *communications parameters* and *external command.*

mode   The operating state in which you place a program by choosing among a set of exclusive operating options. Within a given mode, certain commands and operations are available, but you may need to change modes to use other commands or operations.

Most programs function in two or more modes. For example, Microsoft Word functions in Edit and Command modes. In Edit mode, you can enter and edit text. In Command mode, you choose and carry out commands.

Lotus 1-2-3 always operates in one of the following modes:

Mode	Description
READY	1-2-3 is waiting for you to enter a command or make a cell entry.
VALUE	You are entering a number or formula.
LABEL	You are entering a label.
EDIT	You can edit the cell entry currently displayed on the control panel.
POINT	You can use the arrow keys to expand the highlight and define a range.
FILES	1-2-3 is waiting for you to choose a file name from the list that appears on-screen.

NAMES	1-2-3 is waiting for you to choose a range name from the list that appears on-screen.
MENU	You are choosing an item from the command menu.
HELP	1-2-3 is displaying a help screen.
ERROR	1-2-3 could not carry out the command or operation you requested; you must press Esc or Enter to confirm the message and continue.
WAIT	1-2-3 is carrying out an operation and cannot respond to additional commands or keyboard input.
FIND	1-2-3 is carrying out a data retrieval operation and cannot respond to additional commands or keyboard input.
STAT	1-2-3 is displaying the status of your worksheet.

➜ **Tip:** A key step in learning a program is to understand its modes and how to switch from one mode to another. Beginners may reach a frustrating roadblock when they inadvertently choose an unfamiliar mode and do not know how to exit the mode. Find out where the mode indicator is located on-screen and learn what the messages mean. See *mode indicator*.

mode indicator   An on-screen message that displays the program's current operating mode.

In Lotus 1-2-3, for example, the mode indicator appears in reverse video at the upper right corner of the screen.

model   A mathematical or pictorial representation of an object (the prototype).

The purpose of constructing the model is to gain a better understanding of the prototype in a cost-effective way. By examining or changing the characteristics of the model, you can draw inferences about the prototype's behavior.

In a spreadsheet model of a business enterprise, for example, you can explore the impact of increasing advertising expenditures on market share. Models, however, should be used with caution. A model is only as good as its underlying assumptions. If these assumptions are incorrect, or if important information is missing from the model, it may not reflect the prototype's behavior accurately.

modem A device that converts the digital signals generated by the computer's serial port to the modulated, analog signals required for transmission over a telephone line and transforms incoming analog signals to their digital equivalents. In personal computing, people frequently use modems to exchange programs and data with other computers, and to access on-line information services such as the Dow Jones News/Retrieval Service.

Modem stands for MOdulator/DEModulator. The modulation is necessary because telephone lines were designed to handle the human voice, which warbles between 300 Hz and 3,000 Hz in ordinary telephone conversations (from a growl to a shriek). The speed at which a modem transmits data is measured in units called bits per second (technically not the same as bauds, although the terms are often used interchangeably). See *acoustic coupler, auto-dial/auto-answer modem, direct-connect modem, echoplex, external-modem, full duplex, half duplex, Hayes command set, Hayes-compatible modem, internal modem, Universal Asynchronous Receiver/Transmitter (UART)*.

modified frequency modulation (MFM) recording A method of recording digital information on magnetic media such as tapes and disks by eliminating redundant or blank areas. Because the MFM technique doubles the storage attained under the earlier frequency-modulation (FM) recording technique, MFM recording usually is referred to as double density.

MFM often is used to describe ordinary hard disk controllers, those conforming to the ST506 standard. MFM refers to the method used to pack data on the disk and is not synonymous with disk drive interface standards such as ST506, SCSI, or ESDI. See *double density* and *run-length limited (RLL) recording.*

Modula-2   A high-level programming language that extends Pascal so that the language simultaneous can execute program modules.

Developed in 1980 by the European computer wizard Niklaus Wirth, the creator of Pascal, Modula-2 is an enhanced version of Pascal that supports the separate compilation of program modules and overcomes many other shortcomings of Pascal. A programmer working on a team can write and compile the module he or she has been assigned, testing the module extensively to make sure that it functions correctly.

Modula-2 is a logical extension of Pascal, a prominent feature of which is the setting aside of procedures and functions in program modules (which cannot, however, be compiled separately).

Although Modula-2 is increasingly popular as a teaching language at colleges and universities, professional software development is dominated by the C language. See *C, modular programming*, *Pascal*, and *structured programming.*

modular accounting package   A collection of accounting programs—one for each of the chief accounting functions (general ledger, accounts payable, accounts receivable, payroll, and inventory, for example)—designed to work together, even though they are not integrated into one program.

Modular accounting programs are computerized versions of traditional accounting practices, in which a firm keeps several ledgers—one for accounts receivable, accounts payable, and a general ledger. You update the general ledger in batches at period intervals after carefully proofing the hard copy for errors. Modular packages generally are sold with several separate programs for each of these functions, and you must follow special procedures to make sure that all the transactions are correctly updated.

These programs have not found a large market in personal computing for two reasons: first, because people with professional accounting experience designed them, these programs often do not reflect the way small-business people keep their books. Second, most of these programs are far from easy to use.

Some of these packages, however, are available with automatic links to point-of-sale terminals—for example, Flexware (Microfinancial Corporation) for Macintosh computers and Excalibur (Armour Systems, Inc.) for IBM PC-compatible computers.

modular programming   A programming style that breaks down program functions into modules, each of which accomplishes one function and contains all the code and variables needed to accomplish that function.

Modular programming is a solution to the problem of very large programs that are difficult to debug and maintain. By segmenting the program into modules that perform clearly defined functions, you can determine the source of program errors more easily.

Modula-2 and some other languages can compile modules separately. A member of a team working on a program, therefore, can write and compile his or her module independent of the whole program and of other team members, making sure that the module works properly before adding it to the larger program.

Modular programming principles have clearly influenced the design of object-oriented programming languages such as SmallTalk and HyperTalk, both of which enable you to create fully functional program objects (such as the buttons in HyperCard) which function so independently that you can copy them from one program to another.

modulation   The conversion of a digital signal to its analog equivalent, especially for the purposes of transmitting signals via telecommunications. See *demodulation* and *modem.*

Moiré distortion   Pronounced "mwah´-ray." An optical illusion, perceived as flickering, that sometimes occurs when you place high-contrast line patterns (such as cross-hatching in pie graphs) too close to one another.

▲ **Caution:** Many business graphics programs produce charts and graphs with undesirable Moiré distortions. You can avoid this problem by choosing no more than two or three cross-hatching patterns and separating them with solid white, gray, or black colors. See *cross-hatching.*

monitor   The complete device that produces an on-screen display, including all necessary internal support circuitry. A monitor also is called a video display unit (VDU) or cathode-ray tube (CRT). See *analog monitor, digital monitor, Enhanced Graphics Display, monochrome monitor,* and *multisync monitor.*

monochrome display adapter (MDA)   A single-color display adapter for IBM PC-compatible computers that displays text (but not graphics) with a resolution of 720 pixels horizontally and 350 pixels vertically, placing characters in a matrix of 7-by-9 pixels. See *Hercules Graphics Adapter.*

monochrome monitor   A monitor that displays one color against a black or white background.

Examples include the IBM monochrome monitor that displays green text against a black background and paper-white VGA monitors that display black text on a white background.

monospace   A typeface such as Courier in which the width of all characters is the same, producing output that looks like typed characters. See *proportional spacing.*

MORE   In DOS and OS/2, a filter command that displays one screen of information from a file and pauses while displaying the message - **More** -. When you press any key, the next screen of information appears.

➔ **Tip:** If file names flash by after you use the DIR command, instead of typing DIR only, use the DIR | MORE command to pipe the output to the MORE filter, so that only one page is displayed at a time. See *filter command* and *input/output redirection*.

motherboard   A large, printed, computer circuit board that contains the computer's central processing unit (CPU), microprocessor support chips, random-access memory, and expansion slots. Synonymous with *logic board*.

Motorola 68000   A microprocessor that processes 32 bits internally, although it uses a 16-bit data bus to communicate with the rest of the computer.

The 68000, with its 32-bit address bus, can address up to 32 gigabytes of random-access memory (RAM). Running at 8 MHz, the 68000 powers the entry-level Macintosh Plus computer and the Macintosh SE.

Motorola 68020   A microprocessor electronically similar to the Motorola 68000, except that this microprocessor uses a full 32-bit architecture and runs at a clock speed of 16 MHz.

The 68020 powers the original Macintosh II, displaced by newer models using the Motorola 68030 chip. Macintosh system software limits the amount of usable RAM to 8M (Apple's System 7 should boost this amount to 4 gigabytes).

Motorola 68030   A full 32-bit microprocessor capable of running at substantially higher clock speeds than its predecessors (the Motorola 68000 and 68020). The 68030 includes special features for virtual memory management.

The 68030 incorporates a chip that controls page-mode RAM, so that any 68030-equipped Macintosh can implement the advanced memory management features of System.

➔ **Tip:** If you are buying a Mac, purchase a machine based on the 68030. The chip includes circuits that you need to take full advantage of the next generation of Macintosh software. See *clock speed*, *page-mode RAM*, and *System*.

mouse   An input device, equipped with one or more control buttons, housed in a palm-sized case and designed to roll about on the table next to the keyboard. As the mouse moves, its circuits relay signals that move a pointer on-screen.

The simplest of all mouse functions is repositioning the cursor: you point to the cursor's new location and click the mouse button. You also can use the mouse to choose commands from menus, select text for editing purposes, move objects, and draw pictures on-screen.

The mouse was developed by researchers to make computers easier to use. Instead of forcing users to memorize long lists of keyboard commands, they reasoned, displaying a menu or list of commands on-screen would be easier. The user then could point the cursor at the desired command and click the mouse button.

Most people who have used a mouse agree that it makes the computer easier to use. Others, however, do not like to take their fingers away from the keyboard. Programs that use the mouse often include keyboard equivalents.

Mice are distinguished by the internal mechanism they use to generate their signal and by their means of connection with the computer. Two types of internal mechanisms are popular:

- Mechanical mouse. This mouse has a rubber-coated ball on the underside of the case. As you move the mouse, the ball rotates, and optical sensors detect the motion. (Many companies, therefore, advertise their mice as optomechanical.) You can use a mechanical mouse on virtually any surface, although a mouse pad made of special fabric usually gives the best results.

- Optical mouse. This mouse registers its position by detecting reflections from a light-emitting diode that directs a beam downward. You must have a special metal pad to reflect the beam properly, and you cannot move the mouse beyond the pad.

Mice are connected to the computer in the following three ways:

- Bus mouse. You connect a bus mouse to the computer with an adapter pressed into one of the computer's expansion slots.

- Serial mouse. You connect a serial mouse to the computer with the standard serial port.

- Regular mouse. Most mice are connected to a special mouse port on the computer.

➔ **Tip:** Mechanical mice are prone to collect dirt within their internal mechanisms. If too much debris accumulates, the pointer may behave erratically. You usually can clean a mechanical mouse. Turn the mouse over and rotate the ball-retainer ring. Clean the ball and the ball rollers with a cotton swab moistened in rubbing alcohol. Blow dust out of the ball chamber and reassemble the mouse.

MS-DOS   The standard, single-user operating system of IBM and IBM-compatible computers that runs the computer's microprocessor in real mode.

Introduced in 1981, MS-DOS (short for Microsoft Disk Operating System) is marketed by IBM as PC-DOS; the two systems are almost indistinguishable.

MS-DOS's origins lie in CP/M—the operating system for 8-bit computers popular in the late 1970s. The original version of what was to become MS-DOS was created by a small Seattle firm for experimental purposes. Because Microsoft had landed an IBM contract to create an operating system for the IBM personal computer, Microsoft purchased and developed the program.

The similarity between MS-DOS and CP/M is no accident—MS-DOS was designed to enable an inexpensive and fast conversion of popular CP/M business programs to the new IBM personal computer. IBM analysts thought that their new computer would not succeed unless software publishers could rewrite their programs with a minimum of expense.

The chief advantages of MS-DOS over CP/M are that some commands were improved and the user could not crash the computer by removing a disk before rebooting the system. In addition, Version 2.0 of MS-DOS added UNIX-like directories and subdirectories to the system, enhancing its usefulness with hard disks. Even the most recent versions of MS-DOS are still compatible with Version 2.0.

Although the IBM personal computer architecture supports up to 640K of user RAM, the earliest IBM PCs were sold with 64K (a standard figure in 1981). MS-DOS was designed as an extremely compact operating system that could operate under severely limited memory conditions.

MS-DOS, therefore, provides little in the way of an application program interface (API) or a set of standard routines that applications can use to handle the display of information on-screen. Individual applications are free to configure the screen and keyboard as they like, and the result is a jumble of confusing and mutually incompatible user interfaces.

Operating systems that offer an API—the Macintosh System, for example—encourage the development of programs that use the same user actions and interface procedures for common operations such as selecting and deleting text, using menus, opening and closing applications, and printing.

Recognizing the advantages of an API, Microsoft developed Windows, an optional API for MS-DOS. Very few programs took advantage of the early less-powerful versions of Microsoft Windows.

MS-DOS is a command-line operating system with an interface that requires users to memorize a limited set of commands, arguments, and syntax to use MS-DOS computers successfully.

After mastering MS-DOS commands, however, users can achieve a high degree of control over the operating system's capabilities—including setting file attributes, creating automatically executed batch files, and developing semi-automated backup procedures.

The most severe limitation of MS-DOS is the 640K RAM barrier that the operating system imposes on IBM PC-compatible computing. When the system was devised, 640K seemed like a copious amount of memory. However, the creation of applications such as Lotus 1-2-3 and the advent of terminate-and-stay resident (TSR) programs soon demonstrated that 640K was barely adequate even for a standalone workstation.

The use of TSR programs revealed another severe limitation of MS-DOS: the system was not designed for multiprogramming or running more than one program at a time. MS-DOS, therefore, does not prevent one program from invading the memory space used by another. Such invasions almost invariably result in crashes or unpredictable results.

Concluding that MS-DOS is about to go the way of CP/M, however, would be wrong. Microsoft has developed an operating system called OS/2 to break the 640K RAM barrier. Also, OS/2 simultaneously can run more than one program. The system includes an application-programming interface in the form of Presentation Manager, the OS/2 version of Microsoft Windows.

Software publishers, however, have been reluctant to develop programs for OS/2 because the majority of IBM PC-compatible computers that cannot run the system.

Through the use of extended memory, expanded memory, and memory-management programs, the 640K RAM barrier under MS-DOS has been broken. Microsoft Windows also gives many of OS/2's capabilities to DOS users.

In spite of the confusion about the status of MS-DOS and OS/2 in IBM PC-compatible computing, millions of computer users use MS-DOS daily; even with its limitations, MS-DOS is without question the most widely used operating system in existence.

MultiColor Graphics Array (MCGA) A video display standard of IBM's Personal System/2. MCGA adds 64 gray-scale shades to the CGA standard and provides the EGA standard resolution of 640 x 350 pixels with 16 possible   colors.

MultiFinder A utility program supplied by Apple Computer that extends the Finder's capabilities so that the Macintosh can run more than one application at a time.

The Finder is the Macintosh operating system's shell; the program that handles communication with the user. The Finder can handle only one program at a time.

With MultiFinder, the Macintosh becomes a multiple-loading operating system with some limited capabilities to perform tasks in the background, such as downloading information via telecommunications and carrying out background printing.

Contrary to common belief, MultiFinder is not a true multitasking operating system; when you activate one application, the other application freezes. See *context switching, multiple- loading operating system, multitasking,* and *shell.*

multilaunching   In a local area network, the opening of an application program by more than one user at a time.

multilevel sort   In database management, a sort operation that uses two or more data fields to determine the order in which data records are arranged.

To perform a multilevel sort, you identify two or more fields as sort keys—fields used for ordering records, and you arrange the records in an order of primacy. The first sort key (called the primary sort key) determines the overall order in which data records are arranged.

In a library's bibliographic database, for example, the primary sort key is LAST_NAME. All records are alphabetized by the author's last name. The second sort key—FIRST_NAME—comes into play when two or more records have the same last name. A third sort key—PUB_DATE (publication date)—is used when two or more records have the the same last name and the same first name. The following is a sample of the properly sorted output:

```
Smith, Bill
    1986 French Soups
Smith, Fern
    1982 Organic Gardening
Smith, Jack
    1983 The American Space Program
    1985 The Soviet Space Program
    1987 Private Ventures into Space
```

→ **Tip:** Use a multilevel sort when one sort key cannot resolve the order of two or more records in your database.

MultiMate   A word processing program marketed by Ashton-Tate that emulates the Wang dedicated word processing machines.

multimedia   The presentation of information on a computer using graphics, sound, animation, and text. See *animation*, *computer-assisted instruction (CAI)*, and *hypermedia*.

multiple-loading operating system   An operating system that enables you to start more than one program at a time; only one of the programs is active at any one time, however. You switch from one program to another by pressing a key. See *context switching* and *MultiFinder*.

multiplex   To combine or interleave messages in a communications channel.

multiplexing   In local area networks, the simultaneous transmission of multiple messages in one channel.

A network capable of multiplexing can enable more than one computer to access the network at the same time. Multiplexing increases the cost of a network, however, because multiplexing devices must be included that handle the combination of signals into a single channel for transmission, and the reverse process for receiving. See *frequency division multiplexing*, *local area network (LAN)*, and *time division multiplexing*.

multisync monitor   A color monitor capable of adjusting to a range of input frequencies so that it can work with a variety of display adapters.

multitasking   The execution of more than one program at a time on a computer system. Multitasking should not be confused with multiple program loading, in which two or more programs are present in RAM, but only one program executes at a time.

The active or foreground task responds to the keyboard, while the background task continues to run (but without your active control).

In a multitasking operating system, terminate-and-stay resident (TSR) programs are unnecessary, because you simultaneously can run any programs you want to, as long as the computer has enough memory.

Critics of multitasking operating systems say that users of stand-alone workstations have little need for multi-programming operations. Programs that can print or download files in the background, however, hint at the power of multitasking. Imagine the capability of writing with a word processor while a spreadsheet recalculates and a database sorts.

Among the operating systems or shells that provide multitasking are OS/2 and Microsoft Windows. See *multiple loading operating system.*

multiuser system   A computer system that enables more than one person to access programs and data at the same time.

Each user is equipped with a terminal. If the system has just one central processing unit, a technique called time-sharing provides multiple access. A time-sharing system cycles access to the processing unit among users.

Personal computers equipped with advanced micro-processors such as the Intel 80486 are sufficiently powerful to serve as the nucleus of a multiuser system. Such systems typically are equipped with the UNIX operating system, designed for multiuser systems.

Such technical advances have helped to blur the distinction between personal computers and minicomputers. If a minicomputer is a multiuser system designed to meet the needs of 4 to 100 people, multiuser computers based on 80386 and 80486 chips are legitimate minicomputers. Given such advances, the term personal computer usually is reserved for computers dedicated to stand-alone applications.

➔ **Tip:** If you are considering installing a system that more than one person will use, familiarize yourself with the pros and cons of the two alternatives: multiuser systems and local area networks. See *local area network (LAN)*.

Musical Instrument Digital Interface (MIDI)   Pronounced "middy." A standard communications protocol for the exchange of information between computers and musical synthesizers.

MIDI provides tools that many composers and musicians say are becoming almost indispensable. With a synthesizer and a computer equipped with the necessary software and a MIDI port, a musician can transcribe a composition into musical notation by playing the composition at the keyboard. After being placed into computer-represented form, virtually every aspect of the digitized sound—pitch, attack, delay time, tempo, and more—can be edited and altered.

n

nanosecond (ns)   A unit of time equal to one billionth of a second.

Far beyond the range of human perception, nanoseconds are relevant to computers. For example, an advertisement for 120 ns RAM chips means that the RAM chips respond within 120 nanoseconds.

Macintosh computers with the 68030 microprocessor need faster RAM chips, 80 ns or better. See *millisecond (ms)*.

native code   See *machine language*.

native file format   The default file format an application program uses to store data on disk.

The format is often a proprietary file format that cannot be read by other programs. However, many programs can save data in several formats. See *American Standard Code for Information Interchange (ASCII)*, *file format*, and *proprietary file format*.

natural language   A naturally occurring language such as Spanish, French, German, or Tamil, unlike an artificial language such as a computer programming language.

Computer scientists are working to improve computers so that they can respond to natural language. Human language systems are so complex that no one theoretical model of a natural language grammar system has yet to gain widespread acceptance among linguists. The complexity of human languages, coupled with the lack of understanding about precisely what information is needed to decode naturally occurring human sentences, makes it difficult to devise computer programs to understand natural language input. The recognition of human speech patterns also poses substantial problems in pattern recognition, and progress in solving these problems has been slow.

▲ **Caution:** Computer programs such as Lotus HAL occasionally are marketed with the claim that they can accept natural language input, but the user must exercise caution in phrasing input so that it conforms to fairly strict syntax guidelines. Because no computer program yet devised can understand the meaning of spoken words, natural-language programs must use relatively crude pattern-matching techniques to accept such input.

natural recalculation   In a spreadsheet program, a recalculation order that performs worksheet computations in the manner logically dictated by the formulas you place in cells. If the value of a formula depends on references to other cells that contain formulas, the program calculates the other cells first. See *column-wise recalculation, optimal recalculation*, and *row-wise recalculation*.

near-letter quality (NLQ)   A dot-matrix printing mode that prints typewriter-quality characters. As a result, printers using this mode print slower than other dot-matrix printers.

nested structure   A structure in which one control structure is positioned within another. See *DO/WHILE loop*.

NETNORTH   A Canadian wide-area network fully integrated with BITNET and that performs the same functions as BITNET. See *BITNET*.

NetWare   A network operating system, manufactured by Novell, for local area networks.

NetWare links hardware and accommodates more than 90 types of network interface cards, 30 network architectures, and several communications protocols. Versions are available for IBM PC compatibles and Macintosh computers.

network administrator   In local area networks, the person responsible for maintaining the network and assisting end users.

network architecture   The complete set of hardware, software, and cabling standards that specifies the design of a local area network. See *network topology.*

network interface card   An adapter that enables you to hook a network cable directly to a microcomputer.

Rather than forcing network communications to occur through the serial port, a network interface card takes advantage of a microcomputer's internal bus to make network communications easier (see fig. N.1).

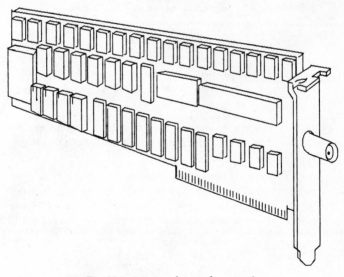

Fig. N.1. A network interface card.

The board includes encoding and decoding circuitry and a receptacle for a network cable connection. Because data is transmitted more rapidly within the computer's internal bus, a network interface card enables the network to operate at higher speeds than it would if delayed by the serial port.

Networks using interface cards (such as EtherNet and ARCnet) can transmit information much faster than networks using serial ports (such as AppleTalk).

network operating system   The system software of a local area network that runs on the file server. The network operating system makes the flow of information among the linked nodes of the network easier.

network server   See *file server.*

network topology   The geometric arrangement of nodes and cable links in a local area network.

Network topologies fall into two categories: centralized and decentralized. In a centralized topology such as a star network, a central computer controls access to the network. This design ensures data security and central management control over the network's contents and activities.

In a decentralized topology such as a bus network or ring network, no central computer controls the network's activities. Rather, each workstation can access the network independently and establish its own connections with other workstations. See *bus network, ring network,* and *star network.*

network version   A version of an application program specifically modified so that the program can function in a network environment.

In a local area network, you cannot place an application program on a file server and expect the application to function when several people try to use it at once. The licensing agreements of most applications prohibit placing the application on a file server. Network versions of programs, however, are designed for concurrent access. Network versions of transactional application programs—such as database management programs—create and maintain shared files. For example, an invoice-processing program has access to a database of accounts receivable.

The network versions of nontransactional programs—such as word processing programs—include file security features. For example, the word processor can lock files to prevent unauthorized users from gaining access to your documents. See *file locking, file server, local area network (LAN), nontransactional application,* and *transactional application.*

New Century Schoolbook   An easily read typeface developed for magazines and school textbooks. New Century Schoolbook often is offered as a built-in font in PostScript laser printers.

newspaper columns   A page format in which two or more columns of text are printed vertically on the page so that the text flows down one column and continues at the top of the next (see fig. N.2).

Sometimes called snaking columns to suggest the flow of text, newspaper columns differ from side-by-side columns in which paragraphs are printed in linked pairs—one to the left and one to the right.

Many word processing programs and all page-layout programs can print multiple-column text, but only the best programs can display multiple columns on-screen while you edit the text. High-end word processing programs such as Microsoft Word and WordPerfect do a good job of producing newspaper columns, but you need a page-layout program such as Ventura Publisher to justify the columns vertically so that all columns align precisely with the bottom margin.

Vertical justification is by no means necessary, but newspapers and magazines often use vertical justification to create a professional-looking effect. You can accomplish vertical justification manually with a word processing program, but the operation is tedious, and the columns may fall out of alignment if you add or delete text.

New Drivers School Location

There's been a change in the location for this year's drivers school for the Windy City Chapter, and I know you'll love this one! Instead of going to Blackhawk Farms, we'll be going up to Road America in beautiful Elkhart Lake, Wisconsin.

This way, all you hotshoes will have about 4.5 miles instead of 2.5 miles to thrash your Bimmers around the track. It'll also be easier on your brakes than Blackhawk, due to the longer straights that'll give them a chance to cool off between turns.

The dates will remain the same, May 21 and 22. Lodging, as always, will be available at Siebkens and Barefoot Bay in Elkhart Lake, or at Motels in Sheboygan or Fond du Lac. Remember, you must make your own reservations. Remember also that Siebkens is basically a summertime resort, which means NO HEAT in the rooms. Also no phones and no credit cards. But LOTS of ATMOSPHERE. The rates at both Siebkens and Barefoot Bay are quite reasonable, $24 and $48 (single/double) at Siebkens and $59.95 at Barefoot Bay for either single or double. Driving directions to Elkhart Lake will be included with your registration package, along with a map of the area.

SATURDAY DINNER

There'll be dinner at Siebkens Saturday night, with a choice of fish, duck or prime rib. The cost will be $15 plus tip. We'll have a cash bar also, but remember you'll want a clear head the next morning or your Bimmer will start playing tricks on you. So go easy on the liquid stuff.

If you want to join us for dinner, let Registration know Saturday morning what your choice of entree is, otherwise there'll be no food waiting for you.

PRETECH AT LEO'S

Pretech will as always be at Leo Franchi's Midwest Motor Sports. The date is April 23. This will give you a chance to get anything fixed before the drivers school. A tech sheet is enclosed with the registration package. Be sure to fill it out and bring it along. There is no charge for the tech inspection. We're planning to start at 9 a.m. and go until everybody is done.

If you miss the tech at Leo's, you'll have to go to your favorite mechanic and bring proof of the inspection and any repairs that were made. Remember, NO TECH - NO TRACK.

We look forward to seeing you all at Elkhart Lake.

Enjoy!

Fig. N.2. Newspaper columns.

➔ **Tip:** Research on legibility demonstrates that a line should have approximately 55 to 60 characters (about nine or 10 words) for optimum readability. If line lengths exceed this amount, break up the text into two or more columns.

New Wave   A DOS-compatible windowing environment and operating shell developed by Hewlett-Packard for its IBM PC-compatible Vectra personal computers.

NeXT   An innovative, UNIX-based professional workstation developed by NeXT, Inc.

Originally conceived as a special-purpose workstation for universities, the NeXT computer is the brainchild of Steve Jobs, the founder of Apple. The NeXT's innovative features include a 256M erasable optical disk drive, a graphical user interface for the UNIX operating system, a PostScript display screen, a PostScript printer that prints at 400 dpi, and high-fidelity sound.

The NeXT computer, however, may not achieve wide-spread success because of its price and because some software publishers have difficulty distributing software on optical disks. The NeXT may find a niche in high-end desktop publishing, where its features and price are competitive.

NLQ   See *near-letter quality (NLQ)*.

no parity   In asynchronous communications, a communications protocol that disables parity checking and leaves no space for the parity bit. See *asynchronous communications communications protocol, parity bit,* and *parity checking.*

node   A connection point in a local area network that can create, receive, or repeat a message.

In personal computer networks, nodes include repeaters, file servers, and shared peripherals. In common usage, however, the term node is synonymous with workstation. See *network topology* and *workstation.*

noise   The extraneous or random electrical content of a communications channel, unlike the signal, which carries information. All communications channels have noise, and if the noise is excessive, data loss can occur.

Telephone lines are particularly noisy. The error-free transmission of data via telecommunications, therefore, requires communications programs that can perform error-checking operations to make sure that the data being received is not corrupted.

nonimpact printer   A printer that forms a text or graphics image by spraying or fusing ink to the page.

Nonimpact printers include inkjet printers, laser printers, and thermal printers. All nonimpact printers are considerably quieter than impact printers, but nonimpact printers cannot print multiple copies using carbon paper. See *impact printer*, *inkjet printer*, *laser printer*, and *thermal printer*.

nonprocedural language   See *declarative language*.

nontransactional application   In a local area network, an application program that produces data that you do not need to record and keep in one common-shared database so that all network participants can have access. (For example, most of the work done with word processing programs is nontransactional).

Norton SI   In IBM PC-compatible computing, a widely-used benchmark measurement of a computer's throughput.

Short for Norton System Information, Norton SI is a program included in the Norton Utilities. The program's composite performance index provides a balanced picture of a computer system's throughput, including its internal-processing speed and the speed of peripherals such as disk drives.

The original IBM XT provides the base reference of 1.0. 80386-based machines operating at clock speeds of 33 MHz can achieve Norton SI ratings of 40 and higher; the 80386 machines run 40 times faster than the original XT. See *benchmark*, *million instructions per second (MIPS)*, and *throughput*.

Norton Utilities   A best-selling package (from Peter Norton Computing) of utility programs for IBM PC-compatible computers, including a benchmark program that measures a computer's throughput, an undelete program that restores files accidentally deleted from the disk, and management utilities for directories and subdirectories.

Novell network   A local area network that uses the Novell NetWare network operating system.

NSFNET   A wide-area network developed by the Office of Advanced Scientific Computing at the National Science Foundation (NSF). NSFNET was developed to take over the civilian functions of the Defense Department's ARPANET, which, for security reasons, has been closed to public access.

NuBus   The high-speed expansion bus of Macintosh II computers. NuBus requires adapters specifically designed for its 96-pin receptacles.

null modem cable   A specially configured serial cable that enables you to connect two computers directly, without the mediation of a modem.

Num Lock key   A toggle key that locks the numeric keypad into a mode in which you can enter numbers. When the Num Lock key is on, the cursor-movement keys are disabled.

On IBM PC-compatible keyboards, the keys on the numeric keypad are labeled with arrows and numbers. You can use these keys to move the cursor and to enter numbers. The gray Num Lock key toggles the keypad back and forth between these two modes.

➔ **Tip:** If you are trying to move the cursor with the cursor-movement keys and you see numbers on-screen, you have pressed Num Lock accidentally. To use the cursor-movement keys, press Num Lock again.

number crunching   Calculation, especially of large amounts of data. (Slang term).

numeric coprocessor   A microprocessor support chip that performs mathematical computations—specifically those using binary-coded decimal (BCD) and floating-point calculations—at speeds of up to 100 times faster than a microprocessor alone.

The Intel numeric coprocessors (8087, 80287, and 80387) are designed to work with their microprocessor counterparts (the 8087 is designed to work the 8088 and 8086, and the 80287 and 80387 are designed to work with the 80286 and 80386, respectively).

Otherwise, all three Intel numeric coprocessors are similar; they are designed to work with 80 bits at a time so that a programmer can express a number of sufficient length to ensure accurate calculations. An innovative feature of the Intel 80486 chip is the numeric coprocessor circuitry on the microprocessor chip.

→ **Tip:** If you work with spreadsheets or any other application that performs calculations intensively, add a numeric coprocessor to your system. You will see substantial gains in the apparent speed of your system without any modification to your software. See *binary coded decimal (BCD)*, *floating-point calculation*, and *microprocessor.*

numeric coprocessor socket   A push-down socket on the motherboard of many personal computers into which you or a dealer can mount a numeric coprocessor, such as the Intel 80287. The coprocessor improves the performance of the computer system when running calculation-intensive applications such as a spreadsheet.

numeric format   In a spreadsheet program, the way in which the program displays numbers in a cell.

With Lotus 1-2-3, for example, you may choose among the following numeric formatting options:

- Fixed. You specify the number of decimal places to display, ranging from 0 to 15. Lotus 1-2-3 rounds numbers that have more decimal places than you chose. If the number of digits exceeds the column width, you see a row of asterisks across the cell.

- Scientific. Displays very large or small numbers using scientific notation (12,460,000,000 appears as 1.25E+11).

- Currency. Displays values with commas and dollar signs. You choose the number of decimal places (0 to 15). If the number of digits exceeds the column width, you see a row of asterisks across the cell.

- Comma. Displays numbers larger than 999 with commas separating thousands; 1-2-3 inserts the commas automatically.

- General. Displays numbers without commas. Does not display trailing zeroes to the right of the decimal point. If the number of digits to the left of the decimal point exceeds the column width, 1-2-3 uses scientific notation. If the number of digits to the right of the decimal point exceeds the column width, 1-2-3 rounds the number.

- +/-. Converts the number to a simple bar graph appearing in the cell, with the number of plus or minus signs equaling the whole-value number of the entry (5 appears as +++++). Plus signs indicate a positive value; negative signs indicate a negative value.

- Percent. Multiplies the value by 100 and adds a percent sign. You choose the number of decimal places (0 to 15). For example, 0.485 appears as 48.5%. If the number of digits exceeds the column width, you see a row of asterisks across the cell.

- Date. Converts a number to a date. The number 32734 is August 14, 1989.

- Text. Displays the formula instead of the value computed by the formula.

- Hidden. Makes the cell entry invisible on-screen. You can see the entry by placing the pointer in the cell and looking at the cell contents indicator. See *cell.*

numeric keypad   A group of keys, usually to the right of the typing area on a keyboard. The keypad is designed for the rapid, touch-typing entry of numerical data.

O

object code   In computer programming, the machine-readable instructions created by a compiler or interpreter from source code.

object-oriented graphic   A graphic image composed of discrete objects such as lines, circles, ellipses, and boxes, that you can move independently.

Object-oriented graphics often are called vector graphics because the program stores them as mathematical formulas for the vectors, or directional lines, that compose the image. Unlike bit-mapped graphics, you can resize object-oriented graphics without introducing distortions.

As figure O.1 shows, increasing the size of a bit-mapped rectangle introduces distortions because you thicken the lines as you increase the overall size. Moreover, the image prints using the printer's highest resolution (up to 300 dpi with laser printers). See *bit-mapped graphic*.

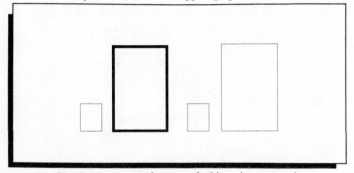

Fig. O.1. A rectangle magnified by a bit-mapped graphics program (left) and an object-oriented graphics program (right).

object-oriented programming language   A nonprocedural programming language in which program elements are conceptualized as objects that can pass messages to each other.

In an object-oriented program, each object has its own data and programming code and is internally self-reliant; the program makes the object part of a larger whole by incorporating it into a hierarchy of layers. Object-oriented programming, therefore, is the ultimate extension of the concept of modular programming.

In object-oriented programming, the modules are independent enough to stand on their own so that you can copy the modules into other programs. This capability raises the possibility of inheritance; you can copy and add some new features to an old object and then move that object to a new program. You do not have to re-create the object.

The objects created in object-oriented programming are excellent tools for program construction because they hide their internal complexity. The objects are self-sufficient and susceptible to copying; you can move the objects around in chunks to compose new programs. Any object-oriented programming language, then, is highly extensible. Object-oriented programming languages also have natural affinities with the graphical user interface. You can display a completed object on-screen as an icon—effectively hiding its complexity—and drag the icon around with a mouse to re-position or copy the object. In HyperCard, for example, when you select and copy a button and paste it on another card, you also copy the script. This technique is extremely powerful and intuitive.

Whether or not object-oriented programming will ever replace conventional programming techniques is far from clear. Object-oriented programming languages require a great deal of memory and execute slowly, compared to languages such as assembly language and C.

The popularity of a language such as C stems from the primitivity of current computing equipment; most people still are working with machines based on Intel 8088 and Motorola 68000 microprocessors, which run so sluggishly that a programmer must find the fastest way of executing an algorithm. In the future, however, a programming language's speed will be less of an issue, and object-oriented programming may find professional applications. See *extensible, modular programming*, and *nonprocedural language*.

oblique Pronounced "oh-bleek." The italic form of a sans-serif typeface. See *sans serif.*

odd parity In asynchronous communications, an error-checking protocol in which the parity bit is set to 1 if the number of 1 bits in a one-byte data item adds up to an odd number. The parity bit is set to 0 if the number of 1 bits adds up to an even number. See *asynchronous communications, communications parameter, communications protocol, even parity* and *parity checking.*

OEM See *original equipment manufacturer (OEM).*

off-line 1. Not directly connected with a computer. A device that is not hooked up to your PC is off-line. 2. In data communications, not connected with another, distant computer. Off-line refers to a workstation that you have temporarily or permanently disconnected from a local area network. 3. A printer that is not turned on or not selected and cannot receive output from the computer is off-line.

off-screen formatting In a word processing program, a formatting technique in which formatting commands are embedded in the text so that they affect printing, but the formatting is not visible on-screen. See *embedded formatting command, on-screen formatting,* and *what-you-see-is-what-you-get (WYSIWYG).*

office automation The use of computers and local area networks to integrate traditional office activities such as conferencing, writing, filing, and sending and receiving messages.

Because many tasks such as filing or word processing can be performed much faster on a computer, many firms hoped to reap huge productivity gains from office automation systems. With some exceptions, these gains have not materialized.

Training employees to use the systems often is expensive and time-consuming, and after the systems are installed, perfectionists may use the technology to do a better job (rather than to do more work). In the days of typewriters, a letter may have been sent out with some imperfections, such as a minor misspelling, because too much work was required to retype the letter, but with today's technology, a secretary may spend more time correcting mistakes until the letter is perfect.

Businesses that have met with success in office automation begin by identifying a specific activity that can be done more cheaply or more rapidly on the computer, and then they develop a system—hardware and software included—for that specific application. For example, an insurance company has realized a major productivity gain by having agents fill out application data directly on portable computers. The software then uploads the applications to the company's main offices via telecommunications.

offset   In word processing, the amount of space added to leave space for binding. Synonymous with *gutter*.

one hundred percent (100%) column graph   A column graph that resembles a pie graph in that each column displays the relative percentage of the data item compared to the total (see fig. O.2). See *stacked column graph*.

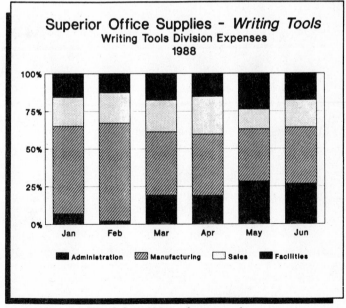

Fig. O.2. A 100% column graph.

on-line 1. Directly connected with a computer. A device that you have successfully hooked up to your PC is on-line. 2. In data communications, connected with another, distant computer. On-line refers to the successful connection with a host computer in a server-client network. 3. A printer turned on, directly connected to the computer, and selected so that it is ready to accept the computer's output is on-line.

on-line help A help utility available on-screen while using a network or an application program.

on-line information service A for-profit firm that makes current news, stock quotes, and other information available to its subscribers via telecommunications linkages. See *bibliographic retrieval service, CompuServe, Dow Jones News/Retrieval Service, GEnie,* and *Prodigy.*

on-screen formatting In a word processing program, a formatting technique in which formatting commands directly affect the text visible on-screen. See *embedded formatting command, off-screen formatting,* and *what-you-see-is-what-you-get (WYSIWYG).*

OOPS (object-oriented programming system) See *object-oriented programming language.*

open architecture A computer system in which all the system specifications are made public so that other companies will develop add-on products such as adapters for the system.

open bus system A computer design in which the computer's expansion bus contains receptacles that readily accept adapters.

An open-architecture system generally has an open bus, but not all systems with open busses have open architectures; the Macintosh is an example of the latter. See *expansion bus.*

Open System Interconnection (OSI) reference model An international standard for the organization of local area networks (LANs) established by the International Standards Organization (ISO) and the Institute of Electrical and Electronic Engineers (IEEE).

The OSI reference model is an important contribution to the conceptual design of local area networks because this model establishes hardware independence. The model separates the communication process into distinct layers: the physical hardware (such as the cabling), the transport layer (the method by which data is communicated via the physical hardware), the presentation layer (the method by which the transmitted data interacts with application programs in each computer), and the application layer (the programs available to all users of the network). Figure O.3 shows the OSI reference model divided into layers.

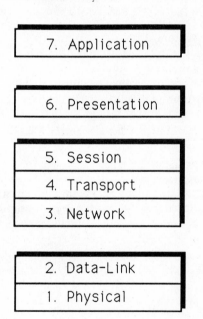

Fig. O.3. The OSI reference model.

Because each layer is at least to some extent independent of the others, you can, in theory, change the cabling (from twisted-pair cable to coaxial cable, for example) without making changes at the other layers. Of course, not all local area networks live up to this level of independence.

From the user's perspective, however, the most important point about the OSI reference model is that you can distinguish between the network hardware and the network software. For example, TOPS, a local area network system, runs on systems physically wired with AppleTalk hardware and twisted-pair cables as well as EtherNet hardware and coaxial cables. See *local area network (LAN)*.

operating system   A master control program for a computer that manages the computer's internal functions and provides you with a means to control the computer's operations.

The most popular operating systems for personal computers include DOS, OS/2, and the Macintosh System.

Operating System/2 (OS/2)   Pronounced "oh ess too" A multitasking operating system for IBM PC-compatible computers that breaks the 640K RAM barrier, provides protection for programs running simultaneously, and enables the dynamic exchange of data between applications.

IBM and Microsoft Corporation jointly developed and introduced OS/2 in 1987; they designed OS/2 as a replacement for MS-DOS.

OS/2 has significant advantages over DOS. Unlike DOS, which uses a maximum of 640K of RAM, OS/2 can use up to 16M of RAM, and by using a technique known as virtual memory, which stores little-used sections of program code on disk, the memory space apparent to programs is expandable to a full 48M.

OS/2 is ideally suited to multitasking (running two or more programs simultaneously). Unlike DOS, which enables programs to invade each other's memory space (a common cause of system crashes), OS/2 takes full advantage of the protected mode of Intel 80286, 80386, and 80486 microprocessors. While running two or more programs simultaneously, moreover, the OS/2 user can move data from one program to another using a temporary parking space called a clipboard.

OS/2's command-line interface closely resembles DOS, and most DOS users do not need much retraining to work with OS/2. Beginning with Version 1.1, OS/2 shipped with Presentation Manager—a shell that resembles Microsoft Windows.

Despite OS/2's many advantages, the system has gained acceptance slowly. Few applications are available in OS/2 versions because software publishers do not want to shut themselves out of the lucrative market for applications that run on the many millions of 8088- and 8086-based personal computers, which cannot run OS/2. The applications available for OS/2, such as Lotus 1-2-3 Release 3, resemble the DOS versions, and many users have no reason to upgrade. If advanced programs that require OS/2 appear, however, this situation may change.

You can run DOS applications in a special DOS-emulation mode, but this mode has few advantages over running DOS programs under MS-DOS. In addition, OS/2 is expensive to run; the system requires approximately 2M of RAM, up to 8M of disk space, and a 80286 or later microprocessor. Few users, therefore, see a clear rationale to upgrade. Multitasking is now available for DOS applications through such shells as DESQview and Microsoft Windows.

optical character recognition (OCR)   The machine recognition of printed or typed text.

optical disk   A secondary storage medium for computers in which you store information of extremely high density on a disk in the form of tiny pits, the presence or absence of which corresponds to a bit of information read by a tightly focused laser beam.

Optical storage technologies are expected to play a significant role in the secondary storage systems of the 1990s. CD-ROM disks and CD-ROM disk drives offer an increasingly economical distribution medium for read-only data and programs. Write-once read-many (WORM) drives enable organizations to create their own huge, in-house databases.

Erasable optical disk drives, such as the 256M drive included with the NeXT computer, offer more secondary storage than hard disks, and the CDs are removable.

Optical storage disk drives, however, are more expensive and much slower than hard disks. See *CD-ROM, interactive videodisc,* and *write-once, read many (WORM).*

optimal recalculation In Lotus 1-2-3 and other advanced spreadsheet programs, a method that speeds automatic recalculation by recalculating only those cells that changed since the last recalculation. See *automatic recalculation.*

ORACLE A program developed by Oracle Corporation, the maker of mainframe and minicomputer relational database programs, that enables users of Macintosh computers and IBM PC-compatibles to access data on large corporate databases.

Many people in the mainframe and minicomputer world know ORACLE as one of the leading relational database management systems (DBMS). In its personal computer form, ORACLE is a connectivity platform—a program designed to enable personal computers to access data kept in large corporate mainframe databases.

Using one of the several versions of ORACLE for personal computers, anyone running Lotus 1-2-3, HyperCard, Super-Card, 4th Dimension, or dBASE III Plus can access the following mainframe databases: ORACLE, DB2, and SQL/DS. Perhaps the most innovative of these programs is ORACLE for the Macintosh, which transforms HyperCard into an exceptionally user-friendly front end for corporate databases. See *connectivity platform* and *relational database program.*

organization chart In presentation graphics, a text chart that you use to diagram the reporting structure of a multilevel organization, such as a corporation or a club (see fig. O.4).

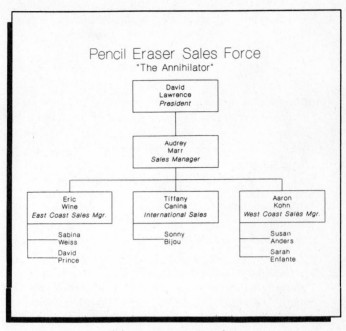

Fig. O.4. An organization chart.

orientation   See *landscape orientation* and *portrait orientation.*

original equipment manufacturer (OEM)   The company that actually manufactures a given piece of hardware, unlike the value-added reseller (VAR)—the company that modifies, configures, repackages, and sells the hardware.

For example, only a few companies such as Canon, Toshiba, and Ricoh make the print engines used in laser printers. These engines are configured and sold by VARs.

orphan   A formatting flaw in which the first line of a paragraph appears alone at the bottom of a page.

Most word processing and page-layout programs suppress widows and orphans; the better programs enable you to switch widow/orphan control on and off and to choose the number of lines for which the suppression feature is effective. See *widow*.

OS/2   See *Operating System/2*.

outline font   A printer or screen font in which a mathematical formula generates each character, producing a graceful and undistorted outline of the character, which the printer then fills in at its maximum resolution.

Mathematical formulas, rather than bit maps, produce the graceful arcs and lines of outline characters (see fig. O.5). You can easily change the type size of an outline font. Unlike bit-mapped fonts, you can scale outline fonts up and down without introducing distortions. (You may need to reduce the weight of small font sizes by using a process called hinting, which keeps the fine detail from being lost).

Because mathematical formulas produce the characters, you need only one font in the printer's memory to use any type size from 2 to 127 points. With bit-mapped fonts, you must download a complete set of characters for each font size into the printer's memory, and you cannot use a type size that you have not downloaded.

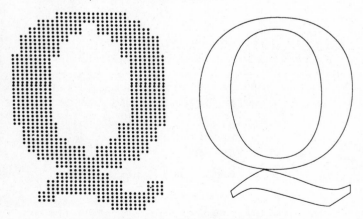

Fig. O.5. A bit-mapped character (left) and an outline character (right).

Outline fonts are available as built-in fonts in many laser printers and as downloadable fonts provided on disk. The leading supplier of outline fonts is Adobe Systems, Inc., which encrypts these fonts (using a proprietary technique) by transforming them into instructions phrased in the Adobe's page description language (PostScript). Adobe's fonts print only on laser or high-resolution printers specifically licensed (at a fee) to contain PostScript decoders. Such fonts are called Type 1 fonts, and PostScript laser printers give these fonts priority in processing operations. See *bit-mapped font* and *hinting*.

outline utility   A mode of some full-featured word processing programs that assists you in planning and organizing a document by equating outline headings with document headings. The program enables you to view the document as an outline or as ordinary text.

This convenient feature is useful for anyone who writes lengthy, complex documents segmented by internal headings and subheadings (scholarly articles, technical reports, and proposals, for example). When you view the document in Outline mode (see fig. O.6), the headings and subheadings appear as they would in an outline. The text beneath the headings collapses (disappears) so that only the headings and subheadings are visible.

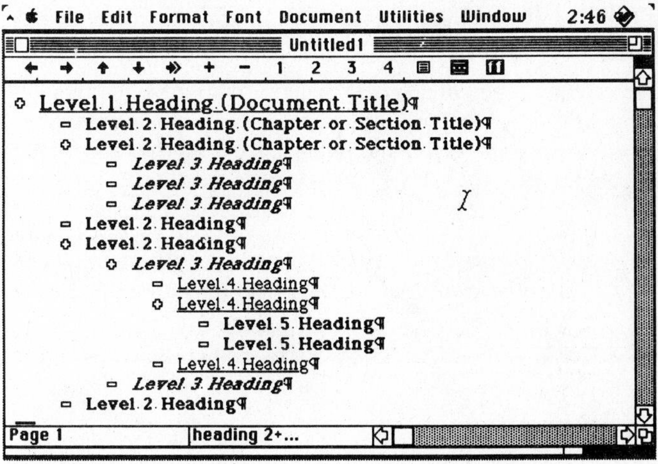

Fig. O.6. Document headings viewed in Outline mode.

In Outline mode, however, you can move the headings and subheadings vertically; if you move the heading, all the hidden text positioned beneath it also moves. The Outline mode provides the tools necessary for reorganizing large text in a document with just a few keystrokes. After you switch back to Document mode (see fig. O.7), the outline format disappears, and the document appears as normal.

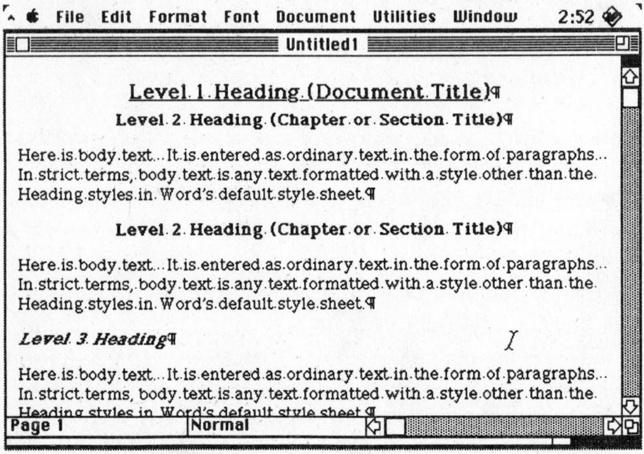

Fig. O.7. Document headings viewed in Document mode.

output   The process of displaying or printing the results of processing operations. See *input.*

overstrike   The printing of a character not found in a printer's character set by printing one character, moving the print head back one space, and printing a second character on top of the first.

Overtype mode   An editing mode in word processing programs and other software that enables you to enter and edit text; the characters you type erase existing characters, if any.

In WordPerfect, the Overtype mode is called the Typeover mode, which you can toggle on and off by pressing the Ins key. See *Insert mode.*

overwrite   To write data on a magnetic disk in the same area where other data is stored (destroying the original data).

p

packaged software   Application programs commercially marketed, unlike custom programs privately developed for a
specific client. Synonymous with off-the-shelf software.

page description language (PDL)   A programming language
that describes printer output in device-independent commands.

Normally, a program's printer output includes printer control codes that vary from printer to printer. A program that
generates output in a PDL can drive any printer containing
an interpreter for the PDL; a PDL, therefore, is device-independent. A program that generates output in the PostScript
page description language, for example, can drive any
printer with a PostScript interpreter—including imagesetters
with 1200 dpi or better resolutions.

PDLs are technically superior to ordinary printing techniques for another reason: the burden of processing the output is transferred from the computer to the printer. To print a
circle using ordinary printing techniques, the computer must
transform the screen image into a bit map and send the bit
map to the computer.

A circle in a PDL, however, is represented mathematically,
and the printer is responsible for constructing the actual image. This technique has a drawback: to interpret the PDL output, the printer must have its own central processing unit
(CPU) and random-access memory (RAM), which makes
PostScript printers expensive.

page layout program   In desktop publishing, an application
program that assembles text and graphics from a variety of
files, with which you can determine the precise placement,
sizing, scaling, and cropping of material in accordance with
the page design represented on-screen.

Page layout programs such as PageMaker and Ventura
Publisher display a graphic representation of the page, in-

cluding nonprinting guides that define areas into which you can insert text and graphics (see fig. P.1). See *PageMaker* and *Ventura Publisher.*

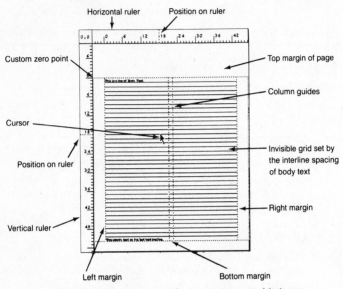

Fig. P.1. Nonprinting guides in Ventura Publisher.

Page-mode RAM   A random-access memory (RAM) chip that segments stored information into a 2K page of rows and columns, and provides fast access to the row or column. Synonymous with *static random-access memory RAM.*

Page-mode RAM is one of several solutions to the problems posed by fast microprocessors outpacing slower memory chips. If the information needed by the central processing unit (CPU) is within the page, even the fastest microcomputers can access the information without wait states. See *cache memory, static random-access memory (RAM),* and *wait state.*

page orientation   See *landscape orientation* and *portrait orientation.*

PageMaker   A leading page layout program for IBM PC compatibles and Macintosh computers that is excellent for documents such as newsletters, brochures, reports, and books.

Introduced in 1985 for the Macintosh, PageMaker (Aldus Corporation) and the Apple LaserWriter printer launched desktop publishing—a term that was, in fact, created by the president of Aldus Corporation, Paul Brainerd. PageMaker continues to dominate the Macintosh market, but Ventura Publisher is more popular in IBM PC-compatible computing.

paint file format   A bit-mapped graphics file format found in programs such as MacPaint and PC Paintbrush.

The standard paint file format in the Macintosh environment is the 72 dots-per-inch format originally used by MacPaint, which is linked to the Mac's bit-mapped screen display. In the IBM PC-compatible environment, no single standard paint format exists. Programs such as Windows Paint and PC Paintbrush create their own proprietary file formats that other programs may not be able to read.

paint program   A program that enables users to paint the screen by switching on or off the individual dots or pixels that make up a bit-mapped screen display.

The first paint program (and the first program for the Macintosh) was MacPaint, the creation of Bill Atkinson at Apple Computer. MacPaint is designed to work with the Mac's bit-mapped display that has a resolution of 72 dots per inch. Graphics created with MacPaint have the same resolution when printed and look rather crude, but you can create some striking effects by varying the patterns of on-and-off pixels.

MacPaint has many imitators in the Macintosh world, such as SuperPaint (Silicon Beach Software). MacPaint-like applications also exist for IBM PC-compatible computers; a leading program in this category is PC Paintbrush. See *MacPaint* and *PC Paintbrush*.

paired bar graph   A bar graph with two different y-axes (values axes).

A paired bar graph is an excellent way to demonstrate the relationship between two data series that share the same x-axis categories but require two different y-axis measurements. As the bars mirror each other, variations become obvious (see fig. P.2). See *dual y-axis graph.*

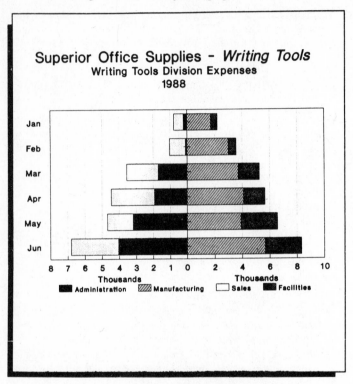

Fig. P.2. A paired bar graph.

Palatino Pronounced "pal-uh-te'-no." A weighty, formal, serif typeface used for body type.

Derived from ancient stone-cut typefaces, Palatino suggests all the dignity and authority of ancient tradition. This typeface is an excellent choice for annual reports and proposals. Palatino is included as a built-in font with many PostScript laser printers (see fig. P.3).

ABCDEFGHIJKLMNOPQRSTUVWXYZ
abcdefghijklmnopqrstuvwxyz 1234567890

Fig. P.3. The Palatino typeface.

palette   In computer graphics, an on-screen display containing the set of colors or patterns that can be used.

Pantone Matching System   A standard color-selection system for professional color printing supported by high-end illustration programs, such as Adobe Illustrator.

paperless office   An office in which the use of paper for traditional purposes, such as sending messages, filling out forms, and maintaining records, has been reduced or eliminated.

When the paperless office was announced as a goal for the office of the future, the future looked bleak indeed for paper manufacturers. Yet, over the past 15 years, paper consumption has exploded and paper manufacturers have experienced record growth and profits. In most offices, computers generate more paper, not less.

A new application for personal computers is the business-form program that enables a person who isn't trained in graphics arts to design and print a business form that can be mass-duplicated using cheap offset techniques.

Paper remains popular as a communication and filing medium for two important reasons. First, paper messages, once received, keep on broadcasting their message unless the user throws the message away, files the message, or answers it. In contrast, electronic mail systems enable people to duck their messages by failing to log on to the system. Second, paper documents have an entrenched legal status; the exchange of first-class letters, for example, has been recognized by the courts to constitute a legal contract. The legal status of computer-based documents is still unclear. Many people fear the storage of important documents on computer systems without hardcopy backup; wiping out a file is easy to do.

Despite these barriers to the acceptance of the paperless office, many valid reasons exist for businesses to seek to reduce the consumption of paper. Filling out forms directly on computer screens, rather than on paper, can save an organization a great deal of money that would have been spent on filing and other clerical tasks.

Paradox   A relational database program originally developed by Ansa Software and offered by Borland International for IBM PC-compatible computers.

Paradox uses query-by-example techniques and an interface reminiscent of Lotus 1-2-3. See *query by example (QBE)*.

parallel columns   See *side-by-side columns*.

parallel interface   See *parallel port*.

parallel port   A port that supports the synchronous, high-speed flow of data along parallel lines to peripheral devices, especially parallel printers.

Essentially an extension of the internal data bus of the computer, the parallel port provides a high-speed connection to printing devices. A parallel port also negotiates with peripheral devices to determine whether they are ready to receive data and reports error messages if a device is not ready. Unlike the serial port, the parallel port provides a trouble-free way to connect a printer to your computer; you usually can install parallel printers easily. As the length of the cable increases, however, so does the risk of crosstalk (interference between the parallel wires). Parallel printer cables, therefore, usually are no longer than 10 to 15 feet.

You can configure the systems of IBM PC-compatible computers with three parallel ports. The device names of the ports are LPT1, LPT2, and LPT3 (the LPT abbreviation stands for line printer). The device named PRN is the same as LPT1.

parallel printer   A printer designed to be connected to the computer's parallel port.

➔ **Tip:** If a printer is available in serial and parallel versions, the parallel version is the better choice unless you must position the printer more than 10 feet away from the computer. Parallel printers are usually easier to install and use than their serial counterparts.

parallel processing   See *multitasking.*

parameter   A value or option that you add or alter when you give a command so that the command accomplishes its task in the way you want. If you do not state a parameter, the program uses a default value or option.

For example, most programs enable you to type the name of the file you want to work with when you start the program. If you type **WORD report1.doc**, for example, Microsoft Word and the document file called REPORT1.DOC load up at the same time. In this case, the file name is the parameter. If you do not type the file name, Word starts and opens a new, blank document file. See *argument.*

parameter RAM   In the Macintosh environment, a small bank of battery-powered memory that stores user configuration choices after you switch the power off.

parent directory   In DOS directories, the directory above the current subdirectory in the tree structure.

➔ **Tip:** You can move quickly to the parent directory by typing **cd..** (two periods) and pressing Enter.

parity bit   In asynchronous communications and primary storage, an extra bit added to a data word for parity checking.

This term becomes relevant to users attempting to use a communications program to contact another computer. For such contact to succeed, the two computers must use the same communications protocol—one of the parameters of this protocol is the parity bit setting.

➔ **Tip:** If you are using a communications program, try setting the parity bit option to no parity and the data bits option to 8 bits. If these settings do not work, try even parity with 7 data bits. See *asynchronous communication* and *parity checking.*

parity checking   A technique used to detect memory or data communication errors. The computer adds up the number of bits in a one-byte data item, and if the parity bit disagrees with the sum of the other bits, the computer reports an error.

When errors occur in a computer's memory or in data communications, a 50 percent chance exists that the sum of the bits in a one-byte data item will change from an odd to an even number, or vice versa.

Parity-checking schemes work by storing a one-bit digit (0 or 1) that indicates whether the sum of the 1 bits in a data item is odd or even. When the data item is read from memory or received by another computer, a parity check occurs. If the parity check reveals that the parity bit is incorrect, the computer displays an error message. See *even parity* and *odd parity.*

parity error   An error that a computer reports when parity checking reveals that one or more parity bits is incorrect, which indicates a probable error in data processing or data transmission.

park   To position a hard drive's read/write head so that the drive is not damaged by jostling during transport.

parse   To separate imported data into separate columns so that it appears correctly in a spreadsheet.

When you import data using 1-2-3's /File Import Text command, for example, the program enters each line of the data as a long label—in other words, each line of data appears in just one cell. Because Lotus 1-2-3 uses soft-cell boundaries, you can see the entire line on-screen, but you cannot use this data for calculations. To render this data usable, you must use the /Data Parse command that separates the data into distinct columns.

partition   A section of a hard disk physically divided from other sections during the formatting operation and treated by the operating system as if it were a separate disk.

In DOS, partitions are used infrequently; they are intended to meet the needs of users who are running two or more operating systems (such as DOS and UNIX).

Macintosh users may partition their drives to separate the Macintosh System and the A/UX version of UNIX, but utility programs are available (such as MultiDisk) that enable the user to create several system partitions. These partitions are treated by the operating system as if they are different disks. These utilities are useful for organizing large hard disks. See *directory*, and *subdirectory*.

Pascal   Pronounced "pass-kal." A high-level programming language that encourages programmers to write well-structured, modular programs. Pascal has gained wide acceptance as a teaching and application-development language.

Developed by the European computer scientist Nicklaus Wirth in the early 1970s, Pascal—named for the seventeenth century French mathematician and philosopher Blaise Pascal—expresses the principles of structured programming. Wirth hoped that the language would be widely adopted as a teaching language and a professional program-development language, and he has succeeded. Pascal is the language of choice for teaching purposes at most colleges and universities, and although the growing popularity of C is beginning to displace Pascal, the language is still frequently used by programming professionals for the creation of small- to medium-sized application programs.

Because Pascal is exclusively a high-level language that does not enable you to include assembly-language statements, the language is too slow for large-scale application program development or systems programming. Pascal is available in interpreted and compiled versions.

Pascal resembles BASIC and FORTRAN in that it is a procedural language: its statements tell the computer what to do. In contrast to these earlier languages, however, Pascal was designed to take full advantage of modern control structures, eliminating spaghetti code and improving program readability.

Unlike BASIC, Pascal does not force programmers to express groups of related data items in arrays; instead, the language has a fully developed record data structure, making it far more suitable for professional program development than any language that lacks this data structure. Another important feature of Pascal is the modular structure; you can express important program functions in mini-programs called procedures, which are set aside from the main program and called by name (compare to Modula-2).

Unlike BASIC and FORTRAN, Pascal is a strongly type-checked language; the program does not use default data types but requires that the programmer declare the data type of all variables and that all input conforms to the types declared. The lack of data typing and type-checking is a major cause of programming errors.

A major disadvantage of Pascal is that its standard version (Standard Pascal) contains many shortcomings. Commercial versions of the language generally include extensions that make them mutually unintelligible. The language's inventor, Wirth, has offered a new language (Modula-2) as a successor to Pascal, and this new language directly addresses Pascal's shortcomings.

In personal computing, Pascal largely lives on due to the influence of Turbo Pascal (Borland International), a high-performance compiler for Pascal that recognizes a number of important and useful extensions to the language. See *Modula-2*.

password   A security tool used to identify authorized users of a computer program or computer network and to define their privileges, such as read-only, reading and writing, or file copying.

password protection   A method of limiting access to a program or a network by requiring the user to enter a password.

▲ **Caution:** Some programs enable you to password-protect your files, but be sure to keep a record of the password. Many users have lost work permanently because they forgot the password, and they cannot find out what the password is. (If a method for retrieving a password was included in software programs, a clever hacker would quickly discover it, and your data would not be secure.)

paste   To insert text or graphics at the cursor's location.

patch   A quick fix, in the form of one or more program state-ments, added to a program to correct bugs or to enhance the program's capabilities.

path   The route a program must follow to physically access data on a secondary storage device.

PATH   In DOS and OS/2, an internal command that tells the operating system which directories to search if a program or batch file is not found in the current directory.

→ **Tip:** Most hard disk users place a PATH command in an AUTOEXEC.BAT (DOS) or STARTUP.CMD (OS/2) file so that the PATH command executes at the beginning of every oper-ating session. The command must include the complete path name for each subdirectory to be searched. See *path name.*

path name   In DOS and OS/2, the name of a DOS subdirec-tory expressed in a way that describes the path DOS can take through the tree structure to reach it.

PAUSE   In DOS and OS/2, a batch command that displays a message such as

```
Press any key to continue
```

   or

```
Strike any key when ready
```

and waits for the user to press a key before carrying out other commands.

PC   See *personal computer.*

PC DOS   See *MS-DOS.*

PC Local Area Network (PC LAN) Program   An IBM network operating system designed for use on IBM's Token-Ring Net-work.

Introduced in 1986, this IBM program provides electronic mail, shared access to printers, and shared access to data and program files.

PC Paintbrush   A popular paint program for IBM PC-compatible computers. See *paint program.*

PC Tools   A popular package of utility programs developed by Central Point Software for IBM PC-compatible and Macintosh computers, including an excellent file recovery (undelete) program.

PDL   See *page description language (PDL).*

peer-to-peer file transfer   A file-sharing technique for local area networks in which each user has access to the public files of all other users in the network located on their respective workstations. (Each user determines which files, if any, he or she wants to make public for network access.) See *TOPS.*

peer-to-peer network   A local area network without a central file server and in which all computers in the network have access to the public files of all other workstations. See *client-server network* and *peer-to-peer file transfer.*

peripheral   A device, such as a printer or disk drive, connected to and controlled by a computer but external to the computer's central processing unit (CPU).

personal computer   A stand-alone computer equipped with all the system, utility, and application software, and the input/output devices and other peripherals that an individual needs to perform one or more tasks.

The idea of personal computing, at least initially, was to free individuals from dependence on tightly controlled, mainframe and minicomputer resources. In a corporate setting, for example, data processing managers once had the sole authority to choose the programs and data formats people used. Even if this choice was made responsibly, it would suit some employees more than others. With the rise of personal computing, people have gained substantially more freedom to choose the applications tailored to their needs.

In recent years, ample reason has been found to reintegrate personal computers (PCs) into the data communications networks of organizations, and this goal can be achieved without forcing people to give up the autonomy that personal computing implies.

PCs can serve, for example, as ideal platforms for the use of common organizational databases, enabling users to access a huge, central-information storehouse. Smaller networks can facilitate productivity and work efficiency among members of a workgroup. By means of electronic mail, the network can serve as a new way of improving communication and exchanging information.

Because PCs increasingly are equipped with the networking and communications hardware they need to participate in such networks, the boundary between PCs and professional workstations has blurred considerably. Professional workstations are powerful, high-performance computers designed to provide professionals such as graphics designers, engineers, and architects with the computing power they need for calculation-intensive applications, such as computer-assisted design (CAD). Generally equipped with communications hardware, workstations clearly provide the model toward which high-end PCs, such as those based on the Intel 80386 and 80486 microprocessors, are evolving.

Similarly blurred is the distinction between PCs and minicomputers. At one time, PCs were synonymous with microcomputers (computers that have a microprocessor as their CPU). Many minicomputers. however, now use microprocessors. Further blurring the issue is the fact that today's high-end PCs can handle a few remote terminals if the PCs have UNIX or some other multiuser operating system. See *professional workstation.*

personal information manager (PIM)   A database-management program such as Lotus Agenda that stores and retrieves a wide variety of personal information, including notes, memos, names and addresses, and appointments.

Unlike a database management program, a PIM is optimized for the storage and retrieval of a variety of personal information.

PFS: Professional Write   A word processing program developed by Software Publishing Corporation for IBM Personal Computers and compatibles. Designed for executives and professional workers, the program is easy to use and does not burden the user with unnecessary features.

PgUp/PgDn keys   On IBM PC-compatible computer keyboards, keys that you press to move the cursor to the preceding screen or the next screen.

Because the precise implementation of these keys is up to the programmer, their functions vary from program to program. Some word processing programs, for example, use PgUp and PgDn keys for moving to the top of the preceding of text as the page will appear when printed, rather than to the preceding screen of text.

phono plug   A connector with a short stem. A phono plug connects home audio devices. For example, the jacks on the back of a high-fidelity amplifier are phono plugs. In computers, phono plugs are used for audio and composite monitor output ports. Synonymous with RCA plug.

phosphor   An electrofluorescent material used to coat the inside face of a cathode ray tube (CRT). After being energized by the electron beam being directed to the inside face of the tube, the phosphors glow for a fraction of a second. The beam must refresh the phosphor many times per second so that a consistent illumination is produced. See *cathode ray tube (CRT)* and *raster display.*

phototypesetter   See *imagesetter.*

physical drive   The disk drive actually performing the read/write operations in a secondary storage system.

A disk drive, such as a floppy disk or a hard disk, may have unique electronic and electromechanical characteristics when compared to the other drives in the system, but these unique characteristics of the physical drive are invisible to the user. In an IBM PC-compatible computer equipped with a floppy drive and a hard disk, for example, you follow exactly the same procedure to save a file to drive A and to drive C—in spite of the fact that the two drives are different items of hardware.

From the user's perspective, you can think of all the drives as logical drives—the drives that appear to have exactly the same characteristics, even though they are physically, electronically, and electromechanically different. See *floppy disk*, *hard disk*, *logical drives*, and *secondary storage*.

physical format   See *low-level format*.

pica   Pronounced "pike'-ah." In typography, a unit of measure equal to approximately 1/6 inch, or 12 points. In typewriting and letter-quality printing, a 12-point monospace font that prints at a pitch of 10 characters per inch (cpi).

Picas usually describe horizontal and vertical measurements on the page, with the exception of type sizes, which are expressed in points.

Although thinking that 6 picas equal one inch is convenient, this comparison is not accurate. In formal typography, a pica is 0.166 of an inch, and 1/6 inch is actually 1.667. Thirty picas, therefore, equal 4.98 inches—a bit less than five inches. Many word processing and page layout programs, however, break with this tradition and define one pica as exactly 1/6 inch.

PICT file format   An object-oriented graphic file format that draws on information available in the Macintosh computer's QuickDraw toolbox, which is part of the Mac's read-only memory (ROM). See *paint file format*.

pie graph   In presentation graphics, a graph that displays a data series as a circle to emphasize the relative contribution of each data item to the whole.

Each slice of the pie appears in a distinctive crosshatching pattern (see fig. P.4), which can produce Moiré distortions if you juxtapose too many patterns. Some programs can produce paired pie graphs that display two data series (see fig. P.5). For presentations, exploding a slice from the whole is a useful technique to add emphasis (see fig. P.6). See *linked pie/column graph, Moiré distortion,* and *proportional pie graph.*

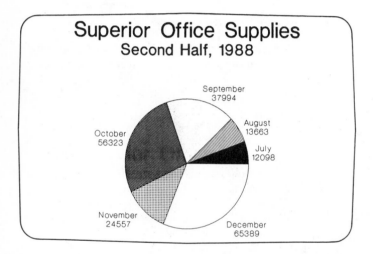

Fig. P.4. A pie graph.

PIF file   A program description file that tells Microsoft Windows the information Windows needs to display an application program. See *Microsoft Windows.*

PILOT   An authoring language for computer-assisted instruction (CAI).

John Starkweather developed PILOT (short for Programmed Inquiry Learning Or Teaching) at the University of California (San Francisco, 1968).

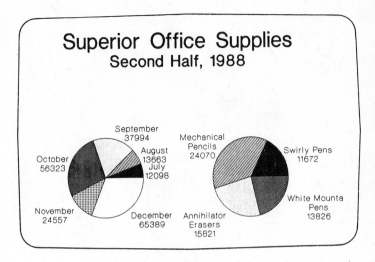

Fig. P.5. A paired pie graph.

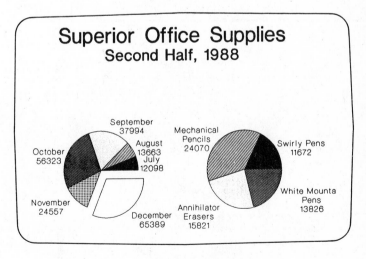

Fig. P.6. A paired pie graph with an exploded slice.

PILOT is exceptionally easy to learn because there are very few commands. Used primarily to develop on-screen instructional materials, PILOT is being displaced by new authoring languages that use graphical user interfaces such as Hyper-Talk. See *computer-assisted instruction (CAI)*.

PIM See *personal information manager (PIM)*.

pin feed See *tractor feed*.

pipe In DOS and OS/2, an operator (a vertical line symbol) that redirects the output of one command so that it becomes the input of another command. See *input/output redirection*.

pitch A horizontal measurement of the number of characters per linear inch in a monospace font, such as those used with typewriters, dot-matrix printers, and daisywheel printers.

By convention, pica pitch (not to be confused with the printer's measurement of approximately 1/6 inch) equals 10 characters per inch, and elite pitch equals 12 characters per inch. See *monospace*, *pica*, and *point*.

pixel Pronounced "picks-ehl." The smallest element (a picture element) that a device can display on-screen and out of which the displayed image is constructed. See *bit-mapped graphic*.

plasma display A display technology used with high-end laptop computers. The display is produced by energizing an ionized gas held between two transparent panels. Synonymous with gas plasma display.

platen In dot-matrix and letter-quality impact printers, the cylinder that guides paper through the printer and provides a surface for the impression of the image onto the page.

platform See *hardware platform*.

platform independence The capability of a local area network to connect computers made by different makers (such as IBM PC-compatibles and Macintosh computers).

platter   Synonymous with *disk*.

plot   To construct an image by drawing lines.

plotter   A printer that produces high-quality output by moving ink pens over the surface of the paper. The printer moves the pens under the direction of the computer, so that printing is automatic. Plotters are commonly used for computer-aided design and presentation graphics.

point   In typography, the fundamental unit of measure. 72 points equal an inch. See *pica* and *pitch*.

pointer   An on-screen symbol, usually an arrow, that shows the current position of the mouse. In database management programs, a record number in an index that stores the actual physical location of the data record. See *cursor*.

pointing device   An input device such as a mouse, trackball, or stylus graphics tablet used to display a pointer on-screen.

polarity   1. In electronics, polarity refers to the negative or positive property of a charge.

2. In computer graphics, polarity refers to the tonal relationship between foreground and background elements. Positive polarity is the printing of black or dark characters on a light or white background, and negative polarity is the printing of white or light characters on a dark or black background.

polling   In local area networks, a method for controlling channel access in which the central computer continuously asks or polls the workstations to determine whether they have a message to transmit.

With polling channel access, you can determine how often, and for how long, the central computer polls the workstations. Unlike CSMA/CD and token-ring channel-access methods, the network manager can establish a form of electronic inequality among the networked workstations, in which some nodes have more access to the network than others. See *carrier sense multiple access with collision (CSMA/CD)* and *token-ring network.*

pop-up menu   An menu that appears on-screen anywhere other than in the standard menu bar location (at the top of the screen). See *pull-down menu.*

port   1. An entry/exit boundary mechanism that governs and synchronizes the flow of data into and out of the central processing unit (CPU) to external devices such as printers and modems. Synonymous with interface. 2. Reprogramming an application so that it runs on another type of computer. See *interface*, *parallel port*, and *serial port.*

portable computer   A computer designed to be transported easily from one location to another.

The first portable personal computers, such as the Osborne I and Compaq II, are best described as "luggables." These computers weigh in at well over 25 pounds and cannot be carried comfortably for more than a short distance. Today's battery-powered laptop computers are much more portable, but a machine weighing over 10 pounds is still too heavy to carry around all day.

portrait orientation   The default printing orientation for a page of text, with the longest measurement oriented vertically (see fig. P.7). See *landscape orientation.*

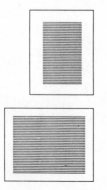

Fig. P.7. Examples of orientation settings.

post In database management, to add data to a data record.

postprocessor A program that performs a final, automatic processing operation after the user has finished working with a file.

Postprocessing programs include text formatters that prepare a document for printing, and page description languages that convert an on-screen document into a set of commands the printer's interpreter can recognize and use to print the document.

PostScript A sophisticated page description language for medium- to high-resolution printing devices.

PostScript, developed by Adobe Systems, Inc., is a programming language that describes how to print a page that blends text and graphics. Because PostScript is a genuine programming language, you can learn to write PostScript instructions and embed them in documents to be printed.

For most users, however, PostScript is invisible and automatic. When you use an application program equipped with a PostScript printer driver, the program generates the PostScript code that goes to the printer. At the printer, a PostScript interpreter reads the instructions and follows them to generate an image of the page in precise accordance with these instructions. The whole operation is transparent to you.

A major benefit of PostScript is its device independence; you can print the PostScript code generated by an application on any printer with a PostScript interpreter—this includes expensive typesetting machines, such as those manufactured by Linotronic, Compugraphic, and Varityper, that are capable of resolutions of up to 2,400 dpi.

PostScript printer output always takes full advantage of the printer's maximum resolution. You can take the disk containing a document you have created with an application such as Microsoft Word or WordPerfect to a service bureau, which can print the document at resolutions equal or surpassing those found in professional publications. See *page description language (PDL)*, and *PostScript laser printer*.

PostScript laser printer   A laser printer that includes the processing circuitry needed to decode and interpret printing instructions phrased in PostScript—a page description language (PDL) widely used in desktop publishing.

Because PostScript laser printers require their own microprocessor circuitry and at least 1M RAM to image each page, they are more expensive than nonPostScript printers.

PostScript laser printers such as the Apple LaserWriter have several advantages over nonPostScript laser printers such as the Hewlett-Packard LaserJet. PostScript printers can print text or graphics in subtle graduations of gray. They can use encapsulated PostScript (EPS) graphics and outline fonts, both of which you can size and scale without introducing distortions. PostScript printers also can produce special effects, such as rotation and overprinting. See *PostScript*.

posture   The slant of the characters in a font. *Italic* characters slant to the right, but the term italic is reserved by conservative typographers for custom-designed (as opposed to electronically produced) serif typefaces.

Italics were designed in the Renaissance by Aldus Manutius, who intended them to be used to mimic the handwriting used in the papal offices. See *italic* and *Roman*.

power-down   To turn off the computer's power switch.

power line filter   An electrical device that smoothes out the peaks and valleys of the voltage delivered at the wall socket.

Every electrical circuit is subject to voltage fluctuations, and if these fluctuations are extreme, they may cause seemingly random computer errors and failures. Flickering lights are a good sign of uneven voltage. If you are using a computer in a circuit shared by heavy appliances, you may need a power line filter to ensure error-free operation. See *surge protector*.

power supply   The electrical component of a computer system that converts standard AC current to the lower-voltage, DC current used by the computer. The amount of current a power supply can provide is rated in watts.

▲ **Caution:** The power supply of early IBM PC-compatible computers (63.5 watts) often proved inadequate after users added several adapters, a hard disk, and other system upgrades. An overloaded power supply can cause erratic operations, such as read or write errors, parity errors, and unexplained system crashes. For systems with hard disks and several adapters, users should have a power supply of at least 200 watts.

power-up To switch on the computer's power switch.

power user A computer user who has gone beyond the beginning and intermediate stages of computer use. Such a person uses the advanced features of application programs, such as software command languages and macros, and can learn new application programs quickly.

PowerPoint A full-featured presentation graphics program for the Macintosh that can produce 35mm transparencies, overhead transparencies, business charts, and flip charts.

Like Harvard Graphics, a similar program available for IBM PC-compatible computers, PowerPoint includes a word processor, spelling checker, and an object-oriented draw program.

precedence The order in which a spreadsheet program performs the operations in a formula. Typically, the program performs exponentiation (such as squaring a number) before multiplication and division; the program then performs addition and subtraction.

precision The number of digits past the decimal that are used to express a quantity. See *accuracy*.

presentation graphics Text charts, column graphs, bar graphs, pie graphs, and other charts and graphs, which you enhance so that they are visually appealing and easily understood by your audience. See *analytical graphics*.

presentation graphics program   An application program designed to create and enhance charts and graphs so that they are visually appealing and easily understood by an audience.

A full-featured presentation graphics package such as Harvard Graphics includes facilities for making text charts, bar graphs, column graphs, pie graphs, high/low/close graphs, and organization charts.

The package also provides facilities for adding titles, legends, and explanatory text anywhere in the chart or graph. A presentation graphics program includes a library of clip art so that you can enliven charts and graphs by adding a picture related to the subject matter (for example, an airplane for a chart of earnings in the aerospace industry). You can print output, direct output to a film recorder, or display output on-screen in a computer slide show.

Presentation Manager   A graphical user interface and application and programming interface (API) for OS/2, jointly developed by Microsoft Corporation and IBM.

Presentation Manager brings to IBM PC-compatible computers running the OS/2 operating system many of the graphical user interface features associated with the Macintosh—multiple on-screen typefaces, pull-down menus, multiple on-screen windows, and desktop accessories.

Presentation Manager is not a version of Microsoft Windows. Presentation Manager clearly reflects its joint development by Microsoft and IBM. Unlike Windows, Presentation Manager conforms to IBM standards such as SAA (Systems Application Architecture). The application programming-interface standards are set by SAA, not by Windows, and programs developed for Windows do not run on Presentation Manager without very substantial modification.

The lack of an easy upgrade path from Windows applications to Presentation Manager is one of the many factors that has delayed the development of programs for OS/2. See *Microsoft Windows* and *Operating System/2*.

primary storage   The computer's main memory directly accessible to the central processing unit (CPU), unlike secondary storage, such as disk drives.

In personal computers, primary storage consists of the random-access memory (RAM) and the read-only memory (ROM). See *internal memory.*

PRINT   In DOS and OS/2, an external command that prints a list of files (called a print queue) without further user intervention.

print engine   Inside a laser printer, the mechanism that uses a laser to create an electrostatic image of a page and fuse that image to a cut sheet of paper.

You can distinguish print engines by their resolution, print quality, longevity, paper-handling features, and speed.

Laser printers generally produce resolutions of 300 dpi, although the trend is toward 400-dpi printers.

High-end laser printers available for professional typesetting purposes are capable of resolutions of up to 600 dpi. (Professional typesetting machines called imagesetters use chemical photo-reproduction techniques to produce resolutions of up to 2,400 dpi.)

Write-white engines expose the portion of the page that does not receive ink (so that toner is attracted to the areas that print black) and generally produce deeper blacks than write-black engines, but this quality varies from engine to engine. Although dozens of retail brands of laser printers are on the market, the print engines are made by just a few Japanese original equipment manufacturers (OEM), such as Canon, Ricoh, Toshiba, and Casio. Canon engines are highly regarded within the desktop publishing industry.

Most print engines have a life of 300,000 copies, but the lifespan ratings among brands vary from 180,000 to 600,000 copies. Because printer longevity is estimated from heavy use over a short period of time, you should consider a printer's longevity rating only if the printer will be used in heavy-demand network applications.

Early laser printers vexed users with thin paper trays capable of holding only 50 or 60 sheets of paper. For convenient use, you should consider a paper tray capacity of at least 100 sheets; 200 or 250 is better.

Print engines often are rated (optimistically) at speeds of up to 10 pages per minute. Such speeds, however, are attained only under ideal conditions; the same sparse page of text is printed over and over, so that the bit map is kept in memory and is zapped out repeatedly. When printing a real manuscript with different text on each page, the printer must pause to construct the image and output is substantially slower. Also, if the printer encounters a graphic, printing may grind to a halt for as long as a minute.

For real-world applications, what determines a print engine's speed is the processing prowess of the controller's microprocessor. The speed demons of laser printing use third-generation microprocessors (such as the Motorola 68020) running at clock speeds of up to 16.7 MHz.

print queue　A list of files that a print spooler prints in the background while the computer performs other tasks in the foreground.

print spooling program　A utility program that prints a file while you continue to work with an application.

printer driver　A file that contains information a program needs to print your work with a given brand and model of printer.

A major difference between the DOS and Macintosh environments is the way printer drivers are handled. In IBM PC-compatible computing, printer drivers are the responsibility of application programs; each program must come equipped with a printer driver for the many dozens of printers available.

These printer drivers work only with the program for which they were written. The WordPerfect printer driver for the HP DeskJet, for example, does not help Microsoft Word print with the DeskJet. If a program does not include a driver for your printer, you may be out of luck. Microsoft

Windows, fortunately, cures the printing deficiencies of DOS by providing printer drivers for all Windows applications.

Printer drivers also are part of the operating environment in the Macintosh. Individual programs do not have printer drivers; instead, they are designed to take advantage of printer drivers provided at the operating system level and stored in the system folder.

A significant advantage of this method for handling printer drivers is that all programs can use the printer—not just the programs that have included a printer driver.

printer font   A font available for printing, unlike screen fonts available for displaying text on-screen.

Ideally, screen fonts and printer fonts should be identical—only then can a computer system claim to offer what-you-see-is-what-you-get text processing. Today's systems are often far from the ideal. Character-based programs running under DOS cannot display typefaces on-screen other than those built into the computer's ROM. In WordPerfect, for example, you can choose many different printer fonts in a document, but you cannot see the font changes on-screen. Many users are quite satisfied with this technology and get excellent results. For others, seeing the fonts on-screen is necessary to avoid printing errors.

Under current windowing environments (such as Microsoft Windows, Presentation Manager, and the Macintosh System), you can display screen fonts that are bit-mapped imitations of what you will get on the printer.

The computing world is clearly headed toward the integration of screen fonts and printer fonts, using outline font technology.

Printer fonts are of three types: built-in fonts, cartridge fonts, and downloadable fonts.

➜ **Tip:** If desktop publishing is among your intended applications, look for a printer with many built-in fonts. Because built-in fonts are available in the printer's ROM, the printer can switch among the fonts almost instantaneously.

Because cartridges contain far fewer font options, you may need to change a cartridge manually during a printing operation.

The least convenient option is downloadable fonts, which you must transfer from the computer to the printer at the beginning of every operating session (or during printing, if you forgot to do so). This operation can require as much as 10 or 15 minutes. Several manufacturers sell cartridges that include dozens of fonts. See *built-in font*, *cartridge font*, and *downloadable font*.

printer port   See *parallel port* and *serial port*.

printer server   In a local area network, a server that provides controlled access to a printer. Using a technique called print spooling, the printer server receives files to be printed from network nodes, stores the files on disk, and places them in a queue based on the order received. The printer server then parcels out the files, one at a time, to the printer.

PRN   In DOS and OS/2, the device that refers to the default printer port (such as LPT1 or COM1, depending on how you have configured your system).

procedural language   A language such as BASIC or Pascal that requires the programmer to specify the procedure the computer has to follow to accomplish the task. See *declarative language* and *nonprocedural language*.

processing   The execution of program instructions by the computer's central processing unit (CPU) so that data is transformed in some way, such as sorting data, selecting some data according to specified criteria, or performing mathematical computations on data.

PROCOMM PLUS   A popular and versatile telecommunications program developed by DATASTORM Technologies for IBM PC-compatible computers. Formerly a shareware program, the commercial version offers enhanced features and thorough documentation. See *telecommunication*.

Prodigy   An on-line information service jointly developed by Sears and IBM that offers (via modem) personal computer users home shopping, news, stock quotes, hobbyist conferences, and so on.

Innovative features of Prodigy include the use of a bit-mapped graphical user interface and unlimited use of the system for a flat fee.

Prodigy, however, has no provisions for software uploading or downloading, and many users complain about its sluggish speed. Part of the screen also is occupied by commercial advertisements. See *on-line information service*.

professional workstation   A high-performance personal computer optimized for professional applications in fields such as digital circuit design, architecture, and technical drawing.

Professional workstations typically offer excellent screen resolution and fast, powerful processing circuits and ample memory. Examples include the workstations made by Sun Microsystems and NeXT, Inc. Professional workstations are more expensive than personal computers, and typically use the UNIX operating system. The boundary between high-end personal computers and professional workstations, however, is eroding as personal computers become more powerful.

program   A list of instructions in a computer-programming language that tell the computer what to do. See *software*.

program generator   A program that enables nonprogrammers to use simple techniques to describe an application that the program generator then codes.

In database management programs, for example, program generation techniques are used to give the user a way to describe the output format graphically. The program generator then uses the user's input as a set of parameters by which the output program code is constructed.

program overlay   A portion of a program kept on disk and called into memory only as required.

programmable   Capable of being controlled through instructions that can be varied to suit the user's needs.

programmable read-only memory (PROM)   A read-only memory (ROM) chip programmed at the factory for use with a given computer.

The alternative to PROM is a ROM chip in which the information is expressed in the actual design of the circuits internal to the chip. This approach is inflexible because the chip can be modified only with difficulty, and if the programming has a bug, or if the firm decides to add a feature to the computer, redesigning and manufacturing the chip is expensive and time-consuming.

A programmable ROM chip gets around this problem by offering the computer manufacturer a write-once chip—a chip that can be programmed just once, after which the programming becomes permanent. The process of programming the chip is called burning the PROM. If it becomes necessary to change the programming, making the alterations and burning the new PROMS with the modified information is simple. See *erasable programmable read-only memory (EPROM)*.

programmer   A person who designs, codes, tests, debugs, and documents a computer program.

Professional programmers often hold B.S. or M.S. degrees in computer science, but a great deal of programming (professional and otherwise) is done by individuals with little or no formal training. More than half the readers of a popular personal computer magazine, for example, stated in a survey that they regularly programmed their personal computers using languages such as BASIC, Pascal, and assembly language.

programmer's switch   A plastic accessory included with all Macintosh computers that, when installed on the side of the computer, enables you to perform a hardware reset and access the computer's built-in debugger.

➔ **Tip:** Every Macintosh user should install the programmer's switch, even if no programming is performed. The programmer's switch enables you to restart the computer after a system crash without flipping the power switch on and off (and subjecting your system to the stress of a start-up power surge). You can perform a soft boot by choosing Restart from the Finder menu, but only if you can get to the Finder. After a crash that freezes the system, the programmer's switch provides the only means to restart the system short of flipping the switch off and on.

programming   The process of providing instructions to the computer that tell the microprocessor what to do.

Stages in programming include design, or making decisions about what the program should accomplish; coding, or using a programming language to express the program's logic in computer-readable form; testing and debugging, in which the program's flaws are discovered and corrected; and documentation, in which a instructional manual for the program is created.

PROLOG   A high-level programming language used in artificial intelligence research and applications, particularly expert systems.

PROLOG (short for PROgramming in LOGic) was developed by French computer scientist Alain Colmerauer and logician Philippe Roussel in the early 1970s. Like LISP, PROLOG is a declarative language; PROLOG does not tell the computer what procedure to follow to solve a problem, as a procedural language does, but enables the programmer to describe the problem to be solved.

The language resembles the query language of a database management system such as SQL; you can use PROLOG to ask a question such as, "Is Foster City in California?" An important difference exists between PROLOG and a database management system (DBMS).

A DBMS query language searches the database to try to match the query terms, using a simple pattern-matching algorithm. PROLOG, however, provides tools by which the programmer can state knowledge about the world as well as a set of rules by which conclusions can be drawn from this knowledge. A database contains information that you can retrieve; a PROLOG program, in contrast, contains knowledge, from which the program can draw inferences about what is true or false.

An example should clarify the significance of this difference between PROLOG and database retrieval systems. In PROLOG, you declare a fact about the world—Susannah likes rock music—in the following way:

```
likes(susannah, rock music)
```

You can create a database of such propositions:

```
likes(susannah, rock music)
likes(billy, susannah)
likes(billy, blues)
likes(susannah, billy)
```

Query operations initiate logical inferences from the knowledge base. For example, we can ask, "Does Susannah like Billy?" The answer is yes—a rule specifies that Susannah likes Billy. We also can ask, "Does Billy like rock music?" The answer is no—no evidence is in the database to infer a yes answer.

Rules embedded in the database specify how you can draw further inferences from the data. For example, we could specify the following rule:

```
X and Y like each other if X likes Y and Y likes X
```

We can ask, "Do Billy and Susannah like each other?" The answer is yes, because Billy likes Susannah and Susannah likes Billy.

Programmers often use PROLOG to develop expert systems at the research system level. A great deal of effort and time is involved in developing a PROLOG expert system. For the development of commercial systems, most expert system programmers prefer to use expert system shells, which free programmers from the task of developing user interfaces, input/output operations, and other procedures tedious to program in PROLOG.

PROM   See *programmable read-only memory (PROM)*.

PROMPT In DOS and OS/2, an internal command that customizes the system prompt.

→ **Tip:** If you are using a hard disk divided into directories, use the following command to change the system prompt to display the current directory and the current drive:

PROMPT pg

prompt A symbol or phrase that appears on-screen informing you that the computer is ready to accept input.

proportional pie graph In presentation graphics, a paired pie graph in which the size of the two pies is adjusted to reflect the difference in their overall magnitude (see fig. P.8).

Proportional pie graphs are useful for comparing two pies when one is significantly larger than the other.

proportional spacing The allocation of character widths proportional to the character shape, so that a narrow character such as i receives less space than a wide character such as m. See *kerning* and *monospace*.

proprietary file format A file format developed by a firm to be used for the storage of data created by its products. A proprietary file format usually is unreadable by other firms' application programs. Microsoft Word, for example, cannot read WordPerfect files.

protected mode In 80286 and later Intel microprocessors for IBM PC-compatible computers, an operating mode in which programs running simultaneously cannot invade each other's memory space or directly access input/output devices, preventing system failures during multitasking operations.

Although most people use personal computers for stand-alone applications, many users find that running more than one program at a time is useful.

For example, if you place a spreadsheet program and a word processing program in memory simultaneously, you can copy and place a spreadsheet in a word processing document quickly and easily. The standard operating mode of IBM PC-compatible computers running DOS, however, does not protect programs from one another. Without such protection, nothing stops one program from accidentally invading another's memory space, which may cause the computer or program to crash.

The most significant advantage of the protected mode is that programs running simultaneously have their own memory space that other programs cannot use. Protected mode programs cannot access peripheral devices directly—a DOS characteristic that can cause system failures. Protected-mode processing enables applications to use more than the 640K RAM limit of DOS. Unfortunately, DOS cannot take advantage of protected mode; a memory-management program such as Microsoft Windows or DESQview is necessary. See *real mode.*

protocol   See *communications protocol* and *file transfer protocol.*

PrtSc   On IBM PC-compatible keyboards, a key that you can use to print an image of the screen display.

➔ **Tip:** If the screen display is currently in a graphics mode, you must run the DOS program GRAPHICS.COM before the screen prints properly.

PS/2   See *IBM Personal System/2.*

pseudocode   An algorithm expressed in English to conceptualize the algorithm before coding it in a programming language. See *algorithm.*

public domain software   Software not copyrighted that can be freely distributed without obtaining permission from the programmer or paying the programmer a fee. See *freeware* and *shareware.*

pull-down menu   A method of providing a command menu that appears on-screen only after you click the menu's name.

To select an option on the menu, press and hold down the mouse button and drag the mouse pointer down the menu until the option you want is highlighted (see fig. P.9).

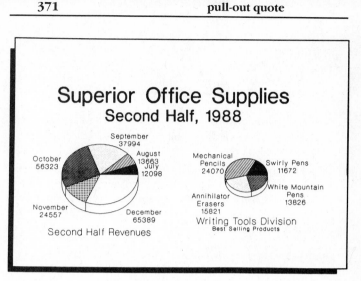

Fig. P.8. A proportional pie graph.

pull-out quote   In desktop publishing, a quotation extracted from the copy of a newsletter or magazine article and printed in larger type in the column, often blocked off with ruled lines.

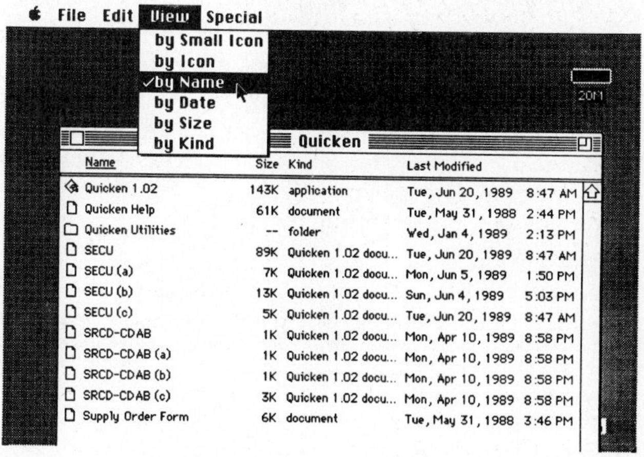

Fig. P.9. A pull-down menu.

q

Q & A   An integrated word processor and flat-file database manager developed by Symantec Corporation for IBM PC-compatible computers.

Designed for novice users, Q & A makes correspondence functions, including mail merging and address label printing, easier. The program also can generate reports and retrieve information based on English-language queries. See *integrated program* and *Microsoft Works*.

quad density   See *high density*.

Quark XPress   A page layout program for the Macintosh computer that allows unlimited document length and includes many word processing functions.

Highly regarded for its typographic capabilities and the capability to float text from a box on one page to a box on another, Quark XPress is gaining steadily on its chief competition, PageMaker. See *page layout program* and *PageMaker*.

Quattro Pro   An innovative, three-dimensional spreadsheet program developed by Borland International, which can run on 640K DOS systems. See *three-dimensional spreadsheet*.

query   In database management, a search question that tells the program what kind of data should be retrieved from the database.

The point of an effective database management system is not to display all the information the system contains but to show you only the information you need for a specific purpose.

A query specifies the criteria by which information is extracted from the database. The query guides the computer toward retrieving the required information (and eliminating information not required). See *data independence, declarative language, query language,* and *Structured Query Language (SQL).*

query by example (QBE)   In database management programs, a query technique that prompts you to type the search criteria into a template resembling the data record.

QBE was developed at IBM's Research Laboratory and is used in the QBE program. As a retrieval technique, QBE is emulated by some personal computer database management programs, such as Paradox.

The advantage of query-by-example retrieval is that you need not learn a query language to frame a query. When you initiate the search, the program displays a screen listing all the data fields that appear on every data record; you enter information that restricts the search to just the specified criteria. The fields left blank, however, will match anything.

Suppose that you are searching for the titles of all the Western videotapes in stock rated PG or PG-13. Using QBE techniques, you can type the following query:

CATEGORY	RATING	TITLE
Western	PG or PG-13	

This query says, "Find all records in which the field CATEGORY contains Western and the field RATING contains PG or PG-13."

The output of such a query is a list like the following:

CATEGORY	RATING	TITLE
Western	PG	Showdown
Western	PG	Tumbleweed
Western	PG-13	Not-So-OK Corral

See *database management programs, data record, Paradox,* and *query language.*

query language   In database management programs, a retrieval and data-editing language that enables you to specify the criteria by which the program retrieves and displays the information stored in a database.

The ideal query language is natural language, or everyday English. Ideally, you could ask the computer, "Using the database called VIDEOS, show me all the records in which the CATEGORY field contains Western and the RATING field contains PG or PG–13."

A good query language enables you to type queries in a format that, although rigid in syntax, approximates English, as follows:

```
SELECT title
FROM videos
WHERE CATEGORY = Western
AND RATING = PG
OR RATING = PG-13
```

The dot-prompt language of dBASE is a full-fledged query language, although it has quirks and odd nomenclature that make it difficult to use. The up-and-coming query language for personal computing is Structured Query Language (SQL), already widely used for minicomputer and mainframe databases. See *database management program, query, query by example (QBE),* and *Structured Query Language (SQL).*

queue See *job queue.*

QuickBASIC A high-performance compiler for programs written in Microsoft BASIC. QuickBASIC recognizes modern control structures and enables programmers to omit line numbers.

QuickBASIC was designed to compile any program written in BASICA or GWBASIC, the versions of BASIC supplied with most IBM Personal Computers and compatibles. However, the compiler enables you to create structured programs, complete with indentations and a full set of control structures.

QuickBASIC programs execute much faster than their interpreted counterparts, making the compiler suitable for the creation of commercial software. See *BASIC, compiler,* and *control structure.*

QuickDraw An application program interface built into the Macintosh System software that defines object-oriented graphic routines so that graphics, windows, and menus can be displayed on-screen in the same way by any application program. See *object-oriented graphic.*

Quicken   A checkbook-management program developed by Intuit for IBM PC-compatibles and Macintosh computers. Quicken is widely used as a complete system for home and small-business accounting.

Quicken simplifies home and small-business accounting by enabling you to carry out tasks such as check writing, check printing, budgeting, and tax accounting in a familiar way. Quicken screens resemble an actual checkbook register (see fig. Q.1).

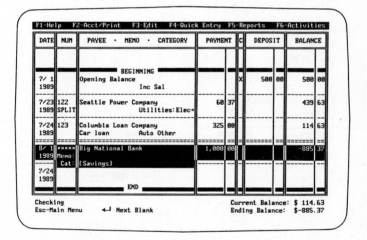

Fig. Q.1. The Quicken Register screen.

Recurring transactions (the payment of the same amounts every month to utilities or creditors) can be automated so that several checks are generated and posted to the register with just one keystroke. The program also can produce a wide variety of reports that enable you to track spending, assess net worth, plan for future cash needs, and list tax-deductible expenditures.

You can accomplish all of these tasks without learning accounting terminology.

QWERTY   Pronounced "kwerty." The standard typewriter keyboard layout also used for computer keyboards.

Alternative keyboard layouts, such as the Dvorak keyboard, speed typing by placing the most commonly used letters on the home row. See *Dvorak keyboard.*

r

r/w   See *read/write.*

radio button   In a graphical user interface, the round option buttons that appear in dialog boxes. Unlike check boxes, radio buttons are mutually exclusive; you can pick only one of the radio button options. See *graphical user interface.*

radio frequency interference (RFI)   The interference with other signals in the radio frequency spectrum caused by the operation of computer equipment or computer peripherals.

All electronic devices generate electromagnetic radiation, but computers are particularly strong emitters of RFI and can disrupt the reception of radio and television signals in nearby houses or apartments.

The U.S. Federal Communications Commission (FCC) regulates commercial computer equipment by requiring that all equipment pass FCC tests before being placed on the market. Two categories of FCC certification are possible, FCC Class A (for businesses) and FCC Class B (the less stringent class for consumer electronics, such as personal computers).

ragged-left alignment   In word processing and desktop publishing, the alignment of each line of text so that the right margin is even, but the left remains ragged. Synonymous with flush right.

ragged-right alignment   In word processing and desktop publishing, the alignment of each line of text so that the left margin is even, but the right remains ragged. Synonymous with flush left.

→ **Tip:** Typographers say that ragged-right alignment is easier to read and more attractive than full justification, in which the left and right margins are aligned. Full justification often is chosen by personal computer users because it produces a more professional appearance, but full-justified documents may be more difficult to read.

RAM   See *random-access memory (RAM)*.

RAM cache   Pronounced "ram cash." A section of random-access memory (RAM) set aside to serve as a buffer between the central processing unit (CPU) and the disk drives.

Because RAM can deliver data and program instructions to the CPU hundreds of times faster than a disk drive, a computer's performance may improve significantly with a RAM cache. A RAM cache stores data and program instructions that an application is likely to require frequently so that this information can be accessed directly from RAM.

The RAM cache also speeds operations by accepting data to be written to disk as fast as the CPU can send data, rather than forcing the CPU to wait until disk-writing operations are completed at the disk's speed. See *central processing unit (CPU), disk cache,* and *random-access memory (RAM)*.

RAM disk   An area of electronic memory configured by a software program to emulate a disk drive. Data stored in a RAM disk can be accessed more quickly than data stored on a disk drive, but this data is erased whenever you turn off or reboot the computer.

RAMDRIVE.SYS   In DOS, a configuration file provided with the operating system that sets aside part of your computer's random-access memory (RAM) so that it acts as a disk drive.

▲ **Caution:** Because virtual disk drives operate much faster than real disk drives, placing programs or data in a virtual disk drive can result in major performance improvements. However, the benefits come at a stiff price.

If you are using a 640K DOS system, you must create the virtual disk out of the available random-access memory (RAM), and because you do not have enough memory to begin with, you may not be able to run your application programs. If you have extended memory or expanded memory, however, you can place the virtual disk in the RAM above 640K, but you still are taking a big risk. When you save work to this disk, you are really writing your work to RAM, and everything in RAM is lost when you switch off the computer. Many computer users have lost hours of important work by failing to copy a document from a virtual disk to a real disk at the end of a session. Synonymous with VDISK.SYS, the name of the driver in IBM releases of DOS. See *configuration file*, *device driver*, *expanded memory*, *extended memory*, and *random-access memory (RAM)*.

random access   An information storage and retrieval technique in which the information can be accessed directly without having to go through a sequence of locations.

This term doesn't imply that information is stored randomly in the memory. The computer does not have to go through a sequence of items (sequential access) to get to the needed information. A better term is direct access, but "random access" has become enshrined in the acronym commonly used to describe a PC's internal memory, random-access memory (RAM).

To understand the distinction between random and sequential access, compare a cassette tape with a long-playing record. To get to the song you want on a cassette tape, you must fast forward through a sequence of songs until you encounter the one you want. To get to the song you want on a record, however, you can move the arm above the surface of the record and go to the track you want. Precisely the same principle is used in computer disk drives. See *random-access memory (RAM)* and *sequential access*.

random-access memory (RAM)   The computer's primary working memory in which program instructions and data are stored so that they are accessible directly to the central processing unit (CPU).

To perform computations at high speeds, the computer's processing circuitry must be able to obtain information from the memory directly and quickly. Computer memories, therefore, are designed to give the processor random access to the contents.

Think of RAM as a checkerboard, with each square on the board capable of holding a byte of data or program instructions. Because many personal computers can hold half a million bytes of internal memory, the computer needs some way to find a given memory location with precision. Every square on the checkerboard, therefore, has an address, like a post office box.

Because each location has a unique address, the CPU can access each memory location directly by specifying the address and activating the circuit that leads directly to that address.

RAM often is called read/write memory to distinguish it from read-only memory (ROM), the other component of a personal computer's primary storage. In RAM, the CPU can write and read data. Most application programs set aside a portion of RAM as a temporary work space for your data, enabling you to modify (rewrite) as needed until the data is ready for printing or storage on disk.

Almost all computers now use volatile semiconductor memory, which does not retain its contents when the power to the computer is switched off.

▲ **Caution:** Save your work frequently. In the event of a system failure or power interruption, you lose all work in RAM that you have not recorded (saved) on a magnetic medium such as a disk drive. See *primary storage, random access, read-only memory (ROM),* and *secondary storage.*

range   In a spreadsheet program, a cell or a rectangular group of cells.

Spreadsheet programs would be tedious to use if you could not perform operations (such as formatting) on groups of cells. For example, you can format one column of numbers with the currency format, even though the rest of the worksheet uses a general format.

All spreadsheet programs enable you to identify ranges of cells. A range can include one cell or thousands, with one restriction: the range must be rectangular in shape and consist of contiguous cells (see fig. R.1). Valid ranges include a single cell, part of a column, part of a row, and a block spanning several columns and several rows.

When using a spreadsheet program, you use range ex-pressions frequently in commands and formulas. A range expression gives you a way to define the boundaries of the rectangular range. See *cell.*

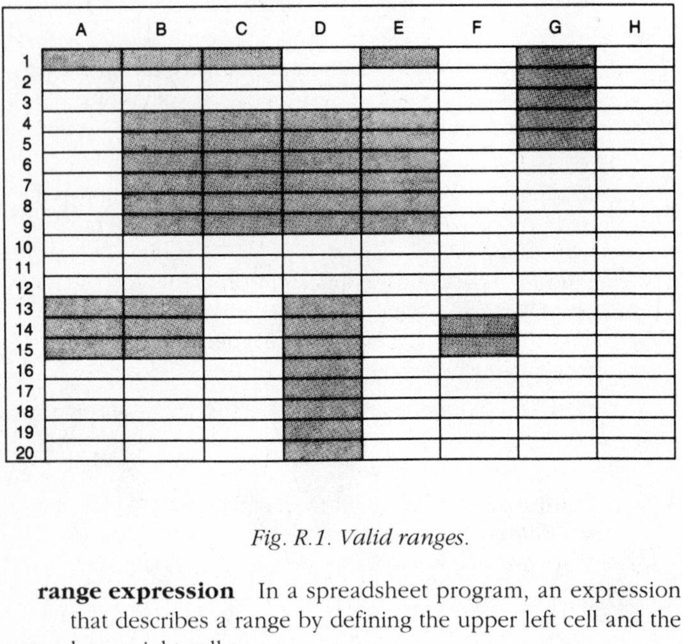

Fig. R.1. Valid ranges.

range expression In a spreadsheet program, an expression that describes a range by defining the upper left cell and the lower right cell.

In Lotus 1-2-3, you write a range expression using the beginning cell..ending cell pattern as in the following example:

A9..B12

The range expression A9..B12 defines a rectangular block that begins with cell A9. Because the ending cell is B12 (one column right and three rows down) the range includes all the following cells:

A9	B9
A10	B10
A11	B11
A12	B12

See *range name.*

range format   In a spreadsheet program, a numeric format or label alignment format that applies to only a range and overrides the global format. See *global format, label alignment, numeric format,* and *range.*

range name   In a spreadsheet program, a range of cells to which you attach a distinctive name.

Remembering a range name is much easier than remembering a range expression. You can name a range of cells and then refer to the range by entering the name. For example, suppose that you create a worksheet in which range E9..E21 contains your company's sales for the first quarter of 1991. After naming the range FQ1991, you use the range name—not the range expression—in formulas. In a formula that totals the column, for example, you type

@SUM(FQ1991)

A second advantage of range naming is that after you have named the range, the name accurately and precisely refers to the entire range. If you type FQ1991, the program unfailingly equates this name with the range E9..E21. If you type this range expression over and over (rather than the range name), however, you may make a typing error, referring once to the range E9..E20 without catching your error. The program cannot detect an error of this sort, and you introduce a significant error into your spreadsheet.

→ **Tip:** To avoid errors in range references, name ranges and use the names in formulas. See *range* and *range expression*.

raster display   The display technology used in television sets and computer monitors. Dozens of times each second, the screen is scanned from top to bottom by a tightly focused electron beam that follows a zig-zag pattern as it moves line-by-line down the screen. See *vector graphics*.

raster image processor (RIP)   Pronounced "rip." In a laser printer, a device that interprets the instructions of a page description language to compose an image of a page and transfer the image to the photosensitive drum of the print engine, line-by-line.

raw data   Unprocessed or unrefined data that has not been arranged, edited, or represented in a form for easy retrieval and analysis.

R:BASE   A relational database-management program developed by MicroRim, Inc., for IBM PC-compatible computers.

RCA plug   See *phono plug*.

RD   See *RMDIR*.

RDBMS   See *relational database management system (RDBMS)*.

read   To retrieve data or program instructions from a peripheral such as a disk drive and place the data into the computer's memory.

read-only   In DOS, a file whose read-only file attribute has been set so that the file can be viewed but not deleted or modified.

➔ **Tip:** In DOS, when you create a template such as a let-terhead or a generic worksheet, use the ATTRIB command to turn the file's read-only attribute on. When you retrieve and modify the file, you cannot overwrite the original file acci-dentally; DOS requires you to save the file with a new file name. You also cannot erase the file accidentally, unless you shut off the read-only attribute. See *ATTRIB*, *file attribute*, *locked file*, and *read/write*.

read-only attribute   In DOS and OS/2, a file attribute stored with a file's directory entry that indicates whether the file can be modified or deleted.

When the read-only attribute is on, you can display the file but cannot modify or erase it. When the read-only attribute is off, you can modify or delete the file.

The ATTRIB command is used to change a file's read-only attribute. See *file attribute*.

read-only memory (ROM)   Pronounced "rahm." The portion of a computer's primary storage that does not lose its con-tents when the current is switched off and contains essential system programs, which neither you nor the computer can erase.

Because the computer's random-access memory (RAM) is volatile (loses information when the current is switched off), the computer's internal memory is blank at power-up, and the computer can perform no functions unless given start-up instructions.

These instructions are provided by the ROM, which may contain only simple programs that tell the disk drive where to find and load the computer's operating system. A growing trend, however, is toward including substantial portions of the operating system on ROM chips, instead of providing the bulk of the operating system on disk.

In the Macintosh, for example, much of the Macintosh System is encoded on ROM chips, including the graphics routines (QuickDraw) that are part of the Mac's application program interface (API). However, upgrading top ROM is more difficult and expensive than supplying new disks. See *application program interface (API)*, *erasable programmable read-only memory (EPROM)*, *programmable read-only memory (PROM)*, and *QuickDraw*.

read/write   The capability of an internal memory or secondary storage device to record data (write) and to play back data previously recorded or saved (read).

read/write file   In DOS, a file whose read-only file attribute is set so that the file can be deleted and modified. See *ATTRIB*, *file attribute*, *locked file*, and *read-only*.

read/write head   In a hard disk or floppy disk drive, the magnetic recording and playback device that travels back and forth across the surface of the disk, storing and retrieving data.

read/write memory   See *random-access memory (RAM)*.

real mode   An operating mode of Intel microprocessors in which a program is given a definite storage location in memory and direct access to peripheral devices.

Real mode is a straightforward way of allocating memory space in a single-user, stand-alone computer system but causes problems when more than one program is loaded into memory simultaneously; programs can invade each other's memory space or try to access peripheral devices simultaneously. In both situations, a system failure may result.

Therefore, the Intel 80286, 80386, and 80486 microprocessors offer an additional operating mode, protected mode, that supervises the allocation of memory and governs access to peripheral devices. See *Intel 80286*, *Intel 80386*, *Intel 80486*, *memory-management program*, and *protected mode*.

real time   The immediate processing of input, such as a point-of-sale transaction or a measurement performed by an analog laboratory device.

recalculation method   In a spreadsheet program, the way the program recalculates cell values after you change the contents of a cell. See *automatic recalculation* and *manual recalculation.*

recalculation order   In a spreadsheet program, the mode currently in effect for recalculating the values in the spreadsheet after you type new values, labels, or formulas.

Early spreadsheet programs offered two recalculation modes, column-wise recalculation and row-wise recalculation. In column-wise recalculation, the program recalculates all the cells in column A before moving to column B, and so on.

In row-wise recalculation, the program recalculates all the cells in row 1 before moving to the beginning of row 2, and so on.

▲ **Caution:** Programs that offer only these two options, such as shareware spreadsheet programs, or very early versions of commercial spreadsheet programs, can produce serious errors.

Suppose that you have created a worksheet in which figures are totaled by column. You place data in columns A, B, and C; in cells A15, B15, and C15, you place a formula to calculate the sum of the column. To show the total of all three columns, you place a formula in cell A14.

However, the sum displayed in this cell may not be accurate. If the program is set to row-wise recalculation order, cell A14 is recalculated before the column totals are recalculated. In most cases, you obtain the correct answer only by changing the recalculation order to column-wise recalculation.

Today's advanced spreadsheet programs, such as Lotus 1-2-3, get around this problem by offering natural recalculation as the default recalculation order. In natural recalculation, a formula is not calculated until all the formulas to which it refers are calculated. The program scans the entire worksheet to determine the logical order of recalculation as established by creating formulas that reference each other. See *column-wise recalculation, natural recalculation, optimal recalculation,* and *row-wise recalculation.*

reboot See *warm boot.*

record See *data record.*

record-oriented database management program A database management program that displays data records as the result of query operations, unlike a table-oriented program in which the result of all data query operations is a table. Purists argue that a true relational database management program always treats data in tabular form, and any program that displays records as the result of queries, such as dBASE, does not deserve to call itself relational even if the program can work with two or more databases at a time.

The rationale for such an attitude is partly academic; the relational model of database management is based on an elegant mathematical foundation so that any departure from its true form (in which data is represented in tables) is an affront to mathematical purity. But the rationale also is practical; a program that retrieves data records as the result of query operations confronts you with much unwanted information, and because most records take up the whole screen, you must page through them.

A table-oriented program, in contrast, succinctly summarizes data in tables displayed on-screen, eliminating all extraneous data not specifically called for in the search query. See *data retrieval, relational database management, Structured Query Language (SQL),* and *table-oriented database management program.*

record pointer In a database management program, the record pointer is an on-screen status message that states the number of the data record currently displayed on-screen (or in which the cursor is positioned).

recover To bring the computer system back to a previous, stable operating state or to restore erased or misdirected data. The recovery, which may require user intervention, is needed after a system or user error occurs, such as instructing the system to write data to a drive not containing a disk. See *undelete utility*.

RECOVER In DOS and OS/2, an external command that recovers the salvageable data or program instructions from a file containing bad sectors.

Use this command with care and attempt to recover only data files. Recopy program files from the original disks if they become damaged on a work disk.

▲ **Caution:** Do not use RECOVER for an entire disk or directory. All file names are converted to FILEnnnn.REC, where nnnn is a number, starting with 0001. You must figure out what each file contains.

recoverable error An error that does not cause the program or system to crash or to erase data irretrievably.

recto The right-hand (odd-numbered) page in two-sided printing. See *verso*.

redirection See *input/output redirection*.

redirection operator In DOS and OS/2, a symbol that routes input or output directions to or from a device other than the console (the keyboard and video display).

You can use the following redirection operators in a DOS or OS/2 command:

> Output redirection. Redirects the output of a command from the console to a file or device. The following command, for example, redirects the contents of LETTER.DOC to the printer:

```
TYPE LETTER.DOC > PRN
```

>> Append redirection. Redirects the output of a command from the console to an existing file and adds the output to the existing file's contents. The following command, for example, redirects the output to DIR.DOC, and appends the information to the end of the file if DIR.DOC exists:

DIR B: >> DIR.DOC

< Input redirection. Changes the input of a command
from the console to a file, so that the contents of
the file are used instead of data input at the
keyboard. The following command, for example,
redirects SORT's input from the file TERMS.DOC:

SORT < TERMS.DOC

See *input/output redirection.*

redlining In word processing, an attribute such as a distinctive color or double underlining that marks the text co-au-
thors have added to a document being produced by a
workgroup. The redlined text is highlighted so that other authors or editors know exactly what has been added to or deleted from the document.

reduced instruction set computer (RISC) Pronounced
"risk." A central processing unit (CPU) in which the number
of instructions the processor can execute is reduced to a
minimum to increase processing speed.

Microprocessors, such as the Intel 80386, recognize well
over one hundred instructions for performing various computations, but the more instructions a chip can handle, the
more slowly it runs for all instructions.

The idea of a RISC architecture is to reduce the instruction
set to the bare minimum, emphasizing the instructions that
are used most of the time, and optimizing them for the fastest
possible execution. The instructions left out of the chip must
be carried out by combining the ones left, but because these
instructions are needed far less frequently, a RISC processor
usually runs 50 to 75 percent faster than its CISC counterpart.

RISC processors also are cheaper to design, debug, and
manufacture because they are less complex. See *central
processing unit (CPU)* and *complex instruction set computer
(CISC).*

reformat In operating systems, to repeat a formatting operation on a secondary storage disk, such as a floppy disk or
hard disk. In word processing or page layout programs, to
change the arrangement of text elements on the page.

refresh To repeat the display or storage of data to keep it from fading or becoming lost. The video display and random-access memory (RAM) must be refreshed constantly.

relational database management An approach to database management in which data is stored in two-dimensional data tables. The program can work with two data tables at the same time, relating the information through links established by a common column or field.

The term relational as applied to database management was introduced in 1970 by Edgar Codd to refer to the storage and retrieval of data in the form of tables, in which the table defines the relation between the items listed in rows (data records) and columns (data fields).

Codd founded his database design on an elegant mathematical theory. A true relational database, one designed solely in accordance with this theory, treats all data as tables, and the result of any query is a new table.

Suppose that a video store database lists customer's phone numbers and names in a table as follows:

Phone_no	Name
325-4321	Smith, Ted
325-4411	Jones, Jane

Another table contains the titles of rented videotapes, the phone number of the person who rented the tape, and the due date:

Title	Phone_no	Due_date
Blues	325-4321	07/16/90
Danger	325-4411	07/19/90

A query may ask, "Show me the name and phone number of customers with tapes due on or before July 19, 1990, and print the film's title." Such a query results in the following table:

Name	Phone_no	Title
Smith, Ted	325-4321	Blues
Jones, Jane	325-4411	Danger

Not all database management programs marketed as relational are true table-oriented programs. Most are record-oriented programs relational only to the extent that they can link data in two databases through a common field. dBASE is such a program; data is stored in records, not tables. However, you can use dBASE as if it is a true relational program.

relational database management system (RDBMS) A relational database management program, especially one that comes with all the necessary support programs and documentation needed to create, install, and maintain custom database applications.

relational model See *relational database management.*

relational operator A symbol used to specify the relation between two numeric values.

In query languages, relational operators frequently are used in specifying search criteria. For example, a video store manager may want to ask the computer, "Show me all the telephone numbers of customers with overdue tapes—due on a date less than or equal to May 7, 1990."

In electronic spreadsheets, relational operators are used to return the number 1 if the expression is true and 0 if the expression is false. In @IF formulas, relational operators can be used to perform tests on data so that different values are displayed depending on the results of the test.

Suppose that you are computing sales bonuses. If a salesperson has sold more than $22,000 worth of merchandise, the normal bonus (5 percent) is increased to 7.5 percent. In the expression @IF(B14>22000, 0.75, 0.5), the program tests cell B14 to see whether the number (total sales) is greater than 22,000. If so, the cell displays 0.75. If not, the cell displays 0.5.

To permit the expression of logical operators in the character-based world of computing, many programs use the following conventions:

Free Issue and a Special Gift.

DBMS, the magazine on increasing database productivity, is the leading publication for professional database developers, serious end users, and DP/MIS managers and staff. *DBMS* is crammed with innovative programming tips and insight on the latest products designed to enhance your database development skills. Your subscription also includes the special *Database Buyers Guide.*

Plus you'll receive a copy of *DBMS TechTips* absolutely FREE! This booklet of database tricks and techniques will save you time and help you create better, faster database applications.

So, what are you waiting for? You have everything to gain and nothing to lose. Examine *DBMS* for yourself by returning the attached postcard today! This special offer won't last long.

DBMS

501 GALVESTON DRIVE
REDWOOD CITY, CALIFORNIA 94063

Dear D. Wolinsky:

I have a _free_ issue reserved in your name. May I send it to you?

You are under no obligation. Just return the above postage-paid card to receive your _free_ sample issue.

Why not take a look?

Kevin Strehlo
Editor-in-Chief

A FREE ISSUE IS RESERVED FOR:

********** **5-DIGIT** 30319
D. Wolinsky
10008 Regencywoods Dr.
Atlanta GA, 30319

=	equal to
<	less than
>	greater than
<=	less than or equal to
=>	greater than or equal to
<>	not equal to

relative addressing   See *relative cell reference.*

relative cell reference   In a spreadsheet program, a formula's cell reference adjusted when you copy the formula to another cell or a range of cells.

To understand what happens when you copy a relative cell reference, you need to know how a spreadsheet program actually records a cell reference. When you type the formula @SUM(C5..C8) in cell C8, the program does not actually record "add cells C5, C6, C7, and C8" in the file (see fig. R.2). Instead, the program records a code that means, "add all the values in the next four cells above the current cell."

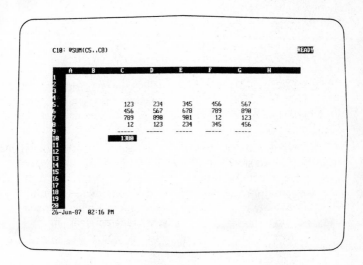

Fig. R.2. Worksheet with one column summed.

When you copy this formula to the next four cells to the right (D10..G10), it still reads, "add all the values in the next four cells above the current cell," and sums each column correctly (see fig. R.3). See *absolute cell reference* and *mixed cell reference*.

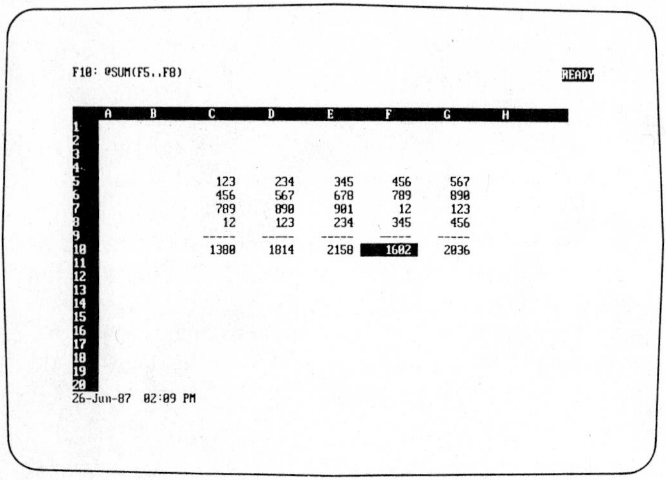

```
F10: @SUM(F5..F8)                                              READY

      A       B       C       D       E       F       G       H
 1
 2
 3
 4
 5            123     234     345     456     567
 6            456     567     678     789     898
 7            789     898     901      12     123
 8             12     123     234     345     456
 9            -----   -----   -----   -----   -----
10           1380    1814    2158    1682    2836
11
12
13
14
15
16
17
18
19
20
26-Jun-87  02:09 PM
```

Fig. R.3. A copied formula with relative cell references.

release number   The number, usually a decimal number, that identifies an incrementally improved version of a program, rather than a major revision, which is numbered using an integer.

A program labeled Version 5.1, for example, is the second release of Version 5 of the program (the first was Version 5.0). This numbering scheme isn't used by all software publishers, and competitive pressures sometimes encourage publishers to jump to a new version number when the program being released is in fact only an incremental improvement over its predecessor. See *version*.

reliability The capability of computer hardware or software to perform as the user expects and to do so consistently, without failures or erratic behavior. See *mean time between failures (MTBF)*.

REM In DOS and OS/2, a batch file command that displays the text that follows the command as an on-screen message. See *batch file*.

remark In a batch file, macro, or source code, explanatory text ignored when the computer executes the commands. See *batch file*.

remote terminal See *terminal*.

removable mass storage A high-capacity secondary storage medium, such as a Bernoulli box or a tape backup system, in which the magnetic disk or tape is encased in a plastic cartridge or cassette and can be removed from the drive for safekeeping.

By this definition, a high-density floppy disk qualifies as a removable mass storage medium, but the term usually is reserved for cartridge-based backup systems with many megabytes of storage capacity. See *Bernoulli box*.

removable storage media A secondary storage device in which the actual storage medium, such as a magnetic disk, can be removed from the drive for safekeeping.

Floppy disks are removable storage media, but the term is more often applied to tape backup units and Bernoulli boxes that use cartridges which can hold dozens of megabytes of data.

REN In DOS and OS/2, an internal command that changes the name of a disk file or files. See *internal command*.

repagination In word processing and desktop publishing, a formatting operation in which pages are renumbered to reflect insertions, deletions, block moves, or other changes to the document's text.

Most programs repaginate automatically as the user inserts and edits text, but some programs require a manual repagination operation before the page count and specific page numbers are correctly displayed on-screen.

repeat key   A key that continues to enter the same character as long as the key is held down.

repeater   In local area networks, a hardware device used to extend the length of network cabling by amplifying and passing along the messages traveling along the network. See *local area network* (LAN).

repeating field   A fundamental error of database design that compromises data integrity by forcing you to type the same data item repeatedly.

Consider the following database design:

TITLE	SUPPLIER_ID	SUPPLIER
Spring Rains	BVS	Big Video Supply
Prince of Doom	AD	Acme Distributors
Warp Drive	AD	Acme Distributors
Fast Buck	AD	Acme Distributors

The SUPPLIER field repeats the data in the SUPPLIER_ID field and forces you to type the SUPPLIER name more than once, because one vendor can supply more than one videotape.

The cure for this problem is to create two databases, TITLES and SUPPLIER. In the TITLES database, you see the following:

TITLE	SUPPLIER_ID
Spring Rains	IGVS
Prince of Doom	AD
Warp Drive	AD
Fast Buck	AD

And in the SUPPLIER database, you see the following:

SUPPLIER_ID	SUPPLIER	ADDRESS
AD	Acme Dist.	8609 Elm Drive
BVS	Big Video Supply	123 24th St.

See *database design, data integrity,* and *data redundancy.*

repeating label   In a spreadsheet program, a character preceded by a label prefix that causes the character to be repeated across the cell.

For example, \ is used in Lotus 1-2-3 to repeat one or more characters across a cell. For example, the entry \- produces a line of hyphens across the cell.

→ **Tip:** You can use repeating labels to create lines across your worksheet. Single lines are created from repeated hyphens, and double lines are made of repeated equal signs. See *label prefix.*

repetitive stress injury (RSI)   A potentially debilitating disease of the hands, wrist, shoulders, upper back, or neck, such as carpal tunnel syndrome or tendonitis, caused by spending too much time performing repetitive motions at a computer terminal or other computer-related equipment, such as a point-of-sale terminal.

RSI is signaled by wrist aches, numbness in the hands, and sharp pains or "pins and needles" in the arms, shoulders, upper back, or neck.

→ **Tip:** Avoid RSI by taking a break, stretching, and exercising at frequent intervals as you work at the computer.

replace   A text processing utility found in most word processing programs that searches for a string and replaces it with another string.

▲ **Caution:** Unless you are absolutely sure you know what you are doing, use the replace utility only in the mode that requests your confirmation. If you permit the utility to do its work without confirmation throughout the document, it may perform incorrect substitutions.

Suppose that you want to delete the vague intensifier "very" throughout your document. You perform the replacement without confirmation. However, the utility also removes the string "very" from the word "every."

With most programs, you can improve the accuracy of the replacement operation by specifying capitalization and whole-word options. If you tell the program to match the capitalization pattern in the search string (such as TREE), the program replaces only those strings that match the characters and the capitalization pattern (TREE is replaced, but not Tree or tree).

If you select the whole-word option when replacing very, the program replaces the string only if it stands alone as a whole word, but not if the string is part of a longer word.

REPLACE   In DOS and OS/2, an external command that selectively replaces files with matching names from one disk to another.

The REPLACE command is more selective than COPY and XCOPY. However, the command confuses many users because it can do two tasks that are exact opposites.

When you copy a file using REPLACE without the /A command parameter, the command copies the file only if a destination file exists with exactly the same name. When used this way, this command replaces a copy of a file with an up-to-date copy. When you use the /A command parameter, REPLACE copies the file only if there is no destination file with the same name. See *external command.*

replaceable parameter   In DOS and OS/2, a symbol used in a batch file that DOS replaces with information you type. The symbol consists of a percent sign and a number from 1 through 9, such as %1.

Suppose that you create a batch file called PRINTNOW .BAT with the following statement:

```
COPY %1 PRN
```

Then, you type the following command:

```
PRINTNOW letter.doc
```

DOS or OS/2 replaces the %1 symbol with the file name you typed and copies LETTER.DOC to the printer. See *batch file* and *FOR*.

report   In database management, printed output usually formatted with page numbers and headings. With most programs, reports can include calculated fields, showing subtotals, totals, averages, and other figures computed from the data. See *calculated field*.

report generator   A program or program function that enables a non-programmer to request printed output from a computer database.

Report Program Generator (RPG)   A programming language for report generation. RPG was developed by IBM.

RPG enables a novice programmer to produce output from a database by describing the format in which the data is to be printed. RPG then generates the necessary programming code.

research network   A wide-area computer network, such as ARPANET or NSFNET, developed and funded by a governmental agency to improve research productivity in areas of national interest.

ResEdit   Pronounced "rez edit." A Macintosh utility program, available free from Apple Computer dealers, that enables you to edit (and copy to other programs) many program features such as menu text, icons, cursor shapes, and dialog boxes.

Every Macintosh file is made up of two parts, the data fork and the resource fork. The data fork contains data, such as text or the data in a database; the resource fork contains a variety of separate program resources, such as dialog boxes, sounds, icons, menus, and graphic images.

With ResEdit, you can edit these resources, thereby customizing the program, or copy the resources to other programs, where they become available as programming resources.

▲ **Caution:** If you are modifying a program file, be sure to work on a backup copy of the program. With ResEdit, modifying icons, menus, and dialog boxes is easy , but you accidentally may make a change that corrupts the program. See *utility program.*

reset key   A key or button that, when pressed, restarts the computer. Usually mounted on the system unit case, this key provides an alternative to switching the power key off and on after a crash so severe that the keyboard does not respond. Synonymous with *hardware reset.* See *programmer's switch.*

resident program   See *terminate-and-stay resident (TSR) program.*

resolution   A measurement—usually expressed in linear dots per inch (dpi), horizontally and vertically—of the sharpness of an image generated by an output device such as a monitor or printer.

In monitors, resolution is expressed as the number of pixels displayed on-screen. For example, a CGA monitor displays fewer pixels than a VGA monitor, and, therefore, a CGA image appears more jagged than a VGA image.

Dot-matrix printers produce output with a lower resolution than laser printers.

response time   The time the computer needs to respond and carry out a request.

Response time is a better measurement of system performance than access time because it more fairly states the system's throughput. See *access time.*

RESTORE   In DOS and OS/2, an external command that copies files backed up with the BACKUP command, restoring the files to the subdirectory from which they were copied. See *BACKUP* and *external command.*

retrieval   All the procedures involved in finding, summarizing, organizing, displaying, or printing information from a computer system in a form useful for the end user.

Return   See *Enter/Return.*

reverse video   In monochrome monitors, a means of highlighting text on the display screen so that normally dark characters are displayed as bright characters on a dark background, or normally bright characters are displayed as dark characters on a bright background. See *highlighting.*

rewrite   Synonymous with *overwrite.*

RGB monitor   A color digital monitor that accepts separate inputs for red, green, and blue, and produces a much sharper image than composite color monitors.

   Although the Enhanced Graphics Display uses RGB techniques, RGB monitor is synonymous in IBM PC-compatible computing with the Color Graphics Adapter (CGA) standard. See *composite color monitor.*

right justification   In word processing, the alignment of text along the right margin and the left margin, producing a superficial resemblance to professionally printed text. The results may be poor, however, if the printer is incapable of proportional spacing; in such cases, right justification can be achieved only by inserting unsightly gaps of two or more spaces between words. For readability, most graphics artists advise computer users to leave the right margin ragged.

RightWriter   A grammar- and punctuation-checking program that can identify dozens of common errors in English usage. The program reads files created by a variety of popular word processing programs. RightWriter uses a built-in set of rules to detect and questionable words, phrases, or sentences that may not conform to accepted standards of English usage for clear, concise business writing.

ring network   In local area networks, a decentralized network topology in which a number of nodes (including workstations, shared peripherals, and file servers) are arranged around a closed loop cable.

Like a bus network, a ring network's workstations send messages to all other workstations. Each node in the ring, however, has a unique address, and its reception circuitry constantly monitors the bus to determine whether a message is being sent. A message sent to the node named Laser Printer is ignored by the other nodes on the network.

Unlike a bus network, each node contains a repeater that amplifies and sends the signal along to the next node. Therefore, ring networks can extend far beyond the geographic limits of bus networks that lack repeaters.

However, the failure of a single node can disrupt the entire network. Fault-tolerance schemes, however, have been devised that enable ring networks to continue to function even if one or more nodes fail.

The ring-like electronic structure of the network may not be immediately obvious from its physical layout, which may resemble a star network or multiple stars; the ring is implemented in the actual electronic connections among the computers, which may or may not be reflected in their actual geographic distribution (see fig. R.4). See *file server, local area network (LAN), network topology,* and *node.*

Fig. R.4. A ring topology.

RIP   See *raster image processor (RIP)*.

ripple-through effect   In a spreadsheet program, the sudden appearance of ERR values throughout the cells of a spreadsheet after a change is made that breaks the linkage among formulas.

If you introduce a change in a spreadsheet that corrupts a formula so that it evaluates to ERR (error) or NA (unavailable value), all the formulas linked to (dependent on) this one also display ERR, and you see the ERR message ripple through the spreadsheet.

If this happens, you may think that you have ruined the whole spreadsheet. But after you locate and repair the problem, all the other formulas are restored.

river   In desktop publishing, a formatting flaw caused by accidental patterns of white space between words that encourage the eye to follow the flow down three or more lines.

Rivers injure what typographers refer to as the color of the page, which should be perceived by the eye as an overall shade of gray without interruption from white spaces, bad word breaks, poor character spacing, or uneven line spacing. See *desktop publishing*.

RLL   See *run length limited (RLL) recording*.

RMDIR   In DOS and OS/2, an internal command that deletes an empty subdirectory from a disk. See *internal command*.

ROM   See *read-only memory (ROM)*.

Roman   1. In typography, an upright serif typeface of medium weight. 2. In proofreading, characters without emphasis. See *emphasis*, *serif*, and *weight*.

root directory   The top-level directory on a disk, the one DOS creates when you format the disk. See *directory*, *parent directory*, and *subdirectory*.

root name   The first, mandatory part of a DOS file name, using from one to eight characters. See *extension* and *file name*.

roughs In desktop publishing, the preliminary page layouts done by the designer using pencil sketches to represent page design ideas. Synonymous with thumbnails. See *desktop publishing*.

row In a spreadsheet program, a horizontal block of cells running across the breadth of the spreadsheet. In most programs, rows are numbered sequentially from the top. In a database, a row is the same as a record or data record.

row-wise recalculation In spreadsheet programs, a recalculation order that calculates all the values in row 1 before moving to row 2 and so on.

▲ **Caution:** If your spreadsheet program does not offer natural recalculation, use row-wise recalculation for worksheets in which rows are summed and the totals are forwarded. Column-wise recalculation may produce an erroneous result. See *column-wise recalculation*, *natural recalculation*, *optimal recalculation*, and *recalculation order*.

RS-232 A standard recommended by the Electronic Industries Association (EIA) concerning the asynchronous transmission of computer data.

The standard widely used in IBM PC-compatible computing is an updated one: Recommended Standard 232C. See *serial port*.

RS-422 A standard recommended by the Electronic Industries Association (EIA) and used as the serial port standard for Macintosh computers, RS-422 governs the asynchronous transmission of computer data at speeds of up to 920,000 bits per second.

rule In computer graphics and desktop publishing, a thin black horizontal or vertical line.

run To execute a program.

run length limited (RLL) recording   A method of storing and retrieving information on a hard disk that, compared to "double density" techniques, increases by at least 50 percent the amount of data a hard disk can store.

The improvement in storage density is achieved by translating the data into a new digital format that can be written more compactly to the disk. The translation is achieved, however, only at the cost of adding complex electronics to the storage device. Therefore, RLL drives are more expensive than their MFM counterparts. See *modified frequency modulation [MFM] recording*.

run-time version   A commercial version of an interpreter or windowing environment that enables the creator of a program to sell an executable version of the program.

Not all users have Microsoft Windows, for example, so some software publishers sell their Windows applications with a run-time version of Windows. This version loads each time the program is used but cannot be used with other programs. See *interpreter* and *windowing environment*.

S

SAA   See *Systems Application Architecture (SAA).*

sans serif   Pronounced "san serr´-if." A typeface that lacks serifs, the fine cross strokes across the ends of the main strokes of a character.

➔ **Tip:** Sans serif typefaces, such as Helvetica, are preferred for display type but are harder to read than serif typefaces, such as Times Roman, when used for body type. See *body type, display type, Helvetica, Roman, serif,* and *typeface.*

satellite   In a multiuser computer system, a terminal or workstation linked to a centralized host computer. See *host.*

sawtooth distortion   See *aliasing*.

scaling   In presentation graphics, the adjustment of the y-axis (values axis) chosen by the program so that differences in the data are highlighted.

Most presentation graphics programs scale the y-axis, but the scaling choice may be unsatisfactory (see fig. S.1). Manually adjusting the scaling produces better results (see fig. S.2). See *presentation graphics* and *y-axis*.

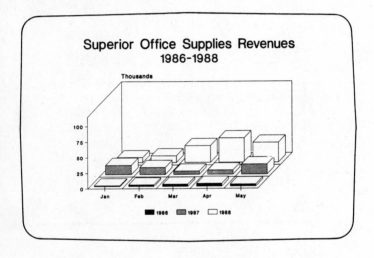

Fig. S.1. Column graph with unsatisfactory scaling.

scanned image   A bit-mapped, or TIFF, image generated by an optical scanner. See *Tagged Image File Format (TIFF)*.

scanner   A peripheral device that digitizes artwork or photographs and stores the image as a file that can be merged with text in many word processing and page layout programs.

Scanners use two techniques for transforming photographs into digitized images (see fig. S.3). The first technique, dithering, simulates a halftone by varying the space between the

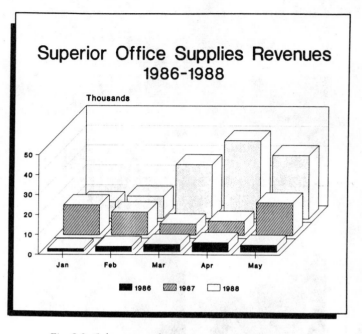

Fig. S.2. Column graph with improved scaling.

dots normally used to create a bit-mapped graphic image. Like all bit-mapped images, the digital halftone cannot be sized without introducing crude distortions, and the quality may be too crude for professional applications.

The second technique, Tagged Image File Format (TIFF), stores the image using a series of 16 gray values and produces better results, but this technique is still inferior to halftones produced by photographic methods. See *bit-mapped graphic*, *halftone*, and *Tagged Image File Format (TIFF)*.

scatter diagram   An analytical graphic in which data items are plotted as points on two numeric axes.

Scatter diagrams show clustering relationships in numeric data. In Lotus 1-2-3, for example, a scatter diagram (an XY graph) shows a clear correlation between sales and advertising funds (see fig. S.4).

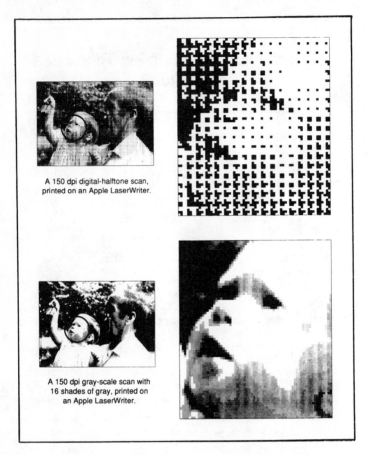

A 150 dpi digital-halftone scan, printed on an Apple LaserWriter.

A 150 dpi gray-scale scan with 16 shades of gray, printed on an Apple LaserWriter.

Fig. S.3. Digital halftone (top) and gray-scale image (bottom).

scatter plot   See *scatter diagram.*

scientific notation   See *floating-point calculation.*

scissoring   In computer graphics, an editing technique in which an image is trimmed to a size determined by a frame, which is sized and then placed over the graphic.

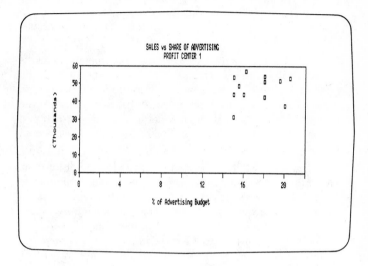

Fig. S.4. A scatter diagram.

scrapbook On the Macintosh, a desk accessory that can hold frequently used graphic images, such as a company letterhead, which can be inserted into new documents as required.

screen capture The storage of a screen display as a text or graphics file on disk.

screen dump A printout of the current screen display.

screen font A bit-mapped font designed to mimic the appearance of printer fonts when displayed on medium-resolution monitors. Modern laser printers can print text with a resolution of 300 dpi or more, but video displays, except for the most expensive, professional units, lack such high resolution and cannot display typefaces with such precision and beauty. What you see isn't necessarily what you get.

In character-based IBM PC-compatible machines running under DOS, no attempt is made to suggest the printer font's typeface. In WordPerfect, for example, you type what appears to be a generic Roman typeface and attach invisible formatting instructions that control the selection of printer fonts.

In graphics-oriented windowing environments (such as Microsoft Windows, OS/2's Presentation Manager, or the Macintosh's System) a low-resolution font can be used to suggest the design of the typeface that appears when the document is printed. Such fonts usually are bit-mapped fonts, which do not resize well without introducing sawtooth and other distortions.

To avoid distortions, keep a complete font on disk for every font size you are likely to use—consuming an inordinate amount of disk space. A trend in end-user computer system design, reflected in the NeXT computer, is the use of high-resolution displays combined with screen fonts using outline (rather than bit-mapped) font technology. See *bit-mapped font, laser printer, NeXT, outline font, printer font, resolution,* and *typeface.*

screen saver utility   A utility program that prolongs the life of your monitor by blanking the screen while you are away from your computer.

Monitors degrade with use, particularly when one image is displayed on-screen continuously. Such images burn into the screen phosphors, resulting in a ghost image. Prolonged use also decreases screen sharpness.

Screen-saver utilities help to prevent burned-in images and to prolong monitor life by blanking the screen while you are away from the computer. The utility can be set so that the blanking occurs after a number of specified minutes, such as 5 or 10.

To alert you that the computer has not been turned off, screen saver utilities display a moving image (such as a clock or stars) on a black background. See *utility program.*

script   In a communications program, a file containing log-on procedures for a specific host, including dialing instructions, access codes, passwords, and initial host commands. The file can be retrieved to automate what otherwise would be a cumbersome and time-consuming procedure.

script font   In typography, a typeface designed to look like fine handwriting (see fig. S.5). See *typeface.*

ABCDEFGHIJKLMNOPQRSTUVWXYZ
abcdefghijklmnopqrstuvwxyz 1234567890

Fig. S.5. The Commercial Script typeface.

scripting   The process of creating a handler, a brief program that traps messages initiated by the user, for an object in an object-oriented programming language, such as HyperTalk. See *handler* and *inheritance.*

scroll   To move the window horizontally or vertically so that its position over a document or worksheet changes.

In some programs, scrolling is clearly distinguished from cursor movement; when you scroll, the cursor stays put. In other programs, however, scrolling the screen also moves the cursor.

scroll bar/scroll box   A method of providing the user with horizontal and vertical scrolling capabilities by placing rectangular scrolling areas on the right and bottom borders of the window. You scroll the document horizontally or vertically by clicking the scroll bar or scroll arrows, or by dragging the scroll bar (see fig. S.6).

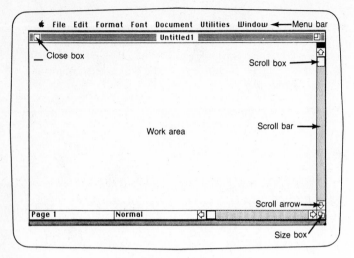

File Edit Format Font Document Utilities Window ◄——Menu bar

Untitled1

Close box

Scroll box ——►

Work area

Scroll bar ——►

Scroll arrow——►

Page 1   Normal

Size box

Fig. S.6. Scroll bars and boxes.

Scroll Lock key On IBM PC-compatible keyboards, a toggle key that switches the cursor-movement keys between two different modes with most programs.

The exact function of this key varies from program to program. In one program, for example, the cursor-movement keys normally move the cursor within the screen. After pressing Scroll Lock, however, the up- and down-arrow keys bring in new lines of text at the top or bottom so that the cursor always remains within two or three lines of the screen's center—and the left- and right-arrow keys do not work at all.

➔ **Tip:** If the cursor-movement keys seem to be doing strange things, you may have pressed the Scroll Lock key accidentally. Toggle it off and try again. See *toggle key.*

SCSI See *Small Computer System Interface (SCSI).*

search and replace See *replace.*

secondary storage   A nonvolatile storage medium such as a disk drive that stores program instructions and data even when the power is switched off. Synonymous with *auxiliary storage* and *external storage*. See *primary storage*.

secondary storage medium   The specific secondary storage technology used to store and retrieve data, such as magnetic disk, magnetic tape, or optical disk.

sector   In a floppy disk or hard disk, a segment of one of the concentric tracks encoded on the disk during a low-level format.

In IBM PC-compatible computing, a sector usually contains 512 bytes of information. See *cluster*.

sector interleave factor   See *interleave factor*.

security   The protection of data so that unauthorized persons cannot examine or copy it.

As business and professional people have discovered, a reasonably competent hacker can get into many computer system, even those that have been protected through such measures as passwords and data encryption. Sensitive data—such as employee performance ratings, customer lists, budget proposals, and confidential memos—can be downloaded on floppy disks that can be carried right out of the office without anyone knowing.

Mainframe computer systems address this problem by keeping the computer and its mass storage media under lock and key; the only way you can use the data is through remote terminals, equipped with a screen but no disk drives.

Writing on the issue of security, some experts argue that personal computer local area networks should be set up the same way. The server should be kept under lock and key, and the workstations should have no disk drives. These experts forget that the excessive centralization of mainframe computer systems was one of the main reasons personal computers were developed.

Concern for security should not prevent a manager from distributing computing power—and computing autonomy—to subordinates. Data encryption and password-protection schemes exist that even a talented hacker cannot penetrate.

seek   In a secondary storage device, to position the read/write head so that data or program instructions can be retrieved.

seek time   In a secondary storage device, the time it takes the read/write head to reach the correct location on the disk. See *access time.*

selection   1. A unit of text, ranging from one character to many pages, highlighted in reverse video for formatting or editing purposes. 2. In programming, a branch or conditional control structure. 3. In database management, the retrieval of records by using a query. See *branch control structure.*

semaphore   A flag indicating the status of a hardware or software operation.

sequence control structure   A control structure that instructs the computer to execute program statements in the order in which the statements are written.

One of three fundamental control structures that govern the order in which program statements are executed; the sequence control structure is the default in all programming languages. Unless instructed otherwise, the computer carries out the tasks in the order in which they are written. The sequence can be altered by using the branch control structure and loop control structure. See *control structure.*

sequential access   An information storage and retrieval technique in which the computer must move through a sequence of stored data items to reach the desired one.

Sequential access media such as cassette tape recorders are much slower than random-access media. See *random access.*

serial   See *asynchronous communication*, *parallel port*, and *parallel processing*.

serial mouse   A mouse designed to be connected directly to one of the computer's serial ports. See *bus mouse* and *mouse*.

serial port   A port that synchronizes and makes asynchronous communication between the computer and devices such as serial printers, modems, and other computers easier.

The function of the serial port is not only to transmit and receive asynchronous data in its one-bit-after-the-other stream; the serial port also negotiates with the receiving device to make sure that transmissions and receptions occur without the loss of data. The negotiation occurs through hardware or software handshaking.

➜ **Tip:** To connect a serial printer to your IBM PC-compatible computer, you may need to use the DOS or OS/2 MODE command. See *asynchronous communication*, *modem*, *port*, *RS-232* and *Universal Asynchronous Receiver/Transmitter (UART)*.

serial printer   A printer designed to be connected to the computer's serial port.

▲ **Caution:** If you are using a serial printer with an IBM PC-compatible system, you must give the correct MODE command to configure your system at the start of each operating session. Almost all users place the necessary command in the AUTOEXEC.BAT file (DOS users) or STARTUP.CMD file (OS/2 users), which the operating system consults when you start your computer. See your printer's manual for more details.

serif   Pronounced "serr´-if." The fine cross strokes across the ends of the main strokes of a character.

➜ **Tip:** Serif fonts are easier to read for body type, but most designers prefer to use sans serif typefaces for display type. See *sans serif*.

server   In a local area network, a computer that provides services for users of the network. The server receives requests for peripheral services and manages the requests so that they are answered in an orderly, sequential manner. Synonymous with network server. See *dedicated file server*, *file server*, *printer server*, and *workstation*.

server-based application   A network version of an application program stored on the network's file server and available to more than one user at a time. See *client-based application* and *file server*.

service bureau   A firm that provides a variety of publication services such as graphics file format conversion, optical scanning of graphics, and typesetting on high-resolution printers such as Linotronics and Varitypers.

setup string   A series of characters that an application program conveys to the printer so that the printer operates in a specified mode. In Lotus 1-2-3, for example, the setup string \027G turns on an Epson printer's double-strike mode.

shadow memory   In 32-bit computers, a portion of random-access memory (RAM) set aside for the storage of ROM routines during an operating session so that these routines can be executed at the microprocessor's fastest possible speed.

Because very few 32-bit microcomputers have a full 32-bit bus architecture, ROM is likely to be placed on a 16-bit bus, where it works at only 50 percent of the speed of the microprocessor and RAM.

Shadow memory solves this problem by setting aside room for the temporary storage of ROM information in RAM while the computer is running. See *random-access memory (RAM)*.

shareware   Copyrighted computer programs made available on a trial basis; if you like and decide to use the program, you are expected to pay a fee to the program's author. See *public domain software*.

sheet feeder   See *cut-sheet feeder*.

shell   A utility program designed to provide an improved (and
often menu-driven) user interface for a program or operating
system generally considered difficult to use. See *user interface* and *utility program*.

shift-click   A Macintosh command technique in which the user
holds down the Shift key before clicking the mouse button.

This technique enables you to select more than one item.

Shift key   A key pressed to enter uppercase letters or punctuation marks.

On early IBM keyboards, the Shift key is labeled with only
a white arrow. Later IBM keyboards and most compatible
keyboards label this key with the word. See *Caps Lock key*.

side-by-side columns   The positioning of unequal blocks of
text side-by-side on a page, so that a given paragraph is kept
parallel with related paragraphs.

Side-by-side columns, often called parallel columns, include paragraphs meant to be positioned adjacent to one
another. Newspaper column formats cannot handle this formatting task, because no relation exists between the paragraphs in one column and the paragraphs in another; on the
contrary, they may move freely and independently of one
another.

Because the paragraphs in a side-by-side format often are
of unequal length, you cannot align them with tabs (see fig.
S.7). The best word processing programs, such as WordPerfect and Microsoft Word, include commands that set up side-
by-side columns and display the format on-screen as you
type and edit. See *newspaper columns*.

SideKick   A popular desktop accessory for IBM Personal Computers and compatibles and the Macintosh developed by
Borland International. The program includes an address
book, an appointment calendar, a notepad, a calculator, and
other utilities.

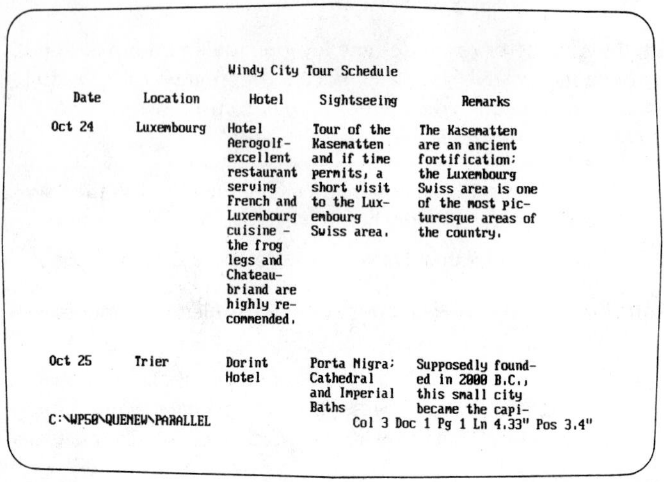

```
                    Windy City Tour Schedule

   Date      Location      Hotel      Sightseeing      Remarks

  Oct 24    Luxembourg    Hotel       Tour of the     The Kasematten
                          Aerogolf-   Kasematten      are an ancient
                          excellent   and if time     fortification;
                          restaurant  permits, a      the Luxembourg
                          serving     short visit     Swiss area is one
                          French and  to the Lux-     of the most pic-
                          Luxembourg  enbourg         turesque areas of
                          cuisine -   Swiss area.     the country.
                          the frog
                          legs and
                          Chateau-
                          briand are
                          highly re-
                          commended.


  Oct 25    Trier         Dorint      Porta Nigra;    Supposedly found-
                          Hotel       Cathedral       ed in 2000 B.C.,
                                      and Imperial    this small city
                                      Baths           became the capi-
 C:\WP50\QUENEW\PARALLEL              Col 3 Doc 1 Pg 1 Ln 4.33" Pos 3.4"
```

Fig. S.7. Parallel columns align side-by-side paragraphs of unequal length.

SIG   See *special interest group.*

signal   The portion of a transmission that coherently represents information, unlike the random and meaningless noise
that occurs in the transmission channel.

silicon chip   See *chip.*

Silicon Valley   An area in California's Santa Clara Valley with
one of the largest concentrations of high-technology businesses in the world.

SIMM   See *single in-line memory module (SIMM).*

simple list text chart   In presentation graphics, a text chart
used to enumerate items in no particular order and with each
item given equal emphasis (see fig. S.8). See *presentation
graphics.*

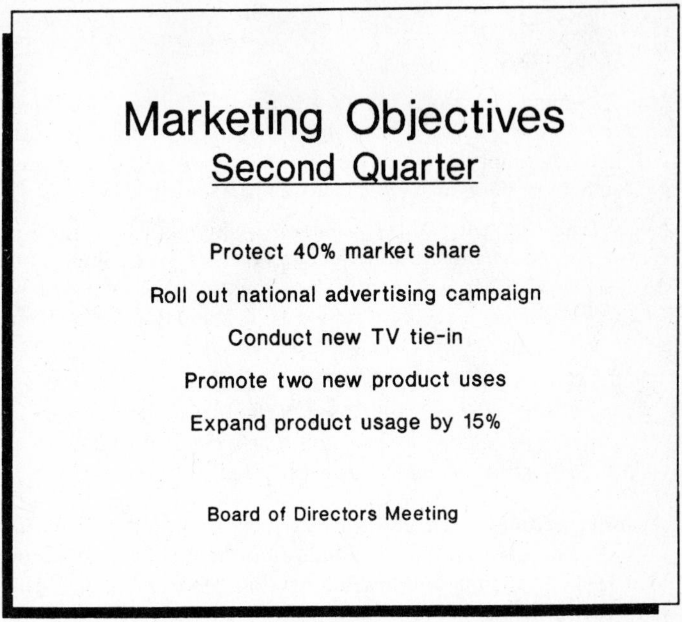

Marketing Objectives
Second Quarter

Protect 40% market share

Roll out national advertising campaign

Conduct new TV tie-in

Promote two new product uses

Expand product usage by 15%

Board of Directors Meeting

Fig. S.8. Simple list text chart.

simulation   An analytical technique used in computer applications, in which a phenomenon's properties are investigated by creating a model of the phenomenon and exploring the model's behavior.

One of the most important contributions the computer is making lies in its provision of new, useful tools for simulation. In aeronautical engineering, for example, the aerodynamic properties of a proposed aircraft could be simulated only through the time-consuming and expensive construction of a series of physical models, which were subjected to wind-tunnel tests.

Now, however, you can design and test thousands of alternative models in short order by using computer simulation techniques. The wind tunnel, therefore, is becoming an anachronism in modern aerospace firms.

In education, simulation techniques are enabling schools that cannot afford laboratory equipment to offer students a chance to engage in simulated, on-screen versions of classic laboratory experiments.

Simulation also is found in computer games, such as Microsoft Flight Simulator. This program is so realistic in its simulation of powered flight that it has been used as a prelude to profession flight instruction in many flight schools.

Users of spreadsheet programs frequently use simulation techniques to create a model of a business. Using simulation, a manager can ask what-if questions such as, "What is the effect on market share if we expend an additional 20 percent on advertising?"

As with any model, however, a simulation is only as good as its underlying assumptions. If these assumptions are not correct, the model does not accurately mimic the behavior of the real-world system being simulated.

single density   The earliest magnetic recording scheme for digital data used a technique called frequency modulation (FM) that resulted in low information densities (such as 90K per disk).

Disk drives designed for FM recording, therefore, could use disks (single-density disks) with relatively large-grained magnetic particles. Single-density recording disks have been superseded by double-density storage devices that use modified frequency modulation (MFM) storage techniques, double-density disks with finer grained partitions, and high-density disks with even finer partitions.

single-sided disk   A floppy disk designed so that only one side of the disk can be used for read/write operations. Single-sided disks have low storage capacities and are used infrequently in today's personal computer systems.

single in-line memory module (SIMM)   Pronounced "sim." A plug-in memory module containing all the chips needed to add 256K or 1M of random-access memory to your computer.

site license   An agreement between a software publisher and an organization that enables the organization to make unlimited copies of the program for internal use. Often a company using a local area network purchases a site license for a program so that all the users on the LAN can access the program. Most site licenses stipulate a numeric limit on the number of copies that can be made. The cost per copy is much less than buying individual copies.

sixteen-bit   See *16-bit computer.*

skip factor   In a graphics program, an increment that specifies how many data points the program should skip as it constructs a chart or graph.

Use a skip factor when a graph looks cluttered with too many thin, spindly columns or when the categories axis is too crowded with headings. A skip factor of 3, for example, displays every third data item, reducing the graph's complexity.

slide show   In presentation graphics, a predetermined list of on-screen charts and graphs displayed one after the other.

Some programs can produce interesting effects, such as fading out one screen before displaying another and enabling you to choose your path through the charts available for display. See *presentation graphics.*

slot   See *expansion slot.*

slug   In word processing and desktop publishing, a code inserted in headers or footers that generates page numbers when the document is printed.

Small Computer System Interface (SCSI)   Pronounced "scuzzy." An interface standard for peripheral devices such as hard disk drives and laser printers.

The most common SCSI device in use is the SCSI hard disk. Unlike ST506 and ESDI drives, the drive contains most of the controller circuitry, leaving the SCSI interface free to communicate with other peripherals. SCSI drivers generally are faster than ST506 drives. See *Enhanced System Device Interface (ESDI)* and *ST506 drive.*

SmallTalk A high-level programming language and programming environment that conceptualizes computations as objects that send messages to one another.

Developed by Alan Kay and others at Xerox Corporation's Palo Alto Research Center (PARC), SmallTalk is unlike all other programming languages because all programming functions are expressed in terms of the dominant metaphor of objects sending messages to one another.

A nonprocedural language, SmallTalk encourages the programmer to define these objects in terms relevant to the intended application, and the language is highly extensible because objects can be created quite easily.

More than a programming language, SmallTalk is a complete programming environment that features a graphical user interface with pull-down menus and mouse support. A major goal of SmallTalk was to make computer programming more accessible to nonprogrammers.

SmallTalk is an important innovation in programming language design and is used in research and development settings.

Because the language requires a great deal of memory to produce efficient, fast-running programs, however, professional programmers continue to prefer languages such as assembly language and C. But SmallTalk inspired HyperTalk, the software command language of HyperCard, an application provided with every Macintosh sold since 1987.

Thousands of hobbyists and professional programmers are learning the object-oriented programming philosophy as they use HyperTalk to create HyperCard applications. In its new guise, SmallTalk has fulfilled its goal of making computer programming more accessible; tens of thousands of Macintosh users have learned to program in HyperTalk. See *high-level programming language* and *object-oriented programming language.*

smart machine Any device containing microprocessor-based electronics that enable the device to branch to alternative operating sequences depending on external conditions, to repeat operations until a condition is fulfilled, and to execute a series of instructions repetitively.

smart terminal   In a multiuser system, a terminal containing its own processing circuitry so that it not only retrieves data from the host computer but also carries out additional processing operations and runs host-delivered programs.

snaking columns   See *newspaper columns.*

snapshot   See *screen dump.*

SNOBOL   Pronounced "snow-ball." A high-level programming language designed for text-processing applications.

Developed at AT&T's Bell Laboratories in 1962, SNOBOL (StriNg-Oriented symBOlic Language) arose from the frustration of its creators (Ralph Griswold, David Farber, and Ivan Polonsky) with numerically oriented programming languages. They sought to create a programming language that could manipulate text, and they hoped to create a language that would interest people who were not mathematicians.

The language they created is especially strong in its textual pattern-matching capabilities and has been used for research work in fields such as language translation, the generation of indexes or concordances to literary works, and text reformatting.

SNOBOL shares with BASIC and FORTRAN, its contemporaries, a lack of structure and an over reliance on GOTO statements, and therefore, is little more than a curiosity. SNOBOL4 is available for IBM PC-compatible personal computers. See *BASIC* and *FORTRAN.*

soft carriage return   In a word processing program, a line break inserted by the program to maintain the margins; the location of the soft carriage return may change if the margins change or if text is inserted or deleted within the line. See *word wrap.*

soft cell boundaries   In a spreadsheet program, a feature that enables you to enter labels longer than the cell's width (unless the adjacent cells are occupied).

soft font   See *downloadable font.*

soft hyphen   A hyphen formatted so that the program does not use it unless the hyphen is needed to improve the spacing on a line. Synonymous with optional hyphen.

soft page break   In a word processing program, a page break inserted by the program based on the current state of the text; the page break may move up or down if insertions, deletions, margin changes, or page size changes occur. See *forced page break.*

soft return   See *soft carriage return.*

soft-sectored disk   A disk that, when new, contains no magnetic patterns of tracks or sectors. The patterns must be added in a process called formatting before the disk can be used. See *formatting.*

soft start   See *warm boot.*

software   System, utility, or application programs expressed in a computer-readable language. See *firmware.*

software command language   A high-level programming language developed to work with an application, such as a spreadsheet or database management program.

Software command languages vary from the simple macro capabilities of word processing programs to full-fledged programming languages, such as the dBASE command language. The best software command languages enable users to create custom applications, complete with iteration, logical branching, and conditional execution of operations.

These languages give the programmer enormous leverage because the package already handles all details related to disk input/output, the user interface, data structures, error handling, and so on. A relatively simple program, therefore, can produce an extremely powerful custom application. See *control structure, dBASE,* and *HyperTalk.*

software compatibility   The capability of a computer system to run a specific type of software. The Commodore 64, for example, is not software-compatible with software written for the Apple II, even though both computers use the MOS Technology 6502 microprocessor.

software engineering   An applied science devoted to improving and optimizing the production of computer software.

software license   A legal agreement included with commercial programs. The software license specifies the rights and obligations of the user who purchased the program and limits the liability of the software publisher.

software package   An application program delivered to the user as a complete, ready-to-run system, including all necessary support and utility programs and documentation.

software piracy   The unauthorized and illegal duplication of copyrighted software without the permission of the software publisher.

Software can be duplicated in a matter of seconds. To the consternation of software publishers, software piracy is extremely common and seems to be an endemic problem of personal computing.

As early as 1976, Bill Gates, a cofounder of Microsoft Corporation, complained that he could not remain in the business of selling a BASIC interpreter for the Altair computer if people kept on making illegal copies of his program. Worse, people who seldom break other moral or legal rules engage in software piracy without hesitation. The computer revolution appears to have happened so quickly that cultural norms and moral values have not had time to adjust accordingly.

Some argue that software piracy has a beneficial effect on the software industry; to motivate people to become registered users, software publishers are forced to make constant improvements to a program. There may be some truth to this claim, although many software revisions are motivated almost exclusively by competitive pressures.

Others argue that software piracy is a way of previewing a program—and a justifiable way, considering that most software retailers don't let you return a program after you have opened the package. If the pirate really likes the program, some argue that he will become a registered user, seeking the benefit of upgrades and documentation. Very few pirates, however, become registered users.

Attempts to stop software piracy through copy-protection schemes backfired on the companies that tried them. Such schemes prevent a casual, unsophisticated user from copying a disk, but they also imposed penalties on valid, registered users of the program, and the major software publishers gave them up.

Software piracy may be common and virtually undetectable when it occurs at home but can become a danger to a business or an organization. More than a few companies have been sued for damages attributable to unauthorized software duplication, and an industry consortium has established a toll-free hotline through which whistle blowers (or disgruntled employees) can report offenders. A wise manager establishes a policy that absolutely no unauthorized copies of software are to be kept near, or used with, company computers.

software protection See *copy protection.*

sort An operation that reorders data in alphabetical or numerical order.

Most application programs can perform sorts. Full-featured word processing programs, such as WordPerfect, provide commands that sort lists, and electronic spreadsheets provide commands that sort the cells in a range.

In database management programs, sorts are distinguished from index operations. A sort performs a physical rearrangement of the data records, resulting in a new, permanently sorted file—consuming much disk space in the process.

The permanently re-sorted records can be used later without repeating the sort operation, but you now have two copies of your database. If you forget to erase the first one, you can become confused about which copy you used to update the data.

An index operation, however, does not physically re-arrange the records. Instead, an index operation creates an index to the records and orders the index rather than the records. The index consumes less disk space than a new copy of the whole database.

Even if you have a huge hard disk, however, indexing provides a much more important advantage; a good database management program (such as dBASE) preserves data integrity by updating all the indexes whenever you add records or update old ones. See *data integrity* and *sort order.*

SORT   In DOS and OS/2, an external filter command that reads lines from a device or file, performs an ASCII sort of the lines, and writes the lines to a device or file. See *filter command.*

sort key   In database management, the data field used to determine the order in which data records are arranged.

In an employee database, for example, the LAST_NAME field or SOCSECNO (social security number) field can be used to arrange the records in alphabetical or numerical order. See *multilevel sort.*

sort order   The order in which a program arranges data when performing a sort. Most programs sort data in the standard order of ASCII characters. Synonymous with collating sequence. See *ASCII sort order, dictionary sort,* and *sort.*

source code   In a high-level programming language, the program as people write and read it, before the program has been compiled or interpreted into machine instructions that the computer can execute.

source file   In many DOS commands, the file from which data or program instructions is copied. See *destination file.*

spaghetti code See *structured programming.*

special interest group (SIG)   Pronounced "sigg." A subgroup of an organization or a computer networking system consisting of members who share a common interest. See *user group.*

speech synthesis   The production by a computer of audio output that resembles human speech.

Computer voice recognition technology is still primitive. Even the best systems can recognize only a few hundred words, and they can can do so only after a lengthy training session in which the computer becomes familiar with an individual's specific voice patterns.

Speech synthesis technology, however, is quite well developed. Existing and inexpensive speech synthesis boards can do an impressive job of reading virtually any file containing English sentences in ASCII script—although, to some listeners, the English sounds as though it is being spoken with a Czechoslovakian accent.

Speech synthesis is improving the lives of blind people by making written material more accessible to them; blind writers can proof and edit their own written work by having the computer read their work to them.

spell checker   A program often incorporated in word processing programs that checks for the correct spelling of words in a document. Each word is compared against a file of correctly spelled words.

A good spell checker displays the correct spelling of a misspelled word and enables you to replace that word. You usually can add words to the spell checker's dictionary.

split screen   A display technique in which the screen is divided into two windows. In word processing programs that have split screen capabilities, independently displaying two parts of the same document is usually possible as is displaying two different documents.

spooler   A program, often included with an operating system's utility programs, that routes printer commands to a file on disk or in RAM instead of to the printer and then feeds the printer commands out of the file when the central processing unit (CPU) is idle.

A print spooler provides a variation on background printing; your program thinks that it is printing to a super-fast printer, but the printer output is being directed to RAM or a disk file. You can continue working with your program, and the spooler guides the printer data to the printer during those moments when the CPU is not busy handling your work.

spreadsheet   See *worksheet.*

spreadsheet program   A program that simulates an accountant's worksheet on-screen and enables you to embed hidden formulas that perform calculations on the visible data.

In 1978, a Harvard Business School student named Dan Bricklin got tired of adding up columns of numbers—and adding them up all over again after a few changes had been made, just to assess the effect of a merger. Bricklin, who knew a little about computers from summer jobs at Wang and other firms, came up with the idea of a spreadsheet program running on a personal computer.

Bricklin's teachers thought the idea was nonsense, but he and a programmer friend, Bob Frankston, produced a program they called VisiCalc for the Apple II computer, and an important new chapter in American enterprise was launched.

A spreadsheet program presents you with a matrix of rows (usually numbered) and columns (usually assigned alphabetical letters), that form individual cells. The on-screen display is called a spreadsheet. Each cell has a distinctive cell address, such as B4 or D19. Into each cell, you can place a value (a number), a hidden formula that performs a calculation, or a label (a heading or explanatory text).

The formulas make a spreadsheet so powerful. A formula can contain constants, such as 2 + 2, but the most useful formulas contain cell references, such as D9 + D10. By placing formulas in a spreadsheet's cells, you can create a complex network of interlinkages among the parts of a spreadsheet. You don't see the formulas, which are hidden behind the cell, but you see the values they generate.

The point of creating a spreadsheet isn't just to find the answer to a problem. When completed, you can enter new values, and the spreadsheet is recalculated. In seconds, you can see how a change in one value ripples through the spreadsheet and affects the bottom line.

This form of sensitivity testing, the changing of values to see how they affect the outcome, is called *what-if analysis* and is one of the main reasons spreadsheet programs have sold so well. Using what-if analysis, a businessman can examine the potential effect of a decision on the business's bottom line.

VisiCalc was a huge success; more than 700,000 copies of the program eventually were sold, and VisiCalc was almost single-handedly responsible for the success of the Apple II personal computer. But VisiCalc met stiff competition from Lotus 1-2-3 in the IBM PC environment, and, by 1984, had disappeared from the market. VisiCalc may be gone, but its influence lives on in many ways; almost all spreadsheet programs use the famous slash key (/) command to bring up the command menu.

Spreadsheets have acquired many new features since VisiCalc's time. Lotus 1-2-3 is an integrated program that combines analytical graphics and database management with what is clearly a clone of VisiCalc's spreadsheet. Recent trends in spreadsheets include the three-dimensional spreadsheet programs, such as 1-2-3 Release 3.0, and graphics-based spreadsheets, such as Microsoft Excel, which bring some desktop publishing technology to spreadsheets.

As useful as spreadsheets are, remember that they are prone to error. Because you cannot see the formulas, you may not notice when one contains a serious error. You also may type a constant into a cell containing a formula while doing what-if analysis and destroy the interlinkages among cells without realizing what you have done. Both errors are very common, and occur even among people who should know better.

A spreadsheet is only a model of a business; any model includes only some of the significant determinants of a firm's behavior, and manipulating the model—as is commonly done in what-if analysis—may lead to serious errors in decision making even if all the formulas are correct. People may be tempted to tweak the assumptions so that they get the right answer.

David Stockman, the director of President Reagan's Office of Management and Budget, was instructed to produce a model of the American economy that would show the results of the President's tax cuts. According to William Greider's book *The Education of David Stockman*, Stockman found that the model suggested huge budget deficits. Because this answer was not the one he was looking for, he introduced a swift decline in prices and a rapid rise in productivity into the model, which then produced the "right" answer.

▲ **Caution:** Do not make business decisions based on a spreadsheet without carefully thinking through what you are doing. First, check all the formulas to see whether they are correct. Many programs include a command that displays the formulas on-screen. Third-party programs such as Spreadsheet Auditor (Cambridge Software) are available for the programs without this command.

Second, use cell protection on every cell containing a formula. Third, never place constants in a formula. Place all the constants in your spreadsheet in a special area at the top of the spreadsheet that contains the key variables. Fourth, bear in mind the limitations of a model; a model can never mimic reality, only part of it.

Fifth, remember that all good decisions aren't necessarily defensible on purely quantitative grounds. A model that suggests saving money may do so at the sacrifice of employee or community good will or of market share, and even though the results look good, they may wind up being catastrophic in the end.

SQL   See *Structured Query Language (SQL)*.

ST506 drive   A hard disk using an interface standard called ST506/412. ST506 drives are slower and cheaper than drives using more recent interface standards. MFM and RLL encoding methods are used with the ST-506/412 interface. MFM has a 5 M/second transfer rate, and RLL has a 7.5 M/second rate.

ST-506 is still the most common interface using the MFM encoding. See Enhanced System Device Interface (ESDI) and Small Computer Systems Interface (SCSI).

stack   In programming, a stack is a data structure in which the first items inserted are the last ones removed. This data structure is used in programs that use branching or procedure/function structures; a stack enables the computer to track what it was doing when it branched or jumped to a procedure.

In HyperCard, stack refers to a file containing one or more cards that share a common background. See *Hypercard.*

stacked column chart   See *stacked column graph.*

stacked column graph   A column graph in which two or more data series are displayed, not adjacent to one another, but on top of one another (see fig S.9). See *histogram.*

stand-alone computer   A computer system dedicated to meeting the computing needs of a person working in isolation.

A stand-alone system contains all the hardware and software a user requires. Links with other computers are incidental to the system's chief purpose. See *distributed processing system, multiuser system*, and *professional workstation.*

star network   In local area networks, a centralized network topology with the physical layout of a star. At the center is a central network processor or wiring concentrator; the nodes are arranged around and connected directly to the central point.

Wiring costs are considerably higher because each workstation requires a cable linking the workstation directly to the central processor (see fig S.10).

start bit   In serial communications, a bit inserted into the data stream to inform the receiving computer that a byte of data is to follow.

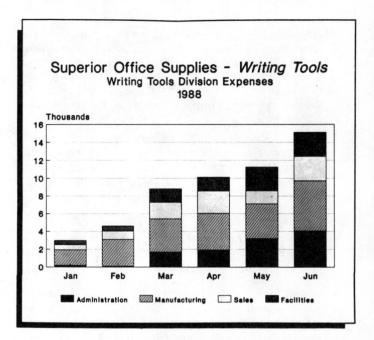

Fig. S.9. A stacked column graph.

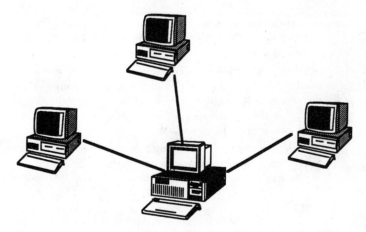

Fig. S.10. A star topology.

startup disk   The disk containing portions of the operating system that you normally use to start your computer. Synonymous with boot disk and *system disk*. See *hard disk*.

startup screen   A Macintosh graphics file that, when placed in the System Folder, is displayed when the computer is turned on or restarted.

Most Macintosh users are content with the "Welcome to Macintosh" message, but you can see virtually anything you want to when you turn on your machine; you can save any bit-mapped graphic image as a startup screen. For example, you can display a bird, a volcano, or even a picture of yourself.

state-of-the-art   An item that is technically sophisticated—containing the latest technology and representing the highest possible level of technical achievement.

statement   In a high-level programming language, a command that trained programmers can read and understand. A statement successfully generates machine language instructions when the program is interpreted or compiled. See *instruction* and *high-level programming language*.

static random-access memory (RAM)   A random-access memory (RAM) chip that holds its contents without constant refreshing from the CPU.

Although as volatile as DRAM chips, static RAM does not require the CPU to refresh its contents several hundred times per second. These chips, therefore, are substantially faster and preferable for high-speed computers based on microprocessors such as the Intel 80386.

They also are significantly more expensive than DRAM chips. See *dynamic random-access memory (DRAM)*, *random-access memory (RAM)*, and *volatility*.

station   See *workstation*.

statistical software   An application program that makes the application of statistical tests and measures to computer-readable data easier.

status indicator   An area of an application program's display screen that describes the state of the program.

Often included in status indicators are the name of the file you currently are modifying and the names of the toggle keys you have pressed, such as Num Lock or Caps Lock.

stem   In typography, the main vertical stroke of a character.

stickup initial   An enlarged initial letter at the beginning of a paragraph that rises above the top of the first line.

▲ **Caution:** You can create initials with many word processing and page layout programs, but to avoid a common formatting error, make sure that the letter aligns precisely at the base of a line of text. See *drop cap*.

stop bit   In serial communications, a bit inserted into the data stream to inform the receiving computer that the transmission of a byte of data is complete.

storage   The retention of program instructions, initial data, and intermediate data within the computer so that this information is available for processing purposes. See *primary storage* and *secondary storage*.

storage device   Any optical or magnetic device that is capable of secondary storage functions in a computer system. See *secondary storage*.

stored program concept   The idea, which underlies the architecture of all modern computers, that the program should be stored in memory with the data.

An insight of the late physician and scientist John von Neumann as he beheld the hard-wired programs of the ENIAC (North America's first digital electronic computer), this concept showed how a program could jump back and forth through instructions instead of executing them sequentially. With this insight, virtually the entire world of modern computing was launched. See *von Neumann bottleneck*.

strikeout An attribute, such as type, struck through with a hyphen to mark text.

Strikeout often is used to mark text to be deleted from a co-authored document so that the other author can see changes easily. See *overstrike, overtype mode,* and *redlining.*

string A series of alphanumeric characters.

string formula In a spreadsheet program, a formula that performs a string operation such as concatenation.

string operation A computation performed on alphanumeric characters.

Computers cannot understand the meaning of words, and they cannot, therefore, process them like people do. However, computers can perform simple processing operations on textual data, such as the following:

- Comparison. Comparing two strings to see whether they are the same.

- Concatenation. Joining two strings together.

- Length calculation. Calculating the number of characters a string occupies.

- Sorting. Arranging strings in ASCII order.

structured programming A set of quality standards that make programs more verbose but more readable, more reliable, and more easily maintained.

The essence of structured programming is the avoidance of spaghetti code, the untrackable interlinkages in a program that result from an over reliance on GOTO statements. Spaghetti code programs are difficult to read, and make tracking the source of difficulties hard to do.

To avoid spaghetti code, structured programming insists that the overall program structure logically reflect what the program is supposed to do, beginning with the first task and proceeding logically. Indentations are used to make the logic clear to anyone reading the program. The programmer is encouraged to use loop and branch control structures and named procedures instead of GOTO statements. A properly designed program does not require line numbers, and the function of the program should be immediately obvious to anyone trained in the language. Languages such as C, Pascal, Modula-2, and the dBASE software command language are inherently structured and encourage the programmer to adopt these good habits.

The earlier versions of languages such as BASIC and FORTRAN are not inherently structured and are seldom used for serious professional program development. See *modular programming.*

Structured Query Language (SQL)   Pronounced "sequel." In database management systems, an IBM-developed query language widely used in mainframe and minicomputer systems. SQL increasingly is being implemented in client/server networks as a way of enabling personal computers to access the resources of corporate databases.

Originally developed by D.D. Chamberlin and other researchers at IBM Research Laboratories, SQL is the up-and-coming query language for microcomputers because the language can be used with a variety of database management packages.

SQL is data independent, because the user does not have to worry about the particulars of how data is accessed physically. At least in theory, SQL is device independent; the same query language can be used to access databases on mainframes, minicomputers, and personal computers. Currently, however, several versions of SQL are competing.

Because of its data and device independence, SQL is a fast-rising star on the personal computer scene. Many companies have purchased hundreds or even thousands of personal computers, which function well as stand-alone workstations, but the problem faced by many companies is how to enable users to access data on corporate minicomputers and mainframes.

SQL, therefore, is fast becoming a common language for computerized database management. A user who knows how to use a personal computer database that uses SQL already has learned the necessary commands and syntax, and the same query language is useful for accessing a database stored on a corporate mainframe.

SQL is an elegant and concise query language with only 30 commands. The four basic commands (SELECT, UPDATE, DELETE, and INSERT) correspond to the four basic functions of data manipulation (data retrieval, data modification, data deletion, and data insertion, respectively).

SQL queries also approximate the structure of an English natural language query. For example, the query, "Show me the TITLE and RATING of those videotapes in the inventory database in which the field CATEGORY contains 'Children' and order the result by TITLE," is represented by the following SQL query:

```
SELECT title, rating
FROM inventory
WHERE category = "children"
ORDER BY title
```

SQL is table-oriented; SQL queries do not display individual data records. Instead, the queries result in the on-screen display of a data table, consisting of columns (corresponding to data fields) and rows (corresponding to data records). See *data deletion, data insertion, data manipulation, data modification, data retrieval, natural language,* and *table-oriented database management program.*

style sheet   In some word processing and page layout programs, a stored collection of user-created text-formatting definitions including two or more formats. A style sheet can be retrieved with a single keystroke.

In the old days of professional typists, the typist interviewed the author and filled out a style sheet listing the author's preferences for all formats (such as titles, footnotes, body text paragraphs, and the like).

In word processing software, the term describes an on-disk collection of formatting definitions you create. For example, if you have a style sheet entry for normal body text paragraphs that includes the following formats: Palatino, 10 point type size, ragged-left indentation, single line spacing, and 0.5-inch first line indentation.

→ **Tip:** When used properly, style sheets can enhance productivity by greatly speeding the reformatting of a document. Suppose that you decide you want to use New Century Schoolbook instead of Palatino for the body type. If you have not defined the body paragraph style in a style sheet, you must go through the document, changing the style of all body paragraphs manually (and carefully skipping over display type and other formats). If you defined a body paragraph style, however, you make just one change to the style sheet, and all the text linked to this style is changed for you.

stylus   A pen-shaped instrument used on a monitor's screen or on a graphics tablet for drawing or selecting menu options.

subdirectory   In DOS, OS/2, and UNIX, a directory listed within a directory that, when opened, reveals another directory containing files and additional subdirectories.

The directory you see when you use the DOS DIR command is an effective guide to a disk's contents until you create more files than one screen can display. With DOS, you operate under stringent limitations on the number of files you can place in one directory. You can place only 112 files in one directory on a 360K or 720K disk. You can place only 512 files in one directory on a hard disk. Subdirectories enable you to create a tree-like, hierarchical structure of nested directories in which you can store many more than 512 files.

To understand how subdirectories are linked, look at a typical root directory created when the disk is formatted—the one you see when you use the DIR command:

```
Volume in Drive A has no label
Directory of A:\
LETTER1   DOC    1651    3-24-89    12:01a
REPORT1   DOC    1102    3-24-89    12:01a
MEMO1     DOC    6462    3-24-89    12:00p
LETTER2   DOC    1651    5-24-89    12:01a
REPORT2   DOC    1102    5-24-89    12:01a
MEMO2     DOC    6462    5-24-89    12:00p
LETTER3   DOC    1651    7-24-89    12:01a
REPORT3   DOC    1102    7-24-89    12:01a
MEMO3     DOC    6462    7-24-89    12:00p
  9 File(s) 280576 byes free
```

Like most of the directories DOS creates, this directory is organized haphazardly. (Imagine what the directory would look like if you had 350 files.) Grouping the LETTER files, REPORT files, and MEMO files would be better than mixing them. You can create three subdirectories—called LETTERS, REPORTS, and MEMOS— and place these files into them.

After you create the subdirectories and move the files, the directory looks different. The DIR command reveals the following directory:

```
Volume in Drive A has no label
Directory of A:\
LETTERS      <DIR>    9-24-89    1:14p
REPORTS      <DIR>    9-24-89    1:15p
MEMOS        <DIR>    9-24-89    1:16p
```

This directory now contains three subdirectories. Using the CHDIR command, you can open one of these subdirectories.

Directories are linked in a tree structure. Think of an upside-down tree. The main directory is like the trunk, and the subdirectories are like branches. The main directory created by DOS is called the root directory. The entire directory structure of the disk grows from this directory.

You also can create subdirectories within subdirectories. In this way, you can organize even a huge hard disk so that you never see more than a few files after typing DIR. See *root directory*.

submenu   A set of lower level commands available when you choose a top-level command.

subroutine   A portion of a program that performs a specific function and is set aside so that it can be used by more than one section of the program.

A subroutine takes care of tasks needed frequently, such as writing a file to disk. In BASIC programs, subroutines are referenced by GOSUB statements.

subscript   In text processing, a number or letter printed slightly below the typing line. See *superscript*.

suitcase   In the Macintosh environment, an icon containing a screen font or desk accessory not yet installed in the System Folder.

SuperPaint   An illustration program for Macintosh computers that combines the bit-mapped graphics of MacPaint with the object-oriented graphics of MacDraw.

Introduced in 1986, the innovative SuperPaint (Silicon Beach Software) separated the paint and draw functions by placing them in a background layer and a foreground layer. The two layers are independent but superimposed, so that you can create a drawing in the background and add transparent paint effects in the foreground.

Because SuperPaint combined the best aspects of MacPaint and MacDraw, this program quickly emerged as the program of choice for amateur illustration purposes. For professional illustration, programs such as Adobe Illustrator and Freehand are preferred.

superscript   A number or letter printed slightly above the typing line.

super VGA   See *Video Graphics Array (VGA).*

support   See *technical support.*

surge   A momentary and sometimes destructive increase in the amount of voltage delivered through a power line.

surge protector   An inexpensive electrical device that prevents high-voltage surges from reaching a computer and damaging its circuitry. See *power line filter.*

swash   A type character that sweeps over or under adjacent characters with a curvilinear flourish.

symbolic coding   The expression of an algorithm in coded form using symbols and numbers that people can understand (rather than the binary numbers that computers use). All modern programming languages use symbolic coding.

Symphony   See i*ntegrated software.*

synchronous communication   Pronounced "sink´-roh-nuss."
The transmission of data at very high speeds using parallel
circuits in which the transfer of data is synchronized by electronic clock signals. Synchronous communication is used
within the computer and in high-speed mainframe computer
networks. See *asynchronous communication.*

syntax   All the rules that specify precisely how a command,
statement, or instruction must be given to the computer so
that the machine can recognize and process the instruction
correctly.

syntax error   An error resulting from the expression of a command in a way that violates a program's syntax rules.

SYSOP   Pronounced "siss´-op." Acronym for SYStem OPerator.
A person who runs a bulletin board.

system   See *computer system.*

System   The operating system for Apple Macintosh computers
contained in the Macintosh's read-only memory and the System File in the System Folder.

system date   The calendar date maintained by the computer
system and updated while the system is in operation.

    Not all personal computers maintain the system date after
the computer is switched off. To do so, the system must be
equipped with a battery.

    Computers without such batteries on their motherboards
must be equipped with a clock-calendar board. If you are
using an IBM PC-compatible computer that lacks battery-
powered system date circuitry, you can set the system date
manually by using the DATE command.

    → **Tip:** Be sure to set the system date. When you create
and save files, the operating system records the date and
time you saved the file. This information can be important
when you are trying to determine which version of a file is
the most recent.

system disk   A disk containing the operating system and all files necessary to start the computer.

Hard disk users normally configure the hard disk to serve as the system disk.

system file A program or data file that contains information needed by the operating system—distinguished from program or data files used by application programs.

System Folder   A folder in the Macintosh desktop environment that contains the System File and the Finder, the two components of the Mac's operating system.

In addition to the System and Finder files, the System Folder also contains all the desk accessories, INITs, CDEV, screen fonts, downloadable printer fonts, and printer drivers to be made available during an operating session.

Because the System Folder is the only folder that the Finder consults when searching for a file, many applications require that configuration files, dictionaries, and other necessary files be placed in this folder so that they can be accessed.

➔ **Tip:** If you frequently see a message informing you that an application cannot find a needed file, place the file in the System Folder. See *CDEV*, *desk accessory (DA)*, *downloadable font*, *Finder*, *INIT*, *printer driver*, and *screen font*.

system prompt   In a command-line operating system, the prompt that indicates the operating system's availability for system maintenance tasks such as copying files, formatting disks, and loading programs. In DOS, the system prompt (a letter designating the disk drive, followed by a greater-than symbol) shows the current drive. When you see the prompt C>, for example, drive C is the current drive, and DOS is ready to accept instructions. You can customize the system prompt by using the PROMPT command. See *command-line operating system*.

systems analyst   A person who designs specifications, calculates feasibility and costs, and implements a business system.

Systems Application Architecture (SAA)   A set of standards for communication among various types of IBM computers, from personal computers to mainframes.

Announced in 1987, SAA was IBM's response to criticisms that its products did not work well together and to the competitive pressure exerted by Digital Electronic Corporation (DEC), which claimed that its products were optimized for easy interconnection.

Although SAA is little more than an evolving set of standards for future development, SAA calls for a consistent user interface and consistent system terminology across all environments. SAA influenced the design of Presentation Manager, the windowing environment jointly developed by Microsoft and IBM for the OS/2 operating system. See *Operating System/2 OS/2, Presentation Manager*, and *windowing environment.*

system software   All the software used to operate and maintain a computer system, including the operating system and utility programs—distinguished from application programs.

system time   The time of day maintained by the computer system that is updated while the system is in operation.

Not all personal computers maintain the system time after the computer has been switched off. To do so, the system must be equipped with a battery. Computers without such batteries on their motherboards must be equipped with a clock-calendar board. If you are using an IBM PC-compatible personal computer that lacks battery-powered system date circuitry, you can set the system time manually by using the TIME command.

➔ **Tip:** Be sure to set the system time. When you create and save files, the operating system records the date and time you saved the file. This information can be important when you are trying to determine which version of a file is the most recent.

system unit   The case that houses the computer's internal processing circuitry, including the power supply, motherboard, disk drives, plug-in boards, and a speaker. Some personal computer system units also contain a monitor.

The system unit often is called the central processing unit (CPU), but this usage is inaccurate. Properly, the CPU consists of the computer's microprocessor and memory, usually housed on the motherboard, but not peripherals such as disk drives.

System V Interface Definition (SVID)   A standard for UNIX operating systems, established by AT&T Bell Laboratories and demanded by corporate buyers, based on UNIX Version 5. See *Berkeley UNIX* and *UNIX*.

tab-delimited file   A data file, usually in ASCII file format, in which the data items are separated by tab keystrokes. See *ASCII file* and *comma-delimited file*.

tab key   A key used to enter a fixed number of blank characters in a document. The tab key often is used to guide the cursor in on-screen command menus.

▲ **Caution:** In a word processing program, don't enter indentations on the first line of paragraphs by pressing Tab unless you have no other way of performing this task. Some programs include first-line indent commands that you should use, because if you change your mind about the amount of the indentation, you can change all of the first-line indentations in one keystroke by resetting the command. If you enter the indentations manually, you must change them all manually.

table   In a relational database management program, the fundamental structure of data storage and display in which data items are linked by the relations formed by placing them in rows and columns.

The rows correspond to the data records of record-oriented database management programs, and the columns correspond to data fields. See *table-oriented database management program*.

table of authorities   A table of legal citations generated by a word processing program from in-text references.

table-oriented database management program   A database management program that displays data tables (rather than records) as the result of query operations. See *data retrieval, record-oriented database management program,* and *Structured Query Language (SQL).*

table utility   In a word processing program, a utility that makes the typing of tables easier by creating a spreadsheet-like matrix of rows and columns, into which text can be inserted without forcing word wrapping.

When you create a table with tab stops, you must type the table line-by-line. If you later find that you have to add a few words to one of the items, the words may not fit, and you succeed only in forcing the rest of the line to wrap down to the next, ruining the column alignment. Table utilities solve this problem by making the cell, not the line, the unit of word wrapping (see fig. T.1).

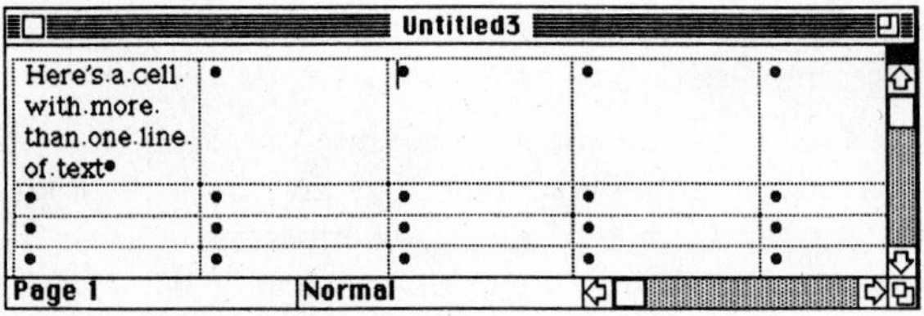

Fig. T.1. A table utility.

Tagged Image File Format (TIFF)   Pronounced "tiff." A bit-mapped graphics format for scanned images with resolutions of up to 300 dpi. TIFF simulates gray-scale shading. See *bit-mapped graphic.*

Tandy Corporation   A Texas-based manufacturer of computer devices and electronic products generally sold through the company's franchised Radio Shack stores.

The Radio Shack TRS-80 Model 1 was one of the first personal computers, and the firm has remained active in the personal computer marketplace. The firm's low-end IBM PC-compatible computers have won broad market acceptance, partly attributable to the provision with each computer of a DeskMate, an easy-to-use DOS shell that includes desk accessories.

tape backup unit   A secondary storage device designed to back up onto magnetic tape all the data on a hard disk at high speeds.

technical support   The provision of technical advice and problem-solving expertise to registered users of a hardware device or program.

telecommunications   The transmission of information, whether expressed by voice or computer signals, via the telephone system. See *asynchronous communication* and *modem.*

Telenet   A commercial wide-area network with thousands of local dial-up numbers. Telenet provides log-on services to a variety of commercial on-line computer services, such as Dialog Information Services and CompuServe.

teletype (TTY) display   A method of displaying characters on a monitor in which characters are generated and sent, one-by-one, to the video display; as the characters are received, the screen fills, line-by-line. When full, the screen scrolls up to accommodate the new lines of characters appearing at the bottom of the screen.

The teletype display mode should be familiar to users of DOS. This mode uses a teletype display for accepting user commands and displaying messages to the user. See *character mapping.*

template   In an application program, a document or worksheet that includes the text or formulas needed for some generic applications and is available repeatedly for customization.

In word processing, templates frequently are used for letterheads; the on-screen version of the file contains the corporate logo, the company's address, and all the formats necessary to write the letter, but no text. You use the template by loading the file, adding the text, and printing.

In spreadsheet programs, templates are available for solving a number of common problems, such as calculating and printing a mortgage amortization schedule.

terabyte Pronounced "terra-bite." A unit of memory measure approximately equal to one trillion bytes (actually 1,099,511,627,776 bytes).

One terabyte equals 1,000 gigabytes, or one million megabytes. See *byte, gigabyte,* and *megabyte (M).*

terminal An input/output device, consisting of a keyboard and video display, commonly used with multiuser systems.

A terminal lacking its own central processing unit (CPU) and disk drives is called a dumb terminal; its use is restricted to interacting with a distant multiuser computer.

A smart terminal has some processing circuitry and, in some cases, a disk drive so that information can be downloaded and displayed later.

A personal computer is in many ways the opposite of a terminal. A terminal centralizes computing resources and denies autonomy to users. A personal computer distributes computing resources and enables users to make their own software choices.

Yet, a personal computer user can have many valid reasons for wanting to take advantage of centralized computer resources. To do so, the computer needs to be transformed into a smart terminal, which is the function of communications software.

Many different brands and models of terminals are in use and their electronic characteristics and capabilities differ. A given on-line service usually expects those contacting its computer to use a specific brand and model of terminal, such as the DEC VT100.

One important function of a communications program, therefore, is to configure the personal computer so that it communicates on-line as a specific terminal would. The better communications programs provide several terminal emulations including TTY (a plain vanilla teletype terminal), DEC VT52, DEC VT 100, and Lear-Siegler ADM/3A.

→ **Tip:** If you are contacting an on-line information service or a bulletin board for the first time, use TTY emulation. See *terminal emulation.*

terminal emulation   The use of a communications program to transform a personal computer into a terminal for the purpose of data communications.

terminate-and-stay-resident (TSR) program   An accessory or utility program designed to remain in the computer's random-access memory (RAM) at all times so that the user can activate it with a keystroke, even if another program also is in memory.

▲ **Caution:** If you are using DOS, use TSR programs with caution. Don't use TSR programs at all if you are working with valuable data or documents.

Using a TSR program all but guarantees a system crash sooner or later because DOS does not operate in protected mode. DOS has no provisions for keeping one program from invading the memory space of another, and such invasions cripple the invaded program or cause crashes.

With its protected mode processing, OS/2 enables the simultaneous execution of two or more programs without the peril of system crashes. See *multitasking, protected mode,* and *real mode.*

text chart   In presentation graphics, a text chart is designed for display to an audience using a slide or transparency. See *bulleted list chart, column text chart, free-form text chart, organization chart,* and *simple list text chart.*

text editor   In computer programming, a program designed for the creation, editing, and storage of object code.

A text editor resembles a word processing program in many respects; a text editor makes the entry and editing of words and numbers easier. Because a text editor is designed for writing computer programs, text editors generally contain only the most primitive facilities for text formatting and printing.

text file   A file consisting of nothing but the standard ASCII characters (with no control characters or higher order characters).

thermal printer   A nonimpact printer that forms an image by moving heated styluses over specially treated paper.

Quiet and fast, thermal printers have one disadvantage: most of them require specially treated paper, which has an unpleasant, waxy feel.

third-party vendor   A firm that markets an accessory hardware product for a given brand of computer equipment.

thirty-two bit computer   See *32-bit computer.*

three-dimensional spreadsheet   A spreadsheet program that can create a worksheet file made up of multiple stacked pages, each page resembling a separate worksheet.

In Lotus 1-2-3 Release 3, you can create one spreadsheet file that contains up to 256 worksheets.

Suppose that your organization has three divisions, each with their own income statements. You create three spreadsheets (called B, C, and D), one for each division. To sum the quarterly and total income amounts, you create a fourth spreadsheet, A. In this spreadsheet, you place formulas that use three-dimensional range statements (see fig. T.2). One statement may look like the following:

@SUM(B:B5..D:B5)

This statement says, "Sum the amounts shown in cell B5 of spreadsheets B, C, and D, and place the total here." See *Quattro Pro.*

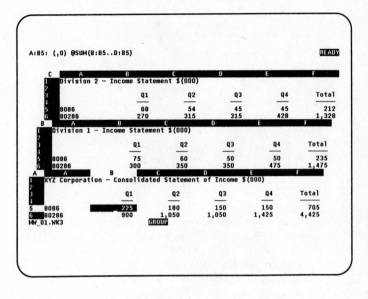

Fig. T.2. A three-dimensional spreadsheet.

throughput A computer's overall performance as measured by its capability to send data through all components of the system, including secondary storage devices, such as disk drives.

Throughput is a much more meaningful indication of system performance than some of the benchmark times commonly reported in computer advertising, which involve the execution of computation-intensive algorithms.

A computer equipped with an Intel 80386 microprocessor and running at 25 MHz, for example, has glowing benchmark speed but may have less-than-spectacular throughput if equipped with slow random-access memory (RAM) chips, lacking cache memory (or some other memory speed-up scheme), and using a slow hard disk.

➔ **Tip:** Before you make a purchasing decision based on benchmarks, find out whether the benchmark includes a full range of computer tasks. *PC Magazine*, for example, tests

CPU instruction mix, floating-point calculation, conventional memory, DOS file access (small and large records), and BIOS disk seek.

TIFF   See *Tagged Image File Format (TIFF)*.

TIME   In DOS and OS/2, an internal command that displays the current system time and prompts you to enter a new time. See *system time*.

timed backup   A desirable application program feature that saves your work at a specified interval, such as every five minutes.

Power outages occur during storms, during periods of heavy demand, and when essential maintenance must be performed on a local circuit. If you don't have an uninterruptable power supply (UPS) or you haven't saved your work to disk, your work is gone forever. Your keyboard also can freeze if you are using a terminate-and-stay-resident (TSR) program that doesn't get along with the current application package.

Because power outages and system crashes can destroy many hours of work, good computer practice calls for saving your work at frequent intervals, but software can perform saves for you. The best word processing programs, such as Microsoft Word 5.0 (IBM PC-compatible version) and WordPerfect, include timed backup features that enable you to specify the interval.

▲ **Caution:** Using a timed backup feature is no substitute for saving your work to disk at the end of a working session. The files created by timed backup utilities are temporary files, designed to restore your work after a system crash or power outage. Use timed backups, but don't forget to save your work.

time division multiplexing   In local area networks, a technique for transmitting two or more signals over the same cable by interleaving them, one after the other. Time division multiplexing is used in baseband (digital) networks. See *baseband*, *frequency division multiplexing*, *local area network (LAN)*, and *multiplexing*.

time-sharing   A technique for sharing a multiuser computer's resources in which each user has the illusion that he or she is the only person using the system.

In the largest mainframe systems, hundreds or even thousands of people can use the system simultaneously without realizing that others are doing so. At times of peak usage, however, system response time tends to decline noticeably.

Times Roman   A highly readable and compact serif typeface designed for body type applications.

With a compact and readable design that makes the typeface especially useful when space is at a premium, Times Roman is a popular choice for newspapers, magazines, and newsletters (see fig T.3). The font often is included with many laser printers.

ABCDEFGHIJKLMNOPQRSTUVWXYZ
abcdefghijklmnopqrstuvwxyz 1234567890

Fig.T.3. The Times Roman typeface.

toggle   To change a program mode by pressing a toggle key. See *toggle key*.

toggle key   A key that switches back and forth between two modes. See *Caps Lock key*, *Num Lock key*, and *Scroll Lock key*.

token passing   In local area networks, a channel access scheme in which a special bit configuration, called a token, is circulated among the workstations. A node gains access to the network only if the node can obtain a free token. The node that obtains the token retains control of the network until the message has been received and acknowledged.

The token can have two values: free or busy. Any workstation wanting to transmit captures a free token, changes the value to busy, and attaches to the token the address of the destination node and the data to be transmitted. Every workstation constantly monitors the network to catch a token addressed to that workstation.

When a workstation receives a token, it attaches an acknowledgment message to the token. When the token comes back to the source node, the token's value is set back to free.

Because token passing rules out the data collisions that occur when two devices begin transmitting at the same time, this channel access method is preferred for large networks that experience high volume. See *carrier sense multiple access with collision detect (CSMA/CD), contention, local area network (LAN)*, and *polling.*

token-ring network   In local area networks, a network architecture that combines token passing with a hybrid star/ring topology.

Developed by IBM and announced in 1986, the IBM Token-Ring Network for uses a Multistation Access Unit at its hub. This unit is wired with twisted-pair cable in a star configuration with up to 255 workstations, but the resulting network is actually a decentralized, ring network. See *local area network (LAN),* and *token passing.*

toner   The electrically charged ink used in laser printers.

toner cartridge   In laser printers, a cartridge containing the electrically charged ink that the printer fuses to the page.

➜ **Tip:** You can save up to 50 percent of the retail cost of new toner cartridges by using recharged toner cartridges.

toolbox   A set of programs that helps programmers develop software without having to create individual routines from scratch.

top-down programming   A method of program design and development in which the design process begins with a statement (in English) of the program's fundamental purpose. This purpose is broken into a set of subcategories that describe aspects of the program's anticipated functions. Each of these subcategories corresponds to a specific program module that can be coded independently.

Structured programming languages, such as Pascal, C, and, Modula-2, and object-oriented programming languages, such as C++, are especially amenable to the top-down approach. See *C, C++, Pascal,* and *structured programming.*

topology   See *network topology.*

TOPS   A file-serving program for local area networks that enables IBM PC compatibles and Macintosh computers to be linked in one distributed processing system. TOPS is designed to work with AppleTalk and EtherNet networks.

File-serving software provides peer-to-peer file transfer in which each user has access to the public files located on the workstations of all other users in the network. (Each user determines which files, if any, are to be made public for network access.)

When a TOPS user decides to make a file public, he or she publishes the file on the network. Every node on the network, therefore, is potentially a file server.

A significant advantage of TOPS is that, when the user of an IBM PC-compatible computer accesses a file on a Macintosh, TOPS displays the file as if it were in a directory on a DOS disk. When the user of a Macintosh computer accesses a file on an IBM PC-compatible machine, the file appears as it normally would on the Finder's desktop display: as an on-screen icon.

Users of IBM PC-compatible computers, therefore, need not learn Macintosh skills, and Macintosh users need not learn IBM PC-compatible skills. See *file server.*

touch screen   See *touch-sensitive display.*

touch-sensitive display   A display technology designed with a pressure-sensitive panel mounted in front of the screen. The user can select options by pressing the screen at the appropriate place. Synonymous with touch screen.

track   In a floppy disk or hard disk, one of several concentric rings, encoded on the disk during the low-level format, that defines a distinct area of data storage on the disk. See *cluster* and *sector.*

trackball   An input device, designed to replace the mouse, that moves the mouse pointer on-screen as the user rotates a ball embedded in the keyboard or in a case adjacent to the keyboard.

tractor feed   A printer paper-feed mechanism in which continuous (fan-fold) paper is pulled (or pushed) into and through the printer using a sprocket wheel. The sprockets fit into prepunched holes on the left and right edges of the paper.

A disadvantage of tractor-feed mechanisms is that when printing is complete, you must tear off the sides of the paper and separate the sheets. For a long document, this job can become tedious, and you can easily tear a page by accident. Dot-matrix printers normally come with tractor-feed mechanisms.

traffic   The volume of messages sent over a communications network.

transactional application   In a local area network, a program that creates and maintains one shared database that contains a master record of all the transactions in which network participants engage, such as filling out invoices or time-billing forms. See *nontransactional application.*

transfer rate   The number of bits of data transferred per second between a disk and the computer after the drive head reaches the place where the data is located.

The maximum transfer rate is controlled by input/output standards such as ESDI or SCSI. See *access time.*

transient command   See *external command.*

translate   To convert a program from one programming language or operating system to another, or to convert a data file from one file format to another. See *file format.*

transparency The quality of a well-designed user interface in which the user does not have to worry how the computer accomplishes a task. Tasks are defined by what needs to be accomplished not by the physical procedures the computer must perform.

Consider the distinction between logical drives and physical drives in secondary storage. Even though you have two different physical devices connected to your computer (a floppy drive and a hard disk), DOS treats the devices the same as far as you are concerned. The same commands work on both drives. See *graphical user interface* and *what-you-see-is-what-you-get (WYSIWYG)*.

transpose To change the order in which characters, words, or sentences are displayed on-screen. Some word processing programs include commands that transpose text. These commands are useful when characters, words, or sentences are in the wrong order.

trapping See *error trapping*.

TREE In DOS and OS/2, an external command that displays the tree structure of directory and subdirectory names.

When you use the TREE command, you see a display like the following in versions prior to DOS 4:

```
DIRECTORY PATH LISTING
Path: A:\LETTERS
Sub-directories: None
Path: A:\DOCUMENTS
Sub-directories: ENGLISH
                 HISTORY
Path: A:\DOCUMENTS\REPORTS
Sub-directories: None
Path: A:\DOCUMENTS\MEMOS
Sub-directories: None
```

You can figure out the tree structure from this listing, but the structure is not immediately apparent. DOS Version 4 displays the tree structure as follows:

```
DIRECTORY PATH LISTING
A:.
|
|
|—LETTERS
|
|—DOCUMENTS
   |
   |—REPORTS
   |
   |—MEMOS
```

tree structure   A way of organizing information into a hierarchical structure with a root and branches. See *directory* and *subdirectory*.

Trojan Horse   A computer program that appears to perform a valid function but contains, hidden in its code, instructions that cause damage (sometimes severe) to the systems on which it runs.

A spectacular Trojan Horse made headlines in late 1989. More than 10,000 copies of a computer disk purportedly containing information about AIDS were mailed from a prestigious London address to corporations, insurance companies, and health professionals throughout Europe and North America.

Ostensibly, the program would help users calculate their risks of exposure to AIDS. Professionally prepared and packaged, the disk and its accompanying documentation would have cost approximately $150,000 to prepare and mail. Recipients who loaded the disks into their computers, however, quickly found that the software was a particularly vicious Trojan Horse that completely wiped out the data on hard disks.

Trojan Horses, unlike computer viruses, cannot replicate themselves.

troubleshooting The process of determining why a computer system or specific hardware device is malfunctioning.

> **→ Tip:** When a computer fails, most people panic and assume that a huge bill is on the way. Most likely, however, the problem is a minor one, such as a loose connection. Turn off the power and carefully inspect all the cables and connections. Remove the computer's lid and press down on the adapter boards to make sure that they are well seated in the expansion slots. You also should check connections at peripheral devices.

True BASIC A modern, structured version of the BASIC programming language developed by its originators (John Kemeny and Thomas Kurtz) in response to criticism of earlier versions of BASIC.

With modern control structures and optional line numbers, True BASIC is a well-structured language used to teach the principles of structured programming. The language, which is interpreted rather than compiled, is not frequently used for professional programming purposes.

truncate To cut off part of a number or character string.

truncation error A rounding error that occurs when part of a number is omitted from storage because it exceeds the capacity of the memory set aside for number storage. See *floating-point calculation.*

TSR See *terminate-and-stay-resident program (TSR).*

TTY See *terminal emulation.*

Turbo Pascal A high-performance compiler for Pascal developed by Borland International. The compiler comes with a full-screen text editor.

Out performing compilers that cost 10 times as much, Borland International's Turbo Pascal took the world of DOS programming by storm when released in 1984 and is now one of the most popular compilers ever written.

Although a compiler, Turbo Pascal is an excellent tool for teaching because it contains a fully integrated, full-screen text editor. If an error is encountered during program compilation, the editor returns on-screen and the cursor points to the error's location.

Turbo Pascal has many of the advantages of an interpreter for teaching but creates executable programs (object code). This compiler is used in hobby and academic environments, and some professional programmers use Turbo Pascal to prepare short- to medium-sized programs.

turnkey system   A computer system developed for a specific application, such as a point-of-sale terminal, and delivered ready-to-run, with all necessary application programs and peripherals.

tutorial   A form of instruction in which the student is guided step-by-step through the application of a program to a specific task, such as developing a budget or writing a business letter. Some application programs come with on-screen tutorials that use computer-based training techniques.

twisted-pair cable   In local area networks, a low band width connecting cable used in telephone systems. The cable includes two insulated wires wrapped around each other to minimize interference from other wires.

TYPE   In DOS and OS/2, an internal command that displays a file on-screen.

typeface   The distinctive design of a set of type, distinguished from its weight (such as bold or italic) and size.

Today's typefaces stem from the columns of ancient Rome, the workshops of Gutenberg and Garamond, and the ultra-modern design philosophy of the Bauhaus school in twentieth-century Germany. Thanks to desktop publishing, personal computer users can lay claim to and use this heritage as another element in an overall communication strategy.

Many laser printers come with as many as a dozen or more typefaces available in the printer's ROM, and literally hundreds more can be downloaded. With this enhanced communicative power, however, comes the responsibility to use typefaces with good taste.

One of the best ways to get help in the selection of typefaces is to look at books, magazines, and brochures from a new viewpoint—the viewpoint of the publication designer. Notice which fonts are used for body type and display type, the message being conveyed by the typeface, the appropriateness of the type for the publication's message, the use of white space as a design element, and the overall "color" of each page. Books in which the design team takes pride often include a colophon, a brief note (often on the last page) that indicates the typefaces chosen and the names of the principal designers.

Typefaces are grouped into two categories, serif and sans serif. Serif typefaces frequently are chosen for body type because they are more legible. Sans serif typefaces are preferred for display type. This rule, however, often is broken by designers striving for unity of design who prefer to use the same typeface (or closely related typefaces) for display and body type.

➜ **Tip:** Even if your system includes dozens of typefaces, professional graphics artists rarely use more than two typefaces in one document. Choose one typeface for display type and a second for body type. See *body type*, *display type*, *font*, and *font family*.

typeover mode See *Overtype mode*.

typeover   See *overtype*.

typesetter   See *imagesetter*.

typesetting   The production of camera-ready copy on a high-end typesetting machine such as a Linotronic or Varityper.

The current crop of office-quality PostScript laser printers can produce 300 dots-per-inch (dpi) output, which is considered crude by professional typesetting standards, but which may be acceptable for many applications such as newsletters, textbooks, instructional manuals, brochures, and pro-

posals. See *resolution*.**type size**   The size of a font, measured in points (approximately 1/72 inch) from the top of the
tallest ascender to the bottom of the lowest descender. See
pitch.

type style   The weight (such as Roman or bold) or posture
(such as italic) of a font—distinguished from a font's typeface
design and type size. See *attribute*, *emphasis*,

typography   The science and art of designing aesthetical-
lypleasing and readable typefaces.

undelete utility   A utility program that can restore a file accidentally erased from disk if no other data has been written to
the disk since the erasure occurred. See *Mace Utilities* and
Norton Utilities.

   Available from commercial and shareware sources, undelete utilities work because disk drives do not actually erase
the file; they delete the file's name from the file allocation
table (FAT).

   The clusters used for the file, however, become available
to the operating system for additional write operations, and if
such operations occur, the file can be erased irretrievably.

   ▲ **Caution:** If you have just deleted a file by error, STOP!
Perform no additional work with your computer that may
result in write operations. Use the undelete utility immediately; if you don't have one, stop working and go buy one.

undo   A program command that restores the program and your
data to the stage they were in just before the last command
was given or the last action was initiated. Undo commands

enable the user to cancel the often catastrophic effects of giving the wrong command.

uninterruptable power supply (UPS)   A battery capable of supplying continuous power to a computer system in the event of a power failure.

The battery, charged by line current, kicks in if the power fails and provides power for up to 10 minutes or more, during which time the computer can be shut down so that the integrity of crucial data is preserved.

→ **Tip:** An uninterruptable power supply is mandatory equipment if a sudden power outage can result in the loss of crucial data.

Universal Asynchronous Receiver/Transmitter (UART) An integrated circuit that transforms the parallel data stream within the computer to the serial, one-after-the-other data stream used in asynchronous communications.

In early IBM Personal Computers, the UART was contained on the Asynchronous Communications Adapter, but the UART now is found on the motherboard in most designs. Serial communication requires, in addition to the UART, a serial port and modem.

UNIX   Pronounced "yoo´-nicks." An operating system for a wide variety of computers, from mainframes to personal computers, that supports multitasking and is ideally suited to multiuser applications.

Written in the highly portable programming language C, UNIX is (like C) the product of work at AT&T Bell Laboratories during the early 1970s. Originally developed by highly advanced research scientists for sophisticated work in computer science, UNIX is a comprehensive programming environment that expresses a unique programming philosophy.

Rather than writing very large programs, each of which performs all functions, creating software tools, each of which performs one (and only one) function, and making these tools part of the operating system is better. Application programs need not rely on their own features to accomplish functions, but can take advantage of the software tools in the programming environment. This philosophy helps programmers keep application programs in manageable bounds.

As appealing as this philosophy may be to programmers, it exacts a heavy toll on end users. The communication of data from one software tool to another is accomplished via a pipe, a user command that couples the output of one command to the input of another. Pipes are highly flexible and enable you to control virtually every aspect of the operating environment; you can extend the command set to create commands for situations not anticipated in the operating system's development.

With more than 200 commands, inadequate error messages, and a cryptic command syntax, however, UNIX imposes heavy burdens on people who do not use the system frequently and have little or no interest in gaining precise control over every conceivable operating system feature. The acceptance of UNIX as a system for end-user computing, therefore, has been prevented and remains restricted to technical and academic environments.

No reason exists why a UNIX operating system cannot be equipped with a shell that makes the system easy to use, and with the development of UNIX shells, the operating system may play a much wider role in computing.

NeXTStep, a shell for the NeXT workstation, is as easy to use and versatile as the Macintosh Finder. NeXTStep aids programmers because it includes an application program interface (API) that handles virtually all screen routines, freeing programmers from the tedious programming required to generate screen images from within an application program. IBM is expected to offer NeXTStep on its own UNIX workstations. NeXTStep is by no means tied to the NeXT workstation and can be made available for 80386 and 80486 computers.

When the user is insulated from the peculiarities of using UNIX at the system level, the operating system's other advantages quickly become apparent. Unlike most personal computer operating systems, UNIX was designed as a multiuser system. With its multitasking capabilities, UNIX can perform more than one function at a time.

In the past, these features have been in little demand by personal computer users, who use stand-alone machines to run one application at a time. UNIX, therefore, is seldom used on personal computers. If the future of personal computing lies in linking workstations to corporate minicomputers and mainframes, however, UNIX operating systems—particularly when equipped with a shell such as NeXTStep—stand a chance of displacing DOS and even OS/2.

Because Bell Laboratories was prohibited from marketing UNIX by the antitrust regulations then governing AT&T, UNIX—the first version to gain significant distribution—was provided without charge to colleges and universities throughout North America, beginning in 1976.

In 1979, the University of California at Berkeley developed an enhanced and technically sophisticated version of UNIX for VAX computers. Much preferred in technical and engineering environments, Berkeley UNIX led to other versions made available commercially. In the early 1980s, AT&T gained the right to market the system and released System V in 1983.

As a result of these independent lines of UNIX development, many alternative and mutually incompatible versions of the system are in use. However, a standard UNIX version clearly is emerging. Although many thought that Berkeley UNIX would establish a standard, AT&T's System V caught up technically with Berkeley UNIX.

With the release of System V, AT&T established a set of UNIX standards called System V Interface Definition (SVID). SVID established a standard toward which most UNIX systems are migrating, especially now that major corporate purchasers are requiring this standard. IBM adopted the SVID standard for its own versions of UNIX. See *input/output redirection*, *NeXT*, *shell*, and *System V Interface Definition (SVID)*.

update   In database management, a fundamental data manipulation that involves adding, modifying, or deleting data records so that data is brought up to date.

upgrade   To purchase a new release or version of a program, or a more recent or more powerful version of a computer or peripheral.

upload   To transmit a file by telecommunications to another computer user or a bulletin board.

UPS   See *uninterruptable power supply (UPS)*.

upward compatibility   Software that functions without modification on later or more powerful versions of a computer system.

USENET   The news distribution and bulletin board channel of UUCP, an international wide-area network that links UNIX computers. See *UUCP*.

user   See *end user*.

user default   A user-defined program operating preference, such as the default margins to be used in every new document that a word processing program creates.

user-defined   Selected or chosen by the user of the computer system.

user-friendly   A program or computer system designed so that persons who lack extensive computer experience or training can use the system without becoming confused or frustrated.

     A user-friendly program usually includes the following elements: menus are used instead of forcing the user to memorize commands; on-screen help is available at the touch of a key; program functions are mapped to the keyboard in a logical order and do not contradict established conventions; error messages contain an explanation of what went wrong and what to do to solve the problem; intermediate and advanced features are hidden from view so that they do not clutter the screen and confuse those who are learning the program; commands that could erase or destroy data display confirmation messages that warn the user of the command's drastic consequences and provide a way to escape without initiating the operation; and clear, concise documentation includes tutorials and reference information.

user group   A voluntary association of users of a specific computer or program who meet regularly to exchange tips and techniques, hear presentations by computer experts, and obtain public domain software and shareware.

user interface   All the features of a program or computer that govern the way people interact with the computer. See *command-driven program* and *graphical user interface.*

utility program   A program that assists you in maintaining and improving the efficiency of a computer system.

In the best of all possible worlds, all the utility programs one needs would be provided with the operating system, but this scenario is rarely the case.

DOS, for example, provides many external commands, including utilities, such as backup programs, but many DOS users purchase additional utilities such as file compression utilities, defragmentation utilities, shells, undelete utilities, and vaccines, which DOS doesn't provide. Because DOS can be difficult to use, many users purchase utilities more user-friendly than existing DOS utilities, such as BACKUP and RESTORE.

UUCP   An international, cooperative wide-area network that links thousands of UNIX computers in the United States, Europe, and Asia. UUCP has electronic mail gateways to BITNET. See *BITNET* and *USENET.*

V

vaccine   A computer program designed to detect the presence of a computer virus in a system.

The vaccine detects the virus by checking for unusual attempts to access vital disk areas and system files and by searching for specific viruses known to afflict many computer systems.

▲ **Caution:** The malevolent authors of computer viruses are aware of vaccines and are busy creating new viruses to thwart them. If your computer is to be used for vital business or professional applications, protect your data by using only fresh, previously unopened copies of software obtained directly from computer software publishers. Synonymous with antivirus program.

value   In a spreadsheet program, a numeric cell entry.

Two kinds of values exist. The first kind, called constants, are values you type directly into a cell. The second kind of value is produced by a formula placed into a cell.

▲ **Caution:** On-screen, the values you enter directly (constants) and the values produced by formulas look alike. You easily can destroy a spreadsheet, therefore, by typing a constant on top of a formula. You see no apparent difference in the spreadsheet, probably, but recalculation produces errors because you have removed a formula. Before changing a value you see on-screen, be sure to check the entry line in the control panel to find out whether a formula is in the cell. See *cell protection* and *label*.

value-added reseller (VAR)   An organization that repackages and improves hardware manufactured by an original-equipment manufacturer (OEM).

A value-added reseller typically improves the original equipment by adding superior documentation, packaging, system integration, and exterior finish. Some VARs, however, do little more than put their name on a device.

vaporware   A program still under development that is heavily marketed even though no one knows for sure whether the development problems will be solved.

The most celebrated vaporware fiasco was Ovation, an integrated program like Symphony or Framework that received a great deal of press attention in 1984. The developer, however, could not overcome development problems, and the program was never released.

variable   In computer programming, a named area in memory that stores a value or string assigned to that variable.

VDT   Acronym for video display terminal. Synonymous with *monitor.*

VDT radiation   The electromagnetic radiation emitted by a video display terminal.

Debate continues in the scientific community about whether VDTs are safe. Computer monitors produce X-rays, ultraviolet radiation, and electromagnetic fields. Studies show conflicting results. Most laboratory studies of these emissions show that they cannot be distinguished from the background radiation present in an average work environment.

Other studies, however, have demonstrated a correlation between VDT use and health problems, particularly miscarriage among pregnant users. Job-related stress, however, may be responsible for these problems. Labor unions continue to charge that the scientific research on VDT radiation is flawed and biased because the research has been conducted by the computer industry or on behalf of the computer industry.

Debate recently has come to focus on extremely low frequency electromagnetic radiation fields, created by strong electrical currents in power lines and electrical equipment. Correlations between the very strong fields emitted by high-voltage electrical power distribution lines and increased risk of cancer have been demonstrated by a number of studies, although other studies show no increased risk.

Some studies indicate that more risk may be involved for much more modest fields, such as those emitted by electric blankets and water bed heaters. A careful study conducted by *PC Magazine,* December 12, 1989, demonstrated that although computers and monitors emit such radiation, the level was below background radiation levels at a distance of 18 inches from the computer and display.

➔ **Tip:** The evidence so far compiled does not suggest that prolonged use of computers and CRT displays is dangerous. To be on the safe side, however, keep your face and body at least 18 inches from the computer and display. If your computer displays varying font sizes, work with a large font such as 14 points while writing and reformat to a smaller font for printing purposes. To avoid repetitive stress injury (RSI), take frequent breaks. See *cathode ray tube (CRT)* and *repetitive stress injury (RSI)*.

VDU   Acronym for video display unit. Synonymous with *monitor*.

vector graphics   A graphics display technology in which images are formed on-screen by directly controlling the motions of the electron gun to form a specific image, such as a line or a circle, rather than requiring the gun to travel across the whole screen line-by-line (as in raster displays). Vector graphics are not used for personal computer displays but are occasionally used for professional workstations in such fields as architectural or engineering design.

Vectra   A line of IBM PC-compatible computers developed and marketed by Hewlett-Packard, Inc., and featuring a windowing environment.

vendor   A seller or supplier of computers, peripherals, or computer-related services.

Ventura Publisher   A page layout program for IBM PC-compatible computers considered excellent for long documents. See *PageMaker*.

VER   In DOS and OS/2, an internal command that displays the version number of DOS currently in use.

verify   To determine the accuracy and completion of a computer operation.

VERIFY   In DOS and OS/2, an internal command that checks the accuracy of data written to disk files to make sure that the information is stored properly.

By default, VERIFY is turned off. When you turn VERIFY on by typing VERIFY ON and pressing Enter, DOS checks the information copied to a disk to make sure that the copy is an exact duplicate of the original file. Storage operations take longer when VERIFY is on.

version A specific release of a software or hardware product.

A large version number indicates a later product release. For example, DOS 4.0 is a more recent product than DOS 3.3. In many cases, as in the DOS example, numbers (3.4–3.9) are skipped. Other products, such as FileMaker, have different versions, not necessarily in sequential order (FileMaker Plus, FileMaker 4, and FileMaker II).

Users are often wary of Version 1.0 products because such releases may lack extensive hands-on testing. Bug fixes often have even smaller intermediate numbers such as Version 1.02 or Version 1.2a.

verso The left-side (even-numbered) page in two-sided printing. See *recto.*

vertical application An application program created for a narrowly defined market, such as the members of a profession or a specific type of retail store.

vertical justification The alignment of newspaper columns by means of feathering (adding vertical space) so that all columns end evenly at the bottom margin.

A page layout program capable of vertical justification inserts white space between frame borders and text, between paragraphs, and between lines so that all columns end evenly on the bottom margin.

Vertical justification is by no means necessary. Vertical justification is common, but not universal, in newspapers and magazines, but many newsletter designers prefer to leave the bottom margin ragged.

very large scale integration (VLSI)   The fabrication on one semiconductor chip of more than 100,000 transistors.

VGA   See *Video Graphics Array (VGA).*

video adapter   The adapter that generates the output required to display computer text (and, with some adapters, graphics) on a monitor. See *Color Graphics Adapter (CGA), Enhanced Graphics Adapter (EGA), Hercules Graphics Adapter, IBM 8514/A display adapter, monochrome display adapter (MDA), multicolor graphics array (MCGA),* and *Video Graphics Array (VGA).*

Video Graphics Array (VGA)   A color bit-mapped graphics display standard, introduced by IBM in 1987 with its PS/2 computers. VGA adapters and analog monitors display as many as 256 continuously variable colors simultaneously with a resolution of 640 pixels horizontally by 480 vertically.

Built into the motherboard of some PS/2 computers, VGA circuitry is downwardly compatible with all previous IBM display standards, including CGA, MDA, and EGA. VGA is superior to the EGA standard not only because of the apparently modest increase in resolution (the increase is perceptually much more significant than the numbers indicate), but, unlike EGA adapters, VGA technology preserves the aspect ratio of on-screen graphics images.

VGA's analog input technology also produces an unlimited number of continuously variable colors; the EGA is a digital monitor technology locked into a fixed number of color intensity levels.

The IBM VGA standard has been pushed to new heights by third-party vendors, who offer VGA adapters that can display two additional graphics modes—an enhanced resolution of 800 by 600 pixels and super VGA with a resolution of 1024 by 768 pixels— with up to 256 colors displayed simultaneously. Many of these adapters, however, are designed to work only with the 16-bit AT expansion bus of 80286 and 80386 computers and cannot be used in 8088- or 8086-based systems.

video monitor   See *monitor.*

video RAM   The random-access memory (RAM) needed by a video adapter to construct and retain a full-screen image of a high-resolution video display. As much as 512K of video RAM may be needed by VGA video adapters.

videodisk   An optical disk used for the storage and retrieval of still pictures or television pictures and sound. A videodisk player is required to play back the videodisk on a standard television monitor.

Coupled with a computer that can control the videodisk player, an application called interactive video becomes possible; the program enables the user to gain controlled access to the information stored on the videodisk for instructional, presentation, or training purposes. A standard videodisk can hold approximately 50,000 still frames or up to two hours of television pictures.

videotext   The transmission of information, such as news headlines, stock quotes, and current movie reviews, through a cable television system. See *on-line information service.*

view   In database management programs, an on-screen display of only part of the information in a database—the part that meets the criteria specified in a query.

Most programs enable you to save a view that can be useful for certain purposes. Suppose that you have created a database of all the videotapes available in your video store. The printout of all the titles is long and expensive to duplicate. Rather than listing all the tapes in every category, you decide to make seven different printouts, sorted by category. The SQL command that produces a view of children's videotapes is as follows:

```
SELECT title, rating
FROM inventory
WHERE category = "children"
ORDER BY title
```

Most database management programs enable you to save views, and the best ones update each view every time you add or edit records.

virtual machine An on-screen simulation of a separate computer, as if the computer really existed and could run programs independently.

This simulation is made possible by a computer with the necessary processing circuitry and a large random-access memory (RAM). The Intel 80386 microprocessor, for example, can run two or more virtual DOS machines, each of which can run DOS programs concurrently in their own 640K memory space.

virtual memory A method of extending the apparent size of a computer's random-access memory (RAM) by using part of the hard disk as an extension of RAM.

Virtual memory has been around in personal computing for a long time; many application programs, such as Microsoft Word, routinely use the disk instead of memory to store data or program instructions. A true virtual memory system, however, is implemented at the operating system level, so that the memory is available to any and all programs. Under virtual memory, even a program such as WordPerfect, which insists that the entire document be placed in RAM, can work with documents of unlimited length (or length limited by the capacity of a hard disk rather than the capacity of RAM).

→ **Tip:** Virtual memory techniques currently are being implemented for most personal computers, but RAM is significantly faster than a hard disk. Virtual memory may result in delays of up to half a minute or more while the microprocessor waits to retrieve needed information from disk. With RAM chip prices at a reasonable level, equip a computer with additional RAM rather than relying on virtual memory techniques.

virtual table See *view*.

virus A computer program, designed as a prank or sabotage, that replicates itself by attaching to other programs and carrying out unwanted and sometimes damaging operations.

When embedded in its host, the virus replicates itself by attaching to other programs in the system, including system software. Like a human virus, the effects of a computer virus may not be detectable for a period of days or weeks, during which time every disk inserted into the system comes away with a hidden copy of the virus.

Eventually, the effects manifest themselves. The consequences range from prank messages to erratic system software performance or catastrophic erasure of all the information on a hard disk.

➔ **Tip:** To protect your system from computer viruses, observe the following rules:

- Do not download executable programs from public bulletin boards unless you are certain they are virus-free (you actually have seen someone else use the program without problems).

- Do not obtain executable programs from mail-order vendors of public domain or shareware programs unless they specifically promise to check each program they sell.

- Never download a recently uploaded program on a bulletin board until the sysop has checked it. When you do download the program, download it to a dual-floppy system so that the program cannot get near your hard disk.

- Don't copy pirated disks of commercial programs, because these disks may contain viruses.

- Purchase and use a vaccine.

See *Trojan Horse* and *vaccine.*

VLSI   See *very large scale integration (VLSI).*

voice mail   In office automation, a communications system in which voice messages are transformed into digital form and stored on a computer network. When the person to whom the message is directed logs on to the system and discovers that a message is waiting, the system plays the message. Synonymous with voice store and forward.

voice recognition   Computer recognition of human speech and the transformation of the recognized words into computer-readable, digitized text.

Computers share with people an unfortunate characteristic: they talk much better than they listen. In the most advanced research systems, computers can recognize only about one or two hundred words, and even this capability is achieved only after the speaker has trained the system to recognize his or her specific voice pattern.

Voice recognition involves some extremely complex pattern-recognition capabilities in the human brain that are not well understood. See *voice synthesis*.

voice store and forward   See *voice mail*.

voice synthesis   The audible output of computer-based text in the form of synthesized speech that people can recognize and understand.

Voice synthesis is much easier to achieve than voice recognition; virtually any personal computer can be equipped to read ASCII text with a minimum of errors. This capability has helped many blind people gain increased access to written works not recorded on cassette tape. However, voice synthesis is seldom used in computer user interfaces. See *voice recognition*.

VOL   In DOS and OS/2, an internal command that displays the volume label of the disk in the current drive. See *Label*.

volatility   The susceptibility of a computer's random-access memory (RAM) to the complete loss of stored information if power is interrupted suddenly.

volume label   In DOS and OS/2, the unique, identifying name assigned to a disk and displayed on the first line of a directory. The name must be no more than 11 characters. You assign the volume label when you format the disk.

➜ **Tip:** To change or delete a volume label or to add one if you didn't do so when you formatted the disk, use the LABEL command.

von Neumann bottleneck   The limitation on processing speed imposed by a computer architecture linking a single processing unit with memory.

This architecture is the product of John von Neumann's discovery of the stored program concept, but its limitations are now apparent. You can create very fast central processing units (CPU) and huge, fast memories, but a seemingly inescapable limitation has emerged: the processor is going to spend more time fetching instructions and data than actually processing the data.

One proposed solution to the von Neumann bottleneck is parallel processing, in which a program's tasks are divided among two or more CPUs. Existing programming languages and techniques, however, cannot handle parallel processing very well, and new languages, such as Occam, that can handle parallel processing involve the programmer in the nitty-gritty procedural details of allocating tasks to the processors.

wait state   A null processing cycle in which nothing occurs. A wait state is programmed into a computer system to allow other components, such as random-access memory (RAM), to catch up with the central processing unit (CPU).

A microprocessor with a fast clock speed, such as 25 MHz, can outrace the main memory, particularly if the memory is composed of dynamic random-access memory (DRAM) chips. Wait states, therefore, are programmed into the machine to rule out the serious errors that can occur if DRAM does not respond to the microprocessor fast enough.

Wait states can be eliminated (resulting in a "zero wait state" machine) by using fast (but expensive) cache memory, interleaved memory, page-mode RAM, or static RAM chips. See *random-access memory (RAM)* and *central processing unit (CPU)*.

warm boot   A system restart performed after the system has been powered and operating; a restart is the electronic equivalent of turning on the system because it clears the memory and reloads the operating system.

A warm boot is preferable to a cold start after a system crash because it places less strain on your system's electrical and electronic components. With IBM PC-compatible computers, you restart the system by pressing Ctrl-Alt-Del, although sometimes this command will not unlock the system.

Some IBM PC-compatible computers have buttons or switches that make a hardware restart possible; Macintosh users must install the programmer's switch before this maneuver is possible. See *live copy/paste* and *warm link*.

warm link   A connection established between two files or data items so that a change in one is reflected by a change in the second. A warm link does not require user intervention and action, such as opening both files and using an updating command, to make sure that the change has occurred; the change is made automatically. See *cold link*.

weight   The overall lightness or darkness of a typeface design, or the gradations of lightness to darkness within a font family.

A type style can be light or dark, and within a type style, you can see several gradations of weight (extra light, light, semilight, regular, medium, semibold, bold, extrabold, and ultrabold). See *typeface*.

Weitek coprocessor   A numeric coprocessor, created for computers that use the Intel 80286 and Intel 80386. This coprocessor offers significantly faster performance than the Intel 80287 and Intel 80387 and is widely used for professional computer-aided design (CAD) applications.

Unlike the Intel 80287 and 80387, however, programs cannot use the Weitek coprocessor unless they are modified to do so. See *computer-aided design (CAD)* and *numeric coprocessor*.

what-if analysis   In spreadsheet programs, an important form of data exploration in which key variables are changed to see the effect on the results of the computation.

What-if analysis provides businessmen and professionals with an effective vehicle for exploring the effect of alternative strategies, such as "What will my profits look like if I were to invest another $10,000 in advertising, assuming past trends hold true?"

what-you-see-is-what-you-get (WYSIWYG) Pronounced "wizzy-wig." A design philosophy for word processing programs in which formatting commands directly affect the text displayed on-screen, so that the screen shows the appearance of the printed text. See *embedded formatting command.*

white space The portion of the page not printed. A good page design involves the use of white space to balance the areas that receive text and graphics.

wide-area network A computer network that uses high-speed, long-distance communications networks or satellites to connect computers over distances greater than the distances (one or two miles) traversed by local area networks.

widow A formatting flaw in which the last line of a paragraph appears alone at the top of a new column or page.

Most word processing and page layout programs suppress widows and orphans; better programs enable you to switch widow/orphan control on and off and to choose the number of lines. See *orphan.*

wild card Characters, such as asterisks and question marks, that stand for any other character that may appear in the same place.

In DOS, you have two wild cards: the asterisk (*), which stands for any character (and any number of characters), and the question mark (?), which stands for any one character.

Wild card	*stands for*
REPORT1.*	REPORT1.DOC
	REPORT1.BAK

REPORT?.DOC   REPORT1.DOC
                 REPORT2.DOC
                 REPORT3.DOC

Winchester drive   See *hard disk*.

window   A rectangular, on-screen frame through which you
can view a document, worksheet, database, or other application.

In most programs, only one window is displayed. This
window functions as a frame through which you can see
your document, database, or worksheet. Some programs can
display two or more parts of the same file, or even two or
more different files, each in its own window.

A windowing environment carries multiple windowing
even further by enabling you to run two or more applications
concurrently, each in its own window.

windowing environment   An applications program interface
(API) that provides the features commonly associated with a
graphical user interface (such as windows, pull-down
menus, on-screen fonts, and scroll bars or scroll boxes), and
makes these features available to programmers of application
packages. See *DESQview* and *Microsoft Windows*.

Windows   See *Microsoft Windows*.

Wingz   Pronounced "wings." A highly innovative spreadsheet
for the Macintosh created by Informix that includes a built-in
draw program and an object-oriented programming language
similar to HyperTalk.

Just as you can include buttons in HyperCard applications
and write scripts for them in HyperTalk, you can use Wingz
to create buttons (see fig. W.1) and write script in Wingz'
programming language, HyperScript. Wingz buttons function
like macros in Lotus 1-2-3 but are easier to create and use.
See *HyperTalk*.

word One unit of memory storage, measured in bits.

The basic unit of memory storage for personal computers is the byte (8 bits). Longer words, however, may be used for number-crunching. See *floating-point calculation* and *numeric coprocessor.*

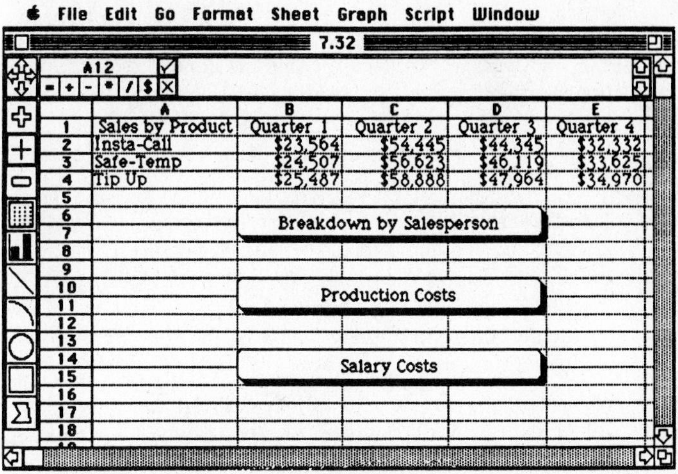

Fig. W.1. A Wingz worksheet with buttons.

WordPerfect A full-featured word processing program for a wide variety of computers, including the Macintosh and IBM PC-compatible computers.

Emphasizing portability and a consistent command structure across a wide variety of computer formats, WordPerfect (from WordPerfect Corporation) is the most widely used word processing program. Its phenomenal success in the IBM PC-compatible marketplace is attributable to its power.

The program includes more features than any other program, with the possible exception of Microsoft Word. WordPerfect also is fast (the entire document is kept in random-access memory, so that scrolling occurs at high speed), and the company's responsiveness to user suggestions is good.

Essentially an on-screen formatting program that operates in the DOS version of a character-based environment, WordPerfect displays most text formats as they appear when printed. The hidden codes that tell the printer how to print these formats, however, can be edited by the user, an unusual feature in this type of program.

WordPerfect strives to make all of its features accessible to the user who wants to gain complete control over the program. The program's critics, however, point out that the user frequently must perform manual edits of these hidden codes when, for one reason or another, the program fails to delete an extraneous code.

In most versions, WordPerfect relies heavily on function keys for the command interface, and this choice also has attracted criticism. In response, WordPerfect Version 5.1 for the IBM PC-compatible computer introduced the use of the mouse and pull-down menus.

The program is available for a wide variety of computers, including mainframe and minicomputers, and one of its strengths lies in its provision of a consistent user interface and file structure across a variety of computing environments. This consistency appeals greatly to organizations, because costs rise as people use a variety of computers to produce documents with mutually unintelligible file formats.

The emphasis on portability, however, has been achieved at some sacrifice of optimizing the program for a given environment. The Macintosh version of WordPerfect, for example, has been criticized because it does not take full advantage of the Mac's graphical user interface, nor does the program recognize many tacit conventions of program functionality that users have come to expect.

word processing program   An application program specifically designed to make the creation, editing, formatting, and printing of text easier.

The boundaries between page-layout programs (such as PageMaker and Ventura Publisher) and word processing programs are narrowing as full-featured word processing programs, such as Microsoft Word and WordPerfect, increasingly include page layout features, such as the capability to position a text or graphic on the page so that text flows around it.

Word processing programs provide the tools a writer needs to create and edit the text (such as outlining, spelling checkers, replace commands, and fast-scrolling text displays); page-layout programs concentrate on providing all the features needed to handle page layout at a professional level.

WordStar   An on-screen word processing program originally developed by MicroPro International (now WordStar International) for CP/M computers and IBM PCs and compatibles.

WordStar originated the term "what-you-see-is-what-you-get," although its WYSIWYG ("wizzy-wig") features are by no means complete; embedded commands still are required for many functions. The program is still preferred by writers with good touch typing skills because almost all commands can be given without taking your fingers off the home position (as you must do with most function keys or a mouse).

word wrap   A feature of word processing programs (and other programs that include text-editing features) that wraps words down to the beginning of the next line if they go beyond the right margin.

▲ **Caution:** If you are just getting started in word processing, remember that you should not press the Enter (or Return) key until you are ready to start a new paragraph. If you press Enter at the end of every line, you may find changing the margins or performing editing operations is difficult after you type the text.

workgroup   A small group of employees assigned to work together on a specific project.

Much of the work accomplished in contemporary corporations is done in workgroups, and if this work is to be done well and in a timely fashion, the workgroup needs to communicate effectively and share resources. Personal computer technology, especially when linked in a local area network (LAN), is thought to enhance workgroup productivity by giving the group additional communication channels (in the form of electronic mail), facilities for the group editing of technical documentation (see *redlining* and *strikeout*), and shared access to a common database.

worksheet In spreadsheet programs, the two-dimensional matrix of rows and columns within which you enter headings, numbers, and formulas. The worksheet resembles the ledger sheet used in accounting. Synonymous with *spreadsheet.*

worksheet window In spreadsheet programs, the portion of the worksheet visible on-screen.

With up to 8,192 rows and 256 columns, modern electronic spreadsheets are larger than a two-car garage in size. The worksheet window displays only a small portion of the total area potentially available (see fig. W.2).

workstation In a local area network, a desktop computer that runs application programs and serves as an access point to shared network resources. See *personal computer, professional workstation,* and *file server.*

WORM See *write-once, read many (WORM).*

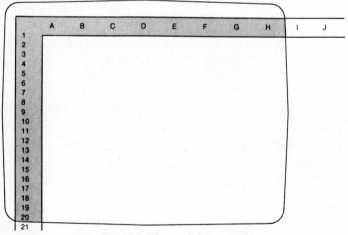

Fig. W.2. The worksheet window.

wrap-around type   Type contoured so that it surrounds a graphic (see fig. W.3).

Because wrap-around type is harder to read than noncontoured type, use wrap-around type sparingly.

write   A fundamental processing operation in which the central processing unit (CPU) records information in the computer's random-access memory (RAM) or the computer's secondary storage media, such as disk drives.

The selected graphic showing
its custom text-wrap boundary.

Dragging the graphic
into place on the page.

Surrounding text automatically
reflows itself around the graphic.

The final page after enlarging
and repositioning the graphic.

Fig. W.3. Text wrapped around a graphic.

In personal computing, the term most often is used in the sense of storing information on disks.

write-black engine   See *print engine*.

write head   See *read/write head*.

write-once, read many (WORM)   Pronounced "worm." An optical disk drive with storage capacities of up to 1 terabyte. This disk becomes a read-only storage medium after data is written to the disk.

WORM drives can store huge amounts of information and have been touted as an excellent technology for organizations that need to publish large databases internally (such as collections of engineering drawings or technical documentation). The advent of fully read/write capable optical disk drives, however, has greatly diminished the appeal of WORM technology. See *CD-ROM* and *erasable optical disk drive*.

write-protect   To modify a floppy disk so that the computer cannot write on the disk or erase the information on it.

write-protect notch   On a 5 1/4-inch floppy disk, a small notch cut out of the disk's protective jacket that, when covered by a piece of tape, prevents the disk drive from performing erasures or write operations to the disk.

With 3 1/2-inch disks, the same function is accomplished by moving a small tab toward the top of the disk's case.

write-white engine   See *print engine*.

WYSIWYG   See *what-you-see-is-what-you-get (WYSIWYG)*.

X

x-axis   In a business graph, the x-axis is the categories axis, which usually is the horizontal axis. See *bar graph, column graph, y-axis,* and *z-axis*.

XCFN   See *external function.*

XCMD   See *external command (XCMD).*

XCOPY   In DOS and OS/2, an external command that selectively copies files from one or more subdirectories.

Using XCOPY, you can back up files from several subdirectories onto one disk or directory. Unlike BACKUP, which performs the same task but preserves the original file's directory location, the path name of the source file is lost when copying occurs.

XENIX   Pronounced "zee´-nicks." An operating system developed by Microsoft Corporation that conforms to the UNIX System V Interface Definition (SVID) and runs on IBM PC-compatible computers. See *UNIX* and *System V Interface Definition (SVID).*

x-height   In typography, the height of a font's lowercase letters that do not have ascenders or descenders (such as x, a, and c).

Because many fonts have unusually long or short ascenders and descenders, the x-height is a better measurement of the actual size of a font than the type size measured in points (see fig. X.1).

Fig. X.1. Letters with the same nominal type size may have different x-heights.

XMODEM   An asynchronous file-transfer protocol for personal computers that makes the error-free transmission of computer files through the telephone system easier.

Developed by Ward Christiansen for 8-bit CP/M computers and placed in the public domain, the XMODEM protocol is included in all personal computer communications programs and commonly is used to download files from computer bulletin boards.

XON/XOFF handshaking   See *handshaking.*

XT   See *IBM Personal Computer XT.*

x-y graph   See *scatter diagram.*

XyWrite   Pronounced "zy´-right." A word processing program developed by XyQuest, Inc., for IBM PC-compatible computers. The program is derived from the Atex typesetting system, which is used in newspaper and magazine publishing.

y

y-axis   In a business graph, the y-axis is the values (vertical) axis. See *bar graph*, *column graph*, *x-axis*, and *z-axis.*

YMCK   Acronym for yellow, magenta, cyan, and black. See *color separation.*

z

zap   Synonymous with erase and delete.

Zapf Chancery   Pronounced "zaff-chance´-er-ee." A typeface developed by Hermann Zapf, a German typeface designer (see fig. Z.1).

Zapf Chancery is beautiful and graceful but should be used sparingly because of its poor legibility. This typeface is an excellent choice for invitations and announcements in which a touch of grace and formality is desired.

abcdefghijklmnopqrstuvwxyz
ABCDEFGHIJKLMNOPQRSTUVWXYZ
1234567890 .,;:'"&!?$

Fig. Z.1. Text in Zapf Chancery.

Zapf Dingbats Pronounced "zaff ding-bats." A set of decorative symbols developed by Hermann Zapf, a German typeface designer.

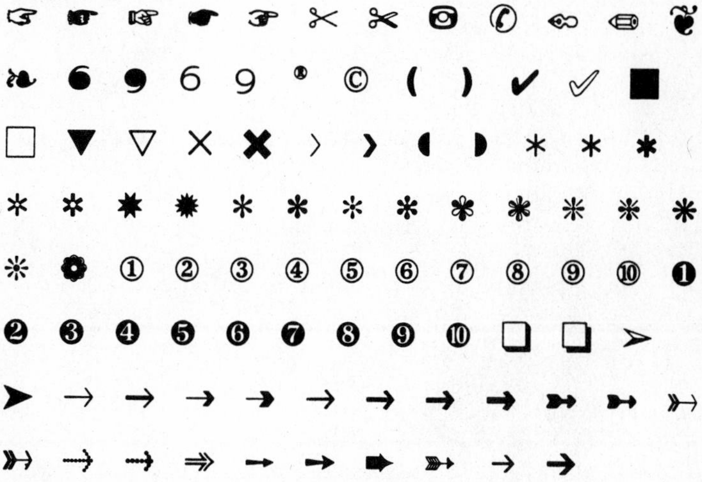

Fig. Z.2. Zapf Dingbats.

z-axis In a three-dimensional graphics image, the third dimension of depth. See *x-axis* and *y-axis*.

zero-slot LAN A local area network designed to use a computer's serial port instead of requiring the user to purchase a network adapter board that occupies one of the computer's expansion slots.

▲ **Caution:** Zero-slot LANS are considerably slower than systems that use network interface cards which take advantage of the computer's high-speed internal bus. Therefore, they are best used for applications in which network applications are limited to occasional access to an infrequently used shared peripheral (such as a plotter) or electronic mail.

zero wait state computer An IBM PC-compatible computer with memory optimized by using a scheme such as cache memory, interleaved memory, page-mode RAM, or static random-access memory (RAM) chips, so that the microprocessor does not have to wait for the memory to catch up with processing operations.

zoom To enlarge a window so that it fills the screen.

zoom box In a graphical user interface, a box (usually positioned on the window border) that you use to zoom the window to full size or restore the window to normal size by clicking the mouse.

THE WORLD'S BEST-SELLING 1-2-3
BOOKS—FROM QUE!

Using 1-2-3 Release 2.2, Special Edition
From the world's leading publisher of 1-2-3 books, this text discusses worksheet basics and advanced 1-2-3 operations. Includes Allways coverage, a Troubleshooting sections, a Command Reference, and a tear-out menu map.
$24.95   **Order #1040**

Using 1-2-3 Release 3
Only the spreadsheet experts at Que can offer this best-selling guide to the commands and operations of 1-2-3 Release 3! Includes a Command Reference, a Troubleshooting section, and easy-to-follow instructions for Release 3 worksheets, graphics, databases, and macros.
$24.95   **Order #971**

Also available from Que:

For more information call
1-800-428-5331

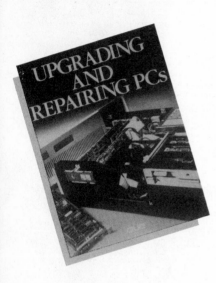

USING DOS IS EASY WITH QUE!

Using DOS

The most helpful DOS book available!
Using DOS is an introductory text that
demonstrates basic DOS operations, then
moves into more advanced file
management techniques. Specially
designed to help you boost your personal
computer productivity.

$22.95   Order #1035

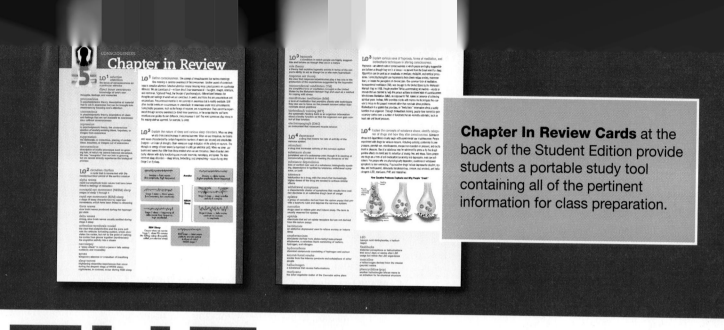

Chapter In Review Cards at the back of the Student Edition provide students a portable study tool containing all of the pertinent information for class preparation.

THE SOLUTION

PSYCH
Are you in?

ONLINE RESOURCES INCLUDED!

 **CourseMate** Engaging. Trackable. Affordable.

CourseMate brings course concepts to life with interactive learning, study, and exam preparation tools that support PSYCH.

FOR INSTRUCTORS:
- Custom Options through 4LTR+ Program
- Instructor's Manual
- Test Bank
- PowerPoint® Slides
- Instructor Prep Cards
- Engagement Tracker

FOR STUDENTS:
- Interactive eBook
- Auto-Graded Quizzes
- Flashcards
- Games: Crossword Puzzles, Beat the Clock
- Videos
- Student Review Cards

Students sign in at
login.cengagebrain.com

WADSWORTH
CENGAGE Learning™

PSYCH Second Edition
Spencer A. Rathus

Senior Publisher: Linda Schreiber-Ganster

Executive Editor: Jon-David Hague

Senior Acquiring/Sponsoring Editor: Jamie Perkins

Developmental Editors: Tangelique Williams and Liana Monari Sarkisian

Assistant Editor: Kelly Miller

Editorial Assistant: Phil Hovanessian

Media Editor: Mary Noel

Marketing Manager: Jessica Egbert

Executive Marketing Communications Manager: Talia Wise

Senior Content Project Manager: Pat Waldo

Design Director: Rob Hugel

Art Director: Vernon Boes

Print Buyer: Judy Inouye

Image and Text Rights Acquisitions Specialist: Don Schlotman

Production Service: Peter Lindstrom, Bill Smith Studio

Text Designer: Beckmeyer Design

Photo Researcher: Scott Rosen, Bill Smith Studio

Text Researcher: Sue C. Howard

Cover Designer: Denise Davidson

Cover Image: Don Farrall/Getty Images

Compositor: Bill Smith Studio

For product information and technology assistance, contact us at **Cengage Learning Customer & Sales Support, 1-800-354-9706.**

For permission to use material from this text or product, submit all requests online at **www.cengage.com/permissions.** Further permissions questions can be emailed to **permissionrequest@cengage.com.**

Library of Congress Control Number: 2010935348

Student Edition:
ISBN-13: 978-1-111-18578-7
ISBN-10: 1-111-18578-6

Wadsworth
20 Davis Drive
Belmont, CA 94002-3098
USA

Cengage Learning is a leading provider of customized learning solutions with office locations around the globe, including Singapore, the United Kingdom, Australia, Mexico, Brazil, and Japan. Locate your local office at **www.cengage.com/global.**

Cengage Learning products are represented in Canada by Nelson Education, Ltd.

To learn more about Wadsworth, visit **www.cengage.com/Wadsworth** Purchase any of our products at your local college store or at our preferred online store **www.cengagebrain.com.**

Printed in the United States of America
1 2 3 4 5 6 7 14 13 12 11 10

PSYCH
Brief Contents

SPEAK UP!

SHE DID

PSYCH2 was built on a simple principle: to create a new teaching and learning solution that reflects the way today's faculty teach and the way you learn.

Through conversations, focus groups, surveys, and interviews, we collected data that drove the creation of the current version of PSYCH2 that you are using today. But it doesn't stop there – in order to make PSYCH2 an even better learning experience, we'd like you to SPEAK UP and tell us how PSYCH2 worked for you.

What did you like about it? What would you change? Are there additional ideas you have that would help us build a better product for next semester's students?

At **www.CengageBrain.com** you'll find all of the resources you need to succeed – **videos, flash cards, interactive quizzes** and more!

Speak Up! Go to **www.CengageBrain.com**.

PSYCH Contents

DAVID BUFFINGTON/GETTY IMAGES

PETER CADE/GETTY IMAGES

ELYSE LEWIN/JUPITER IMAGES

PHOTODISC/JUPITER IMAGES

ENAMUL HOQUE/GETTY IMAGES

ERIK ISAKSON / GETTY IMAGES

LARSEN & TALBERT/JUPITER IMAGES

© 2007 KEVIN ARNOLD/ JUPITERIMAGES CORPORATION

KEITH BROFSKY/GETTY IMAGES

© RUBBERBALL / ALAMY

SCOTT T. BAXTER/GETTY IMAGES

COCOON/GETTY IMAGES

PM IMAGES/GETTY IMAGES

PHOTOLINK/GETTY IMAGES

GETTY IMAGES

MIKE DUNNING/GETTY IMAGES

© IMAGE SOURCE BLACK/JUPITERIMAGES

What *is* Psychology?

Learning Outcomes

LO **1**   Define psychology

LO **2**   Describe the various fields and subfields of psychology

LO **3**   Describe the origins of psychology and identify those who made significant contributions to the field

LO **4**   Identify theoretical perspectives of modern psychologists toward behavior and mental processes

LO **5**   Describe modern approaches to research and practice—critical thinking, the scientific method, and ethical considerations

> ## 66 *What standards or rules should we apply when we are trying to sort out truth from fiction?* 99

Each week, supermarket tabloid headlines exclaim over the latest abductions by extraterrestrials. Isn't it strange that extraterrestrials have the technology to fly between the stars, and yet apparently still need to prod and poke us to figure out how we work? If you can believe the photos and drawings in the tabloids, aliens have been hopping around in the same flying saucers for half a century—a saucer-shaped silver disk with a hump on top. Meanwhile, we inferior humans have progressed. We have evolved our modes of transportation from sleek cars with tail fins to boxy Scions and Elements. We continuously update our iPods with the latest music and download the newest ringtones into our camera cell phones. But the aliens keep flying the same model flying saucers. They're nothing to text home about.

Although we can find some humor in these tales of abduction by aliens, psychologists and other scientists are very interested in the questions these tales raise about human nature and the distinction between sensationalism and science. What do we know about people who claim to have been abducted by aliens? What standards or rules should we apply when we are trying to sort out truth from fiction and decide whether we will believe the "kidnap victims"?

Truth or Fiction?

What do you think?

Folklore, common sense, or nonsense? Place a T for "True" or F for "False" on the lines provided (you'll learn the answers as you read through the text).

__ More than 2,000 years ago, Aristotle wrote a book on psychology, with contents similar to the book you are now holding.

__ The ancient Greek philosopher Socrates suggested a research method that is still used in psychology.

__ Men receive the majority of doctoral degrees in psychology.

__ Even though she had worked to complete all the degree requirements, the first female president of the American Psychological Association turned down the doctoral degree that was offered to her.

__ You could survey millions of voters and still fail to predict the outcome of a presidential election.

__ In many experiments, neither the study participants nor the researchers know who is receiving the real treatment and who is not.

Many psychologists have studied the reported alien kidnappings, and one of their conclusions is that the kidnappings never occurred. However, the people making the claims are not necessarily mentally ill, nor are they even lying (Newman & Baumeister, 1998). These are by and large people who have "remembered" their "experiences" while undergoing therapy, and often under hypnosis. Tales of alien abduction are widely known throughout our culture, so it is not at all surprising that the "memories" of "kidnap victims" would tend to coincide (Lynn & Kirsch, 1996; Patry & Pelletier, 2001).

"Abductees" generally claim that they are awakened in their sleep by the aliens and unable to move. Psychologists know that many of our voluntary muscles—the ones involved in movement—are "paralyzed" when we sleep, which is why we usually don't thrash about when we dream (McNally & Clancy, 2005). *Hallucinations*—that is, seeing and hearing things that are not really there—are quite common as we are waking from a sleep-paralyzed state, and it seems that the reported experiences of "abductees" fit the pattern.

Psychologists also know that people are quite open to suggestion, especially when undergoing hypnosis (Clark & Loftus, 2004). Memories are not perfect snapshots. Sometimes the person interviewing the supposed kidnap victim asks leading questions—that is, questions that might encourage the witnesses to recall events in a certain way—looking for experiences with aliens.

All in all, "UFO memories may be constructed from bits and pieces of sleep-related hallucinations, nightmares, and media attention and fixed solidly into place with the suggestion of hypnosis and the validation of support groups" (Clark & Loftus, 1996). Abductees may also be trying to escape, temporarily, from their humdrum lives—just as buyers of the supermarket tabloids might be doing (Newman and Baumeister, 1998).

Psychologists have thus worked to "explain" how it can be that many people report being abducted by aliens and being subjected to tests by them. But is there evidence that people have been abducted by aliens? In sum, when we subject the stories in the supermarket tabloids to scientific analysis, we usually find that they fall short of any reasonable requirements of evidence.

This book will take you on a journey. It's not a journey into outer space. It's a journey into the inner space of thinking critically about the world around you, about stories and arguments made by other people, about human behavior and mental processes. In our overview of reported alien abductions, we touched on people's memories, the state of consciousness known as sleep, hallucinations, hypnosis, the search for stimulating events, social influences on witnesses, and the effects of social support and the media. All these, and much, much more, lie within the science of psychology. We will see who psychologists are, what they do, what they have learned, and perhaps most importantly, how they sort out truth from fiction. Let us begin by asking, *What is psychology?*

LO¹ Psychology as a Science

Psychology is the scientific study of behavior and mental processes. Topics of interest to psychologists include the nervous system, sensation and perception, learning and memory, intelligence, language, thought, growth and development, personality, stress and health, psychological disorders, ways of treating those disorders, sexual behavior, and the behavior of people in social settings such as groups and organizations.

Sciences have certain goals. Psychology, like other sciences, seeks to describe, explain, predict, and control the events it studies. Psychology thus seeks to describe, explain, predict, and control behavior and mental processes. "Controlling" behavior and mental processes doesn't mean to psychologists what it may sound like to most people. Psychologists are committed to a belief in the dignity of human beings, and human dignity requires that people be free to make their own decisions and choose their own behavior. Psychologists study the influences on human behavior, but they use this knowledge only on request and to help people meet their own goals. For example, a psychologist would wish to help someone who is suffering from anxiety and who asks for help.

When possible, descriptive terms such as *a threat* and concepts such as *anxiety* are interwoven into **theories**. Theories propose reasons for relationships among events, as in perception of *a threat* can arouse feelings of *anxiety*. They allow us to derive explanations and predictions, as in "Dwayne will feel *anxious* if he perceives *a threat*." A theory of hunger should allow us to predict when people will or will not eat. Many psychological theories combine statements about behavior (such as *evading a threat*), mental processes (such as *thinking that the threat may be harmful*), and biological processes (*rapid heart and respiration rates*). If our observations are not adequately explained by or predicted from a theory, we should consider revising or replacing it.

The remainder of this chapter presents an overview of psychology as a science. You will see that psychologists have diverse interests and fields of specialization. We discuss the history of psychology and the perspectives from which today's psychologists view behavior and mental process. Finally, we consider the research methods used by psychologists.

LO^{2}What Psychologists Do

Psychologists share a keen interest in behavior, but in other ways, they may differ markedly. *Just what do psychologists do?* Psychologists engage in research, practice, and teaching. Some researchers engage primarily in basic, or pure research. Pure research has no immediate application to personal or social problems and, therefore, has been characterized as research for its own sake. Others engage in applied research, which is designed to find solutions to specific personal or social problems. Although pure research is sparked by curiosity and the desire to know and understand, today's pure research frequently has applications tomorrow. For example, pure research on learning and motivation in pigeons, rats, and monkeys done early in the 20th century has found applications in school systems. The research has shown, for example, that learning often takes time and repetition and profits from "booster shots" (that is, repetition even after the learning goal has been reached). Pure research into the workings of the nervous system has enhanced knowledge of disorders such as epilepsy, Parkinson's disease, and Alzheimer's disease.

Many psychologists *practice* psychology by applying psychological knowledge to help individuals change their behavior so that they can meet their own goals more effectively. Still other psychologists primarily teach. They share psychological knowledge in classrooms, seminars, and workshops. Some psychologists engage in all three: research, practice, and teaching.

Fields of Psychology

Psychologists are found in different specialties. Although some psychologists wear more than one hat, most of them carry out their functions in the following fields.

Many developmental, educational, and school psychologists observe children's behavior in the classroom—the "natural setting" for important behavior.

Clinical *psychologists* help people with psychological disorders adjust to the demands of life. Clinical psychologists evaluate problems such as anxiety and depression through interviews and psychological tests. They help clients resolve problems and change self-defeating behavior. For example, they may help clients face "threats," such as public speaking, by exposing the clients gradually to situations in which they make presentations to actual or virtual groups (see *virtual therapy* in Chapter 13). Clinical psychologists are the largest subgroup of psychologists (see Figure 1.1 on page 6). *Counseling psychologists,* like clinical psychologists, use interviews and tests to define their clients' problems. Their clients typically have adjustment problems but not serious psychological disorders. For example, clients may have trouble making academic or vocational decisions or making friends in college.

School psychologists help school systems identify and assist students who have problems that interfere with learning. They help schools make decisions about placing students in special classes. *Educational psychologists* research theoretical issues related to learning, measurement, and child development. They study how learning is affected by psychological factors such as motivation and intelligence, sociocultural factors such as poverty and acculturation, and teacher behavior. Some educational psychologists prepare standardized tests such as the SATs.

Developmental psychologists study the changes—physical, cognitive, social, and emotional—that occur across the life span. They try to sort out the effects of heredity and the environment on development.

Personality psychologists identify and measure human traits and determine influences on human thought processes, feelings, and behavior. They are particularly concerned with issues such as anxiety, aggression, and gender roles. *Social psychologists* are concerned with the nature and causes of individuals' thoughts, feelings, and behavior in social situations. Whereas personality psychologists tend to look within the person for explanations of behavior, social psychologists tend to focus on social influences.

Environmental psychologists study the ways in which people and the environment—the natural environment and the human-made environment—influence one another. For example, we know that extremes of temperature and loud noises interfere with learning in school. Environmental psychologists also study ways to encourage people to recycle

OJO IMAGES / JUPITER IMAGES

Figure 1.1

New Doctorates in Psychology (median age = 32)

Demographic Factors	%
Women	78.1
Men	21.7
Asian American/Pacific Islander	4.8
African American	5.6
Latina or Latino American	6.3
Native American	<1.0
European American	76.4
Type of Degree	**%**
Ph.D.	52.9
Psy.D.	47.1
Work Setting	**%**
Academia	20.2
Hospitals	19.6
Other Human Service	16.0
Independent Practice	13.7
Business/Government	13.5
Schools/Educational	7.8
Managed Care	7.3
Primary Work Activity	**%**
Health Service	69.5
Education	13.7
Research	10.2
Administration	4.1
Other	2.5
Selected Subfields	**%**
Clinical Psychology	62.0
Counseling Psychology	11.1
School Psychology	9.5
Clinical Child Psychology	6.4
Other	10.7

Source: Adapted from american psychological association (2009a). Doctoral psychology workforce fast facts. Health service provider subfields. Center for workforce studies. http://research.apa.org/fastfacts-09.pdf. © Copyright 2009 APA center for workforce studies. Washington, DC.

and to preserve bastions of wild=erness.

Experimental psychologists specialize in basic processes such as the nervous system, sensation and perception, learning and memory, thought, motivation, and emotion. For example, experimental psychologists study which areas of the brain are involved in solving math problems or listening to music. They use people or animals such as pigeons and rats to study learning.

Industrial psychologists focus on the relationships between people and work. *Organizational psychologists* study the behavior of people in organizations such as businesses. *Human factors psychologists* make technical systems such as automobile dashboards and computer keyboards more user-friendly. *Consumer psychologists* study the behavior of shoppers in an effort to predict and influence their behavior. They advise store managers how to lay out the aisles of a supermarket in ways that boost impulse buying, how to arrange window displays to attract customers, and how to make newspaper ads and TV commercials more persuasive.

Health psychologists examine the ways in which behavior and attitudes are related to physical health. They study the effects of stress on health problems such as headaches, cardiovascular disease, and cancer. Health psychologists also guide clients toward healthier behavior patterns, such as exercising and quitting smoking.

Sport psychologists help athletes concentrate on their performance and not on the crowd, use cognitive strategies such as positive visualization (imagining themselves making the right moves) to enhance performance, and avoid choking under pressure.

Forensic psychologists apply psychology to the criminal justice system. They deal with legal matters such as whether a defendant was sane when

{ Aristotle }

How do we number Aristotle's contributions to psychology?

1 He argued that science could rationally treat only information gathered by the senses.

2 He numbered the so-called five senses of vision, hearing, smell, taste, and touch.

3 He explored the nature of cause and effect.

4 He pointed out that people differ from other living things in their capacity for rational thought.

5 He outlined laws of *associationism* that have lain at the heart of learning theory for more than 2,000 years.

6 He also declared that people are motivated to seek pleasure and avoid pain—a view that remains as current today as it was in ancient Greece.

he or she committed a crime. Forensic psychologists may also treat psychologically ill offenders, consult with attorneys on matters such as picking a jury, and analyze criminals' behavior and mental processes. Forensic psychologists, like other psychologists, may choose to conduct research on matters ranging from evaluation of eyewitness testimony to interrogation methods.

LO³ Where Psychology Comes From: A History

Have you heard the expression "Know thyself"? It was suggested by the ancient Greek philosopher, Socrates, more than 2,000 years ago. Psychology, which is in large part the endeavor to know ourselves, is as old as history and as modern as today. Knowledge of the history of psychology allows us to appreciate its theoretical conflicts, its place among the sciences, the evolution of its methods, and its social and political roles.

introspection
deliberate looking into one's own cognitive processes to examine one's thoughts and feelings

Who were some of the ancient contributors to psychology? One of them is the ancient Greek philosopher Aristotle (384–322 BCE). Aristotle argued that human behavior, like the movements of the stars and the seas, is subject to rules and laws. Then he delved into his subject matter topic by topic: personality, sensation and perception, thought, intelligence, needs and motives, feelings and emotion, and memory.

Other ancient Greek philosophers also contributed to psychology. Around 400 BCE, Democritus suggested that we could think of behavior in terms of a body and a mind. (Contemporary psychologists talk about the interaction of biological and mental processes.) He pointed out that our behavior is influenced by external stimulation. Democritus was one of the first to raise the question of whether there is free will or choice. Putting the question another way, where do the influences of others end and "our own selves" begin?

Socrates (c. 470–399 BCE) suggested that we should rely on rational thought and introspection—careful examination of one's own thoughts and emotions—to achieve self-knowledge. He also pointed out that people are social creatures who influence one another.

Had we room enough and time, we could trace psychology's roots to thinkers even farther back in time than the ancient Greeks, and we could trace its development through the great thinkers of the Renaissance. As it is, we must move on to the development of psychology as a laboratory science during the second half of the 19th century. Some historians set the marker date at 1860. It was then that Gustav Theodor Fechner (1801–1887) published his landmark book *Elements of Psychophysics*, which showed how physical events (such as lights and sounds) are related to psychological sensation and perception. Fechner also showed how we can scientifically measure the effect of these events. Most historians set the debut of modern psychology as a laboratory science in the year 1879, when Wilhelm Wundt used scientific methods to investigate what were previously philosophical questions in his laboratory in Leipzig, Germany.

Truth

More than 2,000 years ago, Aristotle wrote a book on psychology, *Peri Psyches*, with contents similar to the book you are now holding. Like this book, *Peri Psyches* begins with a history of psychological thought and historical views of the mind and behavior.

Truth

Socrates suggested a research method that is still used in psychology—introspection, which is based on Socrates' advice to "know thyself," which has remained a motto of psychology ever since.

I wished, by treating Psychology like a natural science, to help her become one.

—William James

Structuralism

structuralism
the school of psychology that argues that the mind consists of three basic elements—sensations, feelings, and images—that combine to form experience

functionalism
the school of psychology that emphasizes the uses or functions of the mind rather than the elements of experience

The German psychologist Wilhelm Wundt (1832–1920) looked as if he were going to be a problem child. He did poorly in elementary school—his mind would wander—and he had to repeat a grade. Eventually he attended medical school because he wanted to earn a good living. But he did not like working with patients and dedicated himself to philosophy and psychology.

Like Aristotle, Wundt saw the mind as a natural event that could be studied scientifically, like light, heat, and the flow of blood. Wundt used introspection to try to discover the basic elements of experience.

Wundt and his students founded the school of psychology called structuralism. *What is structuralism?* Structuralism attempted to break down conscious experience into objective sensations, such as sight or taste, and subjective feelings, such as emotional responses, will, and mental images like memories or dreams. Structuralists believed that the mind functions by combining objective and subjective elements of experience.

Functionalism

Toward the end of the 19th century, William James became a major figure in the development of psychology in the United States. He focused on the relation between conscious experience and behavior. He argued, for example, that the stream of consciousness is fluid, and continuous. Introspection convinced him that experience cannot be broken down into objective sensations and subjective feelings as the structuralists maintained.

James was a founder of the school of functionalism. *What is functionalism?* The school of functionalism focused on behavior in addition to the mind or consciousness. Functionalists looked at how our experience

helps us function more adaptively in our environments—for example, how habits help us cope with common situations. (When eating with a spoon, we do not create an individual plan to bring each morsel of food to our mouths.) They also turned to the laboratory for direct observations as a way to supplement introspection. The structuralists tended to ask, "What are the pieces that make up thinking and experience?" In contrast, the functionalists tended to ask, "How do behavior and mental processes help people adapt to the requirements of their lives?"

James was also influenced by Charles Darwin's (1809–1882) theory of evolution. Earlier in the 19th century, the British naturalist Darwin had argued that organisms with adaptive features—that is, the "fittest"—survive and reproduce. Functionalists adopted Darwin's theory and proposed that adaptive behavior patterns are learned and maintained. Maladaptive behavior patterns tend to drop out; only the "fittest" behavior survives. Adaptive behaviors tend to be repeated and become habits. James wrote, "habit is the enormous flywheel of society." Habit keeps the engine of civilization running.

Behaviorism

Imagine you have placed a hungry rat in a maze. It meanders down a pathway that ends in a T. It can turn left or right. If you consistently reward the rat with food for turning right, it will learn to turn right when it arrives there, at least when it is hungry. But what does the rat *think* when it is learning to turn right?

Does it seem absurd to try to place yourself in the "mind" of a rat? So it seemed to John Broadus Watson (1878–1958), the founder of American behaviorism. Watson was asked to consider the contents of a rat's "mind" as one of the requirements for his doctoral degree, which he received from the University of Chicago in 1903. Functionalism was the dominant view of psychology at the University of Chicago, and functionalists were concerned with the stream of consciousness as well as observable behavior.

But Watson (1913) believed that if psychology was to be a natural science, like physics or chemistry, it must limit itself to observable, measurable events—that is, to behavior alone—hence, the term *behaviorism*.

Wilhelm Wundt

William James

Figure 1.2

The Power of Reinforcement

In the photo we see a feathered friend that has learned to drop shapes into their proper places through reinforcement. Behaviorists teach animals complex behaviors such as this by first reinforcing approximations to the goal (or target behavior). As time progresses, closer approximations are demanded before reinforcement is given.

TOM MCHUGH/PHOTO RESEARCHERS, INC.

What is behaviorism? **Behaviorism** is the school of psychology that focuses on learning observable behavior. The term "observable" includes behaviors that are observable by means of instruments, such as the heart rate, blood pressure, and brain waves. These behaviors are *public* in that they can be measured easily and multiple observers would agree about their existence and features. Given their focus on behavior, behaviorists define psychology as the scientific study of *behavior,* not of *behavior and mental processes.*

B. F. Skinner (1904–1990) also contributed to behaviorism. He believed that organisms learn to behave in certain ways because they have been **reinforced** for doing so—that is, their behavior has a positive outcome. He demonstrated that laboratory animals can be trained to carry out behaviors through strategic use of reinforcers, such as food. He trained rats to turn in circles, climb ladders, and push toys across the floor. Because Skinner showed that he could teach animals remarkable combinations of behaviors by means of reinforcement, many psychologists adopted the view that, in principle, one could explain complex human behavior in terms of thousands of instances of learning through reinforcement (see Figure 1.2).

Gestalt Psychology

In the 1920s, another school of psychology—Gestalt psychology—was prominent in Germany. In the 1930s, the three founders of the school—Max Wertheimer (1880–1943), Kurt Koffka (1886–1941), and Wolfgang Köhler (1887–1967)—left Europe to escape the Nazi threat. They carried on their work in the United States, giving further impetus to the growing American ascendance in psychology.

What is Gestalt psychology?

Gestalt psychologists focused on perception and on how perception influences thinking and problem solving. The German word *Gestalt* translates as "pattern" or "organized whole." In contrast to the behaviorists, Gestalt psychologists argued that we cannot understand human nature by focusing only on observable behavior. In contrast to the structuralists, they claimed that we cannot explain human perceptions, emotions, or thought processes in terms of basic units. Perceptions are *more* than the sums of their parts: Gestalt psychologists saw our perceptions as wholes that give meaning to parts, as we see in Figure 1.3.

Gestalt psychologists showed that we tend to perceive separate pieces of information as integrated wholes, depending on the contexts in which they occur. In part A of Figure 1.3, the dots in the centers of the drawings are the same size, yet we may perceive them as being different in size because of their surroundings. The second symbol in each line in part B is identical, but in the top row we may perceive it as a *B* and in the bottom row as the number *13*. The symbol has not changed, but its context

behaviorism
the school of psychology that defines psychology as the study of observable behavior and studies relationships, between stimuli and responses

reinforcement
a stimulus that follows a response and increases the frequency of the response

Gestalt psychology
the school of psychology that emphasizes the tendency to organize perceptions into wholes and to integrate separate stimuli into meaningful patterns

Figure 1.3

The Importance of Context

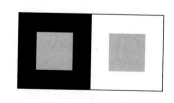

A. Are the dots in the center of the configurations the same size? Why not take a ruler and measure them?

B. Is the second symbol in each line the letter *B* or the number *13*?

C. Which of the gray squares is brighter?

Figure 1.4

Some Insight into Insight

At first, the chimpanzee cannot reach the bananas hanging from the ceiling. After some time has passed, the chimp has an apparent "flash of insight" and piles the boxes on top of one another to reach the fruit.

has. The inner squares in part C are equally bright, but they do not appear so because of their contrasting backgrounds.

Gestalt psychologists believed that learning could be active and purposeful, not merely responsive and mechanical as in Watson's and Skinner's experiments. They found that much learning, especially in problem solving, is accomplished by insight, not by mechanical repetition.

Consider Wolfgang Köhler's research with chimpanzees, as shown in Figure 1.4. At first, the chimpanzee is unsuccessful in reaching for bananas suspended from the ceiling. Then he suddenly stacks the boxes and climbs up to reach the bananas. It seems the chimp has experienced a sudden reorganization of the mental elements of the problem—that is, he has had a "flash of insight." Köhler's findings suggest that people, too, often manipulate the elements of problems until we group them in such a way that we believe we will be able to reach a goal. The manipulations may take quite some time as mental trial and error proceeds. But once the solution has been found, we seem to perceive it all of a sudden.

Psychoanalysis

What is psychoanalysis? **Psychoanalysis**—another school of psychology—is the name of the theory of personality and of the method of therapy developed by Sigmund Freud (1856–1939). As a theory of personality, psychoanalysis was based on the idea that much of our lives is governed by unconscious ideas and impulses that originate in childhood conflicts.

Psychoanalytic theory proposes that most of the mind is unconscious—a seething cauldron of conflicting impulses, urges, and wishes. People are motivated to satisfy these impulses, ugly as some of them are. But at the same time, people are motivated to see themselves as decent, and hence may delude themselves about their true motives. As a physician, Freud's goal was to help individuals who

were suffering from various psychological and social problems. His method of psychotherapy, psychoanalysis, aims to help patients gain insight into many of their deep-seated conflicts and to find socially acceptable ways of expressing wishes and gratifying needs.

LO⁴ How Today's Psychologists View Behavior and Mental Processes

Today we no longer find psychologists who describe themselves as structuralists or functionalists. And, although the school of Gestalt psychology gave birth to current research approaches in perception and problem solving, few would label themselves Gestalt psychologists. But we do find Gestalt therapists who help clients integrate conflicting parts of their personality (making themselves "whole"). The numbers of behaviorists and psychoanalysts have been declining (Robins et al., 1999). Many contemporary psychologists in the behaviorist tradition look on themselves as social cognitive theorists, and many psychoanalysts consider themselves neoanalysts or ego analysts rather than traditional Freudians.

MANSELL/TIME & LIFE PICTURES/GETTY IMAGES

Sigmund Freud

The history of psychological thought has taken many turns, and contemporary psychologists differ in their approaches. Today there are several broad, influential perspectives in psychology: evolutionary and biological, cognitive, humanistic–existential, psychodynamic, learning, and sociocultural. Each emphasizes different topics of investigation. Each approaches its topics in its own way.

The Biological and Evolutionary Perspectives

Psychologists are interested in the roles of heredity and evolution in behavior and mental processes such as psychological disorders, criminal behavior, and thinking. Generally speaking, our heredity provides a broad range of behavioral and mental possibilities. Environmental factors interact with inherited factors to determine specific behavior and mental processes.

What is the biological perspective? Psychologists with a biological perspective seek the links between the activity of the brain, the activity of hormones, and heredity, on the one hand, and behavior and mental processes on the other. Psychologists assume that the thoughts, fantasies, and dreams—and the inborn or instinctive behavior patterns of many species, such as the songs and nest-building of birds—are made possible by the nervous system, and especially the brain. Some biological psychologists—also called *biopsychologists*—focus on evolution.

What is the evolutionary perspective? Evolutionary psychologists focus on the evolution of behavior and mental processes. Charles Darwin argued that in the age-old struggle for existence, only the "fittest" (most adaptive) organisms reach maturity and reproduce. For example, fish that swim faster or people who are naturally immune to certain diseases are more likely to survive and transmit their *genes* to future generations. Individuals die, but species tend to evolve in adaptive directions. Evolutionary psychologists suggest that much human social behavior, such as aggressive behavior and mate selection, has a hereditary basis. People may be influenced by social rules, cultural factors, even personal choice, but evolutionary psychologists believe that inherited tendencies also move us in certain directions. When we ask the question "What evolves?" our answer is the biological processes and structures that make behavior possible.

Charles Darwin

The Cognitive Perspective

What is the cognitive perspective? Psychologists with a cognitive perspective venture into the realm of mental processes to understand human nature. They investigate the ways in which we perceive and mentally represent the world, how we learn, remember the past, plan for the future, solve problems, form judgments, make decisions, and use language. Cognitive psychologists, in short, study those things we refer to as the *mind*.

The cognitive tradition has roots in Socrates' advice to "know thyself" and in his suggested method of introspection. We also find cognitive psychology's roots in structuralism, functionalism, and Gestalt psychology, each of which, in its own way, addressed issues that are of interest to cognitive psychologists.

The Humanistic–Existential Perspective

The humanistic–existential perspective is cognitive in flavor, yet it emphasizes more the role of subjective (personal) experience. *What is the humanistic–existential perspective?* Let us consider each of the parts of this perspective: *humanism* and *existentialism*.

Humanism stresses the human capacity for self-fulfillment and the central roles of consciousness, self-awareness, and decision making. Humanists believe that self-awareness, experience, and choice permit us, to a large extent, to "invent ourselves" as we progress through life. Consciousness—our sense of being in the world—is seen as the force that unifies our personalities. *Existentialism* views people as free to choose and as being responsible for choosing ethical conduct. Grounded in the work of Carl Rogers (1951) and Abraham Maslow (1970), the humanistic–existential perspective has many contemporary adherents (Moss, 2002; Schneider et al., 2003).

The Psychodynamic Perspective

In the 1940s and 1950s, psychodynamic theory dominated the field of psychotherapy and influenced scientific psychology and the arts. Renowned artists and writers consulted psychodynamic therapists to liberate the expression of their unconscious ideas. Today, Freud's influence is still felt, although it no longer dominates psychotherapy. Contemporary psychologists who follow theories derived from Freud are likely to call themselves *neoanalysts*.

Famous neoanalysts such as Karen Horney (1885–1952) and Erik Erikson (1902–1994) focused less on the unconscious and more on conscious choice and self-direction.

Perspectives on Learning

Many contemporary psychologists study the effects of experience on behavior. Learning, to them, is the essential factor in describing, explaining, predicting, and controlling behavior. The term *learning* has different meanings to psychologists of different persuasions, however. Some students of learning find roles for consciousness and insight. Others do not. This distinction is found today among those who adhere to the behavioral and social cognitive perspectives.

What are the two major perspectives on learning? Early proponents of **behaviorism**, like John B. Watson, viewed people as doing things because of their learning histories, their situations, and rewards, not because of conscious choice. Like Watson, contemporary behaviorists emphasize environmental influences and the learning of habits through repetition and reinforcement. Social-cognitive theorists, in contrast, suggest that people can modify and create their environments. They note that people engage in intentional learning by observing others. Since the 1960s, social cognitive theorists have gained influence in the areas of personality development, psychological disorders, and psychotherapy.

The Sociocultural Perspective

The profession of psychology focuses mainly on the individual and is committed to the dignity of the individual. However, many psychologists today believe we cannot understand people's behavior and mental processes without reference to their diversity.

What is the sociocultural perspective? The **sociocultural perspective** addresses many of the ways in which people differ from one another. It studies the influences of ethnicity, gender, culture, and socioeconomic status on behavior and mental processes. Studying cultures other than their own helps psychologists

understand the roles of culture in behavior, beliefs, values, and attitudes.

Ethnicity

One kind of diversity involves people's ethnicity. Members of an ethnic group share their cultural heritage, race, language, or history. The experiences of various ethnic groups in the United States highlight the impact of social, political, and economic factors on human behavior and development (Basic Behavioral Science Task Force, 1996b).

The most well-known African American psychologists may be Kenneth Clark (1914–2005) and Mamie Phipps Clark (1917–1983). The Clarks conducted research that showed the negative effects of school segregation on African American children. In one such study, African American children were shown white and brown dolls and asked to "Give me the pretty doll," or "Give me the doll that looks bad." Most children's choices showed that they preferred the white dolls over the brown ones. The Clarks concluded that the children had swallowed society's preference for European Americans. The Clarks' research was cited by the Supreme Court in 1954 when it overturned the "separate but equal" schools doctrine that had allowed inequalities in school services for various ethnic groups.

A Latino American psychologist, Jorge Sanchez, was among the first to show how intelligence tests are culturally biased—to the disadvantage of Mexican American children. A Latina American, Lillian Comas-Díaz (e.g., 2003), edits a journal on multicultural mental health. An Asian American psychologist, Richard Suinn (Jenkins et al., 2003), studies mental health and the development of identity among Asians and Asian Americans.

Gender

Gender refers to the culturally defined concepts of masculinity and femininity. Gender is not fully defined by anatomic sex. It involves a complex web of cultural expectations and social roles that affect people's self-concepts and hopes and dreams as well as their behavior. Just as members of ethnic minority groups have experienced prejudice, so too have women.

Although American women have attended college only since 1833—when Oberlin College opened its doors to women—most American college students today are, in fact, women. Women now receive nearly three-quarters of the undergraduate and doctoral degrees in psychology (American Psychological Association, 2009a; U.S. Department of Education, 2004).

How did research by Kenneth Clark and Mamie Phipps Clark influence a Supreme Court decision?

Fiction

It is not true that men receive the majority of doctoral degrees in psychology. Women do.

gender
the culturally defined concepts of *masculinity* and *femininity*

Women have made indispensable contributions to psychology. Mary Whiton Calkins (1863–1930) introduced the method of paired associates to study memory (see Chapter 7), discovered the primacy and recency effects, and engaged in research into the role of the frequency of repetition in the vividness of memories. Calkins had studied psychology at Harvard University, which she had to attend as a "guest student," because Harvard was not yet admitting women. When she completed her Ph.D. requirements, Harvard would not award her the degree because of her sex. Instead, Harvard offered to grant her a doctorate from its sister school, Radcliffe. As a form of protest, Calkins declined the offer. Even without the Ph.D., Calkins went on to become president of the American Psychological Association.

In more recent years, Mary Salter Ainsworth (1913–1999) revolutionized our understanding of attachment between parents and children by means of her cross-cultural studies. Elizabeth Loftus (e.g., Loftus, 2004; Loftus & Bernstein, 2005) has shown that our memories are not snapshots of the past. Instead, they often consist of something old (what actually happened), something new (that is, influenced by more recent events), something borrowed (for example, further shaped by our biases and prejudices), and something blue (altered by tinges of color or emotion).

The contributions of members of diverse ethnic groups and women have broadened our understanding of the influences of ethnicity and gender on behavior and mental processes. They have also increased our knowledge of differences among Europeans. For example, Southern Europeans singles (from Italy, Greece, and Portugal, for example) are more likely than Northern European singles (from the United Kingdom, France, Germany, and Scandinavia) to live with their parents until they get married (Giuliano, 2007). The researcher suggests that the family ties of Southern Europeans seem to be relatively stronger.

Truth

The first female president of the American Psychological Association, Mary Whiton Calkins, did turn down the doctoral degree that was offered to her from Radcliffe.

LO⁵ How Psychologists Study Behavior and Mental Processes

Does alcohol cause aggression? Does watching violence on TV cause children to be violent? Why do some people hardly ever think of food, whereas others are obsessed with it and snack all day? Why do some unhappy people attempt suicide, whereas others don't? How does having people of different ethnic backgrounds collaborate in their work affect feelings of prejudice?

Many of us have expressed opinions—maybe strong opinions—on questions like these. But as we saw in our discussion of people who claim to be abducted by aliens from outer space, scientists insist on evidence. Psychologists, like other scientists, use careful means to observe and measure behavior and the factors that influence behavior.

The need for evidence is one of the keys to critical thinking. Critical thinking is a life tool for all of us as well as a pathway toward scientific knowledge.

Critical Thinking

Psychologists are guided by scientific principles, and one hallmark of science is critical thinking. *What is critical thinking?* Critical thinking has many meanings. On one level, it means taking nothing for granted. It means not believing things just because they are in print or because they were uttered by authority figures or celebrities. It means not necessarily believing that it is healthful to express all of your feelings just because a friend in "therapy" urges you to do so. On another level, critical thinking refers to a process of thoughtfully analyzing and probing the questions, statements, and arguments of others.

Principles of Critical Thinking

1 *Be skeptical.* Keep an open mind. Politicians and advertisers try to persuade you. Are some of your own attitudes and beliefs superficial or unfounded? Accept nothing as the truth until you have examined the evidence.

2 *Insist on evidence.* It is not sufficient that an opinion is traditional, that it appears in print or on the Internet, or it is expressed by a doctor or a lawyer. Ask for evidence.

3 *Examine definitions of terms.* Some statements are true when a term is defined in one way but not when it is defined in another way. Consider the statement, "Head Start programs have raised children's IQs." The correctness of the statement depends on the definition of "IQ." (You will see later in the text that *IQ* is not the same thing as *intelligence*.)

4 *Examine the assumptions or premises of arguments.* Consider the statement that one cannot learn about human beings by engaging in research with animals. One premise in the statement seems to be that human beings are not animals. We are, of course.

5 *Be cautious in drawing conclusions from evidence.* For many years, studies had shown that most clients who receive psychotherapy improve. It was therefore generally assumed that psychotherapy worked. Then a psychologist named Hans Eysenck pointed out that most psychologically troubled people who did *not* receive psychotherapy also improved. The question thus becomes whether people receiving psychotherapy are *more* likely to improve than those who do not. Current research on the effectiveness of psychotherapy therefore carefully compares the benefits of therapy techniques to the benefits of other techniques or of no treatment at all. Be especially skeptical of anecdotes. When you hear "I know someone who...," ask yourself whether this one person's reported experience is satisfactory as evidence.

6 *Consider alternative interpretations of research evidence.* Does alcohol cause aggression? Later in the chapter we will report evidence that there is a clear *connection*, or correlation, between alcohol and aggression. For example, many people who commit violent crimes have been drinking. But does the evidence show that drinking causes aggression? Might other factors, such as gender, age, or willingness to take risks, account for both drinking and aggressive behavior?

7 *Do not oversimplify.* Most human behavior involves complex interactions of genetic and environmental influences. Also consider the issue of whether psychotherapy helps people with psychological problems. A broad answer to this question—a simple yes or no—might be oversimplifying. It is more worthwhile to ask, What *type* of psychotherapy, practiced by *whom*, is most helpful for *what kind of problem?*

8 *Do not overgeneralize.* Consider the statement that one cannot learn about human beings by engaging in research with nonhuman animals. Is the truth of the matter an all or nothing issue? Are there certain kinds of information we can obtain about people from research with animals? What kinds of things are you likely to be able to learn only through research with people?

9 *Apply critical thinking to all areas of life.*

The Scientific Method

What is the scientific method? The scientific method is an organized way of using experience and testing ideas in an effort to expand and refine knowledge. Psychologists do not necessarily follow the steps of the scientific method as we might follow a recipe in a cookbook, but research is guided by certain principles.

Psychologists usually begin by *formulating a research question*. Our daily experiences, psychological theory, even folklore all help generate questions for research. Consider some questions that may arise from daily experience. Daily experience in using daycare centers may motivate us to conduct research on whether day care affects the development of social skills or the bonds of attachment between children and mothers. Social cognitive principles of observational learning may prompt research on the effects of TV violence. Research questions may also arise from common knowledge. Consider adages such as "misery loves company," "opposites attract," and "seeing is believing." Psychologists may ask, *Does misery love company? Do opposites attract? Can people believe what they see?*

A research question may be reworded as a hypothesis (see Figure 1.5). A hypothesis is a statement about behavior or mental processes that is tested through research. One hypothesis about day care might be that preschoolers who are placed in day care will acquire greater social skills in relating to peers than preschoolers who are cared for in the home.

Psychologists next examine the research question or *test the hypothesis* through controlled methods such as the experiment. For example, we could take

Figure 1.5

The Scientific Method

The scientific method is a systematic way of organizing and expanding scientific knowledge.

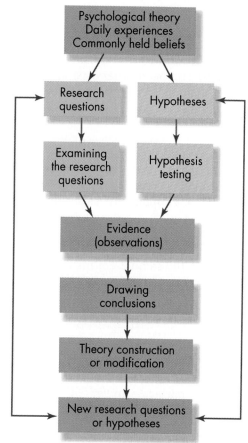

Go to CourseMate for PSYCH at www.cengagebrain.com to access an interactive version of this figure. 🅢

a group of preschoolers who attend day care and another group who do not, and introduce each to a new child in a controlled setting such as a child research center. We could then observe how children in each group interact with the new acquaintance.

Psychologists draw conclusions on the basis of their observations or findings. When their observations do not bear out their hypotheses, they may modify the theories from which the hypotheses were derived. Research findings often suggest refinements to psychological theories and, consequently, new avenues of research. In our research on day care, we would probably find that children in day care show greater social skills than children who are cared for in the home (Belsky et al., 2001).

As psychologists draw conclusions from research evidence, they are guided by principles of critical thinking. For example, they try not to confuse correlations—or associations—between findings with cause and effect. Although more aggressive children apparently spend more time watching violent TV shows, it may be erroneous to conclude from this kind of evidence that TV violence *causes* aggressive behavior. A selection factor may be at work because the children studied choose (select) for themselves what they will watch. Perhaps more aggressive children are more likely than less aggressive children to tune in to violent TV shows.

Samples and Populations

Consider a piece of history that never quite happened: The Republican candidate Alf Landon defeated the incumbent president, Franklin D. Roosevelt, in 1936. Or at least Landon did so in a poll conducted by a popular magazine of the day, the *Literary Digest*. In the actual election, however, Roosevelt routed Landon by a landslide of 11 million votes. In effect, the *Digest* accomplished something like this when they predicted a Landon victory. How was such a difference possible?

The *Digest*, you see, had surveyed voters by phone. Today telephone sampling is a widely practiced and reasonably legitimate polling technique.

hypothesis
in psychology, a specific statement about behavior or mental processes that is tested through research

correlation
an association or relationship among variables, as we might find between height and weight or between study habits and school grades

selection factor
a source of bias that may occur in research findings when participants are allowed to choose for themselves a certain treatment in a scientific study

All generalizations are dangerous, even this one.

—Alexandre Dumas

sample
part of a population

population
a complete group of organisms or events

random sample
a sample drawn so that each member of a population has an equal chance of being selected to participate

stratified sample
a sample drawn so that identified subgroups in the population are represented proportionately in the sample

volunteer bias
a source of bias or error in research reflecting the prospect that people who offer to participate in research studies differ systematically from people who do not

Truth

It is true that you could survey millions of voters and still not predict the outcome of a presidential election.

But the *Digest* poll was taken during the Great Depression, when people who had telephones were much wealthier than those who did not. People at higher income levels are also more likely to vote Republican. No surprise, then, that the overwhelming majority of those sampled said they would vote for Landon.

How do psychologists use samples to represent populations? The *Digest* poll failed because of its method of sampling. Samples must be drawn so that they accurately represent the population they are intended to reflect. Only representative samples allow us to generalize—or extend—our findings from research samples to populations.

In surveys such as that conducted by *Literary Digest*, and in other research methods, the individuals who are studied are referred to as a sample. A sample is a segment of a population (the group that is targeted for study). Psychologists and other scientists need to ensure that the people they observe represent their target population, such as U.S. voters, and not subgroups such as southern Californians or European American members of the middle class.

Does this telephone make me look rich?

Problems in Generalizing from Psychological Research

Many factors must be considered in interpreting the accuracy of the results of scientific research. One is the nature of the research sample. Later in the chapter we consider research in which the participants were drawn from a population of college men who were social drinkers. That is, they tended to drink at social gatherings but not when alone. Who do college men represent, other than themselves? To whom can we extend, or generalize, the results? For one thing, the results may not extend to women, not even to college women. In the chapter on consciousness, for example, we see that alcohol affects women more quickly than men.

Also, compared to the general adult male population, college men tend to be younger and score higher on intelligence tests. We cannot be certain that the findings extend to older men or to those with lower intelligence test scores. Social drinkers may even differ biologically and psychologically from alcoholics, who have difficulty controlling their drinking.

By and large, we must also question whether findings of research with men can be generalized to women and whether research with European American men can be extended to members of ethnic minority groups. For example, personality tests completed by European Americans and by African Americans may need to be interpreted in diverse ways if accurate conclusions are to be drawn.

Random and Stratified Sampling

One way to achieve a representative sample is by means of random sampling. In a random sample, each member of a population has an equal chance of being asked to participate. Researchers can also use a stratified sample, which is selected so that known subgroups in the population are represented proportionately in the sample. For instance, 13% of the American population is African American. A stratified sample would thus be 13% African American. As a practical matter, a large randomly selected sample will show accurate stratification. A random sample of 1,500 people will represent the broad American population reasonably well; a sample of 20,000 European Americans or men will not.

Large-scale magazine surveys of sexual behavior have asked readers to fill out and return questionnaires. Although many thousands of readers completed the questionnaires and sent them in, did the survey respondents represent the American population? Probably not. These studies and similar ones may have been influenced by volunteer bias. People who offer or volunteer to participate in research studies differ systematically from people who do not. In the case of research on sexual behavior, volunteers may represent subgroups of the population—or of readers of the magazines in question—who are willing to disclose intimate information and therefore may also be likely to be more liberal in their sexual behavior (Rathus et al., 2008). Volunteers may also be more interested in research than other people, as well as have more spare time. How might such volunteers differ from the population at large? How might such differences slant or bias the research outcomes?

Methods of Observation

Many people consider themselves experts in psychology. How many times have you or someone else been eager to share a life experience that "proves" some point about human nature?

We see much during our lifetimes, but our personal observations tend to be fleeting and unsystematic. We sift through experience for the things that interest us. We often ignore the obvious because it does not fit our assumptions about the way things ought to be. Scientists, however, have devised more controlled ways of observing others. *What methods of observation are used by psychologists?* In this section we consider three methods of observation widely used by psychologists and other behavioral scientists: the case study, the survey, and naturalistic observation.

Case Study

Case studies collect information about individuals and small groups. Many case studies are clinical; that is, they are detailed descriptions of a person's psychological problems and how a psychologist treated the problems. Case studies are sometimes used to investigate rare occurrences, as in the case of Chris Sizemore, who was diagnosed with multiple personalities (technically termed *dissociative identity disorder*). A psychiatrist identified three distinct personalities in Chris. Her story was made into a more theatrical movie called *The Three Faces of Eve.* One personality, "Eve White," was a mousy, well-meaning woman who had two other "personalities" inside her. One was "Eve Black," a promiscuous personality who emerged now and then to take control of her behavior. The third personality, "Jane," was a well-adjusted woman who integrated parts of Eve White and Eve Black.

Case studies have various sources of inaccuracy. People's memories have gaps and factual inaccuracies (Loftus, 2004). People may also distort their pasts to please the interviewer or because they want to remember things in certain ways.

Interviewers may also have certain expectations and subtly encourage participants to fill in gaps in ways that are consistent with these expectations. Psychoanalysts, for example, have been criticized for guiding people who seek their help into viewing their own lives from the Freudian perspective (Hergenhahn, 2005). No wonder, then, that many people provide "evidence" that is consistent with psychodynamic theory—such as, "My parents' strictness during toilet training is the source of my compulsive neatness." However, interviewers and other kinds of researchers who hold *any* theoretical viewpoint run the risk of indirectly prodding people into saying what they want to hear.

The Survey

Just as computers and pollsters predict election results and report national opinion on the basis of scientifically selected samples, psychologists conduct surveys to learn about behavior and mental processes that cannot be observed in the natural setting or studied experimentally. Psychologists conducting surveys may employ questionnaires and interviews or examine public records. One of the advantages of the survey is that by distributing questionnaires and analyzing answers with a computer, psychologists can study many thousands of people at a time.

The best-known surveys of all time, the so-called Kinsey reports, provided surprising information during the middle of the 20th century, a time of relative sexual repression in the United States. Alfred Kinsey and his colleagues published two surveys of sexual behavior based on extensive interviews: *Sexual Behavior in the Human Male* (1948)

case study
a carefully drawn biography that may be obtained through interviews, questionnaires, and psychological tests

survey
a method of scientific investigation in which a large sample of people answer questions about their atttudes or behavior

naturalistic observation
a scientific method in which organisms are observed in their natural environments

correlation coefficient
a number between +1.00 and −1.00 that expresses the strength and direction (positive or negative) of the relationship between two variables

and *Sexual Behavior in the Human Female* (1953). The nation was shocked to hear that masturbation among his sample of men was virtually universal in a day when masturbation was still widely thought to impair health. During this time, it was also widely believed that virtually all single women were virgins. Nonetheless, Kinsey found that about 1 woman in 3 who was still single at age 25 reported having engaged in sexual intercourse.

Surveys, like case studies, also have sources of inaccuracy. People may recall their behavior inaccurately or lie about it. Some people try to ingratiate themselves with their interviewers by answering in what they think to be the socially desirable direction. The Kinsey studies all relied on male interviewers, for example. It has been speculated that female interviewees might have been more open with female interviewers. Similar problems may occur when interviewers and the people surveyed are from different ethnic backgrounds. Other people may falsify their attitudes and exaggerate their problems to draw attention to themselves or to intentionally foul up the results.

Another bias in the case study and survey methods is social desirability. That is, many people involved in research studies tend to tell the interviewer what they think the interviewer would like to hear and not what they really think. For example, if people brushed their teeth as often as they claimed, and used the amount of toothpaste they indicated, three times as much toothpaste would be sold in the United States than is actually sold. People also appear to overreport church attendance and to underreport abortions (Barringer, 1993).

Naturalistic Observation

You use naturalistic observation—that is, you observe people in their natural habitats—every day. So do psychologists and other scientists. Naturalistic observation has the advantage of allowing psychologists and other scientists to observe behavior where it happens, or "in the field." Observers use unobtrusive measures to avoid interfering with the behaviors they are observing. For example, Jane Goodall has observed the behavior of chimpanzees in their natural environment to learn about their social behavior, sexual behavior, use of tools, and other facts of chimp life. Her observations have shown us that (1) we were incorrect to think that only humans use tools; and (2) kissing on the lips, as a greeting, is apparently used by chimpanzees as well as by humans (Goodall, 2000).

Correlation

Are people with higher intelligence more likely to do well in school? Are people with a stronger need for achievement likely to climb higher up the corporate ladder? What is the relationship between stress and health?

Such questions are often answered by the mathematical method of correlation. *What is the correlational method?* Correlation follows observation. By using the correlational method, psychologists investigate whether an observed behavior or a measured trait is related to, or correlated with, another. Consider the variables of intelligence and academic performance. These variables are assigned numbers such as intelligence test scores and academic averages. Then the numbers are mathematically related and expressed as a correlation coefficient (r). A correlation coefficient is a number that varies from $r = +1.00$ to $r = −1.00$.

In the film biography *Kinsey,* Liam Neeson played Alfred Kinsey, the scientist who investigated human sexuality during a time when even talking about sex was considered indecent.

© PHOTOS 12/ALAMY

Jane Goodall's naturalistic observations revealed that chimpanzees—like humans—use tools and greet one another with a kiss.

© BRUCE COLEMAN INC./ALAMY

Studies report *positive correlations* between intelligence test scores and academic achievement, as measured, for example, by grade point averages. Generally speaking, the higher people score on intelligence tests, the better their academic performance is likely to be. The scores attained on intelligence tests tend to be positively correlated (about $r = +.30$ to $r = +.60$) with academic achievement (see the first panel in Figure 1.6) (Duckworth & Seligman, 2005; Mayes & Calhoun, 2007; Neisser et al., 1996). But factors *other* than performance on intelligence tests also contribute to academic success. These include achievement motivation, self-discipline, and adjustment (Duckworth & Seligman, 2005).

Many correlations are negative; that is, as one variable increases, the other variable decreases. There is a *negative correlation* between stress and health. As the amount of stress affecting us increases, the functioning of our immune system decreases (see Figure 1.6). Under high levels of stress, many people show poorer health.

What kinds of correlations (positive or negative) would you expect to find among behavior patterns such as the following: Churchgoing and crime? Language ability and musical ability? Level of education and incidence of teenage pregnancy? Grades in school and delinquency? Why?

Correlational research may suggest, but does not prove, cause and effect. For example, it may seem logical to assume that high intelligence makes it possible for children to profit from education. Research has also

JUPITERIMAGES

Figure 1.6

Positive and Negative Correlations

When there is a positive correlation between variables, as there is between intelligence and achievement, one increases as the other increases. By and large, the higher people score on intelligence tests, the better their academic performance is likely to be, as in the diagram on the left. (Each dot represents an individual's intelligence test score and grade point average.) But there is a negative correlation between stress and health. As the amount of stress we experience increases, the functioning of our immune system tends to decrease.

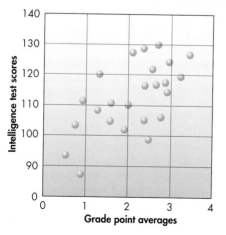

Positive correlation, as found between intelligence and academic achievement

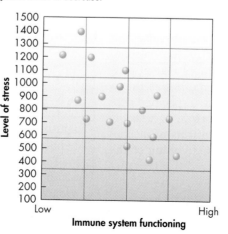

Negative correlation, as found between stress and functioning of the immune system

What kind of correlation would you expect between teenagers' grades in school and their numbers of delinquent acts? Why?

experiment
a scientific method that seeks to confirm cause-and-effect relationships by introducing independent variables and observing their effects on dependent variables

independent variable
a condition in a scientific study that is manipulated so that its effects may be observed

dependent variable
a measure of an assumed effect of an independent variable

experimental groups
in experiments, groups whose members obtain the treatment

control groups
in experiments, groups whose members do not obtain the treatment, while other conditions are held constant

shown, however, that education contributes to higher scores on intelligence tests. Preschoolers who are placed in stimulating Head Start programs later attain higher scores on intelligence tests than age mates who did not have this experience. The relationship between intelligence and academic performance may not be as simple as we might think. What of the link between stress and health? Does stress impair health, or is it possible that people in poorer health encounter more stress?

The Experimental Method

What is the experimental method? Most psychologists agree that the preferred method for answering questions about cause and effect is the experiment. In an experiment, a group of subjects receives a *treatment,* such as a dose of alcohol, a change in room temperature, perhaps an injection of a drug. The subjects are then observed carefully to determine whether the treatment makes a difference in their behavior. Does alcohol alter the ability to take tests, for example? What about differences in room temperatures and level of background noise?

Experiments are used when possible because they allow psychologists to control the experiences of subjects and draw conclusions about cause and effect. A psychologist may theorize that alcohol leads to aggression because it reduces fear of consequences. She or he may then hypothesize that a treatment in which subjects receive a specified dosage of alcohol will lead to increases in aggression. Let us follow the example of the effects of alcohol on aggression to further our understanding of the experimental method.

Independent and Dependent Variables

In an experiment to determine whether alcohol causes aggression, subjects are given an amount of alcohol and its effects are measured. In this case, alcohol is an independent variable. The presence of an independent variable is manipulated by the experimenters so that its effects may be determined. The independent variable of alcohol may be administered at different levels, or doses, from none or very little to enough to cause intoxication or drunkenness.

The measured results, or outcomes, in an experiment are called dependent variables. The presence of dependent variables presumably depends on the independent variables. In an experiment to determine whether alcohol influences aggression, aggressive behavior would be a dependent variable. Other dependent variables of interest might include sexual arousal, visual motor coordination, and performance on cognitive tasks such as defining words.

In an experiment on the relationships between temperature and aggression, temperature would be an independent variable and aggressive behavior would be a dependent variable. We could set temperatures from below freezing to blistering hot, and study its effects on aggression. We could also use a second independent variable such as social provocation; we could insult some participants but not others and see whether insults affect their level of aggression. This method would allow us to study the ways in which two independent variables—temperature and social provocation—affect aggression, by themselves and together.

> Using an *experimental group* and a *control group* enhances researchers' ability to draw conclusions about *cause and effect.*

Experimental and Control Groups

Ideal experiments use "experimental groups" and "control groups." Participants in experimental groups obtain the treatment. Members of control groups do not. Every effort is made to ensure that all other conditions are held constant for both groups. This method enhances the researchers' ability to draw conclusions about cause and effect. The researchers can be more confident that outcomes of the experiment are caused by the treatments and not by chance factors or chance fluctuations in behavior.

For example, in an experiment on the effects of alcohol on aggression, members of the experimental group would ingest alcohol, and members of the control group would not. The researcher would then measure how much aggression was expressed by each group.

Blinds and Double Blinds

One classic experiment on the effects of alcohol on aggression (Boyatzis, 1974) reported that men at parties where beer and liquor were served acted more aggressively than men at parties where only soft drinks were served. But participants in the experimental group *knew* they had drunk alcohol, and those in the control group *knew* they had not. Aggression that appeared to result from alcohol might thus have reflected the participants' *expectations* about the effects of alcohol. People tend to act in stereotypical ways when they believe they have been drinking alcohol. For instance, men tend to become less anxious in social situations, more aggressive, and more sexually aroused. To what extent do these behavior patterns reflect the direct effects of alcohol on the body, and to what extent do they affect people's *beliefs* about the effects of alcohol?

In medicine, physicians sometimes give patients placebos (a fake treatment, often sugar pills, that has the appearance of being genuine) when the patient insists on a medical cure but the physician does not believe that one is necessary. When patients report that placebos have helped them, it is because they expected the pills to be of help and not because of the biochemical effects of the pills. Placebos are not limited to pills made of sugar. As we will see, participants in psychological experiments can be given placebos such as tonic water, but if the participants think they have drunk alcohol, we can conclude that

> The **men's** *belief* about what they drank affected their aggressive behavior more than what they actually consumed.

changes in their behavior stem from their beliefs about the effects of alcohol, not from the alcohol itself.

Well-designed experiments control for the effects of expectations by creating conditions under which participants are unaware of, or blind to, the treatment. Placebos are one way of keeping participants blind to whether they have received a treatment. Yet researchers may also have expectations. They may be "rooting for" a certain treatment. For example, tobacco company executives may wish to show that cigarette smoking is harmless. In such cases, it is useful if the people measuring the experimental outcomes are unaware of which participants have received the treatment. Studies in which neither the participant nor the experimenters know who has obtained the treatment are called double-blind studies. The Food and Drug Administration requires double-blind studies before it allows the marketing of new drugs. In a double-blind study, the drug and the placebo look and taste alike. Experimenters assign the drug or placebo to participants at random. Neither the participants nor the observers know who is taking the drug and who is taking the placebo. After the final measurements have been made, a neutral panel (a group of people who have no personal stake in the outcome of the study) judges whether the

placebo
a bogus treatment that has the appearance of being genuine

blind
in experimental terminology, unaware of whether or not one has received a treatment

double-blind study
a study in which neither the subjects nor the observers know who has received the treatment

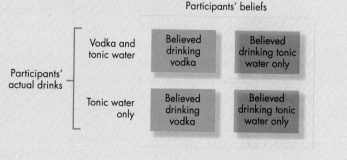

Figure 1.7

The Experimental Conditions in the Lang Study

The taste of vodka cannot be discerned when vodka is mixed with tonic water. For this reason, it was possible for subjects in the Lang study on the effects of alcohol to be kept "blind" as to whether or not they had actually drunk alcohol. Blind studies allow psychologists to control for the effects of subjects' expectations.

	Participants' beliefs	
Participants' actual drinks		
Vodka and tonic water	Believed drinking vodka	Believed drinking tonic water only
Tonic water only	Believed drinking vodka	Believed drinking tonic water only

PURESTOCK/GETTY IMAGES

informed consent
a participants's agreement to participate in research after receiving information about the purposes of the study and the nature of the treatments

debrief
to explain the purposes and methods of a completed procedure to a participant

effects of the drug differed from those of the placebo.

In one classic double-blind study on the effects of alcohol, Alan Lang and his colleagues (1975) pretested a cocktail of vodka and tonic water to make certain that it could not be discriminated by taste from tonic water alone. They recruited college male social drinkers as participants. Some of the men drank vodka and tonic water. Others drank tonic water only. Of those who drank vodka, half were misled into believing they had drunk tonic water only (see Figure 1.7 on page 22). Of those who drank tonic water only, half were misled into believing their drink contained vodka. Thus, half the participants were blind to their treatment. Experimenters who measured the men's aggressive responses were also blind concerning which participants had drunk vodka.

The research team found that men who believed that they had drunk vodka responded "more aggressively" (that is, they chose a higher level of shock and pressed a lever to deliver it) to a provocation than men who believed that they had drunk tonic water only. The actual content of the drink was immaterial. That is, the men's *belief* about what they drank affected their aggressive behavior more than what they actually consumed. The results of the Lang study differ dramatically from those reported by Boyatzis, perhaps because the Boyatzis study did not control for the effects of expectations or beliefs about alcohol.

Truth

It is true that neither the participants nor the researchers know who is receiving the real treatment in many experiments.

Ethics of Research with Humans

If the Lang group were running their experiment today rather than in the 1970s, they might have been denied permission to do so by a university ethics review committee. Why? Because the researchers in the Lang study gave some participants alcohol to drink and deceived the entire group about the purposes and methods of the study. Was their method ethical? We'll return to this question, but let's first address a broader one. *What ethical issues affect research and practice with humans?*

Psychologists adhere to a number of ethical standards that are intended to promote individual dignity, human welfare, and scientific integrity. The standards are also intended to ensure that psychologists do not engage in harmful research methods or treatments. In virtually all institutional settings, including colleges, hospitals, and research foundations, ethics review committees help researchers consider the potential harm of their methods and review proposed studies according to ethical guidelines. When the committees find that proposed research might be unacceptably harmful to subjects, they may withhold approval. The committees also weigh the potential benefits of the research against the potential harm.

Today individuals must provide **informed consent** before they participate in research (American Psychological Association, 2002). A general overview of the research and the opportunity to choose not to participate apparently give potential participants a sense of control and decreases stress (Sieber, 2004). Is there a way in which participants in the Lang study could have provided informed consent? What do you think?

Psychologists keep the records of research participants and clients confidential because they respect people's privacy and because people are more likely to express their true thoughts and feelings when researchers or therapists keep them confidential (Smith, 2003a, 2003c). Sometimes conflicts of interest arise, as when a client threatens to harm someone and the psychologist feels obligated to warn the victim (Follingstad & McCormick, 2002).

Some studies could not be carried out if participants knew what the researchers were trying to learn, or which treatment they had received (e.g., a new medicine or a sugar pill). As you can imagine, psychologists have long debated the ethics of deceiving participants. According to the American Psychological Association's (2002) *Ethical Principles of Psychologists and Code of Conduct,* psychologists may use deception only when they believe the benefits of the research outweigh its potential harm, when they believe the individuals might have been willing to participate if they had understood the benefits of the research, and when participants are debriefed. Debriefing means that the purposes and methods of the research are explained afterward.

Return to the Lang (Lang et al., 1975) study on alcohol and aggression. In this study, the researchers (1) misinformed participants about the beverage they were drinking and (2) misled them into believing they were giving other subjects electric shock when they were actually pressing switches on an unconnected control board. (*Aggression* was defined as pressing these switches.) In the study, students who believed they had drunk vodka selected higher levels of shock than students who believed they had not.

Ethics of Research with Animals

Psychologists and other scientists may use animals to conduct research that cannot be carried out with humans. For example, experiments on the effects of early separation from the mother have been done with monkeys and other animals. Such research has helped psychologists investigate the formation of attachment bonds between parent and child.

What ethical issues affect research with animals? Experiments with infant monkeys highlight some of the ethical issues faced by psychologists and other scientists who contemplate potentially harmful research. Psychologists and biologists who study the workings of the brain destroy sections of the brains of laboratory animals to learn how they influence behavior. For example, a lesion in one part of a brain structure causes a rat to overeat. A lesion elsewhere causes the rat to go on a crash diet. Psychologists generalize to humans from experiments such as these in the hope of finding solutions to problems such as eating disorders. Proponents of the use of animals in research argue that many advances in medicine and psychology could not have taken place without them (Bekoff, 2002). For example, we would know less about how drugs affect tumors or the brain.

According to the ethical guidelines of the American Psychological Association, animals may be harmed only when there is no alternative and when researchers believe that the benefits of the research justify the harm (American Psychological Association, 2002; Smith, 2003b, 2003c).

Now that we have an overview of psychology as a science, we will move on to the connections between psychology and biology in Chapter 2. Psychologists assume that our behaviors and our mental processes are related to biological events. In Chapter 2 we consider the evidence for this assumption.

© BONKERSABOUTSCIENCE / ALAMY

Percent of new doctoral degrees in psychology earned by women > **78**

Percent of American population that is African American > **13**

Year that Wilhelm Wundt established the first psych lab > **1879**

Variation of a correlation coefficient > **−1.00 and +1.00**

0 < As a correlation coefficient, means that there is no linear relationship between the variables

---

Biology *and* Psychology

Learning Outcomes

LO **1** Describe the nervous system, including neurons, neural impulses, and neurotransmitters

LO **2** List the structures of the brain and their functions

LO **3** Explain the role of the endocrine system and list the endocrine glands

LO **4** Describe evolutionary psychology and the connections between heredity, behavior, and mental processes

“Gage is no longer Gage.”

“Gage is no longer Gage,” said those who had known him before the accident.

There are many key characters in the history of psychology, and some of them did not arrive there intentionally. One of these was a promising railroad worker who was helping our young nation stretch from coast to coast. His name was Phineas Gage. Gage was highly admired by his friends and his coworkers. But all that changed one day in 1848. While he was tamping down the blasting powder for a dynamite charge, Gage accidentally set the powder off. The inch-thick metal tamping rod shot upward through his cheek and brain and out the top of his head.

If the trajectory of the rod had been slightly different, Gage would have died. Although Gage fell back in a heap, he was miraculously alive. His coworkers watched in shock as he stood up a few moments later and spoke. While the local doctor marveled at the hole through Gage's head, Gage asked when he'd be able to return to work. Two months later, Gage's external wounds had healed, but the psychological aspects of the wound were now obvious. His former employer, who had regarded him as “the most efficient and capable foreman in their employ previous to his injury” (Harlow, 1868), refused to rehire him because he had changed so much:

The equilibrium or balance, so to speak, between his intellectual faculties and animal propensities, seems to have been destroyed. He is . . . irreverent, indulging at times in the grossest profanity (which was not previously his custom). [He showed little consideration for other people, was] impatient of restraint or advice when it conflicts with his desires . . . obstinate, yet capricious and vacillating, devising many plans of future operation, which are no sooner arranged than they are abandoned in turn for others . . . But all had not been lost in Gage's brain. In fact, many of his intellectual skills were just fine, apparently untouched.

Generations of researchers—psychologists, physicians, biologists, neuroscientists—have wondered how the changes in Gage's

Truth or Fiction?

What do you think?

Folklore, common sense, or nonsense? Place a T for “True” or F for “False” on the lines provided (you'll learn the answers as you read through the text).

__ A single cell can stretch all the way from your spine to your toe.

__ Messages travel in the brain by means of electricity.

__ A brain cell can send out hundreds of messages each second—and manage to catch some rest in between.

__ Fear can give you indigestion.

__ The human brain is larger than that of any other animal.

__ If a surgeon were to stimulate a certain part of your brain electrically, you might swear that someone had stroked your leg.

__ Charles Darwin was nearly excluded from the voyage that led to the development of his theory of evolution because the captain of the ship did not like the shape of his nose.

BSIP / PHOTO RESEARCHERS, INC.

PETE SALOUTOS / CORBIS

neuron
a specialized cell of the nervous system that transmits messages

glial cells
cells that nourish and insulate neurons, direct their growth, and remove waste products from the nervous system

personality might have been caused by the damage to his brain. Perhaps the trajectory of the rod spared parts of the frontal lobes that are involved in language and movement but damaged areas connected with personality and emotional response (Damasio, 2000; Wagar & Thagard, 2004).

In this chapter, we will learn about the frontal lobes of the brain and much more. We will travel from the small to the large—from the microscopic brain cells that hold and transmit information, to the visible structures that provide the basis for functions such as memory, speech, sensation, thought, planning, and voluntary movement.

LO¹ The Nervous System: On Being Wired

The nervous system is a system of nerves involved in thought processes, heartbeat, visual-motor coordination, and so on. The nervous system contains the brain, the spinal cord, and other parts that make it possible for us to receive information from the world outside and to act on that world.

The nervous system is composed of cells, most of which are neurons, which is where we will begin our study of the nervous system.

Neurons: Into the Fabulous Forest

Within our brains lies a fabulous forest of nerve cells, or neurons. *What are neurons?* Neurons are cells that can be visualized as having branches, trunks, and roots—something like trees. As we voyage through this forest, we see that many nerve cells lie alongside one another like a thicket of trees. But neurons can also lie end to end, with their "roots" intertwined with the "branches" of the neurons that lie below. Neurons receive "messages" from a number of sources such as light, other neurons, and pressure on the skin, and they can pass these messages along in a complex biological dance.

We are born with more than 100 billion neurons. Most of them are found in the brain. The nervous system also contains **glial cells**. Glial cells remove dead neurons and waste products from the nervous system, nourish and insulate neurons, and enable them to send messages in waves. But neurons occupy center stage in the nervous system. The messages transmitted by neurons somehow account for phenomena ranging from the perception of an itch from a mosquito bite to the coordination of a skier's vision and muscles to the composition of a concerto to the solution of an algebraic equation.

Figure 2.1

The Anatomy of a Neuron

"Messages" enter neurons through dendrites, are transmitted along the trunk-like axon, and then are sent from axon terminal buttons to muscles, glands, and other neurons. Axon terminal buttons contain sacs of chemicals called *neurotransmitters*. Neurotransmitters are released into the synaptic cleft, where many of them bind to receptor sites on the dendrites of the receiving neuron.

Go to CourseMate for PSYCH at www.cengagebrain.com to access an interactive version of this figure.

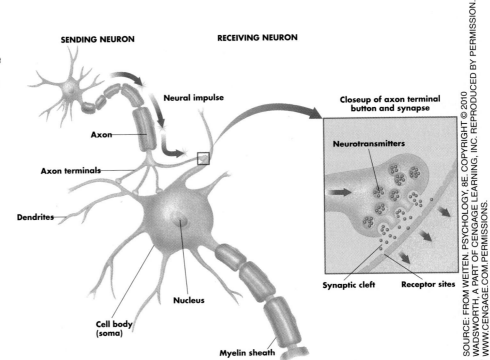

SENDING NEURON · RECEIVING NEURON · Neural impulse · Axon · Axon terminals · Dendrites · Nucleus · Cell body (soma) · Myelin sheath · Closeup of axon terminal button and synapse · Neurotransmitters · Synaptic cleft · Receptor sites

SOURCE: FROM WEITEN. PSYCHOLOGY, 8E. COPYRIGHT © 2010 WADSWORTH, A PART OF CENGAGE LEARNING, INC. REPRODUCED BY PERMISSION. WWW.CENGAGE.COM.PERMISSIONS.

Neurons vary according to their functions and their location. Neurons in the brain may be only a fraction of an inch in length, whereas others in the legs are several feet long. Most neurons include a cell body, dendrites, and an axon (see Figure 2.1). The cell body contains the core or *nucleus* of the cell. The nucleus uses oxygen and nutrients to generate the energy needed to carry out the work of the cell. Anywhere from a few to several hundred short fibers, or dendrites, extend like roots from the cell body to receive incoming messages from thousands of adjoining neurons. Each neuron has an axon that extends like a trunk from the cell body. Axons are very thin, but those that carry messages from the toes to the spinal cord extend several feet.

Like tree trunks, axons can branch off in different directions. Axons end in small bulb-shaped structures called *terminals* or *terminal buttons*. Neurons carry messages in one direction only: from the dendrites or cell body through the axon to the axon terminals. The messages are then transmitted from the terminal buttons to other neurons, muscles, or glands.

As a child matures, the axons of neurons become longer, and the dendrites and terminals proliferate, creating vast interconnected networks for the transmission of complex messages. The number of glial cells also increases as the nervous system develops, contributing to its dense appearance.

Myelin

The axons of many neurons are wrapped tightly with white, fatty myelin that makes them look like strings of sausages under the microscope. The fat insulates the axon from electrically charged atoms, or ions, found in the fluids that surround the nervous system. The myelin sheath minimizes leakage of the electrical current being carried along the axon, thereby allowing messages to be conducted more efficiently.

Myelination is part of the maturation process that leads to the child's ability to crawl and walk during the first year. Infants are not physiologically "ready" to engage in visual–motor coordination and other activities until the coating process reaches certain levels. In people with the disease multiple sclerosis, myelin is replaced with a hard fibrous tissue that throws off the timing of nerve impulses and disrupts muscular control.

Afferent and Efferent Neurons

If someone steps on your toes, the sensation is registered by receptors or sensory neurons near the surface of your skin. Then it is transmitted to the spinal

Truth

It is true that a single cell can stretch all the way from your spine to your toe.

cord and brain through afferent neurons, which are perhaps two to three feet long. In the brain, subsequent messages might be conveyed by associative neurons that are only a few thousandths of an inch long. You experience the pain through this process and perhaps entertain some rather nasty thoughts about the perpetrator, who is now apologizing and begging for understanding. Long before you arrive at any logical conclusions, however, motor neurons (efferent neurons) send messages to your foot so that you withdraw it and begin an impressive hopping routine. Other efferent neurons stimulate glands so that your heart is beating more rapidly, you are sweating, and the hair on the back of your arms has become erect! Being a good sport, you say, "Oh, it's nothing." But considering all the neurons involved, it really is something, isn't it?

In case you think that afferent and efferent neurons will be hard to distinguish because they sound pretty much the SAME to you, remember that they *are* the "SAME." That is, Sensory Afferent, and Motor Efferent.

The Neural Impulse: "The Body Electric"[1]

In the 18th century, the Italian physiologist Luigi Galvani (1737–1798) conducted a shocking experiment in a rainstorm. While his neighbors had the sense to remain indoors, Galvani and his wife were out on the porch connecting lightning rods to the heads of dissected frogs whose legs were connected by wires to a well of water. When lightning blazed above, the frogs' muscles contracted. Galvani was demonstrating that the

***
[1] From Walt Whitman's *Leaves of Grass*.

dendrites
rootlike structures, attached to the cell body of a neuron, that receive impulses from other neurons

axon
a long, thin part of a neuron that transmits impulses to other neurons from branching structures called *terminal buttons*

myelin
a fatty substance that encases and insulates axons, facilitating transmission of neural impulses

afferent neurons
neurons that transmit messages from sensory receptors to the spinal cord and brain. Also called *sensory neurons*

efferent neurons
neurons that transmit messages from the brain or spinal cord to muscles and glands. Also called *motor neurons*

messages (neural impulses) that travel along neurons are electrochemical in nature.

What are neural impulses? Neural impulses are messages that travel within neurons at somewhere between 2 (in nonmyelinated neurons) and 225 miles an hour (in myelinated neurons). This speed is not impressive when compared with that of an electrical current in a toaster oven or a lamp, which can travel at close to the speed of light—over 186,000 miles per second. Distances in the body are short, however, and a message will travel from a toe to the brain in perhaps 1/50th of a second.

An Electrochemical Voyage

The process by which neural impulses travel is electrochemical. Chemical changes take place within neurons that cause an electrical charge to be transmitted along their lengths. Neurons and body fluids contain ions—positively or negatively charged atoms. In a resting state—that is, when a neuron is not being stimulated by its neighbors—negatively charged chloride (Cl⁻) ions are plentiful within the neuron, contributing to an overall negative charge in relation to the outside. The difference in electrical charge readies (polarizes) a neuron for firing by creating an internal negative charge in relation to the

body fluid outside the cell membrane. The electrical potential across the neural membrane when it is not responding to other neurons—its resting potential—is about –70 millivolts in relation to the body fluid outside the cell membrane.

When an area on the surface of the resting neuron is adequately stimulated by other neurons, the cell membrane in the area changes its permeability to allow positively charged sodium ions to enter. Thus the area of entry becomes positively charged, or depolarized with respect to the outside (see Figure 2.2A). The permeability of the cell membrane then changes again, allowing no more sodium ions to enter (see Figure 2.2B).

The electrical impulse that provides the basis for the conduction of a neural impulse along an axon of a neuron is termed its action potential. The inside of the cell axon at the disturbed area has an action potential of 110 millivolts. This action potential, added to the –70 millivolts that characterizes the resting potential, brings the membrane voltage to a positive charge of about +30 to +40 millivolts (see Figure 2.3). This inner change causes the next section of the cell to become permeable to sodium ions. At the same time, other positively charged (potassium) ions are being pumped out of the area of the cell that was previously affected, which returns the area to its resting potential. In this way, the neural impulse is transmitted continuously along an axon. Because the impulse is created anew as it progresses, its strength does not change.

Firing: How Messages Voyage from Neuron to Neuron

The conduction of the neural impulse along the length of a neuron is what is meant by *firing*. When a rifle fires, it sends a bullet speeding through its barrel and discharges it at more than 1,000 feet per second. *What happens when a neuron fires?* Neurons also fire, but instead of a barrel, a neuron has an axon. Instead of discharging a bullet, it releases neurotransmitters.

Some neurons fire in less than 1/1,000th of a second. When they fire,

Figure 2.2

The Neural Impulse

When a section of a neuron is stimulated by other neurons, the cell membrane becomes permeable to sodium ions so that an action potential of about 40 millivolts is induced. This action potential is transmitted along the axon.

A. During an action potential, sodium gates in the neuron membrane open and sodium ions enter the axon, bringing a positive charge with them.

B. After an action potential occurs, the sodium gates close at that point, and open at the next point along the axon. When the sodium gates close, potassium gates open and potassium ions flow out of the axon, carrying a positive charge with them.

A.
Sodium ions
Stimulus
Axon membrane
Flow of charge

B.
Sodium ions
Stimulus
Axon membrane
Potassium ions
Flow of charge

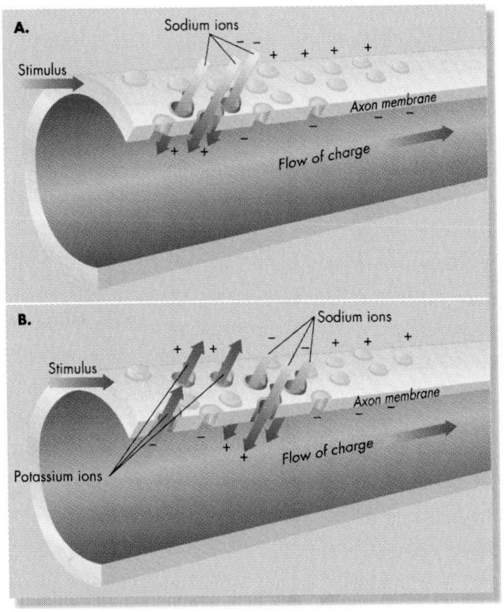

Truth

It is true that messages travel in the brain by means of electricity. These are messages *within* neurons. Communication *between* neurons, however, is carried out quite differently.

Figure 2.3

Changes in Electrical Charges as a Neural Impulse Is Transmitted Across an Axon

The resting potential of a segment of a cell axon is about −70 millivolts. But the inside of the cell axon at the disturbed area has an action potential of about 110 millivolts. When we add this figure to the −70 millivolts that characterizes the resting potential, we bring the membrane voltage to a positive charge of about +30 to +40 millivolts. This inner change causes the next section of the cell to become permeable to sodium ions. In this way, the neural impulse is transmitted continuously along an axon.

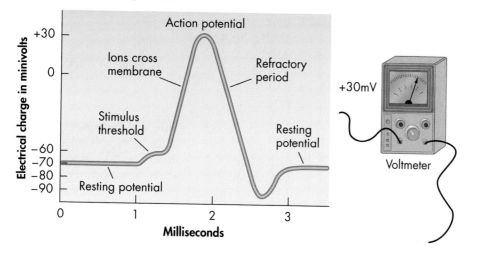

all-or-none principle
the fact that a neuron fires an impulse of the same strength whenever its action potential is triggered

refractory period
a phase following firing during which a neuron is less sensitive to messages from other neurons and will not fire

synapse
a junction between the axon terminals of one neuron and the dendrites or cell body of another neuron

neurotransmitters
chemical substances involved in the transmission of neural impulses from one neuron to another

neurons transmit messages to other neurons, muscles, or glands. However, neurons will not fire unless the incoming messages combine to reach a certain strength, which is defined as the *threshold* at which a neuron will fire. A weak message may cause a temporary shift in electrical charge at some point along the cell membrane, but this charge will dissipate if the neuron is not stimulated to its threshold.

Not only can a neuron fire in less than 1/1,000th of a second, but a neuron may also transmit several hundred messages each second. Every time a neuron fires, it transmits an impulse of the same strength. This occurrence is known as the **all-or-none principle**. That is, either a neuron fires or it doesn't. Neurons fire more often when they have been stimulated by larger numbers of other neurons. Stronger stimuli cause more frequent firing, but again, the strength of each firing remains the same.

For a few thousandths of a second after firing, a neuron is in a **refractory period**; that is, it is insensitive to messages from other neurons and will not fire. This period is a time of recovery during which sodium is prevented from passing through the neuronal membrane. Because such periods of "recovery" might occur hundreds of times per second, it seems a rapid recovery and a short rest indeed.

Truth

It is true that a single brain cell can send out hundreds of messages each second—and manage to catch some rest in between.

The Synapse: On Being Well-Connected

A neuron relays its message to another neuron across a junction called a **synapse**. *What is a synapse?* A synapse consists of an axon terminal button from the transmitting neuron, a dendrite, or the body of a receiving neuron, and a fluid-filled gap between the two that is called the *synaptic cleft* (see Figure 2.1). Although the neural impulse is electrical, it does not jump across the synaptic cleft like a spark. Instead, when a nerve impulse reaches a synapse, axon terminals release chemicals into the synaptic cleft like myriad ships being cast into the sea. Scientists have identified a few dozen of these chemicals to date. In the following section, we consider a few that are usually of the greatest interest to psychologists.

Neurotransmitters: The Chemical Keys to Communication

Sacs called synaptic vesicles in the axon terminals contain neurotransmitters. When a neural impulse (action potential) reaches the axon terminal, the vesicles release varying amounts of **neurotransmitters**—the chemical keys to communication—into the synaptic cleft. From there, they influence the receiving neuron. *Which neurotransmitters are of interest to psychologists? What do they do?*

Dozens of neurotransmitters have been identified. Each has its own chemical structure, and each

receptor site
a location on a dendrite of a receiving neuron tailored to receive a neurotransmitter

acetylcholine (ACh)
a neurotransmitter that controls muscle contractions

hippocampus
a part of the limbic system of the brain that is involved in memory formation

dopamine
a neurotransmitter that is involved in Parkinson's disease and that appears to play a role in schizophrenia

norepinephrine
a neurotransmitter whose action is similar to that of the hormone epinephrine and that may play a role in depression

can fit into a specifically tailored harbor, or receptor site, on the receiving cell. The analogy of a key fitting into a lock is often used to describe this process. Once released, not all molecules of a neurotransmitter find their way into receptor sites of other neurons. "Loose" neurotransmitters are usually either broken down or reabsorbed by the axon terminal (a process called *reuptake*).

Some neurotransmitters act to *excite* other neurons—that is, to cause other neurons to fire. Other neurotransmitters act to *inhibit* receiving neurons. That is, they prevent the neurons from firing. The sum of the stimulation—excitatory and inhibitory—determines whether a neuron will fire and, if so, when neurotransmitters will be released.

Neurotransmitters are involved in physical processes such as muscle contraction and psychological processes such as thoughts and emotions. Excesses or deficiencies of neurotransmitters have been linked to psychological disorders such as depression and schizophrenia. Let us consider the effects of some neurotransmitters that are of interest to psychologists: acetylcholine (ACh), dopamine, norepinephrine, serotonin, GABA, and endorphins.

Acetylcholine (ACh) controls muscle contractions. It is excitatory at synapses between nerves and muscles that involve voluntary movement but inhibitory at the heart and some other locations. The effects of *curare* highlight the functioning of ACh. Curare is a poison that is extracted from plants by South American indigenous people and used in hunting. If an arrow tipped with curare pierces the skin and the poison enters the body, it prevents ACh from binding to the receptor sites on neurons. Because ACh helps muscles move, curare causes paralysis. The victim is prevented from contracting the muscles used in breathing and therefore dies from suffocation. Botulism, a disease that stems from food poisoning,

prevents the release of ACh and has the same effect as *curare*.

ACh is also normally prevalent in a part of the brain called the hippocampus, a structure involved in the formation of memories (Louie & Wilson, 2001). When the amount of ACh available to the brain decreases, as in Alzheimer's disease, memory formation is impaired (Chu et al., 2005). In one experiment, researchers (Egawa et al., 2002) decreased the ACh available to the hippocampi of laboratory rats. As a result, the rats could not learn to navigate a maze, apparently because they could not remember which way to turn at the choice points.

Dopamine acts in the brain and affects ability to perceive pleasure, voluntary movement, and learning and memory (Davis et al., 2004; Heinz, 2004). Deficiencies of dopamine are linked to Parkinson's disease, in which people progressively lose control over their muscles (Olanow, 2000; Swerdlow et al., 2003). They develop muscle tremors and jerky, uncoordinated movements.

The psychological disorder *schizophrenia* is characterized by confusion and false perceptions, and it has been linked to dopamine. People with schizophrenia may have more receptor sites for dopamine in an area of the brain that is involved in emotional responding. For this reason, they may "overutilize" the dopamine available in the brain (Butcher, 2000; Kapur, 2003). Overutilization is connected with hallucinations and disturbances of thought and emotion. The phenothiazines, a group of drugs used in the treatment of schizophrenia, inhibit the action of dopamine by blocking some dopamine receptors (Lidow et al., 2001). Because of their action, phenothiazines may have Parkinson's-like side effects, which are usually treated by lowering the dose, prescribing additional drugs, or switching to another drug.

Norepinephrine is produced largely by neurons in the brain stem, and acts both as a neurotransmitter and as a hormone. It is an excitatory neurotransmitter that speeds up the heartbeat and other body processes and is involved in general arousal, learning and memory, and eating. Excesses and deficiencies of norepinephrine have

The boxer Muhammad Ali and the actor Michael J. Fox are two of the better-known individuals who are afflicted with Parkinson's disease.

STEPHEN JAFFE/AFP/GETTY IMAGES

Figure 2.4

The Divisions of the Nervous System

The nervous system contains two main divisions: the central nervous system and the peripheral nervous system. The central nervous system consists of the brain and spinal cord. The peripheral nervous system contains the somatic and autonomic systems. In turn, the autonomic nervous system has sympathetic and parasympathetic divisions.

Go to CourseMate for PSYCH at www.cengagebrain.com to access an interactive version of this figure.

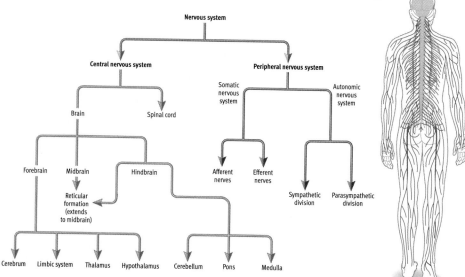

SOURCE: FROM WEITEN. PSYCHOLOGY, 8E. COPYRIGHT © 2010 WADSWORTH, A PART OF CENGAGE LEARNING, INC. REPRODUCED BY PERMISSION. WWW.CENGAGE.COM.PERMISSIONS.

serotonin
a neurotransmitter, deficiencies of which have been linked to affective disorders, anxiety, and insomnia

gamma-aminobutyric acid (GABA)
an inhibitory neurotransmitter that apparently helps calm anxiety

endorphins
neurotransmitters that are composed of amino acids and that are functionally similar to morphine

nerve
a bundle of axons from many neurons

Endorphins occur naturally in the brain and in the bloodstream and are similar to the narcotic morphine in their functions and effects. They lock into receptor sites for chemicals that transmit pain messages to the brain. Once the endorphin "key" is in the "lock," the pain-causing chemicals are locked out. Endorphins may also increase our sense of competence, enhance the functioning of the immune system, and be connected with the pleasurable "runner's high" reported by many long-distance runners (Jonsdottir et al., 2000; Oktedalen et al., 2001).

There you have it—a fabulous forest of neurons in which billions upon billions of axon terminals are pouring armadas of neurotransmitters into synaptic clefts at any given time. The combined activity of all these neurotransmitters determines which messages will be transmitted and which ones will not. You experience your sensations, your thoughts, and your control over your body as psychological events, but the psychological events come from billions upon billions of electrochemical events.

We can think of neurons as the microscopic building blocks of the nervous system. Millions upon millions of these neurons gather together to form larger, visible structures that we think of as the parts of the nervous system. We discuss those parts next.

been linked to mood disorders. Deficiencies of both ACh and norepinephrine particularly impair memory formation (Egawa et al., 2002).

The stimulants cocaine and amphetamine ("speed") boost norepinephrine (as well as dopamine) production, increasing the firing of neurons and leading to persistent arousal. Amphetamines both facilitate the release of these neurotransmitters and prevent their reuptake. Cocaine also blocks reuptake.

Serotonin is involved in emotional arousal and sleep. Deficiencies of serotonin have been linked to eating disorders, alcoholism, depression, aggression, and insomnia. The drug LSD decreases the action of serotonin and is also believed to increase the utilization of dopamine, which may be the mechanism by which it produces hallucinations.

Gamma-aminobutyric acid (GABA) is another neurotransmitter of great interest to psychologists. One reason is that GABA is an inhibitory neurotransmitter that may help calm anxiety reactions (Stroele et al., 2002). Tranquilizers and alcohol may quell anxiety by binding with GABA receptors and amplifying its effects. One class of antianxiety drug may also increase the sensitivity of receptor sites to GABA. Other studies link deficiencies of GABA to depression (Clénet et al., 2005).

Endorphins are inhibitory neurotransmitters. The word *endorphin* is the contraction of *endogenous morphine*. *Endogenous* means "developing from within."

The Parts of the Nervous System

What are the parts of the nervous system? The nervous system consists of the brain, the spinal cord, and the **nerves** linking them to the sensory organs, muscles, and glands. As shown in Figure 2.4, the brain and the spinal cord make up the central nervous system. If you compare your nervous system to a computer, your central nervous system would be your central processing unit (CPU).

The sensory (afferent) neurons, which receive and transmit messages to the brain and spinal cord, and the motor (efferent) neurons, which transmit messages from the brain or spinal cord to the muscles and glands, make up the peripheral nervous system. In the comparison of the nervous system to a computer, the peripheral nervous system makes up the nervous system's peripheral devices—keyboard, mouse, DVD drive, and so on. You would not be able to feed information to your computer's central processing unit without these *peripheral* devices. Other peripheral devices, such as your monitor and printer, allow you to follow what is happening inside your CPU and see what it has done.

> " Autonomic means automatic. "

The Peripheral Nervous System: The Body's Peripheral Devices

What are the divisions and functions of the peripheral nervous system? The peripheral nervous system consists of sensory and motor neurons that transmit messages to and from the central nervous system. Without the peripheral nervous system, our brains would be like isolated CPUs. There would be no keyboards, mouses, CDs, or other ways of inputting information. There would be no monitors, printers, modems, or other ways of displaying or transmitting information. We would be detached from the world. We would not be able to perceive it; we would not be able to act on it. The two main divisions of the peripheral nervous system are the *somatic nervous system* and the *autonomic nervous system*.

The somatic nervous system contains sensory (afferent) and motor (efferent) neurons. It transmits messages about sights, sounds, smells, temperature, body positions, and so on, to the central nervous system. Messages transmitted from the brain and spinal cord to the somatic nervous system control purposeful body movements such as raising a hand, winking, or running, as well as the tiny, almost imperceptible movements that maintain our balance and posture.

The autonomic nervous system (ANS) also has afferent and efferent neurons and regulates the glands and the muscles of internal organs. Thus, the ANS controls activities such as heartbeat, respiration, digestion, and dilation of the pupils. These activities can occur automatically, while we are asleep. But some of them can be overridden by conscious control. You can breathe at a purposeful pace, for example. Methods like biofeedback and yoga also help people gain voluntary control of functions such as heart rate and blood pressure.

The ANS also has two branches, or divisions: sympathetic and parasympathetic. These branches have largely opposing effects. Many organs and glands are stimulated by both branches of the ANS (see Figure 2.5). When organs and glands are simultaneously stimulated by both divisions, their effects can average out to some degree. In general, the sympathetic division is most active during processes that involve spending body energy from stored reserves, such as a fight-or-flight response to a predator or when you find out that your rent is going to be raised. The parasympathetic division is most active during processes that replenish reserves of energy, such as eating. When we are afraid, the sympathetic division of the ANS accelerates the heart rate. When we relax, the parasympathetic division decelerates the heart rate. The parasympathetic division stimulates digestive processes, but the sympathetic branch inhibits digestion. The ANS is of particular interest to psychologists because its activities are linked to various emotions such as anxiety and love.

The Central Nervous System: The Body's Central Processing Unit

What are the divisions and functions of the central nervous system? The central nervous system consists of the spinal cord and the brain. The spinal cord is a true "information superhighway"—a column of nerves as

Truth

It is true that fear can give you indigestion.

The Brain—is wider than the Sky—
For—put them side by side—
The one the other will contain
With ease—and you—beside—

—Emily Dickinson

thick as a thumb. It transmits messages from sensory receptors to the brain and from the brain to muscles and glands throughout the body. The spinal cord also carries out some "local government." That is, it responds to some sources of external stimulation through spinal reflexes. A spinal reflex is an unlearned response to a stimulus that may require only two neurons—a sensory neuron and a motor neuron (see Figure 2.6).

The spinal cord and brain contain gray matter and white matter. Gray matter consists of nonmyelinated neurons. Some of these are involved in spinal reflexes. Others send their axons to the brain. White matter is composed of bundles of longer, myelinated (and thus whitish) axons that carry messages to and from the brain. A cross section of the spinal cord shows that the gray matter, which includes cell bodies, is distributed in a butterfly pattern (see Figure 2.6).

The spinal cord is also involved in reflexes. We blink in response to a puff of air in our faces. We swallow when food accumulates in the mouth. A physician may tap below the knee to elicit the knee-jerk reflex, a sign that the nervous system is operating adequately. Sexual response involves many reflexes. Urinating and defecating are reflexes that occur in response to pressure in the bladder and the rectum. It is your central nervous system that makes you so special. Other species see more sharply, smell more keenly, and hear more acutely. Other species run faster, or fly through the air, or swim underwater—without the benefit of artificial devices such as airplanes and submarines. But it is your central nervous system that enables you to use symbols and language, the abilities that allow people not only to adapt to their environment but also to create new environments and give them names (Bandura, 1999).

spinal reflex
a simple, unlearned response to a stimulus that may involve only two neurons

gray matter
the grayish neurons and neural segments that are involved in spinal reflexes

white matter
axon bundles that carry messages from and to the brain

LO^2 The Brain: Wider Than the Sky

When I was a child, I was told that the human nervous system is more complex than that of any other animal and that our brains are larger than those of any other animal. Now, this last piece of business is not quite true. A human brain weighs about 3 pounds, but the brains of elephants and whales may be four times as heavy. Still, our brains account for a greater part of our body weight than do those of elephants or whales. Our brains weigh about 1/60th of our body weight. Elephant brains weigh about 1/1,000th of their total weight, and whale brains are a paltry 1/10,000th of their weight. Philosophers and scientists have wondered about the functions of the brain throughout history. Scientists today generally agree that the mind is a function of the brain (Bogen, 1998; Dietrich, 2004; Hohwy & Frith, 2004; Roser & Gazzaniga, 2004). Some engage in research that attempts to pinpoint exactly what

Figure 2.5

The Parasympathetic and Sympathetic Branches of the Autonomic Nervous System (ANS)

The parasympathetic branch of the ANS generally acts to replenish stores of energy in the body. The sympathetic branch is most active during activities that expend energy. The two branches of the ANS frequently have antagonistic effects on the organs they service.

Go to CourseMate for PSYCH at www.cengagebrain.com to access an interactive version of this figure.

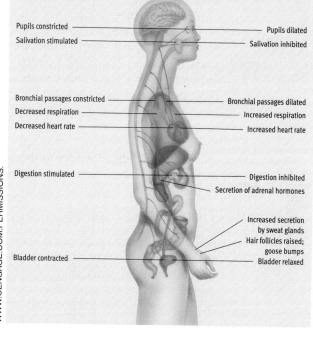

Fiction

It is not true that the human brain is larger than that of any other animal.

IMAGE COPYRIGHT GARY PAUL LEWIS 2010. USED UNDER LICENSE FROM SHUTTERSTOCK.COM

SOURCE: FROM WEITEN. PSYCHOLOGY, 8E. COPYRIGHT © 2010 WADSWORTH, A PART OF CENGAGE LEARNING, INC. REPRODUCED BY PERMISSION. WWW.CENGAGE.COM.PERMISSIONS.

electroencephalo-graph (EEG) a method of detecting brain waves by means of measuring the current between electrodes placed on the scalp

happens in certain parts of the brain when we are listening to music or trying to remember someone's face. At other times—as in the case of Phineas Gage—knowledge has almost literally fallen into their laps. From injuries to the head—some of them minimal, some horrendous—we have learned that brain damage can impair consciousness, perception, memory, and abilities to make plans and decisions. In some cases, the loss of large portions of the brain may result in little loss of function. But the loss of smaller portions in particular locations can cause language problems, memory loss, or death. It has been known for about two centuries that damage to the left side of the brain is connected with loss of sensation or movement on the right side of the body, and vice versa. Thus it has been assumed that the brain's control mechanisms cross over from right to left, and vice versa, as they descend into the body.

Accidents provide unplanned—and uncontrolled—opportunities of studying the brain. Nevertheless, they remain useful (e.g., Baldo et al., 2004; Eslinger et al., 2004). Still, scientists learn more about the brain through methods like experimentation, electroencephalography, and brain scans. *How do researchers learn about the functions of the brain?*

Experimenting with the Brain

The results of disease and accidents (as in the case of Phineas Gage) have shown us that brain injuries can be connected with changes in behavior and mental

Figure 2.7

The Electroencephalograph (EEG)

The EEG detects brain waves that pass between electrodes that are attached to the scalp. It has been used to reveal electrical activity associated with relaxation and the stages of sleep.

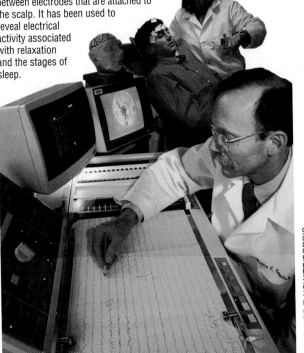

© RICHARD T. NOWITZ/CORBIS

processes. Scientists have also purposefully damaged part of the brain in laboratory animals to observe the results. For example, damaging one part of the hypothalamus causes rats to overeat. Damaging another part of the hypothalamus causes them to stop eating. It is as if parts of the brain contain on–off switches for certain kinds of behavior, at least in lower animals.

Because the brain has no receptors for pain, surgeon Wilder Penfield (1969) was able to stimulate parts of human brains with electrical probes. As a result, his patients reported perceiving certain memories. Electrical stimulation of the brain has also shown that parts of the brain are connected with specific kinds of sensations (as of light or sound) or motor activities (such as movement of an arm or leg).

The Electroencephalograph

Penfield stimulated parts of the brain with an electrical current and asked people to report what they experienced. Researchers have also used the electroencephalograph (EEG) to record the natural electrical activity

Figure 2.6

The Reflex Arc

Reflexes are inborn, stereotyped behavior patterns that have apparently evolved because they help individuals adapt to the environment even before they can understand and purposefully manipulate the environment. Here we see a cross-section of the spinal cord, highlighting a sensory neuron and a motor neuron, which are involved in the knee-jerk reflex. In some reflexes, interneurons link sensory and motor neurons.

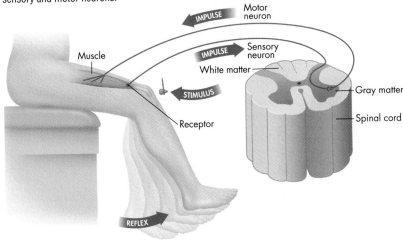

Motor neuron
IMPULSE
IMPULSE
Sensory neuron
Muscle
White matter
STIMULUS
Gray matter
Receptor
Spinal cord
REFLEX

Figure 2.8

Brain Imaging Techniques

Part A shows a CAT scan, part B shows a PET scan, and part C shows an MRI.

A. Computerized axial tomography (the CAT scan) passes a narrow X-ray beam through the head and measures structures that reflect the rays from various angles, enabling a computer to generate a three-dimensional image.

B. Positron emission tomography (the PET scan) injects a radioactive tracer into the bloodstream and assesses activity of parts of the brain according to the amount of glucose they metabolize.

C. Magnetic resonance imaging (MRI) places a person in a magnetic field and uses radio waves to cause the brain to emit signals that reveal shifts in the flow of blood, which, in turn, indicate brain activity.

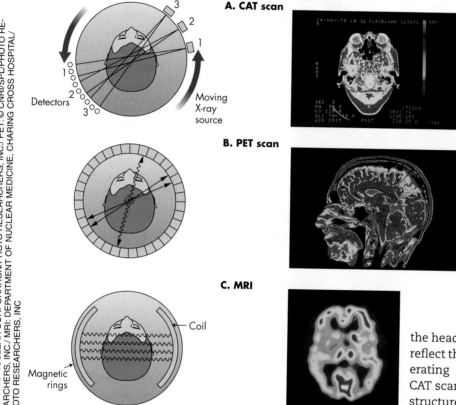

A. CAT scan

B. PET scan

C. MRI

computerized axial tomography (CAT or CT scan) a method of brain imaging that passes a narrow X-ray beam through the head and measures structures that reflect the rays from various angles, enabling a computer to generate a three-dimensional image

positron emission tomography (PET scan) a method of brain imaging that injects a radioactive tracer into the bloodstream and assesses activity of parts of the brain according to the amount of glucose they metabolize

magnetic resonance imaging (MRI) a method of brain imaging that places a person in a magnetic field and uses radio waves to cause the brain to emit signals that reveal shifts in the flow of blood, which, in turn, indicate brain activity

of the brain. The EEG (see Figure 2.7) detects minute amounts of electrical activity—called brain waves—that pass between the electrodes. Certain brain waves are associated with feelings of relaxation, with various stages of sleep, and with neurological problems such as epilepsy.

Brain-Imaging Techniques

When Phineas Gage had his fabled accident, the only ways to look into the brain were to drill holes or crack it open, neither of which would have contributed to the well-being of the subject. But in the latter years of the 20th century, researchers developed imaging techniques that tap the computer's capacity to generate images of the parts of the brain from sources of radiation.

Computerized axial tomography (CAT or CT scan), shown in Figure 2.8A, passes X-rays through the head and measures the structures that reflect the beams from various angles, generating a three-dimensional image. The CAT scan reveals deformities in shape and structure that are connected with blood clots, tumors, and other health problems.

A second method, positron emission tomography (PET scan), shown in Figure 2.8B, forms a computer-generated image of the activity of parts of the brain by tracing the amount of glucose used (or metabolized) by these parts. More glucose is metabolized in more active parts of the brain. To trace the metabolism of glucose, a harmless amount of a radioactive compound, called a *tracer*, is mixed with glucose and injected into the bloodstream. When the glucose reaches the brain, the patterns of activity are revealed by measurement of the positrons—positively charged particles—that are given off by the tracer. The PET scan has been used by researchers to see which parts of the brain are most active when we are, for example, listening to music, working out a math problem, using language, or playing chess.

A third imaging technique is magnetic resonance imaging (MRI), which is shown in Figure 2.8C.

Figure 2.9

The Parts of the Human Brain

The view of the brain, split top to bottom, shows some of the most important structures. The "valleys" in the cerebrum are called fissures.

Go to CourseMate for PSYCH at www.cengagebrain.com to access an interactive version of this figure.

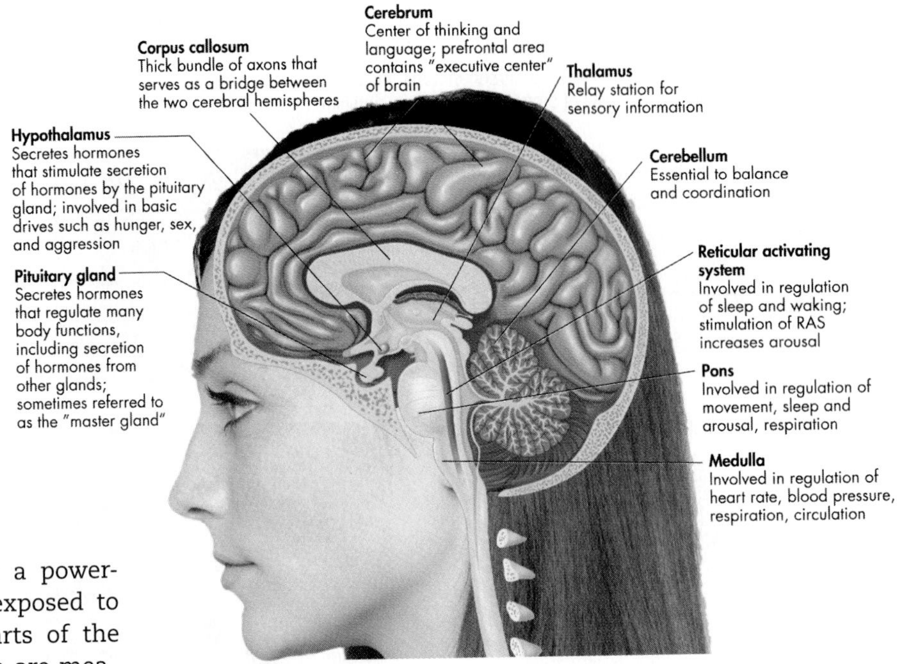

Corpus callosum
Thick bundle of axons that serves as a bridge between the two cerebral hemispheres

Cerebrum
Center of thinking and language; prefrontal area contains "executive center" of brain

Thalamus
Relay station for sensory information

Hypothalamus
Secretes hormones that stimulate secretion of hormones by the pituitary gland; involved in basic drives such as hunger, sex, and aggression

Pituitary gland
Secretes hormones that regulate many body functions, including secretion of hormones from other glands; sometimes referred to as the "master gland"

Cerebellum
Essential to balance and coordination

Reticular activating system
Involved in regulation of sleep and waking; stimulation of RAS increases arousal

Pons
Involved in regulation of movement, sleep and arousal, respiration

Medulla
Involved in regulation of heart rate, blood pressure, respiration, circulation

IMAGE SOURCE/© 2010 JUPITERIMAGES CORPORATION

In MRI, the person lies in a powerful magnetic field and is exposed to radio waves that cause parts of the brain to emit signals, which are measured from multiple angles. MRI relies on subtle shifts in blood flow. (More blood flows to more active parts of the brain, supplying them with oxygen.) MRI can be used to show which parts of the brain are active when we are, say, solving math problems (Rickard et al., 2000) or speaking (Dogil et al., 2002). Functional MRI (fMRI) enables researchers to observe the brain "while it works" by taking repeated scans while subjects engage in activities such as mental processes and voluntary movements.

Some researchers consider the prefrontal cortex to be the "executive center" of the brain, where decisions are made to keep information in working memory and to solve problems. The prefrontal cortex is the part of the frontal lobe (see Figure 2.11 on page 38) that is closest to the front of the brain. Research with the PET scan and MRI supports the view that the prefrontal cortex is where we process much of the information involved in making plans and solving problems (Kroger et al., 2002; Rowe et al., 2001).

A Voyage Through the Brain

What are the structures and functions of the brain? Let us begin our tour of the brain with the hindbrain, where the spinal cord rises to meet the brain (refer to Figure 2.9). Here we find three major structures: the medulla, the pons, and the cerebellum. Many pathways pass through the medulla to connect the spinal cord to higher levels of the brain. The medulla regulates basic functions such as heart rate, blood pressure, and respiration. (In fact, Gage survived his accident because his medulla escaped injury.) The medulla also plays roles in sleeping, sneezing, and coughing. The pons is a bulge in the hindbrain that lies forward of the medulla. *Pons* is the Latin word for "bridge"; the pons is so named because of the bundles of nerves that pass through it. The pons transmits information about body movement and is involved in functions related to attention, sleep and alertness, and respiration.

Behind the pons lies the cerebellum ("little brain" in Latin). The cerebellum has two hemispheres that are involved in maintaining balance and in controlling motor (muscle) behavior. You may send a command from your forebrain to get up and walk to the refrigerator, but your cerebellum is key to organizing the information that enables you to engage in these movements. The cerebellum allows you to place one leg in front of the other and reach your destination without tipping over. Injury to the cerebellum may impair motor coordination and cause stumbling and loss of muscle tone.

As we tour the hindbrain, we also find the lower part of the reticular activating system (RAS). That is where the RAS begins, but it ascends through the midbrain into the lower part of the forebrain. The RAS is vital in the functions of attention, sleep, and arousal. Injury to the RAS may result in a coma. Stimulation of the RAS causes it to send messages to the cerebral cortex (the large wrinkled mass that you think of as your brain), making us more alert to sensory information. In classic neurological research, Giuseppe Moruzzi and Horace Magoun (1949) discovered that electrical stimulation of the reticular formation of a sleeping cat caused it to awaken at once. But when the reticular formation was severed from higher parts of the brain, the cat fell into a coma from which it would not awaken. Drugs known as central nervous system depressants, such as alcohol, are thought to work, in part, by lowering RAS activity.

Key areas of the forwardmost part of the brain, or forebrain, are the thalamus, the hypothalamus, the limbic system, and the cerebrum (see Figure 2.10). The thalamus is located near the center of the brain, and could be said to lie between the forebrain and the midbrain. It consists of two joined egg-shaped structures. The thalamus serves as a relay station for sensory stimulation. Nerve fibers from sensory systems enter from below; their information is then transmitted to the cerebral cortex by fibers that exit from above. For example, the thalamus relays sensory input from the eyes to the visual areas of the cerebral cortex. The thalamus also regulates sleep and attention in coordination with other brain structures, including the RAS.

The hypothalamus lies beneath the thalamus and above the pituitary gland. It weighs only 4 grams, yet it is vital in the regulation of body temperature, concentration of fluids, storage of nutrients, and motivation and emotion. Experimenters learn many of the functions of the hypothalamus by implanting electrodes in parts of it and observing the effects of electrical stimulation. They have found that the hypothalamus is involved in hunger, thirst, sexual behavior, caring for offspring, and aggression. Among lower animals, stimulation of various areas of the hypothalamus can trigger instinctual behaviors such as fighting, mating, or nest building.

Canadian psychologists James Olds and Peter Milner (1954) made a splendid mistake in the 1950s. They were attempting to implant an electrode in a rat's reticular formation to see how stimulation of the area might affect learning. Olds, however, was primarily a social psychologist and not a biological psychologist. He missed his target and found a part of the animal's hypothalamus instead. Olds and Milner dubbed this area the "pleasure center" because the animal would repeat whatever it was doing when it was stimulated. The term pleasure center is not used frequently, because it appears to attribute human emotions to rats. Yet the "pleasure centers" must be doing something right, because rats stimulate themselves in these centers by pressing a pedal several thousand times an hour, until they are exhausted (Olds, 1969).

The hypothalamus is important to humans as well as to lower animals. Unfortunately (or fortunately), our "pleasure centers" are not as clearly defined as those of the rat. Then, too, our responses to messages from the hypothalamus are less automatic and relatively more influenced by higher brain functions—that is, cognitive factors such as thought, choice, and value systems.

The limbic system forms a fringe along the inner edge of the cerebrum and is fully evolved only in mammals (see Figure 2.10). It is made up of several structures, including the amygdala, hippocampus, and parts of the hypothalamus. It is involved in memory and emotion and in the drives of hunger, sex, and aggression. People with hippocampal damage can retrieve old memories but cannot permanently store new information. As a result, they may reread the same newspaper day in and day out without recalling that they read it before. Or they may have to be perpetually reintroduced to people they have met just hours earlier (Squire, 2004).

The amygdala is near the bottom of the limbic system and looks like two little almonds. Studies using lesioning and electrical stimulation show that the amygdala is connected with aggressive behavior

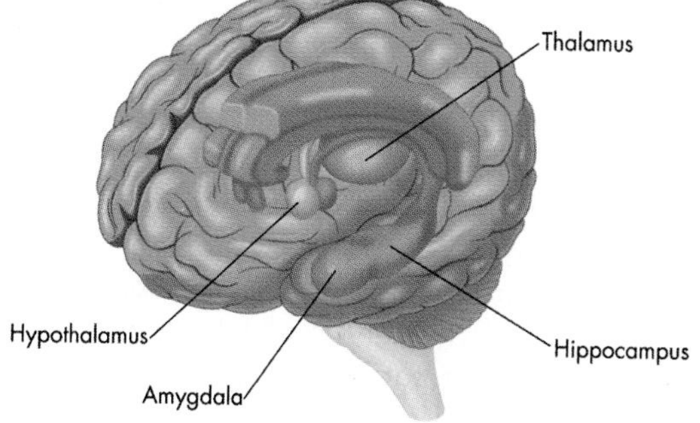

thalamus
an area near the center of the brain involved in the relay of sensory information to the cortex and in the functions of sleep and attention

hypothalamus
a bundle of nuclei below the thalamus involved in body temperature, motivation, and emotion

limbic system
a group of structures involved in memory, motivation, and emotion that forms a fringe along the inner edge of the cerebrum

amygdala
a part of the limbic system that apparently facilitates stereotypical aggressive responses

Figure 2.10

The Limbic System

The limbic system is made up of structures that include the amygdala, the hippocampus, and parts of the hypothalamus. It is evolved fully only in mammals and forms a fringe along the inner edge of the cerebrum. The limbic system is involved in memory and emotion, and in the drives of hunger, sex, and aggression.

Go to CourseMate for PSYCH at www.cengagebrain.com to access an interactive version of this figure.

Thalamus

Hypothalamus

Amygdala

Hippocampus

cerebrum
the large mass of the forebrain, which consists of two hemispheres

cerebral cortex
the wrinkled surface area (gray matter) of the cerebrum

corpus callosum
a thick fiber bundle that connects the hemispheres of the cortex

in monkeys, cats, and other animals. Early in the 20th century, Heinrich Klüver and Paul Bucy (1939) lesioned part of the amygdala of a rhesus monkey. Rhesus monkeys are normally a scrappy lot and try to bite or grab at intruders, but destruction of this animal's amygdala made it docile. No longer did it react aggressively to people. It even allowed people to poke and pinch it. Electrical stimulation of the part of the amygdala that Klüver and Bucy had destroyed, however, triggers a "rage response." For example, it causes a cat to hiss and arch its back in preparation to attack. The amygdala is also connected with a fear response (LeDoux, 1998). If you electrically stimulate another part of the

amygdala, the cat cringes in fear when you cage it with a mouse.

The amygdala is also connected with vigilance. It is involved in emotions, learning, and memory, and it sort of behaves like a spotlight, focusing attention on matters that are novel and important to know more about.

Only in humans does the cerebrum make up such a large part of the brain. The cerebrum is responsible for thinking and language. The surface of the cerebrum—the cerebral cortex—is wrinkled, or convoluted, with ridges and valleys. The convolutions allow a great deal of surface area to be packed into the brain—and surface area is apparently connected with cognitive ability. Valleys in the cortex are called *fissures*. A key fissure almost divides the cerebrum in half, creating two hemispheres with something of the shape of a walnut. The hemispheres are connected by the corpus callosum (Latin for "hard body"), a bundle of some 200 million nerve fibers.

Figure 2.11

The Geography of the Cerebral Cortex

The cortex has four lobes: frontal, parietal, temporal, and occipital. The visual area of the cortex is in the occipital lobe. The hearing or auditory cortex lies in the temporal lobe. The motor and somatosensory areas— shown below—face each other across the central fissure. Note that the face and the hands are "super-sized" in the motor and somatosensory areas. Why do you think this is so?

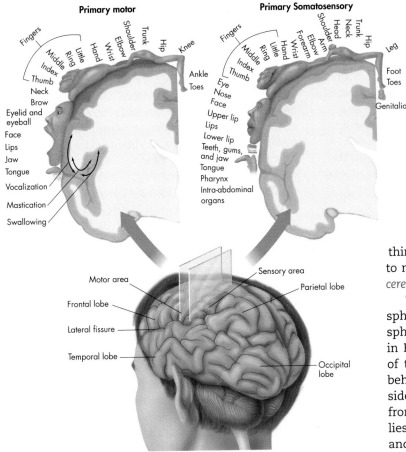

The Cerebral Cortex

The cerebral cortex is the part of the brain that you usually think of as your brain. *Cortex* is a Latin word meaning "bark," as in the bark of a tree. Just as the bark is the outer coating of a tree, the cerebral cortex is the outer coating of the cerebrum. Despite its extreme importance and its creation of a world of civilization and culture, it is only about 1/8" thick.

The cerebral cortex is involved in almost every bodily activity, including most sensations and most responses. It is also the part of the brain that frees people from the tyranny of genetic dictates and instinct. It is the seat of thinking and language, and it enables humans to think deeply about the world outside and to make decisions. *What are the parts of the cerebral cortex?*

The cerebral cortex has two hemispheres, left and right. Each of the hemispheres is divided into four lobes, as shown in Figure 2.11. The *frontal lobe* lies in front of the central fissure and the *parietal lobe* behind it. The *temporal lobe* lies below the side, or lateral, fissure—across from the frontal and parietal lobes. The *occipital lobe* lies behind the temporal lobe and behind and below the parietal lobe.

When light strikes the eyes, neurons in the occipital lobe fire, and as a result, we "see" (that is, the image is projected in the brain). Direct artificial stimulation of the occipital lobe also produces visual sensations. If neurons in the occipital region of the cortex were stimulated with electricity, you would "see" flashes of light even if it were pitch-black or your eyes were covered. The hearing or auditory area of the cortex lies in the temporal lobe along the lateral fissure. Sounds cause structures in the ear to vibrate. Messages are relayed from those structures to the auditory area of the cortex; when you hear a noise, neurons in this area are firing.

Just behind the central fissure in the parietal lobe lies an area called the somatosensory cortex, which receives messages from skin senses all over the body. These sensations include warmth and cold, touch, pain, and movement. Neurons in different parts of the sensory cortex fire, depending on whether you wiggle your finger or raise your leg.

Many years ago it was discovered that patients with injuries to one hemisphere of the brain would show sensory or motor deficits on the opposite side of the body below the head. This led to the recognition that sensory and motor nerves cross in the brain and elsewhere. The left hemisphere controls, acts on, and receives inputs from the right side of the body. The right hemisphere controls, acts on, and receives inputs from the left side of the body. The motor cortex lies in the frontal lobe, just across the valley of the central fissure from the somatosensory cortex. Neurons firing in the motor cortex cause parts of our body to move. More than 100 years ago, German scientists electrically stimulated the motor cortex in dogs and observed that muscles contracted in response (Fritsch & Hitzig, 1870/1960). Since then, neuroscientists have mapped the motor cortex in people and lower animals by inserting electrical probes and seeing which muscles contract. For example, José Delgado (1969) caused one patient to make a fist even though he tried to prevent his hand from closing. The patient said, "I guess, doctor, that your electricity is stronger than my will" (Delgado, 1969, p. 114).

Thinking, Language, and the Cortex

Areas of the cerebral cortex that are not primarily involved in sensation or motor activity are called *association areas*. They make possible the breadth and depth of human learning, thought, memory, and language. *What parts of the cerebral cortex are involved in thinking and language?* The association areas in the *prefrontal* region of the brain—that is, in the frontal lobes, near the forehead—are the brain's executive center. It appears to be where we solve problems and make plans and decisions (Baldo et al., 2004; Buchanan et al., 2004; Shimamura, 2002).

Executive functions like problem-solving also require memory, like the memory in your computer. Association areas also provide the core of your working memory (Chafee & Goldman-Rakic, 2000; Constantinidis et al., 2001). They are connected with various sensory areas in the brain and can tap whatever sensory information is needed or desired. The prefrontal region thus retrieves visual, auditory, and other memories and manipulates them; similarly, a computer retrieves information from files in storage and manipulates it in working memory.

Certain neurons in the visual area of the occipital lobe fire in response to the visual presentation of vertical lines. Others fire in response to presentation of horizontal lines. Although one group of cells may respond to one aspect of the visual field and another group of cells may respond to another, association areas put it all together. As a result, we see a box or an automobile or a road map and not a confusing array of verticals and horizontals.

Language Functions

In some ways, the left and right hemispheres of the brain duplicate each other's functions. In other ways, they differ. The left hemisphere contains language functions for nearly all right-handed people and for two out of three left-handed people (Pinker, 1994b). However, the brain remains "plastic," or changeable, through about the age of 13. As a result, children who lose the left hemisphere of the brain because of medical problems may transfer speech functions to the right hemisphere (Hertz-Pannier et al., 2002).

Two key language areas lie within the hemisphere of the cortex that contains language functions (usually the left hemisphere): Broca's area and Wernicke's area (see Figure 2.12). Damage to either area is likely to cause an aphasia—that is, a disruption of the ability to understand or produce language.

somatosensory cortex
the section of cortex in which sensory stimulation is projected. It lies just behind the central fissure in the parietal lobe

motor cortex
the section of cortex that lies in the frontal lobe, just across the central fissure from the sensory cortex; neural impulses in the motor cortex are linked to muscular responses throughout the body

aphasia
a disruption in the ability to understand or produce language

Truth

It is quite true that if an area of your somatosensory cortex is stimulated with an electrical probe, it might seem to you as if someone were touching your arm or leg.

Wernicke's aphasia
a language disorder characterized by difficulty comprehending the meaning of spoken language

Broca's aphasia
a language disorder characterized by slow, laborious speech

Wernicke's area lies in the temporal lobe near the auditory cortex. It responds mainly to auditory information (sounds). As you are reading this page, however, the visual information is registered in the visual cortex of your occipital lobe. It is then recoded as auditory information as it travels to Wernicke's area. Broca's area is located in the frontal lobe, near the section of the motor cortex that controls the muscles of the tongue, throat, and other areas of the face used when speaking. Broca's area processes the information and relays it to the motor cortex. The motor cortex sends the signals that cause muscles in your throat and mouth to contract. If you are "subvocalizing"—saying what you are reading "under your breath"—that is because Wernicke's area transmits information to Broca's area via nerve fibers.

People with damage to Wernicke's area may show Wernicke's aphasia, which impairs their abilities to comprehend speech and to think of the proper words to express their own thoughts. Ironically, they usually speak freely and with proper syntax. Wernicke's area is essential to understanding the relationships between words and their meanings. When Broca's area is damaged, people usually understand language well enough but speak slowly and laboriously, in simple sentences. This pattern is termed Broca's aphasia.

Some people with Broca's aphasia utter short, meaningful phrases that omit small but important grammatical words such as is, and, and the. Such an individual may laboriously say "walk dog." The phrase can have various meanings, such as "I want to take the dog for a walk" or "Take the dog out for a walk."

Figure 2.12

Broca's and Wernicke's Areas of the Cerebral Cortex

The areas that are most involved in speech are Broca's area and Wernicke's area.

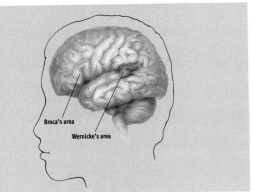

Broca's area

Wernicke's area

A part of the brain called the *angular gyrus* lies between the visual cortex and Wernicke's area. The angular gyrus "translates" visual information, as in perceiving written words, into auditory information (sounds) and sends it on to Wernicke's area. Brain imaging suggests that problems in the angular gyrus can seriously impair reading ability because it becomes difficult for the reader to segment words into sounds (Milne et al., 2002; Ruff et al., 2003).

Left Brain, Right Brain?

What would it mean to be "left-brained" or "right-brained"? The notion is that the hemispheres of the brain are involved in very different kinds of intellectual and emotional functions and responses. According to this view, left-brained people would be primarily logical and intellectual. Right-brained people would be intuitive, creative, and emotional. Those of us who are fortunate enough to have our brains "in balance" would presumably have the best of it—the capacity for logic combined with emotional richness.

Like many other popular ideas, the left-brain–right-brain notion is exaggerated. Research does suggest that in right-handed individuals, the left hemisphere is relatively more involved in intellectual undertakings that require logical analysis and problem-solving, language, and mathematical computation (Corballis et al., 2002; Shenal & Harrison, 2003). The other hemisphere (typically the right hemisphere) is usually superior in visual–spatial functions (it's better at putting puzzles together), recognition of faces, discrimination of colors, aesthetic and emotional responses, understanding metaphors, and creative mathematical reasoning. Despite these differences, the hemispheres of the brain do not act independently such that some people are truly left-brained and others are right-brained (Colvin et al., 2005). The functions of the left and right hemispheres overlap to some degree, and they tend to respond simultaneously as we focus our attention on one thing or another.

Whether we are talking about language functions or being "left-brained" or "right-brained," we are talking about people whose hemispheres of the cerebral cortex communicate back and forth.

Handedness

Being left-handed was once seen as a deficiency. Left-handed students were made to learn to write with their right hands. We are usually labeled right-handed or left-handed on the basis of our handwriting preferences, yet some people write with one hand and pass a football with the other.

Being left-handed appears to provide a somewhat-greater-than-average probability of language problems, such as dyslexia and stuttering, and health problems such as migraine headaches and allergies (Andreou et al., 2002; Geschwind & Galaburda, 1987; Habib & Robichon, 2003). But there may also be advantages to being left-handed. Left-handed people are more likely than right-handed people to be numbered among the ranks of gifted artists, musicians, and mathematicians (Kilshaw & Annett, 1983; Ostatníková et al., 2002).

The origins of handedness have a genetic component. If one of your parents is left-handed, your chances of being right-handed drop to about 80%. And if both of your parents are left-handed, your chances of also being left-handed are about 1 in 2 (Rosenbaum, 2000).

Split-Brain Experiments

A number of people with severe cases of epilepsy have split-brain operations in which much of the corpus callosum is severed (refer back to Figure 2.9). The purpose of the operation is to confine seizures to one hemisphere of the cerebral cortex rather than allowing a neural tempest to reverberate. Split-brain operations do seem to help people with epilepsy. *What happens when the brain is split in two?*

People who have undergone split-brain operations can be thought of as winding up with two brains, yet under most circumstances their behavior remains ordinary enough. Still, some aspects of hemispheres that have stopped talking to each other are intriguing.

As reported by pioneering brain surgeon Joseph Bogen (1969, 2000), each hemisphere may have a "mind of its own." One split-brain patient reported that her hemispheres frequently disagreed on what she should be wearing. What she meant was that one hand might undo her blouse as rapidly as the other was buttoning it.

Another pioneer of split-brain research, Michael Gazzaniga (2002), found that people with split brains whose eyes are closed may be able to verbally describe an object such as a key when they hold it in one hand, but not when they hold it in the other hand. If a person with a split brain handles a key with his left hand behind a screen, tactile impressions of the key are projected into the right hemisphere, which has little or no language ability (see Figure 2.13). Thus, he will not be able to describe the key. If he holds it in his right hand, he will have no trouble describing it because sensory impressions are projected into the left hemisphere of the cortex, which contains language functions. To further confound matters, if the word *ring* is projected into the left hemisphere while the person is asked what he is handling, he will say "ring," not "key."

This discrepancy between what is felt and what is said occurs only in people with split brains. Even so, people who have undergone split-brain operations tend to lead largely normal lives. And for the rest of us, the two hemispheres work together most of the time, such as when we are playing the piano or solving math problems.

epilepsy
temporary disturbances of brain functions that involve sudden neural discharges

Figure 2.13

A Divided-Brain Experiment

In the drawing on the left, we see that visual sensations in the left visual field are projected in the occipital cortex of the right hemisphere. Visual sensations from the right visual field are projected in the occipital cortex in the left hemisphere. In the divided-brain experiment diagrammed on the right, a person with a severed corpus callosum handles a key with his left hand and perceives the written word *key* in his left visual field. The word "key" is projected in the right hemisphere. Speech, however, is usually a function of the left hemisphere. The written word "ring," perceived by the right visual field, is projected in the left hemisphere. So, when asked what he is handling, the divided-brain subject reports "ring," not "key."

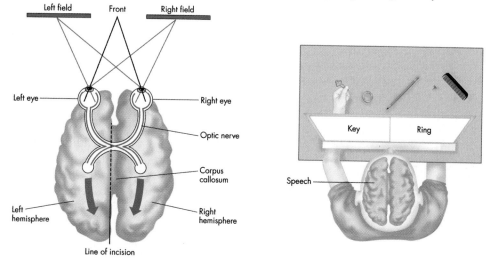

gland
an organ that secretes one or more chemical substances such as hormones, saliva, or milk

endocrine system
the body's system of ductless glands that secrete hormones and release them directly into the bloodstream

hormone
a substance secreted by an endocrine gland that regulates various body functions

pituitary gland
the gland that secretes growth hormone, prolactin, antidiuretic hormone, and other hormones

LO³ The Endocrine System

What is the endocrine system? The body contains two types of glands: glands with ducts and glands without ducts. A *duct* is a passageway that carries substances to specific locations. Saliva, sweat, tears, and breast milk all reach their destinations through ducts. Psychologists are interested in the substances secreted by a number of *ductless* glands because of their effects on behavior and mental processes. The ductless glands make up the endocrine system (see Figure 2.14), and they release hormones into the bloodstream. Hormones are then picked up by specific receptor sites and regulate growth, metabolism, and some forms of behavior. That is, they act only on receptors in certain locations.

Much hormonal action helps the body maintain steady states—fluid levels, blood sugar levels, and so on. Bodily mechanisms measure current levels; when these levels deviate from optimal, they signal glands to release hormones. The maintenance of steady states requires feedback of bodily informa-tion to glands. This type of system is referred to as a *negative feedback loop*. When enough of a hormone has been secreted, the gland is signaled to stop.

The Pituitary and the Hypothalamus

The pituitary gland and the hypothalamus work in close cooperation. The pituitary gland lies below the hypothalamus. Although the pituitary is only about the size of a pea, it is so central to the body's functioning that it has been dubbed the "master gland." The anterior (front) and posterior (back) lobes of the pituitary gland secrete hormones that regulate the functioning of many other glands. *Growth hormone* regulates the growth of muscles, bones, and glands. Children whose growth patterns are abnormally slow may catch up to their age-mates when they obtain growth hormone. *Prolactin* regulates maternal behavior in lower mammals such as rats and stimulates production of milk in women. As a water conservation measure, *vasopressin* (also called *antidiuretic hormone*) inhibits production of urine when the body's fluid levels are low. Vasopressin is also connected with stereotypical paternal behavior in some mammals. *Oxytocin* stimulates labor in pregnant women and is connected with maternal behavior (cuddling and caring for young) in some mammals (Insel, 2000; Taylor et al., 2000b). Obstetricians can induce labor by injecting pregnant women with oxytocin. During nursing, stimulation of the nerve endings of the nipples signals the brain to secrete oxytocin, which then causes the breasts to eject milk.

Although the pituitary gland may be the "master gland," the master has a "commander": the hypothalamus. We know today that the hypothalamus regulates much pituitary activity. The hypothalamus secretes a number of releasing hormones, or "factors," that stimulate the pituitary gland to secrete related hormones. For example, growth hormone releasing factor (hGRF) causes the pituitary to produce growth hormone. Blood vessels between the hypothalamus and the pituitary gland provide a direct route for these factors.

The Pineal Gland

The pineal gland secretes the hormone *melatonin*, which helps regulate the sleep–wake cycle and may affect the onset of puberty. Melatonin may also be connected with aging. In addition, it appears that melatonin is a mild sedative, and some people use it as a sleeping pill (Arendt, 2000; Nagtegaal et al., 2000). Melatonin may also help people adjust to jet lag (Takahashi et al., 2002).

Figure 2.14

The Endocrine Glands

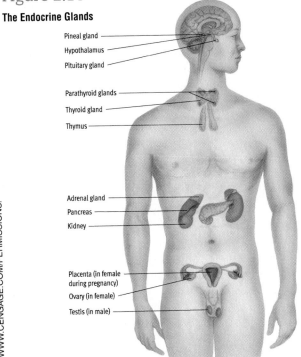

Pineal gland
Hypothalamus
Pituitary gland
Parathyroid glands
Thyroid gland
Thymus
Adrenal gland
Pancreas
Kidney
Placenta (in female during pregnancy)
Ovary (in female)
Testis (in male)

The Thyroid Gland

The thyroid gland could be considered the body's accelerator. It produces *thyroxin,* which affects the body's *metabolism*—the rate at which the body uses oxygen and produces energy. Some people are overweight because of *hypothyroidism,* a condition that results from too little thyroxin. Thyroxin deficiency in children can lead to *cretinism,* a condition characterized by stunted growth and mental retardation. Adults who secrete too little thyroxin may feel tired and sluggish and may put on weight. People who produce too much thyroxin may develop *hyperthyroidism,* which is characterized by excitability, insomnia, and weight loss.

The Adrenal Glands

The adrenal glands, located above the kidneys, have an outer layer, or cortex, and an inner core,

Steroids, Behavior, and Mental Processes

Steroids increase the muscle mass, heighten resistance to stress, and increase the body's energy supply by signaling the liver to release sugar into the bloodstream. The steroid testosterone is connected with the sex drive in both males and females (females secrete some testosterone in the adrenal glands) (Davis, 2000). Anabolic steroids (synthetic versions of the male sex hormone testosterone) have been used, sometimes in tandem with growth hormone, to enhance athletic prowess. Not only do these steroids enhance athletic prowess, but they are also connected with self-confidence, aggressiveness, even memory functioning (Janowsky et al., 2000). Anabolic steroids are generally outlawed in sports, however, the lure of steroids is understandable. Sometimes the difference between an acceptable athletic performance and a great one is rather small. Thousands of athletes try to make it in the big leagues, and the edge offered by steroids—even if minor—can spell the difference between a fumbling attempt and a smashing success. If steroids help, why the fuss? Some of it is related to the ethics of competition—the idea that athletes should "play fair." But steroid use is also linked to liver damage and other health problems.

© ALEX ARDENTI/ALAMY

or medulla. The adrenal cortex is regulated by the pituitary hormone ACTH (adrenocorticotrophic hormone). The adrenal cortex secretes hormones known as *corticosteroids,* or cortical steroids. These hormones regulate the heartbeat, increase resistance to stress, promote muscle development, and cause the liver to release stored sugar, making more energy available in emergencies, such as when you see another car veering toward your own. Epinephrine and norepinephrine are secreted by the adrenal medulla. *Epinephrine,* also known as adrenaline, is manufactured exclusively by the adrenal glands, but norepinephrine (noradrenaline) is also produced elsewhere in the body. (Norepinephrine acts as a neurotransmitter in the brain.) The sympathetic branch of the autonomic nervous system causes the adrenal medulla to release a mixture of epinephrine and norepinephrine that helps arouse the body to cope with threats and stress. Epinephrine is of interest to psychologists because it has emotional as well as physical effects. It intensifies most emotions and is central to the experience of fear and anxiety.

The Testes and the Ovaries

The testes and ovaries also produce steroids, among them testosterone and estrogen. If it were not for the secretion of the male sex hormone *testosterone* about six weeks after conception, we would all develop the external genital organs of females. Testosterone is produced not only by the testes but also in smaller amounts by the adrenal glands. A few weeks after conception, testosterone causes the male's sex organs to develop. During puberty, testosterone stokes the growth of muscle and bone and the development of primary and secondary sex characteristics. *Primary sex characteristics* are directly involved in reproduction and include the increased size of the penis and the sperm-producing ability of the testes. *Secondary sex characteristics* such as the presence of a beard and a deeper voice differentiate males from females but are not directly involved in reproduction.

The ovaries produce *estrogen* and *progesterone* as well as small amounts of testosterone. Estrogen is also produced in smaller amounts by the adrenal glands. Estrogen fosters female reproductive capacity and secondary sex characteristics such as accumulation of fatty tissue in the breasts and hips. Progesterone stimulates growth of the female reproductive organs and prepares the uterus to maintain pregnancy. Estrogen and testosterone have psychological effects as well as biological effects, which we will explore further in Chapter 3.

natural selection
a core concept of the theory of evolution that holds that adaptive genetic variations among members of a species enable individuals with those variations to survive and reproduce

mutation
a sudden variation in an inheritable characteristic, as distinguished from a variation that results from generations of gradual selection

evolutionary psychology
the branch of psychology that studies the ways in which adaptation and natural selection are connected with mental processes and behavior

LO⁴ Evolution and Heredity

Charles Darwin almost missed the boat. Literally. Darwin had volunteered to serve on an expeditionary voyage on the H.M.S. *Beagle*, but the captain, Robert Fitz-Roy, objected to Darwin because of the shape of his nose. Fitz-Roy believed that you could judge a person's character by the outline of his facial features, and Darwin's nose didn't fit the . . . bill. But Fitz-Roy relented, and in the 1830s, Darwin undertook the historic voyage to the Galápagos Islands that led to the development of his theory of evolution.

In 1871 Darwin published *The Descent of Man,* which made the case that humans, like other species, were a product of evolution. He argued that the great apes (chimpanzees, gorillas, and so on) and humans shared a common primate ancestor. Evidence from fossil remains suggests that such a common ancestor might have lived about 13 million years ago (Moyà-Solà et al., 2004). Many people ridiculed Darwin's views because they were displeased with the notion that they might share ancestry with apes. Others argued that Darwin's theory contradicted the Bible's book of Genesis, which stated that humans had been created in one day in the image of God.

What is Darwin's theory of evolution? The concept of a *struggle for existence* lies at the core of Darwin's theory of evolution. At the Galápagos Islands, Darwin found himself immersed in the unfolding of a huge game of "Survivor," with animals and plants competing for food, water, territory, even light. But here the game was for real, and the rewards had nothing to do with fame or fortune. The rewards were reaching sexual maturity and transmitting one's genes into subsequent generations.

As described by evolutionary theory, some creatures have adapted successfully to these challenges, and their numbers have increased. Others have not met the challenges and have fallen back into the distant mists of time. Evidence suggests that 99.99% of all species that ever existed are now extinct (Gould, 2002). Which species prosper and which fade away are determined by natural selection; that is, species that are better adapted to their environment are more likely to survive and reproduce.

When we humans first appeared on Earth, our survival required a different sort of struggle than it does today. We fought or fled from predators such as leopards. We foraged across parched lands for food. But because of the evolution of our intellect, we prevailed. Our numbers have increased. We continue to transmit the traits that led to our selection down through the generations by means of genetic material whose chemical codes are only now being cracked.

Just what is handed down through the generations? The answer is biological, or physiological, structures and processes. Our biology serves as the material base for our behaviors, emotions, and cognitions (our thoughts, images, and plans). Biology somehow gives rise to specific behavioral tendencies in some organisms, such as the chick's instinctive fear of the shadow of the hawk. But the behavior of many species, especially higher species such as humans, is flexible and affected by experience and choice, as well as by heredity.

> Individuals whose traits are better adapted to change are more likely to survive to transmit their traits to the next generation.

According to the theory of evolution, species and individuals compete for the same resources. Natural variations from individual to individual, along with sudden changes in genes (see page 46) called mutations, lead to differences among individuals, differences which affect the ability to adapt to change. Those individuals whose traits are better adapted are more likely to survive (that is, to be "naturally selected"). Survival permits them to reach sexual maturity, to reproduce, and to transmit their features or traits to the next generation. What began as chance variation becomes embedded over the generations—if it fosters survival. Chance variations that hinder survival are likely to disappear from the gene pool.

Evolutionary Psychology: Doing What Comes Naturally

These same concepts of *adaptation* and *natural selection* have also been applied to psychological traits and are key concepts in evolutionary psychology. *What is evolutionary psychology?* Evolutionary psychology studies the ways in which adaptation and natural selection are connected with mental processes and behavior (Buss, 2000; Cory, 2002). Over the eons evolution has provided organisms with advantages such as stronger fins and wings, sharper claws, and camouflage. Human evolution has given rise to various physical traits and also to such diverse activities as language, art, committed relationships, and warfare.

One of the concepts of evolutionary psychology is that not only physical traits but also many patterns of behavior, including social behavior, evolve and can be transmitted genetically from generation to generation. Behavior patterns that help an organism to survive and reproduce may be transmitted to the next generation. Such behaviors are believed to include aggression, strategies of mate selection, even altruism (that is, self-sacrifice of the individual to help perpetuate the family grouping) (Bruene & Ribbert, 2002; McAndrew, 2002). Such behavior patterns are termed *instinctive* or *species-specific* because they evolved within certain species.

What is meant by an "instinct"? An instinct is a stereotyped pattern of behavior that is triggered in a specific situation. Instinctive behavior is nearly identical among the members of the species in which it appears. It tends to resist modification, even when it serves no purpose (as in the interminable barking of some breeds of dogs) or results in punishment. Instinctive behavior also appears when the individual is reared in isolation from others of its kind and thus cannot learn the behavior from experience.

Consider some examples of instinctive behavior. If you place an egg from the nest of a goose a few inches in front of her, she will roll it back to the nest with her beak. However, she won't retrieve it if it's farther away—in the "not my egg" zone. If you rear a white-crowned sparrow in isolation from other sparrows, it will still sing a recognizable species-specific song when it matures. The male stickleback fish instinctively attacks fish (or pieces of painted wood) with the kinds of red bellies that are characteristic of other male sticklebacks. Many psychologists consider language to be "instinctive" among humans. Psychologists are trying to determine what other kinds of human behavior may be instinctive. However, even instinctive behavior can be modified to some degree by learning, and most psychologists agree that the richness and complexity of human behavior are made possible by learning.

Heredity, Genetics, and Behavioral Genetics

What is meant by "heredity"? Heredity defines one's *nature,* which is based on biological structures and processes. Heredity refers to the biological transmission of traits that have evolved from generation to generation. Fish are limited in other ways by their natural traits. Chimpanzees and gorillas can understand many spoken words and express some concepts through nonverbal symbol systems such as American Sign Language. Apes cannot speak, however, apparently because of limitations in the speech areas of the brain.

What is meant by "genetics"? The subfield of biology that studies heredity is called genetics. The field of genetics looks at both species-specific behavior patterns (instincts) and individual differences among the members of a species. *Behavioral genetics* focuses on the contribution of genes to behavior.

Behavioral genetics bridges the sciences of psychology and biology. It is concerned with the genetic transmission of traits that give rise to patterns of behavior. Psychologists are thinking in terms of behavioral genetics when they ask about the inborn reasons why individuals may differ in their behavior and mental processes. For example, some children learn language more quickly than others. Part of the reason may lie in behavioral genetics—their heredity. But some children also experience a richer exposure to language at early ages.

Heredity appears to be a factor in almost all aspects of human behavior, personality, and mental processes (Bouchard & Loehlin, 2001). Examples include sociability, shyness, social dominance, aggressiveness, leadership, thrill seeking, effectiveness as a parent or a therapist, happiness, even interest in arts and crafts (Johnson & Krueger, 2006; Knafo & Plomin, 2006; Leonardo & Hen, 2006).

Heredity is apparently involved in psychological disorders ranging from anxiety and depression to schizophrenia, bipolar disorder, alcoholism, and personality disorders (Farmer et al., 2007; Hill et al., 2007; Metzger et al., 2007; Riley & Kendler, 2005). These disorders are discussed in chapter 12, but here we can note that a study of 794 pairs of female twins by Kendler and his colleagues (2000a) found six aspects of psychological health that were connected with genetic factors: feelings of physical well-being, social relationships, anxiety and depression, substance abuse, use of social support, and self-esteem.

species
a category of biological classification consisting of related organisms who are capable of interbreeding; *homo sapiens*—humans—make up one species

instinct
a stereotyped pattern of behavior that is triggered by a particular stimulus and nearly identical among members of a species, even when they are reared in isolation

heredity
the transmission of traits from parent to offspring by means of genes

genetics
the area of biology that focuses on heredity

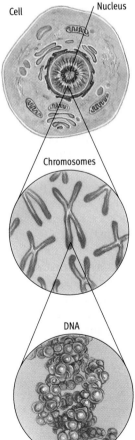

gene
a basic unit of heredity, which is found at a specific point on a chromosome

chromosome
a microscopic rod-shaped body in the cell nucleus carrying genes that transmit hereditary traits from generation to generation; humans normally have 46 chromosomes

DNA
acronym for deoxyribonucleic acid, the substance that forms the basic material of chromosomes; it takes the form of a double helix and contains the genetic code

polygenic
referring to traits that are influenced by combinations of genes

genotype
one's genetic makeup, based on the sequencing of the nucleotides we term A, C, G, and T

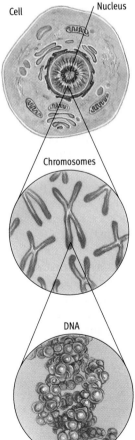

A + T

C + G

The Kendler group also found, however, that the family environment contributed strongly to social relationships, substance abuse, and social support. Although psychological health is influenced by environmental factors, our understanding of the role of heredity continues to expand. Unlocking these mysteries depends on how well we understand genes and chromosomes.

Genes and Chromosomes

Genes are the most basic building blocks of heredity. Genes regulate the development of specific traits. Some traits, such as blood type, are controlled by a single pair of genes. (One gene is derived from each parent.) Other traits are determined by combinations of genes. The inherited component of complex psychological traits, such as intelligence, is believed to be determined by combinations of genes. It is estimated that the cells within your body contain 20,000 to 25,000 genes (Human Genome Sequencing Consortium, 2004).

Genes are segments of chromosomes. That is, chromosomes are made up of strings of genes. Each cell in the body contains 46 chromosomes arranged in 23 pairs. Chromosomes are large complex molecules of DNA (short for *deoxyribonucleic acid*), which has several chemical components. The tightly wound structure of DNA was first demonstrated in the 1950s by James Watson and Francis Crick. DNA takes the form of a double helix—a twisting molecular ladder (see Figure 2.15). The "rungs" of the ladder are made up of chemicals whose names are abbreviated as A, T, C, and G. A always links up with T to complete a rung, and C always combines with G. Therefore, you can describe the *genetic code* in terms of the nucleotides you find along just one of the rungs—e.g., CTGAGTCAC and so on. A single gene can contain hundreds of thousands of base pairs. So if you think of a gene as a word, it can be a few hundred thousand letters long and completely unpronounceable. A group of scientists working together around the globe—referred to as the Human Genome Project—has learned that the sequencing of your DNA consists of about 3 billion DNA sequences spread throughout your chromosomes (Plomin & Crabbe, 2000). These sequences—the order of the chemicals we call A, T, C, and G—caused you to grow arms and not wings, and skin rather than scales. Psychologists debate the extent to which genes influence complex psychological traits such as intelligence, aggressiveness, and happiness, and the appearance of psychological disorders such as schizophrenia. Some traits, such as eye color, are determined by a single pair of genes. Other traits, especially complex psychological traits such as sociability and aggressiveness, are thought to be polygenic—that is, influenced by combinations of genes.

Your genetic code provides your genotype—that is, your full genetic potential, as determined by the sequencing of the chemicals in your DNA.

Cell

Nucleus

Chromosomes

DNA

Figure 2.15

Cells, Chromosomes, and DNA

A. The nuclei of cells contain chromosomes. **B.** Chromosomes are made up of DNA. **C.** Segments of DNA are made up of genes. The genetic code—that is the order of the chemicals A, G, T, and C—determines your species and all those traits that can be inherited, from the color of your eyes to predispositions toward many psychological traits and abilities, including sociability and musical talent.

But the person you see in the mirror was also influenced by your early experiences in the home, injuries, adequacy of nourishment, educational experiences, and numerous other environmental influences. Therefore, you see the outer appearance of your phenotype, including the hairstyles of the day. Your phenotype is the manner in which your genetic code manifests itself because of your experiences and environmental circumstances. Your genotype enables you to acquire language. Your phenotype reveals that you are likely to be speaking English if you were reared in the United States or Spanish if you were reared in Mexico (or both, if you are Mexican American).

Your genotype provides what psychologists refer to as your nature. Your phenotype represents the interaction of your nature (heredity) and your nurture (environmental influences) in the origins of your behavior and mental processes. Psychologists are especially interested in the roles of nature and nurture in intelligence and psychological disorders. Our genotypes provide us with physical traits that set the stage for certain behaviors. But none of us is the result of heredity alone. Environmental factors such as nutrition, learning opportunities, cultural influences, exercise, and (unfortunately) accident and illness also determine our phenotypes, and whether genetically possible behaviors will be displayed. Behavior and mental processes represent the interaction of nature and nurture. A potential Shakespeare who is reared in poverty and never taught to read or write will not create a *Hamlet*.

We normally receive 23 chromosomes from our father's sperm cell and 23 chromosomes from our mother's egg cell (ovum). When a sperm cell fertilizes an ovum, the chromosomes form 23 pairs. The 23rd pair consists of sex chromosomes, which determine whether we are female or male. We all receive an X sex chromosome (so called because of the X shape) from our mother. If we also receive an X sex chromosome from our father, we develop into a female. If we receive a Y sex chromosome (named after the Y shape) from our father, we develop into a male. In the following section, we observe the unfortunate results that may occur when people do not receive the normal complement of chromosomes from their parents.

When people do not have the normal number of 46 chromosomes (23 pairs), physical and behavioral abnormalities may result. Most persons with Down syndrome, for example, have an extra, or third, chromosome on the 21st pair. Persons with Down syndrome have a downward-sloping fold of skin at the inner corners of the eyes, a round face, a protruding tongue, and a broad, flat nose. They are cognitively impaired and usually have physical problems that cause death by middle age (Schupf, 2000).

Kinship Studies

What are kinship studies? Kinship studies are ways in which psychologists compare the presence of traits and behavior patterns in people who are biologically related or unrelated to help determine the role of genetic factors in their occurrence. The more *closely* people are related, the more *genes* they have in common. Identical twins share 100% of their genes. Parents and children have 50% of their genes in common, as do siblings (brothers and sisters). Aunts and uncles related by blood have a 25% overlap with nieces and nephews. First cousins share 12.5% of their genes. If genes are involved in a trait or behavior pattern, people who are more closely related should be more likely to show similar traits or behavior. Psychologists and behavioral geneticists are especially interested in running kinship studies with twins and adopted individuals (Plomin, 2002).

Twin Studies

The fertilized egg cell (ovum) that carries genetic messages from both parents is called a *zygote*. Now and then, a zygote divides into two cells that separate, so that instead of developing into a single person, it develops into two people with the same genetic makeup. Such people are identical, or monozygotic (MZ), twins. If the woman releases two ova in the same month and they are both fertilized, they develop into fraternal, or dizygotic (DZ), twins. DZ twins, like other siblings, share 50% of their genes. MZ twins are important in the study of the relative influences of nature (heredity) and nurture (the environment) because differences between MZ twins are the result of nurture. (They do

phenotype
one's actual development and appearance, as based on one's genotype and environmental influences

nature
the inborn, innate character of an organism

nurture
the sum total of the environmental factors that affect an organism from conception onward

sex chromosomes
the 23rd pair of chromosomes, whose genetic material determines the sex of the individual

Down syndrome
a condition caused by an extra chromosome on the 21st pair and characterized by mental deficiency, a broad face, and slanting eyes

monozygotic (MZ) twins
twins that develop from a single fertilized ovum that divides in two early in prenatal development; MZ twins thus share the same genetic code; also called *identical twins*

dizygotic (DZ) twins
twins that develop from two fertilized ova and who are thus as closely related as brothers and sisters in general; also called *fraternal twins*

not differ in their heredity—that is, their nature—because their genetic makeup is the same.)

Twin studies compare the presence of traits and behavior patterns in MZ twins, DZ twins, and other people to help determine the role of genetic factors in their occurrence. If MZ twins show greater similarity on a trait or behavior pattern than DZ twins, a genetic basis for the trait or behavior is suggested.

Twin studies show how strongly genetic factors influence physical features. MZ twins are more likely to look alike and to be similar in height, even to have more similar cholesterol levels than DZ twins. MZ twins also resemble one another more strongly than DZ twins in intelligence and personality traits like sociability, anxiety, friendliness, and conformity, even happiness (Markon et al., 2002; McCourt et al., 1999; McCrae et al., 2000). MZ twins are also more likely than DZ twins to share psychological disorders such as autism, depression, schizophrenia, and even vulnerability to alcoholism (McGue et al., 1992; Plomin, 2000; Veenstra-Vanderweele & Cook, 2003).

Of course, twin studies are not perfect. MZ twins may resemble each other more closely than DZ twins partly because they are treated more similarly. MZ twins frequently are dressed identically, and parents sometimes have difficulty telling them apart.

One way to get around this difficulty is to find and compare MZ twins who were reared in different homes. Then, any similarities between MZ twins reared apart could not be explained by a shared home environment and would appear to be largely a result of heredity. In the fascinating Minnesota Study of Twins Reared Apart (Bouchard et al., 1990; DiLalla et al., 1999; Markon et al., 2002), researchers have been measuring the physiological and psychologi-

cal characteristics of 56 sets of MZ adult twins who were separated in infancy and reared in different homes.

Research shows that MZ twin sisters begin to menstruate about one to two months apart, whereas DZ twins begin to menstruate about a year apart. MZ twins are more alike than DZ twins in their blood pressure, brain wave patterns, even in their speech patterns, gestures, and mannerisms (Hansell et al., 2001; Lensvelt-Mulders & Hettema, 2001; Lykken et al., 1992).

In sum, MZ twins reared apart are about as similar as MZ twins reared together on a variety of measures of intelligence, personality, temperament, occupational and leisure-time interests, and social attitudes. These traits thus would appear to have a genetic underpinning.

Adoption Studies

The results of kinship studies can be confused when relatives share similar environments as well as genes. Adoption studies overcome some of this problem by comparing children who have been separated from their parents at an early age (or in which identical twins are separated at an early age) and reared in different environments. Psychologists look for similarities between children and their adoptive and natural parents. When children reared by adoptive parents are more similar to their natural parents in a particular trait, strong evidence exists for a genetic role in the development of that trait.

In later chapters we will see that psychologists have been particularly interested in the use of adoption studies to sort out the effects of nature and nurture in the development of personality traits, intelligence, and various psychological disorders. Such traits and disorders apparently represent the interaction of complex groupings of genes as well as environmental influences.

PETER CADE/GETTY IMAGES

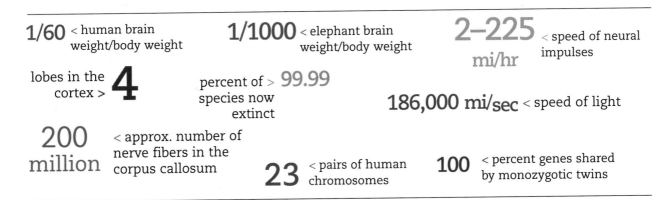

1/60 < human brain weight/body weight

1/1000 < elephant brain weight/body weight

2–225 mi/hr < speed of neural impulses

lobes in the cortex > 4

percent of > 99.99 species now extinct

186,000 mi/sec < speed of light

200 million < approx. number of nerve fibers in the corpus callosum

23 < pairs of human chromosomes

100 < percent genes shared by monozygotic twins

REVIEW

HE DID

PSYCH2 puts a multitude of study aids at your fingertips.
After reading the chapters, check out these resources for further help:

- **Chapter in Review cards**, found in the back of your book, include all learning outcomes, definitions, and visual summaries for each chapter.

- **Online printable flash cards** give you three additional ways to check your comprehension of key concepts.

Other great ways to help you study include **interactive games and online tutorial quizzes with feedback**.

You can find it all at **www.CengageBrain.com**.

CHAPTER 3

Learning Outcomes

LO [1] Explain prenatal development and the role that sex hormones play

LO [2] Explain the physical, cognitive, moral, social, and emotional development of children

LO [3] Explain the physical, cognitive, moral, social, and emotional development of adolescents

LO [4] Explain the physical, cognitive, moral, social, and emotional development of adults

The Voyage *Through* the Life Span

"Billions make the voyage, yet each is unique."

We have a story to tell. An important story. A fascinating story. It is your story. It is about the remarkable voyage you have already taken through childhood and adolescence. It is about the unfolding of your adult life. Billions have made this voyage before. You have much in common with them. Yet you are unique, and things will happen to you, and because of you, that have never happened before.

Developmental psychologists are interested in studying our voyage through the life span for several reasons. The discovery of early influences and developmental sequences helps psychologists understand adults. Psychologists are also interested in the effects of genetic factors, early interactions with parents and siblings, and the school and community on traits such as aggressiveness and intelligence.

Developmental psychologists seek to learn the causes of developmental abnormalities. For example, should pregnant women abstain from smoking and drinking? (Yes.) Is it safe for a pregnant woman to take aspirin for a headache or tetracycline to ward off a bacterial infection? (Perhaps not. Ask your obstetrician.) What factors contribute to child abuse? Some developmental psychologists focus on adult development. For example, what conflicts and disillusionments can we expect as we voyage through our thirties, forties, and fifties? The information acquired by developmental psychologists can help us make decisions about how we rear our children and lead our own lives.

Let us now turn to prenatal developments—the changes that occur between conception and birth. They are spectacular, but they occur "out of sight."

Truth or Fiction?

What do you think?

Folklore, common sense, or nonsense? Place a T for "True" or F for "False" on the lines provided (you'll learn the answers as you read through the text).

___ Your heart started beating when you were only one-fifth of an inch long and weighed a fraction of an ounce.

___ Prior to six months or so of age, "out of sight" is literally "out of mind."

___ The architect Frank Lloyd Wright designed New York's innovative spiral-shaped Guggenheim Museum when he was sixty-five years old.

___ Alzheimer's disease is a normal part of aging.

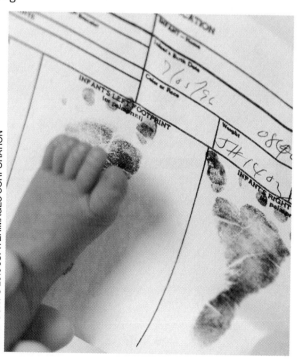

LO¹ Prenatal Development

The most dramatic gains in height and weight occur during prenatal development. *What developments occur from conception through birth?* Within nine months, the newly conceived organism develops from a nearly microscopic cell to a newborn child about twenty inches long. Its weight increases a billion-fold!

During the months following conception, the single cell formed by the union of sperm and egg—the zygote—multiplies, becoming two cells, then four, then eight, and so on.

Conception takes place in a fallopian tube. Following conception, the zygote divides repeatedly as it proceeds on its three- to four-day voyage to the

Figure 3.1

A Human Fetus at Twelve Weeks
By the end of the first trimester, formation of all the major organ systems is complete. Fingers and toes are fully formed, and the sex of the fetus can be determined visually.

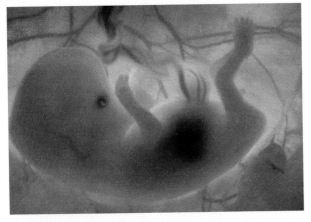

A Human Fetus at Four Months
At this midway point between conception and birth, the fetus is covered with fine, downy hair, called *lanugo.*

> **The heart will continue to beat without rest every minute of every day for most of a century, perhaps longer.**

uterus. The ball-like mass of multiplying cells wanders about the uterus for another three to four days before beginning to implant in the uterine wall. Implantation takes another week or so. The period from conception to implantation is called the germinal stage.

The *embryonic stage* lasts from implantation until about the eighth week of development. During this stage, the major body organ systems take form. As you can see from Figure 3.1, the growth of the head precedes that of other parts of the body. The growth of the organs—heart, lungs, and so on—also precedes the growth of the extremities. The relatively early *maturation* of the brain and the organ systems allows them to participate in the nourishment and further development of the embryo. The heart will continue to beat without rest every minute of every day for most of a century, perhaps longer.

During the second month, the nervous system begins to transmit messages. By five to six weeks, the embryo is only a quarter-inch to a half-inch long, yet nondescript sex organs have formed. By about the seventh week, the genetic code (XY or XX) begins to assert itself, causing the sex organs to differentiate. If a Y sex chromosome is present, testes form and begin to produce *androgens* (male sex hormones), which further masculinize the sex organs. In the absence of these hormones, the embryo develops sex organs typical of the female, regardless of its genetic code. However, individuals with a male genetic code would be sterile. By the end of the second month, the head has become rounded and the facial features distinct—all in an embryo that is about one inch long and weighs one-thirtieth of an ounce.

As it develops, the embryo is suspended within a protective amniotic sac in the mother's uterus. The sac is surrounded by a clear membrane and contains amniotic fluid. The fluid is a sort of natural air bag, allowing the child to move or even jerk around without injury. It also helps maintain an even temperature.

Truth

During the fourth week, a primitive heart begins to beat and pump blood—in an organism that is one-fifth of an inch long.

From now until birth, the embryo exchanges nutrients and wastes with the mother through the placenta. The embryo is connected to the placenta by the umbilical cord. The placenta is connected to the mother by blood vessels in the uterine wall.

The *fetal stage* lasts from the beginning of the third month until birth. By the end of the third month, the major organ systems and the fingers and toes have formed. In the middle of the fourth month, the mother usually detects the first fetal movements. By the end of the sixth month, the fetus moves its limbs so vigorously that mothers often feel that they are being kicked. The fetus opens and shuts its eyes, sucks its thumb, alternates between periods of being awake and sleeping, and responds to light. It also turns somersaults, which can be perceived by the mother.

During the three months prior to birth, the organ systems of the fetus continue to mature. The heart and lungs become increasingly capable of sustaining independent life. The fetus gains about five-and-a-half pounds and doubles in length. Newborn boys average about seven-and-a-half pounds and newborn girls about seven pounds.

LO² Childhood

Childhood begins with birth. When my children are enjoying themselves, I kid them and say, "Stop having fun. You're a child, and childhood is the worst time of life." I get a laugh because they know that childhood is supposed to be the best time of life—a time for play and learning and endless possibilities. In this section we see that childhood is an exciting time of physical, cognitive, and social and emotional developments.

Physical Development

During infancy—the first two years of childhood—dramatic gains in height and weight continue. Babies usually double their birth weight in about five months and triple it by their first birthday (Kuczmarski et al., 2000). Their height increases by about ten inches in the first year. Children grow another four to six inches during the second year and gain some four to seven pounds. After that, they gain about two to three inches a year until they reach the adolescent growth spurt. Weight gains also remain fairly even at about four to six pounds per year until the spurt. Other aspects of physical development in childhood include reflexes and perceptual development.

Reflexes

Soon after you were born, a doctor or nurse probably pressed her fingers against the palms of your hands. Although you would have had no idea what to do

in response, most likely you grasped the fingers firmly—so firmly that you could have been lifted from your cradle!

Grasping at birth is inborn, an example of the importance of nature in human development. Grasping is one of the baby's reflexes. Reflexes are simple, unlearned, stereotypical responses elicited by specific stimuli. Newborn children do not know that it is necessary to eat to survive. Fortunately, rooting and sucking reflexes cause them to eat. They turn their head toward stimuli that prod or stroke the cheek, chin, or corner of the mouth. This is termed rooting. They suck objects that touch their lips. Reflexes are essential to survival and occur automatically—that is, without thinking about them.

Newborns use the withdrawal reflex to avoid painful stimuli. In the startle, or Moro, reflex, they draw up their legs and arch their backs in response to sudden noises, bumps, or loss of support while being held. They grasp objects that press against the palms of their hands (the grasp, or palmar, reflex). They fan their toes when the soles of their feet are stimulated (the Babinski reflex). Pediatricians test these reflexes to assess babies' neural functioning. Babies also breathe, sneeze, cough, yawn, blink, defecate, and urinate reflexively.

Motor Development

The motor development of the child refers to the progression from simple acts like lifting the head to running around. Maturation and experience both

placenta
a membrane that permits the exchange of nutrients and waste products between the mother and her developing child but does not allow the maternal and fetal bloodstreams to mix

umbilical cord
a tube between the mother and her developing child through which nutrients and waste products are conducted

reflex
a simple unlearned response to a stimulus

rooting
the turning of an infant's head toward a touch, such as by the mother's nipple

fixation time
the amount of time spent looking at a visual stimulus

play key roles in motor development (Muir, 2000; Pryce et al., 2001; Roncesvalles et al., 2001). Maturation of the brain is a key to motor development. Motor development provides some of the most fascinating changes in infants, in part because so much seems to happen so quickly—and so much of it during the first year. Children go through a sequence that includes rolling over, sitting up, crawling, creeping, walking, and running. The ages at which infants first engage in these activities vary,

but the sequence generally remains the same (see Figure 3.2). Invariant sequences suggest an unfolding of the genetic code (maturation).

The role of maturation in areas such as physical development (for example, gains in height and weight and the effects of puberty), language development, and motor development is clear. But environmental factors are also involved. Children may have certain genetic potentials for body size and growth rates, but they do not reach them unless environmental factors such as nutrition, relatively clean air, and so on are available. Children do not understand or produce language until their genetic codes spark the development of certain structures and processes in the brain. But the environment is also involved. Children learn the languages used in their homes and communities. They do not speak foreign tongues without being exposed to them.

Perceptual Development

Newborn children spend about sixteen hours a day sleeping and do not have much opportunity to learn about the world. Yet they perceive the world reasonably well soon after birth. Within a couple of days, infants can follow, or "track," a moving light with their eyes (Kellman & von Hofsten, 1992). By three months, they can discriminate most colors (Banks & Shannon, 1993; Teller, 1998). Newborns are nearsighted, but by about four months, infants focus on distant objects about as well as adults do.

The visual preferences of infants are measured by the amount of time, termed **fixation time**, they spend looking at one stimulus instead of another. In classic research by Robert Fantz (1961), two-month-old infants preferred visual

Figure 3.2

Motor Development

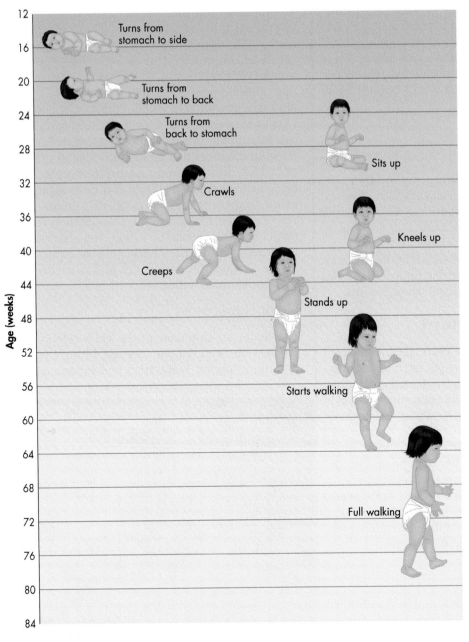

Figure 3.3

Two-Month-Olds' Preferences for Visual Stimuli

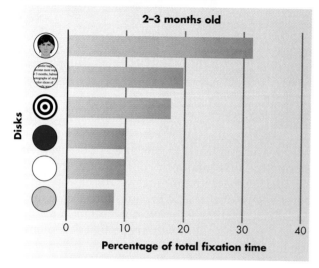

stimuli that resembled the human face to news print, a bull's eye, and featureless red, white, and yellow disks (see Figure 3.3).

Classic research has shown that infants tend to respond to cues for depth by the time they are able to crawl (at about six to eight months). Most also have the good sense to avoid crawling off ledges and table tops into open space (Campos et al., 1978).

Normal newborns hear well. Most newborns reflexively turn their heads toward unusual sounds. This finding, along with findings about visual tracking, suggests that infants are preprogrammed to survey their environments. Speaking or singing softly in a low-pitched tone soothes infants. This is why lullabies help infants fall asleep.

Three-day-old babies prefer their mother's voice to those of other women, but they do not show a preference for their father's voice (DeCasper & Prescott, 1984; Freeman et al., 1993). Babies, of course, have had months of "experience" in the uterus. For at least two or three months before birth, they have been able to hear. Because they are predominantly exposed to sounds produced by their mother, learning may contribute to newborn preferences.

Cognitive Development

The ways in which children mentally represent and think about the world—that is, their *cognitive development*—are explored in this section. Because cognitive functioning develops over many years, young children have ideas about the world that differ considerably from those of adults. Many of these ideas are charming but illogical—at least to adults. Let us consider three views of cognitive development. We will begin with Jean Piaget's stage theory of cognitive development. Then we will turn to the views of the Russian psychologist Lev Semenovich Vygotsky whose approach is quite different from Piaget's but is enjoying a rebirth in popularity. Then we will focus on Lawrence Kohlberg's theory of moral development.

Jean Piaget's Cognitive–Developmental Theory

Jean Piaget (1896–1980) earned his Ph.D. in biology. In 1920 he obtained a job at the Binet Institute in Paris, where work on intelligence tests was being conducted. His first task was to adapt English verbal reasoning items for use with French children. To do so, he had to try out the items on children in various age groups and see whether they could arrive at correct answers. The task was boring until Piaget became intrigued by the children's *wrong* answers. Another investigator might have shrugged them off, but Piaget perceived patterns in the children's "mistakes." The wrong answers reflected consistent, if illogical, cognitive processes. Piaget's observations led to his theory of cognitive development.

Assimilation Piaget described human thought, or intelligence, in terms of the concepts of assimilation and accommodation. Assimilation means responding to a new stimulus through existing cognitive structures.

Jean Piaget

DOUG GOODMAN/PHOTO RESEARCHERS, INC.

schema
according to Piaget, a hypothetical mental structure that permits the classification and organization of new information

accommodation
according to Piaget, the modification of schemas so that information inconsistent with existing schemas can be integrated or understood

object permanence
recognition that objects removed from sight still exist, as demonstrated in young children by continued pursuit

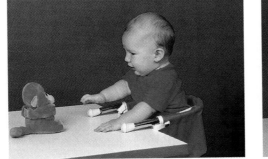 

Figure 3.4

Object Permanence

To this infant, who is in the early part of the sensorimotor stage, out of sight is truly out of mind. Once a sheet of paper is placed between the infant and the toy animal, the infant loses all interest in it. The toy is apparently not yet mentally represented.

Infants, for example, usually try to place new objects in their mouth to suck, feel, or explore. Piaget would say that the child is assimilating a new toy to the sucking schema. A schema is a pattern of action or a "mental structure" involved in acquiring or organizing knowledge.

Accommodation Accommodation is the creation of new ways of responding to objects or looking at the world. In accommodation, children transform existing schemas to incorporate new events. Children (and adults) accommodate to objects and situations that cannot be integrated into existing schemas. For example, children who study biology learn that whales cannot be assimilated into the "fish" schema. They accommodate by constructing new schemas, such as "mammals without legs that live in the sea." The ability to accommodate to novel stimuli advances as a result of maturation and experience. Let us apply these concepts to the stages of cognitive development.

Piaget's Stages of Cognitive Development

What are Piaget's stages of cognitive development? Piaget hypothesized that children's cognitive processes develop in an orderly sequence. Some children may be more advanced than others, but the sequence remains the same. Piaget (1963) identified four major stages of cognitive development: sensorimotor, preoperational, concrete operational, and formal operational.

The Sensorimotor Stage The newborn infant is capable of assimilating novel stimuli only to existing reflexes (or ready-made schemas) such as the rooting and sucking reflexes. But by the time an infant reaches the age of one month, he or she already shows purposeful behavior by repeating behavior patterns that

are pleasurable, such as sucking his or her hand. During the first month or so, an infant apparently does not connect stimuli perceived through different senses. Reflexive turning toward sources of auditory and olfactory stimulation cannot be considered purposeful searching. But within the first few months the infant begins to coordinate vision with grasping, to look at the object being held or touched.

A three- or four-month-old infant may be fascinated by her own hands and legs. The infant may become absorbed in watching herself open and close her fists. The infant becomes increasingly interested in acting on the environment to make interesting results (such as the sound of a rattle) last longer or occur again. Behavior becomes increasingly intentional and purposeful. Between four and eight months of age, the infant explores cause-and-effect relationships such as the thump made by tossing an object or the swinging that results from kicking a hanging toy.

For most infants younger than six months, objects are not yet represented mentally. For this reason, as you can see in Figure 3.4, a child makes no effort to search for an object that has been removed or placed behind a screen. By the age of eight to twelve months, however, infants realize that objects removed from sight still exist and attempt to find them. In this way, they show what is known as object permanence, thereby making it possible to play peekaboo.

Between one and two years of age, children begin to show interest in how things are constructed. It may be for this reason that they persistently touch and finger their parents' faces and their own. Toward the end of the second year, children begin to engage in mental trial and error before they try out overt behaviors. For example, when they look for an object you have removed, they will no longer begin their search in the last place they saw it. Rather, they may follow you, assuming you are carrying the object even though it is not visible. It is as though they are

Truth

It is true that "out of sight" is literally "out of mind" prior to the age of six months or so.

Table 3.1

Examples of Preoperational Thought

Type of Thought	Sample Questions	Typical Answers
Egocentrism	Why does it get dark out? Why does the sun shine? Why is there snow?	So I can go to sleep. To keep me warm. For me to play in.
Animism	Why do trees have leaves? Why do stars twinkle?	To keep them warm. Because they're happy and cheerful.
Artificialism	What makes it rain? Why is the sky blue? What is the wind?	Someone emptying a watering can. Somebody painted it. A man blowing.

anticipating failure in searching for the object in the place where they last saw it.

Because the first stage of development is dominated by learning to coordinate perception of the self and of the environment with motor activity, Piaget termed it the sensorimotor stage. This stage comes to a close with the acquisition of the basics of language at about age two.

The Preoperational Stage The preoperational stage is characterized by the use of words and symbols to represent objects and relationships among them. But be warned—any resemblance between the logic of children between the ages of two and seven and your own logic may be coincidental. Children may use the same words as adults, but this does not mean their views of the world are the same.

To a preoperational child, right is right and wrong is wrong. Why? "Because!"—that's why.

Preoperational children tend to think one-dimensionally—to focus on one aspect of a problem or situation at a time.

One consequence of one-dimensional thinking is egocentrism. Preoperational children cannot understand that other people do not see things the same way they do. When my daughter Allyn was two and a half. I asked her to tell me about a trip to the store with her mother. "You tell me," she replied. It seemed she did not understand that I could not see the world through her eyes.

To egocentric preoperational children, all the world's a stage that has been erected to meet their needs and amuse them. When asked, "What are television sets for?", they may answer, "To watch my favorite shows and cartoons." Preoperational children also show *animism*. They attribute life and consciousness to physical objects like the sun and the moon. They also show *artificialism*. They believe that environmental events like rain and thunder are human inventions. Asked what causes thunder, a four-year-old may reply 'A man grumbling.' Examples of egocentrism, animism, and artificialism are shown in Table 3.1.

To gain further insight into preoperational thinking, find a three- or four-year-old and try these mini-experiments:

- Pour water from a tall, thin glass into a low, wide glass. Now, ask the child whether the low, wide glass contains more, less, or the same amount of water that was in the tall, thin glass. If the child says that they hold the same amount of water, the child is correct. But if the child errs, why do you think this is so?

- Now flatten a ball of clay into a pancake, and ask the child whether you wind up with more, less, or the same amount of clay? If the child errs again, why do you think this is so?

To arrive at the correct answers to these questions, children must understand the law of conservation. This law holds that basic properties of substances such as mass, weight, and volume remain the same—that is, are *conserved*—when one changes superficial properties such as their shape or arrangement.

Conservation requires the ability to think about, or *center* on, two aspects of a situation at once, such as height and width. Conserving the mass, weight, or volume of a substance requires the recognition that a change in one dimension can compensate for a change in another. But the preoperational boy in Figure 3.5 focuses on only one dimension at a time. First he is shown two short, squat glasses of water and agrees that they contain the same amount of water. Then, while he watches, water is poured from a squat glass into a tall, thin glass. Now he is asked which glass contains more water. After mulling over the problem, he points to the tall glass. Why? Because when he looks at the glasses he is "overwhelmed" by the fact that the thinner glass is taller. The preoperational child focuses

sensorimotor stage the first of Piaget's stages of cognitive development, characterized by coordination of sensory information and motor activity, early exploration of the environment, and lack of language

preoperational stage the second of Piaget's stages, characterized by illogical use of words and symbols, spotty logic, and egocentrism

egocentrism according to Piaget, the assumption that others view the world as one does oneself

conservation according to Piaget, recognition that basic properties of substances such as weight and mass remain the same when superficial features change

objective responsibility according to Piaget, the assignment of blame according to the amount of damage done rather than the motives of the actor

concrete operational stage Piaget's third stage, characterized by logical thought concerning tangible objects, conservation, and subjective morality

decentration simultaneous focusing on more than one dimension of a problem, so that flexible, reversible thought becomes possible

subjective moral judgment according to Piaget, moral judgment that is based on the motives of the perpetrator

on the most apparent dimension of the situation—in this case, the greater height of the thinner glass. He does not realize that the increased width of the squat glass compensates for the decreased height. By the way, if you ask him whether any water has been added or taken away in the pouring process, he readily says no. But if you then repeat the question about which glass contains *more* water, he again points to the taller glass. If all this sounds rather illogical, that is because it is illogical—or, in Piaget's terms, preoperational.

Piaget (1997) found that the moral judgment of preoperational children is also one-dimensional. Five-year-olds tend to be slaves to rules and authority. When you ask them why something should be done in a certain way, they may insist, "Because that's the way to do it!" or "Because Mommy says so!" Right is right and wrong is wrong. Why? "Because!"—that's why.

According to most older children and adults, an act is a crime only when there is criminal intent. Accidents may be hurtful, but the perpetrators are usually seen as blameless. But in the court of the one-dimensional, preoperational child, there is objective responsibility. People are sentenced (and harshly!) on the basis of the amount of damage they have done, not their motives or intentions. To demonstrate objective responsibility, Piaget would tell children stories and ask them which character was naughtier and why. John, for example, accidentally breaks fifteen cups when he opens a door. Henry breaks one cup when he sneaks into a kitchen cabinet to find forbidden jam. The preoperational child usually judges John to be naughtier. Why? Because he broke more cups.

The Concrete Operational Stage By about age seven, the typical child is entering the stage of concrete operations. In this stage, which lasts until about age twelve, children show the beginnings of the capacity for adult logic. However, their logical thoughts, or *operations*, generally involve tangible objects rather than abstract ideas. Concrete operational children are capable of decentration; they can center on two dimensions of a problem at once. This attainment has implications for moral judgments, conservation, and other intellectual undertakings.

Children now become subjective in their moral judgments. When assigning guilt, they center on the motives of wrongdoers as well as on the amount of damage done. Concrete operational children judge Henry more harshly than John because John's misdeed was an accident.

Concrete operational children understand the laws of conservation. The boy in Figure 3.5, now a few years older, would say that the squat glass still contains the same amount of juice. If asked why, he might reply, "Because you can pour it back into the other one." Such an answer also suggests awareness of the concept of *reversibility*—the recognition that many processes can be reversed or undone so that things are restored to their previous condition. Centering simultaneously on the height and the width of the glasses, the boy recognizes that the loss in height compensates for the gain in width.

Figure 3.5

Conservation

Children in this stage are less egocentric. They are able to take on the roles of others and to view the world, and themselves, from other people's perspectives. They recognize that people see things in different ways because of different situations and different sets of values.

During the concrete operational stage, children's own sets of values begin to emerge and acquire stability. Children come to understand that feelings of love between them and their parents can endure even when someone is temporarily angry or disappointed. We continue our discussion of Piaget's theory—his stage of formal operations—later in the chapter in the section on adolescence.

Evaluation of Piaget's Theory A number of questions have been raised concerning the accuracy of Piaget's views. Among them are these:

- *Was Piaget's timing accurate?* Some critics argue that Piaget's methods led him to underestimate children's abilities (Bjorklund, 2000; Meltzoff & Gopnik, 1997). Other researchers using different methods have found, for example, that preschoolers are less egocentric and that children are capable of conservation at earlier ages than Piaget thought.

- *Does cognitive development occur in stages?* Cognitive events such as egocentrism and conservation appear to develop more continuously than Piaget thought—that is, they may not occur in stages (Bjorklund, 2000; Flavell, 2000). Although cognitive developments appear to build on previous cognitive developments, the process may be more gradual than stage-like.

- *Are developmental sequences always the same?* Here, Piaget's views have fared better. It seems there is no variation in the sequence in which cognitive developments occur.

In sum, Piaget's theoretical edifice has been rocked, but it has not been reduced to rubble. Now let us consider the views of Vygotsky.

Lev Vygotsky (1896–1934) was a Russian psychologist whose work was banned in communist Russia. Seventy years after his death, his work has been rediscovered. Unlike Piaget, Vygotsky was not a stage theorist. Instead, he saw the transmission of knowledge as cumulative, and focused on the ways in which children's interactions with their elders enhance their cognitive development.

Lev Vygotsky's Sociocultural Theory

The term *sociocultural theory* has different meanings. For example, the term can refer to the roles of factors such as ethnicity and gender in behavior and mental processes. Vygotsky's sociocultural theory focuses instead on the ways in which children's cognitive development is influenced by the cultures in which they are reared and the people who teach them.

Vygotsky's theory (1978) focuses on the transmission of information and cognitive skills from generation to generation. The transmission of skills involves teaching and learning, but Vygotsky was no behaviorist. He did not view learning as a mechanical process that can be described in terms of the conditioning of units of behavior. Rather, he focused more generally on how the child's social interaction with adults, largely in the home, organized a child's learning experiences in such a way that the child can obtain cognitive skills—such as computation or reading skills—and use them to acquire information. Like Piaget, Vygotsky saw the child's functioning as adaptive (Piaget & Smith, 2000), and the child adapts to his or her social and cultural interactions.

What are the key concepts of Vygotsky's theory of cognitive development? Key concepts in Vygotsky's theory include the zone of proximal development and *scaffolding*. The word *proximal* means "nearby" or "close," as in the words *approximate* and *proximity*. The zone of proximal development (ZPD) refers to a range of tasks that a child can carry out with the help of someone who is more skilled (Haenen, 2001). The "zone" refers to the relationship between the child's abilities and what she or he can do with help from others. Adults or older children best guide the child through this zone by gearing their assistance to the child's capabilities (Flavell et al., 2002).

Within the zone we find an apprenticeship in which the child works with, and learns from, others (Meijer & Elshout, 2001). When learning with others, the child tends to internalize—or bring inward—the conversations and explanations that help him or her gain skills (Prior & Welling, 2001; Vygotsky, 1962; Yang, 2000). Children not only learn the meanings of words from teachers but also learn ways of talking to themselves about solving problems within a cultural context (DeVries, 2000). Outer speech becomes inner speech. What was the teacher's becomes the child's. What was a social and cultural context becomes embedded within the child (Moro & Rodriguez, 2000); thus we have the term, *sociocultural theory*.

A *scaffold* is a temporary skeletal structure that enables workers to fabricate a building, bridge, or

> **zone of proximal development (ZPD)** Vygotsky's term for the situation in which a child carries out tasks with the help of someone who is more skilled, frequently an adult who represents the culture in which the child develops

Proximal means "nearby" or "close."

scaffolding Vygotsky's term for temporary cognitive structures or methods of solving problems that help the child as he or she learns to function independently

preconventional level according to Kohlberg, a period during which moral judgments are based largely on expectation of rewards or punishments

other, more permanent, structure. Cognitive scaffolding refers to the temporary support provided by a parent or teacher to a child who is learning to perform a task. Guidance decreases as the child becomes more skilled and self-sufficient (Clarke-Stewart & Beck, 1999; Maccoby, 1992). In Vygotsky's theory, teachers and parents provide children with problem-solving methods that serve as cognitive scaffolding while the child gains the ability to function independently. A child's instructors may offer advice on sounding out letters and words that provide a temporary support until reading "clicks" and the child no longer needs the device. Children may be offered scaffolding that enables them to use their fingers to do calculations. Eventually, the scaffolding is removed and the cognitive structures stand alone.

Piaget's focus was largely maturational. It was assumed that maturation of the brain allowed the child to experience new levels of insights and suddenly develop new kinds of problem-solving. Vygotsky focused on the processes in the teacher–learner relationship. To Vygotsky, cognitive development was about culture and social interaction. Let us now turn to another aspect of cognitive development—the ways in

which children (and adults) arrive at judgments about what is right and what is wrong.

Lawrence Kohlberg's Theory of Moral Development

How do children reason about right and wrong? Cognitive–developmental theorist Lawrence Kohlberg (1981) used the following tale in his research into children's moral reasoning:

> In Europe a woman was near death from a special kind of cancer. There was one drug that the doctors thought might save her. It was a form of radium that a druggist in the same town had recently discovered. The drug was expensive to make, but the druggist was charging ten times what the drug cost him to make. He paid $200 for the radium and charged $2,000 for a small dose of the drug. The sick woman's husband, Heinz, went to everyone he knew to borrow the money, but he could only get together about $1,000, which was half of what it cost. He told the druggist that his wife was dying and asked him to sell it cheaper or let him pay later. But the druggist said: "No, I discovered the drug, and I'm going to make money from it." So Heinz got desperate and broke into the man's store to steal the drug for his wife (Kohlberg, 1969).

Heinz is caught in a moral dilemma. In such dilemmas, a legal or social rule (in this case, the law forbidding stealing) is pitted against a strong human need (his desire to save his wife). Children and adults arrive at yes or no answers for different reasons. According to Kohlberg, the reasons can be classified according to the level of moral development they reflect.

As a stage theorist, Kohlberg argues that the stages of moral reasoning follow a specific sequence. Children progress at different rates, and not all children (or adults) reach the highest stage. But the sequence is always the same: Children must go through stage 1 before they enter stage 2, and so on. According to Kohlberg, there are three levels of moral development and two stages within each level.

When it comes to the dilemma of Heinz, Kohlberg believed that people could justify Heinz's theft of the drug or his decision not to steal it by the reasoning of any level or stage of moral development. In other words, Kohlberg was not as interested in the eventual "yes" or "no" as he was in *how a person reasoned* to arrive at yes or no.

The Preconventional Level The **preconventional level** applies to most children through about the age of nine. Children at this level base their moral judgments on the consequences of behavior. For example, stage 1 is oriented toward obedience and punishment. Good behavior is obedient and allows one to avoid punishment. However, a child in stage 1 can decide that Heinz should or should not steal the drug.

In stage 2, good behavior allows people to satisfy their needs and those of others. (Heinz's wife needs the drug; therefore, stealing it—the only way of obtaining it—is not wrong.)

The Conventional Level In the conventional level of moral reasoning, right and wrong are judged by conformity to conventional (familial, religious, societal) standards of right and wrong. According to the stage 3 "good-boy orientation," moral behavior is that which meets the needs and expectations of others. Moral behavior is what is "normal"—what the majority does. (Heinz should steal the drug because that is what a "good husband" would do. It is "natural" or "normal" to try to help one's wife. Or Heinz should *not* steal the drug because "good people do not steal.")

In stage 4, moral judgments are based on rules that maintain the social order. Showing respect for authority and doing one's duty are valued highly. (Heinz *must* steal the drug; it would be his fault if he let his wife die. He would pay the druggist later, when he had the money.) Many people do not mature beyond the conventional level.

The Postconventional Level Postconventional moral reasoning is more complex and focuses on dilemmas in which individual needs are pitted against the need to maintain the social order and on personal conscience. We discuss the postconventional level later in the chapter in the section on adolescence.

Evaluation of Kohlberg's Theory

As Kohlberg's theory predicts, evidence supports the view that the moral judgments of children develop in an upward sequence (Boom et al., 2007). Postconventional thought, if found at all, first occurs in adolescence. Formal-operational thinking is apparently a prerequisite, and education is likely to play a role (Boom et al., 2007; Patenaude et al., 2003). Postconventional reasoning involves understanding of abstract moral principles and empathy with the views and feelings of others.

Kohlberg believed that the stages of moral development were universal, but he may have underestimated the influence of social, cultural, and educational institutions (Dawson, 2002). Parents are also important. Using reason in discipline and discussing the feelings of others advance moral reasoning (Dawson, 2002).

Social and Emotional Development

Social relationships are crucial to us as children. When we are infants, our very survival depends on them. Later in life, they contribute to our feelings of happiness and satisfaction. In this section we discuss aspects of social development, including Erikson's theory of psychosocial development, attachment, and styles of parenting.

Erik Erikson's Stages of Psychosocial Development

According to Erik Erikson, we undergo several stages of psychosocial development *What are Erikson's stages of psychosocial development?* During Erikson's first stage, trust versus mistrust, we depend on our primary caregivers (usually our parents) and come to expect that our environments will—or will not—meet our needs. During early childhood and the preschool years, we begin to explore the environment more actively and try new things. At this time, our relationships with our parents and friends can encourage us to develop *autonomy* (self-direction) and initiative, or feelings of shame and guilt. During the elementary school years, friends and teachers take on more importance, encouraging us to become industrious or to develop feelings of inferiority. We will return to Erikson's stages of development later in the chapter.

Attachment

Psychologist Mary D. Salter Ainsworth (1913–1999) defined attachment as an emotional tie that is formed between one animal or person and another specific individual. Attachment keeps organisms together—it is vital to the survival of the infant—and it tends to endure. The behaviors that define attachment include (1) attempts to maintain contact or nearness, and (2) shows of anxiety when separated. Babies and children try to maintain contact with caregivers to whom they are attached. They engage in eye contact, pull and tug at them, ask to be picked up, and may even jump in front of them in such a way that they will be "run over" if they are not picked up. *How do feelings of attachment develop? What kinds of experiences affect attachment?*

Mary D. Salter Ainsworth

conventional level according to Kohlberg, a period during which moral judgments largely reflect social conventions; a "law and order" approach to morality

trust versus mistrust Erikson's first stage of psychosocial development, during which children do—or do not—come to trust that primary caregivers and the environment will meet their needs

attachment the enduring affectional tie that binds one person to another

© MARVIN S. ROBERTS

The Strange Situation and Patterns of Attachment

The ways in which infants behave in strange situations are connected with their bonds of attachment with their caregivers. Given this fact, Ainsworth and her colleagues (1978) innovated the *strange situation method* to learn how infants respond to separations and reunions with a caregiver (usually the mother) and a stranger. Using this method, Ainsworth and her colleagues identified three major types of attachment, including secure attachment and two types of insecure attachment:

1 *Secure attachment.* Securely attached infants mildly protest their mother's departure, seek interaction upon reunion, and are readily comforted by her.

2 *Avoidant attachment.* Infants who show avoidant attachment are least distressed by their mother's departure. They play by themselves without fuss and ignore their mothers when they return.

3 *Ambivalent /resistant attachment.* Infants with ambivalent /resistant attachment are the most emotional. They show severe signs of distress when their mother leaves and show ambivalence upon reunion by alternately clinging to and pushing their mother away when she returns.

Attachment is connected with the quality of care that infants receive. The parents of securely attached children are more likely to be affectionate and reliable caregivers (Isabella, 1998; Posada et al., 2002). A wealth of research literature speaks of the benefits of secure attachment. For example, secure children are happier, more sociable, and more cooperative than insecure children (Bohlin et al., 2000). At ages five and six, securely attached children are liked better by their peers and teachers, are more competent, and have fewer behavior problems than insecurely attached children (Granot & Mayseless, 2001; Moss & St-Laurent, 2001). In this vein, we can also note that having the primary caregiver present during stressful situations, such as pediatric exams, helps children cope with these situations (Ybarra et al., 2000).

Stages of Attachment

Ainsworth and her colleagues observed infants in many societies, including the African country of Uganda. She noted the efforts of infants to maintain contact with the mother, their protests when separated from her, and their use of her as a base for exploring their environment. At first, infants show *indiscriminate attachment*. That is, they prefer being held or being with someone to being alone, but they are generally willing to be held by unfamiliar people. Specific attachment to the primary caregiver

begins to develop at about four months of age and becomes intense by about seven months of age. Fear of strangers, which develops in some but not all children, follows one or two months later.

From studies such as these, Ainsworth identified three phases of attachment:

1 *The initial-preattachment phase,* which lasts from birth to about three months and is characterized by indiscriminate attachment.

2 *The attachment-in-the-making phase,* which occurs at about three or four months and is characterized by preference for familiar figures.

3 *The clear-cut-attachment phase,* which occurs at about six or seven months and is characterized by intensified depen-dence on the primary caregiver. Fear of strangers, which develops in some but not all children, follows one or two months later.

Theoretical Views of Attachment

Early in the 20th century, behaviorists argued that attachment behaviors are learned through experience. Caregivers feed their infants and tend to their other physiological needs. Thus, infants associate their caregivers with gratification of needs and learn to approach them to meet their needs. The feelings of gratification associated with the meeting of basic needs generalize into feelings of security when the caregiver is present.

However, classic research by psychologist Harry F. Harlow suggests that skin contact may be more important than learning experiences. Harlow noted that infant rhesus monkeys reared without mothers or companions became attached to pieces of cloth in their cages. They maintained contact with them and showed distress when separated from them. Harlow conducted a series of experiments to find out why (Harlow, 1959).

In one study, Harlow placed infant rhesus monkeys in cages with two surrogate mothers, as shown in Figure 3.6. One "mother" was made of wire mesh from which a baby bottle was extended. The other surrogate mother was made of soft, cuddly terrycloth. The infant monkeys spent most of their time clinging to the cloth mother, even though "she" did not gratify their need for food. Harlow concluded that monkeys—and perhaps humans—have an inborn need for contact comfort that is as basic as the need for food. Gratification of the need for contact comfort, rather than food, might be why infant monkeys (and humans) cling to their mothers.

Other researchers, such as ethologist Konrad Lorenz, argue that for many animals, attachment is an instinct—inborn. (Ethologists study the behavioral characteristics of various species of animals.) Attachment, like other instincts, is theorized to

Figure 3.6

Attachment in Infant Monkeys

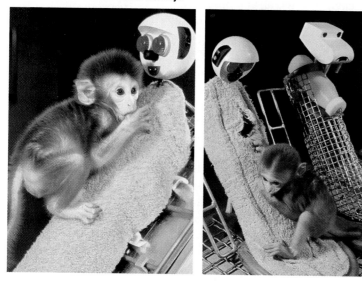

occur in the presence of a specific stimulus and during a critical period of life—that is, a period during which the animal is sensitive to the stimulus.

Some animals become attached to the first moving object they encounter. The formation of an attachment in this manner is therefore called imprinting. Lorenz (1981) became well known when pictures of his "family" of goslings were made public. How did Lorenz acquire his following? He was present when the goslings hatched and during their critical period, and he allowed them to follow him. The critical period for geese and some other animals is bounded, at the younger end, by the age at which they first walk and, at the older end, by the age at which they develop fear of strangers. The goslings followed Lorenz persistently, ran to him when frightened, honked with distress at his departure, and tried to overcome barriers between them. If you substitute crying for honking, it all sounds rather human.

Ainsworth and Bowlby (1991) consider attachment to be instinctive in humans. However, among humans attachment is less related to issues such as locomotion and fear of strangers (which is not universal). Moreover, the critical period with humans is quite extended.

Konrad Lorenz and His Family of Goslings

Parenting Styles

Many psychologists have been concerned about the relationships between parenting styles and the personality development of the child. *What types of parental behavior are connected with variables such as self-esteem, achievement motivation, and independence in children?* Diana Baumrind (1973) has been particularly interested in the connections between parental behavior and the development of *instrumental competence* in their children. (Instrumental competence refers to the ability to manipulate the environment to achieve one's goals.) Baumrind has focused largely on four aspects of parental behavior: (1) strictness; (2) demands for the child to achieve intellectual, emotional, and social maturity; (3) communication ability; and (4) warmth and involvement. She labeled the three parenting styles the *authoritative, authoritarian,* and *permissive* styles. Other researchers also speak of the *uninvolved* style. These four styles are defined in the following ways:

1 *Authoritative parents.* The parents of the most competent children rate high in all four areas of behavior. They are strict (restrictive) and demand mature behavior. But they temper their strictness with desire to reason with their children and with love and support (Galambos et al., 2003). They expect much, but they explain why and offer help. Baumrind labeled these parents **authoritative parents** to suggest that they know what they want but are also loving and respectful to their children.

2 *Authoritarian parents.* **Authoritarian parents** view obedience as a virtue for its own sake. They have strict guidelines about what is right and wrong, and they demand that their children stick to them. Both authoritative and authoritarian parents have strict standards, but authoritative parents explain their demands and are supportive, whereas authoritarian parents rely on force and communicate poorly with their children. Authoritarian parents

critical period
a period of time when an instinctive response can be elicited by a particular stimulus

imprinting
a process occurring during a critical period in the development of an organism, in which that organism responds to a stimulus in a manner that will afterward be difficult to modify

authoritative parents
parents who are strict and warm; authoritative parents demand mature behavior but use reason rather than force in discipline

authoritarian parents
parents who are rigid in their rules and who demand obedience for the sake of obedience

do not respect their children's points of view, and they may be cold and rejecting. When children ask them why they should do this or that, authoritarian parents often answer, "Because I say so!"

3 *Permissive parents.* **Permissive parents** are generally easygoing with their children. As a result, the children do pretty much what the children want. Permissive parents are warm and supportive, but poor at communicating.

4 *Uninvolved parents.* **Uninvolved parents** tend to leave their children on their own. They make few demands and show little warmth or encouragement.

Research evidence shows that the children of warm parents are more likely to be socially and emotionally well adjusted. They are also more likely to internalize moral standards—that is, to develop a conscience (Grusec, 2002; Rudy & Grusec, 2001).

Strictness seems to pay off, provided it is tempered with reason and warmth. Children of authoritative parents have the greatest self-reliance, self-esteem, social competence, and achievement motivation (Galambos et al., 2003; Grusec, 2002; Kim & Rohner, 2002). Children of authoritarian parents are often withdrawn or aggressive and usually do not do as well in school as children of authoritative parents (Kim & Rohner, 2002; Steinberg, 2001). Children of permissive parents seem to be less mature. They are often impulsive, moody, and aggressive. In adolescence, lack of parental monitoring is often linked to delinquency and poor academic performance. Children of uninvolved parents tend to obtain poorer grades than children whose parents make demands on them. The children of uninvolved parents also tend to be more likely to hang out with crowds who "party" a good deal and use drugs (Durbin et al., 1993). The message? Simple enough: Children profit when parents make reasonable demands, show warmth and encouragement, and spend time with them.

LO³ Adolescence

Perhaps no other period of life is as exciting—and as bewildering—as adolescence. Adolescence is bounded by puberty and the assumption of adult responsibilities. Except for infancy, more changes occur during adolescence than during any other time. Like childhood, adolescence entails physical, cognitive, social, and emotional changes.

Physical Development

What physical developments occur during adolescence? One of the most noticeable physical developments of adolescence is a growth spurt that lasts two to three years and ends the gradual changes in height and weight that characterize most of childhood. Within this short span of years, adolescents grow some eight to twelve inches. Most boys wind up taller and heavier than most girls.

In boys, the weight of the muscle mass increases notably. The width of the shoulders and circumference of the chest also increase. Adolescents may eat enormous quantities of food to fuel their growth spurt.

Brain imaging studies show that adolescents' frontal lobes—the seat of executive functioning—are less active than those of adults. Their amygdalas, a part of the limbic system involved in emotions, are more active than adults'. These adolescent-adult differences in brain development may explain, at least in part, why many adolescents do not show the judgment, insight, and reasoning ability of adults.

Puberty: More Than "Just a Phase"?

Puberty is the period during which the body becomes sexually mature. It heralds the onset of adolescence. Puberty begins with the appearance of secondary sex characteristics such as body hair, deepening of the voice in males, and rounding of the breasts and hips in females. In boys, pituitary hormones stimulate the testes to increase the output of testosterone, which in turn causes enlargement of the penis and testes and the appearance of body hair. By the early teens, erections become common, and boys may ejaculate. Ejaculatory ability usually precedes the presence of mature sperm by at least a year. Ejaculation thus is not evidence of reproductive capacity.

In girls, a critical body weight in the neighborhood of 100 pounds is thought to trigger a cascade of hormonal secretions in the brain that cause the ovaries to secrete higher levels of the female sex hormone, estrogen (Frisch, 1997). Estrogen stimulates the growth of breast tissue and tissue in the hips and buttocks. The pelvis widens, rounding the hips. Small amounts of androgens produced by the adrenal glands, along with estrogen, spur the growth of pubic and underarm hair. Estrogen and androgens also stoke the development of female sex organs. Estrogen production becomes cyclical during puberty and regulates the menstrual cycle. The beginning of menstruation, or menarche, usually occurs between eleven and fourteen. Girls cannot become pregnant until they ovulate, however, and ovulation may begin two years after menarche.

Cognitive Development

The adolescent thinker approaches problems differently from the elementary school child. *What cognitive developments occur during adolescence?* Let us begin to answer this question by comparing the child's thought processes to those of the adolescent. The child sticks to the facts, to concrete reality. Speculating about abstract possibilities and what might be is very difficult. The adolescent, on the other hand, is able to deal with the abstract and the hypothetical. In this section we explore some of the cognitive developments of adolescence by referring to the views of Piaget and Kohlberg.

The Stage of Formal Operations

According to Piaget, children undergo three stages of cognitive development prior to adolescence: sensorimotor, preoperational, and concrete operational. The stage of formal operations is the final stage in Piaget's theory, and it represents cognitive maturity. For many children in Western societies, formal operational thought begins at about the beginning of adolescence—the age of eleven or twelve. Some people enter this stage later, however, and some never do.

The major achievements of the stage of formal operations involve classification, logical thought, and the ability to hypothesize. Central features are the ability to think about ideas as well as objects and to group and classify ideas—symbols, statements, entire theories. Adolescents can generally follow arguments from premises to conclusions and back again. They can generally appreciate both the outer environment and the world of the imagination: they engage in hypothetical thinking and deductive reasoning.

Formal operational adolescents (and adults) think abstractly. They solve geometric problems about circles and squares without reference to what the circles and squares may represent in the real world. Adolescents in this stage derive rules for behavior from general principles and can focus, or center, on multiple aspects of a situation at once to solve problems.

In this stage, adolescents tend to emerge as theoretical scientists—even though they may think of themselves as having little interest in science. That is, they can deal with hypothetical situations. They realize that situations can have different outcomes, and they think ahead, imagining those outcomes. Adolescents also conduct social experiments to test their hypotheses. They may try out various tones of voice and ways of treating others to see what works best for them.

Adolescent Egocentrism

Adolescents in the formal operational stage reason deductively. They classify objects or people and then draw conclusions about them. Adolescents can be proud of their new logical abilities, leading to a new sort of egocentrism: They demand acceptance of their logic without recognizing the exceptions or practical problems that may be considered by adults. Consider this example: "It is wrong to hurt people. Company A hurts people" (perhaps through pollution or economic pressures). "Therefore, Company A must be severely punished or shut down." This thinking is logical. But by impatiently demanding major changes or severe penalties, one may not fully consider various practical problems such as the thousands of workers who might be laid off. Adults have often had life experiences that encourage them to see shades of gray rather than black and white.

menarche
the beginning of menstruation

formal operational stage
Piaget's fourth stage, characterized by abstract logical thought and deduction from principles

imaginary
audience
an aspect of adolescent
egocentrism; the belief
that other people are
as concerned with our
thoughts and behaviors
as we are

personal fable
another aspect of ado-
lescent egocentrism;
the belief that our
feelings and ideas are
special and unique and
that we are invulnerable

postconventional
level
according to Kohlberg,
a period during which
moral judgments are
derived from moral
principles and people
look to themselves to
set moral standards

The thought of pre-schoolers is characterized by egocentrism in which they cannot take another's point of view. Adolescent thought is marked by an egocentrism in which they can understand the thoughts of others but still have trouble separating things that are of concern to others and those that are of concern only to them-selves (Elkind, 1967, 1985). Adolescent egocentrism gives rise to two interesting cogni-tive developments: the *imagi-nary audience* and the *personal fable*.

The concept of the imagi-nary audience refers to the belief that other people are as concerned with our thoughts and behavior as we are. Adolescents thus see themselves as the center of attention and assume that other people are also preoccupied with their appearance and behavior (Milstead et al., 1993). Adolescents may feel onstage with all eyes on them. The concept of the imaginary audience may drive the intense adolescent desire for privacy. It helps explain why adolescents are so self-conscious, why they worry about every facial blem-ish and spend hours grooming. Self-consciousness seems to peak at about thirteen and then decline. Girls tend to be more self-conscious than boys (Elkind & Bowen, 1979).

The personal fable is the belief that our feelings and ideas are special, even unique, and that we are invulnerable. The personal fable seems to underlie adolescent showing off and risk taking (Cohn et al., 1995).

The Postconventional Level of Moral Reasoning

Kohlberg's theory of moral reasoning involves three lev-els: preconventional, conven-tional, and postconventional. Individuals can arrive at the same decision as to whether or not Heinz should save his wife by taking the drug with-out paying for it for differ-ent reasons. Deciding not to steal the drug for fear of punishment is less complex than deciding not to because of the belief that doing so will weaken the social order.

None of Kohlberg's levels is tied to a person's age. Although postconventional reasoning is the highest level, most adolescents and adults never reach it. But if postconventional reasoning emerges, it usually does so in adolescence. Kohlberg's (1969) research found postconventional moral judgments were absent among seven- to ten-year-olds. But by age sixteen, stage 5 reasoning is shown by about 20% of adolescents, and stage 6 reasoning by about 5%.

At the postconventional level, moral reasoning is based on the person's own moral standards. Moral judgments are derived from personal values, not from conventional standards or authority figures. In the contractual, legalistic orientation character-istic of stage 5, it is recognized that laws stem from agreed-upon procedures and that the rule of law is in general good for society; therefore, laws should not be violated except under pressing circumstances. (Although it is illegal for Heinz to steal the drug, in this case it is the right thing to do.)

Stage 6 moral reasoning demands adherence to supposedly universal ethical principles such as the sanctity of human life, individual dignity, justice, and the Golden Rule ("Do unto others as you would have them do unto you"). If a law is unjust or contradicts the rights of the individual, it is wrong to obey it.

People at the postconventional level see their conscience as the highest moral authority. This point has created confusion. To some it suggests that it is right to break the law when it is convenient, but this interpretation is wrong. Kohlberg means that people at this level feel they must do what they think is right even if they break the law or must sac-rifice themselves.

Are There Gender Differences in Moral Development?

A number of studies using Heinz's dilemma have found that boys show higher levels of moral reasoning than girls. But Carol Gilligan (1982; Gilligan et al., 1989) argues that this gender difference reflects different pat-terns of socialization for boys and girls—not differences in morality. Gilligan considers eleven-year-old Jake. Jake weighs the scales of justice like a math problem. He shows that life is worth more than property and con-cludes that it is Heinz's duty to steal the drug (stage 4 reasoning). Gilligan also points to eleven-year-old Amy. Amy vacillates. Amy says that stealing the drug and letting Heinz's wife die are both wrong. So Amy looks for alternatives, such as getting a loan, because it wouldn't help Heinz's wife if he went to jail.

Gilligan finds Amy's reasoning to be as sophisticated as Jake's, yet Amy would be rated as having a lower level of moral development in Kohlberg's scheme. Gilligan argues that girls are socialized to focus on the needs of others and forgo simple judgments of right and wrong. Amy is therefore more likely to show stage 3 reasoning, which focuses in part on empathy—or caring for others. Jake has been socialized to make judgments based on logic. He wants to derive clear-cut conclusions from premises.

We could argue endlessly about which form of moral reasoning—Jake's or Amy's—is "higher." Instead, let us note a review of the research that shows only slight tendencies for boys to favor Jake's "justice" approach and girls to favor Amy's "caring" approach (Jaffee & Hyde, 2000). Thus, the justice orientation does not "belong" to boys, and the care orientation does not "belong" to girls.

Social and Emotional Development

What social and emotional developments occur during adolescence? In terms of social and emotional development, adolescence has been associated with turbulence. In the 19th century, psychologist G. Stanley Hall described adolescence as a time of *Sturm und Drang*—storm and stress. Current views challenge the assumption that "storm and stress" is the norm (Griffin, 2001). Many adolescents experience a rather calm and joyous period of development. We need to consider individual differences and cultural variations (Arnett, 1999).

Certainly, many American teenagers abuse drugs, get pregnant, contract sexually transmitted infections, get involved in violence, fail in school, even attempt suicide (CDC, 2000b). The U.S. Centers for Disease Control and Prevention (CDC, 2000b) reported that 72% of all deaths among people aged ten to twenty-four years result from just four causes: motor vehicle crashes (31%), other accidents (11%), homicide (18%), and suicide (12%). Nevertheless, the majority of Americans make it through adolescence quite well.

Striving for Independence

As these biological changes take place, adolescents strive to become more independent from parents, which may lead to bickering (Smetana et al., 2003). Bickering usually concerns homework, chores, money, appearance, curfews, and dating. Disagreements about clothes and friends are common.

Adolescents and parents are often in conflict because adolescents experiment with things that can be harmful to their health. Yet—apparently because of the personal fable—adolescents may not perceive such activities to be as risky as their parents do. Cohn and his colleagues (1995) found, for example, that parents perceived drinking, smoking, failure to use seat belts, drag racing, and a number of other activities to be riskier than did their teenagers.

Some distancing from parents is beneficial (Smetana et al., 2003). After all, adolescents do have to form relationships outside the family. But greater independence does not necessarily mean that adolescents become emotionally detached from parents or fall completely under the spell of peers. Most adolescents continue to feel love, respect, and loyalty toward parents (Eberly & Montemayor, 1999). Adolescents who feel close to their parents actually show more self-reliance and independence than do those who distance themselves. They fare better in school and have fewer adjustment problems (Flouri & Buchanan, 2003). Despite conflict over issues of control, parents and adolescents tend to share social, political, religious, and economic views (Sagrestano et al., 1999). In sum, there are frequent differences between parents and adolescents on issues of personal control. However, there is apparently less of a "generation gap" on broader matters.

Ego Identity Versus Role Diffusion

According to Erik Erikson, we undergo eight stages of psychosocial development. Four of them, beginning with trust versus mistrust, occur in childhood. The fifth, that of *ego identity versus role diffusion,* occurs in adolescence. Ego identity is a firm sense of who one is and what one stands for. It can carry one through difficult times and lend meaning to achievements. Adolescents who do not develop ego identity may experience role diffusion. They spread themselves too thin, running down one blind alley after another and placing themselves at the mercy of leaders who promise to give them the sense of identity they cannot find for themselves.

The creation of an adult identity is a key challenge, involving learning about one's interests and abilities and connecting them with occupations and roles in life. Identity also involves sexual, political, and religious beliefs and commitments. Will the

ego identity
Erikson's term for a firm sense of who one is and what one stands for

role diffusion
Erikson's term for lack of clarity in one's life roles (due to failure to develop ego identity)

menopause
the cessation of
menstruation

individual be monogamous or
sexually active with several
people? Will he or she lean
left or right along the political
spectrum? What role will be played by religion?

Adolescent Sexuality

The changes of puberty make the adolescent body
ready for sexual activity. High hormone levels stir
interest in sex. In today's world, many adolescents
wrestle with issues of how and when to express their
awakening sexuality. To complicate matters, Western
culture sends mixed messages about sex. Teenagers
may be advised to wait until they have married or
entered into meaningful relationships, but they are
also bombarded by sexual messages in films, TV,
print advertising, and virtually every other medium.

About half of American high school students
have engaged in sexual intercourse (CDC, 2000b).
Adolescents usually obtain little advice at home
or in school about how to handle their emerging
sexuality. Peers also influence the sexual behavior of
adolescents. When teenagers are asked why they do
not wait to have sexual intercourse, the most common reason is peer pressure (Dickson et al., 1998). All
in all, about 800,000 teenage girls get pregnant each
year, resulting in 500,000 births ("Less Sex," 2004).

Still, there is encouraging news. Recent research
shows a decline in the teenage pregnancy rate due
largely to educational campaigns in the schools, the
media, churches, and communities ("Less Sex," 2004).

LO⁴ Adulthood

Development continues throughout the life span.
Many theorists believe that adult concerns and
involvements follow observable patterns, so that we
can speak of "stages" of adult development. Others
argue that there may no longer be a standard life
cycle with predictable stages or phases. Age now has
an "elastic quality"—being fifty, sixty, seventy, eighty,
or even ninety no longer necessarily means loss
of cognitive or physical ability, or even wrinkling.
People are living longer than ever before and are
freer than ever to choose their own destiny.

Physical Development

The most obvious aspects of development during
adulthood are physical. *What physical developments
occur during adulthood?* Let us consider the physical
developments that take place in young, or early,
adulthood, which covers the ages between twenty
and forty; the transition to middle adulthood, years

forty to forty-five; middle adulthood, which spans
the ages of forty-five to sixty-five; and late adulthood, which begins at sixty-five.

Young Adulthood

Most young adults are at their height of sensory
sharpness, strength, reaction time, and cardiovascular fitness. On the other hand, women gymnasts find
themselves lacking a competitive edge in their twenties because they are accumulating (normal) body fat
and losing suppleness and flexibility. Other athletes,
such as football, baseball, and basketball players, are
more likely to experience a decline in their thirties.
Most athletes retire by age forty. Sexually speaking, most people in early adulthood become readily
aroused. They tend to attain and maintain erections
as desired and to lubricate readily.

Middle Adulthood

In our middle years, we are unlikely to possess the
strength, coordination, and stamina that we had
during our twenties and thirties. The decline is most
obvious in professional sports, where peak performance is at a premium.

The years between forty and sixty are reasonably stable. There is gradual physical decline, but it is
minor and only likely to be of concern if a person com-
petes with young adults—or with idealized memories
of oneself. There are exceptions. The twenty-year-old
couch potato occasionally becomes the fifty-year-old
marathoner. By any reasonable standard, people in
middle adulthood can maintain excellent cardiore-
spiratory condition. Because the physical decline in
middle adulthood is gradual, people who begin to
exercise and eat more nutritious diets (e.g., decrease
intake of animal fats and increase intake of fruits and
vegetables) may find themselves looking and feeling
better than they did in young adulthood.

For women, menopause is usually considered to be
the single most important change of life that occurs
during middle adulthood. Menopause usually occurs
during the late forties or early fifties. Menopause is
the final phase of the *climacteric,* which is caused by a
decline in secretion of female sex hormones. Ovulation
comes to an end, and there is some loss of breast tissue and of elasticity of the skin. Loss of bone density
can lead to osteoporosis (brittle bones). During the
climacteric, many women experience hot flashes, loss
of sleep, and some anxiety and depression. Women's
experiences during and following the climacteric reflect
the intensity of their physical symptoms—which vary
considerably—and the extent to which their self-concept was wrapped up with their reproductive capacity
(Dennerstein, 2003; Hvas et al., 2004).

Late Adulthood

An *agequake* is coming. With improved health care and knowledge of the importance of diet and exercise, more Americans than ever before are sixty-five or older (Nuland, 2005). In 1900, only one American in thirty was over sixty-five. By 2030, one American in five will be sixty-five or older.

Figure 3.7

The Relentless March of Time

Go to CourseMate for PSYCH at www.cengagebrain.com to access an interactive version of this figure. 🔊

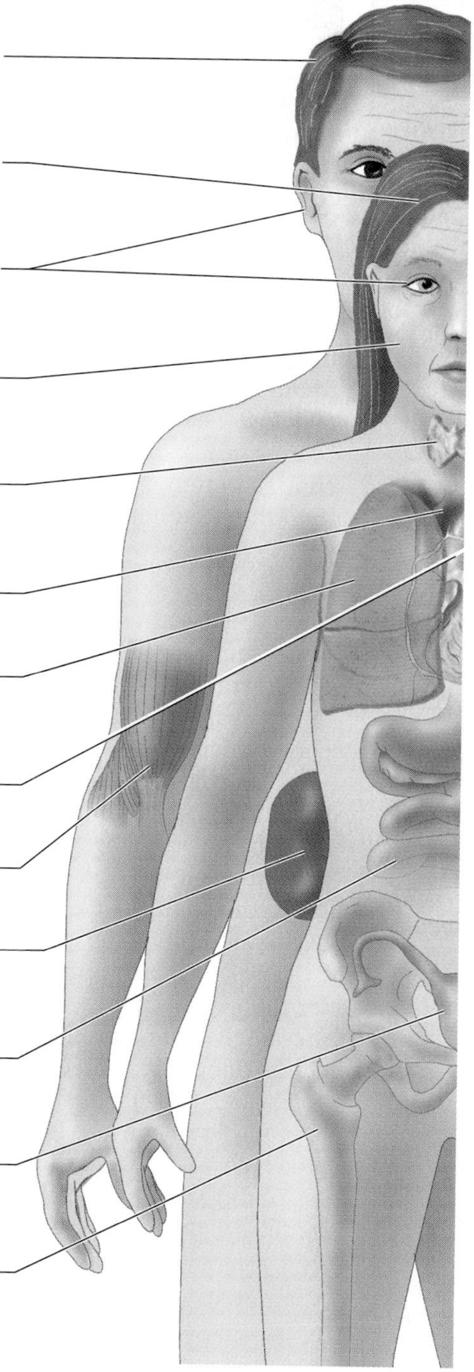

Hair and nails
Hair often turns gray and thins out. Men may go bald. Fingernails can thicken.

Brain
The brain shrinks, but it is not known if that affects mental functions.

The senses
The sensitivity of hearing, sight, taste, and smell can all decline with age.

Skin
Wrinkles occur as the skin thins and the underlying fat shrinks, and age spots often crop up.

Glands and hormones
Levels of many hormones drop, or the body becomes less responsive to them.

Immune system
The body becomes less able to resist some pathogens.

Lungs
It doesn't just seem harder to climb those stairs; lung capacity drops.

Heart and blood vessels
Cardiovascular problems become more common.

Muscles
Strength usually peaks in the 20s, then declines.

Kidneys and urinary tract
The kidneys become less efficient. The bladder can't hold as much, so urination is more frequent.

Digestive system
Digestion slows down as the secretion of digestive enzymes decreases.

Reproductive system
Women go through menopause, and testosterone levels drop for men.

Bones and joints
Wear and tear can lead to arthritic joints, and osteoporosis is common, especially in women.

Various changes—some of them troublesome—do occur during the later years (see Figure 3.7). Changes in calcium metabolism increase the brittleness of the bones and heighten the risk of breaks due to falls. The skin becomes less elastic and subject to wrinkles and folds. Older people see and hear less acutely. Because of a decline in the sense of smell, they may use more spice to flavor their food. Older people need more time to respond to stimuli. Older drivers, for example, need more time to respond to changing road conditions. As we grow older, our immune system functions less effectively, leaving us more vulnerable to disease. Age-related changes impact sexual functioning, yet most people can enjoy sex for a lifetime if they remain generally healthy and adjust their expectations.

Cognitive Development

What cognitive developments occur during adulthood? As in the case of physical development, people are also at the height of their cognitive powers during early adulthood. Cognitive development in adulthood has many aspects—creativity, memory functioning, and intelligence.

People can be creative for a lifetime. At the age of eighty, Merce Cunningham choreographed a dance that made use of computer-generated digital images (Teachout, 2000). Hans Hofmann created some of his most vibrant paintings at eighty-five, and Pablo Picasso was painting in his nineties. Grandma Moses did not even begin painting until she was seventy-eight years old. Giuseppe Verdi wrote his joyous opera *Falstaff* at the age of seventy-nine.

Memory functioning does decline with age. But declines in memory are not usually as large as people assume and are often reversible (Villa & Abeles, 2000). Memory tests usually measure ability to recall meaningless information. Older people show better memory functioning in areas in which they can apply their experience, especially their specialties, to new challenges. For example, who would do a better job of learning and remembering how to solve problems in chemistry—a college history major or a retired professor of chemistry?

You might choose the chemistry professor because of his or her crystallized intelligence, not his or her fluid intelligence.

crystallized intelligence one's lifetime of intellectual achievement, as shown largely through vocabulary and knowledge of world affairs

fluid intelligence mental flexibility as shown in learning rapidly to solve new kinds of problems

Alzheimer's disease a progressive form of mental deterioration characterized by loss of memory, language, problem solving, and other cognitive functions

The Dream in this usage, Levinson's term for the overriding drive of youth to become someone important, to leave one's mark on history

Fiction

It is *not* true that the architect Frank Lloyd Wright designed New York's innovative spiral-shaped Guggenheim Museum when he was sixty-five years old. He was actually eighty-nine.

Crystallized intelligence represents one's lifetime of intellectual attainments. We are using the example of knowledge of chemistry, but crystallized intelligence is shown more generally by vocabulary and accumulated facts about world affairs. Therefore, crystallized intelligence can increase over the decades.

Fluid intelligence is defined as mental flexibility, demonstrated by the ability to process information rapidly, as in learning and solving problems in new areas. It is the sort of intellectual functioning that is typically measured on intelligence tests, especially with problems that have time limits.

Young adults obtain the highest intelligence test scores (Schaie et al., 2004). Yet people tend to retain verbal skills, as demonstrated by vocabulary and general knowledge, into advanced old age. The performance of older people on tasks that require speed and visual–spatial skills, such as piecing puzzles together, tends to decline (Schaie et al., 2004; Zimprich & Martin, 2002).

One of the most severe assaults on intellectual functioning, especially among older people, is Alzheimer's disease, a progressive form of mental deterioration that affects about 1% of people at age sixty and nearly half of people past age eighty-five (Brody, 2005). Although Alzheimer's is connected with aging, it is a disease rather than a normal progression (Yesavage et al., 2002).

Social and Emotional Development

Changes in social and emotional development during adulthood are probably the most "elastic" or fluid. These changes are affected by cultural expectations and individual behavior patterns. As a result, there is much variety. Nevertheless, many developmental theorists suggest that there are enough commonalities that we can speak of trends. One trend is that the outlook for older people has become more

Architect Frank Lloyd Wright with model of his Guggenheim Museum

optimistic over the past generation—not only because of medical advances but also because the behavior and mental processes of many older people are remaining younger than at any other time in history.

There is more good news. Research evidence suggests that people tend to grow psychologically healthier as they advance from adolescence through middle adulthood. Psychologists Constance Jones and William Meredith (2000) studied information on 236 participants in California growth studies who had been followed from early adolescence for about fifty years and found that they generally became more productive and had healthier relationships as time went on. Even some people with a turbulent adolescence showed better psychological health at age sixty-two than they had half a century earlier.

Young Adulthood

What social and emotional developments occur during young adulthood? Many theorists suggest that young adulthood is the period of life during which people tend to establish themselves as independent members of society.

At some point during their twenties, many people become fueled by ambition. Many strive to advance in their careers. Those who seek professional careers may spend much of their twenties acquiring the skills that will enable them to succeed (Levinson et al., 1978; Levinson, 1996). It is largely during the twenties that people become generally responsible for their own support, make their own choices, and are freed from parental influences. Many young adults adopt what theorist Daniel Levinson and his colleagues (1978) call the The Dream—the drive to "become" someone, to leave their mark on history—which serves as a tentative blueprint for life.

During young adulthood, people tend to leave their families of origin and create families of their own. Erik

Fiction

Alzheimer's disease is *not* a normal part of aging.

Erikson (1963) characterized young adulthood as the stage of intimacy versus isolation. Erikson saw the establishment of intimate relationships as central to young adulthood. Young adults who have evolved a firm sense of identity during adolescence are ready to "fuse" their identities with those of other people through marriage and abiding friendships. People who do not reach out to develop intimate relationships risk retreating into isolation and loneliness.

At age thirty or so, many people reassess their lives, asking themselves, "Where is my life going?" "Why am I doing this?" (Levinson et al., 1978). It is not uncommon for them to switch careers or form new intimate relationships. The later thirties are often characterized by settling down—planting roots. They become focused on career advancement, children, and long-term mortgages.

Middle Adulthood

A number of key changes in social and emotional development occur during middle adulthood. *What social and emotional developments occur during middle adulthood?* Consider Erikson's views on the middle years.

Erikson (1963) labeled the life crisis of the middle years generativity versus stagnation. *Generativity* involves doing things that we believe are worthwhile, such as rearing children or producing on the job. Generativity enhances and maintains self-esteem. Generativity also involves making the world a better place through joining church or civic groups. *Stagnation* means treading water, as in keeping the same job at the same pay for thirty years. Stagnation damages self-esteem.

According to Levinson and colleagues (1978), whose research involved case studies of forty men, there is a *midlife transition* at about age forty to forty-five. Previously, men had viewed their age in terms of the number of years that had elapsed since birth. Now they begin to think of their age in terms of the number of years they have left.

Research suggests that women may undergo a midlife transition sooner than men do (Zucker et al., 2002). Why? Much of it has to do with the winding down of the "biological clock"—that is, the abilities to conceive and bear children. For example, once they turn thirty-five women are usually advised to have their fetuses routinely tested for Down syndrome and other chromosomal disorders.

In both sexes, according to Levinson, the midlife transition may trigger a midlife crisis. The middle-level, middle-aged businessperson looking ahead to another ten to twenty years of grinding out accounts in a Wall Street cubbyhole may encounter severe depression. The homemaker with two teenagers, an empty house from 8:00 AM to 4:00 PM, and a fortieth birthday on the way may feel that she or he is coming apart at the seams. Both feel a sense of entrapment and loss of purpose.

Yet many Americans find that these years present opportunities for new direction and fulfillment. Many people are at the height of their productive powers during this period. Many, perhaps most, of today's robust forty-five- to fifty-five-year-olds can look forward to another thirty to forty healthy years.

Late Adulthood

What social and emotional developments occur during late adulthood? Generativity does not end with middle age. Research suggests that many individuals in late adulthood continue to be creative and also to maintain a firm sense of who they are and what they stand for (Webster, 2003). The Greek philosopher Plato was so optimistic about late adulthood that he argued that one could achieve great pleasure in one's later years, engage in meaningful public service, and also achieve wisdom (McKee & Barber, 2001).

According to psychologist Erik Erikson, late adulthood is the stage of ego integrity versus despair. The basic challenge is to maintain the belief that life is meaningful and worthwhile as one ages and faces the inevitability of death. Erikson, like Plato, spoke of the importance of wisdom. He believed that ego integrity derives from wisdom, which can be defined as expert knowledge about the meaning of life, balancing one's own needs and those of others, and pushing toward excellence in one's behavior and achievements (Baltes & Staudinger, 2000; Sternberg, 2000). Erikson also believed that wisdom enables people to accept their life span as occurring at a certain point in the sweep of history and as being limited. We spend most of our lives accumulating objects and relationships, and Erikson argues that adjustment in the later years requires the ability to let go of them. Other views of late adulthood stress the importance of creating new challenges; however, biological and social realities may require older people to become more selective in their pursuits.

intimacy versus isolation
Erikson's life crisis of young adulthood, which is characterized by the task of developing abiding intimate relationships

generativity versus stagnation
Erikson's term for the crisis of middle adulthood, characterized by the task of being productive and contributing to younger generations

midlife crisis
a crisis experienced by many people during the midlife transition when they realize that life may be more than halfway over and they reassess their achievements in terms of their dreams

ego integrity versus despair
Erikson's term for the crisis of late adulthood, characterized by the task of maintaining one's sense of identity despite physical deterioration

CHAPTER 4

Sensation and Perception

Learning Outcomes

LO 1   Define and differentiate between sensation and perception

LO 2   Identify the parts of the eye; explain the properties of light and the theories of color vision

LO 3   Describe how visual perception is organized

LO 4   Identify the parts of the ear; describe the sense of hearing

LO 5   Describe the chemical senses

LO 6   Explain the properties of the skin senses and theoretical explanations for pain

LO 7   Describe the kinesthetic and vestibular senses

LO 8   Explain why psychologists are skeptical about extrasensory perception

"Elephants detected the tsunami before the earth started shaking."

The tsunami that hit the coast of southern Asia in 2004 killed as many as a quarter of a million people. The people were caught off guard, but not the animals.

Along the western coast of Thailand, elephants giving rides to tourists began to trumpet agitatedly hours before the tsunami, just about when the earthquake that fractured the ocean floor sent the big waves rushing toward the shore. An hour before the waves slammed into the area, the elephants began wailing. Before the waves struck, they trooped off to higher ground. Elephants, tigers, leopards, deer, wild boar, water buffalo, monkeys, and reptiles in Sri Lanka's Yala National Park escaped the tsunami unharmed.

People have noticed that animals appear to detect earthquakes, hurricanes, volcanic eruptions, and tsunamis before the earth starts shaking. Some animals are apparently supersensitive to sound, others to temperature, touch, or vibration, which gives them advance warning.

Elephants are particularly sensitive to ground vibrations and probably sensed the earthquake that caused the tsunami in their feet and trunks. Some birds, dogs, tigers, and elephants can sense sound waves whose frequencies are too low for humans to hear. Dogs' superior sense of smell might detect subtle chemical changes in the air that warn them of calamities.

Different animals, then, have different sensory apparatuses, and many of them sense things that people cannot sense. Just how do humans sense the world around them?

Truth or Fiction?

What do you think?

Folklore, common sense, or nonsense? Place a T for "True" or F for "False" on the lines provided (you'll learn the answers as you read through the text).

— People have five senses.

— If we could see waves of light with slightly longer wavelengths, warm-blooded animals would glow in the dark.

— People sometimes hear what they want to hear.

— When we mix blue light and yellow light, we obtain green light.

— Many people experience pain "in" limbs that have been amputated.

— Some people can read other people's minds.

Glossary

sensation
the stimulation of sensory receptors and the transmission of sensory information to the central nervous system

perception
the process by which sensations are organized into an inner representation of the world

absolute threshold
the minimal amount of energy that can produce a sensation

pitch
the highness or lowness of a sound, as determined by the frequency of the sound waves

LO¹ Sensation and Perception

What are sensation and perception? Sensation is the stimulation of sensory receptors and the transmission of sensory information to the central nervous system (the spinal cord or brain). Sensory receptors are located in sensory organs such as the eyes and ears, the skin, and elsewhere in the body. Stimulation of the senses is an automatic process. It results from sources of energy, like light and sound, or from the presence of chemicals, as in smell and taste.

Perception is not automatic. Perception is an active process in which sensations are organized and interpreted to form an inner representation of the world. Perception may begin with sensation, but it also reflects our experiences and expectations as it makes sense of sensory stimuli. A person standing fifteen feet away and a twelve-inch-tall doll right next to you may cast similar-sized images on the back of your eye, but whether you interpret the size to be a foot-long doll or a full-grown person fifteen feet away is a matter of perception that depends on your experience with dolls, people, and distance.

In this chapter you will see that your perception of the world of changing sights, sounds, and other sources of sensory input depends largely on the so-called five senses: vision, hearing, smell, taste, and touch. But touch is just one of several "skin senses," which also include pressure, warmth, cold, and pain. There are also senses that alert you to your own body position without your having to watch every step you take. As we explore each of these senses, we will find that similar sensations may lead to different perceptions in different people—or to different situations in the same person.

Before we begin our voyage through the senses, let us consider a number of concepts that we use to talk about the relationships between sensations and perceptions: *absolute threshold, difference threshold, signal-detection theory,* and *sensory adaptation.* In doing so, we will learn why we can dim the lights gradually to near darkness without anyone noticing.

Fiction

People actually have many more than five senses.

We will also learn why we might become indifferent to the savory aromas of delightful dinners. *How do we know when something is there? How do we know when it has changed?*

Absolute Threshold

Nineteenth-century German psychologist Gustav Fechner used the term absolute threshold to refer to the weakest level of a stimulus that is necessary to produce a sensation. For example, the absolute threshold for light would be the minimum brightness (physical energy) required to activate the visual sensory system.

Psychophysicists look for the absolute thresholds of the senses by exposing individuals to progressively stronger stimuli until they find the minimum stimuli that the person can detect 50% of the time. These absolute thresholds are not all that absolute, however. Some people are more sensitive than others, and even the same person might have a slightly different response at different times. Nevertheless, under ideal conditions, our ability to detect stimuli is quite sensitive. (See the box feature, this page.)

How different our lives would be if the absolute thresholds for the human senses differed! If your ears were sensitive to sounds that are lower in pitch, you might hear the collisions among molecules of air. If you could see light with slightly longer wavelengths, you would see infrared light waves. Your world would be transformed because heat generates infrared light.

Difference Threshold

How much of a difference in intensity between two lights is required before you will detect one as being brighter than the other? The minimum difference in magnitude of two stimuli required to tell them apart

Absolute Thresholds of the Senses

The following are measures of the absolute thresholds for the human senses of vision, hearing, taste, smell, and touch:

- *Vision:* a candle flame viewed from about 30 miles on a clear, dark night.
- *Hearing:* a watch ticking from about 20 feet away in a quiet room.
- *Taste:* 1 teaspoon of sugar dissolved in 2 gallons of water.
- *Smell:* about one drop of perfume diffused throughout a small house (1 part in 500 million).
- *Touch:* the pressure of the wing of a fly falling on a cheek from a distance of about 0.4 inch.

© 2010 THINKSTOCK / JUPITERIMAGES CORPORATION

Truth

If we could see waves of light with slightly longer wavelengths, warm-blooded animals—including other people—would glow in the dark.

is their **difference threshold**. As with the absolute threshold, psychologists agree to the standard of a difference in strength that can be detected 50% of the time.

Psychophysicist Ernst Weber discovered through laboratory research that the threshold for perceiving differences in the intensity of light is about 2% (actually closer to 1/60th) of their intensity. This fraction, 1/60th, is known as **Weber's constant** for light. A related concept is the **just noticeable difference (jnd)**—the minimum difference in stimuli that a person can detect. For example, at least 50% of the time, most people can tell if a light becomes just 1/60th brighter or dimmer. Weber's constant for light holds whether we are comparing moderately bright lights or moderately dull lights. But it becomes inaccurate when we compare extremely bright or extremely dull lights.

Weber's constant for noticing differences in lifted weight is 1/53rd. (Round it off to 1/50th, or 2%.) That means if you are strong enough to heft a 100-pound barbell, you would not notice that it was heavier until about two pounds were added. Yet if you are a runner who carries one-pound dumbbells, you would definitely notice if someone slipped you dumbbells even a pound heavier because the increase would be 100%.

What about sound? People are most sensitive to changes in the pitch (frequency) of sounds. The Weber constant for pitch is 1/333, meaning that on average, people can tell when a tone rises or falls in pitch by an extremely small one-third of 1%. (Even a small error in pitch makes singers sound sharp or flat.) Remember this when friends criticize your singing. The sense of taste is much less sensitive. On average, people cannot detect differences in saltiness of less than 20%. That is why "low-salt" chips that have 15% less salt than your favorite chips do not taste so bad.

Signal-Detection Theory

From the discussion so far, it might seem that people are simply switched on by certain amounts of stimulation. This is not quite so. People are also influenced by psychological factors. **Signal-detection theory** considers these factors. *What is signal-detection theory?*

According to signal-detection theory, the relationship between a physical stimulus and a sensory response is not fully mechanical. People's ability to detect stimuli such as blips on a radar screen depends not only on the intensity of the blips but also on their training (learning), motivation (desire to perceive blips), and psychological states such as fatigue or alertness.

The intensity of the signal is one factor that determines whether people will perceive sensory stimuli (signals) or a difference between signals. Another is the degree to which the signal can be distinguished from background noise. It is easier to hear a friend speaking in a quiet room than in a room in which people are singing and clinking glasses. The sharpness of a person's biological sensory system is still another factor. Is sensory capacity fully developed? Is it diminished by age?

difference threshold the minimal difference in intensity required between two sources of energy so that they will be perceived as being different

Weber's constant the fraction of the intensity by which a source of physical energy must be increased or decreased so that a difference in intensity will be perceived

just noticeable difference (jnd) the minimal amount by which a source of energy must be increased or decreased so that a difference in intensity will be perceived

signal-detection theory the view that the perception of sensory stimuli involves the interaction of physical, biological, and psychological factors

Truth

It is true that people sometimes hear what they want to hear.

feature detectors
neurons in the sensory cortex that fire in response to specific features of sensory information such as lines or edges of objects

sensory adaptation
the processes by which organisms become more sensitive to stimuli that are low in magnitude and less sensitive to stimuli that are constant or ongoing in magnitude

sensitization
the type of sensory adaptation in which we become more sensitive to stimuli that are low in magnitude. Also called *positive adaptation*

desensitization
the type of sensory adaptation in which we become less sensitive to constant stimuli. Also called *negative adaptation*

> I think I can hear a watch ticking on the previous page.

CORTIER CLAUDE/BELPRESS/ANDIA

Sensory Adaptation

Our sensory systems are admirably suited to a changing environment. *How do our sensory systems adapt to a changing environment?* Sensory adaptation refers to the processes by which we become more sensitive to stimuli of low magnitude and less sensitive to stimuli that remain the same, such as the background noises outside the window.

Consider how the visual sense adapts to lower intensities of light. When we first walk into a darkened movie theater, we see little but the images on the screen. As we search for our seats, however, we become increasingly sensitive to the faces around us and to the features of the theater. The process of becoming more sensitive to stimulation is referred to as sensitization, or *positive adaptation*.

But we become less sensitive to constant stimulation. When we live in a city, for example, we become desensitized to sounds of traffic except, perhaps, for the occasional backfire or siren. The process of becoming less sensitive to stimulation is referred to as desensitization, or *negative adaptation*.

Our sensitivities to stimulation provide our brains with information that we use to understand and influence the world outside. Therefore, it is not surprising that psychologists study the ways in which we sense and perceive this information—through vision, hearing, the chemical senses, and still other senses, as we see throughout the remainder of the chapter.

That is, we tend to detect stimuli we are searching for. The place in which you are reading this book may be abuzz with signals. If you are focusing your attention on this page, the other signals recede into the background. One psychological factor in signal detection is focusing on signals one considers important.

Feature Detectors in the Brain

Imagine you are standing by the curb of a busy street as a bus approaches. When neurons in your sensory organs—in this case, your eyes—are stimulated by the approach of the bus, they relay information to the sensory cortex in the brain. Nobel Prize winners David Hubel and Torsten Wiesel (1979) discovered that various neurons in the visual cortex of the brain fire in response to particular features of the visual input. *What are feature detectors?* Many cells in the brain detect (i.e., fire in response to) lines presented at various angles—vertical, horizontal, and in between. Other cells fire in response to specific colors. Because they respond to different aspects or features of a scene, these brain cells are termed feature detectors. In the example of the bus, visual feature detectors respond to the bus's edges, depth, contours, textures, shadows, speed, and kinds of motion (up, down, forward, and back). There are also feature detectors for other senses. Auditory feature detectors, for example, respond to the pitch, loudness, and other aspects of the sounds of the bus.

LO² Vision

Our eyes are our biological "windows on the world." Because vision is our dominant sense, blindness is considered by many to be the most debilitating sensory loss. To understand vision, let us first "look" at light.

Light

Light is fascinating stuff. It radiates. It illuminates. It dazzles. In almost all cultures, light is a symbol of goodness and knowledge. We speak of genius as "brilliance." People who aren't in the know are said to be "in the dark." *Just what is light?*

It is visible light that triggers visual sensations. Yet visible light is just one small part of a spectrum of electromagnetic energy that surrounds us (see Figure 4.1). All forms of electromagnetic energy move in waves, and different kinds of electromagnetic energy have signature wavelengths:

- *Cosmic rays:* The wavelengths of these rays from outer space are only a few *trillionths* of an inch long.

- *Radio waves:* Some radio signals extend for miles.

- *Visible light:* Roses are red, and violets are blue. Why? Different colors have different wavelengths, with violet the shortest at about 400-billionths of a meter in length and red the longest at 700-billionths of a meter.

Sir Isaac Newton, the British scientist, discovered that sunlight could be broken down into different colors by means of a triangular solid of glass called a *prism* (see Figure 4.1). You can remember the colors of the spectrum, from longest to shortest wavelengths, by using the mnemonic device *Roy G. Biv* (red, orange, yellow, green, blue, indigo, violet). The wavelength of visible light determines its color, or hue. The wavelength for red is longer than the wavelength for orange, and so on through the spectrum.

hue
the color of light, as determined by its wavelength

Figure 4.1

The Visible Spectrum

By passing a source of white light, such as sunlight, through a prism, we break it down into the colors of the visible spectrum. The visible spectrum is just a narrow segment of the electromagnetic spectrum. The electromagnetic spectrum also includes radio waves, microwaves, X-rays, cosmic rays, and many others. Different forms of electromagnetic energy have wavelengths that vary from a few trillionths of a meter to thousands of miles. Visible light varies in wavelength from about 400- to 700-billionths of a meter. (One meter = 39.37 inches.)

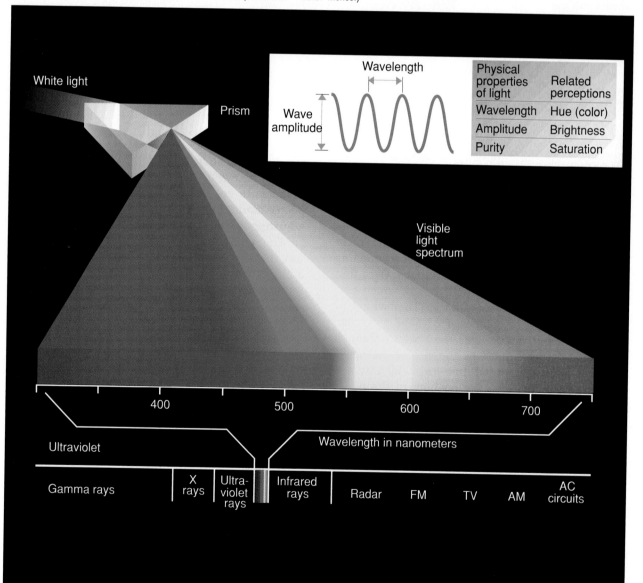

Glossary

cornea
transparent tissue forming the outer surface of the eyeball

iris
a muscular membrane whose dilation regulates the amount of light that enters the eye

pupil
the black-looking opening in the center of the iris, through which light enters the eye

lens
a transparent body behind the iris that focuses an image on the retina

retina
the area of the inner surface of the eye that contains rods and cones

photoreceptors
cells that respond to light

bipolar cells
neurons that conduct neural impulses from rods and cones to ganglion cells

ganglion cells
neurons whose axons form the optic nerve

optic nerve
the nerve that transmits sensory information from the eye to the brain

Figure 4.2   *Go to CourseMate for PSYCH at www.cengagebrain.com to access an interactive version of this figure.*

The Human Eye

In both the eye and a camera, light enters through a narrow opening and is projected onto a sensitive surface. In the eye, the photosensitive surface is called the retina, and information concerning the changing images on the retina is transmitted to the brain. The retina contains photoreceptors called rods and cones. Rods and cones transmit sensory input back through the bipolar neurons to the ganglion neurons. The axons of the ganglion neurons form the optic nerve, which transmits sensory stimulation through the brain to the visual cortex of the occipital lobe.

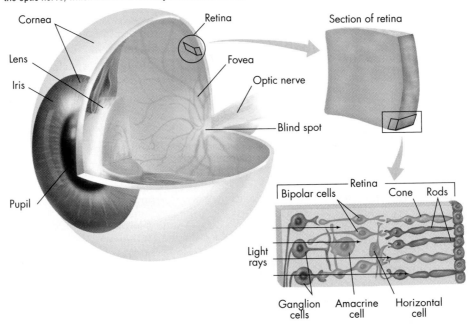

The Eye

How does the eye work? Look at the major parts of the eye, as shown in Figure 4.2. As with a camera, light enters through a narrow opening and is projected onto a sensitive surface. Light first passes through the transparent cornea, which covers the front of the eye's surface. (The "white" of the eye, or *sclera,* is composed of hard protective tissue.) The amount of light that passes through the cornea is determined by the size of the opening of the muscle called the iris, which is the colored part of the eye. The opening in the iris is the pupil. The size of the pupil adjusts automatically to the amount of light present. Therefore, you do not have to purposely open your eyes wider to see better in low lighting—the more intense light, the smaller the opening. Pupil size is also sensitive to your emotions: We can be truly "wide-eyed with fear."

Once light passes through the iris, it encounters the lens. The lens adjusts or accommodates to the image by changing its thickness. Changes in thickness permit a clear image of the object to be projected onto the retina. These changes focus the light according to the distance of the object from the viewer. If you hold a finger at arm's length and slowly bring it toward your nose, you will feel tension in the eye as the thickness of the lens accommodates to keep the retinal image in focus. When people squint to bring an object into focus, they are adjusting the thickness of the lens.

The retina consists of cells called photoreceptors that are sensitive to light (photosensitive). There are two types of photoreceptors: *rods* and *cones.* The retina (see Figure 4.2) contains several layers of cells: the rods and cones, the bipolar cells, and the ganglion cells. All of these cells are neurons. The rods and cones respond to light with chemical changes that create neural impulses that are picked up by the bipolar cells. These then activate the ganglion cells. The axons of the million or so ganglion cells in our retina converge to form the optic nerve. The optic nerve conducts sensory input to the brain, where it is relayed to the visual area of the occipital lobe. As if this were not enough, the eye has additional neurons to enhance this process. Amacrine cells and horizontal cells make sideways connections at a level near the rods and cones and at another level near the ganglion cells. As a result, single bipolar cells can pick up signals from many rods and cones, and, in turn, a single ganglion cell is able to funnel information from multiple bipolar cells. In fact, rods and cones outnumber ganglion cells by more than 100 to 1.

Rods and Cones

Rods and cones are the photoreceptors in the retina (see Figure 4.2). About 125 million rods and 6.4 million cones are distributed across the retina. The cones are most densely packed in a small spot at the center of the retina called the fovea (see Figure 4.2). Visual acuity (sharpness and detail) is greatest at this spot. The fovea is composed almost exclusively of cones. Rods are most dense just outside the fovea and thin out toward the periphery of the retina.

Rods allow us to see in black and white. Cones provide color vision. Rods are more sensitive to dim light than cones are. Therefore, as light grows dim during the evening hours, objects appear to lose their color before their outlines fade from view.

In contrast to the visual acuity of the fovea is the blind spot, which is insensitive to visual stimulation. It is the part of the retina where the axons of the ganglion cells converge to form the optic nerve (see Figure 4.2). Figure 4.3 will help you "view" your blind spot.

Visual acuity (sharpness of vision) is connected with the shape of the eye. People who have to be unusually close to an object to discriminate its details are *nearsighted*. People who see distant objects unusually clearly but have difficulty focusing on nearby objects are *farsighted*. Nearsightedness can result when the eyeball is elongated such that the images of distant objects are focused in front of the retina. When the eyeball is too short, the images of nearby objects are focused behind the retina, causing farsightedness. Eyeglasses or contact lenses help nearsighted people focus distant objects on their retinas. Laser surgery can correct vision by changing the shape of the cornea. Farsighted people usually see well enough without eyeglasses until they reach their middle years, when they may need glasses for reading.

Beginning in middle age—the late thirties to the mid-forties—the lenses of the eye start to grow brittle, making it more difficult to accommodate to, or focus on, objects. This condition is called presbyopia, from the Greek words for "old man" and "eyes." Presbyopia makes it difficult to perceive nearby visual stimuli. People who had normal visual acuity in their youth often require corrective lenses to read in middle adulthood.

Light Adaptation

When we walk out onto a dark street, we may at first not be able to see people, trees, and cars clearly. But as time goes on, we are better able to discriminate the features of people and objects. The process of adjusting to lower lighting is called dark adaptation.

The amount of light needed for detection is a function of the amount of time spent in the dark. The cones and rods adapt at different rates. The cones, which permit perception of color, reach their maximum adaptation to darkness in about ten minutes. The rods, which allow perception of light and dark only, are more sensitive to dim light and continue to adapt for forty-five minutes or so.

Adaptation to brighter lighting conditions takes place more rapidly. For instance, when you emerge from the theater into the brilliance of the afternoon, you may at first be painfully surprised by the featureless blaze around you. But within a minute or so of entering the street, the brightness of the scene dims and objects regain their edges.

Color Vision

For most of us, the world is a place of brilliant colors. Color is an emotional and aesthetic part of our everyday lives. In this section we explore

rods
rod-shaped photoreceptors that are sensitive only to the intensity of light

cones
cone-shaped photoreceptors that transmit sensations of color

fovea
an area near the center of the retina that is dense with cones and where vision is consequently most acute

blind spot
the area of the retina where axons from ganglion cells meet to form the optic nerve

visual acuity
sharpness of vision

presbyopia
a condition characterized by brittleness of the lens

dark adaptation
the process of adjusting to conditions of lower lighting by increasing the sensitivity of rods and cones

Figure 4.3

The Blind Spot

To try a "disappearing act," close your left eye, hold the book close to your face, and look at the boy with your right eye. Slowly move the book away until the pie disappears. The pie disappears because it is being projected onto the blind spot of your retina, the point at which the axons of ganglion neurons collect to form the optic nerve. Note that when the pie disappears, your brain "fills in" the missing checkerboard pattern, which is one reason that you're not usually aware that you have blind spots.

complementary
descriptive of colors of the spectrum that when combined produce white or nearly white light

afterimage
the lingering visual impression made by a stimulus that has been removed

some of the dimensions of color and then examine theories about how we manage to convert different wavelengths of light into perceptions of color. *What are some perceptual dimensions of color?* These include hue, value, and saturation.

The wavelength of light determines its color, or *hue*. The value of a color is its degree of brightness or darkness. The saturation refers to how intense a color appears to us. A fire-engine red is more saturated than a pale pinkish-red.

Colors also have psychological associations within various cultural settings. For example, in the United States a bride may be dressed in white as a sign of purity. In traditional India, the guests would be shocked, because white is the color for funerals. Here we mourn in black.

Warm and Cool Colors

If we bend the colors of the spectrum into a circle, we create a color wheel, as shown in Figure 4.4. Psychologically, the colors on the green–blue side of the color wheel are considered to be cool in temperature. Those colors on the yellow–orange–red side are considered to be warm.

Complementary Colors

The colors across from one another on the color wheel are labeled complementary. Red–green and blue–yellow are the major complementary pairs. If we mix complementary colors together, they dissolve into gray.

"But wait!" you say. "Blue and yellow cannot be complementary because by mixing pigments of blue and yellow we create green, not gray." True enough, but we have been talking about mixing *lights*, not *pigments*. Light is the source of all color. Pigments reflect and absorb different wavelengths of light selectively. The mixture of lights is an *additive* process. The mixture of pigments is *subtractive*. Figure 4.5 shows mixtures of lights and pigments of various colors.

Pigments gain their colors by absorbing light from certain segments of the spectrum and reflecting the rest. For example, we see most plant life as green because the pigment in chlorophyll absorbs most of the red, blue, and violet wavelengths of light. The remaining green is reflected. A red pigment absorbs most of the spectrum but reflects red. White pigments reflect all colors equally. Black pigments reflect very little light.

Afterimages

Try this experiment: Look at the strangely colored American flag on the next page for at least half a minute. Try not to blink as you are doing so. Then look at a sheet of white or light-gray paper. What has happened to the flag? If your color vision is working properly, and if you looked at the miscolored flag long enough, you should see a flag composed of the familiar red, white, and blue. The flag you perceive on the white sheet of paper is an **afterimage** of the first. (If you didn't look at the green, black, and yellow flag long enough the first time, try it again.) In afterimages, persistent sensations of color are followed by perception of the complementary color when the first color is removed. The same holds true for black and white. Staring at one will create an afterimage of the other. The phenomenon of afterimages has contributed to one of the theories of color vision, as we will see.

Theories of Color Vision

Adults with normal color vision can discriminate thousands of colors across the visible spectrum. Different colors have different wavelengths. Although we can vary the physical wavelengths of light in a continuous manner from shorter to longer, many changes in color are discontinuous. Our perception of a color shifts suddenly from blue to green, even though the change in

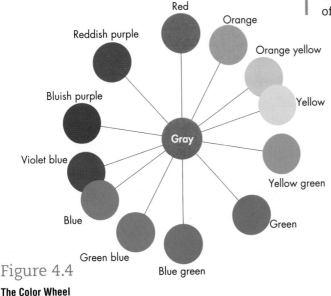

Figure 4.4

The Color Wheel

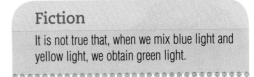

Fiction

It is not true that, when we mix blue light and yellow light, we obtain green light.

Figure 4.5

The mixture of lights is an *additive* process.

The mixture of pigments is *subtractive*.

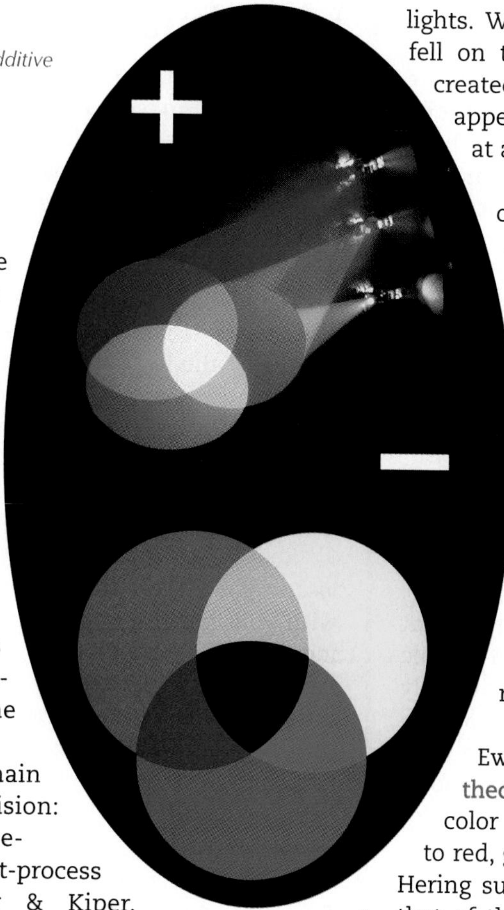

FRITZ GORO/ TIME LIFE PICTURES/GETTY IMAGES

wavelength may be smaller than that between two blues.

How do we perceive color? Why are roses red and violets blue? Our perception of color depends on the physical properties of an object and on the eye's transmission of different messages to the brain when lights with different wavelengths stimulate the cones in the retina.

There are two main theories of color vision: the trichromatic theory and the opponent-process theory (Gegenfurtner & Kiper, 2003). Trichromatic theory is based on an experiment conducted by the British scientist Thomas Young in the early 1800s. As in Figure 4.5, Young projected red, green, and blue-violet lights onto a screen so that they partly overlapped. He found that he could create any color in the visible spectrum by varying the intensities of the three

Figure 4.6

Place a sheet of white paper beneath the book and stare at the black dot in the center of the flag for at least thirty seconds. Then remove the book. The afterimage on the paper beneath will look familiar.

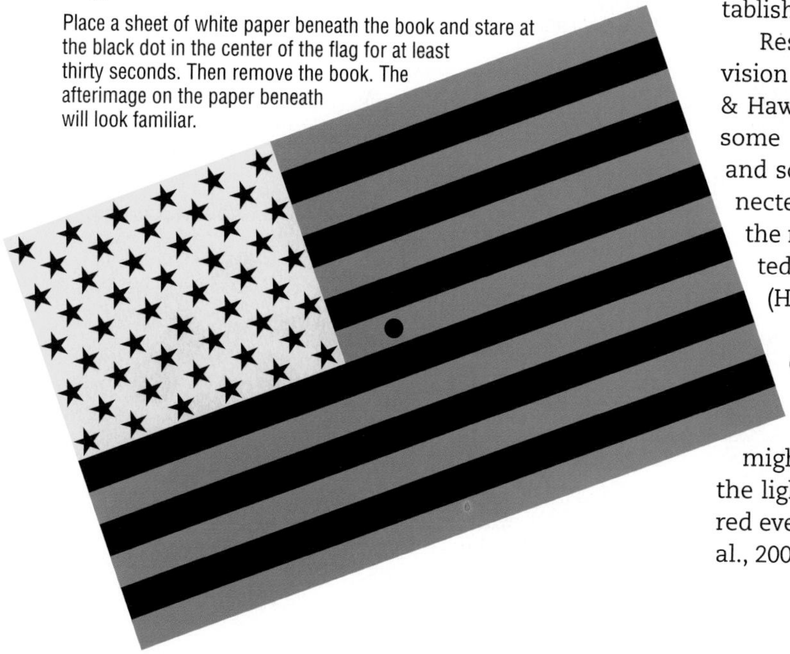

lights. When all three lights fell on the same spot, they created white light, or the appearance of no color at all.

The German physiologist Hermann von Helmholtz saw in Young's discovery an explanation of color vision. Helmholtz suggested that the retina in the eye must have three different types of color photoreceptors or cones. Some cones must be sensitive to red light, some to green, and some to blue. We see other colors when various color receptors are stimulated simultaneously. For example, we perceive yellow when the receptors for red and green are firing.

In 1870, another German physiologist Ewald Hering proposed the opponent-process theory of color vision: There are three types of color receptors, but they are not sensitive only to red, green, and blue, as Helmholtz had claimed. Hering suggested instead that afterimages (such as that of the American flag shown in Figure 4.6) are made possible by three types of color receptors: red–green, blue–yellow, and a type that perceives differences in brightness. According to Hering, a red–green cone cannot transmit messages for red and green at the same time. Therefore, staring at the green, black, and yellow flag for thirty seconds will disturb the balance of neural activity. The afterimage of red, white, and blue would represent the eye's attempt to reestablish a balance.

Research suggests that each theory of color vision is partially correct (Li & DeVries, 2004; Shapley & Hawken, 2002). For example, research shows that some cones are sensitive to blue, some to green, and some to red. However, cones appear to be connected by bipolar and ganglion neurons such that the messages produced by the cones are transmitted to the brain in an opponent-process fashion (Hornstein et al., 2004; Suttle et al., 2002).

A neural rebound effect apparently helps explain the occurrence of afterimages. That is, a green-sensitive ganglion that had been excited by green light for half a minute or so might switch briefly to inhibitory activity when the light is shut off. The effect would be to perceive red even though no red light is present (Hornstein et al., 2004).

trichromatic theory the theory that color vision is made possible by three types of cones, some of which respond to red light, some to green, and some to blue

opponent-process theory the theory that color vision is made possible by three types of cones, some of which respond to red or green light, some to blue or yellow, and some to the intensity of light

trichromat
a person with normal color vision

monochromat
a person who is sensitive to black and white only and hence color-blind

dichromat
a person who is sensitive to black–white and either red–green or blue–yellow and hence partially color-blind

closure
the tendency to perceive a broken figure as being complete or whole

Color Blindness

If you can discriminate among the colors of the visible spectrum, you have normal color vision and are labeled a trichromat. This means that you are sensitive to red–green, blue–yellow, and light–dark. *What is color blindness? Why are some people colorblind?* People who are totally color-blind, called monochromats, are sensitive only to lightness and darkness. Total color blindness is rare. Fully color-blind individuals see the world as trichromats would in a black-and-white movie.

Partial color blindness is a sex-linked trait that affects mostly males. Partially color-blind people are called dichromats. They can discriminate only between two colors—red and green or blue and yellow—and the colors that are derived from mixing these colors (Loop et al., 2003). Figure 4.7 shows the types of tests that are used to diagnose color blindness.

A dichromat might put on one red sock and one green sock, but would not mix red and blue socks. Monochromats might put on socks of any color. They would not notice a difference as long as the socks' colors did not differ in intensity—that is, brightness.

LO³ Visual Perception

What do you see in Figure 4.8—meaningless splotches of ink or a rider on horseback? If you perceive a horse and rider, it is not just because of the visual sensations provided by the drawing. Each of the blobs is meaningless in and of itself, and the pattern is vague. Despite the lack of clarity, however, you may still perceive a horse and rider.

Visual perception is the process by which we organize or make sense of the sensory impressions caused by the light that strikes our eyes. Visual perception involves our knowledge, expectations, and motivations. Whereas sensation may be thought of as a mechanical process (e.g., light stimulating the rods and cones of our retina), perception is an active process through which we interpret the world around us.

How do we organize bits of visual information into meaningful wholes? The answer has something to do with your general knowledge and your desire to fit incoming bits and pieces of information into familiar patterns. In the case of the horse and rider, your integration of disconnected pieces of information into a meaningful whole also reflects the principle of closure—that is, the tendency to perceive a complete or whole figure even when there are gaps in the sensory input.

Perceptual Organization

Early in the 20th century, Gestalt psychologists noted certain consistencies in the way we integrate bits and pieces of sensory stimulation into meaningful

Figure 4.7

Plates from a Test for Color Blindness

Can you see the numbers in these plates from a test for color blindness? A person with red–green color blindness would not be able to see the 6, and a person with blue–yellow color blindness would probably not discern the 12. (Caution: These reproductions cannot be used for actual testing of color blindness.)

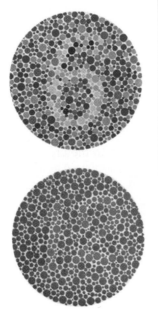

Figure 4.8

Closure

Meaningless splotches of ink, or a horse and rider? This figure illustrates the Gestalt principle of closure.

Figure 4.9

The Rubin Vase: "In parts A, B, and C, is the vase the figure or the ground?"

Go to CourseMate for PSYCH at www.cengagebrain.com to access an interactive version of this figure. ⊙

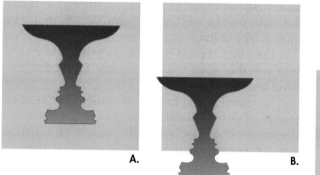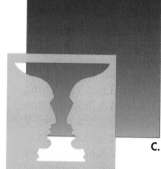

A.　　　　　　B.　　　　　　C.

proximity
nearness; the perceptual tendency to group together objects that are near one another

wholes. They attempted to identify the rules that govern these processes. As a group, these rules are referred to as the laws of perceptual organization.

Figure–Ground Perception

If you look out your window, you may see people, buildings, cars, and streets, or perhaps grass, trees, birds, and clouds. These objects tend to be perceived as figures against backgrounds. For instance, individual cars seen against the background of the street are easier to pick out than cars piled on top of one another in a junkyard.

When figure–ground relationships are *ambiguous*, or capable of being interpreted in various ways, our perceptions tend to be unstable and shift back and forth (Bull et al., 2003).

Figure 4.9 shows a Rubin vase, one of psychologists' favorite illustrations of figure–ground relationships. The figure–ground relationship in part A of the figure is ambiguous. There are no cues that suggest which area must be the figure. For this reason,

our perception may shift from seeing the vase to seeing two profiles. There is no such problem in part B. Because it seems that a blue vase has been brought forward against a colored ground, we are more likely to perceive the vase than the profiles. In part C, we are more likely to perceive the profiles than the vase, because the profiles are complete and the vase is broken against the background. Of course, if we wish to, we can still perceive the vase in part C, because experience has shown us where it is.

Other Gestalt Rules for Organization

Gestalt psychologists have noted that our perceptions are also guided by rules or laws of *proximity*, *similarity*, *continuity*, and *common fate*.

Let's try a mini-experiment. Without reading further, describe part A of Figure 4.10. Did you say it consists of six lines or of three groups of two parallel lines? If you said three sets of lines, you were influenced by the proximity, or nearness, of some of the lines. There is no other reason for perceiving them in pairs or subgroups: All lines are parallel and equal in length.

Now describe part B of Figure 4.10. Did you perceive the figure as a six-by-six grid, or as three columns

Figure 4.10

Some Gestalt Laws of Perceptual Organization

These drawings illustrate the Gestalt laws of proximity, similarity, continuity, and closure.

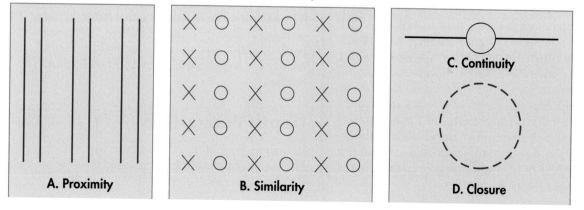

A. Proximity

B. Similarity

C. Continuity

D. Closure

similarity
the perceptual tendency to group together objects that are similar in appearance

continuity
the tendency to perceive a series of points or lines as having unity

common fate
the tendency to perceive elements that move together as belonging together

top-down processing
the use of contextual information or knowledge of a pattern in order to organize parts of the pattern

bottom-up processing
the organization of the parts of a pattern to recognize, or form an image of, the pattern they compose

illusions
sensations that give rise to misperceptions

stroboscopic motion
a visual illusion in which the perception of motion is generated by a series of stationary images that are presented in rapid succession

of 's and three columns of 's? According to the law of similarity, we perceive similar objects as belonging together. For this reason, you may have been more likely to describe part B in terms of columns than in terms of rows or a grid.

What of part C? Is it a circle with two lines stemming from it, or is it a (broken) line that goes through a circle? If you saw it as a single (broken) line, you were probably organizing your perceptions according to the rule of continuity. That is, we perceive a series of points or a broken line as having unity.

According to the law of common fate, elements seen moving together are perceived as belonging together. A group of people running in the same direction appears unified in purpose. Part D of Figure 4.10 provides another example of the law of closure. The arcs tend to be perceived as a circle (or a circle with gaps) rather than as just a series of arcs.

Top-Down Versus Bottom-Up Processing

Imagine that you are trying to put together a 1,000-piece jigsaw puzzle. Now imagine that you are trying to accomplish it after someone has walked off with the box showing the picture formed by the completed puzzle.

If you use the picture on the box, you're engaging in top-down processing—using the completed image to search for the proper pieces. Similarly, we may form more lasting relationships when we search with an idea of the qualities we will find compatible in another person. Or we may make better investments when we have a retirement financial goal and date in mind. With bottom-up processing, we begin with bits and pieces of information and try to assemble them in a pattern—in jigsaw puzzles and, perhaps, by being thrown into a social or vocational situation. In bottom-up processing, we do not have a clear idea of where we are going, and perhaps we try to make the best of things.

Perception of Motion

How do we perceive movement? To understand perception of movement, think of what it is like to be on a train that has begun to pull out of the station while the train on the next track stays still. If your own train does not lurch as it accelerates, it might seem that the other train is moving. Or you might not be sure whether your train is moving forward or the other train is moving back.

The visual perception of movement is based on change of position relative to other objects. To early scientists, whose only tool for visual observation was the naked eye, it seemed logical that the sun circled the earth. You have to be able to imagine the movement of the earth around the sun as seen from a theoretical point in outer space; you cannot observe it directly.

How, then, can you be certain which train is moving? One way is to look for objects that you know are still, such as platform columns, houses, signs, or trees. If your position does not change in relation to them, your train is not moving. You might also try to sense the motion of the train in your body. You probably know from experience how to do these things quite well.

We have been considering the perception of real movement. Psychologists have also studied several types of apparent movement, or illusions of movement. One of these illusions is stroboscopic motion.

Stroboscopic Motion

So-called motion pictures do not really consist of images that move. Rather, the audience is shown sixteen to twenty-two pictures, or *frames*, per second. Each frame differs slightly from the preceding one. Showing the frames in rapid succession provides the illusion of movement. This illusion of motion is termed stroboscopic motion.

At the rate of at least sixteen frames per second, the "motion" in a film seems smooth and natural. With fewer than sixteen or so frames per second, the movement looks jumpy and unnatural. That is why slow motion is usually achieved by filming 100 or more frames per second. When they are played back at about twenty-two frames per second, the movement seems slowed down, but still smooth and natural.

Depth Perception

How do we perceive depth? Monocular and binocular cues help us perceive the depth of objects—that is, their distance from us.

Monocular Cues

Artists use monocular cues called pictorial cues to create an illusion of depth. These cues can be perceived by one eye (*mono* means "one"). They include perspective, relative size, clearness, overlapping, shadows, and texture gradient, and they cause some objects to seem more distant than others even though they are all drawn or painted on a flat surface.

Distant objects stimulate smaller areas on the retina than nearby ones, even though they may be the same size. The distances between far-off objects also appear to be smaller than equivalent distances between nearby objects. For this reason, the phenomenon known as perspective occurs. That is, we tend to perceive parallel lines as coming closer together, or converging, as they recede from us. As we will see when we discuss *size constancy*, however, experience teaches us that distant objects that look small are larger when they are close. In this way, their relative size also becomes a cue to their distance.

Artists normally use *relative size*—the fact that distant objects look smaller than nearby objects of the same size—to suggest depth in their works.

The *clearness* of an object suggests its distance. Experience teaches us that we sense more details of nearby objects. For this reason, artists can suggest that objects are closer to the viewer by depicting them in greater detail.

We also learn that nearby objects can block our view of more distant objects. *Overlapping* is the placing of one object in front of another. Experience teaches us that partly covered objects are farther away than the objects that obscure them (see Figure 4.11).

Additional information about depth is provided by *shadowing* and is based on the fact that opaque objects block light and produce shadows. Shadows and highlights give us information about an object's three-dimensional shape and its relationship to the source of light. For example, in the right part of Figure 4.11, the left circle is perceived as a two-dimensional circle, but the right circle tends to be perceived as a three-dimensional sphere because of the highlight on its surface and the shadow underneath. In the "sphere," the highlighted central area is perceived as closest to us, with the surface receding to the edges.

Another monocular cue is texture gradient. (A gradient is a progressive change.) Closer objects are perceived as having rougher textures.

Motion cues are another kind of monocular cue. If you have ever driven in the country, you have probably noticed that distant objects such as mountains and stars appear to move along with you. Objects at an intermediate distance seem to be stationary, but nearby objects such as roadside markers, rocks, and trees seem to go by quite rapidly. The tendency of objects to seem to move backward or forward as a function of their distance is known as motion parallax. We learn to perceive objects that appear to move with us as being at greater distances.

Earlier we noted that nearby objects cause the lens of the eye to accommodate or bend more in order to bring them into focus. The sensations of tension in the eye muscles also provide a monocular cue to depth, especially when we are within about four feet of the objects.

monocular cues stimuli suggestive of depth that can be perceived with only one eye

perspective a monocular cue for depth based on the convergence (coming together) of parallel lines as they recede into the distance

texture gradient a monocular cue for depth based on the perception that closer objects appear to have rougher (more detailed) surfaces

motion parallax a monocular cue for depth based on the perception that nearby objects appear to move more rapidly in relation to our own motion

Figure 4.11

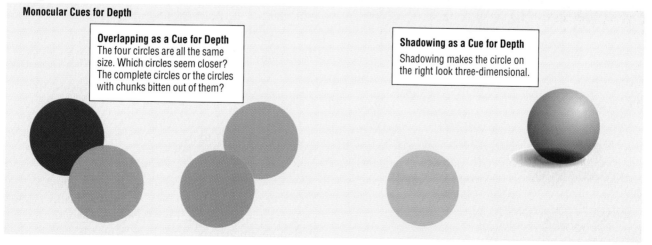

Monocular Cues for Depth

Overlapping as a Cue for Depth
The four circles are all the same size. Which circles seem closer? The complete circles or the circles with chunks bitten out of them?

Shadowing as a Cue for Depth
Shadowing makes the circle on the right look three-dimensional.

© 2010 ENAMUL HOQUE/ JUPITERIMAGES CORPORATION

Figure 4.12

Brightness Constancy

The orange squares within the blue squares are the same hue, yet the orange within the dark blue square is perceived as brighter. Why?

Binocular Cues

Binocular cues, or cues that involve both eyes, also help us perceive depth. Two binocular cues are *retinal disparity* and *convergence*.

Try an experiment. Hold your right index finger at arm's length. Now hold your left index finger about a foot closer, but in a direct line. If you keep your eyes relaxed as you do so, you will see first one finger and then the other. An image of each finger will be projected onto the retina of each eye, and each image will be slightly different because the finger will be seen from different angles. The difference between the projected images is referred to as **retinal disparity** and serves as a binocular cue for depth perception. Note that in the case of the closer finger, the "two fingers" appear to be farther apart. Closer objects have greater retinal disparity.

If we try to maintain a single image of the closer finger, our eyes must turn inward, or converge on it, making us cross-eyed. **Convergence** causes feelings of tension in the eye muscles and provides another binocular cue for depth. (After convergence occurs, try looking at the finger first with one eye closed, then the other. You will readily see how different the images are in each eye.) The binocular cues of retinal disparity and convergence are strongest when objects are close.

Perceptual Constancies

Think how confusing it would be if you believed that a door was a trapezoid and not a rectangle because it is ajar. Fortunately, perceptual constancies enable us to recognize objects even when their apparent shape or size differs. *What are perceptual constancies?*

Size Constancy

There are a number of perceptual constancies, including that of **size constancy**. The image of a dog seen from twenty feet away occupies about the same amount of space on your retina as an inch-long insect crawling on your hand. Yet you do not perceive the dog to be as small as the insect. Through your visual experiences you have acquired size constancy—that is, the tendency to *perceive* an object as the same size even though the size of its image on your retina varies as a function of its distance. Experience teaches us about perspective—that the same object seen at a distance appears to be smaller than when it is nearby.

Color Constancy

Color constancy is the tendency to perceive objects as retaining their color even though lighting conditions may alter their appearance. Your bright-yellow car may edge toward gray as the hours wend their way through twilight. But when you finally locate the car in the parking lot, you may still think of it as yellow. You expect to find a yellow car and still judge it to be "more yellow" than the (twilight-faded) red and green cars on either side of it.

Brightness constancy is similar to color constancy. Consider Figure 4.12. The orange squares within the blue squares are equally bright, yet the one within the dark-blue square is perceived as brighter. Why? Again,

consider the role of experience. If it were nighttime, we would expect orange to fade to gray. The fact that the orange within the dark square stimulates the eye with equal intensity suggests that it must be much brighter than the orange within the lighter square.

Shape Constancy

Shape constancy is the tendency to perceive objects as maintaining their shape, even if we look at them from different angles so that the shape of their image on the retina changes dramatically. You perceive the top of a coffee cup or a glass to be a circle even though it is a circle only when seen from above. When seen from an angle, it is an ellipse. When the cup or glass is seen on edge, its retinal image is the same as that of a straight line. So why do you still describe the rim of the cup or glass as a circle? Perhaps for two reasons: First, experience has taught you that the cup will look circular when seen from above. Second, you may have labeled the cup as circular or round.

Let us return to the door that "changes shape" when it is ajar. The door is a rectangle only when viewed straight on. When we move to the side or open it, the left or right edge comes closer and appears to be larger, changing the retinal image to a trapezoid. Yet we continue to think of doors as rectangles. In the photo on the previous page, we see a woman with a very large hand, but because of experience, we recognize that the hand only appears to be out of proportion to the rest of her because it is pushed toward us.

Visual Illusions

The principles of perceptual organization make it possible for our eyes to "play tricks" on us. That is, the perceptual constancies trick the eye through *visual illusions.*

The Hering–Helmholtz and Müller–Lyer illusions (see Figure 4.13) are named after the people who devised them. In the Hering–Helmholtz illusion (part A), the horizontal lines are straight and parallel. However, the radiating lines cause them to appear to be bent outward near the center. The two lines in the Müller–Lyer illusion (part B) are the same length, but the line on the right, with its reversed arrowheads, looks longer.

Let us try to explain these illusions. Because of our experience and lifelong use of perceptual cues, we tend to perceive the Hering–Helmholtz drawing as three-dimensional. Because of our tendency to perceive bits of sensory information as figures against grounds, we perceive the blue area in the center as a circle in front of a series of radiating lines, all of which lie in front of a blue ground. Next, because of our experience with perspective, we perceive the radiating lines as parallel. We perceive the two horizontal lines as intersecting the "receding" lines, and we know that they would have to appear bent out at the center if they were to be equidistant at all points from the center of the circle.

Experience probably compels us to perceive the vertical lines in the Müller–Lyer illusion as the corners of a building (see Figure 4.13, part B). We interpret the length of the lines based on our experience with corners of buildings.

> **shape constancy**
> the tendency to perceive an object as being the same shape although the retinal image varies in shape as it rotates

LO⁴ Hearing

Consider the advertising slogan for the classic science fiction film *Alien:* "In space, no one can hear you scream." It's true. Space is an almost perfect vacuum. Hearing requires a medium through which

Figure 4.13

The Hering–Helmholtz and Müller–Lyer Illusions

In the Hering–Helmholtz illusion, are the horizontal lines straight or curved? In the Müller–Lyer illusion, are the vertical lines equal in length?
Go to CourseMate for PSYCH at www.cengagebrain.com to access an interactive version of this figure. ⊙

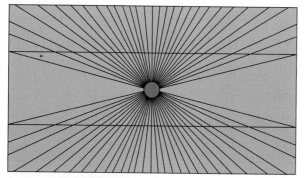

A. The Hering–Helmholtz Illusion

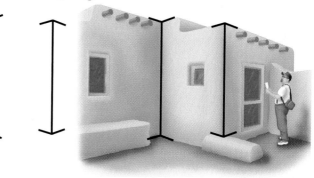

B. The Müller–Lyer Illusion

hertz (Hz)
a unit expressing the frequency of sound waves. One hertz equals one cycle per second

decibel (dB)
a unit expressing the loudness of a sound

sound can travel, such as air or water. *What is sound?*

Sound, or auditory stimulation, is the vibration of molecules in a medium such as air or water. Sound travels through the medium like waves, or like ripples in a pond when you toss in a pebble. The molecules of the medium are alternately compressed and expanded like the movements of an accordion. If you were listening under water, you would also hear the splash because of changes in the pressure of the water. In either case, the changes in pressure are vibrations that approach your ears in waves. These vibrations—sound waves—can also be created by a ringing bell, your vocal cords, guitar strings, or the slam of a book thrown down on a desk. A single cycle of compression and expansion is one wave of sound. Sound waves can occur many times in one second. The human ear is sensitive to sound waves with frequencies of from twenty to 20,000 cycles per second.

Pitch and Loudness

Pitch and loudness are two psychological dimensions of sound. The pitch of a sound is determined by its frequency, or the number of cycles per second as expressed in the unit hertz (Hz). One cycle per second is 1 Hz. The greater the number of cycles per second (Hz), the higher the pitch of the sound.

Figure 4.14

Sound Waves of Various Frequencies and Amplitudes

Which sounds have the highest pitch? Which are loudest?

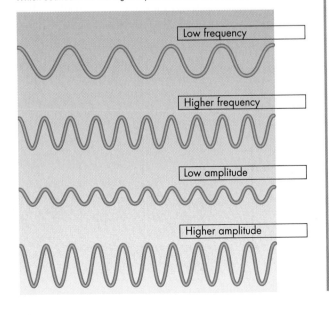

Low frequency

Higher frequency

Low amplitude

Higher amplitude

The pitch of women's voices is usually higher than that of men's voices because women's vocal cords are usually shorter and therefore vibrate at a greater frequency. Also, the strings of a violin are shorter than those of a viola or double bass. Pitch detectors in the brain allow us to tell differences in pitch.

The loudness of a sound roughly corresponds to the height, or amplitude, of sound waves. Figure 4.14 shows records of sound waves that vary in frequency and amplitude. Frequency and amplitude are independent. That is, both high- and low-pitched sounds can be either high or low in loudness. The loudness of a sound is expressed in decibels (dB). Zero dB is equivalent to the threshold of hearing—the lowest sound that the typical person can hear. How loud is that? It's about as loud as the ticking of a watch twenty feet away in a very quiet room.

The decibel equivalents of familiar sounds are shown in Figure 4.15. Twenty-five dB is equivalent in

Figure 4.15

Decibel Ratings of Familiar Sounds

Zero dB is the threshold of hearing. You may suffer hearing loss if you incur prolonged exposure to sounds of 85 to 90 dB.

Typical decibel level		Dangerous time exposure	Examples
	180		Space Shuttle launch
	170		
	160	Hearing loss certain	Shotgun blast
	150		Jet airplane
	140	Any exposure dangerous	Siren at 50 feet / Stereo headset (full volume) / Threshold of pain
Extremely loud	130	Immediate danger	Thunder, rock concert, basketball or hockey crowd
	120		Riveter
	110		Factory noise, chain saw
	100	Less than 8 hours	Subway, tractor, power mower, screaming child
Very loud	90		Bus, motorcycle, snowmobile
	80	More than 8 hours	Loud home stereo, food blender / Heavy traffic
	70		Average automobile
	60		Normal conversation
	50		Quiet auto
Quiet	40		Quiet office
	30		
Very quiet	20		Whisper at 5 feet
	10		Broadcast studio when quiet
Just audible	0		

© 2010 PHOTODISC / JUPITERIMAGES CORPORATION / © PRNEWSFOTO/MURRAY INC.

loudness to a whisper at five feet. Thirty dB is roughly the limit of loudness at which your librarian would like to keep your college library. You may suffer hearing damage if you are exposed to sounds of 85 to 90 dB for long periods.

The Ear

How does the ear work? The ear is shaped and structured to capture sound waves, vibrate in sympathy with them, and transmit them to the brain. In this way, you not only hear something, you can also figure out what it is. The ear has three parts: the outer ear, the middle ear, and the inner ear (see Figure 4.16).

The outer ear is shaped to funnel sound waves to the *eardrum*, a thin membrane that vibrates in response to sound waves, and thereby transmits them to the middle and inner ears. The middle ear contains the eardrum and three small bones, which also transmit sound by vibrating. These bones were given their Latin names (*malleus, incus,* and *stapes* [pronounced STAYpeas], which translate as "hammer," "anvil," and "stirrup") because of their shapes. The middle ear functions as an amplifier, increasing the pressure of the air entering the ear.

The stirrup is attached to another vibrating membrane, the *oval window*. The oval window works in conjunction with the round window, which balances the pressure in the inner ear (see Figure 4.16). The round window pushes outward when the oval window pushes in, and is pulled inward when the oval window vibrates outward.

The oval window transmits vibrations into the inner ear, the bony tube called the cochlea (from the Greek word for "snail"). The cochlea, which is shaped like a snail shell, contains two longitudinal membranes that divide it into three fluid-filled chambers. One of the membranes that lies coiled within the cochlea is called the basilar membrane. Vibrations in the fluids within the chambers of the inner ear press against the basilar membrane.

The organ of Corti, sometimes referred to as the "command post" of hearing, is attached to the basilar membrane. Some 25,000 receptor cells—called hair cells because they project like hair from the organ of Corti—are found in each ear. Hair cells "dance" in response to the vibrations of the basilar membrane. Their movements generate neural impulses, which are transmitted to the brain via the auditory nerve. Auditory input is then projected onto the hearing areas of the temporal lobes of the cerebral cortex.

Locating Sounds

How do we locate sounds? There is a resemblance between balancing a set of stereo speakers and

cochlea the inner ear; the bony tube that contains the basilar membrane and the organ of Corti

basilar membrane a membrane that lies coiled within the cochlea

organ of Corti the receptor for hearing that lies on the basilar membrane in the cochlea

auditory nerve the axon bundle that transmits neural impulses from the organ of Corti to the brain

Figure 4.16

The Human Ear

Go to CourseMate for PSYCH at www.cengagebrain.com to access an interactive version of this figure.

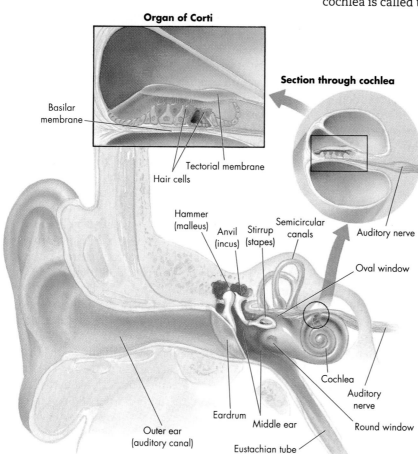

Organ of Corti

Basilar membrane

Tectorial membrane

Hair cells

Section through cochlea

Hammer (malleus)

Anvil (incus)

Stirrup (stapes)

Semicircular canals

Auditory nerve

Oval window

Cochlea

Auditory nerve

Eardrum

Middle ear

Round window

Outer ear (auditory canal)

Eustachian tube

locating sounds. A sound that is louder in the right ear is perceived as coming from the right. A sound coming from the right also reaches the right ear first. Both loudness and the sequence in which the sounds reach the ears provide directional cues.

But it may not be easy to locate a sound coming from in front or in back of you or above. Such sounds are equally distant from each ear and equally loud. So what do we do? Simple—we turn our head slightly to determine in which ear the sound increases. If you turn your head to the right and the loudness increases in your left ear, the sound is likely coming from in front.

Perception of Loudness and Pitch

Sounds are heard because they cause vibration in parts of the ear and information about these vibrations is transmitted to the brain. *How do we perceive loudness and pitch?* The loudness and pitch of sounds appear to be related to the number of receptor neurons on the organ of Corti that fire and how often they fire. Psychologists generally agree that sounds are perceived as louder when more of these sensory neurons fire.

It takes two processes to explain perception of color: *trichromatic theory* and *opponent-process theory*. Similarly, it takes at least two processes to explain perception of sound waves that vary in frequency from twenty to 20,000 cycles per second: *place theory* and *frequency theory*.

Hermann von Helmholtz helped develop the place theory of pitch discrimination as well as the trichromatic theory of color vision. Place theory holds that the pitch of a sound is sensed according to the place along the basilar membrane that vibrates in response to it. In research that led to the award of a Nobel Prize, Georg von Békésy (1957) found that receptors at different sites along the membrane fire in response to tones of differing frequencies. Receptor neurons appear to be lined up along the basilar membrane like piano keys. The higher the pitch of a sound, the closer the responsive neurons lie to the oval window (Larkin, 2000). However, place theory appears to apply only to pitches that are at least 5,000 Hz. But what about lower pitches? That's where frequency theory comes in.

Frequency theory notes that for us to perceive lower pitches, we need to match the frequency of the sound waves with our neural impulses. That is, in response to low pitches—say twenty to 1,000 cycles per second—hair cells on the basilar membrane fire at the same frequencies as the sound waves. However, neurons cannot fire more frequently. Therefore, frequency theory best explains perception of pitches between twenty and 1,000 cycles per second.

It takes at least two processes to explain how people perceive pitch. The perception of sounds between 1,000 and 5,000 cycles per second depends both on the part of the basilar membrane that vibrates (as in place theory), and the frequency with which it vibrates (as in frequency theory). The processes apparently work together to enable us to hear pitches in the intermediate range (Goldstein, 2004).

Deafness

More than one in ten Americans have a hearing impairment, and one in 100 cannot hear at all (Canalis & Lambert, 2000). *What is deafness? What can we do about it?*

Two major types of deafness are conductive deafness and sensorineural deafness. *Conductive deafness* stems from damage to the structures of the middle ear—either to the eardrum or to the bones that conduct (and amplify) sound waves from the outer ear to the inner ear (Canalis & Lambert, 2000). This is the hearing impairment often found among older people. Hearing aids amplify sound and often help people with conductive deafness.

Sensorineural deafness usually stems from damage to the structures of the inner ear, most often the loss of hair cells. Sensorineural deafness can also stem from damage to the auditory nerve, caused by such factors as disease or exposure to very loud sounds. In sensorineural deafness, people tend to be more sensitive to some pitches than others. In so-called Hunter's notch, the loss is limited to the frequencies of the sound waves generated by a gun firing. Prolonged exposure to 85 dB can cause hearing loss. People who attend rock concerts, where sounds may reach 140 dB, risk damaging their ears, as do workers who run pneumatic drills or drive noisy vehicles. The ringing sensation that often follows exposure to loud sounds probably means that hair cells in the inner ear have been damaged.

Cochlear implants, or "artificial ears," contain microphones that sense sounds and electronic equipment that transmits sounds past damaged hair cells to stimulate the auditory nerve. Such implants have helped many people with sensorineural deafness (Geers et al., 2002), but they cannot assume the functions of damaged auditory nerves.

Apples and onions are similar in taste, but their flavors differ greatly.

LO⁵ The Chemical Senses: Smell and Taste

Smell and taste are the chemical senses. In vision and hearing, physical energy strikes our sensory receptors. In smell and taste, we sample molecules of substances.

Smell

Smell has an important role in human behavior. It contributes to the flavor of foods, for example. If you did not have a sense of smell, an onion and an apple might taste the same to you. People's sense of smell may be deficient when compared with that of a dog, but we can detect the odor of 1 one-millionth of a milligram of vanilla in a liter of air.

How does the sense of smell work? Smell detects odors. An *odor* is a sample of molecules of a substance in the air. Odors trigger firing of receptor neurons in the olfactory membrane high in each nostril. Receptor neurons can detect even a few molecules of the substance in gaseous form. The receptor neurons transmit information about odors to the brain via the olfactory nerve.

What's that SCENT you're wearing?

Taste

How does the sense of taste work? As in the case of smell, taste samples molecules of a substance. Taste is sensed through taste cells—receptor neurons located on taste buds. You have about 10,000 taste buds, most of which are located near the edges and back of your tongue. Some tastebuds are more responsive to sweetness, whereas others react to several tastes. Other taste receptors are found in the roof, sides, and back of the mouth, and in the throat. Buds in the mouth are evolutionarily adaptive because they can warn of bad food before it is swallowed (Brand, 2000).

Researchers generally agree on at least four primary taste qualities: sweet, sour, salty, and bitter. Some argue for a fifth basic taste, which is termed *umami* (pronounced *oohmommy*) in Japanese and means "meaty" or "savory." Regardless of the number of basic tastes, the flavor of a food is more complex than taste alone. *Flavor* depends on odor, texture, and temperature as well as on taste. Apples and onions are similar in taste, but their flavors differ greatly.

Just as some people see better than others, some people taste better than others—but their superiority may be limited to one or more basic tastes. Those of us with low sensitivity for sweetness may require twice the sugar to sweeten our food as those who are more sensitive. Those of us who claim to enjoy bitter foods may actually be taste-blind to them (Lanier et al., 2005). Sensitivities to various tastes have a genetic component (Bartoshuk, 2000; Duffy et al., 2004).

flavor
a complex quality of food and other substances that is based on their odor, texture, and temperature as well their taste

olfactory nerve
the nerve that transmits information concerning odors from olfactory receptors to the brain

taste cells
receptor cells that are sensitive to taste

taste buds
the sensory organs for taste. They contain taste cells and are located mostly on the tongue

LO⁶ The Skin Senses

What are the skin senses? How do they work? The skin senses include touch, pressure, warmth, cold, and pain. We have distinct sensory receptors for pressure, temperature, and pain, but some nerve endings may receive more than one type of sensory input. Here let's focus on touch, pressure, temperature, and pain.

Touch and Pressure

Sensory receptors embedded in the skin fire when the surface of the skin is touched. There may

Talk to me about nerve endings and the sensory cortex.

be several kinds of receptors for touch, some that respond to constant pressure, some that respond to intermittent pressure, as in tapping the skin. *Active touching* means continually moving your hand along the surface of an object so that you continue to receive sensory input from the object (O'Dell & Hoyert, 2002). If you are trying to "get the feel of" a fabric or the texture of a friend's hair, you must move your hand over it. Otherwise the sensations quickly fade. If you pass your hand over the fabric or hair and then hold it still, the sensations of touching will fade. Active touching receives information concerning pressure, temperature, texture, and feedback from the muscles involved in movements of our hands.

Different parts of the body are more sensitive to touch and pressure than others. The parts of the body that "cover" more than their fair share of somatosensory cortex are most sensitive to touch. These parts include the hands, face, and some other regions of the body. Our fingertips, lips, noses, and cheeks are more sensitive than our shoulders, thighs, and calves. Why the difference in sensitivity? First, nerve endings are more densely packed in the fingertips and face than in other locations. Second, more sensory cortex is devoted to the perception of sensations in the fingertips and face (see Figure 2.11 on page 38).

Temperature

The receptors for temperature are neurons located just beneath the skin. When skin temperature increases, the receptors for warmth fire. Decreases in skin temperature cause receptors for cold to fire.

Sensations of temperature are relative. When we are at normal body temperature, we might perceive another person's skin as warm. When we are feverish, though, the other person's skin might seem cool. We also adapt to differences in temperature. When we enter a swimming pool, the water may seem cold because it is below body temperature. Yet after a few moments an 80°F pool may seem quite warm. In fact, we may chide a newcomer for not diving right in.

Pain

For most people, pain is a frequent visitor. Headaches, backaches, toothaches—these are only a few of the types of pain that most of us encounter from time to time. According to a national Gallup survey of more than 2,000 adults (Arthritis Foundation, 2000), 89% experience pain at least once a month. More than half (55%) of people aged sixty-five and above say they experience pain daily. People aged sixty-five and above are most likely to attribute pain to getting older (88%) and to assume they can do nothing about disabilities such as arthritis. By contrast, people aged eighteen to thirty-four are more likely to attribute pain to tension or stress (73%), overwork (64%), or their lifestyle (51%). When we assume that there is nothing we can do about pain, we are less likely to try. Yet 43% of Americans say that pain curtails their activities, and 50% say that pain puts them in a bad mood. *What is pain? What can we do about it?*

Pain results when neurons called *nociceptors* in the skin are stimulated. Evolutionary psychologists would point out that pain is adaptive, if unpleasant, because it motivates us to do something about it. For some of us, however, chronic pain—pain that lasts once injuries or illnesses have cleared—saps our vitality and interferes with the pleasures of everyday life (Turk & Okifuji, 2002).

We can sense pain throughout most of the body, but pain is usually sharpest where nerve endings are densely packed, as in the fingers and face. Pain can also be felt deep within the body, as in the cases of abdominal pain and back pain. Even though headaches may seem to originate deep inside the head, there are no nerve endings for pain in the brain.

Pain usually originates at the point of contact, as when you bang a knee. But it reverberates throughout the nervous system. The pain message to the brain is initiated by the release of chemicals such as prostaglandins, bradykinin, and P (yes, P stands for "pain"). *Prostaglandins* facilitate transmission of the pain message to the brain and heighten circulation to the injured area, causing the redness and swelling that we call inflammation. Inflammation attracts infection-fighting blood cells to the injury to protect it against invading germs. Pain-relieving drugs such as aspirin and ibuprofen help by inhibiting production of prostaglandins.

The pain message is relayed from the spinal cord to the thalamus and then projected to the cerebral cortex, making us aware of the location and intensity of the damage. Ronald Melzack (1999) speaks of a "neuromatrix" that includes these chemical reactions but involves other aspects of our physiology and psychology in our reaction to pain. For example, visual and other sensory inputs tell us what is happening and affect our interpretation of the situation. Our emotional response affects the degree of pain, and so do the ways in which we respond to stress. If, for instance, the pain derives from an object we fear, perhaps a knife or a needle, we may experience more pain. If we perceive that there is nothing we can do to change the situation, perception of pain may increase. If we have self-confidence and a history of successful response to stress, perception of pain may diminish.

Phantom Limb Pain

One of the more intriguing topics in the study of pain is phantom limb pain. About two out of three combat veterans with amputated limbs report feeling pain in such missing, or "phantom," limbs (Kooijman et al., 2000). Although the pain occurs in the absence of the limb, it is real enough. It sometimes involves activation of nerves in the stump of the missing limb, but local anesthesia does not always eliminate the pain. Researchers have found that many people who experience phantom limb pain have also undergone reorganization of the motor and somatosensory cortex that is consistent with the pain (Mackert et al., 2003).

> **Truth**
>
> Many people do appear to experience pain "in" limbs that have been amputated (Horgan & MacLachlan, 2004).

Gate Theory

Simple remedies like rubbing a banged knee frequently help relieve pain. Why? One possible answer lies in the *gate theory* of pain originated by Ronald Melzack and Patrick Wall (Sufka & Price, 2002). Gate theory proposes that the nervous system can process only a limited amount of stimulation at a time. Rubbing the knee transmits sensations to the brain that "compete" for the attention of neurons. Many nerves are thus prevented from transmitting pain messages to the brain. It is like shutting down a "gate" in the spinal cord, or like a switchboard being flooded with calls. Flooding prevents any calls from getting through.

Acupuncture

Thousands of years ago, the Chinese began mapping the body to learn where pins might be placed to deaden pain. This practice is termed acupuncture. Traditional acupuncturists believe that the practice balances the body's flow of energy, but research has shown that it stimulates nerves that reach the hypothalamus and may also cause the release of *endorphins* (Ulett & Wedding, 2003). Endorphins are neurotransmitters that are similar to the narcotic morphine in their chemical structure and effects.

LO⁷ Kinesthesis and the Vestibular Sense

Try an experiment. Close your eyes, and then touch your nose with your finger. If you weren't right on target, I'm sure you came close. But how? You didn't see your hand moving, and you didn't hear your arm swishing through the air. Humans and many other animals have senses that alert them to their movements and body position without relying on vision, including kinesthesis and the vestibular sense.

Kinesthesis

What is kinesthesis? Kinesthesis is the sense that informs you about the position and motion of parts of the body. The term is derived from the ancient Greek words for "motion" (kinesis) and "perception" (aisthesis). In kinesthesis, sensory information is fed back to the brain from sensory organs in the joints, tendons, and muscles. You were able to bring your finger to your nose easily by employing your kinesthetic sense. When you make a muscle in your arm, the sensations of tightness and hardness are also provided by kinesthesis.

> **kinesthesis**
> the sense that informs us about the positions and motion of parts of our bodies

vestibular sense
the sense of equilibrium that informs us about our bodies' positions relative to gravity

Imagine going for a walk without kinesthesis. You would have to watch the forward motion of each leg to be certain you had raised it high enough to clear the curb. And if you had tried the brief nose-to-finger experiment without the kinesthetic sense, you would have had no sensory feedback until you felt the pressure of your finger against your nose (or cheek, or eye, or forehead), and you probably would have missed dozens of times.

The Vestibular Sense

It is your vestibular sense that provides your brain with information as to whether or not you are physically upright.

How does the vestibular sense work? Sensory organs located in the semicircular canals and elsewhere in the ears monitor your body's motion and position in relation to gravity. They tell you whether you are falling and provide cues to whether your body is changing speed, such as when you are in an accelerating airplane or automobile.

LO^8 ESP: Is There Perception Without Sensation?

Our sensory organs are the peripheral devices that feed information into our central processing units—our brains. What if there were such as thing as extra sensory perception (ESP)? What if sensation were bypassed, and we directly perceived things in the world outside? Although the actual research evidence comes down hard against ESP, 60% of the American public believes that some people have psychic powers or ESP (National Science Foundation, 2002). Therefore, it is useful to understand the issue and examine the type of research that psychologists conduct to determine whether it has validity. Let us begin by defining precognition and other topics in ESP.

Precognition, Psychokinesis, Telepathy, and Clairvoyance

Imagine the wealth you could amass if you had *precognition*, that is, if you were able to perceive future events in advance. Perhaps you would check the next week's stock market reports and know what to buy or sell. Or you could bet with confidence on who would win the next Super Bowl or World Series. Or think of the power you would have if you were capable of *psychokinesis*, that is, of mentally manipulating or moving objects. You may have gotten a glimpse of the possibilities in films like *The Matrix*, *The Sixth Sense*, and *Star Wars*. Precognition and psychokinesis are two concepts associated with ESP. Two other theoretical forms of ESP are *telepathy* or direct transmission of thoughts or ideas from one person to another, and *clairvoyance*, or the perception of objects that do not stimulate the sensory organs. An example of clairvoyance is "seeing" what card will be dealt next, even though it is still in the deck and unseen even by the dealer.

Many psychologists do not believe that ESP is an appropriate area for scientific inquiry. Other psychologists, however, believe that there is nothing wrong with investigating ESP. The issue for them is whether its existence can be demonstrated in the laboratory. *Does ESP really exist?*

A well-known ESP researcher was Joseph Banks Rhine of Duke University, who studied ESP for several decades, beginning in the 1920s. In a typical experiment in clairvoyance, Rhine would use a pack of twenty-five cards, which contained five sets of simple symbols. Pigeons pecking patterns at random to indicate which one was about to be turned up would be "correct" 20% of the time. Rhine found that some people guessed correctly significantly more often than the 20% chance rate. He concluded that these people might have some degree of ESP.

A more current method for studying telepathy is the *ganzfeld procedure* (Dalkvist, 2001; Parker, 2001). In this method, one person acts as a "sender" and the other as a "receiver." The sender views randomly selected visual stimuli such as photographs or videotapes, while the receiver, who is in another room and whose eyes are covered and ears are blocked, tries to mentally tune in to the sender. After a session, the receiver is shown four visual stimuli and asked to select the one transmitted by the sender. A person guessing which stimulus was "transmitted" would be correct 25% of the time (one time in four) by chance alone. An analysis of twenty-eight experiments using the ganzfeld procedure, however, found that receivers correctly identified the visual stimulus 38% of the time (Honorton, 1985), a percentage unlikely to be due to chance. A series of eleven more studies with the ganzfeld procedure obtained similar results (Bem & Honorton, 1994; Honorton et al., 1990).

Overall, however, there are reasons to be skeptical. First is the *file-drawer problem*. Buyers of supermarket tabloids tend to forget the predictions of "psychics" when the predictions fail to come true (that is, they have "filed" them away). Similarly, ESP researchers are more likely to "file away" research results that show failure. Therefore, we would expect unusual findings (for example, a subject with a high success rate on experimental tasks over a few days) to appear in the research literature. In other words, if you flip a coin indefinitely, eventually you will flip ten heads in a row. The odds against it are high, but if you report your eventual success and do not report the weeks of failure, you may give the impression that you have unique coin-flipping ability.

It has also been difficult to replicate experiments in ESP. People who have "demonstrated" ESP with one researcher have failed to do so with another, or they have refused to participate in other studies. Also, the findings in one study are usually absent in follow-ups or under careful analysis. For example, Milton and Wiseman (1999) reviewed the research reported by Bem and Honorton (1994). They weighed the results of thirty ganzfeld ESP studies from seven laboratories. They found no evidence—zero—that subjects in these studies scored above chance levels on the ESP task. From all of these studies, *not one person has emerged who can reliably show ESP from one occasion to another and from one researcher to another.* Research has not identified one single indisputable telepath or clairvoyant. In sum, most psychologists do not grant ESP research much credibility. They prefer to study perception that involves sensation. After all, what is life without sensation?

Fiction

There is no adequate scientific evidence that people can read other people's minds.

1/60 < Weber's constant for light

Weber's constant for lifted weight > 1/53

Weber's constant for pitch > 1/333

wavelength of violet light in nanometers > 400

700 < wavelength of red light in nanometers

125 < million rods in the retina

6.4 < million cones in the retina

16–22 < frames/second in movie film playback

0 < equivalent to the threshold of hearing in dB

Consciousness

Learning Outcomes

LO¹ Define consciousness

LO² Explain the nature of sleep and various sleep disorders

LO³ Explain various uses of hypnosis, forms of meditation, and biofeedback techniques in altering consciousness

LO⁴ Explain the concepts of substance abuse; identify categories of drugs and how they alter consciousness

When you talk to yourself, who talks, and who listens?

This is the type of question posed by philosophers and scientists who study consciousness. Although it might seem that psychologists, who study the brain and mental processes, are best equipped to look into consciousness, they banished this topic from their field for many years. In 1904, for example, William James wrote an article with the intriguing title "Does Consciousness Exist?" James did not think consciousness was a proper area of study for psychologists because scientific methods could not directly observe or measure another person's consciousness.

John Watson, the "father of modern behaviorism," agreed. Watson insisted that only observable, measurable behavior is the province of psychology: "The time seems to have come when psychology must discard all references to consciousness" (1913, p. 163). When Watson became the president of the American Psychological Association in 1914, his view was further cemented in the minds of many psychologists.

But the past few decades have seen a cognitive revolution, and thousands of psychologists now believe we cannot capture the richness of human experience without referring to consciousness (Schultz & Schultz, 2008). We are flooded with studies of consciousness by psychologists, biologists, neuroscientists, physicists, even computer scientists. Yet we still cannot directly observe the consciousness of another person, and so we rely on self-reports of consciousness as we observe events such as neural activity in the brain.

Truth or Fiction?

What do you think?

Folklore, common sense, or nonsense? Place a T for "True" or F for "False" on the lines provided (you'll learn the answers as you read through the text).

—— We act out our forbidden fantasies in our dreams.

—— Insomnia can be caused by trying too hard to fall asleep.

—— It is dangerous to awaken a sleepwalker.

—— You can be hypnotized against your will.

—— You can teach a rat to raise or lower its heart rate.

—— Many health professionals calm down hyperactive children by giving them a stimulant.

—— Coca-Cola once "added life" to its signature drink through the use of a powerful—but now illegal—stimulant.

—— The number of people who die from smoking-related causes is greater than the number lost to motor-vehicle accidents, abuse of alcohol and all other drugs, suicide, homicide, and AIDS *combined.*

LO¹ What Is Consciousness?

Mental concepts such as consciousness acquire scientific status by being tied to observable behavior whenever possible. *What is consciousness?* The concept of consciousness has various meanings, and psychologists use it in many ways.

selective attention
the focus of consciousness on a particular stimulus

direct inner awareness
knowledge of one's own thoughts, feelings, and memories

preconscious
in psychodynamic theory, descriptive of material that is not in awareness but can be brought into awareness by focusing one's attention

Consciousness as Awareness

One meaning of consciousness is *sensory awareness* of the environment. The sense of vision enables us to see, or be *conscious* of, the sun gleaming on the snow. The sense of hearing allows us to hear, or be conscious of, a concert. Yet sometimes we are not aware of sensory stimulation. We may be unaware, or unconscious, of sensory stimulation when we do not pay attention to it. The world is abuzz with signals, yet you are conscious of or focusing on only the words on this page (I hope).

Therefore, another aspect of consciousness is selective attention. Selective attention means focusing one's consciousness on a particular stimulus. Selective attention is a key to self-control. To keep your car on the road, you must pay more attention to driving conditions than to your hunger pangs or a cell-phone call.

Adaptation to our environment involves learning which stimuli must be attended to and which can be safely ignored. Selective attention makes our senses keener (Vorobyev et al., 2004). This is why we can pick out the speech of a single person across a room at a

How do we define consciousness?

cocktail party, a phenomenon aptly termed the *cocktail party effect*. Selective attention also plays a role in the advertisements and marketing ploys we notice.

How do advertisers of running shoes, automobiles, or beer use these facts to get "into" our consciousness and, they hope, our pocketbooks? Think of some TV commercials that captured your attention. What kinds of stimuli made them front and center in your awareness?

Yet another meaning of consciousness is that of direct inner awareness. Close your eyes and imagine spilling a can of bright-red paint across a black tabletop. Watch it spread across the black, shiny surface and then spill onto the floor. Although this image may be vivid, you did not "see" it literally. Neither your eyes nor any other sensory organs were involved. You were conscious of the image through direct inner awareness.

We are conscious of—or have direct inner awareness of—thoughts, images, emotions, and memories. However, we may not be able to measure direct inner awareness scientifically. Nevertheless, many psychologists would argue that if you have it, you know it. Self-awareness is connected with the firing of billions of neurons hundreds of times per second. Even so, we detect psychological processes but not neural events (Roth, 2000).

Conscious, Preconscious, Unconscious, and Nonconscious

Sigmund Freud, the founder of psychoanalysis, differentiated between thoughts and feelings of which we are conscious and those that are preconscious and unconscious.

Preconscious material is not currently in awareness but is readily available. If you answer the following questions, you will summon up "preconscious"

© 2010 ANDERSEN ROSS / JUPITERIMAGES CORPORATION

Selective attention makes our senses keener.

DIGITAL VISION/ JUPITER IMAGES

information: What did you eat for breakfast? What is your phone number? You can make these pre-conscious bits of information conscious by directing your attention to them.

Still other mental events are unconscious, or unavailable to awareness under most circumstances. Freud believed that some painful memories and sexual and aggressive impulses are unacceptable to us, so we *automatically* (unconsciously) eject them from awareness. That is, we *repress* them. Repression allows us to avoid feelings of anxiety, guilt, or shame.

Related, non-Freudian concepts include *suppression* and *nonconscious*. When people choose to stop thinking about unacceptable ideas or distractions, they are using suppression. When we consciously eject unwanted mental events from awareness, we are using suppression. We may suppress thoughts of an upcoming party when we need to study for a test. We may also try to suppress thoughts of the test while we are at the party!

Some bodily processes, such as the firing of neurons, are nonconscious. They cannot be experienced through sensory awareness or direct inner awareness. Growing hair and carrying oxygen in the blood are nonconscious. We can see that our hair has grown, but we have no sense receptors that provide sensations of growing. We feel the need to breathe but do not experience the exchange of carbon dioxide and oxygen.

Consciousness as Personal Unity

As we develop, we differentiate ourselves from that which is not us. We develop a sense of being persons, individuals. There is a totality to our impressions, thoughts, and feelings that makes up our consciousness—our continuing sense of self in the world. That self forms intentions and guides behavior. In this usage of the word, consciousness is self.

Consciousness as the Waking State

The word *conscious* also refers to the waking state as opposed, for example, to sleep. From this perspective, sleep, meditation, the hypnotic "trance," and the distorted perceptions that can accompany use of consciousness-altering drugs are considered *altered states of consciousness*.

In the remainder of this chapter, we explore various types of altered states of consciousness, including sleep and dreams; hypnosis, meditation, and biofeedback; and, finally, the effects of psychoactive drugs.

unconscious in psychodynamic theory, descriptive of ideas and feelings that are not available to awareness; also: without consciousness

repression in psychodynamic theory, the unconscious ejection of anxiety-evoking ideas, impulses, or images from awareness

suppression the deliberate, or conscious, placing of certain ideas, impulses, or images out of awareness

nonconscious descriptive of bodily processes such as growing hair, of which we cannot become conscious. We may "recognize" that our hair is growing, but we cannot directly experience the biological process

LO^2 Sleep and Dreams

Sleep is a fascinating topic. After all, we spend about one-third of our adult lives asleep. Sleep experts recommend that adults get eight hours of sleep a night, but according to the National Sleep Foundation (2008), adults in the United States typically get a bit less than seven. About one-third get six hours or less of sleep a night during the workweek. One-third admit that lack of sleep impairs their ability to function during the day, and nearly one in five admits to falling asleep at the wheel sometime during the past year.

Yes, we spend one-third of our lives in sleep—or would if we could. As you can see in Figure 5.1, on p. 100, some animals get much more sleep than we do, and some obtain much less. Why? It might have something to do with evolutionary forces. Animals who are most at risk of being hunted by predators tend to sleep less—an adaptive response to the realities of life and death. Individuals who slept more might have been killed by predators, eliminating their genes from the gene pool of their species.

Biological and Circadian Rhythms

Our lives are connected with the rhythms of the universe at large. Planet Earth rotates in about twenty-four hours. The earth revolves around the sun once a year.

We and other animals are also subject to rhythms,

circadian rhythm
a cycle that is connected with the twenty-four-hour period of the earth's rotation

alpha waves
rapid low-amplitude brain waves that have been linked to feelings of relaxation

nonrapid eye movement (NREM) sleep
stages of sleep 1 through 4

rapid eye movement (REM) sleep
a stage of sleep characterized by rapid eye movements, which have been linked to dreaming

and they are related to the rotation and revolutions of the planet. Many birds (and people who can afford it!) migrate south in the fall and north in the spring. A number of animals hibernate for the winter and emerge when buds are about to blossom again.

Alternating periods of wakefulness and sleep reflect an internally generated *circadian rhythm. What is a circadian rhythm?* A circadian rhythm is a cycle that is connected with the twenty-four-hour period of the earth's rotation. A cycle of wakefulness and sleep is normally twenty-four hours long. When people are removed from cues that signal day or night, however, a cycle tends to become extended to about twenty-five hours, and people sleep nearly ten of them (National Sleep Foundation, 2008). Why? We do not know. And during a night of sleep, we typically

undergo a series of ninety-minute cycles in which we run through the stages of sleep. In the morning, the shining sun adjusts the timing of the circadian clock by activating proteins in the retinas of the eyes. The proteins then signal tiny structures in the hypothalamus called the *suprachiasmatic nucleas (SCN)*. In turn, the SCN stimulates the pineal gland to decrease its output of the hormone melatonin, which promotes sleep.

Some of us, "morning people," function best in the morning, others in the afternoon. Some of us are "night owls," who are at our best when most neighbors are sound asleep.

Why do we sleep? Why do we dream? Let us explore the nature of sleep, dreams, and sleep disorders.

The Stages of Sleep

When we sleep, we slip from consciousness to unconsciousness. When we are conscious, our brains emit waves characterized by certain *frequencies* (numbers of waves per second) and *amplitudes* (heights—an index of strength). Brain waves indicate the activity of neurons. The strength or energy of brain waves is expressed in volts (an electrical unit). When we sleep our brain waves differ from those emitted when we are conscious. The electroencephalograph (EEG; see Figure 2.7 on page 34) has enabled researchers to measure brain waves. Figure 5.2 shows EEG patterns that reflect the frequency and strength of brain waves during the waking state, when we are relaxed, and when we are in the various stages of sleep. Brain waves, like other waves, are cyclical. The printouts in Figure 5.2 show what happens during a period of 15 seconds or so. *How do we describe the various stages of sleep?*

High-frequency brain waves are associated with wakefulness. When we move deeper into sleep, their frequency decreases and their amplitude (strength) increases. When we close our eyes and begin to relax before going to sleep, our brains emit alpha waves—low-amplitude brain waves of about eight to thirteen cycles per second.

Figure 5.2 shows five stages of sleep. The first four sleep stages are considered nonrapid eye movement (NREM) sleep. These contrast with the fifth stage, rapid eye movement (REM) sleep, so called because our eyes dart back and forth beneath our eyelids.

As we enter stage 1 sleep, our brain waves slow down from the alpha rhythm

Figure 5.1

Sleep Times for Mammals

Different mammals require different amounts of sleep. Reasons remain uncertain, but evolution apparently plays a role: Animals that are more prone to being attacked by predators sleep less.

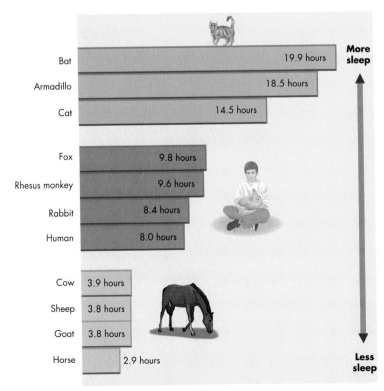

Bat	19.9 hours
Armadillo	18.5 hours
Cat	14.5 hours
Fox	9.8 hours
Rhesus monkey	9.6 hours
Rabbit	8.4 hours
Human	8.0 hours
Cow	3.9 hours
Sheep	3.8 hours
Goat	3.8 hours
Horse	2.9 hours

More sleep ↑

Less sleep ↓

Figure 5.2

The Stages of Sleep

This figure illustrates typical EEG patterns for the stages of sleep. During REM sleep, EEG patterns resemble those of the waking state. For this reason, REM sleep is often termed *paradoxical sleep.* As sleep progresses from stage 1 to stage 4, brain waves become slower, and their amplitude increases. Dreams, including normal nightmares, are most vivid during REM sleep. More disturbing sleep terrors tend to occur during deep stage 4 sleep.

Go to CourseMate for PSYCH at www.cengagebrain.com to access an interactive version of this figure.

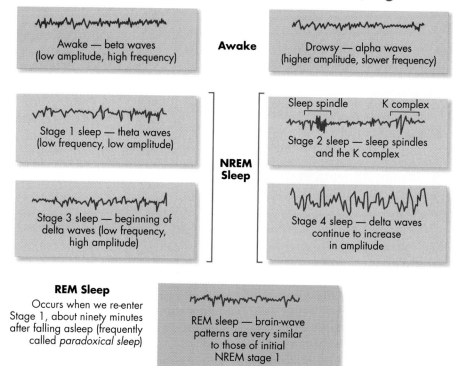

Awake — beta waves
(low amplitude, high frequency)

Awake

Drowsy — alpha waves
(higher amplitude, slower frequency)

Stage 1 sleep — theta waves
(low frequency, low amplitude)

NREM Sleep

Sleep spindle   K complex

Stage 2 sleep — sleep spindles
and the K complex

Stage 3 sleep — beginning of
delta waves (low frequency,
high amplitude)

Stage 4 sleep — delta waves
continue to increase
in amplitude

REM Sleep

Occurs when we re-enter
Stage 1, about ninety minutes
after falling asleep (frequently
called *paradoxical sleep*)

REM sleep — brain-wave
patterns are very similar
to those of initial
NREM stage 1

theta waves
slow brain waves produced during the hypnagogic state

delta waves
strong, slow brain waves usually emitted during stage 4 sleep

and enter a pattern of theta waves. Theta waves, with a frequency of about six to eight cycles per second, are accompanied by slow, rolling eye movements. The transition from alpha waves to theta waves may be accompanied by a *hypnagogic state* during which we may experience brief but vivid dreamlike images. Stage 1 sleep is the lightest stage of sleep. If we are awakened from stage 1 sleep, we may feel we were not sleeping at all.

After thirty to forty minutes of stage 1 sleep, we undergo a steep descent into stages 2, 3, and 4 (see Figure 5.3 on page 102). During stage 2, brain waves are medium in amplitude with a frequency of about four to seven cycles per second, but these are punctuated by *sleep spindles.* Sleep spindles have a frequency of twelve to sixteen cycles per second and represent brief bursts of rapid brain activity.

During deep sleep stages 3 and 4, our brains produce slower delta waves, which reach relatively great amplitude. During stage 3, the delta waves have a frequency of one to three cycles per second. Stage 4 is the deepest stage of sleep, from which it is the most difficult to be awakened. During stage 4 sleep, the delta waves slow to about 0.5 to 2 cycles

per second, and their amplitude is greatest.

After perhaps half an hour of deep stage 4 sleep, we begin a relatively rapid journey back upward through the stages until we enter REM sleep (see Figure 5.3). During REM sleep, we produce relatively rapid, low-amplitude brain waves that resemble those of light stage 1 sleep. REM sleep is also called *paradoxical sleep* because the EEG patterns observed suggest a level of arousal similar to that of the waking state (see Figure 5.2). However, it is difficult to awaken a person during REM sleep. When people are awakened during REM sleep, they report dreaming about 80% of the time. We also dream during NREM sleep but only about 20% of the time.

Each night we tend to undergo five cycles through the stages of sleep (see Figure 5.3). Five cycles include five periods of REM sleep. Our first journey through stage 4 sleep is usually the longest. Sleep tends to become lighter as the night wears on; periods of REM sleep lengthen and we may not enter the deepest stages of sleep. Toward morning our last period of REM sleep may last about half an hour.

The Functions of Sleep

Why do we sleep? Researchers do not have all the answers as to why we sleep, but sleep seems to serve several purposes: It rejuvenates the body, helps us recover from stress, helps us consolidate learning, and may promote development of infants' brains.

Consider the hypothesis that sleep helps rejuvenate a tired body. Most of us have had the experience of going without sleep for a night and feeling "wrecked" or "out of it" the following day. Perhaps the next evening we went to bed early to "catch up on our sleep." What happens to you if you do not

Sleep deprivation is connected with 100,000 vehicular crashes and 1,500 deaths each year.

ADAM GAULT/GETTY IMAGES

Why Do You Need the Amount of Sleep You Need?

The amount of sleep we need seems to be in part genetically determined (National Sleep Foundation, 2008). People also need more sleep when they are under stress, such as a change of job or an episode of depression (National Sleep Foundation, 2008). Sleep helps us recover from stress.

Newborn babies may sleep sixteen hours a day, and teenagers may sleep "around the clock" (twelve hours or more). It is widely believed that older people need less sleep than younger adults do, but sleep in older people is often interrupted by physical discomfort or the need to go to the bathroom. To make up for sleep lost at night, older people may "nod off" during the day.

Sleep, Learning, and Memory

REM sleep and deep sleep are both connected with the consolidation of learning and memory (Gais & Born, 2004; Ribeiro & Nicolelis, 2004). Fetuses have periods of waking and sleeping, and REM sleep may foster the development of the brain before birth (Fifer & Moon, 2003). In some studies, animals or people have been deprived of REM sleep. Under deprivation of REM sleep, animals and people learn more slowly and forget what they have learned more quickly (Kennedy, 2002; Ribeiro & Nicolelis, 2004). REM-sleep-deprived people and animals tend to show *REM rebound,* meaning that they spend more time in REM sleep during subsequent sleep periods. They "catch up."

sleep for one night? For several nights? Compare people who are highly sleep-deprived with people who have been drinking heavily. Sleepless people's abilities to concentrate and perform may be seriously impaired, but they may not recognize their limitations.

Many students can pull "all-nighters" during which they cram for a test through the night and perform reasonably well the following day (Horowitz et al., 2003). But they begin to show deficits in psychological functions such as learning and memory if they go sleepless for more than one night (Ohno et al., 2002; Taylor & McFatter, 2003). Sleep deprivation makes for dangerous driving (Stutts et al., 2003). The National Sleep Foundation (2008) estimates that sleep deprivation is connected with 100,000 vehicular crashes and 1,500 deaths each year. To combat sleep deprivation during the week, many people sleep late or nap on their days off (National Sleep Foundation, 2008).

Figure 5.3

Sleep Cycles

This figure illustrates the alternation of REM and non-REM sleep for the typical sleeper. There are about five periods of REM sleep during an eight-hour night. Sleep is deeper earlier in the night, and REM sleep tends to become prolonged toward morning.

| Sleep stage | A | 1 | 2 | 3 | 4 | 3 | 2 | REM | 1 | 2 | 3 | 4 | 3 | 2 | 3 | 2 | REM |

Dreams

What are dreams? Dreams are imagery in the absence of external stimulation and can seem real. In college I had repeated "anxiety dreams" the night before a test. I would dream that I had taken the test and it was all over. Imagine my disappointment when I awakened and realized the test still lay before me!

Dreams are most likely to be vivid during REM sleep. Images are vaguer and more fleeting during NREM sleep. If you sleep for eight hours and undergo five sleep cycles, you may have five dreams. Dreams may compress time the way a movie does, by skipping hours or days to a future time, but the actual action tends to take place in "real time." Fifteen minutes of events fills about fifteen minutes of dreaming (Hall, 1953). Furthermore, your dream theater is quite flexible. You can dream in black and white or in full color.

Some dreams are nightmares. One common nightmare is that you are falling. Another is that you are trying to run away from a threat but cannot gain your footing or coordinate your legs. Nightmares, like most pleasant dreams, are products of REM sleep.

Why do we dream what we dream? There are many theories about why we dream what we dream. Some are psychological, and others are more biologically oriented.

Dreams as "the Residue of the Day"

You may recall dreams involving fantastic adventures, but most dreams involve memories of the day gone by—or, poetically, "the residue of the day" (Domhoff, 2001, 2003). If we are preoccupied with illness or death, sex or aggression, or moral dilemmas, we are likely to dream about them. The characters in our dreams are more likely to be friends and neighbors than spies, monsters, and princes.

Traumatic events, however, can spawn nightmares, as reported in the aftermath of the terrorist attacks on the World Trade Center and Pentagon in 2001 (Gorman, 2001; Singareddy & Balon, 2002). People who have frequent nightmares are more likely than others to also have feelings of anxiety and depression (Blagrove et al., 2004; Levin & Fireman, 2002).

Dreams as the Expression of Unconscious Desires

In the Disney film *Cinderella*, a song lyric goes, "A dream is a wish your heart makes." Freud theorized that dreams reflect unconscious wishes and urges. He argued that dreams express impulses we would censor during the day. Moreover, he said that the content of dreams is symbolic of unconscious fantasized objects such as the genitals. In his method of psychoanalysis, Freud would interpret his clients' dreams. Dreams do, however, seem to be consistent with gender roles; that is, males are more likely than females to have dreams with aggressive content (Schredl et al., 2004).

The Activation–Synthesis Model of Dreams

There are also biological views of the "meanings" of dreams (Domhoff, 2003). According to the activation–synthesis model, acetylcholine (a neurotransmitter) and the pons (see Figure 2.11 on page 38) stimulate responses that lead to dreaming (Hobson, 2003; Ogawa et al., 2002). One is *activation* of the reticular activating system (RAS; see Figure 2.11), which arouses us, but not to waking. During the waking state, firing of these cells is linked to movement, particularly in walking, running, and other physical acts. But during REM sleep, neurotransmitters tend to inhibit activity so we usually do not thrash about

> **activation–synthesis model** the view that acetylcholine and the pons activate the reticular activating system, which stimulates the cortex, but not to the point of waking; the cortex then pieces together (synthesizes) the cognitive activity into a dream

Fiction

There is no evidence that we act out forbidden fantasies in our dreams.

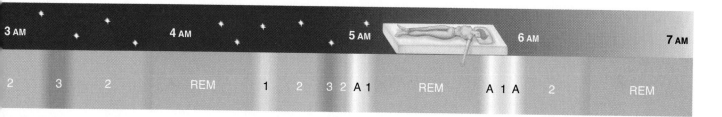

narcolepsy
a "sleep attack" in which a person falls asleep suddenly and irresistibly

(Bassetti et al., 2000). In this way, we save ourselves— and our bed partners—wear and tear. But the eye muscles are stimulated and show the REM activity associated with dreaming. The RAS also stimulates parts of the cortex involved in memory. The cortex then *synthesizes*, or pieces together, these sources of stimulation to yield the stuff of dreams (Anderson & Horne, 2004). Because recent events are most likely to be reverberating in our brains, we are most likely to dream about them. With the brain cut off from the world outside, learning experiences and memories are replayed and consolidated during sleep (Siegel, 2002; Stickgold et al., 2001). It's useful to get a night of sleep between studying and test-taking, if you can.

Sleep Disorders

Although nightmares are unpleasant, they do not qualify as sleep disorders. The term *sleep disorder* is reserved for other problems that can seriously interfere with our functioning.

What kinds of sleep disorders are there? Some sleep disorders, like insomnia, are all too familiar, experienced by at least half of American adults. Others,

like apnea (pauses in breathing) affect fewer than 10% of us (National Sleep Foundation, 2008). In this section we discuss insomnia and less common sleep disorders: narcolepsy, apnea, sleep terrors, bed-wetting, and sleepwalking.

Insomnia

According to the National Sleep Foundation (2008), more than half of American adults and about two-thirds of older adults are affected by insomnia in any given year. Trying to get to sleep compounds their sleep problems by creating autonomic activity and muscle tension. You cannot force or will yourself to go to sleep. You can only set the stage for sleep by relaxing when you are tired.

Narcolepsy

A person with narcolepsy falls asleep suddenly. Narcolepsy afflicts as many as 100,000 people in the United States and seems to run in families. The "sleep attack" may last fifteen minutes or so, after which

> **Truth**
> Many people have insomnia because they try too hard to fall asleep at night.

Most dreams involve memories of the day gone by—or, poetically, "the residue of the day."

the person feels refreshed. Nevertheless, sleep attacks are dangerous and upsetting. They can occur while driving or working with sharp tools. They may be accompanied by the collapse of muscle groups or the entire body—a condition called *sleep paralysis*. In sleep paralysis, the person cannot move during the transition from consciousness to sleep, and hallucinations (as of a person or object sitting on the chest) occur.

Narcolepsy is thought to be a disorder of REM-sleep functioning. Stimulants and antidepressant drugs have helped many people with the problem (Schwartz, 2004).

Apnea

Apnea is a dangerous sleep disorder in which the air passages are obstructed. People with apnea stop breathing periodically, up to several hundred times per night (National Sleep Foundation, 2008). Obstruction may cause the sleeper to sit up and gasp for air before falling back asleep. People with apnea are stimulated nearly, but not quite, to waking by the buildup of carbon dioxide. Some 10 million Americans have apnea, and it is associated with obesity and chronic snoring (National Sleep Foundation, 2008). Apnea can lead to high blood pressure, heart attacks, and strokes.

Causes of apnea include anatomical deformities that clog the air passageways, such as a thick palate, and problems in the breathing centers in the brain. Apnea is treated by such measures as weight loss, surgery, and *continuous positive airway pressure*, which is supplied by a mask that provides air pressure that keeps the airway open during sleep.

Deep-Sleep Disorders: Sleep Terrors, Bed-Wetting, and Sleepwalking

Sleep terrors, bed-wetting, and sleepwalking all occur during deep (stage 3 or 4) sleep. They are more common among children and may reflect immaturity of the nervous system (Kataria, 2004). **Sleep terrors** are similar to, but more severe than, nightmares, which occur during REM sleep. Sleep terrors usually occur during the first two sleep cycles of the night, whereas nightmares are more likely to occur toward morning. Experiencing a surge in the heart and respiration rates, the person may suddenly sit up, talk incoherently, and thrash about. He or she is never

> ### Fiction
> Contrary to myth, there is no evidence that sleepwalkers become violent if they are awakened, although they may be confused and upset.

fully awake, returns to sleep, and may recall a vague image as of someone pressing on his or her chest. (Memories of nightmares tend to be more detailed.) Sleep terrors are often decreased by a minor tranquilizer at bedtime, which reduces the amount of time spent in stage 4 sleep (Mason II & Pack, 2005).

Bed-wetting probably reflects immaturity of the nervous system. In most cases it resolves itself before adolescence, often by age eight. Methods that condition children to awaken when they are about to urinate have been helpful (Kainz, 2002; Mellon & McGrath, 2000). The drug imipramine often helps. Sometimes all that is needed is reassurance that no one is to blame for bed-wetting and that most children "outgrow" it.

Perhaps half of children talk in their sleep now and then. Adults occasionally do so, too. Surveys suggest that some 7% to 15% of children walk in their sleep (Neveus et al., 2002). Only 2% of adults do (Ohayon et al., 1999). Sleepwalkers may roam about nightly while their parents fret about possible accidents. Sleepwalkers typically do not remember their excursions, although they may respond to questions while they are up and about. Mild tranquilizers and maturity typically put an end to it.

LO³ Altering Consciousness Through Hypnosis, Meditation, and Biofeedback

Perhaps you have watched a fellow student try to place a friend in a "trance" after reading a book on hypnosis. Or perhaps you have seen an audience member hypnotized in a nightclub act. If so, chances are the person acted as if he or she had returned to childhood, imagined that a snake was about to have a nip, or lay rigid between two chairs for a while. In this section we deal with three altered states of consciousness: hypnosis, meditation, and biofeedback. In each of these, we focus on stimuli that are not common parts of our daily lives.

Hypnosis

Of these altered states, the one we hear of most is hypnosis. *What is hypnosis?* The word **hypnosis** is derived from the Greek word for sleep. It is an altered state of consciousness in which people are

> **apnea**
> temporary absence or cessation of breathing
>
> **sleep terrors**
> frightening dreamlike experiences that occur during the deepest stage of NREM sleep; nightmares, in contrast, occur during REM sleep
>
> **hypnosis**
> a condition in which people are highly suggestible and behave as though they are in a trance

role theory
a theory that explains hypnotic events in terms of the person's ability to act *as though* he or she were hypnotized

suggestible and behave as though they are in a trance. Modern hypnosis evolves from the ideas of Franz Mesmer in the 18th century. Mesmer asserted that everything in the universe was connected by forms of magnetism—which may not be far off the mark. However, he also claimed that people, too, could be drawn to one another by "animal magnetism." Not so. Mesmer used bizarre props to bring people under his "spell" and managed a respectable cure rate for minor ailments. Scientists now attribute his successes to the placebo effect, not animal magnetism.

Today hypnotism is more than a nightclub act. It is also used as an anesthetic in dentistry, childbirth, and medical procedures (Patterson, 2004; Shenefelt, 2003). Some psychologists use hypnosis to help clients reduce anxiety, overcome fears, or lessen the perception of chronic pain (Jensen et al., 2005; Pinnell & Covino, 2000). A study with 241 surgery patients shows how hypnosis can help people deal with pain and anxiety. The patients had procedures with local anesthetics (Lang et al., 2000). They could use as much pain medication as they wished. Patients who were hypnotized needed less additional pain medication and experienced less anxiety as measured by blood pressure and heart rate. The hypnotized patients focused on pleasant imagery rather than the surgery. Hypnosis helps people relax to cope with stress and enhance the functioning of their immune systems (Kiecolt-Glaser et al., 2001). Hypnosis can also be useful in helping people control their weight and stop smoking (Lynn et al., 2003). Some police departments use hypnosis to prompt the memories of witnesses.

The state of consciousness called the *hypnotic trance* has traditionally been induced by asking people to narrow their attention to a small light, a spot on the wall, an object held by the hypnotist, or the hypnotist's voice. The hypnotist usually suggests that the person's limbs are becoming warm, heavy, and relaxed. People may also be told that they are becoming sleepy or falling asleep. But hypnosis is *not* sleep, as shown by differences between EEG recordings for the hypnotic trance and the stages of sleep. (Subjects understand that the word *sleep* suggests a hypnotic trance.) Researchers are also studying changes in the brain that result from hypnosis. For example, Rainville and his colleagues (2002) used PET scans on people being hypnotized and found that mental absorption and mental relaxation are associated with changes in blood flow in the cerebral cortex (absorption) and parts of the brain involved in arousal and attention (relaxation).

Fiction

It is extremely unlikely that someone could be hypnotized against his or her will (Barber, 2000).

People who are easily hypnotized are said to have *hypnotic suggestibility*. Part of "suggestibility" is knowledge of what is expected during the "trance state." Generally speaking, suggestible people are prone to fantasy and want to cooperate with the hypnotist (Barber, 2000). As a result, they pay close attention to the instructions.

Explaining Hypnosis

Hypnotism is no longer explained in terms of animal magnetism, but others have offered explanations. According to Freud, hypnotized adults permit themselves to return to childish modes of responding that emphasize fantasy and impulse rather than fact and logic. Modern views of hypnosis are quite different. *How do psychologists explain the effects of hypnosis?*

Theodore Sarbin offers a **role theory** view of hypnosis (Sarbin & Coe, 1972). He points out that the changes in behavior attributed to the hypnotic trance can be successfully imitated when people are instructed to behave *as though* they were hypnotized.

" Hypnosis is *not* sleep, as shown by differences between EEG recordings for the hypnotic trance and the stages of sleep. "

For example, people can lie rigid between two chairs whether they are hypnotized or not. Also, people cannot be hypnotized unless they are familiar with the hypnotic "role"—the behavior that constitutes the trance. Sarbin is not saying that subjects *fake* the hypnotic role. Instead, Sarbin is suggesting that people *allow* themselves to enact this role under the hypnotist's directions.

The response set theory of hypnosis is related to role theory. It suggests that expectations play a role in the production of experiences suggested by the hypnotist (Kirsch, 2000). A positive response to each suggestion of the hypnotist sets the stage—creates a *response set*—in which the subject is more likely to follow further suggestions (Barrios, 2001).

Role theory and response set theory appear to be supported by research evidence that "suggestible" people want to be hypnotized, are good role players, have vivid imaginations, and know what is expected of them (Barber, 2000; Kirsch, 2000). By making suggestions that the subject follows, the hypnotist gets his or her "foot in the door," increasing the likelihood that the subject will follow additional suggestions. The fact that the behaviors shown by hypnotized people can be mimicked by people who know what is expected of them means that we need not resort to the concept of the "hypnotic trance"—an unusual and mystifying altered state of awareness—to explain hypnotic events.

Let us now consider two other altered states of consciousness that involve different ways of focusing our attention: meditation and biofeedback.

Meditation

What is meditation? The dictionary defines *meditation* as the act or process of thinking. But the concept usually suggests thinking deeply about the universe or about one's place in the world, often within a spiritual context. As the term is commonly used by psychologists, however, meditation refers to various ways of focusing one's consciousness to alter one's relationship to the world. In this use, ironically, *meditation* can also refer to a process by which people seem to suspend thinking and allow the world to fade away.

The kinds of meditation that helping professionals speak of tend to refer to rituals, exercises, even passive observation—activities that alter the normal relationship between the person and the environment. They are methods of suspending problem solving, planning, worries, and awareness of the events of the day. These methods alter consciousness—the normal focus of attention—and help people cope with stress by inducing feelings of relaxation.

One common form of meditation, transcendental meditation (TM), was brought to the United States by the Maharishi Mahesh Yogi in 1959. People practice TM by concentrating on *mantras*—words or sounds that are claimed to help the person achieve an altered state of consciousness. TM has some goals that cannot be assessed scientifically, such as expanding consciousness to encompass spiritual experiences, but there are also measurable goals, such as reducing anxiety and lowering blood pressure. For example, Herbert Benson (1975) found that TM lowered the heart and respiration rates and also produced what he labeled a *relaxation response*. The blood pressure of people with hypertension—a risk factor in cardiovascular disease—decreased.

A research program at the College of Maharishi Vedic Medicine in Fairfield, Iowa, has focused

response set theory the view that response expectancies play a key role in the production of the experiences suggested by the hypnotist

transcendental meditation (TM) the simplified form of meditation brought to the United States by the Maharishi Mahesh Yogi and used as a method for coping with stress

mindfulness meditation (MM) a form of meditation that provides clients with techniques they can use to focus on the present moment rather than ruminate about problems

biofeedback training (BFT) the systematic feeding back to an organism information about a bodily function so that the organism can gain control of that function

on older African Americans, a group prone to hypertension (Ready, 2000). Two studies compared the effects of TM, muscle relaxation, and a "health education" placebo on high blood pressure (Alexander et al., 1996; Schneider et al., 1995). They found that TM was significantly more effective at reducing blood pressure than relaxation or the placebo. A third study reported that TM practiced regularly by African American adults was significantly more likely than the health education placebo to slow hardening of the arteries (Castillo-Richmond et al., 2000).

Psychologist Jon Kabat-Zinn, founder of the Stress Reduction Clinic at the University of Massachusetts Medical Center, has promoted the use of mindfulness meditation (MM) in cognitive and behavior therapy. MM, as opposed to TM, makes no pretense of achieving spiritual goals. Instead, MM provides clients with mantra-like techniques they can use to focus on the present moment rather than ruminate about problems (Heidenreich & Michalak, 2003; Salmon et al., 2004). MM holds promise for helping clients cope with problems such as depression as well as reducing stress (Ramel et al., 2004). Brain imaging also shows

that meditation activates neural structures involved in attention and in control of the autonomic nervous system, helping produce feelings of relaxation (Lazar et al., 2000).

Biofeedback

Psychologist Neal E. Miller (1909–2002) trained laboratory rats to increase or decrease their heart rates. How? His procedure was simple but ingenious. As discovered by James Olds and Peter Milner (1954), there is a "pleasure center" in the rat's hypothalamus. A small burst of electricity in this center is strongly reinforcing: Rats learn to do what they can, such as pressing a lever, to obtain this "reward."

Miller (1969) implanted electrodes in the rats' pleasure centers. Some rats were then given a burst of electricity whenever their heart rates happened to increase. Other rats received the burst when their heart rates decreased. After a ninety-minute training session, the rats learned to alter their heart rates by as much as 20% in the direction for which they had been rewarded.

Truth

It is true that you can teach a rat to raise or lower its heart rate.

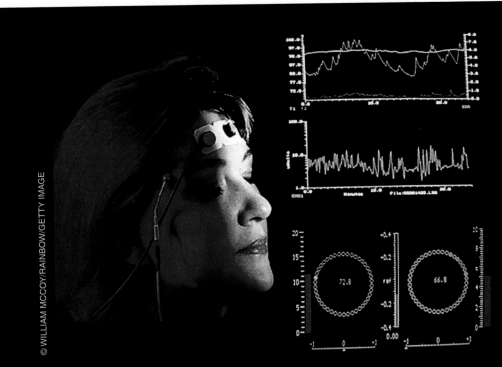

© WILLIAM McCOY/RAINBOW/GETTY IMAGE

Biofeedback is a system that provides, or "feeds back," information about a bodily function to an organism. Through biofeedback training, people have learned to gain voluntary control over a number of functions that are normally automatic, such as heart rate and blood pressure.

Miller's research was an example of biofeed-back training (BFT). *What is biofeedback training?* Biofeedback is a system that provides, or "feeds back," information about a bodily function. Miller used electrical stimulation of the brain to feed back information to rats when they had engaged in a targeted bodily response—in this case, raised or lowered their heart rates. Somehow the rats used this feedback to raise or lower their heart rates voluntarily.

Similarly, people have learned to change some bodily functions voluntarily, including heart rate, that were once considered beyond conscious control. Electrodes are not implanted in people's brains. Rather, people hear a "blip" or receive some other signal that informs them when they are showing the targeted response.

How is biofeedback training used? BFT is used in many ways, including helping people combat stress, tension, and anxiety. For example, people can learn to emit alpha waves through EEG feedback and feel more relaxed. The psychologist asks the person to "make the blip go faster." A blip may blink faster whenever alpha waves are being emitted. An electromyograph (EMG) monitors muscle tension. The EMG can be used to help people become more aware of muscle tension in the forehead, fingers, and elsewhere and to learn to lower tension (Martin, 2002). Through the use of other instruments, people have learned to lower their heart rates, blood pressure, and sweating (Nagourney, 2002). Biofeedback is widely used by sports psychologists to teach athletes how to relax muscle groups that are unessential to the task at hand so that the athletes can control anxiety and tension.

LO⁴ Altering Consciousness Through Drugs

The world is a supermarket of drugs. The United States is flooded with drugs that distort perceptions and change mood—drugs that take you up, let you down, and move you across town. Some of these drugs are legal, others illegal. Some are used recreationally, others medically. Some are safe if used correctly and dangerous if they are not. Some people use drugs because their friends do or because their parents tell them not to. Some are seeking pleasure; others are seeking inner truth or escape.

Young people often become involved with drugs that impair their ability to learn at school and are connected with reckless behavior (Centers for Disease Control and Prevention, 2005). Alcohol is the most popular drug on high school and college cam-

puses (Johnston et al., 2009). More than 40% of college students have tried marijuana, and one in six or seven smokes it regularly (Johnston et al., 2006). Many Americans take depressants to get to sleep at night and stimulants to get going in the morning. Cocaine was once a toy of the well-to-do, but price breaks have brought it into the lockers of high school students.

Substance Abuse and Dependence

Where does drug use end and abuse begin? *What are substance abuse and dependence?* The American Psychiatric Association (2000) defines substance abuse as repeated use of a substance despite the fact that it is causing or compounding social, occupational, psychological, or physical problems. If you are missing school or work because you are drunk or "sleeping it off," you are abusing alcohol. The amount you drink is not as crucial as the fact that your pattern of use disrupts your life.

Substance dependence is more severe than substance abuse and has behavioral and biological aspects (American Psychiatric Association, 2000). Behaviorally, dependence is characterized by loss of control over use of the sub-stance. Dependent people may organize their lives around getting and using a substance. Biological or physiological dependence is typified by tolerance, withdrawal symptoms, or both. Tolerance is the body's habituation to a substance so that, with regular usage, higher doses are needed to achieve similar effects. There are withdrawal symptoms when the level of usage suddenly drops off. Withdrawal symptoms for alcohol include anxiety, tremors, restlessness, rapid pulse, and high blood pressure.

When doing without a drug, people who are *psychologically* dependent show signs of anxiety such as shakiness, rapid pulse, and sweating that may be similar to withdrawal symptoms. Because of these signs, they may believe that they are physiologically dependent on—or addicted to—a drug when

electromyograph (EMG) an instrument that measures muscle tension

depressant a drug that lowers the rate of activity of the nervous system

stimulant a drug that increases activity of the nervous system

substance abuse persistent use of a substance even though it is causing or compounding problems in meeting the demands of life

substance dependence loss of control over use of a substance; biologically speaking, dependence is typified by tolerance, withdrawal symptoms, or both

tolerance habituation to a drug, with the result that increasingly higher doses of the drug are needed to achieve similar effects

withdrawal symptoms a characteristic cluster of symptoms that results from sudden decrease in an addictive drug's level of usage

they are psychologically dependent. But symptoms of withdrawal from some drugs are unmistakably physiological. One is delirium tremens ("the DTs"), experienced by some chronic alcoholics when they suddenly lower their intake of alcohol. People with DTs have heavy sweating, restlessness, disorientation, and frightening hallucinations—often of crawling animals.

Causal Factors in Substance Abuse and Dependence

What are the causes of substance abuse and dependence? Substance abuse and dependence usually begin with experimental use in adolescence (Lewinsohn et al., 2000a). People experiment with drugs for various reasons, including curiosity, conformity to peer pressure, parental use, rebelliousness, escape from boredom or pressure, and excitement or pleasure (Griffin et al., 2004; Wilkinson & Abraham, 2004). Let us have a look at some theories of substance abuse.

Social–cognitive theorists suggest that people often try alcohol and tranquilizers such as Valium (the generic name is diazepam) on the basis of a recommendation or observation of others. Expectations about the effects of a substance predict its use (Cumsille et al., 2000).

Use of a substance may be reinforced by peers or by the drug's positive effects on mood and its reduction of anxiety, fear, and stress (Griffin et al., 2004). Many people use drugs as a form of self-medication for anxiety and depression, even

low self-esteem (Dierker et al., 2001). For people who are physiologically dependent, avoidance of withdrawal symptoms is also reinforcing. Carrying a supply of the substance is reinforcing because one need not worry about going without it. Parents who use drugs may increase their children's knowledge of drugs. They also, in effect, show their children when to use them—for example, by drinking alcohol to cope with tension or to lessen the anxiety associated with meeting people at parties and other get-togethers (Power et al., 2005).

Certain people apparently have a genetic predisposition toward physiological dependence on certain substances, such as alcohol, opioids, cocaine, and nicotine (Chen et al., 2004; Nurnberger et al., 2004; Radel et al., 2005). The biological children of alcoholics who are reared by nonalcoholic adoptive parents are more likely to develop alcohol-related problems than the biological children of the adoptive parents. An inherited tendency toward alcoholism may involve greater sensitivity to alcohol (that is, greater enjoyment of it) and greater tolerance (Pihl et al., 1990). Greater tolerance is shown by studies in which college students with alcoholic parents show better muscular control and visual–motor coordination when they drink than other college students do (Pihl et al., 1990). People with a family history of alcoholism are also more sensitive to the stimulating effects of alcohol, which occur at lower levels of intoxication (Conrad et al., 2001).

Now that we have learned about substance abuse

The amount you drink is not as crucial as the effects of drinking on your life in deciding whether or not you are abusing alcohol.

© NOBLE STOCK/JUPITERIMAGES

and dependence, let us turn to a discussion of the different kinds of psychoactive drugs. Some are depressants, others stimulants, and still others hallucinogens. Let us consider the effects of these drugs on consciousness, beginning with depressants.

Depressants

Depressants generally act by slowing the activity of the central nervous system. There are also effects specific to each depressant. In this section we consider the effects of alcohol, opiates, and barbiturates.

Alcohol—The Swiss Army Knife of Psychoactive Substances

No drug has meant so much to so many as alcohol. Alcohol is our dinnertime relaxant, our bedtime sedative, our cocktail-party social facilitator. We use alcohol to celebrate holy days, applaud our accomplishments, and express joyous wishes. The young assert their maturity with alcohol. Alcohol is used at least occasionally by the majority of high school and college students (Bachman et al., 2008). Alcohol even kills germs on surface wounds.

People use alcohol like a Swiss Army knife. It does it all. It is the all-purpose medicine you can buy without prescription. It is the relief from anxiety, depression, or loneliness that you can swallow in public without criticism or stigma (Bonin et al., 2000; Swendsen et al., 2000). A man who takes a Valium tablet may look weak. It is "macho" to down a bottle of beer.

But the army knife also has a sharp blade. No drug has been so abused as alcohol. Ten million to 20 million Americans are alcoholics. In contrast, 750,000 to 1 million use heroin regularly, and about 800,000 use cocaine regularly (O'Brien, 1996). Excessive drinking has been linked to lower productivity, loss of employment, and downward movement in social status. Yet, half of all Americans use alcohol regularly.

About four college students die *each day* from alcohol-related causes (Hingson et al., 2002). Binge drinking—having five or more drinks in a row for a male, or four or more for a female (Naimi et al., 2003b)—is connected with aggressive behavior, poor grades, sexual promiscuity, and accidents (Birch et al., 2007; Keller et al., 2007). Nevertheless, 44% of college students binge at least twice a month (Hingson et al., 2002). The media pay more attention to deaths due to heroin and cocaine overdoses, but more college students die each year from causes related to drinking, including accidents and overdoses (Hingson et al., 2002).

What are the effects of alcohol? The effects of alcohol vary with the dose and duration of use. Low doses may be stimulating because alcohol dilates blood vessels, which ferry sugar through the body. Higher doses have a sedative effect, which is why alcohol is classified as a depressant. Alcohol relaxes people and deadens minor aches and pains. Alcohol impairs cognitive functioning, slurs the speech, and impairs coordination.

Alcohol lowers inhibitions. Drinkers may do things they would not do if they were sober, such as having unprotected sex (Donohue et al., 2007). When drunk, people may be less able to foresee the consequences of their behavior. They may also be less likely to summon up their moral beliefs. Then, too, alcohol induces feelings of elation and euphoria that may wash away doubts. Alcohol is also associated with a liberated social role in our culture. Drinkers may place the blame on alcohol ("It's the alcohol, not me"), even though they choose to drink.

Men are more likely than women to become alcoholics. Why? A cultural explanation is that tighter social constraints are usually placed on women. A biological explanation is that alcohol hits women harder, discouraging them from overindulging. Alcohol "goes to women's heads" faster than to men's, because women metabolize less of it in the stomach (Lieber, 1990). Alcohol reaches women's bloodstreams and brains relatively intact. Asians and Asian Americans are less likely than Europeans and European Americans to drink to excess because they are more likely to show an unpleasant "flushing response" to alcohol, as evidenced by redness of the face, rapid heart rate, dizziness, and headaches (Fromme et al., 2004).

Regardless of how or why one starts drinking, regular drinking can lead to physiological dependence. People are then motivated to

opiates
a group of narcotics
derived from the opium
poppy that provide
a euphoric rush and
depress the nervous
system

narcotics
drugs used to relieve
pain and induce sleep.
The term is usually
reserved for opiates

opioids
chemicals that act on
opiate receptors but are
not derived from the
opium poppy

barbiturate
an addictive depressant
used to relieve anxiety
or induce sleep

About four college students die *each day* from alcohol-related causes.

© 2010 DIGITAL VISION / JUPITERIMAGES CORPORATION

drink to avoid withdrawal symptoms. Still, even when alcoholics have "dried out"—withdrawn from alcohol—many return to drinking. Perhaps they still want to use alcohol as a way of coping with stress or as an excuse for failure.

Opiates

Opiates are a group of narcotics derived from the opium poppy, from which they obtain their name. The ancient Sumerians gave the opium poppy its name: It means "plant of joy." Opioids are similar in chemical structure but made in a laboratory. Opiates include morphine, heroin, codeine, Demerol, and similar drugs. *What are the effects of opiates?* The major medical application of opiates is relief from pain.

Heroin can provide a strong euphoric "rush." Users claim that it is so pleasurable it can eradicate thoughts of food or sex. High doses can cause drowsiness and stupor, alter time perception, and impair judgment. With regular use of opiates, the brain stops producing neurotransmitters that are chemically similar to opiates—the pain-relieving endorphins.

As a result, people can become physiologically dependent on opiates, such that going without them can be agonizing. Withdrawal syndromes may begin with flu-like symptoms and progress through tremors, cramps, chills alternating with sweating, rapid pulse, high blood pressure, insomnia, vomiting, and diarrhea. This information seems to have gotten through to high school students; most disapprove of using heroin (Johnston et al., 2006).

Heroin was once used as a cure for addiction to morphine. Now we have methadone, a human-made opioid that is used to treat physiological dependence on heroin. Methadone is slower acting than heroin and does not provide the thrilling rush, but it does prevent withdrawal symptoms.

Barbiturates

What are the effects of barbiturates? Barbiturates like Nembutal and Seconal are depressants with several medical uses, including relief from anxiety, tension, and pain, and treatment of epilepsy, high blood pressure, and insomnia. With regular use, barbiturates lead rapidly to physiological and psychological dependence. Physicians therefore provide them with caution.

Barbiturates are popular as street drugs because they are relaxing and produce mild euphoria. High doses result in drowsiness, motor impairment, slurred speech, irritability, and poor judgment. A highly physiologically dependent person who is withdrawn abruptly from barbiturates may experience convulsions and die. Because of additive effects, it is dangerous to mix alcohol and other depressants.

Stimulants

Stimulants increase the activity of the nervous system. Some of their effects can be positive. For example, amphetamines stimulate cognitive activity and apparently help people control impulses. Some stimulants are appealing as street drugs because they contribute to feelings of euphoria and self-confidence. But they also have their risks. In this section we discuss amphetamines, cocaine, and nicotine.

Amphetamines and Related Stimulants

What are the effects of amphetamines? Amphetamines were first used by soldiers during World War II to help them stay alert at night. Truck drivers also use them to drive through the night. Students use amphetamines for all-night cram sessions. Dieters use them because they reduce hunger.

Amphetamines are often abused for the euphoric rush high doses can produce. Some people swallow amphetamines in pill form or inject liquid Methedrine, the strongest form, into their veins. As a result, they may stay awake and high for days on end. But such highs must end. People who have been on prolonged highs sometimes "crash," or fall into a deep sleep or depression. Some commit suicide when crashing.

Although some critics believe that Ritalin is prescribed too freely, Ritalin has been shown to increase the attention span, decrease aggressive and disruptive behavior, and lead to academic gains (Evans et al., 2001; Pelham et al., 2002). Why should Ritalin, a stimulant, calm children? Hyperactivity may be connected with immaturity of the cerebral cortex, and Ritalin may stimulate the cortex to exercise control over more primitive parts of the brain.

Tolerance for amphetamines and Ritalin develops quickly, and users can become dependent on them, especially when they use them to self-medicate themselves for depression. Whether these stimulants cause physical addiction has been a subject of controversy (Shen et al., 2007). High doses can cause restlessness, insomnia, loss of appetite, hallucinations, paranoid delusions (e.g., false ideas that others are eavesdropping or intend them harm), and irritability.

Cocaine

Cocaine is derived from coca leaves—the plant from which the soft drink took its name. Do you recall commercials claiming that "Coke adds life"? Given its caffeine and sugar content, "Coke"—Coca-Cola, that is—should provide quite a lift. But Coca-Cola hasn't been "the real thing" since 1906, when the company stopped using cocaine in its formula.

What are the effects of cocaine? The stimulant cocaine produces euphoria, reduces hunger, deadens pain, and boosts self-confidence. As shown in Figure 5.4, cocaine apparently works by binding to sites on sending neurons that normally reuptake molecules of the neurotransmitters norepinephrine, dopamine, and serotonin. As a result, molecules of these transmitters remain longer in the synaptic cleft, enhancing their mood-altering effects and producing a "rush." But when cocaine levels drop, lower absorption of neurotransmitters by receiving neurons causes the user's mood to "crash." Cocaine may be brewed from coca leaves as a "tea," snorted in powder form, or injected in liquid form. Repeated snorting constricts blood vessels in the nose, drying the skin and sometimes exposing cartilage and perforating the nasal septum. These problems require cosmetic surgery. The potent cocaine derivatives known as "crack" and "bazooka" are inexpensive because they are unrefined.

Physical dangers include sudden rises in blood pressure, which constricts the coronary arteries and decreases the oxygen supply to the heart, and quickens the heart rate events that can lead to respiratory and cardiovascular collapse, as in the sudden deaths of some young athletes (Mitchell, 2006). Overdoses can cause restlessness and insomnia, tremors, headaches, nausea, convulsions, hallucinations, and delusions. Use of crack has been connected with strokes. Only about 4% of adolescents aged fifteen to nineteen use cocaine regularly, and most believe that it is harmful (Johnston et al., 2006). Cocaine causes physiological as well as psychological dependence.

Cocaine—also called *snow* and *coke*—has been used as a local anesthetic since the early 1800s. In 1884 it came to the attention of Sigmund Freud, who used it to fight his own depression and published an article about it: "Song of Praise." Freud's early ardor was tempered when he learned that cocaine is habit-forming and can cause hallucinations and delusions.

> **IRONICALLY, HEROIN WAS ONCE USED AS A CURE FOR ADDICTION TO MORPHINE.**

amphetamines stimulants derived from alpha-methyl-beta-phenyl-ethylamine, a colorless liquid consisting of carbon, hydrogen, and nitrogen

Truth

It is true that many health professionals calm hyperactive children by giving them a stimulant—the stimulant methylphenidate (Ritalin).

Truth

It is true that Coca-Cola once "added life" through the use of a powerful, then-legal but now-illegal stimulant: cocaine.

Figure 5.4

How Cocaine Produces Euphoria and Why People "Crash"

Go to CourseMate for PSYCH at www.cengagebrain.com to access an interactive version of this figure.

A. In the normal functioning of the nervous system, neurotransmitters are released into the synaptic cleft by vesicles in terminal buttons of sending neurons. Many are taken up by receptor sites in receiving neurons.

B. In the process called reuptake, sending neurons typically reabsorb excess molecules of neurotransmitters.

C. Molecules of cocaine bind to the sites on sending neurons that normally reuptake molecules of neurotransmitters. As a result, molecules of norepinephrine, dopamine, and serotonin remain longer in the synaptic cleft, increasing their typical mood-altering effects and providing a euphoric "rush." When the person stops using cocaine, the lessened absorption of neurotransmitters by receiving neurons causes his or her mood to "crash."

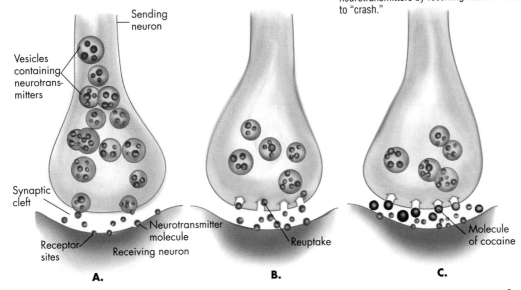

Nicotine

Nicotine is the stimulant in tobacco smoke. *What are the effects of nicotine?* Nicotine stimulates discharge of the hormone adrenaline and the release of neurotransmitters, including dopamine, acetylcholine, GABA, and endorphins (Brody, 2008). Adrenaline creates a burst of autonomic activity that accelerates the heart rate and pours sugar into the blood.

Acetylcholine is vital in memory formation, and nicotine appears to enhance memory and attention; improve performance on simple, repetitive tasks; and enhance the mood (Gentry, et al., 2000; Rezvani & Levin, 2001). Although it is a stimulant, because of GABA and endorphins, nicotine has a relaxing effect. It depresses the appetite and raises the metabolic rate. Thus, some people smoke cigarettes to control their weight.

The perils of cigarette smoking are widely known today. One surgeon general declared that cigarette smoking is the chief preventable cause of death in the United States. The numbers of Americans who die from smoking are comparable to the number of lives that would be lost if two jumbo jets crashed *every day*. If flying were that unsafe, would the government ground all flights? Would the public continue to make airline reservations?

STOCKBYTE/GETTY IMAGES

Table 5.1

Snapshot, U.S.A.: Gender, Level of Education, and Smoking		
Factor	Group	Percent Who Smoke
Gender	Women	18.3
	Men	23.1
Level of education	Fewer than 12 years	27.5
	16 years and above	10.6

Data based on reports of persons aged 18 and above.

Source: Dube, S. R., Asman, K., Malarcher, A., & Carabollo, R. (2009). Cigarette Smoking among adults and trends in smoking cessation—United States, 2008. *Morbidity and Mortality Weekly Report, 58*(44), 1227–1232.

Nicotine creates the physiological dependence on tobacco products (American Lung Association, 2008). Symptoms of withdrawal include nervousness, drowsiness, loss of energy, headaches, irregular bowel movements, lightheadedness, insomnia, dizziness, cramps, palpitations, tremors, and sweating.

It's no secret. Cigarette packs sold in the United States carry messages like "Warning: The Surgeon General Has Determined That Cigarette Smoking Is Dangerous to Your Health." Cigarette advertising has been banned on radio and television. Nearly 430,000 Americans die from smoking-related illnesses each year (American Lung Association, 2008). This number is greater than the equivalent of two jumbo jets colliding in midair each day with all passengers lost.

The carbon monoxide in cigarette smoke impairs the blood's ability to carry oxygen, causing shortness of breath. The **hydrocarbons** ("tars") in cigarette and cigar smoke lead to lung cancer (American Lung Association, 2008). Cigarette smoking also stiffens arteries (Mahmud & Feely, 2003) and is linked to death from heart disease, chronic lung and respiratory diseases, and other health problems. Women who smoke show reduced bone density, increasing the risk of fracture of the hip and back. Pregnant women who smoke have a higher risk of miscarriage, preterm births, stillborn babies, and children with learning problems (American Lung Association, 2008).

Secondhand smoke—smoke inhaled from other people's tobacco products—is also connected with respiratory illnesses, asthma, and other health problems.

Truth

The number of smoking-related deaths in the U.S. is higher than the number of people who die each year from motor vehicle accidents, alcohol and drug abuse, suicide, homicide, and AIDS *combined*.

Prolonged exposure to secondhand smoke during childhood is a risk factor for lung cancer (American Cancer Society, 2008). Because of the effects of second-hand smoke, smoking has been banished from many airplanes and restaurants.

Why, then, do people smoke? For many reasons—such as the desire to look sophisticated (although these days smokers may be more likely to be judged foolish than sophisticated), to have something to do with their hands, and—of course—to take in nicotine.

The incidence of smoking is connected with gender and level of education (see Table 5.1). Better-educated people are less likely to smoke and more likely to quit if they do smoke.

hydrocarbons
chemical compounds consisting of hydrogen and carbon

second-hand smoke
smoke from the tobacco products and exhalations of other people

hallucinogen
a substance that causes hallucinations

marijuana
the dried vegetable matter of the *Cannabis sativa* plant

Hallucinogens

Hallucinogens are so named because they produce hallucinations—that is, sensations and perceptions in the absence of external stimulation. Hallucinogens may also have additional effects such as relaxation, euphoria, or, in some cases, panic.

Marijuana

Marijuana is produced from the *Cannabis sativa* plant, which grows wild in many parts of the world. *What are the effects of marijuana?* Marijuana helps some people relax and can elevate their mood. It also sometimes produces mild hallucinations, which is why we discuss it as a hallucinogen. The major psychedelic substance in marijuana is delta-9-tetrahydrocannabinol, or THC. THC is found in the branches and leaves of the plant, but it is highly concentrated in the resin. *Hashish*, or "hash," is derived from the resin and is more potent than marijuana.

Marijuana carries a number of health risks. For example, it impairs the perceptual–motor coordination used in driving and operating machines. It impairs short-term memory and slows learning (Egerton 35 al., 2006).

Some users report that marijuana helps them socialize. Moderate to strong intoxication is linked to reports of sharpened perceptions, increases in self-insight, creative thinking, and empathy for others. Time seems to slow. A song might seem to last an hour rather than minutes. There is increased awareness of bodily sensations such as heartbeat. Marijuana users also report that strong intoxication heightens sexual sensations. Visual hallucinations may occur, and strong intoxication may cause disorientation. If the smoker's mood is euphoric, disorientation may be interpreted as "harmony" with the universe, but some users find disorientation threatening and fear they will not regain their identity (Bonn-Miller et al., 2007). Rapid heart rate and heightened awareness of bodily sensations lead some users to fear their hearts will "run away" with them. Strong intoxication can cause nausea and vomiting. Regular users may experience tolerance and withdrawal symptoms (Budney et al., 2007). Brain imaging studies suggest that males who begin using marijuana in adolescence may have smaller brains and less gray matter than other males (Ashtari et al., 2009). Both males and females who started marijuana use early may be generally smaller in height and weight than other people. These differences may reflect the effect of marijuana on pituitary and sex hormones.

LSD is a hallucinogen that can give rise to a vivid parade of colors and visual distortions. Some users claim to have achieved great insights while "tripping," but typically they have been unable to recall or apply them afterward.

LSD and Other Hallucinogens

LSD is the abbreviation for lysergic acid diethylamide, a synthetic hallucinogen. *What are the effects of LSD and other kinds of hallucinogens?* Users of "acid" claim that it "expands consciousness" and opens up new worlds to them. Sometimes people say they have achieved great insights while using LSD, but when it wears off they cannot apply or recall them. LSD produces vivid, colorful hallucinations.

Some LSD users have flashbacks—distorted perceptions or hallucinations that mimic the LSD "trip" but occur days, weeks, or longer after usage. The experiencing of flashbacks is more technically termed hallucinogen persisting perception disorder (HPPD) by the American Psychiatric Association (2000). The psychological explanation of "flashbacks" is that people who would use LSD regularly are also more likely to allow flights of fancy. But research with 38 people with HPPD suggests that following extensive use of LSD, the brain may fail to inhibit internal sources of visionlike experiences when the eyes are closed (Abraham & Duffy, 2001).

Other hallucinogens include mescaline (derived from the peyote cactus) and phencyclidine (PCP). PCP was developed as an anesthetic and an animal tranquilizer. It goes by the street names "angel dust," "ozone," "wack," and "rocket fuel." The street terms "killer joints" and "crystal super grass" refer to PCP combined with marijuana.

Regular use of hallucinogens may lead to tolerance and psychological dependence, but is not known to create physiological dependence. High doses may impair coordination, cloud judgment, change the mood, and cause frightening hallucinations and delusions. Table 5.2 summarizes the effects of various psychoactive drugs.

Table 5.2

Drugs and Their Effects

Drug	Type	How Taken	Desired Effects	Tolerance	Abstinence Syndrome	Side Effects
Alcohol	Depressant	By mouth	Relaxation, euphoria, lowered inhibitions	Yes	Yes	Impaired coordination, poor judgment, hangover*
Heroin	Depressant	Injected, smoked, by mouth	Relaxation, euphoria, relief from anxiety and pain	Yes	Yes	Impaired coordination and mental functioning, drowsiness, lethargy*
Barbiturates and Methaqualone	Depressants	By mouth, injected	Relaxation, sleep, euphoria, lowered inhibitions	Yes	Yes	Impaired coordination and mental functioning, drowsiness, lethargy*
Amphetamines	Stimulants	By mouth, injected	Alertness, euphoria	Yes	†	Restlessness, loss of appetite, psychotic symptoms
Cocaine	Stimulant	By mouth, snorted, injected	Euphoria, self-confidence	Yes	Yes	Restlessness, loss of appetite, convulsions, strokes, psychotic symptoms
Nicotine (cigarettes)	Stimulant	By tobacco (smoked, chewed, or sniffed)	Relaxation, stimulation, weight control	Yes	Yes	Cancer, heart disease, lung and respiratory diseases
Marijuana	Hallucinogenic	Smoked, by mouth	Relaxation, perceptual distortions, enhancement of experience	†	†	Impaired coordination, learning, respiratory problems, panic
MDMA "Ecstasy"	Stimulant/ Hallucinogenic	By mouth	Alertness, self-confidence, hallucinations	?	?	Impaired memory, increased heart rate, anxiety, confusion, possible depression
LSD, PCP	Hallucinogenic	By mouth	Perceptual distortions, vivid hallucinations	Yes	No	Impaired coordination, psychotic symptoms, panic

*Overdose can result in death.
†Recent research suggests the answer is yes, although some might consider the "jury still to be out."

1/3 < portion of adult life spent in sleep

minutes/cycle in each of the sleep stages > 90

cycles/second delta waves in stage 4 sleep > 0.5 to 2

50 < percent American adults affected by insomnia

 750,000-1,000,000 < the number of people in the U.S. who regularly use heroin.

10,000,000-20,000,000 < the number of alcoholics in the U.S.

1 to 3 < cycles/second delta waves in stage 3 sleep

100,000 < yearly vehicular crashes connected to sleep deprivation

6

Learning

Learning Outcomes

LO **1**   Describe the learning process according to classical conditioning

LO **2**   Describe the learning process according to operant conditioning

LO **3**   Describe cognitive factors in learning

> ## "What do we learn *from video games?* Aggressive skills, violent thoughts?"

Dylan Klebold and Eric Harris were engrossed in violent video games for hours at a time. They were particularly keen on a game named *Doom*. Harris had managed to reprogram *Doom* so that he, the player, became invulnerable and had an endless supply of weapons. He would "mow down" all the other characters in the game. His program caused some of the characters to ask God why they had been shot as they lay dying. Later on, Klebold and Harris asked some of their shooting victims at Columbine High School in Colorado whether they believed in God. One of the killers also referred to his shotgun as Arlene, the name of a character in *Doom* (Saunders, 2003).

In the small rural town of Bethel, Alaska, Evan Ramsey shot four people, killing two and wounding two. Afterward, he said his favorite video games—*Doom, Die Hard,* and *Resident Evil*—taught him that being shot would reduce a player's "health factor" but probably not be lethal.

The debate about whether violence in media such as films, television, and video games fuels violence in the real world has been going on for more than forty years. Psychologist Craig A. Anderson (2003, 2004), who has carried out extensive research in this area, argues that studies show that media violence is a risk factor for increasing emotional arousal, aggressive behavior, and violent thoughts.

One reason to be particularly concerned about violent video games is that they require audience participation (Anderson et al., 2004). Players don't passively watch; they *participate*. Violent games like *Grand Theft Auto* have grown increasingly popular. Some games reward players for killing police, prostitutes, and bystanders. Virtual

Truth or Fiction?

What do you think?

Folklore, common sense, or nonsense? Place a T for "True" or F for "False" on the lines provided (you'll learn the answers as you read through the text).

___ A single nauseating meal can give rise to a taste aversion that lasts for years.

___ Psychologists helped a young boy overcome his fear of rabbits by having him eat cookies while a rabbit was brought closer and closer.

___ During World War II, a psychologist created a missile that would use pigeons to guide the missile to its target.

___ Slot-machine players pop coins into the machines most rapidly when they have no idea when they might win.

___ You can train a rat to climb a ramp, cross a bridge, climb a ladder, pedal a toy car, and do several other tasks—all in proper sequence.

___ You have to make mistakes to learn.

___ Despite all the media hoopla, no scientific connection has been established between violence in the media and real-life aggression.

learning (1) according to behaviorists, a relatively permanent change in behavior that results from experience (2) according to cognitive theorists, the process by which organisms make relatively permanent changes in the way they represent the environment because of experience

classical conditioning a simple form of learning in which a neutral stimulus comes to evoke the response usually evoked by another stimulus by being paired repeatedly with the other stimulus

weapons include guns, knives, flamethrowers, swords, clubs, cars, hands, and feet. Sometimes the player assumes the role of a hero, but it is also common for the player to assume the role of a criminal.

What do we *learn* from video games and other media, such as television, films, and books? The research suggests that we learn a great deal—not only aggressive skills, but also the idea that violence is the normal state of affairs.

We will return to this controversial issue later in the chapter. This is the chapter that deals with the psychology of learning. Most of what we learn may be helpful and adaptive. But there are exceptions, as in the case of violent video games.

What is learning? Learning as defined in psychology is more than listening to teachers, honing skateboard jumps, or mastering the use of an iPod. From the strict behaviorist perspective, **learning** is a relatively permanent change in behavior that arises from practice or experience. The behaviorist perspective plays down the roles of cognition and choice. It suggests that players of violent video games went on rampages because they had been rewarded or reinforced for similar behavior in games.

Cognitive psychologists define learning as a mental change that may or may not be associated with changes in behavior. These mental changes may affect, but do not directly cause, changes in behavior. From this perspective, the participants in the video games had acquired skills that enabled them to attack people, but they had then chosen to attack others. Learning, for cognitive psychologists, may be *shown* by changes in behavior, but learning itself is a mental process. Cognitive psychologists suggest that people choose whether or not to imitate the aggressive and other behaviors they observe, and that people are most likely to imitate behaviors that are consistent with their values.

Sometimes learning experiences are direct, as when we are praised for doing something properly. But we can also learn from the experiences of others—by watching their behavior and hearing their life stories. We learn, too, from books and audiovisual media. In this chapter we consider various kinds of learning, including conditioning and learning in which cognition plays a more central role.

What do we *learn* from violence in video games and other media? The research suggests that we learn a great deal—not only aggressive skills, but also the idea that violence is the normal state of affairs.

LO¹ Classical Conditioning: Learning What Is Linked to What

Classical conditioning involves ways in which we learn to associate events with other events. It is involuntary, automatic learning. For example, we generally prefer grades of A to grades of F and are more likely to stop for red lights than green lights. Why? We are not born with instinctive attitudes toward letter grades or stoplights. Rather, we learn the meanings of these symbols because they have been associated with other events. A's are associated with the approval of our teachers and caregivers. Because of experience in crossing streets or riding in cars, we associate green lights with the word "go" and red lights with "stop."

What is classical conditioning? **Classical conditioning** is a simple form of associative learning that enables organisms to anticipate events. If the name Ivan Pavlov rings a bell with us, it is most likely because of his research in learning with dogs. *What is the contribution of Ivan Pavlov to the psychology of learning?* Ivan Pavlov (1927) made his great contribution to the psychology of learning by accident. Pavlov was actually attempting to identify neural receptors in the mouth that triggered a response from the salivary glands. But his efforts were hampered by the dogs' annoying tendency to salivate at undesired times, such as when a laboratory assistant was clumsy and banged the metal food trays.

Just as you salivate after you've taken a big bite of cake, a dog salivates if meat powder is placed on its tongue. Pavlov was dosing his dogs with meat powder for his research because he knew that salivation in response to meat powder is a reflex. Reflexes are unlearned and evoked by certain **stimuli**. Pavlov discovered that reflexes can also be learned, or *conditioned,* by association. His dogs began salivating in response to clanging food trays because clanging, in the past, had been repeatedly paired with arrival of food. The dogs would also salivate when an assistant entered the laboratory. Why? In the past, the assistant had brought food.

Pavlov at first viewed the extra salivation of his dogs as a hindrance to his research. But then it dawned on him that this "problem" might be worth looking into. He found out that he could train, or condition, his dogs to salivate in response to any stimulus.

In his initial experiments, Pavlov trained dogs to salivate when he sounded a tone. Pavlov termed these trained salivary responses "conditional reflexes." The reflexes were *conditional* on the repeated pairing of a previously neutral stimulus (such as the clanging of a food tray) and a stimulus (in this case, food) that evoked the target response (in this case, salivation). Today, conditional reflexes are generally referred to as *conditioned responses.*

Pavlov demonstrated conditioned responses by showing that when meat powder was placed on a dog's tongue, the dog salivated. Pavlov repeated the process several times, with one difference. He preceded the meat powder by half a second or so with the sounding of a tone on each occasion. After several pairings of the meat powder and the tone, Pavlov sounded the tone but did **not** follow it with the meat powder. Still the dog salivated. It had learned to salivate in response to the tone.

stimulus
an environmental condition that elicits a response

Explaining Classical Conditioning

Behaviorists explain the outcome of *classical conditioning* in terms of the publicly observable conditions of learning. For them, classical conditioning is a simple form of learning in which one stimulus comes to evoke the response usually evoked by another stimulus. Why? Because the stimuli are paired repeatedly. In Pavlov's demonstration, the dog learned to salivate in response to the tone *because* the tone had been paired with meat powder. Behaviorists do *not* say that the dog "knew" food was on the way. How can we guess what a dog "knows"? We can only outline the conditions under which targeted behaviors occur.

Cognitive psychologists view classical conditioning as the learning of relationships among events. The relationships allow organisms to mentally represent their environments and make predictions (Pickens & Holland, 2004). In Pavlov's demonstration, the dog salivated in response to the tone *because* the tone became mentally connected with the meat. The cognitive focus is on *the information learned by the organism.* Organisms are seen as seekers of information that generate and test rules about relationships among events.

Ivan Pavlov and His Associates—Including a "Professional Furry Salivator" (the Dog).

© BETTMANN/CORBIS

unconditioned stimulus (UCS) a stimulus that elicits an unconditioned response

unconditioned response (UCR) a natural, usually unvarying response elicited by a stimulus without learning or conditioning

orienting reflex an unlearned response in which an organism attends to a stimulus

conditioned stimulus (CS) a previously neutral stimulus that, after repeated association with an unconditioned stimulus, elicits the response elicited by the unconditioned stimulus.

conditioned response (CR) a response that becomes associated with a previously unrelated stimulus as a result of pairing the stimulus with another stimulus that normally elicits the response

Stimuli and Responses in Classical Conditioning

In Pavlov's experiment, the meat powder is an **unconditioned stimulus (UCS)**. Salivation in response to the meat powder is an unlearned or **unconditioned response (UCR)**. The tone was at first a meaningless or neutral stimulus. It might have caused the dog to look in the direction of the sound—an **orienting reflex**. But the tone was not yet associated with food. Then, through repeated association with the meat powder, the tone became a learned or **conditioned stimulus (CS)** for the salivation response. Salivation in response to the tone (or conditioned stimulus) is a learned or **conditioned response (CR).** Therefore, salivation can be either a conditioned response or an unconditioned response, depending on the method used to evoke the response (see Figure 6.1).

Here is a mini-experiment that many adults have tried. They smile at infants, say something like "kitchie-coo" (don't ask me why), and then tickle the infant's foot. Perhaps the infant laughs and perhaps curls or retracts the foot. After a few repetitions—which psychologists call "trials"—the adult's simply saying "kitchie-coo" is likely to be enough to cause the infant to laugh and retract its foot.

Taste Aversion

When I was a child in the Bronx, my friends and I would go to the movies on Saturday mornings. One day my friends dared me to eat two huge containers of buttered popcorn by myself. I had no problem with the first

> IN CLASSICAL CONDITIONING, ORGANISMS LEARN TO CONNECT STIMULI,
>
> **SUCH AS THE SOUNDING OF A TONE WITH FOOD.**

Figure 6.1

A Schematic Representation of Classical Conditioning

Prior to conditioning, food elicits salivation. The tone, a neutral stimulus, elicits either no response or an orienting response. During conditioning, the tone is sounded just before meat powder is placed on the dog's tongue. After several repetitions, the tone, now a CS, elicits salivation, the CR.

Go to CourseMate for PSYCH at www.cengagebrain.com to access an interactive version of this figure.

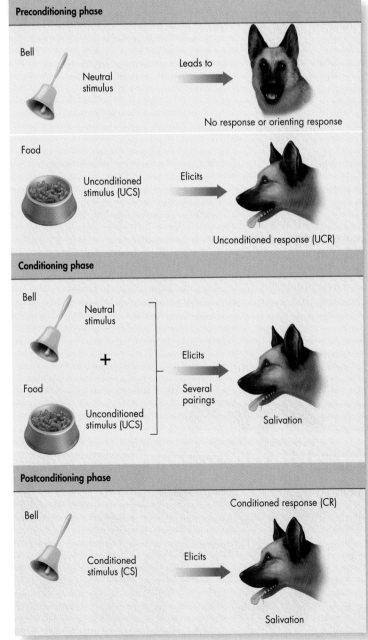

enormous basket of buttered popcorn. More slowly—much more slowly—I forced down the second basket. I felt bloated and nauseated. The taste of the butter, corn, and salt lingered in my mouth and nose, and my head spun. It was obvious to me that no one could talk me into even another handful of popcorn that day. But I was surprised that I couldn't face buttered popcorn again for a year.

Years later I learned that psychologists refer to my response to buttered popcorn as a *taste aversion*. Many decades have now passed, and the distinctive odor of buttered popcorn still turns my stomach.

What are taste aversions? Why are they of special interest to psychologists? Taste aversions are intriguing examples of classical conditioning. They are adaptive because they motivate organisms to avoid harmful foods. Taste aversions differ from other kinds of classical conditioning in a couple of ways. First, only one association may be required. A single overdose of popcorn left me with a lifetime aversion. Second, whereas most kinds of classical conditioning require that the unconditioned stimulus and conditioned stimulus be close together in time, in taste aversion the unconditioned stimulus (in this case, nausea) can occur hours after the conditioned stimulus (in this case, the flavor of food).

The Evolution of Taste Aversion

Research on taste aversion also challenges the view that organisms learn to associate any stimuli that are linked in time. In reality, not all stimuli are created equal. The evolutionary perspective suggests that animals (and humans) would be biologically predisposed to develop aversions that are adaptive in their environments (Garcia et al., 1989). Those of us who acquire taste aversions quickly are less likely to eat bad food, more likely to survive, and more likely to contribute our genes to future generations.

In a classic study, Garcia and Koelling (1966) conditioned two groups of rats. Each group was exposed to the same three-part conditioned stimulus: a taste of sweetened water, a light, and a clicker. Afterward, one group of rats was induced to experience nausea by radiation or poison, and the other group received electric shock. After conditioning, the rats who had been nauseated showed an aversion for sweetened water but not to the light or clicker. Although all three stimuli had been presented at the same time, *the rats had acquired only the taste aversion.* After conditioning, the rats that had been shocked avoided both the light and the clicker, *but they did not show a taste aversion to the sweetened water.* For each group of rats, learning was adaptive. In the natural scheme of things, nausea is more likely to stem from poisoned food than from lights or sounds. So, for nauseated rats, acquiring the taste aversion was appropriate. Sharp pain, in contrast, is more likely to stem from natural events involving lights (e.g., fire, lightning) and sharp sounds (e.g., twigs snapping, things falling). Therefore, it was more appropriate for the shocked animals to develop an aversion to the light and the clicker than the sweetened water.

In classical conditioning, organisms learn to connect stimuli, such as the sounding of a tone with food. Now let us consider various

Formation of a Taste Aversion?
Taste aversions can be acquired by means of a single pairing of the US and the CS. Evolutionary psychologists point out that the rapid acquisition of a taste aversion makes it more likely that a human or an animal will survive and reproduce.

© JUPITERIMAGES

IMAGE COPYRIGHT GELPI 2010. USED UNDER LICENSE FROM SHUTTERSTOCK.COM

factors in classical conditioning, beginning with what happens when the connection between stimuli is broken.

Extinction and Spontaneous Recovery

Figure 6.2

Learning and Extinction Curves

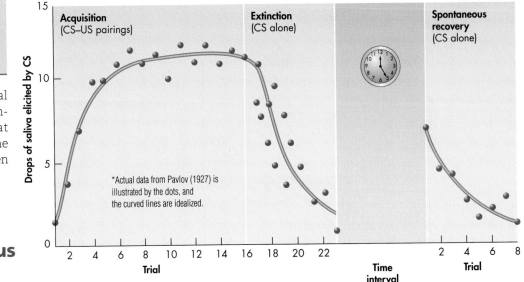

Acquisition (CS–US pairings)

Extinction (CS alone)

Spontaneous recovery (CS alone)

Drops of saliva elicited by CS

*Actual data from Pavlov (1927) is illustrated by the dots, and the curved lines are idealized.

Trial

Time interval

Trial

Extinction and spontaneous recovery are aspects of conditioning that help us adapt by updating our expectations or representations of a changing environment. For example, a child may learn to connect hearing a car pull into the driveway (a conditioned stimulus) with the arrival of his or her parents (an unconditioned stimulus). Thus, the child may squeal with delight when he or she hears the car.

What is the role of extinction in classical conditioning? Extinction enters the picture when times—and the relationships between events—change. After moving to a new house, the child's parents may commute by public transportation. The sound of a car in a nearby driveway may signal a neighbor's, not a parent's, homecoming. When a conditioned stimulus (such as the sound of a car) is no longer followed by an unconditioned stimulus (a parent's homecoming), the conditioned stimulus loses its ability to elicit a conditioned response. The organism adapts to change.

In classical conditioning, **extinction** is the process by which conditioned stimuli lose the ability to elicit conditioned responses, because the conditioned stimuli are no longer associated with unconditioned stimuli. That is, the toddler is no longer gleeful at the sounds of the car in the driveway. From the cognitive perspective, extinction changes the child's mental representation of its environment, because the conditioned stimulus no longer allows the child to make the same prediction.

In experiments on the extinction of conditioned responses, Pavlov found that repeated presentations of the conditioned stimulus (in this case, the

Evolution would favor the survival of animals that associate a water hole with the thirst drive from time to time so that they return to it when it once more holds water.

tone) without the unconditioned stimulus (in this case, meat powder) led to extinction of the conditioned response (salivation in response to the tone). Basically, the dog stopped salivating at the sound of the tone. Interestingly, Figure 6.2 shows that a dog was conditioned to begin to salivate in response to a tone after two or three pairings of the tone with meat powder. Continued pairings of the stimuli led to increased salivation (measured in number of drops of saliva). After seven or eight trials, salivation leveled off at eleven to twelve drops.

In the next series of experiments, salivation in response to the tone was extinguished by trials in which the tone was presented without the meat powder. After about ten extinction trials, the animal no longer salivated. It no longer showed the conditioned response when the tone was sounded.

What is the role of spontaneous recovery in classical conditioning? We asked what would happen if we were to allow a day or two to pass after we had extinguished salivation in Pavlov's dog and then again sounded the tone. Where would you place your bet? Would the dog salivate or not?

If you bet that the dog would again show the conditioned response (in this case, salivation in response to the tone), you were correct. Organisms tend to show **spontaneous recovery** of extinguished conditioned responses as a function of the passage of time. For this reason, the term *extinction* may be a bit misleading. When a species of animal becomes extinct, all members of that species capable of reproducing have died. The species vanishes. But the experimental extinction of conditioned responses does not lead to their permanent eradication. Rather, it seems to *inhibit* them. The response remains available for the future under the "right" conditions.

Evolutionary psychologists note that spontaneous recovery, like extinction, is adaptive. What would happen if the child heard no car in the driveway for several months? It could be that the next time a car entered the driveway the child would associate the sounds with a parent's homecoming rather than with the arrival of a neighbor. This expectation could be appropriate. After all, *something* had changed when no car entered the driveway for so long. In the wild, a water hole may contain water for only a couple of months during the year. Evolution would favor the survival of animals that associate the water hole with the thirst drive from time to time so that they return to it when it once more holds water.

As time passes and seasons change, things sometimes follow circular paths and arrive where they were before. Spontaneous recovery helps organisms adapt to situations that recur from time to time.

Generalization and Discrimination

No two things are exactly alike. Traffic lights are hung at slightly different heights, and shades of red and green differ a little. The barking of two dogs differs, and the sound of the same animal differs slightly from one bark to the next. Rustling sounds in the undergrowth differ, but evolution would favor the survival of rabbits and deer that flee when they perceive any one of many possible rustling sounds. Adaptation requires us to respond similarly (or *generalize*) to stimuli that are equivalent in function and to respond differently to (or *discriminate* between) stimuli that are not.

What is the role of generalization in classical conditioning? Pavlov noted that responding to different stimuli as though they were functionally equivalent—*generalizing*—is adaptive for animals. **Generalization** is the tendency for a conditioned response to be evoked by stimuli that are similar to the stimulus to which the response was conditioned. For example, Pavlov demonstrated generalization by getting his dog to salivate when it was shown a circle. Then later the dog salivated in response to being shown closed geometric figures—even squares. The more closely the figure resembled a circle, however, the greater the *strength* of the response (as measured by drops of saliva).

But what happens if food follows the presentation of a circle but not a square? *What is the role of discrimination in classical conditioning?* Organisms must also learn that (1) many stimuli perceived as being similar are functionally different, and (2) they must respond adaptively to each. During the first couple of months of life, for example, babies can discriminate their mother's voice from those of other women. They often stop crying when they hear their mother but not when they hear a stranger.

Pavlov showed that a dog conditioned to salivate in response to circles could be trained *not* to salivate in response to ellipses. After a while, the dog no longer salivated in response to the ellipses. Instead, it showed **discrimination**: It salivated only in response to circles. Pavlov found that increasing the difficulty of the discrimination task apparently tormented the dog. After the dog was trained to salivate in response to circles but not ellipses, Pavlov showed it a series of

spontaneous recovery the recurrence of an extinguished response as a function of the passage of time

generalization in conditioning, the tendency for a conditioned response to be evoked by stimuli that are similar to the stimulus to which the response was conditioned

discrimination in conditioning, the tendency for an organism to distinguish between a conditioned stimulus and similar stimuli that do not forecast an unconditioned stimulus

higher-order conditioning
a classical conditioning procedure in which a previously neutral stimulus comes to elicit the response brought forth by a *conditioned* stimulus by being paired repeatedly with that conditioned stimulus

progressively rounder ellipses. Eventually the dog could no longer distinguish the ellipses from circles. The animal was so stressed that it urinated, defecated, barked profusely, and snapped at laboratory personnel.

How do we explain the dog's belligerent behavior? In *Frustration and Aggression,* a classic work written more than sixty-five years ago, a group of behaviorally oriented psychologists suggested that frustration induces aggression (Dollard et al., 1939). Rewards—such as food— are usually contingent on correct discrimination. That is, if the dog errs, it doesn't eat. Cognitive theorists, however, disagree (Rescorla, 1988). They would say that in Pavlov's experiment, the dog's loss of the ability to adjust its mental map of the environment was frustrating.

Daily life requires generalization and discrimination. No two hotels are alike, but when we travel from one city to another it is adaptive to expect to stay in a hotel. It is encouraging that a green light in Washington has the same meaning as a green light in Paris. Returning home requires the ability to discriminate among our home from others. Imagine the confusion that would reign if we could not discriminate among our friends, mates, or coworkers from other people.

Higher-Order Conditioning

Consider a child who is burned by touching a hot stove. After this experience, the sight of the stove may evoke fear. And because hearing the word *stove* may evoke a mental image of the stove, just hearing the word may evoke fear.

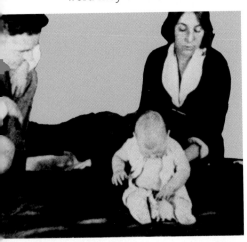

Watson and Rayner conditioned 'Little Albert' to fear a rat by clanging steel bars behind his head when he played with the rat.

Do you recall the mini-experiment in which an adult smiles, says "kitchie-coo," and then tickles an infant's foot? After a few repetitions, just smiling at the infant may cause the infant to retract its foot. In fact, just walking into the room may have the same effect! The experiences with touching the hot stove and tickling the infant's foot are examples of higher-order conditioning. *What is higher-order conditioning?*

In **higher-order conditioning**, a previously neutral stimulus (for example, hearing the word *stove* or seeing the adult who had done the tickling enter the room) comes to serve as a learned or conditioned stimulus after being paired repeatedly with a stimulus that has already become a learned or conditioned stimulus (for example, seeing the stove or hearing the phrase "kitchie-coo"). Pavlov demonstrated higher-order conditioning by first conditioning a dog to salivate in response to a tone. He then repeatedly paired the shining of a light with the sounding of the tone. After several pairings, shining the light (the higher-order conditioned stimulus) came to evoke the response (salivation) that had been elicited by the tone (the first-order conditioned stimulus).

Applications of Classical Conditioning

Some of the most important applications of classical conditioning involve the conditioning of fear and the counterconditioning or extinction of fear. The fear-reduction methods we discuss are part of behavior therapy, which we elaborate in Chapter 13.

"Little Albert": Classical Conditioning of Emotional Responses

In 1920, John B. Watson and his future wife, Rosalie Rayner, published an article describing their demonstration that emotional reactions such as fears can be acquired through principles of classical conditioning. The subject of their demonstration was a lad known in psychological literature by the name of Little Albert. Albert was a phlegmatic fellow at the age of eleven months, not given to ready displays of emotion. But prior to the study, the infant did enjoy playing with a laboratory rat.

Using a method that some psychologists have criticized as unethical, Watson startled Little Albert by clanging steel bars behind his head when he played with the rat. After seven pairings, Albert showed fear of the rat even though clanging was suspended. Albert's fear was also generalized to objects similar in appearance to the rat, such as a rabbit and the fur collar on his mother's coat. Albert's conditioned fear of rats may never have become extinguished because extinction would have required perceiving rats (the conditioned stimuli) without painful consequences (in the absence of the unconditioned stimuli). But Albert's mother removed him from the laboratory before Watson and Rayner could attempt to countercondition the boy's acquired fear. And once outside the laboratory, fear might have prevented Albert from facing furry animals. And as we shall see in the section on operant conditioning, avoiding furry animals might have been *reinforced* by reduction of fear.

Counterconditioning

The reasoning behind counterconditioning is this: If fears, as Watson had shown, could be conditioned by painful experiences like a clanging noise, perhaps fears could be **counterconditioned** by substituting pleasant experiences. In 1924, Watson's protégé Mary Cover Jones attempted to countercondition fear in a two-year-old boy named Peter.

Peter had an intense fear of rabbits. Jones had a rabbit gradually brought closer to Peter while he munched candy and cookies. Jones first placed the rabbit in a far corner of the room while Peter munched and crunched. Peter cast a wary eye, but he continued to consume the treats. Gradually the animal was brought closer until Peter simultaneously ate and touched the rabbit. Jones theorized that the joy of eating was incompatible with fear and counterconditioned it.

> ### Truth
> It is true that psychologists helped a young boy overcome his fear of rabbits by having him eat cookies while a rabbit was brought progressively closer.

Flooding and Systematic Desensitization

If Mary Cover Jones had simply plopped the rabbit on Peter's lap rather than bring it gradually closer, she would have been using the method of

COPYRIGHT © MICHAEL NEWMAN / PHOTO EDIT

flooding. Flooding and systematic desensitization, like counterconditioning, are behavior therapy methods for reducing fears. They are based on the classical conditioning principle of extinction. In flooding, the client is exposed to the fear-evoking stimulus until fear is extinguished. Little Albert, for example, might have been placed in close contact with a rat until his fear had become extinguished. In extinction, the conditioned stimulus (in this case, the rat) is presented repeatedly in the absence of the unconditioned stimulus (the clanging of the steel bars) until the conditioned response (fear) is no longer evoked.

Although flooding is usually effective, it is unpleasant. (When you are fearful of rats, being placed in a room with one is no picnic.) For this reason, behavior therapists frequently prefer to use **systematic desensitization**, in which the client is gradually exposed to fear-evoking stimuli under circumstances in which he or she remains relaxed. For example, while feeling relaxed, Little Albert might have been given an opportunity to look at photos of rats or to see rats from a distance before they were brought closer. Systematic desensitization takes longer than flooding but is not as unpleasant.

In any event, people can learn by means of simple association. In terms of the evolutionary perspective, organisms that can learn by several routes—including conditioning and conscious reflection—would stand a greater chance of survival than organisms whose learning is limited to conditioning.

LO² Operant Conditioning: Learning What Does What to What

Through classical conditioning, we learn to associate stimuli. As a result, a simple, usually passive response made to one stimulus is then made in response to the other. In the case of Little Albert, clanging noises were associated with a rat. As a result, the rat came to elicit the fear caused by the clanging. However, classical conditioning is only one kind of learning that occurs in these situations. After Little Albert acquired his fear of the rat, his voluntary behavior changed:

counterconditioning
a fear-reduction technique in which pleasant stimuli are associated with fear-evoking stimuli so that the fear-evoking stimuli lose their aversive qualities

flooding
a behavioral fear-reduction technique based on principles of classical conditioning; fear-evoking stimuli (CSs) are presented continuously in the absence of actual harm so that fear responses (CRs) are extinguished

systematic desensitization
a behavioral fear-reduction technique in which a hierarchy of fear-evoking stimuli is presented while the person remains relaxed

reinforce
to follow a response
with a stimulus that
increases the frequency
of the response

operant behavior
voluntary responses
that are reinforced

operant
conditioning
a simple form of learn-
ing in which an organ-
ism learns to engage in
behavior because it is
reinforced

Fiction

During World War II, Skinner *proposed* that pigeons be trained to guide missiles to their targets, but his proposal was never acted on.

He tried to avoid the rat. Thus, Little Albert engaged in another kind of learning—*operant conditioning*. In operant conditioning, organisms learn to do things—or *not* to do things—because of the consequences of their behavior. For example, I avoided buttered popcorn to prevent nausea. But we also seek fluids when we are thirsty, sex when we are aroused, and an ambient temperature of 68° to 70° F when we feel too hot or too cold. *Classical conditioning focuses on how organisms form anticipations about their environments. Operant conditioning focuses on what they do about them.* Let us consider the key contributions of B. F. Skinner to operant conditioning.

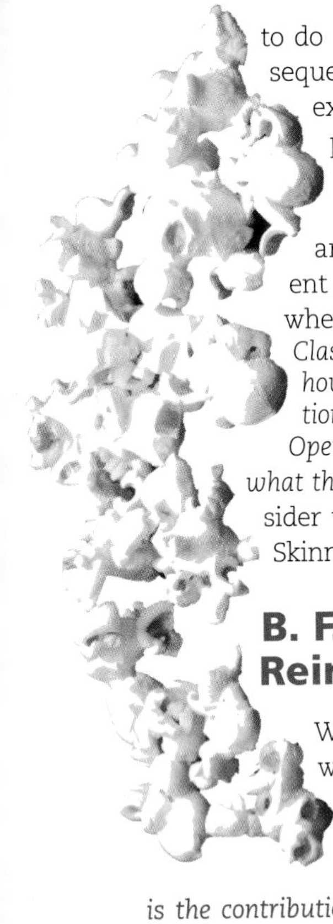

B. F. Skinner and Reinforcement

When it comes to unusual war stories, few will top that of B. F. Skinner. One of Skinner's wartime efforts was "Project Pigeon." *What is the contribution of B. F. Skinner to the psychology of learning?* In their training, the pigeons would be **reinforced** with food pellets for pecking at targets projected onto a screen (see Figure 6.3). Once trained, the pigeons would be placed in missiles. Their pecking at similar targets displayed on a screen would correct the missile's flight path, resulting in a "hit" and a sacrificed pigeon. Plans for building the necessary missile—for some reason called the *Pelican* and not the *Pigeon*—were scrapped, however. The pigeon equipment was too bulky, and Skinner's suggestion was not taken seriously.

Project Pigeon may have been scrapped, but Skinner's ideas have found wide

Figure 6.3

Project Pigeon

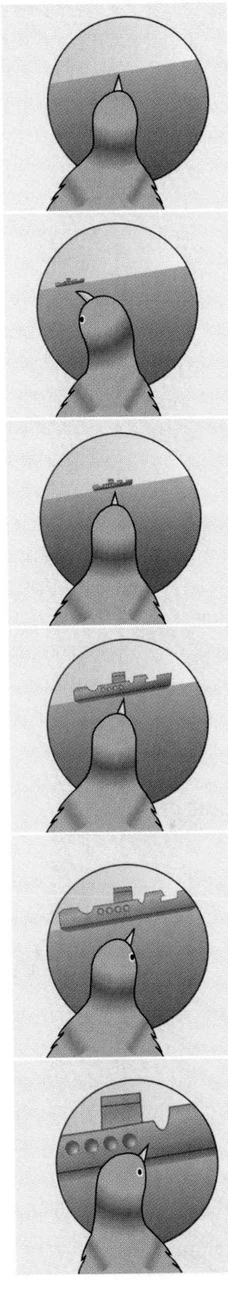

application. In operant conditioning, an organism learns to *do* something because of the effects or consequences of the behavior.

Skinner taught pigeons and other animals to engage in **operant behavior**, behavior that operates on, or manipulates, the environment. In classical conditioning, involuntary responses such as salivation or eyeblinks are often conditioned. In operant conditioning, *voluntary* responses such as pecking at a target, pressing a lever, or skills required for playing tennis are acquired, or conditioned. *What is operant conditioning?*

Operant conditioning is defined as a simple form of learning in which an organism learns to engage in certain behavior because of the effects of that behavior. In operant conditioning, we learn to engage in behaviors that result in presumably desirable consequences such as food, a hug, an A on a test, attention, or social approval. Some children learn to conform to social rules to earn the attention and approval of their parents and teachers. Ironically, other children may learn to "misbehave" because misbehavior also gets attention. In particular, children may learn to be "bad" when their "good" behavior is routinely ignored. Some children who do not do well in school seek the approval of deviant peers (Patterson et al., 2000).

Methods of Operant Conditioning

Skinner (1938) made many theoretical and technological innovations. Among them was his focus on discrete behaviors, such as lever pressing, as the *unit*, or type, of behavior to be studied. Other psychologists might focus on how organisms think or "feel." Skinner focused on measurable things they do. Many psychologists have found these kinds of behavior inconsequential, especially when it comes to explaining and predicting human behavior. But Skinner's supporters point out that focusing on discrete behavior creates the potential for helpful changes. For example, in helping people combat depression, one psychologist might focus on their "feelings." A Skinnerian would focus on cataloging (and modifying) the types of things that "depressed people" *do*. Directly modifying depressive behavior might also brighten clients' self-reports about their "feelings of depression."

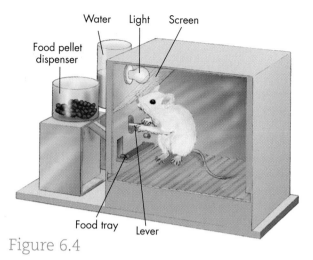

Water   Light   Screen

Food pellet
dispenser

Figure 6.4

The Effects of Reinforcement

NINA LEEN/TIME LIFE PICTURES/GETTY IMAGES

Food tray   Lever

To study operant behavior, Skinner devised an animal cage (or "operant chamber") that has been dubbed the *Skinner box*. (Skinner himself repeatedly requested that his operant chamber *not* be called a Skinner box, but history has thus far failed to honor his wishes.) Such a box is shown in Figure 6.4. The cage is ideal for laboratory experimentation because experimental conditions can be carefully introduced and removed, and their effects on laboratory animals can be observed.

The rat in Figure 6.4 was deprived of food and placed in a Skinner box with a lever at one end. At first it sniffed its way around the cage and engaged in random behavior. The rat's first pressing of the lever was accidental. But because of this action, a food pellet dropped into the cage. The arrival of the food pellet increased the probability that the rat would press the lever again. The pellet is thus said to have *reinforced* lever pressing.

In operant conditioning, it matters little why or how the first "correct" response is made. The animal can happen on it by chance or be physically guided to make the response. You may command your dog to "Sit!" and then press its backside down until it is sitting. Finally you reinforce sitting with food or a pat on the head and a kind word. Animal trainers use physical guiding or coaxing to bring about the first "correct" response. Can you imagine how long it would take to train your dog if you waited for it to sit or roll over and then seized the opportunity to command it to sit or roll over?

People, of course, can be verbally guided into desired responses when they are learning tasks such as spelling, adding numbers, or operating a machine. But they need to be informed when they have made the correct response. Knowledge of results often is all the reinforcement people need to learn new skills.

Types of Reinforcers

A reinforcer is any stimulus that increases the probability that the responses preceding it— whether pecking a button in a Skinner box or studying for a quiz—will be repeated. *What are the various kinds of reinforcers?* Reinforcers include food pellets when an animal has been deprived of food; water when it has been deprived of liquid; the opportunity to mate; the sound of a tone that has previously been associated with eating. Skinner distinguished between positive and negative reinforcers.

Positive and Negative Reinforcers

Positive reinforcers increase the probability that a behavior will occur when they are applied. Food and approval usually serve as positive reinforcers. **Negative reinforcers** increase the probability that a behavior will occur when the reinforcers are *removed* (see Figure 6.5).

Skinner himself repeatedly requested that his operant chamber not be called a Skinner box, but history has thus far failed to honor his wishes.

primary reinforcer
an unlearned reinforcer

secondary reinforcer
a stimulus that gains reinforcement value through association with established reinforcers

conditioned reinforcer
another term for a secondary reinforcer

Figure 6.5

Positive Versus Negative Reinforcers

Procedure	Behavior	Consequence	Change in behavior
Use of positive reinforcement	Behavior (Studying)	Positive reinforcer (Teacher approval) is *presented* when student studies	Frequency of behavior *increases* (Student studies more)
Use of negative reinforcement	Behavior (Studying)	Negative reinforcer (Teacher disapproval) is *removed* when student studies	Frequency of behavior *increases* (Student studies more)

Go to CourseMate for PSYCH at www.cengagebrain.com to access an interactive version of this figure.

People often learn to plan ahead so that they need not fear that things will go wrong. In such cases fear acts as a negative reinforcer; *removal* of fear increases the probability that planning ahead will be repeated.

Immediate Versus Delayed Reinforcers

Immediate reinforcers are more effective than delayed reinforcers. Therefore, the short-term consequences of behavior often provide more of an incentive than the long-term consequences.

Some students socialize when they should be studying because the pleasure of socializing is immediate. Studying may not pay off until the final exam or graduation. (This is why younger students do better with frequent tests.) It is difficult to quit smoking cigarettes because the reinforcement of nicotine is immediate and the health hazards of smoking are more distant. Focusing on short-term reinforcement is also connected with risky sex, such as engaging in sexual activity with a stranger or failing to prevent pregnancy (Caffray & Schneider, 2000; Fuertes et al., 2002). One of the aspects of being human is the ability to foresee the long-range consequences of one's behavior and to make choices. But immediate reinforcers—such as those cookies staring in the face of the would-be dieter—can be powerful temptations indeed.

Nicotine Creates Short-Term Reinforcement

It is difficult to quit smoking cigarettes because the reinforcement of nicotine is immediate and the health hazards of smoking are more distant.

© 2010 C. SHERBURNE/PHOTOLINK / GETTY IMAGES

Primary and Secondary Reinforcers

We can also distinguish between primary and secondary, or conditioned, reinforcers. **Primary reinforcers** are effective because of the organism's biological makeup. For example, food, water, warmth (positive reinforcers), and pain (a negative reinforcer) all serve as primary reinforcers. **Secondary reinforcers** acquire their value through being associated with established reinforcers. For this reason they are also termed **conditioned reinforcers**. We may seek money because we have learned that it may be exchanged for primary reinforcers.

Extinction and Spontaneous Recovery in Operant Conditioning

Keisha's teacher writes "Good" on all of her homework assignments before returning them. One day, her teacher no longer writes anything on the assignments—the reinforcement ends. Reinforcers are used to strengthen responses. What happens when reinforcement stops? *What is the role of extinction in operant conditioning?*

In Pavlov's experiment, the meat powder was the event that followed and confirmed the appropriateness of salivation. In Keisha's situation, seeing "Good" written on her assignments confirmed the appropriateness of the way in which she did her homework. In operant conditioning, the ensuing events are reinforcers. The extinction of learned responses results from the repeated performance of operant behavior without reinforcement. Keisha might stop doing her homework if she is not reinforced for completing it. In other words, reinforcers maintain operant behavior or strengthen habitual behavior in operant conditioning. With humans, fortunately, people can reinforce

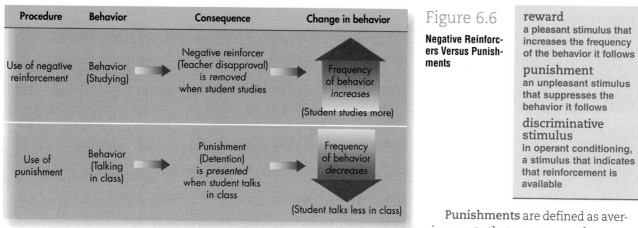

Procedure	Behavior	Consequence	Change in behavior
Use of negative reinforcement	Behavior (Studying)	Negative reinforcer (Teacher disapproval) is *removed* when student studies	Frequency of behavior *increases* (Student studies more)
Use of punishment	Behavior (Talking in class)	Punishment (Detention) is *presented* when student talks in class	Frequency of behavior *decreases* (Student talks less in class)

Figure 6.6

Negative Reinforcers Versus Punishments

Go to CourseMate for PSYCH at www.cengagebrain.com to access an interactive version of this figure.

themselves for desired behavior by telling themselves they did a good job—or in Keisha's case, she may tell herself that she is doing the right thing regardless of whether her teacher recognizes it.

What is the role of spontaneous recovery in operant conditioning? Spontaneous recovery of learned responses occurs in operant conditioning as well as in classical conditioning. Spontaneous recovery is adaptive in operant conditioning as well as in classical conditioning. Reinforcers may once again become available after time elapses, just as there are new tender sprouts on twigs when the spring arrives.

Reinforcers Versus Rewards and Punishments

Reinforcers are defined as stimuli that increase the frequency of behavior. *Why did Skinner make a point of distinguishing between reinforcers on the one hand and rewards and punishments on the other?* Reinforcers are known by their effects, whereas **rewards** and punishments are known by how they feel. It may be that most reinforcers—food, hugs, having the other person admit to starting the argument, and so on—feel good, or are pleasant events. Yet things that we might assume would feel bad, such as a slap on the hand, disapproval from a teacher, even suspensions and detention may be positively reinforcing to some people—perhaps because such experiences confirm negative feelings toward teachers or one's belonging within a deviant subculture (Atkins et al., 2002).

Skinner preferred the concept of reinforcement to that of reward because reinforcement does not suggest trying to "get inside the head" of an organism (whether a human or lower animal) to guess what it would find pleasant or unpleasant. A list of reinforcers is arrived at scientifically and *empirically*—that is, by observing what sorts of stimuli increase the frequency of the behavior.

Punishments are defined as aversive events that suppress or decrease the frequency of the behavior they follow (see Figure 6.6). Punishment can rapidly suppress undesirable behavior (Gershoff, 2002) and may be warranted in "emergencies," such as when a child tries to run into the street.

Discriminative Stimuli

B. F. Skinner might not have been able to get his pigeons into the drivers' seats of missiles, but he had no problem training them to respond to traffic lights. Imagine yourself trying the following experiment.

Place a pigeon in a Skinner box with a button on the wall. Deprive it of food for a while. Drop a food pellet into the cage whenever it pecks the button. Soon it will learn to peck the button. Now you place a small green light in the cage and turn it on and off intermittently throughout the day. Reinforce button pecking with food whenever the green light is on, but not when the light is off. It will not take long for the pigeon to learn that it will gain as much by grooming itself or cooing and flapping around as it will by pecking the button when the light is off.

The green light has become a **discriminative stimulus**. *What are discriminative stimuli?* Discriminative stimuli, such as green or red lights, indicate whether behavior (in the case of the pigeon, pecking a button) will be reinforced (by a food pellet being dropped into the cage). Behaviors that are not reinforced tend to be extinguished. For the pigeon in our experiment, the behavior of pecking the button *when the light is off* is extinguished.

A moment's reflection will suggest many ways in which discriminative stimuli influence our behavior. Isn't it more efficient to answer the telephone when it is ringing? Do you think it is wise to ask someone for a favor when she or he is displaying anger and disapproval toward you?

We noted that a pigeon learns to peck a button if food drops into its cage when it does so. What if you want the pigeon to continue to peck the button, but

continuous reinforcement
a schedule of reinforcement in which every correct response is reinforced

partial zreinforcement
one of several reinforcement schedules in which not every correct response is reinforced

fixed-interval schedule
a schedule in which a fixed amount of time must elapse between the previous and subsequent times that reinforcement is available

variable-interval schedule
a schedule in which a variable amount of time must elapse between the previous and subsequent times that reinforcement is available

you're running out of food? Do not despair. As we see in the following section, you can keep that bird pecking away indefinitely, even as you hold up on most of the food.

Schedules of Reinforcement

In operant conditioning, some responses are maintained by means of **continuous reinforcement**. You probably become warmer every time you put on heavy clothing. You probably become less thirsty every time you drink water. Yet if you have ever watched people toss their money down the maws of slot machines, you know that behavior can also be maintained by means of **partial reinforcement**. *What are the various schedules of reinforcement? How do they affect behavior?*

Folklore about gambling is consistent with learning theory. You can get a person "hooked" on gambling by fixing the game to allow heavy winnings at first. Then you gradually space out the winnings (reinforcements) until gambling is maintained by infrequent winning—or even no winning at all. Partial reinforcement schedules can maintain gambling, like other behavior, for a great deal of time, even though it goes unreinforced (Pulley, 1998).

Responses that have been maintained by partial reinforcement are more resistant to extinction than responses that have been maintained by continuous reinforcement (Rescorla, 1999). From the cognitive perspective, we could suggest that organisms that have experienced partial reinforcement do not expect reinforcement every time they engage in a response. Therefore, they are more likely to persist in the absence of reinforcement.

There are four basic reinforcement schedules: *fixed-interval, variable-interval, fixed-ratio,* and *variable-ratio.*

Interval Schedules

In a **fixed-interval schedule**, a fixed amount of time—say, a minute—must elapse before the correct response will result in a reinforcer. With a fixed-interval schedule, an organism's response rate falls off after each reinforcement and then picks up again as the time when reinforcement will occur approaches. For example, in a one-minute fixed-interval schedule, a rat is reinforced with, say, a food pellet for the first operant—for example, the first pressing of a lever—that occurs after a minute has elapsed. After each reinforcement, the rat's rate of lever pressing slows down, but as the end of the one-minute interval draws near, lever pressing increases in frequency, as suggested in Figure 6.7. It is as if the rat has learned that it must wait a while before it is reinforced. The resultant record on the cumulative recorder shows a typical series of upward waves, or scallops, which are called *fixed-interval scallops.*

Car dealers use fixed-interval reinforcement schedules when they offer incentives for buying up the remainder of the year's line in summer and fall. In a sense, they are suppressing buying at other times, except for consumers whose current cars are in their death throes or those with little self-control. Similarly, you learn to check your e-mail only at a certain time of day if your correspondent writes at that time each day.

Reinforcement is more unpredictable in a **variable-interval schedule**. Therefore, the response rate is steadier but lower. If the boss calls us in for a weekly report, we probably work hard to pull things together just before the report is to be given, just as we might cram the night before a weekly quiz. But if we know that the boss might call us in for a report on the progress of a certain project at any time (variable-interval schedule), we are likely to keep things in a state of reasonable readiness at all times. However,

Truth

For gamblers, the unpredictability of winning also maintains a high response rate.

Figure 6.7

The Fixed-Interval Scallop

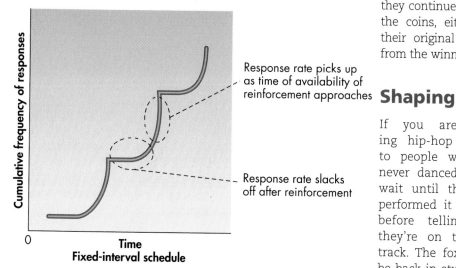

Response rate picks up as time of availability of reinforcement approaches

Response rate slacks off after reinforcement

Cumulative frequency of responses

0

Time
Fixed-interval schedule

our efforts are unlikely to have the intensity they would in a fixed-interval schedule (for example, a weekly report). Similarly, we are less likely to cram for unpredictable pop quizzes than to study for regular quizzes. But we are likely to do at least some studying on a regular basis. Likewise, if you receive e-mail from your correspondent regularly, you are likely to check your e-mail regularly, but with less eagerness.

Ratio Schedules

In a **fixed-ratio schedule**, reinforcement is provided after a fixed number of correct responses have been made. In a **variable-ratio schedule**, reinforcement is provided after a variable number of correct responses have been made. In a 10:1 ratio schedule, the mean number of correct responses that would have to be made before a subsequent correct response would be reinforced is ten, but the ratio of correct responses to reinforcements might be allowed to vary from, say, 1:1 to 20:1 on a random basis.

Fixed- and variable-ratio schedules maintain a high response rate. With a fixed-ratio schedule, it is as if the organism learns that it must make several responses before being reinforced. It then "gets them out of the way" as rapidly as possible. Consider the example of piecework. If a worker must sew five shirts to receive ten dollars, he or she is on a fixed-ratio (5:1) schedule and is likely to sew at a uniformly high rate, although there might be a brief pause after each reinforcement. With a variable-ratio schedule, reinforcement can come at any time. Slot machines tend to pay off on variable-ratio schedules, and players can be seen popping coins into them and yanking their "arms" with barely a pause. I have seen players who do

not even stop to pick up their winnings. Instead, they continue to pop in the coins, either from their original stack or from the winnings tray.

Shaping

If you are teaching hip-hop dancing to people who have never danced, do not wait until they have performed it precisely before telling them they're on the right track. The foxtrot will be back in style before they have learned a thing.

We can teach complex behaviors by **shaping**. *How can we use shaping to teach complex behavior patterns?* Shaping reinforces progressive steps toward the behavioral goal. At first, for example, it may be wise to smile and say, "Good," when a reluctant newcomer gathers the courage to get out on the dance floor, even if your feet are flattened by his initial clumsiness. If you are teaching someone to drive a car with a standard shift, at first generously reinforce the learner simply for shifting gears without stalling.

But as training proceeds, we come to expect more before we are willing to provide reinforcement. We reinforce **successive approximations** of the goal. If you want to train a rat to climb a ladder, first reinforce it with a food pellet when it turns toward the ladder. Then wait until it approaches the ladder before giving it a pellet. Then do not drop a pellet into the cage until the rat touches the ladder. In this way, the rat will reach the top of the ladder more quickly than if you had waited for the target behavior to occur at random.

fixed-ratio schedule a schedule in which reinforcement is provided after a fixed number of correct responses

variable-ratio schedule a schedule in which reinforcement is provided after a variable number of correct responses

shaping a procedure for teaching complex behaviors that at first reinforces approximations of the target behavior

successive approximations behaviors that are progressively closer to a target behavior

© 2007 JUPITERIMAGES CORPORATION

Have you ever driven home and suddenly realized that you couldn't recall exactly how you got there? Your entire trip may seem "lost." Were you in great danger? How could you allow such a thing to happen? Actually, your driving and your responses to the demands of the route may have become so habitual that you did not have to focus on them. As you drove, you were able to think about dinner, work, or the weekend. But if something unusual had occurred on the way, such as an engine problem or a rainstorm, you would have devoted as much attention to your driving as was needed to arrive home. Your trip was probably quite safe after all.

> **Truth**
>
> Through use of shaping, one can indeed train a rat to climb a ramp, cross a bridge, climb a ladder, and so on in a desired sequence.

Applications of Operant Conditioning

Operant conditioning, like classical conditioning, is not just an exotic laboratory procedure. We use it every day in our efforts to influence other people. Parents and peers induce children to acquire so-called gender-appropriate behavior patterns through rewards and punishments. Parents also tend to praise their children for sharing their toys and to punish them for being too aggressive. Peers participate in the socialization process by playing with children who are generous and nonaggressive and often by avoiding those who are not (Warman & Cohen, 2000).

Operant conditioning also plays a role in attitude formation. Adults often reward children for expressing attitudes that coincide with their own and punish or ignore them for expressing contradictory attitudes. Let us now consider some specific applications of operant conditioning.

Biofeedback Training

Biofeedback training (BFT) is based on principles of operant conditioning. BFT has enabled people and lower animals to learn to control autonomic responses to attain reinforcement (Miller, 1969; Vernon et al., 2003).

Through BFT, people can gain control of autonomic functions such as the flow of blood in a finger. They can also learn to improve their control over functions that can be manipulated voluntarily, such as muscle tension. When people receive BFT, reinforcement is given in the form of *information*. Perhaps

a sound changes in pitch or frequency of occurrence to signal that they have modified the autonomic function in the desired direction. For example, we can learn to emit alpha waves—the kind of brain wave associated with feelings of relaxation—through feedback from an electroencephalograph (EEG, an instrument that measures brain waves). People use other instruments to learn to lower their muscle tension, heart rates, and blood pressure.

BFT is also used with people who have lost neuromuscular control of parts of their body as a result of an accident. A "bleep" sound informs them when they have contracted a muscle or sent an impulse down a neural pathway. By concentrating on changing the bleeps, they may gradually regain voluntary control over the damaged function.

Behavior Modification in the Classroom: Accentuating the Positive

Remember that reinforcers are defined as stimuli that increase the frequency of behavior—not as pleasant events. Ironically, adults frequently reinforce undesirable behavior in children by paying attention to them, or punishing them, when they misbehave but ignoring them when they behave in desirable ways. Similarly, teachers who raise their voices when children misbehave may be unintentionally conferring hero status on those pupils in the eyes of their peers. To the teacher's surprise, some children may then go out of their way to earn disapproval.

Teacher preparation and in-service programs show teachers how to use behavior modification to reverse these response patterns. Teachers are taught to reinforce children when they are behaving

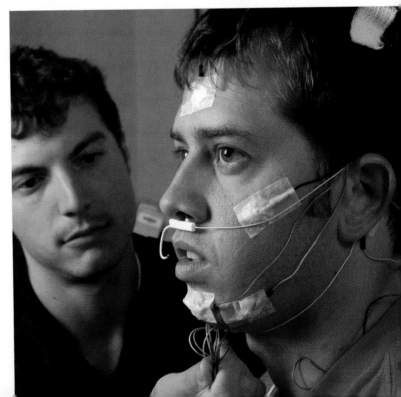
© ROBIN NELSON / ALAMY

appropriately and, when possible, to extinguish misbehavior by ignoring it.

Among older children and adolescents, peer approval may be a more powerful reinforcer than teacher approval. Peer approval may maintain misbehavior, and ignoring misbehavior may only allow students to become more disruptive. In such cases it may be necessary to separate troublesome children.

Teachers also frequently use time out from positive reinforcement to discourage misbehavior. In this method, children are placed in a drab, restrictive environment for a specified period, usually about ten minutes, when they behave disruptively. While they are isolated, they cannot earn the attention of peers or teachers, and no reinforcers are present.

Programmed Learning: Step by Step

B. F. Skinner developed an educational method called *programmed learning* that is based on operant conditioning. This method assumes that any complex task involving conceptual learning as well as motor skills can be broken down into a number of small steps. These steps can be shaped individually and then combined in sequence to form the correct behavioral chain.

Programmed learning does not punish errors. Instead, correct responses are reinforced, usually with immediate feedback. Every child earns a 100, but at her or his own pace. Programmed learning also assumes it is the task of the teacher (or program) to structure the learning experience in such a way that errors will not be made.

Fiction

Actually, one can learn *without* making mistakes.

LO³ Cognitive Factors in Learning

Classical and operant conditioning were originally conceived of as relatively simple forms of learning. Much of conditioning's appeal is that it can be said to meet the behaviorist objective of explaining behavior in terms of observable events—in this case, laboratory conditions. Building on this theoretical base, some psychologists have suggested that the most complex human behavior involves the summation of a series of instances of conditioning. Many psychologists believe, however, that conditioning is too mechanical a process to explain all instances of learned behavior, even in laboratory rats. They turn to cognitive factors to describe and explain additional findings in the psychology of learning. *How do we explain what happens during classical conditioning from a cognitive perspective?*

In addition to concepts such as association and reinforcement, cognitive psychologists use concepts such as mental structures, schemas, templates, and information processing. Cognitive psychologists see people as searching for information, weighing evidence, and making decisions. Let us consider some classic research that points to cognitive factors in learning, as opposed to mechanical associations. These cognitive factors are not necessarily limited to humans—although, of course, people are the only species that can talk about them.

> Remember that **reinforcers** are defined as stimuli that increase the frequency of behavior—not as pleasant events.

Latent Learning: Forming Cognitive Maps

Many behaviorists argue that organisms acquire only responses for which they are reinforced. E. C. Tolman, however, showed that rats also learn about their environment in the absence of reinforcement. In doing so, he showed that rats must form cognitive maps of their surroundings. *What is the evidence that people and lower animals form cognitive maps of their environments?*

Tolman trained some rats to run through mazes for food goals. Other rats were allowed to explore the same mazes for several days without food goals or other rewards. After the unrewarded rats had been allowed to explore the mazes for ten days, food rewards were placed in a box at the far end of the

latent
hidden or concealed

contingency theory
the view that learning occurs when stimuli provide information about the likelihood of the occurrence of other stimuli

observational learning
the acquisition of knowledge and skills through the observation of others (who are called *models*) rather than by means of direct experience

maze. The previously unrewarded rats reached the food box as quickly as the rewarded rats after only one or two trials (Tolman & Honzik, 1930).

Tolman concluded that the rats had learned about the mazes by exploring them even when they went unrewarded by food. He distinguished between *learning* and *performance*. Rats apparently created a cognitive map of a maze. Even though they were not externally motivated to follow a rapid route through the maze, they would learn fast routes just by exploring it. Yet this learning might remain hidden, or **latent**, until food motivated them to take the rapid routes.

Contingency Theory

Behaviorists and cognitive psychologists interpret classical conditioning in different ways. Behaviorists explain it in terms of the pairing of stimuli. Cognitive psychologists explain classical conditioning in terms of the ways in which stimuli provide information that allows organisms to form or revise mental representations of their environment. Robert Rescorla's **contingency theory** suggests that learning occurs only when the conditioned stimulus (CS) provides *information* about the unconditioned stimulus (US).

In classical conditioning of dogs, Rescorla (1967) obtained some results that are difficult to explain without reference to cognitive concepts. Each phase of his work paired a tone (a CS) with an electric shock (a US), but in different ways. With one group of animals, the shock was consistently presented after the tone. The dogs in this group learned to show a fear response when the tone was presented.

A second group of dogs heard an equal number of tones and received an equal number of electric shocks, but the shock did not immediately follow the tone. In other words, the tone and the shock were not paired. Now, from the behaviorist perspective, the dogs should not have learned to associate the tone and the shock, because one did not predict the other. Actually, the dogs learned quite a lot: They learned that they had nothing to fear when the tone was sounded! They showed vigilance and fear when the laboratory was quiet—for the shock might come at any time—but they were calm in the presence of the tone itself.

The third group of dogs also received equal numbers of tones and shocks, but the stimuli were presented at random. Occasionally they were paired, but most often they were not. According to Rescorla, behaviorists might argue that intermittent pairing of the tones and shocks should have brought about some learning. Yet it did not. The animals showed no fear in response to the tone. Rescorla suggests that the animals in this group learned nothing because the tones did not allow them to make predictions about electric shock. Rescorla concluded that learning occurs only when the CS (in this case, the tone) provides information about the US (in this case, the shock).

Observational Learning

How many things have you learned from watching other people in real life, in films, and on television? From films and television, you may have gathered vague ideas about how to skydive, ride a surfboard, climb sheer cliffs, run a pattern to catch a touchdown pass in the Super Bowl, and dust for fingerprints, even if you have never tried them yourself. How do people learn by observing others?

In experiments on **observational learning**, Albert Bandura and his colleagues conducted experiments (e.g., Bandura et al., 1963) that show that we can acquire skills by observing the behavior of others. Observational learning occurs when, as children, we watch our parents cook, clean, or repair a broken appliance. Observational learning takes place when we watch teachers solve problems on the blackboard or hear them speak in a foreign language. Observational learning is not mechanically acquired

To what degree are gender roles learned by observation?

© STOCKBYTE/FIRST LIGHT

through reinforcement. We can learn through observation without engaging in overt responses at all. It appears sufficient to pay attention to the behavior. We may need some practice to refine the skills we acquire. We may also allow these skills to lie dormant or latent. For example, we may not imitate aggressive behavior unless we are provoked and believe that we are more likely to be rewarded than punished for it.

In the terminology of observational learning, a person who engages in a response that is imitated is a **model**. When we see modeled behavior being reinforced, we are said to be *vicariously* reinforced. Engaging in the behavior thus becomes more likely for us as well as for the model.

Violence in the Media and Aggression

We learn by observing parents and peers, attending school, reading books, and watching media such as television and films. Movies and the Internet are also key sources of informal observational learning. Children are routinely exposed to scenes of murder, beating, and sexual assault—just by turning on the TV set (Huesmann et al., 2003). If a child watches two to four hours of TV a day, she or he will have seen 8,000 murders and another 100,000 acts of violence *by the time she or he has finished elementary school* (Eron, 2000). Are kids less likely to be exposed to violence by going to the movies? No. One study found that virtually all G-rated animated films have scenes of violence, with a mean duration of nine to ten minutes per film (Yokota & Thompson, 2000). Other media with violent content include films, music, music videos, video games, the Internet, and comic books (Anderson, 2004).

Bandura: Effects of Violence in the Media

A classic experiment by Bandura, Ross, and Ross (1963) suggests the influence of aggressive models. One group of preschool children observed a film of an adult model hitting and kicking an inflated Bobo doll, while a control group saw an aggression-free film. The experimental and control groups were then left alone in a room with the same doll, as hidden observers recorded their behavior. The children who had observed the aggressive model showed significantly more aggressive behavior toward the doll themselves (see Figure 6.8 on the following page). Many children imitated bizarre attacks they would not have thought up themselves.

Violence tends to be glamorized in the media. Superheroes battle villains who are trying to destroy or take over the world. Violence is often portrayed as having only temporary or minimal effects. (How often

has Wile E. Coyote fallen from a cliff and been pounded into the ground by a boulder, only to bounce back and pursue the Road Runner once more?) In the great majority of violent TV shows, there is no remorse, criticism, or penalty for violent behavior. Few TV programs show harmful long-term consequences of aggressive behavior.

> **model**
> an organism that engages in a response that is then imitated by another organism

Seeing the perpetrator of the violence go unpunished increases the chances that the child will act aggressively (Krcmar & Cooke, 2001). Children may not even view death as much of a problem. As killer Evan Ramsey said, being shot might reduce a person's "health factor." How often do videogame characters "die"— only to be reborn to fight again?

Why all this violence? Simple: Violence sells. But does violence do more than sell? That is, does media violence *cause* real violence? If so, what can parents and educators do to prevent the fictional from spilling over into the real world?

> **Fiction**
>
> Actually, numerous scientific connections have been established between violence in the media and real-life aggression.

Consensus on the Effects of Violence in the Media?

In any event, most organizations of health professionals agree that media violence contributes to aggression (Anderson, 2004; Huesmann et al., 2003). Consider a number of ways in which depictions of violence make such a contribution:

- *Observational learning.* Children learn from observation. TV violence models aggressive "skills," which children may acquire. Media violence also provides viewers with aggressive scripts— that is, ideas about how to behave in situations like those they have observed.

- *Disinhibition.* Punishment inhibits behavior. Conversely, media violence may disinhibit aggressive behavior, especially when media characters "get away" with violence or are rewarded for it.

- *Increased arousal.* Media violence and aggressive video games increase viewers' emotional arousal. That is, media "work them up." We are more likely to be aggressive when we are aroused.

- *Priming of aggressive thoughts and memories.* Media violence triggers aggressive ideas and memories.

- *Habituation.* We become "habituated to," or used to, repeated stimuli. Repeated exposure to TV violence may decrease viewers' sensitivity to real violence. If children come to perceive violence as the norm, they may become more tolerant of it and place less value on restraining aggressive urges.

Figure 6.8

Classic Research on the Imitation of Aggressive Models

On the other hand, viewers are more likely to imitate media violence when they identify with the characters and when the portrayal of violence is realistic (Huesmann et al., 2003). Therefore, viewers may be more likely to imitate violence when the perpetrator looks like them and lives in a similar environment than when it is perpetrated by Wile E. Coyote.

Playing violent video games increases aggressive thoughts and behavior in the laboratory (Anderson, 2003, 2004). It is also connected with a history of juvenile delinquency. However, males are relatively more likely than females to act aggressively after playing violent video games and are more likely to see the world as a hostile place (Bartholow & Anderson, 2002). But students who obtain higher grades are *less* likely than their lower-achieving peers to act aggressively after exposure to violent media games. Thus, gender roles, possible biological gender differences, and psychological factors such as achievement motivation also figure into the effects of media violence.

There seems to be a circular relationship between exposure to media violence and aggressive behavior (Anderson & Dill, 2000; Anderson et al., 2003; Haridakis, 2002). Yes, violence in the media contributes to aggressive behavior, but aggressive youngsters are also more likely to seek out this kind of entertainment. Figure 6.9 explores the possible connections between media violence and aggressive behavior.

The family also affects the likelihood that children will imitate media violence. Studies find that parental substance abuse, paternal physical punishments, and single parenting contribute to the likelihood of aggression in early childhood (Brook et al., 2001; Gupta et al., 2001). Parental rejection and use of physical punishment further increase the likelihood of aggression in children (Eron, 1982). These family factors suggest that the parents of aggressive children may be absent or unlikely to help young children understand that the kinds of socially inappropriate behaviors they see in the media are not for them. A harsh home life may also confirm the TV viewer's or game player's vision of the world as a violent place.

If children believe violence to be inappropriate for them, they will be less likely to act aggressively, even if they have acquired aggressive skills from exposure to the media or other sources. It would be of little use to talk about learning if we couldn't remember what we learn from second to second or from day to day. In the next chapter, we turn our attention to memory. In Chapter 8, we see how learning is intertwined with thinking, language, and intelligence.

Teaching Children *Not* to Imitate Media Violence

Children are going to be exposed to media violence—if not in Saturday-morning cartoon shows, then in evening dramas and in the news. Or they'll hear about violence from friends, watch other children get into fights, or read about violence in the newspapers. If all those sources of violence were somehow hidden from view, they would learn about violence in *Hamlet, Macbeth,* and the Bible. The notion of preventing children from being exposed to violent models may be impractical.

What, then, should be done? Parents and educators can do many things to tone down the impact of media violence. Children who watch violent shows may act less aggressively when they are informed that:

- The violent behavior they observe in the media does not represent the behavior of most people.

- The apparently aggressive behaviors they watch are not real. They reflect camera tricks, special effects, and stunts.

- Most people resolve conflicts by nonviolent means.

- The real-life consequences of violence are harmful to the victim and often to the aggressor.

Despite our history of evolutionary forces, and despite the fact that in most species, successful aggression usually wins individuals the right to transmit their genes to future generations, humans are thinking beings. If children consider violence to be inappropriate for them, they will be less likely to act aggressively, even when they have acquired aggressive skills from exposure to the media or other sources.

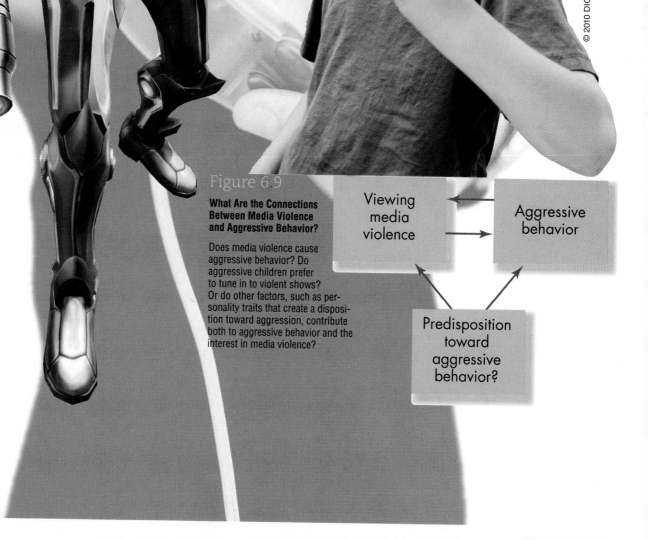

Figure 6.9

What Are the Connections Between Media Violence and Aggressive Behavior?

Does media violence cause aggressive behavior? Do aggressive children prefer to tune in to violent shows? Or do other factors, such as personality traits that create a disposition toward aggression, contribute both to aggressive behavior and the interest in media violence?

Viewing media violence

Aggressive behavior

Predisposition toward aggressive behavior?

CHAPTER 7

Memory:
Remembrance of Things Past—and Future

Learning Outcomes

LO **1**   Define memory and differentiate between types of memories

LO **2**   Explain the process of memory

LO **3**   Explain the stages of memory

LO **4**   Identify contributors to forgetting

LO **5**   Describe the biological aspects of memory

> ## 66 *Without your memory, there is no past.* 99

Jeff would never forget his sudden loss of memory. He watched in horror as his flip phone slipped from his pocket and fell to the floor of the Blockbuster store in Boston. Before he could grab it, it shattered into pieces. A New York college student, Jeff experienced the trauma of phone loss on his winter break.

Why was the loss traumatic? Why was it a memory problem? Simple: There was no way for Jeff to retrieve his phone book. "I was at the store and it was snowing out and I suddenly realized that I had no way of getting in touch with anyone," he explains (Metz, 2005). Jeff now copies every cell-phone entry in a little black book—made of paper. Other people back up their phone books—and their pictures and downloads—on servers provided by cellular telephone operating companies or cell-phone manufacturers.

What's the problem with remembering all those phone numbers? The answer lies partly in their length. Psychologist George Miller (1956) researched the amount of information people can keep in mind at once, and he found that the average person is comfortable with digesting about seven digits at a time. Most people have little trouble recalling five pieces of information, as in a ZIP code. Some can remember nine, which is, for most, an upper limit. So seven pieces of information, plus or minus one or two, is the "magic" number.

Truth or Fiction?

What do you think?

Folklore, common sense, or nonsense? Place a T for "True" or F for "False" on the lines provided (you'll learn the answers as you read through the text).

— A woman who could not remember who she was automatically dialed her mother's number when the police gave her a telephone.

— Learning must be meaningful if we are to remember it.

— If you can see, you have a photographic memory.

— All of our experiences are permanently imprinted on the brain, so the proper stimulus can cause us to remember them exactly.

— It may be easier for you to recall the name of your first-grade teacher than the name of someone you just met at a party.

— You may always recall where you were and what you were doing on the morning of September 11, 2001.

— If you study with the stereo on, you would probably do better to take the test with the stereo on.

— Learning Spanish can make it harder to remember French—and vice versa.

This chapter is all about the "backup assistant" in your brain—your memory. Without your memory, there is no past. Without your memory, experience is trivial and learning is lost. Let us see what psychologists have learned about the ways in which we remember things—beyond keying them into our handheld device's memory storage.

Five Memory Challenges

Let's challenge your memory. This is not an actual memory test of the sort used by psychologists to determine whether people's memory functioning is within normal limits. Instead, it will provide you with some insight into how your memory works and may also be fun.

explicit memory
memory that clearly and distinctly expresses (explicates) specific information

episodic memory
memories of events experienced by a person or that take place in the person's presence

semantic memory
general knowledge, as opposed to episodic memory

implicit memory
memory that is suggested (implied) but not plainly expressed, as illustrated in the things that people *do* but do not state clearly

Directions: Find four sheets of blank paper and number them 1 through 4. Also use a watch with a second hand. Then follow these instructions:

1. Following are ten letters. Look at them for fifteen seconds. Later in the chapter I will ask you if you can write them on sheet number 1. (No cheating! Don't do it now.)

THUNSTOFAM

2. Look at these nine figures for thirty seconds. Then try to draw them in the proper sequence on sheet number 2, right after you have finished looking at them. (We'll talk about your drawings later.)

3. Look at the list of seventeen letters for sixty seconds and then see whether you can reproduce it on sheet number 3.

GMC-BSI-BMA-TTC-IAF-BI

4. Which of these pennies is an accurate reproduction of the Lincoln penny? This time there's nothing to draw on another sheet; just circle or put a check mark by the penny that you think resembles the ones you see every day.

A   B   C   D   E   F

5. Examine the following drawings for one minute. Then copy the *names* of the figures on sheet number 4. When you're finished, just keep reading. Soon I'll be asking you to draw those figures.

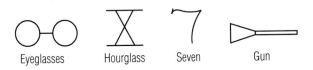

Eyeglasses   Hourglass   Seven   Gun

LO¹ Memory Systems

Jeff remembered a thing he had personally done, like drop his cell phone in Boston on a blustery day in January. Remembering dropping one's cell phone is an *episodic memory*—a memory of an event in one's life. According to psychologists who have extensively researched memory, episodic memory is one kind of memory system (Dobbins et al., 2004; Schacter, 2000). There are several, most of which address information from the past, but one—prospective

memory—which involves keeping the things we intend to do in mind. Let us begin by distinguishing between explicit memories and implicit memories. As you will see, for all practical purposes, implicit memories may last for a lifetime.

Explicit Versus Implicit Memories

Explicit Memory

What is meant by explicit memory? Explicit memory—also referred to as *declarative memory*—is memory for specific information. Things that are *explicit* are clear, or clearly stated or explained. The use of the term *declarative* indicates that these memories state or reveal (i.e., *declare*) specific information. The information may be autobiographical or refer to general knowledge.

Two kinds of explicit memories are described by psychologist Endel Tulving (1985): episodic and semantic. They are identified according to the type of information they hold.

Episodic Memory (I remember...) What is *meant by episodic memory?* Episodic memories are types of explicit memories. They are memories of the things that happen to us or take place in our presence. Episodic memory is also referred to as *autobiographical memory.* Your memories of what you ate for breakfast and of what your professor said in class today are episodic memories. We tend to use the phrase "I remember ..." when we are referring to episodic memories, as in "I remember the blizzard of 2004."

Semantic Memory (I know ...) What is *meant by semantic memory?* General knowledge is referred to as semantic memory—another kind of explicit memory. *Semantics* concerns meanings. You can "know" that the United States has fifty states without visiting them and personally adding them up. You "know" who authored *Hamlet,* although you were not looking over Shakespeare's shoulder as he did so. These are examples of semantic memory.

Your future recollection that there are several memory systems is more likely to be semantic than episodic. In other words, you are more likely to "know" that there are several types of memory than to recall where you were and how you were sitting. We are more likely to say "I know ..." in reference to semantic memories, as in "I *know* about—" (or "I heard about—") "—the blizzard of 1898."

Implicit Memory

What is meant by implicit memory? Implicit memory—also referred to as *nondeclarative*

> **"You *remember* what you had for breakfast, but you *know* that Shakespeare wrote *Hamlet*."**

memory—is memory of how to perform a procedure or skill; it is the act itself, doing something, like riding a bike, accessing your cell-phone contacts list, and texting a message (Schacter et al., 1993). Implicit memories are suggested (or implied) but not plainly stated or verbally expressed. Implicit memories are illustrated by the things that people *do* but not by the things they state clearly. Implicit memories involve procedures and skills, cognitive and physical, and are also referred to as *procedural* or *skill memories*.

Implicit memories can endure even when we have not used them for years. Getting to class "by habit"—without paying attention to landmarks or directions—is another instance of implicit memory. If someone asked you what two times two is, the number four would probably "pop" into mind without conscious calculation. After going over the alphabet or multiplication tables hundreds of times, our memory of them becomes automatic or implicit. We need not focus on them to use them.

Your memory of the alphabet or the multiplication tables reflects repetition that makes associations automatic. This phenomenon is called priming. Brain imaging shows that priming makes it possible for people to carry out mental tasks with less neural activity (Savage et al., 2001; Schacter et al., 2004). Years of priming help people make complete words out of the word fragments (Schacter et al., 1999). Even though the cues in the following fragments are limited, you might make them into words:

PYGY   TXT   BUFL

Sample answers are "pygmy," "text," and "buffalo." Can you think of others?

Daniel Schacter (1992) illustrates implicit memory with the story of a woman with amnesia who was wandering the streets. The police picked her up and found that she could not remember who she was and that she had no identification. After fruitless interviewing, the police hit on the idea of asking her to dial phone numbers—"any number at all." When asked for the phone numbers of people she knew, she had had no answer. She could not *declare* her mother's phone number. She could not make the number *explicit*. She could not even remember her mother's name, or whether she had a mother. But dialing her mother's phone number was a habit, and she did it "on automatic pilot."

ERIK ISAKSON / GETTY IMAGES

Retrospective Memory Versus Prospective Memory

Retrospective memory is the recalling of information that has been previously learned. *Episodic, semantic,* and *implicit memories* involve remembering things that were learned. Prospective memory refers to remembering to do things in the future, such as remembering to pay your bills or to withdraw some cash.

Most of us have had failures of prospective memory in which we feel we were supposed to do something but can't remember what. Prospective memory may fail when we are preoccupied, distracted, or "stressed out" about time (Schacter, 1999).

There are various kinds of prospective memory tasks. *Habitual tasks* such as getting to class on time are easier to remember than occasional tasks such as meeting someone for coffee at an arbitrary time (d'Ydewalle et al., 1999). Motivation also plays a role. You are more likely to remember the coffee date if the person you are meeting excites you. Psychologists also distinguish between event-based and time-based prospective memory tasks (Fortin et al., 2002). *Event-based tasks* are triggered by events, such as remembering to take one's medicine at breakfast or to brush one's teeth after eating. *Time-based tasks* are to be performed at a certain time or after a certain amount of time has elapsed between occurrences, such as tuning in to a favorite news program at 7:30 p.m. or taking a pill every four hours (Marsh et al., 2005).

An age-related decline takes place in retrospective and prospective memories (Brigman & Cherry, 2002; Reese &

priming
the activation of specific associations in memory, often as a result of repetition and without making a conscious effort to access the memory

retrospective memory
memory for past events, activities, and learning experiences, as shown by explicit (episodic and semantic) and implicit memories

prospective memory
memory to perform an act in the future, as at a certain time or when a certain event occurs

Truth

Although the woman did not "know" what she was doing, she dialed her mother's number.

encoding
modifying information so that it can be placed in memory; the first stage of information processing

storage
the maintenance of information over time; the second stage of information processing

maintenance rehearsal
mental repetition of information to keep it in memory

metamemory
self-awareness of the ways in which memory functions, allowing the person to encode, store, and retrieve information effectively

elaborative rehearsal
the kind of coding in which new information is related to information that is already known

Cherry, 2002). The decline in older adults may be related to their speed of cognitive processing rather than the "loss" of information per se. In the case of prospective memory, older adults take longer to respond to the cues or reminders (West & Craik, 1999).

Moods and attitudes affect prospective memory (Villa & Abeles, 2000). For example, depressed people are less likely to push to remind themselves to do what they intend to do (Rude et al., 1999).

Before moving to the next section, turn to sheet number 4 and draw the figures from memory. Hold onto the drawings. We'll talk about them soon.

LO² Processes of Memory

Both psychologists and computer scientists speak of processing information. Think of using a computer to write a term paper. Once the system is up and operating, you begin to enter information. You can enter information by, for example, typing alphanumeric characters on a keyboard or—in the case of voice recognition technology—speaking. But if you were to do some major surgery on your computer and open up its memory, you wouldn't find these characters or sounds inside it. This is because the computer is programmed to change the characters or sounds—the information you have entered—into a form that can be placed in its electronic memory. Similarly, when we perceive information, we must change it into a form that can be remembered if we are to place it in our memory.

Encoding

Information about the outside world reaches our senses in the form of physical and chemical stimuli. The first stage of information processing is changing information so that we can place it in memory: encoding. *What is the role of encoding in memory?* When we encode information, we transform it into psychological formats that can be

represented mentally. To do so, we commonly use visual, acoustic, and semantic codes.

Let us illustrate the uses of coding by referring to the list of letters you first saw in the section on challenges to memory. Try to write the letters on sheet number 1. Go on, take a minute and then come back.

If you had used a *visual code* to try to remember the list, you would have mentally represented it as a picture. That is, you would have maintained—or attempted to maintain—a mental image of the letters.

You may also have decided to read the list of letters to yourself—that is, to silently say them in sequence: "t," "h," "u," and so on. By so doing, you would have been using an *acoustic code*, or representing the stimuli as a sequence of sounds. You may also have read the list as a three-syllable word, "thun-sto-fam." This is an acoustic code, but it also involves the "meaning" of the letters, in the sense that you are interpreting the list as a word. This approach has elements of a semantic code.

Semantic codes represent stimuli in terms of their meaning. Our ten letters were meaningless in and of themselves. However, they can also serve as an acronym—a term made up of the first letters of a phrase that is pronounced as a word—for the familiar phrase "THe UNited STates OF AMerica." This observation lends them meaning.

Storage

The second memory process is *storage*. *What is the role of storage in memory?* Storage means maintaining information over time. If you were given the task of storing the list of letters—that is, told to remember it—how would you attempt to place it in storage? One way would be by maintenance rehearsal—by mentally repeating the list, or saying it to yourself. Our awareness of the functioning of our memory, referred to by psychologists as metamemory, becomes more sophisticated as we develop.

You could also encode the list of letters by relating it to something that you already know. This coding is called elaborative rehearsal. You are "elaborating" or extending the semantic meaning of the letters you are trying to remember. For example, as mentioned above, the list of ten letters is an acronym for "The United States of America." That is, you take the first two letters of each of the words in the phrase and string them together to make up the ten letters of THUNSTOFAM. If you had recognized this, storage of the list of letters might have been almost instantaneous, and it would probably have been permanent. But enough maintenance rehearsal can do the job.

Retrieval

The third memory process is *retrieval*. *What is the role of retrieval in memory?* The retrieval of stored information means locating it and returning it to consciousness. With well-known information such as our names and occupations, retrieval is effortless and rapid. But when we are trying to remember large amounts of information, or information that is not perfectly understood, retrieval can be difficult or fail. It is easiest to retrieve information stored in a computer by using the name of the file. Similarly, retrieval of information from our memories requires knowledge of the proper cues.

If you had encoded THUNSTOFAM as a three-syllable word, your retrieval strategy would involve recollection of the word and rules for decoding. In other words, you would say the "word" *thun-sto-fam* and then decode it by spelling it out. You might err in that "thun" sounds like "thumb" and "sto" could also be spelled "stow." However, using the semantic code, or recognition of the acronym for "The United States of America," could lead to flawless recollection.

I predicted that you would immediately and permanently store the list if you recognized it as an acronym. Here, too, there would be recollection (of the name of a nation) and rules for decoding. That is, to "remember" the ten letters, you would have to envision the phrase ("The United States of America") and read off the first two letters of each word. In this case, you are actually reconstructing the list of ten letters.

But what if you were not able to remember the list of ten letters? What would have gone wrong? In terms of the three processes of memory, it could be that you had (1) not encoded the list in a useful way, (2) not entered the encoded information into storage, or (3) stored the information but forgotten the cues for remembering it—such as the phrase "The United States of America" or the rule for decoding the phrase.

You may have noticed that we have come a long way into this chapter, but I have not yet *defined* memory. No apologies—we weren't ready. Now that we have explored some basic concepts, let us give it a try: **Memory** is the processes by which information is encoded, stored, and retrieved.

LO³ Stages of Memory

William James (1890) was intrigued by the fact that some memories are unreliable. They would "go in one ear and out the other," while other memories stuck for a lifetime. The world is a dazzling array of sights and sounds and other sources of sensory information, but only some of it is remembered. Psychologists Richard Atkinson and Richard Shiffrin (1968) suggested a model for how some information is lost immediately, other information is held briefly, and still other information is held for a lifetime. *What is the Atkinson–Shiffrin model of memory?* As shown in Figure 7.1 on page 146, they proposed three stages of memory that determine whether (and how long) information is retained: *sensory memory, short-term memory* (STM), and *long-term memory* (LTM).

Sensory Memory

When we look at a visual stimulus, our impressions may seem fluid enough. Actually, however, they consist of a series of eye fixations referred to as *saccadic eye movements*. These movements jump from one point to another about four times each second. Yet the visual sensations seem continuous, or stream-like, because of sensory memory. Sensory memory is the type or stage of memory that is first encountered by a stimulus. Although sensory memory holds impressions briefly, it is long enough so that a series of perceptions seem to be connected. *How does sensory memory function?*

To explain the functioning of sensory memory, let us return to our list of letters: THUNSTOFAM. If the list were flashed on a screen for a fraction of a second, the visual impression, or memory trace, of the stimulus would also last for only a fraction of a second afterward. Psychologists speak of the memory trace of the list as being held in a visual *sensory register*.

If the letters had been flashed on a screen for, say, a tenth of a second, your ability to remember them on the basis of sensory memory alone would be limited. Your memory would be based on a single eye fixation, and the trace of the image would vanish before a single second had passed. A century ago, psychologist William McDougall (1904) engaged in research in which he showed people one to twelve letters

retrieval
the location of stored information and its return to consciousness; the third stage of information processing

memory
the processes by which information is encoded, stored, and retrieved

sensory memory
the type or stage of memory first encountered by a stimulus

memory trace
an assumed change in the nervous system that reflects the impression made by a stimulus

arranged in rows—just long enough to allow a single eye fixation. Under these conditions, people could typically remember only four or five letters. Thus, recollection of THUNSTOFAM, a list of ten letters arranged in a single row, would probably depend on whether one had encoded it so that it could be processed further.

George Sperling (1960) modified McDougall's experimental method and showed that there is a difference between what people can see and what they can report. McDougall had used a *whole-report procedure,* in which people were asked to report every letter they saw in the array. Sperling used a modified *partial-report procedure,* in which people were asked to report the contents of one of three rows of letters. In a typical procedure, Sperling flashed three rows of letters like the following on a screen for 50 milliseconds (1/20th of a second):

A G R E
V L S B
N K B T

Using the whole-report procedure, people could report an average of four letters from the entire display (one out of three). But if immediately after presenting the display Sperling pointed an arrow at a row he wanted viewers to report, they usually reported most of the letters in the row successfully.

If Sperling presented six letters arrayed in two rows, people could usually report either row without error. If people were flashed three rows of four letters

Figure 7.1

Three Stages of Memory: The Atkinson–Shiffrin Model

The Atkinson–Shiffrin model proposes that there are three stages of memory: (a) sensory memory, (b) short-term memory, and (c) long-term memory. Part A shows that sensory information impacts the registers of sensory memory. Memory traces are held briefly in sensory memory before decaying. If we attend to the information, much of it can be transferred to short-term memory (STM). Part B Information may be maintained in STM through maintenance rehearsal or elaborative rehearsal. Otherwise, it may decay or be displaced. Part C: Once information is transferred to long-term memory (LTM), it may be filed away indefinitely. However, if the information in LTM is organized poorly, or if we cannot find cues to retrieve it, it can be lost.

Go to CourseMate for PSYCH at www.cengagebrain.com to access an interactive version of this figure.

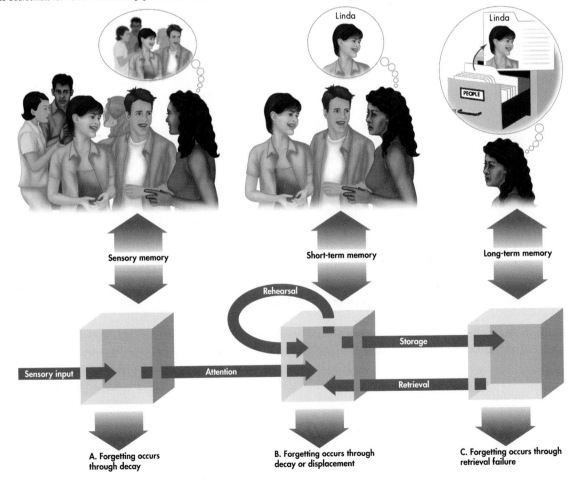

A. Forgetting occurs through decay

B. Forgetting occurs through decay or displacement

C. Forgetting occurs through retrieval failure

each—a total of twelve—they reported correctly an average of three of four letters in the designated row, suggesting that about nine of the twelve letters had been perceived.

Sperling found that the amount of time that elapsed before he pointed to the row to be reported affected people's memory. If he delayed pointing for a few fractions of a second after showing the letters, people were less successful in reporting the letters in the row. If he allowed a full second to elapse, the arrow did not help people remember at all. Sperling concluded that the memory trace of visual stimuli *decays* within a second (see Figure 7.1). With a single eye fixation, people can *see* most of a display of twelve letters clearly, as shown by their ability to immediately read off most of the letters in a designated row. Yet as fractions of a second are elapsing, the trace of the letters is fading. By the time a full second elapses, the trace is gone.

Iconic Memory

Psychologists believe we possess a sensory register for each sense. The mental representations of visual stimuli are referred to as icons. The sensory register that holds icons is labeled iconic memory. Iconic memories are accurate, photographic memories. But these memories are brief. What most of us usually think of as a photographic memory—the ability to retain exact mental representations of visual stimuli over long periods—is technically termed eidetic imagery. Only a few people are capable of eidetic imagery.

Iconic Memory and Saccadic Eye Movements

As mentioned previously, saccadic eye movements occur about four times a second. But iconic memory holds icons for up to a second. For this reason, the flow of visual information seems smooth and continuous. Your impression that the words you are reading flow across the page, rather than jumping across in spurts, is a product of your iconic memory. Similarly, motion pictures present sixteen to twenty-two separate frames, or still images, each second, but iconic memory allows you to perceive the imagery in the film as being seamless (G. R. Loftus, 1983).

Truth

Those of us who see and mentally represent visual stimuli do have "photographic memories."

Echoic Memory

Mental representations of sounds, or auditory stimuli, are called echoes. Echoic memory is the sensory register that holds echoes.

The memory traces of auditory stimuli—echoes—can last for several seconds, many times longer than the traces of visual stimuli (icons). This difference is one of the reasons that acoustic codes aid in the retention of information that has been presented visually—or why saying the letters or syllables of THUNSTOFAM makes the list easier to remember.

Short-Term Memory

Imagine that you are completing a writing assignment and you key or speak words and phrases into your word-processing program. They appear on your monitor as a sign that your computer has them in *memory.* Your word-processing program allows you to add words, delete words, check whether they are spelled correctly, add images, and move paragraphs from place to place. Although you can manipulate the information in your computer's memory, it isn't saved. It hasn't been entered into storage. If the program or the computer crashes, the information is gone. The computer's memory is a short-term affair. To maintain a long-term connection with the information, you have to save it. Saving it means naming it—hopefully with a name that you will remember so that you can later find and retrieve the information—and instructing your computer to save it (keep it in storage until told otherwise).

If you focus on a stimulus in the sensory register, you will tend to retain it in your own short-term memory—also referred to as working memory—for a minute or so after the trace of the stimulus decays. *How does short-term memory function?* As one researcher describes it, "Working memory is the

> The memory traces of auditory stimuli —echoes—can last for several seconds, many times longer than the traces of visual stimuli (icons).

icon
a mental representation of a visual stimulus that is held briefly in sensory memory

iconic memory
the sensory register that briefly holds mental representations of visual stimuli

eidetic imagery
the maintenance of detailed visual memories over several minutes

echo
a mental representation of an auditory stimulus (sound) that is held briefly in sensory memory

echoic memory
the sensory register that briefly holds mental representations of auditory stimuli

short-term memory
the type or stage of memory that can hold information for up to a minute or so after the trace of the stimulus decays

working memory
another term for *short-term memory*

mental glue that links a thought through time from its beginning to its end" (Goldman-Rakic, 1995). When you are given a phone number by the information operator and write it down or immediately dial the number, you are retaining the number in your short-term memory. When you are told the name of someone at a party and then use that name immediately in addressing that person, you are retaining the name in short-term memory. In short-term memory, the image tends to fade significantly after ten to twelve seconds if it is not repeated or rehearsed. It is possible to focus on maintaining a visual image in the short-term memory, but it is more common to encode visual stimuli as sounds, or auditory stimuli. Then the sounds can be rehearsed, or repeated.

Once information is in our short-term memories, we can work on it. Like the information in the word-processing program, we can manipulate it. But it isn't necessarily saved. If we don't do something to save—such as write down a new telephone number or key it into your cell phone's contact list—it can be gone forever.

You need to rehearse new information to "save" it, but you may need only the proper cue to retrieve information from long-term memory.

Let us now return to the task of remembering the first list of letters in the challenges to memory at the beginning of the chapter. If you had encoded the letters as the three-syllable word THUN-STO-FAM, you would probably have recalled them by mentally rehearsing (saying

to yourself) the three-syllable "word" and then spelling it out from the sounds. A few minutes later, if someone asked whether the letters had been uppercase (THUNSTOFAM) or lowercase (thunstofam), you might not have been able to answer with confidence. You used an acoustic code to help recall the list, and uppercase and lowercase letters sound alike.

Because it can be pronounced, THUNSTOFAM is not too difficult to retain in short-term memory. But what if the list of letters had been TBXLFNTSDK? This list of letters cannot be pronounced as it is. You would have to find a complex acronym to code these letters, and do so within a fraction of a second—most likely an impossible task. To aid recall, you would probably choose to try to repeat the letters rapidly—to read each one as many times as possible before the memory trace fades. You might visualize each letter as you say it and try to get back to it (that is, to run through the entire list) before it decays.

Let us assume that you encoded the letters as sounds and then rehearsed the sounds.

When asked to report the list, you might mistakenly say T-V-X-L-F-N-T-S-T-K. This would be an understandable error because the incorrect V and T sounds are similar, respectively, to the correct B and D sounds.

The Serial-Position Effect

If asked to recall the list of letters TBXLFNTSDK, you would be likely to recall the first and last letters in the series, T and K, more accurately than the others. *Why are we most likely to remember the first and last items in a list?* The tendency to recall the first and last items in a series is known as the serial-position effect. This effect may occur because we

Memorizing a Script by Rehearsing Echoic Memories
As actors work on memorizing scripts, they first encode visual information (printed words) as echoes (their corresponding sounds within the brain). Then they commit the echoes to memory by rehearsing (repeating) them, referring back to the visual information as necessary. Eventually, the lines of other actors become cues that trigger memory of an actor's own lines.

pay more attention to the first and last stimuli in a series. They serve as the boundaries for the other stimuli. It may also be that the first items are likely to be rehearsed more frequently (repeated more times) than other items. The last items are likely to have been rehearsed most recently and hence are most likely to be retained in short-term memory.

Chunking

Rapidly rehearsing ten meaningless letters is not an easy task. With TBXLFNTSDK there are ten discrete elements, or chunks, of information that must be kept in short-term memory. When we encode THUNSTOFAM as three syllables, there are only three chunks to memorize at once.

As noted at the beginning of the chapter, psychologist George Miller (1956) found that the average person is comfortable with remembering about seven integers at a time, the number of integers in a telephone number. *Is seven a magic number, or did the phone company get lucky?*

Businesses pay the phone company hefty premiums so that they can attain numbers with two or three zeroes or repeated digits—for example, 592-2000 or 277-3333. These numbers include fewer chunks of information and so are easier to remember. Customer recollection of business phone numbers increases sales. One financial services company uses the toll-free number CALL-IRA, which reduces the task to two chunks of information that also happen to be meaningfully related (semantically coded) to the nature of the business.

Return to the third challenge to memory presented earlier. Were you able to remember the six groups of letters? Would your task have been simpler if you had grouped them differently? How about moving the dashes forward by a letter, so that they read GM-CBS-IBM-ATT-CIA-FBI? If we do this, we have the same list of letters, but we also have six chunks of information that can be coded semantically (according to what they mean). You may have also been able to generate the list by remembering a rule, such as "big corporations and government agencies."

Reconsider the second challenge to memory presented earlier. You were asked to remember nine chunks of visual information. Perhaps you could have used the acoustic codes "L" and "Square" for chunks three and five, but no obvious codes are available for the seven other chunks. Now look at Figure 7.2. If you had recognized that the elements in the challenge could be arranged as the familiar tic-tac-toe grid, remembering the nine elements might have required two chunks of information. The first would have been the men-

tal image of the grid, and the second would have been the rule for decoding: Each element corresponds to the shape of a section of the grid if read like words on a page (from upper left to lower right). The number sequence 1 through 9 would not in itself present a problem, because you learned this series by rote many years ago and have rehearsed it in countless calculations since then.

Interference in Short-Term Memory

In a classic experiment with college students, Lloyd and Margaret Peterson (1959) demonstrated how prevention of rehearsal can wreak havoc with short-term memory. They asked students to remember three-letter combinations such as HGB—normally, three easy chunks of information. They then had the students count backward from an arbitrary number, such as 181, by threes (that is, 181, 178, 175, 172, and so on). The students were told to stop counting and to report the letter sequence after the intervals of time shown in Figure 7.3 on page 150. The percentage of correctly recalled letter combinations fell dramatically within seconds. After eighteen seconds of interference, counting had dislodged the letter sequences in almost all students' memories.

Figure 7.2

A Familiar Grid

The nine drawings in the second challenge to memory form this familiar tic-tac-toe grid when the numbers are placed inside them and they are arranged in order. This method for recalling the shapes collapses nine chunks of information into two. One is the tic-tac-toe grid. The second is the rule for decoding the drawings from the grid.

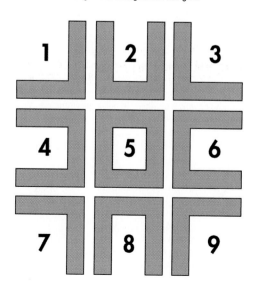

displace
in memory theory, to cause information to be lost from short-term memory by adding new information

long-term memory
the type or stage of memory capable of relatively permanent storage

repression
in Freud's psychodynamic theory, the ejection of anxiety-evoking ideas from conscious awareness

schema
a way of mentally representing the world, such as a belief or an expectation, that can influence perception of persons, objects, and situations

Psychologists say that the appearance of new information in short-term memory displaces the old information. Remember: Only a few bits of information can be retained in short-term memory at the same time.

Long-Term Memory

Long-term memory is the third stage of information processing (Refer back to Figure 7.1.). Think of your long-term memory as a vast storehouse of information containing names, dates, places, what Johnny did to you in second grade, and what Susan said about you when you were twelve. *How does long-term memory function?*

Some psychologists (Freud was one) used to believe that nearly all of our perceptions and ideas are stored permanently. We might not be able to retrieve all of them, however.

Some memories might be "lost" because of lack of proper cues, or they might be kept unconscious by the forces of repression. Adherents to this view often pointed to the work of neurosurgeon Wilder Penfield (1969). When parts of their brains were electrically stimulated, many of Penfield's patients reported the appearance of images that had something of the feel of memories.

Today most psychologists view this notion as exaggerated. Memory researcher Elizabeth Loftus,

for example, notes that the "memories" stimulated by Penfield's probes lacked detail and were sometimes incorrect (Loftus & Loftus, 1980; E. F. Loftus, 1983). Now let us consider some other questions about long-term memory.

How Accurate Are Long-Term Memories?

Psychologist Elizabeth Loftus notes that memories are distorted by our biases and needs—by the ways in which we conceptualize our worlds. We represent much of our world in the form of schemas. A *schema* is a way of mentally representing the world, such as a belief or expectation, that can influence our perception of persons, objects, and situations.

Now, retrieve sheet number 4. You drew the figures "from memory" according to instructions on page 142. Now look at Figure 7.4. Are your drawings closer in form to those in group 1 or to those in group 2? I wouldn't be surprised if they were more like those in group 1—if, for example, your first drawing looked more like eyeglasses than a dumbbell. After all, they were labeled like the drawings in group 1. The labels serve as *schemas* for the drawings—ways of organizing your knowledge of them—and these schemas may have influenced your recollections.

> 66 Long-term memory is reconstructive rather than photographic. 99

How Much Information Can Be Stored in Long-Term Memory?

How many "gigabytes of storage" are there in your most personal computer—your brain? Unlike a computer, the human ability to store information is, for all practical purposes, unlimited (Goldman-Rakic et al., 2000b). Even the largest hard drives fill up when we save Web pages, photos, songs, and movies. Yet how many "movies" of the past have you saved in your own long-term memory? How many thousands of scenes and stories can you rerun at will? And, assuming that you have an intact sensory system, the movies in your personal storage bins not only have color and sound, but also aromas, tactile sensations, and more. *Your long-term memory is a biochemical "hard drive" with no known limits on the amount of information it can store.*

New information may replace older information in short-term memory, but there is no evidence that long-term memories—those in "storage"—are lost by

Figure 7.3

The Effect of Interference on Short-Term Memory

In this experiment, college students were asked to remember a series of three letters while they counted backward by threes. After just three seconds, retention was cut by half. Ability to recall the words was almost completely lost by fifteen seconds.

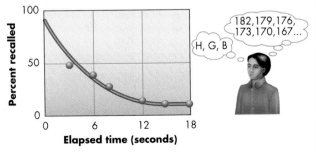

Fiction

It has *not* been shown that all our experiences are permanently imprinted on the brain.

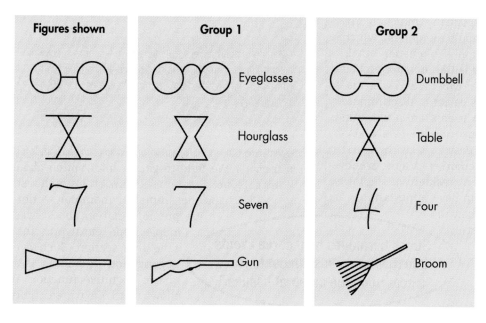

Figures shown	Group 1		Group 2	
⊙—⊙	⊙⊙	Eyeglasses	⊙—⊙	Dumbbell
⋈	⋈	Hourglass	⋈	Table
7	7	Seven	4	Four
⊳—	⊳—	Gun	⋰	Broom

Figure 7.4

Memory as Reconstructive

In their classic experiment, Carmichael, Hogan, and Walter (1932) showed people the figures in the left box and made remarks as suggested in the other boxes. For example, the experimenter might say, "This drawing looks like eyeglasses [or a dumbbell]." When people later reconstructed the drawings, they were influenced by the labels.

displacement. Long-term memories may endure a lifetime. Now and then it may seem that we have forgotten, or "lost," a long-term memory such as the names of elementary-school classmates, yet it may be that we cannot find the proper cues to retrieve them. However, if you drive by your elementary school (a cue) you might suddenly recall the long-lost names of schoolteachers.

Levels of Processing Information

People who use elaborative rehearsal to remember things are *processing information at a deeper level* than people who use maintenance rehearsal. *What is the levels-of-processing model of memory?* Fergus Craik and Robert Lockhart (1972) pioneered the levels-of-processing model of memory, which holds that memories tend to endure when information is processed *deeply*—attended to, encoded carefully, pondered, and related to things we already know. Remembering relies on how *deeply* people process information, not on whether memories are transferred from one *stage* of memory to another.

Think of all the math problems we solved in high school. Each problem is an application of a procedure and, perhaps, of certain formulas. By repeatedly applying the procedures and formulas in slightly different contexts, we rehearse them elaboratively. As a result, we are more likely to remember them.

Truth

It is true that it may be easier for you to recall the name of your first-grade teacher than the name of someone you just met at a party.

Biologically oriented research connects deep processing with activity in certain parts of the brain, notably the prefrontal area of the cerebral cortex (Constantinidis et al., 2001). One reason that older adults show memory loss is that they tend not to process information quite as deeply as younger people do (Grady et al., 1999). Deep processing requires sustained attention, and older adults, along with people who have suffered brain injuries and strokes, apparently cannot focus as well as they once did (Winocur et al., 2000).

Flashbulb Memories

Why is it that some events, like the attack of September 11, 2001, can be etched in memory for a lifetime? It appears that we tend to remember events that are surprising,

AP PHOTO/CARMEN TAYLOR

important, and emotionally stirring more clearly. Such events can create "flashbulb memories," which preserve experiences in detail (Finkenauer et al., 1998; Otani et al., 2005). Why is the memory etched when the "flashbulb" goes off? One factor is the distinctness of the memory. It is easier to discriminate stimuli that stand out. Such events are striking in themselves. The feelings caused by them are also special. It is thus relatively easy to pick them out from the storehouse of memories. Major events such as the assassination of a president or the loss of a close relative also tend to have important effects on our lives. We are likely to dwell on them and form networks of associations. That is, we are likely to rehearse them elaboratively. Our rehearsal may include great expectations, or deep fears, for the future.

Stress hormones help carve events into memory—"as almost to leave a scar upon the cerebral tissues."

Biology is intimately connected with psychology. Strong feelings are connected with the secretion of stress hormones, and stress hormones help carve events into memory—"as almost to leave a scar upon the cerebral tissues," as noted by William James.

Organization in Long-Term Memory

The storehouse of long-term memory is usually well organized. Items are not just piled on the floor or

thrown into closets. *How is knowledge organized in long-term memory?* We tend to gather information about rats and cats into a certain section of the storehouse, perhaps the animal or mammal section. We put information about oaks, maples, and eucalyptus into the tree section. Such categorization of stimuli is a basic cognitive function. It allows us to make predictions about specific instances and to store information efficiently.

We tend to organize information according to a *hierarchical structure*, as shown in Figure 7.5. A *hierarchy* is an arrangement of items (or chunks of information) into groups or classes according to common or distinct features. As we work our way up the hierarchy shown in the figure, we find more encompassing, or *superordinate*, classes to which the items below them belong. For example, all mammals are animals, but there are many types of animals other than mammals.

Figure 7.5

The Hierarchical Structure of Long-Term Memory

Where are whales filed in the hierarchical cabinets of your memory? Your classification of whales may influence your answers to these questions: Do whales breathe underwater? Are they warm-blooded? Do they nurse their young? A note to biological purists: This figure is not intended to represent phyla, classes, orders, and so on accurately. Rather, it shows how an individual's classification scheme might be organized.

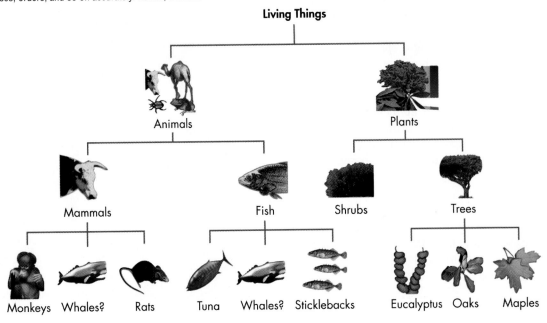

When items are correctly organized in long-term memory, you are more likely to recall—or know—accurate information about them. For example, do you "remember" whether whales breathe underwater? If you did not know that whales are mammals (or in Figure 7.5, *subordinate* to mammals), or if you knew nothing about mammals, a correct answer might depend on some remote instance of rote learning. That is, you might be depending on chancy episodic memory rather than on reliable semantic memory. For example, you might recall some details from a TV documentary on whales. If you *did* know that whales are mammals, however, you would also know—or remember—that whales do not breathe underwater. How? You would reconstruct information about whales from knowledge about mammals, the group to which whales are subordinate. Similarly, you would know, or remember, that because they are mammals, whales are warm-blooded, nurse their young, and are a good deal more intelligent than, say, tunas and sharks, which are fish. Had you incorrectly classified whales as fish, you might have searched your memory and constructed the incorrect answer that they do breathe underwater.

The Tip-of-the-Tongue Phenomenon

Having something on the tip of your tongue can be a frustrating experience. Psychologists term this experience the **tip-of-the-tongue (TOT) phenomenon**, or the *feeling-of-knowing experience*. *Why do we sometimes feel that the answer to a question is on the tip of our tongue?*

Research provides insight into the TOT phenomenon (Brown & McNeill, 1966; James & Burke, 2000). In classic research, Brown and McNeill (1966) defined some rather unusual words for students, such as *sampan*, a small riverboat used in China and Japan. The students were then asked to recall the words they had learned. Some of the students often had the right word "on the tip of their tongue" but reported words with similar meanings such as *junk, barge,* or *houseboat*. Still other students reported words that sounded similar, such as *Saipan, Siam, sarong,* and *sanching*. Why?

To begin with, the words were unfamiliar, so elaborative rehearsal did not take place. The students did not have an opportunity to relate the words to other things they knew. Brown and McNeill also suggested that our storage systems are indexed according to cues that include both the sounds and the meanings of words—that is, according to both acoustic and semantic codes. By scanning words similar in sound and meaning to the word on the tip of the tongue, we sometimes find a useful cue and

retrieve the word for which we are searching.

Sometimes an answer seems to be on the tip of our tongue because our learning of the topic is incomplete. We may not know the exact answer, but we know something. (As a matter of fact, if we have good writing skills, we may present our incomplete knowledge so forcefully that we earn a good grade on an essay question on the topic!) At such times, the problem lies not in retrieval but in the original processes of learning and memory—that is, encoding and storage.

Context-Dependent Memory

The context in which we acquire information can also play a role in retrieval. I remember walking down the halls of the apartment building where I had lived as a child. Cooking odors triggered a sudden assault of images of playing under the staircase, of falling against a radiator, of the shrill voice of a former neighbor calling for her child at dinnertime. Odors, it turns out, are particularly likely to trigger related memories (Pointer & Bond, 1998).

My experience was an example of a **context-dependent memory**. My memories were particularly clear in the context in which they were formed. *Why might it be useful to study in the same room in which we will be tested?* One answer is that being in the proper context—for example, studying in the exam room or under the same conditions—can dramatically enhance recall (Isarida & Isarida, 1999).

According to a study with twenty bilingual Cornell students, the "context" for memory extends to language (Marian & Neisser, 2000). The students were in

tip-of-the-tongue (TOT) phenomenon the feeling that information is stored in memory although it cannot be readily retrieved

context-dependent memory information that is better retrieved in the context in which it was encoded and stored, or learned

PHOTODISC/GETTY IMAGES

state-dependent memory information that is better retrieved in the physiological or emotional state in which it was encoded and stored, or learned

nonsense syllables meaningless sets of two consonants, with a vowel sandwiched in between, that are used to study memory

their early twenties and had emigrated from Russia an average of eight years earlier. They were asked to recall the details of experiences in Russia and the United States. When they were interviewed in Russian, they were better able to retrieve experiences from their lives in Russia. Similarly, when they were interviewed in English, they were better able to recall events that happened in the United States.

State-Dependent Memory

State-dependent memory is an extension of context-dependent memory. We sometimes retrieve information better when we are in a biological or emotional state similar to the one in which we encoded and stored the information. Feeling the rush of love may trigger other images of falling in love. The grip of anger may prompt memories of incidents of frustration. The research in this area extends to states in which we are sober or inebriated.

LO⁴ Forgetting

What do DAL, RIK, BOF, and ZEX have in common? They are all nonsense syllables. Nonsense syllables are meaningless sets of two consonants with a vowel sandwiched in between. They were first used by Hermann Ebbinghaus (1885/1913) to study memory and forgetting. Because nonsense syllables

are intended to be meaningless, remembering them should depend on simple acoustic coding and maintenance rehearsal rather than on elaborative rehearsal, semantic coding, or other ways of making learning meaningful. They are thus well suited for use in the measurement of forgetting. *What types of memory tasks are used in measuring forgetting?*

Memory Tasks Used in Measuring Forgetting

Three basic memory tasks have been used by psychologists to measure forgetting: recognition, recall, and relearning. Nonsense syllables have been used in studying each of them. The study of these memory tasks has led to several conclusions about the nature of forgetting.

Recognition

One aspect of forgetting is failure to recognize something we have experienced. There are many ways of measuring *recognition*. In many studies, psychologists ask subjects to read a list of nonsense syllables. The subjects then read a second list of nonsense syllables and indicate whether they recognize any of the syllables as having appeared on the first list. Forgetting is defined as failure to recognize a syllable that has been read before.

In another kind of recognition study, Harry Bahrick and his colleagues (1975) studied high-school graduates who had been out of school for various lengths of time. They interspersed photos of the graduates' classmates with four times as many photos of strangers. Recent graduates correctly recognized former classmates 90% of the time. Those who had been out of school for forty years recognized former classmates 75% of the time. A chance level of recognition would have been only 20% (one photo in five was of an actual classmate). Thus, even older people showed rather solid long-term recognition ability.

Recognition is the easiest type of memory task. This is why multiple-choice tests are easier than fill-in-the-blank or essay tests.

> **Truth**
>
> If you study with the stereo on, you would probably do better to take the test with the stereo on.

Recall

In his own studies of *recall*, another memory task, Ebbinghaus (1885/1913) would read lists of nonsense syllables aloud to the beat of a metronome and then see how many he could produce from memory. After reading through a list once, he usually would be able to recall seven syllables—the typical limit for short-term memory.

Psychologists also often use lists of pairs of nonsense syllables, called **paired associates**, to measure recall. A list of paired associates is shown in Figure 7.6. Subjects read through the lists pair by pair. Later they are shown the first member of each pair and are asked to recall the second. Recall is more difficult than recognition. In a recognition task, one simply indicates whether an item has been seen before or which of a number of items is paired with a stimulus (as in a multiple-choice test). In a recall task, the person must retrieve a syllable, with another syllable serving as a cue.

Retrieval is made easier if the two syllables can be meaningfully linked—that is, encoded semantically—even if the "meaning" is stretched. Consider the first pair of nonsense syllables in Figure 7.6. The image of a WOMan smoking a CEG-arette may make CEG easier to retrieve when the person is presented with the cue WOM.

Relearning

Relearning is a third method of measuring retention. Do you remember having to learn all of the state capitals in grade school? What were the capitals of Wyoming and Delaware? Even when we cannot recall or recognize material that had once been learned, such as Cheyenne for Wyoming and Dover for Delaware, we can relearn it more rapidly the second time.

To study the efficiency of relearning, Ebbinghaus (1885/1913) devised the **method of savings**. First he recorded the number of repetitions required to learn a list of nonsense syllables or words. Then he recorded the number of repetitions required to relearn the list after a certain amount of time had elapsed. Next he computed the difference in the number of repetitions to determine the **savings**. If a list had to be repeated twenty times before it was learned, and twenty times again after a year had passed, there were no savings. Relearning, that is, was as tedious as the initial learning. If the list could be learned with only ten repetitions after a year had elapsed, however, half the number of repetitions required for learning had been saved.

Figure 7.7 on page 156 shows Ebbinghaus's classic curve of forgetting. As you can see, there was no loss of memory as measured by savings immediately after a list had been learned. However, recollection dropped quite a bit, by half, during the first hour after learning a list. Losses of learning then became more gradual. It took a month (thirty-one days) for retention to be cut in half again. Forgetting occurred most rapidly right after material was learned.

paired associates
nonsense syllables presented in pairs in experiments that measure recall

method of savings
a measure of retention in which the difference between the number of repetitions originally required to learn a list and the number of repetitions required to relearn the list after a certain amount of time has elapsed is calculated

savings
the difference between the number of repetitions originally required to learn a list and the number of repetitions required to relearn the list after a certain amount of time has elapsed

interference theory
the view that we may forget stored material because other learning interferes with it

Figure 7.6

Paired Associates

Interference Theory

When we do not attend to, encode, and rehearse sensory input, we may forget it through decay of the trace of the image. Material in short-term memory, like material in sensory memory, can be lost through decay. It can also be lost through displacement, as may happen when we try to remember several new names at a party.

Why can learning Spanish make it harder to remember French? The answer may be found in **interference theory**. According to this view, we also forget material in short-term and long-term memory because newly learned material interferes with it. The two basic types of interference are retroactive interference (also called *retroactive inhibition*) and proactive interference (also called *proactive inhibition*).

retroactive
interference
the interference of new
learning with the abil-
ity to retrieve material
learned previously

proactive
interference
the interference by old
learning with the abil-
ity to retrieve material
learned recently

dissociative
amnesia
amnesia thought to
stem from psychologi-
cal conflict or trauma

Figure 7.7

Ebbinghaus's Classic Curve of Forgetting

Recollection of lists of words drops precipitously during the first hour after learning. Loss of learning then becomes more gradual. Retention drops by half within the first hour. It takes a month (thirty-one days), however, for retention to be cut in half again.

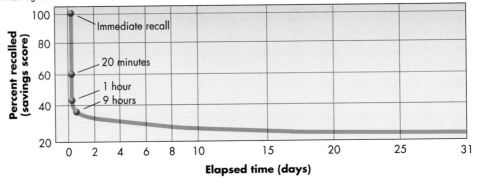

Retroactive Interference

In retroactive interference, new learning interferes with the retrieval of old learning. For example, a medical student may memorize the names of the bones in the leg through rote repetition. Later he or she may find that learning the names of the bones in the arm makes it more difficult to retrieve the names of the leg bones, especially if the names are similar in sound or in relative location on each limb.

Proactive Interference

In proactive interference, older learning interferes with the capacity to retrieve more recently learned material. High-school Spanish may pop in when you are trying to retrieve college French or Italian words. All three are Romance languages, with simi-lar roots and spellings. Previously learned Japanese words probably would not interfere with your ability to retrieve more recently learned French or Italian, because the roots and sounds of Japanese differ considerably from those of the Romance languages.

> **Truth**
>
> It is true that learning Spanish can make it harder to remember French—and vice versa.

Repression

According to Sigmund Freud, we are motivated to forget painful memories and unacceptable ideas because they produce anxiety, guilt, and shame. *What is the Freudian concept of repression?* Repression, according to Freud, is the automatic ejection of painful memories and unacceptable urges from conscious awareness. It is motivated by the desire to avoid facing painful memories and emotions.

Psychoanalysts believe that repression is at the heart of disorders such as dissociative amnesia (see Chapter 12). There is a current controversy in psy-chology about whether repression (motivated forget-ting) exists and, if it does, how it works.

There is much research on repression, often in the form of case studies that are found in psychoanalytic journals (e.g., Eagle, 2000). Much has been made of case studies in which veterans have supposedly for-gotten traumatic battlefield experiences, developed post-traumatic stress disorder (once called "battle-field neurosis"), and then "felt better" once they recalled and discussed the traumatic events (Karon & Widener, 1998). Critics argue that the evidence for such repression and recovery of memories is weak and that this kind of "memory" can be implanted by the suggestions of interviewers (Loftus, 2001). The issue remains controversial, as we see next.

Do People Really Recover Repressed Memories of Childhood?

Despite shaky scientific support, there are cases of so-called recovered memories, especially memories of childhood sexual abuse by a relative, teacher, or friend. The question is whether these memories are induced by therapists who foster beliefs that become so deeply ingrained they seem like authen-tic memories. "We don't know what percent of these recovered memories are real and what percent are pseudomemories," notes psychiatrist Harold Lief (cited in Brody, 2000), one of the first to challenge such memories.

Psychologist Elizabeth Loftus has engaged in numerous studies that show how easy it is to implant false memories through leading questions. In one study, researchers were able to readily convince half the subjects that they had been lost in a mall or hos-pitalized with severe pain as children.

Infantile Amnesia

Can children remember events from the first couple of years of life? When he interviewed people about their early experiences, Freud discovered that they could not recall episodes that had happened prior to the age of three or so and that recall was cloudy through the age of five. This phenomenon is referred to as infantile amnesia.

Infantile amnesia has little to do with the fact that the episodes occurred in the distant past. Middle-aged and older people have vivid memories from the ages of six through ten, yet the events happened many decades ago. But eighteen-year-olds show steep declines in memory when they try to recall episodes that occurred earlier than the age of six, even though they happened less than eighteen years earlier (Wetzler & Sweeney, 1986).

Freud believed that young children have aggressive impulses and perverse lusts toward their parents. He attributed infantile amnesia to repression of these impulses. The episodes lost to infantile amnesia, however, are not weighted in the direction of such "primitive" impulses. In fact, infantile amnesia probably reflects the interaction of physiological and cognitive factors. For example, a structure of the limbic system (the hippocampus) that is involved in the storage of memories does not become mature until we are about two years old (Squire, 2004). Also, myelination of brain pathways is incomplete for the first few years, contributing to the inefficiency of information processing and memory formation.

There are also cognitive explanations for infantile amnesia:

- Infants are not particularly interested in remembering the past (Neisser, 1993).

- Infants, in contrast to older children, tend not to weave episodes together into meaningful stories of their own lives. Information about specific episodes thus tends to be lost. Research shows that when parents reminisce about the past with children, the children's memories of being infants are strengthened (Peterson, 2002).

- Infants do not make reliable use of language to symbolize or classify events (Wang, 2003). Their ability to *encode* sensory input—that is, to apply the auditory and semantic codes that facilitate memory formation—is therefore limited. Yet research shows that young infants can recall events throughout the period when infantile amnesia is presumed to occur if they are now and then exposed to objects they played with or photos of events (Rovee-Collier, 1999).

> "We are unlikely to remember episodes from early childhood unless we are reminded of them from time to time."

In any event, we are unlikely to remember episodes from early childhood unless we are reminded of them from time to time as we develop. Many early childhood memories that seem so clear today might be reconstructed and hold many inaccuracies. They might also be memories of events that occurred later than we thought. Yet there is no evidence that such early memories are systematically repressed.

infantile amnesia inability to recall events that occur prior to the age of two or three; also termed *childhood amnesia*

hippocampus a structure in the limbic system that plays an important role in the formation of new memories

anterograde amnesia failure to remember events that occur after physical trauma because of the effects of the trauma

Anterograde and Retrograde Amnesia

Adults also experience amnesia, although usually for biological reasons, as in the cases of anterograde and retrograde amnesia (Kopelman, 2002). *Why do people frequently have trouble recalling being in accidents?* In so-called anterograde amnesia, there are memory lapses for the period following a trauma such as a

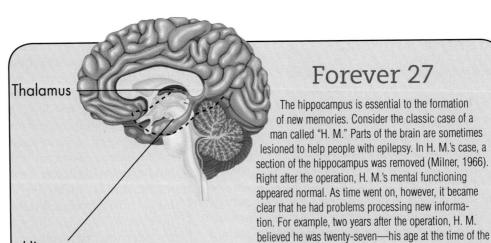

retrograde amnesia
failure to remember events that occur prior to physical trauma because of the effects of the trauma

engram
(1) an assumed electrical circuit in the brain that corresponds to a memory trace (2) an assumed chemical change in the brain that accompanies learning (from the Greek *en-*, meaning "in" and *gramma*, meaning "something that is written or recorded")

Forever 27

The hippocampus is essential to the formation of new memories. Consider the classic case of a man called "H. M." Parts of the brain are sometimes lesioned to help people with epilepsy. In H. M.'s case, a section of the hippocampus was removed (Milner, 1966). Right after the operation, H. M.'s mental functioning appeared normal. As time went on, however, it became clear that he had problems processing new information. For example, two years after the operation, H. M. believed he was twenty-seven—his age at the time of the operation. When his family moved to a new address, H. M. could not find his new home or remember the new address. He responded with appropriate grief to the death of his uncle, yet he then began to ask about his uncle and why he did not visit. Each time he was reminded of his uncle's passing, he grieved as if he were hearing it for the first time. H. M.'s operation apparently prevented him from transferring information from short-term to long-term memory.

Thalamus

Hippocampus

COURTESY OF DANA COPELAND

blow to the head, an electric shock, or an operation. In some cases the trauma seems to interfere with all the processes of memory. The ability to pay attention, the encoding of sensory input, and rehearsal are all impaired. A number of investigators have linked certain kinds of brain damage—such as damage to the hippocampus—to amnesia (Eichenbaum & Fortin, 2003; Spiers et al., 2001).

In **retrograde amnesia**, the source of trauma prevents people from remembering events that took place before the accident (Wheeler & McMillan, 2001). In one well-known case of retrograde amnesia, a man received a head injury in a motorcycle accident (Baddeley, 1982). When he regained consciousness, he had lost memory for all events that had occurred after the age of eleven. In fact, he appeared to believe that he was still eleven years old. During the next few months he gradually recovered more knowledge of his past. He moved toward the present year by year, up until the critical motorcycle ride.

But he never did recover the events just prior to the accident. The accident had apparently prevented the information that was rapidly unfolding before him from being transferred to long-term memory. In terms of stages of memory, it may be that our perceptions and ideas need to consolidate, or rest undisturbed for a while, if they are to be transferred to long-term memory (Nader et al., 2000).

LO⁵ The Biology of Memory

Psychologists assume that mental processes such as the encoding, storage, and retrieval of information—that is, memory—are accompanied by changes in the brain. Early in the 20th century, many psychologists used the concept of the **engram** in their study of memory. Engrams were viewed as electrical circuits in the brain that corresponded to memory traces—neurological processes that paralleled experiences. Yet biological psychologists such as Karl Lashley (1950) spent many fruitless years searching for such circuits or for the structures of the brain in which they might be housed. Much research on the biology of memory focuses today on the roles of stimulants, neurons, neurotransmitters, hormones, and structures in the brain.

Neural Activity and Memory

What neural events are connected with memory? Rats who are reared in stimulating environments provide some answers. The animals develop more dendrites and synapses in the cerebral cortex than rats reared in impoverished environments (Neisser, 1997a). Moreover, visually stimulating rats increases the number of synapses in their visual cortex (Battaglia et al., 2004; Bilkey, 2004). Therefore, the storage of experience does involve avenues of communication among brain cells.

Information received through other senses is just as likely to lead to corresponding changes in the cortical regions that represent them. For example, sounds may similarly cause changes in the auditory cortex. Experiences perceived by several senses are apparently stored in numerous parts of the cortex. The recall of sensory experiences apparently involves neural activity in related regions of the brain.

Research with sea snails such as *Aplysia* and *Hermissenda* offers more insight into the biology of memory. *Aplysia* has only some 20,000 neurons compared with humans' billions. As a result, researchers have been able to study how experience is reflected at the synapses of specific neurons. The sea snail will reflexively withdraw its gills when it receives electric shock, in the way a person will reflexively withdraw a hand from a hot stove or a thorn. In one kind of experiment, researchers precede the shock with a squirt of water. After a few repetitions, the sea snail becomes conditioned to withdraw its gills when squirted with the water. When sea snails are conditioned, they release more serotonin at certain synapses. As a consequence, transmission at these synapses becomes more efficient as trials (learning) progress (Kandel, 2001). This greater efficiency is termed long-term potentiation (LTP). As shown in Figure 7.8, dendrites can also participate in LTP by sprouting new branches that attach to the transmitting axon. Rats who are given substances that enhance LTP learn mazes with fewer errors; that is, they are less likely to turn down the wrong alley (Uzakov et al., 2005).

Serotonin and many other naturally occurring chemical substances, including adrenaline, noradrenaline, acetylcholine, glutamate, antidiuretic hormone, even the sex hormones estrogen and testosterone have been shown to play roles in memory.

The hippocampus is not a storage bin. It is involved in relaying sensory information to parts of the cortex.

Brain Structures and Memory

What structures in the brain are connected with memory? Memory does not reside in a single structure of the brain; it relies on complex neural networks that draw on various parts of the brain (Nyberg et al., 2000). However, some parts of the brain play more specific roles in memory. The hippocampus is vital in storing new information even if we can retrieve old information without it (Fields, 2005). But the hippocampus is not a storage bin. Rather, it is involved in relaying sensory information to parts of the cortex.

Where are the storage bins? The brain stores parts of memories in the appropriate areas of the sensory cortex. Sights are stored in the visual cortex, sounds in the auditory cortex, and so on. The limbic system is largely responsible for integrating these pieces of information when we recall an event. The frontal lobes apparently store information about where and when events occur (Goldman-Rakic et al., 2000a).

But what of the decision to try to recall something? What of the spark of consciousness that drives us to move

long-term potentiation (LTP) enhanced efficiency in synaptic transmission that follows brief, rapid stimulation

Figure 7.8

One Avenue to Long-Term Potentiation (LTP)

LTP can occur via the action of neurotransmitters such as serotonin and glutamate at synapses. Structurally, LTP can also occur as shown in Parts A and B, when dendrites sprout new branches that connect with transmitting axons, increasing the amount of stimulation they receive.

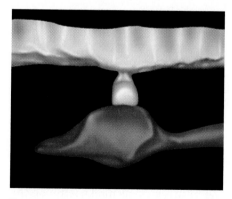

Part A.

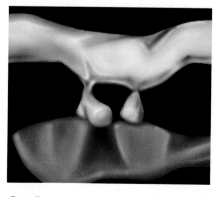

Part B.

Jean Piaget, the investigator of children's cognitive development, distinctly remembered an attempt to kidnap him from his baby carriage as he was being wheeled along the Champs Élysées. He recalled the excited throng, the abrasions on the face of the nurse who rescued him, the police officer's white baton, and the flight of the assailant. Although they were graphic, Piaget's memories were false. Years later, the nurse admitted that she had made up the tale.

Can eyewitness testimony be trusted? Is there reason to believe that the statements of eyewitnesses are any more factual than Piaget's? Legal professionals and psychologists are concerned about the accuracy of our long-term memories as reflected in eyewitness testimony (Cutler, 2009; Cutler & Kovera, 2010; Wright & Loftus, 2008). Let us consider what can go wrong—and what can go right—with eyewitness testimony.

One problem with eyewitness testimony is that the words chosen by an experimenter—and those chosen by a lawyer interrogating a witness—have been shown to influence the reconstruction of memories (Cutler & Kovera, 2010). For example, an attorney for the plaintiff might ask the witness, "How fast was the defendant's car going when it *smashed into* the plaintiff's car?" In such a case, the car might be reported as going faster than if the question had been: "How fast was the defendant's car going when the accident occurred?" Could the attorney for the defendant claim that use of the word *smashed* biased the witness? What about jurors who heard the word *smashed*? Would they be biased toward assuming that the driver had been reckless?

Children tend to be more suggestible witnesses than adults, and preschoolers are more suggestible than older children. But when questioned properly, even young children may be able to provide accurate and useful testimony (Ceci et al., 2007; Krähenbühl et al., 2009).

There are also problems in the identification of criminals by eyewitnesses. For one thing, witnesses may pay more attention to the suspect's clothing than to more meaningful characteristics such as facial features, height, and weight.

Other problems with eyewitness testimony include the following (Cutler & Kovera, 2010):

Identification is less accurate when suspects belong to ethnic or racial groups that differ from that of the witness.

Identification of suspects is compromised when interrogators make misleading suggestions.

TOM MERTON / OJO IMAGES / JUPITER IMAGES

"Psychologist Eilzabeth Loftus showed that our testimony can be affected by the concepts that attorneys use when they ask questions. For example, eyewitnesses assumed that cars were going faster if the attorney asked, "How fast were the cars going when they *smashed* into each other?" as opposed to "How fast were they going when they *hit* one another?"

Witnesses are seen as more credible when they claim to be certain in their testimony, but there is little evidence that claims of certainty are accurate.

There are thus many problems with eyewitness testimony. Yet even Elizabeth Loftus (e.g., Wright & Loftus, 2008), who has extensively studied the accuracy of eyewitness testimony, agrees that it is a valuable tool in the courtroom. After all, identifications made by eyewitnesses are frequently correct, and what, Loftus asks, would be the alternative to the use of eyewitnesses? If we were to prevent eyewitnesses from testifying, how many criminals would go free?

Sources: Ceci, S. J., Kulkofsky, S., Klemfuss, J. Z., Sweeney, C. D., & Bruck, M. (2007). Unwarranted assumptions about children's testimonial accuracy. *Annual Review of Clinical Psychology, 3,* 311–328.

Cutler, B. L. (2009). *Expert testimony on the psychology of eyewitness identification.* New York: Oxford University Press.

Cutler, B. L. & Kovera, M. B. (2010). *Evaluating eyewitness identification.* New York: Oxford University Press.

Krähenbühl, S., Blades, M., & Eiser, C. (2009). The effect of repeated questioning on children's accuracy and consistency in eyewitness testimony. *Legal and Criminological Psychology, 14*(2), 263–278.

Wright, D. B., & Loftus, E. F. (2008). In G. Cohen & M. A. Conway. (Eds.). *Memory in the real world, 3rd edition.* New York: Psychology Press.

backward in time or to strive to remember to do something in the future? The prefrontal cortex (see Figure 7.9 on page 161) is the executive center in memory (Buckner et al., 2001; Wheeler & Treisman, 2002). It appears to empower people with consciousness—the ability to mentally represent and become aware of experiences that occur in the past, present, and future. It enables people to mentally travel back in time to reexperience the personal, autobiographical past. It enables people to focus on the things they intend to do in the future, such as mail a letter on the way to class or brush their teeth before going to bed.

The hippocampus is also involved in the where and when of things (Eichenbaum & Fortin, 2003). The hippocampus does not become mature until we are about two years old. Immaturity may be connected

Figure 7.9

The Prefrontal Cortex of the Brain

The prefrontal cortex comes in pairs. One is found in each hemisphere, a bit above the outer edge of the eyebrow. The prefrontal cortex is highly active during visual and spatial problem-solving. Your sense of self—your continuous sense of being in and operating on the world—may also reside largely in the prefrontal cortex.

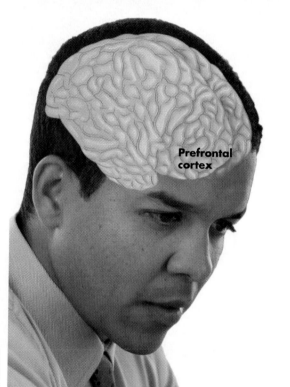

Prefrontal cortex

© CORBIS

with infantile amnesia. Adults with hippocampal damage may be able to form new procedural memories, even though they cannot form new episodic ("where and when") memories (Fields, 2005). They can develop new skills even though they cannot recall the practice sessions (Reed & Squire, 1997).

The thalamus is involved in the formation of verbal memories. Part of the thalamus of an Air Force cadet known as N. A. was damaged in a fencing accident. Afterward, N. A. could no longer form verbal memories, but he could form visual memories (Squire, 2004). (One might measure visual memory by showing people pictures, allowing time to pass, and then asking them to point out those they have been shown.)

The encoding, storage, and retrieval of information thus involve biological activity. As we learn, new synapses are developed, and changes occur at existing synapses. Parts of the brain are also involved in the formation of memories. In the next chapter, we see how people manipulate information they have stored to adapt to the environment or create new environments.

Thinking, Language, *and* Intelligence

Learning Outcomes

LO [1] Define thinking and the various concepts involved in thinking

LO [2] Describe how language develops

LO [3] Identify the concept of intelligence and the techniques used to measure intelligence

LO [4] Describe the controversy surrounding intelligence testing

> # ❝ *Intelligence may be the most controversial topic in psychology.* ❞

What form of life is so adaptive that it can survive in desert temperatures of 120°F or Arctic climes of –40°F? What form of life can run, walk, climb, swim, live underwater for months on end, and fly to the moon and back? I won't keep you in suspense any longer. We are that form of life. Yet our unclad bodies do not allow us to adapt to these extremes of temperature. Brute strength does not allow us to live underwater or travel to the Moon. Rather, it is our cognitive processes that allow us to adapt to these conditions and surpass our physical limitations.

In this chapter we explore thinking, language, and intelligence. Thinking enables us to pose problems and solve them, and to make judgments and decisions. Humans use language not only in communicating, but also in thinking. Humans attach words and sentences to the objects and concepts they think about, taking them into abstract realms. Intelligence may be the most controversial topic in psychology. Psychologists do not agree on exactly what intelligence is or exactly how people develop intelligence. By and large, however, psychologists view intelligence as the underlying ability to understand the world and cope with its challenges.

Truth or Fiction?

What do you think?

Folklore, common sense, or nonsense? Place a T for "True" or F for "False" on the lines provided (you'll learn the answers as you read through the text).

— Only humans can use insight to solve problems.

— Crying is an early form of language.

— Young children say things like "Daddy goed away" and "Mommy sitted down" because they *do* understand rules of grammar.

— "Street smarts" are a sign of intelligence.

— Creative people are highly intelligent.

— Highly intelligent people are creative.

— Two children can answer exactly the same items on an intelligence test correctly, yet one child can be above average in IQ, and the other can be below average.

— Intelligence tests measure many things other than intelligence.

LO¹ Thinking

The Greek philosopher Aristotle pointed out that people differ from lower organisms in their capacity for rational thinking. *What is thinking?* Thinking means paying attention to information, representing it mentally, reasoning about it, and making judgments and decisions about it. Thinking refers to conscious, planned attempts to make sense of and change the world. By contrast, mental processes such as dreaming and daydreaming do not represent thinking; they may be unplanned and proceed more or less on their own.

We begin with concepts, which provide many of the building blocks for thinking.

thinking
paying attention to information, mentally representing it, reasoning about it, and making decisions about it

concept
a mental category
that is used to class
together objects, rela-
tions, events, abstrac-
tions, or qualities that
have common proper-
ties

prototype
a concept of a category
of objects or events
that serves as a good
example of the category

exemplar
a specific example

Concepts

Concepts are mental categories used to group together
objects, relations, events,
abstractions, or qualities that
have common properties.
Concepts are crucial to cognition. Concepts can represent
objects, events, and activities—and visions of things
that never were or cannot
be measured, such as Middle
Earth in *The Lord of the Rings* or
the Land of Oz in *The Wizard of Oz*.

Labels for objects depend on experience with
them and on one's cultural setting (Sloman et al.,
2002). Squares, circles, and triangles are not all that
common in nature, and some peoples, such as the
Himba of northern Namibia, have no concepts of
them (Roberson et al., 2002). But these shapes are
concepts that are basic to geometry. Much thinking has to do with categorizing new concepts and
manipulating relationships among concepts, as in
problems in geometry.

We tend to organize concepts in *hierarchies*. For
example, the newspaper category includes objects
such as your school paper and the *Los
Angeles Times*. Newspapers, college textbooks, and catalogs
can be combined into
higher-order cat-
egories such as
printed matter or
printed devices

that store information. If you add hard drives and
DVDs, you can create a still higher category—*objects
that store information.* Now consider a question that
requires categorical thinking: How are a newspaper
and a DVD alike? Answers to such questions entail
supplying the category that includes both objects.
In this case, we can say that both objects store
information. Their functions are alike, even if their
technology differs.

Prototypes are good examples. They best match
the key features of categories. Which animal seems
more birdlike to you: a robin or an ostrich? Why?
Which better fits the prototype of a fish: a sea horse
or a tuna? Why?

Many simple prototypes, such as *dog* and *red*,
are taught by means of examples, or exemplars.
Research suggests that it is more efficient for most
of us to learn what *fruits* and *vegetables* are from
experience with exemplars of each, rather than by
working from definitions of them (Smits et al., 2002).
We point to a dog and tell a child "dog" or "This is a
dog." Dogs are *positive instances* of the dog concept.
Negative instances—things that are *not* dogs—are
then shown to the child while we say, "This is *not* a
dog." Negative instances of one concept may be positive instances of another. So, in teaching a child, we
may be more likely to say, "This is not a dog—it's a
cat" than simply, "This is not a dog."

Children may at first include horses and
other four-legged animals within the dog
concept until the differ-
ences between dogs
and horses are

© ARIADNE VAN ZANDBERGEN / GETTY IMAGES

Circles, squares, and triangles are found only
rarely in nature and not among the Himba of
northern Namibia. It is not surprising, then,
that they have no words for these concepts.

pointed out. In language development, such overinclusion of instances in a category (reference to horses as dogs) is labeled *overextension*.

Children's prototypes become refined after children are shown positive and negative instances and given explanations. Abstract concepts such as *bachelor* or *square root* tend to be formed through explanations that involve more basic concepts.

Problem-Solving

Problem-solving is an important aspect of thinking. Here's a problem for you to solve. What are the next two letters in this series?

> OTTFFSSE__?

How did you try to find the answer? Did you search your personal memory banks and ask yourself what O can stand for, then T, and so on? Did you try to think of some phrase the letters might represent? Perhaps the first letters of the stars in a constellation? [If you don't resort to a search engine answer and do not arrive at the answer on your own, I'll be discussing it within a few pages.]

Understanding the Problem

Successful understanding of a problem generally requires three features:

- *The parts or elements of our mental representation of the problem relate to one another in a meaningful way.* If we are trying to solve a problem in geometry, our mental triangles, like actual triangles, should have angles that total 180 degrees.

- *The elements of our mental representation of the problem correspond to the elements of the problem in the outer world.* If we are assessing a patient in the emergency room of a hospital, we want to arrive at a diagnosis of what might be wrong before we make a treatment plan. To do so, we take the patient's "vital signs," including heart rate, temperature, and blood pressure, so that our mental picture of the patient conforms to what is going on in his or her body.

- *We have a storehouse of background knowledge that we can apply to the problem.* We have the necessary experience or course work to solve the problem.

The Use of Algorithms

An algorithm is a specific procedure for solving a type of problem. An algorithm invariably leads to the solution—if it is used properly, that is. Mathematical formulas like the Pythagorean theorem are examples of algorithms. They yield correct answers to problems *as long as the right formula is used.* Finding the right formula to solve a problem may require scanning one's memory for all formulas that contain variables that represent one or more of the elements in the problem. The Pythagorean theorem concerns right triangles. Therefore, it is appropriate to consider using this formula for problems concerning right triangles, but not others.

If you are going to be meeting someone for the first time and want to make a good impression, you consider the nature of the encounter (for example, a job interview or a "blind date") and then consider how to dress and behave for the encounter. If it's a job interview, the algorithm may be to dress neatly, be well-groomed, and not to wear too much cologne or perfume. If it's a date, you may ditch the suit but hike up the cologne or perfume a notch. In either case, smile and make eye contact—it's all part of the formula.

Anagrams are scrambled words. *Korc* is an anagram for *rock* or *cork*. The task in anagram problems is to try to reorganize jumbles or groups of letters into words. Some anagram problems require us to use every letter from the pool of letters; others allow us to use only some of the letters. How many words can you make from the pool of letters *DWARG?* If you were to use the systematic random search algorithm, you would list every possible letter combination, using from one to all five letters. You could use a dictionary or a spell-checking program to see whether each result is, in fact, a word. The method might take awhile, but it would work.

The Use of Heuristic Devices

Is it best to use a tried-and-true formula to solve a problem? Sometimes people use shortcuts to "jump to conclusions"—and these are often correct conclusions. The shortcuts are called heuristics, or heuristic devices—rules of thumb that help us simplify and solve problems. Heuristics are often based on strategies that worked in the past (Klaczynski, 2001).

In contrast to algorithms, heuristics do not guarantee a correct solution. But when they work, they permit more rapid solutions. A heuristic device for solving the anagram problem would be to look for familiar letter combinations and then check the remaining letters for words that include these combinations. In *DWARG,* for example, we find some familiar combinations: *dr* and *gr.* We may then quickly find *draw, drag,* and *grad.* The drawback to this method is that we might miss some words.

One type of heuristic device is the means–end analysis. In using this heuristic device, we assess the difference between our current situation and our goals

algorithm
a systematic procedure for solving a problem that works invariably when it is correctly applied

systematic random search
an algorithm for solving problems in which each possible solution is tested according to a particular set of rules

heuristics
rules of thumb that help us simplify and solve problems

means–end analysis
a heuristic device in which we try to solve a problem by evaluating the difference between the current situation and the goal

and do what we can to reduce this difference. Let's say that you are out in your car and have gotten lost. One heuristic device based on analysis of what you need to do to get to where you want to go might be to ask for directions. This approach requires no "sense of direction." An algorithm might be more complicated and require some scientific knowledge. For example, if you know your destination is west of your current location you might try driving toward the setting sun.

The Use of Analogies

An *analogy* is a partial similarity among things that are different in other ways. The analogy heuristic applies the solution of an earlier problem to the solution of a new one. We use the analogy heuristic whenever we try to solve a new problem by referring to a previous problem (Halpern et al., 1990).

Let us see whether you can use the analogy heuristic to your advantage in the following number-series problem. Look at the following series of numbers and find the rule that governs their order:

8, 5, 4, 9, 1, 7, 6, 3, 2, 0

This is rather abstract and mathematical. Actually, you use the analogy heuristic regularly. For example, when you begin a new term with a new instructor, you probably consider who the instructor reminds you of. Then, perhaps, you recall the things that helped you get along with the analogous instructor and try them on the new one. We tend to look for things that helped us in the past in similar situations. When we considered OTTFFSSENT, we used the first letters of the numbers one through ten. When we consider the first ten digits in the following order—8, 5, 4, 9, 1, 7, 6, 3, 2, and 0—we can again think of their first letters when they are spelled out. It happens that they are in alphabetical order (*e*ight, *f*ive, *f*our, and so on).

Factors That Affect Problem-Solving

The way you approach a problem is central to how effective you are at solving it. Other factors also influence your effectiveness. *What factors make it easier or harder to solve problems?* Three such factors reside within you: your level of expertise, whether you fall prey to a mental set, and whether you develop insight into the problem.

Expertise To appreciate the role of expertise in problem-solving, unscramble the following anagrams, taken from Novick and Coté (1992). In each case use all of the letters to form an actual English word:

DNSUO
RCWDO
IASYD

How long did it take you to unscramble each anagram ("sound," "crowd," and "daisy")? Would a person whose native language is English—that is, an "expert"—unscramble each anagram more efficiently than a bilingual person who spoke another language in the home? Why or why not?

Experts solve problems more efficiently and rapidly than novices do. Generally speaking, people who are experts at solving a certain kind of problem share the following characteristics (Szala, 2002; Gorodetsky & Klavir, 2003):

- They know the particular area well.
- They have a good memory for the elements in the problems.
- They form mental images or representations that facilitate problem-solving.
- They relate the problem to similar problems.
- They are more goal-directed and have efficient methods for problem-solving.

These factors are interrelated. Art historians, for example, acquire a database that permits them to understand the intricacies of paintings. As a result, their memory for details of paintings mushrooms.

Novick and Coté (1992) found that the solutions to the anagram problems seemed to "pop out" in under two seconds among experts. The experts apparently used more efficient methods than the novices. Experts seemed to use *parallel processing*. That is, they dealt simultaneously with two or more elements of the problems. In the case of DNSUO, for example, they may have played with the order of the vowels (*UO* or *OU*) at the same time that they tested which consonant (D, N, or S) was likely to precede them, arriving quickly at *sou* and *sound*. Novices were more likely to engage in *serial processing*—that is, to handle one element of the problem at a time.

Mental Sets The tendency to respond to a new problem with the same approach that helped solve similar problems is termed a **mental set**. Mental sets usually make our work easier, but they can mislead us when the similarity between problems is illusory.

Insight To gain insight into the role of **insight** in problem-solving, consider the following problem, posed by Metcalfe (1986):

A stranger approached a museum curator and offered him an ancient bronze coin. The coin had an authentic appearance and was marked with the date 544 BCE. The curator had happily made acquisitions from suspicious sources before, but this time he promptly called the police and had the stranger arrested. Why?

I'm not going to give you the answer to this problem. But I'll make a guarantee. When you arrive at the solution, it will hit you all at once. You'll think "Of course!" It will seem as though the pieces of information in the problem have suddenly been reorganized so that the solution leaps out—in a flash.

Bismarck, one of psychologist N. R. F. Maier's rats, appeared to suddenly reorganize the pieces of information in a problem with which he was presented, showing evidence of insight in his species. (Maier & Schneirla, 1935). Bismarck had been trained to climb a ladder to a tabletop where food was placed. On one occasion, Maier used a mesh barrier to prevent the rat from reaching his goal. But, as shown in Figure 8.1, a second ladder was provided and was visible to the animal. At first Bismarck sniffed and scratched and tried to find a path through the mesh. Then he spent some time washing his face, an activity that may signal frustration in rats. Suddenly he jumped into the air, turned, ran down the familiar ladder and around to the new ladder, ran up the new ladder, and claimed his just desserts. Did Bismarck suddenly perceive the relationships between the elements of the problem so that the solution occurred by insight? He seems to have had what Gestalt psychologists have termed an "Aha! experience."

Incubation An incubator warms chicken eggs so that they will hatch. Incubation in problem-solving refers to standing back from the problem for a while as some process within may continue to work on it. Later, the answer may come to us in a flash of insight. Standing back from the problem may help by distancing us from unprofitable but persistent mental sets (Both et al., 2004; Segal, 2004).

incubation
in problem-solving, a hypothetical process that sometimes occurs when we stand back from a frustrating problem for a while and the solution "suddenly" appears

functional fixedness
tendency to view an object in terms of its name or familiar usage

Functional Fixedness Functional fixedness may hinder problem-solving. For example, first ask yourself what a pair of pliers is. Is it a tool for grasping, a paperweight, or a weapon?

A pair of pliers could function as any of these, but your tendency to think of it as a grasping tool is fostered by your experience with it. You have probably used pliers only for grasping things. Functional fixedness is the tendency to think of an object in terms of its name or its familiar function. It can be similar to a mental set in that it makes it difficult to use familiar objects to solve problems in novel ways.

Judgment and Decision-Making

How do people make judgments and decisions? You might like to think that people are so rational that they carefully weigh the pros and cons when they make judgments or decisions. Or you might think that they insist on finding and examining all the relevant information. Actually, people make most of their decisions on the basis of limited information. They take shortcuts. They use heuristic devices—rules of thumb—in judgments and decision-making just as they do in problem-solving (Gilovich et al., 2002). For example, they may let a financial advisor select stocks for them rather than research the companies themselves. Or they may see a doctor recommended by a friend rather than look at the doctor's credentials. In this section we consider various factors in judgment and decision-making.

> **Fiction**
> It appears that humans are not the only species who use insight to solve problems.

Figure 8.1

Bismarck Uses a Cognitive Map to Claim His Just Desserts

Bismarck has learned to reach dinner by climbing ladder *A*. But now the food goal (*F*) is blocked by a wire-mesh barrier *B*. Bismarck washes his face for a while, but then, in an apparent flash of insight, he runs back down ladder *A* and up new ladder *N* to reach the goal.

Heuristics in Decision-Making

Let us begin by asking you to imagine that you flip a coin six times. In the following three possible outcomes, H stands for heads and T for tails. Circle the most likely sequence:

H	H	H	H	H	H
H	H	H	T	T	T
T	H	H	T	H	T

Did you select T H H T H T as the most likely sequence of events? Most people do. Why? There are two reasons. First, people recognize that the sequence of six heads in a row is unlikely. (The probability of achieving it is $1/2 \times 1/2 \times 1/2 \times 1/2 \times 1/2 \times 1/2$, or 1/64th.) Three heads and three tails are more likely than six heads (or six tails). Second, people recognize that the sequence of heads and tails ought to appear random. T H H T H T has a random look to it, whereas H H H T T T does not.

People tend to select T H H T H T because of the **representativeness heuristic**. According to this decision-making heuristic, people make judgments about events (samples) according to the populations of events that they appear to represent (Kahneman & Frederick, 2002; Shepperd & Koch, 2005). In this case, the sample of events is six coin tosses. The "population" is an infinite number of random coin tosses. But guess what? *Each* sequence is equally likely (or unlikely). If the question had been whether six heads or three heads and three tails had been more likely, the correct answer would have been three and three.

If the question had been whether heads and tails would be more likely to be consecutive or in random order, the correct answer would have been random order. But each of the three sequences is a *specific* sequence. What is the probability of attaining the *specific* sequence T H H T H T? The probability that the first coin toss will result in a tail is 1/2. The probability that the second will result in a head is 1/2, and so on. Thus, the probability of attaining the exact sequence T H H T H T is identical to that of achieving any other specific sequence: $1/2 \times 1/2 \times 1/2 \times 1/2 \times 1/2 \times 1/2 = 1/64$th. (Try this out on a friend.)

Another heuristic device used in decision-making is the **availability heuristic**. According to this heuristic, our estimates of frequency or probability are based on how easy it is to find examples of relevant events. Let me ask you whether there are more art majors or sociology majors at your college. Unless you are familiar with the enrollment statistics, you will probably answer on the basis of the numbers of art majors and sociology majors that you know.

The **anchoring and adjustment heuristic** suggests that there can be a good deal of inertia in our judgments. In forming opinions or making estimates, we have an initial view, or presumption. This is the anchor. As we receive additional information, we make adjustments, sometimes grudgingly. That is, if you grow up believing that one religion or one political party is the "right" one, that belief serves as a cognitive anchor. When inconsistencies show up in your religion or political party, you may adjust your views of them, but perhaps not very willingly.

Let us illustrate further with a math problem. Write each of the following multiplication problems on a separate piece of paper:

A. 8 x 7 x 6 x 5 x 4 x 3 x 2 x 1
B. 1 x 2 x 3 x 4 x 5 x 6 x 7 x 8

Show problem A to a few friends. Give them each five seconds to estimate the answer. Show problem B to some other friends and give them five seconds to estimate the answer.

The answers to the multiplication problems are the same because the order of quantities being multiplied does not change the outcome. When Tversky and Kahneman (1982) showed these problems to high-school students, the average estimate given by students who were shown version A was significantly higher than that given by students who were shown version B. Students who saw 8 in the first position offered an average estimate of 2,250. Students who saw 1 in the first position gave an average estimate of 512. That is, the estimate was larger when 8 served as the anchor. By the way, what is the correct answer to the multiplication problems? Can you use the anchoring and adjustment heuristic to explain why both groups were so far off?

The Framing Effect

What is the framing effect? The **framing effect** refers to the way in which wording, or the context in which information is presented, affects decision-making (Gonzalez et al., 2005; Tetlock & McGraw, 2005). Political groups, like advertisers, are aware of the *framing effect* and choose their words accordingly. For example, proponents of legalized abortion refer to themselves as "pro-choice" and opponents refer to themselves as "pro-life." Each group frames itself in a

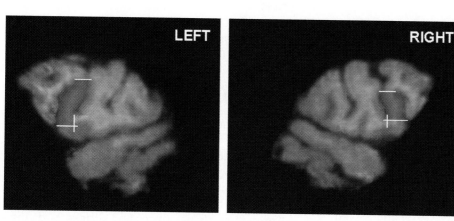

LEFT

RIGHT

Figure 8.2

MRI Results of the Left and Right Hemispheres of the Cerebral Cortexes of a Great Ape

In their MRI study of the brains of twenty-five chimpanzees and two gorillas, Cantalupo and Hopkins found that the great majority, twenty, showed larger areas similar to Broca's area in the left hemisphere. So do most humans. Six apes showed larger areas in the right hemisphere. Only one showed no difference. It would thus appear that chimpanzees and gorillas have some rudimentary language structures in their brains, even if they are not "wired" for speech.

positive way ("pro" something) and refers to a popular value (freedom or life).

Overconfidence

Whether our decisions are correct or incorrect, most of us tend to be overconfident about them. We also tend to view our situations with twenty-twenty hindsight. When we are proven wrong, we frequently find a way to show that we "knew it all along." We also become overconfident that we would have known the actual outcome if we had had access to the information that became available after the event. For example, if we had known that a key player would pull a hamstring muscle, we would have predicted a different outcome for the football game. If we had known that it would be blustery on Election Day, we would have predicted a smaller voter turnout and a different outcome. *Why do people tend to be convinced that they are right, even when they are dead wrong?* There are several reasons for overconfidence, even when our judgments are wrong:

- We tend to be unaware of how flimsy our assumptions may be.

- We tend to focus on examples that confirm our judgments and ignore those that do not.

- Because our working memories have limited space, we tend to forget information that runs counter to our judgments.

- We work to bring about the events we believe in, so they sometimes become self-fulfilling prophecies.

LO^2 Language

Communication by Nonhumans

In recent years the exclusive human claim to language has been brought into question by studies of communication with various animal species. The African Grey parrot, like many other parrots, can mimic human speech, but it is also suspected of being intelligent enough to understand some of the words it imitates. It has long been suspected that spontaneous language development occurs among many species of dolphins and whales, but we lack solid scientific evidence. Monkeys signal the peril of nearby predators with characteristic hoots. But none of these sounds contains *symbols*.

A language is a system of symbols along with rules that are used to manipulate the symbols. Symbols such as words stand for or represent other objects, events, or ideas. Because chimpanzees and gorillas have been taught to communicate by making signs with their hands, the question as to whether or not they are actually using language in the way that humans do is much more complex.

Chimpanzees are our closest genetic relatives, sharing an estimated 98.42% of their genetic code with humans (Zimmer, 2002–2003). MRI studies with chimpanzees and gorillas show that most of them, like humans, show enlargement in the left hemisphere of the cerebral cortex, in part of Broca's area (Cantalupo & Hopkins, 2001; see Figure 8.2). The differences that remain between humans and chimps are at least in part associated with capabilities such as fine control of the mouth and larynx that are not found in apes (Enard et al., 2002). The genetic codes of chimps and humans are apparently similar enough to give chimps some ability to use language, but different enough to prevent chimps from speaking.

Do Apes Really Use Language?

Although apes do not speak, they have been taught to use American Sign Language and other symbol systems. For example, a chimpanzee named Washoe, who was a pioneer in the effort to teach apes to use language, was using 181 signs by the age of thirty-two. Loulis, a baby chimp adopted by Washoe, gained the ability to use signs just by observing Washoe and some other chimps who had been trained in sign language (Fouts, 1997). Other chimps have used plastic symbols or pressed keys on a computer keyboard to communicate.

Sue Savage-Rumbaugh and her colleagues (1993; Shanker et al., 1999) believe that pygmy chimpanzees

language
the communication of information by means of symbols arranged according to rules of grammar

can understand some of the semantic subtleties of language. She claims that one chimp, Kanzi, picked up language from observing another chimp being trained and has the grammatical abilities of a two-and-a-half-year-old child. Kanzi also understands several words spoken by humans. Kanzi held a toy snake to a toy dog's mouth when asked to make the dog bite the snake.

Critics of the view that apes can learn to produce language, such as Herbert Terrace (1979) and Steven Pinker (1994a), note the following:

• Apes can string together signs in a given sequence to earn rewards, but animals lower on the evolutionary ladder, such as pigeons, can also peck buttons in a certain sequence to obtain a reward.

• It takes apes longer to learn new signs than it takes children to learn new words.

• Apes are unreliable in their sequencing of signs, suggesting that by and large they do not comprehend rules of grammar.

• People observing apes signing may be subject to *observer bias*—that is, they may be seeing what they want to see.

Scientists will continue to debate how well chimpanzees and gorillas understand and produce language, but there is little doubt that they have learned to use symbols to communicate (Savage-Rumbaugh & Fields, 2000).

What Is Language?

As you can see from the discussion of apes and language, the way in which one defines language is no small matter. *Just how do we define language?* If we define language simply as a system of communication, many animals have language, including the birds and the bees.

Through particular chirps and shrieks, birds may communicate that they have taken possession of a tree or bush. The waggle dances of bees inform other bees of the location of a food source or a predator. None of these are instinctive communication patterns, or what we mean by language.

In language, sounds or signs are symbols for objects and actions. Apes have been taught to use symbols to communicate, but is such usage an adequate definition of language? Many language experts require one more piece. They define **language** as the communication of thoughts and feelings by means of symbols *that are arranged according to rules of grammar*. Instinctive waggle dances and shrieks have no symbols and no grammar.

SUSAN KUKLIN / PHOTO RESEARCHERS

Joyce Butler of Columbia University shows chimpanzee "Nim Chimpsky" —named humorously after linguist Noam Chomsky—the sign for "drink," and Nim imitates her.

By these rigorous rules, only humans use language. Whether apes can handle rules of grammar is under debate.

Language makes it possible for one person to communicate knowledge to another and for one generation to communicate to another. It creates a vehicle for recording experiences. It allows us to put ourselves in the shoes of other people, to learn more than we could learn from direct experience. Language also provides many units of thinking.

True language is distinguished from the communication systems of lower animals by properties such as semanticity, infinite creativity, and displacement (Hoff, 2005):

- **Semanticity:** The sounds (or signs) of a language have meaning. Words serve as symbols for actions, objects, relational concepts (*over, in, more,* and so on), and other ideas. The communication systems of the birds and the bees lack semanticity.

- **Infinite creativity:** The capacity to create rather than imitate sentences.

- **Displacement:** The capacity to communicate information about events and objects in another time or place. Language makes it possible to transmit knowledge from one person to another and from one generation to another, furthering human adaptation.

Language and Cognition

The relationships between language and thinking are complex and not always obvious. For example, can you think *without* using language? Would you be able to solve problems without using words or sentences?

Jean Piaget (Inhelder & Piaget, 1958) believed that language reflects knowledge of the world but that much knowledge can be acquired without language. For example, it is possible to understand the concepts of roundness or redness even when we do not know or use the words *round* or *red*.

Language and Culture

Different languages have different words for the same concepts, and concepts do not necessarily overlap. Concepts expressed in our own language (such as *square* and *triangle*) may not exist in the language of another culture—and vice versa. Is it possible for English speakers to share the thoughts experienced by people who speak other languages? The answer is probably yes in many or most cases, but in some cases, no. In any event, the question brings us to the linguistic-relativity hypothesis.

How many words do you know for snow?

The Linguistic-Relativity Hypothesis

The linguistic-relativity hypothesis was proposed by Benjamin Whorf (1956). Whorf believed that language structures the way we perceive the world. That is, the categories and relationships we use to understand the world are derived from our language. Therefore, speakers of various languages conceptualize the world in different ways.

The Inuit (Eskimos) have many words for snow. The words differ according to whether the snow is hard-packed, falling, melting, and so on. In English, in contrast, we have fewer words to choose from and must choose descriptive adjectives to describe snow. Are English speakers limited in their ability to think about skiing conditions? Probably not. English-speaking skiers who are concerned about different skiing conditions have developed a comprehensive vocabulary about snow, including the terms *powder, slush, ice, hard-packed,* and *corn snow,* that allows them to communicate and think about snow. When a need to expand a language's vocabulary arises, the speakers of that language apparently have little trouble meeting the need.

In English, we have hundreds of words to describe colors. Shona-speaking people use only three words for colors, and Bassa speakers use only two words for colors, corresponding to light and dark. Nevertheless, a study of a hundred languages spoken in nonindustrialized societies finds overlaps for white, black, red, green,

semanticity
meaning; the quality of language in which words are used as symbols for objects, events, or ideas

infinite creativity
the capacity to combine words into original sentences

displacement
the quality of language that permits one to communicate information about objects and events in another time and place

linguistic-relativity hypothesis
the view that language structures the way in which we view the world

holophrase
a single word used
to express complex
meanings

yellow, and blue (Regier et al., 2005). Moreover, people who use only a few words to distinguish among colors seem to perceive the same color variations as people with more words. For example, the Dani of New Guinea have just two words for colors: one that refers to yellows and reds and one that refers to greens and blues. Yet performance on matching and memory tasks shows that the Dani can discriminate the many colors of the spectrum.

Most cognitive scientists no longer accept the linguistic-relativity hypothesis (Pinker, 1990). For one thing, adults use images and abstract logical propositions, as well as words, as units of thought. Infants, moreover, display considerable intelligence before they have learned to speak. Another criticism is that a language's vocabulary suggests the range of concepts that the speakers of the language have traditionally found important, not their cognitive limits. For example, people who were magically lifted from the 19th century and placed inside an airplane probably would not think they were flying inside a bird or a large insect, even if their language lacked a word for airplane.

Language Development: The Two-Year Explosion

How does language develop? Languages around the world develop in a specific sequence of steps, beginning with the *prelinguistic* vocalizations of crying, cooing, and babbling. These sounds are not symbols. That is, they do not represent objects or events. Therefore, they are *prelinguistic*, not linguistic.

Prelinguistic Vocalizations

As parents are well aware, newborn children have one inborn, highly effective form of verbal expression: crying—and more crying. But crying does not represent language; it is a prelinguistic event. During the second month, babies begin *cooing*, another form of prelinguistic expression that appears to be linked to feelings of pleasure. By the fifth or sixth month, children begin to *babble*. Children babble sounds that occur in many languages, including the throaty German *ch*, the clicks of certain African languages, and rolling *r*'s. Babies' babbling frequently combines consonants and vowels, as in "ba," "ga," and,

Fiction

Crying does *not* represent language; it is a prelinguistic event.

sometimes, the much-valued "dada." "Dada" at first is purely coincidental (sorry, dads), despite the family's delight over its appearance.

Babbling, like crying and cooing, is inborn and prelinguistic. Deaf children babble, and children from cultures whose languages sound very different all seem to babble the same sounds (Hoff, 2005). But children single out the sounds used in the home within a few months. By the age of nine or ten months they are repeating the sounds regularly, and foreign sounds are dropping out. In fact, early experience in acquiring the phonemes native to one's own language can make it difficult to pronounce and even discriminate the phonemes used in other languages later in life (Iverson et al., 2003).

Children tend to utter their first word at about one year of age, but many parents miss it, often because it is not pronounced clearly or because pronunciation varies from one usage to the next (Nelson et al., 1993). The growth of vocabulary is slow at first. It may take children three to four months to achieve a ten-word vocabulary after they have spoken their first word. By about eighteen months, children are producing a couple of dozen words.

For both children with normal hearing and deaf children, gesturing tends to develop ahead of words (Guidetti & Nikoladis, 2008). Babies can wave bye-bye to Grandma months before they can talk, for instance, and can also be taught to use signs in the second half of the first year. The researcher of children's language development, Elizabeth Bates (2004), noted that the development of sign language "has to do with how easily one can imitate and reproduce something with a great big fat hand as opposed to the mini, delicate hundreds of muscles that control the tongue… You can also see somebody using a hand, which you can't do with a tongue." The areas in the brain that control the mouth and speech and the areas that control the hands and gestures overlap a great deal and develop together (Bates, 2001; Bernardis et al., 2008; Guidetti & Nikoladis, 2008).

Development of Grammar

The first linguistic utterances of children around the globe are single words that can express complex meanings. These initial utterances of children are called holophrases. For example, *mama* may be used by the child to signify meanings as varied as "There goes Mama," "Come here, Mama," and "You are my Mama." Similarly, *cat* can signify "There is a cat," "That stuffed animal looks just like my cat," or "I want you to give me my cat right now!" Most children show their parents what they intend by augmenting their holophrases with gestures and intonations. That is, they act delighted when parents do as requested and howl when they do not.

Toward the end of the second year, children begin to speak two-word sentences. These sentences are termed *telegraphic speech* because they resemble telegrams. Telegrams cut out the "unnecessary" words. "Home Tuesday" might stand for "I expect to be home on Tuesday." Two-word utterances seem to appear at about the same time in the development of all languages (Slobin, 1983). Two-word utterances are brief but grammatically correct. The child says, "Sit chair" to tell a parent to sit in a chair, not "Chair sit." The child says, "My shoe," not "Shoe my," to show possession. "Mommy go" means Mommy is leaving. "Go Mommy" expresses the wish for Mommy to go away.

There are different kinds of two-word utterances. Some, for example, contain nouns or pronouns and verbs ("Daddy sit"). Others contain verbs and objects ("Hit ball"). The sequence of emergence of the various kinds of two-word utterances is also apparently the same in all languages—languages as diverse as English, Luo (an African tongue), German, Russian, and Turkish (Slobin, 1983). The invariance of this sequence has implications for theories of language development, as we will see.

Overregularization

Overregularization is an important development for understanding the roles of nature and nurture in language development. In English, we add *d* or *ed* to make the past tense of regular verbs and *s* or *z* sounds to make regular nouns plural. Thus, *walk* becomes *walked*, and *look* becomes *looked*. *Cat* becomes *cats*, and *doggy* becomes *doggies*. There are also irregular verbs and nouns. For example, *see* becomes *saw*, *sit* becomes *sat*, and *go* becomes *went*. *Sheep* remains *sheep* (plural) and *child* becomes *children*.

At first children learn irregular verbs and nouns by imitating older people. Two-year-olds tend to form them correctly—at first! Then they become aware of the grammatical rules for forming the past tense and plurals. As a result, they tend to make charming errors (Pinker, 1997). A three- to five-year-old, for example, may be more likely to say "I seed it" than "I saw it," and more likely to say "Mommy sitted down" than "Mommy sat down." They are likely to talk about the "gooses" and "sheeps" they "seed" on the farm and about all the "childs" they ran into at the playground. This tendency to regularize the irregular is what is meant by overregularization.

Should parents be concerned about overregularization? Not at all. Overregularization reflects knowledge of grammar, not faulty language development. In another year or two, *mouses* will be boringly transformed into *mice*, and Mommy will no longer have *sitted* down. Parents might as well enjoy overregularization while they can.

Other Developments

By the age of six, children's vocabularies have expanded to 10,000 words, give or take a few thousand. By seven to nine, most children realize that words can have more than one meaning, and they are entertained by riddles and jokes that require some sophistication with language.

Between the elementary school and high school years, language grows more complex, and children rapidly add to their vocabularies. Vocabulary, in fact, can grow for a lifetime, especially in one's fields of specialization and interest.

> ### Truth
> Young children say things like "Daddy goed away" and "Mommy sitted down" because they *do* understand rules of grammar.

Nature and Nurture in Language Development

Billions of children have acquired the languages spoken by their parents and passed them down, with minor changes, from generation to generation. Language development, like many other areas of development, apparently reflects the interactions between nature and nurture. *What are the roles of nature and nurture in language development?*

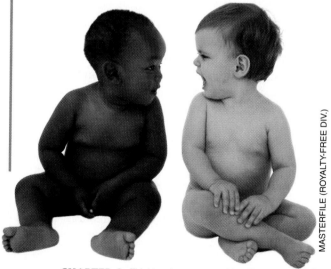

MASTERFILE (ROYALTY-FREE DIV.)

> **overregularization**
> the application of regular grammatical rules for forming inflections (e.g., past tense and plurals) to irregular verbs and nouns

Learning Theory and Language Development

Learning theorists see language as developing according to laws of learning (Hoff, 2005). They usually refer to the concepts of imitation and reinforcement. From a social-cognitive perspective, parents serve as *models*. Children learn language, at least in part, through observation and imitation. Many words, especially nouns and verbs (including irregular verbs), are apparently learned by imitation.

Children initially repeat the irregular verb forms they have heard accurately, apparently as a result of modeling. Modeling, however, does not explain all of the events in language learning. As noted previously, children later overregularize irregular verb forms because they have developed an understanding of grammar. Nor can learning by imitation explain how children come to utter phrases and sentences they have *not* observed. Parents, for example, are unlikely to model utterances such as "Bye-bye sock" and "All gone Daddy," but children say them.

Learning theory cannot account for the unchanging sequence of language development and the spurts in children's language acquisition. Even the types of two-word utterances emerge in a consistent pattern in diverse cultures. Although timing differs from one child to another, the types of questions used, passive versus active sentences, and so on, all emerge in the same order.

The Nativist Approach to Language Development

The nativist theory of language development holds that the innate factors—which make up children's *nature*—cause children to attend to and acquire language in certain ways. From this perspective, children bring neurological "prewiring" to language learning (Newport, 1998; Pinker, 1994a, 1999).

According to psycholinguistic theory, language acquisition involves the interaction of environmental influences—such as exposure to parental speech and reinforcement—and the inborn tendency to acquire language. Noam Chomsky (1980, 1991) refers to the inborn tendency as a language acquisition device (LAD). Evidence for an LAD is found in the universal-

ity of human language abilities and in the specific sequence of language development (Baker, 2001).

The LAD prepares the nervous system to learn grammar. On the surface, languages differ a great deal. However, the LAD serves children all over the world because languages share what Chomsky refers to as a "universal grammar"—an underlying set of rules for turning ideas into sentences (Pinker, 1994a).

In the following section we see that some aspects of language development—particularly vocabulary development—are strongly related to intelligence. Numerous researchers suggest that language learning occurs during one or more *sensitive periods*, which begin at about eighteen to twenty-four months and last until puberty (Bates, 2001). During these sensitive periods, neural development (as in the differentiating of brain structures) provides plasticity that facilitates language learning (Bates, 2001). Evidence for a sensitive period is found in recovery from brain injuries in some people. Injuries to the hemisphere that controls language (usually the left hemisphere) can impair or destroy the ability to speak. But before puberty, children suffering left-hemisphere injuries frequently recover a good deal of speaking ability. Lenneberg (1967) suggested that in young children, left-hemisphere damage may encourage the development of language functions in the right hemisphere. But adaptation ability wanes in adolescence, when brain tissue has reached adult levels of differentiation.

LO³ Intelligence

The concept of intelligence is closely related to thinking. Whereas thinking involves the understanding and manipulating of information, intelligence is the underlying ability to understand the world and cope with its challenges. Although these concepts overlap, psychologists tend to be concerned with *how* we think, but laypeople and psychologists are often concerned with *how much* intelligence we have. Although intelligence, like thinking, cannot be directly seen or touched, psychologists tie the concept to achievements such as school performance and occupational status (Pind et al., 2003; Wagner, 1997).

Theories of Intelligence

Although psychologists have engaged in thousands of studies on intelligence, they do not quite agree on what intelligence is. Psychologists have therefore developed theories to help them understand and define intelligence.

Factor Theories

Many investigators have viewed intelligence as consisting of one or more *factors*. Factor theories argue that intelligence is made up of a number of mental abilities, ranging from one kind of ability to hundreds.

In 1904, British psychologist Charles Spearman suggested that the behaviors we consider intelligent have a common underlying factor that he labeled *g*, for "general intelligence" or broad reasoning and problem-solving abilities. Spearman supported his view by noting that people who excel in one area (such as vocabulary) are also likely to excel in others (such as math). But he also noted that even the most capable people are relatively superior in some areas—such as music or business or poetry. For this reason, he suggested that specific, or *s*, factors account for specific abilities.

Contemporary psychologists continue to use the term *g* in research, speaking, for example, of the extent to which they believe a particular kind of test, such as the SATs, measure *g* (Gignac & Vernon, 2003; Rushton et al., 2003).

The American psychologist Louis Thurstone (1938) analyzed tests of specific abilities and concluded that Spearman had oversimplified intelligence. Thurstone's data suggested the presence of nine specific factors, which he labeled primary mental abilities (see Table 8.1). Thurstone's primary mental abilities contain the types of items measured on the most widely used intelligence tests today. The question remains as to whether his primary mental abilities are distinct or whether they are different ways of assessing *g*.

The Theory of Multiple Intelligences

Thurstone wrote about various factors or components of intelligence. Howard Gardner (1983/1993), instead, proposes that there are a number of *intelligences*, not just one. *What is meant by multiple intelligences?* Gardner refers to each kind of intelligence in his theory as "an intelligence" because they can differ so much. Two of these "intelligences" are familiar ones: language ability and logical–mathematical ability. Gardner also refers, however, to bodily-kinesthetic talents (of the sort shown by dancers and athletes), musical talent, spatial–relations skills, and two kinds of personal intelligence: awareness of one's own inner feelings and sensitivity to other people's feelings. Gardner (2001) has recently added "naturalist intelligence" and "existential intelligence." Naturalist intelligence refers to the ability to look at natural events, such as kinds of animals and plants, or the stars above, and to develop insights into their nature and the laws that govern their behavior. Existential intelligence means dealing with the larger philosophical issues of life. According to Gardner, one can compose symphonies or advance mathematical theory yet be average in, say, language and personal skills.

Critics of Gardner's view agree that people function more intelligently in some aspects of life than in others. They also agree that many people have special talents, such as bodily–kinesthetic talents, even if their overall intelligence is average. But these critics question whether such talents are best thought of as "intelligences" (Neisser et al., 1996). Language skills, reasoning ability, and ability to solve math problems seem to be more closely related than musical or gymnastic talent to what most people mean by intelligence.

The Triarchic Theory of Intelligence

Psychologist Robert Sternberg (2000; Sternberg et al., 2003) has constructed a three-pronged, or *triarchic*, theory of intelligence that resembles a view proposed by the Greek philosopher Aristotle (Tigner & Tigner, 2000). *What is Sternberg's triarchic model of intelligence?* These types of intelligence are *analytical*, *creative*, and *practical* (see Figure 8.3 on page 176).

Analytical intelligence is similar to Aristotle's "theoretical intelligence" and can be defined as academic ability. It enables us to solve problems and

g
Spearman's symbol for general intelligence, which he defined as broad reasoning and problem-solving abilities

s
Spearman's symbol for *specific* factors, or *s factors*, which he believed accounted for individual abilities

primary mental abilities
according to Thurstone, the basic abilities that make up intelligence; examples include word fluency and numerical ability

Table 8.1

Primary Mental Abilities, According to Thurstone

Ability	Definition
Visual and spatial abilities	Visualizing forms and spatial relationships
Perceptual speed	Grasping perceptual details rapidly, perceiving similarities and differences between stimuli
Numerical ability	Computing numbers
Verbal meaning	Knowing the meanings of words
Memory	Recalling information (e.g., words and sentences)
Word fluency	Thinking of words quickly (e.g., rhyming and doing crossword puzzles)
Deductive reasoning	Deriving examples from general rules
Inductive reasoning	Inferring general rules from examples

acquire new knowledge. It is the type of intelligence measured by standard intelligence tests. Problem-solving skills include encoding information, combining and comparing bits of information, and generating a solution. Consider Sternberg's analogy problem:

> *Washington* is to 1 as *Lincoln* is to
> (a) 5, (b) 10, (c) 15, (d) 50?

To solve the analogy, we must first correctly *encode* the elements—*Washington, 1,* and *Lincoln*—by identifying them and comparing them to other information. We can first encode *Washington* and *Lincoln* as the names of presidents and then try to combine *Washington* and 1 in a meaningful manner. (There are other possibilities: Both are also the names of memorials and cities, for example.) If we do encode the names as presidents, two possibilities quickly come to mind. Washington was the first president, and his picture is on the one-dollar bill. We can then generate two possible solutions and try them out. First, was Lincoln the fifth, tenth, fifteenth, or fiftieth president? Second, on what bill is Lincoln's picture found? (Do you need to consult a history book or peek into your wallet at this point?) The answer is (a) 5, because Lincoln's likeness is found on the five-dollar bill. (He was the nation's 16th president, not 15th president.)

Creative intelligence is similar to Aristotle's "productive intelligence" and is defined by the ability to cope with novel situations and generate many possible solutions to problems.

It is creative to quickly relate novel situations to familiar situations (that is, to perceive similarities and differences). Psychologists who consider creativity to be separate from analytical intelligence or academic ability note that there is only a moderate relationship between academic ability and creativity (Simonton, 2000). To Sternberg, however, creativity is a form of intelligence.

Aristotle and Sternberg both speak of practical intelligence ("street smarts"). Practical intelligence enables people to deal with other people, including difficult people, and to meet the demands of their environment. For example, keeping a job by adapting one's behavior to the employer's requirements is adaptive. But if the employer is making unreasonable demands, finding a more suitable job is also adaptive. Street smarts appear to help people get by in the real world, especially with other people, but are not particularly predictive of academic success.

Truth

It is true that street smarts are a sign of intelligence—at least according to Aristotle and Sternberg.

Emotional Intelligence

Psychologists Peter Salovey and John Mayer developed the theory of emotional intelligence, which was popularized by psychologist Daniel Goleman (1995). The theory holds that social and emotional skills, like academic skills, are a form of intelligence. *Just what is "emotional intelligence"?*

Figure 8.3

Sternberg's Theory of Intelligence

According to Robert Sternberg, there are three types of intelligence: analytical (academic ability), creative, and practical ("street smarts"). Psychologists discuss the relationships between intelligence and creativity, but within Sternberg's model, creativity is a *type* of intellectual functioning.

Analytical intelligence
(Academic ability)
Abilities to solve problems, compare and contrast, judge, evaluate, and criticize

Creative intelligence
(Creativity and insight)
Abilities to invent, discover, suppose, or theorize

Practical intelligence
("Street smarts")
Abilities to adapt to the demands of one's environment, apply knowledge in practical situations

Emotional intelligence resembles two of Gardner's "intelligences"—intrapersonal skills and interpersonal skills (including insight into the feelings of other people). It also involves self-insight and self-control—the abilities to recognize and regulate one's moods (Salovey et al., 2002).

Failure to develop emotional intelligence is connected with poor ability to cope with stress, depression, and aggressive behavior (Salovey et al., 2002; Wang, 2002).

But *is* emotional intelligence a form of intelligence? Psychologist Ulric Neisser (1997b) says that "the skills that Goleman describes . . . are certainly important for determining life outcomes, but nothing is to be gained by calling them forms of intelligence."

There are thus many views of intelligence—what intelligence is and how many kinds of intelligence there may be. We do not yet have the final word on the nature of intelligence, but I would like to share David Wechsler's definition. Wechsler originated the most widely used series of intelligence tests, and he defined intelligence as the "capacity of an individual to understand the world [and the] resourcefulness to cope with its challenges" (1975, p. 139).

Creativity and Intelligence

Think of artists, musicians, poets, scientists who innovate research methods, and other creative individuals. *What is creativity? How is it connected to intelligence?*

Like the concept of intelligence, the concept of creativity has been difficult to define. One issue is whether creativity is distinct from intelligence, or is, as Sternberg suggests, a type of intelligence. For example, we would not ask the question, "Do creative people tend to be intelligent?" unless we saw creativity as distinct from intelligence. If you consider creativity to be an aspect of intelligence, then the two concepts—intelligence and creativity—overlap. But if you think of intelligence as more closely related to academic ability, it is not always true that a highly intelligent person is creative or that a creative person is highly intelligent. Research findings suggest that the relationship between intelligence test scores and standard measures of creativity is only moderate (Simonton, 2000; Sternberg & Williams, 1997).

Within his triarchic theory, Sternberg defines creativity as the ability to do things that are novel and useful (Sternberg, 2001). Other psychologists note that creative people can solve problems to which there are no preexisting solutions and no proven formulas (Simonton, 2000). According to Sternberg and Lubart (1995, 1996), creative people take chances. They refuse to accept limitations. They appreciate art and music. They use common materials to make unique things. They challenge social norms and take unpopular stands. They challenge ideas that other people accept at face value.

Many psychologists see creativity as the ability to make unusual, sometimes remote, associations to the elements of a problem to generate new combinations. An essential aspect of a creative response is the leap from the elements of the problem to the novel solution.

Creative problem-solving demands divergent rather than convergent thinking. In convergent thinking, thought is limited to present facts; the problem-solver narrows his or her thinking to find the best solution. (You use convergent thinking to arrive at the right answer to a multiple-choice question.) In divergent thinking, the problem-solver associates freely to the elements of the problem, allowing "leads" to run a nearly limitless course. (You may use divergent thinking when you are trying to generate ideas to answer an essay question on a test.)

Problem-solving can involve both kinds of thinking. At first divergent thinking helps generate many possible solutions. Convergent thinking is then used to select likely solutions and reject others.

Intelligence test questions usually require analytical, convergent thinking to focus in on the one right answer. Tests of creativity determine how flexible a person's thinking is (Simonton, 2000). Here is an item from a test used by Getzels and Jackson (1962) to measure associative ability, a factor in creativity: "Write as many meanings as you can for each of the following words: (a) duck; (b) sack; (c) pitch; (d) fair." Those who write several meanings for each word, rather than only one, are rated as potentially more creative.

Now that we have begun speaking of scores on intelligence tests, let's see how psychologists go about measuring intelligence. We will also see how psychologists attempt to *validate* their measures of intelligence—that is, how they try to demonstrate that they are in fact measuring intelligence.

creativity the ability to generate novel and useful solutions to problems

convergent thinking a thought process that narrows in on the single best solution to a problem

divergent thinking a thought process that attempts to generate multiple solutions to problems

Truth/Fiction (depends)

The answer to whether an intelligent person is creative or a creative person is intelligent partly depends on definitions of the terms.

mental age (MA)
the accumulated months of credit that a person earns on the Stanford–Binet Intelligence Scale

intelligence quotient (IQ)
(1) originally, a ratio obtained by dividing a child's score (or mental age) on an intelligence test by chronological age (2) generally, a score on an intelligence test

The Measurement of Intelligence

Although psychologists disagree about the nature of intelligence, laypeople and educators are concerned with "how much" intelligence people have, because the issue affects educational and occupational choices. In this section we consider two of the most widely used intelligence tests.

The Stanford–Binet Intelligence Scale

Many of the concepts of psychology have their origins in common sense. The commonsense notion that academic achievement depends on children's intelligence led Alfred Binet and Theodore Simon to invent measures of intelligence.

What is the Stanford–Binet Intelligence Scale? Early in the 20th century, the French public school system was looking for a test that could identify children who were unlikely to benefit from regular classroom instruction. If these children were identified, they could be given special attention. The first version of that test, the Binet–Simon scale, came into use in 1905. Since that time it has undergone extensive revision and refinement. The current version is the Stanford–Binet Intelligence Scale (SBIS).

Binet assumed that intelligence increases with age, so older children should get more items right than younger children. Binet therefore included a series of age-graded questions, as in Table 8.2, arranged in order of difficulty.

The Binet–Simon scale yielded a score called a *mental age (MA)*. The MA shows the intellectual level at which a child is functioning. For example, a child with an MA of 6 is functioning intellectually like the average six-year-old. In taking the test, children earned "months" of credit for each correct answer. Their MA was determined by adding up the years and months of credit they attained.

Louis Terman adapted the Binet–Simon scale for use with American children at Stanford University. The first version of the resultant Stanford–Binet Intelligence Scale was published in 1916. The SBIS included more items than the original test and was used with children aged two to sixteen. The SBIS also yielded an <u>intelligence quotient (IQ)</u> rather than an MA. As a result, American educators developed interest in learning the IQs of their pupils. The SBIS is used today with children from the age of two upward and with adults.

The IQ reflects the relationship between a child's mental age and his or her actual or chronological age (CA). Use of this ratio reflects the fact that the same MA score has different implications for children of different ages. That is, an MA of 8 is an above-average score for a six-year-old but below average for a ten-year-old. In 1912 the German psychologist Wilhelm Stern suggested the IQ as a way to deal with this problem. Stern computed IQ using the formula

$$IQ = \frac{\text{Mental age (MA)}}{\text{Chronological age (CA)}} \times 100.$$

According to this formula, a child with an MA of 6 and a CA of 6 would have an IQ of 100. Children who can handle intellectual problems as well as older children do have IQs above 100. For example, an eight-year-old who does as well on the SBIS as the average ten-year-old would attain an IQ of 125. Children who do not answer as many items correctly as other children of the same age attain MAs lower than their CAs. Thus, their IQ scores are below 100.

IQ scores on the SBIS today are derived by comparing their results to those of other people of the same age. People who answer more items correctly than the average for people of the same age attain IQ scores above 100. People who answer fewer items correctly than the average for their age attain scores below 100. Therefore, two children can answer exactly the same items on an intelligence test correctly, yet one can be above average in IQ. This is because the ages of the children may differ. The more intelligent child would be the younger of the two.

Truth

Two children can answer exactly the same items on an intelligence test correctly, yet one can be above average and the other below average in IQ.

The Wechsler Scales

In contrast to the SBIS, David Wechsler developed a series of scales for use with children and adults. *What is different about the Wechsler scales of intelligence?* The Wechsler scales group test questions into a number of separate subtests (see Figure 8.4). Each subtest measures a different intellectual task. For this reason, the test shows how well a person does on one type of task (such as defining words) as compared with another (such as using blocks to construct geometric designs). In this way, the Wechsler scales highlight children's relative strengths and

Table 8.2

Items Similar to Those on the Stanford–Binet Intelligence Scale

Level (Years)	Item
2	1. Children show knowledge of basic vocabulary words by identifying parts of a doll, such as the mouth, ears, and hair.
	2. Children show counting and spatial skills along with visual–motor coordination by building a tower of four blocks to match a model.
4	1. Children show word fluency and categorical thinking by filling in the missing words when they are asked questions such as: "Father is a man; mother is a _____?" "Hamburgers are hot; ice cream is _____?"
	2. Children show comprehension by answering correctly when they are asked questions such as: "Why do people have automobiles?" "Why do people have medicine?"
9	1. Children can point out verbal absurdities, as in this question: "In an old cemetery, scientists unearthed a skull which they think was that of George Washington when he was only five years of age. What is silly about that?"
	2. Children display fluency with words, as shown by answering these questions: "Can you tell me a number that rhymes with snore?" "Can you tell me a color that rhymes with glue?"
Adult	1. Adults show knowledge of the meanings of words and conceptual thinking by correctly explaining the differences between word pairs like "sickness and misery," "house and home," and "integrity and prestige."
	2. Adults show spatial skills by correctly answering questions like: "If a car turned to the right to head north, in what direction was it heading before it turned?"

weaknesses, as well as measure overall intellectual functioning.

Wechsler described some of his scales as measuring *verbal* tasks and others as assessing *performance* tasks. In general, verbal subtests require knowledge of verbal concepts, whereas performance subtests require familiarity with spatial–relations concepts. Wechsler's scales permit the computation of verbal and performance IQs. Nontechnically oriented college students often attain higher verbal than performance IQs. Less-well-educated people often obtain higher performance than verbal IQs.

Wechsler also introduced the concept of the *deviation IQ*. Instead of dividing mental age by chronological age to compute an IQ, he based IQ scores on how a person's answers compared with those attained by people in the same age group. The average test result at any age level is defined as an IQ score of 100. Wechsler distributed IQ scores so that the middle 50% were defined as the "broad average range" of 90 to 110. As you can see in Figure 8.5, IQ scores cluster around the average. Only 4% of the population have IQ scores of above 130 or below 70.

Group Tests

The SBIS and Wechsler scales are administered to one person at a time. This one-to-one ratio is optimal because it allows the examiner to observe the test taker closely. Examiners are alerted to factors that impair performance, such as language difficulties, illness, or a noisy or poorly lit room. But large institutions with few trained examiners, such as the public schools and armed forces, require tests that can be administered simultaneously to large groups.

Group tests for children were first developed during World War I. At first these tests were hailed as remarkable instruments because they helped school administrators place children. As the years passed, however, group tests came under attack because many administrators relied on them exclusively and did not seek other sources of information about children's abilities.

At their best, intelligence tests provide only one source of information about individual children. Numbers alone, and especially IQ scores, cannot adequately define children's special abilities and talents.

Differences in Intellectual Functioning

The average IQ score in the United States is very close to 100. Yet for some socioeconomic and ethnic groups in the United States, the average is higher, and for others, it is lower. Questions have also been raised about whether males or females are more intelligent overall, and whether there are gender

Figure 8.4

Items Similar to Those on the Wechsler Adult Intelligence Scale

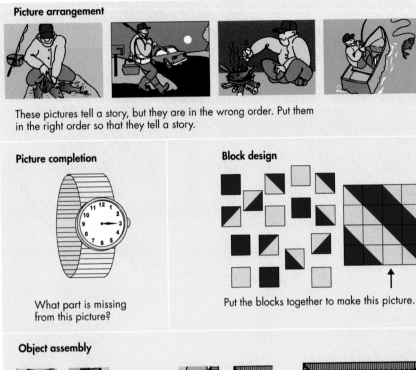

Picture arrangement

These pictures tell a story, but they are in the wrong order. Put them in the right order so that they tell a story.

Picture completion

What part is missing from this picture?

Block design

Put the blocks together to make this picture.

Object assembly

Put the pieces together as quickly as you can.

differences in the kinds of intellectual or cognitive skills valued in society. Tests of intellectual functioning have thus been seen as divisive and as maintaining a class system or social order that is based on prejudices and "tradition" as much as on science. In this section we discuss (1) socioeconomic and ethnic differences and (2) gender differences in cognitive skills.

Socioeconomic and Ethnic Differences

There is a body of research suggestive of differences in intelligence—or, more precisely, intelligence test scores—between socioeconomic and ethnic groups. *What are the socioeconomic and ethnic differences in intelligence?* Lower-class U.S. children obtain IQ scores some ten to fifteen points lower than those obtained by middle- and upper-class children. African American children tend to obtain IQ scores some fifteen points lower than those obtained by their European American age-mates (Neisser

et al., 1996). Latino and Latina American and Native American children also tend to score below the norms for European Americans (Neisser et al., 1996).

Many studies of IQ confuse the factors of social class and ethnicity because disproportionate numbers of African Americans, Latino and Latina Americans, and Native Americans are found among the lower socioeconomic classes (Neisser et al., 1996). When we limit our observations to particular ethnic groups, we still find an effect for social class. That is, middle-class European Americans outscore poorer European Americans. Middle-class African Americans, Latino and Latina Americans, and Native Americans outscore poorer members of their own ethnic groups.

There may also be intellectual differences between Asians and Caucasians. Asian Americans, for example, frequently outscore European Americans on the math portion of the Scholastic Aptitude Test. Students in China (Taiwan) and Japan also outscore European Americans on achievement tests in math and science (Stevenson et al., 1986). In the United States, moreover, people of Asian Indian, Korean, Japanese, Filipino, and Chinese descent are more likely than European Americans, African Americans, and Latino and Latina Americans to graduate from high school and complete college (Xie & Goyette, 2003; Yeh & Chang, 2004). They are also highly over represented in competitive colleges and universities.

Most psychologists believe that such ethnic differences reflect cultural attitudes toward education rather than inborn racial differences (Neisser et

Truth

Many psychologists and social critics argue that intelligence tests measure many things other than intelligence—including familiarity with the dominant middle-class culture in the United States and motivation to perform well.

Figure 8.5

Approximate Distribution of IQ Scores

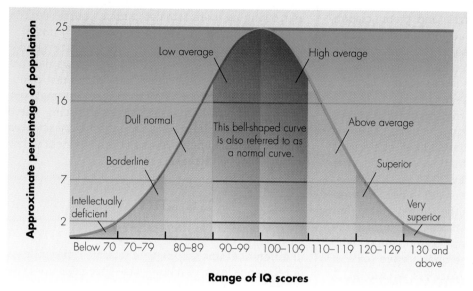

Because children reared in African American or Latino and Latina American neighborhoods may be at a cultural disadvantage in intelligence testing (Helms, 1992; Kwate, 2001), many psychologists, including Raymond B. Cattell (1949) and Florence Goodenough (Goodenough & Harris, 1950), have tried to construct culture-free intelligence tests. Cattell's Culture-Fair Intelligence Test evaluates reasoning through the child's ability to understand and use the rules that govern a progression of geometric designs (see Figure 8.6). Goodenough's Draw-A-Person test is based on the premise that children from all cultural backgrounds have had the opportunity to observe people and note the relationships between the parts and the whole. Her instructions simply require children to draw a picture of a man or woman.

Ironically, European American children outperform African American children on "culture-free" tests (Rushton et al., 2003), perhaps because they are more likely than disadvantaged children to have played with blocks (practice relevant to the Cattell test) and to have sketched animals, people, and things (practice relevant to the Goodenough test). Nor do culture-free tests predict academic success as well as other intelligence tests.

al., 1996). That is, the Asian children may be more motivated to work in school (Fuligni & Witkow, 2004; Xie & Goyette, 2003). Research shows that Chinese and Japanese students and their mothers tend to attribute academic successes to hard work (Randel et al., 2000). European Americans are more likely to attribute their children's academic successes to "natural" ability (Basic Behavioral Science Task Force, 1996b). Steinberg and his colleagues (1996) claim that parental encouragement and supervision in combination with peer support for academic achievement partially explain the superior performances of European Americans and Asian Americans as compared with African Americans and Latino and Latina Americans.

These ethnic differences lead us to ask: *Do intelligence tests contain cultural biases against ethnic minority groups and immigrants? Are the tests valid when used with ethnic minority groups or people who are poorly educated?*

Gender Differences

It was once widely believed that males were more intelligent than females because of their greater knowledge of world affairs and their skills in science and industry. But these differences did not reflect differences in cognitive ability. Rather, they reflected exclusion of females from world affairs, science, and industry. Moreover, intelligence tests do not show overall gender differences in cognitive abilities (Halpern & LaMay, 2000).

Do males and females differ in intellectual functioning? Reviews of the research suggest that girls are

Figure 8.6

Sample Items from Cattell's Culture-Fair Intelligence Test

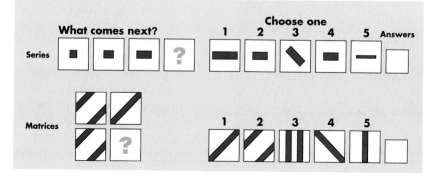

somewhat superior to boys in verbal abilities, such as vocabulary, ability to generate sentences and words that are similar in meaning to other words, spelling, knowledge of foreign languages, and pronunciation (Halpern, 2003). Girls seem to acquire language somewhat faster than boys do. Also, in the United States, more boys than girls have reading problems, ranging from reading below grade level to severe disabilities (Liederman et al., 2005; Skelton, 2005).

Males seem to do somewhat better at manipulating visual images in working memory. Males as a group excel in visual–spatial abilities of the sort used in math, science, and map-reading (Collaer & Nelson, 2002; Halpern & LaMay, 2000).

There are no overall gender differences in average scores on math tests in the United States, but males are more likely than females to perform at the extremes, as in the percentage of individuals who obtain scores over 700 on the quantitative scale of the SAT (Else-Quest, N. M., Hyde, J. S., & Linn, M. C. (2010). Cross-national patterns of gender differences in mathematics: A meta-analysis. Psychological Bulletin, 136(1), 103-127).

But note that the reported gender differences are *group* differences. There is greater variation in these skills between individuals *within* the groups than between males and females (Halpern, 2003). That is, there may be a greater difference in, say, verbal skills between two women than between the typical woman and the typical man. Millions of females outdistance the "average" male in math and spatial abilities. Men have produced their verbally adept Shakespeares. Moreover, Hyde and Plant

(1995) assert that in most cases, gender differences in cognitive skills are small. Differences in verbal, math, and visual–spatial abilities also appear to be narrowing as more females pursue course work in fields that had been typically populated by males.

While scholars sit around and debate gender differences in intellectual functioning, women are voting on the issue by flooding fields once populated almost exclusively by men (Cox & Alm, 2005). Figure 8.7 shows that women are tossing these stereotypes out the window by entering the sciences and professional fields ranging from business to law to medicine in increasing numbers.

LO⁴ Nature and Nurture in Intelligence

If different ethnic groups tend to score differently on intelligence tests, psychologists— like educators and other people involved in public life—want to know why. We will see that this is one debate that can make use of key empirical findings. Psychologists can point with pride to a rich mine of research on the roles of nature (genetic influences) and nurture (environmental influences) in the development of intelligence.

Genetic Influences on Intelligence

What are the genetic influences on intelligence? Research on genetic influences has employed kinship studies, twin studies, and adoptee studies (Neisser et al., 1996). Let us consider each of these to see whether heredity affects intellectual functioning.

We can examine the IQ scores of closely and distantly related people who have been reared together or apart. If heredity is involved in human intelligence, closely related people ought to have more similar IQs than distantly related or unrelated people, even when they are reared separately (Petrill & Deater-Deckard, 2004).

Figure 8.8 is a composite of the results of more than a hundred studies of IQ and heredity in human beings (Bouchard et al., 1990). The IQ scores of identical (monozygotic, or MZ)

Figure 8.7

Women Flood Professions Once Populated Almost Exclusively by Men

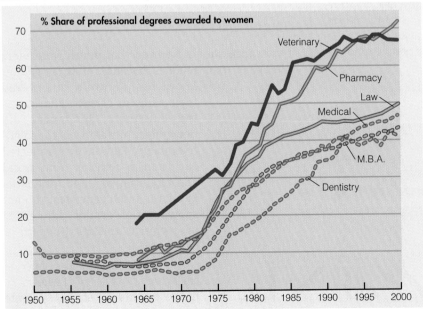

twins are more alike than scores for any other pairs, even when the twins have been reared apart. There are moderate correlations between the IQ scores of fraternal (dizygotic, or DZ) twins, between those of siblings, and between those of parents and their children. Correlations between the scores of children and their foster parents and between those of cousins are weak.

The results of large-scale twin studies are consistent with the data in Figure 8.8. A classic study of 500 pairs of MZ and DZ twins in Louisville, Kentucky (Wilson, 1983), found that the correlations in intelligence for MZ twins were higher than those for DZ twins. The correlations in intelligence between DZ twin pairs was the same as that between other siblings. The MacArthur Longitudinal Twin Study examined the intellectual abilities of 200 fourteen-month-old pairs of twins (Plomin et al., 1993). The study found that MZ twins were more similar than DZ twins in spatial memory, ability to categorize things, and word comprehension.

In sum, studies generally suggest that the heritability of intelligence is between 40% and 60% (Neisser et al., 1996). In other words, about half of the difference between your IQ score and the IQ scores of other people can be explained by heredity.

Note, too, that genetic pairs (such as MZ twins) who were reared together show higher correlations in their IQ scores than similar genetic pairs (such as other MZ twins) who were reared apart. This finding holds for DZ twins, siblings, parents and their children, and unrelated people. Being reared together is, therefore, related with similarities in IQ. *For this reason, the same group of studies used to demonstrate a role for the heritability of IQ scores also suggests that the environment plays a role in determining IQ scores.*

Another strategy for exploring genetic influences on intelligence is to compare the correlations between the IQ scores of adopted children and those of their biological and adoptive parents. When children are separated from their biological parents at an early age, one can argue that strong relationships between their IQs and those of their natural parents reflect genetic influences. Strong relationships between the children's IQs and those of their adoptive parents might reflect environmental influences.

Several studies with one- and two-year-old children in Colorado (Baker et al., 1983), Texas (Horn, 1983), and Minnesota (Scarr & Weinberg, 1983) have found a stronger relationship between the IQ scores of adopted children and those of their biological parents than between the children's scores and those of their adoptive parents.

heritability
the degree to which the variations in a trait from one person to another can be attributed to, or explained by, genetic factors

Environmental Influences on Intelligence

What are the environmental influences on intelligence? To answer this question we must consider studies of environmental influences, which also employ a variety of research strategies. These include observation of the role of the home environment and evaluation of the effects of educational programs.

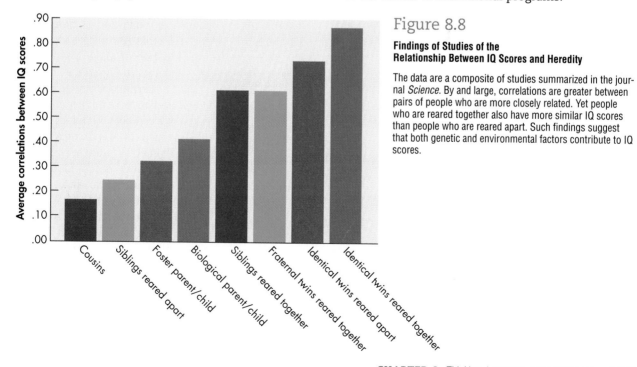

Figure 8.8

Findings of Studies of the Relationship Between IQ Scores and Heredity

The data are a composite of studies summarized in the journal *Science*. By and large, correlations are greater between pairs of people who are more closely related. Yet people who are reared together also have more similar IQ scores than people who are reared apart. Such findings suggest that both genetic and environmental factors contribute to IQ scores.

The Home Environment

The home environment and styles of parenting also affect IQ scores (Han et al., 2004; Molfese et al., 2003). Children of parents who are emotionally and verbally responsive, furnish appropriate play materials, are involved with their children, encourage independence, and provide varied daily experiences obtain higher IQ scores later on (Molfese et al., 1997). Organization and safety in the home have also been linked to higher IQs and achievement test scores (Bradley et al., 1989; Petrill et al., 2004).

Other studies support the view that children's early environment is linked to IQ scores and academic achievement. For example, Victoria Molfese and her colleagues (1997) found that the home environment was the single most important predictor of scores on IQ tests among children aged three to eight.

Education

Although intelligence is viewed as permitting people to profit from education, education also apparently contributes to intelligence. Government-funded efforts to provide preschoolers with enriched early environments have led to intellectual gains. Head Start programs, for example, enhance the IQ scores, achievement test scores, and academic skills of disadvantaged children (Stipek & Hakuta, 2007) by exposing them to materials and activities that middle-class children take for granted. These include letters and words, numbers, books, exercises in drawing, pegs and pegboards, puzzles, toy animals, and dolls. Head Start also helps poor children get medical and dental care, serves nutritious meals, and helps children develop the social skills necessary to succeed in school.

Preschool intervention programs can have long-term positive effects on children. During the elementary and high school years, graduates of preschool programs are less likely to be held back or placed in classes for slow learners. They are more likely to graduate from high school, go on to college, and earn higher incomes.

Later schooling also contributes to IQ. When children of about the same age start school a year apart because of admissions standards related to their date of birth, children who have been in school longer obtain higher IQ scores (Neisser et al., 1996). Moreover, test scores tend to decrease during the summer vacation (Neisser et al., 1996).

The findings on intelligence, the home environment, and educational experiences show that much indeed can be done to enhance intellectual functioning in children.

The Flynn Effect

Philosopher and researcher John Flynn (2003) found that IQ scores in the Western world increased substantially between 1947 and 2002, some 18 points in the United States. Psychologist Richard Nisbett (2007) argues that our genetic codes could not possibly have changed enough in half a century to account for this enormous difference and concludes that social and cultural factors such as the effects of improved educational systems and the penetration of the mass media must be among the reasons for the change.

If such environmental factors are capable of producing changes of this magnitude over time for the entire American population, they can also produce significant differences between subpopulations, such as between African Americans and European Americans. For example, the difference in IQ scores between the two racial groups has decreased from 15 points to 9.5 points over the past thirty years (Nisbett, 2007), which is again too large a difference to reflect genetic factors. Instead, it would suggest that the educational gap between the races may be narrowing.

All in all, intellectual functioning appears to reflect the interaction of a complex web of genetic, physical, personal, and sociocultural factors (Bartels et al., 2002; Bishop et al., 2003), as suggested in Figure 8.9.

Perhaps we need not be so concerned with whether we can sort out exactly how much of a person's intelligence is due to heredity and how much is due to environmental influences. Psychology has traditionally supported the dignity of the individual. It might be more appropriate for us to try to identify children of all ethnic groups who are at risk of failure and to do what we can to enrich their environments.

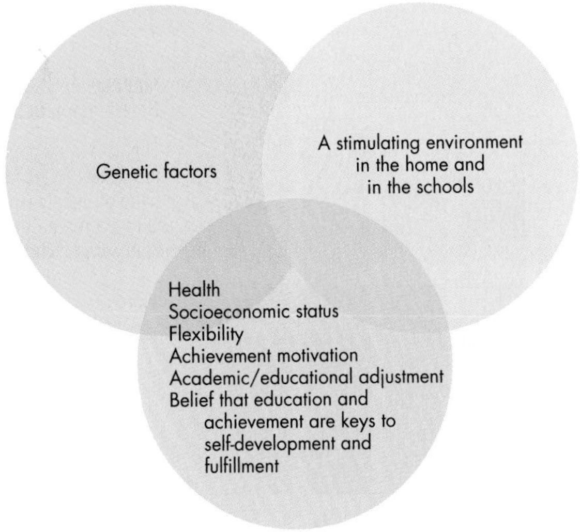

Genetic factors

A stimulating environment in the home and in the schools

Health
Socioeconomic status
Flexibility
Achievement motivation
Academic/educational adjustment
Belief that education and achievement are keys to self-development and fulfillment

Figure 8.9

The Complex Web of Factors That Affect Intellectual Functioning

Intellectual functioning appears to be influenced by the interaction of genetic factors, health, personality, and sociocultural factors.

Theories of Intelligence Summary Chart

Theory	Basic Information	Comments
General versus specific factors (proponent: Charles Spearman) © ARCHIVES OF THE HISTORY OF AMERICAN PSYCHOLOGY—THE UNIVERSITY OF AKRON	■ Spearman created factor analysis to study intelligence. ■ There is strong evidence for the general factor (g) in intelligence. ■ s factors are specific abilities, skills, and talents.	■ Concept of g remains in use today—a century later.
Primary mental abilities (proponent: Louis Thurstone) TIME & LIFE PICTURES/ GETTY IMAGES	■ Thurstone used factor analysis. ■ There are many "primary" abilities. ■ All abilities and factors are academically oriented.	■ Other researchers (e.g., Guilford) claim to have found hundreds of factors. ■ The more factors that are claimed, the more they overlap.
Triarchic theory (proponent: Robert Sternberg) COURTESY OF TUFTS UNIVERSITY	■ Intelligence is three-pronged—with analytical, creative, and practical components. ■ Analytical intelligence is analogous to academic ability.	■ The theory coincides with the views of Aristotle. ■ Critics do not view creativity as a component of intelligence.
Multiple intelligences (proponent: Howard Gardner) © 2003 JAY GARDNER	■ Gardner theorized distinct "intelligences." ■ Intelligences include academic intelligences, personal and social intelligences, talents, and philosophical intelligences. ■ The theory posits different bases in the brain for different intelligences.	■ Proponents continue to expand the number of "intelligences." ■ Critics see little value in theorizing "intelligences" rather than aspects of intelligence. ■ Most critics consider musical and bodily skills to be special talents, not "intelligences."

Motivation
and
Emotion

Learning Outcomes

LO[1] Define motivation including needs, drives, and incentives

LO[2] Identify the theories of motivation

LO[3] Describe the biological and psychological contributions to hunger

LO[4] Explain the role of sex hormones and the sexual response cycle in human sexuality

LO[5] Describe achievement motivation

LO[6] Identify the theoretical explanations of emotions

> ## " When a prophecy fails, how do its believers respond? Why? "

The Seekers had received word that the world was coming to an end on December 21st. A great flood would engulf their city and the rest of the Earth. Now they were gathered around their leader, Marian Keech, in her home, as she recorded messages that she said were sent to her by the Guardians from outer space. The messages were received through "automatic writing"; that is, the Guardians communicated through Ms. Keech, who wrote down their words without awareness. Another message brought good news, however. Because of their faith, the Seekers would be saved by flying saucers at the stroke of midnight on the 21st.

In their classic observational study, Leon Festinger and his colleagues (1956) described how they managed to be present in Ms. Keech's household at the fateful hour by pretending to belong to the group. Their purpose was to observe the behavior of the Seekers during and following the prophecy's failure. The cognitive theory of motivation that Festinger was working on—*cognitive-dissonance theory*—suggested that there would be a discrepancy or conflict between two key cognitions: (1) Ms. Keech is a prophet, and (2) Ms. Keech is wrong.

Truth or Fiction?

What do you think?

Folklore, common sense, or nonsense? Place a T for "True" or F for "False" on the lines provided (you'll learn the answers as you read through the text).

__ Getting away from it all by going on a vacation from all sensory input for a few hours is relaxing.

__ People feel hunger due to contractions ("pangs") in the stomach.

__ Fashion magazines can contribute to eating disorders among women.

__ Money can't buy you happiness.

__ You may be able to fool a lie detector by squiggling your toes.

How might the conflict be resolved? One way would be for the Seekers to lose faith in Ms. Keech. But the researchers expected that according to their theory, the Seekers could also be motivated to resolve the conflict by going out to spread the word and find additional converts. Otherwise the group would be painfully embarrassed.

Let us return to the momentous night. Many members of the group had quit their jobs and gone on spending sprees before the anticipated end. Now, as midnight approached they fidgeted, awaiting the flying saucers. Midnight came, but there were no saucers. Anxious glances were exchanged. There was silence, and then some coughs. Minutes passed, torturously slowly. Watches were checked, more glances exchanged.

At 4:00 a.m., a bitter and frantic Ms. Keech complained that she sensed that members of the group were doubting her. At 4:45 a.m., however, she seemed suddenly relieved. Still another message was arriving, and Ms. Keech was spelling it out through automatic writing! The Seekers, it turned out, had managed to save the world through their faith. The universal powers had decided to let the world travel on along its sinful way for a while longer. Why? Because of the faith of the Seekers, there was hope!

ERIK ISAKSON / JUPITER IMAGES

motive
a hypothetical state within an organism that propels the organism toward a goal (from the Latin *movere*, meaning "to move")

need
a state of deprivation

drive
a condition of arousal in an organism that is associated with a need

physiological drives
unlearned drives with a biological basis, such as hunger, thirst, and avoidance of pain

incentive
an object, person, or situation that can satisfy a need

instinct
an inherited disposition to activate specific behavior patterns that are designed to reach certain goals

With their faith restored, the followers called wire services and newspapers to spread the word. The three psychologists from the University of Minnesota went home, weary but enlightened. They wrote a book entitled *When Prophecy Fails,* which serves as one of the key documents of their theory.

LO¹ The Psychology of Motivation

The psychology of motivation is concerned with the *why* of behavior. Why do we eat? Why do some of us strive to get ahead? Why do some of us ride motorcycles at breakneck speeds? Why are some people aggressive? Why were the Seekers in a state of discomfort when the prophecy failed? In order to answer these questions, psychologists use concepts such as motives, needs, drives, and incentives. *What are motives, needs, drives, and incentives?* **Motives** are hypothetical states that activate behavior, propelling us toward goals. We call these states hypothetical because motives are not seen and measured directly. They are inferred from behavior. Motives may take the form of *needs, drives,* and *incentives,* which are also inferred from behavior.

We have physiological and psychological **needs**. We must meet physiological needs to survive—for example, the needs for oxygen, food, drink, pain avoidance, proper temperature, and elimination of waste products. Some physiological needs, such as hunger and thirst, are states of physical deprivation. When we have not eaten or drunk for a while, we develop needs for food and water. The body also needs oxygen, vitamins, and so on.

Psychological needs include needs for achievement, power, self-esteem, social approval, and belonging. Psychological needs are not necessarily based on states of deprivation. A person with a need for achievement may already have a history of successful achievements. Because people's biological makeups are similar, we share similar physiological needs. But because we are influenced by our cultural settings, our needs may be expressed in different ways. We all need food, but some prefer a vegetarian diet whereas others prefer meat. Because learning enters into psychological needs, they can differ markedly from one person to another.

Needs give rise to **drives**. Depletion of food gives rise to the hunger drive, and depletion of liquids gives rise to the thirst drive. **Physiological drives** are the counterparts of physiological needs. When we have gone without food and water, our body may *need* these substances. However, our *experience* of the drives of hunger and thirst is psychological. Drives arouse us to action and tend to be stronger when we have been deprived longer. We are hungrier when we haven't eaten for ten hours than one hour.

Psychological needs for approval, achievement, and belonging also give rise to drives. We can have a drive to get ahead in the business world just as we have a drive to eat. Psychologists are working to learn more about the origins of these drives. We do know that we can also be driven to obtain *incentives*. An **incentive** is an object, a person, or a situation that can satisfy a need or is desirable for its own sake. Money, food, a sexually attractive person, social approval, and attention can all act as incentives.

LO² Theories of Motivation

Although psychologists agree that it is important to understand why humans and lower animals do things, they do not agree about the precise nature of motivation. Let us consider various theoretical perspectives on motivation.

The Evolutionary Perspective

The evolutionary perspective notes that many animals are neurally "prewired"—that is, born with preprogrammed tendencies—to respond to certain situations in certain ways. Spiders spin webs instinctively. Bees "dance" instinctively to communicate the location of food to other bees.

These instinctive behaviors are found in particular species. They are *species-specific. What is meant by species-specific behaviors?* **Species-specific** behaviors are also called **instincts** and are inborn. They are genetically transmitted from generation to generation.

Psychologists have asked whether humans have instincts, and if so, how many. A century ago, psychologists William James (1890) and William McDougall (1908) argued that humans have instincts that foster survival and social behavior. James numbered love, sympathy, and modesty as social instincts. McDougall compiled twelve "basic" instincts, including hunger, sex, and self-assertion. Other psychologists have made longer lists, and still others deny that

Spiders spin webs instinctively

people have instincts. The question of whether people have instincts—and what they might be—remains unresolved.

Drive-Reductionism and Homeostasis

Sigmund Freud believed that tension motivates us to behave in ways that restore us to a resting state. His views are similar to those of the drive-reduction theory of learning, as set forth by psychologist Clark Hull in the 1930s. *What is drive-reduction theory?*

According to Hull, *primary drives* such as hunger, thirst, and pain trigger arousal (tension) and activate behavior. We learn to engage in behaviors that reduce the tension. We also acquire drives—called *acquired drives*—through experience. We may acquire a drive for money because money enables us to obtain food, drink, and homes, which protect us from crime and extremes of temperature. We might acquire drives for social approval and affiliation because other people, and their goodwill, help us reduce primary drives, especially as infants. In all cases, reduction of tension is the goal. Yet some people appear to acquire what could be considered excessive drives for money.

> What motivates children to spend hour after hour playing video games?

They gather money long after their material needs have been met.

Primary drives like hunger are triggered when we are in a state of deprivation. Sensations of hunger motivate us to act in ways that will restore the bodily balance. This tendency to maintain a steady state is called homeostasis. Homeostasis works like a thermostat. When the temperature in a room drops below the set point, the furnace turns on. The furnace stays on until the set point is reached. Similarly, most animals eat until they are no longer hungry. But many people eat "recreationally"—as when they see an appealing dessert—suggesting there is more to eating than drive reduction.

The Search for Stimulation

Physical needs give rise to drives like hunger and thirst. In such cases, we are motivated to *reduce* the tension or stimulation that impinges on us. *Are all motives aimed at the reduction of tension?*

In the case of *stimulus motives,* organisms seek to *increase* stimulation. A study conducted at McGill University in Montreal during the 1950s suggests the importance of sensory stimulation and activity. Some "lucky" students were paid $20 a day (which, with inflation, would now be more like $200) for doing nothing—literally. Would you like to "work" by doing nothing for $200 a day? Don't answer too quickly. According to the results of this study you might not like it at all. In this experiment, student volunteers were placed in quiet cubicles and blindfolded (Bexton et al., 1954). Their arms were bandaged; they could hear nothing but the dull, continuous hum of air conditioning. Many slept for a while, but after a few hours of sensory-deprived wakefulness, most felt bored and irritable. As time went on, many grew more uncomfortable. Many students quit the experiment during the first day despite the financial incentive. Many of those who remained for a few

Fiction

Generally, it is not true that getting away from it all by going on a vacation from all sensory input for a few hours is relaxing.

days found it hard to concentrate on simple problems for days afterward. For many, the experiment did not provide a relaxing vacation. Instead, it produced boredom, discomfort, and disorientation.

Humans and other animals appear motivated to seek novel stimulation. Even when they have been deprived of food, rats may explore unfamiliar arms of mazes rather than head straight for the food source. Animals that have just copulated and thereby reduced their primary sex drives often show renewed interest in sex when presented with a novel sex partner. People (and nonhumans) take in more calories at buffets and smorgasbords than when fewer kinds of food are available (Raynor & Epstein, 2001). Children spend hour after hour playing video games for the pleasure of zapping virtual people or monsters. Infants play with "busy boxes"—boxes filled with objects that honk, squeak, rattle, and buzz when manipulated in certain ways. Finding ways to control the gadgets is apparently reinforcing, even though learning is not rewarded with desserts or parental hugs.

Stimulus motives provide an evolutionary advantage. Animals that are active and motivated to explore and manipulate their environment are more likely to survive. If you know where the nearest tall tree is, you're more likely to escape a leopard and transmit your genes to future generations.

Humanistic Theory

Humanistic psychologists such as Abraham Maslow (1908–1970) suggest that human behavior is more than mechanical and more than aimed toward tension-reduction and survival. *How does humanistic theory differ from other theories of motivation?* Maslow believed that people are also motivated by a conscious desire for personal growth. Humanists note that people tolerate pain, hunger, and many other kinds of tension to seek personal fulfillment.

Maslow believed that we are separated from other animals by our capacity for **self-actualization**, or self-initiated striving to become what we believe we are capable of being. Maslow considered self-actualization to be as vital a need in humans as hunger. The need for self-actualization pushes people to strive to become concert pianists, chief executive officers, or best-selling authors—even when they have plenty of money to live on.

Maslow (1970) organized human needs into a hierarchy. *What is Maslow's hierarchy of needs?* Maslow's hierarchy ranges from physiological needs such as hunger and thirst, through self-actualization (see Figure 9.1). He believed that we naturally strive to climb this hierarchy.

Critics of Maslow's theory argue that there is too much individual variation for the hierarchy of motives to apply to everyone. Some people whose physiological, safety, and love needs are met show little interest in achievement and recognition. And some artists devote themselves fully to their craft, even if they have to pass up the comforts of a warm home or alienate their families.

Cognitive Perspectives on Motivation

Cognitive theorists note that people represent their worlds mentally. As in Piaget's cognitive developmental theory, they see people as natural scientists who strive to understand the world so that they can predict and control events. Therefore, people try to eliminate inconsistencies—or, as we saw in the case of the Seekers at the beginning of the chapter—discrepancies in information so that their ability to make sense of the world remains whole.

Children also attempt to create consistency between their own gender and what experience teaches them that boys and girls are expected to do in their cultural settings. As soon as they come to understand whether they are male or female, they begin to imitate the behavior of older people of the same gender (Ruble et al., 2006). According to cognitive-dissonance theory, people are generally motivated to hold consistent beliefs and to justify their behavior. That is why we are generally more likely to appreciate what we must work to obtain.

Each theory of motivation may have something to offer. Drive-reduction theory may explain why we drink when thirsty, but stimulus motives might explain why we go clubbing and drink alcohol. Each theory might apply to certain aspects of behavior. As the chapter progresses, we will describe research that lends support to each theory. Let us first consider the hunger drive. Hunger is based on physiological needs, and drive reduction would appear to explain some—although not all—eating behavior. Then we consider two powerful motives that push us ahead in life and sometimes to the front of the line: aggression and achievement. Psychologist Henry Murray (1938) called aggression and achievement social motives. He believed that people acquired aggressive and achievement-oriented behavior patterns to meet psychological needs. But evolutionary psychologists believe that "genetic whisperings" also influence aggression, achievement, and other aspects of personality and social behavior (Buss, 2003; Plomin, 2002).

Figure 9.1

Maslow's Hierarchy of Needs

Maslow believed we progress toward higher psychological needs once basic survival needs have been met. Where do you fit in this picture?

Go to CourseMate for PSYCH at www.cengagebrain.com to access an interactive version of this figure.

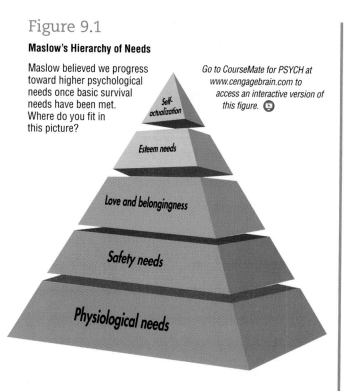

LO³ Hunger

We need food to survive, but food means more than survival. Food is a symbol of family togetherness and caring. We associate food with the nurturance of the parent–child relationship, with visits home on holidays. Friends and relatives offer us food when we enter their homes, and saying no may be viewed as a personal rejection. Bacon and eggs, coffee with cream and sugar, meat and mashed potatoes—all seem to be part of sharing American values and abundance. *How is the hunger drive regulated?*

Biological Influences on Hunger

In considering the bodily mechanisms that regulate hunger, let us begin with the mouth. (After all, we are talking about eating.) After we chew and swallow a certain amount, we receive signals of satiety. We also get signals of satiety from the digestive tract, although these signals take longer to reach the brain.

To demonstrate that chewing and swallowing provide feelings of satiety, researchers conducted classic "sham feeding" experiments with dogs. They implanted a tube in the animals' throats so that any food swallowed fell out of the body. Even though no food reached the stomach, the animals stopped feeding after a while (Janowitz & Grossman, 1949). The dogs in the study, however, resumed feeding

© 2007 JUPITERIMAGES

sooner than animals whose food did reach the stomach. Let us proceed to the stomach, too, as we seek further regulatory factors in hunger.

An empty stomach leads to stomach contractions, which we call *hunger pangs*. Classic research suggested that stomach contractions are crucial to hunger. A man (A. L. Washburn) swallowed a balloon that was inflated in his stomach. His stomach contractions squeezed the balloon, so the contractions could be recorded by observers. Washburn also pressed a key when he felt hungry, and the researchers found a correspondence between his stomach contractions and his feelings of hunger (Cannon & Washburn, 1912).

Medical observations and classic research find that humans and nonhumans whose stomachs have been removed still regulate food intake so as to maintain a normal weight (Tsang, 1938). (Food is absorbed through their intestines.) This finding led to the discovery of other mechanisms that regulate hunger, including the hypothalamus, blood sugar level, and receptors in the liver. When we are deprived of food, the level of sugar in the blood drops. The drop is communicated to the hypothalamus, which stokes the hunger drive.

Two parts of the hypothalamus have been found to be important to the hunger drive. When a

We know that pizza can taste good, but what other factors contribute to her eating?

ventromedial nucleus (VMN) a central area on the underside of the hypothalamus that appears to function as a stop-eating center

hyperphagic characterized by excessive eating

lateral hypothalamus an area at the side of the hypothalamus that appears to function as a start-eating center

aphagic characterized by undereating

researcher destroys the ventromedial nucleus (VMN) of a rat's hypothalamus during surgery, the rat will grope toward food as soon as its eyes open. Then it eats vast quantities of Purina Rat Chow or whatever. The VMN seems to be able to function like a "stop-eating center" in the rat's brain. If the VMN is electrically stimulated—that is, "switched on"—the rat stops eating until the current is turned off. When the VMN is destroyed, the rat becomes hyperphagic (see Figure 9.2). That is, it continues to eat until it has about doubled its normal weight. Then it will level off its eating rate and maintain the higher weight. It is as if the set point of the stop-eating center has been raised to a higher level. Some people develop tumors near the base of the brain that damage the VMN and apparently lead them to overeat (Miller, 1995).

The lateral hypothalamus may function like a "start-eating center" by producing hormones that signal the rat to eat (Chua, 2004). If you destroy the lateral hypothalamus, the rat may stop eating altogether—that is, become aphagic.

Psychological Influences on Hunger

Although many areas of the body work in concert to regulate the hunger drive, this is only part of the story. In human beings, the hunger drive is more complex. Psychological as well as physiological factors play an important role. How many times have you been made hungry by the sight or aroma of food? How many times have you eaten not because you were hungry but because you were at a relative's home or hanging around a cafeteria or coffee shop? Or because you felt anxious or depressed? Or simply because you were bored? One study confirmed what most of us already assumed—that watching television increases the amount of food we eat (Higgs & Woodward, 2009). One reason is that watching television can distract us from bodily changes that signal fullness and from cognitive awareness of how much we have already eaten. The same reason seems to hold true for gorging on popcorn, candy, and soft drinks at the movies. Watching television also interferes with memory formation of how much we have eaten, making us vulnerable to overeating at subsequent meals.

Obesity: A Serious and Pervasive Problem

Consider some facts about obesity:

- More than two out of three adult Americans are overweight, and one in three is obese (Flegal et al., 2010).

- Problems with unhealthy weight gain have been on the upswing in the United States; for example, 68% of Americans were overweight in 2008 as compared with 60% in 1988–1994 (Flegal et al., 2010).

- More than 78% of African American women and 81% of Latina Americans, age 40 and above, are overweight, and about half are obese (Flegal et al., 2010).

- Obesity is a risk in various chronic medical conditions including diabetes, hypertension (high blood pressure), high cholesterol levels, stroke, heart disease, some cancers, and arthritis (Flegal et al., 2010).

Figure 9.2

A Hyperphagic Rat

This rodent winner of the basketball look-alike contest went on a binge after it received a lesion in the ventromedial nucleus (VMN) of the hypothalamus. It is as if the lesion pushed the "set point" for the body weight up several notches; the rat's weight is now about five times normal. But now it eats only enough to maintain its pleasantly plump figure, so you need not be concerned that it will eventually burst. If the lesion had been made in the lateral hypothalamus, the animal might have become the Calista Flockhart of the rat world.

DR. NEAL MILLER/YALE UNIVERSITY

Table 9.1

Years of Life Lost by an Extremely Obese, Non-smoking, 40-year-old, Compared with a Normal-Weight Person of the Same Age

	European American	African American
Male	9	8
Female	7	5

Source of data: Finkelstein, E. A., Brown, D. S., Wrage, L. A., Allaire, B. T. & Hoerger, T. J. (2010). Individual and Aggregate Years-of-life-lost Associated with Overweight and Obesity. *Obesity, 18*(2), 333–339.

© 2010 MARK ANDERSEN/ JUPITERIMAGES CORPORATION

• Weight control is elusive for most people, who regain most of the weight they have lost, even when they have dieted "successfully" (Apovian, 2010; Heber, 2010).

American culture idealizes slender heroes and heroines. For those who want to "measure up" to TV and film idols, food may have replaced sex as the central source of guilt. Obese people encounter more than their fair share of health problems, including hypertension, heart disease, diabetes, gallbladder disease, osteoarthritis, sleep apnea and respiratory problems, and certain kinds of cancer (Centers for Disease Control and Prevention, 2005a). A study using data collected by the federal government found that severely obese young adults (those with a BMI above 45) live shorter lives than people who are normal in weight (Fontaine et al., 2003; see Table 9.1). With all the health problems connected to obesity, why are so many people obese?

Origins of Obesity

Many biological and psychological factors are involved in obesity. Overweight runs in families. Studies of monkeys (Kavanagh et al., 2007) and of human twins (Silventoinen et al., 2007) suggest there are strong roles for heredity. Efforts by overweight and obese people to maintain a slender profile may be sabotaged by an adaptive mechanism that would help preserve life in times of famine—*adaptive thermogenesis*. This mechanism causes the body to produce less energy (burn fewer calories) when someone goes on a diet (Major et al., 2007). This does not mean that overweight people will not lose weight by dieting; it means that it will take longer than expected.

Fatty tissue in the body also metabolizes (burns) food more slowly than muscle. For this reason, a person with a high fat-to-muscle ratio metabolizes food more slowly than a person of the same weight with more muscle. That is, two people of the same weight may metabolize food at different rates, depending on their distribution of muscle and fat. The average man is 40% muscle and 15% fat, whereas the average woman is 23% muscle and 25% fat. Therefore, if a typical man and woman are equal in weight, the woman has to eat less to maintain that weight.

Psychological factors, such as observational learning, stress, and emotional states also contribute to obesity. People in the United States are exposed to thousands of food commercials a year—many of them for fatty fast foods, sweetened cereals, and sugar-laden soft drinks. Situations such as family celebrations, watching TV, arguments, and tension at work can all lead to overeating or falling off a diet (Fletcher et al., 2007). Negative emotions such as depression and anxiety can trigger binge eating (Reas & Grilo, 2007).

anorexia nervosa a life-threatening eating disorder characterized by dramatic weight loss and a distorted body image

Eating Disorders

The *eating disorders* are characterized by persistent, gross disturbances in eating patterns. In this section we focus on an eating disorder in which individuals are too thin, *anorexia nervosa*, and one in which the person may be normal in weight, but certainly not in the methods used to maintain that weight—*bulimia nervosa*.

Consider some facts about eating and eating disorders in the United States, as reported by the National Eating Disorders Association (2010):

— Over half of teenage girls and nearly one-third of teenage boys use unhealthful methods to try to control their weight, including fasting, skipping meals, smoking cigarettes, vomiting, and using laxatives.

— About two out of five first to third grade girls would like to be thinner.

— More than four out of five 10-year-old girls report fear of being fat.

— Nearly half of 9- to 11-year old girls are "sometimes" or "very often" dieting.

— More than 90% of college women have dieted at some time.

Anorexia Nervosa

Anorexia nervosa is a life-threatening eating disorder characterized by extreme fear of being too heavy, dramatic weight loss, a distorted body image, and resistance to eating enough to reach or maintain a healthful weight.

© 2010 BRAND X PICTURES / JUPITERIMAGES CORPORATION

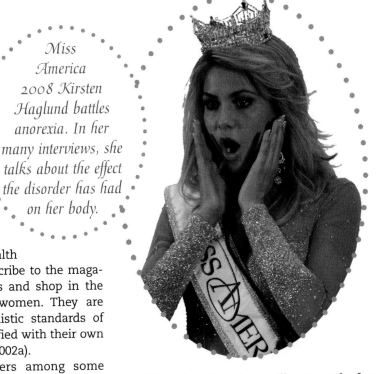

Miss America 2008 Kirsten Haglund battles anorexia. In her many interviews, she talks about the effect the disorder has had on her body.

STEVE MARCUS/REUTERS/LANDOV

Anorexia nervosa mostly afflicts women during adolescence and young adulthood. The typical person with anorexia is a young European American female of higher socioeconomic status (McLaren, 2002).

Affluent females have greater access to fitness centers and health clubs and are more likely to subscribe to the magazines that idealize slender bodies and shop in the boutiques that cater to svelte women. They are regularly confronted with unrealistic standards of slimness that make them dissatisfied with their own figures (Neumark-Sztainer et al., 2002a).

We also find eating disorders among some males, particularly among males who are compelled by their chosen activities—for example, wrestling or dancing—to keep their weight at a certain limit (Bailey, 2003a; Goode, 2000). But women with these disorders outnumber men who have them by more than six to one (Striegel-Moore & Cachelin, 2001).

Females with anorexia nervosa can drop 25% or more of their weight within a year. Severe weight loss can prevent ovulation and cause general health to deteriorate. Females with anorexia are also at risk for premature development of osteoporosis (Jacoangeli et al., 2002). Given these problems, the mortality rate for females with anorexia nervosa is approximately 5%.

In one common pattern, the girl sees that she has gained some weight after reaching puberty, and she resolves that she must lose it. But even after the weight is gone, she maintains her pattern of dieting and, in many cases, exercises at a fever pitch. This pattern continues as she plunges below her "desirable" weight. Girls with the disorder are in denial about health problems; some point to feverish exercise routines as evidence of strength. Distortion of the body image is a major feature of the disorder (Striegel-Moore et al., 2004).

Bulimia Nervosa

Bulimia nervosa entails repeated cycles of binge eating and purging. Binge eating often follows efforts to diet (Corwin, 2000). There are various methods of purging, including vomiting, strict dieting or fasting, laxatives, and prolonged exercise. Individuals with eating disorders will not settle for less than their idealized body shape and weight. Bulimia, like anorexia, triggers hormonal imbalances: One study found that nearly half of women with bulimia nervosa have irregular menstrual cycles (Gendall et al., 2000). Bulimia nervosa, like anorexia nervosa, tends to afflict mainly women during adolescence and young adulthood (Lewinsohn et al., 2000b).

Origins of the Eating Disorders

What are the origins of the eating disorders? Health professionals have done a great deal of research into the origins of eating disorders, but they admit that many questions about them remain unanswered (Striegel-Moore & Cachelin, 2001).

Many parents are obsessed with getting their children—especially their infants—to eat. Thus some psychologists suggest that children may use refusal to eat as a way of resisting or punishing parents. ("You have to eat something!" "I'm not hungry!") Parents in such families often have issues with eating and dieting themselves. They also "act out" against their daughters—letting them know that they consider them unattractive and that they should slim down (Baker et al., 2000; Cooper et al., 2001).

A particularly disturbing risk factor for eating disorders in adolescent females is a history of child abuse, particularly sexual abuse (Ackard et al., 2001; Leonard et al., 2003). One study found a history of childhood sexual abuse in about half of women with bulimia nervosa, as opposed to a rate of about 7% among women without the disorder (Deep et al., 1999).

The sociocultural climate also affects eating behavior (Williams et al., 2003). Slimness is idealized in the United States. When you check out current fashion magazines and catalogs, you are looking at models who, on average, are 9% taller and 16% thinner than the typical female—and who still manage to have ample bustlines. Miss America, the annually renewed American role model, has also been slenderizing across the years. Over the past eighty years, the winner has added only 2% in height but has lost twelve pounds in weight. In the 1920s, Miss America's weight relative to her height yielded a Body Mass Index (BMI) of 20 to 25, which is considered normal by the World Health Organization (WHO). WHO labels people as malnourished when their BMIs are lower than 18.5. Recent Miss Americas, however, come in at a BMI near 17 (Rubinstein & Caballero, 2000). So Miss America adds to the woes of "normal" young women.

As the cultural ideal slenderizes, women with average body weights according to the health charts feel overweight, and more-than-average women feel gargantuan (Utter et al., 2003; Williams et al., 2003).

Truth

It is true that fashion magazines can contribute to eating disorders among women.

LO⁴ Sexual Motivation

What triggers the sex drive? Many factors contribute to the sex drive. People vary greatly in the cues that excite them sexually and in the frequency with which they experience sexual thoughts and feelings. Sex hormones and cultural beliefs also influence sexual behavior and the pleasure people find—or do not find—in sex. Sexual motivation may be natural, but this natural function is strongly influenced by religious and moral beliefs, cultural tradition, folklore, and superstition.

Regardless of our ethnicity, our levels of education, and cultural influences, our sex drives are connected with sex hormones. *What are the effects of sex hormones on sexual motivation?*

Hormones and Sexual Motivation

Sex hormones can be said to fuel the sex drive. Research with men who produce little testosterone—due to age or health problems—shows that their sex drive increases when they receive testosterone replacement therapy (Seidman, 2003). The most common sexual problem among women is lack of sexual desire or interest, and the sex drive in women is also connected to testosterone levels (Apperloo et al., 2003). Although men produce ten to twenty times the testosterone produced by women, women produce androgens ("male" sex hormones) in the adrenal glands. Testosterone injections, patches, or pills can heighten the sex drive in women who do not produce enough of the hormone (Van Anders et al., 2005).

Sex hormones promote the development of male and female sex organs and regulate the menstrual cycle. They also have activating and organizing effects on sexual behavior. **Activating effects** involve the sex drive. Female mice, rats, cats, and dogs are receptive to males only during **estrus**, when female sex hormones are plentiful. During estrus, female rats respond to males by hopping, wiggling their ears, and arching their backs with their tails to one side, thus enabling males to penetrate them. Sex hormones also have directional or **organizing effects**. That is, they predispose lower animals toward stereotypical masculine or feminine mating patterns. Sex hormones are thus likely candidates for influencing the development of sexual orientation (Lalumière et al., 2000).

Sex hormones may further "masculinize" or "feminize" the brain by creating predispositions consistent with some gender-role tendencies (Collaer & Hines, 1995; Crews, 1994). For example, male rats are generally superior to females in maze-learning ability, a task that requires spatial skills. But female rats that are exposed to androgens in the uterus (e.g., because they have several male siblings in the uterus with them) or soon after birth learn maze routes as rapidly as males (Vandenbergh, 1993).

Sexual Response

What happens to the body when people are sexually aroused? Men show more interest in sex than women do (Peplau, 2003). Women are more likely to want to combine sex with a romantic relationship (Fisher, 2000). A survey of more than 1,000 undergraduates found that men reported being more interested than women in casual sex and multiple sex partners (Schmitt et al., 2001).

activating effect
the arousal-producing effects of sex hormones that increase the likelihood of sexual behavior

estrus
the periodic sexual excitement of many female mammals, as governed by levels of sex hormones

organizing effect
the directional effect of sex hormones—for example, along stereotypically masculine or feminine lines

sexual response cycle
Masters and Johnson's model of sexual response, which consists of four stages or phases

vasocongestion
engorgement of blood vessels with blood, which swells the genitals and breasts during sexual arousal

myotonia
muscle tension

excitement phase
the first phase of the sexual response cycle, which is characterized by muscle tension, increases in the heart rate, and erection in the male and vaginal lubrication in the female

plateau phase
the second phase of the sexual response cycle, which is characterized by increases in vasocongestion, muscle tension, heart rate, and blood pressure in preparation for orgasm

ejaculation
propulsion of seminal fluid (semen) from the penis by contraction of muscles at the base of the penis

orgasm
the height or climax of sexual excitement, involving involuntary muscle contractions, release of sexual tensions, and, usually, subjective feelings of pleasure

resolution phase
the fourth phase of the sexual response cycle, during which the body gradually returns to its prearoused state

refractory period
in the sexual response cycle, a period of time following orgasm during which an individual is not responsive to sexual stimulation

Although we may be more culturally attuned to focus on sex differences rather than similarities, William Masters and Virginia Johnson (1966) found that the biological responses of males and females to sexual stimulation are quite similar. Masters and Johnson use the term *sexual response cycle* to describe the changes that occur in the body as men and women become sexually aroused. They divide the sexual response cycle into four phases: *excitement, plateau, orgasm,* and *resolution.*

The cycle is characterized by *vasocongestion* and *myotonia*. Vasocongestion is the swelling of the genital tissues with blood, causing erection of the penis and swelling of the area surrounding the vaginal opening. The testes and the nipples swell as blood vessels dilate in these areas. Myotonia is muscle tension, which causes grimaces, spasms in the hands and feet, and the spasms of orgasm.

Erection, vaginal lubrication, and orgasm are all reflexes. That is, they occur automatically in response to adequate sexual stimulation.

Excitement Phase

Vasocongestion during the excitement phase can cause erection in young men within a few seconds after sexual stimulation begins. The scrotal skin thickens, becoming less baggy. The testes increase in size and become elevated.

In the female, excitement is characterized by vaginal lubrication, which may start 10 to 30 seconds after sexual stimulation begins. Vasocongestion swells the clitoris and flattens and spreads the vaginal lips. The inner part of the vagina expands. The breasts enlarge, and blood vessels near the surface become more prominent. The nipples may erect in both men and women. Heart rate and blood pressure increase.

Plateau Phase

The level of sexual arousal remains somewhat stable during the plateau phase. Because of vasocongestion, the circumference of the head of the penis increases somewhat. The testes are elevated into position for ejaculation and may reach one-and-a-half times their unaroused size.

In women, vasocongestion swells the outer part of the vagina, contracting the vaginal opening in preparation for grasping the penis. The inner part of the vagina expands further. The clitoris withdraws beneath the clitoral hood and shortens.

Breathing becomes rapid, like panting. Heart rate may increase to 100 to 160 beats per minute. Blood pressure continues to rise.

Orgasmic Phase

During orgasm in the male, muscle contractions propel semen from the body. Sensations of pleasure tend to be related to the strength of the contractions and the amount of seminal fluid. The first three to four contractions are generally most intense and occur at 0.8-second intervals (five contractions every four seconds). Additional contractions are slower.

Orgasm in the female is manifested by three to fifteen contractions of the pelvic muscles that surround the vaginal barrel. The contractions first occur at 0.8-second intervals. Weaker and slower contractions follow.

Blood pressure and heart rate reach a peak, with the heart beating up to 180 times per minute. Respiration may increase to forty breaths per minute.

Resolution Phase

In the resolution phase, after orgasm, the body returns to its unaroused state. Erection and clitoral swelling subside. Blood pressure, heart rate, and breathing return to normal levels.

Unlike women, men enter a refractory period during which they cannot experience another orgasm or ejaculate. The refractory period of adolescent males may last only minutes, whereas that of men age fifty and above may last from hours to a day. Women do not undergo a refractory period and therefore can become quickly rearoused to the point of repeated (multiple) orgasm if they desire and receive continued sexual stimulation.

The sexual response cycle describes what happens when females and males are exposed to sexual stimulation. But what kinds of sexual experiences do people seek? How many sex partners do they have? Who are their partners? *What do we know about the sex lives of people in the United States?*

Surveys of Sexual Behavior

The well-known Kinsey reports (Kinsey et al., 1948, 1953) interviewed 5,300 males and 5,940 females in the United States between 1938 and 1949. Interviewers asked about sexual experiences including masturbation, oral sex, and premarital sex. The nation was astounded to learn that most males masturbated and had had sexual intercourse prior to marriage. Moreover, significant minorities of females reported these behaviors. But Kinsey had not obtained a random sample of the population. His samples underrepresented people of color, people in rural areas, older people, poor people, Catholics, and Jews. There is thus no way of knowing whether or not Kinsey's results accurately mirrored general American sexual behavior at the time. But the *relationships* Kinsey uncovered, such as the positive link between level of education and premarital sex, may be accurate enough.

A more recent survey—the National Health and Social Life Survey (NHSLS)—interviewed 3,432 people (Laumann et al., 1994) and may provide our most accurate information. Of this number, 3,159 were English-speaking adults aged eighteen to fifty-nine. The other 273 respondents were obtained by purposefully oversampling African American and Hispanic American households to obtain more information about these ethnic groups.

The sample probably represents the overall U.S. adult population quite well, but it may include too few Asian Americans, Native Americans, and Jews to offer much information about these groups. The NHSLS team identified households in various locales and obtained an overall participation rate of close to 80%.

The NHSLS considered the sociocultural factors of sex, level of education, religion, and race/ethnicity in many aspects of people's sexual behavior, including their number of sex partners (see Figure 9.3 on page 198). Males in the survey reported higher numbers of sex partners than females did. For example, one male in three (33%) reported having eleven or more sex partners. This compares with fewer than one woman in ten (9%). On the other hand, most Americans limit their sex partners to a handful or fewer.

Education appears to be a liberating influence on sexual behavior. People with some college, or who have completed college, report more sex partners than those who attended only grade school or high school. Conservative religious experience, on the other hand, acts as a restraint. Liberal Protestants and people who say they have no religion report higher numbers of sex partners than Catholics and more conservative Protestants.

Ethnicity is also connected with sexual behavior. The research findings in Figure 9.3 suggest that European Americans and African Americans have the highest numbers of sex partners. Asian Americans appear to be the most sexually restrained ethnic group.

Sexual Orientation

The great majority of people have a heterosexual orientation; they are sexually attracted to and interested in forming romantic relationships with people of the other sex. Some people, however, have a homosexual orientation; they are attracted to and interested in forming romantic relationships with people of their own sex. Males with a homosexual orientation are referred to as *gay males*. Homosexual females are referred to as *lesbians*. *Bisexual* people are attracted to both females and males.

Surveys find that about 3% of the males and 2% of the females in the United States identify themselves as homosexual (Mosher et al., 2005; Savin-

heterosexual referring to people who are sexually aroused by and interested in forming romantic relationships with people of the other sex

homosexual referring to people who are sexually aroused by and interested in forming romantic relationships with people of the same sex (derived from the Greek *homos*, meaning "same," not from the Latin *homo*, meaning "man")

WALTER LOCKWOOD / GETTY IMAGES

sexual orientation the directionality of one's sexual and romantic interests; that is, whether one is sexually attracted to and desires to form a romantic relationship with members of the other sex or of one's own sex

Williams, 2006). However, it is estimated that anywhere from 2% to 10% of the population is gay male or lesbian (Martins et al., 2005). Theories of the origins of sexual orientation look both at nature and nurture—the biological makeup of the individual and environmental influences. Several theories bridge the two. *What do we know about the origins of gay male and lesbian sexual orientations?*

Learning theorists look for the roles of factors such as reinforcement and observational learning. From this perspective, reinforcement of sexual behavior with members of one's own sex—as in reaching orgasm with them when members of the other sex are unavailable—might affect one's sexual orientation. Similarly, childhood sexual abuse by someone of the same sex could lead to fantasies about sex with people of one's own sex and affect sexual orientation. Observation of others engaged in enjoyable male–male or female–female sexual encounters could also affect the development of sexual orientation. But critics point out that most individuals become aware of their sexual orientation before they have sexual contacts with other people of either sex (Laumann et al., 1994). Moreover, in a society that generally condemns homosexuality, young people are unlikely to believe that male–male or female–female contacts will have positive effects for them.

Figure 9.3

Number of Sex Partners as Found in the National Health and Social Life Survey*

	Number of Sex Partners (%)					
	0	1	2–4	5–10	11–20	21+
Gender						
Male	3	20	21	23	16	17
Female	3	32	36	20	6	3
Education						
Less than high school	4	27	36	19	9	6
High school graduate	3	30	29	20	10	7
Some college	2	24	29	23	12	9
College graduate	2	24	26	24	11	13
Advanced degree	4	25	26	23	10	13
Religion						
None	3	16	29	20	16	16
Liberal, moderate Protestant	2	23	31	23	12	8
Conservative Protestant	3	30	30	20	10	7
Catholic	4	27	29	23	8	9
Race/Ethnicity						
European American	3	26	29	22	11	9
African American	2	18	34	24	11	11
Latino and Latina American	3	36	27	17	8	9
Asian American**	6	46	25	14	6	3
Native American**	5	28	35	23	5	5

Source: From Laumann, E. O., Gagnon, J. H., Michael, R. T., & Michaels, S. (1994). The social organization of sexuality: Sexual practices in the United States. Chicago: University of Chicago Press. Copyright © 1994 by University of Chicago Press. Reprinted by permission.
*Conducted by a research team centered at the University of Chicago.
**These sample sizes are quite small.

There is evidence for genetic factors in sexual orientation (Dawood et al., 2000; Kendler et al., 2000c). One study found that 22% of the brothers of fifty-one gay men were gay or bisexual, although one would expect to find only 3% of the brothers to be gay if the relationship were coincidental (Pillard & Weinrich, 1986). Twin studies also support a role for genes. About 52% of identical (MZ) twin pairs are "concordant" (in agreement) for a gay male sexual orientation, as compared with 22% for fraternal (DZ) twins (Bailey & Pillard, 1991).

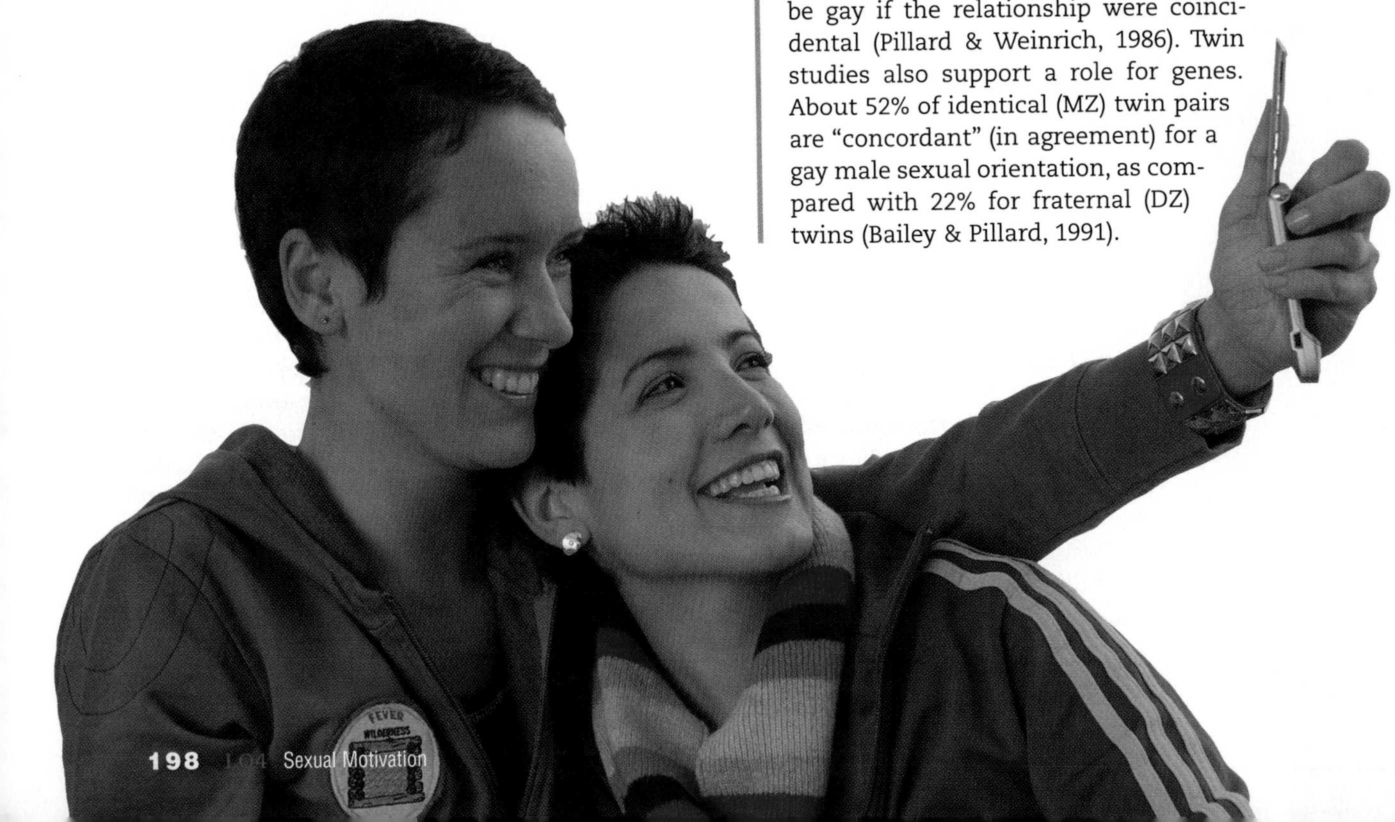

RYAN PIERSE / GETTY IMAGES

In many species, sexual motivation is governed by sex hormones. Are humans ruled by hormones or do social experiences and personal choice come into play?

TITUS LACOSTE/GETTY IMAGES

In many species, there is little room for thinking about sex and deciding whether an individual will pursue sexual relationships with males or females. Sexual motivation comes under the governance of sex hormones (Hill et al., 2005; Holmes et al., 2005). And much sexual motivation is determined by whether the brains and sex organs of fetuses are bathed in large doses of testosterone in the uterus. In male fetuses, testosterone is normally produced by the developing testes. Yet female fetuses are exposed to testosterone when they share the uterus with many male siblings. Researchers have also injected male sex hormones into the uteruses of rodents. When they do, the sex organs of females become masculinized in appearance, and they show a tendency toward masculine-type behavior patterns at maturity, including mating with other females (Crews, 1994).

It has been shown, then, that sex hormones predispose nonhumans to stereotypical masculine or feminine mating patterns. Do sex hormones influence the developing human embryo and fetus as they affect

rodents? We're not sure, but it is possible that the brains of some gay males were feminized in utero and that the brains of some lesbians were masculinized in utero (Collaer & Hines, 1995). We have to conclude by confessing that much about the development of sexual orientation remains speculative.

LO⁵ Achievement Motivation

Many students persist in studying despite being surrounded by distractions. Many people strive relentlessly to get ahead, to "make it," to earn large sums of money, to invent, to accomplish the impossible. *Why do some people strive to get ahead?* Psychological research suggests that these people have *achievement motivation* (Robbins et al., 2005).

Psychologist David McClelland (1958) helped pioneer the assessment of achievement motivation through evaluation of fantasies. One method involves the Thematic Apperception Test (TAT), developed by Henry Murray. The TAT contains cards with pictures and drawings that are subject to various interpretations. Individuals are shown one or more TAT cards and asked to construct stories about the pictured theme: to indicate what led up to it, what the characters are thinking and feeling, and what is likely to happen.

One TAT card is similar to the image shown below. The meaning of the card is ambiguous—unclear. Is the girl sleeping, thinking about the book, wishing she were out with friends?

Consider two stories that could be told about this card:

- *Story 1:* "She's upset that she's got to read the book because she's behind in her assignments and doesn't particularly like to work. She'd much rather be out with her friends, and she may very well sneak out to do just that."

- *Story 2:* "She's thinking, 'Someday I'll be a great scholar. I'll write books like this, and everybody will be proud of me.' She reads all the time."

The second story suggests the presence of more achievement motivation than the first. Classic studies find that people with high achievement motivation earn higher grades than people with comparable learning ability but lower achievement motivation. They are more likely to earn high salaries and be promoted than less motivated people with similar opportunities (Aronoff & Litevin, 1971; Orpen, 1995).

McClelland (1965) used the TAT to sort college students into groups—students with high achievement motivation and students with low achievement motivation. He found that 83% of college graduates with high achievement motivation found jobs in occupations characterized by risk, decision-making, and the chance for great success, such as business management, sales, or self-employment. Most (70%) of the graduates who chose non-entrepreneurial positions showed low achievement motivation. People with high achievement motivation seem to prefer challenges and are willing to take moderate risks to achieve their goals.

Extrinsic Versus Intrinsic Motives

Do you want to do well in this course? If you do, why? Carol Dweck (e.g., Molden & Dweck, 2000) finds that achievement motivation can be driven by performance or learning goals, or both. For example, are you motivated mainly by performance goals, such as your grade in the course? If so, it may be in part because your motives concern tangible rewards such as getting into graduate school, landing a good job, reaping approval from your parents or your instructor, or avoiding criticism. Performance goals are usually met through extrinsic rewards such as praise and income. Research suggests that tangible rewards, such as money, can serve as an incentive for maintaining good grades. These rewards tend to have a more lasting effect, however, when students look upon incentives as signs that they are intelligent and capable (Spencer et al., 2005).

Or is it learning goals that mainly motivate you to do well? That is, is your central motive the enhancing of your knowledge and skills—your ability to understand and master the subject matter? Learning goals usually lead to intrinsic rewards, such as self-satisfaction. Students who develop learning goals often have parents with strong achievement motivation who encourage their children to think and act independently. Parents and teachers help children develop learning goals by showing warmth and praising them for their efforts to learn, exposing them to novel and stimulating experiences, and encouraging persistence (Dweck, 2002a). Children who are stimulated in this way tend to set high standards for themselves, associate their achievements with self-worth, and attribute their achievements to their own efforts rather than to chance or to the intervention of others (Dweck, 2002b; Marshall & Brown, 2004).

Many of us strive to meet both performance and learning goals in our courses as well as in other areas of life. Grades are important because they are connected with tangible benefits, but learning for its own sake is also of value and can provide great pleasure.

LO⁶ Emotion

Emotions color our lives. We are green with envy, red with anger, blue with sorrow. Positive emotions such as love and desire can fill our days with pleasure. Negative emotions such as fear, depression, and anger can fill us with dread and make each day a chore. *Just what is an emotion?*

An emotion can be a response to a situation, in the way that fear is a response to a threat. An emotion can motivate behavior, as anger can motivate us to act aggressively. An emotion can also be a goal in itself. We may behave in ways that will lead us to experience happiness or love. Emotions are thus intertwined with motivation. We are driven by emotions, and meeting—or failing to meet—our needs can have powerful emotional results.

Emotions are defined as feeling states with physiological, cognitive, and behavioral components (Carlson & Hatfield, 1992). Strong emotions arouse the autonomic nervous system (Gomez et al., 2005; see Chapter 2). The greater the arousal, the more intense the emotion. It also appears that the type of arousal affects the emotion being experienced. Although the word *emotion* might seem to be about feeling and not about thinking, cognitions—particularly interpretations of the meanings of events—are important aspects of emotions. *Fear,* which usually occurs in response to a threat, involves cognitions that one is in danger as well as arousal of the sympathetic nervous system (e.g., rapid heartbeat and breathing, sweating, muscle tension). Emotions also involve behavioral tendencies. Fear is connected with behavioral tendencies to avoid or escape a situation (see Table 9.2). As a response to a social provocation, *anger* involves cognitions that the provocateur should be paid back, arousal of both the sympathetic and

Figure 9.4

Photographs Used in Research by Paul Ekman

Ekman's research suggests that the facial expressions connected with several important emotions such as happiness, anger, surprise, and fear are universally recognized.

© 1976 PAUL EKMAN/HUMAN INTERACTION LABORATORY

parasympathetic nervous systems, and tendencies to attack. *Depression* usually involves cognitions of helplessness and hopelessness, parasympathetic arousal, and tendencies toward inactivity—or sometimes self-destruction. *Happiness, grief, jealousy, disgust, embarrassment, liking*—all have cognitive, physiological, and behavioral components.

The Expression of Emotions

Happiness and sadness are found in all cultures, but, *How can we tell when other people are happy or sad?* It turns out that the expression of many emotions may be universal (Ekman, 2003). Smiling is apparently a universal sign of friendliness and approval. Baring the teeth, as noted by Charles Darwin (1872) in the 19th century, may be a universal sign of anger. As the originator of the theory of evolution, Darwin believed that the universal recognition of facial expressions would have survival value. In the absence of language, facial expressions could signal the approach of enemies (or friends).

Table 9.2

Components of Emotions

Emotion	Physiological	Cognitive	Behavioral
Fear	Sympathetic arousal	Belief that one is in danger	Avoidance tendencies
Anger	Sympathetic and parasympathetic arousal	Frustration or belief that one is being mistreated	Attack tendencies
Depression	Parasympathetic arousal	Thoughts of helplessness, hopelessness, worthlessness	Inactivity, possible self-destructive tendencies

Most investigators (e.g., Ekman, 2003; Izard, 1994) concur that certain facial expressions suggest the same emotions in all people. Moreover, people in diverse cultures recognize the emotions indicated by certain facial expressions. Paul Ekman (1999) describes his classic research in which he took photographs of people exhibiting anger, disgust, fear, happiness, sadness, and surprise (see Figure 9.4). He then asked people around the world to say what emotions were being depicted. Those queried ranged from European college students to members of the Fore, a tribe that dwells in the New Guinea highlands.

All groups, including the Fore, who had almost no contact with Western culture, agreed on the emotions. The Fore also displayed familiar facial expressions when asked how they would respond if they were the characters in stories that called for basic emotional responses. Ekman and his colleagues (1987) obtained similar results in a study of ten cultures. In that study, participants were allowed to identify more than one emotion in facial expressions. The participants generally agreed on which two emotions were being shown and which emotion was more intense.

On the other hand, there is no perfect one-to-one relationship between facial expressions and emotions. Facial expressions sometimes occur in the absence of the emotion they are thought to accompany (Camras, 2000). As noted by psychologist Joseph Campos (2000), the voice, posture, and gestures also provide clues to what people are feeling and are about to do.

parasympathetic nervous system the branch of the autonomic nervous system that is most active during processes that restore reserves of energy to the body, such as relaxing and eating

Positive Psychology

Ted Lewis, the Great Depression–era bandleader, used to begin his act by asking, "Is evvvvrybody happy?" Well, everybody is not happy, but surveys do suggest that most people in developed nations are satisfied with their lives (Cummins & Nistico, 2002). Many people might think that psychologists are interested only in negative emotions such as anxiety, depression, and anger. Not at all. An area of psychology called positive psychology deals with positive emotions such as happiness and love, optimism and hope, and joy and sensual pleasures.

What factors contribute to happiness? Are some people just "born happy" or do life experiences determine happiness? What factors interfere with happiness? Some psychologists, such as David Lykken (Lykken & Csikszentmihalyi, 2001), believe that genetic factors play a powerful role in happiness. They note that happiness tends to run in families and that we tend to have a more or less stable level of happiness throughout much of our lives. Positive events such as learning that the person we love also loves us, having a loved one support our goals, or recognition at work can certainly raise our level of happiness at the moment (Feeney, 2004). Similarly, negative life events, such as the loss of a loved one, financial reverses, or injuries can depress us—and understandably so. Yet we may tend to bounce back to a more or less characteristic level of happiness, as did the actor Christopher Reeve following the accident—being thrown from a horse—that paralyzed him.

Which life experiences contribute to happiness? U.S. surveys reveal more evidence for a role for social and socioeconomic factors in happiness. For example, European Americans tend to be happier than African Americans, and well-educated people tend to be happier than those who are not (Easterlin, 2001). The persistence of differences according to race and education suggests that socioeconomic circumstances are in fact important contributors to happiness (Easterlin, 2001). Money might not make people happy in itself, but when we have enough money, at least we don't have to worry about money (Cummins, 2000).

People who are married (Tsou & Liu, 2001) and who have social support tend to be happier than "loners" (Feeney, 2004). Happy people also tend to be open to new experiences; they are more willing to risk becoming involved in new relationships (Rath, 2002).

Research has also suggested that religious people are happier than those who are not, as was found to be the case in studies of Americans, Chinese people, and Israelis (Francis et al., 2004; Swinyard et al., 2001). The Swinyard study found that one's inner life—one's feeling of connectedness to important things outside oneself—was found to be a greater contributor to happiness than material possessions. Chinese college students tend to think about happiness in terms of feelings of contentment, inner harmony, personal achievement, physical wellness, spiritual enrichment, hopefulness about the future, generosity, and self-development (Lu, 2001).

Then there are the attitudinal aspects of happiness (Cheng & Furnham, 2001; Cummins & Nistico, 2002). People at any income level can make themselves miserable when they compare their incomes to those who bring in more money (Stutzer, 2004). Happiness also tends to be accompanied by optimism—a cognitive bias toward assuming that things will work out (Diener et al., 2000; Keyes & Haidt, 2003). But the "bias" is not groundless, because happy people often believe in their ability to effect change. Thus, they try harder. They are also willing to pat themselves on the back for their successes and are not quick to blame themselves when things go wrong—attitudes that contribute to self-esteem, another factor in happiness.

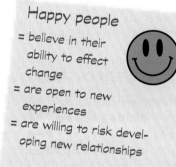

Happy people
= believe in their ability to effect change
= are open to new experiences
= are willing to risk developing new relationships

Fiction

Despite the saying that "money can't buy you happiness," surveys in the United States, Russia, China, and Latin America suggest that people tend to be happier when they live in affluent societies or earn decent incomes (Lever, 2004; Schyns, 2001).

The Facial-Feedback Hypothesis

The face has a special place among visual stimuli. Social animals like humans need to be able to differentiate and recognize members of their group, and in people, the face is the most distinctive key to identity (Parr et al., 2000). Faces are also a key to social communication. Facial expressions reflect emotional states, and our ability to "read" these expressions enables us to interact appropriately with other people.

It is known that various emotional states give rise to certain patterns of electrical activity in the facial muscles and in the brain (Cacioppo et al., 1988). But can it work the other way around? The facial-feedback hypothesis argues that facial expressions can also affect our emotional state. *Can smiling give rise to feelings of goodwill? Can frowning produce anger?* Perhaps they can.

Psychological research has yielded some interesting findings concerning the facial feedback hypothesis. Inducing people to smile, for example, leads them to report more positive feelings and to rate cartoons as more humorous (Soussignan, 2002). When induced to frown, they rate cartoons as more aggressive. When people exhibit pain through facial expressions, they rate electric shocks as more painful.

facial-feedback hypothesis
the view that stereotypical facial expressions can contribute to stereotypical emotions

What are the possible links between facial feedback and emotion? One is arousal. Intense contraction of facial muscles such as those used in signifying fear heightens arousal, which, in turn, boosts emotional response. Feedback from the contraction of facial muscles may also induce emotions. Engaging in the "Duchenne smile," characterized by "crow's feet wrinkles around the eyes and a subtle drop in the eye cover fold so that the skin above the eye moves down slightly toward the eyeball" (Ekman, 2003) can induce pleasant feelings (Soussignan, 2002).

You may have heard the British expression "Keep a stiff upper lip" as a recommendation for handling stress. It might be that a "stiff" lip suppresses emotional response—as long as the lip is relaxed rather than quivering with fear or tension. But when the lip is stiffened through strong muscle tension, facial feedback may heighten emotional response.

Smiling is usually a response to feeling good within, but experimental research into the facial-feedback hypothesis suggests that the act of smiling can also enhance our moods.

Theories of Emotion

David, 32, is not sleeping well. He wakes before dawn and cannot get back to sleep. His appetite is off, his energy level is low, and he has started smoking again. He has a couple of drinks at lunch and muses that it's lucky that any more alcohol makes him sick to his stomach—otherwise, he'd probably be drinking too much, too. Then he thinks, "So what difference would it make?" Sometimes he is sexually frustrated; at other times he wonders whether he has any sex drive left. Although he's awake, each day it's getting harder to drag himself out of bed in the morning. This week he missed one day of work and was late twice. His supervisor has suggested in a nonthreatening way that he "do something about it." David knows that her next warning will not be nonthreatening. It's been going downhill since Sue walked out. Suicide has even crossed David's mind. He wonders if he's going crazy.

David is experiencing the emotion of depression, and seriously so. Depression is to be expected following a loss, such as the end of a relationship, but David's feelings have lingered. His friends tell him that he should get out and do things, but David is so down that he hasn't the motivation to do much at all. After much prompting by family and friends,

© C SQUARED STUDIOS/GETTY IMAGES

David consults a psychologist who ironically also pushes him to get out and do things—the things he used to enjoy. The psychologist also shows David that part of his problem is that he sees himself as a failure who cannot make meaningful changes.

How do the physiological, situational, and cognitive components of emotions interact to produce feelings and behavior? Some psychologists argue that physiological arousal is a more basic component of emotional response than cognition and that the type of arousal we experience strongly influences our cognitive appraisal and our labeling of the emotion (e.g., Izard, 1984). For these psychologists, the body takes precedence over the mind. Do David's bodily reactions— for example, his loss of appetite and energy—take precedence over his cognitions? Other psychologists argue that cognitive appraisal and physiological arousal are so strongly intertwined that cognitive processes may determine the emotional response. Are David's ideas that he is helpless to change things more at the heart of his feelings of depression?

The "commonsense theory" of emotions is that something happens (a situation) that is cognitively appraised (interpreted) by the person, and the feeling state (a combination of arousal and thoughts) follows. For example, you meet someone new, you appraise that person as delightful, and feelings of attraction follow. Or, as in the case of David, a social relationship comes to an end, you recognize your loss, feel powerless to change it, and feel down in the dumps.

However, both historic and contemporary theories of how the components of emotions interact are at variance with this commonsense view. Let us consider a number of theories and see whether we can arrive at some useful conclusions.

The James–Lange Theory

A century ago, William James suggested that our emotions follow, rather than cause, our behavioral responses to events. At about the same time this view was also proposed by the Danish physiologist Karl G. Lange. It is therefore termed the James–Lange theory of emotion.

According to James and Lange, certain external stimuli instinctively trigger specific patterns of arousal and action, such as fighting or fleeing (see Figure 9.5, part A). We then become angry *because* we are acting aggressively or become afraid *because* we are running away. Emotions are simply the cognitive representations (or by-products) of automatic physiological and behavioral responses.

The James–Lange theory is consistent with the facial-feedback hypothesis. That is, smiling apparently can induce pleasant feelings, even if the effect may not be strong enough to overcome feelings of sadness (Ekman, 1993). The theory also suggests that we may be able to change our feelings by changing our behavior. Changing one's behavior to change one's feelings is one aspect of behavior therapy. When David's psychologist urges him to get out and do things, she is assuming that by changing his behavior, David can have a positive effect on the way he feels.

Walter Cannon (1927) criticized the James–Lange assertion that each emotion has distinct physiological correlates. He argued that the physiological arousal associated with emotion A is not as distinct from the arousal associated with emotion B as the theory asserts.

Figure 9.5

Theories of Emotion

Go to CourseMate for PSYCH at www.cengagebrain.com to access an interactive version of this figure.

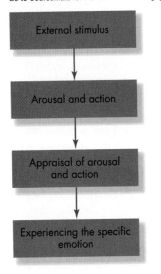

A. James–Lange

Events trigger specific arousal patterns and actions. Emotions result from our appraisal of our body responses.

B. Cannon–Bard

Events are first processed by the brain. Body patterns of arousal, action, and our emotional responses are then triggered simultaneously.

C. Cognitive appraisal

Events and arousal are appraised by the individual. The emotional response stems from the person's appraisal of the situation and his or her level of arousal.

The Cannon–Bard Theory

Walter Cannon (1927) and Philip Bard (1934) suggested that an event might *simultaneously* trigger bodily responses (arousal and action) and the experience of an emotion. As shown in Figure 9.5 (part B), when an event is perceived (processed by the brain), the brain stimulates autonomic and muscular activity (arousal and action) *and* cognitive activity (experience of the emotion). Thus, according to the Cannon–Bard theory, emotions *accompany* bodily responses. They are not *produced by* bodily changes, as in the James–Lange theory.

The central criticism of the Cannon–Bard theory focuses on whether bodily responses (arousal and action) and emotions are in fact stimulated simultaneously. For example, pain or the perception of danger may trigger arousal before we begin to feel distress or fear. Also, many of us have had the experience of having a "narrow escape" and becoming aroused and shaky afterward, when we have had time to consider the damage that might have occurred. What is needed is a theory that allows for an ongoing interaction of external events, physiological changes (such as autonomic arousal and muscular activity), and cognitive activities.

The Theory of Cognitive Appraisal

More recent theoretical approaches to emotion stress cognitive factors. Among those who argue that thinking comes first are Gordon Bower, Richard Lazarus, Stanley Schachter, Jerome Singer, and Robert Zajonc.

Schachter asserts that emotions are associated with similar patterns of bodily arousal that vary in strength, but that the way we label an emotion depends largely on our appraisal of the situation. Cognitive appraisal is based on many factors, including our perception of events and the ways other people respond to those events (see Figure 9.5, part C). When other people are present, we engage in social comparison to arrive at a response.

In a classic experiment, Schachter and Singer (1962) showed that arousal can be labeled quite differently, depending on the situation. The investigators told participants they wanted to determine the effects of a vitamin on vision. Half the participants received an injection of adrenaline, a hormone that stimulates the sympathetic branch of the autonomic nervous system. A control group received an injection of a placebo. Those who had been given adrenaline received one of three "cognitive manipulations." Group 1 was told nothing about possible emotional effects of the "vitamin." Group 2 was deliberately misinformed; members of this group were led to expect itching, numbness, or other irrelevant symptoms. Group 3 was informed accurately about the increased arousal they would experience. Group 4 was a control group injected with a placebo and given no information about its effects.

After receiving injections and cognitive manipulations, the participants were asked to wait in pairs while the experimental apparatus was being set up. The participants did not know that the person with whom they were waiting was a confederate of the experimenter. The confederate's purpose was to respond in a way that the participant would believe was caused by the injection.

Some participants waited with a confederate who acted happy-go-lucky. He flew paper airplanes about the room and tossed paper balls into a wastebasket. Other participants waited with a confederate who acted angry. He complained about the experiment, tore up a questionnaire, and stormed out of the room. As the confederates worked for their Oscar awards, the real participants were observed through a one-way mirror.

The people in groups 1 and 2 were likely to imitate the behavior of the confederate. Those who were exposed to the happy-go-lucky confederate acted jovial and content. Those who were exposed to the angry confederate imitated that person's complaining, aggressive behavior. But those in groups 3 and 4 were less influenced by the confederate's behavior.

Schachter and Singer concluded that participants in groups 1 and 2 were in an ambiguous situation. Members of these groups felt arousal from the adrenaline injection but couldn't label it as a specific emotion. Social comparison with a confederate led them to attribute their arousal either to happiness or to anger. Members of group 3 expected arousal from the injection, but no particular emotional consequences. These participants did not imitate the confederate's display of happiness or anger because they were not in an ambiguous situation; they knew their arousal was caused by adrenaline. Members of group 4 had no arousal for which they needed an attribution, except perhaps for some arousal induced by observing the confederate. Nor did they imitate the behavior of the confederate.

Now, happiness and anger are very different emotions. Yet Schachter and Singer suggest that the bodily differences between these two emotions are slight enough that different views of the situation can lead one person to label arousal as happiness and another person to label it as anger. The Schachter–Singer view could not be further removed from the James–Lange theory, which holds that each emotion is associated with specific and readily recognized body sensations. The truth, it happens, may lie somewhere in between.

In science, it must be possible to replicate experiments and attain identical or similar results; otherwise, a theory cannot be considered valid. The Schachter and Singer study has been replicated, but with *different* results (Ekman, 1993). For example, some studies found that participants were less likely to imitate the behavior of the confederate and were likely to perceive unexplained arousal negatively, attributing it to nervousness or anger (Zimbardo et al., 1993).

The connections between arousal and emotions have led to the development of many kinds of lie detection, as we see in the following section.

The Polygraph: Just What Do Lie Detectors Detect?

Lying—for better or worse—is a part of life. A *New York Times* poll found that 60% of American adults believe that it is sometimes necessary to lie, especially to protect people's feelings (Smiley, 2000). Political leaders lie to get elected. Many people lie to get dates or initiate sexual relations—for example, about other relationships, making professions of love, or in the case of the Internet, about one's appearance or age (Suler, 2005). People also lie about their qualifications to get jobs, and, of course, some people lie in denying guilt for crimes. Although we are unlikely

to subject political leaders and lovers to lie-detector tests, such tests are frequently used in hiring and in criminal investigations.

Facial expressions often offer clues to deceit, but some people can lie with a straight face—or a smile. As Shakespeare pointed out in *Hamlet,* "One may smile, and smile, and be a villain." The use of devices to detect lies has a long, if not laudable, history:

> The Bedouins of Arabia . . . until quite recently required conflicting witnesses to lick a hot iron; the one whose tongue was burned was thought to be lying. The Chinese, it is said, had a similar method for detecting lying: Suspects were forced to chew rice powder and spit it out; if the powder was dry, the suspect was guilty. (Kleinmuntz & Szucko, 1984, pp. 766–767)

These methods may sound primitive, even bizarre, but they are broadly consistent with modern psychological knowledge. Anxiety about being caught in a lie is linked to arousal of the sympathetic division of the autonomic nervous system. One sign of sympathetic arousal is lack of saliva, or dryness in the mouth. The emotions of fear and guilt are also linked to sympathetic arousal and hence to dryness in the mouth.

How do lie detectors work? How reliable are they? Modern polygraphs monitor indicators of sympathetic arousal during an interrogation: heart rate, blood pressure, respiration rate, and electrodermal response (sweating). But questions have been raised about the validity of assessing truth or fiction by means of polygraphs (Branaman & Gallagher, 2005).

The American Polygraph Association claims that use of the polygraph is 85% to 95%

© KEITH BROFSKY/GETTY IMAGES

accurate. Critics find polygraph testing to be less accurate and claim that it is sensitive to more than lies (Saxe & Ben-Shakhar, 1999). Tense muscles, drugs, and previous experience with polygraph tests can significantly reduce their accuracy rate. In one experiment, people were able to reduce the accuracy of polygraph-based judgments to about 50% by biting their tongue (to produce pain) or pressing their toes against the floor (to tense muscles) while being interrogated (Honts et al., 1985). You might thus give the examiner the impression that you are lying even when you are telling the truth, throwing off the test's results.

It appears that no specific pattern of bodily responses pinpoints lying (*Nature* editorial, 2004). Because of validity problems, results of polygraph examinations are no longer admitted as evidence in many courts. But the lure of technology to determine lying remains strong. Research is under way in the development of techniques that measure brain waves, heat patterns in the face, and other biological events (*Nature* editorial, 2004).

Truth

It is true that you might be able to fool a lie detector by wiggling your toes.

Evaluation

What can we make of all this? First of all, stronger emotions are connected with higher levels of arousal (Gomez et al., 2005), but research by Paul Ekman (1993) suggests that the patterns of arousal connected with various emotions are more specific than suggested by Schachter and Singer. They are, however, apparently less specific than suggested by James and Lange. Brain imaging suggests that different emotions, such as happiness and sadness, involve different structures within the brain (Goleman, 1995). Moreover, lack of control over our emotions and lack of understanding of what is happening to us are disturbing experiences (Zimbardo et al., 1993). Thus our cognitive appraisals of situations affect our emotional responses, even if not quite in the way envisioned by Schachter.

In sum, various components of an experience—cognitive, physiological, and behavioral—contribute to our emotional responses. Our bodies may become aroused in a given situation, but as we saw in the classic research of Schachter and Singer, people also appraise those situations so that arousal alone does not appear to directly cause one emotion or another. The fact that none of the theories of emotion we have discussed applies to all people in all situations is comforting. Apparently our emotions are not quite as easily understood, manipulated, or—as in the case of the polygraph—even detected as some theorists have suggested.

3/10 < fraction that represents the number of obese American adults

total number of additional calories Americans consume **200 billion** than needed to maintain their weights each day >

total number of daily calories needed to feed a nation of 80 million people > **200 billion**

percent muscle of the average man > **40**

23 < percent muscle of the average woman

6:1 < ratio of women with an eating disorder, compared to men

3 and 2 < percent of U.S. males and females, respectively, that identify themselves as homosexual

60 < percent of Americans that believe it is sometimes necessary to lie

percent of APA respondents who believe that polygraph results should not be admitted as evidence in courts of law > **74**

Personality:
Theory and Measurement

Learning Outcomes

LO **1** Describe the psychoanalytical perspective and how it contributed to the study of personality

LO **2** Explain the trait perspective and the "Big Five" trait model

LO **3** Identify the contributions of learning theory to understanding personality

LO **4** Describe the humanistic perspective on personality

LO **5** Describe the sociocultural perspective on personality

LO **6** Describe the different kinds of tests psychologists use to measure personality

"Can there ever be one true portrait of human personality?"

Nearly 1,000 years ago, an Islamic theologian told his pupils the fable of *The Blind Men and the Elephant:*

Once upon a time, a group of blind men heard that an unusual animal called an elephant had come to their country. Since they had no idea what an elephant looked like and had never even heard its name, they resolved that they would obtain a "picture" of sorts, and the knowledge they sought, by feeling the animal. After all, that was the only possibility available to them. They sought out the elephant, and its handler kindly permitted them to touch the beast. One blind man stroked its leg, the other a tusk, the third an ear, and believing that they now had knowledge of the elephant, they returned home satisfied. But when they were questioned by others, they provided very different descriptions. The one who had felt the leg said that the elephant was firm, strong, and upright, like a pillar. The one who had felt the tusk disagreed. He described the elephant as hard and smooth, clearly not as stout as a pillar, and sharp at the end. Now spoke the third blind man, who had held the ear of the elephant. "By my faith," he asserted, "the elephant is soft and rough." It was neither pillar-like nor hard and smooth. It was broad, thick, and leathery. And so the three argued about the true nature of the beast. Each was right in part, but none grasped the real nature of the elephant. Yet each was fervent in his belief that he knew the animal.

Each of the blind men had come to know the elephant from a different angle. Each was bound by his first experience and blind to the beliefs of his fellows and to the real nature of the beast—not just because of his physical limitations, but also because his initial encounter led him to think of the elephant in a certain way.

Truth or Fiction?

What do you think?

Folklore, common sense, or nonsense? Place a T for "True" or F for "False" on the lines provided (you'll learn the answers as you read through the text).

___ Biting one's fingernails or smoking cigarettes is a sign of conflict experienced during early childhood.

___ Twenty-five hundred years ago, a Greek physician devised a way of looking at personality that—with a little "tweaking"—remains in use today.

___ Bloodletting and vomiting were once recommended as ways of coping with depression.

___ Actually, there are no basic personality traits. We are all conditioned by society to behave in certain ways.

___ The most well-adjusted immigrants are those who abandon the language and customs of their country of origin and become like members of the dominant culture in their new host country.

___ Psychologists can determine whether a person has told the truth on a personality test.

___ There is a psychological test made up of inkblots, and test-takers are asked to say what the blots look like to them.

personality
the distinct patterns of behavior, thoughts, and feelings that distinguish people from one another

psychoanalytic theory
Sigmund Freud's perspective, which emphasizes the importance of unconscious motives and conflicts as forces that determine behavior

Our own conceptions about people, and about ourselves, may be similarly bound up with our own perspectives and initial beliefs. Some think of personality as consisting of the person's most striking traits, as in "This person has an outgoing personality" or "That person has an agreeable personality." But many psychological theorists look deeper. Those schooled in the Freudian tradition look at personality as consisting of underlying mental structures that jockey for supremacy outside the range of our ordinary awarenss. Other theorists focus on how personality is shaped by learning. And to the humanistic theorists, personality is not something people *have* but rather something they *create*, to give meaning and direction to their lives. Then, too, sociocultural theorists remind us that we must always consider the influences of culture, race, and ethnicity on personality.

Sometimes even psychologists prefer the first theory of personality they learn about. The Islamic theologian taught his pupils the legend of the blind men and the elephant to illustrate that no person can have a complete view of religious truths; we must therefore remain flexible in our thinking and open to new ideas. It may also be that none of the views of personality presented in this chapter will offer the one true portrait of human personality, but each may have something to contribute to our understanding of personality. So let us approach our study with an open mind, because years from now psychologists may well be teaching new ideas about personality.

While the blind men could touch the elephant, researchers cannot touch a personality; therefore, personality is even harder to describe and understand. Before we discuss psychologists' various approaches to personality, let us define our subject matter: personality refers to the reasonably stable patterns of emotions, motives, and behavior that distinguish one person from another.

LO¹ The Psychoanalytic Perspective

Where do we get the idea that there is something like an unconscious mind that can exert control over our behavior? One source is psychoanalytic theory.

There are several psychoanalytic theories of personality, each of which owes its origin to Sigmund Freud. Each teaches that personality is characterized by conflict. At first the conflict is external: Drives like sex, aggression, and the need for superiority come into conflict with laws, social rules, and moral codes. But at some point laws and social rules are brought inward—that is, *internalized*. The conflict is then between opposing *inner* forces.

At any given moment our behavior, our thoughts, and our emotions represent the outcome of these inner contests. *What is Freud's psychoanalytic theory?*

Sigmund Freud's Theory of Psychosexual Development

Sigmund Freud (1856–1939) was a mass of contradictions. Some have lauded him as one of the greatest thinkers of the 20th century. Others have criticized him as overrated. He preached liberal views on sexuality but was himself a model of sexual restraint. He invented a popular form of psychotherapy but experienced lifelong psychologically related problems such as migraine headaches, fainting under stress, hatred of the telephone, and an addiction to cigars. He smoked 20 cigars a day and could not break the habit even after he developed cancer of the jaw.

Freud was trained as a physician. Early in his practice, he was surprised to find that some people apparently experienced loss of feeling in a hand or paralysis of the legs even though they have no medical disorder. These odd symptoms often disappeared once the person recalled and discussed stressful events and feelings of guilt or anxiety that seemed to be related to the symptoms. Although these events and feelings lay hidden beneath the surface of awareness, they could influence behavior.

From this sort of clinical evidence, Freud concluded that the mind is like an iceberg. Only the tip of an iceberg rises above the surface of the water; the great mass of it lies hidden in the deep (see Figure 10.1). Freud came to believe that people, similarly, are aware of only a small part of the ideas and impulses that dwell within their minds. He thought that a larger portion of the mind—one that contained our deepest images, thoughts, fears, and urges—lies beneath the surface of awareness, where little light illumines them.

Figure 10.1

The Human Iceberg According to Freud

According to psychoanalytic theory, only the tip of human personality rises above the surface of the mind into conscious awareness. Material in the preconscious can become conscious if we direct our attention to it. Unconscious material tends to remain shrouded in mystery.

Go to Coursemate for PSYCH at www.cengagebrain.com to access an interactive version of this figure.

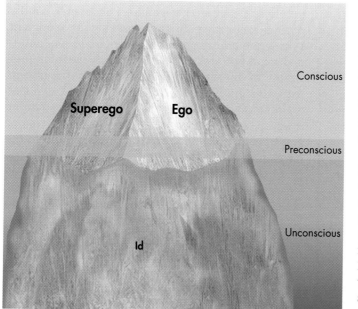

Freud labeled the region that pokes into the light of awareness the conscious part of the mind. He called the regions below the surface the *preconscious* and the *unconscious*. The preconscious mind contains ideas that are out of awareness but can be made conscious by focusing on them. The unconscious mind contains primitive instincts such as sex and aggression. Some unconscious urges cannot be experienced consciously because mental images and words cannot portray them in all their color and fury. Other unconscious urges may be kept below the surface by repression because they would create anxiety. *Repression* is defined as the automatic ejection of anxiety-evoking ideas from awareness. People forget many ugly experiences, and some research evidence suggests that people *might* repress them (Furnham et al., 2003; Myers & Brewin, 1994). Other investigators allow that forgetting and distortion of memory occurs, but view the concept of repression as nothing but a myth (Kihlstrom, 2002).

In the unconscious mind, primitive drives seek expression, while learned values try to keep them in check. The conflict can arouse emotional outbursts and psychological problems. To explore the unconscious mind, Freud used a form of mental detective work called *psychoanalysis*. In psychoanalysis, people are encouraged to talk about anything that pops into their mind while they remain comfortable and relaxed.

The Structure of Personality

Freud spoke of mental or *psychic structures* to describe the clashing forces of personality. Psychic structures cannot be seen or measured directly, but their presence is suggested by behavior, expressed thoughts, and emotions. Freud believed that there are three psychic structures: the id, the ego, and the superego.

The **id** is present at birth. It represents biological drives and is unconscious. Freud described the id as "a chaos, a cauldron of seething excitations" (1927/1964, p. 73). The conscious mind might find it inconsistent to love and hate the same person, but such conflicting emotions can dwell side by side in the id. In the id, one can hate one's mother for failing to gratify immediately all of one's needs, while also loving her. The id seeks instant gratification without consideration for law, social custom, or other people.

The **ego** begins to develop during the first year of life, largely because a child's demands for gratification cannot all be met immediately. The ego stands for reason and good sense, for rational ways of coping with frustration. It curbs the appetites of the id and seeks ways to find gratification yet avoid social disapproval. The id informs you that you are hungry, but the ego decides to microwave enchiladas. The ego takes into

id
the psychic structure, present at birth, that represents physiological drives and is fully unconscious

ego
the second psychic structure to develop, characterized by self-awareness, planning, and delay of gratification

Sigmund Freud

IMAGNO/GETTY IMAGES

superego
the third psychic structure, which functions as a moral guardian and sets forth high standards for behavior

identification
in psychoanalytic theory, the unconscious adoption of another person's behavior

psychosexual development
in psychoanalytic theory, the process by which libidinal energy is expressed through different erogenous zones during different stages of development

oral stage
the first stage of psychosexual development, during which gratification is hypothesized to be attained primarily through oral activities

anal stage
the second stage of psychosexual development, when gratification is attained through anal activities

account what is practical along with what is urged by the id. The ego also provides the conscious sense of self.

Although most of the ego is conscious, some of its business is carried out unconsciously. For example, the ego also acts as a censor that screens the impulses of the id. When the ego senses that improper impulses are rising into awareness, it may use psychological defenses to prevent them from surfacing. Repression is one such psychological defense, or *defense mechanism.*

The **superego** develops as the child incorporates the moral standards and values of parents and other members of the community. The child does so through **identification**, by trying to become like these people. The superego holds up shining models of an ideal self and monitors the intentions of the ego, handing out judgments of right and wrong. It floods the ego with feelings of guilt and shame when the verdict is negative.

Freud believed that a healthy personality has found ways to gratify most of the id's demands without seriously offending the superego. Most of these demands are contained or repressed. If the ego is not a good problem solver, or if the superego is too stern, the ego will have a hard time of it.

Stages of Psychosexual Development

Freud stirred controversy by arguing that sexual impulses are a central factor in personality development, even among children. Freud believed that sexual feelings are closely linked to children's basic ways of relating to the world, such as nursing and moving their bowels.

Freud believed that a major instinct, *eros,* aims to preserve and perpetuate life. Eros is fueled by psychological, or psychic, energy, which Freud labeled *libido.* Libidinal energy involves sexual impulses, so Freud considered it to be *psychosexual.* As the child develops, this energy is expressed through sexual feelings in different parts of the body, or *erogenous zones.* To Freud, human development involves the transfer of libidinal energy from one erogenous zone to another. He hypothesized five periods of

psychosexual development: oral, anal, phallic, latency, and genital.

During the first year of life a child experiences much of her or his world through the mouth. If it fits, into the mouth it goes. This is the oral stage. Freud argued that oral activities such as sucking and biting give the child sexual gratification as well as nourishment.

Freud believed that children encounter conflict during each stage of psychosexual development. During the oral stage, conflict centers on the nature and extent of oral gratification. Early weaning (cessation of breastfeeding) can lead to frustration. Excessive gratification, on the other hand, can lead an infant to expect that it will routinely get anything it wants. Insufficient or excessive gratification in any stage could lead to *fixation* in that stage and to the development of traits that are characteristic of the stage. Oral traits include dependency, gullibility, and excessive optimism or pessimism (depending on the child's experiences with gratification).

Freud theorized that adults with an *oral fixation* could experience exaggerated desires for "oral activities," such as smoking, overeating, alcohol abuse, and nail biting. Like the infant whose survival depends on the mercy of an adult, adults with oral fixations may desire clinging, dependent relationships.

The anal stage begins in the second year. During the anal stage, gratification is attained through contraction and relaxation of the muscles that control elimination of waste products. Elimination, which is reflexive during most of the first year, comes under voluntary muscular control, even if such control is

Freud believed that the first year of life was the oral stage of development. During this time, if it fits, into the mouth it goes.

not reliable at first. During the anal stage children learn to delay the gratification that comes from eliminating whenever they feel the urge. The general issue of self-control may bring conflict between parent and child. *Anal fixations* may stem from this conflict and lead to either of two sets of traits in adulthood. *Anal-retentive* traits involve excessive use of self-control: perfectionism, a strong need for order, and exaggerated neatness and cleanliness. *Anal-expulsive* traits, on the other hand, "let it all hang out": carelessness, messiness, even sadism.

Children enter the phallic stage during the third year. The major erogenous zone is the penis in boys and the clitoris in girls. Parent–child conflict is likely to develop over masturbation, to which parents may respond with threats or punishment. During this stage children may develop strong sexual attachments to the parent of the other sex and begin to view the parent of the same sex as a rival for the other parent's affections. Thus boys may want to marry their mothers, and girls may want to marry their fathers.

Children have difficulty dealing with feelings of lust and jealousy. These feelings, therefore, remain unconscious, but their influence is felt through fantasies about marriage with the parent of the other sex and hostility toward the parent of the same sex. In boys, this conflict is labeled the Oedipus complex, after the legendary Greek king who unwittingly killed his father and married his mother. Similar feelings in girls give rise to the Electra complex. According to Greek legend, Electra was the daughter of the king Agamemnon. She longed for him after his death and sought revenge against his slayers— her mother and her mother's lover.

The Oedipus and Electra complexes are resolved by about the ages of five or six. Children repress their hostilities toward the parent of the same sex and begin to identify with her or him. In psychoanalytic theory, identification is the key to gender-typing: It leads children to play the gender roles of the parent of the same sex and to internalize his or her values.

Sexual feelings toward the parent of the other sex are repressed for several years. When the feelings reemerge during adolescence, they are displaced, or transferred, to socially appropriate members of the other sex.

Freud believed that by the age of five or six, children have been in conflict with their parents over sexual feelings for several years. The pressures of the Oedipus and Electra complexes cause them to repress all sexual urges. In so doing, they enter a period of latency, during which their sexual feelings remain unconscious, they prefer playmates of their own sex, and they focus on schoolwork.

Freud believed that we enter the final stage of psychosexual development, the genital stage, at puberty. Adolescent males again experience sexual urges toward their mother, and adolescent females experience such urges toward their father. But the *incest taboo* causes them to repress these impulses and displace them onto other adults or adolescents of the other sex. Boys might seek girls "just like the girl that married dear old Dad." Girls might be attracted to boys who resemble their fathers.

People in the genital stage prefer to find sexual gratification through intercourse with a member of the other sex. In Freud's view, oral or anal stimulation, masturbation, and sexual activity with people of the same sex all represent *pregenital* fixations and immature forms of sexual conduct.

Other Psychoanalytic Theorists

Freud had several intellectual heirs. Their theories, like his, include conflict and defense mechanisms. In other respects, they differ considerably. *Who are some other psychoanalytic theorists? What are their views on personality?*

Carl Jung

Carl Jung (1875–1961) was a Swiss psychiatrist who had been a member of Freud's inner circle. He fell into disfavor with Freud when he developed his own psychoanalytic theory—analytical psychology. Jung downplayed the importance of sex, which he saw as one of several important instincts.

Jung, like Freud, was intrigued by unconscious processes. He believed that we not only have a *personal* unconscious that contains repressed memories and impulses, but also a collective unconscious containing primitive images, or archetypes, that

phallic stage
the third stage of psychosexual development, characterized by a shift of libido to the phallic region (from the Greek *phallos*, referring to an image of the penis; however, Freud used the term *phallic* to refer both to boys and girls)

Oedipus complex
a conflict of the phallic stage in which the boy wishes to possess his mother sexually and perceives his father as a rival in love

Electra complex
a conflict of the phallic stage in which the girl longs for her father and resents her mother

latency
a phase of psychosexual development characterized by repression of sexual impulses

genital stage
the mature stage of psychosexual development, characterized by preferred expression of libido through intercourse with an adult of the other gender

analytical psychology
Jung's psychoanalytic theory, which emphasizes the collective unconscious and archetypes

collective unconscious
Jung's hypothesized store of vague memories that represent the history of humankind

inferiority complex feelings of inferiority hypothesized by Adler to serve as a central motivating force

creative self according to Adler, the self-aware aspect of personality that strives to achieve its full potential

individual psychology Adler's psychoanalytic theory, which emphasizes feelings of inferiority and the creative self

reflect the history of our species. Examples of archetypes are the all-powerful God, the young hero, the fertile and nurturing mother, the wise old man, the hostile brother—even fairy godmothers, wicked witches, and themes of rebirth or resurrection. Archetypes themselves remain unconscious, but Jung believed they affect our thoughts and feelings and cause us to respond to cultural themes in the media.

Alfred Adler

Alfred Adler (1870–1937), another follower of Freud, also felt that Freud had placed too much emphasis on sex. Adler believed that people are basically motivated by an inferiority complex. In some people, feelings of inferiority may be based on physical problems and the need to compensate for them. Adler believed, however, that all of us encounter some feelings of inferiority because of our small size as children, and that these feelings give rise to a drive for superiority. As a child, Adler was crippled by rickets and suffered from pneumonia, and it may

be that his theory developed in part from his own striving to overcome bouts of illness.

Adler believed that self-awareness plays a major role in the formation of personality. He spoke of a creative self, a self-aware aspect of personality that strives to overcome obstacles and develop the person's potential. Because each person's potential is unique, Adler's views have been termed individual psychology.

Karen Horney

Karen Horney (1885–1952) was criticized by the New York Psychoanalytic Institute because she took issue with the way in which psychoanalytic theory portrayed women. Early in the century, psychoanalytic theory taught that a woman's place was in the home. Women who sought to compete with men in the business world were assumed to be suffering from unconscious penis envy. Psychoanalytic theory taught that little girls feel inferior to boys when they learn that boys have a penis and they do not. But Horney argued that little girls do *not* feel inferior to boys and that these views were founded on Western cultural prejudice, not scientific evidence.

Horney agreed with Freud that childhood experiences are important in psychological development. Like other neoanalysts, however, she asserted that unconscious sexual and aggressive impulses are less important than social relationships. She also

{ Why Do We Need to Have Sports Heroes? }

What have psychologists learned about the appeal of celebrities, and especially sports celebrities? Many people form deep and enduring bonds of attachment with athletes and sports teams. Once they identify with a team, their self-esteem rises and falls with the team's wins and losses (Wann et al., 2000). Wins lead to a surge of testosterone in males (Bernhardt et al., 1998), which is connected with aggressiveness and self-confidence. Wins increase the optimism of both males and females.

Psychoanalytic theory suggests that children identify with parents and other "big" people in their lives because big people seem to hold the keys to the resources they need for sustenance and stimulation or

excitement. Athletes and entertainers—the rich and famous—have their fan clubs, filled with people who tie their own lights to the brilliant suns of their stars.

Teams and sports heroes provide both entertainment and the kind of gutsy competition that evolutionary psychologists believe whispers to us from our genes, pushing us toward aggression and dominance. If we can't do it on our own, we can do it *through* someone else. In some kind of psychological sense, we can *be* someone who is more effective at climbing the heap of humankind into the sun.

VISIONS OF AMERICA/JOE SOHM/GETTY IMAGES

Karen Horney

Horney, like many of Freud's intellectual descendants, took issue with Freud on many issues. For one thing, Horney did not believe that little girls had penis envy or felt inferior to boys in any other way. She also believed that children's social relationships are more important in their development than unconscious sexual and aggressive impulses.

believed that genuine and consistent love can alleviate the effects of a traumatic childhood.

Erik Erikson

Like many other modern psychoanalysts, Erik Erikson (1902–1994) believed that Freud had placed undue emphasis on sex. Like Horney, he believed that social relationships are more important than sex. Erikson also believed that to a large extent we are the conscious architects of our own personalities.

Erikson, like Freud, is known for devising a comprehensive theory of personality development. But whereas Freud proposed stages of psycho*sexual* development, Erikson proposed stages of psycho*social* development. The first stage of psychosocial development is labeled the stage of trust versus mistrust because two outcomes are possible: (1) a warm, loving relationship with the mother and others during infancy might lead to a sense of basic trust in people and the world; or (2) a cold, ungratifying relationship with the mother and others might generate a general sense of mistrust. For Erikson, the goal of adolescence is the attainment of ego identity, not genital sexuality. The focus is on who we see ourselves as being and what we stand for, not on sexual interests.

Evaluation of the Psychoanalytic Perspective

Psychoanalysis has tremendous appeal. It is rich in concepts and seems to explain many human traits. *What are the strengths and weaknesses of the psychoanalytic perspective?*

On the positive side, Freud fought for the idea that personality is subject to scientific analysis. He developed his theory at a time when many people viewed psychological problems as signs of possession by the devil or evil spirits. Freud argued that psychological

disorders stem from psychological problems—not spirits. His views contributed to the development of compassion for people with psychological disorders and to methods of psychotherapy.

Psychoanalytic theory also focused attention on the far-reaching effects of childhood events and suggested that parents respond to the emotional needs of their children.

Freud taught us that sexual and aggressive urges are common, and that recognizing them is not the same as acting on them. As W. Bertram Wolfe put it, "Freud found sex an outcast in the outhouse, and left it in the living room an honored guest."

Critics note that "psychic structures"—id, ego, and superego—are too vague to measure scientifically (Hergenhahn, 2009). Nor can they be used to predict behavior. Nor have the stages of psychosexual development escaped criticism. Children begin to masturbate as early as the first year, not in the phallic stage. As parents know from discovering their children playing "doctor," the latency stage is not as sexually latent as Freud believed.

The evidence for Erikson's developmental views seems sturdier. For example, people who fail to develop ego identity in adolescence seem to have problems with intimate relationships later on.

Freud's clinical method of gathering evidence is also suspect (Hergenhahn, 2009). Therapists may subtly guide clients into producing memories and

> **psychosocial development**
> Erikson's theory of personality and development, which emphasizes social relationships and eight stages of growth
>
> **ego identity**
> a firm sense of who one is and what one stands for

Erik Erikson
Like other modern-day analysts, Erikson believed that Freud had placed too much emphasis on sex and unconscious conflict. Erikson believed that social relationships were the key to healthful development.

trait
a relatively stable aspect of personality that is inferred from behavior and assumed to give rise to consistent behavior

introversion
a trait characterized by intense imagination and the tendency to inhibit impulses

extraversion
a trait characterized by tendencies to be socially outgoing and to express feelings and impulses freely

Fiction

No, there is no evidence that biting one's nails or smoking cigarettes signifies an oral fixation.

Truth

It is true that some 2,500 years ago, Hippocrates, the Greek physician, devised a way of looking at personality that could be said to remain in use today.

feelings they expect to find. Also, most psychoanalytic theorists restricted their evidence gathering to case studies with individuals who sought help, particularly people from the middle and upper classes. People who seek therapy differ from the general population.

Psychoanalytic theory focused on reasons that people develop certain traits. We next discuss trait theory, which is not so much concerned with the origins of traits as with their description and categorization.

LO² The Trait Perspective

The notion of traits is familiar enough. If I asked you to describe yourself, you would probably do so in terms of traits such as bright, sophisticated, and witty. (That is you, is it not?) We also describe other people in terms of traits. *What are traits?*

Traits are reasonably stable elements of personality that are inferred from behavior. If you describe a friend as "shy," it may be because you have observed anxiety or withdrawal in that person's social encounters. Traits are assumed to account for consistent behavior in different situations. You probably expect your "shy" friend to be retiring in most social confrontations.

From Hippocrates to the Present

What is the history of the trait perspective? The trait perspective dates at least to the Greek physician Hippocrates (ca. 460–377 BCE). It has generally been assumed that traits are embedded in people's bodies. Hippocrates believed they were embedded in bodily fluids. In his view, a person's personality depends on the balance of four basic fluids, or "humors," in the body. Yellow bile is associated with a choleric (quick-tempered) disposition; blood with a sanguine (warm, cheerful) one; phlegm with a phlegmatic

> In most of us by the age of thirty, the character has set like plaster, and will never soften again.
> —William James

(sluggish, calm, cool) disposition; and black bile with a melancholic (gloomy, pensive) temperament. Disease was believed to reflect an imbalance among the humors. Depression, for example, represented an excess of black bile. Although Hippocrates' theory was speculative, the terms *choleric, sanguine,* and so on remain in use.

More contemporary trait theories assume that traits are heritable and are embedded in the nervous system. These theories rely on the mathematical technique of factor analysis to determine which traits are basic to others.

Early in the 20th century, Gordon Allport and a colleague (Allport & Oddbert, 1936) catalogued some 18,000 human traits from a search through word lists like dictionaries. Some were physical traits such as *short, weak,* and *brunette.* Others were behavioral traits such as *shy* and *emotional.* This exhaustive list has served as the basis for personality research by many other psychologists. *How have psychologists reduced Allport's traits to more manageable lists?*

Hans Eysenck's Trait Theory

British psychologist Hans J. Eysenck (1916–1997) focused much of his research on the relationships between two personality traits: introversion–extraversion and emotional stability–instability (Eysenck & Eysenck, 1985). (Emotional instability is also called *neuroticism*). Carl Jung was the first to distinguish between introverts and extraverts. Eysenck added the dimension of emotional stability–instability to introversion–extraversion. He catalogued various personality traits according to where they are situated along these dimensions (see Figure 10.2). For example, an anxious person would be high in both introversion and neuroticism—that is, preoccupied with his or her own thoughts and emotionally unstable.

Eysenck acknowledged that his scheme is similar to Hippocrates'. According to Eysenck's dimensions, the choleric type would be extraverted and unstable; the sanguine type, extraverted and stable; the phlegmatic type, introverted and stable; and the melancholic type, introverted and unstable.

The "Big Five": The Five-Factor Model

More recent research suggests that there may be five basic personality factors, not two. These include the two found by Eysenck—extraversion and neuroticism—along with conscientiousness, agreeableness, and openness to experience (see Table 10.1).

Many personality theorists, especially Robert McCrae and Paul T. Costa, Jr., have developed the five-factor model. Cross-cultural research has found that these five factors appear to define the personality

Figure 10.2

Eysenck's Personality Dimensions and Hippocrates' Personality Types

Various personality traits shown in the outer ring fall within the two major dimensions of personality suggested by Hans Eysenck. The inner circle shows how Hippocrates' four major personality types—choleric, sanguine, phlegmatic, and melancholic—fit within Eysenck's dimensions.

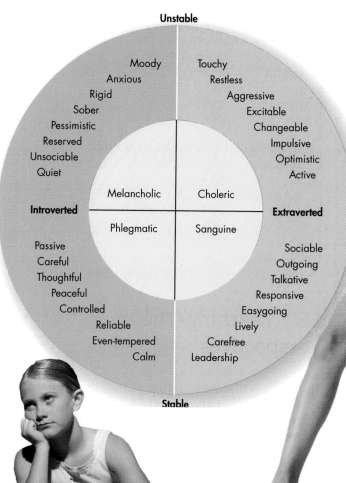

Unstable

Moody
Anxious
Rigid
Sober
Pessimistic
Reserved
Unsociable
Quiet

Touchy
Restless
Aggressive
Excitable
Changeable
Impulsive
Optimistic
Active

Melancholic | Choleric

Introverted | **Extraverted**

Phlegmatic | Sanguine

Passive
Careful
Thoughtful
Peaceful
Controlled
Reliable
Even-tempered
Calm

Sociable
Outgoing
Talkative
Responsive
Easygoing
Lively
Carefree
Leadership

Stable

Truth

Methods such as bloodletting and vomiting were recommended to restore the balance of humors (Maher & Maher, 1994).

structure of American, German, Portuguese, Israeli, Chinese, Korean, Japanese, and Philippine people (Katigbak et al., 2002; McCrae & Costa, 1997). A study of more than 5,000 German, British, Spanish, Czech, and Turkish people suggests that the factors are related to people's basic temperaments, which are considered to be largely inborn (McCrae et al., 2000). The researchers interpreted the results to suggest that our personalities tend to mature over time rather than be shaped by environmental conditions, although the expression of personality traits is certainly affected by culture.

The five-factor model—also known as the "Big Five" model—is quite popular. There are hundreds of studies correlating scores on the five factors, according to a psychological test constructed by Costa and McCrae (the *NEO Five-Factor Inventory*), with various behavior patterns, psychological disorders, and kinds of "personalities." Consider driving. Significant negative correlations have been found between the numbers of traffic citations people receive and the accidents they get into, on the one hand, and the factor of agreeableness on the other (Cellar et al., 2000). In other words, it's safer to share the freeway with agreeable people. People who are

Fiction

Actually, there may be several basic personality traits, as suggested by trait theory.

Table 10.1

The "Big Five": The Five-Factor Model

Factor	Name	Traits
I	Extraversion	Contrasts talkativeness, assertiveness, and activity with silence, passivity, and reserve
II	Agreeableness	Contrasts kindness, trust, and warmth with hostility, selfishness, and distrust
III	Conscientiousness	Contrasts organization, thoroughness, and reliability with carelessness, negligence, and unreliability
IV	Neuroticism	Contrasts nervousness, moodiness, and sensitivity to negative stimuli with coping ability
V	Openness to experience	Contrasts imagination, curiosity, and creativity with shallowness and lack of perceptiveness

not judgmental—who will put up with your every whim—tend to score low on conscientiousness (they don't examine you closely) and high on agreeableness (you can be yourself) (Bernardin et al., 2000). Despite the stereotype that older people, especially men, are "crotchety," assessment of sixty-five- to one-hundred-year-olds using the NEO *Five-Factor Inventory* suggests that people, especially men, become more agreeable as they grow older (Weiss et al., 2005). People who are anxious or depressed tend to score higher on the trait of neuroticism (Bienvenu et al., 2005). Introverts are more likely than extraverts to fear public gatherings and public speaking (Bienvenu et al., 2005).

Evaluation of the Trait Perspective

What are the strengths and weaknesses of trait theory? Trait theorists have focused much attention on the development of personality tests. They have also given rise to theories about the fit between personality and certain kinds of jobs (Holland, 1996). The qualities that suit a person for various kinds of work can be expressed in terms of abilities, personality traits, and interests. By using interviews and tests to learn about an individual's abilities and traits, testing and counseling centers can make helpful predictions about that person's chances of success and personal fulfillment in certain kinds of jobs.

One limitation of trait theory is that it has tended to be more descriptive than explanatory. It has historically focused on describing traits rather than on tracing their origins or seeking ways to modify maladaptive personality traits and behavior.

{ Virtuous Traits: Positive Psychology and Trait Theory }

Trait theory has applications within positive psychology, a field that studies character strengths and virtues, such as those in the table below—how they come into being and how they are related to life satisfaction. Christopher Peterson and Martin E. P. Seligman (2004) summarized many of the research findings in their book, *Character Strengths and Virtues: A Handbook and Classification* (the *CSV*). The handbook lists six major virtuous traits found in 40 different countries as different as Azerbaijan and Venezuela, along with the United States and other developed nations. These virtues were widely recognized and valued, despite cultural and religious differences (Park et al., 2005).

The *CSV* was partly developed as a counterpoint to the *DSM*, which is the *Diagnostic and Statistical Manual of the Mental Disorders* of the American Psychiatric Association (2000). Whereas the *DSM* is a catalogue of (nearly) everything that can go wrong with people, the *CSV* is a catalogue of things that go right. Fortunately, there are many of them.

Virtue	Corresponding Character Strengths
Wisdom and knowledge	Creativity, curiosity, open-mindedness, love of learning, perspective (ability to provide other people with sound advice)
Courage	Authenticity (speaking one's mind), bravery, persistence, zest
Humanity	Kindness, love, social intelligence (see emotional intelligence, discussed in Chapter 8)
Justice	Fairness, leadership, teamwork
Temperance	Forgiveness, modesty, prudence, self-regulation
Transcendence	Appreciation of beauty and excellence, gratitude (when appropriate), hope, humor, religiousness (having a belief system about the meaning of life)

Source: Peterson & Seligman, 2004.

LO³ Learning-Theory Perspectives

Trait theory focused on enduring personality characteristics that were generally presumed to be embedded in the nervous system. Learning theorists tend not to theorize in terms of traits. They focus instead on behaviors and presume that those behaviors are largely learned.

That which is learned is also, in principle, capable of being unlearned. As a result, learning theory and personality theory may not be a perfect fit. Nevertheless, learning theorists—both behaviorists and social cognitive theorists—have contributed to the discussion of personality. *What does behaviorism contribute to our understanding of personality?*

Behaviorism

At Johns Hopkins University in 1924, John B. Watson sounded the battle cry of the behaviorist movement:

Give me a dozen healthy infants, well-formed, and my own specified world to bring them up in, and I'll guarantee to take any one at random and train him to become any type of specialist I might suggest—doctor, lawyer, merchant-chief and, yes, even beggar-man and thief, regardless of his talents, penchants, tendencies, abilities, vocations, and the race of his ancestors. (p. 82)

This proclamation underscores the behaviorist view that personality is plastic—that situational or environmental influences, not internal, individual variables, are the key shapers of personality. In contrast to the psychoanalysts and structuralists of his day, Watson argued that unseen, undetectable mental structures must be rejected in favor of that which can be seen and measured. In the 1930s Watson's flag was carried onward by B. F. Skinner, who agreed that psychologists should avoid trying to see into the "black box" of the organism and instead emphasize the effects of reinforcements on behavior.

The views of Watson and Skinner largely ignored the notions of personal freedom, choice, and self-direction. Most of us assume that our wants originate within us. Watson and Skinner suggested that environmental influences such as parental approval and social custom shape us into *wanting* certain things and *not wanting* others.

In his novel *Walden Two,* Skinner (1948) described a Utopian society in which people are happy and content because they are allowed to do as they please. From early childhood, however, they have been trained or conditioned to be cooperative. Because of their reinforcement histories, they *want* to behave in decent, kind, and unselfish ways. They see themselves as free because society makes no effort to force them to behave in particular ways. The American poet Robert Frost wrote, "You have freedom when you're easy in your harness." Society in Skinner's *Walden Two* made children "easy" in their "harnesses," but the harnesses were very real.

Some object to behaviorist notions because they play down the importance of consciousness and choice. Others argue that humans are not blindly ruled by pleasure and pain. In some circumstances people have rebelled against the so-called necessity of survival by choosing pain and hardship over pleasure, or suicide. Many people have sacrificed their own lives to save those of others; and some commit suicide as a weapon. The behaviorist "defense" might be that the apparent choice of pain or death is forced on some just as conformity to social custom is forced on others.

Social Cognitive Theory

Social cognitive theory was developed by Albert Bandura (1986, 1999, 2002) and other psychologists (e.g., Mischel & Shoda, 1995). *How does social cognitive theory differ from the behaviorist view?* In contrast to behaviorism, which focuses on observable behavior and the situations in which behavior occurs, social cognitive theory focuses on learning by observation and on the cognitive processes that underlie personal differences. Social cognitive theorists see people as influencing their environment just as their environment affects them. Social cognitive theorists agree with behaviorists that discussions of human nature should be tied to observable behavior, but they assert that variables within people—*person variables*—must also be considered if we are to understand people. *Situational variables* include rewards and punishments. Person variables include knowledge and skills, ways of interpreting experience, expectancies, emotions, and self-regulatory systems and plans (Bandura & Locke, 2003; Mischel & Shoda, 1995; see Figure 10.3).

Figure 10.3

Situational and Personal Variables

Neither situational variables nor personal variables enable us to fully understand people and predict behavior. Social cognitive theorists look to their interaction to tell the tale.

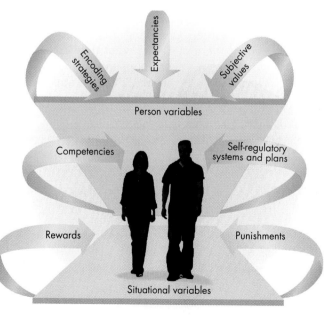

gender-typing
The process by which males and female come to display behavior patterns consistent with stereotypical masculine and feminine gender roles.

gender-schema theory
a cognitive view of gender-typing that proposes that once girls and boys become aware of their anatomic sex, they begin to blend their self-expectations and self-esteem with the ways in which they fit the gender roles prescribed in a given culture

We cannot predict behavior from situational variables alone. Whether a person will behave in a certain way also depends on the person's *expectancies* about the outcomes of that behavior and the perceived or *subjective values* of those outcomes. There are various kinds of expectancies. Some are predictions about what will follow what. For example, people might predict other people's behavior on the basis of body language such as "tight lips" or "shifty eyes." *Self-efficacy expectations* are beliefs that we can accomplish certain things, such as doing a backflip into a swimming pool or solving math problems (Bandura & Locke, 2003). People with positive self-efficacy expectations tend to have high self-esteem (Sanna & Meier, 2000) and achievement motivation (Heimpel et al., 2002). Psychotherapy often motivates people to try new things by changing their self-efficacy expectations from "I can't" to "Perhaps I can" (Bandura, 1999).

Observational Learning

Observational learning (also termed *modeling* or *cognitive learning*) is one of the foundations of social cognitive theory. It refers to acquiring knowledge by observing others. For operant conditioning to occur, an organism must first engage in a response, and that response must be reinforced. But observational learning occurs even when the learner does not perform the observed behavior. Direct reinforcement is not required either. Observing others extends to reading about them or seeing what they do and what happens to them in books, TV, film, and the Internet.

Social Cognitive Theory and Gender-Typing

There seems to be little question that hormonal influences and organization of the brain contribute to gender-typing. Social cognitive theorists, however, suggest that children also learn what is considered masculine or feminine by observational learning. Research evidence shows that children's views of what is masculine and feminine are related to those of their parents (Tenenbaum & Leaper, 2002).

Parents and other adults—even other children—inform children about how they are expected to behave. They reinforce or reward children for behavior they consider appropriate for their anatomic sex. They punish (or fail to reinforce) children for behavior they consider inappropriate.

Girls, for example, are given dolls while they are still sleeping in their cribs. They are encouraged to use the dolls to rehearse caretaking behaviors in preparation for traditional feminine adult roles. Reinforcement helps, but, according to social cognitive theorists, not mechanically. Rather, reinforcement provides information about what behaviors people consider to be proper for girls and boys.

Gender-schema theory further emphasizes the role of cognition in gender-typing (Martin et al., 2002; Martin & Ruble, 2004). Cultures tend to polarize males and females into opposing groups because social life is organized around exclusive gender roles. For example, girls often accept their roles as nurturant (playing with dolls). Unless parents or unusual events encourage them to challenge the validity of gender polarization, children attempt to construct identities that are consistent with the "proper" script. Most children reject behavior that deviates. Children's self-esteem becomes wrapped up in the ways in which they measure up to the gender schema. For example, many boys tie their self-esteem to prowess in sports.

SOMOS/VEER/JUPITER IMAGES

Many males tie their self-esteem to prowess in sports.

Once children understand the labels *boy* and *girl*, they have a basis for blending their self-concepts with the gender schema of their culture. No external pressure is required. Children who have developed a sense of being male or being female, which usually occurs by the age of three, seek to learn what is considered appropriate for them by observing other people (Tenenbaum & Leaper, 2002).

Evaluation of the Learning Perspective

Psychoanalytic theorists and trait theorists propose the existence of psychological structures that cannot be seen and measured directly. Learning theorists—particularly behaviorists—have dramatized the importance of referring to publicly observable variables, or behaviors, if psychology is to be accepted as a science.

Similarly, psychoanalytic theorists and trait theorists focus on internal variables such as unconscious conflict and traits to explain and predict behavior. Learning theorists emphasize the importance of environmental conditions, or situational variables, as determinants of behavior. They have also elaborated on the conditions that foster learning, including automatic kinds of learning. They have shown that we can learn to do things because of reinforcements and that many behaviors are learned by observing others.

Social cognitive theory does not account for self-awareness, and, like its intellectual forebear, behaviorism, it may not pay enough attention to genetic variation in explaining individual differences in behavior.

LO⁴ The Humanistic Perspective

Humanists dwell on the meaning of life. Self-awareness is the hub of the humanistic search for meaning. *What is humanism?*

Humanism puts people and self-awareness at the center of consideration and argues that they are capable of free choice, self-fulfillment, and ethical behavior. It became a third force in American psychology in the 1950s and 1960s, partly in response to the predominant psychoanalytic and behavioral models. Psychoanalysis put people at the mercy of unconscious conflict, and behaviorism argued that people were shaped by the environment.

Abraham Maslow and the Challenge of Self-Actualization

Freud wrote that people are basically motivated to gratify biological drives and that their perceptions are distorted by their psychological needs. *How do humanistic psychologists differ from psychoanalytic theorists?* The humanistic psychologist Abraham Maslow—whose hierarchy of needs we described in Chapter 9—argued that people also have a conscious need for **self-actualization**, or to become all that they can be. Because people are unique, they must follow unique paths to self-actualization. People are not at the mercy of unconscious, primitive impulses. Rather, the main threat to individual personality development is control by other people. We must each be free to get in touch with and actualize our selves. But self-actualization requires taking risks. Many people are more comfortable with the familiar. But people who adhere to the "tried and true" may find their lives slipping into monotony and mediocrity.

Carl Rogers's Self Theory

The humanistic psychologist Carl Rogers (1902–1987) wrote that people shape themselves through free choice and action. *What is your self?* Rogers defined the *self* as the center of experience. Your self is your ongoing sense of who and what you are, your sense of how and why you react to the environment and how you choose to act on the environment. Your choices are made on the basis of your values, and your values are also part of your self. *What is self theory?* Rogers's self theory focuses on the nature of the self and the conditions that allow the self to develop freely. Two of his major concerns are the self-concept and self-esteem.

The Self-Concept and Frames of Reference

Our self-concepts consist of our impressions of ourselves and our evaluations of our adequacy. It may be helpful to think of us as rating ourselves according to various scales or dimensions such as good–bad, intelligent–unintelligent, strong–weak, and tall–short.

Rogers believed that we all have unique ways of looking at ourselves and the world—that is, unique frames of reference. It may be that we each use a different set of dimensions in defining ourselves and

humanism
the view that people are capable of free choice, self-fulfillment, and ethical behavior

self-actualization
in humanistic theory, the innate tendency to strive to realize one's potential

that we judge ourselves according to different sets of values. To one person, achievement–failure may be the most important dimension. To another person, the most important dimension may be decency–indecency. A third person may not even think in these terms.

Self-Esteem and Positive Regard

Rogers assumed that we all develop a need for self-regard, or self-esteem. At first, self-esteem reflects the esteem in which others hold us. Parents help children develop self-esteem when they show them unconditional positive regard—that is, when they accept them as having intrinsic merit regardless of their behavior at the moment. But when parents show children conditional positive regard—that is, when they accept them only when they behave in a desired manner—children may develop conditions of worth. Therefore, children may come to think that they have merit only if they behave as their parents wish them to behave.

Because each individual has a unique potential, children who develop conditions of worth must be somewhat disappointed in themselves. They cannot fully live up to the wishes of others and be true to themselves. This does not mean that the expression of the self inevitably leads to conflict. Rogers believed that we hurt others or act in antisocial ways only when we are frustrated in our efforts to develop our potential. When parents and others are loving and tolerant of our differentness, we, too, are loving—even if our preferences, abilities, and values differ from those of our parents.

Children in some families, however, learn that it is bad to have ideas of their own, especially about sexual, political, or religious matters. When they perceive their caregivers' disapproval, they may come to see themselves as rebels and label their feelings as selfish, wrong, or evil. If they wish to retain a consistent self-concept and self-esteem, they may have to deny their feelings or disown parts of themselves. In this way their self-concept becomes distorted. According to Rogers, anxiety often stems from recognition that people have feelings and desires that are inconsistent with their distorted self-concept. Because anxiety is unpleasant, people may deny the existence of their genuine feelings and desires.

Rogers believed that the path to self-actualization requires getting in touch with our genuine feelings, accepting them, and acting on them. This is the goal of Rogers's method of psychotherapy, *client-centered therapy*. Rogers also believed that we have mental images of what we are capable of becoming. These are termed self-ideals. We are motivated to reduce the difference between our self-concepts and our self-ideals.

Evaluation of the Humanistic Perspective

What are the strengths and weaknesses of humanistic theory? The humanistic perspective has tremendous appeal for college students because of its focus on the importance of personal experience. We tend to treasure our conscious experiences (our "selves"). For most nonhumans, to live is to move, to process food, to exchange oxygen and carbon dioxide, and to reproduce. But for humans, an essential aspect of life is conscious experience—the sense of oneself as progressing through space and time.

Ironically, the primary strength of the humanistic approach—its focus on conscious experience—is also its main weakness. Conscious experience is private and subjective. Therefore, the validity of formulating theories in terms of consciousness has been questioned.

Humanistic theories, like learning theories, have little to say about the development of traits and personality types. They assume that we are all unique, but they do not predict the sorts of traits, abilities, and interests we will develop.

You are unique,
and if
that is not
fulfilled, then
something has
been lost.
—Martha Graham

LO⁵ The Sociocultural Perspective

Thirteen-year-old Hannah brought her lunch tray to the table in the cafeteria. Her mother, Julie, eyed with horror the french fries, the plate of mashed potatoes in gravy, the bag of potato chips, and the large paper cup brimming with soda. "You can't eat that!" she said. "It's garbage!"

"Oh come on, Mom! Chill, okay?" Hannah rejoined before taking her tray to sit with some friends rather than with us.

This scene occurred one Saturday at the Manhattan School of Music. I was sitting with other parents whose children studied piano, voice, or another instrument.

Julie and Hannah are Korean Americans. Flustered, Julie shook her head and said, "I've now been in the United States longer than I was in Korea, and I still can't get used to the way children act here." Dimitri, a Russian American parent, chimed in, "I never would have spoken to my parents the way Michael speaks to me. I would have been . . . whipped or beaten."

"I try to tell Hannah she is part of the family," Julie continued. "She should think of other people. When she talks that way, it's embarrassing."

"Over here children are not part of the family," said Ken, an African American parent. "They are either part of their own crowd or they are 'individuals.'"

"Being an individual does not mean you have to talk back to your mother," Julie said.

Why is the sociocultural perspective important to the understanding of personality? In our multicultural society, personality cannot be understood without reference to the sociocultural perspective. According to a *New York Times* poll, 91% of people in the United States agree that "being an American is a big part" of who they are (Powers, 2000). Seventy-nine percent say that their religion has played a big role or some role in making them who they are, and 54% say that their race has played either a big role or some role (Powers, 2000). Different cultural groups within the United States have different attitudes, beliefs, norms, self-definitions, and values (Phinney, 2000, 2005).

Hannah's traits included exceptional academic ability and musical talent, which were at least partly determined by her heredity. Clearly, she was consciously striving to become a great violinist. We could also detail the ways in which she had learned to play the violin. But we could not fully understand her personality without also considering the sociocultural influences acting on her.

Hannah, a teenager, was strongly influenced by her peers—she was completely at home with blue jeans and french fries. She was also a daughter in an Asian American immigrant group that views education as the key to success in our culture (Leppel, 2002). Belonging to this ethnic group had probably contributed to her ambition. But being a Korean American had not prevented her from becoming an outspoken American teenager. Her outspoken behavior had struck her mother as brazen and inappropriate.

Let us consider how sociocultural factors can affect one's sense of self.

sociocultural perspective
the view that focuses on the roles of ethnicity, gender, culture, and socioeconomic status in personality formation, behavior, and mental processes

individualist
a person who defines herself or himself in terms of personal traits and gives priority to her or his own goals

collectivist
a person who defines herself or himself in terms of relationships to other people and groups and gives priority to group goals

Individualism Versus Collectivism: Who Am I (in This Cultural Setting)?

One could say that Julie's complaint was that Hannah saw herself as an individual and an artist to a greater extent than as a family member and a Korean girl. *What is meant by individualism and collectivism?* Cross-cultural research reveals that people in the United States and many northern European nations tend to be individualistic. Individualists tend to define themselves in terms of their personal identities and to give priority to their personal goals (Triandis, 2005). When asked to complete the statement "I am. . . ," they are likely to respond in terms of their personality traits ("I am outgoing," "I am artistic") or their occupations ("I am a nurse," "I am a systems analyst") (Triandis & Suh, 2005). In contrast, many people from cultures in Africa, Asia, and Central and South America tend to be collectivistic. Collectivists tend to define themselves in terms of the groups to which they belong and to give priority to the group's goals (Bandura, 2003; Triandis, 2005). They feel complete in terms of their relationships with others (see Figure 10.4 on page 224). They are more likely than individualists to conform to group norms and judgments. When asked to complete the statement "I am. . . ," collectivists are more likely to respond in terms of their families, gender, or nation ("I am a father," "I am a Buddhist," "I am a Japanese") (Triandis, 2005).

The seeds of individualism and collectivism are found in the culture in which a person grows up. The capitalist system fosters individualism to some degree. It assumes that individuals are entitled to amass personal fortunes and that the process of

acculturation
the process of adaptation in which immigrants and native groups identify with a new, dominant culture by learning about that culture and making behavioral and attitudinal changes

doing so creates jobs and wealth for large numbers of people. The individualist perspective is found in the self-reliant heroes and antiheroes of Western literature and mass media—from Homer's Odysseus to James Bond. The traditional writings of the East have exalted people who resist personal temptations to do their duty and promote the welfare of the group.

Another issue from the sociocultural perspective is *acculturation*. Just how much acculturation is good for you? *How does acculturation affect the psychological well-being of immigrants and their families?*

Acculturation, Adjustment, and Self-Esteem

Should Hindu women who emigrate to the United States surrender the sari in favor of California Casuals? Should Russian immigrants try to teach their children English at home? Should African American children be acquainted with the music and art of African peoples or those of Europe? Such activities are examples of acculturation, the process by which immigrants become acclimated to the customs and behavior patterns of their new host culture.

Self-esteem has been shown to be connected with patterns of acculturation among immigrants (Berry et al., 2006; Phinney, 2005). Those patterns

take various forms. Some immigrants are completely assimilated by the dominant culture. They lose the language and customs of their country of origin and identify with the dominant culture in the new host country. Others maintain almost complete separation. They retain the language and customs of their country of origin and never acclimate to those of the new country. Still others become bicultural. They remain fluent in the language of their country of origin but also become conversant in the language of their new country. They blend the customs and values of both cultures. They can switch "mental gears"; they apply the values of one culture under some circumstances and apply the values of the other culture under others. Perhaps they relate to other people in one way at work or in school, and in another way at home or in the neighborhood.

Research evidence suggests that people who do not surrender their traditional backgrounds have relatively higher self-esteem than those who do. African American and Mexican Americans who are bicultural are less likely to be anxious and depressed than their peers who identify fully either with the majority culture or their subculture (Kim et al., 2003; Phinney & Devich-Navarro, 1997).

Fiction

Actually, research evidence suggests that people who do not fully surrender their traditional backgrounds have higher self-esteem than those who do.

Figure 10.4

The Self in Relation to Others from the Individualist and Collectivist Perspectives

To an individualist, the self is separate from other people (part A). To a collectivist, the self is complete only in terms of relationships to other people (part B). (Based on Markus & Kitayama, 1991).

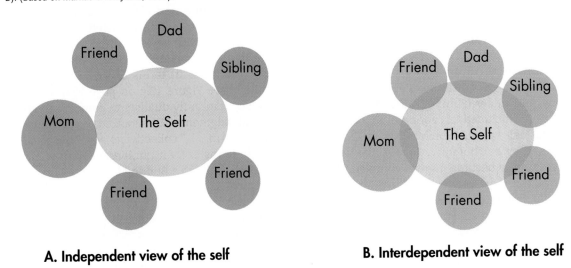

A. Independent view of the self

B. Interdependent view of the self

Evaluation of the Sociocultural Perspective

The sociocultural perspective provides valuable insights into the roles of ethnicity, gender, culture, and socioeconomic status in personality formation. It enhances our sensitivity to cultural differences and expectations and allows us to appreciate the richness of human behavior and mental processes.

LO⁶ Measurement of Personality

Physicians have an easy time of it measuring heart rate and blood pressure. Psychologists, biologists, and neuroscientists find it easier to measure electricity in the brain or substances in the blood than to measure psychological concepts such as intelligence, depression, extraversion, or emotional stability. It may take time, money, and expertise to develop and operate the proper instruments, but once you have them, the measurements tend to be accurate enough.

In Chapter 8 we saw that many critics argue that "intelligence tests" measure many things other than intelligence, including motivation and familiarity with European American middle-class culture. In Chapter 9 we saw that "lie detectors" measure four physiological variables and detect much more than lies. The reliability and validity of intelligence tests and lie detectors have been brought into question. So too have the reliability and validity of personality tests.

The validity of a test is the extent to which it measures what it is supposed to measure. We usually assess the validity of personality tests by comparing test results to external criteria or standards. For example, a test of hyperactivity might be compared with teachers' reports about whether or not children in their classes are hyperactive. The reliability of a test is the stability of one's test results from one testing to another. We usually determine the reliability of tests by comparing testing results on different occasions or at different ages. A reliable IQ test should provide scores during childhood that remain reasonably similar in adolescence and adulthood. Test standardization is a process that checks out the scores, validity, and reliability of a test with people of various ages and from various groups. We cannot assess the intellectual functioning of an individual without relating it to other people in the same age group. Such information is made available when tests are professionally developed and scored.

Behavior-rating scales assess behavior in settings such as classrooms or mental hospitals. With behavior-rating scales, trained observers usually check off each occurrence of a specific behavior within a certain time frame—say, fifteen minutes. Standardized objective and projective tests, however, are used more frequently, and we focus on them in this section.

How are personality measures used? Measures of personality are used to make important decisions, such as whether a person is suited for a certain type of work, a particular class in school, or a drug to reduce agitation. As part of their admissions process, graduate schools often ask professors to rate prospective students on scales that assess traits such as intelligence, emotional stability, and cooperation. Students may take tests to measure their *aptitudes* and interests to gain insight into whether they are suited for certain occupations. It is assumed that students who share the aptitudes and interests of people who function well in certain positions are also likely to function well in those positions.

Let us consider the two most widely used types of personality tests: objective tests and projective tests.

Objective Tests

What are objective personality tests? Objective tests present respondents with a standardized group of test items in the form of a questionnaire. Respondents are limited to a specific range of answers. One test might ask respondents to indicate whether items are true or false for them. Another might ask respondents to select the preferred activity from groups of three.

validity in psychological testing, the degree to which a test measures what it is supposed to measure

reliability in psychological testing, the consistency or stability of test scores from one testing to another

standardization in psychological testing, the process by which one obtains and organizes test scores from various population groups, so that the results of a person's completing a test can be compared to those of others of his or her sex, in his or her age group, and so on

objective tests tests whose items must be answered in a specified, limited manner; tests whose items have concrete answers that are considered correct

Some tests have a *forced-choice format*, in which respondents are asked to indicate which of two or more statements is more true for them or which of several activities they prefer. The respondents are not usually given the option of answering "none of the above." Forced-choice formats are frequently used in interest inventories, which help predict whether the person would function well in a certain occupation. They are typically the only means of responding to online assessments because the test-taker is usually required to "click" the chosen answer. The following item is similar to those found in occupational interest inventories:

I would rather
a. be a forest ranger.
b. work in a busy office.
c. play a musical instrument.

The Minnesota Multiphasic Personality Inventory (MMPI[3]) contains hundreds of items presented in a true–false format. The MMPI is designed to be used by clinical and counseling psychologists to help diagnose psychological disorders. Accurate measurement of an individual's problems should point to appropriate treatment. The MMPI is the most widely used psychological test in clinical work and is widely used in psychological research.

Fiction

No, psychologists cannot guarantee that they can detect deception on a personality test.

The MMPI is usually scored for the four *validity scales* and ten *clinical scales* described in Table 10.2. The validity scales suggest whether answers actually represent the person's thoughts, emotions, and behaviors.

The validity scales in Table 10.2 assess different response sets, or biases, in answering the questions. People with high L scores, for example, may be attempting to present themselves as excessively moral and well-behaved individuals. People with high F scores may be trying to seem bizarre or are answering haphazardly. Many personality measures have some kind of validity scale. The clinical scales of the MMPI assess the problems shown in Table 10.2, as well as stereotypical masculine or feminine interests and introversion.

The MMPI scales were constructed and validated *empirically*—that is, on the basis of actual clinical data rather than psychological theory. A test-item bank of several hundred items was derived from questions that are often asked in clinical interviews. Here are some examples of the kinds of items that were used:

Table 10.2

Minnesota Multiphasic Personality Inventory (MMPI) Scales

Scale	Abbreviation	Possible Interpretations
Validity scales		
Question	?	Corresponds to number of items left unanswered
Lie	L	Lies or is highly conventional
Frequency	F	Exaggerates complaints or answers items haphazardly; may have bizarre ideas
Correction	K	Denies problems
Clinical scales		
Hypochondriasis	Hs	Has bodily concerns and complaints
Depression	D	Is depressed; has feelings of guilt and helplessness
Hysteria	Hy	Reacts to stress by developing physical symptoms; lacks insight
Psychopathic deviate	Pd	Is immoral, in conflict with the law; has stormy relationships
Masculinity/femininity	Mf	High scores suggest interests and behavior considered stereotypical of the other gender
Paranoia	Pa	Is suspicious and resentful, highly cynical about human nature
Psychasthenia	Pt	Is anxious, worried, high-strung
Schizophrenia	Sc	Is confused, disorganized, disoriented; has bizarre ideas
Hypomania	Ma	Is energetic, restless, active, easily bored
Social introversion	Si	Is introverted, timid, shy; lacks self-confidence

PHOTODISC/GETTY IMAGES

Truth

There are actually a number of psychological tests made up of inkblots, and test-takers are indeed asked to say what the blots look like to them.

My father was a good man.	T	F
I am very seldom troubled by headaches.	T	F
My hands and feet are usually warm enough.	T	F
I have never done anything dangerous for the thrill of it.	T	F
I work under a great deal of tension.	T	F

The items were administered to people with previously identified symptoms, such as depressive or schizophrenic symptoms. Items that successfully set these people apart were included.

Projective Tests

How do projective tests differ from objective tests? In **projective tests** there are no clear, specified answers. People are shown ambiguous stimuli such as inkblots or ambiguous drawings and asked to say what they look like or to tell stories about them. There is no one correct response. It is assumed that people *project* their own personalities into their responses. The meanings they attribute to these stimuli are assumed to reflect their personalities as well as the drawings or blots themselves.

The Rorschach Inkblot Test

There are a number of psychological tests made up of inkblots, and test-takers are asked to say what the blots look like to them. The best known of these is the Rorschach inkblot test, named after its originator, Hermann Rorschach.

People are handed the inkblots, one by one, and are asked what they look like or what they could be. A response that reflects the shape of the blot is considered a sign of adequate *reality testing.* A response that richly integrates several features of the blot is considered a sign of high intellectual functioning. Supporters of the Rorschach believe that it provides insight into a person's intelligence, interests, cultural background, personality traits, psychological disorders, and many other variables. Critics argue that there is little empirical evidence to support the test's validity (Garb et al., 2005).

projective test a psychological test that presents ambiguous stimuli onto which the test taker projects his or her own personality in making a response

Although there is no single "correct" response to the inkblot shown in Figure 10.5, some responses are not in keeping with the features of the blots and reveal to the examiner that the test-taker is projecting his or her personality onto the test stimuli. The shape of the inkblot in Figure 10.5 might commonly suggest a butterfly or a flower, or many other things. A test-taker who makes unusual or uncommon responses to the features of the blot may be revealing personality problems.

The Thematic Apperception Test

The Thematic Apperception Test (TAT) was developed in the 1930s by Henry Murray and Christiana Morgan. It consists of drawings, like the one shown on page 199, that are open to various interpretations. Individuals are given the cards one at a time and asked to make up stories about them.

The TAT is widely used in research on motivation and in clinical practice. The assumption is that we are likely to project our own needs into our responses to ambiguous situations, even if we are unaware of them or reluctant to talk about them. The TAT is also widely used to assess attitudes toward other people, especially parents and intimate partners.

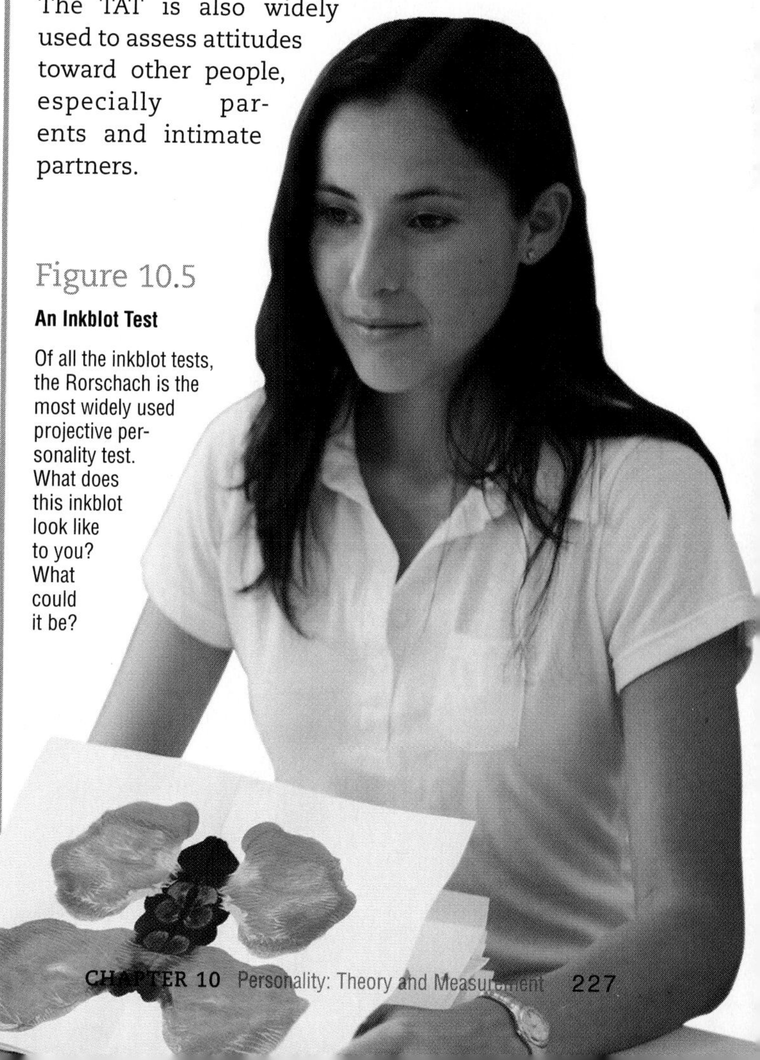

Figure 10.5

An Inkblot Test

Of all the inkblot tests, the Rorschach is the most widely used projective personality test. What does this inkblot look like to you? What could it be?

MASTERFILE (ROYALTY-FREE DIV.)

CHAPTER 11

Stress, Health, and Adjustment

Learning Outcomes

LO [1]   Define stress and identify various sources of stress

LO [2]   Identify the psychological moderators of stress

LO [3]   Describe the impact of stress on the body

LO [4]   Explain the relationships between psychology and health

> ## "Then it dawned on them that people around them were screaming for help."

Katrina came through the door of a home in a New Orleans suburb at ten o'clock on Monday morning. She didn't knock. She flowed underneath the door, and then she began to come in through the windows, the rising waters of a tempest whose winds had tossed torrents against the shore at close to 150 miles per hour.

Gail, a nurse, and her husband Earl, a machinist, had socked away some money for the future and nearly owned their one-story brick home free and clear. They had been looking forward to spending more time with their grandchildren.

But in minutes Katrina changed their lives forever. Before they fully comprehended what was happening, water was sloshing up against their waists.

The front door normally opened out, but Katrina held it shut. Gail and Earl managed to climb out a window against Katrina's onrushing fury.

Gail and Earl, like many of their neighbors, owned a boat—a seventeen-foot Sunbird. They slogged to the boat through the sudden river and the pouring rain, to where it was parked under the roof of the carport. They pulled themselves up onto it, and then they realized that the keys to the engine were still in the house.

Truth or Fiction?

What do you think?

Folklore, common sense, or nonsense? Place a T for "True" or F for "False" on the lines provided (you'll learn the answers as you read through the text).

__ Some stress is good for us.

__ Vacations can be stressful.

__ Searching for social approval or perfection is an excellent way of making yourself miserable.

__ Type A people achieve more than Type B people, but they are less satisfied with themselves.

__ Humor helps us cope with stress.

__ At any given moment, countless microscopic warriors within our bodies are carrying out search-and-destroy missions against foreign agents.

__ If you have a family history of heart disease or cancer, there is little or nothing you can do to prevent developing the illness yourself.

Gail and Earl looked at each other. Earl knew what he had to do. He slid back into the water. There was no more reaching the ground to walk through it. He swam back to the house. Once he was in the house, the water continued to rise.

"The boat was just about touching the roof of the carport," Gail said. "I'm screaming for him to hurry up. Because if we got stuck under there, you know, we would have died" (Herbert, 2005).

Somehow Earl found the keys and worked his way back to the boat and they got the engine going. By the time they left the carport, the water was up to the roof of the house. They could barely see through the rain, much less maneuver, but they managed to move the boat two blocks to the shelter of the roof of the drive-through lane of a bank. But about an hour later they had to return to the storm because the boat was bouncing up against the roof of the drive-through.

Fortunately, the rain eased and Gail and Earl piloted the Sunbird out across the alien waterscape. There was no refilling the engine with gasoline. The gas stations were

stress
the demand that is made on an organism to adapt

eustress
(YOU-stress)
stress that is healthful

health psychology
the field of psychology that studies the relationships between psychological factors (e.g., attitudes, beliefs, situational influences, and behavior patterns) and the prevention and treatment of physical illness

underwater. Even locating themselves had turned eerie, with the street signs underwater. Cars and trucks bobbed by like strange logs in a stream.

Then it dawned on them that people around them were screaming for help. Drenched people stood on rooftops or leaned out of upper-story windows, waving and yelling. Gail and Earl took as many as they could in the Sunbird and found their way to a shelter in a local high school.

Then they turned about and went out for more people. Others—police, firefighters, civilians—were also out in boats doing their part. Local officials managed to find them gasoline. They rode the waters and ferried people to the shelter for two days, bringing in 150. Hungry, unwashed despite the flooding, and exhausted, Gail and Earl were then evacuated themselves to Baton Rouge, where they rested for a couple of days and then made their way to relatives in Florida. It never occurred to them that they were heroes.

Their home is gone. So, too, are their jobs. They lost a car and a truck. Yet they were lucky. "If we did not have family," Gail said, "we'd be living under a bridge." When asked how the ordeal had affected her psychologically, Gail said, "Don't ask me now. It's too early." Later she added, "Listen, everybody's depressed and kind of still in shock. Everybody who's been through this thing. It's hard to believe it happened" (Herbert, 2005).

Disasters like Katrina have their emotional toll as well as their physical toll (Carey, 2005; Leitch, 2005). Studies of communities devastated by hurricanes, oil spills, earthquakes, tsunamis, fires, and other disasters suggest that most survivors eventually come to live with their memories and their grief. But many have lingering nightmares, flashbacks, depression, and irritability that suggest deeper effects of stress.

This chapter is about stress—its origins, its psychological and physical effects, and ways of coping. *What is stress?*

LO¹ Stress: What It Is, Where It Comes From

In physics, stress is defined as a pressure or force exerted on a body. Tons of rock pressing on the earth, one car smashing into another, a rubber band stretching—all are types of physical stress. Psychological forces, or stresses, also press, push, or pull. We may feel "crushed" by the weight of a big decision, "smashed" by adversity, or "stretched" to the point of snapping. In the case of the victims of Katrina, physical events had psychological as well as physical consequences. As we will see throughout the chapter, those psychological consequences can also affect our health.

Psychologists define **stress** as the demand made on an organism to adapt, cope, or adjust. Some stress is healthful and necessary to keep us alert and occupied. Stress researcher Hans Selye (1980) referred to such healthful stress as **eustress**. We may experience eustress when we begin a sought-after job or are trying to choose the color of an iPod. But intense or prolonged stress, such as that caused by Hurricane Katrina or social or financial problems, can overtax our adjustive capacity, affect our moods, impair our ability to experience pleasure, and harm the body (Kiecolt-Glaser et al., 2002a, 2002b; Schneiderman et al., 2005).

Stress is one of the key topics in health psychology. **Health psychology**

AP PHOTO/ERIC GAY

studies the relationships between psychological factors and the prevention and treatment of physical health problems. Health psychologists investigate how

- psychological factors such as stress, behavior patterns, and attitudes can lead to or aggravate illness;

- people can cope with stress;

- stress and pathogens (disease-causing organisms such as bacteria and viruses) interact to influence the immune system;

- people decide whether or not to seek health care; and

- psychological interventions such as health education (for example, concerning nutrition, smoking, and exercise) and behavior modification can contribute to physical health.

Daily Hassles and Life Changes

What are daily hassles? *Daily hassles* are the stresses of everyday life, which can pile up until we can no longer deal with them. Lazarus and his colleagues (1985) analyzed a scale that measures daily hassles and their opposites—termed *uplifts*—and found that hassles could be grouped as follows:

- *Household hassles:* preparing meals, shopping, and home maintenance

- *Health hassles:* physical illness, concern about medical treatment, side effects of medication

- *Time-pressure hassles:* having too many things to do and not enough time

- *Inner concern hassles:* being socially isolated, lonely

- *Environmental hassles:* crime, neighborhood deterioration, noise, pollution

- *Financial responsibility hassles:* concern about owing money, such as mortgage payments and loans

- *Work hassles:* job dissatisfaction

- *Security hassles:* concerns about job security, terrorism, investments, retirement

pathogen
a microscopic organism (e.g., bacterium or virus) that can cause disease

What are life changes? Life changes differ from daily hassles in two ways:

- Many life changes are positive, whereas all hassles are negative.

- Hassles occur regularly, whereas life changes occur at irregular intervals.

Peggy Blake and her colleagues (1984) constructed a scale of "life-change units" to measure the impact of life changes among college students. Surveys with students revealed that death of a spouse or parent were considered the most stressful life changes (94 and 88 life-change units, respectively). Academic failure (77 units) and graduation from college (68 units) were also considered highly stressful, even though graduation from college is a positive event—considering the alternative. Positive life changes such as an outstanding personal achievement (49 units) and going on vacation (30 units) also made the list.

A worker tries to capture some of the oil washing on to a beach in the Gulf of Mexico following the Deepwater Horizon oil spill of 2010. The oil spill killed rig workers, decimated animal life in and around the Gulf, and financially devastated communities whose livelihoods depended on fishing and tourism.

JOE RAEDLE/GETTY IMAGES

Hassles, Life Changes, and Health Problems

Hassles and life changes—especially negative life changes—can cause us to worry and can affect our moods (Lavee & Ben-Ari, 2003). Stressors such as hassles and life changes also predict physical health problems such as heart disease and athletic injuries (Schneiderman et al., 2005). Holmes and Rahe (1967) found that people who "earned" 300 or more life-change units within a year, according to their scale, were at greater risk for health problems. Eight of ten developed health problems, compared with only one of three people whose totals of life-change units for the year were below 150.

Stress in America: The American Psychological Association Survey

Each year the American Psychological Association (2009) has been commissioning surveys of stress in America. In 2009, Harris Interactive conducted an online survey of a nationally representative sample of Americans. The figures for sex, age, race and ethnicity, level of education, region, and household income were adjusted as necessary so that they were brought into line with their actual percentages of the American population at large.

As you see in Figure 11.1, the respondents overwhelmingly reported that money and work were their major sources of stress. We will see later

that "job strain" is a key contributor to heart disease. When we add in the costs of housing, which are mentioned by nearly half the sample, we find another area in which finances contribute to stress. Health is another major area of concern, mentioned in various ways by more than half of the sample. Finally, Figure 11.1 shows that intimate relationships are also a source of stress for half (51%) of the sample. One might think that intimate relationships would serve as a buffer against external sources of stress for people, *and perhaps they do*. (Life is complex.) However, these relationships can also contribute to stress.

Respondents reported many symptoms of stress, both physical and psychological. As shown in Figure 11.2, nearly half the respondents (45%) reported that stress made them irritable or angry. Stress made more than two in five respondents (43%) tired, and about one-third (34%) reported having them headaches. More than one in four (27%) had indigestion, and about one in four (24%) felt tense. Two in five lacked interest in things, and about one-third felt depressed (34%) or as though they could cry (32%).

Figure 11.3 shows that the most commonly reported methods of coping with stress were listening to music (49%), exercising or going for walks (44%0, and reading (41%). Watching TV or movies was tied (36%) with spending time with friends or family. About one-third (32%) reported napping or praying. One in seven (14%) smoke or drank.

Figure 11.1

Significant Sources of Stress

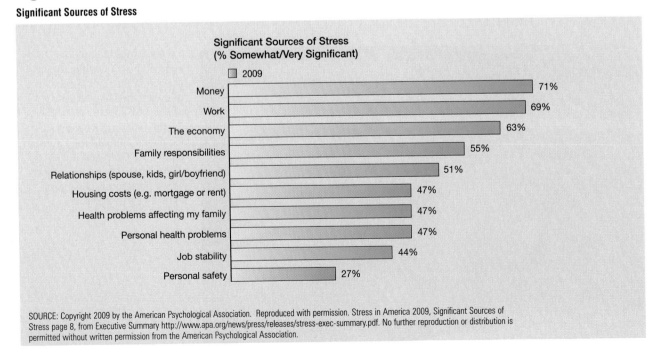

Figure 11.2

Symptoms of Stress

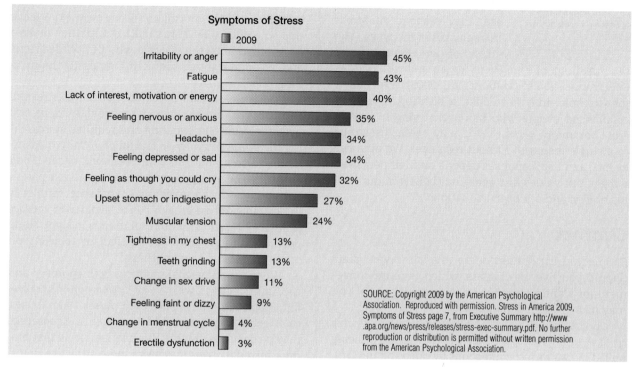

Symptoms of Stress

☐ 2009

Symptom	Percentage
Irritability or anger	45%
Fatigue	43%
Lack of interest, motivation or energy	40%
Feeling nervous or anxious	35%
Headache	34%
Feeling depressed or sad	34%
Feeling as though you could cry	32%
Upset stomach or indigestion	27%
Muscular tension	24%
Tightness in my chest	13%
Teeth grinding	13%
Change in sex drive	11%
Feeling faint or dizzy	9%
Change in menstrual cycle	4%
Erectile dysfunction	3%

SOURCE: Copyright 2009 by the American Psychological Association. Reproduced with permission. Stress in America 2009, Symptoms of Stress page 7, from Executive Summary http://www.apa.org/news/press/releases/stress-exec-summary.pdf. No further reproduction or distribution is permitted without written permission from the American Psychological Association.

Figure 11.3

Stress Management Techniques Used by Americans

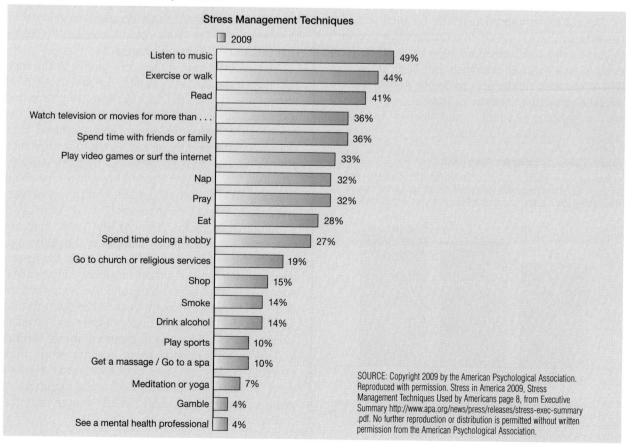

Stress Management Techniques

☐ 2009

Technique	Percentage
Listen to music	49%
Exercise or walk	44%
Read	41%
Watch television or movies for more than . . .	36%
Spend time with friends or family	36%
Play video games or surf the internet	33%
Nap	32%
Pray	32%
Eat	28%
Spend time doing a hobby	27%
Go to church or religious services	19%
Shop	15%
Smoke	14%
Drink alcohol	14%
Play sports	10%
Get a massage / Go to a spa	10%
Meditation or yoga	7%
Gamble	4%
See a mental health professional	4%

SOURCE: Copyright 2009 by the American Psychological Association. Reproduced with permission. Stress in America 2009, Stress Management Techniques Used by Americans page 8, from Executive Summary http://www.apa.org/news/press/releases/stress-exec-summary.pdf. No further reproduction or distribution is permitted without written permission from the American Psychological Association.

conflict
being torn in different directions by opposing motives; feelings produced by being in conflict

Not all people report that the same events cause them stress, or course. And, as we see, they respond to stress in many different ways. The stress of an event reflects the meaning of the event to an individual (CNS Spectrums, 2005; Gaab et al., 2005). Pregnancy, for example, may seem like a blessing to a well-established couple who has been trying to have a child for many years, but it may seem disastrous to a single teenager without resources. We appraise events, and our responses depend on their perceived danger, our values and goals, our beliefs in our coping ability, and our social situations.

Conflict

Should you eat dessert or try to stick to your diet? Should you live on campus, which is more convenient, or should you rent an apartment, where you may have more independence?

Choices like these can place us in conflict. *What is conflict?* In psychology, conflict is the feeling of being pulled in two or more directions by opposing motives. Conflict is frustrating and stressful. Psychologists often classify conflicts into four types: approach–approach, avoidance–avoidance, approach–avoidance, and multiple approach–avoidance.

Classic experimental research by Neal E. Miller (1944) and others suggests that the *approach–approach conflict* is the least stressful type of conflict. Here each of two goals is desirable, and both are within reach. You may not be able to decide between pizza or tacos, or a trip to Nassau or Hawaii. I recently had such a conflict in which I was "forced" to choose

between triple-chocolate fat-free frozen yogurt and coffee chocolate-chip fat-free frozen yogurt. Such conflicts are usually resolved by making a decision (I took the triple chocolate). Those who experience this type of conflict may vacillate until they make a decision, as shown by people who put off decisions and ruminate about conflicting goals (Emmons & King, 1988).

Avoidance–avoidance conflict is more stressful because you are motivated to avoid each of two negative goals. But avoiding one requires approaching the other. You may be fearful of visiting the dentist but also afraid that your teeth will decay if you do not make an appointment and go. Each potential outcome in an avoidance–avoidance conflict is undesirable. When an avoidance–avoidance conflict is highly stressful and no resolution is in sight, some people withdraw from the conflict by focusing on other matters or doing nothing.

When the same goal produces both approach and avoidance motives, we have an *approach–avoidance conflict*. People and things have their pluses and minuses, their good points and their bad points. Cheesecake may be delicious, but oh, the calories! Goals that produce mixed motives may seem more attractive from a distance but undesirable from up close (Miller, 1944). Many couples who repeatedly break up and reunite recall each other fondly when apart and swear that they could make the relationship work if they got together again. But after they do spend time together, they again wonder, "How could I ever have believed that this so-and-so would change?"

The most complex form of conflict is the *multiple approach–avoidance conflict*, in which each of several alternative courses of action has pluses and minuses. This sort of conflict might arise on the eve of an examination, when you are faced with the choice of studying or, say, going to a film. Each alternative has both positive and negative aspects: "Studying's a bore, but I won't have to worry about flunking. I'd love to see the movie, but I'd just be worrying about how I'll do tomorrow."

Research by Robert Emmons and Laura King has connected internal conflict with various health problems. In one study (Emmons & King, 1988), the researchers enlisted eighty-eight college undergraduates and surveyed their personal goals and the degree of conflict experienced between them. They used diaries to assess the students' emotional lives and physical symptoms. Students who reported more conflict and more ambivalence about conflict more often reported feeling anxious and depressed, reported more physical complaints, and made significantly more visits to the college health center over the course of two years.

Figure 11.4

Impact of Stress on Eating and Sleep Habits

In their survey on stress in America, the American Psychological Association found that respondents reported that stress caused them to disrupt their usual eating and sleep habits, as shown in this figure.

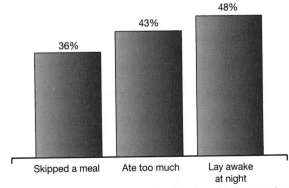

SOURCE: Copyright 2009 by the American Psychological Association. Reproduced with permission. Stress in America 2009, Impact of Stress on Sleep and Eating Habits page 9, from Stress in America 2007 Executive Summary http://www.apa.org/pubs/info/reports/2007-stress.doc. No further reproduction or distribution is permitted without written permission from the American Psychological Association.

Table 11.1

Irrational Beliefs: Cognitive Doorways to Distress

Irrational Belief 1:	You must have sincere love and approval almost all the time from the people who are important to you.
Irrational Belief 2:	You must prove yourself to be thoroughly competent, adequate, and achieving at something important.
Irrational Belief 3:	Things must go the way you want them to go. Life is awful when you don't get your first choice in everything.
Irrational Belief 4:	Other people must treat everyone fairly and justly. When people act unfairly or unethically, they are rotten.
Irrational Belief 5:	When there is danger or fear in your world, you must be preoccupied with and upset by it.
Irrational Belief 6:	People and things should turn out better than they do. It's awful and horrible when you don't find quick solutions to life's hassles.
Irrational Belief 7:	Your emotional misery stems from external pressures that you have little or no ability to control. Unless these external pressures change, you must remain miserable.
Irrational Belief 8:	It is easier to evade life's responsibilities and problems than to face them and undertake more rewarding forms of self-discipline.
Irrational Belief 9:	Your past influenced you immensely and must therefore continue to determine your feelings and behavior today.
Irrational Belief 10:	You can achieve happiness by inertia and inaction, or by just enjoying yourself from day to day.

JUPITERIMAGES / GETTY IMAGES

catastrophize
to interpret negative events as being disastrous; to "blow out of proportion"

Irrational Beliefs

Psychologist Albert Ellis noted that our beliefs about events, as well as the events themselves, can be stressors (Ellis, 2002, 2004a, 2004b). Consider a case in which a person is fired from a job and is anxious and depressed about it. It may seem logical that losing the job is responsible for the misery, but Ellis pointed out how the individual's beliefs about the loss compounded his or her misery.

How do irrational beliefs create or compound stress? Let us examine this situation according to Ellis's A→B→C approach: Losing the job is an *activating event* (A). The eventual outcome, or *consequence* (C), is misery. Between the activating event (A) and the consequence (C), however, lie *beliefs* (B), such as these: "This job was the most important thing in my life," "What a no-good failure I am," "My family will starve," "I'll never find a job as good," "There's nothing I can do about it." Beliefs such as these compound misery, foster helplessness, and divert us from planning and deciding what to do next. The belief that "There's nothing I can do about it" fosters helplessness. The belief that "I am a no-good

failure" internalizes the blame and may be an exaggeration. The belief that "My family will starve" may also be an exaggeration.

Let's diagram the situation:

> Activating events →Beliefs →Consequences
> or A→B→C

Anxieties about the future and depression over a loss are normal and to be expected. The beliefs of the person who lost the job, however, tend to **catastrophize** the extent of the loss and contribute to anxiety and depression—and thus raise the person's blood pressure (Dunkley et al., 2003; Melmed, 2003). By heightening the individual's emotional reaction to the loss and fostering feelings of helplessness, these beliefs also impair coping ability. They lower the person's self-efficacy expectations.

Ellis proposed that many of us carry with us the irrational beliefs shown in Table 11.1. They are our personal doorways to distress. In fact, they can give rise to problems in themselves. When problems assault us from other sources, these beliefs can magnify their effect.

Truth

Research findings confirm the connections between irrational beliefs (e.g., excessive dependence on social approval and perfectionism) and feelings of anxiety and depression (Ciarrochi, 2004; Rice & Dellwo, 2001; Wiebe & McCabe, 2002).

Ellis found it understandable that we would want the approval of others but irrational to believe that we cannot survive without it. It would be nice to be competent in everything we do, but it's unreasonable to *expect* it. Sure, it would be nice to be able to serve and volley like a tennis pro, but most of us haven't the time or natural ability to perfect the game. Demanding perfection prevents us from going out on the court on weekends and batting the ball back and forth just for fun (Ciarrochi, 2004). The belief that one must be preoccupied by threats is a prescription for perpetual emotional upheaval. Believing that we cannot overcome the influences of the past leads to feelings of helplessness and demoralization. Sure, Ellis might say, childhood experiences can explain the origins of irrational beliefs, but it is our own cognitive appraisal—here and now—that causes us to be miserable.

The Type A Behavior Pattern

Some people create stress for themselves through the Type A behavior pattern. *What is Type A behavior?* Type A people are highly driven, competitive, impatient, hostile, and aggressive—so much so that they are prone to getting into auto accidents (Ben-Zur, 2002; Karlberg et al., 1998; Magnavita et al., 1997). They feel rushed and pressured and keep one eye glued to the clock (Conte et al., 2001). They are not only prompt for appointments but often early. They eat, walk, and talk rapidly. They grow restless when others work slowly. They attempt to dominate group discussions. Type A people find it difficult to surrender control or share power. They are reluctant to delegate authority in the workplace and thus increase their own workloads. They watch their form, perfect their strokes, and strive for continual self-improvement. They require

Truth

It is true that Type A people achieve more than Type B people but are less satisfied with themselves.

themselves to achieve in everything they do. Type B people relax more readily than Type A people and focus more on the quality of life. They are less ambitious and less impatient, and they pace themselves. Type A people earn higher grades and more money than Type B's who are equal in intelligence, but Type A people are more likely to continue to strive for more and more.

LO² Psychological Moderators of Stress

Five out of six respondents to the *Stress in America* survey reported that stress caused some physical symptom or some psychological symptom, but there is no one-to-one relationship between stress and physical or psychological health problems. Some people inherit predispositions to specific health problems. Psychological factors can also play a role (Melmed, 2003). In the next section we discuss several psychological factors that can influence, or *moderate*, the effects of stress.

Self-Efficacy Expectations: "The Little Engine That Could"

Our self-efficacy expectations affect our abilities to withstand stress and make things happen.

JOSE LUIS PELAEZ INC/BLEND IMAGES/JUPITER IMAGES

Self-efficacy is the ability to make things happen. Our self-efficacy expectations affect our ability to withstand stress (Basic Behavioral Science Task Force, 1996a; Maciejewski et al., 2000). *How do our self-efficacy expectations affect our ability to withstand stress?*

A classic experiment by Albert Bandura and his colleagues (1985) shows that high self-efficacy expectations are accompanied by relatively *lower* levels of adrenaline and noradrenaline in the bloodstream when we are faced with fear-inducing objects. The Bandura group assessed subjects' self-efficacy, exposed them to fearful stimuli, and monitored the levels of adrenaline and noradrenaline in their bloodstreams as they did so. Adrenaline and noradrenaline are secreted when we are under stress. They arouse the body in several ways, such as accelerating the heart rate and releasing glucose from the liver. As a result, we may have "butterflies in the stomach" and feel nervous. Excessive arousal can also distract us from coping with the tasks at hand.

People who are self-confident are less prone to be disturbed by adverse events (Kaslow et al., 2002; Lang & Heckhausen, 2001). People with higher self-efficacy expectations are more likely to lose weight or quit smoking and less likely to relapse afterward (E. S. Anderson et al., 2000, 2001; Shiffman et al., 2000). They are better able to function in spite of pain (Lackner et al., 1996). A study of Native Americans found that alcohol abuse was correlated with self-efficacy expectations (Walle, A. H., 2004). That is, individuals with feelings of powerlessness were more likely to abuse alcohol, perhaps as a way of lessening stress.

People are more likely to comply with medical advice when they believe that it will work (Schwartzer & Renner, 2000). Women, for example, are more likely to engage in breast self-examination when they believe that they will really be able to detect abnormal growths (Miller et al., 1996). People are more likely to try to quit smoking when they believe that they can do so successfully (Segan et al., 2002).

Psychological Hardiness

Psychological hardiness also helps people resist stress (Kaddour, 2003; Richardson, 2002). Our understanding of hardiness is derived largely from the pioneering work of Suzanne Kobasa and her colleagues (1994). They studied business executives who seemed able to resist illness despite stress. In one phase of the research, executives completed a battery of psychological tests. Kobasa (1990) found that the psychologically hardy executives had three key characteristics. *What characteristics are connected with psychological hardiness?* The characteristics

include commitment, challenge, and control.

- Kobasa found that psychologically hardy executives were high in *commitment*. They tended to involve themselves in, rather than feel alienated from, whatever they were doing or encountering. A Slovakian study found that psychologically hardy secondary school students try to actively solve problems rather than avoid them (Baumgartner, 2002).

psychological hardiness
a cluster of traits that buffer stress and are characterized by commitment, challenge, and control

locus of control
the place (locus) to which an individual attributes control over the receiving of reinforcers—either inside or outside the self

- They were also high in *challenge*. They believed that change, rather than stability, is normal in life. They appraised change as an interesting incentive to personal growth, not as a threat to security.

- They were high in perceived *control* over their lives. A sense of control is one of the keys to psychological hardiness (Folkman & Moskowitz, 2000b; Tennen & Affleck, 2000). Hardy participants felt and behaved as though they were influential, rather than helpless, in facing the various rewards and punishments of life. Psychologically hardy people tend to have what Julian B. Rotter (1990) terms an internal **locus of control**.

Hardy people may be more resistant to stress because they *choose* to face it (Baumgartner, 2002; Kobasa, 1990). They also interpret stress as making life more interesting. For example, they see a conference with a supervisor as an opportunity to persuade the supervisor rather than as a risk to their position.

Sense of Humor

The idea that humor lightens the burdens of life and helps people cope with stress has been with us for millennia. Consider the biblical maxim, "A merry heart doeth good like a medicine" (Proverbs 17: 22). *Is there any evidence that humor helps us cope with stress?* Research suggests that humor can moderate the effects of stress (Godfrey, 2004). In one classic study, for example, students completed a checklist of negative life events and a measure of mood disturbance (Martin &

A sense of humor can lighten the burdens of the day.

Truth

Research suggests that humor can indeed moderate the effects of stress.

internals
people who perceive the ability to attain reinforcements as being largely within themselves

externals
people who perceive the ability to attain reinforcements as being largely outside themselves

Lefcourt, 1983). The measure of mood disturbance yielded a stress score. The students also rated their sense of humor. Students were asked to try to produce humor in an experimental stressful situation, and their ability to do so was rated by the researchers. Students who had a greater sense of humor and were capable of producing humor in the stressful experimental condition were less affected by the stress than other students. In other experiments, Lefcourt (1997) found that exposing students to humorous videotapes raised the level of immunoglobin A (a measure of the functioning of the immune system) in their saliva.

How does humor help people cope with stress? We are uncertain, but there are many possibilities. One is that laughter stimulates the output of endorphins, which might enhance the functioning of the immune system. Another is that the benefits of humor may be explained in terms of the positive cognitive shifts they entail and the positive emotions that accompany them.

Predictability and Control

The ability to predict a stressor apparently moderates its impact. *How do predictability and control help us cope with stress?* Predictability allows us to brace ourselves for the inevitable and, in many cases, plan ways of coping with it. Control—even the illusion of being in control—allows us to feel that we are not at the mercy of the fates (Folkman & Moskowitz, 2000b; Tennen & Affleck, 2000). There is also a relationship between the desire to assume control over one's situation and the usefulness of information about impending stressors. Predictability is of greater benefit to internals—that is, to people who wish to exercise control over their situations—than to externals. People who want information about medical procedures and what they will experience cope better with pain when they undergo those procedures (Ludwick-Rosenthal & Neufeld, 1993).

Social Support

People are social beings, and social support also seems to act as a buffer against the effects of stress (Cohen et al., 2003; Folkman & Moskowitz, 2000a). The concept of social support has many definitions:

- *Emotional concern:* listening to people's problems and expressing feelings of sympathy, caring, understanding, and reassurance.

- *Instrumental aid:* the material supports and services that facilitate adaptive behavior. For example, after a disaster the government may arrange for low-interest loans so that survivors can rebuild. Relief organizations may provide food, medicines, and temporary living quarters.

- *Information:* guidance and advice that enhance people's ability to cope.

- *Appraisal:* feedback from others about how one is doing. This kind of support involves helping people interpret, or "make sense of," what has happened to them.

- *Socializing:* conversation, recreation, going shopping with someone. Socializing is beneficial even when it is not oriented toward solving problems.

Does social support help people cope with stress? Yes, research does support the value of social support. Introverts, people who lack social skills, and people who live by themselves seem more prone to developing infectious diseases such as colds under stress (Cohen et al., 2003). Social support helps Mexican Americans and other immigrants to cope with the stresses of acculturation (Hovey, 2000). Social support helped children cope with the stresses of Hurricane Andrew (Vernberg et al., 1996) and Chinese villagers cope with an earthquake (X. Wang et al., 2000). Stress is less likely to lead to high blood pressure or alcohol abuse in people who have social support (Linden et al., 1993). Even online social support helps people cope with the stresses of cancer and other health problems (Broom, 2005; Hoybye et al., 2005).

How does stress contribute to the development of physical health problems? In the next section, we consider the effects of stress on the body.

LO^3 Stress and the Body

Stress is more than a psychological event. It is more than "knowing" it is there; it is more than "feeling" pushed and pulled. Stress also has very definite effects on the body which, as we will see, can lead to psychological and physical health problems. Stress researcher Hans Selye outlined a number of the bodily effects in his concept of the general adaptation syndrome (GAS).

The General Adaptation Syndrome

Hans Selye suggested that under stress the body is like a clock with an alarm that does not shut off until the clock shakes apart or its energy has been depleted. The body's response to different stressors shows certain similarities whether the stressor is a bacterial invasion, perceived danger, or a major life change (Selye, 1976). For this reason, Selye labeled this response the general adaptation syndrome (GAS). *What is the general adaptation syndrome?* The GAS is a group of bodily changes that occur in three stages: an alarm reaction, a resistance stage, and an exhaustion stage. These changes mobilize the body for action and—like that alarm that goes on ringing—can eventually wear out the body.

The Alarm Reaction

The alarm reaction is triggered by perception of a stressor. This reaction mobilizes or arouses the body, biologically speaking. Early in the 20th century, physiologist Walter B. Cannon (1932) argued that this mobilization was the basis for an instinctive fight-or-flight reaction. The fight-or-flight response kicks the endocrine, cardiovascular, and musculoskeletal systems into action to enable survival. Short-term stress can enhance the functioning of the immune system as well, thus helping prevent infection from wounds, but chronic or long-term stress can impair the functioning of the immune system (Dhabhar, 2009).

Stress has a domino effect on the endocrine system (Bauer et al., 2003; Melmed, 2003; see Figure 11.5). The hypothalamus secretes corticotrophin-releasing hormone (CRH). CRH causes the pituitary gland to secrete adrenocorticotrophic hormone (ACTH). ACTH then causes the adrenal cortex to secrete cortisol and other corticosteroids (steroidal hormones produced by the adrenal cortex). Corticosteroids help protect the body by combating allergic reactions (such as difficulty in breathing) and producing inflammation (Leonard, 2005). (However, corticosteroids can be harmful to the cardiovascular system, which is one reason that chronic stress can impair one's health and why athletes who use steroids to build the muscle mass can experience cardiovascular problems.) Inflammation increases circulation to parts of the body that are injured. It ferries in hordes of white blood cells to fend off invading pathogens.

Two other hormones that play a major role in the alarm reaction are secreted by the adrenal medulla. The sympathetic division of the ANS activates the adrenal medulla, causing it to release a mixture of adrenaline and noradrenaline. This mixture arouses the body by accelerating the heart rate and causing the liver to release glucose (sugar). This provides the energy that fuels the fight-or-flight reaction, which activates the body so that it is prepared to fight or flee from a predator.

The fight-or-flight reaction stems from a period in human prehistory when many stressors were life

general adaptation syndrome (GAS) Selye's term for a hypothesized three-stage response to stress

alarm reaction the first stage of the GAS, which is triggered by the impact of a stressor and characterized by sympathetic activity

fight-or-flight reaction an innate adaptive response to the perception of danger

Figure 11.5

Stress and the Endocrine System

Stress has a domino effect on the endocrine system, leading to the release of corticosteroids and a mixture of adrenaline and noradrenaline. Corticosteroids combat allergic reactions (such as difficulty in breathing) and cause inflammation. Adrenaline and noradrenaline arouse the body to cope by accelerating the heart rate and providing energy for the fight-or-flight reaction.

Go to CourseMate for PSYCH to access an interactive version of this figure.

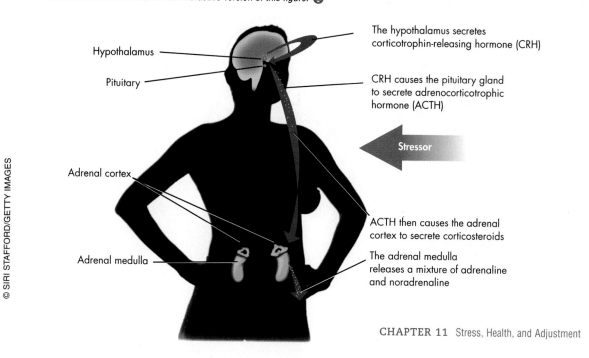

© SIRI STAFFORD/GETTY IMAGES

Hypothalamus

Pituitary

Adrenal cortex

Adrenal medulla

The hypothalamus secretes corticotrophin-releasing hormone (CRH)

CRH causes the pituitary gland to secrete adrenocorticotrophic hormone (ACTH)

Stressor

ACTH then causes the adrenal cortex to secrete corticosteroids

The adrenal medulla releases a mixture of adrenaline and noradrenaline

threatening. It was triggered by the sight of a predator at the edge of a thicket or by a sudden rustling in the undergrowth. Today it may be aroused when you are caught in stop-and-go traffic or learn that your mortgage payments are going to increase. Once the threat is removed, the body returns to a lower state of arousal. Many of the bodily changes that occur in the alarm reaction are outlined in Table 11.2.

Many contemporary theorists do not believe that the fight-or-flight reaction is universal. Shelley Taylor and her colleagues (2000) report evidence that many women engage in a tend-and-befriend response to threats, rather than a fight-or-flight response. Margaret Kemeny and her colleagues (e.g., Updegraff et al., 2002) also observe that some people attempt to respond productively to stress by pulling back from the situation to better appraise it and conserve their resources while they are doing so. This response pattern to stress is described by two theories that are currently under development: cognitive adaptation theory and conservation of resources theory.

The Resistance Stage

According to Selye's theory, if the alarm reaction mobilizes the body and the stressor is not removed, we enter the adaptation or resistance stage of the GAS. Levels of endocrine and sympathetic activity are lower than in the alarm reaction but still higher than normal. (It's as if the alarm is still on, but a bit softer.) But make no mistake: The person feels tense, and the body remains under a heavy burden.

The Exhaustion Stage

If the stressor is still not dealt with adequately, we may enter the exhaustion stage of the GAS. Individual capacities for resisting stress vary, but anyone will eventually become exhausted when stress continues indefinitely. The muscles become fatigued. The body is depleted of the resources required for combating stress. With exhaustion, the parasympathetic division of the ANS may predominate. As a result, our heartbeat and respiration rate slow down, and many aspects of sympathetic activity are reversed. It might sound as if we would profit from the respite, but remember that we are still under stress—possibly an external threat. Continued stress in the exhaustion stage may lead to what Selye terms "diseases of adaptation." These are connected with constriction of blood vessels and

COCOON/PHOTODISC/JUPITER IMAGES

Table 11.2

Components of the Alarm Reaction*

Corticosteroids are secreted.
Adrenaline is secreted.
Noradrenaline is secreted.
Respiration rate increases.
Heart rate increases.
Blood pressure increases.
Muscles tense.
Blood shifts from internal organs to the skeletal musculature.
Digestion is inhibited.
Sugar is released from the liver.
Blood coagulability increases.

*The alarm reaction is triggered by stressors. It is defined by the release of corticosteroids and adrenaline and by activity of the sympathetic branch of the autonomic nervous system.

alternation of the heart rhythm, and can range from allergies to hives and coronary heart disease (CHD)—and, ultimately, death.

Discussion of the effects of stress on the immune system paves the way for understanding the links between psychological factors and physical illness.

Effects of Stress on the Immune System

Research shows that stress suppresses the immune system, as measured by the presence of various substances in the blood that make up the immune system (Antoni et al., 2005; Hawkley & Cacioppo, 2004). Psychological factors such as feelings of control and social support moderate these effects (Cohen et al., 2001a).

The Immune System

Given the complexity of the human body and the fast pace of scientific change, we often feel that we are dependent on trained professionals to cope with illness. Yet we actually do most of this coping by ourselves, by means of the immune system. *How does the immune system work?*

The immune system combats disease in several ways (Delves & Roitt, 2000; Leonard, 2005). One way is the production of white blood cells, which engulf and kill pathogens such as bacteria, fungi, and viruses, and worn-out and cancerous body cells. The technical term for white blood cells is leukocytes. They engage in search-and-destroy missions in which they "recognize" and eradicate foreign agents and unhealthy cells.

Leukocytes recognize foreign substances, or antigens, by their shapes. The body reacts to antigens by generating specialized proteins, or antibodies. Antibodies attach themselves to the antigens, deactivating them and marking them for destruction. The immune system "remembers" how to battle antigens by maintaining their

immune system
the system of the body that recognizes and destroys foreign agents (antigens) that invade the body

leukocytes
white blood cells (derived from the Greek words *leukos*, meaning "white," and *kytos*, literally meaning "a hollow" but used to refer to cells)

antigen
a substance that stimulates the body to mount an immune system response to it (short for *antibody generator*)

antibodies
substances formed by white blood cells that recognize and destroy antigens

Truth

Leukocytes carry on microscopic warfare.

{ Are There Gender Differences in Response to Stress? }

For a century, it has been widely believed that humans are prewired to experience what biologist Walter Cannon labeled a "fight-or-flight" reaction to stress. Cannon believed we are instinctively pumped up to fight like demons or, when advisable, to beat a hasty retreat.

Or are we? Not all of us, according to UCLA psychologist Shelley E. Taylor and her colleagues (2000b). Taylor found that women under stress are more likely to tend to the kids or "interface" with family and friends than either fight or flee. The "woman's response" to stress, the "tend-and-befriend" response, involves nurturing and seeking social support rather than fighting or fleeing. When females face a threat, a disaster, or even an especially bad day at the office, they often respond by caring for their children and seeking social contact and support from others, especially other women.

This response may be prewired in female humans and in females of other mammalian species. Evolutionary psychologists suggest that the tend-and-befriend response might have become sealed in human genes because it promotes the survival of females who are tending their young. Females who choose to fight might die or be separated from their young—no evolutionary brass ring there.

Males may be more aggressive than females under stress because of the balance of hormones in their bodies. Due to such differences, women tend to outlive men. "Men are more likely than women to respond to stressful experiences by developing certain stress-related disorders, including hypertension, aggressive behavior, or abuse of alcohol or hard drugs," Taylor added in a press release (May 2000).

PLAINPICTURE/CORBIS

antibodies in the bloodstream, often for years.[1]

Inflammation is another function of the immune system. When injury occurs, blood vessels in the area first contract (to stem bleeding) and then dilate. Dilation increases the flow of blood, cells, and natural chemicals to the damaged area, causing the redness, swelling, and warmth that characterize inflammation (Leonard, 2005). The increased blood supply also floods the region with white blood cells to combat invading microscopic life-forms such as bacteria, which otherwise might use the local damage as a port of entry into the body.

Stress and the Immune System

One of the reasons that stress eventually exhausts us is that it stimulates the production of steroids. Steroids suppress the functioning of the immune system. Suppression has negligible effects when steroids are secreted occasionally. But persistent secretion of steroids decreases inflammation and interferes with the formation of antibodies. As a consequence, we become more vulnerable to infections, including the common cold (Barnard et al., 2005; Cohen et al., 2001b, 2003).

In one study, dental students showed lower immune system functioning, as measured by lower levels of antibodies in their saliva, during stressful periods of the school year than immediately following vacations (Jemmott et al., 1983). In contrast, social support buffers the effects of stress and enhances the functioning of the immune system (Cohen et al., 2001a, 2001b). In the Jemmott study, students who had many friends showed less suppression of immune system functioning than students with few friends.

Other studies with students show that the stress of exams depresses the immune system's response to the Epstein-Barr virus, which causes fatigue and other problems (Glaser et al., 1993). Here, too, lonely students showed greater suppression of the immune system than students who had social support. All in all, however, there is only modest evidence that psychological interventions enhance the functioning of the immune system. A review of the research found that hypnosis (intended to help people relax), stress management methods, and conditioning methods were of some use, but less than reliable (Miller & Cohen, 2001).

❋ ❋ ❋

[1] A vaccination introduces a weakened form of an antigen (usually a bacteria or a virus) into the body to stimulate the production of antibodies. Antibodies can confer immunity for many years, in some cases for a lifetime.

LO⁴ Psychology and Chronic Health Problems

© 2010 GOODSHOOT/ JUPITERIMAGES CORPORATION

Why do people become ill? Why do some people develop cancer? Why do others have heart attacks? Why do still others seem to be immune to these illnesses? *What is the biopsychosocial approach to health?* The biopsychosocial approach recognizes that there is no single, simple answer to these questions. The likelihood of contracting an illness—be it a case of the flu or cancer—can reflect the interaction of many factors, including biological, psychological, and sociocultural factors (Schneiderman et al., 2005).

Biological factors such as pathogens, inoculations, injuries, age, gender, and a family history of disease may strike us as the most obvious causes of illness. Genetics, in particular, tempts some people to assume that there is little they can do about their health. Some cases of health problems are unavoidable for people with certain genes. However, if you have a family history of heart disease or cancer, it is *not* true that there is little or nothing you can do to prevent developing the disease. In many cases, especially with heart problems and cancer, genes only create *predispositions* toward the health problem. The life choices we make—the behaviors we select—also affect our likelihood of becoming ill (Hoover, 2000).

Genetic predispositions interact with the environment to express themselves (Kéri, 2003). For example, genetic factors are involved in breast cancer. However, rates of breast cancer among women who have recently emigrated to the United States from rural Asia are similar to those in their countries of origin and nearly 80% lower than the rates among third-generation Asian American women, whose rates are similar to those of European American

Fiction

It is *not* true that if you have a family history of heart disease or cancer, there is little or nothing you can do to prevent developing the illness yourself.

women (Hoover, 2000). Thus, factors related to one's lifestyle are also intimately connected with the risk of breast cancer—and most other kinds of cancer.

Biological, psychological (behavior and personality), sociocultural factors, and stressors all play roles in health and illness. Many health problems are affected by psychological factors, such as attitudes, emotions, and behavior (Kiecolt-Glaser et al., 2002b; Salovey et al., 2000). Table 11.3 reveals that nearly one million deaths each year in the United States are preventable (Health, United States, 2002). Stopping smoking, eating right, exercising, and controlling alcohol use would prevent nearly 80% of these. Psychological states such as anxiety and depression can impair the functioning of the immune system, rendering us more vulnerable to physical disorders ranging from viral infections to cancer (McGuire et al., 2002; Salovey et al., 2000).

Let us now discuss the chronic health problems of heart disease and cancer. Each involves biological, psychological, and environmental factors—including the social and technological environments. Although these are medical problems, we also explore ways in which psychologists have contributed to their prevention and treatment.

Coronary Heart Disease

Coronary heart disease (CHD) is the leading cause of death in the United States, most often from heart attacks (American Heart Association, 2005b). *What are the major risk factors for coronary heart disease?* Let us begin by considering the risk factors for CHD. (American Heart Association, 2008):

- *Family history:* People with a family history of CHD are more likely to develop the disease themselves.

- *Physiological conditions:* Obesity, high *serum cholesterol* levels, and *high blood pressure* are risk factors for CHD. About one American in five has hypertension, or abnormally high blood pressure, which can lead to CHD. When high blood pressure has no identifiable cause, it is referred to as *essential hypertension.* This condition has a genetic component. Blood pressure is also, however, connected with emotions like depression and anxiety. It also rises when we inhibit the expression of strong feelings or are angry or on guard against threats. When we are under stress, we may believe that we can feel our blood pressure "pounding through the roof," but this notion is usually false. Most people cannot recognize hypertension. Therefore, it is important to check the blood pressure regularly.

- *Patterns of consumption:* Patterns include heavy drinking, smoking, and overeating. On the other hand, a little alcohol seems to be good for the heart.

WOMEN MARRIED TO A SMOKER HAVE A 91% GREATER RISK OF HEART DISEASE.

SECONDHAND SMOKE. STILL WANT TO BREATHE IT?

Table 11.3

Annual Preventable Deaths in the United States*

- Elimination of tobacco use could prevent 400,000 deaths each year from cancer, heart and lung diseases, and stroke.

- Improved diet and exercise could prevent 300,000 deaths from conditions like heart disease, stroke, diabetes, and cancer.

- Control of underage and excess drinking of alcohol could prevent 100,000 deaths from motor vehicle accidents, falls, drownings, and other alcohol-related injuries.

- Immunizations for infectious diseases could prevent up to 100,000 deaths.

- Safer sex or sexual abstinence could prevent 10,000–20,000 deaths from sexually transmitted infections (STIs).

*Other measures for preventing needless deaths include improved worker training and safety to prevent accidents in the workplace, wider screening for breast and cervical cancer, and control of high blood pressure and elevated blood cholesterol levels.

- *Type A behavior:* Most studies suggest that there is at least a modest relationship between Type A behavior and CHD. Research suggests that alleviating Type A behavior may reduce the risk of *recurrent* heart attacks.

- *Hostility and holding in feelings of anger:* Hostility seems to be the component of the Type A behavior pattern that is most harmful to physical health. People who are highly prone to anger are about three times as likely as other people to have heart attacks (Williams et al., 2000). The stress hormones connected with anger can constrict blood vessels to the heart, leading to a heart attack. Highly hostile young adults—as young as 18 to 30—are already at greater risk for hardening of the arteries, which increases the risk of heart attacks (Iribarren et al., 2000).

- *Job strain:* Overtime work, assembly line labor, and exposure to conflicting demands can all contribute to CHD. High-strain work, which makes heavy demands on workers but gives them little personal control, puts workers at the highest risk (Bishop et al., 2003; Krantz et al., 1988; Smith & Ruiz, 2002).

- *Chronic fatigue, stress, anxiety, depression, and emotional strain*

- *Sudden stressors:* After the 1994 Los Angeles earthquake there was an increased incidence of death from heart attacks in people with heart disease (Leor et al., 1996).

- *A physically inactive lifestyle.*

African Americans are more likely than any other ethnic group in the United States to have heart attacks and to die from them (National Center for Health Statistics, 2009). Figure 11.6 compares the death rates from heart disease of American men and women of various ethnic backgrounds. Asian Americans, Native Americans, and Latina and Latino Americans are less likely than Europeans or African Americans to die from heart disease. Early diagnosis and treatment might help decrease the racial gap.

Measures such as the following may help reduce the risk of coronary heart disease: stopping smoking; eating fewer saturated fats and more fruits, vegetables, and whole grains; reducing hypertension and lowering LDL (harmful) serum cholesterol, through medicine if necessary; modifying Type A behavior; managing feelings of anger; and exercising regularly (get a medical checkup first).

Figure 11.6

Deaths from Heart Disease per 100,000 People, All Ages

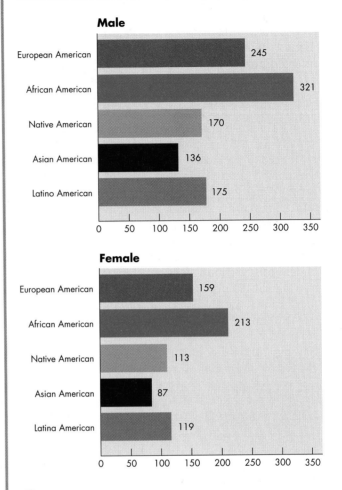

Male

European American	245
African American	321
Native American	170
Asian American	136
Latino American	175

Female

European American	159
African American	213
Native American	113
Asian American	87
Latina American	119

Cancer

According to the National Vital Statistics Reports, cancer is the second-leading cause of death in the United States (Minino et al., 2007). Cancer is characterized by the development of abnormal, or mutant, cells that may take root anywhere in the body: in the blood, bones, digestive tract, lungs, and sex organs. If their spread is not controlled early, the cancerous cells may *metastasize*—that is, establish colonies elsewhere in the body. It appears that our bodies develop cancerous cells frequently. However, these are normally destroyed by the immune system. People whose immune system is damaged by physical or psychological factors may be more likely to develop tumors (Antoni, 2003, 2009).

Risk Factors

What are the major risk factors for cancer? As with many other disorders, people can inherit a disposition toward cancer (American Cancer Society, 2005a; Hoover, 2000). Carcinogenic genes may remove the

BLEND IMAGES/ROLF BRUDERER/DIGITAL RAILROAD

brakes from cell division, allowing cells to multiply wildly. Or they may allow mutations to accumulate unchecked. Many behavior patterns, however, markedly heighten the risk for cancer. These include smoking, drinking alcohol (especially in women), and sunbathing (which may cause skin cancer due to exposure to ultraviolet light). Prolonged psychological conditions such as depression or stress may heighten the risk of some kinds of cancer by depressing the functioning of the immune system (Bauer et al., 2003; McGuire et al., 2002; Salovey et al., 2000).

African Americans are more likely than European Americans to contract most forms of cancer (American Cancer Society, 2005b). Possibly because of genetic factors, the incidence of lung cancer is significantly higher among African Americans than European Americans (American Cancer Society, 2005b). Once they contract cancer, African Americans are more likely than European Americans to die from it (American Cancer Society, 2005b). The results for African Americans are connected with their lower socioeconomic status and relative lack of access to health care (Altman, 2005; Whitfield et al., 2002).

Also consider cultural differences in health. Death rates from cancer are higher in such nations as the Netherlands, Denmark, England, Canada, and—yes—the United States, where average rates of animal fat intake are high (Bray & Atkin, 2004). Death rates from cancer are lower in such nations as Thailand, the Philippines, and Japan, where fat intake is lower and people eat more fruits and vegetables. However, studies in the United States have brought into question the usefulness of eating fruits and vegetables in preventing cancer.

For example, Karin Michels and her colleagues (2000) followed some 80,000 women and 40,000 men over several years and found little connection between eating fruits and vegetables and the risk of colon and rectal cancers. Arthur Schatzkin and his colleagues (2000) studied some 2,000 women and men who had had precancerous growths removed from their colons. The subjects were randomly assigned to eat low-fat diets that were high in fiber, fruits, and vegetables and were assessed four years later. There were no differences in the incidence of new precancerous growths in the colons of the two groups.

Researchers have also suggested possible links between stress and cancer (Salovey et al., 2000). For example, Rachel Yehuda (2003) suggests that stress sometimes lowers levels of cortisol and impairs the ability of the immune system to destroy cancer cells. But here, too, the research evidence calls these theoretical links into question.

For example, Polly Newcomb (2005), head of a Seattle cancer prevention program, interviewed nearly 1,000 women, some of whom had developed breast cancer and others who had not. The women were asked about the incidence of major life changes over a five-year period. There were no differences in the incidence of these life events between the cancer patients and the other women.

Does stress cause cancer, then? "I have no idea, and nobody else does, either," replies Ohio State psychologist Barbara Andersen (2005), who researches stress reduction in cancer patients. "If somebody suggested that they know, I would question them."

Measures such as the following may help reduce the risk of developing or dying from cancer: getting regular medical checkups to detect cancer early; stopping smoking; eating fewer saturated fats and more fruits, vegetables, and whole grains; and exercising regularly (get a medical checkup first). Cancer is most curable when it is detected early, before it metastasizes.

---

51 < percent of people report being stressed by their children

percent of people report being stressed out by money > **71**

percent of people report having stress-related headaches > **34**

percent of people report having stress-related upset stomachs or indigestion > **27**

47 < percent of people report being stressed about their health

28 < percent of people killed by heart disease

24 < percent of people killed by cancer

Psychological Disorders

Learning Outcomes

LO 1   Define psychological disorders and describe their prevalence

LO 2   Describe the symptoms, types, and possible origins of schizophrenia

LO 3   Describe the symptoms and possible origins of mood disorders

LO 4   Describe the symptoms and possible origins of anxiety disorders

LO 5   Describe the symptoms and possible origins of somatoform disorders

LO 6   Describe the symptoms and possible origins of dissociative disorders

LO 7   Describe the symptoms and possible origins of personality disorders

" The devil made me do it. "

Let's listen in on part of an interview with Etta:

Etta: Well . . . ah . . . Jesus was giving me all these cracks, window cracks, and screen crack sounds telling me that they was going to break into the house. So I put the camera stereo in the room where they jiggled the window off to come through the window. And the camera stereo, the security guards picked that up, the message by putting that camera in that room.

Interviewer: Were you in danger?

Etta: Well, if anyone gets into the house they said I'd get shot.

Interviewer: Who said?

Etta: That's The Eagle.

Interviewer: Can you say a little something about The Eagle?

Etta: The Eagle works through General Motors. It has something to do with my General Motors check I get every month.

Interviewer: And you get that check because it's part of your husband's work with GM?

Etta: Yes.

Interviewer: Say something about the relationship between GM and The Eagle.

Etta: Well . . . ah . . . when you do the twenty-five of the clock it means that you leave the house after one to mail letters so that they can check on you what how you're mailing the mail and they know when you're at that time.

Interviewer: And who's "they"?

Etta: That's The Eagle.

Truth or Fiction?

What do you think?

Folklore, common sense, or nonsense? Place a T for "True" or F for "False" on the lines provided (you'll learn the answers as you read through the text).

___ In the Middle Ages, people suspected of witchcraft were drowned as a way of proving that they were possessed.

___ People with schizophrenia may see and hear things that are not really there.

___ Feeling elated is not always a good thing.

___ Some people have more than one personality dwelling within them, and each one may have different allergies and eyeglass prescriptions.

___ Some people can kill or maim others without any feelings of guilt.

If you have the feeling that Etta is not making sense, you are quite correct. Etta has been diagnosed with the psychological disorder termed schizophrenia. Schizophrenia is a thought disorder—meaning that Etta's thoughts are not coherent. Normally our thoughts are rather tightly knit, having a beginning, a middle, and an end. Etta's thoughts—the way things are associated with one another—have come loose. She jumps from Jesus to cracks in the window to her "camera stereo" to "The Eagle" to General Motors to twenty-five o'clock (which does not exist) and the mail.

Etta also sees herself as being under attack. "They" are trying to break into the house. There's some kind of plot afoot having to do with The Eagle and General Motors. "They" are checking on her. Etta

schizophrenia
a psychotic disorder characterized by loss of control of thought processes and inappropriate emotional responses

KATRINA WITTKAMP/TAXI/GETTY IMAGES

delusions
false, persistent beliefs that are unsubstantiated by sensory or objective evidence

affect (AFF-ekt)
feeling or emotional response, particularly as suggested by facial expression and body language

psychological disorders
patterns of behavior or mental processes that are connected with emotional distress or significant impairment in functioning

has false beliefs, or delusions, that she is being observed and persecuted. Yet for someone who believes she is being persecuted, Etta doesn't appear to be all that upset. Her affect—that is, her emotional response—is "flat" and inappropriate to the situation.

Schizophrenia is a psychological disorder, perhaps the most severe of psychological disorders. Fortunately—or unfortunately—it affects only about 1% of the population.

If Etta had lived in Salem, Massachusetts, in 1692, just 200 years after Columbus set foot in the New World, she might have been hanged as a witch. At that time, most people assumed that the strange behaviors that we associate with psychological disorders were caused by possession by the devil. A score of people were executed in Salem that year for allegedly practicing the arts of Satan.

Possession could stem from retribution, in which God allowed the devil to possess a person's soul as punishment for committing certain kinds of sins. Agitation and confusion were ascribed to such retribution. Possession was also believed to result from deals with the devil, in which people traded their souls for earthly gains. Such individuals were called witches. Witches were held responsible for unfortunate events ranging from a neighbor's infertility to a poor harvest. During the Middle Ages in Europe, as many as 500,000 accused witches were killed (Hergenhahn, 2009). The goings on at Salem were trivial by comparison.

A document authorized by Pope Innocent VIII, *The Hammer of Witches*, proposed ingenious "diagnostic" tests, such as the water-float test, to identify those who were possessed. The water-float test was based on the principle that pure metals sink to the bottom during smelting. Impurities float to the surface. Suspects were thus placed in deep water. Those who sank to the bottom (and drowned) were judged to be pure. Those who managed to keep their heads above water were assumed to be "impure" and in league with the devil. Then they were in real trouble. This ordeal is the origin of the phrase, "Damned if you do, and damned if you don't."

Truth

A document authorized by Pope Innocent VIII proposed tests, such as the water-float test, to identify those who were possessed.

Exorcism
This medieval woodcut represents the practice of exorcism, in which a demon is expelled from a person who has been "possessed."

Few people in the United States today would claim that unusual or unacceptable behavior is caused by demons. Still, we continue to use "demonic" language. How many times have you heard the expressions "Something got into me" or "The devil made me do it"?

Sometimes unusual and unacceptable behavior is a result of a psychological disorder. *What exactly are psychological disorders?*

LO¹ What Are Psychological Disorders?

Psychology is the study of behavior and mental processes. Psychological disorders are behaviors or mental processes that are connected with distress or disability. They are not predictable responses to specific events.

Some psychological disorders are characterized by anxiety, but many people are anxious now and then without being considered disordered. It is appropriate to be anxious before an important date or on the eve of a midterm exam. When then are feelings like anxiety deemed to be abnormal or signs of a psychological disorder?

For one thing, anxiety may suggest a disorder when it does not fit the situation. For example, there is (usually) little or no reason to be anxious when entering an elevator or looking out of a fourth-story window. The magnitude of the problem may also suggest disorder. Some anxiety can be expected before a job interview. However, feeling that your heart is pounding so intensely that it might leap out of your chest—and then avoiding the interview—are not.

Behaviors or mental processes are suggestive of psychological disorders when they meet some combination of the following standards:

- *Is the behavior unusual?* Etta's thoughts and her speech patterns were quite unusual, found only among a small minority of the population. Yet uncommon behavior or mental processes are not necessarily abnormal in themselves. Only one person holds the record for running or swimming the fastest mile. That person is different from you and me but is not abnormal. Thus, rarity or statistical deviance is not sufficient for behavior or mental processes to be labeled abnormal. We must also consider the situation. Although many of us feel "panicked" when we realize that a term paper or report is due the next day, most of us do not have panic attacks "out of the blue." Unpredictable panic attacks are thus a psychological disorder.

- *Does the behavior suggest faulty perception or interpretation of reality?* Etta's beliefs about The Eagle and General Motors suggested faulty interpretation of reality. Hearing voices and seeing things that are not there are considered **hallucinations**. **Ideas of persecution**, such as believing that the Mafia or the FBI is "out to get you," are also considered signs of disorder. (Unless, of course, they *are* out to get you.)

- *Is the person's emotional response appropriate to the situation?* Irrational fears, such as intense fear of injections and depression among people with "good lives," may be considered inappropriate and thus abnormal. Etta, on the other hand, showed **flat affect**—too little emotional response—when she reported imaginary events that should have been frightening.

- *Is the behavior self-defeating?* Behavior or mental processes that cause misery rather than happiness and fulfillment may suggest psychological disorder. Chronic drinking impairs one's health and may therefore be deemed abnormal. Fear of needles is more likely to be considered abnormal if it prevents one from receiving necessary medical treatment.

- *Is the behavior dangerous?* Behavior or mental processes that are hazardous to the self or others may be considered suggestive of psychological disorders. People who threaten or attempt suicide may be considered abnormal, as may people who threaten or attack others. But aggressive behavior in athletics—within certain limits, as in contact sports—is not considered disordered.

- *Is the behavior socially unacceptable?* We must consider the cultural context of a behavior pattern in judging whether or not it is normal.

Classifying Psychological Disorders

Classification is at the heart of science. Without classifying psychological disorders, investigators would not be able to communicate with each other and scientific progress would come to a halt. The most widely used classification scheme for psychological disorders is the *Diagnostic and Statistical Manual of Mental Disorders (DSM–IV–TR)* of the American Psychiatric Association (2000). *How are psychological disorders classified?*

The current edition of the *DSM* is the *DSM-IV-TR* (fourth edition, text revision), and it provides information about a person's overall functioning as well as a diagnosis. People may receive diagnoses for clinical syndromes or personality disorders, or for both. It also includes information about people's medical conditions, psychosocial problems, and a global assessment of functioning. Medical conditions include physical disorders or problems that may affect people's response to psychotherapy or drug treatment. Psychosocial and environmental problems include difficulties that may affect the diagnosis, treatment, or outcome of a psychological disorder. The global assessment of functioning allows the clinician to compare the client's current level of functioning with her or his highest previous level of functioning to help set goals for restoring functioning.

Although the *DSM* is widely used, researchers have some concerns about it. Two of them concern the *reliability* and *validity* of the diagnostic standards. The *DSM* might be considered *reliable* if different interviewers or raters would make the same diagnosis when they evaluate the same people. The *DSM* might be considered *valid* if the diagnoses described in the manual correspond to clusters of behaviors observed in the real world. In the case of Etta, the *DSM* might be considered reliable if various evaluators who were using the manual arrived at the same diagnosis—schizophrenia. Referring once more to Etta, the *DSM* might be considered valid if the diagnosis of schizophrenia, described in the manual, fits Etta's actual behavior. A specific type of validity, called predictive validity, means that if a diagnosis is valid, we should be able to predict what will happen to the person over time (that is, the *course* of the disorder) and what type of treatment may be of help.

Prevalence of Psychological Disorders

At first glance, psychological disorders might seem to affect only a few of us. Relatively few people are admitted to psychiatric hospitals. Most people will never seek the help of a psychologist or psychiatrist.

Classification is at the heart of science.

hallucination
a perception in the absence of sensory stimulation that is confused with reality

ideas of persecution
erroneous beliefs that one is being victimized or persecuted

flat affect
a severe reduction in emotional expressiveness, found among many people with schizophrenia or serious depression

predictive validity
in this usage, the extent to which a diagnosis permits one to predict the course of a disorder and the type of treatment that may be of help

Table 12.1

Past-Year and Lifetime Prevalences of Psychological Disorders

	Anxiety Disorders	Mood Disorders	Bipolar Disorders	Substance Use Disorders	Any Disorders
Prevalence during past year	18.1%	9.5%	2.8%	3.8%	26.2%
Lifetime prevalence	28.8%	20.8%	4.4%	14.6%	46.4%
Median age of onset	11 years	30 years	21 years	20 years	14 years

Sources: Kessler et al., 2005, Merikangas, K. R., et al. (2007).

Note: The data in this table are based on a nationally representative sample of 9,282 English-speaking U.S. residents aged 18 and above. Respondents could report symptoms of more than one type of disorder. For example, anxiety and mood disorders are often "comorbid"—that is, go together. Anxiety and mood disorders are discussed in this chapter. Substance use disorders include abuse of or dependence on alcohol or other drugs, as described in Chapter 5.

And the insanity plea—though well publicized—is a rarity in the criminal justice system. Many of us have "eccentric" relatives or friends, but most of them are not considered to be literally "crazy." Nonetheless, psychological disorders affect us all in one way or another.

About half of us will meet the criteria for a DSM-IV disorder at some time or another in our lives, with the disorder most often first beginning in childhood or adolescence (Kessler et al., 2005a; see Table 12.1). Slightly more than one-quarter of us will experience a psychological disorder in any given year (Kessler et al., 2005c); (see Table 12.1). But if we include the problems of family members, friends, and coworkers, add in the number of those who foot the bill in terms of health insurance and taxes, and factor in increased product costs due to lost productivity, perhaps everyone is affected.

Let us now consider the various kinds of psychological disorders. We begin with schizophrenia, the disorder with which Etta was diagnosed.

LO² Schizophrenia

When interviewers listened to Etta's incoherent story about Jesus and cracks in the window and her "camera stereo," they suspected that she could be diagnosed with schizophrenia. *What is schizophrenia?* Schizophrenia is a severe psychological disorder that touches every aspect of a person's life. It is characterized by disturbances in thought and language, perception and attention, motor activity, and mood, and by social withdrawal and absorption in daydreams or fantasy (Heinrichs, 2005).

Schizophrenia has been referred to as the worst disorder affecting people. It afflicts nearly 1% of the population worldwide. Its onset occurs relatively early in life, and it tends to endure.

People with schizophrenia have problems in memory, attention, and communication. Their thinking and communication ability becomes unraveled (Kerns & Berenbaum, 2002). Unless we allow our thoughts to wander, our thinking is normally tightly knit. We start at a certain point, and thoughts are logically connected. But people with schizophrenia often think illogically. As with Etta, their speech may be jumbled. They may combine parts of words into new words or make meaningless rhymes. They may jump from topic to topic, conveying little useful information. They usually do not recognize that their thoughts and behavior are abnormal.

Many people with schizophrenia, like Etta, have delusions—for example, delusions of grandeur, persecution, or reference. In the case of delusions of grandeur, a person may believe that he is a famous historical figure such as Jesus, or a person on a special mission. He may have grand, illogical plans for saving the world. Delusions tend to be unshakable even in the face of evidence that they are not true. People with delusions of persecution, like Etta, may believe that they are sought by the Mafia, CIA, FBI, or some other group. A woman with delusions of reference said that news stories contained coded information about her. A man with such delusions complained that neighbors had "bugged" his walls with "radios." Other people with schizophrenia have had delusions that they have committed unpardonable sins, that they were rotting away from disease, or that they or the world did not exist.

People with schizophrenia may see or hear things that are not really there. Their perceptions often include hallucinations—imagery in the absence of external stimulation that the person cannot distinguish from reality. Other people who experience hallucinations may see colors or even obscene words spelled out in midair. Auditory hallucinations are most common.

In individuals with schizophrenia, motor activity may become wild or so slowed that the person is said to be in a stupor—that is, a condition in which the senses, thought, and movement are inhibited. There may be strange gestures and grimaces. The person's emotional responses may be flat or blunted, or inappropriate—as in giggling upon hearing bad news. People with schizophrenia tend to withdraw from social contacts, and become wrapped up in their own thoughts and fantasies.

Positive Versus Negative Symptoms

Many investigators find it useful to distinguish between positive and negative symptoms of schizophrenia. *What are the positive and negative symptoms of schizophrenia?* The positive symptoms are the excessive and sometimes bizarre symptoms, including hallucinations, delusions, and looseness of associations. The negative symptoms are the deficiencies we find among people with schizophrenia, such as lack of emotional expression and motivation, loss of pleasure in activities, social withdrawal, and poverty of speech.

Etta showed an abundance of positive symptoms, including delusions, along with negative symptoms, such as flat affect. The distinction is useful not only in terms of description, but also in terms of development of the disorder and likely outcome. For example, people with mainly positive symptoms are more likely to experience an abrupt onset of the disorder and tend to preserve their intellectual abilities. The positive symptoms also respond more favorably to antipsychotic medication (Roth et al., 2004; Walker et al., 2004). People with mainly negative symptoms tend to experience a more gradual development of the disorder and severe intellectual impairments in attention, memory, and so on. The negative symptoms also respond more poorly to antipsychotic drugs.

It may be that positive and negative symptoms represent different but related biological processes. Positive symptoms may involve deficiency in the brain mechanisms that normally inhibit excessive or bizarre behaviors. They may reflect a disturbance in regulation of dopamine in the brain, because drugs

stupor
a condition in which the senses, thought, and movement are dulled

positive symptoms
the excessive and sometimes bizarre symptoms of schizophrenia, including hallucinations, delusions, and loose associations

negative symptoms
the deficiencies among people with schizophrenia, such as flat affect, lack of motivation, loss of pleasure, and social withdrawal

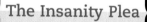

The Insanity Plea

In 1982, John Hinckley, Jr., was found not guilty of the assassination attempt on President Reagan's life, even though the shooting was witnessed by millions on television. Expert witnesses testified that he should be diagnosed with schizophrenia. Hinckley was found not guilty by reason of insanity and committed to a psychiatric institution, where he remains to this day. What does it mean to be "insane"? What is the "insanity plea"?

In pleading insanity, lawyers use the M'Naghten rule, named after Daniel M'Naghten, who tried to assassinate the British prime minister, Sir Robert Peel, in 1843. He killed Peel's secretary in the attempt. M'Naghten had delusions that Peel was persecuting him. The court found M'Naghten not guilty by reason of insanity. The M'Naghten rule states that the accused did not understand what she or he was doing at the time of the act or did not realize it was wrong. (Follingstad & McCormick, 2002; McSherry, 2005; Nagtegaal, 2004).

Many people would like to ban the insanity plea because they equate it with people's "getting away with murder." But there may not be all that much cause for concern. The insanity defense is raised in only about 1% of cases (Silver, 1994). Moreover, people found to be not guilty by reason of insanity are institutionalized for indefinite terms—supposedly until they are no longer insane.

While on trial, John Hinckley, Jr., looks on while his father cries and claims responsibility for "John's tragedy" because he prevented his son from coming home when he desperately needed help.

Truth

It is true that people with schizophrenia may see and hear things that are not really there.

that regulate dopamine levels generally reduce bizarre behavior. Negative symptoms may reflect structural damage to the brain. Even so, positive and negative symptoms can coexist in the same person. Thus, these groups of symptoms have descriptive value but do not appear to represent distinct types of schizophrenia. *What types of schizophrenia are there?*

All types of schizophrenia involve a thought disorder. There are, however, various "types" with different emphases on positive and negative symptoms, including paranoid, disorganized, and catatonic schizophrenia.

Paranoid Schizophrenia

People with paranoid schizophrenia, such as Etta, have systematized delusions and, frequently, related auditory hallucinations. They usually have delusions of grandeur and persecution, but they may also have delusions of jealousy, in which they believe that a spouse or lover has been unfaithful. They may show agitation, confusion, and fear, and may experience vivid hallucinations that are consistent with their delusions. People with paranoid schizophrenia often construct complex or systematized delusions involving themes of wrongdoing or persecution. John Nash, whose life was depicted in the movie *A Beautiful Mind*, believed that the government was recruiting him to decipher coded messages by our Cold War enemies.

Disorganized Schizophrenia

People with disorganized schizophrenia show incoherence, loosening of associations, disorganized behavior, disorganized delusions, fragmentary delusions or hallucinations, and flat or highly inappropriate emotional responses. Extreme social impairment is common. People with this type of schizophrenia may also exhibit silliness and giddiness of mood,

giggling, and nonsensical speech. They may neglect their appearance and personal hygiene and lose control of their bladder and bowels.

Catatonic Schizophrenia

People with catatonic schizophrenia show striking impairment in motor activity. It is characterized by a slowing of activity into a stupor that may suddenly change into an agitated phase. Catatonic people may maintain unusual and even difficult postures for hours, even as their limbs grow swollen or stiff. A striking feature of this condition is waxy flexibility, in which the person maintains positions into which he or she has been manipulated by others. Catatonic individuals may also show mutism, but afterward they usually report that they heard what others were saying at the time.

Schizophrenia is thus characterized by extremely unusual behavior. *What is known about the origins of schizophrenia?*

Explaining Schizophrenia

Biological, psychological, and sociocultural factors may all contribute to schizophrenia.

Biological Perspectives

Schizophrenia appears to be a brain disorder (Heinrichs, 2005). Many studies have been done to determine how the brains of schizophrenic people may differ from those of others. Studies have

Catatonic Schizophrenia
People with catatonic schizophrenia show striking motor impairment and may hold unusual positions for hours.

GRUNNITUS STUDIO / PHOTO RESEARCHERS, INC.

focused on the amount of gray matter in the brain, the size of ventricles (hollow spaces), activity levels in the brain, and brain chemistry.

One avenue of brain research connects the major deficits we find in schizophrenia—problems in attention, working memory, abstract thinking, and language—with dysfunction in the prefrontal cortex of the brain (Heinrichs, 2005). Brain imaging has shown that some but not all people with schizophrenia have less gray matter than other people (Heinrichs, 2005; Kasai et al., 2003; Thompson et al., 2001; see Figure 12.1). Many have smaller brains and, in particular, a smaller prefrontal region of the cortex (Heinrichs, 2005; Selemon et al., 2003). They also tend to have larger ventricles in the brain than other people (Keller et al., 2003). Brain scans suggest that people with schizophrenia also tend to have a lower level of activity in the frontal region of the brain (Lahti, et al., 2001; Meyer-Lindenberg et al., 2001). Still other research connects the lower activity levels with a loss in synapses in the region (Glantz & Lewis, 2000; Selemon et al., 2003; Wolkin et al., 2003).

What might account for differences in brain structure and functioning? Heredity, complications during pregnancy and birth, and birth during winter are all risk factors for schizophrenia. Schizophrenia, like many other psychological disorders, runs in families (Conklin & Iacono, 2002; Hwu et al., 2003). People with schizophrenia make up about 1% of the population. Yet children with one parent who has been diagnosed with schizophrenia have about a 10% chance of being diagnosed with schizophrenia themselves. Children with two such parents have about a 35% to 40% chance of being so diagnosed (Gottesman, 1991;

Straube & Oades, 1992). Twin studies also find about a 45% matching rate for the diagnosis among pairs of identical (MZ) twins, whose genetic codes are the same, compared with a 17% rate among pairs of fraternal (DZ) twins, who share half their genetic code (Plomin & Crabbe, 2000). Moreover, adoptee studies find that the biological parent typically places the child at greater risk for schizophrenia than the adoptive parent—even though the child has been reared by the adoptive parent (Gottesman, 1991). Sharing genes with relatives who have schizophrenia apparently places a person at risk of developing the disorder. Many studies have been carried out to try to isolate the gene or genes involved in schizophrenia. Some studies find locations for multiple genes on several chromosomes.

Many people with schizophrenia have undergone complications during pregnancy and birth (Heinrichs, 2005). For example, the mothers of many people with schizophrenia had the flu during the sixth or seventh month of pregnancy (Brown & Susser, 2002). An interaction between biology and the sociocultural setting is found in the link between poor maternal nutrition and schizophrenia (Hulshoff et al., 2000; Pol et al., 2000). Complications during childbirth, especially prolonged labor, seem to be connected with the larger ventricles we find among people with schizophrenia (McNeil et al., 2000). People with schizophrenia are also somewhat more likely to have been born during winter than would be predicted by chance (Pol et al., 2000; Suvisaari et al., 2002). Alcohol abuse may also lead to differences in brain structures among people with schizophrenia (E. V. Sullivan et al., 2000). On the

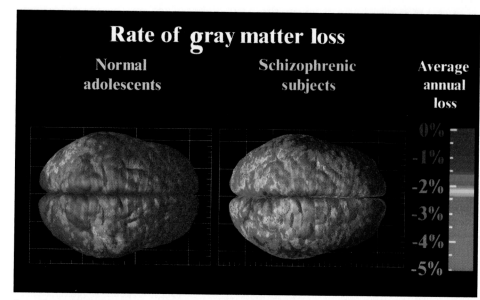

Rate of gray matter loss

Normal adolescents — Schizophrenic subjects — Average annual loss

0% −1% −2% −3% −4% −5%

Source: Thompson et al., 2001.

Figure 12.1

Average Rates of Loss of Gray Matter Among Normal Adolescents and Adolescents Diagnosed with Schizophrenia

High-resolution MRI scans show rates of gray matter loss in normal thirteen- to eighteen-year-olds and among adolescents of the same age diagnosed with schizophrenia. Maps of brain changes reveal profound, progressive loss in schizophrenia (right). Loss also occurs in normal adolescents (left), but at a slower rate.

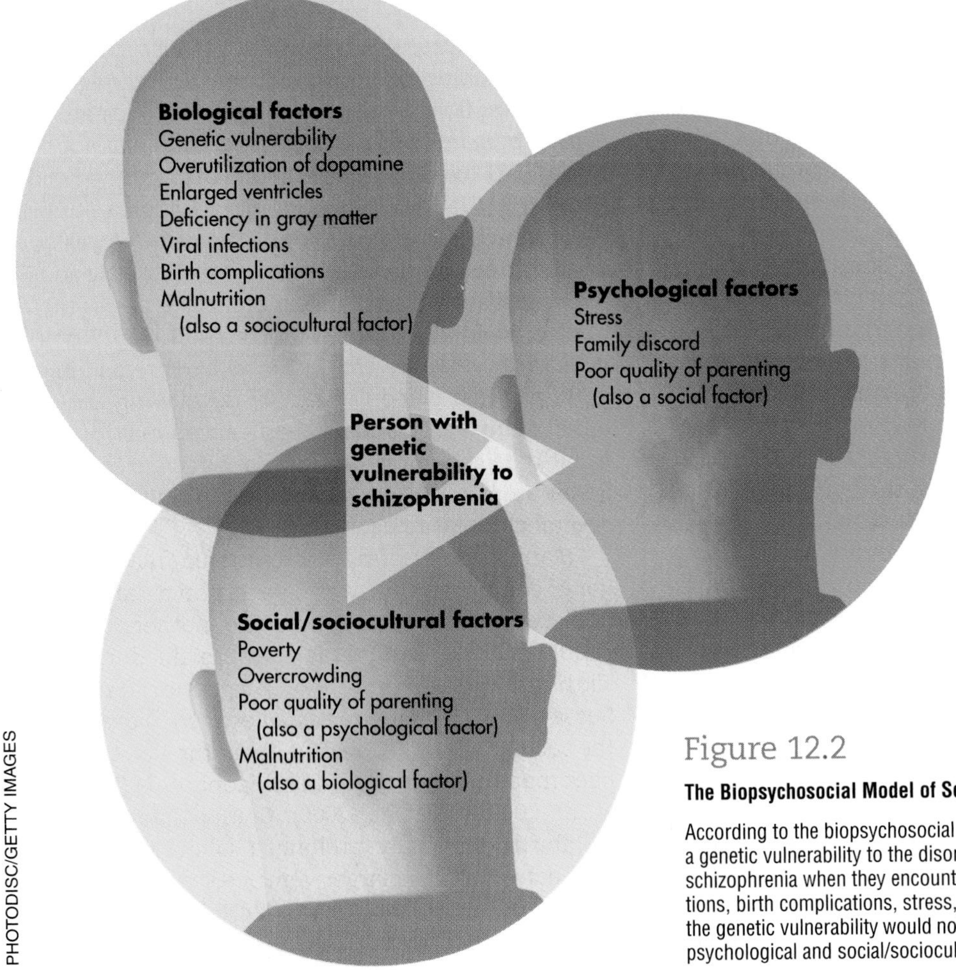

Biological factors
Genetic vulnerability
Overutilization of dopamine
Enlarged ventricles
Deficiency in gray matter
Viral infections
Birth complications
Malnutrition
  (also a sociocultural factor)

Psychological factors
Stress
Family discord
Poor quality of parenting
  (also a social factor)

Person with genetic vulnerability to schizophrenia

Social/sociocultural factors
Poverty
Overcrowding
Poor quality of parenting
  (also a psychological factor)
Malnutrition
  (also a biological factor)

Figure 12.2

The Biopsychosocial Model of Schizophrenia

According to the biopsychosocial model of schizophrenia, people with a genetic vulnerability to the disorder experience increased risk for schizophrenia when they encounter problems such as viral infections, birth complications, stress, and poor parenting. People without the genetic vulnerability would not develop schizophrenia despite psychological and social/sociocultural problems.

other hand, research evidence is mixed about whether viral infections in childhood are connected with schizophrenia (Suvisaari et al., 2003). But taken together, these risk factors suggest that schizophrenia involves faulty development of the central nervous system.

Problems in the nervous system may involve brain chemistry as well as brain structures, and research along these lines has led to the dopamine theory of schizophrenia. According to the dopamine theory, people with schizophrenia overutilize dopamine (use more of it than other people do) although they may not produce more of it (Gijsman et al., 2002; Tsai & Coyle, 2002). Why? Research suggests that people with schizophrenia have increased concentrations of dopamine at the synapses in the brain and also larger numbers of dopamine receptors (Butcher, 2000). It's a sort of "double hit" of neural transmission that may be connected with the confusion that characterizes schizophrenia.

Sociocultural Perspectives

Many investigators have considered whether and how social and cultural factors such as poverty, discrimination, and overcrowding contribute to schizophrenia—especially among people with a genetic vulnerability. Classic research in New Haven, Connecticut, showed that the rate of schizophrenia was twice as high in the lowest socioeconomic class as in the next-higher class on the socioeconomic ladder (Hollingshead & Redlich, 1958). Poor-quality housing may contribute to schizophrenia (Mueser & McGurk, 2004). Some sociocultural theorists therefore suggest that "treatment" of schizophrenia requires alleviation of poverty and other social ills.

Critics of this view suggest that low socioeconomic status may be a result, rather than a cause, of schizophrenia. People with schizophrenia may drift toward low social status because they lack the social skills and cognitive abilities to function at higher social-class levels. Thus, they may wind up in poor neighborhoods or among the homeless in disproportionately high numbers.

Evidence for the hypothesis that people with schizophrenia drift downward in socioeconomic status is mixed. Many people with schizophrenia do drift downward occupationally in comparison with their fathers' occupations. Many others, however, were reared in families in which the father came from the lowest socioeconomic class. Because poverty may play a role in the development of schizophrenia, many researchers are interested in the possible interactions between biological and psychosocial factors (Buckley et al., 2000; Sawa & Snyder, 2002).

Quality of parenting is also connected with the development of schizophrenia (Buckley et al., 2000), but critics note that many people who are reared in socially punitive settings are apparently immune to the extinction of socially appropriate behavior. Other people develop schizophrenic behavior without having had opportunities to observe other people with schizophrenia.

The Biopsychosocial Perspective

Because biological, psychological, and sociocultural factors are implicated in schizophrenia, most investigators today favor the biopsychosocial model. According to this model, genetic factors create a predisposition toward or vulnerability to schizophrenia (see Figure 12.2). Genetic vulnerability to the disorder interacts with other factors, such as complications of pregnancy and birth, stress, quality of parenting, and social conditions to give rise to the disorder (Buckley et al., 2000; Sawa & Snyder, 2002).

LO³ Mood Disorders

Mood disorders are characterized by disturbance in expressed emotions. The disruption generally involves sadness or elation. Most instances of sadness are normal, or "run-of-the-mill." If you have failed an important test, if you have lost money in a business venture, or if your closest friend becomes ill, it is understandable and fitting for you to be sad about it. It would be odd, in fact, if you were *not* affected by adversity.

What kinds of mood disorders are there? In this section we discuss two mood disorders: major depression and bipolar disorder.

ROMAN MAKHMUTOV/GETTY IMAGES

Major Depression

People with run-of-the-mill depression may feel sad, blue, or "down in the dumps." They may complain of lack of energy, loss of self-esteem, difficulty concentrating, loss of interest in activities and other people (Nezlek et al., 2000), pessimism, crying, and thoughts of suicide.

These feelings are more intense in people with major depressive disorder (MDD). According to a nationally representative sample of 9,000 English-speaking adults in the United States, MDD affects 6% to 7% of men and about 12% of women within any given year, and one person in five to six over the course of a lifetime (Kessler et al., 2005a, 2005c). About half of those with MDD experience severe symptoms such as poor appetite, serious weight loss, and agitation or psychomotor retardation. They may be unable to concentrate and make decisions. They may say that they "don't care" anymore and in some cases attempt suicide. A minority may display faulty perception of reality—so-called psychotic behaviors. These include delusions of unworthiness, guilt for imagined wrongdoings, even the notion that one is rotting from disease. There may also be delusions, as of the devil administering deserved punishment, or hallucinations, as of strange bodily sensations.

Bipolar Disorder

People with bipolar disorder, formerly known as *manic–depressive disorder,* have mood swings from ecstatic elation to deep depression. The cycles seem to be unrelated to external events. The manic person may also be argumentative. The manic person may show excessive energy, lessened need for sleep, and inflated self-esteem. He or she may also be argumentative, show poor judgment, destroy property, make huge contributions to charity,

major depressive disorder (MDD) a serious to severe depressive disorder in which the person may show loss of appetite, psychomotor retardation, and impaired reality testing

psychomotor retardation slowness in motor activity and (apparently) in thought

bipolar disorder a disorder in which the mood alternates between two extreme poles (elation and depression); also referred to as *manic depression*

manic elated, showing excessive excitement

Truth

In the case of bipolar disorder, feeling elated is not a good thing because in the elated, or manic phase, the person may show excessive excitement or silliness, carrying jokes too far.

rapid flight of ideas
rapid speech and topic changes, characteristic of manicky behavior

neuroticism
a personality trait characterized largely by persistent anxiety

learned helplessness
a model for the acquisition of depressive behavior, based on findings that organisms in aversive situations learn to show inactivity when their operants go unreinforced

attributional style
the tendency to attribute one's behavior to internal or external factors, stable or unstable factors, and so on

or give away expensive possessions. People often find manic individuals abrasive and avoid them. They are often oversexed and too restless to sit still or sleep restfully. They often speak rapidly (showing "pressured speech") and jump from topic to topic (showing rapid flight of ideas). It can be hard to get a word in edgewise.

Depression is the other side of the coin. People with bipolar depression often sleep more than usual and are lethargic. People with major (or unipolar) depression are more likely to have insomnia and agitation. Those with bipolar depression also exhibit social withdrawal and irritability. Some people with bipolar disorder attempt suicide when the mood shifts from the elated phase toward depression (Jamison, 2000). They will do almost anything to escape the depths of depression that lie ahead.

Explaining Mood Disorders

What is known about the origins of mood disorders?

Biological Perspectives

Researchers are searching for biological factors in mood disorders. Depression, for example, is often associated with the trait of neuroticism, which is heritable (Chioqueta & Stiles, 2005; Khan et al., 2005). Anxiety is also connected with neuroticism, and mood and anxiety disorders are frequently found in the same person (Khan et al., 2005). Genetic factors appear to be involved in major depression and bipolar disorder, as suggested by twin and adoption studies (Evans et al., 2005; Farmer et al., 2005).

Psychological Perspectives

Many learning theorists suggest that depressed people behave as though they cannot obtain reinforcement. For example, they appear to be inactive and apathetic. Many people with depressive disorders have an *external locus of control*. That is, they do not believe they can control events so as to achieve reinforcements (Tong, 2001; Weinmann et al., 2001).

Research conducted by learning theorists has also found links between depression and learned

helplessness. In classic research, psychologist Martin Seligman taught dogs that they were helpless to escape an electric shock. The dogs were prevented from leaving a cage in which they received repeated shocks. Later, a barrier to a safe compartment was removed, offering the animals a way out. When they were shocked again, however, the dogs made no effort to escape. They had apparently learned that they were helpless. Seligman's dogs were also, in a sense, reinforced for doing nothing. That is, the shock *eventually* stopped when the dogs were showing helpless behavior—inactivity and withdrawal. "Reinforcement" might have increased the likelihood of repeating the "successful behavior"—that is, doing nothing—in a similar situation. This helpless behavior resembles that of people who are depressed.

Other cognitive factors contribute to depression. For example, perfectionists set themselves up for depression by making irrational demands on themselves. They are likely to fall short of their (unrealistic) expectations and to feel depressed as a result (Flett & Hewitt, 2002).

Cognitive psychologists also note that people who ruminate about feelings of depression are more likely to prolong the feelings (Spasojevic & Alloy, 2001). Women are more likely than men to ruminate about feelings of depression (Nolen-Hoeksema, 2001). Men are more likely than women to fight negative feelings by distracting themselves or turning to alcohol (Nolen-Hoeksema, 2001). They thus expose themselves and their families to further problems.

Still other cognitions involve the ways in which people explain their failures and shortcomings to themselves (Hankin et al., 2005). Seligman (1996) suggests that when things go wrong we may think of the causes of failure as either *internal* or *external, stable* or *unstable, global* or *specific*. These various attributional styles can be illustrated using the example of having a date that does not work out. An internal attribution involves self-blame, as in "I really loused it up." An external attribution places the blame elsewhere (as in "Some couples just don't take to each other," or, "She was the wrong person for me"). A stable attribution ("It's my personality") suggests a problem that cannot be changed. An unstable attribution ("It was because I had a head cold") suggests a temporary condition. A global attribution of failure ("I have no idea what to do when I'm with other people") suggests that the problem is quite large. A specific attribution ("I have problems making small talk at the beginning of a relationship") chops the problem down to a manageable size. Research has shown that people who are depressed are more likely to attribute the causes of their failures to internal, stable, and global factors—factors that they are relatively powerless to change (Riso et al., 2003).

An internal attribution involves self-blame, as in "I really loused it up." An external attribution places the blame elsewhere.

Let's add one remarkable note about attributional styles and the mind–body connection. Shelley Taylor and her colleagues (2000a) found that self-blame for negative events is connected with poorer functioning of the immune system. Too much self-blame, in other words, is not only depressing; it may also be able to make us physically ill.

The Biopsychosocial Perspective

Relationships between mood disorders and biological factors are complex and under intense study. Even if people are biologically predisposed toward depression, self-efficacy expectations and attitudes—particularly attitudes about whether one can change things for the better—may also play a role.

Although the mood disorders are connected with processes within the individual, many kinds of situations are also connected with depression. For example, depression may be a reaction to loss or stress (Cowen, 2002). Sources of chronic strain such as marital discord, physical discomfort, incompetence, and failure or pressure at work all contribute to depression. We tend to be more depressed by things we bring on ourselves, such as academic problems, financial problems, unwanted pregnancy, conflict with the law, arguments, and fights. Some people recover from depression less readily than others, however. People who remain depressed have lower self-esteem, are less likely to be able to solve social problems, and have less social support.

Suicide

Why do people commit suicide? We will deal with suicide terrorism in Chapter 14. Here let us talk about people who choose to take their lives to escape feelings of depression, hopelessness, and helplessness. We may think many of these people have "so much to live for." Apparently, they disagree. So do the thousands of others who take their own lives each year.

In any given year, about 3% of the American population considers suicide (Nock et al., 2008). About 31,000 Americans commit suicide each year (Nock et al., 2008). Suicide is the third- or fourth-leading cause of death among older teenagers (Nock et al., 2008). Who is most at risk of attempting or committing suicide?

Risk Factors in Suicide

Most suicides are linked to feelings of depression and hopelessness (Beautrais, 2003). Jill Rathus and her colleagues (Miller et al., 2000) found that suicidal adolescents experience four areas of psychological problems: (1) confusion about the self, (2) impulsiveness, (3) emotional instability, and (4) interpersonal problems. Some suicidal teenagers, like suicidal adults, are highly achieving, rigid perfectionists who have set impossibly high expectations for themselves (Miller et al., 2000). Many people throw themselves into feelings of depression and hopelessness by comparing themselves negatively with others, even when the comparisons are inappropriate (Barber, 2001). For example, some people criticize themselves for being hired at a lower salary than others were, even though the financial climate of a company has changed.

Suicide attempts are more common following stressful life events, especially "exit events" (Beautrais, 2003). Exit events entail loss of social support, as in the death of a parent or friend, divorce, or a family member's leaving home. These exit events result in what Shneidman (2001) refers to as psychological pain, or "psychache." Other contributors to suicidal behavior among adolescents include concerns over sexuality, grades in school, problems at home, and substance abuse (Cuellar & Curry, 2007). It is not always a stressful event itself that precipitates suicide but can also be the individual's anxiety or fear of being "found out" about something, such as failing a course or getting arrested (Marttunen, 1998).

There is a tendency for suicide to run in families (Miller et al., 2007). Many suicide attempters have family members with serious psychological problems, and about 25% have family members who have taken their lives (Segal & Roy, 2001; Sorenson

& Rutter, 1991). The causal connections are unclear, however. Do people who attempt suicide inherit disorders that can lead to suicide? Does the family environment subject family members to feelings of hopelessness? Does the suicide of a family member give a person the idea of committing suicide, or create the impression that he or she is destined to commit suicide? These possibilities and others—such as poor problem-solving ability—form a complex web of contributors.

Sociocultural Factors in Suicide

Suicide is connected not only with feelings of depression and stressful events, but also with age, educational status, ethnicity, and gender.

> Although teenage suicides loom large in the media spotlight, older people are actually more likely to commit suicide.

Consider some facts about suicide:

• Suicide is the third-leading cause of death among young people aged fifteen to twenty-four (Miller et al., 2007). More teenagers and young adults die from suicide than from cancer, heart disease, AIDS, birth defects, stroke, pneumonia and influenza, and chronic lung disease combined (National Center for Health Statistics, 2005).

• Suicide is more common among college students than among people of the same age who do not attend college.

• Although teenage suicides loom large in the media spotlight, older people are actually more likely to commit suicide (National Center for Health Statistics, 2005). The suicide rate among older people who are single is twice that of older people who are married (National Center for Injury Prevention and Control, 2005).

Rates of suicide and suicide attempts also vary among different ethnic groups and according to gender. For example, about one in six Native Americans (17%) has attempted suicide—

{ Women and Depression }

Women are nearly twice as likely to be diagnosed with depression as men (Keyes & Goodman, 2006). This sex difference begins to emerge during adolescence, at about the age of thirteen. In any given year, about 12% of women and 7% of men in the United States are diagnosed with depression. It was once assumed that depression was most likely to accompany menopause in women, because women could no longer carry out their "natural" function of childbearing. However, women are more likely to encounter depression during the childbearing years (Deecher et al., 2008; Keyes & Goodman, 2006).

Many people assume that biological sex differences largely explain why women are more likely to become depressed (Deecher et al., 2008). Low levels of estrogen are widely seen as the culprit. Estrogen levels plummet prior to menstruation, and the deficit may trigger psychological changes. How often do we hear degrading remarks such as "It must be that time of the month" when a woman expresses feelings of anger or irritation? Some theorists

suggest that women may also have a "cognitive vulnerability" to depression, connected with greater tendencies than men to ruminate about stresses and other negative events (Hankin & Abramson, 2001).

Some of the sex difference may also reflect the greater stresses placed on women, which tend to be maximized when they are working a triple shift—one in the workforce and the others meeting the demands of homemaking, child rearing, and aging parents (Plaisier et al., 2008; Rathus, 2009-2010). Women are more likely to experience physical and sexual abuse, poverty, single parenthood, and sexism. Single mothers, in particular, have lower socioeconomic status than men, and depression and other psychological disorders are more common among poor people (Nicholson et al., 2008). A part of treatment for depressed women, then, is to modify the demands on women. The pain may lie in the individual, but the cause often lies in society.

GERARD FRITZ/GETTY IMAGES

a rate higher than that of other Americans (Blum et al., 1992). About one in eight Latino and Latina Americans has attempted suicide and three in ten have considered it (National Center for Health Statistics, 2005). European Americans are next, with 8% attempting and 28% contemplating suicide. African Americans are least likely to attempt suicide (6.5%) or to consider it (20%). The suicide rates for African Americans are only about two-thirds of those for European Americans, even though African Americans are more likely to live in poverty and suffer discrimination (National Center for Health Statistics, 2005).

About three times as many females as males attempt suicide, but about four times as many males "succeed," in part because males are likely to choose more deadly methods (National Center for Injury Prevention and Control, 2005). Males are more likely to shoot or hang themselves; females more often use drugs, such as overdoses of tranquilizers or sleeping pills, or poisons. Females often do not take enough of these chemicals. It also takes awhile for the chemicals to work, giving others the opportunity to find the person and intervene.

Myths About Suicide

Some believe that those who fail at suicide attempts are only seeking attention. But many people who commit suicide have made prior attempts (Jackson & Nuttall, 2001; Waters, 2000). Contrary to widespread belief, discussing suicide with a person who is depressed does not prompt the person to attempt suicide (National Center for Injury Prevention and Control, 2005). Extracting a promise not to commit suicide before calling or visiting a helping professional seems to prevent some suicides.

Some believe that only "insane" people (meaning people who are out of touch with reality) would take their own lives. However, suicidal thinking is not necessarily a sign of bizarre thinking. Instead, people may consider suicide when they think they have run out of options (Nock & Kazdin, 2002; Townsend et al., 2001).

LO⁴ Anxiety Disorders

Anxiety has psychological and physical symptoms. Psychological symptoms include worrying, fear of the worst things happening, fear of losing control, nervousness, and inability to relax. Physical symptoms reflect arousal of the sympathetic branch of the autonomic nervous system. They include trembling, sweating, a pounding or racing heart, elevated blood pressure (a flushed face), and faintness. Anxiety is an appropriate response to a real threat. It can be abnormal, however, when it is excessive or when it comes out of nowhere—that is, when events do not seem to warrant it. *What kinds of anxiety disorders are there?*

There are different kinds of anxiety disorders, but all of them are characterized by excessive or unwarranted anxiety. The anxiety disorders include phobias, panic disorder, generalized anxiety, obsessive–compulsive disorder, and stress disorders.

specific phobia
persistent fear of a specific object or situation

claustrophobia
fear of tight, small places

acrophobia
fear of high places

social phobia
an irrational, excessive fear of public scrutiny

agoraphobia
fear of open, crowded places

Phobias

Phobias include specific phobias, social phobia, and agoraphobia. They can be detrimental to one's quality of life. Specific phobias are irrational fears of specific objects or situations, such as spiders, snakes, or heights. One specific phobia is fear of elevators. Some people will not enter elevators despite the hardships they incur as a result (such as walking up ten flights of steps). Yes, the cable *could* break. The ventilation *could* fail. One *could* be stuck in midair waiting for repairs. But these problems are uncommon, and it affects one's quality of life to walk up and down several flights of stairs to elude them. Similarly, some people with a specific phobia for hypodermic needles will not have injections, even to treat serious illness. Injections can be painful, but most people with a phobia for needles would gladly suffer an even more painful pinch if it would help them fight illness. Other specific phobias include claustrophobia (fear of tight or enclosed places), acrophobia (fear of heights), and fear of mice, snakes, and other creepy crawlies. Social phobias are persistent fears of scrutiny by others or of doing something that will be humiliating or embarrassing. Fear of public speaking is a common social phobia.

Agoraphobia is also widespread among adults.

© GOODSHOOT/JUPITERIMAGES

panic disorder
the recurrent experiencing of attacks of extreme anxiety in the absence of external stimuli that usually elicit anxiety

generalized anxiety disorder
feelings of dread and foreboding and sympathetic arousal of at least six months' duration

obsession
a recurring thought or image that seems beyond control

Agoraphobia is derived from the Greek words meaning "fear of the marketplace," or fear of being out in open, busy areas. Persons with agoraphobia fear being in places from which it might be difficult to escape or in which help might not be available if they get upset. In practice, people who receive this diagnosis often refuse to venture out of their homes, especially by themselves. They find it difficult to hold a job or to maintain an ordinary social life.

Panic Disorder

Panic disorder is an abrupt attack of acute anxiety that is not necessarily triggered by a specific object or situation. People with panic disorder have strong physical symptoms such as shortness of breath, heavy sweating, tremors, and pounding of the heart. They are particularly aware of cardiac sensations. It is not unusual for them to think they are having a heart attack. People with the disorder may also experience choking sensations, nausea, numbness or tingling, flushes or chills, and fear of going crazy or losing control. Panic attacks may last minutes or hours. Afterward, the person usually feels drained.

Many people panic now and then. The diagnosis of panic disorder is reserved for those who undergo a series of attacks or live in fear of attacks.

Panic attacks seem to come from nowhere. Thus, some people who have had them stay home for fear of having an attack in public. They are diagnosed as having panic disorder with agoraphobia.

Generalized Anxiety Disorder

The central feature of generalized anxiety disorder is persistent anxiety. As with panic disorder, the anxiety cannot be attributed to a phobic object, situation, or activity. Rather, it seems to be free floating. The core of the disorder appears to be pervasive worrying about numerous problems. Features of the disorder include motor tension (shakiness, inability to relax, furrowed brow, fidgeting); autonomic overarousal (sweating, dry mouth, racing heart, light-headedness, frequent urinating, diarrhea); and excessive vigilance, as shown by irritability, insomnia, and a tendency to be easily distracted.

The central symptom of generalized anxiety disorder is persistent anxiety.

Obsessive–Compulsive Disorder

Obsessions are recurrent, anxiety-provoking thoughts or images that seem irrational and beyond control. They are so compelling and recurrent that they disrupt daily life. They may include doubts about whether one has locked the doors and shut the windows, or images such as one mother's repeated fantasy that her children had been run over on the way home from school. One woman became obsessed with the idea that she had contaminated her hands with Sani-Flush and that the chemicals were spreading to everything she touched. A sixteen-year-old boy complained that he was distracted by "numbers in my head" when he was about to study or take a test. The more he tried to ignore them, the louder they became.

© 2010 GEORGE DOYLE / JUPITERIMAGES CORPORATION

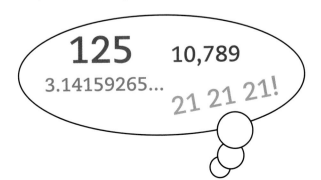

Compulsions are thoughts or behaviors that tend to reduce the anxiety connected with obsessions. They are seemingly irresistible urges to engage in specific acts, often repeatedly, such as elaborate washing after using the bathroom or repeatedly checking that one has locked the door or turned off the gas burners before leaving home. The impulse is recurrent and forceful, interfering with daily life.

Stress Disorders

Sharia dreamed of a man assaulting her in the night at the Superdome in New Orleans, after she had been moved to this "refuge" following Hurricane Katrina in the summer of 2005. Darla, who lives in Oregon, dreamed that she was trapped in a World Trade Center tower when it was hit by an airplane on September 11, 2001. About one in six Iraq or Afghanistan veterans has nightmares and flashbacks to buddies being killed by snipers or explosive devices (Hoge et al., 2004). These all-too-real nightmarish events have caused many bad dreams. Such dreams are part of the experience of posttraumatic stress disorder.

Post-traumatic stress disorder (PTSD) is characterized by a rapid heart rate and feelings of anxiety and helplessness that are caused by a traumatic experience. Such experiences may include a natural or human-made disaster, a threat or assault, or witnessing a death. PTSD may occur months or years after the event. It frequently occurs among firefighters, combat veterans, and people whose homes and communities have been swept away by natural disasters or who have been victims of accidents or violence (DeAngelis, 2008).

The traumatic event is revisited in the form of intrusive memories, recurrent dreams, and flashbacks—the sudden feeling that the event is recurring. People with PTSD typically try to avoid thoughts and activities connected to the traumatic event. They may find it more difficult to enjoy life and have sleep problems, irritable outbursts, difficulty concentrating, extreme vigilance, and an intensified "startle" response (Griffin, 2008). The attacks of September 11, 2001, took their toll on sleep. According to a poll taken by the National Sleep Foundation (2001) two months afterward, nearly half of Americans had difficulty falling asleep, as compared with about one-quarter of Americans before the attacks (see Figure 12.3).

Acute stress disorder, like PTSD, is characterized by feelings of anxiety and helplessness that are caused by a traumatic event. PTSD, however, can occur six months or more after the traumatic event and tends to persist. Acute stress disorder occurs within a month of the event and lasts from two days to four weeks. Women who have been raped, for example, experience acute distress that tends to peak in severity a few weeks after the assault. Yet the same women often go on to experience PTSD (Koss et al., 2002).

compulsion
an irresistible urge to repeat an act or engage in ritualistic behavior such as hand washing

post-traumatic stress disorder (PTSD)
a disorder that follows a distressing event outside the range of normal human experience and that is characterized by features such as intense fear, avoidance of stimuli associated with the event, and reliving of the event

acute stress disorder
a disorder, like PTSD, that is characterized by feelings of anxiety and helplessness and caused by a traumatic event; acute stress disorder occurs within a month of the event and lasts from two days to four weeks

Figure 12.3

Sleep Problems Among Americans Before and After September 11, 2001

Insomnia is one of the symptoms of stress disorders. A poll by the National Sleep Foundation found that Americans had a greater frequency of sleep problems after the terrorist attacks of September 11, 2001.

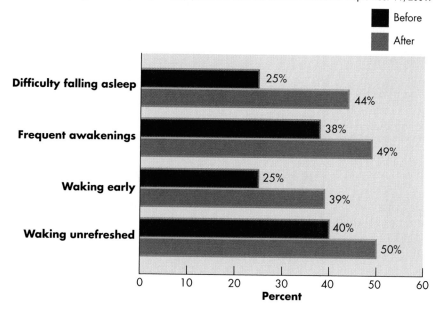

- Before
- After

Difficulty falling asleep: 25% / 44%
Frequent awakenings: 38% / 49%
Waking early: 25% / 39%
Waking unrefreshed: 40% / 50%

Percent: 0 10 20 30 40 50 60

Explaining Anxiety Disorders

What is known about the origins of anxiety disorders?

Biological Perspectives

Biological factors play a role in anxiety disorders. Genetic factors are implicated in most psychological disorders, including anxiety disorders (Low et al., 2008). Anxiety disorders tend to run in families. Twin studies find a higher rate of match for anxiety disorders among identical twins than among fraternal twins (Kendler et al., 2001). Studies of adoptees who are anxious similarly show that the biological parent places the child at risk for anxiety and related traits.

Perhaps a predisposition toward anxiety—in the form of a highly reactive autonomic nervous system—can be inherited. What might make a nervous system "highly reactive"?

In the case of panic disorder, faulty regulation of levels of serotonin and norepinephrine may be involved. Other anxiety disorders may involve the neurotransmitter glutamate, and receptor sites in the brain may not be sensitive enough to gamma-aminobutyric acid (GABA), a neurotransmitter that may counteract glutamate (Kalin, 2003). The benzodiazepines, a class of drugs that reduce anxiety, may work by increasing the sensitivity of receptor sites to GABA.

Psychological and Social Perspectives

Some learning theorists—particularly behaviorists—consider phobias to be conditioned fears that were acquired in early childhood. Therefore, their origins are beyond memory. Avoidance of feared stimuli is reinforced by the reduction of anxiety.

Other learning theorists—social cognitive theorists—dwell on the social aspects of developing phobias (Basic Behavioral Science Task Force, 1996b). If parents squirm, grimace, and shudder at the sight of mice, blood, or dirt on the kitchen floor, children might assume that these stimuli are awful and imitate their parents' behavior.

Cognitive theorists note that people's appraisals of the magnitude of threats help determine whether they are traumatic and can lead to PTSD (Folkman & Moskowitz, 2000a; Koss et al., 2002). People with panic attacks tend to overreact to physical sensations. Obsessions and compulsions may serve to divert attention from more frightening issues, such as "What am I going to do with my life?" When anxieties are acquired at a young age, we may later interpret them as enduring traits and label ourselves as "people who fear _____" (you fill it in). We then live up to the labels. We also entertain thoughts that heighten and perpetuate anxiety such as "I've got to get out of here," or "My heart is going to leap out of my chest." Such ideas intensify physical features of anxiety, disrupt planning, make stimuli seem worse than they are, motivate avoidance, and lower self-efficacy expectations. The belief that we will not be able to handle a threat heightens anxiety. The belief that we are in control reduces anxiety (Bandura et al., 1985).

The Biopsychosocial Perspective

Many cases of anxiety disorders reflect the interaction of biological, psychological, and social factors. In panic disorder, biological imbalances may initially trigger attacks. However, subsequent fear of attacks—and of the bodily cues that signal their onset—may heighten discomfort and give one the idea that nothing can be done about them (Craske & Zucker, 2001). Moreover, panic attacks are likely to occur in social situations, especially in crowds. Feelings of helplessness increase fear. People with panic disorder can be helped by methods that reduce physical discomfort—including regular breathing—and show them that there are ways to cope with attacks (Craske & Zucker, 2001). They are also sometimes taken into social settings, such as crowded streets or stores, by psychologists who offer them social support and show them that they can tolerate such situations.

LO⁵ Somatoform Disorders

People with **somatoform disorders** complain of physical problems such as paralysis, pain, or a persistent belief that they have a serious disease. But health professionals can find no evidence of a physical abnormality. *What kinds of somatoform disorders are there?* In this section we discuss three somatoform disorders: conversion disorder, hypochondriasis, and body dysmorphic disorder.

Conversion Disorder

Conversion disorder is characterized by a major change in or loss of physical functioning, although there are no medical findings to explain the loss of functioning. The behaviors are not intentionally produced. That is, the person is not faking. Conversion disorder is so named because it appears to "convert" a source of stress into a physical difficulty.

If you lost the ability to see at night, or if your legs became paralyzed, you would understandably show concern. But some people with conversion disorder show indifference to their symptoms, a remarkable feature referred to as la belle indifférence.

During World War II, some bomber pilots developed night blindness. They could not carry out their nighttime missions, although no damage to the optic nerves was found. In rare cases, women with large families have been reported to become paralyzed in the legs, again with no medical findings. More recently, a Cambodian woman who had witnessed atrocities became blind as a result.

Hypochondriasis

Another more common type of somatoform disorder is hypochondriasis (also called *hypochondria*). People with this disorder insist that they are suffering from a serious physical illness, even though no medical evidence of illness can be found. They become preoccupied with minor physical sensations and continue to believe that they are ill despite the reassurance of physicians that they are healthy. They may run from doctor to doctor, seeking the one who will find the causes of the sensations. Fear of illness may disrupt their work or home life.

Body Dysmorphic Disorder

People with body dysmorphic disorder are preoccupied with a fantasized or exaggerated physical defect in their appearance. They may spend hours examining themselves in the mirror and go to extreme lengths to correct the "problem," including cosmetic surgery. Others remove all mirrors from their homes so as not to be reminded of the "flaw." People with the disorder may assume that others see them as deformed. They may compulsively groom themselves or pay close attention to styling every strand of hair.

Explaining Somatoform Disorders

What is known about the origins of somatoform disorders? The somatoform disorders offer a fascinating study in the biopsychosocial perspective. Psychologically speaking, the somatoform disorders have much

to do with what one focuses on—actual social and financial problems, for example, or one's body. Some investigators consider conversion disorder to be a form of self-hypnosis (Roelofs et al., 2002), and they note that there is research evidence that people with conversion disorder are highly susceptible to being hypnotized. The idea here would be that people with conversion disorder focus on an imaginary physical problem to the point where they exclude conflicting information.

In the case of hypochondriasis, people may misinterpret run-of-the-mill physical sensations—or symptoms—as signifying deadly illness. There is research evidence that people who develop hypochondriasis are particularly sensitive to bodily sensations and tend to ruminate about them (Lecci & Cohen, 2002). Moreover, enacting the role of a sick person has the "benefits" of relieving one of ordinary responsibilities and concerns. For example, how can one focus on work or family life when one believes he or she is rotting away with disease?

Certainly the social value of personal attractiveness can contribute to dissatisfaction with one's body. But people with body dysmorphic disorder may focus irrationally on an exaggerated blemish or other minor feature, suggestive of perfectionistic and ruminative tendencies.

Biologically speaking, tendencies toward perfectionism and rumination, which are found among many people with somatoform disorders, are thought to be at least partly heritable. Squeamishness about one's body may be too much of a good thing from the evolutionary perspective. That is, concern about bodily harm will presumably encourage one to avoid danger and provide advantages in survival and reproduction. But too much concern may lead to useless preoccupations.

LO⁶ Dissociative Disorders

During one long fall semester, the Ohio State University campus lived in terror. Four college women were kidnapped, forced to take out cash from ATMs,

la belle indifférence
a French term descriptive of the lack of concern for their (imagined) medical problem sometimes shown by people with conversion disorders

hypochondriasis
a somatoform disorder characterized by persistent belief that one is ill despite lack of medical findings

body dysmorphic disorder
a somatoform disorder characterized by preoccupation with an imagined or exaggerated physical defect in one's appearance

dissociative disorders
disorders in which there are sudden, temporary changes in consciousness or self-identity

dissociative amnesia
a dissociative disorder marked by loss of memory or self-identity; skills and general knowledge are usually retained

dissociative fugue
a dissociative disorder in which one experiences amnesia and then flees to a new location

dissociative identity disorder
a disorder in which a person appears to have two or more distinct identities or personalities that may alternately emerge

multiple personality disorder
the previous term for *dissociative identity disorder*

and raped. A mysterious phone call led to the arrest of a twenty-three-year-old drifter—let's call him "William"—who had been dismissed from the Navy.

William was not the boy next door.

Psychologists and psychiatrists who interviewed William concluded that ten personalities—eight male and two female—dwelled in him (Keyes, 1995). His personality had been "fractured" by an abusive childhood. His several personalities displayed distinct facial expressions, speech patterns, and memories. They performed differently on psychological tests.

Arthur, the most rational personality, spoke with a British accent. Danny and Christopher were quiet adolescents. Christine was a three-year-old girl. Tommy, a sixteen-year-old, had enlisted in the Navy. Allen was eighteen and smoked. Adelena, a nineteen-year-old lesbian personality, had committed the rapes. Who had placed the mysterious phone call? Probably David, nine, an anxious child.

The defense claimed that William's behavior was caused by *dissociative identity disorder*. Of the identities or personalities dwelling within him, some were aware of the others. Some believed they were unique. As a child, Billy, the core identity, had learned to sleep to avoid his father's abuse. A psychiatrist asserted that Billy had also been "asleep," or in a "psychological coma," during the abductions. Billy should therefore be found not guilty by reason of insanity.

William was found not guilty. He was committed to a psychiatric institution and released six years later.

Dissociative identity disorder is one of the **dissociative disorders**. In dissociative disorders, there is a splitting of psychological processes such as thoughts, emotions, identity, memory, or consciousness—the processes that make the person feel whole. *What kinds of dissociative disorders are there?* The dissociative disorders include dissociative amnesia, dissociative fugue, and William's disorder: dissociative identity disorder (also termed *multiple personality disorder*).

Dissociative Amnesia

In **dissociative amnesia**, the person is suddenly unable to recall important personal information (that is, explicit episodic memories). The loss of memory cannot be attributed to biological problems such as a blow to the head or excessive drinking. It is thus a psychological disorder and not an organic one. In the most common example, the person cannot recall events for a number of hours after a stressful incident, as in warfare or in the case of an uninjured survivor of an accident. In generalized amnesia, people forget their entire lives. Amnesia may last for hours or years.

Dissociative Fugue

In **dissociative fugue**, the person abruptly leaves his or her home or place of work and travels to another place, having lost all memory of his or her past life. While at the new location, the person either does not think about the past or reports a past filled with invented memories. The new personality is often more outgoing and less inhibited than the "real" identity. Following recovery, the events that occurred during the fugue are not recalled.

Dissociative Identity Disorder

In **dissociative identity disorder** (formerly termed **multiple personality disorder**), two or more identities or personalities, each with distinct traits and memories, "occupy" the same person. Each identity may or may not be aware of the others or of events experienced by the others.

The different personalities might have different eyeglass prescriptions (Braun, 1988). Braun reports cases in which assorted identities showed different allergic responses. In one person, an identity named Timmy was not sensitive to orange juice. But when another identity drank

orange juice, he would break out with hives. Hives would also erupt if another identity emerged while the juice was being digested. If Timmy reappeared when the allergic reaction was present, the itching of the hives would cease and the blisters would start to subside. In other cases reported by Braun, different identities within a person might show various responses to the same medicine. Or one identity might exhibit color blindness while others have normal color vision.

Explaining Dissociative Disorders

The dissociative disorders are some of the odder psychological disorders. *What is known about the origins of dissociative disorders?* Biopsychosocial factors may well be involved in dissociative disorders. According to learning and cognitive psychologists, people with dissociative disorders may have learned *not to think* about bad memories or disturbing impulses in an effort to avoid feelings of anxiety, guilt, and shame. Dissociative disorders may help people keep disturbing ideas out of mind.

What might such memories contain? The answer is painful interpersonal— or social—information. Research suggests that many cases of dissociative disorders involve memories of sexual or physical abuse during childhood, usually by a relative or caretaker (Martinez-Taboas & Bernal, 2000; Migdow, 2003).

Truth

The personalities of people with dissociative identity disorder can be very different from one another.

On a biological level, research with abused children and adolescents suggests that the trauma-related dissociation observed in dissociative disorders may have a neurological basis (Diseth, 2005). Child abuse may lead to some permanent neurochemical and structural abnormalities in parts of the brain involved in cognition and memory. Although it seems that the nature of the trauma in such cases is interpersonal, it need not necessarily be sexual in nature. In any event, one might expect resultant impairments in the recall of personal information.

personality disorders enduring patterns of maladaptive behavior that are sources of distress to the individual or others

paranoid personality disorder a personality disorder characterized by persistent suspiciousness, but not involving the disorganization of paranoid schizophrenia

schizotypal personality disorder a personality disorder characterized by oddities of thought and behavior, but not involving bizarre psychotic behaviors

LO⁷ Personality Disorders

Personality disorders, like personality traits, are characterized by enduring patterns of behavior. Personality disorders, however, are inflexible and maladaptive. They impair personal or social functioning and are a source of distress to the individual or to other people. *What kinds of personality disorders are there?* There are a number of personality disorders. They include the paranoid, schizotypal, schizoid, antisocial, and avoidant personality disorders.

Paranoid Personality Disorder

The defining trait of the paranoid personality disorder is a tendency to interpret other people's behavior as threatening or demeaning. People with the disorder do not show the grossly disorganized thinking of paranoid schizophrenia. They are mistrustful of others, however, and their relationships suffer for it. They may be suspicious of coworkers and supervisors, but they can generally hold a job.

Schizotypal and Schizoid Personality Disorders

Schizotypal personality disorder is characterized by peculiarities of thought, perception, or behavior, such as excessive fantasy and suspiciousness, feelings of being unreal, or odd usage of words. The bizarre behaviors that characterize schizophrenia are absent, so this disorder is schizo*typal,* not schizo*phrenic.*

The schizoid personality is defined by indifference to relationships and flat emotional response. People with this disorder are "loners." They do not develop warm, tender feelings for others. They have few friends and rarely maintain long-term relationships. Some people with schizoid personality disorder do very well on the job, provided that continuous social interaction is not required. They do not have hallucinations or delusions.

Borderline Personality Disorder

People with borderline personality disorder show instability in their relationships, self-image, and mood, and lack of control over impulses. They tend to be uncertain of their values, goals, loyalties, careers, choices of friends, sometimes even their sexual orientations. Instability in self-image or identity may leave them with feelings of emptiness and boredom. Many cannot tolerate being alone and make desperate attempts to avoid feelings of abandonment. They may be clinging and demanding in social relationships, but clinging often pushes away the people on whom they depend. They alternate between extremes of adulation in their relationships (when their needs are met) and loathing (when they feel scorned). They tend to view other people as all good or all bad, shifting abruptly from one extreme to the other. As a result, they may flit from partner to partner in brief and stormy relationships. People whom they had idealized are treated with contempt when they feel the other person has failed them.

Instability of moods is a central characteristic of borderline personality disorder. Moods run the gamut from anger and irritability to depression and anxiety, with each lasting from a few hours to a few days. People with the disorder have difficulty controlling anger and are prone to fights or smashing things. They often act on impulse, such as eloping with someone they have just met. This impulsive and unpredictable behavior is often self-destructive and linked to a risk of suicidal attempts and gestures. It may involve spending sprees, gambling, drug abuse, engaging in unsafe sexual activity, reckless driving, binge eating, or shoplifting. People with the disorder may also engage in self-mutilation, such as scratching their wrists or burning cigarettes on their arms. Self-mutilation is sometimes a means of manipulating others, particularly in times of stress. Frequent self-mutilation is also associated with suicide attempts.

Antisocial Personality Disorder

People with antisocial personality disorder often show a superficial charm and are at least average in intelligence. They fail to learn to improve their behavior from punishment, and they do not form meaningful bonds with other people. Though they are often heavily punished by their parents and rejected by peers, they continue in their impulsive, careless styles of life. While women are more likely than men to have anxiety and depressive disorders, men are more likely than women to have antisocial personality disorder.

Table 12.2

Characteristics of People Diagnosed with Antisocial Personality Disorder

Key Characteristics
History of delinquency and truancy
Persistent violation of the rights of others
Impulsiveness
Poor self-control
Lack of remorse for misdeeds
Lack of empathy
Deceitfulness and manipulativeness
Irresponsibility
Glibness; superficial charm
Exaggerated sense of self-worth
Other Common Characteristics
Lack of loyalty or of formation of enduring relationships
Failure to maintain good job performance over the years
Failure to develop or adhere to a life plan
Sexual promiscuity
Substance abuse
Inability to tolerate boredom
Low tolerance for frustration
Irritability

Sources: Levenston et al., 2000; Romero et al., 2001.

Avoidant Personality Disorder

People with avoidant personality disorder are generally unwilling to enter a relationship without some assurance of acceptance because they fear rejection and criticism. As a result, they may have few close relationships outside their immediate families. Unlike people with schizoid personality disorder, however, they have some interest in, and feelings of warmth toward, other people.

Explaining Personality Disorders

What is known about the origins of personality disorders? Numerous biological, psychological, and sociocultural factors have been implicated in the personality disorders.

Biological Factors

Genetic factors are apparently involved in some personality disorders (Rutter & Silberg, 2002). Personality traits are to some degree heritable (Plomin, 2000), and many personality disorders seem to be extreme variations of normal personality traits. An analysis of fifty-one twin and adoption studies estimated that genetic factors were the greatest influences on antisocial behavior (Rhee & Waldman, 2002). Referring to the five-factor model of personality, people with schizoid personalities tend to be highly introverted (Ross et al., 2002; Widiger & Costa, 1994). People with avoidant personalities tend to be both introverted and emotionally unstable (Ross et al., 2002; Widiger & Costa, 1994).

Perhaps the genetics of antisocial personality involve the prefrontal cortex of the brain, a part of the brain connected with emotional responses.

There is some evidence that people with antisocial personality, as a group, have less gray matter (associative neurons) in the prefrontal cortex of the brain than other people do (Damasio, 2000; Yang et al., 2005). The lesser amount of gray matter could lessen the level of arousal of the nervous system. As a result, it could be more difficult to condition fear responses (Blair & James, 2003). People with the disorder would then be unlikely to show guilt for their misdeeds and would seem to be unafraid of punishment. But a biological factor such as a lower-than-normal level of arousal might not in itself cause the development of an antisocial personality (Rutter & Silberg, 2002). Perhaps a person must also be reared under conditions that do not foster the self-concept of a law-abiding citizen.

Psychological Factors

Learning theorists suggest that childhood experiences can contribute to maladaptive ways of relating to others in adulthood—that is, can lead to personality disorders. Cognitive psychologists find that antisocial adolescents encode social information in ways that bolster their misdeeds. For example, they tend to interpret other people's behavior as threatening, even when it is not (Crick & Dodge, 1994). Aggressive individuals often find it difficult to solve social problems in useful ways (McMurran et al., 2002). Cognitive therapists have encouraged some antisocial male adolescents to view social provocations as problems to be solved rather than as threats to their "manhood," with some favorable initial results (Lochman & Dodge, 1994).

Sociocultural Factors

The label of borderline personality has been applied to people as diverse as Marilyn Monroe and Lawrence of Arabia. Some theorists believe we live in fragmented and alienating times that tend to create problems in forming a stable identity and stable relationships. "Living on the edge," or border, can be seen as a metaphor for an unstable society.

Although the causes of many psychological disorders remain in dispute, various methods of therapy have been devised to deal with them. Those methods are the focus of Chapter 13.

Methods of Therapy

Learning Outcomes

LO 1 Define psychotherapy and describe the history of treatment of psychological disorders

LO 2 Describe traditional psychoanalysis and short-term psychodynamic therapies

LO 3 Define humanistic therapy and contrast its two main approaches

LO 4 Define behavior therapy and identify various behavioral approaches to therapy

LO 5 Define cognitive therapy and describe Beck's approach and REBT

LO 6 Identify various types of group therapy and discuss their advantages and disadvantages

LO 7 Explain whether psychotherapy works and who benefits from it

LO 8 Describe methods of biological therapy-- their benefits and side effects

> ## " Had she broken her leg, her treatment would have followed a fairly standard course. "

Jasmine, a nineteen-year-old college sophomore, has been crying almost without letup for several days. She feels that her life is falling apart. Her college aspirations lie in shambles. She believes that she has brought shame upon her family. Thoughts of suicide have crossed her mind. She can barely drag herself out of bed in the morning. She is avoiding friends. She can pinpoint some sources of stress in her life: a couple of less-than-shining grades, an argument with a boyfriend, friction with roommates. Still, her misery seemed to descend on her from nowhere.

Jasmine is depressed—she feels so down that family and friends have finally prevailed upon her to seek professional help. Had she broken her leg, her treatment would have followed a fairly standard course. Yet treatment of psychological problems and disorders like depression is sometimes approached from different perspectives. Depending on the therapist Jasmine sees, she may be

Truth or Fiction?

What do you think?

Folklore, common sense, or nonsense? Place a T for "True" or F for "False" on the lines provided (you'll learn the answers as you read through the text).

__ Residents of London used to visit the local insane asylum for a fun night out on the town.

__ Some psychotherapists let their clients take the lead in psychotherapy.

__ Some psychotherapists tell their clients exactly what to do.

__ Lying in a reclining chair and fantasizing can be an effective way of confronting fears.

__ Smoking cigarettes can be an effective method for helping people stop smoking cigarettes.

__ There is no scientific evidence that psychotherapy helps people with psychological disorders.

__ The originator of a surgical technique to reduce violence learned that it was not always successful when one of his patients shot him.

- Lying on a couch, talking about anything that pops into awareness, and exploring the possible meaning of her recurrent dreams;

- Sitting face to face with a warm, gentle therapist who expresses faith in Jasmine's ability to manage her problems;

- Listening to a frank, straightforward therapist assert that Jasmine's problems stem from self-defeating attitudes and perfectionistic beliefs;

- Taking medication; or

- Participating in some combination of these approaches.

These methods, although very different, all represent methods of therapy. In this chapter we explore various methods of psychotherapy and biological therapy. *What is psychotherapy?*

Glossary

psychotherapy
a systematic interaction between a therapist and a client that brings psychological principles to bear on influencing the client's thoughts, feelings, or behavior to help the client overcome abnormal behavior or adjust to problems in living

asylum
an institution for the care of the mentally ill

LO¹ What Is Psychotherapy?

There are many kinds of psychotherapy, but they all have certain common characteristics.

Psychotherapy is a systematic interaction between a therapist and a client that applies psychological principles to affect the client's thoughts, feelings, or behavior in an effort to help the client overcome psychological disorders, adjust to problems in living, or develop as an individual.

Quite a mouthful? True. But note the essentials:

✔ *Systematic interaction*
Psychotherapy is a systematic interaction between a client and a therapist. The therapist's theoretical point of view interacts with the client's to determine how the therapist and client relate to each other.

✔ *Psychological principles*
Psychotherapy is based on psychological theory and research in areas such as personality, learning, motivation, and emotion.

✔ *Thoughts, feelings, and behavior*
Psychotherapy influences clients' thoughts, feelings, and behavior. It can be aimed at any or all of these aspects of human psychology.

✔ *Psychological disorders, adjustment problems, and personal growth*
Psychotherapy is often used with people who have psychological disorders. Other people seek help in adjusting to problems such as shyness, weight problems, or loss of a life partner. Still other clients want to learn more about themselves and to reach their full potential as individuals, parents, or creative artists.

The History of Therapies

Historically speaking, "treatments" of psychological disorders often reflected the assumption that people who behaved in strange ways were possessed by demons. *How have people with psychological problems and disorders been treated throughout the ages?* Because of this belief, treatment tended to involve cruel practices such as exorcism and execution. Some people who could not meet the demands of everyday life were tossed into prisons. Others begged in the streets, stole food, or became prostitutes. A few found their way to monasteries or other retreats that offered a kind word and some support. Generally speaking, they died early.

Asylums

Asylums originated in European monasteries. They were the first institutions meant primarily for people with psychological disorders. But their function was warehousing, not treatment. Their inmate populations mushroomed until the stresses created by noise, overcrowding, and disease aggravated the problems they were meant to ease. Inmates were frequently chained and beaten.

The word *bedlam* derives from St. Mary's of *Bethlehem*, the London asylum that opened its gates in 1547. Here unfortunate people with psychological disorders were chained, whipped, and allowed to lie in their own waste.

Humanitarian reform movements began in the 18th century. In Paris, the physician Philippe Pinel unchained the patients at La Salpêtrière. Rather than run amok, as had been feared, most patients profited from kindness and freedom. Many eventually reentered society. Later movements to reform institutions were led by William Tuke in England and Dorothea Dix in America.

> **Truth**
>
> The ladies and gentlemen of the British upper class might stroll by on a lazy afternoon to be amused by asylum inmates' antics. The price of admission was one penny.

Mental Hospitals

In the United States mental hospitals gradually replaced asylums. In the mid-1950s more than a million people resided in state, county, Veterans Administration, or private facilities. The mental hospital's function is treatment, not warehousing.

Still, because of high patient populations and understaffing, many patients received little attention. Even today, with somewhat improved conditions, one psychiatrist may be responsible for the welfare of several hundred residents on the weekend when other staff are absent.

The Community Mental Health Movement

Since the 1960s, efforts have been made to maintain people with serious psychological disorders in their communities. Community mental health centers attempt to maintain new patients as outpatients and to serve patients who have been released from mental hospitals. Today most people with chronic psychological disorders live in the community, not in the hospital. Social critics note that many people who had resided in hospitals for decades were suddenly discharged to "home" communities that seemed foreign and forbidding to them. Many do not receive adequate follow-up care. Many join the ranks of the homeless.

LO² Psychoanalytic Therapies

Psychoanalytic therapies are based on the thinking of Sigmund Freud, the founder of psychoanalytic theory. These therapies assume that psychological problems reflect early childhood experiences and internal conflicts. According to Freud, these conflicts involve the shifting of psychic energy among the id, ego, and superego. These shifts of psychic energy determine our behavior. When primitive urges threaten to break through from the id or when the superego floods us with excessive guilt, defenses are established and distress is created. Freud's therapy method—psychoanalysis—aims to bulwark the ego against the torrents of energy loosed by the id and the superego. With impulses and feelings of guilt and shame placed under greater control, clients are freer to develop adaptive behavior.

How do psychoanalysts conduct a traditional Freudian psychoanalysis?

Traditional Psychoanalysis

Imagine your therapist asking you to lie on a couch in a slightly darkened room. She or he would sit behind you and encourage you to talk about anything that comes to mind, no matter how trivial, no matter how personal. To avoid interfering with your self-exploration, she or he might say little or nothing for session after session. That would be par for the course. A traditional psychoanalysis can extend for months, even years.

Psychoanalysis is the clinical method devised by Sigmund Freud. It aims to provide *insight* into the conflicts that are presumed to lie at the roots of a person's problems. Insight means many things, including knowledge of the experiences that lead to conflicts and maladaptive behavior, recognition of unconscious feelings and conflicts, and conscious evaluation of one's thoughts, feelings, and behavior.

Psychoanalysis also aims to help the client express feelings and urges that have been repressed.

psychoanalysis
Freud's method of psychotherapy; (also the name of Freud's theory of personality)

The Unchaining of the Patients at La Salpêtrière
Philippe Pinel sparked the humanitarian reform movement by unchaining the patients at this asylum in Paris.

A View of Freud's Consulting Room
Freud would sit in a chair by the head of the couch while a client free-associated. The basic rule of free association is that no thought is censored. Freud did not believe that free association was really "free"; he assumed that significant feelings would rise to the surface and demand expression.

FREUD MUSEUM, LONDON

By so doing, Freud believed that the client spilled forth the psychic energy that had been repressed by conflicts and guilt. He called this "spilling forth" catharsis. Catharsis would provide relief by alleviating some of the forces assaulting the ego. Freud also sought to replace impulsive and defensive behavior with coping behavior. In this way, for example, a man with a phobia for knives might discover that he had been repressing the urge to harm someone who had taken advantage of him. He might also find ways to confront the person verbally.

Early in his career as a therapist, Freud found that hypnosis allowed his clients to focus on repressed conflicts and talk about them. He also found, however, that some clients denied the accuracy of this material once they were out of the trance. Others found the memories to be brought out into the open prematurely and painfully. Freud therefore turned to free association, a more gradual method of breaking through the walls of defense that block a client's insight into unconscious processes. In free association, the client is made comfortable—for example, by lying on a couch—and asked to talk about any topic that comes to mind. No thought is to be censored—that is the basic rule. Psychoanalysts ask their clients to wander "freely" from topic to topic, but they do not believe that the process occurring *within* the client is fully free. Repressed impulses clamor for release.

The ego persists in trying to repress unacceptable impulses and threatening conflicts. As a result, clients might show resistance to recalling and discussing threatening ideas. The therapist observes the dynamic struggle between the compulsion to talk about disturbing ideas and resistance. Through discreet comments and questions, the analyst hopes to encourage the client to discuss his or her problems. Talking helps the client gain insight into his or her true wishes and explore ways of fulfilling them.

Transference

Freud believed that clients not only responded to him as an individual but also in ways that reflected their attitudes and feelings toward other people in their lives. He labeled this process transference. For example, a young woman client might respond to him as a father figure and displace her feelings toward her father onto Freud, perhaps seeking affection and wisdom.

> Analyzing and working through transference has been considered a key aspect of psychoanalysis.

Analyzing and working through transference has been considered a key aspect of psychoanalysis. Freud believed that clients reenact their childhood conflicts with their parents when they are in therapy.

Dream Analysis

Freud often asked clients to jot down their dreams upon waking so they could discuss them in therapy. Freud considered dreams the "royal road to the unconscious." He believed that the content of dreams is determined by unconscious processes as well as by the events of the day. Unconscious impulses were expressed in dreams as wish fulfillment.

Short-Term Dynamic Therapies

How do modern psychoanalytic approaches differ from traditional psychoanalysis? Although some psychoanalysts still adhere to Freud's techniques, shorter-term dynamic therapies have been devised. Modern psychoanalytic therapy is briefer and less intense and makes treatment available to clients who do not have the time or money to make therapy part of their lifestyle.

Some modern psychoanalysts continue to focus on revealing unconscious material and breaking through psychological defenses. Nevertheless, they differ from traditional psychoanalysis in several ways (Prochaska & Norcross, 2007). One is that the client and therapist usually sit face to face (i.e., the client does not lie on a couch). The therapist may be directive. That is, modern therapists often suggest helpful behavior instead of focusing on insight alone. Finally, there is more focus on the ego as the "executive" of personality and less emphasis on the id. For this reason, many modern psychoanalysts are called ego analysts.

Interpersonal Psychotherapy

One contemporary dynamic therapy, interpersonal psychotherapy (ITP), focuses on clients' current relationships rather than their childhoods and usually lasts no longer than 9 to 12 months. Developers of ITP view problems such as anxiety and depression as often occurring within social relationships. They therefore focus on clients' relationships and also try to directly alleviate feelings of anxiety and depression (de Mello et al., 2005; Kirschenbaum & Jourdan, 2005).

LO³ Humanistic Therapies

Psychoanalytic therapies focus on internal conflicts and unconscious processes. Humanistic therapies focus on the quality of the client's subjective, conscious experience. Traditional psychoanalysis focuses on early childhood experiences. Humanistic therapies are more likely to focus on what clients are experiencing here and now.

Carl Rogers believed that our psychological well-being is connected with our freedom to develop our unique frames of reference and potentials. Do you think you can separate your "real self" from your sociocultural experiences and religious training?

© ROGER RESSMEYER/CORBIS

Client-Centered Therapy

What is Carl Rogers's method of client-centered therapy? Rogers believed that we are free to make choices and control our destinies, despite the burdens of the past. He also believed that we have natural tendencies toward health, growth, and fulfillment. Psychological problems arise from roadblocks placed in the path of self-actualization—that is, what Rogers believed was an inborn tendency to strive to realize one's potential. If, when we are young, other people approve of us only when we are doing what they want us to do, we may learn to disown the parts of ourselves to which they object. We may learn to be seen but not heard—not even by ourselves. As a result, we may experience stress and discomfort and the feeling that we—or the world—are not real.

Client-centered therapy aims to provide insight into the parts of us that we have disowned so that we can feel whole. It creates a warm, therapeutic atmosphere that encourages self-exploration and self-expression. The therapist's acceptance of the client is thought to foster self-acceptance and self-esteem. Self-acceptance frees the client to make choices that develop his or her unique potential.

Client-centered therapy is nondirective. An effective client-centered therapist has several qualities:

1 *Unconditional positive regard:* respect for clients as human beings with unique values and goals.

2 *Empathy:* recognition of the client's experiences and feelings. Therapists view the world through the client's *frame of reference* by setting aside their own values and listening closely.

3 *Genuineness:* Openness and honesty in responding to the client. Client-centered therapists must be able to tolerate differentness because they believe that every client is different in important ways.

The following excerpt from a therapy session shows how Carl Rogers uses empathetic understanding and paraphrases a client's (Jill's) feelings. His goal is to help her recognize feelings that she has partially disowned:

Jill: I'm having a lot of problems dealing with my daughter. She's twenty years old; she's in

ego analyst
a psychoanalyst therapist who focuses on the conscious, coping behavior of the ego instead of the hypothesized, unconscious functioning of the id

interpersonal psychotherapy (ITP)
a short-term dynamic therapy that focuses on clients' relationships and direct alleviation of negative emotions such as anxiety and depression

client-centered therapy
Carl Rogers's method of psychotherapy, which emphasizes the creation of a warm, therapeutic atmosphere that frees clients to engage in self-exploration and self-expression

Gestalt therapy Fritz Perls' form of psychotherapy, which attempts to integrate conflicting parts of the personality through directive methods designed to help clients perceive their whole selves

Truth

It is true that in client-centered therapy, the client takes the lead, stating and exploring problems.

college; I'm having a lot of trouble letting her go.... And I have a lot of guilt feelings about her; I have a real need to hang on to her.

C. R.: A need to hang on so you can kind of make up for the things you feel guilty about. Is that part of it?

Jill: There's a lot of that.... Also, she's been a real friend to me, and filled my life. . . . And it's very hard. . . . a lot of empty places now that she's not with me.

C. R.: The old vacuum, sort of, when she's not there.

Jill: Yes. Yes. I also would like to be the kind of mother that could be strong and say, you know, "Go and have a good life," and this is really hard for me, to do that.

C. R.: It's very hard to give up something that's been so precious in your life, but also something that I guess has caused you pain when you mentioned guilt.

Jill: Yeah. And I'm aware that I have some anger toward her that I don't always get what I want. I have needs that are not met. And, uh, I don't feel I have a right to those needs. You know . . . she's a daughter; she's not my mother. Though sometimes I feel as if I'd like her to mother me . . . it's very difficult for me to ask for that and have a right to it.

C. R.: So, it may be unreasonable, but still, when she doesn't meet your needs, it makes you mad.

Jill: Yeah, I get very angry, very angry with her.

C. R.: (*Pauses*) You're also feeling a little tension at this point, I guess.

Jill: Yeah. Yeah. A lot of conflict.... (C. R.: M-hm.) A lot of pain.

C. R.: A lot of pain. Can you say anything more about what that's about? (Farber et al., 1996, pp. 74 –75)

Client-centered therapy is practiced widely in college and university counseling centers, not just to help students experiencing, say, anxieties or depression but also to help them make decisions. Many

By showing the qualities of unconditional positive regard, empathic understanding, and genuineness, client-centered therapists create an atmosphere in which clients can explore their feelings.

college students have not yet made career choices, or wonder whether they should become involved with particular people or in sexual activity. Client-centered therapists do not tell clients what to do. Instead, they help clients arrive at their own decisions.

Gestalt Therapy

Gestalt therapy was originated by Fritz Perls (1893–1970). *What is Fritz Perls's method of Gestalt therapy?* Like client-centered therapy, Gestalt therapy assumes that people disown parts of themselves that might meet with social disapproval or rejection. People also don social masks, pretending to be things that they are not. Therapy aims to help individuals integrate conflicting parts of their personality. Perls used the term *Gestalt* to signify his. The German word *Gestalt* means "unified whole." Perls adopted the term because he wanted to help clients integrate conflicting parts of their personalities.

Although Perls's ideas about conflicting personality elements owe much to psychoanalytic theory, his form of therapy, unlike psychoanalysis, focuses on the here and now. Exercises heighten clients' awareness of their current feelings and behavior. Perls also believed, along with Rogers, that people are free to make choices and to direct their personal growth. But the charismatic and forceful Perls was unlike the gentle and accepting Rogers in temperament (Prochaska & Norcross, 2007). Thus, unlike client-centered therapy, Gestalt therapy is directive. The therapist leads the client through planned experiences.

© ANGELO CAVALLI/CORBIS

LO⁴ Behavior Therapy

Psychoanalytic and humanistic forms of therapy tend to focus on what people think and feel. Behavior therapists tend to focus on what people *do*. *What is behavior therapy?* **Behavior therapy**—also called *behavior modification*—applies principles of learning to directly promote desired behavioral changes. Behavior therapists rely heavily on principles of conditioning and observational learning. They help clients discontinue self-defeating behavior patterns such as overeating, smoking, and phobic avoidance of harmless stimuli. They help clients acquire adaptive behavior patterns such as the social skills required to start social relationships or say no to insistent salespeople.

Behavior therapists may help clients gain "insight" into maladaptive behaviors such as feelings of anxiety by helping the person become aware of the circumstances in which the behaviors occur. They do not help unearth the childhood origins of problems and the symbolic meanings of maladaptive behaviors as psychoanalysts do. Behavior therapists, like other therapists, may also build warm, therapeutic relationships with clients, but they see the effectiveness of behavior therapy as deriving from specific, learning-based procedures (Rachman, 2000). They insist that their methods be established by experimentation and that results be assessed in terms of measurable behavior. In this section we consider some frequently used behavior-therapy techniques.

> **Truth**
>
> Gestalt therapists and behavior therapists may use specific procedures—telling their clients what to do.

Fear-Reduction Methods

Many people seek therapy because of fears and phobias that interfere with their functioning. This is one of the areas in which behavior therapy has made great inroads. *What are some behavior-therapy methods for reducing fears?* These include flooding (see Chapter 6), systematic desensitization, virtual therapy, and modeling.

Systematic Desensitization

Adam has a phobia for receiving injections. His behavior therapist treats him as he reclines in a comfortable padded chair. In a state of deep muscle relaxation, Adam observes slides projected on a screen. A slide of a nurse holding a needle has just been shown three times, thirty seconds at a time. Each time

Adam has shown no anxiety. So now a slightly more discomforting slide is shown: one of the nurse aiming the needle toward someone's bare arm. After fifteen seconds, our armchair adventurer notices twinges of discomfort and raises a finger as a signal (speaking might disturb his relaxation). The projector operator turns off the light, and Adam spends 2 minutes imagining his "safe scene"— lying on a beach beneath the tropical sun. Then the slide is shown again. This time Adam views it for thirty seconds before feeling anxiety.

Adam is undergoing **systematic desensitization**, a method for reducing phobic responses originated by psychiatrist Joseph Wolpe (1915–1997). Systematic desensitization is a gradual process in which the client learns to handle increasingly disturbing stimuli while anxiety to each one is being counter-conditioned. About ten to twenty stimuli such as slides are arranged in a sequence, or **hierarchy**, according to their "fear factor"—their capacity to trigger anxiety. In imagination or by being shown photos, the client travels gradually up through this hierarchy, approaching the target behavior. In Adam's case, the target behavior was the ability to receive an injection without undue anxiety.

> **behavior therapy**
> systematic application of the principles of learning to the direct modification of a client's problem behaviors
>
> **systematic desensitization**
> Wolpe's method for reducing fears by associating a hierarchy of images of fear-evoking stimuli with deep muscle relaxation
>
> **hierarchy**
> an arrangement of stimuli according to the amount of fear they evoke

> **Truth**
>
> Using systematic desensitization, Adam is in effect confronting his fear while lying in a recliner and relaxing.

Virtual Therapy

Virtual therapy may use more elaborate equipment than slides, but the principle is desensitization. New York Fire Chief Stephen King was in the north tower at the World Trade Center on September 11, 2001, which was hit first by the airplanes. The experience led him to retire from the department, avoid bridges and tunnels, and stay out of Manhattan (King, 2005). "Where I was and what I saw that day—the many people that jumped, the magnitude of it—was just overwhelming."

But virtual therapy has helped King face the past—and his future. Using the technology we find in video games, programs mimic traumatic settings and events—public speaking in an auditorium, flying in an airplane, spiders, or, in King's case, images of the World Trade Center. "The idea behind the treatment,"

modeling
a behavior-therapy technique in which a client observes and imitates a person who approaches and copes with feared objects or situations

Figure 13.1

A Program Containing Images of the World Trade Center Intended to Help People with Post-Traumatic Stress Disorder

Virtual therapy clients are exposed to virtual stimuli that represent their source of anxiety and stress to help them gradually confront their fears.

explains Dr. JoAnn Difede (2005), "is to systematically expose the patient to aspects of their experience in a graded fashion so they can confront their fear of the trauma" (see Figure 13.1). Psychologist Albert Rizzo has developed scenes from classrooms and parties to help people overcome social anxieties. "To help people deal with their problems, you must get them exposed to what they fear most," Rizzo (2004) notes.

Atlanta-based company Virtually Better focuses on creating virtual environments that therapists can use to treat phobias, substance abuse, and post-traumatic stress disorder (Virtually Better, 2010). Virtually Better has developed scenes of a bridge and a glass elevator to desensitize patients to fear of heights, a virtual airplane cabin for people who fear flying, and a virtual thunderstorm to help people lessen fear of tempestuous weather. "Virtual Iraq" is available to help therapists teach veterans how to cope with the stresses of wartime Iraq. Virtual exposure to alcohol, drugs, and cigarettes can evoke cravings that patients can learn to resist. Virtually Better's contributions include scenes of a virtual crack house and a virtual bar.

Psychologist Hunter Hoffman (2004) describes a virtual environment, *SpiderWorld*, that helps people with spider phobias overcome their aversion by gradually approaching virtual spiders and reaching out to touch them. A toy spider and a device that tracks the patient's hand movements provide tactile sensations akin to touching a real spider (see Figure 13.2).

Modeling

Modeling relies on observational learning. In this method clients observe and then imitate people who approach and cope with the objects or situations that the clients fear. Bandura and his colleagues (1969) found that modeling worked as well as systematic desensitization—and more rapidly—in reducing fear of snakes. Clients observed models handling snakes. In the same session, they were able to touch the snakes, pick them up, and let them crawl on their bodies. Like systematic desensitization, modeling is likely to increase self-efficacy expectations in coping with feared stimuli.

Aversive Conditioning

Many people also seek behavior therapy because they want to break bad habits, such as smoking, excessive drinking, nail-biting, and the like. One

Figure 13.2

Dr. Hunter Hoffman of the University of Washington Uses Virtual Therapy to Treat "Miss Muffet"

Miss Muffet is the name playfully given by Hoffman to a woman with a phobia for spiders. She is wearing virtual-reality headgear and sees the scene displayed on the monitor, which shows a large and hairy—but virtual—tarantula.

behavior-therapy approach to helping people do so is aversive conditioning. *How do behavior therapists use aversive conditioning to help people break bad habits?* Aversive conditioning is a controversial procedure in which painful or aversive stimuli are paired with unwanted impulses, such as desire for a cigarette or desire to engage in antisocial behavior, in an effort to make the impulse less appealing. For example, to help people control alcohol intake, tastes of different alcoholic beverages can be paired with drug-induced nausea and vomiting or with electric shock.

Aversive conditioning has been used with problems as diverse as cigarette smoking, sexual abuse, and retarded children's self-injurious behavior. Rapid smoking is an aversive conditioning method designed to help smokers quit. In this method, the would-be quitter inhales every six seconds. In another method the hose of a hair dryer is hooked up to a chamber containing several lit cigarettes. Smoke is blown into the quitter's face as he or she also smokes a cigarette. A third method uses branching pipes so that the smoker draws in smoke from several cigarettes at the same time. In these methods, overexposure makes once-desirable cigarette smoke aversive. The quitter becomes motivated to avoid, rather than seek, cigarettes. Interest in aversive conditioning for quitting smoking has waned, however, because of side effects such as raising blood pressure and the availability of nicotine-replacement techniques.

> { **Eye-Movement Desensitization and Reprocessing** }
>
> Helping professionals are often inspired to develop therapy methods based on their personal experiences. Such was the case with Francine Shapiro. As she paints it, Shapiro (1989) had troubling thoughts on her mind when she strolled into a park one day. But as her eyes darted about, taking in the scene, she found her troubled thoughts disappearing. Thus she developed a therapy method called **eye-movement desensitization and reprocessing (EMDR)**, which has joined the arsenal of therapeutic weapons against stress disorders. In this method, the client is asked to imagine a traumatic scene while the therapist moves a finger rapidly back and forth before his or her eyes for about twenty to thirty seconds. The client follows the finger while keeping the troubling scene in mind. Evidence from a number of studies suggests that EMDR helps decrease the anxiety associated with traumatic events.
>
> Devilly (2002) allows that EMDR is often effective, but his review finds other exposure therapies to be more effective. Research even challenges the idea that eye movements are a necessary part of therapy (May, 2005; Devilly, 2002). Skeptics have tried EMDR—or a cousin of it—using finger tapping rather than finger wagging, or instructing clients to keep their eyes straight ahead, and the results have remained the same.
>
> Clients receiving EMDR may profit from a "therapeutic alliance" with the helping professional and from expectations of success. Moreover, the client *is* to some degree being exposed to the trauma that haunts him or her, and under circumstances in which the client believes he or she will be able to manage the trauma.
>
> Conclusion? Exposure helps people cope with trauma. Eye movements may not be needed.

Operant Conditioning Procedures

We tend to repeat behavior that is reinforced. Behavior that is not reinforced tends to become extinguished. Behavior therapists have used these principles of operant conditioning with psychotic patients as well as with clients with milder problems. *How do behavior therapists apply principles of operant conditioning in behavior modification?*

The staff at one mental hospital was at a loss about how to encourage withdrawn schizophrenic patients to eat regularly. Ayllon and Haughton (1962) observed that staff members were making the problem worse by coaxing patients into the dining room and even feeding them. Staff attention apparently reinforced the patients' lack of cooperation. Some rules were changed. Patients who did not arrive at the dining hall within thirty minutes after serving were locked out. Staff could not interact with patients at mealtime. With uncooperative behavior no longer reinforced, patients quickly changed their eating habits. Then patients were required to pay one penny

aversive conditioning a behavior therapy technique in which undesired responses are inhibited by pairing repugnant or offensive stimuli with them

rapid smoking an aversive conditioning method for quitting smoking in which the smoker inhales rapidly, thus rendering once-desirable cigarette smoke aversive

eye-movement desensitization and reprocessing (EMDR) a method of treating stress disorders by having clients visually follow a rapidly oscillating finger while they think of the traumatic events connected with the disorders

Truth

In the method of rapid smoking, behavior therapists use smoking as a way of making cigarette smoke unappealing to smokers, helping them to stop smoking.

to enter the dining hall. Pennies were earned by interacting with other patients and showing other socially appropriate behaviors. These target behaviors also became more frequent.

Health professionals are concerned about whether people who are, or have been, dependent on alcohol can exercise control over their drinking. One study showed that rewards for remaining abstinent from alcohol can exert a powerful effect (Petry et al., 2000). In the study, one group of alcohol-dependent veterans was given a standard treatment while another group received the treatment *plus* the chance to win prizes for remaining alcohol-free, as measured by a Breathalyzer test. By the end of the eight-week treatment period, 84% of the veterans who could win prizes remained in the program, as compared with 22% of the standard treatment group. The prizes had an average value of $200, far less than what alcohol-related absenteeism from work and other responsibilities can cost.

The Token Economy

Many psychiatric wards and hospitals use token economies in which patients need tokens such as poker chips to purchase TV viewing time, extra visits to the canteen, or a private room (Comaty et al., 2001). The tokens are dispensed as reinforcers for productive activities such as making beds, brushing teeth, and socializing. Token economies have not eliminated all symptoms of schizophrenia but have increased patients' activity and cooperation. Tokens have also been used to modify the behavior of children with conduct disorders.

Successive Approximations

The operant conditioning method of successive approximations is often used to help clients build good habits. For example: You want to study three hours each evening but can concentrate for only half an hour. Rather than attempting to increase your study time all at once, you could do so gradually by adding, say, five minutes each evening. After every hour or so of studying, you could reinforce yourself with five minutes of people-watching in a busy section of the library.

Biofeedback Training

Through biofeedback training (BFT), therapists help clients become more aware of, and gain control over, various bodily functions. Therapists attach clients to devices that measure bodily functions such as heart rate. "Bleeps" or other electronic signals are used to indicate (and thereby reinforce) changes ("operants") in the desired direction—for example, a slower heart rate. (Knowledge of results is a powerful reinforcer.) One device, the electromyograph (EMG), monitors muscle tension. It has been used to increase control over muscle tension in the forehead and elsewhere, thereby alleviating anxiety, stress, and headaches (Nestoriuc et al., 2008).

BFT also helps clients voluntarily regulate functions once thought to be beyond conscious control, such as heart rate and blood pressure. Hypertensive clients use a blood-pressure cuff and electronic signals to gain control over their blood pressure. The electroencephalograph (EEG) monitors brain waves and can be used to teach people how to produce alpha waves, which are associated with relaxation. Some people have overcome insomnia by learning to produce the kinds of brain waves associated with sleep.

Social Skills Training

In social skills training, behavior therapists decrease social anxiety and build social skills through operant-conditioning procedures that employ self-monitoring, coaching, modeling, role-playing, behavior rehearsal, and feedback. Social skills training has been used to help formerly hospitalized mental patients maintain jobs and apartments in the community.

For example, a worker can rehearse politely asking a supervisor for assistance or asking a landlord to fix the plumbing in an apartment. Social skills training is effective in groups. Group members can role-play important people—such as parents, spouses, or potential dates—in the lives of other members.

LO⁵ Cognitive Therapies

What thoughts do you have when things go wrong at school or on the job? Do you tell yourself that you're facing a problem that needs a solution? That you've successfully solved problems before and will be able to create a solution this time? Or do you think, "Oh no! This is awful! It's going to get worse, and I'm going to flunk (or get fired)!" If you go the "This is awful" route, you are probably heightening your discomfort and impairing your coping ability. Cognitive therapy focuses directly on your thoughts and encourages ideas that will help you solve problems rather than blow them out of proportion and magnify your discomfort.

What is cognitive therapy? Cognitive therapy focuses on changing the beliefs, attitudes, and automatic types of thinking that create and compound people's problems. Cognitive therapists, like psychoanalytic and humanistic therapists, aim to foster self-insight, but they mainly aim to help make people more aware of their *current cognitions*. Cognitive therapists also aim to directly change maladaptive thoughts in an effort to reduce negative feelings and help clients solve problems.

Many behavior therapists incorporate cognitive procedures in their methods. For example, techniques such as systematic desensitization, covert sensitization, and covert reinforcement ask clients to focus on visual imagery. Behavioral methods for treating bulimia nervosa focus on clients' irrational attitudes toward their weight and body shape as well as foster good eating habits. Let us look at the approaches and methods of the cognitive therapists Aaron Beck and Albert Ellis.

Aaron Beck's Cognitive Therapy

Psychiatrist Aaron Beck began his professional life as a psychoanalyst. He became impatient, however, with analysis's lengthy methods and reluctance to offer specific advice. In his own life he had successfully defeated his fear of blood by assisting in surgical operations and argued himself out of irrational fear of driving through tunnels. Similarly, his methods of cognitive therapy focus on arguing clients out of beliefs that are making them miserable and exposing them to situations they avoid because of irrational fear (Berk et al.,

2004; Warman et al., 2005). *What is Aaron Beck's method of cognitive therapy?* Beck encourages clients to become their own personal scientists and challenge feelings and beliefs that make no sense.

Beck encourages clients to see the irrationality of their ways of thinking. For example, depressed people tend to minimize their accomplishments and to assume that the worst will happen. Minimizing accomplishments and expecting the worst are (usually) distortions of reality that lead to feelings of depression. Cognitive distortions can be fleeting and automatic, difficult to detect. Beck's methods help clients become aware of such distortions and challenge them.

Beck notes a number of "cognitive errors" that contribute to clients' miseries:

1 Clients may *selectively perceive* the world as a harmful place and ignore evidence to the contrary.

2 Clients may *overgeneralize* on the basis of a few examples. For example, they may perceive themselves as worthless because they were laid off at work or as unattractive because they were refused a date.

3 Clients may *magnify,* or blow out of proportion, the importance of negative events. They may catastrophize failing a test by assuming they will flunk out of college or catastrophize losing a job by believing that they will never find another one and that serious harm will befall their family as a result.

4 Clients may engage in *absolutist thinking,* or looking at the world in black and white rather than in shades of gray. In doing so, a rejection on a date takes on the meaning of a lifetime of loneliness; an uncomfortable illness takes on life-threatening proportions.

Becoming aware of cognitive errors and modifying catastrophizing thoughts help us cope with stress. Internal, stable, and global attributions of failure lead to depression and feelings of helplessness. Cognitive therapists also alert clients to cognitive errors or irrational thoughts so that the clients can change their attitudes and pave the way for more effective overt behavior.

cognitive therapy
a form of therapy that focuses on how clients' cognitions (e.g., expectations, attitudes, beliefs) lead to distress and may be modified to relieve distress and promote adaptive behavior

Aaron Beck (left) and Albert Ellis (right)

Rational Emotive Behavior Therapy

What is Albert Ellis's method of rational emotive behavior therapy (REBT)? In rational emotive behavior therapy (REBT), Albert Ellis (1913–2007) pointed out that our beliefs *about* events, not only the events themselves, shape our responses to them. Moreover, many of us harbor a number of irrational beliefs that can give rise to problems or magnify their impact. Two of the most important ones are the belief that we must have the love and approval of people who are important to us and the belief that we must prove ourselves to be thoroughly competent, adequate, and achieving.

Albert Ellis, like Aaron Beck, began his career as a psychoanalyst. And, also like Beck, he became disturbed by the passive role of the analyst and by the slow rate of obtaining results—if they were obtained at all. Ellis's REBT methods are active and directive. He did not sit back like the traditional psychoanalyst and occasionally offer an interpretation. Instead, he urged clients to seek out their irrational beliefs, which can be unconscious, though not as deeply buried as Freud believed. Nevertheless, they can be hard to pinpoint without some direction. Ellis showed clients how those beliefs lead to misery and challenged clients to change them. When Ellis saw clients behaving according to irrational beliefs, he refuted the beliefs by asking "Where is it written that you must . . . ?" or "What evidence do you have that . . . ?" According to Ellis, we need less misery and less blaming in our lives, and more action.

Toward a Cognitive-Behavioral Therapy

Many theorists consider cognitive therapy to be a collection of techniques that are a part of behavior therapy. Aaron Beck himself appears to be comfortable referring to his approach as *cognitive* in one article and *cognitive-behavioral* in another (Berk et al., 2005; Warman & Beck, 2003). We are apparently headed toward an integration of the two approaches that is termed cognitive-behavioral therapy (CBT).

Ellis straddled behavioral and cognitive therapies. He originally dubbed his method of therapy *rational-emotive therapy,* because his focus was on the cognitive—irrational beliefs and how to change them. However, Ellis also always promoted behavioral changes to cement cognitive changes. In keeping with his broad philosophy, he recently changed the name of rational-emotive therapy to rational-emotive *behavior* therapy.

LO⁶ Group Therapies

When a psychotherapist has several clients with similar problems—anxiety, depression, adjustment to divorce, lack of social skills—it often makes sense to treat them in a group rather than in individual sessions. The methods and characteristics of the group reflect the needs of the members and the theoretical orientation of the leader. In group psychoanalysis, clients might interpret one another's dreams. In a client-centered group, they might provide an accepting atmosphere for self-exploration. Members of behavior therapy groups might be jointly desensitized to anxiety-evoking stimuli or might practice social skills together. *What are the advantages and disadvantages of group therapy?*

Group therapy has the following advantages:

1 It is economical. It allows the therapist to work with several clients at once.

2 Compared with one-to-one therapy, group therapy provides more information and life experience for clients to draw on.

3 Appropriate behavior receives group support. Clients usually appreciate an outpouring of peer approval.

4 When we run into troubles, it is easy to imagine that we are different from other people or inferior to them. Affiliating with people with similar problems is reassuring.

5 Group members who show improvement provide hope for other members.

6 Many individuals seek therapy because of problems in relating to other people. People who seek therapy for other reasons also may be socially inhibited. Members of groups have the opportunity to practice social skills in a relatively nonthreatening atmosphere. In a group consisting of men and women of different ages, group members can role-play one another's employers, employees, spouses, parents, children, and friends. Members can role-play asking one another out on dates, saying no (or yes), and so on.

But group therapy is not for everyone. Some clients fare better with individual treatment. Many prefer not to disclose their problems to a group. They may be overly shy or want individual attention. It is the responsibility of the therapist to insist that group disclosures be kept confidential, to establish a supportive atmosphere, and to ensure that group members obtain the attention they need.

Many types of therapy can be conducted either individually or in groups. Couple therapy and family therapy are conducted only with groups.

Couple Therapy

Couple therapy helps couples enhance their relationship by improving their communication skills and helping them manage conflict (Prochaska & Norcross, 2007). There are often power imbalances in relationships, and couple therapy helps individuals find "full membership" in the couple. Correcting power imbalances increases happiness and can decrease the incidence of domestic violence. Ironically, in situations of domestic violence, the partner with *less* power in the relationship is usually the violent one. Violence sometimes appears to be a way of compensating for inability to share power in other aspects of the relationship (Rathus & Sanderson, 1999).

Today the main approach to couple therapy is cognitive-behavioral (Rathus & Sanderson, 1999). It teaches couples communications skills (such as how to listen and how to express feelings), ways of handling feelings like depression and anger, and ways of solving problems.

Family Therapy

What is family therapy? Family therapy is a form of group therapy in which one or more families constitute the group. Family therapy may be undertaken from various theoretical viewpoints. One is the systems approach, in which family interaction is studied and modified to enhance the growth of individual family members and of the family unit as a whole (Prochaska & Norcross, 2007).

Family members with low self-esteem often cannot tolerate different attitudes and behaviors in other family members. Faulty communication within the family also creates problems. In addition, it is not uncommon for the family to present an "identified patient"—that is, the family member who has *the* problem and is *causing* all the trouble. Yet family therapists usually assume that the identified patient is a scapegoat for other problems within and among family members. It is a sort of myth: Change

the "bad apple," or identified patient, and the "barrel," or family, will be functional once more. The family therapist—often a specialist in this field—attempts to teach the family to communicate more effectively and encourage growth and autonomy in each family member.

LO⁷ Does Psychotherapy Work?

In 1952, the British psychologist Hans Eysenck published a review of psychotherapy research—"The Effects of Psychotherapy"—that sent shock waves through the psychotherapy community. On the basis of his review of the research, Eysenck concluded that the rate of improvement among people in psychotherapy was no greater than the rate of "spontaneous remission"—that is, the rate of improvement that would be shown by people with psychological disorders who received no treatment at all. Eysenck was not addressing people with schizophrenia, who typically profit from biological forms of therapy, but he argued that whether or not people with problems such as anxiety and depression received therapy, two of three reported substantial improvement within two years.

That was half a century ago. There is now quite a bit of research evidence—with many studies employing a sophisticated statistical averaging method called meta-analysis—that show that psychotherapy is effective (Luborsky et al., 2002; Shadish et al., 2000). *What, then, has research shown about the effectiveness of psychotherapy?*

Fiction

Actually, there is now quite a bit of research evidence that shows that psychotherapy is effective.

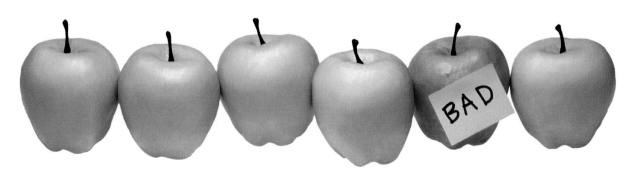

It is a sort of myth: Change the "bad apple," or identified patient, and the "barrel," or family, will be functional once more.

In their classic early use of meta-analysis, Mary Lee Smith and Gene Glass (1977) analyzed the results of dozens of outcome studies of various types of therapies. They concluded that people who obtained psychoanalytic therapy showed greater well-being, on the average, than 70% to 75% of those who did not obtain treatment. Similarly, nearly 75% of the clients who obtained client-centered therapy were better off than people who did not obtain treatment. Psychoanalytic and client-centered therapies appear to be most effective with well-educated, verbal, strongly motivated clients who report problems with anxiety, depression (of light to moderate proportions), and interpersonal relationships. Neither form of therapy appears to be effective with people with psychotic disorders such as major depression, bipolar disorder, and schizophrenia. Smith and Glass (1977) found that people who obtained Gestalt therapy showed greater well-being than about 60% of those who did not obtain treatment. The effectiveness of psychoanalysis and client-centered therapy thus was reasonably comparable. Gestalt therapy fell behind.

Smith and Glass (1977) did not include cognitive therapies in their meta-analysis because at the time of their study many cognitive approaches were relatively new. Because behavior therapists also incorporate many cognitive techniques, it can be difficult to sort out which aspects—cognitive or otherwise—of behavioral treatments are most effective. Many meta-analyses of cognitive–behavioral therapy have been conducted since the early work of Smith and Glass, however. Their results are encouraging (e.g., DeRubeis et al., 2005; Hollon et al., 2005). A meta-analysis of ninety studies by William R. Shadish and his colleagues (2000) concurred that psychotherapy is generally effective. Generally speaking, the more therapy, the better; that is, people who have more psychotherapy tend to fare better than people who have less of it. Therapy also appears to be more effective when the outcome measures reflect the treatment (e.g., when the effects of treatment aimed at fear-reduction are measured in terms of people's ability to approach fear-inducing objects and situations).

Studies of cognitive therapy have shown that modifying irrational beliefs of the type described by Albert Ellis helps people with problems such as anxiety and depression (Engels et al., 1993; Haaga & Davison, 1993). Modifying self-defeating beliefs of the sort outlined by Aaron Beck also frequently alleviates anxiety and depression (Butler & Beck, 2001). Cognitive therapy has also helped people with personality disorders (Beck et al., 2001; Trull et al., 2003).

Behavioral and cognitive therapies have provided strategies for treating anxiety disorders, social-skills deficits, and problems in self-control. These therapies—which are often integrated as cognitive-behavioral therapy (CBT)—have also provided empirically supported methods for helping couples and families in distress (Baucom et al., 1998), and for modifying behaviors related to health problems such as headaches, smoking, chronic pain, and bulimia nervosa (Agras et al., 2000). Cognitive-behavioral therapists have also innovated treatments for sexual dysfunctions for which there were no effective treatments.

Cognitive-behavioral therapy has been used to help anorexic and bulimic individuals challenge their perfectionism and their attitudes toward their bodies. It has also been used to systematically reinforce appropriate eating behavior. Studies that compare the effectiveness of CBT and antidepressants find them to be comparably effective, with CBT sometimes showing a slight advantage (e.g., De Maat et al., 2006). Drugs, after all, do not directly "attack" people's perfectionist attitudes and their distorted body images. They ease the presence of negative feelings and may help individuals enlist their own psychological resources, but pills do not offer advice or even a sympathetic ear.

The combination of cognitive therapy or CBT and drug therapy has helped many people with schizophrenia modify their delusional beliefs and behave in more socially acceptable ways (Turkington et al., 2004; Warman et al., 2005). But psychological therapy alone is apparently inadequate to treat the quirks of thought exhibited in people with severe psychotic disorders.

Thus, it is not enough to ask which type of therapy is most effective. We must ask which type is most effective for a particular problem and a particular patient. What are its advantages? Its limitations? Clients may successfully use systematic desensitization or virtual therapy to overcome stage fright, but if they also want to know *why* they have stage fright, behavior therapy alone will not provide the answer. But, then again, insight-oriented forms of therapy might also be unable to provide the answer.

All in all, despite Han Eysenck's skepticism noted at the beginning of the section, research suggests that psychotherapy appears to be effective more often than not. But, we might wonder, does psychotherapy help

> It is not enough to ask which type of therapy is most effective. We must ask which type is most effective for a particular problem and a particular patient.

because of specific factors and treatment methods or because a client is receiving the support of an educated and trained helping professional?

So-called nonspecific factors in therapy, such as the formation of the client-therapist "alliance," are connected with better therapeutic results (Scaturo, 2005). However, specific techniques—such as specific cognitive and behavioral methods—appear to be much more effective than the therapist-client relationship in bringing about helpful changes (Stevens et al., 2000).

Psychotherapy and Race/Ethnicity

Multiculturalism raises other issues concerning the effectiveness of psychotherapy. Most of the "prescriptions" for psychotherapy discussed in this chapter were originated by, and intended for use with, European Americans. Let us note that people from different racial or ethnic backgrounds are less likely than European Americans to seek therapy for psychological problems for reasons such as the following:

- lack of awareness that therapy would help
- lack of information about the availability of professional services, or inability to pay for them
- distrust of professionals, particularly European American professionals and (for women) male professionals
- language barriers
- reluctance to open up about personal matters to strangers—especially strangers who are not members of one's own ethnic group
- cultural inclinations toward other approaches to problem solving, such as religious approaches and psychic healers
- negative experiences with professionals and authority figures

Clinicians need to be sensitive to the cultural heritage, language, and values of the people they see in therapy (Chen & Davenport, 2005). Let us consider some of the issues involved in conducting psychotherapy with African Americans, Asian Americans, Latino and Latina Americans, and Native Americans.

African Americans

In addition to addressing the psychological problems of African American clients, therapists often need to help them cope with the effects of prejudice and discrimination. Some African Americans develop low self-esteem because they internalize negative stereotypes (Boyd-Franklin, 2001).

African Americans often are reluctant to seek psychological help because of cultural assumptions that people should manage their own problems and because of mistrust of the therapy process. They tend to assume that people are supposed to solve their own problems. Signs of emotional weakness such as tension, anxiety, and depression are stigmatized (Ivey & Brooks-Harris, 2005).

Many African Americans are also suspicious of their therapists—especially when the therapist is a European American. They may withhold personal information because of the society's history of racial discrimination.

Asian Americans

Asian Americans tend to stigmatize people with psychological disorders. As a result, they may deny problems and refuse to seek help for them (Chen & Davenport, 2005). Asian Americans, especially recent immigrants, also may not understand or believe in Western approaches to psychotherapy. For example, Western psychotherapy typically encourages people to express their feelings openly. This mode of behavior may conflict with the Asian tradition of restraint in public. Many Asians prefer to receive concrete advice rather than Western-style encouragement

specific factors those factors in psychotherapy that are specific to a given approach, such as free association in psychoanalysis or systematic desensitization in behavior therapy

nonspecific factors those factors in psychotherapy that are common to many approaches, such as the "therapeutic alliance" with the client

> CLINICIANS NEED TO BE SENSITIVE TO THE CULTURAL HERITAGE, LANGUAGE, AND VALUES OF THE PEOPLE THEY SEE IN THERAPY.

© 2010 ALVIS UPITIS / JUPITERIMAGES CORPORATION

rebound anxiety
anxiety that can occur when one discontinues use of a tranquilizer

to develop their own solutions (Chen & Davenport, 2005).

Because of a cultural tendency to deny painful thoughts, many Asians experience and express psychological problems as physical symptoms (Chen & Davenport, 2005). Rather than thinking of themselves as being anxious, they may focus on physical features of anxiety such as a pounding heart and heavy sweating. Rather than thinking of themselves as depressed, they may focus on fatigue and low energy levels.

Latino and Latina Americans

Therapists need to be aware of potential conflicts between the traditional Latino and Latina American value of interdependency in the family and the typical European American belief in independence and self-reliance (Anger-Díaz et al., 2004). Measures like the following may help bridge the gaps between psychotherapists and Latino and Latina American clients:

- Interacting with clients in the language requested by them or, if this is not possible, referring them to professionals who can do so.

- Using methods that are consistent with the client's values and levels of acculturation, as suggested by fluency in English and level of education.

- Developing therapy methods that incorporate clients' cultural values (Cervantes & Parham, 2005). Malgady and his colleagues (1990), for example, use *cuento therapy* with Puerto Ricans. *Cuento therapy* uses Latino and Latina folktales (*cuentos*) with characters who serve as models for adaptive behavior.

Native Americans

Many psychological disorders experienced by Native Americans involve the disruption of their traditional culture caused by European colonization (Walle, 2004). Native Americans have also been denied full access to key institutions in Western culture. Loss of cultural identity and social disorganization have set the stage for problems such as alcoholism, substance abuse, and depression (Walle, 2004). If psychologists are to help Native Americans cope with psychological disorders, they need to do so in a way that is sensitive to their culture, customs, and values. Efforts to prevent such disorders should focus on strengthening Native American cultural identity, pride, and cohesion.

LO 8 Biological Therapies

The kinds of therapy we have discussed are psychological in nature—forms of *psychotherapy.* Psychotherapies apply *psychological* principles to treatment, principles based on psychological

knowledge of matters such as learning and motivation. People with psychological disorders are also often treated with biological therapies. Biological therapies apply what is known of people's *biological* structures and processes to the amelioration of psychological disorders. For example, they may work by altering events in the nervous system, as by changing the action of neurotransmitters. In this section, we discuss three biological, or medical, approaches to treating people with psychological disorders: drug therapy, electroconvulsive therapy, and psychosurgery. *What kinds of drug therapy are available for psychological disorders?*

Drug Therapy

In the 1950s Fats Domino popularized the song "My Blue Heaven." Fats was singing about the sky and happiness. Today "blue heavens" is one of the street names for the 10-milligram dose of the antianxiety drug Valium. Clinicians prescribe Valium and other drugs for people with various psychological disorders.

Antianxiety Drugs

Most antianxiety drugs, such as Valium and Serax, belong to the chemical class known as *benzodiazepines.* Antianxiety drugs are usually prescribed for outpatients who complain of generalized anxiety or panic attacks, although many people also use them as sleeping pills. Valium and other antianxiety drugs depress the activity of the central nervous system (CNS). The CNS, in turn, decreases sympathetic activity, reducing the heart rate, respiration rate, and nervousness and tension.

Many people come to tolerate antianxiety drugs very quickly. When tolerance occurs, dosages must be increased for the drug to remain effective.

Sedation (feeling of being tired or drowsy) is the most common side effect of antianxiety drugs. Problems associated with withdrawal from these drugs include rebound anxiety. That is, some people who have been using these drugs regularly report that their anxiety becomes worse than before once they discontinue them. Antianxiety drugs can induce physical dependence, as evidenced by withdrawal symptoms such as tremors, sweating, insomnia, and rapid heartbeat.

Antipsychotic Drugs

People with schizophrenia are often given antipsychotic drugs (also called *major tranquilizers*). In most cases these drugs reduce agitation, delusions, and hallucinations. Many antipsychotic drugs, including phenothiazines (e.g., Thorazine) and clozapine

(Clozaril) are thought to act by blocking dopamine receptors in the brain. Research along these lines supports the theory that schizophrenia is connected with overactivity of the neurotransmitter dopamine.

Antidepressants

People with major depression often take so-called antidepressant drugs. These drugs are also helpful for some people with eating disorders, panic disorder, obsessive–compulsive disorder, and social phobia. Problems in the regulation of noradrenaline and serotonin may be involved in eating and panic disorders as well as in depression. Antidepressants are believed to work by increasing levels of these neurotransmitters, which can affect both depression and the appetite. As noted in the section on the effectiveness of psychotherapy, however, cognitive therapy addresses irrational attitudes concerning weight and body shape, fosters normal eating habits, and helps people resist the urges to binge and purge, often making therapy more effective than drugs for people with bulimia. But when cognitive therapy does not help people with bulimia nervosa, drug therapy may do so.

There are various antidepressants. Each increases the concentration of noradrenaline or serotonin in the brain. Selective serotonin-reuptake inhibitors (SSRIs) such as Prozac and Zoloft block the reuptake of serotonin by presynaptic neurons. As a result, serotonin remains in the synaptic cleft longer, influencing receiving neurons.

Antidepressant drugs must usually build up to a therapeutic level over several weeks. Because overdoses can be lethal, some people stay in a hospital during the buildup to prevent suicide attempts. There are also side effects such as nausea, agitation, and weight gain. The nausea and agitation tend to dissipate after patients have been using the drugs for a day or two.

Lithium

The ancient Greeks and Romans were among the first to use the metal lithium as a psychoactive drug. They prescribed mineral water—which contains lithium—for people with bipolar disorder. They had no inkling as to why this treatment sometimes helped. A salt of the metal lithium (lithium carbonate), in tablet form, flattens out cycles of manic behavior and depression in most people. It is not known exactly how lithium works, although it affects the functioning of neurotransmitters.

People with bipolar disorder may have to use lithium indefinitely, as a person with diabetes must use insulin to control the illness. Lithium also has been shown to have side effects such as hand tremors, memory impairment, and excessive thirst and urination. Memory impairment is reported as the main reason why people discontinue lithium.

Does Drug Therapy Work?

There are thus a number of drugs available to treat psychological disorders. There is little question that drug therapy has helped many people with severe psychological disorders. For example, antipsychotic drugs largely account for the reduced need for the use of restraint and supervision (e.g., padded cells, straitjackets,

antidepressant acting to relieve depression

selective serotonin-reuptake inhibitors (SSRIs) antidepressant drugs that work by blocking the reuptake of serotonin by presynaptic neurons

electroconvulsive therapy (ECT) treatment of disorders like major depression by passing an electric current (that causes a convulsion) through the head

sedative a drug that relieves nervousness or agitation or puts one to sleep

psychosurgery surgery intended to promote psychological changes or to relieve disordered behavior

prefrontal lobotomy the severing or destruction of a section of the frontal lobe of the brain

hospitalization, and so on) with people diagnosed with schizophrenia. Antipsychotic drugs have allowed hundreds of thousands of former mental hospital residents to lead largely normal lives in the community, hold jobs, and maintain family lives. Most of the problems related to these drugs concern their side effects.

But many comparisons of psychotherapy (in the form of cognitive therapy) and drug therapy for depression suggest that cognitive therapy is as effective as or more effective than antidepressants (DeRubeis et al., 2005; De Maat et al., 2006). Cognitive therapy appears to provide coping skills that reduce the risk of recurrence of depression once treatment ends (Hollon et al., 2005).

Many psychologists and psychiatrists are comfortable with the short-term use of antianxiety drugs in helping clients manage periods of unusual anxiety or tension. Many people, however, use antianxiety drugs routinely to dull the arousal stemming from anxiety-producing lifestyles or interpersonal problems. Rather than make the often painful decisions required to confront their problems and change their lives, they prefer to take a pill.

One study found that both tranquilizers and CBT (stress management training plus imagined exposure to the fearful stimuli) helped phobic people get through a dental session. However, 70% of those who received cognitive-behavioral therapy continued to go for dental treatment, as compared with only 20% of those who took the tranquilizer (Thom et al., 2000). CBT apparently taught people in the study coping skills, whereas the tranquilizers afforded only temporary relief.

In sum, drug therapy is effective for some disorders that do not respond to psychotherapy alone. Yet common sense and research evidence suggest that psychotherapy is preferable for problems such as anxiety and mild depression. No chemical can show a person how to change an idea or solve an interpersonal problem.

Electroconvulsive Therapy

What is electroconvulsive therapy? Electroconvulsive therapy (ECT) is a biological form of therapy for psychological disorders that was introduced by the Italian psychiatrist Ugo Cerletti in 1939. Cerletti had noted that some slaughterhouses used electric shock to render animals unconscious. The shocks also produced convulsions. Along with other European researchers of the period, Cerletti erroneously believed that convulsions were incompatible with schizophrenia and other major psychological disorders.

ECT was originally used for a variety of psychological disorders. Because of the advent of antipsychotic drugs, however, it is now used mainly for people with major depression who do not respond to antidepressants.

People typically obtain one ECT treatment three times a week for up to ten sessions. Electrodes are attached to the temples and an electrical current strong enough to produce a convulsion is induced. The shock causes unconsciousness, so the patient does not recall it. Nevertheless, patients are given a sedative so that they are asleep during the treatment.

ECT is controversial for many reasons, such as the fact that many professionals are distressed by the thought of passing an electric shock through a patient's head and producing convulsions. There are also side effects, including memory problems.

Psychosurgery

Psychosurgery is more controversial than ECT. *What is psychosurgery? How is it used to treat psychological disorders?* The best-known modern technique, prefrontal lobotomy, has been used with people with severe disorders. In this method, a pick-like instrument severs the nerve pathways that link the prefrontal lobes of the brain to the thalamus. It is intended to sever thought from emotion and enable severely disturbed patients to regain control.

The method was pioneered by the Portuguese neurologist Antonio Egas Moniz and was brought to the United States in the 1930s. The theoretical rationale for the operation was vague and misguided, and Moniz's reports of success were exaggerated. Nevertheless, by 1950 prefrontal lobotomies had been performed on thousands of people in an effort to reduce violence and agitation. Anecdotal evidence of the method's unreliable outcomes is found in an ironic footnote to history: one of Dr. Moniz's patients returned to shoot him.

Truth

One of Dr. Moniz's "failures" did indeed shoot him, leaving a bullet lodged in his spine and paralyzing his legs.

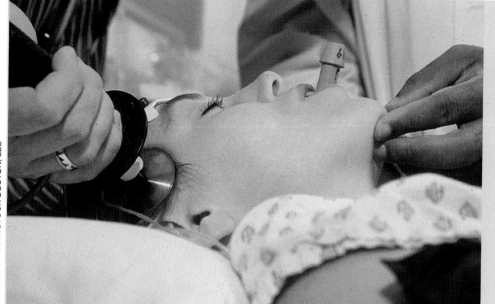

NAJILAH FEANNY/STOCK BOSTON, LLC

Electroconvulsive Therapy
In ECT, electrodes are placed on each side of the patient's head and a current is passed between them, inducing a seizure. ECT is used mainly in cases of major depression when antidepressant drugs and psychotherapy are not sufficient.

Prefrontal lobotomy also has side effects, including hyperactivity and distractibility, impaired learning ability, overeating, apathy and withdrawal, epileptic-type seizures, reduced creativity, and, now and then, death. Because of these side effects, and because of the advent of antipsychotic drugs, this method has been largely discontinued in the United States.

Social Psychology

Learning Outcomes

LO¹ Define social psychology

LO² Define attitude and discuss factors that shape it

LO³ Define social perception and describe the factors that contribute to it

LO⁴ Explain why people obey authority figures and conform to social norms

LO⁵ Describe how and why people behave differently as group members than as individuals

> ## "People can be goaded by social influences into doing things that are not necessarily consistent with their personalities."

Consider some news from the early years of the 21st century. On December 27, 2007, Benazir Bhutto, the two-time prime minister of Pakistan, was killed by a suicide bomber during a political rally as she was campaigning to hold that post for a third time. On July 7, 2005, four suicide bombers blew themselves up aboard three London commuter trains and a bus, killing more than fifty people and wounding 700. And, of course, in the United States there were the nineteen suicide terrorists who used fully fueled airplanes as bombs on September 11, 2001, and flew them into the World Trade Center and the Pentagon, killing 3,000.

Although you might think of suicide terrorism as a recent phenomenon, it dates back thousands of years (Pastor, 2004). But we have become most recently aware of suicide terrorism by strikes throughout the Muslim world, in Israel, and—with the attacks on New York, Washington, D.C., Madrid, and London—in the Western world. The word "suicide" in the phrase "suicide bomber" leads people to turn to psychologists for understanding, with the idea that something must be very wrong psychologically with these terrorists (Pastor, 2004). But many social scientists assert that suicide terrorists have no telltale psychological profile (Consortium of Social Science Associations, 2003; Lester et al., 2004). Social psychologist Philip Zimbardo (2008) argues that we must look to social influence to understand suicide terrorism.

One area of social psychology studies the ways in which people can be goaded by social influences into doing things that are not necessarily consistent with their personalities. In particular, Zimbardo (2004) has investigated the relative ease with which "ordinary" men and women can be incited to behave in evil ways.

Truth or Fiction?

What do you think?

Folklore, common sense, or nonsense? Place a T for "True" or F for "False" on the lines provided (you'll learn the answers as you read through the text).

__ People act in accord with their consciences.

__ We appreciate things more when we have to work for them.

__ Beauty is in the eye of the beholder.

__ Opposites attract.

__ We tend to hold others responsible for their misdeeds but to see ourselves as victims of circumstances when we misbehave.

__ Most people will torture an innocent person if they are ordered to do so.

__ Seeing is believing.

__ Nearly forty people stood by and did nothing while a woman was being stabbed to death.

LO¹ What Is Social Psychology?

The situationist perspective is part of the field of social psychology. *What is social psychology?* Social psychology studies the nature and causes of behavior and mental processes in social situations. The

social psychology
the field of psychology that studies the nature and causes of people's thoughts and behavior in social situations

© BEAU LARK/CORBIS

social psychological topics we discuss in this chapter include attitudes, social perception, social influence, and group behavior. As we explore each of these, we will ask what they might offer to those of us who have difficulty imagining why people would surrender their own lives to take the lives of others.

{ Suicide Bombers: Evil? Ordinary? }

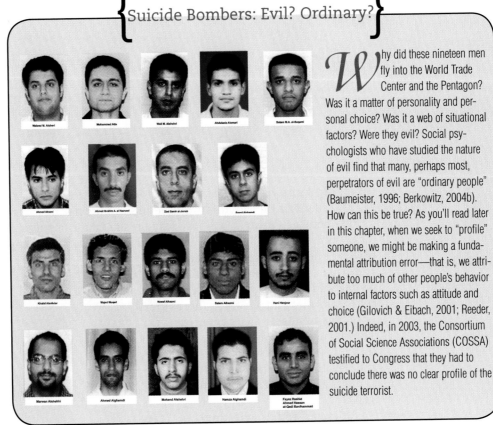

GETTY IMAGES

Why did these nineteen men fly into the World Trade Center and the Pentagon? Was it a matter of personality and personal choice? Was it a web of situational factors? Were they evil? Social psychologists who have studied the nature of evil find that many, perhaps most, perpetrators of evil are "ordinary people" (Baumeister, 1996; Berkowitz, 2004b). How can this be true? As you'll read later in this chapter, when we seek to "profile" someone, we might be making a fundamental attribution error—that is, we attribute too much of other people's behavior to internal factors such as attitude and choice (Gilovich & Eibach, 2001; Reeder, 2001.) Indeed, in 2003, the Consortium of Social Science Associations (COSSA) testified to Congress that they had to conclude there was no clear profile of the suicide terrorist.

LO² Attitudes

How do you feel about abortion, stem cell research, and exhibiting the Ten Commandments in courthouses? These are hot-button topics because people have strong attitudes toward them. They each give rise to cognitive evaluations (such as approval or disapproval), feelings (such as liking, disliking, or something stronger), and behavioral tendencies (such as approach or avoidance). Although I asked you how you "feel," attitudes are not just feelings or emotions. Many psychologists view thinking—or judgment—as more basic. Feelings and behavior follow. *What are attitudes?* Attitudes are behavioral and cognitive tendencies that are expressed by evaluating particular people, places, or things with favor or disfavor.

Attitudes are largely learned, and they affect behavior. They can foster love or hate. They can give rise to helping behavior or to mass destruction. They can lead to social conflict or to the resolution of conflicts. Attitudes can change, but not easily. Most people do not change their religion or political affiliation without serious reflection or coercion.

The A–B Problem

Is our behavior consistent with our attitudes—that is, with our beliefs and feelings? *Do people do as they think? (For example, do people really vote their consciences?)* When we are free to do as we wish, the answer is often yes. But, as indicated by the term **A–B problem**, there are exceptions. For example, research reveals that attitudes toward health-related behaviors such as excessive drinking, smoking, and drunken driving do not necessarily predict these behaviors (Stacy et al., 1994).

Several factors affect the likelihood that we can predict behavior from attitudes:

1 *Specificity.* We can better predict specific behavior from specific attitudes than from global attitudes. For example, we can better predict church attendance by knowing people's attitudes toward church attendance than by knowing whether they are Christian.

2 *Strength of attitudes.* Strong attitudes are more likely

Fiction

Actually, people do not always act in accord with their consciences. The links between attitudes (A) and behaviors (B) tend to be weak to moderate.

to determine behavior than weak attitudes (Huskinson & Haddock, 2004; Petty et al., 1997). A person who believes that the nation's destiny depends on Democrats taking control of Congress is more likely to vote than a person who leans toward that party but does not believe that elections make much difference.

3 *Vested interest.* People are more likely to act on their attitudes when they have a vested interest in the outcome. People are more likely to vote for (or against) unionization of their workplace when they believe that their job security depends on it (Lehman & Crano, 2002).

4 *Accessibility.* People are more likely to behave in accord with their attitudes when they are accessible—that is, when they are brought to mind (Kallgren et al., 2000; Petty et al., 1997). This is why politicians attempt to "get out the vote" by means of media blitzes just prior to an election. It does little good to have supporters who forget them on Election Day. Attitudes with a strong emotional impact are more accessible, which is one reason that politicians strive to get their supporters "worked up" over issues.

Attitude Formation

You were not born a Republican or a Democrat. You were not born a Catholic, Jew, or Muslim—although your parents may have prac-

ticed one of these religions when you came along. *Where do attitudes come from?* Political, religious, and other attitudes are learned or derived from cognitive processes.

Conditioning may play a role in attitude formation (Walther et al., 2005). Laboratory experiments have shown that attitudes toward national groups can be influenced by associating them with positive words (such as *gift* or *happy*) or negative words (such as *ugly* or *failure*) (De Houwer et al., 2001). Parents often reward children for saying and doing things that agree with their own attitudes. Patriotism is encouraged by showing children approval when they sing the national anthem or wave the flag.

Attitudes formed through direct experience may be stronger and easier to recall, but we also acquire attitudes by observing, listening to, or reading the works of other people. The approval or disapproval of peers leads adolescents to prefer short or long hair, baggy jeans, or preppy sweaters. How do the things you read in newspapers or hear on the radio influence your attitudes?

Cognitive Appraisal

Nevertheless, attitude formation is not fully mechanical. People are also motivated to understand the environment so that they can make predictions and exercise some control over it (Bizer et al.,

Politicians participate in media blitzes just prior to an election so that they will be "accessible" to their voters on election day.

2004; Wood, 2000). People also sometimes form or change attitudes on the basis of new information (Dovidio et al., 2004; Petty et al., 1999; Walther et al., 2005). For example, we may believe that a car is more reliable than we had thought if a survey by *Consumer Reports* finds that it has an excellent repair record. Even so, initial attitudes act as cognitive anchors (Wegener et al., 2001; Wood, 2000). We often judge new ideas in terms of how much they deviate from our existing attitudes. Accepting larger deviations requires more information processing—in other words, more intellectual work (Petty et al., 1999; Tormala & Petty, 2004). For this reason, perhaps, great deviations—such as changes from liberal to conservative attitudes, or vice versa—are apt to be resisted.

Changing Attitudes Through Persuasion

Will Rogers's comment below sounds on the mark, but he was probably wrong. It does little good to have a wonderful product if it remains a secret. *Can you really change people's attitudes and behavior?*

The elaboration likelihood model describes the ways in which people respond to persuasive messages (Crano, 2000; Salovey & Wegener, 2003). Consider two routes to persuading others to change attitudes. The first, or central, route inspires thoughtful consideration of arguments and evidence. The second, or peripheral, route associates objects with positive or negative cues. When politicians avow, "This bill is supported by liberals (or conservatives)," they are seeking predictable, knee-jerk reactions rather than careful consideration of a bill's merits. Other cues are rewards (such as a smile or a hug), punishments (such as parental disapproval), and such factors as the trustworthiness and attractiveness of the communicator.

Advertisements, which are a form of persuasive communication, also rely on central and peripheral routes. Some ads focus on the quality of the product (central route). Others attempt to associate the product with appealing images (peripheral route). Ads for Total cereal, which highlight its nutritional benefits, provide information about the quality of the product. So, too, did the "Pepsi Challenge" taste-

Let advertisers spend the same amount of money improving their product that they do on advertising and they wouldn't have to advertise it.
—Will Rogers

test ads, which claimed that Pepsi tastes better than Coca-Cola. Ads that show football players heading for Disney World or choosing a brand of beer offer no information about the product itself.

In this section we look at one central factor in persuasion—the nature of the message—and three peripheral factors: the messenger, the context of the message, and the audience.

The Persuasive Message

How do we respond when TV commercials are repeated until we have memorized the dimples on the actors' faces? Research suggests that familiarity breeds content, not contempt (Zajonc, 2001; Zizak & Reber, 2004). It appears that repeated exposure to people and things as diverse as the following enhances their appeal:

- political candidates (who are seen in repeated TV commercials)
- photos of African Americans
- photos of college students
- abstract art
- classical music

When trying to persuade someone, is it helpful or self-defeating to alert them to the arguments presented by the opposition? In two-sided arguments, the communicator recounts the arguments of the opposition in an effort to refute them. In research concerning a mock trial, college undergraduates were presented with two-sided arguments—those of the prosecution and those of the defendant (McKenzie et al., 2002). When one argument was weak, the college "jurors" expressed more confidence in their decision than when they did not hear the other side at all. Theologians and politicians sometimes forewarn their followers about the arguments of the opposition and then refute each one. Forewarning creates a kind of psychological immunity to them (Jacks & Devine, 2000).

It would be nice to think that people are too sophisticated to be persuaded by emotional factors in attitude formation, but they usually aren't (DeSteno et al., 2004). Consider the fear appeal: Women who are warned of the dire risk they run if they fail to be screened for breast cancer are more likely to obtain mammograms than women who are informed of the *benefits* of mammography (Ruiter et al., 2001). Interestingly, although sun tanning has been shown to increase the likelihood of skin cancer, warnings against sun tanning were shown to be more effective when students were warned of risks to their *appearance* (e.g., premature aging, wrinkling, and scarring of the skin) than when the warning dealt with the risk to their health. That is, students informed of tanning's cosmetic effects were more likely to say they would protect themselves from the sun than were students informed about the risk of cancer. Fear appeals are most effective when the audience believes that the risks are serious—as in causing wrinkles!—and that the audience members can change their behavior to avert the risks—as in preventing cancer or wrinkling.

Audiences also tend to believe arguments that appear to run counter to the vested interests of the communicator (Lehman & Crano, 2002). If the president of Ford or General Motors said that Toyotas and Hondas were superior, you can bet that we would prick up our ears.

The Persuasive Communicator

Would you go to a doctor who admitted that he or she was behind the times? Would you buy a used car from a person who had been convicted of larceny? Research shows that persuasive communicators are characterized by expertise, trustworthiness, attractiveness, or similarity to their audiences (Petty et al., 1997). Because of the adoration of their fans, sports superstars such as Peyton Manning are the most valuable endorsers. Some companies who had used Tiger Woods as a spokesperson dropped him when news of his infidelities emerged. He was no longer as much of a role model.

People find it painful when they are confronted with information that counters their own views (Foerster et al., 2000). Therefore, they often show selective avoidance and selective exposure (Lavine et al., 2005). That is, they tend to watch news channels that endorse their own views and switch channels when the news coverage counters their own attitudes. They also seek communicators who share their views.

The Context of the Message

You are too shrewd to let someone persuade you by buttering you up, but perhaps someone you know would be influenced by a sip of wine, a bite of cheese,

We often selectively expose ourselves to opinions with which we agree—and vice versa.

and a sincere compliment. Aspects of the immediate environment, such as music, increase the likelihood of persuasion. When we are in a good mood, we apparently are less likely to evaluate the situation carefully (Petty et al., 1997).

It is also counterproductive to call your friends foolish when they differ with you—even though their ideas are bound to be "foolish" if they do not agree with yours. Agreement and praise are more effective ways to encourage others to embrace your views.

selective avoidance diverting one's attention from information that is inconsistent with one's attitudes

selective exposure deliberately seeking and attending to information that is consistent with one's attitudes

cognitive-dissonance theory the view that we are motivated to make our cognitions or beliefs consistent

The Persuaded Audience

Why can some people say no to salespeople? Why do others enrich the lives of every door-to-door salesperson? It may be that people with high self-esteem and low social anxiety are more likely to resist social pressure (Ellickson et al., 2001).

A classic study by Schwartz and Gottman (1976) describes the cognitive nature of the social anxiety that can make it difficult to refuse requests. They found that people who comply with unreasonable requests are more apt to report thoughts such as:

- "I was worried about what the other person would think of me if I refused."
- "It is better to help others than to be self-centered."
- "The other person might be hurt or insulted if I refused."

People who refuse unreasonable requests reported thoughts like these:

- "It doesn't matter what the other person thinks of me."
- "I am perfectly free to say no."
- "This request is unreasonable."

Changing Attitudes and Behavior by Means of Cognitive Dissonance

What is cognitive-dissonance theory? According to cognitive-dissonance theory, people are thinking creatures who seek consistency in their behaviors and their attitudes—that is, their views of the world. People must apparently mentally represent the world accurately to predict and control events. Consistency in beliefs, attitudes, and behavior helps make the world seem like a predictable place. Therefore, if we

© 2010 STOCK4B / JUPITERIMAGES CORPORATION

attitude-discrepant behavior
behavior inconsistent with an attitude that may have the effect of modifying an attitude

effort justification
in cognitive-dissonance theory, the tendency to seek justification (acceptable reasons) for strenuous efforts

stereotype
a fixed, conventional idea about a group

find ourselves in the uncomfortable spot where two cherished ideas conflict, we are motivated to reduce the discrepancy.

In the first and still one of the best-known studies on cognitive dissonance, one group of participants received one dollar (worth about ten dollars today) for telling someone else that a boring task was interesting (Festinger & Carlsmith, 1959). Members of a second group received twenty dollars (worth about $200 today) to describe the chore positively. Both groups were paid to engage in attitude-discrepant behavior—that is, behavior that ran counter to what they actually thought. After presenting their fake enthusiasm for the boring task, the participants were asked to rate their own liking for it. Ironically, those who were paid *less* rated the task as actually more interesting than their better-paid colleagues reported. Similarly, being compelled by the law to recycle can lead to people's supporting recycling as opposed to throwing out all trash and garbage in a bundle.

Learning theorists (see Chapter 6) might predict a different outcome—that the more we are reinforced for doing something (given more money, for example), the more we should like it (not find the task quite as boring, that is). But that is not what happened here. Cognitive-dissonance theorists rightly predicted that because the ideas (cognitions) of (a) "I was paid very little" and (b) "I told someone that this assignment was interesting" are dissonant, people will tend to engage in effort justification. The discomfort of cognitive dissonance motivates people to explain their behavior to themselves in such a way that unpleasant undertakings seem worth it. Participants who were paid only a dollar may have justified their lie by concluding that they may not have been lying in the first place.

> By and large, we assume that "good things come in pretty packages."

Prejudice and Discrimination

Prejudice is an attitude toward a group that leads people to evaluate members of that group negatively—even though they have never met them. On a cognitive level, prejudice is linked to expectations that members of the target group will behave poorly, say, in the workplace, or engage in criminal behavior or terrorism. On an emotional level, prejudice is associated with negative feelings such as fear, dislike, or hatred (No, 2004).

Truth

We do tend to appreciate things more when we have to work for them. This is an example of effort justification.

In behavioral terms, prejudice is connected with avoidance, aggression, and discrimination. Prejudice is the most troubling kind of attitude. It is connected with the genocide of millions of people. One form of behavior that results from prejudice is discrimination. Discrimination takes many forms, including denial of access to jobs, housing, and the voting booth.

Stereotypes

Are Jewish Americans shrewd and ambitious? Are African Americans superstitious and musical? Are gay men and lesbians unfit for military service? Such ideas are stereotypes—fixed, conventional attitudes toward certain groups that lead people to view members of those groups in a biased fashion.

Some stereotypes are positive rather than negative, such as the cultural stereotypes about physically attractive people. By and large, we assume that "good things come in pretty packages." Attractive children and adults are judged and treated more positively than their unattractive peers (Langlois et al., 2000). We expect attractive people to be poised, sociable, popular, intelligent, mentally healthy, fulfilled, persuasive, and successful in their jobs.

Sources of Prejudice

The sources of prejudice are many and varied:

1 *Dissimilarity*. We are apt to like people who share our attitudes. In forming impressions of others, we are influenced by attitudinal similarity and dissimilarity (Duckitt et al., 2002). People of different religions and races often have different backgrounds, however, giving rise to dissimilar attitudes. Even when people of different races share important values, they may assume that they do not.

2 *Social conflict*. There is often social and economic conflict between people of different races and religions (Duckitt & Fisher, 2003).

3 *Social learning.* Children acquire some attitudes from other people, especially their parents. Children tend to imitate their parents, and parents reinforce their children for doing so (Duckitt et al., 2002). In this way prejudices can be transmitted from generation to generation.

4 *Information processing.* Prejudices act as cognitive filters through which we view the social world. We tend to think of people as "familiar" or "foreign," or "good" or "bad." Our feelings and reactions toward others may be biased by these perceptions (Crisp & Nicel, 2004).

5 *Social categorization.* We also tend to divide our social world into "us" and "them." People usually view those who belong to their own groups—the "in-group"—more favorably than those who do not—the "out-group" (Förster et al., 2004; Smith & Weber, 2005). Isolation from the out-group makes it easier to maintain our stereotypes.

Interpersonal Attraction

Attitudes of liking and loving can lead to important, lasting relationships. They are the flip side of the coin of prejudice—positive attitudes that are associated with interpersonal attraction rather than avoidance. *What factors contribute to attraction in our culture?* Among the factors contributing to attraction are physical appearance, similarity, and reciprocity (Smith & Weber, 2005).

Physical Appearance

Physical appearance is a key factor in attraction and in the consideration of romantic partners (Langlois et al., 2000). What determines physical allure? Are our standards subjective—that is, "in the eye of the beholder"? Or is there general agreement on what is appealing?

Many standards for beauty appear to be cross-cultural (Langlois et al., 2000; Little & Perrett, 2002). For example, a study of people in England and Japan found that both British and Japanese men consider

Figure 14.1

What Features Contribute to Facial Attractiveness?

In both England and Japan, features such as large eyes, high cheekbones, and narrow jaws contribute to perceptions of the attractiveness of women. Part A shows a composite of the faces of fifteen women rated as the most attractive of a group of sixty. Part B is a composite in which the features of these fifteen women are exaggerated—that is, developed further in the direction that separates them from the average of the entire sixty.

A.

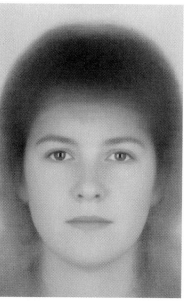

B.

women with large eyes, high cheekbones, and narrow jaws to be most attractive (Perrett, 1994). In his research, Perrett created computer composites of the faces of sixty women and, as shown in part A of Figure 14.1, of the fifteen women who were rated the most attractive. He then used computer enhancement to exaggerate the differences between the composite of the sixty and the composite of the fifteen most attractive women. He arrived at the image shown in part B of Figure 14.1. Part B, which shows higher cheekbones and a narrower jaw than Part A, was rated as the most attractive image. Similar results were found for the image of a Japanese woman. Works of art suggest that the ancient Greeks and Egyptians favored similar facial features.

Gender Differences in Selection of a Partner

Physical appearance may be a major factor in the selection of a romantic partner, but cross-cultural studies on mate selection find that women tend to place greater emphasis on traits such as professional status, consideration, dependability, kindness, and fondness for children. Men tend to place relatively greater emphasis on physical allure, cooking ability, even thrift (Buss, 1994).

Susan Sprecher and her colleagues (1994) surveyed more than 13,000 Americans, attempting to represent the ethnic diversity we

Fiction

Although there may be individual preferences, it does not seem that standards for beauty are so flexible that they are fully "in the eye of the beholder."

© SCIENCE PHOTO LIBRARY/PHOTO RESEARCHERS, INC

find in the United States. They found that women were more willing than men to marry someone who was not good-looking, but less willing to marry someone who did not hold a steady job (see Figure 14.2).

Why do males tend to place relatively more emphasis than females on physical appearance in mate selection? Why do females tend to place relatively more emphasis on personal factors such as financial status and reliability? Evolutionary psychologists believe that evolutionary forces favor the survival of women who desire status in their mates and men who emphasize physical allure because these preferences provide reproductive advantages. According to the "parental investment model," a woman's appeal is more strongly connected with her age and health, both of which are markers of reproductive capacity. The value of men as reproducers, however, is more intertwined with factors that contribute to a stable environment for child rearing—such as social standing and reliability (Schmitt, 2003).

The Attraction–Similarity Hypothesis

The *attraction–similarity hypothesis* holds that people tend to develop romantic relationships with people who are similar to themselves in physical attractiveness and other traits (Morry & Gaines, 2005). Researchers have found that people who are involved in committed relationships are most likely to be similar to their partners in their attitudes and cultural attributes (Amodio & Showers, 2005).

Our partners tend to be like us in race and ethnicity, age, level of education, and religion. Note some facts and trends:

- Ninety-five percent of marriages and nearly 90% of cohabiting unions were between partners of the same race at the time of the most recent census (Batson et al., 2006).

- Even so, highly educated people are more likely than poorly educated people to marry people of other races (Batson et al., 2006).

- African Americans are less likely than Native Americans, Asian Americans and Latino and Latina Americans to marry European Americans (Batson et al., 2006)

- As non-European immigrants become assimilated over the generations, they become more likely to intermarry with people of other races. For example, third-generation Asian Americans are more likely than recent Asian immigrants to marry or cohabit with European Americans (Brown et al., 2008).

- Puerto Rican men and women have the highest percentage of intermarriage with European Americans (Batson et al., 2006).

Figure 14.2

Gender Differences in Preferences for Mates

The study by Sprecher and her colleagues found that women are more likely than men to be willing to marry someone who is older, makes more money, is better educated, but not good-looking. Men, on the other hand, are less willing to marry someone who is not good-looking. Men are also more willing to have partners who are younger, earn less, and are less well-educated. How would you interpret these findings?

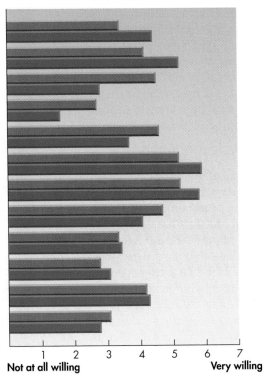

How willing would you be to marry someone who . . .

was not "good looking"?
was older than you by five or more years?
was younger than you by five or more years?
was not likely to hold a steady job?
would earn much less than you?
would earn much more than you?
had more education than you?
had less education than you?
had been married before?
already had children?
was of a different religion?
was of a different race?

Men
Women

1   2   3   4   5   6   7
Not at all willing   Very willing

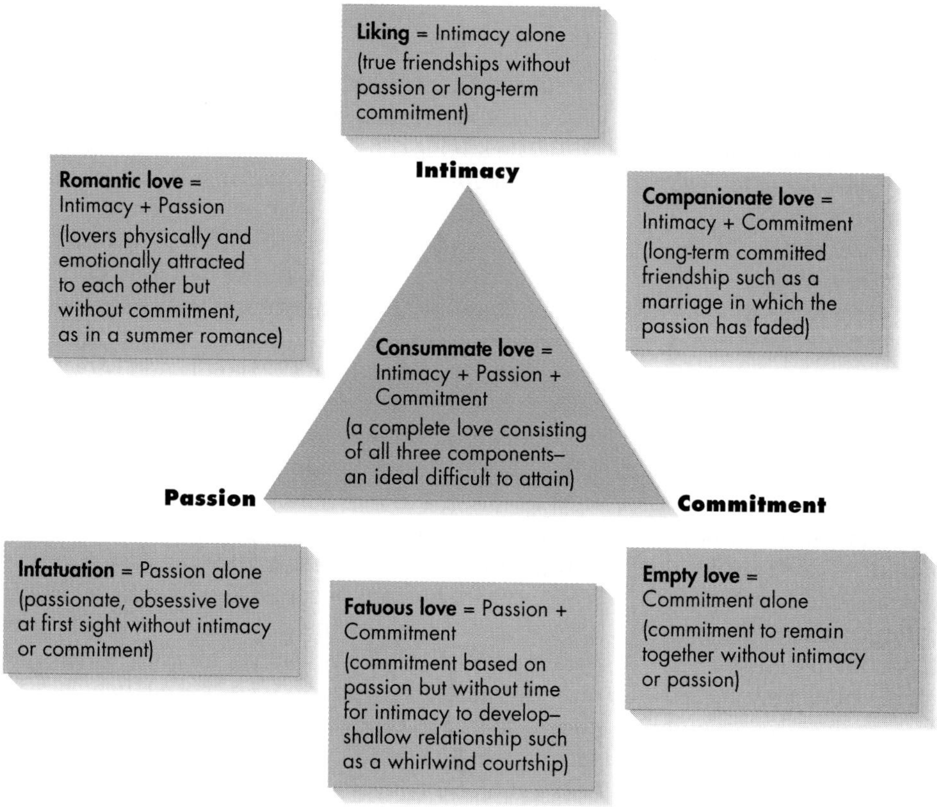

Figure 14.3

The Triangular Model of Love

According to this model, love has three components: intimacy, passion, and commitment. The ideal of consummate love consists of romantic love plus commitment.

Source: From *The Psychology of Love* by R. J. Sternberg. Copyright 1988 Yale University Press. Reprinted by permission of the publisher.

Similarity in Attitudes

We are actually less apt to be attracted to people who disagree with our views and tastes than to people who share them (Singh et al., 2007).

Why do the great majority of us have partners from our own backgrounds? One reason is *propinquity*, or nearness. Although mobility has increased in Western societies in recent decades, we tend to live among people who are reasonably similar to us in background and thus come into contact with them. Another is that we are drawn to people who are similar in their attitudes. People similar in background are more likely to be similar in their attitudes. Similarity in attitudes and tastes is a key contributor to attraction, friendships, and love relationships (Morry & Gaines, 2005).

Let us also note a sex difference. Evidence shows that women place greater weight on attitude

Fiction

Actually, it is not true that "opposites attract." People who share attitudes are more likely to be attracted to one another.

similarity as a determinant of attraction to a stranger of the other sex than do men, whereas men place more value on physical attractiveness (Laumann et al., 1994). We also tend to assume that people we find attractive share our attitudes (Morry, 2005). Although similarity may be important in determining initial attraction, compatibility appears to be a stronger predictor of maintaining an intimate relationship (Amodio & Showers, 2005).

Love

Just what is love? Love is a strong positive emotion. We had a look at love between children and parents in Chapter 3. Here we will focus on that most dramatic, heated, passionate love we label *romantic love.*

There are a number of theories about romantic love. One theory is Robert Sternberg's (1988) **triangular model of love**, which can be thought of as a love triangle. This love triangle does not refer to two men wooing the same woman. It refers to Sternberg's view that love involves three components: intimacy, passion, and commitment (see Figure 14.3).

Intimacy refers to a couple's closeness, to their mutual concern and sharing of feelings and resources. **Passion** means romance and sexual feelings. **Commitment** is the decision to maintain a relationship. Passion is most crucial in short-term relationships. Intimacy and commitment are more important

consummate love
the ideal form of love within Sternberg's model, which combines passion, intimacy, and commitment

romantic love
an intense, positive emotion that involves sexual attraction, feelings of caring, and the belief that one is in love

social perception
a subfield of social psychology that studies the ways in which we form and modify impressions of others

primacy effect
the tendency to evaluate others in terms of first impressions

recency effect
the tendency to evaluate others in terms of the most recent impression

attribution
a belief concerning why people behave in a certain way

dispositional attribution
an assumption that a person's behavior is determined by internal causes such as personal attitudes or goals

situational attribution
an assumption that a person's behavior is determined by external circumstances such as the social pressure found in a situation

in enduring relationships. The ideal form of love—consummate love—combines all three. Consummate love is made up of romantic love plus commitment.

Romantic love, in Sternberg's scheme, is characterized by passion and intimacy. Passion involves fascination (preoccupation with the loved one), sexual craving, and the desire for exclusiveness (a special relationship with the loved one). Intimacy involves caring—championing the interests of the loved one, even if it entails sacrificing one's own. People are cognitively biased toward evaluating their partners positively (Loving & Agnew, 2001). That is, we idealize those we love.

LO³ Social Perception

An important area of social psychology concerns the ways in which we perceive other people—for example, the importance of the first impressions they make on us. Next we explore some factors that contribute to social perception: the primacy and recency effects, attribution theory, and body language.

Primacy and Recency Effects

Why do you wear a suit to a job interview? Why do defense attorneys make sure that their clients dress neatly and get their hair cut before they are seen by the jury? *Do first impressions really matter?* Apparently first impressions do matter—a great deal.

What are the primacy and recency effects? Whether we are talking about the business or social worlds, or even the relationship between a therapist and a client, first impressions are important (Bidell et al., 2002). First impressions are an example of the primacy effect.

Subjects in a classic experiment on the primacy effect read different stories about "Jim" (Luchins, 1957). The stories consisted of one or two paragraphs. The one-paragraph stories portrayed Jim as either friendly or unfriendly. These paragraphs were also used in the two-paragraph stories, but in this case the paragraphs were read in the reverse order. Of those reading only the "friendly" paragraph, 95% rated Jim as friendly. Of those who read just the "unfriendly" paragraph, 3% rated him as friendly. Seventy-eight percent of those who read two-paragraph stories in the "friendly-unfriendly" order labeled Jim as friendly. When they read the paragraphs in the reverse order, only 18% rated Jim as friendly.

How can we encourage people to pay more attention to impressions occurring after the first encounter? Abraham Luchins accomplished this by allowing time to pass between the presentations of the two paragraphs. In this way, fading memories allowed more recent information to take precedence. This is known as the recency effect. Luchins also found a second way to counter first impressions: He simply asked subjects to avoid making snap judgments and to weigh all the evidence.

Attribution Theory

What is attribution theory? Why do we assume that other people intend the mischief that they do? An attribution is an assumption about why people do things. When you assume that one child is mistreating another child because she is "mean," you are making an attribution. This section focuses on *attribution theory*, or the processes by which people draw conclusions about the factors that influence one another's behavior. Attribution theory is important because attributions lead us to perceive others either as purposeful actors or as victims of circumstances.

Dispositional and Situational Attributions

Social psychologists describe two types of attributions. Dispositional attributions ascribe a person's behavior to internal factors such as personality traits and free will. Situational attributions attribute a person's actions to external factors such as social influence or socialization. If you assume that one child is mistreating the other because her parents have given her certain attitudes toward the other child, you are making a situational attribution.

The Actor–Observer Effect

When we see people (including ourselves) doing things that we do not like, we tend to see the others as willful actors but to see ourselves as victims of circumstances (Baron et al., 2006; Stewart, 2005). The

FLYING COLOURS LTD / GETTY IMAGES

actor–observer effect the tendency to attribute our own behavior to situational factors but to attribute the behavior of others to dispositional factors

fundamental attribution error the assumption that others act predominantly on the basis of their dispositions, even when there is evidence suggesting the importance of their situations

self-serving bias the tendency to view one's successes as stemming from internal factors and one's failures as stemming from external factors

The Actor-Observer Effect
Who is at fault here? People tend to make dispositional attributions for other people's behavior, but they tend to see their own behavior as motivated by situational factors. Thus, people are aware of the external forces acting on themselves when they behave, but tend to attribute other people's behavior to choice and will.

tendency to attribute other people's behavior to dispositional factors and our own behavior to situational influences is called the actor–observer effect.

Parents and teenagers often argue about the teen's choice of friends or partners. When they do, the parents tend to infer traits from behavior and to see the teens as stubborn and resistant. The teenagers also infer traits from behavior. Thus, they may see their parents as bossy and controlling. Parents and teens alike attribute the others' behavior to internal causes. That is, both make dispositional attributions about other people's behavior.

How do the parents and teenagers perceive themselves? The parents probably see themselves as being forced into combat by their children's foolishness. If they become insistent, it is in response to the teens' stubbornness. The teenagers probably see themselves as responding to peer pressures. Both parents and children make situational attributions for their own behavior.

The Fundamental Attribution Error

In cultures that view the self as independent, such as ours, people tend to attribute other people's behavior primarily to internal factors such as personality, attitudes, and free will (Gilovich & Eibach, 2001; Reeder, 2001). This bias is known as the fundamental attribution error. If a teenager gets into trouble with the law, individualistic societies are more likely to blame the teenager than the social environment in which the teenager lives.

One reason for the fundamental attribution error is that we tend to infer traits from behavior. But in collectivist cultures that stress interdependence, such as Asian cultures, people are more likely to attribute other people's behavior to that person's social roles and obligations (Basic Behavioral Science Task Force, 1996c). For example, Japanese people might be more likely to attribute a businessperson's extreme competitiveness to the "culture of business" rather than to his or her personality.

> **Truth**
>
> We do tend to hold others responsible for their misdeeds and to see ourselves as victims of circumstances when we misbehave.

The Self-Serving Bias

There is also a self-serving bias in the attribution process. We are likely to ascribe our successes to internal, dispositional factors but our failures to external, situational influences (Smith & Weber, 2005).

A study with twenty-seven college wrestlers found that they tended to attribute their wins to stable and internal conditions such as their abilities, but their losses to unstable and external conditions such as an error by a referee (De Michele et al., 1998). Sports fans fall into the same trap. They tend to attribute their team's victories to internal conditions and their losses to external conditions (Wann & Shrader, 2000).

Another interesting attribution bias is a gender difference in attributions for friendly behavior. Men are more likely than women to interpret a woman's smile or friendliness toward a man as flirting (Abbey, 1987).

Body Language

Body language is important in social perception. *What is body language?* Body language is nonverbal language; it refers to the meanings we infer from the ways in which people carry themselves and the gestures they make. The way people carry themselves provides cues to how they feel and are likely to behave. When people are emotionally "uptight," they may also be rigid and straight-backed. People who are relaxed are more likely to "hang loose." Factors such as eye contact, posture, and the distance between two people provide cues to their moods and their feelings toward one another. When people face us and lean toward us, we may assume that they like us or are interested in what we are saying.

Touching

Women are more likely than men to touch other people when they are interacting with them (Stier & Hall, 1984). In one "touching" experiment, Kleinke (1977) showed that appeals for help can be more effective when the distressed person makes physical contact with people who are asked for aid. A woman obtained more coins for phone calls when she touched the arm of the person she was asking for money. In another experiment, waitresses obtained higher tips when they touched patrons on the hand or the shoulder while making change (Crusco & Wetzel, 1984).

Gazing and Staring

When other people "look us squarely in the eye," we may assume that they are being assertive or open with us. Avoidance of eye contact may suggest deception or depres-

sion. Gazing is interpreted as a sign of liking or friendliness (Kleinke, 1986). In one study, men and women were asked to gaze into each other's eyes for two minutes (Kellerman et al., 1989). After doing so, they reported having passionate feelings toward one another.

A gaze is not the same thing as a persistent hard stare. A hard stare is interpreted as a provocation or a sign of anger. Adolescent males sometimes engage in staring contests as an assertion of dominance. The male who looks away first loses the contest. In a classic series of field experiments, Phoebe Ellsworth and her colleagues (1972) subjected drivers stopped at red lights to hard stares by riders of motor scooters (see Figure 14.4). When the light changed, people who were stared at crossed the intersection more rapidly than people who were not. People who are stared at experience higher levels of physiological arousal than people who are not (Strom & Buck, 1979).

LO⁴ Social Influence

Other people and groups can exert enormous pressure on us to behave according to their norms. Social influence is the area of social psychology that studies the ways in which people alter the thoughts, feelings, and behavior of others. Let us describe a couple of

Figure 14.4

Diagram of an Experiment in Hard Staring and Avoidance

A 1978 study by Greenbaum and Rosenfeld found that the confederate of the experimenter stared at some drivers and not at others. Recipients of the stares drove across the intersection more rapidly once the light turned green. Why?

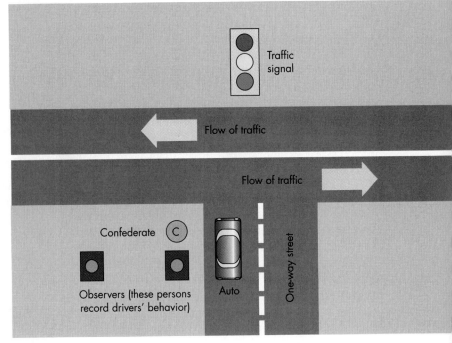

classic experiments that demonstrate how people influence others to engage in destructive obedience or conform to social norms.

Obedience to Authority

Throughout history soldiers have followed orders—even when it comes to slaughtering innocent civilians. The Turkish slaughter of Armenians, the Nazi slaughter of Jews, the mutual slaughter of Hutus and Tutsis in Rwanda—these are all examples of the tragedies that can arise from simply following orders. We may say we are horrified by such crimes, and we cannot imagine why people engage in them. But how many of us would refuse to follow orders issued by authority figures? *Why will so many people commit crimes against humanity if they are ordered to do so? (Why don't they refuse?)*

The Milgram Studies

Yale University psychologist Stanley Milgram also wondered how many people would resist immoral requests made by authority figures. To find out, he undertook a series of classic experiments at the university that have become known as the Milgram studies on obedience.

In an early phase of his work, Milgram (1963) placed ads in local newspapers for people who would be willing to participate in studies on learning and memory. He enlisted forty people ranging in age from twenty to fifty—teachers, engineers, laborers, salespeople, people who had not completed elementary school, and people with graduate degrees.

Let's suppose that you have answered the ad. You show up at the university in exchange for a reasonable fee ($4.50, which in the early 1960s might easily fill your gas tank) and to satisfy your own curiosity. You might be impressed. After all, Yale is a venerable institution that dominates the city. You are no less impressed by the elegant labs, where you meet a distinguished behavioral scientist dressed in a white coat and another person who has responded to the ad. The scientist explains that the purpose of the experiment is to study the *effects of punishment on learning*. The experiment requires a "teacher" and a "learner." By chance, you are appointed the teacher and the other recruit, the learner.

You, the scientist, and the learner enter a laboratory room containing a threatening chair with dangling straps. The scientist straps the learner in. The learner expresses some concern, but this is, after all, for the sake of science. And this is Yale, isn't it? What could happen to a person at Yale?

You follow the scientist to an adjacent room, from which you are to do your "teaching." This teaching promises to have an impact. You are to punish the learner's errors by pressing levers marked from fifteen to 450 volts on a fearsome-looking console. Labels describe twenty-eight of the thirty levers as running the gamut from "Slight Shock" to "Danger: Severe Shock." The last two levers are simply labeled "XXX." Just in case you have no idea what electric shock feels like, the scientist gives you a sample forty-five-volt shock. It stings. You pity the person who might receive more.

Your learner is expected to learn pairs of words, which are to be read from a list. After hearing the list once, the learner is to produce the word that pairs with the stimulus word from a list of four alternatives. This is done by pressing a switch that lights one of four panels in your room. If it is the correct panel, you proceed to the next stimulus word. If not, you are to deliver an electric shock. With each error, you are to increase the voltage of the shock (see Figure 14.5).

You probably have some misgivings. Electrodes

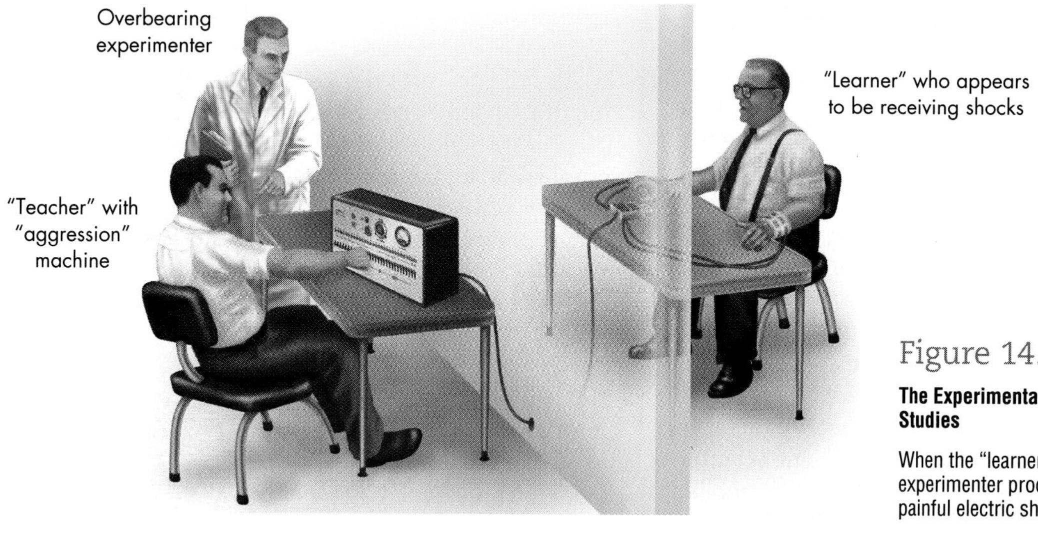

Overbearing experimenter

"Learner" who appears to be receiving shocks

"Teacher" with "aggression" machine

Figure 14.5

The Experimental Setup in the Milgram Studies

When the "learner" makes an error, the experimenter prods the "teacher" to deliver a painful electric shock.

have been strapped to the learner's wrists, and the scientist has applied electrode paste "to avoid blisters and burns." You have also been told that the shocks will cause "no permanent tissue damage," although they might be painful. Still, the learner is going along. And after all, this is Yale.

The learner answers some items correctly and then makes some errors. With mild concern you press the levers up through forty-five volts. You've tolerated that much yourself. Then a few more mistakes are made. You press the sixty-volt lever, then seventy-five. The learner makes another mistake. You pause and look at the scientist, who is reassuring: "Although the shocks may be painful, there is no permanent tissue damage, so please go on." The learner makes more errors, and soon you are up to a shock of 300 volts. But now the learner is pounding on the other side of the wall! Your chest tightens, and you begin to perspire. "Damn science and the $4.50!" you think. You hesitate and the scientist says, "The experiment requires that you continue." After the delivery of the next stimulus word, the learner chooses no answer at all. What are you to do? "Wait for five to ten seconds," the scientist instructs, "and then treat no answer as a wrong answer." But after the next shock the pounding on the wall resumes! Now your heart is racing, and you are convinced you are causing extreme pain and discomfort. Is it possible that no lasting damage is being done? Is the experiment that important, after all? What to do? You hesitate again, and the scientist says, "It is absolutely essential that you continue." His voice is very convincing. "You have no other choice," he says, "you *must* go on." You can barely think straight, and for some unaccountable reason you feel laughter rising in your throat. Your finger shakes above the lever. *What are you to do?*

Milgram had foreseen that some "teachers" in his experiment would hesitate. He had therefore conceived standardized statements that his assistants would use when subjects balked—for example: "Although the shocks may be painful, there is no permanent tissue damage, so please go on." "The experiment requires that you continue." "It is absolutely essential that you continue." "You have no other choice: you *must* go on."

To repeat: If you are a teacher in the Milgram study, what do you do? Milgram (1963, 1974) found out what most people in his sample would do. The sample was a cross-section of the male population of New Haven. Of the forty men in this phase of his research, only five refused to go beyond the 300-volt level, the level at which the learner first pounded the wall. Nine other "teachers" defied the scientist within the 300-volt range. But 65% of the subjects complied with the scientist throughout the series, believing they were delivering 450-volt, XXX-rated shocks.

Were these subjects unfeeling? Not at all. Milgram was impressed by their signs of stress. They trembled, they stuttered, they bit their lips. They groaned, they sweated, they dug their fingernails into their flesh. Some had fits of laughter, although laughter was inappropriate. One salesperson's laughter was so convulsive that he could not continue with the experiment.

Milgram's initial research on obedience was limited to a sample of New Haven men.

Could he generalize his findings to other men or to women? Would college students, who are considered to be independent thinkers, show more defiance? A replication of Milgram's study with a sample of Yale men yielded similar results. What about women, who are supposedly less aggressive than men? In subsequent research, women, too, administered shocks to the learners. All this took place in a nation that values independence and free will.

On Deception and Truth

I have said that the "teachers" in the Milgram studies *believed* that they were shocking other people when they pressed the levers on the console. They weren't. The only real shock in this experiment was the forty-five-volt sample given to the teachers. Its purpose was to make the procedure believable.

The learners in the experiment were actually confederates of the experimenter. They had not answered the newspaper ads but were in on the truth from the start. The "teachers" were the only real subjects. They were led to believe they had been chosen at random for the teacher role, but the choice was rigged so that newspaper recruits would always become teachers.

Milgram debriefed his subjects after the experiment was complete. He explained the purpose and methods of his research in detail. He emphasized the fact that they had not actually harmed anyone. But of course the subjects did believe that they were hurting other people as the experiment was being carried out. As you can imagine, the ethics of the Milgram studies have been debated by psychologists for decades. College and university review committees might prevent them from being conducted today.

Truth

It appears to be true that most people will torture an innocent person, just because they are ordered to do so.

Why Did People in the Milgram Studies Obey the Experimenters?

Many people obey the commands of others even when they are required to perform immoral tasks. But *why?* Why did Germans "just follow orders" during the Holocaust? Why did "teachers" obey the experimenter in Milgram's study? We do not have all the answers, but we can offer a number of hypotheses:

1 *Socialization.* Despite the expressed American ideal of independence, we are socialized from early childhood to obey authority figures such as parents and teachers (Blass, 1999).

2 *Lack of social comparison.* In Milgram's experimental settings, experimenters displayed command of the situation, but teachers (subjects), did not have the opportunity to compare their ideas and feelings with those of other people in the same situation.

3 *Perception of legitimate authority.* An experimenter at Yale might have appeared to be a highly legitimate authority figure— as might a government official or a high-ranking officer in the military (Blass & Schmitt, 2001). Yet further research showed that the university setting contributed to compliance but was not fully responsible for it. The percentage of individuals who complied with the experimenter's demands dropped from 65% to 48% when Milgram (1974) replicated the study in a dingy storefront in a nearby town. At first glance, this finding might seem encouraging. But the main point of the Milgram studies is that most people are willing to engage in morally reprehensible acts at the behest of a legitimate-looking authority figure. Hitler and his henchmen were authority figures in Nazi Germany. "Science" and Yale University legitimized the authority of the experimenters in the Milgram studies.

4 *Foot-in-the-door.* In the **foot-in-the-door technique,** social pressure is gradually increased so that the recipient complies with small requests before complying with large requests. Once teachers had begun to deliver shocks to learners, they might have conceptualized themselves as people who help researchers and found it progressively more difficult to extricate themselves from the situation (Rodafinos et al., 2005).

5 *Inaccessibility of values.* Most people believe that it is wrong to harm innocent people. But strong emotions interfere with clear thinking. As the teachers in the Milgram experiments became more aroused, their values might thus have become less "accessible."

6 *Buffers.* Several buffers decreased the effect of the learners' pain on the teachers. For example, the "learners" were in another room. When they were in the same room with the teachers, the teachers' compliance rate dropped from 65% to 40%. Moreover, when the teacher held the learner's hand on the shock plate, the compliance rate dropped to 30%.

> **foot-in-the-door technique**
> a method for inducing compliance in which a small request is followed by a larger request

Conformity

We are said to *conform* when we change our behavior to adhere to *social norms.* Explicit social norms are often made into rules and laws such as those that require us to whisper in libraries and to slow down when driving past a school. There are also unspoken or implicit social norms, such as those that cause us to face the front in an elevator or to be "fashionably late" for social gatherings. Can you think of some instances in which you have conformed to social pressure?

The tendency to conform to social norms is often good. Many norms have evolved because they promote comfort and survival. Group pressure can also promote maladaptive behavior, as when people engage in risky behavior because "everyone is doing it." *Why do so many people tend to follow the crowd?* To answer this question, let us look at a classic experiment on conformity conducted by Solomon Asch in the early 1950s.

The Asch Study

Can you believe what you see with your own eyes? Seeing is believing, isn't it? Not if you were a subject in Asch's (1952) study.

Let's say you entered a laboratory room with seven other subjects, supposedly taking part in an experiment on visual discrimination. At the front of the room stood a man holding cards with lines drawn on them.

The eight of you were seated in a series. You were given the seventh seat, a minor fact at the time. The man explained the task. There was a single line on the card on the left. Three lines were drawn on the card at the right (see Figure 14.6). One line on the right card

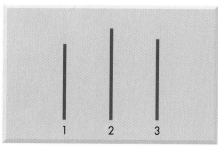

Figure 14.6

Cards Used in the Asch Study on Conformity

Which line on card B (1, 2, or 3) is the same length as the line on card A? Line 2, right? But would you say "2" if you were a member of a group and six people answering ahead of you all said "3"? Are you sure?

A. Standard line

B. Comparison lines

social facilitation the process by which a person's performance is increased when other members of a group engage in similar behavior

was the same length as the line on the left card. You and the other subjects were to call out, one at a time, which of the three lines—1, 2, or 3—was the same length as the one on the card on the left. Simple.

The subjects to your right spoke out in order: "3," "3," "3," "3," "3," "3." Now it was your turn. Line 3 was clearly the same length as the line on the first card, so you said "3." The fellow after you then chimed in: "3." That's all there was to it. Then two other cards were set up at the front of the room. This time line 2 was clearly the same length as the line on the first card. The answers were "2," "2," "2," "2," "2," "2." Again it was your turn. You said "2," and perhaps your mind began to wander. Your stomach was gurgling a bit. The fellow after you said "2." Another pair of cards was held up. Line 3 was clearly the correct answer. The six people on your right spoke in turn: "1," "1 . . ." Wait a second! ". . . 1," "1." You forgot about dinner and studied the lines briefly. No, line 1 was too short by a good half-inch. But the next two subjects said "1" and suddenly it was your turn. Your hands had become sweaty, and there was a lump in your throat. You wanted to say "3," but was it right? There was really no time, and you had already paused noticeably. You said "1," and so did the last fellow.

Now your attention was riveted on the task. Much of the time you agreed with the other seven judges, but sometimes you did not. And for some reason beyond your understanding, they were in perfect agreement even when they were wrong—assuming you could trust your eyes. The experiment was becoming an uncomfortable experience, and you began to doubt your judgment.

The discomfort in the Asch study was caused by the pressure to conform. Actually, the other seven recruits were confederates of the experimenter. They prearranged a number of incorrect responses. The sole purpose of the study was to see whether you would conform to the erroneous group judgments.

How many people in Asch's study caved in? How many went along with the crowd rather than give what they thought to be the right answer? Seventy-five percent. *Three out of four agreed with the majority's wrong answer at least once.*

Fiction

Seeing is not always believing—especially when the group sees things differently.

Factors That Influence Conformity

Several factors increase the tendency to conform, including belonging to a collectivist rather than an individualistic society, the desire to be liked by other members of the group (but valuing being right over being liked decreases the tendency to conform), low self-esteem, social shyness, and lack of familiarity with the task (Phalet & Schoenpflug, 2001; Santee & Maslach, 1982). Other factors in conformity include group size and social support. The likelihood of conformity, even to incorrect group judgments, increases rapidly as group size grows to five members, then rises more slowly as the group grows to about eight members. At about that point the maximum chance of conformity is reached. Yet finding one other person who supports your minority opinion is apparently enough to encourage you to stick to your guns (Morris et al., 1977).

LO⁵ Group Behavior

To be human is to belong to groups. Groups have much to offer us. They help us satisfy our needs for affection, attention, and belonging. They empower us to do things we could not manage by ourselves. But groups can also pressure us into doing things we might not do if we were acting alone, such as taking great risks or attacking other people.

This section considers ways in which people behave differently as group members than they would as individuals. We begin with social facilitation.

Social Facilitation

When you are given a group assignment, do you work harder or less hard than you would alone? Why? One effect of groups on individual behavior is social facilitation. Runners and bicycle riders tend to move faster when they are members of a group. Research suggests that the presence of other people

JULIAN FINNEY/GETTY IMAGES

© GUY CALI/CORBIS

Group Decision Making

Organizations use groups such as committees or juries to make decisions in the belief that group decisions are more accurate than individual decisions (Gigone & Hastie, 1997). *How do groups make decisions?* Social psychologists have discovered a number of "rules," or social decision schemes, that govern much of group decision making (Stasser, 1999). Here are some examples:

increases our levels of arousal, or motivation (Platania & Moran, 2001; Thomas et al., 2002). At high levels of arousal, our performance of simple tasks is facilitated. Our performance of complex responses may be impaired, however. For this reason, a well-rehearsed speech may be delivered masterfully before a larger audience, while an impromptu speech may be hampered by a large audience.

+ = −

Social facilitation may be influenced by evaluation apprehension as well as arousal—that is, by concern that they are evaluating us (Platania & Moran, 2001; Thomas et al., 2002). When giving a speech, we may "lose our thread" if we are distracted by the audience and focus too much on its apparent reaction. If we believe that we have begun to flounder, evaluation apprehension may skyrocket. As a result, our performance may falter even more.

The presence of others can also impair performance—not when we are acting *before* a group but when we are anonymous members *of* a group (Guerin, 1999). Workers, for example, may "goof off" or engage in *social loafing*—that is failure to make a significant effort because others have made or are making such an effort—when they believe they will not be found out and held accountable. Under these group conditions there is no evaluation apprehension, but rather there may be diffusion of responsibility in groups. Each person may feel less obligation to help because others are present, especially if the others are perceived as being capable of doing the job (Hart et al., 2001). Group members may also reduce their efforts if an apparently capable member makes no contribution but "rides free" on the efforts of others.

"Smart people working collectively can be dumber than the sum of their brains."
—Schwartz & Wald, 2003

1 *The majority-wins scheme.* In this commonly used scheme, the group arrives at the decision that was initially supported by the majority. This scheme appears to guide decision making most often when there is no single objectively correct decision. An example is a decision about which car models to build when their popularity has not been tested in the court of public opinion.

2 *The truth-wins scheme.* In this scheme, as more information is provided and opinions are discussed, the group comes to recognize that one approach is objectively correct. For example, a group deciding whether to use SAT scores in admitting students to college would profit from information about whether the scores do predict college success.

3 *The two-thirds majority scheme.* Juries tend to convict defendants when two-thirds of the jury initially favors conviction.

4 *The first-shift rule.* In this scheme, the group tends to adopt the decision that reflects the first shift in opinion expressed by any group member. If a jury is deadlocked, the members may eventually follow the lead of the first juror to switch his position.

Polarization and the "Risky Shift"

Are group decisions more risky or more conservative than those of the individual members of the group? We might think that a group decision would be more conservative than an individual decision. After all, shouldn't there be an effort to compromise, to "split the difference"? We might also expect that a few mature individuals would be able to balance the opinions of daredevils.

Groups do not always appear to work as we

groupthink
a process in which group members are influenced by cohesiveness and a dynamic leader to ignore external realities as they make decisions

might expect, however. Consider the *polarization* effect. As an individual, you might recommend that your company risk an investment of $500,000 to develop or market a new product. Other company executives, polled individually, might risk similar amounts. If you were gathered together to make a group decision, however, you would probably recommend either an amount well above this figure or nothing at all (Kamalanabhan et al., 2000). This group effect is called *polarization*, or the taking of an extreme position. If you had to gamble on which way the decision would go, however, you would do better to place your money on movement toward the higher sum—that is, to bet on a *risky shift*. Why?

One possibility is that one member of the group may reveal information that the others were not aware of. This information may clearly point in one direction or the other. With doubts removed, the group moves decisively in the appropriate direction. It is also possible that social facilitation occurs in the group setting and that the resulting greater motivation prompts more extreme decisions.

Why, however, do groups tend to take *greater* risks than those their members would take as individuals? One answer is diffusion of responsibility (Kamalanabhan et al., 2000). If the venture flops, the blame will not be placed on you alone.

Groupthink

Groupthink, a concept originated by Irving Janis (1982), is a problem that sometimes arises in group decision making. *What is groupthink?* In **groupthink**, group members tend to be more influenced by group cohesiveness and a dynamic leader than by the realities of the situation (Turner et al., 2007). Group problem solving may degenerate into groupthink when a group senses an external threat (Underhill, 2008). Groupthink is usually fueled by a dynamic group leader. The threat heightens the cohesiveness of the group and is a source of stress. Under stress, group members tend not to consider all their options carefully and frequently make flawed decisions.

Groupthink has been connected with fiascos such as the Bay of Pigs invasion of Cuba, the escalation of the Vietnam War, the Watergate scandal, and NASA's decision to launch the *Challenger* and *Columbia* space shuttles despite engineers' warnings about the dangers created by cold weather and falling foam (Brownstein, 2003; Schwartz & Wald, 2003). Janis (1982) and other researchers (Pratkanis, 2007) note several characteristics of groupthink that contribute to flawed group decisions:

1 *Feelings of invulnerability.* Each decision-making group might have believed that it was beyond the reach of critics or the law.

2 *The group's belief in its rightness.* These groups apparently believed in the rightness of what they were doing.

3 *Discrediting of information contrary to the group's decision.* The government group involved in the Iran-Contra affair knowingly broke the law. Its members apparently discredited the law by (a) deciding that it was inconsistent with the best interests of the United States, and (b) enlisting private citizens to do the dirty work so that the government was not directly involved.

4 *Pressures on group members to conform.* Striving for unanimity overrides the quest for realism, and authority can trump expertise.

5 *Stereotyping of members of the out-group.* Members of the group that broke the law in the Iran-Contra affair reportedly stereotyped people who would oppose them as "communist sympathizers" and "knee-jerk liberals."

Groupthink can be averted if group leaders encourage members to remain skeptical about options and to feel free to ask probing questions and disagree with one another.

{ **Strength in Numbers? Maybe Not.** }

In their classic experiment, Darley and Latané (1968) had male subjects perform meaningless tasks in cubicles. Then, while they were working they heard a (convincing) recording of a person apparently having an epileptic seizure. When the men thought that four other persons were immediately available, only 31% tried to help the victim. When they thought that no one else was available, however, 85% of them tried to help.

As in other areas of group behavior, it seems that diffusion of responsibility inhibits helping behavior in groups or crowds. When we are in a group, we are often willing to let George (or Georgette) do it. When George isn't around, we are more willing to help others ourselves.

Mob Behavior and Deindividuation

Have you ever done something as a member of a group that you would not have done as an individual? What was it? What motivated you? How do you feel about it?

The Frenchman Gustave Le Bon (1895–1960) branded mobs and crowds as irrational, resembling a "beast with many heads." Mob actions such as race riots and lynchings sometimes seem to operate on a psychology of their own. *How is it that mild-mannered people commit mayhem when they are part of a mob?*

Deindividuation

When people act as individuals, fear of consequences and self-evaluation tend to prevent them from engaging in antisocial behavior. But in a mob, they may experience deindividuation, a state of reduced self-awareness and lowered concern for social evaluation. Many factors lead to deindividuation, including anonymity, diffusion of responsibility, arousal due to noise and crowding, and a focus on emerging group norms rather than on one's own values (Baron et al., 2006). Under these circumstances crowd members behave more aggressively than they would as individuals.

Altruism and the Bystander Effect

Altruism—selfless concern for the welfare of others—is connected with some heroic behavior. Humans have sacrificed themselves to ensure the survival of their children or of comrades in battle. So how, one might ask, could the murder of twenty-eight-year-old Kitty Genovese have happened? It took place in New York City more than forty years ago (Rasenberger, 2004). Murder was not unheard of in the Big Apple, but Kitty had screamed for help as her killer stalked her for more than half an hour and stabbed her in three separate attacks. Thirty-eight neighbors heard the commotion. Twice, the assault was interrupted by their voices and bedroom lights. Each time the attacker returned. Yet nobody came to the victim's aid. No one even called the police.

Why? Some witnesses said matter-of-factly that they did not want to get involved. One said that he was tired. Still others said, "I don't know." As a nation,

> ## Truth
>
> It is true that nearly forty people stood by and did nothing while a woman was being stabbed to death.

are we a callous bunch who would rather watch than help when others are in trouble?

The Helper

Why do people come to the aid of others, or ignore them? It turns out that many factors are involved in helping behavior:

1 Observers are more likely to help when they are in a good mood (Baron et al., 2006; Sprecher et al., 2007). Perhaps good moods impart a sense of personal power—the feeling that we can handle the situation.

2 People who are empathic are more likely to help people in need (Decety & Batson, 2009). Women are more likely than men to be empathic and thus more likely to help people in need (Trobst et al., 1994).

3 Bystanders may not help unless they believe that an emergency exists (Baron et al., 2006).

4 Observers must assume the responsibility to act (Baron et al., 2006). A lone person may have been more likely to try to help Kitty Genovese. *Diffusion of responsibility* may inhibit helping behavior in crowds.

5 Observers must know what to do. Observers who are not sure that they can take charge of the situation may stay on the sidelines for fear of making a social blunder or of getting hurt themselves.

6 Observers are more likely to help people they know (Hopkins & Powers, 2009). Evolutionary psychologists suggest that altruism is selfish from an evolutionary point of view when it helps close relatives or others who are similar to us to survive (Bruene & Ribbert, 2002). It helps us perpetuate a genetic code similar to our own. This view suggests that we are more likely to be altruistic with our relatives rather than strangers, however.

7 Observers are more likely to help people who are similar to themselves. Being able to identify with the person in need promotes helping behavior (Cialdini et al., 1997).

Ordinary People in Extraordinary Times

But let us not end this chapter and this book on a negative note. Let us think, instead, about the altruism of the firefighters, police officers, and ordinary people who came to the aid of the victims of the suicide terrorism of September 11, 2001. Following the attacks, thousands evacuated lower Manhattan by ferry to New Jersey. Residents of New Jersey drove up and down the streets near the ferry, asking if they could give evacuees rides or help in any other way. And people heading away from the devastation in Manhattan were happy to share their taxicabs, even with strangers. If you know a little about New York City, you know that's rather special—but it's also something done by ordinary people in extraordinary times.

> **deindividuation**
> the process by which group members may discontinue self-evaluation and adopt group norms and attitudes
>
> **altruism**
> unselfish concern for the welfare of others

Statistics

Learning Outcomes

LO[1] Explain how statistics are used in psychology

LO[2] Calculate values using descriptive statistics

LO[3] Describe and apply the normal curve

LO[4] Calculate values using the correlation coefficient

LO[5] Explain the logic behind inferential statistics

> ## "To what degree do you think the people in your school represent the population of the United States? North America? The world?"

LO¹ Statistics

Imagine that some visitors from outer space arrive outside Madison Square Garden in New York City. Their goal this dark and numbing winter evening is to learn all they can about planet Earth. They are drawn inside the Garden by lights, shouts, and warmth. The spotlighting inside rivets their attention to a wood-floored arena where the New York Big Apples are hosting the California Quakes in a briskly contested basketball game.

Our visitors use their sophisticated instruments to take some measurements of the players. Some interesting statistics are sent back to their planet of origin: It appears that (1) 100% of Earthlings are male and (2) the height of Earthlings ranges from 6'1" to 7'2".

Truth or Fiction?

What do you think?

Folklore, common sense, or nonsense? Place a T for "True" or F for "False" on the lines provided (you'll learn the answers as you read through the text).

___ Basketball players could be said to be abnormal.

___ Being a "ten" is not always a good thing.

___ You should not assume that you can walk across a river with an average depth of four feet.

___ Adding people's incomes and then dividing them by the number of people can be an awful way of showing the average income.

___ Psychologists express your IQ score in terms of how deviant you are.

___ An IQ score of 130 is more impressive than an SAT score of 500.

These measurements are called statistics. *What is statistics?* Statistics is the name given the science concerned with obtaining and organizing numerical information or measurements. Our imagined visitors have sent home statistics about the gender and size of human beings that are at once accurate and misleading. Although they accurately measured the basketball players (we have translated their units of measurement into feet and inches for readers' convenience), their small sample of Earth's population was, shall we say, distorted.

What are samples and populations? A population is a complete group of people, other animals, or measures from which a sample is drawn. For example, all people on Earth could be defined as the population of interest. So could all women, or all women in the United States. A sample is a group of measures drawn from a population. Fortunately for us Earthlings, about half of the world's population is female. And the range of heights observed by the aliens, of 6'1" to 7'2", is both restricted and too high—much too high. People vary in height by more than 1 foot and

statistics
numerical facts assembled in such a manner that they provide useful information about measures or scores; (from the Latin *status*, meaning "standing" or "position")

sample
part of a population

population
a complete group from which a sample is selected

range
a measure of variability defined as the high score in a distribution minus the low score

average
the central tendency of a group of measures, expressed either as the mean, median, or mode of a distribution

descriptive statistics
the branch of statistics that is concerned with providing descriptive information about a distribution of scores

1 inch. And our average height is not between 6'1" and 7'2"; rather, it is a number of inches below.

Psychologists, like our imagined visitors, are vitally concerned with measuring human as well as animal characteristics and traits—not just physical characteristics as height, but also psychological traits such as intelligence, sociability, aggressiveness, neatness, anxiety, and depression. By observing the central tendencies (averages) and variations in measurement from person to person, psychologists can say that one person is average or above average in intelligence, or that someone else is less anxious than, say, 60% of the population.

But psychologists, unlike our aliens, attempt to select a sample that accurately represents the entire population. Professional basketball players do not represent the entire human species. Their "abnormalities" are assets to them, of course, not deficits.

In this appendix we survey some of the statistical methods used by psychologists to draw conclusions about the measurements they take in research. First we discuss *descriptive statistics* and learn what types of statements we can make about height and other human traits. Then we discuss the *normal curve* and learn why basketball players are abnormal—at least in terms of height. We explain *correlation coefficients* and provide you with some less-than-shocking news: As a group, students who study obtain higher grades than students who do not study. Finally, we have a look at *inferential statistics,* and we see why we can be bold enough to say that the difference in height between basketball players and other people

is not a chance fluctuation or fluke. Basketball players are in fact *statistically significantly* taller than the general population.

LO^2 Descriptive Statistics

Being told that someone is a ten may sound great at first. However, it is not very descriptive unless you know something about how the scores on the scale are distributed and how frequently one finds a ten. Fortunately—for tens, if not for the rest of us—one usually means that the person is a ten on a scale of from one to ten, and that ten is the highest possible score on the scale. If this is not sufficient, one will also be told that tens are few and far between—rather unusual statistical events.

The idea of the scale from one to ten may not be very scientific, but it does suggest something about *descriptive statistics. What is descriptive statistics?* (Why isn't it always good to be a ten?) Descriptive statistics is the branch of statistics that provides information about distributions of scores. We can use descriptive statistics to clarify our understanding of a distribution of scores such as heights, test grades, IQs, or even

© IMAGE SOURCE BLACK/JUPITERIMAGES

Table A.1

Roster of Quakes Versus Big Apples at New York

A glance at the rosters for a recent basketball game in which the New York Big Apples "entertained" the California Quakes shows that the heights of the team members, combined, ranged from 6'1" to 7'2". Do the heights of the team members represent those of the general male population? What do you think?

CALIFORNIA QUAKES		NEW YORK BIG APPLES	
2 Callahan	6'7"	3 Roosevelt	6'1"
5 Daly	6'11"	12 Chaffee	6'5"
6 Chico	6'2"	13 Baldwin	6'9"
12 Capistrano	6'3"	25 Delmar	6'6"
21 Brentwood	6'5"	27 Merrick	6'8"
25 Van Nuys	6'3"	28 Hewlett	6'6"
31 Clemente	6'9"	33 Hollis	6'9"
32 Whittier	6'8"	42 Bedford	6'5"
41 Fernando	7'2"	43 Coram	6'2"
43 Watts	6'9"	45 Hampton	6'10"
53 Huntington	6'6"	53 Ardsley	6'10"

The Frequency Distribution

What is a frequency distribution? A frequency distribution takes scores or items of raw data, puts them into order from the lowest to the highest, and indicates how often a score appears. A frequency distribution groups data according to class intervals, although the class may be a single unit (one), as in Table A.2. Table A.1 shows the rosters for a increases or decreases in measures of aggressive behavior following the drinking of alcohol. For example, descriptive statistics can help us determine measures of central tendency (averages) and to determine how much fluctuation or variability there is in the scores. Being a ten loses much of its charm if the average score is an eleven. Being a 10 is more remarkable in a distribution whose scores range from 1 to 10 than it is in a distribution whose scores range from 9 to 11.

Let us now consider some of the concerns of descriptive statistics: the frequency distribution, measures of central tendency (types of averages), and measures of variability.

frequency distribution
an ordered set of data that indicates the frequency (how often) with which scores appear

Table A.2

Frequency Distribution of Basketball Players (Quakes and Big Apples Combined), with a One-Inch Class Interval

CLASS INTERVAL	NUMBER OF PLAYERS IN CLASS
6'1"–6'1.9"	1
6'2"–6'2.9"	2
6'3"–6'3.9"	2
6'4"–6'4.9"	0
6'5"–6'5.9"	3
6'6"–6'6.9"	3
6'7"–6'7.9"	1
6'8"–6'8.9"	2
6'9"–6'9.9"	4
6'10"–6'10.9"	2
6'11"–6'11.9"	1
7'0"–7'0.9"	0
7'1"–7'1.9"	0
7'2"–7'2.9"	1

frequency histogram
a graphic representation of a frequency distribution that uses rectangular solids (bars) to represent the frequency with which scores appear

frequency polygon
a graphic representation of a frequency distribution that connects the points that show the frequencies with which scores appear, thereby creating a multisided geometric figure

recent basketball game between the California Quakes and the New York Big Apples. The players are listed according to the numbers on their uniforms. Table A.2 shows a frequency distribution of the heights of the players, with the two teams combined. The class interval in Table A.2 is 1 inch.

It would also be possible to use other class intervals, such as 3 inches, as shown in Table A.3. In determining the size of a class interval, the researcher tries to collapse the data into a small enough number of classes to ensure that they will be meaningful at a glance. But the researcher also tries to keep a large enough number of categories (classes) to ensure that important differences are not obscured.

Table A.3 obscures the fact that no players are 6'4" tall. If the researcher believes that this information is extremely important, a class interval of 1 inch may be maintained.

Figure A.1 shows two methods of graphing the information in Table A.3: the frequency histogram and the frequency polygon. Students sometimes have difficulty interpreting graphs, but the purpose of graphs is to reveal key information about frequency distributions at a glance. Note that in both kinds of graph, the frequency histogram and the frequency polygon, the class intervals are usually

drawn along the horizontal line. The horizontal line is also known as the x-axis. The numbers of cases (scores, persons, or events) in each class interval are shown along the vertical line, which is also known as the y-axis. In the histogram, the number of scores in each class interval is represented by a bar—a rectangular solid—so that the graph looks like a series of steps. In the polygon, the number of scores in each class interval is plotted as a point. The points are connected to form a many-sided geometric figure (polygon). Note that empty class intervals were added at each end of the frequency polygon so that the sides of the figure could be brought down to the x-axis to close the geometric figure.

Table A.3

Frequency Distribution of Heights of Basketball Players, Using a Three-Inch Class Interval

CLASS INTERVAL	NUMBER OF PLAYERS IN CLASS
6'1"–6'3.9"	5
6'4"–6'6.9"	6
6'7"–6'9.9"	7
6'10"–7'0.9"	3
7'1"–7'3.9"	1

Measures of Central Tendency

What are measures of central tendency? Measures of central tendency are "averages" that show the center or balancing points of a frequency distribution. There are three commonly used types of measures of central tendency: the *mean*, the *median*, and the *mode*. Each attempts to describe something about

Figure A.1

Two Graphical Representations of the Data in Table A.3

The graph on the left is called a frequency histogram, or bar graph. The graph on the right is called a frequency polygon.

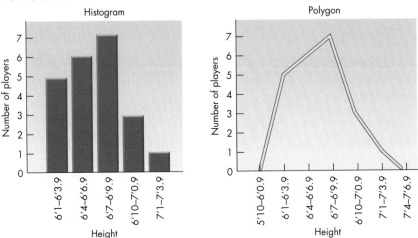

the scores in a frequency distribution through the use of a typical or representative number.

The mean is what most people think of as "the average." We obtain the mean of a distribution by adding up the scores and then dividing the sum by the number of scores. In the case of the basketball players, it would be advisable to first convert the heights into a single unit, such as inches (6'1" becomes 73", and so on). If we add all the heights in inches and then divide by the number of players (22), we obtain a mean height of 78.73". If we convert that number back into units of feet and inches, we obtain 6'6.73".

The median is the score of the middle case in a distribution. It is the score beneath which 50% of the cases fall. In a distribution with an even number of cases, such as the distribution of the heights of the 22 basketball players as shown in Table A.2, we obtain the median by finding the mean of the two middle cases. When we list the 22 cases in ascending order (moving from lowest to highest), the 11th case is 6'6" and the 12th case is 6'7". Therefore, the median of the distribution is (6'6" + 6'7") /2, or 6'6.5".

When we analyze the heights of the basketball players, we find that the mean and the median are similar. Either one serves as a useful indicator of the central tendency of the data. But suppose we are trying to find the average savings of 30 families living on a suburban block. Let us assume that 29 of the 30 families have savings between $8,000 and $12,000, adding up to $294,000. But the 30th family has savings of $1,400,000! The mean savings for a family on this block would thus be $56,467. The mean can be greatly distorted by one or two extreme scores. An IQ score of 145 would similarly distort the mean of the IQ scores of a class of 20 students, among whom the other 19 IQ scores ranged from 93 to 112. Then, too, if a few basketball players signed up for one

Never try to walk across a river just because it has an average depth of four feet.
—Martin Friedman

of your classes, the mean of the students' heights would be distorted in an upward direction.

When there are a few extreme scores in a distribution, the median is a better indicator of central tendency. The median savings on our hypothetical block would lie between $8,000 and $12,000. Thus it would be more representative of the central tendency of savings. Studies of the incomes of families in the United States usually report median rather than mean incomes just to avoid the distortion of findings that would occur if the incomes of a handful of billionaires were treated in the same way as more common incomes. On the other hand, one could argue that choosing the median as the average obscures or hides the extreme scores, which are just as "real" as the other scores. Perhaps it is best to use the median and a footnote—a rather big footnote.

The mode is simply the most frequently occurring score or measure in a distribution. The mode of the data in Table A.1 is 6'9" because this height occurs most often among the players on the two teams. The median class interval for the data shown in Table A.3 is 6'6.5" to 6'9.5". With this particular distribution, the mode is somewhat higher than the mean or the median.

In some cases the mode is a more appropriate description of the central tendency of a distribution than the mean or the median. Figure A.2 shows a bimodal distribution—that is, a distribution with two modes. This is a hypothetical distribution of test scores obtained by a class. The mode at the left indicates the most common class interval (45 to 49) for students who did not study, and the mode to the right shows the most common class interval (65 to 69) for students who did study. (Don't be alarmed. I'm sure that the professor, who is extremely fair, will be delighted to curve the grades so that the interval of 75 to 79 is an A+ and the interval of 65 to 69 is at least a B.) The mean and median test scores would probably lie within the 55 to 59 class interval, yet use of that interval as the measure of central tendency could obscure rather than reveal the important aspects of this distribution of test scores. It might suggest that the test was too hard, not that a number of students chose not to study. Similarly, one of the distribution's modes might be a bit larger than the other, so one

mean
a type of average that is calculated by adding all the scores and then dividing by the number of scores

median
the central score in a frequency distribution; the score beneath which 50% of the cases fall

mode
the most frequently occurring number or score in a distribution

bimodal
having two modes

standard deviation
a measure of the variability of a distribution, obtained by the formula
$$S.D. = \sqrt{\frac{\text{Sum of } d^2}{N}}$$

could follow the exact rule for finding the mode and report just one of them. But this approach would also hide the meaning of this particular distribution of scores. All in all, it is clearly best to visualize this distribution of scores as bimodal. Even when the modes are not exactly equal, it is often most accurate to report distributions as bimodal, or, when there are three or more modes, as multimodal. One chooses one's measure or measures of central tendency to describe the essential features of a frequency distribution, not to hide them.

Figure A.2

A Bimodal Distribution

This hypothetical distribution represents students' scores on a test. The mode at the left represents the central tendency of the test scores of students who did not study. The mode at the right represents the mode of the test scores of students who did study.

Measures of Variability

Our hypothetical class obtained test scores ranging from class intervals of 35 to 39 to class intervals of 75 to 79. That is, the scores *varied* from the lower class interval to the higher class interval. Now, if all the students had obtained scores from 55 to 59 or from to 65 to 69, the scores would not have varied as much; that is, they would have clustered closer to one another and would have had lower variability.

What are measures of variability? The measures of the variability of a distribution inform us about the spread of scores—that is, about the typical distances of scores from the average score. Two commonly used measures of variability are the *range* of scores and the *standard deviation* of scores.

The range of scores in a distribution is defined as the difference between the highest score and the lowest score. The range is obtained by subtracting the lowest score from the highest score. The range of heights in Table A.2 is obtained by subtracting 6'1" from 7'2", or 1'1". It is useful to know the range of temperatures when we move to an area with a different climate so that we may anticipate the weather and dress for it appropriately. A teacher must have some understanding of the range of abilities or skills in a class in order to teach effectively. An understanding of the range of human heights can be used to design doorways, beds, and headroom in automobiles. Even so, the typical doorway is 6'8" high; and, as we saw with the California Quakes and New York Big Apples, some people will have to duck to get through.

The range is an imperfect measure of variability because of the manner in which it is influenced by extreme scores. The range of savings of the 30 families on our suburban block is $1,400,000 minus $8,000, or $1,392,000. This is a large number, and it is certainly true. However, it tells us little about the *typical* variation of savings accounts, which lie within a more restricted range of $8,000 to $12,000.

The standard deviation is a statistic that does a better job of showing how the scores in a distribution are distributed (spread) about the mean. It is usually better than the range because it considers every score in the distribution, not just the extreme (highest and lowest) scores. Consider Figure A.3. Each distribution in the figure has the same number of scores, the same mean, and the same range of scores. However, the scores in the distribution on the right side cluster more closely about the mean. Therefore, the standard deviation of the distribution on the right is smaller. That is, the typical score deviates less from the mean score.

Figure A.3

Hypothetical Distributions of Student Test Scores

Each distribution has the same number of scores, the same mean, even the same range, but the standard deviation (a measure of variability) is greater for the distribution on the left because the scores tend to be farther from the mean.

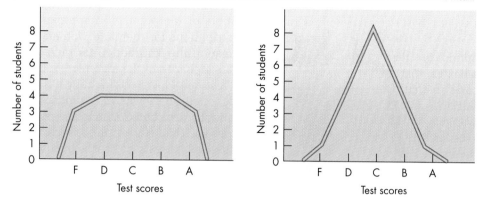

Test scores (left graph, x-axis: F D C B A; y-axis: Number of students 0–8)

Test scores (right graph, x-axis: F D C B A; y-axis: Number of students 0–8)

The standard deviation is usually abbreviated as S.D. It is calculated by the formula

$$S.D. = \sqrt{\frac{\text{Sum of } d^2}{N}}$$

where d equals the deviation of each score from the mean of the distribution and N equals the number of scores in the distribution.

Let us find the mean and standard deviation of the IQ scores listed in column 1 of Table A.4. To obtain the mean we add all the scores, attain 1,500, and then divide by the number of scores (15) to obtain a mean of 100. We obtain the deviation score (d) for each IQ score by subtracting the score from 100. The d for an IQ score of 85 equals 100 minus 85, or 15, and so on. Then we square each d and add the squares. The S.D. equals the square root of the sum of squares (1,426) divided by the number of scores (15), or 9.75.

As an additional exercise, we can show that the S.D. of the test scores on the left (in Figure A.3) is greater than that for the scores on the right. First we assign the grades a number according to a 4.0 system. Let A = 4, B = 3, C = 2, D = 1, and F = 0. The S.D. for each distribution is computed in Table A.5. The larger S.D. for the

Table A.4

Hypothetical Scores Obtained from an IQ Testing

IQ SCORE	d (DEVIATION SCORE)	d^2 (DEVIATION SCORE SQUARED)
85	15	225
87	13	169
89	11	121
90	10	100
93	7	49
97	3	9
97	3	9
100	0	0
101	−1	1
104	−4	16
105	−5	25
110	−10	100
112	−12	144
113	−13	169
117	−17	289

Sum of IQ scores = 1,500   Sum of d^2 scores = 1,426

$$\text{Mean} = \frac{\text{Sum of scores}}{\text{Number of scores}} = \frac{1,500}{15} = 100$$

$$\text{Standard Deviation (S.D.)} = \sqrt{\frac{\text{Sum of } d^2}{N}} = \sqrt{\frac{1.426}{15}} = \sqrt{95.07} = 9.75$$

Table A.5

Computation of Standard Deviations for Test-Score Distributions in Figure A.3

DISTRIBUTION AT LEFT			DISTRIBUTION TO THE RIGHT		
GRADE	d	d^2	GRADE	d	d^2
A (4)	2	4	A (4)	2	4
A (4)	2	4	B (3)	1	1
A (4)	2	4	B (3)	1	1
B (3)	1	1	B (3)	1	1
B (3)	1	1	B (3)	1	1
B (3)	1	1	C (2)	0	0
C (2)	0	0	C (2)	0	0
C (2)	0	0	C (2)	0	0
C (2)	0	0	C (2)	0	0
D (1)	−1	1	C (2)	0	0
D (1)	−1	1	C (2)	0	0
D (1)	−1	1	D (1)	−1	1
D (1)	−1	1	D (1)	−1	1
F (0)	−2	4	D (1)	−1	1
F (0)	−2	4	D (1)	−1	1
F (0)	−2	4	F (0)	−2	4

Sum of grades = 36   Sum of grades = 36
Mean grade = 36/18 = 2   Mean grade = 36/18 = 2
Sum of d^2 = 32   Sum of d^2 = 16
Sum of grades = 36   Sum of grades = 36
Mean grade = 36/18 = 2   Mean grade = 36/18 = 2
Sum of d^2 = 32   Sum of d^2 = 16
S.D. = $\sqrt{32/18}$ = 1.33   S.D. = $\sqrt{16/18}$ = 0.94

normal distribution
a symmetrical distribution that is assumed to reflect chance fluctuations; approximately 68% of cases lie within a standard deviation of the mean

normal curve
graphic presentation of a normal distribution, which shows a characteristic bell shape

Truth

Psychologists may express your IQ score in terms of how deviant you are from the average or mean score.

distribution on the left indicates that the scores in that distribution are more variable, or tend to be farther from the mean.

LO³ The Normal Curve

Many human traits and characteristics including height and intelligence seem to be distributed in a pattern known as a normal distribution. *What is a normal distribution?* In a **normal distribution**, the mean, the median, and the mode all fall at the same data point or score. Scores cluster most heavily about the mean, fall off rapidly in either direction at first (as shown in Figure A.4), and then taper off more gradually.

The curve in Figure A.4 is bell-shaped. This type of distribution is also called a **normal curve** or bell-shaped curve. This curve is hypothesized as the distribution of variables in which different scores are determined by chance variation. Height is thought to be largely determined by chance combinations of genetic material. A distribution of the heights of a random sample of the population approximates normal distributions for men and women, with the mean of the distribution for men a few inches higher than the mean for women.

Test developers traditionally assumed that intelligence was also randomly or normally distributed among the population. For that reason, they constructed intelligence tests so that scores would be distributed as close to "normal" as possible. In actuality, IQ scores are also influenced by environmental factors and chromosomal abnormalities, so that the resultant curves are not perfectly normal. The means of most IQ tests are defined as scores of 100 points. The Wechsler scales are constructed to have standard deviations of 15 points, as shown in Figure A.4. A standard deviation of 15 points causes 50% of the Wechsler scores to fall between 90 and 110, which is called the "broad average" range. About 68% of scores (two out of three) fall between 85 and 115 (within a standard deviation of the mean), and more than 95% fall between 70 and 130—that is, within two standard deviations of the mean. The more extreme high (and low) IQ scores deviate more from the mean score.

The Scholastic Assessment Tests (SATs) were constructed so that the mean scores would be 500 points and the S.D. would be 100 points. Thus a score of 600 would equal or excel that of some 84% to 85% of the test takers. Because of the complex interaction of variables that determine SAT scores, their distribution is not exactly normal either. Moreover, the actual mean scores and standard deviations tend to vary from year to year, and, in the case of the SAT IIs, from test to test. The normal curve is an idealized curve.

MIKE DUNNING / GETTY IMAGES

Figure A.4

A Bell-Shaped or Normal Curve

In a normal curve, approximately two out of three cases (68%) lie within a standard deviation (S.D.) from the mean. The mean, median, and mode all lie at the same score. IQ tests and the Scholastic Assessment Tests (SATs) are constructed so that their distributions approximate the normal curve.

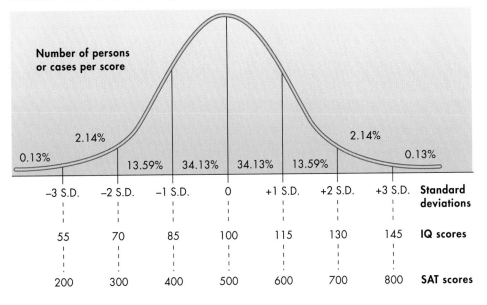

Number of persons or cases per score

| 0.13% | 2.14% | 13.59% | 34.13% | 34.13% | 13.59% | 2.14% | 0.13% |

Standard deviations	−3 S.D.	−2 S.D.	−1 S.D.	0	+1 S.D.	+2 S.D.	+3 S.D.
IQ scores	55	70	85	100	115	130	145
SAT scores	200	300	400	500	600	700	800

The IQ score of 130 is two standard deviations above the mean and exceeds that of more than 97% of the population. An SAT score of 500 is the mean SAT score and thus equals or excels that of about 50% of the population.

Truth

An IQ score of 130 is more impressive than an SAT score of 500. The IQ score is two standard deviations above the mean, and the SAT score is the mean for that test.

LO⁴ The Correlation Coefficient

What is the relationship between intelligence and educational achievement? Between cigarette smoking and lung cancer among humans? Between the personality trait of introversion and numbers of dates among college students? We cannot run experiments to determine whether the relationships between these variables are causal, because we cannot manipulate the independent variable. That is, we cannot assign high or low intelligence at random. Nor can we (ethically) assign some people to smoke cigarettes and others not to smoke. People must be allowed to make their own decisions, so it is possible that the same factors that lead some people to smoke—or to continue to smoke after they have experimented with cigarettes—also lead to lung cancer. (Even if we were to assign a group of people to a nonsmoking condition, could we monitor them continuously to make sure that they weren't sneaking puffs?) Nor can we designate who will be introverted and who will be extraverted. True, we could encourage people to act as if they are introverted or extraverted, but behavior is not the same thing as a personality trait. We cannot run true experiments to answer any of these questions, but the correlation coefficient can be used to reveal whether there is a relationship between intelligence and achievement,

a relationship between smoking and cancer, or a relationship between personality and dating. Correlational research shows that smoking and cancer are related but does not reveal cause and effect. However, experimental research with animals does strongly suggest that smoking will cause cancer in humans.

What is the correlation coefficient? The correlation coefficient is a statistic that describes the relationship between two variables. A correlation coefficient can vary from +1.00 to −1.00. A correlation coefficient of +1.00 is called a perfect positive correlation, and it describes the relationship between temperatures as measured by the Fahrenheit and Centigrade scales. A correlation coefficient of −1.00 is a perfect negative correlation, and a correlation of 0 (zero) reveals no relationship between variables.

As suggested by Figures A.5 and A.6, most correlation coefficients in psychological research are less than perfect. The left graph in Figure A.5 reveals a positive relationship between time spent studying and grade point averages. Because there is a positive correlation between the variables but the relationship is not perfect, the correlation coefficient will lie between 0.00 and +1.00. Perhaps it is about +0.60 or +0.70. However, we cannot absolutely predict what

> **correlation coefficient** a number between −1.00 and +1.00 that indicates the direction (negative or positive) and extent (from none to perfect) of the relationship between two variables

Figure A.5

Positive and Negative Correlations

When there is a positive correlation between variables, as there is between intelligence and achievement, one increases as the other increases. By and large, the more time students spend studying, the better their grades are likely to be, as suggested in the diagram to the left. (Each dot represents the amount of time a student spends studying each week and his or her grade point average.) But there is a negative correlation between grades and juvenile delinquency. As the number of delinquent acts per year increases, one's grade point average tends to decline. Correlational research may suggest but does not demonstrate cause and effect.

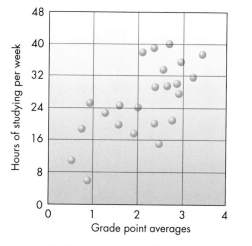

Positive correlation, as found between intelligence and academic achievement

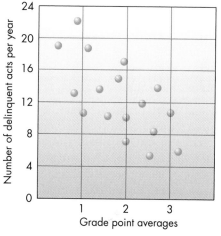

Negative correlation, as found between delinquency and academic achievement

Figure A.6

Correlational Relationships, Cause and Effect

Correlational relationships may suggest but do not demonstrate cause and effect. In part A, there is a correlation between variables X and Y. Does this mean that either variable X causes variable Y or that variable Y causes variable X? Not necessarily. Other factors could affect both variables X and Y. Consider the examples of academic grades (variable X) and time spent studying (variable Y) in part B. There is a positive correlation between the two. Does this mean that studying contributes to good grades? Perhaps. Does it mean that good grades encourage studying? Again, perhaps. But there could also be other variables—such as cultural belief in the value of education, enjoyment of learning, even parental pressure to do well—that contribute both to time spent studying and good grades.

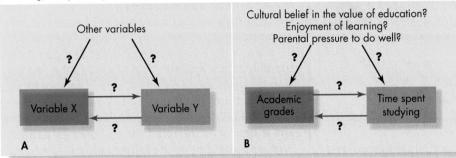

a person's GPA will be if we know the hours per week that he or she spends studying (nor can we predict exactly how much time the person spends studying on the basis of his or her GPA). Nevertheless, it would seem advisable to place oneself among those who spend a good deal of time studying if one wishes to achieve a good GPA.

The right drawing in Figure A.5 reveals a negative relationship between number of delinquent acts committed per year and GPA. The causal connection is less than perfectly clear. Does delinquency interfere with studying and academic achievement? Does poor achievement weaken a student's commitment to trying to get ahead through work? Do feelings of distance from "the system" contribute both to delinquent behavior and a low GPA? The answers are not to be found in Figure A.5, but the negative correlation between delinquent behavior and GPA does suggest that it is worthwhile to study the issues involved and—for a student—to distance himself or herself from delinquent behavior if he or she wishes to achieve in the academic world.

LO⁵ Inferential Statistics

Head Start programs have apparently raised children's intellectual functioning, as reflected in their grades and IQ scores. In one such study, children enrolled in a Head Start program obtained a mean IQ score of 99, whereas children similar in background who were not enrolled in Head Start obtained a mean IQ score of 93. Is this difference of six points in IQ *significant*, or does it represent a chance fluctuation in scores? In a study reported in Chapter 1, college students were provoked by people in league with the researchers. Some of the students believed they had drunk alcohol (in a cocktail with tonic water); others believed they had drunk tonic water only. The students were then given the opportunity to shock the individuals who had provoked them. Students who believed they had drunk alcohol chose higher levels of shock than students who believed they had drunk tonic water only. Did the mean difference in shock level chosen by the two groups of students represent actual differences between the groups, or might it have been a chance fluctuation? The individuals in the Head Start study were a sample of young children. The individuals in the alcohol study were a sample of college students. Inferential statistics help us determine whether we can conclude that the differences between such samples reflect real differences that are found in the populations that they represent.

Figure A.7

Distribution of Heights for Random Samples of Men and Women

Note that the mean height of the men is greater than that of the women. Is the group mean difference in height statistically significant? Researchers use a tool called inferential statistics to determine the answer.

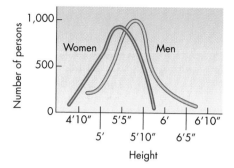

Descriptive statistics enables us to provide descriptive information about samples of scores. *What are inferential statistics?* **Inferential statistics** assist us in determining whether we can generalize differences among samples to the populations that they represent.

Figure A.7 shows the distribution of heights of 1,000 men and 1,000 women who were selected at random from the general U.S. population. The mean height for men is greater than the mean height for women. Can we conclude, or **infer**, that this difference in height is not just a chance fluctuation but represents an actual difference between the general populations of men and women? Or must we avoid such an inference and summarize our results by stating only that the mean height of the sample of men in the study was greater than the mean height of the sample of women in the study?

If we could not draw inferences about populations from studies of samples, our research findings would be limited indeed. We could speak only about the specific individuals studied. There would be no point to learning about any study in which you did not participate because it would not apply to you! Fortunately, that is not the case. Inferential statistics permits us to extend findings with samples to the populations from which they were drawn.

Statistically Significant Differences

We asked whether the differences in height between our samples of men and women were simply a chance fluctuation or whether they represented actual differences between the heights of men and women. Researchers tend not to talk about "real differences" or "actual differences" between groups, however. Instead, they speak of statistically significant differences. Similarly, researchers asked whether differences in IQ scores between children in Head Start programs and other children from similar backgrounds were chance fluctuations or statistically significant differences. *What are "statistically significant" differences?* Statistically significant differences are differences that are unlikely to be due to chance fluctuation. Psychologists usually do not accept a difference as being statistically significant unless the probability (*p*) that it is due to chance fluctuation is less than 1 in 20 (i.e., *p* <.05). They are more comfortable labeling a difference as statistically significant when the probability (*p*) that it is due to chance fluctuation is less than 1 in 100 (i.e., *p* <.01).

Psychologists use formulas involving the means (e.g., mean IQ scores of 93 versus 99) and the standard deviations of sample groups to determine whether differences in means are statistically significant. As you can see in Figure A.8, the farther apart group means are, the more likely it is that they are statistically significant. In other words, if the men are on the average five inches taller than the women, it is more likely that the difference is statistically significant than if the men are only one-quarter of an inch taller on average. *Principle 1: Everything else being equal, the greater the difference between means, the greater the probability that the difference is statistically significant.* This makes common sense. After all, if you were told that your neighbor's car had gotten one-tenth of a mile more per gallon of gas than your car in the past year, you would probably attribute the difference to chance fluctuation. But if the difference were greater, say fourteen miles per gallon, you would probably assume that the difference reflected an actual difference in driving habits or the efficiency of the automobile.

As you can see in Figure A.9, the smaller the standard deviations (a measure of variability) of the groups, the more likely it is that the difference between means is statistically significant. Consider the extreme example in which there is *no* variability within each group. That is, imagine that every woman in the randomly selected sample of 1,000 women is exactly 5'5" tall. Similarly, imagine that every man in the randomly selected sample of 1,000

> **Statistically significant differences are differences that are unlikely to be due to chance fluctuation.**

inferential statistics
the branch of statistics that is concerned with confidence with which conclusions drawn about samples can be extended to the populations from which the samples were drawn

infer
to go from the particular to the general; to draw a conclusion

Figure A.8

Decreasing and Increasing the Mean Group Difference in Heights

Everything else being equal, the greater the difference in group means, the greater the probability that the difference is statistically significant. The distribution on the right shows a greater difference in group means; therefore, there is a greater probability that the difference is statistically significant.

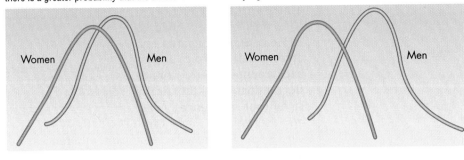

We have been "eyeballing" the data and making assumptions. We have been relying on what one professor of mine called the "Wow!" effect. As noted, psychologists and other researchers actually use mathematical techniques that take group means and standard deviations into account to determine whether group differences are statistically significant. It is often the case that eyeballing real data does not yield clear results or even good guesses.

men is exactly 5'10" tall. In such a case the heights of the men and women would not overlap at all, and it would appear that the differences were statistically significant. Consider the other extreme—one with unnaturally large variability. Imagine that the heights of the women vary from 2' to 14' and that the heights of the men vary from 2'1" to 14'3". In such a case we might be more likely to assume that the difference in group means of 5" was a chance fluctuation. *Principle 2: Everything else being equal, the smaller the variability of the distributions of scores, the greater the probability that the difference in group means is statistically significant.*

> It is often the case that eyeballing real data does not yield clear results or even good guesses.

Therefore, we cannot conclude that men are taller than women unless we know the average heights of men and women and how much the heights within each group vary. We must know both the central tendencies (means) and variability of the two distributions of heights in order to infer that the mean heights are statistically significantly different.

Samples and Populations

Inferential statistics are mathematical tools that psychologists apply to samples of scores to determine whether they can generalize or extend their findings to populations of scores. They must, therefore, be quite certain that the samples involved actually represent the populations from which they were drawn. Sampling techniques are crucial. Random sampling is the best method, and sampling is random only if every member of the target population has an equal chance of being selected.

It matters little how sophisticated our statistical methods are if the samples studied do not represent the target populations. We could use a variety of sophisticated statistical techniques to analyze the heights of the New York Big Apples and the California Quakes, but none of these methods would tell us much about the height of the general population. Or about the height of women. (Or about the height of people who can't pass the ball, shoot, or play defense.)

Figure A.9

Decreasing and Increasing the Variability of the Distributions of Scores

Everything else being equal, the smaller the variability in group scores, the greater the probability that the difference in groups means is statistically significant. The distribution on the right shows a greater difference in the variability of the groups; therefore, there is a *lower* probability that the difference in group means is statistically significant.

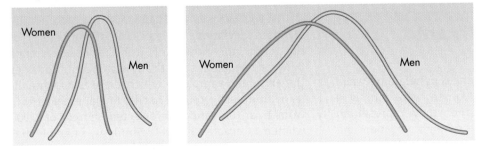

References

A

Abbey, A. (1987). Misperceptions of friendly behavior as sexual interest. *Psychology of Women Quarterly,* 11, 173–194.

Abraham, H. D.,& Duffy, F.H. (2001). EEG coherence in post-LSD visual hallucinations. *Psychiatry Research: Neuroimaging, 107*(3), 151–163.

Ackard, D. M., Neumark-Sztainer, D., Hannan, P. J., French, S., & Story, M. (2001). Binge and purge behavior among adolescents: Associations with sexual and physical abuse in a nationally representative sample: The Commonwealth Fund survey. *Child Abuse & Neglect, 25*(6), 771–785.

Agras, W. S., Walsh, T., Fairburn, C. G., Wilson, G. T., & Kraemer, H. C. (2000). A multicenter comparison of cognitive-behavioral therapy and interpersonal psychotherapy for bulimia nervosa.

Ainsworth, M. D. S., & Bowlby, J. (1991). An ethological approach to personality development. *American Psychologist, 46,* 333–341.

Ainsworth, M. D. S., Blehar, M. C., Waters, E., & Wall, S. (1978). *Patterns of attachment: A psychological study of the strange situation.* Hillsdale, NJ: Erlbaum.

Alexander, C. N., et al. (1996). Trial of stress reduction for hypertension in older African Americans: II. Sex and risk subgroup analysis. *Hypertension, 28,* 228–237.

Allport, G. W., & Oddbert, H. S. (1936). Trait names: A psycholexical study. *Psychological Monographs, 47,* 1–36.

Altman, L. K. (2005, May 16). Studies find disparity in U.S. cancer care. *The New York Times online.*

Altran, S. (Accessed 2005, May). Genesis and future of suicide terrorism. http://www.interdisci plines.org/ terrorism /papers/1.

American Cancer Society. (2005a). Cancer facts & figures 2005. http://www.cancer.org.

American Cancer Society. (2005c; accessed 2005, September 23). Alcohol increases breast cancer risk. http://www. cancer.org/docroot/NWS/content/NWS_1_1x_Alcohol_ Increases_Breast_Cancer_Risk.asp.

American Heart Association. (2005b). Leading causes of death—Statistics. http://www.americanheart.org/ presenter.jhtml?identifier_30009 63.

American Heart Association. (2008). www.americanheart.org

American Lung Association (2008). http://www. lungusa.org.

American Psychological Association (2002). Ethical principles of psychologists and code of conduct. *American Psychologist, 57*(12), 1060–1073.

American Psychologist, 47(4), 559–569.

Amodio, D. M., & Showers, C. J. (2005). "Similarity breeds liking" revisited: The moderating role of commitment. *Journal of Social and Personal Relationships,* 22(6), 817–836.

Andersen, B. L. (2002). Biobehavioral outcomes following psychological interventions for cancer patients. *Journal of Consulting & Clinical Psychology, 70*(3), 590–610.

Andersen, B. L., Kiecolt-Glaser, J. K., & Glaser, R. (1994). A biobehavioral model of cancer stress and disease course. *American Psychologist, 49,* 389–404.

Anderson, C. A. (2004). An update on the effects of violent video games. *Journal of Adolescence, 27,* 113–122.

Anderson, C. A., & Dill, K. E. (2000). Video games and aggressive thoughts, feelings, and behavior in the laboratory and in life. *Journal of Personality and Social Psychology, 78*(4), 772–790.

Anderson, C. A., Berkowitz, L., Donnerstein, E., Huesmann, R. L., Johnson, J., Linz, D., Malamuth, N., & Wartella, E. (2003). The influence of media violence on youth. *Psychological Science in the Public Interest, 4,* 81–110.

Anderson, C. A., et al. (2004). Violent video games: Specific effects of violent content on aggressive thoughts and behavior. *Advances in Experimental Social Psychology, 36,* 199–249.

Anderson, C., & Horne, J. A. (2004). Presleep relaxed 7–8 Hz EEG from left frontal region: Marker of localised neuropsychological performance? *Physiology & Behavior, 81*(4), 657–664.

Anderson, E. S., Winett, R. A., & Wojcik, J. R. (2000). Social-cognitive determinants of nutrition behavior among supermarket food shoppers: A structural equation analysis. *Health Psychology, 19*(5), 479–486.

Anderson, E. S., Winett, R. A., Wojcik, J. R., Winett, S. G., & Bowden, T. (2001). A computerized social cognitive intervention for nutrition behavior: Direct and mediated effects on fat, fiber, fruits and vegetables, self-efficacy and outcome expectations among food shoppers. *Annals of*

Behavioral Medicine, 23(2), 88–100.

Anderson, K. P., LaPorte, D. J., & Crawford, S. (2000). Child abuse and bulimic symptomology: Review of specific abuse variables. *Child Abuse and Neglect 24*(11), 1495–1502.

Anderson, O. (1995). The buzz on exercise. *Men's Health, 10,* 88–89. This article discusses the Runner's High, what contributes to it and how a person might experience it.

Andreasen, N. C. (2003). From molecule to mind: Genetics, genomics, and psychiatry. *American Journal of Psychiatry, 160,* 613.

Andreou, G., et al. (2002). Handedness, asthma, and allergic disorders: Is there an association? *Psychology, Health & Medicine, 7*(1), 53–60.

Anger-Díaz, B., Schlanger, K., Rincon, C., & Abbey, A. (1987). Misperceptions of friendly behavior as sexual interest. *Psychology of Women Quarterly, 11,* 173–194.

Ansburg, P. I. (2000). Individual differences in problem solving via insight. *Current Psychology, 19,* 143. This article describes insight and the differences seen in individuals.

Antoni, M. H., et al. (2005). Increases in a marker of immune system reconstitution are predated by decreases in 24-h urinary cortisol output and depressed mood during a 10-week stress management intervention in symptomatic HIV-infected men. *Journal of Psychosomatic Research, 58*(1), 3–13.

Antoni, M. H. (2009). Stress management effects on biobehavioral processes in breast cancer. *Brain, Behavior, and Immunity, 23*(Suppl. 2), S26.

Apovian, C. M. (2010). The causes, prevalence, and treatment of obesity revisited in 2009: What have we learned so far? *American Journal of Clinical Nutrition 91*(1), 277S-279S.

Apperloo, M. J. A., Van Der Stege, J. G., Hoek, A., & Weijmar Schultz, W. C. M. (2003). In the mood for sex: The value of androgens. *Journal of Sex & Marital Therapy, 29*(2), 87–102.

Arendt, J. (2000). Melatonin, circadian rhythms, and sleep. *The New England Journal of Medicine online, 343*(15).

Arnett, J. J. (1999). Adolescent storm and stress, reconsidered. *American Psychologist, 54*(5), 317–326.

Aronoff, J., & Litevin, G. H. (1971). Achievement motivation training and executive advancement. *Journal of Applied Behavioral Science, 7*(2), 215–229. *Psychological Bulletin, 131*(3), 410–411.

Asch, S. E. (1952). *Social psychology.* Englewood Cliffs, NJ: Prentice-Hall.

Ashtari, M., et al. (2009). Diffusion abnormalities in adolescents and young adults with a history of heavy cannabis use. *Journal of Psychiatric Research, 43*(3), 189-204.

Atkins, M. S., et al. (2002). Suspensions and detention in an urban, low-income school: Punishment or reward? *Journal of Abnormal Child Psychology, 30*(4), 361–371.

Atkinson, R. C., & Shiffrin, R. M. (1968). Human memory: A proposed system and its control processes. In K. Spence (Ed.), *The psychology of learning and motivation* (Vol. 2). New York: Academic Press.

Ayllon, T., & Haughton, E. (1962). Control of the behavior of schizophrenic patients by food. *Journal of the Experimental Analysis of Behavior, 5,* 343–352.

B

Baddeley, A. (1982). *Your memory: A user's guide.* New York: Macmillan.

Bahrick, H. P., Bahrick, P. O., & Wittlinger, R. P. (1975). Fifty years of memory for names and faces. *Journal of Experimental Psychology: General, 104,* 54–75.

Bailey, J. M. (2003a). Personal communication.

Bailey, J. M., & Pillard, R. C. (1991). A genetic study of male sexual orientation. *Archives of general psychiatry 48,* 1089–1096.

Baker, C. W., Whisman, M. A., & Brownell, K. D. (2000). Studying intergenerational transmission of eating attitudes and behaviors: Methodological and conceptual questions. *Health Psychology, 19*(4), 376–381.

Baker, L. A., DeFries, J. C., & Fulker, D. W. (1983). Longitudinal stability of cognitive ability in the Colorado adoption project. *Child Development, 54,* 290–297.

Baker, M. C. (2001). *The atoms of language: The mind's hidden rules of grammar.* New York: Basic Books.

Baldo, J. V., Delis, D. C., Wilkins, D. P., & Shimamura, A. P. (2004). Is it bigger than a breadbox? Performance of patients with prefrontal lesions on a new executive function test. *Archives of Clinical Neuropsychology, 19*(3), 407–419.

Baltes, P. B., & Staudinger, U. M. (2000). Wisdom: A meta-heuristic (pragmatic) to orchestrate mind and virtue toward excellence. *American Psychologist, 55,* 122–136.

Bandura, A. (1986). *Social foundations of thought and action: A social-cognitive theory.* Englewood Cliffs, NJ: Prentice-Hall.

Bandura, A. (1999). Social cognitive theory: An agentic perspective. *Asian Journal of Social Psychology, 2*(1), 21–41.

Bandura, A. (2002). Social cognitive theory in cultural context. *Applied Psychology: An International Review, 51*(2), 269–290.

Bandura, A., & Locke, E. A. (2003). Negative selfefficacy and goal effects revisited. *Journal of Applied Psychology, 88*(1), 87–99.

Bandura, A., Barbaranelli, C., Vittorio Caprara, G., & Pastorelli, C. (2001). Self-efficacy beliefs as shapers of children's aspirations and career trajectories. *Child Development, 72*(1), 187–206.

Bandura, A., Blanchard, E. B., & Ritter, B. (1969). The relative efficacy of desensitization and modeling approaches for inducing behavioral, affective, and cognitive changes.

Journal of Personality and Social Psychology, 13, 173–199. 274–281.

Bandura, A., Pastorelli, C., Barbaranelli, C., & Caprara, G. V. (1999). Self-efficacy pathways to childhood depression. *Journal of Personality & Social Psychology, 76*(2), 258–269.

Bandura, A., Ross, S. A., & Ross, D. (1963). Imitation of film-mediated aggressive models. *Journal of Abnormal and Social Psychology, 66,* 3–11.

Bandura, A., Taylor, C. B., Williams, S. L., Medford, I. N., & Barchas, J. D. (1985). Catecholamine secretion as a function of perceived coping self-efficacy. *Journal of Consulting and Clinical Psychology, 53,* 406–414.

Banks, M. S., & Shannon, E. (1993). Spatial and chromatic visual efficiency in human neonates. In C. E. Granrud (Ed.), *Visual perception and cognition in infancy.* Hillsdale, NJ: Erlbaum.

Barber, J. G. (2001). Relative misery and youth suicide. *Australian & New Zealand Journal of Psychiatry, 35*(1), 49–57.

Barber, T. X. (2000). A deeper understanding of hypnosis: Its secrets, its nature, its essence. *American Journal of Clinical Hypnosis, 42*(3–4), 208–272.

Barbor, C. (2001). The science of meditation. *Psychology Today, 34,* 54. This article discusses research efforts at Harvard Medical School using MRI to investigate brain processing changes that occur while meditating.

Bard, P. (1934). The neurohumoral basis of emotional reactions. In C. A. Murchison (Ed.), *Handbook of general experimental psychology.* Worcester, MA: Clark University Press.

Barnard, C. J., Collins, S. A., Daisley, J. N., & Behnke, J. M. (2005). Maze performance and immunity costs in mice. *Behaviour, 142*(2), 241–263.

Baron, R. A., Byrne, D., & Branscombe, N. R. (2006). *Social psychology* (11th ed.). Boston: Allyn & Bacon.

Barringer, F. (1993, April 1). Some traps of surveys. *The New York Times,* pp. A1, B9.

Barrios, A. A. (2001). A theory of hypnosis based on principles of conditioning and inhibition. *Contemporary Hypnosis, 18*(4), 163–203.

Bartels, M., Rietveld, M. J. H., Van Baal, G. C. M., & Boomsma, D. I. (2002). Genetic and environmental influences on the development of intelligence. *Behavior Genetics, 32*(4), 237–249.

Bartholow, B. D., & Anderson, C. A. (2002). Effects of violent video games on aggressive behavior: Potential sex differences. *Journal of Experimental Social Psychology, 38,* 283–290.

Bartoshuk, L. M. (2000). Psychophysical advances aid the study of genetic variation in taste. *Appetite, 34*(1), 105.

Basic Behavioral Science Task Force of the National Advisory Mental Health Council. (1996b). Basic behavioral science research for mental health: Perception, attention, learning

and memory. *American Psychologist, 51,*133–142.

Basic Behavioral Science Task Force of the National Advisory Mental Health Council. (1996c). Basic behavioral science research for mental health: Sociocultural and environmental practices. *American Psychologist, 51,* 722–731.

Bassetti, C., Vella, S., Donati, F., Wielepp, P., & Weder, B. (2000). SPECT during sleepwalking. *Lancet, 356,* 484–485.

Bates, E. (2001) Plasticity, localization and language development. In S. T. Parker, J. Langer & C. Milbrath (Eds.), *Biology and knowledge revisited* (pp. 205-254). London: Routledge.

Bates, E. (2004). In J. Berck, Before baby talk, signs and signals. *The New York Times online.*

Batson, C. D., Qian, Z., & Lichter, D. T. (2006). Interracial and intraracial patterns of mate selection among America's diverse black populations. *Journal of Marriage and the Family, 68,* 658-672.

Battaglia, F. P., Sutherland, G. R., & McNaughton, B. L. (2004). Local sensory cues and place cell directionality: Additional evidence of prospective coding in the hippocampus. *Journal of Neuroscience, 24*(19), 4541–4550.

Baucom, D. H., Shoham, V., Mueser, K. T., Daiuto, A. D., & Stickle, T. R. (1998). Empirically supported couple and family interventions for marital distress and adult mental health problems. *Journal of Consulting and Clinical Psychology, 66,* 53–88.

Bauer, M. E., et al. (2003). Altered glucocorticoid immunoregulation in treatment resistant depression. *Psychoneuroendocrinology, 28*(1), 49–65.

Baumeister, R. F. (1996). *Evil: Inside human cruelty and violence.* New York: W. H. Freeman /Times Books/ Henry Holt & Co.

Baumgartner, F. (2002). The effect of hardiness in the choice of coping strategies in stressful situations. *Studia Psychologica, 44*(1), 69–75.

Beautrais, A. L. (2003). Suicide and serious suicide attempts in youth: A multiple-group comparison study. *American Journal of Psychiatry, 160,* 1093–1099.

Beck, A. T., et al. (2001). Dysfunctional beliefs discriminate personality disorders. *Behaviour Research & Therapy, 39*(10), 1213–1225.

Bekoff, M. (2002). *Minding animals: Awareness, emotions, and heart.* New York: Oxford University Press.

Belsky, J., Weinraub, M., Owen, M., & Kelly, J. (2001, April). Quantity of child care and problem behavior. In J. Belsky (Chair), *Early childcare and children's development prior to school entry.* Symposium conducted at the 2001 Biennial Meetings of the Society for Research in Child Development, Minneapolis, MN.

Bem, D. J., & Honorton, C. (1994). Does Psi exist? Replicable evidence for an anomalous process of information transfer. *Psychological Bulletin, 115,* 4–18.

Bem, D. J., Palmer, J., & Broughton, R. S. (2001).Updating the ganzfeld database: A victim of its own success? *Journal of Parapsychology, 65*(3), 207–218.

Benson, H. (1975). *The relaxation response.* New York: Morrow.

Ben-Zur, H. (2002). Associations of type A behavior with the emotional traits of anger and curiosity. *Anxiety, Stress & Coping: An International Journal, 15*(1), 95–104.

Bergen, A. W., et al. (2003). Candidate genes for anorexia nervosa in the 1p33–36 linkage region: Serotonin 1D and delta opioid receptor loci exhibit significant association to anorexia nervosa.

Berk, M. S., Henriques, G. R., Warman, D. M., Brown, G. K., & Beck, A. T. (2004). A cognitive therapy intervention for suicide attempters: An overview. *Cognitive and Behavioral Practice. 11*(3), 265–277.

Berkowitz, L. (2004b). Two views of evil: Evil is not only banal. *PsycCRITIQUES.*

Bernardin, H. J., Cooke, D. K., & Villanova, P. (2000). Conscientiousness and agreeableness as predictors of rating leniency. *Journal of Applied Psychology, 85*(2), 232–236.

Bernardis, P. et al. (2008). Manual actions affect vocalizations of infants. *Experimental Brain Research 184*(4), 599-603.

Bernhardt, P. C., Dabbs, J. M., Jr., Fielden, J. A., & Lutter, C. D. (1998). Testosterone changes during vicarious experiences of winning and losing among fans at sporting events. *Physiology & Behavior, 65*(1), 59–62.

Berry, J. W., Phinney, J. S., Sam, D. L., & Vedder, P. (Eds.) (2006). *Immigrant youth in cultural transition.* Mahwah, NJ: Erlbaum.

Bexton, W. H., Heron, W., & Scott, T. H. (1954). Effects of decreased variation in the sensory environment. *Canadian Journal of Psychology, 8,* 70–76.

Bidell, M. P., Turner, J. A., & Casas, J. M. (2002). First impressions count: Ethnic/racial and lesbian /gay/ bisexual content of professional psychology application materials. *Professional Psychology: Research & Practice, 33*(1), 97–103.

Bienvenu, O. J., et al. (2005). Anxiety and depressive disorders and the five-factor model of personality: A higher- and lower-order personality trait investigation in a community sample. *Depression & Anxiety, 20*(2), 92–97.

Bilkey, D. K. (2004). Neuroscience: In the place space. *Science, 305,* 1245–1246.

Birch, C. D., Stewart, S. H., & Brown, C. G. (2007). Exploring differential patterns of situational risk for binge eating and heavy drinking. *Addictive Behaviors, 32*(3), 433.

Bishop, G. D., et al. (2003). Job demands, decisional control, and cardiovascular responses. *Journal of Occupational Health Psychology, 8*(2), 146–156.

Bizer, G. Y., et al. (2004). The impact of personality on cognitive, behavioral, and affective political processes: The effects of need to evaluate. *Journal of Personality, 72*(5), 995–1027.

Bjorklund, D. F. (2000). *Children's thinking* (3rd ed). Pacific Grove, CA: Brooks/Cole.

Blagrove, M., Farmer, L., & Williams, E. (2004). The relationship of nightmare frequency and nightmare distress to well-being. *Journal of Sleep Research, 13*(2), 129–136.

Blair, R. , & James, R. (2003). Neurobiological basis of psychopathy. *British Journal of Psychiatry, 182,* 5–7.

Blanchard, E. B., et al. (2003). A controlled evaluation of cognitive behavioral therapy for posttraumatic stress in motor vehicle accident survivors. *Behaviour Research & Therapy, 41*(1), 79–96.

Blass, T. (1999). The Milgram paradigm after 35 years: Some things we now know about obedience to authority. *Journal of Applied Social Psychology, 29*(5), 955–978.

Blass, T., & Schmitt, C. (2001). The nature of perceived authority in the Milgram paradigm: Two replications. *Current Psychology: Developmental, Learning, Personality, Social, 20*(2), 115–121.

Blum, R. W., Harmon, B., Harris, L., & Bergeisen, L (1992). American Indian–Alaska Native youth health. Journal of the American Medical Association, *268*(7), 874.

Blumenthal, J. A., et al. (2005). Effects of exercise and stress management training on markers of cardiovascular risk in patients with ischemic heart disease: A randomized controlled trial. *Journal of the American Medical Association, 293*(13), 1626–1634.

Bogen, J. E. (1969). The other side of the brain II: An appositional mind. *Bulletin of the Los Angeles Neurological Society, 34,* 135–162.

Bogen, J. E. (1998). My developing understanding of Roger Wolcott Sperry's philosophy. *Neuropsychologia, 36*(10), 1089–1096.

Bogen, J. E. (2000). Split-brain basics: Relevance for the concept of one's other mind. *Journal of the American Academy of Psychoanalysis, 28*(2), 341–369.

Bohlin, G., Hagekull, B., & Rydell, A. (2000). Attachment and social functioning: A longitudinal study from infancy to middle childhood. *Social Development, 9*(1), 24–39.

Bonds-Raacke, J. M., Fryer, L. S., Nicks, S. D., and Durr, R. T. (2001). Hindsight bias demonstrated in the prediction of a sporting event. *The Journal of Social Psychology, 141,* 349. This article describes a research study in which students predict a sporting event outcome to illustrate the hindsight bias.

Bonin, M. F., McCreary, D. R., & Sadava, S. W. (2000). Problem drinking behavior in two community- based samples of adults: Influence of gender, coping, loneliness, and depression. *Psychology of Addictive Behaviors, 14*(2), 151–161.

Bonn-Miller, M. O., Zvolensky, M. J., & Bernstein, A. (2007). Marijuana use motives: Concurrent relations to frequency of past 30-day use and anxiety sensitivity among young adult marijuana smokers. *Addictive Behaviors, 32*(1) 49–62.

Boom, J., Wouters, H., & Keller, M. (2007). A cross cultural validation of stage development. A Rasch re-analysis of longitudinal socio-moral reasoning data. *Cognitive Development, 22*(2), 213–229.

Both, L., Needham, D., & Wood, E. (2004). Examining tasks that facilitate the experience of incubation while problem-solving. *Alberta Journal of Educational Research, 50*(1), 57–67.

Bouchard, T. J., Jr., & Loehlin, J. C. (2001). Genes, evolution, and personality. *Behavior Genetics, 31*(3), 243–273.

Bouchard, T. J., Jr., Lykken, D. T., McGue, M., Segal, N. L., & Tellegen, A. (1990). Sources of human psychological differences: The Minnesota study of twins reared apart. *Science, 250,* 223–228.

Bouchard, T. J., Jr., Lykken, D. T., McGue, M., Segal, N. L., & Tellegen, A. (1990). Sources of human psychological differences: The Minnesota study of twins reared apart. *Science, 250,* 223–228.

Bower, B. (2000). Certain mental ills may be tied to violence. *Science News, 158,* 279. This article discusses mental disorders that are tied to violence.

Boyd-Franklin, N. (2001). Using the multisystems model with an African American family: Crossracial therapy and supervision. In S. H. McDaniel, et al. (Eds.), *Casebook for integrating family therapy: An ecosystemic approach* (pp. 395–400). Washington, DC: American Psychological Association.

Bradley, R. H., et al. (1989). Home environment and cognitive development in the first 3 years of life. *Developmental Psychology, 25,* 217–235.

Branaman, T. F., & Gallagher, S. N. (2005). Polygraph testing in sex offender treatment: A review of limitations. American *Journal of Forensic Psychology,* 23(1), 45–64.

Brand, J. (2000). Cited in McFarling, U. L. (2000, August 27). Sniffing out genes' role in our senses of taste and smell. *The Los Angeles Times online.*

Braun, B. G. (1988). *Treatment of multiple personality disorder.* Washington, DC: American Psychiatric Press.

Bray, F., & Atkin, W. (2004). International cancer patterns in men: Geographical and temporal variations in cancer risk and the role of gender. *Journal of Men's Health & Gender, 1*(1), 38–46.

Brigman, S., & Cherry, K. E. (2002). Age and skilled performance: Contributions of working memory and processing speed. *Brain & Cognition, 50*(2), 242–256.

Brissette, I., Scheier, M. F., & Carver, C. S. (2002). The role of optimism in social network development, coping, and psychological adjustment during a life transition. *Journal of Personality & Social Psychology,* 82(1), 102–111.

Brody, J. E. (2000, April 25). Memories of things that never were. *The New York Times,* p. F8.

Brody, J. E. (2008, May 20). Trying to break nicotine's grip. *The New York Times online.*

Brook, J. S., Zheng, L., Whiteman, M., & Brook, D. W. (2001). Aggression in toddlers: Associations with parenting and marital relations. *Journal of Genetic Psychology, 162*(2), 228–241.

Broom, A. (2005). The eMale: Prostate cancer, masculinity and

online support as a challenge to medical expertise. *Journal of Sociology, 41*(1), 87–104.

Brown, A. S., & Susser, E. S. (2002). In utero infection and adult schizophrenia. *Mental Retardation & Developmental Disabilities Research Reviews, 8*(1), 51–57.

Brown, R., & McNeill, D. (1966). The tip-of-the tongue phenomenon. *Journal of Verbal Learning and Verbal Behavior, 5,* 325–337.

Brown, S. L., Van Hook, J., & Glick, J. E. (2008). Generational differences in cohabitation and marriage in the U.S. *Population Research and Policy Review, 27*(5), 531-550.

Brownstein, A. L. (2003). Biased predecision processing. *Psychological Bulletin, 129*(4), 545–568.

Bruene, M., & Ribbert, H. (2002). Grundsaetzliches zur Konzeption einer evolutionaeren Psychiatrie. *Schweizer Archiv für Neurologie und Psychiatrie, 153*(1), 4–11.

Buchanan, R. W., Pearlson, G., & Tamminga, C. A. (2004). Prefrontal cortex, structural analysis: Segmenting the prefrontal cortex. *American Journal of Psychiatry, 161*(11), 1978.

Buckley, P. F., Buchanan, R. W., Tamminga, C. A., & Schulz, S. C. (2000). Schizophrenia research. *Schizophrenia Bulletin, 26*(2), 411–419.

Buckner, R. L., Wheeler, M. E., & Sheridan, M. A. (2001). Encoding processes during retrieval tasks. *Journal of Cognitive Neuroscience, 13*(3), 406–415.

Budney, A. J., Vandrey, R. G., Hughes, J. R., Moore, B. A., & Bahrenburg, B. (2007). Oral delta-9-tetrahydrocannabinol suppresses cannabis withdrawal symptoms. *Drug and Alcohol Dependence, 86*(1), 22–29.

Bull, N. J., Hunter, M., & Finlay, D. C. (2003). Cue gradient and cue density interact in the detection and recognition of objects defined by motion, contrast, or texture. *Perception,* 32(1), 29–39.

Bullough, V. L. (1998). Alfred Kinsey and the Kinsey Report: Historical overview and lasting contributions. *The Journal of Sex Research, 35,* 127–131. This article summarizes the contributions that Kinsey made to the field of sex research.

Buss, D. M. (1994). *The evolution of desire.* New York: Basic Books.

Buss, D. M. (2000). The evolution of happiness. *American Psychologist, 55,* 15–23.

Buss, D. M. (2003). Sexual strategies: A journey into controversy. *Psychological Inquiry, 14*(3–4), 219–226.

Butcher, J. (2000). Dopamine hypothesis gains further support. *The Lancet, 356,* 139–146.

Butler, A. C., & Beck, J. S. (2001). Cognitive therapy outcomes. A review of meta-analyses. *Tidsskrift for Norsk Psykologforening, 38*(8), 698–706.

C

Cacioppo, J. T., Martzke, J. S., Petty, R. E., & Tassinary, L. G. (1988). Specific forms of facial EMG response index emotions during an interview.

Caffray, C. M., & Schneider, S. L. (2000). Why do they do it? Affective motivators in adolescents' decisions to participate in risk behaviours. *Cognition & Emotion, 14*(4), 543–576.

Cailhol, S., & Mormede, P. (2002). Conditioned taste aversion and alcohol drinking: Strain and gender differences. *Journal of Studies on Alcohol, 63*, 91–99. This article discusses research conducted with rats to determine etiological basis for alcohol abuse.

Campos, J. J., Hiatt, S., Ramsey, D., Henderson, C., & Svejda, M. (1978). The emergence of fear on the visual cliff. In M. Lewis & L. Rosenblum (Eds.), *The origins of affect.* New York: Plenum.

Camras, L. (2000). Cited in Azar, B. (2000). What's in a face? *Monitor on Psychology, 31*(1), 44–45.

Canalis, R. F., & Lambert, P. R. (2000). *The ear: Comprehensive otology.* Philadelphia: Lippincott Williams & Wilkins.

Cannon, W. B. (1927). The James-Lange theory of emotions: A critical examination and an alternative theory. *American Journal of Psychology, 39*, 106–124.

Cannon, W. B. (1932). *The wisdom of the body.* New York: Norton.

Cannon, W. B., & Washburn, A. (1912). An explanation of hunger. *American Journal of Physiology, 29*, 441–454.

Cantalupo, C., & Hopkins, W. D. (2001). Asymmetric Broca's area in great apes: A region of the ape brain is uncannily similar to one linked with speech in humans. *Nature, 414*(6863), 505.

Carey, B. (2005, January 4). After food and shelter, help in coping with unbearable loss. *The New York Times online.*

Carlson, J. G., & Hatfield, E. (1992). *Psychology of emotion.* Fort Worth: Harcourt Brace Jovanovich.

Carpenter, S. (2001, March). Everyday fantasia: The world of synesthesia. *Monitor on Psychology, 32.* Retrieved May 22, 2003, from the World Wide Web: http://www.apa. org/monitor.mar01/synesthesia.html This article discusses the interesting condition known as synesthesia.

Carroll, D. (2004). *Psychology of language* (4th ed.). Belmont, CA: Wadsworth Publishing Company.

Cassaday, H. J., et al. (2003). Intraventricular 5,7- dihydroxytryptamine lesions disrupt acquisition of working memory task rules but not performance once learned. *Progress in Neuro-Psychopharmacology & Biological Psychiatry, 27*(1), 147–156.

Castillo-Richmond, A., et al. (2000). Effects of stress reduction on carotid atherosclerosis in hypertensive African Americans. *Stroke, 31,* 568.

Cattell, R. B. (1949). *The culture-free intelligence test.* Champaign, IL: Institute for Personality and Ability Testing.

Ceci, S. J., & Bruck, M. (1993). Suggestibility of the child witness. *Psychological Bulletin, 113,* 403–439.

Cellar, D. F., Nelson, Z. C., & Yorke, C. M. (2000). The five-factor model and driving behavior: Personality and involvement in vehicular accidents. *Psychological Reports, 86*(2), 454–456.

Centers for Disease Control and Prevention. (2000b). Suicide in the United States. Page updated January 28, 2000.

http://www.cdc.gov/ ncipc/factsheets/suifacts.htm.

Centers for Disease Control and Prevention. (2005). National Center for Health Statistics. *America's children, 2005. America's children: Key national indicators of well-being 2005.* Childstats.gov.

Centers for Disease Control and Prevention. (2005a, April 21). Overweight and obesity: Health consequences. http://www. cdc.gov/nccd php/dnpa/obesity/consequences.htm.

Cervantes, J. M., & Parham, T. A. (2005). Toward a meaningful spirituality for people of color: Lessons for the counseling practitioner. *Cultural Diversity & Ethnic Minority Psychology, 11*(1), 69–81.

Cervilla, J. A., et al. (2000). Long-term predictors of cognitive outcome in a cohort of older people with hypertension. *British Journal of Psychiatry, 177,* 66–71.

Chafee, M. V., & Goldman-Rakic, P. S. (2000). Inactivation of parietal and prefrontal cortex reveals interdependence of neural activity during memory-guided saccades. *Journal of Neurophysiology, 83*(3), 1550–1566.

Chang, D. F., & Sue, S. (2003). The effects of race and problem type on teachers' assessments of student behavior. *Journal of Consulting & Clinical Psychology, 71*(2), 235–242.

Chen, C., et al. (2004). Association analysis of dopamine D2-like receptor genes and methamphetamine abuse. *Psychiatric Genetics, 14*(4), 223–226.

Chen, S. W., & Davenport, D. S. (2005). Cognitive behavioral therapy with Chinese American clients: Cautions and modifications. *Psychotherapy: Theory, Research, Practice, Training, 42*(1), 101–110.

Cheng, H., & Furnham, A. (2001). Attributional style and personality as predictors of happiness and mental health. *Journal of Happiness Studies, 2*(3), 307–327.

Chioqueta, A. P., & Stiles, T. C. (2005). Personality traits and the development of depression, hopelessness, and suicide ideation. *Personality & Individual Differences, 38*(6), 1283–1291.

Chomsky, N. (1980). Rules and representations. *Behavioral and Brain Sciences, 3,* 1–16.

Chomsky, N. (1991). Linguistics and cognitive science. In A. Kasher (Ed.), *The Chomskyan turn.* Cambridge, MA: Blackwell.

Chu, L., Ma, E. S. K., Lam, K. K. Y., Chan, M. F., & Lee, D. H. S. (2005). Increased alpha 7 nicotinic acetylcholine receptor protein levels in Alzheimer's disease patients. *Dementia & Geriatric Cognitive Disorders, 19*(2–3), 106–112.

Chua, S. C., Jr. (2004). Molecular and cellular correlates of the developmental acquisition of mechanisms modulating ingestive behavior. *Physiology & Behavior, 82*(1), 145–147.

Cialdini, R. B. (2000). Cited in McKinley, J. C., Jr. (2000, August 11). It isn't just a game: Clues to avid rooting. *The New York Times online.*

Cialdini, R. B., & Goldstein, N. J. (2004). Social influence: Compliance and conformity. *Annual Review of Psychology, 55,* 591–621.

Cialdini, R. B., et al. (1997). Reinterpreting the empathy-altruism relationship: When one into one equals oneness. *Journal of Personality & Social Psychology, 73*(3), 481–494.

Ciarrochi, J. (2004). Relationships between dysfunctional beliefs and positive and negative indices of well-being: A critical evaluation of the common beliefs survey–III. *Journal of Rational- Emotive & Cognitive Behavior Therapy, 22*(3), 171–188.

Clark, S. E., & Loftus, E. F. (1996). The construction of space alien abduction memories. *Psychological Inquiry, 7*(2), 140–143.

Clark, S. E., & Loftus, E. F. (2004). The psychological pay dirt of space alien abduction memories.

Clarke-Stewart, K. A., & Beck, R. J. (1999). Maternal scaffolding and children's narrative retelling of a movie story. *Early Childhood Research Quarterly, 14*(3), 409–434.

Clayton, E. C., & Williams, C. L. (2000). Adrenergic activation of the nucleus tractus solitarius potentiates amygdala norepinephrine release and enhances retention performance in emotionally arousing and spatial memory tasks. *Behavioural Brain Research. 112*(1–2), 151–158.

Clènet, F., Hascoët, M., Fillion, G., Galons, H., & Bourin, M. (2005). Role of GABA-ergic and serotonergic systems in the anxiolytic-like mechanism of action of a 5-HT-moduline antagonist in the mouse elevated plus maze. *Behavioural Brain Research, 158*(2), 339–348.

Cohen, L. L. (2002). Reducing infant immunization distress through distraction. *Health Psychology, 21*(2), 207–211.

Cohen, S., Doyle, W. J., Turner, R., Alper, C. M., & Skoner, D. P. (2003). Sociability and susceptibility to the common cold. *Psychological Science, 14*(5), 389–395.

Cohen, S., Gottlieb, B. H., & Underwood, L. G. (2001a). Social relationships and health: Challenges for measurement and intervention. *Advances in Mind-Body Medicine, 17*(2), 129–141.

Cohen, S., Miller, G. E., & Rabin, B. S. (2001b). Psychological stress and antibody response to immunization: A critical review of the human literature. *Psychosomatic Medicine, 63*(1), 7–18.

Cohn, L. D., Macfarlane, S., Yanez, C., & Imai, W. K. (1995). Risk-perception: Differences between adolescents and adults. *Health Psychology, 14,*217–222.

Collaer, M. L., & Hines, M. (1995). Human behavioral sex differences: A role for gonadal hormones during early development? *Psychological Bulletin, 118,* 55–107.

Collaer, M. L., & Nelson, J. D. (2002). Large visuospatial sex difference in line judgment: Possible role of attentional factors. *Brain & Cognition, 49*(1), 1–12.

Coltraine, S., & Messineo, M. (2000). The perpetuation of subtle prejudice: Race and gender imagery in 1990s television advertising. *Sex Roles, 42*(5–6), 363–389.

Colvin, M. K., Funnell, M. G., & Gazzaniga, M. S. (2005). Numerical processing in the two hemispheres: Studies of a split-brain patient. *Brain & Cognition, 57*(1), 43–52.

Comas-Díaz, L. (2003). The Black Madonna: The psychospiritual feminism of Guadeloupe, Kali, and Monserrat. In L. B. Silverstein & T. J. Goodrich (Eds.), *Feminist family therapy: Empowerment in social context* (pp. 147–160).

Comaty, J. E., Stasio, M., & Advokat, C. (2001). Analysis of outcome variables of a token economy system in a state psychiatric hospital: A program evaluation. *Research in Developmental Disabilities, 22*(3), 233–253.

Concar, D. (2002, April 20). Ecstasy on the brain. http://www.NewScientist.com.

Conklin, H. M., & Iacono, W. G. (2002). Schizophrenia: A neurodevelopmental perspective. *Current Directions in Psychological Science, 11*(1), 33–37.

Conrad, P. J., Peterson, J. B., & Pihl, R. O. (2001). Reliability and validity of alcohol-induced heart rate increase as a measure of sensitivity to the stimulant properties of alcohol. *Psychopharmacology, 157*(1), 20–30.

Consortium of Social Science Associations. (2003, May 23). McQueary testifies to Homeland Security Science Subcommittee. *Washington Update, 22*(10), 1–7.

Constantinidis, C., Franowicz, M. N., & Goldman- Rakic, P. S. (2001). Coding specificity in cortical microcircuits: A multiple-electrode analysis of primate prefontal cortex. *Journal of Neuroscience, 21*(10), 3646–3655.

Conte, J., M., Schwenneker, H. H., Dew, A. F., & Romano, D. M. (2001). Incremental validity of time urgency and other Type A subcomponents in predicting behavioral and health criteria. *Journal of Applied Social Psychology, 31*(8), 1727–1748.

Cooper, M., Galbraith, M., & Drinkwater, J. (2001). Assumptions and beliefs in adolescents with anorexia nervosa and their mothers. *Eating Disorders: The Journal of Treatment & Prevention, 9*(3), 217–223.

Cooper, Z., & Fairburn, C. G. (2001). A new cognitive behavioural approach to the treatment of obesity. *Behaviour Research & Therapy, 39*(5), 499–511.

Corballis, P. M., Funnell, M. G., & Gazzaniga, M. S. (2002). Hemispheric asymmetries for simple visual judgments in the split brain. *Neuropsychologia, 40*(4), 401–410.

Corwin, R. L. (2000). Biological and behavioral consequences of food restriction. *Appetite, 34*(1), 112.

Cory, G. A. (2002). MacLean's evolutionary neuroscience, the CSN model and Hamilton's rule: Some developmental, clinical, and social policy implications. *Brain & Mind, 3*(1), 151–181.

Courtenay, W. H. (2000). Engendering health: A social constructionist examination of men's health beliefs and behaviors. *Psychology of Men & Masculinity, 1*(1), 4–15.

Cowen, P. J. (2002). Cortisol, serotonin and depression: All stressed out? *British Journal of Psychiatry, 180*(2), 99–100.

Cox, W. M., & Alm, R. (2005, February 25). Scientists are made, not born. *The New York Times online.*

Craig, J. C., & Rollman, G. B. (1999, Annual). Somesthesis.

Annual Review of Psychology, p. 305. This article is an in-depth article focusing on the skin senses (Somesthesis).

Craik, F. I. M., & Lockhart, R. S. (1972). Levels of processing. *Journal of Verbal Learning and Verbal Behavior, 11,* 671–684.

Crano, W. D. (2000) Milestones in the psychological analysis of social influence. *Group Dynamics, 4*(1), 68–80.

Craske, M. G., & Zucker, B. G. (2001). Consideration of the APA practice guideline for the treatment of patients with panic disorder: Strengths and limitations for behavior therapy. *Behavior Therapy, 32*(2), 259–281.

Crews, D. (1994). Animal sexuality. *Scientific American, 270*(1), 108–114.

Crick, N. R., & Dodge, K. A. (1994). A review and reformulation of social information-processing mechanisms in children's social adjustment. *Psychological Bulletin, 115,* 74–101.

Crisp, R. J., & Nicel, J. K. (2004). Disconfirming intergroup evaluations: Asymmetric effects for ingroups and out-groups. *Journal of Social Psychology, 144*(3), 247–271.

Crusco, A. H., & Wetzel, C. G. (1984). The Midas touch: The effects of interpersonal touch on restaurant tipping. *Personality and Social Psychology Bulletin, 10,* 512–517.

Cuellar, J. C., & Curry, T. R. (2007). The prevalence and comorbidity between delinquency, drug abuse, suicide attempts, physical and sexual abuse, and self-mutilation among delinquent Hispanic females. *Hispanic Journal of Behavioral Sciences, 29*(1), 68-82.

Cummins, R. A., & Nistico, H. (2002). Maintaining life satisfaction: The role of positive cognitive bias. *Journal of Happiness Studies, 3*(1), 37–69.

Cumsille, P. E., Sayer, A. G., & Graham, J. W. (2000). Perceived exposure to peer and adult drinking as predictors of growth in positive alcohol expectancies during adolescence. *Journal of Consulting and Clinical Psychology, 68*(3), 531–536.

Curry, K. (1993, October 22). Male menopause: Is it myth, or a reality of aging. *Knight Ridder/Tribune News Service.* This article discusses the possibility of male menopause and provides expert opinion.

D

d'Ydewalle, G., Luwel, K., & Brunfaut, E. (1999). The importance of on-going concurrent activities as a function of age in time- and event-based prospective memory. *European Journal of Cognitive Psychology, 11*(2), 219–237.

Dabbs, J. M., Jr., Chang, E-L., Strong, R. A., & Milun, R. (1998). Spatial ability, navigation strategy, and geographic knowledge among men and women. *Evolution & Human Behavior, 19*(2), 89–98.

Dalkvist, J. (2001). The ganzfeld method: Its current status. *European Journal of Parapsychology, 16,* 19–22.

Damasio, A. R. (2000). A neural basis for sociopathy. *Archives of General Psychiatry online, 57*(2).

Darley, J. M., & Latané, B. (1968). Bystander intervention in emergencies: Diffusion of responsibility. *Journal of Personality and Social Psychology, 8,* 377–383.

Darwin, C. A. (1872). *The expression of the emotions in man and animals.* London: J. Murray.

Davis, C., Strachan, S., & Berkson, M. (2004). Sensitivity to reward: Implications for overeating and overweight. *Appetite, 42*(2), 131–138.

Davis, S. (2000). Testosterone and sexual desire in women. *Journal of Sex Education & Therapy, 25*(1), 25–32.

Dawood, K., Pillard, R. C., Horvath, C., Revelle, W., & Bailey, J. M. (2000). Familial aspects of male homosexuality. *Archives of Sexual Behavior, 29*(2), 155–163.

Dawson, T. L. (2002). New tools, new insights: Kohlberg's moral judgement stages revisited. *International Journal of Behavioral Development, 26*(2), 154–166.

De Houwer, J., Thomas, S., & Baeyens, F. (2001). Associative learning of likes and dislikes: A review of 25 years of research on human evaluative conditioning. *Psychological Bulletin, 127*(6), 853–869.

De Maat, S., Dekker, J., Schoevers, R., & De Jonghe, F. (2006). Relative efficacy of psychotherapy and pharmacotherapy in the treatment of depression: A meta-analysis. *Psychotherapy Research, 16*(5), 562-572.

de Mello, M. F., et al. (2005). A systematic review of research findings on the efficacy of interpersonal therapy for depressive disorders. *European Archives of Psychiatry & Clinical Neuroscience, 255*(2), 75–82.

De Michele, P. E., Gansneder, B., & Solomon, G. B. (1998). Success and failure attributions of wrestlers: Further evidence of the self-serving bias. *Journal of Sport Behavior, 21*(3), 242–255.

DeAngelis, T. (2002). A genetic link to anorexia. *APA Monitor, 33*(3), 34–36.

DeAngelis, T. (2008). PTSD treatments grow in evidence, effectiveness. *Monitor on Psychology, 39*(1). Also delete references: Blanchard 2003 and Vasterling 2002.

DeCasper, A. J., & Prescott, P. A. (1984). Human newborns' perception of male voices. *Developmental Psychobiology, 17,* 481–491.

Decety, J., & Batson, C. D. (2009). Empathy and morality: Integrating social and neuroscience approaches. In J. Verplaetse et al. (Eds.). *The moral brain.* (pp. 109-127). New York: Springer.

Deecher, D., Andree, T. H., Sloan, D., & Schechter, L. E. (2008). From menarche to menopause: Exploring the underlying biology of depression in women experiencing hormonal changes. *Psychoneuroendocrinology,* 33(1), 3–17.

Deep, A. L., et al. (1999). Sexual abuse in eating disorder subtypes and control women: The role of comorbid substance dependence in bulimia nervosa. Activating the ZPD: Mutual scaffolding in L2 peer revision. *Modern Language Journal, 84*(1), 51–68.

Dehghani, M., Sharpe, L., & Nicholas, M. K. (2004). Modification of attentional biases in chronic pain patients: A preliminary study. *European Journal of Pain, 8*(6), 585–594.

Delgado, J. M. R. (1969). *Physical control of the mind.* New York: Harper & Row.

Delves, P. J., & Roitt, I. M. (2000). Advances in immunology: The immune system. *The New England Journal of Medicine online, 343*(1).

Dennerstein, L. L. (2003). The sexual impact of menopause. In S. B. Levine, et al. (Eds.), *Handbook of clinical sexuality for mental health professionals* (pp. 187–198). New York: Brunner- Routledge.

DeRubeis, R. J., et al. (2005). Cognitive therapy vs. medications in the treatment of moderate to severe depression. *Archives of General Psychiatry, 62*(4), 409–416.

DeSteno, D., Petty, R. E., Rucker, D. D., Wegener, D. T., & Braverman, J. (2004). Discrete emotions and persuasion: The role of emotion induced expectancies. *Journal of Personality & Social Psychology, 86*(1), 43–56.

Devilly, G. J. (2002). Eye movement desensitization and reprocessing: A chronology of its development and scientific standing. *Scientific Review of Mental Health Practice, 1*(2), 113–138.

DeVries, R. (2000). Vygotsky, Piaget, and education: A reciprocal assimilation of theories and educational practices. *New Ideas in Psychology, 18*(2–3), 187–213.

Dhabhar, F. S. (2009). A hassle a day may keep the pathogens away: The fight-or-flight stress response and the augmentation of immune function. *Integrative and Comparative Biology, 49*(3), 215-236.

Dickson, N., Paul, C., Herbison, P., & Silva, P. (1998). First sexual intercourse: age, coercion, and later regrets reported by a birth cohort. *British Medical Journal, 316,* 29–33.

Diener, E., Napa Scollon, C. K., Oishi, S., Dzokoto, V., Suh, E. M. (2000). Positivity and the construction of life satisfaction judgments: Global happiness is not the sum of its parts. *Journal of Happiness Studies, 1*(2), 159–176.

Dierker, L. C., et al. (2001). Association between psychiatric disorders and the progression of tobacco use behaviors. *Journal of the American Academy of Child & Adolescent Psychiatry, 40*(10), 1159–1167.

Dietrich, A. (2004). Neurocognitive mechanisms underlying the experience of flow. *Consciousness & Cognition: An International Journal, 13*(4), 746–761.

DiLalla, D. L., Carey, G., Gottesman, I. I., & Bouchard, T. J., Jr. (1996). Heritability of MMPI personality indicators of psychopathology in twins reared apart. *Journal of Abnormal Psychology, 105,* 491–499.

Diseth, T. H. (2005). Dissociation in children and adolescents as reaction to trauma—An overview of conceptual issues and neurobiological factors. *Nordic Journal of Psychiatry, 59*(2), 79–91.

Dobbins, I. G., Simons, J. S., & Schacter, D. L. (2004). fMRI evidence for separable and lateralized prefrontal memory monitoring processes. *Journal of Cognitive Neuroscience, 16*(6), 908–920.

Doblin, R. (2002). A clinical plan for MDMA (ecstasy) in the treatment of posttraumatic stress disorder (PTSD): Partnering with the FDA. *Journal of Psychoactive Drugs, 34*(2), 185–194.

Dogil, G., et al. (2002). The speaking brain: A tutorial introduction to fMRI experiments in the production of speech, prosody and syntax. *Journal of Neurolinguistics, 15*(1), 59–90.

Dollard, J., Doob, L. W., Miller, N. E., Mowrer, O. H., & Sears, R. R. (1939). *Frustration and aggression.* New Haven, CT: Yale University Press.

Domhoff, G. W. (2001). A new neurocognitive theory of dreams. *Dreaming: Journal of the Association for the Study of Dreams, 11*(1), 13–33.

Domhoff, G. W. (2003). *The scientific study of dreams: Neural networks, cognitive development, and content analysis.* Washington, DC: American Psychological Association.

Donohue, K. F., Curtin, J. J., Patrick, C. J., & Lang, A. R. (2007). Intoxication level and emotional response. *Emotion, 7*(1), 103–112.

Donovan, C. A., & Smolkin, L. B. (2002). Children's genre knowledge: An examination of K-5 student's performance on multiple tasks providing differing levels of scaffolding. *Reading Research Quarterly, 37,* 428–466. This article discusses cognitive scaffolding in K-5 age children.

Dovidio, J. F., et al. (2004). Perspective and prejudice: Antecedents and mediating mechanisms. *Personality & Social Psychology Bulletin, 30*(12), 1537–1549.

Duckitt, J., & Fisher, K. (2003). The impact of social threat on world view and ideological attitudes. *Political Psychology, 24*(1), 199–222.

Duckworth, A. L., & Seligman, M. E. P. (2005). Self-discipline outdoes IQ in predicting academic performance of adolescents. *Psychological Science, 16*(12), 939-944.

Duffy, V. B., Peterson, J. M., & Bartoshuk, L. M. (2004). Associations between taste genetics, oral sensation and alcohol intake. *Physiology & Behavior, 82*(2–3), 435–445.

Dunkley, D. M., Zuroff, D. C., & Blankstein, K. R. (2003). Self-critical perfectionism and daily affect: Dispositional and situational influences on stress and coping. *Journal of Personality & Social Psychology, 84*(1), 234–252.

Durbin, D. L., Darling, N., Steinberg, L., & Brown, B. B. (1993). Parenting style and peer group membership among European American adolescents. *Journal of Research on Adolescence, 3*(1), 87–100.

Dweck, C. S. (2002a). Messages that motivate: How praise molds students' beliefs, motivation, and performance (in surprising ways). In J. Aronson, (Ed.), *Improving academic achievement: Impact of psychological factors on education* (pp. 37–60). San Diego: Academic Press.

Dweck, C. S. (2002b). The development of ability conceptions. In A. Wigfield & J. S. Eccles (Eds.), *Development of achievement motivation* (pp. 57–88). San Diego: Academic Press.

Dweck, C. S. (2002b). The development of ability conceptions. In A. Wigfield & J. S. Eccles (Eds.), *Development of achievement motivation* (pp. 57–88). San Diego: Academic Press.

E

Eagle, M. (2000). Repression, part I of II. *Psychoanalytic Review, 87*(1), 1–38.

Easterlin, R. A. (2002). Is reported happiness five years ago comparable to present happiness? A cautionary note. *Journal of Happiness Studies, 3*(2), 193–198.

Ebbinghaus, H. (1913). *Memory: A contribution to experimental psychology.* (H. A. Roger & C. E. Bussenius, Trans.). New York: Columbia University Press. (Original work published 1885).

Eberly, M. B., & Montemayor, R. (1999). Adolescent affection and helpfulness toward parents: A 2–year follow-up. *Journal of Early Adolescence, 19*(2), 226–248.

Egawa, T., et al. (2002). Impairment of spatial memory in kaolin-induced hydrocephalic rats is associated with changes in the hippocampal cholinergic and noradrenergic contents. *Behavioural Brain Research, 129*(1–2), 31–39.

Egerton, A., Allison, C., Brett, R. R., & Pratt, J. A. (2006). Cannabinoids and prefrontal cortical function: Insights from preclinical studies. *Neuroscience & Biobehavioral Reviews, 30*(5), 680–695.

Eichenbaum, H., & Fortin, N. (2003). Episodic memory and the hippocampus: It's about time. *Current Directions in Psychological Science,* 12(2), 53–57.

Ekman, P. (1999). Facial expressions. In T. Dalgleish & M. J. Power (Eds.), *Handbook of cognition and emotion* (pp. 301–320). New York: John Wiley & Sons.

Ekman, P. (2003). Cited in Foreman, J. (2003, August 5). A conversation with: Paul Ekman: The 43 facial muscles that reveal even the most fleeting emotions. *The New York Times online.*

Ekman, P., et al. (1987). Universals and cultural differences in the judgments of facial expressions of emotion. *Journal of Personality and Social Psychology, 53,* 712–717.

Elkind, D. (1967). Egocentrism in adolescence. *Child Development, 38,* 1025–1034.

Elkind, D. (1985). Egocentrism redux. *Developmental Review, 5,* 218–226.

Elkind, D., & Bowen, R. (1979). Imaginary audience behavior in children and adolescents. *Developmental Psychology, 15*(1), 38–44.

Ellickson, P. L., Tucker, J. S., Klein, D. J., & McGuigan, K. A. (2001). Prospective risk factors for alcohol misuse in late adolescence. *Journal of Studies on Alcohol, 62*(6), 773–782.

Ellis, A. (2004a). How my theory and practice of psychotherapy has influenced and changed other psychotherapies. *Journal of Rational-Emotive & Cognitive Behavior Therapy, 22*(2), 79–83.

Ellis, A. (2004b). Why rational emotive behavior therapy is the most comprehensive and effective form of behavior therapy. *Journal of Rational- Emotive & Cognitive Behavior Therapy, 22*(2), 85–92.

Ellsworth, P. C., Carlsmith, J. M., & Henson, A. (1972). The stare as a stimulus to flight in human subjects. *Journal of Personality and Social Psychology, 21,* 302–311.

Emmons, R. A., & King, L. A. (1988). Conflict among personal strivings: Immediate and longterm implications for psychological and physical well-being. *Journal of Personality & Social Psychology, 54*(6), 1040–1048.

Enard, W., et al. (2002). Molecular evolution of FOXP2, a gene involved in speech and language. *Nature, 418*(6900), 869–872.

Engels, G. I., Garnefski, N., & Diekstra, R. F. W. (1993). Efficacy of rational-emotive therapy. *Journal of Consulting and Clinical Psychology, 61,* 1083–1090.

Erikson, E. H. (1963). *Childhood and society.* New York: W. W. Norton.

Eron, L. D. (1982). Parent–child interaction, television violence, and aggression of children. *American Psychologist, 37,* 197–211.

Eron, L. D. (2000). A psychological perspective. In V. B. Van Hasselt & M. Hersen, (Eds.), *Aggression and violence: An introductory text* (pp. 23–39). Needham Heights, MA: Allyn & Bacon.

Erskine, A., Markham, R., & Howie, P. (2001). Children's script-based inferences: Implications for eyewitness testimony. *Cognitive Development, 16*(4), 871–887.

Eslinger, P. J., Flaherty-Craig, C. V., & Benton, A. L. (2004). Developmental outcomes after early prefrontal cortex damage. *Brain & Cognition, 55*(1), 84–403.

Evans, L., et al. (2005). Familiality of temperament in bipolar disorder: Support for a genetic spectrum. *Journal of Affective Disorders, 85*(1–2), 153–168.

Evans, S. W., et al. (2001). Dose-response effects of methylphenidate on ecologically valid measures of academic performance and classroom behavior in adolescents with ADHD. *Experimental & Clinical Psychopharmacology, 9*(2), 163–175.

Eysenck, H. J., & Eysenck, M. W. (1985). *Personality and individual differences.* New York: Plenum.

F

Fairburn, C. G., & Harrison, P. J. (2003). Eating disorders. *The Lancet, 361,* 407. This article is an in-depth look at anorexia and bulimia including diagnostic criteria and treatment options.

Fantz, R. L. (1961). The origin of form perception. *Scientific American, 204*(5), 66–72.

Farber, B. A., Brink, D. C., & Raskin, P. M. (1996). *The psychotherapy of Carl Rogers: Cases and commentary* (pp. 74–75). New York: Guilford Press.

Farmer, A., Eley, T. C., & McGuffin, P. (2005). Current strategies for investigating the genetic and environmental risk factors for affective disorders. *British Journal of Psychiatry, 186*(3), 179–181.

Farooqi, I. S., et al. (2003). Clinical spectrum of obesity and mutations in the melanocortin 4 receptor gene. *New England Journal of Medicine, 348*(12), 1085–1095.

Favaro, A. (2005). The relationship between temperament and impulsive behaviors in eating disordered subjects. *Eating Disorders: The Journal of Treatment & Prevention, 13*(1), 61–70.

Feeney, B. C. (2004). A secure base: Responsive support of goal strivings and exploration in adult intimate relationships. *Journal of Personality & Social Psychology, 87*(5), 631–648. Lever, J. P. (2004). Poverty and subjective well-being in Mexico. *Social Indicators Research, 68*(1), 1–33.

Feingold, A. (1992a). Gender differences in mate selection preferences. *Psychological Bulletin, 112,*

Festinger, L., & Carlsmith, J. M. (1959). Cognitive consequences of forced compliance. *Journal of Abnormal and Social Psychology, 58,* 203–210.

Fields, R. D. (2005, February). Making memories stick. *Scientific American,* 75–81.

Fifer, W. P., & Moon, C. (2003). Prenatal development. In A. Slater & G. Bremner (Eds.), *An introduction to developmental psychology* (pp. 95–114). Malden, MA: Blackwell Publishers.

Finkenauer, C., et al. (1998). Flashbulb memories and the underlying mechanisms of their formation: Toward an emotional-integrative model. *Memory & Cognition, 26*(3), 516–531.

Fisher, H. E. (2000). Brains do it: Lust, attraction and attachment. *Cerebrum, 2,* 23–42.

Flavell, J. H. (2000). Development of children's knowledge about the mental world. *International Journal of Behavioral Development, 24*(1), 15–23.

Flegal, K. M., Carroll, M. D., Ogden, C. L., & Curtin, L. R. (2010). Prevalence and trends in obesity among U.S. adults, 1999-2008. *Journal of the American Medical Association, 303*(3), 235-241.

Flegal, K. M., Carroll, M. D., Ogden, C. L., & Johnson, C. L. (2002). Prevalence and trends in obesity among U.S. adults, 1999–2000. *Journal of the American Medical Association, 288*(14), 1723–1727.

Fletcher, B., Pine, K. J., Woodbridge, Z., & Nash, A. (2007). How visual images of chocolate affect the craving and guilt of female dieters. *Appetite, 48*(2), 211–217.

Flett, G. L., Madorsky, D., Hewitt, P. L., & Heisel, M. J. (2002). Perfectionism cognitions, rumination, and psychological distress. *Journal of Rational-Emotive & Cognitive Behavior Therapy, 20*(1), 33–47.

Flouri, E., & Buchanan, A. (2003). The role of father involvement and mother involvement in adolescents' psychological well-being. *British Journal of Social Work, 33*(3), 399–406.

Foerster, J., Higgins, E. T., & Strack, F. (2000). When stereotype disconfirmation is a personal threat: How prejudice and prevention focus moderate incongruency effects. *Social Cognition, 18*(2), 178–197.

Folkman, S., & Moskowitz, T. (2000). Positive affect and the other side of coping. *American Psychologist, 55*(6), 647–654.

Follingstad, D., & McCormick, M. (2002). *Law and mental health professionals.* Washington, DC: American Psychological Association.

Fontaine, K. R., Redden, D. T., Wang, C., Westfall, A. O., & Allison, D. B. (2003). Years of life lost due to obesity. *Journal of the American Medical Association, 289(2),* 187–193.

Förster, J., Higgins, E. T., & Werth, L. (2004). How threat from stereotype disconfirmation triggers self-defense. *Social Cognition,* 22(1), 54–74.

Fortin, S., Godbout, L., & Braun, C. M. J. (2002). Strategic sequence planning and prospective memory impairments in frontally lesioned head trauma patients performing activities of daily living. *Brain & Cognition, 48*(2–3), 361–365.

Fouts, R. S. (1997). *Next of kin: What chimpanzees have taught me about who we are.* New York: Morrow.

Francis, L. J., Katz, Y. J., Yablon, Y., & Robbins, M. (2004). Religiosity, personality, and happiness: A study among Israeli male undergraduates. *Journal of Happiness Studies, 5(4),* 315–333.

Freeman, M. S., Spence, M. J., & Oliphant, C. M. (1993, June). *Newborns prefer their mothers' lowpass filtered voices over other female filtered voices.* Paper presented at the annual convention of the American Psychological Society, Chicago.

Freese, T. E., Miotto, K., & Reback, C. J. (2002). The effects and consequences of selected club drugs. *Journal of Substance Abuse Treatment, 23*(2), 151–156.

Freud, S. (1998). The baby and the bathwater: Some thoughts on Freud as a postmodernist. *Families in Society: The Journal of Contemporary Human Services, 79,* 455–464. This article suggests that there are aspects of Freud's theory that continue to have relevance today.

Freud, S. (1927). A religious experience. In *Standard edition of the complete psychological works of Sigmund Freud* (Vol. 21). London: Hogarth Press, 1964.

Friedman, M., & Ulmer, D. (1984). *Treating Type A behavior and your heart.* New York: Fawcett Crest.

Frisch, R. (1997). Cited in Angier, N. (1997). Chemical tied to fat control could help trigger puberty. *The New York Times,* pp. C1, C3.

Fritsch, G., & Hitzig, E. (1960). On the electrical excitability of the cerebrum. In G. von Bonin (Ed.), *Some papers on the cerebral cortex.* Springfield, IL: Charles C. Thomas. (Original work published 1870)

Fromme, K., et al. (2004). Biological and behavioral markers of alcohol sensitivity. *Alcoholism: Clinical & Experimental Research, 28*(2), 247–256.

Fuertes, A., et al. (2002). Factores asociados a las conductas sexuales de reigso en la adolencia. *Infancia y Aprendizaje, 25*(3), 347–361.

Fuligni, A. J., & Witkow, M. (2004). The postsecondary educational progress of youth from immigrant families. *Journal of Research on Adolescence, 14*(2), 159–183.

Furnham, A., Petrides, K. V., Sisterson, G., & Baluch, B. (2003). Repressive coping style and positive self-presentation. *British Journal of Health Psychology, 8*(2), 223–249.

Fuster, J. M. (2000). The prefrontal cortex of the primate: A synopsis. *Psychobiology, 28*(2), 125–131.

G

Gaab, J., Rohleder, N., Nater, U. M., & Ehlert, U. (2005). Psychological determinants of the cortisol stress response: The role of anticipatory cognitive appraisal. *Psychoneuroendocrinology, 30*(6), 599–610.

Gais, S., & Born, J. (2004). Declarative memory consolidation: Mechanisms acting during human sleep. *Learning & Memory, 11*(6), 679–685.

Galambos, N. L., Barker, E. T., & Almeida, D. M. (2003). Parents do matter: Trajectories of change in externalizing and internalizing problems in early adolescence. *Child Development, 74*(2), 578–594.

Garb, H. N., Wood, J. M., Lilienfeld, S. O., & Nezworski, M. T. (2005). Roots of the Rorschach controversy. *Clinical Psychology Review, 25*(1), 97–118.

Garcia, J., & Koelling, R. A. (1966). Relation of cue to consequences in avoidance learning. *Psychonomic Science 4,* 123–124.

Gould, S. J. (2002). *The structure of evolutionary theory.* Cambridge, MA: Belknap Press /Harvard University Press.

Garcia, J., Brett, L. P., & Rusiniak, K. W. (1989). Limits of Darwinian conditioning. In S. B. Klein & R. R. Mowrer (Eds.), *Contemporary learning theories: Instrumental conditioning theory and the impact of biological constraints on learning.* Hillsdale, NJ: Erlbaum.

Gardner, H. (1983/1993). *Frames of mind.* New York: Basic Books.

Gardner, H. (2001, April 5). Multiple intelligence. *The New York Times,* p. A20.

Gay, M., Philippot, P., & Luminet, O. (2002). Differential effectiveness of psychological interventions for reducing osteoarthritis pain: A comparison of Erickson hypnosis and Jacobson relaxation. *European Journal of Pain, 6*(1), 1–16.

Gay, P. (1999). Psychoanalyst: Sigmund Freud. *Time, 153,* 66. This article summarizes the work of Sigmund Freud and the contributions he made to psychology and the world.

Geers, A., Spehar, B., & Sedey, A. (2002). Use of speech by children from total communication programs who wear cochlear implants. *American Journal of Speech-Language Pathology, 11*(1), 50–58.

Gegenfurtner, K. R., & Kiper, D. C. (2003). Color vision. *Annual Review of Neuroscience, 26,* 181–206.

Gendall, K. A., Bulik, C. M., Joyce, P. R., McIntosh, V. V., &

Carter, F. A. (2000). Menstrual cycle irregularity in bulimia nervosa: Associated factors and changes with treatment. *Journal of Psychosomatic Research, 49*(6), 409–415.

Gentry, M. V., et al. (2000). Nicotine patches improve mood and response speed in a lexical decision task. *Addictive Behaviors, 25*(4), 549–557.

Gershoff, E. T. (2002). Corporal punishment by parents and associated child behaviors and experiences: A meta-analytic and theoretical review. *Psychological Bulletin, 128*(4), 539–579.

Gershon, J., Zimand, E., Pickering, M., Rothbaum, B. O., & Hodges, L. (2004). A pilot and feasibility study of virtual reality as a distraction for children with cancer. *Journal of the American Academy of Child & Adolescent Psychiatry, 43*(10), 1243–1249. Video games calm kids before surgery. (2004, December 10). Associated Press.

Geschwind, N., & Galaburda, A. M. (1987). *Cerebral lateralization: Biological mechanisms, associations, and pathology.* Cambridge, MA: Harvard University Press.

Getzels, J. W., & Jackson, P. W. (1962). *Creativity and intelligence.* New York: Wiley.

Gignac, G., & Vernon, P. A. (2003). Digit symbol rotation: A more g-loaded version of the traditional digit symbol subtest. *Intelligence, 31*(1), 1–8.

Gigone, D., & Hastie, R. (1997). Proper analysis of the accuracy of group judgments. *Psychological Bulletin, 121,* 149–167.

Gijsman, H. J., et al. (2002). A dose-finding study on the effects of branch chain amino acids on surrogate markers of brain dopamine function. *Psychopharmacology, 160*(2), 192–197.

Gill, T. M., DiPietro, L., & Krumholz, H. M. (2000). Role of exercise stress testing and safety monitoring for older persons starting an exercise person. *Journal of the American Medical Association, 284,* 342–349.

Gilligan, C. (1982). *In a different voice.* Cambridge, MA: Harvard University Press.

Gilligan, C., Ward, J. V., & Taylor, J. M. (1989). *Mapping the moral domain: A contribution of women's thinking to psychological theory and education.* Cambridge, MA: Harvard University Press.

Gilovich, T., & Eibach, R. (2001). The fundamental attribution error where it really counts. *Psychological Inquiry, 12*(1), 23–26.

Gilovich, T., et al. (Eds.). (2002). *Heuristics and biases: The psychology of intuitive judgment* (pp. 348–366). New York: Cambridge University Press.

Glantz, L. A., & Lewis, D. A. (2000). Decreased dendritic spine density on prefrontal cortical pyramidal neurons in schizophrenia. *Archives of General Psychiatry, 57*(1), 65–73.

Glaser, R., et al. (1993). Stress and the memory Tcell response to the Epstein-Barr virus. *Health Psychology, 12,* 435–442.

Godfrey, J. R. (2004). Toward optimal health: The experts discuss therapeutic humor. *Journal of Women's Health, 13*(5), 474–479.

Goldman-Rakic, P. S. (1995). Cited in Goleman, D. (1995, May 2). Biologists find site of working memory. *The New York Times,* pp. C1, C9.

Goldman-Rakic, P. S., et al. (2000b). Memory. In M. S. Gazzaniga (Ed.), *The new cognitive neurosciences* (2nd ed., pp. 733–840). Cambridge, MA: MIT Press.

Goldman-Rakic, P. S., Muly, E. C., III, & Williams, G. V. (2000a). D-sub-1 receptors in prefrontal cells and circuits. *Brain Research Reviews, 31*(2–3), 295–301.

Goldstein, E. B. (2004). *Sensation and perception, media edition.* (6th ed.). Belmont, CA: Wadsworth Publishing Company.

Goleman, D. J. (1995). *Emotional intelligence.* New York: Bantam Books.

Gomez, P., Zimmermann, P., Guttormsen-Schär, S., & Danuser, B. (2005). Respiratory responses associated with affective processing of film stimuli. *Biological Psychology, 68*(3), 223–235.

Gonzalez, C., Dana, J., Koshino, H., & Just, M. (2005). The framing effect and risky decisions: Examining cognitive functions with fMRI. *Journal of Economic Psychology, 26*(1), 1–20.

Goode, E. (2000, June 25). Thinner: The male battle with anorexia. *The New York Times,* p. MH8.

Goodenough, F. L., & Harris, D. B. (1950). Studies in the psychology of children's drawings: II 1928–1949. *Psychological Bulletin, 47,* 369–433.

Goodwin, P. J., et al. (2001). The effect of group psychosocial support on survival in metastatic breast cancer. *New England Journal of Medicine, 345*(24), 1719–1726.

Gordon, B. N., Baker-Ward, L., & Ornstein, P. A. (2001). Children's testimony: A review of research on memory for past experiences. *Clinical Child & Family Psychology Review, 4*(2), 157–181.

Gorman, J. M. (2001). A call to action: Overcoming anxiety through active coping. *American Journal of Psychiatry, 158*(12), 1953–1955.

Gorodetsky, M., & Klavir, R. (2003). What can we learn from how gifted /average pupils describe their processes of problem solving? *Learning & Instruction, 13*(3), 305–325.

Gottesman, I. I. (1991). *Schizophrenia genesis.* New York: Freeman.

Grady, C. L., McIntosh, A. R., Rajah, M. N., Beig, S., & Craik, F. I. M. (1999). The effects of age on the neural correlates of episodic encoding. *Cerebral Cortex, 9*(8), 805–814.

Granot, D., & Mayseless, O. (2001). Attachment security and adjustment to school in middle childhood. *International Journal of Behavioral Development, 25*(6), 530–541.

Greenberg, J. (1985). Small family size has a number of apparently positive effects on a child's intellectual development. *Science News, 127*(22), 340–341.

Greenberger, E., Chen, C., Tally, S. R., & Dong, Q. (200). Family, peer, and individual correlates of depressive symptomology among U.S. and Chinese adolescents. *Journal of Consulting and Clinical Psychology, 68,* 209–219.

Griffin, C. (2001). Imagining new narratives of youth. Childhood: *A Global Journal of Child Research,* 8(2), 147–166.

Griffin, K. W., Botvin, G. J., Nichols, T. R., & Scheier, L. M. (2004). Low perceived chances for success in life and binge drinking among inner-city minority youth. *Journal of Adolescent Health, 34*(6), 501–507.

Griffin, M. G. (2008). A prospective assessment of auditory startle alterations in rape and physical assault survivors. *Journal of Traumatic Stress, 21*(1), 91–99.

Gross, R. (2002). The prison simulation experiment. *Psychology Review, 8,* 15–17. This article summarizes the classic prison simulation study conducted by Zimbardo.

Grusec, J. E. (2002). Parenting socialization and children's acquisition of values. In M. H. Bornstein (Ed.), *Handbook of parenting: Vol. 5: Practical issues in parenting* (2nd ed., pp. 143–167).

Guerin, B. (1999). Social behaviors as determined by different arrangements of social consequences: Social loafing, social facilitation, deindividuation, and a modified social loafing. *Psychological Record, 49*(4), 565–578.

Guidetti, M. & Nikoladis, E. (2008). Gestures and communication development. *First Language, 28*(2), 107-115.

Gupta, V. B., Nwosa, N. M., Nadel, T. A., & Inamdar, S. (2001). Externalizing behaviors and television viewing in children of low-income minority parents. *Clinical Pediatrics, 40*(6), 337–341.

H

Haaga, D. A. F., & Davison, G. C. (1993). An appraisal of rational-emotive therapy. *Journal of Consulting and Clinical Psychology, 61,* 215–220.

Habib, M., & Robichon, F. (2003). Structural correlates of brain asymmetry: Studies in left-handed and dyslexic individuals. In K. Hugdahl & R. J. Davidson (Eds.), *The asymmetrical brain* (pp. 681–716). Cambridge, MA: MIT Press.

Haenen, J. (2001). Outlining the teaching–learning process: Piotr Gal'perin's contribution. *Learning & Instruction, 11*(2), 157–170.

Hakim, A. A., et al. (1998). Effects of walking on mortality among nonsmoking retired men. *New England Journal of Medicine, 338,* 94–99.

Hall, Calvin S. *The Meaning of Dreams.* New York: Harper & Brothers, 1953

Halpern, D. F. (2003). Sex differences in cognitive abilities. *Applied Cognitive Psychology, 17*(3), 375–376

Halpern, D. F., & LaMay, M. L. (2000). The smarter sex: A critical review of sex differences in intelligence. *Educational Psychology Review, 12*(2), 229–246.

Halpern, D. F., Hansen, C., & Riefer, D. (1990). Analogies as an aid to understanding and memory. *Journal of Educational Psychology, 82,* 298–305.

Hamilton, N. A., Karoly, P., & Kitzman, H. (2004). Self-regulation and chronic pain: The role of emotion. *Cognitive Therapy & Research, 28*(5), 559–576.

Han, W., Leventhal, T., & Linver, M. R. (2004). The Home Observation for Measurement of the Environment (HOME) in middle childhood: A study of three large-scale data sets. *Parenting: Science & Practice, 4*(2–3), 189–210.

Hankin, B. L., & Abramson, L. Y. (2001). Development of gender differences in depression: An elaborated cognitive vulnerability-transactional stress theory. *Psychological Bulletin, 127*(6), 773–796.

Hankin, B. L., Fraley, R. C., & Abela, J. R. Z. (2005). Daily depression and cognitions about cognitive style and the prediction of depressive symptoms in a prospective daily diary study. *Journal of Personality and Social Psychology, 88*(4), 673–685.

Hansell, N. K., et al. (2001). Genetic influence on ERP slow wave measures of working memory. *Behavior Genetics, 31*(6), 603–614.

Haridakis, P. M. (2002). Viewer characteristics, exposure to television violence, and aggression. *Media Psychology, 4*(4), 323–352.

Harker, L., & Keltner, D. (2001). Expressions of positive emotion in women's college yearbook pictures and their relationship to personality and life outcomes across adulthood. *Journal of Personality and Social Psychology, 80*(1), 112–124.

Harley, K., & Reese, E. (1999). Origins of autobiographical memory. *Developmental Psychology, 35*(5), 1338–1348.

Harlow, H. F. (1959). Love in infant monkeys. *Scientific American, 200,* 68–86.

Harlow, J. M. (1868). Recovery from the passage of an iron bar through the head. *Publication of the Massachusetts Medical Society, 2,* 327.

Hart, J. W., Bridgett, D. J., & Karau, S. J. (2001). Coworker ability and effort as determinants of individual effort on a collective task. *Group Dynamics, 5*(3), 181–190.

Hawkley, L. C., & Cacioppo, J. T. (2004). Stress and the aging immune system. *Brain, Behavior & Immunity, 18*(2), 114–119.

Health, United States (2002). http:/www.cdc.gov/ nchs (National Center for Health Statistics).

Heber, D. (2010). An integrative view of obesity. *American Journal of Clinical Nutrition 91*(1), 280S-283S.

Heidenreich, P. A. (2003). Understanding and modifying physician behavior for prevention and management of cardiovascular disease. *Journal of General Internal Medicine, 18*(12), 1060–1061.

Heidenreich, T., & Michalak, J. (2003). Mindfulness as a treatment principle in behavior therapy. *Verhaltenstherapie, 13(4),* 264–274.

Heimpel, S. A., Wood, J. V., Marshall, M. A., & Brown, J. D. (2002). Do people with low self-esteem really want to feel better? Self-esteem differences in motivation to repair negative moods. *Journal of Personality & Social Psychology, 82*(1), 128–147.

Heinrichs, R. W. (2005). The primacy of cognition in schizophrenia. *American Psychologist, 60*(3), 229–242.

Heinz, A. (2004). Reward and dependence—A psychological and neurobiological analysis of reward mechanisms and of their role in dependence (European University Studies, Vol. 685). *Addiction, 99*(11), 1482.

Helms, J. E. (1992). Why is there no study of cultural equivalence of standardized cognitive ability testing? *American Psychologist, 47,* 1083–1101.

Hensley, W. E. (1981). The effects of attire, location, and sex on aiding behavior. *Journal of Nonverbal Behavior, 6,* 3–11.

Herbert, B. (2005, September 26). A waking nightmare. *The New York Times online.*

Hergenhahn, B. R. (2009). *History of psychology* (6th ed.). Belmont, CA: Wadsworth Publishing Company.

Hertz-Pannier, L., et al. (2002). Late plasticity for language in a child's non-dominant hemisphere: A pre- and post-surgery fMRI study. *Brain, 125*(2), 361–372.

Hill, W. L., Ballard, S., Coyer, M. J., & Rowley, T. (2005). The interaction of testosterone and breeding phase on the reproductive behavior and use of space of male zebra finches. *Hormones & Behavior, 47*(4), 452–458.

Hingson, R., et al. (2002). A call to action: Changing the culture of drinking at U.S. colleges. National Institutes of Health: National Institute of Alcohol Abuse and Alcoholism. Washington, DC.

Hobson, J. A. (2003). *Dreaming: An introduction to the science of sleep.* New York: Oxford University Press.

Hoff, E. (2005). *Language development* (3rd ed.). Belmont, CA: Wadsworth Publishing Company.

Hoge, C. W., et al. (2004). Combat duty in Iraq and Afghanistan, mental health problems, and barriers to care. *New England Journal of Medicine, 351*(1), 13–22.

Hohwy, J., & Frith, C. (2004). Can neuroscience explain consciousness? *Journal of Consciousness Studies, 11*(7–8), 180–198.

Holland, J. L. (1996). Exploring careers with a typology. *American Psychologist, 51,* 397–406.

Hollinger, L. M., & Buschmann, M. B. (1993).Factors influencing the perception of touch by elderly nursing home residents and their health caregivers. *International Journal of Nursing Studies, 30,* 445–461.

Hollingshead, A. B., & Redlich, F. C. (1958). *Social class and mental illness.* New York: Wiley.

Hollon, S. D., et al. (2005). Prevention of relapse following cognitive therapy vs. medications in moderate to severe depression. *Archives of General Psychiatry, 62*(4), 417–422.

Holmes, M. M., Putz, O., Crews, D., & Wade, J. (2005). Normally occurring intersexuality and testosterone induced plasticity in the copulatory system of adult leopard geckos. *Hormones & Behavior, 47*(4), 439–445.

Holmes, T. H., & Rahe, R. H. (1967). The social readjustment rating scale. *Journal of Psychosomatic Research, 11,* 213–218.

Honorton, C. (1985). Meta-analysis of psi Ganzfeld research.

Journal of Parapsychology, 49, 51–91.

Honorton, C., et al. (1990). Psi communication in the Ganzfeld. *Journal of Parapsychology, 54,* 99–139.

Honts, C. R., Hodes, R. L., & Raskin, D. C. (1985). Effects of physical countermeasures on the physiological detection of deception. *Journal of Applied Psychology, 70*(1), 177–187.

Hoover, R. N. (2000). Cancer: Nature, nurture, or both. *New England Journal of Medicine, 343,* 135–136.

Hopkins, R. A., & Powers, T. L. (2009). Development and test of new dimensions of altruistic buying behavior. *Journal of Consumer Marketing, 26*(3), 185-199.

Horgan, O., & MacLachlan, M. (2004). Psychosocial adjustment to lower-limb amputation: A review. *Disability & Rehabilitation: An International Multidisciplinary Journal, 26*(14–15), 837–850.

Horn, J. M. (1983). The Texas adoption project. *Child Development, 54,* 268–275.

Hornstein, E. P., Verweij, J., & Schnapf, J. L. (2004). Electrical coupling between red and green cones in primate retina. *Nature Neuroscience, 7*(7), 745–750.

Horowitz, T. S., Cade, B. E., Wolfe, J. M., & Czeisler, C. A. (2003). Searching night and day: A dissociation of effects of circadian phase and time awake on visual selective attention and vigilance. *Psychological Science, 14*(6), 549–557.

Hoybye, M. T., Johansen, C., & Tjornhoj-Thomsen, T. (2005). Online interaction. Effects of storytelling in an Internet breast cancer support group. *Psycho-Oncology, 14*(3), 211–220.

Huesmann, L. R., Moise-Titus, J., Podolski, C., & Eron, L. D. (2003). Longitudinal relations between children's exposure to TV violence and their aggressive and violent behavior in young adulthood: 1977–1992. *Developmental Psychology, 39*(2), 201–221.

Hulshoff, P., et al. (2000). Prenatal exposure to famine and brain morphology in schizophrenia. *American Journal of Psychiatry, 157*(7), 1170–1172.

Human Genome Sequencing Consortium. (2004, October 29). Cited in "Number of genes in human genome lower than previously estimated." News Office, Massachusetts Institute of Technology. http://web.mit.edu /newsoffice/ 2004/ humangenome.html.

Hunter, B.T. (2002). How food communicates with your taste buds: The chemistry of perception. *Consumers' Research Magazine, 85,* 26–28. This article describes the complex interaction of taste and smell. The article also discusses taste modifiers and blockers.

Huskinson, T. L. H., & Haddock, G. (2004). Individual differences in attitude structure: Variance in the chronic reliance on affective and cognitive information. *Journal of Experimental Social Psychology, 40*(1), 82–90.

Hvas, L., Reventlow, S., & Malterud, K. (2004). Women's needs and wants when seeing the GP in relation to menopausal issues. *Scandinavian Journal of Primary Health Care, 22*(2), 118–121.

Hwu, H., Liu, C., Fann, C. S., Ou-Yang, W., & Lee, S. F. (2003).

Linkage of schizophrenia with chromosome 1q loci in Taiwanese families. *Molecular Psychiatry, 8*(4), 445–452.

Hyde, J. S., & Plant, E. A. (1995). Magnitude of psychological gender differences. *American Psychologist, 50,* 159–161.

Hypnosis: Theory and application Part I. (2002, May). *Harvard Mental Health Letter, 18,* NA. This article discusses the theoretical component to hypnosis including subject experience and hypnotizability.

Hypnosis: Theory and application Part II. (2002, June). *Harvard Mental Health Letter, 18,* NA. This article continues the series on hypnosis and discusses hypnotherapy, hypnosis used to control pain and hypnosis and memory.

I

Iacono, W. G., & Lykken, D. T. (1997). The validity of the lie detector: Two surveys of scientific opinion. *Journal of Applied Psychology, 82*(3), 426–433.

Iidaka, T., Anderson, N. D., Kapur, S., Cabeza, R., & Craik, F. I. M. (2000). The effect of divided attention on encoding and retrieval in episodic memory revealed by positron emission tomography. *Journal of Cognitive Neuroscience, 12*(2), 267–280.

Inhelder, B., & Piaget, J. (1958). *The growth of logical thinking from childhood to adolescence.* Chicago: University of Chicago Press.

Insel, T. R. (2000). Toward a neurobiology of attachment. *Review of General Psychology, 4*(2), 176–185.

Iribarren, C., et al. (2000). Association of hostility with coronary artery calcification in young adults: The CARDIA study. *Journal of the American Medical Association, 283,* 2546–2551.

Isabella, R. A. (1998). Origins of attachment: The role of context, duration, frequency of observation, and infant age in measuring maternal behavior. *Journal of Social & Personal Relationships, 15*(4), 538–554.

Isarida, T., & Isarida, T. (1999). Effects of contextual changes between class and intermission on episodic memory. *Japanese Journal of Psychology, 69*(6), 478–485.

Iverson, P., et al. (2003). A perceptual interference account of acquisition difficulties for non-native phonemes. *Cognition, 87*(1), B47–B57.

Ivey, A. E., & Brooks-Harris, J. E. (2005). Integrative psychotherapy with culturally diverse clients. In J. C. Norcross & M. R. Goldfried (Eds.), *Handbook of psychotherapy integration* (2nd ed., pp. 321–339). London: Oxford University Press.

Izard, C. E. (1984). Emotion-cognition relationships and human development. In C. E. Izard, J.

Izard, C. E. (1994). Basic emotions, relations among emotions, and emotion-cognition relations. *Psychological Bulletin, 115,* 561–565.

J

Jacks, J. Z., & Devine, P. G. (2000). Attitude importance, forewarning of message content, and resistance to persuasion.

Basic & Applied Social Psychology, 22(1), 19–29.

Jackson, H., & Nuttall, R. L. (2001). Risk for preadolescent suicidal behavior: An ecological model. *Child & Adolescent Social Work Journal, 18*(3), 189–203.

Jacoangeli, F., et al. (2002). Osteoporosis and anorexia nervosa: Relative role of endocrine alterations and malnutrition. *Eating & Weight Disorders, 7*(3), 190–195.

Jaffee, S., & Hyde, J. S. (2000). Gender differences in moral orientation. *Psychological Bulletin, 126*(5), 703–726.

James, L. E., & Burke, D. M. (2000). Phonological priming effects on word retrieval and tip-of-the tongue experiences in young and older adults. *Journal of Experimental Psychology— Learning, Memory, and Cognition, 26*(6), 1378–1391.

James, W. (1890). *The principles of psychology.* New York: Henry Holt.

Jamison, K. R. (2000). Suicide and bipolar disorder. *Journal of Clinical Psychiatry, 61*(Suppl. 9), 47–51.

Janis, I. L. (1982). *Groupthink* (2nd ed.). Boston: Houghton Mifflin.

Janowitz, H. D., & Grossman, M. I. (1949). Effects of variations in nutritive density on intake of food in dogs and cats. *American Journal of Physiology, 158,* 184–193. 1400–1402.

Janowsky, J. S., Chavez, B., & Orwoll, E. (2000). Sex steroids modify working memory. *Journal of Cognitive Neuroscience, 12,* 407–414.

Jemmott, J. B., et al. (1983). Academic stress, power motivation, and decrease in secretion rate of salivary secretory immunoglobin A. *Lancet, 1,* 1400–1402.

Jensen, M. P., et al. (2005). Hypnotic analgesia for chronic pain in persons with disabilities: A case series. *International Journal of Clinical & Experimental Hypnosis, 53*(2), 198–228.

Johnson, W., & Krueger, R. F. (2006). How money buys happiness: Genetic and environmental processes linking finances and life satisfaction. *Journal of Personality and Social Psychology, 90*(4) 680–691.

Johnston, L. D., O'Malley, P. M., Bachman, J. G. & Schulenberg, J. E. (2009). *Monitoring the future national results on adolescent drug use: Overview of key findings, 2008* (NIH Publication No. 09-7401). Bethesda, MD: National Institute on Drug Abuse

Jonsdottir, I. H., Hellstrand, K., Thoren, P., & Hoffman, P. (2000). Enhancement of natural immunity seen after voluntary exercise in rats. Role of central opioid receptors. *Life Sciences, 66*(13), 1231–1239.

Jorgensen, R. S., Johnson, B. T., Kolodziej, M. E., & Schreer, G. E. (1996). Elevated blood pressure and personality. *Psychological Bulletin, 120,* 293–320.

Journal of Happiness Studies, 2(2), 173–204.

K

Kaddour, J. (2003). Psychological endurance (hardiness): Definitional, nomological, and critical aspects. *European Review of Applied Psychology, 53*(3–4), 227–

237.

Kagan, & R. B. Zajonc (Eds.), *Emotions, cognition, and behavior.* New York: Cambridge University Press.

Kahneman, D., & Frederick, S. (2002). Representativeness revisited: Attribute substitution in intuitive judgment. In T. Gilovich, et al. (Eds.), *Heuristics and biases: The psychology of intuitive judgment* (pp. 49–81). New York: Cambridge University Press.

Kainz, K. (2002). A behavioral conditioning program for treatment of nocturnal enuresis. *Behavior Therapist, 25*(10), 185–187.

Kalin, N. H. (2003). Nonhuman primate studies of fear, anxiety, and temperament and the role of benzodiazepine receptors and GABA systems. *Journal of Clinical Psychiatry, 64*(Suppl. 3), 41–44.

Kallgren, C. A., Reno, R. R., & Cialdini, R. B. (2000). A focus theory of normative conduct: When norms do and do not affect behavior. *Personality & Social Psychology Bulletin, 26*(8), 1002–1012.

Kamalanabhan, T. J., Sunder, D. L., & Vasanthi, M. (2000). An evaluation of the Choice Dilemma Questionnaire as a measure of risk-taking propensity. *Social Behavior & Personality, 28*(2), 149–156.

Kandel, E. R. (2001). The molecular biology of memory storage: A dialogue between genes and synapses. *Science, 294,* 1030–1038.

Kapur, S. (2003). Psychosis as a state of aberrant salience: A framework linking biology, phenomenology, and pharmacology in schizophrenia. *American Journal of Psychiatry, 160*(1), 13–23.

Karlberg, L., et al. (1998). Is there a connection between car accidents, near accidents, and Type A drivers? *Behavioral Medicine, 24*(3), 99–106.

Karon, B. P., & Widener, A. (1998). Repressed memories: The real story. *Professional Psychology: Research & Practice, 29*(5), 482–487.

Karwautz, A., et al. (2001). Individual-specific risk factors for anorexia nervosa: A pilot study using a discordant sister-pair design. *Psychological Medicine, 31*(2), 317–329.

Kasai, K., et al. (2003). Progressive decrease of left Heschl gyrus and planum temporale gray matter volume in first-episode schizophrenia: A longitudinal magnetic resonance imaging study. *Archives of General Psychiatry, 60*(8), 766–775.

Kashima, Y. (2000). Maintaining cultural stereotypes in the serial reproduction of narratives. *Personality & Social Psychology Bulletin, 26*(5), 594–604.

Kaslow, N. J., et al., (2002). Risk and protective factors for suicidal behavior in abused African American women. *Journal of Consulting & Clinical Psychology, 70*(2), 311–319.

Kataria, S. (2004). A clinical guide to pediatric sleep: Diagnosis and management of sleep problems. *Journal of Developmental & Behavioral Pediatrics, 25*(2), 132–133.

Katigbak, M. S., Church, A. T., Guanzon- Lapena, M. A., Carlota, A. J., & del Pilar, G. H. (2002). Are indigenous personality dimensions culture specific? Philippine inventories and the five-factor model. *Journal of Personality & Social Psychology, 82*(1), 89–101.

Kauff, N. D., & Offit, K. (2007). Modeling genetic risk of breast cancer. *Journal of the American Medical Association, 297*, 2637–2639.

Kavanagh, K., et al. (2007). Characterization and heritability of obesity and associated risk factors in vervet monkeys. *Obesity, 15*(7), 1666–1674.

Kaye, W. H., et al. (2004). Genetic analysis of bulimia nervosa: Methods and sample description. *International Journal of Eating Disorders, 35*(4), 556–570.

Kazuomi Kario, J. E., et al. (2001). Gender differences in associations of diurnal blood pressure variation, awake physical activity, and sleep quality with negative affect: The Work Site Blood Pressure Study. *Hypertension, 38*, 997–1002.

Kéri, S. (2003). Genetics, psychology, and determinism. *American Psychologist, 58*(4), 319.

Keller, A., et al. (2003). Progressive loss of cerebellar volume in childhood-onset schizophrenia. *American Journal of Psychiatry, 160,* 128–133.

Keller, S., Maddock, J. E., Laforge, R. G., Velicer, W. F., & Basler, H-D. (2007). Binge drinking and health behavior in medical students. *Addictive Behaviors, 32*(3), 505–515.

Kellerman, J., Lewis, J., & Laird, J. D. (1989). Looking and loving: The effects of mutual gaze on feelings of romantic love. *Journal of Research in Personality, 23,* 145–161.

Kellman, P. J., & von Hofsten, C. (1992). The world of the moving infant. In C. Rovee-Collier & L. P. Lipsitt (Eds.), *Advances in Infancy Research* (Vol. 7). Norwood, NJ: Ablex.

Kendler, K. S., et al. (2000a). Illicit psychoactive substance use, heavy use, abuse, and dependence in a U.S. population-based sample of male twins. *Archives of General Psychiatry, 57,* 261–269.

Kendler, K. S., Myers, J., Prescott, C. A., & Neale, M. C. (2001). The genetic epidemiology of irrational fears and phobias in men. *Archives of General Psychiatry, 58*(3), 257–265.

Kendler, K. S., Thornton, L. M., Gilman, S. E., & Kessler, R. C. (2000c). Sexual orientation in a U.S. national sample of twin and nontwin sibling pairs. *American Journal of Psychiatry, 157,* 1843–1846.

Kennedy, C. H. (2002). Effects of REM sleep deprivation on a multiple schedule of appetitive reinforcement. *Behavioural Brain Research, 128*(2), 205–214.

Kerns, J. G., & Berenbaum, H. (2002). Cognitive impairments associated with formal thought disorder in people with schizophrenia. *Journal of Abnormal Psychology, 111*(2), 211–224.

Kessler, R. C., Berglund, P., Borges, G., Nock, M., & Wang, P. S. (2005b). Trends in suicide ideation, plans, gestures, and attempts in the United States, 1990–1992 to 2001–2003. *Journal of the American Medical Association, 293,* 2487–2495.

Kessler, R. C., Chiu, W. T., Demler, O., & Walters, E. E. (2005c).

Prevalence, severity, and comorbidity of 12-month *DSM–IV* disorders in the National Comorbidity Survey Replication. *Archives of General Psychiatry, 62*(6), 617–627.

Kessler, R. C., et al. (2005a) Lifetime prevalence and age-of-onset distributions of DSM–IV disorders in the National Comorbidity Survey Replication. *Archives of General Psychiatry, 62*(6), 593–602.

Keyes, C. L. M., & Goodman, S. H. (Eds.). (2006). *Women and depression: A handbook for the social, behavioral, and biomedical sciences.* New York: Cambridge University Press.

Keyes, C. L. M., & Haidt, J. (2003). *Flourishing: Positive psychology and the life well-lived.* Washington, DC: American Psychological Association.

Keyes, D. (1995). *The minds of Billy Milligan.* New York: Bantam Books.

Khan, A. A., Jacobson, K. C., Gardner, C. O., Prescott, C. A., & Kendler, K. S. (2005). Personality and comorbidity of common psychiatric disorders. *British Journal of Psychiatry, 186*(3), 190–196.

Kiecolt-Glaser, J. K., Marucha, P. T., Atkinson, C., & Glaser, R. (2001). Hypnosis as a modulator of cellular immune dysregulation during acute stress. *Journal of Consulting & Clinical Psychology, 69*(4), 674–682. *Annual Review of Psychology, 53*(1), 83–107.

Kiecolt-Glaser, J. K., McGuire, L., Robles, T. F., & Glaser, R. (2002a). Psychoneuroimmunology and psychosomatic medicine: Back to the future.

Kiecolt-Glaser, J. K., McGuire, L., Robles, T. F., & Glaser, R. (2002b). Emotions, morbidity, and mortality: New perspectives from psychoneuroimmunology.

Kihlstrom, J. F. (2002). No need for repression. *Trends in Cognitive Sciences, 6*(12), 502.

Kilshaw, D., & Annett, M. (1983). Right- and lefthand skill: Effects of age, sex, and hand preferences showing superior in left-handers. *British Journal of Psychology, 74,* 253–268.

Kim, B. S. K., Brenner, B. R., Liang, C. T. H., & Asay, P. A. (2003). A qualitative study of adaptation experiences of 1.5-generation Asian Americans. *Cultural Diversity & Ethnic Minority Psychology, 9*(2), 156–170.

Kim, K., & Rohner, R. P. (2002). Parental warmth, control, and involvement in schooling: Predicting academic achievement among Korean American adolescents. *Journal of Cross-Cultural Psychology, 33*(2), 127–140.

King, S. (2005). In Lake, M. (2005, May 2). Virtual reality heals 9/11 wounds. http://www.cnn.com/2005/TECH/04/29/spark.virtual /index.html.

Kingsbury, S.J. (1997). What is solution-focused therapy? *Harvard Mental Health Letter, 13,* 8. This article describes solution-focused therapy.

Kinsey, A. C., Pomeroy, W. B., & Martin, C. E. (1948). *Sexual behavior in the human male.* Philadelphia: W. B. Saunders.

Kinsey, A. C., Pomeroy, W. B., Martin, C. E., & Gebhard, P. H. (1953). *Sexual behavior in the human female.* Philadelphia:

W. B. Saunders.

Kirsch, I. (2000). The response set theory of hypnosis. *American Journal of Clinical Hypnosis, 42*(3–4), 274–292.

Kirsch, I., Lynn, S. J., Vigorito, M., & Miller, R. R. (2004). The role of cognition in classical and operant conditioning. *Journal of Clinical Psychology, 60*(4), 369–392.

Kirschenbaum, H., & Jourdan, A. (2005). The current status of Carl Rogers and the person-centered approach. *Psychotherapy: Theory, Research, Practice, Training, 42*(1), 37–51.

Klaczynski, P. A. (2001). Framing effects on adolescent task representations, analytic and heuristic processing and decision making. Implications for the normative /descriptive gap. *Journal of Applied Developmental Psychology, 22*(3), 289–309.

Kleinke, C. L. (1977). Compliance to requests made by gazing and touching experimenters in field settings. *Journal of Experimental Social Psychology, 13*, 218–223.

Kleinke, C. L. (1986). Gaze and eye contact. *Psychological Review, 100*, 78–100.

Kleinmuntz, B., & Szucko, J. J. (1984). Lie detection in ancient and modern times. *American Psychologist, 39*, 766–776.

Knafo, A., Iervolino, A. C., & Plomin, R. (2005). Masculine girls and feminine boys: Genetic and environmental contributions to atypical gender development in early childhood. *Journal of Personality & Social Psychology, 88*(2), 400–412.

Kobasa, S. C. O. (1990). Stress-resistant personality. In R. E. Ornstein & C. Swencionis (Eds.), *The healing brain* (pp. 219–230). New York: Guilford Press.

Kobasa, S. C. O., Maddi, S. R., Puccetti, M. C., & Zola, M. A. (1994). Effectiveness of hardiness, exercise, and social support as resources against illness. In A. Steptoe & J. Wardle (Eds.), *Psychosocial processes and health* (pp. 247–260).

Kohlberg, L. (1969). *Stages in the development of moral thought and action.* New York: Holt, Rinehart and Winston.

Kohlberg, L. (1981). *The philosophy of moral development.* San Francisco: Harper & Row.

Kooijman, C. M., et al. (2000). Phantom pain and phantom sensations in upper limb amputees: An epidemiological study. *Pain, 87*(1), 33–41.

Kopelman, M. D. (2002). Disorders of memory. *Brain, 125*(10), 2152–2190.

Koss, M. P., Figueredo, A. J., & Prince, R. J. (2002). Cognitive mediation of rape's mental, physical and social health impact: Tests of four models in cross-sectional data. *Journal of Consulting & Clinical Psychology, 70*(4), 926–941.

Kramer, P. D. (2003, June 22). Your Zoloft might prevent a heart attack. *The New York Times,* p. WK3.

Krantz, D. S., Contrada, R. J., Hill, D. R., & Friedler, E. (1988). Environmental stress and biobehavioral antecedents of coronary heart disease. *Journal of Consulting and Clinical Psychology, 56*, 333–341.

Krcmar, M., & Cooke, M. C. (2001). Children's moral reasoning and their perceptions of television violence. *Journal of Communication, 51*(2), 300–316.

Kroger, J. K., et al. (2002). Recruitment of anterior dorsolateral prefrontal cortex in human reasoning: A parametric study of relational complexity. *Cerebral Cortex, 12*(5), 477–485.

Kuczmarski, R. J., et al. (2000, December 4). CDC Growth charts: United States. Advance data from vital and health statistics, no. 314. Hyattsville, MD: National Center for Health Statistics.

Kwate, N. O. A. (2001). Intelligence or misorientation? Eurocentrism in the WICS-III. *Journal of Black Psychology, 27*(2), 221–238. Washington, DC: American Psychological Association.

L

Labiano, L. M., & Brusasca, C. (2002). Psychological treatments in arterial hypertension. *Interdisciplinaria, 19*(1), 85–97.

Lackner, J. M., Carosella, A. M., & Feuerstein, M. (1996). Pain expectancies, pain, and functional self-efficacy expectancies as determinants of disability in patients with chronic low back disorders. *Journal of Consulting and Clinical Psychology, 64*, 212–220.

Lahti, A. C., et al. (2001). Abnormal patterns of regional cerebral blood flow in schizophrenia with primary negative symptoms during an effortful auditory recognition task. *American Journal of Psychiatry, 158*, 1797–1808.

Lalumére, M. L., Blanchard, R., & Zucker, K. J. (2000). Sexual orientation and handedness in men and women: A meta-analysis. *Psychological Bulletin, 126*(4), 575–592.

Lam, A. G., & Sue, S. (2001). Client diversity. *Psychotherapy: Theory, Research, Practice, Training, 38*(4), 479–486.

Lang, A. R., Goeckner, D. J., Adesso, V. J., & Marlatt, G. A. (1975). Effects of alcohol on aggression in male social drinkers. *Journal of Abnormal Psychology, 84*, 508–518.

Lang, E. V., et al. (2000). Adjunctive non-pharmacological analgesia for invasive medical procedures: a randomised trial. *The Lancet, 355*, 1486–1490.

Lang, F. R., & Heckhausen, J. (2001). Perceived control over development and subjective wellbeing: Differential benefits across adulthood. *Journal of Personality & Social Psychology, 81*(3), 509–523.

Langlois, J. H., et al. (2000). Maxims or myths of beauty? A meta-analytic and theoretical review. *Psychological Bulletin, 126*(3), 390–423.

Lanier, S. A., Hayes, J. E., & Duffy, V. B. (2005). Sweet and bitter tastes of alcoholic beverages mediate alcohol intake in of-age undergraduates. *Physiology & Behavior, 83*(5), 821–831.

Larkin, M. (2000). Can lost hearing be restored? *The Lancet, 356*, 741–748.

Lashley, K. S. (1950). In search of the engram. In *Symposium of the Society for Experimental Biology* (Vol. 4). New York: Cambridge University Press.

Laumann, E. O., Gagnon, J. H., Michael, R. T., & Michaels,

S. (1994). *The social organization of sexuality.* Chicago: University of Chicago Press.

Lavee, Y., & Ben-Ari, A. (2003). Daily stress and uplifts during times of political tension: Jews and Arabs in Israel. *American Journal of Orthopsychiatry, 73*(1), 65–73.

Lavine, H., Lodge, M., & Freitas, K. (2005). Threat, authoritarianism, and selective exposure to information. *Political Psychology, 26*(2), 219–244.

Lawson, T. J., & Reardon, M. (1997). A humorous demonstration of in vivo systematic desensitization: The case of eraser phobia. *Teaching of Psychology, 24,* 270–271. This article describes a humorous teaching demonstration to aid students in their understanding of systematic desensitization.

Lazar, S. W., et al. (2000). Functional brain mapping of the relaxation response and meditation. *Neuroreport: For Rapid Communication of Neuroscience Research, 11*(7), 1581–1585.

Lazarus, R. S., DeLongis, A., Folkman, S., & Gruen, R. (1985). Stress and adaptational outcomes. *American Psychologist, 40,* 770–779.

Le Bon, G. (1960). *The crowd.* New York: Viking. (Original work published 1895)

Leahey, E., & Guo, G. (2001). Gender differences in mathematical trajectories. *Social Forces, 80*(2), 713–732.

Lecci, L., & Cohen, D. J. (2002). Perceptual consequences of an illness-concern induction and its relation to hypochondriacal tendencies. *Health Psychology, 21*(2), 147–156.

LeDoux, J. E. (1998). Fear and the brain: Where have we been, and where are we going? *Biological Psychiatry, 44*(12), 1229–1238.

LeDoux, J. E. (1998). Fear and the brain: Where have we been, and where are we going? *Biological Psychiatry, 44*(12), 1229–1238.

Lefcourt, H. M. (1997). Cited in Clay, R. A. (1997). Researchers harness the power of humor. *APA Monitor, 28*(9), 1, 18.

Lenneberg, E. H. (1967). *Biological foundations of language.* New York: Wiley.

Liebman, B., & Schardt, D. (2002). Tangled memories: Alzheimer's disease: The story so far. *Nutrition Action Healthletter, 29,* 1–8. This article discusses Alzheimer's disease including symptoms, possible causes and possible preventative measures.

Leitch, M. L. (2005, May 31). Just like bodies, psyches can drown in disasters. *The New York Times online.*

Lehman, B. J., & Crano, W. D. (2002). The pervasive effects of vested interest on attitude-criterion consistency in political judgment. *Journal of Experimental Social Psychology, 38*(2), 101–112.

Lensvelt-Mulders, G., & Hettema, J. (2001). Genetic analysis of autonomic reactivity to psychologically stressful situations. *Biological Psychology, 58*(1), 25–40.

Leonard, B. E. (2005). Mind over matter: Regulation of peripheral inflammation by the CNS. *Human Psychopharmacology: Clinical & Experimental, 20*(1), 71–72.

Leonard, S., Steiger, H., & Kao, A. (2003). Childhood and adulthood abuse in bulimic and nonbulimic women: Prevalences and psychological correlates. *International Journal of Eating Disorders, 33*(4), 397–405.

Leonardo, E. D., & Hen, R. (2006). Genetics of affective and anxiety disorders. *Annual Review of Psychology, 57,* 117–137.

Leor, J., Poole, K., & Kloner, R. A. (1996). Sudden cardiac death triggered by an earthquake. *New England Journal of Medicine, 334,* 413–419.

Leppel, K. (2002). Similarities and differences in the college persistence of men and women. *Review of Higher Education: Journal of the Association for the Study of Higher Education, 25*(4), 433–450.

Less sex, more protection, fewer pregnancies. (2004, March 7). *The New York Times,* p. 36N.

Lester, D., Yang, B., & Lindsay, M. (2004). Suicide bombers: Are psychological profiles possible?

Lever, J. P. (2004). Poverty and subjective well-being in Mexico. *Social Indicators Research, 68*(1), 1–33.

Levin, R., & Fireman, G. (2002). Nightmare prevalence, nightmare distress, and self-reported psychological disturbance. *Sleep: Journal of Sleep & Sleep Disorders Research, 25*(2), 205–212.

Levinson, D. J. (1996). *The seasons of a woman's life.* New York: Knopf.

Levinson, D. J., Darrow, C. N., Klein, E. B., Levinson, M. H., & McKee, B. (1978). *The seasons of a man's life.* New York: Knopf.

Levy, D., et al. (2000). Evidence for a gene influencing blood pressure on chromosome 17: Genome scan linkage results for longitudinal blood pressure phenotypes in subjects from the Framingham Heart Study. *Hypertension, 36,* 477–483.

Lewinsohn, P. M., Brown, R. A., Seeley, J. R., & Ramsey, S. E. (2000a). Psychological correlates of cigarette smoking abstinence, experimentation, persistence, and frequency during adolescence. *Nicotine & Tobacco Research, 2*(2), 121–131.

Li, G., Baker, S. P., Smialek, J. E., & Soderstrom, C. A. (2001). Use of alcohol as a risk factor for bicycling injury. *Journal of the American Medical Association, 284,* 893–896.

Li, W., & DeVries, S. H. (2004). Separate blue and green cone networks in the mammalian retina.

Lidow, M. S., et al. (2001). Antipsychotic treatment induces alterations in dendrite- and spine-associated proteins in dopamine-rich areas of the primate cerebral cortex. *Biological Psychiatry, 49*(1), 1–12.

Lieber, C. S. (1990). Cited in Barroom biology: How alcohol goes to a woman's head (January 14). *The New York Times,* p. E24.

Liebman, B., & Schardt, D. (2002). Tangled memories: Alzheimer's disease: The story so far. *Nutrition Action Healthletter, 29,* 1–8. This article discusses Alzheimer's disease including symptoms, possible causes and possible preventative measures.

Liederman, J., Kantrowitz, L., & Flannery, K. (2005). Male vulnerability to reading disability is not likely to be a myth: A call for new data. *Journal of Learning Disabilities, 38*(2), 109–129.

Linden, W., Chambers, L., Maurice, J., & Lenz, J. W. (1993). Sex differences in social support, selfdeception, hostility, and ambulatory cardiovascular activity. *Health Psychology, 12*, 376–380.

Little, A. C., & Perrett, D. I. (2002). Putting beauty back in the eye of the beholder. *Psychologist, 15*(1), 28–32.

Lochman, J. E., & Dodge, K. A. (1994). Social-cognitive processes of severely violent, moderately aggressive, and nonaggressive boys. *Journal of Consulting and Clinical Psychology, 62*, 366–374.

Loftus, E. F. (1983). Silence is not golden. *American Psychologist, 38*, 564–572.

Loftus, E. F. (2001). Imagining the past. *Psychologist, 14*(11), 584–587.

Loftus, E. F. (2004). Memories of things unseen. *Current Directions in Psychological Science, 13*(4), 145–147.

Loftus, E. F., & Bernstein, D. M. (2005). Rich false memories: The royal road to success. In A. F. Healy (Ed.), *Experimental cognitive psychology and its applications* (pp. 101–113). Washington, DC: American Psychological Association.

Loftus, G. R. (1983). The continuing persistence of the icon. *Behavioral and Brain Sciences, 6*, 28.

Loftus, G. R., & Loftus, E. F. (1976). *Human memory.*

Loop, M. S., Shows, J. F., Mangel, S. C., & Kuyk, T. K. (2003). Colour thresholds in dichromats and normals. *Vision Research, 43*(9), 983–992.

Lorenz, K. Z. (1981). *The foundations of ethology.* New York: Springer-Verlag.

Los Angeles Unified School District. (2000). Youth Suicide Prevention Information. http://www.sanpedro.com /spyc/suicide.htm.

Louie, K., & Wilson, M. A. (2001). Temporally structured replay of awake hippocampal ensemble activity during rapid eye movement sleep. *Neuron, 29*(1), 145–156.

Loving, T. J., & Agnew, C. R. (2001). Socially desirable responding in close relationships: A dualcomponent approach and measure. *Journal of Social & Personal Relationships, 18*(4), 551–573.

Low, N. C. P., Cui, L., & Merikangas, K. R. (2008). Specificity of familial transmission of anxiety and comorbid disorders. *Journal of Psychiatric Research. 42*(7), 596-604.

Lu, L. (2001). Understanding happiness: A look into the Chinese folk psychology. *Journal of Happiness Studies, 2*(4), 407–432.

Luborsky, L., et al. (2002). The dodo bird verdict is alive and well—mostly. *Clinical Psychology: Science & Practice, 9*(1), 2–12.

Luchins, A. S. (1957). Primacy-recency in impression formation. In C. I. Hovland (Ed.), *The order of presentation in persuasion.* New Haven, CT: Yale University Press.

Ludwick-Rosenthal, R., & Neufeld, R. W. J. (1993). Preparation for undergoing an invasive medical procedure. *Journal of Consulting and Clinical Psychology, 61,* 156–164.

Lupton, D. (2002). Road rage: Driver's understandings and experiences. *Journal of Sociology, 38,* 275–291. This article discusses a qualitative research study designed to explore the phenomenon of road rage.

Lykken, D. T., & Csikszentmihalyi, M. (2001). Happiness—stuck with what you've got? *Psychologist, 14*(9), 470–472.

Lykken, D. T., McGue, M., Tellegen, A., & Bouchard, T. J., Jr. (1992). Emergenesis: Genetic traits that may not run in families. *American Psychologist, 47,* 1565–1577.

Lynn, S. J., Shindler, K., & Meyer, E. (2003). Hypnotic suggestibility, psychopathology, and treatment outcome. *Sleep & Hypnosis, 5*(1), 2–10.

M

Maccoby, E. E. (1992). The role of parents in the socialization of children: An historical overview. *Developmental Psychology, 28,* 1006–1017.

MacGregor, J. (2005). *Sunday money.* New York: HarperCollins.

Maciejewski, P. K., Prigerson, H. G., & Mazure, C. M. (2000). Self-efficacy as a mediator between stressful life events and depressive symptoms: Differences based on history of prior depression. *British Journal of Psychiatry, 176,* 373–378.

Mackert, B., et al. (2003). The eloquence of silent cortex: Analysis of afferent input to deafferented cortex in arm amputees. *Neuroreport: For Rapid Communication of Neuroscience Research, 14*(3), 409–412.

MacNeill, I. (2003). Stressed: Warning signs that you could be hitting the danger zone. *BC Business, 31,* 60–63. This article presents physiological warning signs of stress and negative side effects of stress.

Magnavita, N., et al. (1997). Type A behaviour pattern and traffic accidents. *British Journal of Medical Psychology, 70*(1), 103–107.

Maher, B. A., & Maher, W. B. (1994). Personality and psychopathology. *Journal of Abnormal Psychology, 103,* 72–77.

Mahmud, A., & Feely, F. (2003). Effect of smoking on arterial stiffness and pulse pressure amplification. *Hypertension, 41,* 183–187.

Maier, N. R. F., & Schneirla, T. C. (1935). *Principles of animal psychology.* New York: McGraw-Hill.

Major, G. C., etal. (2007). Clinical significance of adaptive thermogenesis. *International Journal of Obesity, 31*(2), 204–212.

Malgady, R. G., Rogler, L. H., & Costantino, G. (1990). Hero/heroine modeling for Puerto Rican adolescents. *Journal of Consulting and Clinical Psychology, 58,* 469–474.

Malkin, E. (2004, November 11). In health care, gap between rich and poor persists, W.H.O. says. *The New York Times online.*

Maltby, J., & Day, L. (2001). The relationship between exercise motives and psychological well-being. *The Journal of Psychology, 135,* 651–660. This article describes research in an attempt to identify the motivations for exercise. The article focuses on both intrinsic and extrinsic motivation.

Mamtani, R., & Cimino, A. (2002). A primer of complementary and alternative medicine and its relevance in the treatment of mental health problems. *Psychiatric Quarterly, 73*(4), 367–381.

Marian, V., & Neisser, U. (2000). Language-dependent recall of autobiographical memories. *Journal of Experimental Psychology: General, 129*(3), 361–368.

Markon, K. E., Krueger, R. F., Bouchard, T. J., Jr., & Gottesman, I. I. (2002). Normal and abnormal personality traits: Evidence for genetic and environmental relationships in the Minnesota Study of Twins Reared Apart. *Journal of Personality, 70*(5), 661–693.

Marks, I. M., & Dar, R. (2000). Fear reduction by psychotherapies: Recent findings, future directions. *The British Journal of Psychiatry, 176,* 507–511.

Markus, H., & Kitayama, S. (1991). Culture and the self. *Psychological Review, 98*(2), 224–253.

Marsh, R. L., Hicks, J. L., & Cook, G. I. (2005). On the relationship between effort toward an ongoing task and cue detection in event-based prospective memory. *Journal of Experimental Psychology: Learning, Memory & Cognition, 31*(1), 68–75.

Marshall, M. A., & Brown, J. D. (2004). Expectations and realizations: The role of expectancies in achievement settings. *Motivation & Emotion, 28*(4), 347–361.

Martin, C. L., & Ruble, D. (2004). Children's search for gender cues: Cognitive perspectives on gender development. *Current Directions in Psychological Science, 13*(2), 67–70.

Martin, S. (2002). Easing migraine pain. *Monitor on Psychology, 33*(4), 71.

Martinez-Taboas, A., & Bernal, G. (2000). Dissociation, psychopathology, and abusive experiences in a nonclinical Latino university student group. *Cultural Diversity & Ethnic Minority Psychology, 6*(1), 32–41.

Martins, Y., et al. (2005). Preference for human body odors is influenced by gender and sexual orientation. *Psychological Science, 16*(9), 694-701.

Marttunen, M. J., et al. (1998). Completed suicide among adolescents with no diagnosable psychiatric disorder. *Adolescence, 33*(131), 669–681.

Maslow, A. H. (1970). *Motivation and personality* (2nd ed.). New York: Harper & Row.

Mason II, T. & Pack, A. (2005). Sleep terrors in childhood. *The Journal of Pediatrics, 147*(3), 388-392.

Masters, W. H., & Johnson, V. E. (1966). *Human sexual response.* Boston: Little, Brown.

May, R. (2005). How do we know what works? *Journal of College Student Psychotherapy, 19*(3), 69–73.

Mayes, S. D., & Calhoun, S. L. Wechsler Intelligence Scale for Children-Third and -Fourth Edition predictors of academic achievement in children with attention-deficit/hyperactivity disorder. *School Psychology Quarterly, 22*(2), 234-249.

McAndrew, F. T. (2002). New evolutionary perspectives on altruism: Multilevel-selection and costly-signaling theories. *Current Directions in Psychological Science, 11*(2), 79–82.

McCormick, M. J. (2001). Self-efficacy and leadership effectiveness: Applying social cognitive theory to leadership. *Journal of Leadership Studies, 8,* 22–33. This article describes a model of effective leadership utilizing social cognitive theory.

McCourt, K., et al. (1999). Authoritarianism revisited: Genetic and environmental influences examined in twins reared apart and together. *Personality & Individual Differences, 27*(5), 985–1014.

McCrae, R. R., & Costa, P. T., Jr. (1997). Personality trait structure as a human universal. *American Psychologist, 52,* 509–516.

McCrae, R. R., et al. (2000). Nature over nurture: Temperament, personality, and life span development. *Journal of Personality & Social Psychology, 78*(1), 173–186.

McDaniel, M. A., Glisky, E. L., Guynn, M. J., & Routhieaux, B. C. (1999). Prospective memory: A neuropsychological study. *Neuropsychology, 13*(1), 103–110.

McDougall, W. (1904). The sensations excited by a single momentary stimulation of the eye. *British Journal of Psychology, 1,* 78–113.

McDougall, W. (1908). *An introduction to social psychology.* London: Methuen.

McGaugh, J. L., McIntyre, C. K., & Power, A. E. (2002). Amygdala modulation of memory consolidation: Interaction with other brain systems. *Neurobiology of Learning & Memory. 78*(3), 539–552.

McGovern, C. M. (1993). Asylum: The complex and controversial story of mental institutions in the U.S.A. *Journal of Social History, 26,* 668–669. This article is a review of a movie that focuses on the history of mental institutions and the controversy surrounding them.

McGrath, P. (2004). Psychological methods of pain control: Basic science and clinical perspectives. *Pain Research & Management, 9*(4), 217–217.

McGraw, A. P., Mellers, B. A., & Ritov, I. (2004). The affective costs of overconfidence. *Journal of Behavioral Decision Making, 17*(4), 281–295.

McGue, M., Pickens, R. W., & Svikis, D. S. (1992). Sex and age effects on the inheritance of alcohol problems: A twin study. *Journal of Abnormal Psychology, 101,* 3–17.

McKee, P., & Barber, C. E. (2001). Plato's theory of aging. *Journal of Aging & Identity, 6*(2), 93–104.

McKenzie, C. R. M., Lee, S. M., & Chen, K. K. (2002). When negative evidence increases confidence: Changes in belief after hearing two sides of a dispute. *Journal of Behavioral Decision Making, 15*(1), 1–18.

McLaren, L. (2002). Cited in Wealthy women most troubled by poor body image. (2002, February 11). Reuters online.

McMurran, M., Blair, M., & Egan, V. (2002). An investigation of the correlations between aggression, impulsiveness, social problem-solving, and alcohol use. *Aggressive Behavior, 28,* 439–445.

McNally, R. J., & Clancy, S. A. (2005). Sleep paralysis, sexual abuse, and space alien abduction. *Transcultural Psychiatry, 42*(1), 113–122.

McNeil, T. F., Cantor-Graae, E., & Weinberger, D. R. (2000). Relationship of obstetric complications and differences in size of brain structures in monozygotic twin pairs discordant for schizophrenia. *American Journal of Psychiatry, 157,* 203–212.

McSherry, B. (2005). Men behaving badly: Current issues in provocation, automatism, mental impairment and criminal responsibility. *Psychiatry, Psychology and Law, 12*(1), 15–22.

Meijer, J., & Elshout, J. J. (2001). The predictive and discriminant validity of the zone of proximal development. *British Journal of Educational Psychology, 71*(1), 93–113.

Mellon, M. W., & McGrath, M. L. (2000). Empirically supported treatments in pediatric psychology: Nocturnal enuresis. *Journal of Pediatric Psychology, 25*(4), 193–214.

Melmed, R. N. (2003). Mind, body, and medicine: An integrative text. *American Journal of Psychiatry, 160*(3), 605–606.

Meltzoff, A. N., & Gopnik, A. (1997). *Words, thoughts, and theories.* Cambridge, MA: MIT Press.

Melzack, R. (1999, August). From the gate to the neuromatrix. *Pain* (Suppl. 6), S121–S126.

Merikangas, K. R., et al. (2007). Lifetime and 12-month prevalence of bipolar spectrum disorder in the national comorbidity survey replication. *Archives of General Psychiatry, 64*(5), 432-552.

Metcalfe, J. (1986). Premonitions of insight predict impending error. *Journal of Experimental Psychology: Learning, Memory, and Cognition, 12,* 623–634.

Metz, R. (2005, March 10). Think of a number . . .Come on, think! *The New York Times online.*

Metzger, B. L. (2003). The effect of a genetic variant for obesity and type 2 diabetes on the therapeutic potential of exercise and calorie restrictive diets in Zucker rats. *Research and Theory for Nursing Practice: An International Journal, 17*(4) 321–333.

Meyer-Lindenberg, A., et al. (2001). Evidence for abnormal cortical functional connectivity during working memory in schizophrenia. *American Journal of Psychiatry, 158,* 1809–1817.

Michael, R. T., Gagnon, J. H., Laumann, E. O., & Kolata, G. (1994). *Sex in America: A definitive survey.* Boston: Little, Brown.

Michels, K. B., et al. (2000). Prospective study of fruit and vegetable consumption and incidence of colon and rectal cancers. *Journal of the National Cancer Institute, 92*(21), 1740–1752.

Migdow, J. (2003). The problem with pleasure. *Journal of Trauma & Dissociation, 4*(1), 5–25.

Miles, J. (2005, May 22). Nascar nation. *The New York Times Book Review,* pp. 1, 10–11.

Milgram, S. (1963). Behavioral study of obedience. *Journal of Abnormal and Social Psychology, 67,* 371–378.

Milgram, S. (1974). *Obedience to authority.* New York: Harper & Row.

Milius, S. (2002). Rescue Rat: Could wired rodents save the day? *Science News Online.* http://www .phschool.com /science /science_news/articles / rescue_rat.html.

Miller, A. L., Rathus, J. H., & Linehan, M. M. (2007). *Dialectical behavior therapy with suicidal adolescents.* New York: Guilford Press.

Miller, A. L., Wyman, S. E., Huppert, J. D., Glassman, S. L., & Rathus, J. H. (2000). Analysis of behavioral skills utilized by suicidal adolescents receiving dialectical behavior therapy. *Cognitive & Behavioral Practice, 7*(2), 183–187.

Miller, G. A. (1956). The magical number seven, plus or minus two: Some limits on our capacity for processing information. *Psychological Review, 63,* 81–97.

Miller, N. E. (1969). Learning of visceral and glandular responses. *Science, 163,* 434–445.

Miller, N. E. (1995). Clinical-experimental interactions in the development of neuroscience. *American Psychologist, 50,* 901–911.

Milne, R. D., Syngeniotis, A., Jackson, G., & Corballis, M. C. (2002). Mixed lateralization of phonological assembly in developmental dyslexia. *Neurocase, 8*(3), 205–209.

Milner, B. R. (1966). Amnesia following operation on temporal lobes. In C. W. M. Whitty & O. L.

Milstead, M., Lapsley, D., & Hale, C. (1993, March). *A new look at imaginary audience and personal fable.* Paper presented at the meeting of the Society for Research in Child Development, New Orleans, LA.

Milton, J., & Wiseman, R. (1999). Does psi exist? Lack of replication of an anomalous process of information transfer. *Psychological Bulletin, 125*(4), 387–391.

The mind and the immune system-part I. (2002). *Harvard Mental Health Letter, 18,* NA. This article discusses the immune system and how the immune system can learn. Also discussed are hormonal effects on stress.

Minino, A. M., Heron, M. P., Murphy, S. L., & Kochanek, K. D. (2007, October 10). Deaths: Final data for 2004. National vital statistics reports, 55(19). http://www.cdc.gov/nchs/data/nvsr/nvsr55/nvsr55_19.pdf.

Mischel, W., & Shoda, Y. (1995). A cognitive-affective system theory of personality. *Psychological Review, 102,* 246–268.

MIT researchers ID gene involved in memory retrieval. (2002, June 21). *Genomics & Genetics Weekly,* p. 4. This article discusses comparative research conducted with mice that implicates the hippocampus in memory retrieval.

Mitchell, A. L. (2006). Medical consequences of cocaine. *Journal of Addictions Nursing, 17*(4), 249.

Mittal, M., & Wieling, E. (2004). The influence of therapists' ethnicity on the practice of feminist family therapy: A pilot study. *Journal of Feminist Family Therapy, 16*(2), 25–42.

Molden, D. C., & Dweck, C. S. (2000). Meaning and motivation. In C. Sansone & J. M. Harackiewicz (Eds.), *Intrinsic and extrinsic motivation: The search for optimal motivation and performance,* (pp. 131–159). San Diego: Academic Press.

Molfese, V. J., DiLalla, L. F., & Bunce, D. (1997). Prediction of the intelligence test scores of 3–to 8–year-old children by home environment, socioeconomic status, and biomedical risks. *Merrill- Palmer Quarterly, 43*(2), 219–234.

Molfese, V. J., Modglin, A., & Molfese, D. L. (2003). The role of environment in the development of reading skills: A longitudinal study of preschool and school-age measures. *Journal of Learning Disabilities, 36*(1), 59–67.

Montgomery, G. H., DuHamel, K. N., & Redd, W. H. (2000). A meta-analysis of hypnotically induced analgesia: How effective is hypnosis? *International Journal of Clinical & Experimental Hypnosis, 48(2),* 138–153.

Moore, C. C., Romney, A. K., & Hsia, T. (2002). Cultural, gender, and individual differences in perceptual and semantic structures of basic colors in Chinese and English. *Journal of Cognition & Culture, 2*(1), 1–28.

Moro, C., & Rodriguez, C. (2000). La creation des representations chez l'enfant au travers des processus de semiosis. *Enfance, 52*(3), 287–294.

Morris, E. J. (1991). Classroom demonstration of behavioral effects of the split-brain operation. *Teaching of Psychology, 18 (4),* 226–228. This article discusses a fun activity to demonstrate what it must be like for those who undergo brain surgery that results in a split brain.

Morris, W. N., Miller, R. S., & Spangenberg, S. (1977). The effects of dissenter position and task difficulty on conformity and response conflict. *Journal of Personality, 45,* 251–256.

Morry, M. M. (2005). Relationship satisfaction as a predictor of similarity ratings: A test of the attraction-similarity hypothesis. *Journal of Social and Personal Relationships, 22*(4), 561–584.

Mosher, W. D., Chandra, A., & Jones, J. (2005, September 15). Sexual behavior and selected health measures: Men and women 15–44 years of age in the U.S., 2002. Advance Data Number 362. Hyattsville, MD: National Center for Health Statistics.

Moss, D. P. (2002). Cited in Clay, R. A. (2002). A renaissance for humanistic psychology. *Monitor on Psychology, 33*(8), 42–43.

Moss, E., & St-Laurent, D. (2001). Attachment at school age and academic performance. *Developmental Psychology, 37*(6), 863–874.

Moyà-Solà, S., Köhler, M., Alba, D. M., Casanovas-Vilar, I., & Galindo, J. (2004). Pierolapithecus catalaunicus, a new middle Miocene great ape from Spain. *Science, 19,* 1339–1344.

Mozaffarian, D., et al. (2003). Cereal, fruit, and vegetable fiber intake and the risk of cardiovascular disease in elderly individuals. *Journal of the American Medical Association, 289,* 1659–1666.

Mueser, K. T., & McGurk, S. R. (2004). Schizophrenia. *Lancet, 363*(9426), 2063–2072.

Muir, G. D. (2000). Early ontogeny of locomotor behaviour: A comparison between altricial and precocial animals. *Brain Research Bulletin, 53*(5), 719–726.

Mukamal, K. J., Maclure, M., Muller, J. E., Sherwood, J. B., & Mittleman, M. A. (2001). Prior alcohol consumption and mortality following acute myocardial infarction. *Journal of the American Medical Association, 285*(15), 1965–1970.

Murray, H. A. (1938). *Explorations in personality.* New York: Oxford University Press.

Muscari, M. (2002). Media violence: Advice for parents. *Pediatric Nursing, 28,* 585–591. This article provides suggestions for parents to help in mediating the effects that media violence can have on children.

Myers, L. B., & Brewin, C. R. (1994). Recall of early experience and the repressive coping style. *Journal of Abnormal Psychology, 103,* 288–292.

N

Nader, K., Schafe, G. E., & Le Doux, J. E. (2000). Fear memories require protein synthesis in the amygdala for reconsolidation after retrieval. *Nature, 406*(6797), 722–726.

Nagourney, E. (2002, April 2). Neal E. Miller is dead at 92; studied brain and behavior. *The New York Times,* p. A21.

Nagtegaal, J. E., et al. (2000). Effects of melatonin on the quality of life in patients with delayed sleep phase syndrome. *Journal of Psychosomatic Research, 48*(1), 45–50.

Naimi, T. S., et al. (2003b). Definitions of binge drinking. *Journal of the American Medical Association, 289*(13), 1636.

National Center for Health Statistics. *Health, United States, 2009: With Special Feature on Medical Technology.* Hyattsville, MD. 2010. Table 32. (Accessed March 15, 2010). http://www.cdc.gov/nchs/data/hus/hus09.pdf#032.

National Center for Health Statistics. (2005, June 19). Self-inflicted injury/suicide. Atlanta: Centers for Disease Control and Prevention. http://www.cdc.gov/nchs/fastats/suicide.htm.

National Center for Injury Prevention and Control. (2005, June 19). Suicide: Fact sheet. http://www.cdc.gov/ncipc /factsheets /suifacts .htm.

National Eating Disorders Associations (2010). (Accessed 3 March 2010). http://www.nationaleatingdisorders.org/information-resources/general-information.php

National Science Foundation (2002). Science and technology: Public attitudes and public understanding. http://www.nsf.gov/sbe/srs / seind02/c7/c7h.htm.

National Sleep Foundation (2001, November 19). Events of 9–11 took their toll on Americans' sleep, particularly for women, according to new National Sleep Foundation poll.

http:// www.sleepfoundation.org/whatsnew/crisis_poll.html.

National Sleep Foundation (2008). *2005 Sleep in America Poll.* Washington, DC: National Sleep Foundation. http://www.sleepfoundation.org.

Nature editorial. (2004). *True lies. Nature, 428*(6984), 679.

Nature Neuroscience, 7(7), 751–756.

Navarro, J. F., & Maldonado, E. (2002). Acute and subchronic effects of MDMA ("ecstasy") on anxiety in male mice tested in the elevated plus-maze. *Progress in Neuro-Psychopharmacology & Biological Psychiatry, 26*(6), 1151–1154.

Neisser, U. (1993). Cited in Goleman, D. J. (1993, April 6). Studying the secrets of childhood memory. *The New York Times,* pp. C1, C11.

Neisser, U., et al. (1996). Intelligence: Knowns and unknowns. *American Psychologist, 51*(2), 77-101.

Neisser, U. (1997a). Never a dull moment. *American Psychologist, 52,* 79–81.

Neisser, U. (1997b). Cited in Sleek, S. (1997). Can "emotional intelligence" be taught in today's schools? *APA Monitor, 28*(6), 25.

Nelson, K., Hampson, J., & Shaw, L. K. (1993). Nouns in early lexicons: Evidence, explanations, and implications. *Journal of Child Language, 20,* 228.

Nestoriuc, Y., Rief, W., & Martin, A. (2008). Meta-analysis of biofeedback for tension-type headache: Efficacy, specificity, and treatment moderators. *Journal of Consulting and Clinical Psychology, 76*(3), 379-396.

Neumark-Sztainer, D., et al. (2002a). Ethnic/ racial differences in weight-related concerns and behaviors among adolescent girls and boys: Findings from Project EAT. *Journal of Psychosomatic Research, 53*(5), 963–974.

Neumark-Sztainer, D., et al. (2002a). Ethnic/ racial differences in weight-related concerns and behaviors among adolescent girls and boys: Findings from Project EAT. *Journal of Psychosomatic Research, 53*(5), 963–974.

Neveus, T., Cnattingius, S., Olsson, U., & Hetta, J. (2002). Sleep habits and sleep problems among a community sample of schoolchildren. *Journal of the American Academy of Child & Adolescent Psychiatry, 41*(7), 828.

Newman, L. S., & Baumeister, R. F. (1998). Abducted by aliens: Spurious memories of interplanetary masochism. In S. J. Lynn & K. M. Mc- Conkey (Eds), *Truth in memory* (pp. 284–303).

Newport, E. L. (1998). Cited in Azar, B. (1998). Acquiring sign language may be more innate than learned. *APA Monitor, 29*(4), 12.

Nezlek, J. B., Hampton, C. P., & Shean, G. D. (2000). Clinical depression and day-to-day social interaction in a community sample. *Journal of Abnormal Psychology, 109*(1), 11–19.

Nicholson, A. (2008). Socio-economic status over the life-course and depressive symptoms in men and women in Eastern Europe. *Journal of Affective Disorders, 105*(1-3), 125–136.

Nickell, J. (2001). Exorcism! Driving out the nonsense. *Skeptical Inquirer, 25,* 20. This article describes that one reason attributed to psychological disorders was demon possession. Exorcism was an attempt to help people possessed. This article describes this historical perspective.

No, S. (2004). From prejudice to intergroup emotions: Differentiated reactions to social groups. *Asian Journal of Social Psychology, 7*(1), 119–122.

Nock, M. K., et al. (2008). Suicide and suicidal behavior. *Epidemiologic Reviews, 30*(1), 133-154.

Nock, M. K., & Kazdin, A. E. (2002). Examination of affective, cognitive, and behavioral factors and suicide-related outcomes in children and young adolescents. *Journal of Community Psychology, 31*(1), 48–58.

Nolen-Hoeksema, S. (2001). Gender differences in depression. *Current Directions in Psychological Science, 10*(5), 173–176.

Norton, A. (2000, July 21). A drink a day keeps brain in tip-top shape. Reuters News Agency online.

Novick, L. R., & Coté, N. (1992). The nature of expertise in anagram solution. In *Proceedings of the Fourteenth Annual Conference of the Cognitive Science Society.* Hillsdale, NJ: Erlbaum.

Nowakowska, C., Strong, C. M., Santosa, C. M., Wang, P. W., & Ketter, T. A. (2005). Temperamental commonalities and differences in euthymic mood disorder patients, creative controls, and healthy controls. *Journal of Affective Disorders, 85*(1–2), 207–215.

Nuland, S. (2005, February). Do you want to live forever? *MIT Technology Review, 108*(2), 36–45.

Nurnberger, J. I., Jr., et al. (2004). A family study of alcohol dependence: Coaggregation of multiple disorders in relatives of alcohol-dependent probands. *Archives of General Psychiatry, 61*(12), 1246–1256.

Nyberg, L., et al. (2000). Large scale neurocognitive networks underlying episodic memory. *Journal of Cognitive Neuroscience, 12*(1), 163–173.

O

O'Dell, C. D., & Hoyert, M. D. (2002). Active and passive touch: A research methodology project. *Teaching of Psychology, 29*(4), 292–294.

Ogawa, K., Nittono, H., & Hori, T. (2002). Brain potential associated with the onset and offset of rapid eye movement (REM) during REM sleep. *Psychiatry & Clinical Neurosciences, 56*(3), 259–260.

Ohayon, M. M., Guilleminault, C., & Priest, R.G. (1999). Night terrors, sleepwalking, and confusional arousals in the general population: Their frequency and relationship to other sleep and mental disorders. *Journal of Clinical Psychiatry, 60*(4), 268–276.

Ohno, H., Urushihara, R., Sei, H., & Morita, Y. (2002). REM sleep deprivation suppresses acquisition of classical eye-blink conditioning. *Sleep: Journal of Sleep Research & Sleep Medicine, 25*(8), 877–881.

Oktedalen, O., Solberg, E. E., Haugen, A. H., & Opstad, P. K. (2001). The influence of physical and mental training on plasma beta-endorphin level and pain perception after intensive physical exercise. *Stress & Health: Journal of the International Society for the Investigation of Stress, 17*(2), 121–127.

Olanow, W. M. (2000, July). Clinical and pathological perspective on Parkinsonism. Paper presented to the World Alzheimer Congress 2000, Washington, DC.

Olds, J., & Milner, P. (1954). Positive reinforcement produced by electrical stimulation of the septal area and other regions of the rat brain. *Journal of Comparative and Physiological Psychology, 47,* 419–427.

Omer, H., & Elitzur, A. C. (2001). What would you say to the person on the roof ? A suicide prevention text. *Suicide & Life-Threatening Behavior, 31*(2), 129–139.

Orpen, C. (1995). The Multifactorial Achievement Scale as a predictor of salary growth and motivation among middle-managers. *Social Behavior & Personality, 23*(2), 159–162.

Ostatníková, D., et al. (2002). Biological aspects of intellectual giftedness. *Studia Psychologica, 44*(1), 3–13.

Otani, H., et al. (2005). Remembering a nuclear accident in Japan: Did it trigger flashbulb memories? *Memory, 13*(1), 6–20.

P

Pappas, G., Queen, S., Hadden, W., & Fisher, G. (1993). The increasing disparity of mortality between socioeconomic groups in the United States, 1960 and 1986. *New England Journal of Medicine, 329,* 103–109.

Park, N., Peterson, C., & Seligman, M. E. P. (2005). *Character strengths in forty nations and fifty states.* Unpublished manuscript, University of Rhode Island.

Parker, A. (2001). The ganzfeld: Suggested improvements of an apparently successful method for psi research. *European Journal of Parapsychology, 16,* 23–29.

Parr, L. A., Winslow, J. T., Hopkins, W. D., & de Waal, F. B. M. (2000). Recognizing facial cues: Individual discrimination by chimpanzees (*Pan troglodytes*) and Rhesus monkeys (Macaca mulatta).

Parrott, A. (Ed.) (2003). Cognitive deficits and cognitive normality in recreational cannabis and ecstasy/MDMA users. *Human Psychopharmacology: Clinical & Experimental, 18*(2), 89–90.

Pastor, L. H. (2004). Countering the psychological consequences of suicide terrorism. *Psychiatric Annals, 34*(9), 701–707.

Patenaude, J., Niyonsenga, T., & Fafard, D. (2003). Changes in students' moral development during medical school: A cohort study. *Canadian Medical Association Journal, 168*(7), 840–844.

Patry, A. L., & Pelletier, L. G. (2001). Extraterrestrial beliefs and experiences: An application of the theory of reasoned action. *Journal of Social Psychology, 141*(2), 199–217.

Patterson, D. R. (2004). Treating pain with hypnosis. *Current Directions in Psychological Science, 13*(6), 252–255.

Patterson, G. R., Dishion, T. J., & Yoerger, K. (2000). Adolescent growth in new forms of problem behavior: Macro- and micro-peer dynamics.

Pavlov, I. (1927). *Conditioned reflexes.* London: Oxford University Press.

Pelham, W. E., et al. (2002). Effects of methyphenidate and expectancy on children with ADHD: Behavior, academic performance, and attributions in a summer treatment program and regular classroom settings. *Journal of Consulting & Clinical Psychology, 70*(2), 320–335.

Penfield, W. (1969). Consciousness, memory, and man's conditioned reflexes. In K. H. Pribram (Ed.), *On the biology of learning.* New York: Harcourt Brace Jovanovich.

Pentney, A. R. (2001). An exploration of the history and controversies surrounding MDMA and MDA. *Journal of Psychoactive Drugs, 33*(3), 213–221.

Peplau, L. A. (2003). Human sexuality: How do men and women differ? *Current Directions in Psychological Science, 12*(2), 37–40.

Peters, M., et al. (2004). Migraine and chronic daily headache management: A qualitative study of patients' perceptions. *Scandinavian Journal of Caring Sciences, 18*(3), 294–303.

Peterson, C. (2002). Children's long-term memory for autobiographical events. *Developmental Review, 22*(3), 370–402.

Peterson, L. R., & Peterson, M. J. (1959). Shortterm retention of individual verbal items. *Journal of Experimental Psychology, 58,* 193–198.

Petrill, S. A., & Deater-Deckard, K. (2004). The heritability of general cognitive ability: A withinfamily adoption design. *Intelligence, 32*(4), 403–409.

Petrill, S. A., Pike, A., Price, T., & Plomin, R. (2004). Chaos in the home and socioeconomic status are associated with cognitive development in early childhood: Environmental mediators identified in a genetic design. *Intelligence, 32*(5), 445–460.

Petry, N. M., Martin, B., Cooney, J. L., & Kranzler, H. R. (2000). Give them prizes and they will come: Contingency management for treatment of alcohol dependence. *Journal of Consulting and Clinical Psychology, 68,* 250–257.

Petty, R. E., Fleming, M. A., & White, P. H. (1999). Stigmatized sources and persuasion: Prejudice as a determinant of argument scrutiny. *Journal of Personality & Social Psychology, 76*(1), 19–34.

Petty, R. E., Wegener, D. T., & Fabrigar, L. R. (1997). Attitudes and attitude change. *Annual Review of Psychology, 48,* 609–647.

Phalet, K., & Schoenpflug, U. (2001). Intergenerational transmission of collectivism and achievement values in two acculturation contexts: The case of Turkish families in Germany and Turkish and Moroccan families in the Netherlands. *Journal of Cross-Cultural Psychology, 32*(2), 186–201.

Phinney, J. S. (2000). Identity formation across cultures: The interaction of personal, societal, and historical change. *Human Development, 43*(1), 27–31.

Phinney, J. S. (2005). Ethnic identity in late modern times. *Identity, 5*(2), 187–194.

Phinney, J. S., Cantu, C. L., & Kurtz, D. A. (1997). Ethnic and American identity as predictors of self-esteem among African American, Latino, and White adolescents. *Journal of Youth & Adolescence, 26*(2), 165–185.

Phinney, J. S., & Devich-Navarro, M. (1997). Variations in bicultural identification among African American and Mexican American adolescents. *Journal of Research on Adolescence, 7*(1), 3–32.

Piaget, J. (1963). *The origins of intelligence in children.* New York: W. W. Norton.

Piaget, J., & Smith, L. (Trans). (2000). Commentary on Vygotsky's criticisms of language and thought of the child and judgment and reasoning in the child. *New Ideas in Psychology, 18*(2–3), 241–259.

Pickens, C. L., & Holland, P. C. (2004). Conditioning and cognition. *Neuroscience & Biobehavioral Reviews, 28*(7), 651–661.

Pihl, R. O., Peterson, J. B., & Finn, P. (1990). Inherited predisposition to alcoholism. *Journal of Abnormal Psychology, 99,* 291–301.

Pillard, R. C., & Weinrich, J. D. (1986). Evidence of familial nature of male homosexuality. *Archives of General Psychiatry, 43*(8), 808–812.

Pind, J., Gunnarsdottir, E. K., & Johannesson, H. S. (2003). Raven's Standard Progressive Matrices: New school age norms and a study of the test's validity. *Personality and Individual Differences, 34*(3), 375–386.

Pinel, J. P. J., Assanand, S., & Lehman, D. R. (2000). Hunger, eating, and ill health. *American Psychologist, 55*(10), 1105–1116.

Pinker, S. (1990). Language acquisition. In D. N. Osherson & H. Lasnik (Eds.), *An invitation to cognitive science: Language* (Vol. 1). Cambridge, MA: MIT Press, a Bradford Book.

Pinker, S. (1994a). *The language instinct.* New York: William Morrow.

Pinker, S. (1997). Words and rules in the human brain. *Nature, 387*(6633), 547–548.

Pinker, S. (1999). Out of the minds of babes. *Science, 283*(5398), 40–41

Pinnell, C. M., & Covino, N. A. (2000). Empirical findings on the use of hypnosis in medicine: A critical review. *International Journal of Clinical & Experimental Hypnosis, 48*(2), 170–194.

Plaisier, I., et al. (2008). Work and family roles and the association with depressive and anxiety disorders: Differences between men and women. *Journal of Affective Disorders, 105*(1-3), 63–72.

Platania, J., & Moran, G. P. (2001). Social facilitation as a function of mere presence of others. *Journal of Social Psychology, 141*(2), 190–197.

Plomin, R. (2000). Behavioural genetics in the 21st century. *International Journal of Behavioral Development, 24*(1), 30–34.

Plomin, R. (Ed.). (2002). *Behavioral genetics in the postgenomic era.* Washington, DC: American Psychological Association.

Plomin, R. (Ed.). (2002). *Behavioral genetics in the postgenomic era.* Washington, DC: American Psychological Association.

Plomin, R., & Crabbe, J. (2000). DNA. *Psychological Bulletin, 126*(6), 806–828.

Plomin, R., Emde, R., Braungart, J. M., & Campos. (1993). Genetic change and continuity from fourteen to twenty months: The MacArthur Longitudinal Twin Study. *Child Development, 64*(5), 1354–1376.

Pointer, S. C., & Bond, N. W. (1998). Context-dependent memory: Colour versus odor. *Chemical Senses, 23*(3), 359–362.

Pol, H. E. H., et al. (2000). Prenatal exposure to famine and brain morphology in schizophrenia. *American Journal of Psychiatry, 157,* 1170–1172.

Porter, R. (1997). Bethlem/Bedlam: Methods of madness? *History Today, 47,* 41–46. This article is an excellent history of perhaps the most famous mental institution in psychology.

Posada, G., et al. (2002). Maternal caregiving and infant security in two cultures. *Developmental Psychology, 38*(1), 67–78.

Power, T. G., Stewart, C. D., Hughes, S. O., & Arbona, C. (2005). Predicting patterns of adolescent alcohol use: A longitudinal study. *Journal of Studies on Alcohol, 66*(1), 74–81.

Powers, R. (2000, May 7). American dreaming. *The New York Times Magazine,* pp. 66–67.

Prevention Science, 1(1), 3–13.

Pratkanis, A. R. (Ed.). (2007). *The science of social influence: Advances and future progress.* New York: Psychology Press.

Prior, S. M., & Welling, K. A. (2001). "Read in your head": A Vygotskian analysis of the transition from oral to silent reading. *Reading Psychology, 22*(1), 1–15.

Prochaska, J. O., & Norcross, J. C. (2007). *Systems of psychotherapy* (6th ed.). Belmont, CA: Wadsworth.

Pryce, C. R., Bettschen, D., Bahr, N. I., & Feldon, J. (2001). Comparison of the effects of infant handling, isolation, and nonhandling on acoustic startle, prepulse inhibition, locomotion, and HPA activity in the adult rat. *Behavioral Neuroscience, 115*(1), 71–83.

Psychodynamic perspective. (1999). *Psychology Review, 6,* 32. This article provides a succinct summary of the psychodynamic perspective.

Psychology & Health, 17(5), 611–627.

Psychosomatic Medicine, 64(1), 15–28.

Pulley, B. (1998, June 16). Those seductive snake eyes: Tales of growing up gambling. *The New York Times,* A1, A28.

R

Rachman, S. (2000). Joseph Wolpe (1915–1997): Obituary. *American Psychologist, 55*(4), 431–432.

Radel, M., et al. (2005). Haplotype-based localization of an alcohol dependence gene to the 5q34 y-aminobutyric acid type A gene cluster. *Archives of General Psychiatry, 62*(1), 47–55.

Rainville, P., et al. (2002). Hypnosis modulates activity in brain structures involved in the regulation of consciousness. *Journal of Cognitive Neuroscience, 14*(6), 887–901.

Ramel, W., Goldin, P. R. Carmona, P. E., & Mc- Quaid, J. R. (2004). The effects of mindfulness meditation on cognitive processes and affect in patients with past depression. *Cognitive Therapy & Research, 28*(4), 433–455.

Ramsey, J. L., & Langlois, J. H. (2002). Effects of the "beauty is good" stereotype on children's information processing. *Journal of Experimental Child Psychology, 81*(3), 320–340.

Ramsey, J. L., et al. (2004). Origins of a stereotype: Categorization of facial attractiveness by 6–month-old infants. *Developmental Science, 7*(2), 201–211.

Randel, B., Stevenson, H. W., & Witruk, E. (2000). Attitudes, beliefs, and mathematics achievement of German and Japanese high school students. *International Journal of Behavioral Development, 24*(2), 190–198.

Rasenberger, J. (2004, February 8). Kitty, 40 years later. *The New York Times online.*

Rath, N. (2002). The power to feel fear and the one to feel happiness are the same. *Journal of Happiness Studies, 3*(1), 1–21.

Rathus, J. H., & Sanderson, W. C. (1999). *Marital distress: Cognitive behavioral interventions for couples.* Northvale, NJ: Jason Aronson.

Rathus, S. A. (2008-2009). *HDEV.* Mason, OH: 4LTR Press/ Cengage Learning.

Raynor, H., A., & Epstein, L. H. (2001). Dietary variety, energy regulation, and obesity. *Psychological Bulletin, 127*(3), 325–341.

Ready, T. (2000, June 7). Meditation apparently good for the heart as well as the mind. Healtheon /WebMD.

Reas, D. L., & Grilo, C. M. (2007). Timing and sequence of the onset of overweight, dieting, and binge eating in overweight patients with binge eating disorder. International *Journal of Eating Disorders, 40*(2), 165-170.

Reed, J. M., & Squire, L. R. (1997). Impaired recognition memory in patients with lesions limited to the hippocampal formation. *Behavioral Neuroscience, 111*(4), 667–675.

Reeder, G. D. (2001). On perceiving multiple causes and inferring multiple internal attributes. *Psychological Inquiry, 12*(1), 34–36.

Reese, C. M., & Cherry, K. E. (2002). The effects of age, ability, and memory monitoring on prospective memory task performance.

Aging, Neuropsychology & Cognition, 9(2), 98–113.

Reeve, C. L. (2002). Race and intelligence: Separating science from myth. (Book Review). *Personnel Psychology, 55,* 778–781. This article presents an attempt at uncovering the myths surrounding race and intelligence and includes such topics as defining race and the bell curve.

Regier, T., Kay, P., & Cook, R. S. (2005). Focal colors are universal after all. *Proceedings of the National Academy of Sciences, 102*(23), 8386–8391.

The relation of child care to cognitive and language development. (2000). *Child Development, 71,* 960. This article discusses the contributors to children's language and cognitive development and the differences seen with children who experience various types of care.

Rescorla, R. A. (1967). Inhibition of delay in Pavlovian fear conditioning. *Journal of Comparative & Physiological Psychology, 64*(1), 114–120.

Rescorla, R. A. (1988). Pavlovian conditioning: It's not what you think it is. *American Psychologist, 43,* 151–160.

Rescorla, R. A. (1999). Partial reinforcement reduces the associative change produced by nonreinforcement.

Rezvani, A. H., & Levin, E. D. (2001). Cognitive effects of nicotine. *Biological Psychiatry, 49*(3), 258–267.

Rhee, S. H., & Waldman, I. D. (2002). Genetic and environmental influences on antisocial behavior: A meta-analysis of twin and adoption studies. *Psychological Bulletin, 128*(3), 490–529.

Ribeiro, S., & Nicolelis, M. A. L. (2004). Reverberation, storage, and postsynaptic propagation of memories during sleep. *Learning & Memory, 11*(6), 686–696.

Ricciardelli, L. A., & McCabe, M. P. (2001, February). Self-esteem and negative affect as moderators of sociocultural influences on body dissatisfaction, strategies to decrease weight, and strategies to increase muscles among adolescent boys and girls. *Sex Roles: A Journal of Research,* 189. This article discusses the complex interactions of self-esteem, sociocultural influences and body image.

Rice, K. G., & Dellwo, J. P. (2001). Within-semester stability and adjustment correlates of the Multidimensional Perfectionism Scale. *Measurement & Evaluation in Counseling & Development, 34*(3), 146–156.

Richards, J. C., Hof, A., & Alvarenga, M. (2000). Serum lipids and their relationships with hostility and angry affect and behaviors in men. *Health Psychology, 19*(4), 393–398.

Richardson, G. E. (2002). The metatheory of resilience and resiliency. *Journal of Clinical Psychology, 58*(3), 307–321.

Rickard, T. C., et al. (2000). The calculating brain: An fMRI study. *Neuropsychologia, 38*(3), 325–335. Riley & Kendler, 2005.

Riley, B., & Kendler, K. S. (2005). Genetics of Schizophrenia: Linkage and Association Studies. In K. S. Kendler, & L. J. Eaves (Eds.). *Psychiatric genetics.* (pp. 95-140). *Review of psychiatry series, 24*(1). Washington, DC: American Psychiatric Publishing, Inc.

Riniolo, T. C., Koledin, M., Drakulic, G. M., & Payne, R. A. (2003).

An archival study of eyewitness memory of the Titanic's final plunge. *The Journal of General Psychology, 130,* 89–95. This article presents a study which examined the eyewitness accounts of the Titanic disaster to determine the veracity of eyewitness testimony in traumatic events.

Riso, L. P., et al. (2003). Cognitive aspects of chronic depression. *Journal of Abnormal Psychology, 112*(1), 72–80.

Robbins, S. B., Le, H., & Lauver, K. (2005). Promoting successful college outcomes for all students.

Roberson, D., Davidoff, J., & Shapiro, L. (2002). Squaring the circle: The cultural relativity of good shape. *Journal of Cognition & Culture, 2*(1), 29–51.

Robins, R. W., Gosling, S. D., & Craik, K. H. (1999). An empirical analysis of trends in psychology. *American Psychologist, 54*(2), 117–128.

Rodafinos, A., Vucevic, A., & Sideridis, G. D. (2005). The effectiveness of compliance techniques: Foot in the door versus door in the face. *Journal of Social Psychology, 145*(2), 237–239.

Roelofs, K., et al. (2002). Hypnotic susceptibility in patients with conversion disorder. *Journal of Abnormal Psychology, 111*(2), 390–395.

Romero, E., Luengo, M. A., & Sobral, J. (2001). Personality and antisocial behaviour: Study of temperamental dimensions. *Personality & Individual Differences, 31*(3), 329–348.

Roncesvalles, M. N. C., Woollacott, M. H., & Jensen, J. L. (2001). Development of lower extremity kinetics for balance control in infants and young children. *Journal of Motor Behavior, 33*(2), 180–192.

Rosenbaum, M. (2002). Ecstasy: America's new "reefer madness." *Journal of Psychoactive Drugs, 34*(2), 137–142.

Rosenthal, E. (1993, July 20). Listening to the emotional needs of cancer patients. *The New York Times,* pp. C1, C7.

Roser, M., & Gazzaniga, M. S. (2004). Automatic brains—Interpretive minds. *Current Directions in Psychological Science, 13*(2), 56–59.

Reeve, C. L. (2002). Race and intelligence: Separating science from myth. (Book Review). *Personnel Psychology, 55,* 778–781. This article presents an attempt at uncovering the myths surrounding race and intelligence and includes such topics as defining race and the bell curve.

Ross, S. E., Niebling, B. C., & Heckert, T. M. (1999). Sources of stress among college students. *College Student Journal, 33,* 312. This article presents the results of a study conducted to determine stressful life events college students experience.

Ross, S. R., Lutz, C. J., & Bailley, S. E. (2002). Positive and negative symptoms of schizotypy and the Five-Factor Model: A domain and facet level analysis. *Journal of Personality Assessment, 79*(1), 53–72.

Roth, B. L., Hanizavareh, S. M., & Blum, A. E. (2004). Serotonin receptors represent highly favorable molecular targets for cognitive enhancement in schizophrenia and other disorders. *Psychopharmacology, 174*(1), 17–24.

Roth, G. (2000). The evolution and ontogeny of consciousness. *Neural correlates of consciousness: Empirical and conceptual questions.* Cambridge, MA: MIT Press.

Rothbaum, F., Rosen, K., Ujiie, T., & Uchida, N. (2002). Family systems theory, attachment theory, and culture. *Family Process, 41,* 328–350. This article compares and contrasts family systems theory and attachment theory. These theories are discusses in the context of non-western cultures.

Rotter, J. B. (1990). Internal versus external control of reinforcement. *American Psychologist, 45,* 489–493.

Rovee-Collier, C. (1999). The development of infant memory. *Current Directions in Psychological Science, 8*(3), 80–85.

Rowe, J. B., Owen, A. M., Johnsrude, I. S., & Passingham, R. E. (2001). Imaging the mental components of a planning task. *Neuropsychologia, 39*(3), 315–327.

Rubinstein, S., & Caballero, B. (2000). Is Miss America an undernourished role model? *Journal of the American Medical Association online, 283*(12).

Rude, S. S., Hertel, P. T., Jarrold, W., Covich, J., & Hedlund, S. (1999). Depression-related impairments in prospective memory. *Cognition & Emotion, 13*(3), 267–276.

Rudy, D., & Grusec, J. E. (2001). Correlates of authoritarian parenting in individualist and collectivist cultures and implications for understanding the transmission of values. *Journal of Cross-Cultural Psychology, 32*(2), 202–212.

Ruff, S., et al. (2003). Neural substrates of impaired categorical perception of phonemes in adult dyslexics: An fMRI study. *Brain & Cognition, 53*(2) 331–334.

Ruiter, R. A. C., Abraham, C., & Kok, G. (2001). Scary warnings and rational precautions: A review of the psychology of fear appeals. *Psychology & Health, 16*(6), 613–630.

Rushton, J. P., Skuy, M., & Fridjhon, P. (2003). Performance on Raven's Advanced Progressive Matrices by African, East Indian, and White engineering students in South Africa. *Intelligence, 31*(2), 123–137.

Rutkowski, G. K., Gruder, C. L., & Romer, D. (1983). Group cohesiveness, social norms, and bystander intervention. *Journal of Personality and Social Psychology, 44,* 545–552.

Rutter, M., & Silberg, J. (2002). Gene-environment interplay in relation to emotional and behavioral disturbance. *Annual Review of Psychology, 53*(1), 463–490.

S

Sacks, F. M., et al. (2001). Effects on blood pressure of reduced dietary sodium and the Dietary Approaches to Stop Hypertension (DASH) Diet. *The New England Journal of Medicine, 344*(1), 3–10.

Sagrestano, L. M., McCormick, S. H., Paikoff, R. L., & Holmbeck, G. N. (1999). Pubertal development and parent-child conflict in low-income, urban, African American adolescents. *Journal of Research on Adolescence, 9*(1), 85–107.

Salmon, P., et al. (2004). Mindfulness meditation in clinical practice. *Cognitive & Behavioral Practice, 11*(4), 434–446.

Salovey, P., & Wegener, D. T. (2003). Communicating about health: Message framing, persuasion and health behavior. In J. Suls & K. A. Wallston (Eds.), *Social psychological foundations of health and illness* (pp. 54–81). Malden, MA: Blackwell Publishers.

Salovey, P., Stroud, L. R., Woolery, A., & Epel, E. S. (2002). Perceived emotional intelligence, stress reactivity, and symptom reports: Further explorations using the trait meta-mood scale.

Sanders, G. S. (1984). Effects of context cues on eyewitness identification responses. *Journal of Applied Social Psychology, 14,* 386–397.

Sanna, L. J., & Meier, S. (2000). Looking for clouds in a silver lining: Self-esteem, mental simulations, and temporal confidence changes. *Journal of Research in Personality, 34*(2), 236–251.

Santee, R. T., & Maslach, C. (1982). To agree or not to agree: Personal dissent amid social pressure to conform. *Journal of Personality and Social Psychology, 42*(4), 690–700.

Sarbin, T. R., & Coe, W. C. (1972). *Hypnosis.* New York: Holt, Rinehart and Winston.

Saunders, K. W. (2003). Regulating youth access to violent video games: Three responses to First Amendment concerns. http://www.law.msu.edu/lawrev/2003–1/2–Saunders.pdf.

Savage, C. R., et al. (2001). Prefrontal regions supporting spontaneous and directed application of verbal learning strategies. Evidence from PET. *Brain, 124*(1), 219–231.

Savage-Rumbaugh, E. S., & Fields, W. M. (2000). Linguistic, cultural and cognitive capacities of bonobos (Pan paniscus). *Culture & Psychology, 6*(2), 131–153.

Savage-Rumbaugh, E. S., et al. (1993). *Monographs of the Society for Research in Child Development, 58*(3–4), v-221.

Sawa, A., & Snyder, S. H. (2002, April 26). Schizophrenia: Diverse approaches to a complex disease. *Science,* pp. 692–695.

Saxe, L., & Ben-Shakhar, G. (1999). Admissibility of polygraph tests: The application of scientific standards post-Daubert. *Psychology, Public Policy & Law, 5*(1), 203–223.

Scarr, S., & Weinberg, R. A. (1976). IQ test performance of Black children adopted by White families.

Schachter, S., & Singer, J. E. (1962). Cognitive, social, and physiological determinants of emotional state. *Psychological Review, 69,* 379–399.

Schacter, D. L. (1992). Understanding implicit memory: A cognitive neuroscience approach.

Schacter, D. L. (1999). The seven sins of memory: Insights from psychology and cognitive neuroscience. *American Psychologist, 54*(3), 182–203.

Schacter, D. L. (2000). Memory: Memory systems. In A. E. Kazdin (Ed.), *Encyclopedia of psychology* (Vol. 5, pp. 169–172). Washington, DC: American Psychological Association.

Schacter, D. L., Cooper, L. A., & Treadwell, J. (1993). Preserved priming of novel objects across size transformation in amnesic patients. *Psychological Science, 4*(5), 331–335.

Schacter, D. L., Dobbins, I. G., & Schnyer, D. M. (2004). Specificity of priming: A cognitive neuroscience perspective. *Nature Reviews Neuroscience, 5*(11), 853–862.

Schaie, K. W., Willis, S. L., & Caskie, G. I. L. (2004). The Seattle longitudinal study: Relationship between personality and cognition. *Aging, Neuropsychology & Cognition, 11*(2–3), 304–324.

Schiffman, S. S. (2000). Taste quality and neural coding: Implications from psychophysics and neurophysiology. *Physiology and Behavior, 69*(1–2), 147–159.

Schiffman, S. S., et al. (2003). Effect of repeated presentation on sweetness intensity of binary and ternary mixtures of sweeteners. *Chemical Senses, 28*(3), 219–229.

Schmitt, D. P. (2003). Universal sex differences in the desire for sexual variety: Tests from 52 nations, 6 continents, and 13 islands. *Journal of Personality and Social Psychology, 85*(1), 85–104.

Schmitt, D. P., Shackelford, T. K., Duntley, J., Tooke, W., & Buss, D. M. (2001). The desire for sexual variety as a key to understanding basic human mating strategies. *Personal Relationships, 8*(4), 425–455.

Schneider, K. J., Bugental, J. F. T., & Pierson, J. F. (Eds). (2003). The handbook of humanistic psychology: Leading edges in theory, research, and practice. *Psychotherapy Research, 13*(1), 119–121.

Schneider, R. H., et al. (1995). A randomized controlled trial of stress reduction for hypertension in older African Americans. *Hypertension, 26,* 820.

Schneiderman, N., Ironson, G., & Siegel, S. D. (2005). Stress and health: Psychological, behavioral, and biological determinants. *Annual Review of Clinical Psychology, 1*(1), 607–628

Schredl, M., Ciric, P., Go¨tz, S., & Wittmann, L. (2004). Typical dreams: Stability and gender differences. *Journal of Psychology: Interdisciplinary & Applied, 138*(6), 485–494.

Schupf, N. (2000, July). Epidemiology of dementia in Down syndrome. Paper presented to the World Alzheimer Congress 2000, Washington, DC.

Schultz, D. P., & Schultz, S. E. (2008). *A history of modern psychology,* 9th Edition. Belmont, CA: Cengage.

Schuster, M. A., et al. (2001). A national survey of stress reactions after the September 11, 2001, terrorist attacks. *New England Journal of Medicine, 345*(20), 1507–1512.

Schwartz, J. R. L. (2004). Pharmacologic management of daytime sleepiness. *Journal of Clinical Psychiatry, 65*(Suppl. 16), 46–49.

Schwartz, J., & Wald, M. L. (2003, March 9). NASA's curse? "Groupthink" is 30 years old, and still going strong. *The New York Times online.*

Schwartz, R. M., & Gottman, J. M. (1976). Toward a task analysis of assertive behavior. *Journal of Consulting and Clinical Psychology, 44,* 910–920.

Schwartzer, R., & Renner, B. (2000). Social-cognitive predictors of health behavior: Action selfefficacy and coping self-efficacy. *Health Psychology, 19*(5), 487–495.

Schyns, P. (2001). Income and satisfaction in Russia. *Journal of Happiness Studies, 2*(2), 173–204.

Scott, T. R. (2001). The role of taste in feeding. *Appetite, 37*(2), 111–113.

Scruggs, T. E., & Mastropieri, M. A. (1992). Remembering the forgotten art of memory. *American Educator, 16*(4), 31–37.

Second thoughts. (1989). *The Economist, 313,* 69. This article focuses on the remarkable comeback of asylums in Britain.

Segal, E. (2004). Incubation in insight problem solving. *Creativity Research Journal, 16*(1), 141–148.

Segal, N. L., & Roy, A. (2001). Suicidal attempts and ideation in twins whose co-twins' deaths were non-suicides: Replication and elaboration. *Personality & Individual Differences, 31*(3), 445–452.

Segan, C. J., Borland, R., & Greenwood, K. M. (2002). Do transtheoretical model measures predict the transition from preparation to action in smoking cessation? *Psychology & Health, 17*(4), 417–435.

Seidman, S. M. (2003). The aging male: Androgens, erectile dysfunction, and depression. *Journal of Clinical Psychiatry, 64*(Suppl. 10), 31–37.

Selemon, L. D., Mrzljak, J., Kleinman, J. E., Herman, M. M., & Goldman-Rakic, P. S. (2003). Regional specificity in the neuropathologic substrates of schizophrenia: A morphometric analysis of Broca's area 44 and area 9. *Archives of General Psychiatry, 60*(1), 69–77.

Seligman, M. E. P. (1996, August). Predicting and preventing depression. Master lecture presented to the meeting of the American Psychological Association, Toronto.

Selye, H. (1976). *The stress of life* (Rev. ed.). New York: McGraw-Hill. Kutash, et al. (Eds.), *Handbook on stress and anxiety.* San Francisco: Jossey-Bass.

Selye, H. (1980). The stress concept today. In I. L. *Sex & Marital Therapy, 31*(3), 173–185.

Shadish, W. R., Matt, G. E., Navarro, A. M., & Phillips, G. (2000). The effects of psychological therapies under clinically representative conditions: A meta-analysis. *Psychological Bulletin, 126*(4), 512–529.

Shafran, R., Cooper, Z., & Fairburn, C. (2002). Clinical perfectionism: A cognitive–behavioural analysis. *Behaviour Research and Therapy, 40*(7), 773–791.

Shanker, S. G., Savage-Rumbaugh, E. S., & Taylor, T. J. (1999). Kanzi: A new beginning. *Animal Learning & Behavior, 27*(1), 24–25.

Shapiro, F. (1989). Efficacy of the eye movement desensitization procedure in the treatment of traumatic memories. *Journal of Traumatic Stress, 2,* 199–223.

Shapley, R., & Hawken, M. (2002). Neural mechanisms for color perception in the primary visual cortex. *Current Opinion in Neurobiology, 12*(4), 426–432.

Shen, R-Y, Choong, K-C, & Thompson, A. C. (2007). Long-term reduction in ventral tegmental area dopamine neuron population activity following repeated stimulant or ethanol treatment. *Biological Psychiatry, 61*(1), 93–100.

Shenal, B. V., & Harrison, D. W. (2003). Investigation of the laterality of hostility, cardiovascular regulation, and auditory recognition. *International Journal of Neuroscience, 113*(2), 205–222.

Shenefelt, P. D. (2003). Hypnosis-facilitated relaxation using self-guided imagery during dermatologic procedures. *American Journal of Clinical Hypnosis, 45*(3), 225–232.

Shepperd, J. A., & Koch, E. J. (2005). Pitfalls in teaching judgment heuristics. *Teaching of Psychology, 32*(1), 43–46.

Sherrington, J. M., Hawton, K. E., Fagg, J., Andrews, B., & Shiffman, S., et al. (2000). Dynamic effects of self-efficacy on smoking lapse and relapse. *Health Psychology, 19*(4), 315–323.

Shimamura, A. P. (2002). Memory retrieval and executive control processes. In D. T. Stuss & R. T. Knight (Eds.), *Principles of frontal lobe function* (pp. 210–220). London: Oxford University Press.

Shneidman, E. S. (2001). *Comprehending suicide.* Washington, DC: American Psychological Association.

Sieber, J. E. (2004). Using our best judgment in conducting human research. *Ethics & Behavior, 14*(4), 297–304.

Siegel, J. M. (2002). The REM sleep–memory consolidation hypothesis. *Science, 294*(5544), 1058–1063.

Siesta time; Power napping. (2002, June 1). *The Economist.* This article discusses a research study where subjects took afternoon naps and were subsequently tested on a visual perception task.

Silventoinen, K., et al. (2007). Genetic and environmental factors in relative weight from birth to age 18: The Swedish young male twins study. *International Journal of Obesity, 31*(4), 615-621.

Silver, E. (1994). Cited in DeAngelis, T. (1994). Experts see little impact from insanity plea ruling. *APA Monitor, 25*(6), 28.

Simonton, D. K. (2000). Creativity: Cognitive, personal, developmental, and social aspects. *American Psychologist, 55,* 151–158

Simpson, M. L., Olejnik, S., Tam, A. Y., & Supattathum, S. (1994). Elaborative verbal rehearsals and college students' cognitive performance. *Journal of Educational Psychology, 86,* 267–278.

Singareddy, R. K., & Balon, R. (2002). Sleep in posttraumatic stress disorder. *Annals of Clinical Psychiatry, 14*(3), 183–190.

Singh, R., Yeo, S. E-L., Lin, P. K. F., & Tan, L. (2007). Multiple mediators of the attitude similarity-attraction relationship: Dominance of inferred attraction and subtlety of affect. *Basic and Applied Social Psychology, 29*(1), 61–74.

Singletary, K. W., & Gapstur, S. M. (2001). Alcohol and breast cancer: Review of epidemiologic and experimental evidence and potential mechanisms. *Journal of the American Medical Association, 286*(17), 2143–2151.

Skelton, C. (2005). Boys and schooling in the early years. *International Journal of Early Years Education, 13*(1), 83–84

Skinner, B. F. (1938). *The behavior of organisms: An experimental analysis.* New York: Appleton.

Skinner, B. F. (1948). *Walden Two.* New York: Macmillan.

Sleep and dreams. (2002). *Science Weekly, 19,* 1–12. This article is geared towards helping children understand the various aspects of sleep.

Slobin, D. I. (1983). Crosslinguistic evidence for basic child grammar. Paper presented to the biennial meeting of the Society for Research in Child Development, Detroit.

Sloman, S. A., Harrison, M. C., & Malt, B. C. (2002). Recent exposure affects artifact naming. *Memory & Cognition, 30*(5), 687–695.

Smetana, J. G., Daddis, C., & Chuang, S. S. (2003). "Clean your room!" A longitudinal investigation of adolescent–parent conflict and conflict resolution in middle-class African American families. *Journal of Adolescent Research, 18*(6), 631–650.

Smiley, J. (2000, May 7). The good life. *The New York Times magazine,* pp. 58–59.

Smith, D. (2001). Outcome of women admitted to hospital for depressive illness: Factors in the prognosis of severe depression. *Psychological Medicine, 31*(1), 115–125.

Smith, D. (2003b). Five principles for research ethics. *Monitor on Psychology, 34*(1), 56–60.

Smith, D. (2003c). What you need to know about the new code: The chair of APA's Ethics Code Task Force highlights changes to the 2002 Ethics Code. *Monitor on Psychology online, 34*(1).

Smith, J. F. (2001). Biological evidence for evolution. *Journal of the Idaho Academy of Science, 37,* 102–104. This article discusses considerations for the biological evidence for evolution.

Smith, M. L., & Glass, G. V. (1977). Meta-analysis of psychotherapy outcome studies. *American Psychologist, 32,* 752–760.

Smith, R. A., & Weber, A. L. (2005). Applying social psychology in everyday life. In F. W. Schneider, et al. (Eds.), *Applied social psychology: Understanding and addressing social and practical problems* (pp. 75–99). Thousand Oaks, CA: Sage Publications.

Smith, T. W., & Ruiz, J. M. (2002). Course of coronary heart disease: Current status and implications for research and practice. *Journal of Consulting and Clinical Psychology, 70*(3), 548–568.

Smith, V. (2000, February 16). Female heart, geography link shown. The Associated Press.

Smits, T., Storms, G., Rosseel, Y., & De Boeck, P. (2002). Fruits and vegetables categorized: An application of the generalized context model. *Psychonomic Bulletin & Review, 9*(4), 836–844.

Soll, J. B., & Klayman, J. (2004). Overconfidence in interval estimates. *Journal of Experimental Psychology: Learning, Memory & Cognition, 30*(2), 299–314.

Sorenson, S. B., & Rutter, C. M. (1991). Transgenerational patterns of suicide attempt. *Journal of Consulting and Clinical Psychology, 59,* 861–866.

Soussignan, R. (2002). Duchenne smile, emotional experience, and autonomic reactivity: A test of the facial feedback hypotheses. *Emotion, 2*(1), 52–74.

Spasojevic, J., & Alloy, L. B. (2001). Rumination as a common mechanism relating depressive risk factors to depression. *Emotion, 1*(1), 25–37.

Spencer, M. B., Noll, E., & Cassidy, E. (2005). Monetary incentives in support of academic achievement: Results of a randomized field trial involving high-achieving, low-resource, ethnically diverse urban adolescents. *Evaluation Review, 29*(3), 199–222.

Speranza, M., et al. (2001). Obsessive compulsive disorders in eating disorders. *Eating Behaviors, 2*(3), 193–207.

Sperling, G. (1960). The information available in brief visual presentations. *Psychological Monographs, 74,* 1–29.

Sperry, R. W. (1982). Some effects of disconnecting the cerebral hemispheres. *Science, 217*(4566), 1223–1226.

Spiers, H. J., Maguire, E. A., & Burgess, N. (2001). Hippocampal amnesia. *Neurocase, 7*(5), 357–382.

Sprecher, S., Fehr, B., & Zimmerman, C. (2007). Expectation for mood enhancement as a result of helping: The effects of gender and compassionate love. *Sex Roles, 56*(7-8), 543-549.

Sprecher, S., Sullivan, Q., & Hatfield, E. (1994). Mate selection preferences. *Journal of Personality and Social Psychology, 66*(6), 1074–1080.

Squire, L. R. (2004). Memory systems of the brain: A brief history and current perspective. *Neurobiology of Learning & Memory, 82*(3), 171–177.

Squire, L. R. (2004). Memory systems of the brain: A brief history and current perspective. *Neurobiology of Learning & Memory, 82*(3), 171–177.

Stacy, A. W., Bentler, P. M., & Flay, B. R. (1994). Attitudes and health behavior in diverse populations. *Health Psychology, 13,* 73–85.

Stampfer, M. J., Kang, J. H., Chen, J., Cherry, R., & Grodstein, F. (2005). Effects of moderate alcohol consumption on cognitive function in women. *New England Journal of Medicine, 352*(3), 245–253.

Stasser, G. (1999). A primer of social decision scheme theory: Models of group influence, competitive model-testing, and prospective modeling. *Organizational Behavior & Human Decision Processes, 80*(1), 3–20.

Steenari, R., Vuontela, V., Paavonen, E. J., Carlson, S., Fjallberg, M., & Aronen, E.T. (2003). Working memory and sleep in

6 to 13-year old schoolchildren. *Journal of the American Academy of Child and Adolescent Psychiatry, 42,* 85–92. This article reports the results of a study showing that lack of sleep can impair memory performance.

Steinberg, L. (1996). *Beyond the classroom.* New York: Simon & Schuster.

Steinberg, L. (2001). We know some things: Parent–adolescent relationships in retrospect and prospect. *Journal of Research on Adolescence, 11*(1), 1–19.

Sternberg, R. J. (1988). Triangulating love. In R. J.Sternberg & M. J. Barnes (Eds.), *The psychology of love.* New Haven, CT: Yale University Press.

Sternberg, R. J. (2000). Wisdom as a form of giftedness. *Gifted Child Quarterly, 44*(4), 252–260.

Sternberg, R. J. (2001). What is the common thread of creativity? *American Psychologist, 56*(4), 360–362.

Sternberg, R. J., & Lubart, T. I. (1996). Investing in creativity. *American Psychologist, 51,* 677–688.

Sternberg, R. J., & Williams, W. M. (1997). Does the Graduate Record Examination predict meaningful success in the graduate training of psychologists?

Sternberg, R. J., Lautrey, J., & Lubart, T. I. (2003). *Models of intelligence: International perspectives.*

Stevens, S. E., Hynan, M. T., & Allen, M. (2000). A meta-analysis of common factor and specific treatment effects across the outcome domains of the phase model of psychotherapy. *Clinical Psychology: Science and Practice, 7,* 273–290.

Stevenson, H. W., Lee, S. Y., & Stigler, J. W. (1986). Mathematics achievement of Chinese, Japanese, and American children. *Science, 231,* 693–699.

Stewart, A. E. (2005). Attributions of responsibility for motor vehicle crashes. *Accident Analysis & Prevention. 37*(4), 681–688.

Stickgold, R., Hobson, J. A., Fosse, R., & Fosse, M. (2001). Sleep, learning, and dreams: Off-line memory reprocessing. *Science, 294*(5544), 1052–1057.

Stier, D. S., & Hall, J. A. (1984). Gender differences in touch. *Journal of Personality and Social Psychology, 47,* 440–459.

Stipek, D., & Hakuta, K. (2007). Strategies to ensure that no child starts from behind. In Aber, J. L., et al. (Eds.). *Child development and social policy: Knowledge for action, APA Decade of Behavior volumes.* (pp. 129–145). Washington, DC: American Psychological Association.

Stocker, S. (1994). Stop a headache in 5 minutes. *Prevention, 46,* 65–72. This article discusses the importance of relaxation when faced with a tension headache and suggests that if a person relaxes for five minutes in the early stages of the headache, that it will go away.

Storm, L., & Ertel, S. (2001). Does psi exist? Comments on Milton and Wiseman's (1999) metaanalysis of Ganzfeld research. *Psychological Bulletin, 127*(3), 424–433.

Storm, L., & Ertle, S. (2002). The Ganzfeld debate continued: A response to Milton & Wiseman (2001). *Journal of Parapsychology, 66*(1), 73–82.

Straube, E. R., & Oades, R. D. (1992). *Schizophrenia.* San Diego: Academic Press.

Strickland, T. L., & Gray, G. (2000). Neurobehavioral disorders and pharmacologic intervention: The significance of ethnobiological variation in drug responsivity. In E. Fletcher-Janzen, et al. (Eds.), Handbook of cross-cultural neuropsychology (pp. 361–369). Dordrecht, Netherlands: Kluwer Academic Publishers.

Striegel-Moore, R. H., & Cachelin, F. M. (2001). Etiology of eating disorders in women. *Counseling Psychologist, 29*(5), 635–661.

Striegel-Moore, R. H., et al. (2003). Eating disorders in White and Black women. *American Journal of Psychiatry, 160,* 1326–1331.

Striegel-Moore, R. H., et al. (2004). Changes in weight and body image over time in women with eating disorders. *International Journal of Eating Disorders, 36*(3), 315–327.

Stroele, A., et al. (2002). GABA-sub(A) receptormodulating neuroactive steroid composition in patients with panic disorder before and during paroxetine treatment. *American Journal of Psychiatry, 159*(1), 145–147.

Strom, J. C., & Buck, R. W. (1979). Staring and participants' sex. *Personality and Social Psychology Bulletin, 5,* 114–117.

Strote, J., Lee, J. E., & Wechsler, H. (2002). Increasing MDMA use among college students: Results of a national survey. *Journal of the American Academy of Child & Adolescent Psychiatry, 41*(10), 1215.

Stroud, M. W., Thorn, B. E., Jensen, M. P., & Boothby, J. L. (2000). The relation between pain beliefs, negative thoughts, and psychosocial functioning in chronic pain patients. *Pain, 84*(2–3), 347–352.

Studies in Conflict & Terrorism, 27(4), 283–295.

Stutts, J. C., Wilkins, J. W., Osberg, J. S., & Vaughn, B. V. (2003). Driver risk factors for sleep-related crashes. *Accident Analysis & Prevention, 35*(3), 321–331.

Stutzer, A. (2004). The role of income aspirations in individual happiness. *Journal of Economic Behavior & Organization, 54*(1), 89–109.

Sufka, K. J., & Price, D. D. (2002). Gate control theory reconsidered. *Brain & Mind, 3*(2), 277–290.

Suler, J. (2005, March 29). Psychological qualities of cyberspace. http://www.rider.edu/suler/psycyber/netself.html.

Suttle, C. M., Banks, M. S., & Graf, E. W. (2002). FPL and sweep VEP to tritan stimuli in young human infants. *Vision Research, 42*(26), 2879–2891.

Suvisaari, J., Mautemps, N., Haukka, J., Hovi, T., & Löönnqvist, J. (2003). Childhood central nervous system viral infections and adult schizophrenia. *American Journal of Psychiatry, 160,* 1183–1185.

Swendsen, J. D., et al. (2000). Mood and alcohol consumption: An experience sampling test of the self-medication hypothesis. *Journal of Abnormal Psychology, 109*(2), 198–204.

Swerdlow, N. R., et al. (2003). Prestimulus modification of the startle reflex: Relationship to personality and psychological markers of dopamine function. *Biological Psychology, 62*(1), 17–26.

Swinyard, W. R., Kau, A., & Phua, H. (2001). Happiness, materialism, and religious experience in the U.S. and Singapore. *Journal of Happiness Studies, 2*(1), 13–32.

Szala, M. (2002). Two-level pattern recognition in a class of knowledge-based systems. *Knowledge-Based Systems, 15*(1–2), 95–101.

T

Taffe, M. A., et al. (2002). Cognitive performance of MDMA-treated rhesus monkeys: Sensitivity to serotonergic challenge. *Neuropsychopharmacology, 27*(6), 993–1005.

Tait, R. C. (2005). Mind matters: Psychological interventions for chronic pain. *Clinical Journal of Pain, 21*(1), 106–107.

Takahashi, T., et al. (2002). Melatonin alleviates jet lag symptoms caused by an 11-hour eastward flight. *Psychiatry & Clinical Neurosciences, 56*(3), 301–302.

Takemura, K. (1994). Influence of Elaboration on the Framing of Decision. *The Journal of Psychology, 128,* 33–39. This article presents a demonstration of the framing effect.

Tanasescu, M., et al. (2002). Exercise type and intensity in relation to coronary heart disease in men. *Journal of the American Medical Association, 288,* 1994–2000.

Taylor, D. J., & McFatter, R. M. (2003). Cognitive performance after sleep deprivation: Does personality make a difference? *Personality & Individual Differences, 34*(7), 1179–1193.

Taylor, S. E. (2000). Cited in Goode, E. (2000, May 19). Response to stress found that's particularly female. *The New York Times,* p. A20.

Taylor, S. E., et al. (2000b). Biobehavioral responses to stress in females: Tend-and-befriend, not fight-or-flight. *Psychological Review, 107*(3), 411–429.

Teachout, T. (2000, April 2). For more artists, a fine old age. *The New York Times online.*

Teller, D. Y. (1998). Spatial and temporal aspects of infant color vision. *Vision Research, 38*(21), 3275–3282.

Tenenbaum, H. R., & Leaper, C. (2002). Are parents' gender schemas related to their children's gender-related cognitions? A meta-analysis. *Developmental Psychology, 38*(4), 615–630.

Tennen, H., & Affleck, G. (2000). The perception of personal control: Sufficiently important to warrant careful scrutiny. *Personality & Social Psychology Bulletin, 26*(2), 152–156.

Terrace, H. S. (1979, November). How Nim Chimpsy changed my mind. *Psychology Today,* pp. 65–76.

Tetlock, P. E., & McGraw, A. P. (2005). Theoretically framing relational framing. *Journal of Consumer Psychology, 15*(1), 35–37.

Thom, A., Sartory, G., & Jo¨hren, P. (2000). Comparison between one-session psychological treatment and benzodiazepine in dental phobia. *Journal of Consulting and Clinical Psychology, 68*(3), 378–387.

Thomas, A. K., & Loftus, E. F. (2002). Creating bizarre false memories through imagination. *Memory & Cognition, 30*(3), 423–431.

Thompson, B. R., & Thornton, H. J. (2002). The transition from extrinsic to intrinsic motivation in the college classroom: A first year experience. *Education, 122,* 785–782. This article describes the difficulties some college students have as they move from an extrinsically based high school motivation to an intrinsically based college experience.

Thompson, P. M., et al. (2001). Mapping adolescent brain change reveals dynamic wave of accelerated gray matter loss in very early-onset schizophrenia.

Thurstone, L. L. (1938). Primary mental abilities. *Psychometric Monographs, 1.*

Tigner, R. B., & Tigner, S. S. (2000). Triarchic theories of intelligence: Aristotle and Sternberg. *History of Psychology, 3*(2), 168–176.

Tkachuk, G. A., & Martin, G. L. (1999). Exercise therapy for patients with psychiatric disorders: Research and clinical implications. *Professional Psychology: Research and Practice, 30*(3), 275–282.

Tolman, E. C., & Honzik, C. H. (1930). Introduction and removal of reward, and maze performance in rats. *University of California Publications in Psychology, 4,* 257–275.

Tong, H. (2001). Loneliness, depression, anxiety, and the locus of control. *Chinese Journal of Clinical Psychology, 9*(3), 196–197.

Tormala, Z. L., & Petty, R. E. (2004). Source credibility and attitude certainty: A metacognitive analysis of resistance to persuasion. *Journal of Consumer Psychology, 14*(4), 427–442.

Townsend, E., et al. (2001). The efficacy of problem-solving treatments after deliberate selfharm. Meta-analysis of randomizes controlled trials with respect to depression, hopelessness and improvement in problems. *Psychological Medicine,* 31(6), 979–988.

Triandis, H. C. (2005). Issues in individualism and collectivism research. In R. M. Sorrentino, et al. (Eds.). *Cultural and social behavior: The Ontario Symposium, 10.* (pp. 207–225). Mahwah, NJ: Erlbaum.

Triandis, H. C., & Suh, E. M. (2002). Cultural influences on personality. *Annual Review of Psychology, 53*(1), 133–160.

Trobst, K. K., Collins, R. L., & Embree, J. M. (1994). The role of emotion in social support provision. *Journal of Social and Personal Relationships, 11,* 45–62.

Trull, T. J., Stepp, S. D., & Durrett, C. A. (2003). Research on borderline personality disorder: An update. *Current Opinion in Psychiatry, 16*(1), 77–82.

Tsai, G., & Coyle, J. T. (2002). Glutamatergic mechanisms in schizophrenia. *Annual Review of Pharmacology & Toxicology, 42,* 165–179.

Tsang, Y. C. (1938). Hunger motivation in gastrectomized rats. *Journal of Comparative Psychology, 26,* 1–17.

Tsou, M., & Liu, J. (2001). Happiness and domain satisfaction in Taiwan. *Journal of Happiness Studies, 2*(3), 269–288.

Tulving, E. (1985). How many memory systems are there? *American Psychologist, 40,* 385–398.

Turk, D. C., & Okifuji, A. (2002). Psychological factors in chronic pain: Evolution and revolution. *Journal of Consulting and Clinical Psychology, 70*(3), 678–690.

Turkington, D., Dudley, R., Warman, D. M., & Beck, A. T. (2004). Cognitive-behavioral therapy for schizophrenia: A review. *Journal of Psychiatric Practice, 10*(1), 5–16.

Turner, M. E., Pratkanis, A. R., & Struckman, C. K. (2007). Groupthink as social identity maintenance. In A. R. Pratkanis (Ed.). *The science of social influence: Advances and future progress.* (pp. 223-246). New York: Psychology Press.

Tversky, A., & Kahneman, D. (1982). Judgment under uncertainty. In D. Kahneman, P. Slovic, & A. Tversky (Eds.), *Judgment under uncertainty: Heuristics and biases.* New York: Cambridge University Press.

Tyrka, A. R., Waldron, I., Graber, J. A., & Brooks-Gunn, J. (2002). Prospective predictors of the onset of anorexic and bulimic syndromes. *International Journal of the Eating Disorders, 32*(3), 282–290.

U

U.S. Department of Education, NCES. (2004).

Ulett, G. A., & Wedding, D. (2003). Electrical stimulation, endorphins, and the practice of clinical psychology. *Journal of Clinical Psychology in Medical Settings, 10*(2), 129–131.

Underhill, J. B. (2008). The politics of crisis management: Public leadership under pressure and Lessons on leadership by terror: Finding Shaka Zulu in the attic. *Political Psychology, 29*(1), 139-143.

Updegraff, J. A., Taylor, S. E., Kemeny, M. E., & Wyatt, G. E. (2002). Positive and negative effects of HIV infection in women with low socioeconomic resources. *Personality & Social Psychology Bulletin, 28*(3), 382–394.

Utter, J., Neumark-Sztainer, D., Wall, M., & Story, M. (2003). Reading magazine articles about dieting and associated weight control behaviors among adolescents. *Journal of Adolescent Health, 32*(1), 78–82.

Uzakov, S., Frey, J. U., & Korz, V. (2005). Reinforcement of rat hippocampal LTP by holeboard training. *Learning & Memory, 12,* 165–171.

V

Van Anders, S. M., Chernick, A. B., Chernick, B. A., Hampson, E., & Fisher, W. A. (2005). Preliminary clinical experience with androgen administration for pre- and postmenopausal women with hypoactive sexual desire. *Journal of Sex & Marital Therapy, 31*(3), 173–185.

van de Wetering, S., Bernstein, D. M., & Loftus, E. F. (2002). Public education against false memories: A modest proposal. *International Journal of Cognitive Technology, 7*(2), 4–7.

Vandenbergh, J. G. (1993). Cited in Angier, N. (1993, August 24). Female gerbil born with males is found to be begetter of sons. *The New York Times,* p. C4.

Vasterling, J. J., et al. (2002). Attention, learning, and memory performances and intellectual resources in Vietnam veterans: PTSD and no disorder comparisons. *Neuropsychology, 16*(1), 5–14.

Veenstra-Vanderweele, J., & Cook, E. H. (2003). Genetics of childhood disorders: XLVI. Autism, part 5: Genetics of autism. *Journal of the American Academy of Child and Adolescent Psychiatry, 42*(1), 116–118.

Velting, D. M., Rathus, J. H., & Miller, A. L. (2000). MACI personality scale profiles of depressed adolescent suicide attempters: A pilot study. *Journal of Clinical Psychology, 56*(10), 1381–1385.

Vernon, D., et al. (2003). The effect of training distinct neurofeedback protocols on aspects of cognitive performance. *International Journal of Psychophysiology, 47*(1), 75–85.

Villa, K. K., & Abeles, N. (2000). Broad spectrum intervention and the remediation of prospective memory declines in the able elderly. *Aging & Mental Health, 4*(1), 21–29.

Virtually Better. (2010, January 13). *Splash page.* (Accessed March 15, 2010). http://www.virtuallybetter.com/

Vorobyev, V. A., et al. (2004). Linguistic processing in visual and modality-nonspecific brain areas: PET recordings during selective attention. *Cognitive Brain Research, 20*(2), 309–322.

Vygotsky, L. (1978). *Mind in society: The development of higher psychological processes.* Cambridge, MA: Harvard University Press.

Vygotsky, L. S. (1962). *Thought and language.* Cambridge, MA: MIT Press.

W

Wagar, B. M., & Thagard, P. (2004). Spiking Phineas Gage: A neurocomputational theory of cognitive-affective integration in decision making. *Psychological Review, 111*(1), 67–79.

Wagner, R. K. (1997). Intelligence, training, and employment. *American Psychologist, 52*(10), 1059–1069.

Walker, E., Kestler, L., Bollini, A., & Hochman, K. M. (2004). Schizophrenia: Etiology and course. *Annual Review of Psychology, 55,* 401–430.

Walle, A. H. (2004). Native Americans and alcoholism therapy: The example of Handsome Lake as a tool of recovery. *Journal of Ethnicity in Substance Abuse, 3*(2), 55–79.

Walther, E., Nagengast, B., & Trasselli, C. (2005). Evaluative conditioning in social psychology: Facts and speculations. *Cognition & Emotion, 19*(2), 175–196.

Wang, C. (2002). Emotional intelligence, general self-efficacy, and coping style of juvenile delinquents.

Wang, J., Lin, W., & Chen, Z. (2002). The effects of psychological intervention on chemotherapy of cancer patients. *Psychological Science* (China), *25*(5), 517–519.

Wang, Q. (2003). Infantile amnesia reconsidered: A cross-cultural analysis. *Memory, 11*(1), 65–80.

Wang, X., et al. (2000). Longitudinal study of earthquake-related PTSD in a randomly selected community sample in North China. *American Journal of Psychiatry, 157,* 1260–1266.

Wann, D. L., & Schrader, M. P. (2000). Controllability and stability in the self-serving attributions of sport spectators. *Journal of Social Psychology, 140*(2), 160–168.

Wann, D. L., Royalty, J., & Roberts, A. (2000). The self-presentation of sports fans: Investigating the importance of team identification and self-esteem. *Journal of Sport Behavior, 23*(2), 198–206.

Warman, D. M., & Beck, A. T. (2003). Cognitive behavioral therapy for schizophrenia: An overview of treatment. *Cognitive & Behavioral Practice, 10*(3), 248–254.

Warman, D. M., & Cohen, R. (2000). Stability of aggressive behaviors and children's peer relationships. *Aggressive Behavior, 26*(4), 277–290.

Warman, D. M., Grant, P., Sullivan, K., Caroff, S., & Beck, A. T. (2005). Individual and group cognitive-behavioral therapy for psychotic disorders: A pilot investigation. *Journal of Psychiatric Practice, 11*(1), 27–34.

Washington, DC: American Psychological Association.

Waters, M. (2000). Psychologists spotlight growing concern of higher suicide rates among adolescents. *Monitor on Psychology, 31*(6), 41.

Watson, J. B. (1913). Psychology as the behaviorist views it. *Psychological Review, 20,* 158–177.

Weaver, C. A., III, & Krug, K. S. (2004). Consolidation- like effects in flashbulb memories: Evidence from September 11, 2001. *American Journal of Psychology, 117*(4), 517–530.

Webster, J. D. (2003). An exploratory analysis of a self-assessed wisdom scale. *Journal of Adult Development, 10*(1), 13–22.

Wechsler, D. (1975). Intelligence defined and undefined. *American Psychologist, 30,* 135–139.

Wegener, D. T., Petty, R. E., Detweiler-Bedell, B. T., & Jarvis, W. B. G. (2001). Implications of attitude change theories for numerical anchoring: Anchor plausibility and the limits of anchor effectiveness. *Journal of Experimental Social Psychology, 37*(1), 62–69.

Weinmann, M., Bader, J., Endrass, J., & Hell, D. (2001). Sind Kompetenz- und Kontrollueberzeugungen depressionsabhaengig? Eine Verlaufsuntersuchung. *Zeitschrift fuer Klinische Psychologie und Psychotherapie,* 30(3), 153–158.

Weiss, A., et al. (2005). Cross-sectional age differences in personality among Medicare patients aged 65 to 100. *Psychology and Aging, 20*(1), 182–185.

Wells, G. L., & Olsen, E. A. (2003). Eyewitness testimony. *Annual Review of Psychology, 54,* 277–295.

West, R., & Craik, F. I. M. (1999). Age-related decline in pro-spective memory: The roles of cue accessibility and cue sensitivity. *Psychology & Aging, 14*(2), 264–272.

Wetzler, S. E., & Sweeney, J. A. (1986). Childhood amnesia. In D. C. Rubin (Ed.), *Autobiographical memory.* New York: Cambridge University Press.

Wheeler, M. A., & McMillan, C. T. (2001). Focal retrograde amnesia and the episodic-semantic distinction. *Cognitive, Affective & Behavioral Neuroscience, 1*(1), 22–36.

Wheeler, M. E., & Treisman, A. M. (2002). Binding in short-term visual memory. *Journal of Experimental Psychology: General, 131*(1), 48–64.

Whitfield, K. E., Weidner, G., Clark, R., & Anderson, N. B. (2002). Sociodemographic diversity and behavioral medicine. *Journal of Consulting and Clinical Psychology, 70*(3), 463–481.

Whorf, B. (1956). *Language, thought, and reality.* New York: Wiley.

Widiger, T. A., & Costa, P. T., Jr. (1994). Personality and personality disorders. *Journal of Abnormal Psychology, 103,* 78–91.

Wiebe, R. E., & McCabe, S. B. (2002). Relationship perfectionism, dysphoria, and hostile interpersonal behaviors. *Journal of Social & Clinical Psychology, 21*(1), 67–91.

Wilkinson, D., & Abraham, C. (2004). Constructing an integrated model of the antecedents of adolescent smoking. *British Journal of Health Psychology, 9*(3), 315–333.

Willett, W. C. (2002). Balancing lifestyle and genomics research for disease prevention. *Science, 296*(5568), 695–698.

Williams, J. E., et al. (2000). Anger proneness predicts coronary heart disease risk : Prospective analysis from the Atherosclerosis Risk In Communities (ARIC) study. *Circulation, 101*(17), 2034–2039.

Williams, M. S., Thomsen, S. R., & McCoy, J. K. (2003). Looking for an accurate mirror: A model for the relationship between media use and anorexia. *Eating Behaviors, 4*(2), 127–134.

Williams, S. M., et al. (2000). Combinations of variations in multiple genes are associated with hypertension. *Hypertension, 36,* 2–6.

Wilson, K. D., & Farah, M. J. (2003). When does the visual system use viewpoint-invariant representations during recognition? *Cognitive Brain Research, 16*(3), 399–415.

Wilson, R. S. (1983). The Louisville twin study: Developmental synchronies in behavior. *Child Development, 54,* 298–316.

Winocur, G., et al. (2000). Cognitive rehabilitation in clinical neuropsychology. *Brain & Cognition, 42*(1), 120–123. *American Journal of Psychiatry, 160,* 572–574.

Wolkin, A., et al. (2003). Inferior frontal white matter anisotropy and negative symptoms of schizophrenia: A diffusion tensor imaging study.

Woloshyn, V. E., Paivio, A., & Pressley, M. (1994). Use of elaborative interrogation to help students acquire information consistent with prior knowledge and information inconsistent with prior knowledge. *Journal of Educational Psychology, 86,* 79–89.

Wood, W. (2000). Attitude change: Persuasion and social influence. *Annual Review of Psychology, 51,* 539–570.

Wooten, P. (1996). Humor: An antidote for stress. *Holistic Nursing Practice, 10,* 49–56. This article describes how stress can impact occupational functioning and suggests ways of dealing with stress including humor and laughter.

X

Xie, Y., & Goyette, K. (2003). Social mobility and the educational choices of Asian Americans. *Social Science Research, 32*(3), 467–498.

Y

Yacoubian, G. S. (2003). Correlates of ecstasy use among high school seniors surveyed through Monitoring the Future. *Drugs: Education, Prevention & Policy, 10*(1), 65–72.

Yang, Y., et al. (2005). Volume reduction in prefrontal gray matter in unsuccessful criminal psychopaths. *Biological Psychiatry, 57*(10), 1103–1108.

Yatham, L. N., et al. (2000). Brain serotonin2 receptors in major depression: A positron emission tomography study. *Archives of General Psychiatry, 57,* 850–858.

Ybarra, G. J., Passman, R. H., & Eisenberg, C. S. L. (2000). The presence of security blankets or mothers (or both) affects distress during pediatric examinations. *Journal of Consulting and Clinical Psychology, 68,* 322–330.

Yeh, C., & Chang, T. (2004). Understanding the multidimensionality and heterogeneity of the Asian American experience. *PsycCRITIQUES.*

Yesavage, J. A., et al. (2002). Modeling the prevalence and incidence of Alzheimer's disease and mild cognitive impair-

ment. *Journal of Psychiatric Research, 36*(5), 281–286.

Yokota, F., & Thompson, K. M. (2000). Violence in G-rated animated films. *Journal of the American Medical Association, 283,* 2716–2720.

Young, E. A., et al. (2003). Mineralocorticoid receptor function in major depression. *Archives of General Psychiatry, 60,* 24–28.

Z

Zahavi, A. (2003). Anniversary essay: Indirect selection and individual selection in sociobiology: My personal views on theories of social behavior. *Animal Behaviour, 65*(5), 859–863.

Zajonc, R. B. (2001). Mere exposure: A gateway to the subliminal. *Current Directions in Psychological Science, 10*(6), 224–228.

Zangwill (Eds.), *Amnesia.* London: Butterworth.

Zimbardo, P. G. (2004). A situationist perspective on the psychology of evil: Understanding how good people are transformed into perpetrators.

Zimbardo, P. G. (2008). The journey from the Bronx to Stanford to Abu Ghraib. In R. Levine, A. Rodrigues & L. Zelezny. (Eds.). *Journeys in social psychology: Looking back to inspire the future.* (pp. 85-104). New York: Psychology Press.

Zimbardo, P. G., LaBerge, S., & Butler, L. D. (1993). Psychophysiological consequences of unexplained arousal. *Journal of Abnormal Psychology, 102,* 466–473.

Zimmer, C. (2002–2003). Searching for your inner chimp. *Natural History, 112*(December, 2002–January, 2003).

Zimprich, D., & Martin, M. (2002). Can longitudinal changes in processing speed explain longitudinal age changes in fluid intelligence? *Psychology & Aging, 17*(4), 690–695.

Zizak, D. M., & Reber, A. S. (2004). Implicit preferences: The role(s) of familiarity in the structural mere exposure effect. *Consciousness & Cognition: An International Journal, 13*(2), 336–362.

Zucker, A. N., Ostrove, J. M., & Stewart, A. J. (2002). College-educated women's personality development in adulthood: Perceptions and age differences. *Psychology & Aging, 17*(2), 236–244.

Name Index

Clénet, F., 31
Coe, W. C., 106
Cohen, D. J., 263
Cohen, R., 134
Cohen, S., 238, 241, 242
Cohn, L. D., 66
Collaer, M. L., 182, 195, 199
Colvin, M. K., 40
Comaty, J. E., 278
Conklin, H. M., 253
Conrad, P. J., 110
Constantinidis, C., 39, 151
Conte, J. M., 236
Cook, E. H., 48
Cooke, M. C., 137
Cooper, M., 194
Corballis, P. M., 40
Corwin, R. L., 194
Cory, G. A., 45
Costa, Paul T., 217, 267
Coté, N., 166
Covino, N. A., 106
Cowen, P. J., 257
Cox, W. M., 182
Coyle, J. T., 254
Crabbe, J., 45, 46, 253
Craik, Fergus I. M., 144, 151
Crano, W. D., 291, 292, 293
Craske, M. G., 262
Crews, D., 195, 199
Crick, Francis, 46
Crick, N. R., 267
Crisp, R. J., 295
Crusco, A. H., 300
Csikszentmihalyi, M., 202
Cuellar, J. C., 257
Cummins, R. A., 202
Cumsille, P. E., 110
Curry, T. R., 257
Cutler, B. L., 160

D

Dalkvist, J., 94
Damasio, A. R., 26, 267
Darley, J. M., 306, 307
Darwin, Charles, 8, 11, 44, 201
Davenport, D. S., 283, 284
Davis, C., 30
Davis, S., 43
Davison, G. C., 282
Dawood, K., 198
Dawson, T. L., 61
DeAngelis, T, 261
DeCasper, A. J., 55
Decety, J., 307
Deecher, D., 258
Deep, A. L., 194
De Houwer, J., 291
Delgado, José, 39
Dellwo, J. P., 236

Delves, P. J., 241
De Maat, S., 282, 286
de Mello, M. F., 273
De Michele, P. E., 300
Dennerstein, L. L., 68
DeRubeis, R. J., 282, 286
DeSteno, D., 292
Devich-Navarro, M., 224
Devilly, G. J., 277
Devine, P. G., 292
DeVries, R., 59
DeVries, S. H., 81
Dhabhar, F. S., 239
Diaz, Lillian Comas, 13
Dickson, N., 68
Diener, E., 202
Dierker, L. C., 110
Dieter-Deckard, K., 182
Dietrich, A., 33
Difede, JoAnn, 276
DiLalla, D. L., 48
Dill, K. E., 138
Diseth, T. H., 265
Dobbins, I. G., 142
Dodge, K. A., 267
Dogil, G., 36
Dollard, J., 126
Domhoff, G. W., 103
Donohue, K. F., 111
Dovidio, J. F., 292
Dube, S. R., 115
Duckitt, J., 294, 295
Duckworth, 19
Duffy, F. H., 116
Duffy, V. B., 91
Dunkley, D. M., 235
Durbin, D. L., 64
Dweck, Carol, 200
d'Ydewalle, G., 143

E

Eagle, M., 156
Easterlin, R. A., 202
Ebbinghaus, Hermann, 154, 155
Egawa, T., 30, 31
Egerton, A., 115
Eibach, R., 290, 299
Eichenbaum, H., 158, 160
Eisner, C., 160
Ekman, Paul, 201, 203, 204, 206, 207
Elkind, D., 66
Ellickson, P. L., 293
Ellis, Albert, 235, 236, 279, 280, 282
Else-Quest, N. M., 182
Elshout, J. J., 59
Emmons, Robert, 234
Enard, W., 169
Engels, G. I., 282

Epstein, L. H., 190
Erikson, Erik, 12, 61, 67, 71, 215
Eron, L. D., 137, 138
Eslinger, P. J., 34
Evans, L., 256
Evans, S. W., 113
Eysenck, Hans J., 216, 217, 281, 282
Eysenck, M. V., 216

F

Fantz, Robert, 54
Farber, B. A., 274
Farmer, A., 45, 256
Fechner, Gustav Theodor, 7, 74
Feely, F., 115
Feeney, B. C., 202
Festinger, Leon, 187, 190, 294
Fields, R. D., 161
Fields, W. M., 170
Fifer, W. P., 102
Finkelstein, E. A., 193
Finkenauer, C., 152
Fireman, G., 103
Fisher, H. E., 195
Fisher, K., 294
Flavell, J. H., 59
Flegal, K. M., 192
Fletcher, B., 193
Flett, G. L., 256
Flouri, E., 67
Flynn, John, 184
Folkman, S., 237, 238, 262
Follingstad, D., 22, 251
Fontaine, K. R., 193
Forester, J., 293
Förster, J., 295
Fortin, N., 158, 160
Fortin, S., 143
Fouts, R. S., 169
Francis, L. J., 202
Frederick, S., 168
Freeman, M. S., 55
Freud, Sigmund, 10, 113, 150, 156, 210, 211, 212, 213, 215, 271, 272
Frisch, R., 64
Frith, C., 33
Fritsch, G., 39
Fromme, K., 111
Fuertes, A., 130
Fuligni, A. J., 181
Furnham, A., 202, 211

G

Gaab, J., 234
Gage, Phineas, 25, 33, 34, 36
Gaines, 296, 297
Gais, S., 102

Galaburda, A., 41
Galambos, N. L., 63, 64
Gallagher, S. N., 206
Galvani, Luigi, 27
Garb, H. N., 227
Garcia, J., 123
Gardner, Howard, 175
Gazzaniga, M. S., 33, 41
Geers, A., 90
Gegenfurtner, K. R., 81
Gendall, K. A., 194
Gentry, M. V., 114
Gershoff, E. T., 131
Geschwind, N., 41
Getzels, J. W., 177
Gignac, G., 175
Gijsman, H. J., 254
Gilligan, Carol, 66, 67
Gilovich, T., 167, 290, 299
Giuliano, 13
Glaser, R., 242
Glass, Gene, 282
Godfrey, J. R., 237
Goldman-Rakic, P. S., 39, 148, 150, 159
Goldstein, E. B., 90
Goleman, Daniel, 176, 177, 207
Gomez, P., 200, 207
Gonzalez, C., 168
Goodall, Jane, 18, 19
Goode, E., 194
Goodenough, Florence L., 181
Goodman, S. H., 258
Gopnik, A., 59
Gorman, J. M., 103
Gorodetsky, M., 166
Gottesman, I. I., 253
Gottman, J. M., 293
Gould, S. J., 44
Goyette, K., 181
Grady, C. L., 151
Granot, D., 62
Griffin, C., 67
Griffin, K. W., 110
Griffin, M. G., 261
Grilo, C. M., 193
Grossman, M. I., 191
Grusec, J. E., 64
Guerin, B., 305
Guidetti, M., 172
Gupta, V. B., 138

H

Haaga, D. A. F., 282
Habib, M., 41
Haddock, G., 290
Haidt, J., 202
Hakuta, K., 184
Hall, C. S., 103

Subject Index

mean, **313**, 313
means-end analysis, **165**
median, **313**, 313
media violence and aggression, 137–138, *138, 139*
meditation, 107–108
medulla, **36,** *36,* 36
memory, **145**
   biology of, 158, *158,* 159–161, *161*
   echoic, 147
   explicit, 142
   eyewitness testimony, 160
   five challenges, 141–142, *142*
   "flashbulb," 151–152
   forgetting, 154–158
   iconic, 147
   implicit, 142–143
   long-term, 150–154
   processes of, 144–145
   prospective, 143–144
   as reconstructive, *151*
   repression of, 156
   retrospective, 143–144
   sensory, 145–147
   short-term, 147–150
   and sleep, 102
   stages of, 145–154
   systems, 142–144
   working, 147–148
memory trace, **145**
men. *See* Gender
menarche, **65**
menopause, **68**
mental age (MA), **178,** 178
mental hospitals, 270
mental sets, **166,** 166
mescaline, **116,** 116, *117*
meta-analysis, **281**
metamemory, **144**
method of savings, **155**
middle adulthood, 68, 71
midlife crisis, **71,** 71
Milgram studies, 301–303, *301*
mindfulness meditation (MM), **108,** 108
Minnesota Multiphasic Personality Inventory (MMPI₃), 226, *226*
mob behavior, 307
mode, **313,** 313
model, **137**
modeling, **276,** 276
monochromat, **82**
monocular cues, **85,** 85, *85*
monozygotic (MZ) twins, **47**
mood disorders, 255
   biological perspective, 256
   biopsychosocial perspective, 257
   bipolar disorder, 255–256

major depression, 255
   psychological perspective, 256–257
   suicide and. *See* Suicide
moral development
   gender differences in, 66–67
   Kohlberg's theory, 60–61
motion parallax, **85**
motion perception, 84
motivation, 187, 190
   achievement, 199–200
   cognitive perspectives, 190–191
   drive-reductionism, 189
   evolutionary perspective, 188–189
   extrinsic motives, 200
   homeostasis, 189
   humanistic theory of, 190
   intrinsic motives, 200
   psychology of, 188
   sexual, 195–199
   stimulus motives, 189–190
   theories of, 188–191
motive, **188**
motor cortex, **39,** 39
motor development, 53–54, *54*
MRIs, **35,** 35–36, *35, 169*
Müller-Lyer illusion, 87, *87*
multiple approach-avoidance conflict, 234
multiple intelligences, 175, 185
multiple personality disorder, **264**
mutations, **44,** 44
mutism, **252**
myelin, **27**
myotonia, **196,** 196

N

narcolepsy, **104,** 104–105
narcotics, **112.** *See also* Drugs
naturalistic observation, 18, *18*
natural selection, **44,** 44
nature, **47**
nearsightedness, 79
needs, **188,** 188
negative reinforcers, **129,** 129–130, *130*
negative symptoms, **251,** 251–252
nerve, **31**
nervous system, 26–33, *31, 33*
neural activity and memory, 158–159
neural impulses, 27–29, *28,* **28,** *29*
neurons, *26,* **26,** 26–27
neuroticism, **256**
neurotransmitters, **29,** 29–31
nicotine, 114–115, *114, 115, 117*
   annual preventable deaths in the U.S., *243*

   as short-term reinforcement, 130
nonconscious, **99,** 99
nonrapid eye movement (NREM) sleep, **100,** 100
nonsense syllables, **154**
nonspecific factors, **283**
norepinephrine, **30,** 43
normal curve, **316,** 316–317, *316*
normal distribution, **316**
NREM sleep, 100
nurture, **47**

O

obedience to authority, 301–303
obesity, 192–193
objective personality tests, 225–227
objective responsibility, **58**
objective tests, **225**
object permanence, **56**
observational learning, **136,** 136
   and personality, 220
observation methods, 17–18
obsession, **260–261**
obsessive-compulsive disorder, 260–261
Oedipus complex, **213,** 213
olfactory nerve, **91**
operant behavior, **128**
operant conditioning, 120–127, **128**
   therapeutic procedures, 277–278
opiates, **112,** 112, *117*
opioids, **112**
opponent-process theory, **81,** 81, *81*
optic nerve, **78**
oral fixation, 212
oral stage, **212,** 212
organizational psychologists, 6
organizing effect, **195**
organ of Corti, **89,** 89
orgasmic phase, 196
orienting reflex, **122**
ovaries, 43
overregulation, **173**

P

pain, sensation of, 92–93
paired associates, **155**
panic disorder, **260,** 260
paranoid personality disorder, **265,** 265
paranoid schizophrenia, **252,** 252
parasympathetic, **32**
parasympathetic nervous system, **201**
parenting styles, 63–64

partial reinforcement, **132**
passion, **297**
pathogen, **231**
Pavlov's dogs, 120–121, *122*
PCP, **116,** 116, *117*
perception, **74,** 74–76
   of depth, 84–86
   extrasensory (ESP), 94–95
   of loudness, 90
   of motion, 84
   of pitch, 90
   social, 298–300
   visual, 82–87
perceptual constancies, 86–87
perceptual development, 54–55, *55*
perceptual organization, 82–84
peripheral nervous system, 32, **32**
permissive parents, **64,** 64
personal fable, **66**
personality, 209–210, **210**
   disorders. *See* Personality disorder(s)
   humanistic perspective, 221–222
   learning-theory perspectives, 218–219
   measurement of, 225–227
   psychoanalytic perspective, 210–216
   sociocultural perspective, 223–225
   trait perspective, 216–218
personality disorder(s), **265,** 265
   antisocial, 266, *266*
   avoidant, 266, 267
   biological factors, 267
   borderline, 266
   origins of, 266–267 paranoid, 265
   psychological factors, 267
   schizoid, 265–266
   schizotypal, 265–266
   sociocultural factors, 267
personality psychologists, 5
perspective, **85**
persuaded audience, 293
persuasive communicator, 293
persuasive message, 292–293
PET scans, **35,** 35, *35*
phallic stage, **213,** 213
"phantom" limb pain, 93
phencyclidine (PCP), **116,** 116, *117*
phenotype, **47**
phobias, 259–260
photoreceptors, **78**
physical appearance, 295
physical development
   adolescence, 64–65
   adulthood, 68–69

What's Changed? What's New? What's Different?

Chapter 1:

- "Participants" now used instead of "subjects"
- New figure providing information on demographics of new doctorates in psychology
- Revised section on The Biological and Evolutionary Perspectives
- New statistic at end of chapter to indicate the percent of new doctorate degrees earned by women

Chapter 2

- New definition provided for "neuron"
- New figure of the Parasympathetic and Sympathetic Branches of the Automatic Nervous System
- New figure of Broca's and Wernicke's Areas of the Cerebral Cortex
- New figure of the Endocrine Glands
- New figure of Cells, Chromosomes, and DNA

Chapter 3

- Updated example for *animism*
- New photo of Mary D. Salter Ainsworth
- New photo of Frank Lloyd Wright

Chapter 4

- Revised section on top-down and bottom-up processing

Chapter 5

- New definition of activation-synthesis model
- Updated table providing information about the gender, level of education, and percentage of those Americans who smoke
- New statistics about the number of Americans who regularly use heroin and the number of alcoholics in the U.S.

Chapter 6

- Updated definition of unconditioned stimulus (UCS)
- Updated definition of unconditioned response (UCR)
- Updated definition of conditioned stimulus (CS)
- Updated definition of conditioned response (CR)
- New section on Teaching Children *Not* to Imitate Media Violence

Chapter 7

- New box feature on trusting eyewitness testimony

Chapter 8

- New information about *sensitive periods*
- New Theories of Intelligence Summary Chart

Chapter 9

- Updated facts about obesity
- New photo of hyperphagic rats
- Updated table providing information on the number of years lost by an extremely obese person compared to a normal-weight person

© BEAU LARK/CORBIS

Chapter 10

- Formerly Chapter 11 (in the previous edition)
- Revised section/definition of personality
- Addition of *gender-typing* to running glossary

Chapter 11

- Formerly Chapter 10 (in previous edition)
- Revised section on Stress in America
- Updated figure on the number of deaths from heart disease

Chapter 12

- Bipolar Disorder added to Table 12.1 (prevalence of psychological disorders)

Chapter 13

- New information about Virtually Better

Chapter 14

- Deleted situationist perspective as a key term
- Updated facts about people choosing partners that are like them in race, ethnicity, age, level of education, and religion

IMAGES.COM/CORBIS

ZENSHUI/ALIX MINDE/PHOTOALTO AGENCY
RF COLLECTIONS/GETTY IMAGES

Chapter in Review

1

LO¹ **psychology**
the science that studies behavior and mental processes

theory
a formulation of relationships underlying observed events

LO² **pure research**
research conducted without concern for immediate applications

applied research
research conducted in an effort to find solutions to particular problems

LO³ **introspection**
deliberate looking into one's own cognitive processes to examine one's thoughts and feelings

structuralism
the school of psychology that argues that the mind consists of sations, feelings, to form experience

functionalism
the school of psy uses or functions of the mind rather than the elements of experience

behaviorism
the school of psychology that defines psychology as the study of observable behavior and studies relationships between stimuli and responses

reinforcement
a stimulus that follows a response and increases the frequency of the response

Gestalt psychology
the school of psychology that emphasizes the tendency to organize perceptions into wholes and to integrate separate stimuli into meaningful patterns

psychoanalysis
the school of psychology that emphasizes the importance of unconscious motives and conflicts as deter

LO⁴ **cog**
hav
such as sens
intelligence, l
solving

social-cogn
a school of p
tradition that
the explanati
formerly term

sociocultur
the view that
gender, cultu
behavior and

gender
the culturally
and *feminit*

> **Here, you'll find the key terms and definitions in the order they appear in the chapter.**

> ### How to Use the Card:
>
> 1. Look over the card to preview the new concepts you'll be introduced to in the chapter.
>
> 2. Read your chapter to fully understand the material.
>
> 3. Go to class (and pay attention).
>
> 4. Review the card one more time to make sure you've registered the key concepts.
>
> 5. Don't forget, this card is only one of many PSYCH learning tools available to help you succeed in your psychology course.

LO¹ Define psychology. Psychology is the scientific study of behavior and mental processes. Topics of interest to psychologists include the nervous system, sensation and perception, learning and memory, intelligence, language, thought, growth and development, personality, stress and health, psychological disorders, ways of treating these disorders, sexual behavior, and the behavior of people in social settings such as gr of the psychologist, like other scientists, is to describe, explain, pr or she studies—in this case, behavior and mental processes.

> **In this column, you'll find summary points supported by exhibits from the chapters.**

LO² Describe the various fields and subfields of psychology. Psychologists are found in a number of different specialties:

Clinical psychologists help people with psychological disorders adjust to the demands of life.

Counseling psychologists typically see clients with adjustment problems but not serious psychological disorders.

School psychologists help school systems identify and assist students who have problems that interfere with learning.

Educational psychologists research theoretical issues related to learning, measurement, and child development.

Developmental psychologists study the changes—physical, cognitive, social, and personality—that occur throughout the life span.

Personality psychologists identify and measure human traits and determine influences on human thought processes, feelings, and behavior.

Social psychologists are concerned with the nature and causes of individuals' thoughts, feelings, and behavior in social situations.

Environmental psychologists study the ways in which people and the environment influence one another.

Experimental psychologists specialize in basic processes such as the nervous system, sensation and perception, learning and memory, thought, motivation, and emotion.

Industrial psychologists focus on the relationships between people and work.

Organizational psychologists study the behavior of people in organizations such as businesses.

Human factors psychologists make technical systems more user-friendly.

Consumer psychologists study the behavior of shoppers in an effort to predict and influence their behavior.

Health psychologists examine the ways in which behavior and attitudes are related to physical health.

Sport psychologists help people improve their performance in sports.

Forensic psychologists apply principles of psychology to the criminal justice system.

LO³ Describe the origins of psychology and identify those who made significant contributions to the field. An ancient contributor to the modern field of psychology, Aristotle argued that human behavior, like the movements of the stars and the seas, is subject to rules and laws. Today, as then, the subject matter of the study of human behavior includes the study of personality, sensation and perception, thought, intelligence, needs and motives, feelings and emotion, and memory. The following is a list of the historic schools of psychology and the major proponent(s) of each: *Structuralism:* Wilhelm Wundt; *Functionalism:* William James; *Behaviorism:* John B. Watson and B. F. Skinner; *Gestalt Psychology:* Max Wertheimer, Kurt Koffka, and Wolfgang Köhler; and *Psychoanalysis:* Sigmund Freud, Carl Jung, Alfred Adler, Karen Horney, and Erik Erikson.

LO⁴ Identify theoretical perspectives of modern psychologists toward behavior and mental processes. There are several influential perspectives in contemporary psychology: biological and evolutionary, cognitive, humanistic–existential, psychodynamic, learning, and sociocultural.

• *Evolutionary psychologists* focus on the evolution of behavior and mental processes.

> **When it's time to prepare for exams, use the Card and the technique to the left to ensure successful study sessions.**

PSYCH was designed for students just like you—busy people who want choices, flexibility, and multiple learning options.

PSYCH delivers concise, focused information in a fresh and contemporary way. In addition to your tear-out review cards, PSYCH offers a variety of learning materials designed with you in mind. Visit CourseMate for PSYCH at www.cengagebrain.com to access multiple PSYCH resources to help you succeed.

- *Printable Flash Cards* Our extensive research shows that almost all students use flash cards to reinforce their understanding of core psychology concepts. To help you prepare flash cards that fit your specific study needs, the website provides three varieties of downloadable flash cards: 1) term only, 2) definition only, or 3) term and definition. Each set of cards is formatted to fit the standard Avery business card template.
- *Interactive Flashcards* Key terms are also available as interactive flash cards that allow you to shuffle the deck, remove a card, view the term first, or view the definition first.
- *PowerVisuals* Important concepts covered in images and graphs from PSYCH are provided as interactive visuals.
- *Learning Outcomes* Downloadable learning outcomes from PSYCH.
- *Build a Summary* You can select a chapter and check your understanding of text concepts by filling in the blanks of these paragraphs.
- *Glossary* Select a chapter to view glossary terms and definitions.
- *Tutorial Quizzes* You can practice before chapter tests, midterms, and finals by taking these interactive quizzes.
- *Web Links* Select a chapter to view web links that reinforce or extend concepts from the text.
- *Study Games* Fun study practice with Sort-It-Out and Crossword puzzles.

psychology

Chapter 1

The science that studies behavior and mental processes.

Chapter 1

YOU TOLD US HOW YOU LIKE TO STUDY, AND

WE LISTENED.

Chapter in Review

1

LO¹ psychology
the science that studies behavior and mental processes

theory
a formulation of relationships underlying observed events

LO² pure research
research conducted without concern for immediate applications

applied research
research conducted in an effort to find solutions to particular problems

LO³ introspection
deliberate looking into one's own cognitive processes to examine one's thoughts and feelings

structuralism
the school of psychology that argues that the mind consists of three basic elements—sensations, feelings, and images—that combine to form experience

functionalism
the school of psychology that emphasizes the uses or functions of the mind rather than the elements of experience

behaviorism
the school of psychology that defines psychology as the study of observable behavior and studies relationships between stimuli and responses

reinforcement
a stimulus that follows a response and increases the frequency of the response

Gestalt psychology
the school of psychology that emphasizes the tendency to organize perceptions into wholes and to integrate separate stimuli into meaningful patterns

psychoanalysis
the school of psychology that emphasizes the importance of unconscious motives and conflicts as determinants of human behavior

LO⁴ cognitive
having to do with mental processes such as sensation and perception, memory, intelligence, language, thought, and problem solving

social-cognitive theory
a school of psychology in the behaviorist tradition that includes cognitive factors in the explanation and prediction of behavior; formerly termed *social learning theory*

sociocultural perspective
the view that focuses on the roles of ethnicity, gender, culture, and socioeconomic status in behavior and mental processes

gender
the culturally defined concepts of *masculinity* and *femininity*

LO¹ Define psychology.
Psychology is the scientific study of behavior and mental processes. Topics of interest to psychologists include the nervous system, sensation and perception, learning and memory, intelligence, language, thought, growth and development, personality, stress and health, psychological disorders, ways of treating those disorders, sexual behavior, and the behavior of people in social settings such as groups and organizations. The goal of the psychologist, like other scientists, is to describe, explain, predict, and control the events he or she studies—in this case, behavior and mental processes.

LO² Describe the various fields and subfields of psychology.
Psychologists are found in a number of different specialties:

Clinical psychologists help people with psychological disorders adjust to the demands of life.

Counseling psychologists typically see clients with adjustment problems but not serious psychological disorders.

School psychologists help school systems identify and assist students who have problems that interfere with learning.

Educational psychologists research theoretical issues related to learning, measurement, and child development.

Developmental psychologists study the changes—physical, cognitive, social, and personality—that occur throughout the life span.

Personality psychologists identify and measure human traits and determine influences on human thought processes, feelings, and behavior.

Social psychologists are concerned with the nature and causes of individuals' thoughts, feelings, and behavior in social situations.

Environmental psychologists study the ways in which people and the environment influence one another.

Experimental psychologists specialize in basic processes such as the nervous system, sensation and perception, learning and memory, thought, motivation, and emotion.

Industrial psychologists focus on the relationships between people and work.

Organizational psychologists study the behavior of people in organizations such as businesses.

Human factors psychologists make technical systems more user-friendly.

Consumer psychologists study the behavior of shoppers in an effort to predict and influence their behavior.

Health psychologists examine the ways in which behavior and attitudes are related to physical health.

Sport psychologists help people improve their performance in sports.

Forensic psychologists apply principles of psychology to the criminal justice system.

LO³ Describe the origins of psychology and identify those who made significant contributions to the field.
An ancient contributor to the modern field of psychology, Aristotle argued that human behavior, like the movements of the stars and the seas, is subject to rules and laws. Today, as then, the subject matter of the study of human behavior includes the study of personality, sensation and perception, thought, intelligence, needs and motives, feelings and emotion, and memory. The following is a list of the historic schools of psychology and the major proponent(s) of each: *Structuralism:* Wilhelm Wundt; *Functionalism:* William James; *Behaviorism:* John B. Watson and B. F. Skinner; *Gestalt Psychology:* Max Wertheimer, Kurt Koffka, and Wolfgang Köhler; and
Psychoanalysis: Sigmund Freud, Carl Jung, Alfred Adler, Karen Horney, and Erik Erikson.

LO⁴ Identify theoretical perspectives of modern psychologists toward behavior and mental processes.
There are several influential perspectives in contemporary psychology: biological and evolutionary, cognitive, humanistic–existential, psychodynamic, learning, and sociocultural.

• *Evolutionary psychologists* focus on the evolution of behavior and mental processes.

LO⁵ hypothesis
in psychology, a specific statement about behavior or mental processes that is tested through research

correlation
an association or relationship among variables, as we might find between height and weight or between study habits and school grades

selection factor
a source of bias that may occur in research findings when subjects are allowed to choose for themselves a certain treatment in a scientific study

sample
part of a population

population
a complete group of organisms or events

random sample
a sample drawn so that each member of a population has an equal chance of being selected to participate

stratified sample
a sample drawn so that identified subgroups in the population are represented proportionately in the sample

volunteer bias
a source of bias or error in research reflecting the prospect that people who offer to participate in research studies differ systematically from people who do not

case study
a carefully drawn biography that may be obtained through interviews, questionnaires, and psychological tests

survey
a method of scientific investigation in which a large sample of people answer questions about their attitudes or behavior

naturalistic observation
a scientific method in which organisms are observed in their natural environments

correlation coefficient
a number between +1.00 and −1.00 that expresses the strength and direction (positive or negative) of the relationship between two variables

experiment
a scientific method that seeks to confirm cause-and-effect relationships by introducing independent variables and observing their effects on dependent variables

independent variable
a condition in a scientific study that is manipulated so that its effects may be observed

dependent variable
a measure of an assumed effect of an independent variable

experimental groups
in experiments, groups whose members obtain the treatment

control groups
in experiments, groups whose members do not obtain the treatment, while other conditions are held constant

placebo
a bogus treatment that has the appearance of being genuine

blind
in experimental terminology, unaware of whether or not one has received a treatment

double-blind study
a study in which neither the subjects nor the observers know who has received the treatment

informed consent
a subject's agreement to participate in research after receiving information about the purposes of the study and the nature of the treatments

debrief
to explain the purposes and methods of a completed procedure to a participant

---

- Psychologists with a *cognitive perspective* investigate the ways in which we perceive and mentally represent the world by learning, memory, planning, problem solving, decision making, and language.
- *The humanistic–existential perspective* is cognitive in flavor, yet emphasizes more the role of subjective (personal) experience.
- Neoanalysts with a *psychodynamic perspective* focus less on the unconscious—as was done in Freud's day—and more on conscious choice and self-direction.
- The first of two learning perspectives, *behaviorists* emphasize environmental influences and the learning of habits through repetition and reinforcement. *Social-cognitive theorists,* in contrast, suggest that people can modify and create their environments, and engage in intentional learning by observing others.
- A psychologist with a *sociocultural perspective* studies the influences of ethnicity, gender, culture, and socioeconomic status on behavior and mental processes.

LO⁵ Describe modern approaches to research and practice—critical thinking, the scientific method, and ethical considerations. Psychologists, like

other scientists, must use careful means to observe and measure behavior and the factors that influence behavior. Psychologists use evidence and critical thinking—the process of thoughtfully analyzing and probing the questions, statements, and arguments of others. The scientific method is a systematic way of organizing and expanding scientific knowledge. Daily experiences, common beliefs, and scientific observations all contribute to the development of theories. Psychological theories explain observations and lead to hypotheses about behavior and mental processes. Observations can then confirm the theory or lead to its refinement or abandonment. Many factors—such as the nature of the research sample—must be considered in interpreting the accuracy of the results of scientific research. Psychologists must also adhere to a number of ethical standards that are intended to promote individual dignity, human welfare, and scientific integrity. The standards are also intended to ensure that psychologists do not engage in harmful research methods or treatments.

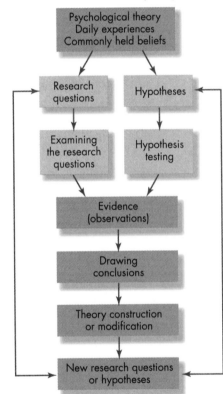

Chapter in Review

LO¹ neuron
a specialized cell of the nervous system that transmits messages

glial cells
cells that nourish and insulate neurons, direct their growth, and remove waste products from the nervous system

dendrites
rootlike structures, attached to the cell body of a neuron, that receive impulses from other neurons

axon
a long, thin part of a neuron that transmits impulses to other neurons from branching structures called *terminal buttons*

myelin
a fatty substance that encases and insulates axons, facilitating transmission of neural impulses

afferent neurons
neurons that transmit messages from sensory receptors to the spinal cord and brain. Also called *sensory neurons*

efferent neurons
neurons that transmit messages from the brain or spinal cord to muscles and glands. Also called *motor neurons*

neural impulse
the electrochemical discharge of a nerve cell, or neuron

polarize
to ready a neuron for firing by creating an internal negative charge in relation to the body fluid outside the cell membrane

resting potential
the electrical potential across the neural membrane when it is not responding to other neurons

depolarize
to reduce the resting potential of a cell membrane from about 70 millivolts toward zero

action potential
the electrical impulse that provides the basis for the conduction of a neural impulse along an axon of a neuron

all-or-none principle
the fact that a neuron fires an impulse of the same strength whenever its action potential is triggered

refractory period
a phase following firing during which a neuron is less sensitive to messages from other neurons and will not fire

synapse
a junction between the axon terminals of one neuron and the dendrites or cell body of another neuron

neurotransmitters
chemical substances involved in the transmission of neural impulses from one neuron to another

receptor site
a location on a dendrite of a receiving neuron tailored to receive a neurotransmitter

LO¹ Describe the nervous system, including neurons, neural impulses, and neurotransmitters.
The nervous system regulates the body and is involved in thought processes, emotional responses, heartbeat, and motor activity. The central nervous system contains the brain and the spinal cord. The somatic system transmits sensory information about skeletal muscles, skin, and joints and controls skeletal muscular activity. The autonomic system regulates glands and activities like digestion. Neurons transmit information through electrochemical neural impulses. Their dendrites receive messages and their axons conduct messages, transmitting them to other cells via neurotransmitters.

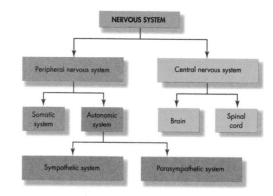

The Anatomy of a Neuron. "Messages" enter neurons through dendrites, are transmitted along the trunk-like axon, and then are sent from axon terminal buttons to muscles, glands, and other neurons. Axon terminal buttons contain sacs of chemicals called *neurotransmitters*. Neurotransmitters are released into the synaptic cleft, where many of them bind to receptor sites on the dendrites of the receiving neuron.

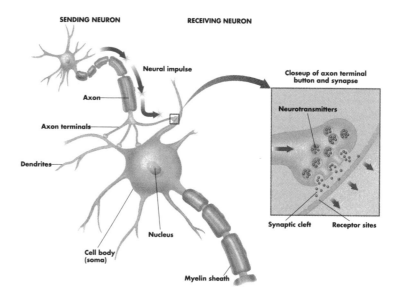

The Parasympathetic and Sympathetic Branches of the Autonomic Nervous System (ANS). The parasympathetic branch of the ANS generally acts to replenish stores of energy in the body. The sympathetic branch is most active during activities that expend energy. The two branches of the ANS frequently have antagonistic effects on the organs they service.

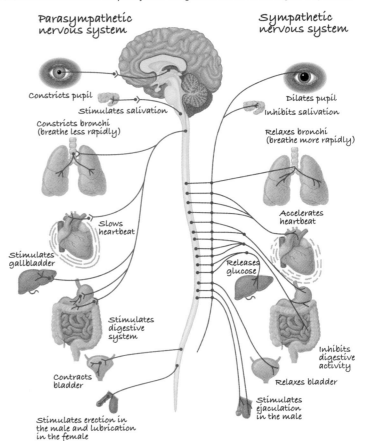

LO 2 List the structures of the brain and their functions. The hindbrain includes the medulla, the pons, and the cerebellum. The reticular activating system begins in the hindbrain and continues into the forebrain. Important structures of the forebrain include the thalamus, which serves as a relay station for sensory stimulation; the hypothalamus, which regulates body temperature and influences motivation and emotion; the limbic system, which is involved in memory, emotion, and motivation; and the cerebrum, which handles thinking and language. The outer fringe of the cerebrum is the cerebral cortex, which is divided into four lobes: frontal, parietal, temporal, and occipital.

The Parts of the Human Brain
The view of the brain, split top to bottom, shows some of the most important structures. The "valleys" in the cerebrum are called fissures.

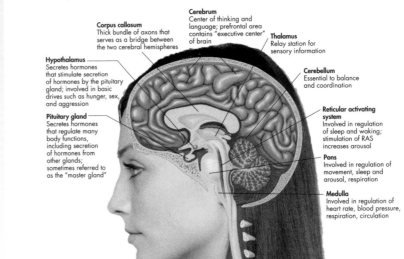

Chapter in Review

2

LO^2 **electroencephalograph (EEG)**
a method of detecting brain waves by means of measuring the current between electrodes placed on the scalp

computerized axial tomography (CAT scan)
a method of brain imaging that passes a narrow X-ray beam through the head and measures structures that reflect the rays from various angles, enabling a computer to generate a three-dimensional image

positron emission tomography (PET scan)
a method of brain imaging that injects a radioactive tracer into the bloodstream and assesses activity of parts of the brain according to the amount of glucose they metabolize

magnetic resonance imaging (MRI)
a method of brain imaging that places a person in a magnetic field and uses radio waves to cause the brain to emit signals that reveal shifts in the flow of blood which, in turn, indicate brain activity

functional MRI (fMRI)
a form of MRI that enables researchers to observe the brain "while it works" by taking repeated scans

medulla
a oblong area of the hindbrain involved in regulation of heartbeat and respiration

pons
a structure of the hindbrain involved in respiration, attention, and sleep and dreaming

cerebellum
a part of the hindbrain involved in muscle coordination and balance

reticular activating system (RAS)
a part of the brain involved in attention, sleep, and arousal

thalamus
an area near the center of the brain involved in the relay of sensory information to the cortex and in the functions of sleep and attention

hypothalamus
a bundle of nuclei below the thalamus involved in body temperature, motivation, and emotion

limbic system
a group of structures involved in memory, motivation, and emotion that forms a fringe along the inner edge of the cerebrum

amygdala
a part of the limbic system that apparently facilitates stereotypical aggressive responses

cerebrum
the large mass of the forebrain, which consists of two hemispheres

cerebral cortex
the wrinkled surface area (gray matter) of the cerebrum

corpus callosum
a thick fiber bundle that connects the hemispheres of the cortex

The geography of the cerebral cortex. The cortex has four lobes: frontal, parietal, temporal, and occipital. The visual area of the cortex is in the occipital lobe. The hearing or auditory cortex lies in the temporal lobe. The motor and somatosensory areas—shown below—face each other across the central fissure. Note that the face and the hands are "super-sized" in the motor and somatosensory areas. Why do you think this is so?

Primary motor
Fingers
Middle
Index
Ring
Little
Hand
Wrist
Elbow
Shoulder
Trunk
Hip
Knee
Thumb
Neck
Brow
Eyelid and eyeball
Face
Lips
Jaw
Tongue
Vocalization
Mastication
Swallowing
Ankle
Toes

Primary Somatosensory
Fingers
Middle
Index
Ring
Little
Hand
Forearm
Arm
Elbow
Wrist
Shoulder
Head
Neck
Trunk
Hip
Leg
Thumb
Eye
Nose
Face
Upper lip
Lips
Lower lip
Teeth, gums, and jaw
Tongue
Pharynx
Intra-abdominal organs
Foot
Toes
Genitalia

Motor area
Sensory area
Frontal lobe
Parietal lobe
Lateral fissure
Temporal lobe
Occipital lobe

LO^3 Explain the role of the endocrine system and list the endocrine glands. The glands of the endocrine system secrete hormones regulating development and activity. The pituitary gland secretes growth hormone, prolactin, and oxytocin. The thyroid regulates metabolism. The adrenal cortex produces steroids. The adrenal medulla secretes epinephrine, which increases the metabolic rate and stimulates general emotional arousal. The sex hormones are responsible for sexual differentiation and regulate the menstrual cycle in females.

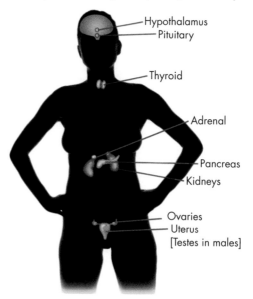

Hypothalamus
Pituitary
Thyroid
Adrenal
Pancreas
Kidneys
Ovaries
Uterus
[Testes in males]

somatosensory cortex
the section of cortex in which sensory stimulation is projected. It lies just behind the central fissure in the parietal lobe

motor cortex
the section of cortex that lies in the frontal lobe, just across the central fissure from the sensory cortex. Neural impulses in the motor cortex are linked to muscular responses throughout the body

aphasia
a disruption in the ability to understand or produce language

Wernicke's aphasia
a language disorder characterized by difficulty comprehending the meaning of spoken language

Broca's aphasia
a language disorder characterized by slow, laborious speech

epilepsy
temporary disturbances of brain functions that involve sudden neural discharges

LO³ gland
an organ that secretes one or more chemical substances such as hormones, saliva, or milk

endocrine system
the body's system of ductless glands that secrete hormones and release them directly into the bloodstream

hormone
a substance secreted by an endocrine gland that regulates various body functions

pituitary gland
the gland that secretes growth hormone, prolactin, antidiuretic hormone, and other hormones

LO⁴ Describe evolutionary psychology and the connections between heredity, behavior, and mental processes. Evolutionary psychology studies the way natural selection influences mental processes and behavior. Evolutionary psychologists suggest that behavior evolves as it is transmitted from generation to generation. Evolutionarily advantageous behaviors like aggression, strategic mate selection, and familial altruism are often influenced by heredity.

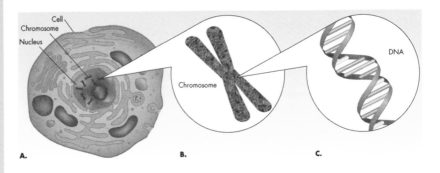

LO⁴ natural selection
a core concept of the theory of evolution that holds that adaptive genetic variations among members of a species enable individuals with those variations to survive and reproduce

mutation
a sudden variation in an inheritable characteristic, as distinguished from a variation that results from generations of gradual selection

evolutionary psychology
the branch of psychology that studies the ways in which adaptation and natural selection are connected with mental processes and behavior

species
a category of biological classification consisting of related organisms who are capable of interbreeding. *Homo sapiens*—humans—make up one species

instinct
a stereotyped pattern of behavior that is triggered by a particular stimulus and nearly identical among members of a species, even when they are reared in isolation

heredity
the transmission of traits from parent to offspring by means of genes

genetics
the area of biology that focuses on heredity

gene
a basic unit of heredity, which is found at a specific point on a chromosome

chromosome
a microscopic rod-shaped body in the cell nucleus carrying genes that transmit hereditary traits from generation to generation. Humans normally have 46 chromosomes

DNA
acronym for deoxyribonucleic acid, the substance that forms the basic material of chromosomes. It takes the form of a double helix and contains the genetic code

polygenic
referring to traits that are influenced by combinations of genes. Genotype One's genetic makeup, based on the sequencing of the nucleotides we term A, C, G, and T

phenotype
one's actual development and appearance, as based on one's genotype and environmental influences

nature
the inborn, innate character of an organism

nurture
the sum total of the environmental factors that affect an organism from conception onward

sex chromosomes
the 23rd pair of chromosomes, whose genetic material determines the sex of the individual

Down syndrome
a condition caused by an extra chromosome on the 21st pair and characterized by mental deficiency, a broad face, and slanting eyes

monozygotic (MZ) twins
twins that develop from a single fertilized ovum that divides in two early in prenatal development. MZ twins thus share the same genetic code. Also called *identical twins*

dizygotic (DZ) twins
twins that develop from two fertilized ova and who are thus as closely related as brothers and sisters in general. Also called *fraternal twins*

Chapter in Review

3

LO¹ zygote
a fertilized ovum (egg cell)

germinal stage
the first stage of prenatal development, during which the dividing mass of cells has not become implanted in the uterine wall

amniotic sac
a sac within the uterus that contains the embryo or fetus

placenta
a membrane that permits the exchange of nutrients and waste products between the mother and her developing child but does not allow the maternal and fetal bloodstreams to mix

umbilical cord
a tube between the mother and her developing child through which nutrients and waste products are conducted

LO² reflex
a simple unlearned response to a stimulus

rooting
the turning of an infant's head toward a touch, such as by the mother's nipple

fixation time
the amount of time spent looking at a visual stimulus

assimilation
according to Piaget, the inclusion of a new event into an existing schema

schema
according to Piaget, a hypothetical mental structure that permits the classification and organization of new information

accommodation
according to Piaget, the modification of schemas so that information inconsistent with existing schemas can be integrated or understood

object permanence
recognition that objects removed from sight still exist, as demonstrated in young children by continued pursuit

sensorimotor stage
the first of Piaget's stages of cognitive development, characterized by coordination of sensory information and motor activity, early exploration of the environment, and lack of language

preoperational stage
the second of Piaget's stages, characterized by illogical use of words and symbols, spotty logic, and egocentrism

egocentrism
according to Piaget, the assumption that others view the world as one does oneself

conservation
according to Piaget, recognition that basic properties of substances such as weight and mass remain the same when superficial features change

objective responsibility
according to Piaget, the assignment of blame according to the amount of damage done rather than the motives of the actor

LO¹ Explain prenatal development and the role that sex hormones play.
The fetal stage lasts from the beginning of the third month until birth. By the end of the third month, the major organ systems and the fingers and toes have formed. In the middle of the fourth month, the mother usually detects the first fetal movements. By the end of the sixth month, the fetus moves its limbs so vigorously that mothers often feel that they are being kicked. The fetus opens and shuts its eyes, sucks its thumb, alternates between periods of being awake and sleeping, and responds to light. It also turns somersaults, which can be perceived by the mother. During the three months prior to birth, the organ systems of the fetus continue to mature. The heart and lungs become increasingly capable of sustaining independent life. The fetus gains about five-and-a-half pounds and doubles in length. Newborn boys average about seven-and-a-half pounds and newborn girls about seven pounds.

LO² Explain the physical, cognitive, moral, social, and emotional development of children.
Childhood begins with birth. During infancy—the first two years of childhood—dramatic gains in height and weight continue. Babies usually double their birth weight in about five months and triple it by their first birthday. Their height increases by about ten inches in the first year. Children grow another four to six inches during the second year and gain some four to seven pounds. After that, they gain about two to three inches a year until they reach the adolescent growth spurt. Other aspects of physical development in childhood include reflexes and perceptual development. Theories in cognitive development include Piaget's stage theory, Vygotsky's sociocultural theory, and Kohlberg's theory of moral development. Erikson's theory of psychosocial development and Ainsworth's attachment studies explore critical aspects of social and emotional development in childhood.

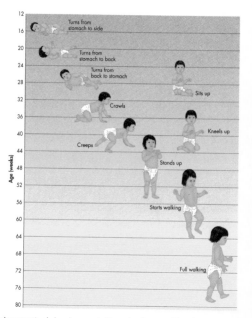

LO³ Explain the physical, cognitive, moral, social, and emotional development of adolescents.
Adolescence is bounded by the onset of puberty—the period during which the body becomes sexually mature—and the assumption of adult responsibilities. Except for infancy, more changes occur during adolescence than during any other time. One of the most noticeable physical developments of adolescence is a growth spurt that lasts two to three years and ends the gradual changes in height and weight that characterize most of childhood. Within this short span of years, adolescents grow some eight to twelve inches. According to Piaget, children undergo three stages of cognitive development prior to adolescence: sensorimotor, preoperational, and concrete operational. The stage of formal operations is the final stage in Piaget's theory, and it represents cognitive maturity. Formal operational thought generally begins at about the beginning of adolescence. The major achievements of the stage of formal operations involve classification, logical thought, and the ability to hypothesize. Central features are the ability to think about ideas as well as objects and to group and classify ideas, such as symbols and statements. Kohlberg's research around the levels of moral reasoning found postconventional moral judgments were absent until about age sixteen, when stage 5 reasoning is shown by about 20% of adolescents. According to Erik Erikson's eight stages of psychosocial development, the fifth stage—ego identity versus role diffusion—occurs in adolescence.

concrete operational stage
Piaget's third stage, characterized by logical thought concerning tangible objects, conservation, and subjective morality

decentration
simultaneous focusing on more than one dimension of a problem, so that flexible, reversible thought becomes possible

subjective moral judgment
according to Piaget, moral judgment that is based on the motives of the perpetrator

zone of proximal development (ZPD)
Vygotsky's term for the situation in which a child carries out tasks with the help of someone who is more skilled, frequently an adult who represents the culture in which the child develops

scaffolding
Vygotsky's term for temporary cognitive structures or methods of solving problems that help the child as he or she learns to function independently

preconventional level
according to Kohlberg, a period during which moral judgments are based largely on expectation of rewards or punishments

conventional level
according to Kohlberg, a period during which moral judgments largely reflect social conventions; a "law and order" approach to morality

trust versus mistrust
Erikson's first stage of psychosocial development, during which children do—or do not—come to trust that primary caregivers and the environment will meet their needs

attachment
the enduring affectional tie that binds one person to another

contact comfort
a hypothesized primary drive to seek physical comfort through contact with another

ethologist
a scientist who studies the characteristic behavior patterns of species of animals

critical period
a period of time when an instinctive response can be elicited by a particular stimulus

imprinting
a process occurring during a critical period in the development of an organism, in which that organism responds to a stimulus in a manner that will afterward be difficult to modify

authoritative parents
parents who are strict and warm; authoritative parents demand mature behavior but use reason rather than force in discipline

authoritarian parents
parents who are rigid in their rules and who demand obedience for the sake of obedience

permissive parents
parents who impose few, if any, rules and who do not supervise their children closely

uninvolved parents
parents who generally leave their children to themselves

LO³ adolescence
the period of life bounded by puberty and the assumption of adult responsibilities

puberty
the period of physical development during which sexual reproduction first becomes possible

LO⁴
Explain the physical, cognitive, moral, social, and emotional development of adults. A number of physical changes occur during the later years. The reasons for aging, however, are not yet completely understood. People can also affect the pace of their aging by eating properly, exercising, maintaining a positive outlook, and finding and meeting challenges that are consistent with their abilities. People are at the height of their cognitive powers during early adulthood. Cognitive development in adulthood has many aspects—creativity, memory functioning, and intelligence. Changes in social and emotional development during adulthood are probably the most "elastic" or fluid. According to Erik Erikson, young adulthood is characterized by the task of developing abiding intimate relationships; middle adulthood involves being productive and contributing to younger generations; the challenge for late adulthood is to maintain one's sense of identity despite physical deterioration.

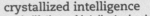

Hair and nails
Hair often turns gray and thins out. Men may go bald. Fingernails can thicken.

Brain
The brain shrinks, but it is not known if that affects mental functions.

The senses
The sensitivity of hearing, sight, taste, and smell can all decline with age.

Skin
Wrinkles occur as the skin thins and the underlying fat shrinks, and age spots often crop up.

Glands and hormones
Levels of many hormones drop, or the body becomes less responsive to them.

Immune system
The body becomes less able to resist some pathogens.

Lungs
It doesn't just seem harder to climb those stairs; lung capacity drops.

Heart and blood vessels
Cardiovascular problems become more common.

Muscles
Strength usually peaks in the twenties, then declines.

Kidneys and urinary tract
The kidneys become less efficient. The bladder can't hold as much, so urination is more frequent.

Digestive system
Digestion slows down as the secretion of digestive enzymes decreases.

Reproductive system
Women go through menopause, and testosterone levels drop for men.

Bones and joints
Wear and tear can lead to arthritic joints, and osteoporosis is common, especially in women.

secondary sex characteristics
characteristics that distinguish the sexes, such as distribution of body hair and depth of voice, but that are not directly involved in reproduction

menarche
the beginning of menstruation

formal operational stage
Piaget's fourth stage, characterized by abstract logical thought and deduction from principles

imaginary audience
an aspect of adolescent egocentrism; the belief that other people are as concerned with our thoughts and behaviors as we are

personal fable
another aspect of adolescent egocentrism; the belief that our feelings and ideas are special and unique and that we are invulnerable

postconventional level
according to Kohlberg, a period during which moral judgments are derived from moral principles and people look to themselves to set moral standards

ego identity
Erikson's term for a firm sense of who one is and what one stands for

role diffusion
Erikson's term for lack of clarity in one's life roles (due to failure to develop ego identity)

LO⁴ menopause
the cessation of menstruation

crystallized intelligence
one's lifetime of intellectual achievement, as shown largely through vocabulary and knowledge of world affairs

fluid intelligence
mental flexibility as shown in learning rapidly to solve new kinds of problems

Alzheimer's disease
a progressive form of mental deterioration characterized by loss of memory, language, problem solving, and other cognitive functions

dream
in this usage, Levinson's term for the overriding drive of youth to become someone important, to leave one's mark on history

intimacy versus isolation
Erikson's life crisis of young adulthood, which is characterized by the task of developing abiding intimate relationships

generativity versus stagnation
Erikson's term for the crisis of middle adulthood, characterized by the task of being productive and contributing to younger generations

midlife crisis
a crisis experienced by many people during the midlife transition when they realize that life may be more than halfway over and they reassess their achievements in terms of their dreams

ego integrity versus despair
Erikson's term for the crisis of late adulthood, characterized by the task of maintaining one's sense of identity despite physical deterioration

Chapter in Review

4

LO¹ sensation
the stimulation of sensory receptors and the transmission of sensory information to the central nervous system

perception
the process by which sensations are organized into an inner representation of the world

absolute threshold
the minimal amount of energy that can produce a sensation

pitch
the highness or lowness of a sound, as determined by the frequency of the sound waves

difference threshold
the minimal difference in intensity required between two sources of energy so that they will be perceived as being different

Weber's constant
the fraction of the intensity by which a source of physical energy must be increased or decreased so that a difference in intensity will be perceived

just noticeable difference (jnd)
the minimal amount by which a source of energy must be increased or decreased so that a difference in intensity will be perceived

signal-detection theory
the view that the perception of sensory stimuli involves the interaction of physical, biological, and psychological factors

feature detectors
neurons in the sensory cortex that fire in response to specific features of sensory information such as lines or edges of objects

sensory adaptation
the processes by which organisms become more sensitive to stimuli that are low in magnitude and less sensitive to stimuli that are constant or ongoing in magnitude

sensitization
the type of sensory adaptation in which we become more sensitive to stimuli that are low in magnitude; also called *positive adaptation*

desensitization
the type of sensory adaptation in which we become less sensitive to constant stimuli. Also called *negative adaptation*

LO² hue
the color of light, as determined by its wavelength

cornea
transparent tissue forming the outer surface of the eyeball

iris
a muscular membrane whose dilation regulates the amount of light that enters the eye

pupil
the black-looking opening in the center of the iris, through which light enters the eye

lens
a transparent body behind the iris that focuses an image on the retina

LO¹ Define and differentiate between sensation and perception.
Stimulation of the senses is an automatic process. It results from sources of energy, like light and sound, or from the presence of chemicals, as in smell and taste. Perception is an active process. Perception may begin with sensation, but it also reflects our experiences and expectations as it makes sense of sensory stimuli.

LO² Identify the parts of the eye; explain the properties of light and the theories of color vision.
It is visible light that triggers visual sensations. Yet visible light is just one small part of a spectrum of electromagnetic energy that surrounds us. All forms of electromagnetic energy move in waves, and different kinds of electromagnetic energy have signature wavelengths.

In both the eye and a camera, light enters through a narrow opening and is projected onto a sensitive surface. In the eye, the photosensitive surface is called the retina, and information concerning the changing images on the retina is transmitted to the brain.

LO³ Describe how visual perception is organized.
Visual perception is the process by which we organize or make sense of the sensory impressions caused by the light that strikes our eyes. The attempt to identify the rules that govern these processes resulted in what are referred to as the laws of perceptual organization: *figure-ground perception,* and the laws of *proximity, similarity, continuity,* and *common fate.*

LO⁴ Identify the parts of the ear; describe the sense of hearing.
Sound, or auditory stimulation, travels through the air like waves. A single cycle of compression and expansion is one wave of sound, which can occur many times in a second. The ear has three parts: the outer ear, middle ear, and inner ear. The outer ear funnels sound to the eardrum. Inside the eardrum, vibrations transmit sound to the inner ear. Vibrations in the cochlea transmit the sound to the auditory nerve.

LO⁵ Describe the chemical senses.
In smell and taste, we sample molecules of substances. An odor is a sample of molecules of a substance in the air. Odors trigger firing of receptor neurons in the olfactory membrane high in each nostril. Taste is sensed through taste cells—receptor neurons located on taste buds.

LO⁶ Explain the properties of the skin senses and theoretical explanations for pain.
The skin senses include touch, pressure, warmth, cold, and pain. Pain results when neurons called nociceptors in the skin are stimulated. The pain message to the brain is initiated by the release of chemicals such as prostaglandins, bradykinin, and P.

LO⁷ Describe the kinesthetic and vestibular senses.
Kinesthesis and the vestibular sense alert us to our movements and body position without relying on vision. In kinesthesis, sensory information is fed back to the brain from sensory organs in the joints, tendons, and muscles. The vestibular sense makes use of sensory organs located in the semicircular canals and elsewhere in the ears to monitor the body's motion and position in relation to gravity.

LO⁸ Explain why psychologists are skeptical about extrasensory perception.
One method for studying telepathy is the ganzfeld procedure. However, when Milton and Wiseman weighed the results of 30 ganzfeld ESP studies from seven laboratories, they found no evidence that subjects in these studies scored above chance levels on the ESP task. It has also been difficult to replicate experiments in ESP.

retina
the area of the inner surface of the eye that contains rods and cones

photoreceptors
cells that respond to light

bipolar cells
neurons that conduct neural impulses from rods and cones to ganglion cells

ganglion cells
neurons whose axons form the optic nerve

optic nerve
the nerve that transmits sensory information from the eye to the brain

rods
rod-shaped photoreceptors that are sensitive only to the intensity of light

cones
cone-shaped photoreceptors that transmit sensations of color

fovea
an area near the center of the retina that is dense with cones and where vision is consequently most acute

blind spot
the area of the retina where axons from ganglion cells meet to form the optic nerve

visual acuity
sharpness of vision

presbyopia
a condition characterized by brittleness of the lens

dark adaptation
the process of adjusting to conditions of lower lighting by increasing the sensitivity of rods and cones

complementary
descriptive of colors of the spectrum that when combined produce white or nearly white light

afterimage
the lingering visual impression made by a stimulus that has been removed

trichromatic theory
the theory that color vision is made possible by three types of cones, some of which respond to red light, some to green, and some to blue

opponent-process theory
the theory that color vision is made possible by three types of cones, some of which respond to red or green light, some to blue or yellow, and some to the intensity of light

trichromat
a person with normal color vision

monochromat
a person who is sensitive to black and white only and hence color-blind

dichromat
a person who is sensitive to black–white and either red–green or blue–yellow and hence partially color-blind

LO³ closure
the tendency to perceive a broken figure as being complete or whole proximity nearness; the perceptual tendency to group together objects that are near one another

proximity
nearness; the perceptual tendency to group together objects that are near one another

similarity
the perceptual tendency to group together objects that are similar in appearance

continuity
the tendency to perceive a series of points or lines as having unity

common fate
the tendency to perceive elements that move together as belonging together

top-down processing
the use of contextual information or knowledge of a pattern in order to organize parts of the pattern

bottom-up processing
the organization of the parts of a pattern to recognize, or form an image of, the pattern they compose

illusions
sensations that give rise to misperceptions

stroboscopic motion
a visual illusion in which the perception of motion is generated by a series of stationary images that are presented in rapid succession

monocular cues
stimuli suggestive of depth that can be perceived with only one eye

perspective
a monocular cue for depth based on the convergence (coming together) of parallel lines as they recede into the distance

texture gradient
a monocular cue for depth based on the perception that closer objects appear to have rougher (more detailed) surfaces

motion parallax
a monocular cue for depth based on the perception that nearby objects appear to move more rapidly in relation to our own motion

binocular cues
stimuli suggestive of depth that involve simultaneous perception by both eyes

retinal disparity
a binocular cue for depth based on the difference in the image cast by an object on the retinas of the eyes as the object moves closer or farther away

convergence
a binocular cue for depth based on the inward movement of the eyes as they attempt to focus on an object that is drawing nearer

size constancy
the tendency to perceive an object as being the same size even as the size of its retinal image changes according to the object's distance

color constancy
the tendency to perceive an object as being the same color even though lighting conditions change its appearance

brightness constancy
the tendency to perceive an object as being just as bright even though lighting conditions change its intensity

shape constancy
the tendency to perceive an object as being the same shape although the retinal image varies in shape as it rotates

LO⁴ hertz (Hz)
a unit expressing the frequency of sound waves; one hertz equals one cycle per second

decibel (dB)
a unit expressing the loudness of a sound

cochlea
the inner ear; the bony tube that contains the basilar membrane and the organ of Corti

basilar membrane
a membrane that lies coiled within the cochlea

organ of Corti
the receptor for hearing that lies on the basilar membrane in the cochlea

auditory nerve
the axon bundle that transmits neural impulses from the organ of Corti to the brain

place theory
the theory that the pitch of a sound is determined by the section of the basilar membrane that vibrates in response to the sound

frequency theory
the theory that the pitch of a sound is reflected in the frequency of the neural impulses that are generated in response to the sound

LO⁵ flavor
a complex quality of food and other substances that is based on their odor, texture, and temperature as well as their taste

olfactory nerve
the nerve that transmits information concerning odors from olfactory receptors to the brain

taste cells
receptor cells that are sensitive to taste

taste buds
the sensory organs for taste. They contain taste cells and are located mostly on the tongue

LO⁷ kinesthesis
the sense that informs us about the positions and motion of parts of our bodies

vestibular sense
the sense of equilibrium that informs us about our bodies' positions relative to gravity

Chapter in Review

5

LO¹ selective attention
the focus of consciousness on a particular stimulus

direct inner awareness
knowledge of one's own thoughts, feelings, and memories

preconscious
in psychodynamic theory, descriptive of material that is not in awareness but can be brought into awareness by focusing one's attention

unconscious
in psychodynamic theory, descriptive of ideas and feelings that are not available to awareness; also: without consciousness

repression
in psychodynamic theory, the unconscious ejection of anxiety-evoking ideas, impulses, or images from awareness

suppression
the deliberate, or conscious, placing of certain ideas, impulses, or images out of awareness

nonconscious
descriptive of bodily processes such as growing hair, of which we cannot become conscious. We may "recognize" that our hair is growing, but we cannot directly experience the biological process

LO² circadian rhythm
a cycle that is connected with the twenty-four-hour period of the earth's rotation

alpha waves
rapid low-amplitude brain waves that have been linked to feelings of relaxation

nonrapid eye movement (NREM) sleep
stages of sleep 1 through 4

rapid eye movement (REM) sleep
a stage of sleep characterized by rapid eye movements, which have been linked to dreaming

theta waves
slow brain waves produced during the hypnagogic state

delta waves
strong, slow brain waves usually emitted during stage 4 sleep

activation–synthesis model
the view that acetylcholine and the pons activate the reticular activating system, which stimulates the cortex, but not to the point of waking; the cortex then pieces together (synthesizes) the cognitive activity into a dream

narcolepsy
a "sleep attack" in which a person falls asleep suddenly and irresistibly

apnea
temporary absence or cessation of breathing

sleep terrors
frightening dreamlike experiences that occur during the deepest stage of NREM sleep; nightmares, in contrast, occur during REM sleep

LO¹ Define consciousness. The concept of consciousness has various meanings. One meaning is *sensory awareness* of the environment. Another aspect of consciousness is *selective attention*. Selective attention means focusing one's consciousness on a particular stimulus. We are conscious of—or have *direct inner awareness* of—thoughts, images, emotions, and memories. Sigmund Freud, the founder of psychoanalysis, differentiated between the thoughts and feelings of which we are *conscious*, or aware, and those that are preconscious and unconscious. *Preconscious* material is not currently in awareness but is readily available. Still other mental events are *unconscious*, or unavailable, to awareness under most circumstances. Some bodily processes, such as the firings of neurons, are *nonconscious*. They cannot be experienced through sensory awareness or direct inner awareness. In the sense that the *self* forms intentions and guides its own behavior, consciousness is *self*. The word conscious also refers to the *waking state* as opposed, for example, to sleep.

LO² Explain the nature of sleep and various sleep disorders. When we sleep, we slip from consciousness to unconsciousness. When we are conscious, our brains emit waves characterized by certain frequencies (numbers of waves per second) and amplitudes (heights—an index of strength). Brain waves are rough indicators of the activity of neurons. The strength or energy of brain waves is expressed in volts (an electrical unit). When we sleep, our brains emit waves that differ from those emitted when we are conscious. Sleep disorders seriously interfere with daily functioning and include insomnia, narcolepsy, and apnea. The less-common sleep disorders—sleep terrors, bedwetting, and sleepwalking—occur during deep (stage 3 or 4) sleep.

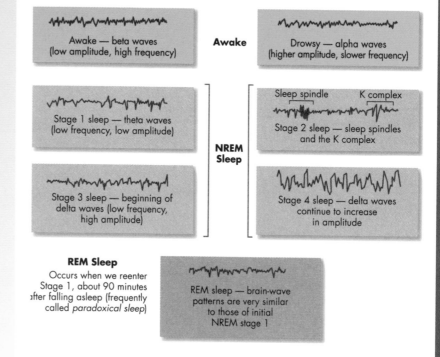

Awake — beta waves (low amplitude, high frequency)

Awake

Drowsy — alpha waves (higher amplitude, slower frequency)

Stage 1 sleep — theta waves (low frequency, low amplitude)

NREM Sleep

Sleep spindle   K complex
Stage 2 sleep — sleep spindles and the K complex

Stage 3 sleep — beginning of delta waves (low frequency, high amplitude)

Stage 4 sleep — delta waves continue to increase in amplitude

REM Sleep
Occurs when we reenter Stage 1, about 90 minutes after falling asleep (frequently called *paradoxical sleep*)

REM sleep — brain-wave patterns are very similar to those of initial NREM stage 1

LO³ hypnosis
a condition in which people are highly suggestible and behave as though they are in a trance

role theory
a theory that explains hypnotic events in terms of the person's ability to act *as though* he or she were hypnotized

response set theory
the view that response expectancies play a key role in the production of the experiences suggested by the hypnotist

transcendental meditation (TM)
the simplified form of meditation brought to the United States by the Maharishi Mahesh Yogi and used as a method for coping with stress

mindfulness meditation (MM)
a form of meditation that provides clients with techniques they can use to focus on the present moment rather than ruminate about problems

biofeedback training (BFT)
the systematic feeding back to an organism information about a bodily function so that the organism can gain control of that function

electromyograph (EMG)
an instrument that measures muscle tension

LO⁴ depressant
a drug that lowers the rate of activity of the nervous system

stimulant
a drug that increases activity of the nervous system

substance abuse
persistent use of a substance even though it is causing or compounding problems in meeting the demands of life

substance dependence
loss of control over use of a substance; biologically speaking, dependence is typified by tolerance, withdrawal symptoms, or both

tolerance
habituation to a drug, with the result that increasingly higher doses of the drug are needed to achieve similar effects

withdrawal symptoms
a characteristic cluster of symptoms that results from sudden decrease in an addictive drug's level of usage

opiates
a group of narcotics derived from the opium poppy that provide a euphoric rush and depress the nervous system

narcotics
drugs used to relieve pain and induce sleep. The term is usually reserved for opiates

opioids
chemicals that act on opiate receptors but are not derived from the opium poppy

barbiturate
an addictive depressant used to relieve anxiety or induce sleep

amphetamines
stimulants derived from *alpha-methyl-beta-phenyl-ethylamine,* a colorless liquid consisting of carbon, hydrogen, and nitrogen

hydrocarbons
chemical compounds consisting of hydrogen and carbon

second-hand smoke
smoke from the tobacco products and exhalations of other people

hallucinogen
a substance that causes hallucinations

marijuana
the dried vegetable matter of the *Cannabis sativa* plant

LO³ Explain various uses of hypnosis, forms of meditation, and biofeedback techniques in altering consciousness.
Hypnosis—an altered state of consciousness in which people are highly suggestible and behave as though they are in a trance—is derived from the Greek word for sleep. Hypnotism can be used as an anesthetic in dentistry, childbirth, and medical procedures. Some psychologists use hypnosis to help clients reduce anxiety, overcome fears, or lessen the perception of chronic pain. One common form of meditation, transcendental meditation (TM), was brought to the United States by the Maharishi Mahesh Yogi in 1959. People practice TM by concentrating on mantras—words or sounds that are claimed to help the person achieve an altered state of consciousness. Mindfulness Meditation (MM), as opposed to TM, makes no pretense of achieving spiritual goals. Instead, MM provides clients with mantra-like techniques they can use to focus on the present moment rather than ruminate about problems. Biofeedback is a system that provides, or "feeds back," information about a bodily function to an organism. Through biofeedback training, people have learned to gain voluntary control over a number of functions that are normally automatic, such as heart rate and blood pressure.

LO⁴ Explain the concepts of substance abuse; identify categories of drugs and how they alter consciousness. Substance abuse and dependence usually begin with experimental use in adolescence. People experiment with drugs for various reasons, including curiosity, conformity to peer pressure, parental use, rebelliousness, escape from boredom or pressure, and excitement or pleasure. Use of a substance may be reinforced by peers or by the drug's positive effects on mood and its reduction of anxiety, fear, and stress. Many people use drugs as a form of self-medication for anxiety and depression, even low self-esteem. For people who are physiologically dependent, avoidance of withdrawal symptoms is also reinforcing. Psychoactive drugs include depressants (alcohol, opiates, and barbiturates), stimulants (amphetamines, cocaine, and nicotine), and hallucinogens (LSD, marijuana, PHP, and mescaline).

How Cocaine Produces Euphoria and Why People "Crash"

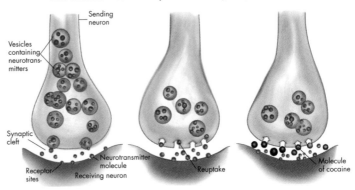

LSD
lysergic acid diethylamide; a hallucinogen

flashbacks
distorted perceptions or hallucinations that occur days or weeks after LSD usage but mimic the LSD experience

mescaline
a hallucinogen derived from the mescal (peyote) cactus

phencyclidine (pcp)
another hallucinogen whose name is an initialism for its chemical structure

Chapter in Review

LO¹ learning

(1) according to behaviorists, a relatively permanent change in behavior that results from experience (2) according to cognitive theorists, the process by which organisms make relatively permanent changes in the way they represent the environment because of experience

classical conditioning
a simple form of learning in which a neutral stimulus comes to evoke the response usually evoked by another stimulus by being paired repeatedly with the other stimulus

stimulus
an environmental condition that elicits a response

unconditioned stimulus (UCS)
a stimulus that elicits an unconditioned response

unconditioned response (UCR)
a natural, usually unvarying response elicited by a stimulus without learning or conditioning

orienting reflex
an unlearned response in which an organism attends to a stimulus

conditioned stimulus (CS)
a previously neutral stimulus that, after repeated association with an unconditioned stimulus, elicits the response elicited by the unconditioned stimulus

conditioned response (CR)
a response that becomes associated with a previously unrelated stimulus as a result of pairing the stimulus with another stimulus that normally elicits the response

extinction
an experimental procedure in which stimuli lose their ability to evoke learned responses because the events that had followed the stimuli no longer occur

spontaneous recovery
the recurrence of an extinguished response as a function of the passage of time

generalization
in conditioning, the tendency for a conditioned response to be evoked by stimuli that are similar to the stimulus to which the response was conditioned

discrimination
in conditioning, the tendency for an organism to distinguish between a conditioned stimulus and similar stimuli that do not forecast an unconditioned stimulus

higher-order conditioning
a classical conditioning procedure in which a previously neutral stimulus comes to elicit the response brought forth by a *conditioned* stimulus by being paired repeatedly with that conditioned stimulus

counterconditioning
a fear-reduction technique in which pleasant stimuli are associated with fear-evoking stimuli so that the fear-evoking stimuli lose their aversive qualities

LO¹ Describe the learning process according to classical conditioning.
Classical conditioning is a simple form of associative learning that teaches animals to anticipate events. When a neutral stimulus (like a bell ringing) and one that evokes a response (like dog food) are paired together repeatedly, the conditioned neutral stimulus will begin to trigger a response (like salivation) on its own.

KIND OF LEARNING: Classical conditioning
Major theorists: Ivan Pavlov (known for basic research with dogs); John B. Watson (known as the originator of behaviorism)

WHAT IS LEARNED
Association of events; anticipations, signs, expectations; automatic responses to new stimuli

HOW IT IS LEARNED
A neutral stimulus is repeatedly paired with a stimulus (an unconditioned stimulus, or UCS) that elicits a response (an unconditioned response, or UCR) until the neutral stimulus produces a response (conditioned response, or CR) that anticipates and prepares for the unconditioned stimulus. At this point, the neutral stimulus has become a conditioned stimulus (CS).

LO² Describe the learning process according to operant conditioning.
Under operant conditioning, animals learn to engage in behavior because of the way it is reinforced. Positive reinforcement encourages the learner to repeat a behavior more frequently. Negative reinforcement discourages the learner from repeating a behavior.

KIND OF LEARNING: Operant conditioning
Major theorist: B. F. Skinner

WHAT IS LEARNED
Behavior that operates on, or affects, the environment to produce consequences

HOW IT IS LEARNED
A response is rewarded or reinforced so that it occurs with greater frequency in similar situations.

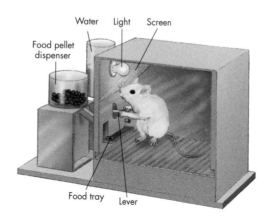

Water   Light   Screen

Food pellet
dispenser

Food tray   Lever

flooding
a behavioral fear-reduction technique based on principles of classical conditioning; fear-evoking stimuli (CSs) are presented continuously in the absence of actual harm so that fear responses (CRs) are extinguished

systematic desensitization
a behavioral fear-reduction technique in which a hierarchy of fear-evoking stimuli is presented while the person remains relaxed

LO² reinforce
to follow a response with a stimulus that increases the frequency of the response

operant behavior
voluntary responses that are reinforced

operant conditioning
a simple form of learning in which an organism learns to engage in behavior because it is reinforced

positive reinforcer
a reinforcer that when *presented* increases the frequency of an operant

negative reinforcer
a reinforcer that when *removed* increases the frequency of an operant

primary reinforcer
an unlearned reinforcer

secondary reinforcer
a stimulus that gains reinforcement value through association with established reinforcers

conditioned reinforcer
another term for a secondary reinforcer

reward
a pleasant stimulus that increases the frequency of the behavior it follows

punishment
an unpleasant stimulus that suppresses the behavior it follows

discriminative stimulus
in operant conditioning, a stimulus that indicates that reinforcement is available

continuous reinforcement
a schedule of reinforcement in which every correct response is reinforced

partial reinforcement
one of several reinforcement schedules in which not every correct response is reinforced

fixed-interval schedule
a schedule in which a fixed amount of time must elapse between the previous and subsequent times that reinforcement is available

variable-interval schedule
a schedule in which a variable amount of time must elapse between the previous and subsequent times that reinforcement is available

fixed-ratio schedule
a schedule in which reinforcement is provided after a fixed number of correct responses

variable-ratio schedule
a schedule in which reinforcement is provided after a variable number of correct responses

shaping
a procedure for teaching complex behaviors that at first reinforces approximations of the target behavior

LO³ Describe cognitive factors in learning.
Learning is often more complex than association and reinforcement; it involves searching for information, weighing evidence, and making decisions. Cognitive psychologists study mental structures, schemas, templates, and information processing to prove that learning can occur without conditioning. Latent learning—like a cognitive map of a maze—may not be revealed without motivation. Contingency theory suggests that learning occurs when a conditioned stimulus provides information about the unconditioned stimulus. Finally, observational learning makes it possible to acquire skills and knowledge by watching others rather than through direct experience.

KIND OF LEARNING:
Observational learning
Major theorists: Albert Bandura; Julian Rotter; Walter Mischel

WHAT IS LEARNED
Expectations (if–then relationships), knowledge, and skills

HOW IT IS LEARNED
A person observes the behavior of another person (live or through media such as films, television, or books) and its effects

successive approximations
behaviors that are progressively closer to a target behavior

LO³ latent
hidden or concealed

contingency theory
the view that learning occurs when stimuli provide information about the likelihood of the occurrence of other stimuli

observational learning
the acquisition of knowledge and skills through the observation of others (who are called *models*) rather than by means of direct experience

model
an organism that engages in a response that is then imitated by another organism

MEMORY: REMEMBRANCE OF THINGS PAST—AND FUTURE

Chapter in Review

LO¹ explicit memory
memory that clearly and distinctly expresses (explicates) specific information

episodic memory
memories of events experienced by a person or that take place in the person's presence

semantic memory
general knowledge, as opposed to episodic memory

implicit memory
memory that is suggested (implied) but not plainly expressed, as illustrated in the things that people *do* but do not state clearly

priming
the activation of specific associations in memory, often as a result of repetition and without making a conscious effort to access the memory

retrospective memory
memory for past events, activities, and learning experiences, as shown by explicit (episodic and semantic) and implicit memories

prospective memory
memory to perform an act in the future, as at a certain time or when a certain event occurs

LO² encoding
modifying information so that it can be placed in memory; the first stage of information processing

storage
the maintenance of information over time; the second stage of information processing

maintenance rehearsal
mental repetition of information to keep it in memory

metamemory
self-awareness of the ways in which memory functions, allowing the person to encode, store, and retrieve information effectively

elaborative rehearsal
the kind of coding in which new information is related to information that is already known

retrieval
the location of stored information and its return to consciousness; the third stage of information processing

memory
the processes by which information is encoded, stored, and retrieved

LO³ sensory memory
the type or stage of memory first encountered by a stimulus

memory trace
an assumed change in the nervous system that reflects the impression made by a stimulus

icon
a mental representation of a visual stimulus that is held briefly in sensory memory

LO¹ Define memory and differentiate between types of memories.
Memory is the processes by which information is encoded, stored, and retrieved. *Explicit memory*—also referred to as declarative memory—is memory for specific information. Two kinds of explicit memories are identified according to the type of information they hold: episodic memories are memories of the things that happen to us or take place in our presence ("I remember…") and semantic memory refers to general knowledge ("I know…") *Implicit memory*—also referred to as nondeclarative memory—is memory of how to perform a procedure or skill; it is the act itself, doing something, like riding a bike.

Retrospective memory is the recalling of information that has been previously learned. Explicit and implicit memories involve remembering things that were learned. *Prospective memory* refers to remembering to do things in the future.

LO² Explain the process of memory.
The first stage of information processing is changing information so that we can place it in memory: encoding. When we encode information, we transform it into psychological formats that can be represented mentally. To do so, we commonly use visual, auditory, and semantic codes. The second memory process is storage. Storage means maintaining information over time. The third memory process is retrieval. The retrieval of stored information means locating it and returning it to consciousness. The phrase below might be more easily recalled if you think of it as an acronym of the first two letters of the name of a nation (hint, hint).

> **THUNSTOFAM**

LO³ Explain the stages of memory.
The Atkinson–Shiffrin model proposes that there are three stages of memory: (a) sensory memory, (b) short-term memory, and (c) long-term memory. Part a shows that sensory information impacts on the registers of sensory memory. Memory traces are held briefly in sensory memory before decaying. If we attend to the information, much of it can be transferred to short-term memory (STM). Part b: Information may be maintained in STM through maintenance rehearsal or elaborative rehearsal. Otherwise, it may decay or be displaced. Part c: Once information is transferred to long-term memory (LTM), it may be filed away indefinitely. However, if the information in LTM is organized poorly, or if we cannot find cues to retrieve it, it can be lost.

Three Stages of Memory: The Atkinson–Shiffrin Model

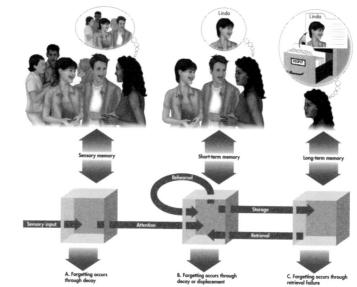

iconic memory
the sensory register that briefly holds mental representations of visual stimuli

eidetic imagery
the maintenance of detailed visual memories over several minutes

echo
a mental representation of an auditory stimulus (sound) that is held briefly in sensory memory

echoic memory
the sensory register that briefly holds mental representations of auditory stimuli

short-term memory
the type or stage of memory that can hold information for up to a minute or so after the trace of the stimulus decays

working memory
another term for *short-term memory*

serial-position effect
the tendency to recall more accurately the first and last items in a series

chunk
a stimulus or group of stimuli that are perceived as a discrete piece of information

displace
in memory theory, to cause information to be lost from short-term memory by adding new information

long-term memory
the type or stage of memory capable of relatively permanent storage

repression
in Freud's psychodynamic theory, the ejection of anxiety-evoking ideas from conscious awareness

schema
a way of mentally representing the world, such as a belief or an expectation, that can influence perception of persons, objects, and situations

tip-of-the-tongue (TOT) phenomenon
the feeling that information is stored in memory although it cannot be readily retrieved

context-dependent memory
information that is better retrieved in the context in which it was encoded and stored, or learned

state-dependent memory
information that is better retrieved in the physiological or emotional state in which it was encoded and stored, or learned

LO⁴ nonsense syllables
meaningless sets of two consonants, with a vowel sandwiched in between, that are used to study memory

paired associates
nonsense syllables presented in pairs in experiments that measure recall

method of savings
a measure of retention in which the difference between the number of repetitions originally required to learn a list and the number of repetitions required to relearn the list after a certain amount of time has elapsed is calculated

savings
the difference between the number of repetitions originally required to learn a list and the number of repetitions required to relearn the list after a certain amount of time has elapsed

interference theory
the view that we may forget stored material because other learning interferes with it

retroactive interference
the interference of new learning with the ability to retrieve material learned previously

---

LO⁴ Identify contributors to forgetting. Recognition, recall, and relearning are three basic memory tasks that have been used by psychologists to measure forgetting. Nonsense syllables have been used in studying each of them. According to interference theory, we forget material in short-term and long-term memory because newly learned material interferes with it. The two basic types of interference are retroactive interference and proactive interference. According to Sigmund Freud, we are motivated to repress painful memories and unacceptable ideas because they produce anxiety, guilt, and shame. Freud also believed that young children repress memories of aggressive impulses and perverse lusts toward their parents, which would explain why people could not recall episodes in their early childhoods (infantile amnesia). Adults also experience amnesia, although usually for biological reasons, as in the cases of anterograde and retrograde amnesia.

Ebbinghaus's Classic Curve of Forgetting
Recollection of lists of words drops precipitously during the first hour after learning. Losses of learning then becomes more gradual. Retention drops by half within the first hour. It takes a month (thirty-one days), however, for retention to be cut in half again.

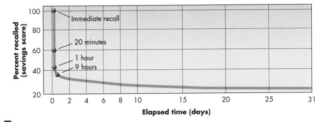

LO⁵ Describe the biological aspects of memory. Psychologists assume that mental processes such as the encoding, storage, and retrieval of information—that is, memory—are accompanied by changes in the brain. Much research on the biology of memory focuses today on the roles of stimulants, neurons, neurotransmitters, hormones, and structures in the brain.

One Avenue to Long-Term Potentiation (LTP)

LTP can occur via the action of neurotransmitters such as serotonin and glutamate at synapses. Structurally, LTP can also occur as shown in Parts A and B, when dendrites sprout new branches that connect with transmitting axons, increasing the amount of stimulation they receive.

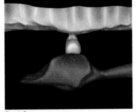
Part A

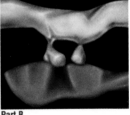
Part B

---

proactive interference
the interference by old learning with the ability to retrieve material learned recently

dissociative amnesia
amnesia thought to stem from psychological conflict or trauma

infantile amnesia
inability to recall events that occur prior to the age of two or three; also termed *childhood amnesia*

hippocampus
a structure in the limbic system that plays an important role in the formation of new memories

anterograde amnesia
failure to remember events that occur after physical trauma because of the effects of the trauma

retrograde amnesia
failure to remember events that occur prior to physical trauma because of the effects of the trauma

LO⁵ engram
(1) an assumed electrical circuit in the brain that corresponds to a memory trace (2) an assumed chemical change in the brain that accompanies learning (from the greek *en-*, meaning "in," and *gramma*, meaning "something that is written or recorded")

long-term potentiation (LTP)
enhanced efficiency in synaptic transmission that follows brief, rapid stimulation

Chapter in Review

8

LO¹

thinking
paying attention to information, mentally representing it, reasoning about it, and making decisions about it

concept
a mental category that is used to class together objects, relations, events, abstractions, or qualities that have common properties

prototype
a concept of a category of objects or events that serves as a good example of the category

exemplar
a specific example

algorithm
a systematic procedure for solving a problem that works invariably when it is correctly applied

systematic random search
an algorithm for solving problems in which each possible solution is tested according to a particular set of rules

heuristics
rules of thumb that help us simplify and solve problems

means–end analysis
a heuristic device in which we try to solve a problem by evaluating the difference between the current situation and the goal

mental set
the tendency to respond to a new problem with an approach that was successfully used with similar problems

insight
in Gestalt psychology, a sudden perception of relationships among elements of the "perceptual field," permitting the solution of a problem

incubation
in problem solving, a hypothetical process that sometimes occurs when we stand back from a frustrating problem for a while and the solution "suddenly" appears

functional fixedness
tendency to view an object in terms of its name or familiar usage

representativeness heuristic
a decision-making heuristic in which people make judgments about samples according to the populations they appear to represent

availability heuristic
a decision-making heuristic in which our estimates of frequency or probability of events are based on how easy it is to find examples

LO¹ Define thinking and the various concepts involved in thinking. Thinking entails attending to information, representing it mentally, reasoning about it, and making judgments and decisions about it; thinking means making conscious, planned attempts to make sense of our world, as well as categorizing new concepts and manipulating relationships among concepts. Three factors that affect problem solving include: level of expertise; whether you fall prey to a mental set; and whether you develop insight into the problem.

LO² Describe how language develops. Language is the communication of thoughts and feelings by means of symbols that are arranged according to rules of grammar. True language is distinguished from the communication systems of lower animals by properties such as semanticity, infinite creativity, and displacement. Language development reflects the interactions between the influences of heredity (nature) and the environment (nurture). Learning theorists see language developing according to imitation and reinforcement, where parents serve as models.

LO³ Identify the concept of intelligence and the techniques used to measure intelligence. Intelligence is broadly thought of as the underlying ability to understand the world and cope with its challenges. Intelligence allows people to: think, understand complex ideas, reason, solve problems, learn from experience, and adapt to the environment.

Approximate Distribution of IQ Scores

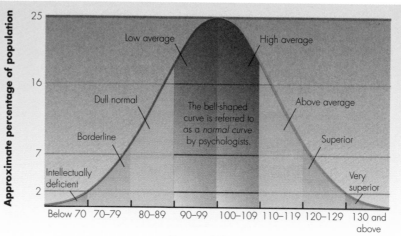

Primary Mental Abilities, According to Thurstone

Ability	Definition
Visual and spatial abilities	Visualizing forms and spatial relationships
Perceptual speed	Grasping perceptual details rapidly, perceiving similarities and differences between stimuli
Numerical ability	Computing numbers
Verbal meaning	Knowing the meanings of words
Memory	Recalling information (e.g., words and sentences)
Word fluency	Thinking of words quickly (e.g., rhyming and doing crossword puzzles)
Deductive reasoning	Deriving examples from general rules
Inductive reasoning	Inferring general rules from examples

anchoring and adjustment heuristic
a decision-making heuristic in which a presumption or first estimate serves as a cognitive anchor; as we receive additional information, we make adjustments but tend to remain in the proximity of the anchor

framing effect
the influence of wording, or the context in which information is presented, on decision making

LO 2 language
the communication of information by means of symbols arranged according to rules of grammar

semanticity
meaning; the quality of language in which words are used as symbols for objects, events, or ideas

infinite creativity
the capacity to combine words into original sentences

displacement
the quality of language that permits one to communicate information about objects and events in another time and place

linguistic-relativity hypothesis
the view that language structures the way in which we view the world

holophrase
a single word used to express complex meanings

overregularization
the application of regular grammatical rules for forming inflections (e.g., past tense and plurals) to irregular verbs and nouns

psycholinguistic theory
the view that language learning involves an interaction between environmental factors and an inborn tendency to acquire language

language acquisition device (LAD)
in psycholinguistic theory, neural "prewiring" that facilitates the child's learning of grammar

LO 3 intelligence
a complex and controversial concept; according to David Wechsler (1975), the "capacity . . . to understand the world [and] resourcefulness to cope with its challenges"

g
Spearman's symbol for general intelligence, which he believed underlay more specific abilities

s
Spearman's symbol for *specific* factors, or *s factors,* which he believed accounted for individual abilities

primary mental abilities
according to Thurstone, the basic abilities that make up intelligence

creativity
the ability to generate novel and useful solutions to problems

LO 4 Describe the controversy surrounding intelligence testing. The role that nature and nurture play in intellectual functioning is a controversial topic in psychology. Education contributes to intelligence. For example, Head Start programs enhance IQ scores, achievement scores, and academic skills of disadvantaged children. Adoptee studies suggest a genetic influence on intelligence. But they also suggest a role for environmental influence. All in all, studies generally suggest that the heritability of intelligence is between 40% and 60%. Intellectual functioning would appear to reflect the interaction of genetic, physical, personal, and sociocultural factors.

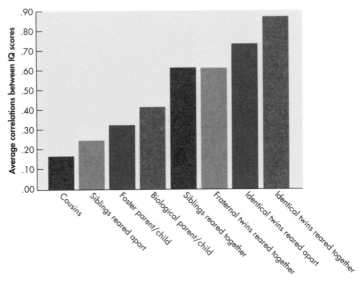

Findings of Studies of the Relationship between IQ Scores and Heredity

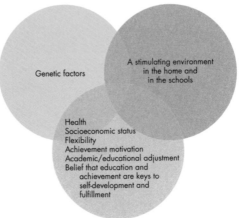

The Complex Web of Factors That Affect Intellectual Functioning

convergent thinking
a thought process that narrows in on the single best solution to a problem

divergent thinking
a thought process that attempts to generate multiple solutions to problems

mental age (MA)
the accumulated months of credit that a person earns on the Stanford–Binet intelligence scale

intelligence quotient (IQ)
(1) originally, a ratio obtained by dividing a child's score (or mental age) on an intelligence test by chronological age (2) generally, a score on an intelligence test

LO 4 heritability
the degree to which the variations in a trait from one person to another can be attributed to, or explained by, genetic factors

Chapter in Review

LO¹ motive
a hypothetical state within an organism that propels the organism toward a goal (from the latin *movere*, meaning "to move")

need
a state of deprivation

drive
a condition of arousal in an organism that is associated with a need

physiological drives
unlearned drives with a biological basis, such as hunger, thirst, and avoidance of pain

incentive
an object, person, or situation perceived as being capable of satisfying a need

LO² instinct
an inherited disposition to activate specific behavior patterns that are designed to reach certain goals

drive-reduction theory
the view that organisms learn to engage in behaviors that have the effect of reducing drives

homeostasis
the tendency of the body to maintain a steady state

self-actualization
according to Maslow and other humanistic psychologists, self-initiated striving to become what one is capable of being

LO³ satiety
the state of being satisfied; fullness

ventromedial nucleus (VMN)
a central area on the underside of the hypothalamus that appears to function as a stop-eating center

hyperphagic
characterized by excessive eating

lateral hypothalamus
an area at the side of the hypothalamus that appears to function as a start-eating center

aphagic
characterized by under-eating

anorexia nervosa
a life-threatening eating disorder characterized by dramatic weight loss and a distorted body image

bulimia nervosa
an eating disorder characterized by repeated cycles of binge eating and purging

activating effect
the arousal-producing effects of sex hormones that increase the likelihood of sexual behavior

estrus
the periodic sexual excitement of many female mammals, as governed by levels of sex hormones

LO¹ Define motivation including needs, drives, and incentives. The psychology of motivation concerns the *whys* of behavior. Motives are hypothetical states that activate behavior toward goals and may take the form of needs, drives, and/or incentives. *Needs* come in two types: physiological (needs necessary for survival) and psychological (needs for achievement, power, self-esteem, etc.). Physiological and psychological needs differ in two ways: psychological needs are not necessarily based on deprivation; psychological needs may be acquired through experience. Needs give rise to *drives* that arouse us to action. *Incentives* are objects, persons, or situations viewed as capable of satisfying a need or as desirable for their own sake.

LO² Identify the theories of motivation. Psychologists do not agree about the precise nature of motivation. The evolutionary perspective holds that animals are naturally prewired to respond to certain stimuli in certain ways. The drive reductionism and homeostasis perspective holds that primary drives trigger arousal (tension) and activate behavior. Organisms engage in behaviors that reduce tension and are motivated to maintain a steady state (homeostasis). Other theorists hold with the stimulus motivation perspective—that an organism is motivated to increase stimulation, not reduce a drive. Stimulus motivation provides an evolutionary advantage: Animals that are active and motivated to learn about their environment are more likely to survive. A humanistic theorist, Abraham Maslow believed that people are motivated by the conscious desire for personal growth. Maslow's hierarchy of needs ranges from physiological needs such as hunger and thirst through self-actualization (self-initiated striving to become whatever we believe we are capable of being). Critics argue that there is too much individual variation for the hierarchy of motives to apply to everyone.

Self-actualization

Esteem needs

Love and belongingness

Safety needs

Physiological needs

LO³ Describe the biological and psychological contributions to hunger. Biological mechanisms that regulate hunger include stomach pangs associated with stomach contractions, the functions of the hypothalamus, blood sugar level, and receptors in the liver. The ventromedial nucleus of the hypothalamus is the "stop-eating" center of the brain; the lateral hypothalamus is the "start-eating" center of the brain. Some psychological factors that influence hunger include the aroma of food, because a person feels anxious or depressed, or bored.

Problems associated with unhealthy weight are on the upswing. The origins of eating disorders aren't entirely clear. Exposure to cultural standards and role models that emphasize excessive slenderness plays a major role. Eating disorders are also more common when the family environment is negative—possibly a history of child abuse or exposure to high parental expectations. Genetic factors might not directly cause eating disorders but are likely to involve obsessionistic and perfectionistic personality traits.

LO⁴ Explain the role of sex hormones and the sexual response cycle in human sexuality. Sexual motivation, although natural, is also strongly influenced by religious and moral beliefs, cultural tradition, folklore, and superstition. What is considered "normal" depends on the society in which one lives. Level of education is connected with sexual behavior. Much about the development of sexual orientation remains speculative. Sex hormones have activating effects: they affect the sex drive and promote sexual response. Sex hormones also have organizing effects: they motivate lower animals toward masculine or feminine mating patterns.

LO⁵ Describe achievement motivation. Henry Murray developed the Thematic Apperception Test (TAT) in an attempt to assess motivation. The TAT contains cards with pictures and drawings that are subject to various interpretations. Subjects are to construct stories about the picture.

Performance goals are usually met through extrinsic or intrinsic rewards. Examples of extrinsic rewards include praise and income, while self-satisfaction is an example of an intrinsic reward. Extrinsic, or tangible, rewards can serve as an incentive for maintaining good grades. An intrinsic goal—e.g., feeling capable and intelligent—tends to have more long-lasting effects.

LO⁶ Identify the theoretical explanations of emotions. Emotions are feeling states with physiological, cognitive, and behavioral components. A physiological reaction can involve the sympathetic nervous system and result in rapid heartbeat, breathing, sweating, or muscle tension. Behavioral tendencies occur with emotions. For example, fear leads to avoidance or escape, and anger may lead to "pay-back" behaviors. Parasympathetic nervous system arousal can also occur. Joy, grief, jealousy, disgust, and so on all have cognitive, physiological, and behavioral components.

Various perspectives hold that cognitive processes—or a combination of arousal and thoughts—may determine the emotional response (see graphic below). All three theories have aspects of correctness but none fully explain emotions.

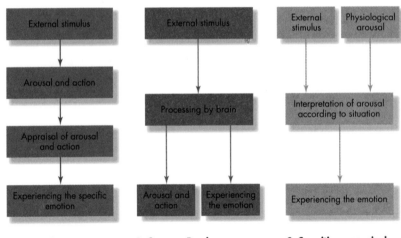

A. James–Lange   **B. Cannon–Bard**   **C. Cognitive appraisal**

Chapter in Review

10

LO¹

personality
the distinct patterns of behavior, thoughts, and feelings that characterize a person's adaptation to life

psychoanalytic theory
Sigmund Freud's perspective, which emphasizes the importance of unconscious motives and conflicts as forces that determine behavior

id
the psychic structure, present at birth, that represents physiological drives and is fully unconscious

ego
the second psychic structure to develop, characterized by self-awareness, planning, and delay of gratification

superego
the third psychic structure, which functions as a moral guardian and sets forth high standards for behavior

identification
in psychoanalytic theory, the unconscious adoption of another person's behavior

psychosexual development
in psychoanalytic theory, the process by which libidinal energy is expressed through different erogenous zones during different stages of development

oral stage
the first stage of psychosexual development, during which gratification is hypothesized to be attained primarily through oral activities

anal stage
the second stage of psychosexual development, when gratification is attained through anal activities

phallic stage
the third stage of psychosexual development, characterized by a shift of libido to the phallic region; (from the greek *phallos*, referring to an image of the penis; however, Freud used the term *phallic* to refer both to boys and girls)

Oedipus complex
a conflict of the phallic stage in which the boy wishes to possess his mother sexually and perceives his father as a rival in love

Electra complex
a conflict of the phallic stage in which the girl longs for her father and resents her mother

latency
a phase of psychosexual development characterized by repression of sexual impulses

LO¹ Describe the psychoanalytical perspective and how it contributed to the study of personality.

Focus of Research
- Unconscious conflict
- Drives such as sex, aggression, and the need for superiority come into conflict with law, social rules, and moral codes

View of Personality
- Three structures of personality—id, ego, superego
- Five stages of psychosexual development—oral, anal, phallic, latency, genital
- Ego analysts—or *neoanalysts*—focus more on the role of the ego in making meaningful, conscious decisions

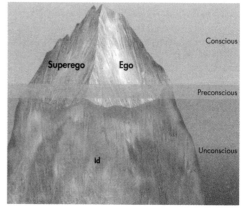

LO² Explain the trait perspective and the "Big Five" trait model.

Focus of Research
- Use of mathematical techniques to catalogue and organize basic human personality traits

View of Personality
- Based on theory of Hippocrates and work of Gordon Allport
- Eysenck's two-dimensional model: introversion–extraversion and emotional stability–instability
- Current emphasis on the five-factor model (the "Big Five")—extraversion, agreeableness, conscientiousness, neuroticism, openness to experience

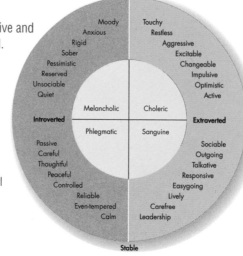

LO³ Identify the contributions of learning theory in understanding personality.

Focus of Research
- Behaviorists focus on situational factors that determine behavior
- Social cognitive emphasis on observational learning and person variables—competencies, encoding strategies, expectancies, emotions, and self-regulation

View of Personality
- Watson saw personality as plastic and determined by external, situational variables
- Skinner believed that society conditions individuals into wanting what is good for society
- Bandura believes in reciprocal determinism—that people and the environment influence one another—and in the role of making conscious choices

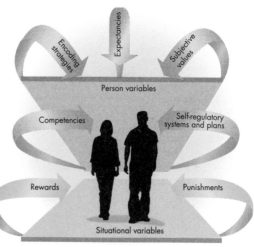

genital stage
the mature stage of psychosexual development, characterized by preferred expression of libido through intercourse with an adult of the other gender

analytical psychology
Jung's psychoanalytic theory, which emphasizes the collective unconscious and archetypes

collective unconscious
Jung's hypothesized store of vague memories that represent the history of humankind

inferiority complex
feelings of inferiority hypothesized by Adler to serve as a central motivating force

creative self
according to Adler, the self-aware aspect of personality that strives to achieve its full potential

individual psychology
Adler's psychoanalytic theory, which emphasizes feelings of inferiority and the creative self

psychosocial development
Erikson's theory of personality and development, which emphasizes social relationships and eight stages of growth

ego identity
a firm sense of who one is and what one stands for

LO⁴ Describe the humanistic perspective on personality.

Focus of Research
- The experience of being human and developing one's unique potential within an often hostile environment

View of Personality
- People have inborn drives to become what they are capable of being
- Unconditional positive regard leads to self-esteem, which facilitates individual growth and development.

LO⁵ Describe the sociocultural perspective on personality.

Focus of Research
- The roles of ethnicity, gender, culture, and socioeconomic status in personality formation and behavior

View of Personality
- Development differs in individualistic and collectivist societies
- Discrimination, poverty, and acculturation affect self-concept and self-esteem

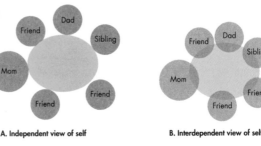

A. Independent view of self   B. Interdependent view of self

LO⁶ Describe the different kinds of tests psychologists use to measure personality.

The two most widely used types of personality tests are objective tests and projective tests. Objective tests present respondents with a standardized group of test items in the form of a questionnaire. Responses are limited to a specific range of answers. The MMPI is the most widely used objective test. It is usually scored for four validity scales and ten clinical scales. The validity scales suggest whether answers actually represent the person's thoughts, emotions, and behaviors.

In projective tests, people are shown ambiguous stimuli such as inkblots or drawings and asked to say what they look like. People project their own personalities into their responses. The Thematic Apperception Test (TAT) is an example of a projective test.

LO² trait
a relatively stable aspect of personality that is inferred from behavior and assumed to give rise to consistent behavior

introversion
a trait characterized by intense imagination and the tendency to inhibit impulses

extraversion
a trait characterized by tendencies to be socially outgoing and to express feelings and impulses freely

LO³ social cognitive theory
a cognitively oriented learning theory in which observational learning and person variables such as values and expectancies play major roles in individual differences

gender-schema theory
a cognitive view of gender-typing that proposes that once girls and boys become aware of their anatomic sex, they begin to blend their self-expectations and self-esteem with the ways in which they fit the gender roles prescribed in a given culture

LO⁴ humanism
the view that people are capable of free choice, self-fulfillment, and ethical behavior

self-actualization
in humanistic theory, the innate tendency to strive to realize one's potential

unconditional positive regard
a persistent expression of esteem for the value of a person, but not necessarily an unqualified acceptance of all of the person's behaviors

conditional positive regard
judgment of another person's value on the basis of the acceptability of that person's behaviors

conditions of worth
standards by which the value of a person is judged

LO⁵ sociocultural perspective
the view that focuses on the roles of ethnicity, gender, culture, and socioeconomic status

in personality formation, behavior, and mental processes

individualist
a person who defines herself or himself in terms of personal traits and gives priority to her or his own goals

collectivist
a person who defines herself or himself in terms of relationships to other people and groups and gives priority to group goals

acculturation
the process of adaptation in which immigrants and native groups identify with a new, dominant culture by learning about that culture and making behavioral and attitudinal changes

validity
in psychological testing, the degree to which a test measures what it is supposed to measure

reliability
in psychological testing, the consistency or stability of test scores from one testing to another

LO⁶ standardization
in psychological testing, the process by which one obtains and organizes test scores from various population groups, so that the results of a person's completing a test can be compared to those of others of his or her sex, in his or her age group, and so on

objective tests
tests whose items must be answered in a specified, limited manner; tests whose items have concrete answers that are considered correct

response set
a tendency to answer test items according to a bias—for example, to make oneself seem perfect or bizarre

projective test
a psychological test that presents ambiguous stimuli onto which the test taker projects his or her own personality in making a response

Chapter in Review

LO¹ stress
the demand that is made on an organism to adapt

eustress (YOU-stress)
stress that is healthful

health psychology
the field of psychology that studies the relationships between psychological factors (e.g., attitudes, beliefs, situational influences, and behavior patterns) and the prevention and treatment of physical illness

pathogen
a microscopic organism (e.g., bacterium or virus) that can cause disease

conflict
being torn in different directions by opposing motives; feelings produced by being in conflict

catastrophize
to interpret negative events as being disastrous; to "blow out of proportion"

type A behavior
behavior characterized by a sense of time urgency, competitiveness, and hostility

LO² self-efficacy expectations
our beliefs that we can bring about desired changes through our own efforts

psychological hardiness
a cluster of traits that buffer stress and are characterized by commitment, challenge, and control

locus of control
the place (locus) to which an individual attributes control over the receiving of reinforcers—either inside or outside the self

internals
people who perceive the ability to attain reinforcements as being largely within themselves

externals
people who perceive the ability to attain reinforcements as being largely outside themselves

LO¹ Define stress and identify various sources of stress. Psychological factors such as stress, behavior patterns, and attitudes can lead to or aggravate illness. People can cope with stress, and in fact there is such a thing as healthful stress (eustress). Small stressors, such as daily hassles, can threaten or harm our well-being and lead to nervousness, worrying, inability to get started, feelings of sadness, and feelings of loneliness. Hassles can predict health problems such as heart disease, cancer, and athletic injuries.

Conflict is the feeling of being pulled in two or more directions by opposing motives and can be frustrating and stressful. There are four types of conflict as illustrated in the figure below: *Approach-approach conflict* (A) is the least stressful type. Each of two goals is desirable and both are within reach. *Avoidance-avoidance conflict* (B) is more stressful. A person is motivated (M) to avoid each of two negative goals. Avoiding one of them requires approaching the other. In *approach-avoidance conflict,* (C), the same goal produces both approach and avoidance motives. *Multiple approach-avoidance conflict* (D) occurs when each of several alternative courses of action has pluses and minuses. Decision-making can be stressful—especially when there is no clear correct choice.

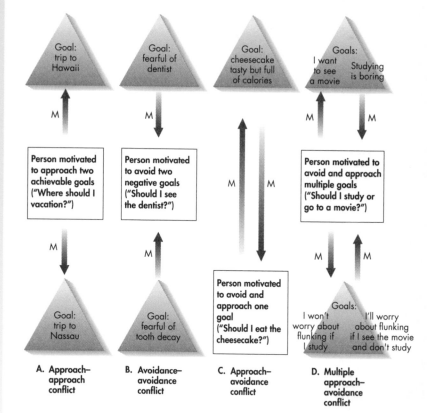

A. Approach–approach conflict

B. Avoidance–avoidance conflict

C. Approach–avoidance conflict

D. Multiple approach–avoidance conflict

LO² Identify the psychological moderators of stress. Psychological factors can influence or moderate the effects of stress. For example, self-efficacy expectations affect our ability to withstand stress (high self-efficacy expectations are accompanied by relatively lower levels of adrenaline and noradrenaline in the bloodstream). People who are self-confident are less prone to be disturbed by adverse events. Humor, laughter, and feelings of happiness may have beneficial effects on the immune system. On the other hand, there is a significant relationship between negative life events and stress scores, although the ability to predict a stressor apparently moderates its impact. Control and even the illusion of control can also moderate impact. Social support also seems to act as a buffer against the effects of stress. Sources of social support include: emotional concern, instrumental aid, information, appraisal, and socializing.

LO³ Describe the impact of stress on the body. The General Adaptation Syndrome, proposed by Selye, is a cluster of bodily changes that occur in three stages—alarm, resistance, and exhaustion. The alarm reaction is triggered by perception of a stressor. The reaction mobilizes or arouses the body. This mobilization is the basis for the instinctive fight-or-flight reaction. The alarm reaction involves bodily changes that are initiated by the brain and regulated by the endocrine system and the sympathetic division of the autonomic nervous system (ANS). If the stressor isn't removed, we enter the adaptation or resistance stage, in which the body attempts to restore lost energy and repair bodily damage. If the stressor isn't dealt with, we may enter the exhaustion stage—the body is depleted of the resources required for combating stress.

Stress suppresses the immune system. Feelings of control and social support can moderate these effects. The immune system has several functions that combat disease. One function is production of white blood cells (leukocytes). These cells recognize and eradicate foreign agents and unhealthy cells. Foreign substances are called antigens. The body generates specialized proteins or antibodies to fight antigens. Inflammation is another function of the immune system. This is increased blood supply, which floods the region with white blood cells. One of the reasons stress exhausts us is that it stimulates the production of steroids. Steroids suppress the functioning of the immune system. Persistent secretion of steroids decreases inflammation and interferes with the formation of antibodies. We become more vulnerable to various illnesses.

Hypothalamus

Pituitary

The hypothalamus secretes corticotrophin-releasing hormone (CRH)

CRH causes the pituitary gland to secrete adrenocorticotrophic hormone (ACTH)

Stressor

Adrenal cortex

Adrenal medulla

ACTH then causes the adrenal cortex to secrete corticosteroids

The adrenal medulla releases a mixture of adrenaline and noradrenaline

LO⁴ Explain the relationships between psychology and health. The biopsychosocial approach to health recognizes that there are complex factors (biological, psychological, and sociocultural factors) that contribute to health and illness and that there is no single, simple answer. Biological factors such as pathogens, inoculations, injuries, age, gender, and a family history of disease may be the most obvious cause of disease, although genetics certainly plays a role. Coronary heart disease (CHD) is the leading cause of death in the United States. Risks for CHD include: family history, physiological conditions, patterns of consumption, Type A behavior, hostility and holding in feelings of anger, job strain, chronic fatigue and chronic emotional strain, sudden stressors, and a physically inactive lifestyle. Cancer is the number-one killer of women in the United States and the number-two killer of men. Cancer is characterized by the development of abnormal, or mutant, cells that may take root anywhere in the body. If not controlled early, the cancerous cells may metastasize—establish colonies elsewhere in the body. Risk factors for cancer include heredity and behaviors such as smoking, drinking alcohol, eating animal fats, sunbathing, and prolonged psychological conditions such as depression.

Chapter in Review

LO¹ schizophrenia
a psychotic disorder characterized by loss of control of thought processes and inappropriate emotional responses

delusions
false, persistent beliefs that are unsubstantiated by sensory or objective evidence

affect (AFF-ekt)
feeling or emotional response, particularly as suggested by facial expression and body language

psychological disorders
patterns of behavior or mental processes that are connected with emotional distress or significant impairment in functioning

hallucination
a perception in the absence of sensory stimulation that is confused with reality

ideas of persecution
erroneous beliefs that one is being victimized or persecuted

flat affect
a severe reduction in emotional expressiveness, found among many people with schizophrenia or serious depression

predictive validity
in this usage, the extent to which a diagnosis permits one to predict the course of a disorder and the type of treatment that may be of help

LO² stupor
a condition in which the senses, thought, and movement are dulled

positive symptoms
the excessive and sometimes bizarre symptoms of schizophrenia, including hallucinations, delusions, and loose associations

negative symptoms
the deficiencies among people with schizophrenia, such as flat affect, lack of motivation, loss of pleasure, and social withdrawal

paranoid schizophrenia
a type of schizophrenia characterized primarily by delusions—commonly of persecution—and vivid hallucinations

disorganized schizophrenia
a type of schizophrenia characterized by disorganized delusions, vivid hallucinations, and inappropriate affect

catatonic schizophrenia
a type of schizophrenia characterized by striking motor impairment

waxy flexibility
a feature of catatonic schizophrenia in which people can be molded into postures that they maintain for quite some time

mutism
refusal to talk

LO¹ Define psychological disorders and describe their prevalence.
Psychological disorders are characterized by unusual behavior, socially unacceptable behavior, faulty perception of reality, personal distress, dangerous behavior, or self-defeating behavior. The American Psychiatric Association groups disorders on the basis of clinical syndromes and factors related to adjustment. About half of us will experience a psychological disorder at one time or another.

Past-Year and Lifetime Prevalences of Psychological Disorders

	Anxiety Disorders	Mood Disorders	Bipolar Disorder	Substance Use Disorders	Any Disorders
Prevalence during past year	18.1%	9.5%	2.8%	3.8%	26.2%
Lifetime prevalence	28.8%	20.8%	4.4%	14.6%	46.4%
Median age of onset	11 years	30 years	21 years	20 years	14 years

Sources: Kessler et al., 2005a; Kessler et al., 2005c; Merikangas et al, 2007.

LO² Describe the symptoms, types, and possible origins of schizophrenia.
Schizophrenia is characterized by disturbances in thought and language, perception and attention, motor activity, mood, and social interaction. Schizophrenia is connected with smaller brains in some people, especially fewer synapses in the prefrontal region, and larger ventricles. A genetic vulnerability to schizophrenia may interact with other factors, such as stress, complications during pregnancy and childbirth, and quality of parenting, to cause the disorder to develop. People with schizophrenia may also use more dopamine than other people do.

LO³ Describe the symptoms and possible origins of mood disorders. Mood disorders involve disturbances in expressed emotions. Major depression is characterized by persistent feelings of sadness, loss of interest, feelings of worthlessness or guilt, and inability to concentrate. Bipolar disorder is characterized by mood swings between elation and depression. Genetic factors may be involved in mood disorders. Research emphasizes possible roles for learned helplessness, attributional styles, and underutilization of serotonin in depression. People who are depressed are more likely than other people to make internal, stable, and global attributions for failures. Most people who commit suicide do so because of depression.

LO⁴ Describe the symptoms and possible origins of six types of anxiety disorders. Anxiety disorders are characterized by feelings of dread and sympathetic arousal. They include phobias, panic disorder, generalized anxiety, obsessive–compulsive disorder, and stress disorders. Some people may be genetically predisposed to acquire certain fears. Cognitive theorists focus on ways in which people interpret threats.

LO⁵ Describe the symptoms and possible origins of somatoform disorders. People with somatoform disorders display or complain of physical problems, although no medical evidence for them can be found. They include conversion disorder, hypochondriasis, and body dysmorphic disorder. Somatoform disorders may reflect the relative benefits of focusing on physical symptoms or features rather than life problems that most people would consider to be more important.

LO³ major depressive disorder (MDD)
a serious to severe depressive disorder in which the person may show loss of appetite, psychomotor retardation, and impaired reality testing

psychomotor retardation
slowness in motor activity and (apparently) in thought

bipolar disorder
a disorder in which the mood alternates between two extreme poles (elation and depression); also referred to as *manic depression*

manic
elated, showing excessive excitement

neuroticism
a personality trait characterized largely by persistent anxiety

rapid flight of ideas
rapid speech and topic changes, characteristic of manicky behavior

learned helplessness
a model for the acquisition of depressive behavior, based on findings that organisms in aversive situations learn to show inactivity when their operants go unreinforced

attributional style
the tendency to attribute one's behavior to internal or external factors, stable or unstable factors, and so on

LO⁴ specific phobia
persistent fear of a specific object or situation

claustrophobia
fear of tight, small places

acrophobia
fear of high places

social phobia
an irrational, excessive fear of public scrutiny

agoraphobia
fear of open, crowded places

panic disorder
the recurrent experiencing of attacks of extreme anxiety in the absence of external stimuli that usually elicit anxiety

generalized anxiety disorder
feelings of dread and foreboding and sympathetic arousal of at least six months' duration

obsession
a recurring thought or image that seems beyond control

compulsion
an irresistible urge to repeat an act or engage in ritualistic behavior such as hand washing

post-traumatic stress disorder (PTSD)
a disorder that follows a distressing event outside the range of normal human experience and that is characterized by features such as intense fear, avoidance of stimuli associated with the event, and reliving of the event

acute stress disorder
a disorder, like PTSD, that is characterized by feelings of anxiety and helplessness and caused by a traumatic event; acute stress disorder occurs within a month of the event and lasts from two days to four weeks

LO⁵ somatoform disorders
disorders in which people complain of physical (somatic) problems even though no physical abnormality can be found

LO⁶ Describe the symptoms and possible origins of dissociative disorders. Dissociative disorders are characterized by sudden, temporary changes in consciousness or self-identity. They include dissociative amnesia, dissociative fugue, and dissociative identity disorder (multiple personality). Dissociative disorders may help people keep disturbing memories or ideas out of mind, especially memories of child abuse.

LO⁷ Describe the symptoms and possible origins of personality disorders. Personality disorders are inflexible, maladaptive behavior patterns that impair personal or social functioning. Genetic factors may be involved in personality disorders. Antisocial personality disorder may develop from some combination of genetic vulnerability (less gray matter in the prefrontal cortex of the brain, which may provide lower-than-normal levels of arousal), inconsistent discipline, and a cynical worldview.

conversion disorder
a somatoform disorder in which anxiety or unconscious conflicts are "converted" into physical symptoms that often have the effect of helping the person cope with anxiety or conflict

la belle indifférence
a French term descriptive of the lack of concern for their (imagined) medical problem sometimes shown by people with conversion disorders

hypochondriasis
a somatoform disorder characterized by persistent belief that one is ill despite lack of medical findings

body dysmorphic disorder
a somatoform disorder characterized by preoccupation with an imagined or exaggerated physical defect in one's appearance

LO⁶ dissociative disorders
disorders in which there are sudden, temporary changes in consciousness or self-identity

dissociative amnesia
a dissociative disorder marked by loss of memory or self-identity; skills and general knowledge are usually retained

dissociative fugue
a dissociative disorder in which one experiences amnesia and then flees to a new location

dissociative identity disorder
a disorder in which a person appears to have two or more distinct identities or personalities that may alternately emerge

multiple personality disorder
the previous term for *dissociative identity disorder*

LO⁷ personality disorders
enduring patterns of maladaptive behavior that are sources of distress to the individual or others

paranoid personality disorder
a personality disorder characterized by persistent suspiciousness, but not involving the disorganization of paranoid schizophrenia

schizotypal personality disorder
a personality disorder characterized by oddities of thought and behavior, but not involving bizarre psychotic behaviors

schizoid personality disorder
a personality disorder characterized by social withdrawal

borderline personality disorder
a personality disorder characterized by instability in relationships, self-image, mood, and lack of impulse control

antisocial personality disorder
the diagnosis given a person who is in frequent conflict with society, yet who is undeterred by punishment and experiences little or no guilt and anxiety

avoidant personality disorder
a personality disorder in which the person is unwilling to enter relationships without assurance of acceptance because of fears of rejection and criticism

LO¹ psychotherapy
a systematic interaction between a therapist and a client that brings psychological principles to bear on influencing the client's thoughts, feelings, or behavior to help the client overcome abnormal behavior or adjust to problems in living

asylum
an institution for the care of the mentally ill

LO² psychoanalysis
Freud's method of psychotherapy; (also the name of Freud's theory of personality)

catharsis
release of emotional tension, as after a traumatic experience, that has the effect of restoring one's psychological well-being

free association
in psychoanalysis, the uncensored uttering of all thoughts that come to mind

resistance
the tendency to block the free expression of impulses and primitive ideas—a reflection of the defense mechanism of repression

transference
responding to one person (such as a spouse or the psychoanalyst) in a way that is similar to the way one responded to another person (such as a parent) in childhood

wish fulfillment
a primitive method used by the id to attempt to gratify basic instincts

ego analyst
a psychoanalyst therapist who focuses on the conscious, coping behavior of the ego instead of the hypothesized, unconscious functioning of the id

interpersonal psychotherapy (ITP)
a short-term dynamic therapy that focuses on clients' relationships and direct alleviation of negative emotions such as anxiety and depression

LO³ client-centered therapy
Carl Rogers's method of psychotherapy, which emphasizes the creation of a warm, therapeutic atmosphere that frees clients to engage in self-exploration and self-expression

Gestalt therapy
Fritz Perls' form of psychotherapy, which attempts to integrate conflicting parts of the personality through directive methods designed to help clients perceive their whole selves

LO⁴ behavior therapy
systematic application of the principles of learning to the direct modification of a client's problem behaviors

systematic desensitization
Wolpe's method for reducing fears by associating a hierarchy of images of fear-evoking stimuli with deep muscle relaxation

LO¹ Define psychotherapy and describe the history of treatment. Psychotherapy uses psychological principles to help clients overcome psychological disorders or problems. Throughout most of history it has been generally assumed that psychological disorders represent possession, and cruel "treatment" methods such as exorcism have been used. Asylums, mental hospitals, and community treatment are relatively recent innovations.

LO² Describe traditional psychoanalysis and short-term psychodynamic therapies. The main method of a Freudian psychoanalysis is free association, but dream analysis and interpretations are also used. Modern approaches are briefer and more directive, and the therapist and client usually sit face to face.

LO³ Define humanistic therapy and contrast its two main approaches. Rogers' client-centered therapy uses nondirective methods: The therapist shows unconditional positive regard, empathy, and genuineness. Perls's directive method of Gestalt Therapy provides exercises aimed at helping people integrate conflicting parts of their personality.

LO⁴ Define behavior therapy and identify various behavioral approaches to therapy. Behavior therapy relies on principles of learning to help clients develop adaptive behavior patterns and discontinue maladaptive ones. These include flooding, systematic desensitization, and modeling. Virtual therapy is a new method for desensitizing patients to fears. Operant conditioning methods include token economies, successive approximation, social skills training, and biofeedback training.

LO⁵ Define cognitive therapy and describe Beck's approach and REBT. Cognitive therapy aims to give clients insight into irrational beliefs and cognitive distortions and replace them with rational beliefs and accurate perceptions. Beck notes that clients may develop depression because they minimize accomplishments and catastrophize failures. Ellis originated rational emotive behavior therapy (REBT), which holds that people's irrational beliefs about events shape their responses to them.

LO⁶ Identify advantages, disadvantages, and types of group therapy. Group therapy is more economical than individual therapy. Moreover, group members benefit from the social support and experiences of other members. However, some clients cannot disclose their problems to a group or risk group disapproval. Specialized methods include couple therapy and family therapy.

hierarchy
an arrangement of stimuli according to the amount of fear they evoke

modeling
a behavior-therapy technique in which a client observes and imitates a person who approaches and copes with feared objects or situations

aversive conditioning
a behavior therapy technique in which undesired responses are inhibited by pairing repugnant or offensive stimuli with them

rapid smoking
an aversive conditioning method for quitting smoking in which the smoker inhales rapidly, thus rendering once-desirable cigarette smoke aversive

eye-movement desensitization and reprocessing (EMDR)
a method of treating stress disorders by having clients visually follow a rapidly oscillating finger while they think of the traumatic events connected with the disorders

token economy
a controlled environment in which people are reinforced for desired behaviors with tokens (such as poker chips) that may be exchanged for privileges

successive approximations
in operant conditioning, a series of behaviors that gradually become more similar to a target behavior

biofeedback training (BFT)
the systematic feeding back to an organism of information about a bodily function so that the organism can gain control of that function

self-monitoring
keeping a record of one's own behavior to identify problems and record successes

behavior rehearsal
practice

feedback
in assertiveness training, information about the effectiveness of a response

LO 5 cognitive therapy
a form of therapy that focuses on how clients' cognitions (e.g., expectations, attitudes, beliefs) lead to distress and may be modified to relieve distress and promote adaptive behavior

rational emotive behavior therapy (REBT)
Albert Ellis's form of therapy that encourages clients to challenge and correct irrational expectations and maladaptive behaviors

cognitive-behavior therapy (CBT)
an approach to therapy that uses cognitive and behavioral techniques that have been validated by research

LO 7 meta-analysis
a method for combining and averaging the results of individual research studies

specific factors
those factors in psychotherapy that are specific to a given approach, such as free association in psychoanalysis or systematic desensitization in behavior therapy

nonspecific factors
those factors in psychotherapy that are common to many approaches, such as the "therapeutic alliance" with the client

LO 8 rebound anxiety
anxiety that can occur when one discontinues use of a tranquilizer

antidepressant
acting to relieve depression

selective serotonin-reuptake inhibitors (SSRIs)
antidepressant drugs that work by blocking the reuptake of serotonin by presynaptic neurons

LO 7 Explain whether psychotherapy works and who benefits from it. Statistical analyses such as meta-analysis show that people who obtain most forms of psychotherapy fare better than people who do not. Psychoanalytic and client-centered approaches are most helpful with highly verbal and motivated individuals. Cognitive and behavior therapies are probably the most effective. People from various cultural backgrounds may profit from different kinds of treatment.

LO 8 Describe methods of biological therapy and their benefits and side effects. Antipsychotic drugs help many people with schizophrenia by blocking the action of dopamine. Antidepressants help many people by increasing the action of serotonin. Lithium often helps people with bipolar disorder. The use of antianxiety drugs for daily tensions is controversial because people build tolerance and do not learn to solve their problems. ECT, another controversial treatment, induces a seizure and frequently relieves severe depression. The prefrontal lobotomy attempts to alleviate agitation by severing nerve pathways in the brain but has been largely discontinued because of side effects.

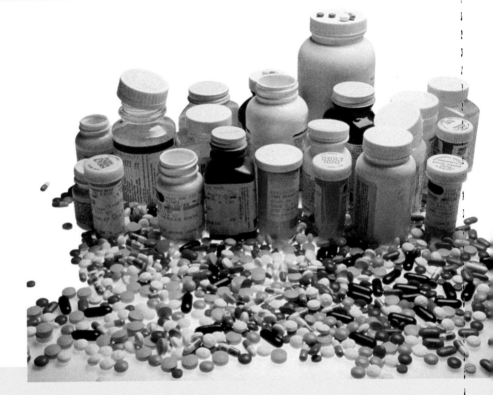

electroconvulsive therapy (ECT)
treatment of disorders like major depression by passing an electric current (that causes a convulsion) through the head

sedative
a drug that relieves nervousness or agitation or puts one to sleep

psychosurgery
surgery intended to promote psychological changes or to relieve disordered behavior

prefrontal lobotomy
the severing or destruction of a section of the frontal lobe of the brain

Chapter in Review

14

LO¹ social psychology
the field of psychology that studies the nature and causes of people's thoughts and behavior in social situations

LO² attitude
an enduring mental representation of a person, place, or thing that evokes an emotional response and related behavior

A–B problem
the issue of how well we can predict behavior on the basis of attitudes

elaboration likelihood model
the view that persuasive messages are evaluated (elaborated) on the basis of central and peripheral cues

fear appeal
a type of persuasive communication that influences behavior on the basis of arousing fear instead of rational analysis of the issues

selective avoidance
diverting one's attention from information that is inconsistent with one's attitudes

selective exposure
deliberately seeking and attending to information that is consistent with one's attitudes

cognitive-dissonance theory
the view that we are motivated to make our cognitions or beliefs consistent

attitude-discrepant behavior
behavior inconsistent with an attitude that may have the effect of modifying an attitude

effort justification
in cognitive-dissonance theory, the tendency to seek justification (acceptable reasons) for strenuous efforts

stereotype
a fixed, conventional idea about a group

attraction
in social psychology, an attitude of liking or disliking (negative attraction)

triangular model of love
Sternberg's view that love involves combinations of three components: intimacy, passion, and commitment

intimacy
close acquaintance and familiarity; a characteristic of a relationship in which partners share their inmost feelings

passion
strong romantic and sexual feelings

commitment
the decision to maintain a relationship

LO¹ Define social psychology. One area of social psychology studies the ways in which people can be goaded by social influences into doing things that are not necessarily consistent with their personalities. Social psychology studies the nature and causes of behavior and mental processes in social situations. Topics covered in social psychology include: attitudes, conformity, persuasion, social perception, interpersonal attraction, social influence, group conformity, and obedience.

LO² Define attitude and discuss factors that shape it. Attitudes are comprised of cognitive evaluations, feelings, and behavioral tendencies. A number of factors influence the likelihood that we can predict behavior from attitudes: specificity, strength of attitudes, vested interest, and accessibility. Attitudes with a strong emotional impact are more accessible. People attempt to change other people's attitudes and behavior by means of persuasion. According to the elaboration likelihood model, persuasion occurs through central and peripheral routes. Repeated messages generally "sell" better than messages delivered once. People tend to respond more to fear appeals than the purely factual presentation. Persuasive communicators tend to show expertise, trustworthiness, attractiveness, or similarity to the audience.

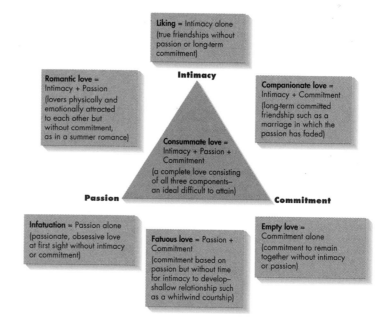

LO³ Define social perception and describe the factors that contribute to it. The primacy effect refers to the fact that we often judge people in terms of our first impressions. The recency effect appears to be based on the fact that recently learned information is easier to remember. The attribution process is the tendency to infer the motives and traits of others through observation of their behavior. In dispositional attributions, we attribute people's behavior to internal factors. In situational attributions, we attribute people's behavior to external forces. According to the actor–observer effect, we tend to attribute the behavior of others to internal, dispositional factors, but we tend to attribute our own behavior to external, situational factors. The fundamental attribution error is the tendency to attribute too much of other people's behavior to dispositional factors.

consummate love
the ideal form of love within Sternberg's model, which combines passion, intimacy, and commitment

romantic love
an intense, positive emotion that involves sexual attraction, feelings of caring, and the belief that one is in love

LO³ social perception
a subfield of social psychology that studies the ways in which we form and modify impressions of others

primacy effect
the tendency to evaluate others in terms of first impressions

recency effect
the tendency to evaluate others in terms of the most recent impression

attribution
a belief concerning why people behave in a certain way

dispositional attribution
an assumption that a person's behavior is determined by internal causes such as personal attitudes or goals

situational attribution
an assumption that a person's behavior is determined by external circumstances such as the social pressure found in a situation

actor–observer effect
the tendency to attribute our own behavior to situational factors but to attribute the behavior of others to dispositional factors

fundamental attribution error
the assumption that others act predominantly on the basis of their dispositions, even when there is evidence suggesting the importance of their situations

self-serving bias
the tendency to view one's successes as stemming from internal factors and one's failures as stemming from external factors

LO⁴ social influence
the area of social psychology that studies the ways in which people influence the thoughts, feelings, and behavior of others

foot-in-the-door technique
a method for including compliance in which a small request is followed by a larger request

LO⁵ social facilitation
the process by which a person's performance is increased when other members of a group engage in similar behavior

evaluation apprehension
concern that others are evaluating our behavior

diffusion of responsibility
the spreading or sharing of responsibility for a decision or behavior within a group

social decision schemes
rules for predicting the final outcome of group decision making on the basis of the members' initial positions

groupthink
a process in which group members are influenced by cohesiveness and a dynamic leader to ignore external realities as they make decisions

deindividuation
the process by which group members may discontinue self-evaluation and adopt group norms and attitudes

altruism
unselfish concern for the welfare of others

LO⁴ Explain why people obey authority figures and conform to social norms.
Other people and groups can exert enormous pressure on us to behave according to their norms. In fact, classic experiments have demonstrated that people influence others to engage in destructive obedience or conform to social norms. For example, the majority of subjects in the Milgram studies complied with the demands of authority figures, even when the demands required that they hurt innocent people by means of electric shock. Factors contributing to obedience include socialization, lack of social comparison, perception of legitimate authority figures, the foot-in-the-door technique, inaccessibility of values, and buffers between perpetrator and victim. Asch's research in which subjects judged the lengths of lines suggests that most people will follow the crowd, even when the crowd is wrong. Personal factors such as desire to be liked by group members, low self-esteem, high self-consciousness, and shyness contribute to conformity. Group size also contributes.

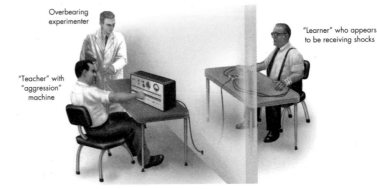

Overbearing experimenter

"Learner" who appears to be receiving shocks

"Teacher" with "aggression" machine

LO⁵ Describe how and why people behave differently as group members than as individuals.
The concept of social facilitation refers to the effects on performance that result from the presence of other people. The presence of others may facilitate performance for reasons such as increased arousal and evaluation apprehension. Anonymous group members, however, may experience diffusion of responsibility and performance may fall off, as in social loafing. Social psychologists have identified several decision-making schemes, including the majority-wins scheme, the truth-wins scheme, the two-thirds majority scheme, and the first-shift rule. Group decisions tend to be more polarized and riskier than individual decisions, largely because groups diffuse responsibility. Group decisions may be highly productive when group members are knowledgeable, there is an explicit procedure for arriving at decisions, and there is a process of give and take.